P9-CAJ-097

HANDBOOKS

NEW ENGLAND

MICHAEL BLANDING & ALEXANDRA HALL

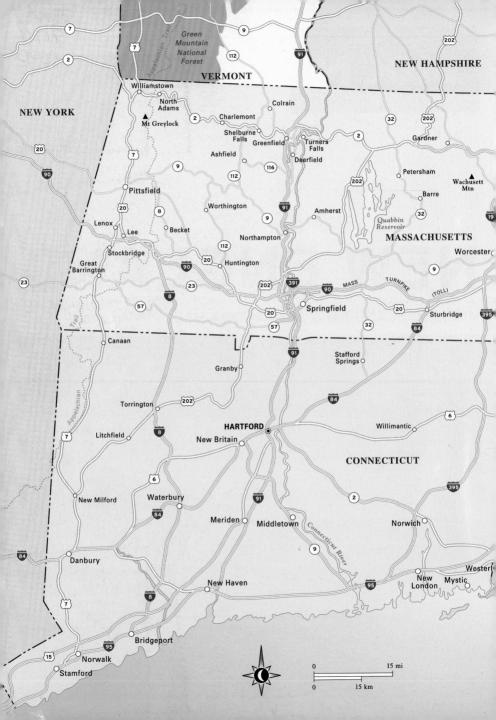

MASSACHUSETTS, RHODE ISLAND, AND CONNECTICUT

101

3

93

95

1A

Newburyport

495

Merrimack River

Nashua

Lawrence

1A

Ipswich

127

3

95

Andover

1

Essex

Gloucester

Lowell

28

127

128

2

93

95

3

Salem

Marblehead

ATLANTIC
OCEAN

495

Lexington

1A

Concord

95

2

20

Massachusetts
Bay

290

9

Wellesley

BOSTON

90

135

Framingham

Quincy

109

1

28

3

Blackstone
Valley

95

Brockton

Cape   Cod

495

24

Provincetown

Cape Cod National Seashore

6

PROVIDENCE

295

Pawtucket

Taunton

495

3

Plymouth

Wellfleet

Bay

95

195

24

28

Sandwich

6A

Warwick

140

Dennis

6A

Bristol

Fall River

195

6

6A

Barnstable

Chatham

RHODE
ISLAND

6

New
Bedford

28

Hyannis

Yarmouth

6

28

Buzzards
Bay

Nantucket
Sound

Newport

Woods Hole

Elizabeth
Islands

Vineyard Haven

1

Edgartown

Nantucket
Island

Martha's
Vineyard

Nantucket

ATLANTIC

Block
Island

OCEAN

© AVALON TRAVEL

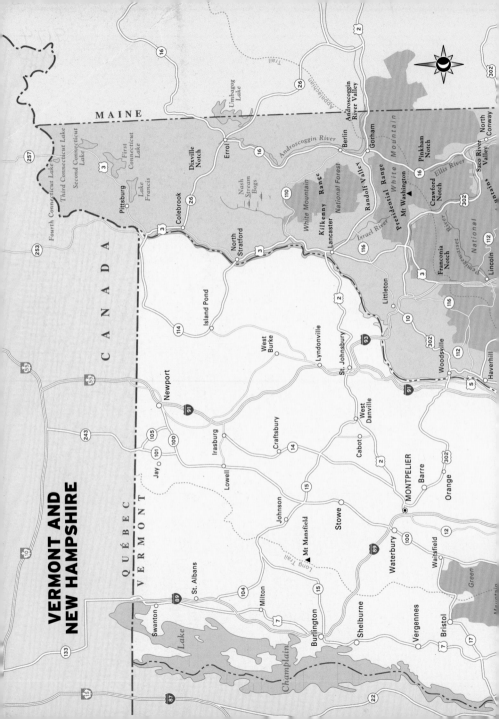

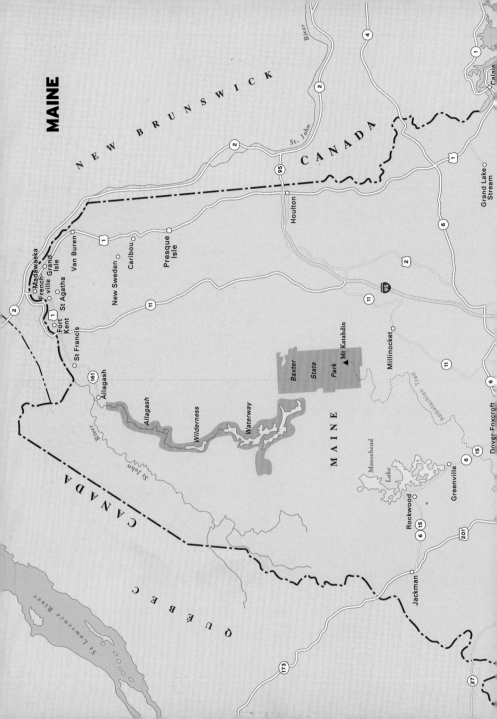

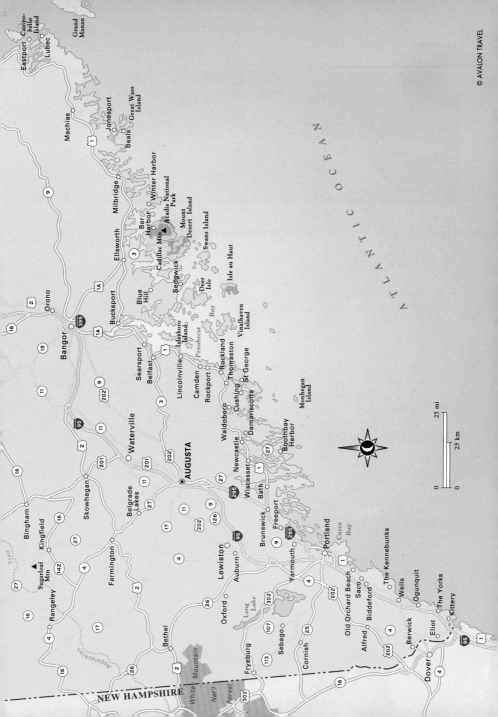

© AVALON TRAVEL

Contents

Discover New England

"The Yankee," Ralph Waldo Emerson once observed of his fellow New Englanders, "is one who, if he gets his teeth set on a thing, all creation can't make him let go." That sentiment only begins to describe the spirit of independent thinking that binds the residents of the six northeastern states. From the Harvard professor researching a novel economic theory to the Vermont farmer stubbornly holding onto his grandfather's dairy farm, New Englanders don't like to be told what to do — or for that matter, that it can't be done.

A stubborn independence was what made the Pilgrims tough it out through New England winters in one of the first permanent settlements in North America. It's what made the Minutemen flock to Lexington 150 years later to kick off the American Revolution. And today, it's what has led New Englanders to preserve much of the region's historic character.

Walking down the gaslit streets of Beacon Hill in downtown Boston, you can almost hear the clip-clop of Paul Revere's horse on the cobblestones. Even in the most remote corner of New Hampshire or Vermont, you are likely to find an inn where Washington or some other patriot (allegedly) slept, or a musket piece fired at the Battle of Bunker Hill taking pride of place in a historical museum.

As rich as it is in colonial history, New England's spirit of independence didn't end on Independence Day. Shrines to a number of creative

freethinkers lie throughout the region – celebrating the likes of Emily Dickinson, Nathaniel Hawthorne, Robert Frost, and Jack Kerouac.

Then there is the land. Whether it's a lonely lighthouse on a rocky cliff, a weather-beaten farmhouse surrounded by black-and-white spotted Holsteins, or the quintessential town common with the white-steepled church, this landscape is one of the most recognizable in the world. Driving down back roads there are constant excuses to pull over for a photo op – especially when the region mounts its annual tour-de-force of fall foliage.

There are plenty of unexpected pleasures as well: a museum in Connecticut devoted to big-top king P. T. Barnum; an island artist colony in Maine where electricity is rare and cars are forbidden; an "underwater state park" in Lake Champlain littered with shipwrecks; and a museum full of giant papier-mâché puppets in a converted Vermont farmhouse.

In these and thousands of other ways, New Englanders show off their independent ways of thinking, making a trip to this six-state region inspiring in countless ways.

Planning Your Trip

▶ WHERE TO GO

MASSACHUSETTS

The heart of New England both geographically and spiritually, Massachusetts sets the tone that the region follows. Plan to spend at least some time in the state, which abounds in historic and literary sites—especially in its capital, Boston. While Massachusetts doesn't enjoy as much stunning scenery as its northern neighbors, it has its own outdoor attractions in the stark coastline of Cape Cod and the roller-coaster slopes of the Berkshires.

RHODE ISLAND

Founded by religious heretics, Rhode Island has always been New England's "black sheep," maintaining a low profile compared to the other states in the region. But that's just the way residents like it. Otherwise, they'd have to share their miles of beaches and quaint coastal villages with the tourists. And the nation's smallest state holds its own can't-miss urban attractions in the arts mecca of Providence, and the picturesque yachting capital of Newport.

CONNECTICUT

Sandwiched between New York and New England, Connecticut residents boast that they have the best of both worlds. Mansions front Long Island Sound, where espresso-gulping residents daily board the train for Gotham daily. Further up the coast, the literati flock to New Haven, synonymous with Yale University; and tourists raise the rigging at the reconstructed seaport of Mystic. The rest of the state is classic New England, with farmhouses and foliage decorating the rolling Litchfield Hills and the Connecticut River Valley.

IF YOU HAVE . . .

- **A WEEKEND:** Visit Boston, with a road trip to Concord or Plymouth for the historic sights.

- **5 DAYS:** Add a trip to Cape Cod or hike the White Mountains of New Hampshire.

- **A WEEK:** Add the back roads of Vermont or the culture of Providence and Newport.

- **TWO WEEKS:** Add Mystic, New Haven, and the Berkshires; or a drive up the rocky Maine coast.

VERMONT

Woods, mountains, and ice cream—Vermont has just about everything a traveler could want, short of a city. More than any of their neighbors, Vermonters have taken pains to preserve the rural character of their state. In the fall, the state's Green Mountains are known for some of the most colorful foliage in the world. And while the state doesn't have as many

through the New Hampshire psyche holds itself in proud contrast to its liberal-leaning neighbors. The state's terrain, formed around the backbone of the White Mountains, is just as rugged, drawing thousands of rock climbers and hikers every year to scale the peaks of the Presidential Range. Almost as popular is the summer paradise of Lake Winnepesauke (bonus points for spelling) and the state's sliver of coast, packed with amusements and the architectural gem of Portsmouth.

MAINE

There's a reason they call them "Maine-iacs." The folks in the Northeast's northernmost state are a breed apart; quirky, inscrutable, and—when you break the ice—the most down-to-earth people you could meet. This is where to meet real people doing real work, from lobster fishing to lumber cutting. The state's other reputation as "Vacationland" is well deserved: Of all the New England states, its rocky coastline is the most picturesque, while inland lakes and mountains offer enormous tracts of silent wilderness broken only by the cries of loons.

official "attractions" as other states, it makes up for it with the profusion of galleries, craft shops, maple syrup farms, and cheese-making shops that spring from every curve in the road.

NEW HAMPSHIRE

The famous libertarian streak that runs

▶ WHEN TO GO

As Mark Twain famously said about weather in New England, "There is only one thing certain about it: you are certain there is going to be plenty of it." But at least some generalizations are possible.

For many, the best time of year is the fall, when the famed foliage is in full splendor and days are crisp and cool, but not cold. If you plan on leaf-peeping, be sure to check ahead and find out where the foliage is most dramatic, as the color can vary enormously with time and latitude. In general, the leaves

LEAF-PEEPING

The term may evoke comical images of tourists sneaking up on unsuspecting fallen leaves to ogle them, but come autumn in New England, "leaf-peeping" is serious business. It's the basis for the state's second-biggest tourist season (behind winter ski season), drawing visitors in droves from around the country and, often, the globe to witness the glorious color palette of fall. But the phenomenon of leaves changing color is less about beauty than it is science. Leaves begin to change from bright green to red, orange, and yellow as a way of getting ready for winter, when there is not enough light or water for photosynthesis. Trees use winter as a time to rest, living off the food they have stored up during summertime rather than on the food created by their leaves. As the green chlorophyll disappears from their leaves, the green fades into yellow, red, purple, brown, and orange hues – many of which are amplified by the leftover glucose trapped in the leaves after the tree has stopped photosynthesizing.

start changing in Maine in late September, and work their way down to the Connecticut coast by late October. Summer is arguably the second-best time for a trip, especially if you're spending time on the coast. Because of cold Atlantic currents, beaches don't come into their own until late July and August. If you plan on traveling inland, however, be forewarned that August's infamous humidity can make for a sticky time of it.

Winter brings the added appeal of skiing and other outdoor sports, and a fresh layer of snow can make rural areas quite romantic. The only time that New England lacks luster is in the spring, a brief season of mud and raw weather through which most locals grit their teeth. Or, as Twain put it: "Every year (New Englanders) kill a lot of poets for writing about 'Beautiful Spring.'" Note that except around ski resorts, many hotels and museums also close during the low season of January-March (the last month of which is known as "mud season" in Vermont and New Hampshire).

a herd of Jersey cows at Billings Farm in Woodstock

▶ BEFORE YOU GO

In general, New Englanders dress casually. Even in Boston, jeans are fine in all but the most upscale restaurants and hotels. When in doubt, anything from the L.L.Bean catalog will do. Sweaters and heavy coats are a must in winter—supplemented with long underwear and wool socks if you plan on being comfortable during long stints outdoors. A light jacket and several layers are often the best choice in spring and fall, when temperatures can change dramatically over the course of a day. T-shirts and shorts are standard in summer, but even in August be sure to pack a light jacket or sweater, as nights can sometimes be quite cool, especially on the coast. There is only one item of clothing that you wear at your peril: a New York Yankees cap!

pumpkins on a New Hampshire stone wall

Invest in a good road-map book if you are going to be doing a lot of driving in rural areas, where roads can be confusing and locals less than helpful. (The classic joke in Maine: A man stops to ask directions. "Can you take this road to Bangor?" Local responds (in a thick Maine accent): "Ayuh, but I think they already got some theah.") Sunscreen is recommended in summer for those with fair skin who don't want to look as red as the lobster they're eating. Bug repellent is also essential when visiting for outdoor areas, especially during black fly season in early summer in New Hampshire and Maine—not that it will help, but it's good to know that at least you are doing everything you can.

skiing at Sunday River, Maine

Explore New England

▶ RUMBLINGS OF REVOLUTION

From the landing of the Pilgrims at Plymouth Rock to the Boston Tea Party and shot heard 'round the world at Concord Bridge, this is where it all began. Don't be surprised if you feel a stirring of patriotism in your breast as you tour some of the most important sites in the history of the United States. Less well-known are the sites dedicated to the many literary lights who hail from New England, including the Concord transcendentalists; novelists Mark Twain, Nathaniel Hawthorne, and Herman Melville; and beloved poets Emily Dickinson and Robert Frost. This two-week trip takes in many of the highlights in an easygoing circle around the region.

Day 1

Arrive in historic Boston, and orient yourself

The Freedom Trail connects Boston's most famous historic sights.

with an all-day amble along the Freedom Trail, taking in Old North Church, Paul Revere's House, the USS Constitution, and other sites that played an important role in the nation's struggle for freedom. At night, have an Italian dinner in the North End—Boston's oldest neighborhood.

Day 2

In the morning, visit the replica of the Tea Party Ship. In the afternoon, cross the river to Cambridge, where you can tour Harvard University and visit Longfellow Historic Site, which was both home to the poet and headquarters for General Washington.

Day 3

Drive a half hour west along Route 2 to Lexington and visit the site of the opening battle of the American Revolution, the Battle Green. Follow the "battle road" to Concord, where the patriots were victorious at Old North Bridge. Book a room for the night at the historic Longfellow's Wayside Inn.

Day 4

Take a literary tour of Concord center, visiting the homes of the transcendentalist writers—The Emerson House, Bronson Alcott's Orchard House, and the site of Henry David Thoreau's cabin at Walden Pond. If the weather is warm enough, take a dip just like Thoreau.

Day 5

Head southeast along I-95 and Route 3 to Plymouth (2 hours) and back into an even earlier time with a tour of the painstakingly constructed

FAMILY MATTERS

Traveling with kids isn't always as easy as the guidebooks make it sound, but New England is, in fact, as ideal a place to do it as any, thanks to its balance of education and fun. For every historical town, there is a wax museum full of witches; for every Concord Bridge, a Basketball Hall of Fame. There is no bad time to pack up the minivan, either: Spring is wonderful for outside strolls in the parks; summer begs for cooling dips at the beach; fall is foliage and festival time; and winter is when to head for the indoor museums – or hit the ski trails. Following are the top sights and activities for kids, by state.

MASSACHUSETTS

- **Children's Museum** (Boston) puts the "act" in interactive.

- **Fire Museum** (Boston) teaches wee ones about the history of firefighting.

- **Museum of Science** (Boston) is an enormous building spotlighting everything from live lightning shows and an Omni theatre to fossil exhibits.

- **Public Garden** (Boston) is where tykes love to ride on the famous **swan boats** and pay homage to the *Make Way for Ducklings* statue.

- **Salem Maritime Historic Site** (Salem) is the place to pace the decks of the tall ships.

- **Wolf Hollow** (Ipswich) is a howl – quite literally; a quasi-natural setting in which to visit and learn about wolves.

- **Minuteman National Historic Park** (Concord) captures the opening battles of the Revolutionary War. Later, take a swim (and visit Thoreau's cabin) at **Walden Pond.**

VERMONT

- **ECHO Lake Aquarium** (Burlington) guarantees that kids will get wet as they learn about frogs, snakes, and the resident sea monster, Champ.

- **Fairbanks Museum** (Fairmont) is a treasure trove of mummies, dinosaur fossils, stuffed animals, and Civil War memorabilia, along with an interactive weather center for budding meteorologists.

- **Vermont Toy and Train Museum** (Quechee) has case after case of toys from yesteryear to bring back memories, and some from today for kids to play with.

- **The Retreat Farm** (Brattleboro) is a working farm with a petting barn that encourages tykes to feed and groom the animals.

NEW HAMPSHIRE

- **Hampton Beach** (Hampton) is a veritable kid magnet; parents can relax on the sand while they play arcade games and eat cotton candy to their hearts' content.

RHODE ISLAND

- **Watch Hill** (Watch Hill) is a family-friendly throwback to the Victorian era, with a beautiful beach, a carousel for the kids, and plenty of upscale shops for parents to explore.

pre-colonial village at Plimoth Plantation. Don't miss Hobbamock's Homesite to see how the other half—the Native Americans—lived. Stay the night in Plymouth.

Day 6

Drive south along Routes 44 and 140 to New Bedford (one hour), and learn about a time when spermaceti oil and whalebones drove the world's economy at the impressive Whaling Museum. While there, take a pilgrimage to the Seaman's Bethel church, featured in the opening chapter of Herman Melville's *Moby-Dick*. Continue on down Routes I-195 and 114 and cross over into Rhode Island to spend the night in Newport (45 minutes).

a marker for Boston's Freedom Trail

Day 7

For an upscale diversion, take a tour of Newport's stunning cliff-side mansions, once the playground for the rich and famous. If you'd like, include a visit to the replica of the USS *Providence,* the sloop involved in the first naval engagement of the Revolution.

Day 8

Shoot down I-95 to New Haven (2.5 hours), where you can take an afternoon tour of Yale University, Harvard's academic and athletic rival. While there, head to the waterfront to see the *Amistad* Memorial, which commemorates the slave-ship rebellion that inspired the eponymous Spielberg movie. Stay the night in New Haven.

Day 9

Venture up I-91 to Hartford (45 minutes) and pay homage to two literary giants at the Mark Twain House and the Harriet Beecher Stowe House. Or learn about the history of African Americans in New England through the Amistad collection at the Wadsworth Atheneum. Push on up the highway to spend the night in Amherst, Massachusetts (one hour).

Day 10

In Amherst, visit the Emily Dickinson Homestead and any of the five colleges in the area. In the afternoon, browse the bookstores and cafés of neighboring Northampton. Spend another night in Amherst.

Day 11

Head south on I-91 and west on I-90, then north on Route 7 to Pittsfield (1.5 hours), where you can visit the thoroughly landlocked home at Arrowhead where Herman Melville wrote *Moby-Dick.* On your way through town, stop at the Berkshire Athenaeum to peruse its stunning collection of Melville memorabilia. Then push up Route 7 to spend the night in Bennington, Vermont (one hour).

Day 12

Visit the Bennington Battle Monument, where ragtag patriots beat off the British and turned the tide of the northern campaign of the war. Learn more about the conflict at the Bennington Museum. Then take a short drive up Route 7 to the Stone House, where poet Robert Frost penned "Stopping By the Woods on a Snowy Evening."

Day 13

Off to New Hampshire! Take Routes 9 and 101 to the small town of Derry (2.5 hours). Continue your homage to Frost at the Frost Farm, where you can hike along the trails that inspired some of his poems. Then continue down into Massachusetts and head up Route 128 to spend the night in Salem (one hour), site of the infamous Witch Trials. After dinner, take a late-night visit to the cheesy but spooky Witch Museum, before spending the night in Salem—if you dare.

Day 14

Spend the day exploring Salem's fascinating history, with a visit to the Witch House, the

Peabody Essex Museum, and the House of Seven Gables, which inspired Nathaniel Hawthorne's book of the same name.

Be sure to check out the waterfront, where you can learn about Salem's other historical legacy at the Salem Maritime National Historic Site. Head back down Route 128 and Route 1 to Boston (one hour). Or, if you have time, take the long way back along Route 114 and Route 1A and stop off to browse historic downtown Marblehead. There, you can view the famous painting *The Spirit of '76,* something you are sure to be full of after two weeks drenched in American history.

▶ ARTISTIC EXPRESSION

Boston isn't called the "Athens of America" for nothing—it's one of the country's premier outlets of art and culture. You can craft a whole itinerary from the art and theater in New England's cities and college towns. Boston's art scene gets hopping in the fall and spring; in the summer, the action moves to the southern shores and the Berkshires.

Days 1-2

Spend your first day in Boston taking in the world-class collection at the Museum of Fine Arts. At night, take in a pre-Broadway show in the Theater District or a show at a rock club.

On your second day, stroll along Newbury Street in the morning, checking out its many art galleries. In the afternoon, visit the one-of-a-kind Isabella Stewart Gardner Museum or the new waterfront Institute of Contemporary Art.

Day 3

Head south along I-95 to Providence (one

Boston's Museum of Fine Arts

Museum of Art, Rhode Island School of Design

the season, you can catch the Boston Symphony Orchestra at their summer home of Tanglewood, a performance at the annual Jacob's Pillow Dance Festival, or a production by the Commonwealth Shakespeare Company at their reconstructed Rose Playhouse. While there, don't miss the flower gardens at The Mount, a work of art to rival any museum.

Day 6

Another day, another college—head up Route 7 to Williamstown (one hour) and tour beautiful Williams College. While there, take in the college art museum and the spectacular collection at the Clark Art Museum. If you're lucky, you'll catch a performance at the Williamstown Theatre Festival, which has drawn such actors as Ethan Hawke and Marisa Tomei.

Day 7

While staying in Williamstown, take a side trip down Route 2 to North Adams (20 minutes), a rejuvenated mill town that's home to the gargantuan Massachusetts Museum of Contemporary Art and countless galleries. After dinner, stick around for the town's funky nightlife.

hour), where you can check out the cutting-edge modern art museum at Rhode Island School of Design and browse the funky shops around Brown University. At night, catch an experimental performance at the acclaimed Trinity Repertory Theatre or, if the timing is right, attend the Waterfire performance on the river.

Day 4

Head up Interstates 295, 90, and 91 back into Massachusetts to visit Northampton (2.5 hours), one of the most delightful college towns in New England. Visit Smith College, treat yourself to a wide selection of ethnic food, and take in a folk music performance at night.

Day 5

Head down I-90 and up Route 20 to Lenox (2 hours), where, depending on

Day 8

Drive up Route 7 to Bennington (30 minutes) and check out the famous folk art of Grandma Moses at the Bennington Museum. Then cross southern Vermont along Route 9 to Brattleboro (one hour), home to a thriving café and gallery scene. If the season's right, take in a traditional music concert in Marlboro, or one of the acclaimed barn concerts in Putney, before bedding down in Brattleboro. Tomorrow, take the express trip back to Boston, along I-91 and Route 2 (2 hours). Leave room in your luggage for your own unique art finds!

THE *NEW* NEW ENGLAND DINING

Boston was once known as the home of the cod and the bean, but thankfully, things have significantly progressed since then. These days, those beans might easily be mixed up with Latin spices or Italian-inspired stews. And that cod might be dressed up with organic tomatoes over potato-basil puree. Here are just a few of the best ways to discover the region's bounty and specialties.

CLAM SHACK CHIC

With New England's incredible supply of fresh seafood, you could go to almost any beachside seafood shanty and get a great meal. But today, many restaurants are shaking up the seafood shack genre with newfangled and vibrant ways to cook the ocean's offerings. In Boston, **Legal Sea Foods** complements its classic seafood chowder with an adventurous menu of South Indian-spiced shrimp, tuna, and salmon. On Nantucket, **The Pearl** turns oysters into a revelation, with a cilantro sauce that leaves even the most jaded bivalve lovers addicted. Their salt-and-pepper wok-fried lobster is equally phenomenal. The menu at Newport's **Cheeky Monkey Cafe** works its way around the oceans of the world – with choices like calamari with prosciutto and pepper sauce, and a to-die-for tuna with lemongrass.

Seafood's always on the menu.

TRADITIONAL NEW ENGLAND

Even tried-and-true New England cuisine has gotten a reworking of late. To wit: **The Fireplace,** just outside of Boston. Go for the cozy room, stay for the maple-glazed pork ribs. Portland's much-loved heavy-hitter, **Fore Street,** packs people in with straight-from-the-farm dishes like wood-oven roasted mussels and grilled hanger steak – all from local sources, all inspired by simple, full-flavored New England classics. The same goes for **The White Barn Inn,** though you'll find the results far fancier. Housed in an antique-dotted old barn, the candlelit setting is downright lovely – as is the ever-changing regional menu with options like halibut over slow-cooked fennel, bacon-wrapped pork loin with butternut squash, and wild Maine blueberry cobbler.

► INTO THE WILD

The mountains and lakes of northern New England have long called to the intrepid among us to test their slopes and waters. This tour takes in the best of the rugged outdoors, concentrating on the wilder country of New Hampshire and Maine. It can be done as soon as the snow finishes thawing in April, but is best experienced in summer and fall.

Day 1

Begin in Boston to orient yourself and buy supplies. Then spend the afternoon driving

Acadia National Park

Days 4-5

Take a long drive through the western mountains of Maine to Greenville, along the shores of remote Moosehead Lake. For the most direct route, take Route 302 east to I-95, then take the exit for Route 201 north, and finally take Route 6/15 to Greenville (4 hours).

Spend the next day on the lake, canoeing, kayaking, or taking a seaplane ride. If you haven't yet seen your moose, be sure to book a moose cruise.

Days 6-7

Ask a local for directions along the bumpy back roads north to Baxter State Park (3 hours). See where the Appalachian Trail begins at Mount Katahdin, and get your hiking boots dirty on 175 miles of trails that hold something for every interest and skill level. Give yourself at least two days to enjoy the solitude of this wilderness park. Be sure to book ahead for a campsite.

up I-95 and scenic Route 16 into the heart of the White Mountains, basing yourself at Conway.

Days 2-3

Get up at the crack of dawn to climb Mount Washington, the highest peak in the Northeast. If that's too much mountain for you, you can take the cog railway to the top. Spend the night at the scenic Lake in the Clouds.

The next day, nurse sore muscles with a hike among the many outlet shops here. Or, if you can't wait to get back out into the hills, take your rock climbing gear to Cathedral Ledge, known for the best climbing in the Northeast.

Days 8-9

Backtrack down the back roads to I-95 South, then take Route 1A and 3 to the coast for a stay in breathtaking Acadia National Park (4 hours). On the first day, explore Bar Harbor or one of the small lobstering villages on the southern coast of Mount Desert Island. On the second day, drive the Park Loop, giving yourself enough time to hike along the rocky cliffs that plunge straight into the ocean.

Day 10

On the way back down the scenic Maine coast, stop off at Ogunquit for a relaxing day at the beach and a big lobster dinner before returning to Boston—you've earned it!

▶ A SHORE THING

The remote lighthouse at the end of a sandy beach is just as much a symbol of New England as Paul Revere on his horse. After the long winter, southern New England positively explodes with beach bums and boaters, who flock to the Atlantic for fun in the sun. Pristine beaches, maritime history, and plenty of greasy seafood await. . . .

Day 1

Starting out in Boston, get up close and personal with sealife at the New England Aquarium, one of the best in the world. At night, take a harbor cruise to see the city skyline the way it was meant to be seen—from the water.

Days 2-3

Book ahead to take your car on the fast ferry across Massachusetts Bay to the funky town of Provincetown (1.5 hours), known locally as P-Town, for breathtaking views, art galleries, and eclectic shops. When you tire of shopping, relax at Race Point Beach. (If you forget to book ahead for the ferry, you can drive to P-Town along I-95, I-495, and Route 6; 3 hours.)

On your second day in P-Town, take a whale-watch or deep sea-fishing charter onto the rough waves of the Atlantic. In the afternoon, tour the remote dune shacks where artists and writers have found inspiration among the shifting sands.

Day 4

Drive down Route 6 along the scenic Cape Cod Seashore to Hyannis (1.5 hours), the heart of the Cape and summer retreat of the Kennedys.

Days 5-6

In the morning, leave the car on shore and

Trees top the masts of historic vessels at Old Mystic Seaport.

take a ferry across to one of two island desti-nations, the proper and quaint Nantucket (2 hours) or the downbeat and trendy Martha's Vineyard (1 hour). Spend your first day in town exploring the quaint downtowns of Nantucket Town or Oak Bluffs. On day two, rent a bicycle and take a ride out to 'Sconset or Gay Head for a picnic on the beach. In the afternoon, visit the Nantucket Whaling Museum or go celebrity-hunting on the streets of Edgartown.

Day 7

After taking the ferry back to land, drive down the coast, along Route 6, I-95, and Route 114, to the yachting capital of Newport (1 hour). Take a walk along the dramatic Cliff Walk, and tour one of the impressive mansions.

Day 8

It's time to hit the beach, with an all-day excursion across the East Bay to the quiet sands of Sakonnet Point (1 hour), perhaps taking time out for a free sample at Sakonnet Vineyards. After you've had your fill of the beach, drive back to Newport for the night.

Day 9

Head down I-95 along the Rhode Island coast and cross into Connecticut to base yourself at the charming fishing village of Stonington (1 hour). Then take the rest of the day to raise the rigging at the reconstructed 19th-century maritime village of Old Mystic Seaport, a hands-on museum of maritime history. Be sure to grab a slice at Mystic Pizza before returning to Stonington for the night.

Day 10

One more day to get out onto the water. Drive up I-95 to the little village of Stony Creek (1 hour), where you can rent a kayak for a tour of the Thimble Islands and come face-to-face with shorebirds and maybe even a dolphin. Spend the night in Stony Creek. The next day, take I-95 back up to Boston with a boatload of happy memories (2.5 hours).

MASSACHUSETTS

BOSTON

There is something about Boston that seems to set it apart from the rest of the country. To visitors, it often feels more like a European city, with a walkable downtown littered with parks and brownstone buildings. And even while the city has erected skyscrapers to keep pace with its high-tech economy, it has kept its older buildings intact. Businessmen and bicycle messengers race past white-steepled churches and historic houses that played essential roles in the war for American Independence.

While Greater Boston ranks as the seventh-largest urban area in the country, with more than three million people, the city itself barely breaks the top 25, with just 600,000 people. To Bostonians, that makes the city exactly the right size, thank you very much—big enough that you can find most everything you need,

but small enough to get to know the major people and places in town quickly. Among them are the cultural institutions that give Boston its identity: the Boston Pops on the Fourth of July, the swan boats in the Public Garden, and the recent world-champion Boston Red Sox at Fenway Park. New symbols mark the city's drive into the 21st century, including the breathtaking Zakim Bridge and the "Big Dig"—the city's ambitious attempt to put the central expressway underground (which unfortunately has been recently beset by engineering problems).

Indeed, the city has come a long way from the days of scrod and clam chowder. The resurgence started in the late 1990s with the dot-com boom, for which Boston, with its educated populace and venture capital companies,

© TIM GRAFFT/MOTT

MASSACHUSETTS

HIGHLIGHTS

(Freedom Trail: Follow the redbrick road from Boston Common to Bunker Hill (page 30).

(New England Aquarium: Sharks, penguins, and other ocean-dwellers await at this waterfront museum (page 44).

(Mapparium: A 30-foot-wide stained-glass globe of the world is one of the more unusual spaces in the city (page 51).

(Fenway Park: From the Green Monster to the bleachers, this ball field is a living shrine (page 52).

(Museum of Fine Arts: The French Impressionist paintings and Asian sculpture here are among the best anywhere (page 53).

(Isabella Stewart Gardner Museum: This Victorian jewel-box of a museum is as acclaimed for its building as for its art (page 54).

(Harvard Museum of Natural History: Meticulously hand-blown glass flowers are just the beginning of the wonders on display here (page 62).

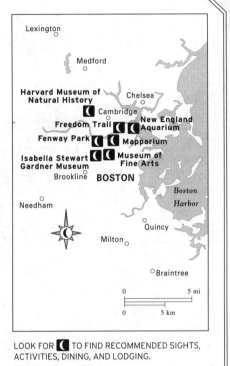

LOOK FOR (TO FIND RECOMMENDED SIGHTS, ACTIVITIES, DINING, AND LODGING.

was especially poised. Even after the dot-com bubble popped, however, the revitalization of downtown has continued, with million-dollar condos springing up on block after block and a bumper crop of inventive restaurants, hip lounges, and international boutiques. The result is a new cosmopolitan air that has improved upon, not replaced, the historic charms of the city and made Boston one of the most enjoyable cities in (or not in) America.

PLANNING YOUR TIME
You could spend a week exploring all that Boston has to offer. The city's small size, however, makes it easy to see different parts of the city on the same trip, no matter how much time you have. The only mandatory sightseeing is a

walk along the **Freedom Trail,** which connects all of downtown's Revolutionary War sites. The city's cultural attractions, for the most part, are grouped on the outskirts of downtown in the Back Bay, South End, and Fenway districts. Art buffs can choose between several very different museums—the world-class **Museum of Fine Arts,** the charming **Isabella Stewart Gardner Museum,** and the cutting-edge **Institute of Contemporary Art.** For sports fans of any age, a tour of **Fenway Park** is essential. And in planning meals, it's important to note that while nearly all restaurants are open year-round, many of the city's upscale dining rooms do not serve lunch and many do not serve breakfast. When in doubt, call ahead.

Even on a short trip, it's worth getting across

MASSACHUSETTS

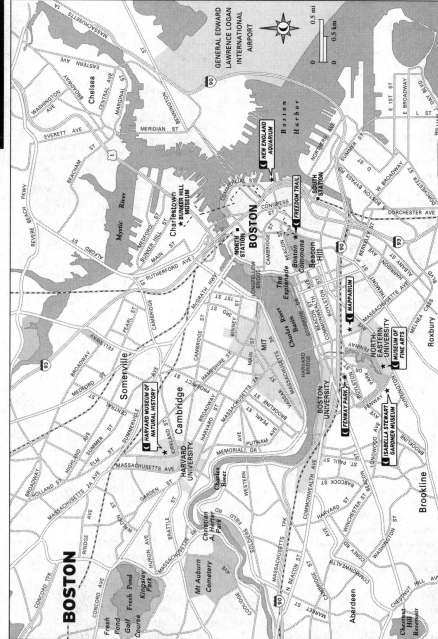

BOSTON

GENERAL EDWARD
LAWRENCE LOGAN
INTERNATIONAL
AIRPORT

0.5 mi
0   0.5 km

© AVALON TRAVEL

Chelsea

Boston Harbor

NEW ENGLAND AQUARIUM

BUNKER HILL MUSEUM

Charlestown

FREEDOM TRAIL

SOUTH STATION

BOSTON

NORTH STATION

Boston Commons

Beacon Hill

The Esplanade

MAPPARIUM

NORTH EASTERN UNIVERSITY

MUSEUM OF FINE ARTS

Roxbury

Somerville

HARVARD MUSEUM OF NATURAL HISTORY

Cambridge

HARVARD UNIVERSITY

BOSTON UNIVERSITY

FENWAY PARK

ISABELLA STEWART GARDNER MUSEUM

Brookline

Charles River

Christian A. Herter Park

Mt. Auburn Cemetery

Kingsley Park

Fresh Pond

Fresh Pond Golf Course

Aberdeen

Chestnut Hill Reservoir

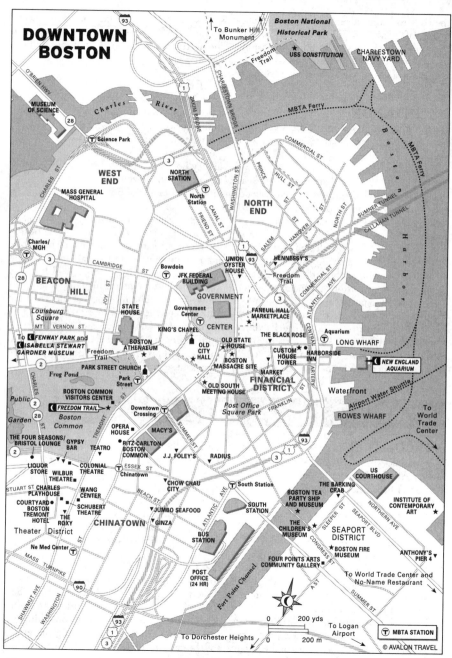

DOWNTOWN BOSTON

To Bunker Hill Monument

Boston National Historical Park

Freedom Trail

USS *CONSTITUTION*

CHARLESTOWN NAVY YARD

O'BRIEN HWY

MUSEUM OF SCIENCE

Charles River

CHARLES ST

28 Science Park

WEST END

MASS GENERAL HOSPITAL

NORTH STATION

North Station

ZAKIM BRIDGE

CHARLESTOWN BRIDGE

WASHINGTON ST

MBTA Ferry

COMMERCIAL ST

PRINCE ST

HULL ST

HANOVER ST

SALEM ST

NORTH END

NORTH ST

SUMNER TUNNEL

CALLAHAN TUNNEL

Boston Harbor

MBTA Ferry

Charles/MGH

BEACON HILL

CAMBRIDGE ST

JOY ST

Bowdoin

JFK FEDERAL BUILDING

UNION OYSTER HOUSE

HENNESSY'S

93

Freedom Trail

COMMERCIAL ST

ATLANTIC AVE

CANAL ST

FRIEND ST

Louisburg Square

MT. VERNON ST

STATE HOUSE

GOVERNMENT

Government Center

CENTER

FANEUIL HALL MARKETPLACE

CENTRAL ARTERY

To FENWAY PARK and ISABELLA STEWART GARDNER MUSEUM

Freedom Trail

BOSTON ATHENAEUM

KING'S CHAPEL

OLD CITY HALL

OLD STATE HOUSE

THE BLACK ROSE

Aquarium

LONG WHARF

CUSTOM HOUSE TOWER

HARBORSIDE INN

NEW ENGLAND AQUARIUM

PARK STREET CHURCH

Frog Pond

Park Street

BOSTON MASSACRE SITE

MARKET

FINANCIAL DISTRICT

Waterfront

Public

BOSTON COMMON VISITORS CENTER

OLD SOUTH MEETING HOUSE

Post Office Square Park

Airport Water Shuttle

Garden

FREEDOM TRAIL

Boston Common

Downtown Crossing

FRANKLIN

ROWES WHARF

To World Trade Center

OPERA HOUSE

MACY'S

SUMMER ST

TREMONT ST

93

THE FOUR SEASONS/BRISTOL LOUNGE

GYPSY BAR

RITZ-CARLTON BOSTON COMMON

TEATRO

J.J. FOLEY'S

RADIUS

US COURTHOUSE

LIQUOR STORE

WILBUR THEATRE

COLONIAL THEATRE

ESSEX ST

Chinatown

CHOW CHAU CITY

South Station

THE BARKING CRAB

INSTITUTE OF CONTEMPORARY ART

STUART ST

CHARLES PLAYHOUSE

WANG CENTER

BEACH ST

BOSTON TEA PARTY SHIP AND MUSEUM

SLEEPER ST

SEAPORT BLVD

NORTHERN AVE

COURTYARD BOSTON TREMONT HOTEL

SCHUBERT THEATRE

JUMBO SEAFOOD

SOUTH STATION

ATLANTIC AVE

THE CHILDREN'S MUSEUM

SEAPORT DISTRICT

THE ROXY

GINZA

CHINATOWN

Theater District

Ne Med Center

BUS STATION

CONGRESS ST

BOSTON FIRE MUSEUM

ANTHONY'S PIER 4

MASS TURNPIKE

SHAWMUT AVE

WASHINGTON ST

90

POST OFFICE (24 HR)

Fort Point Channel

FOUR POINTS ARTS COMMUNITY GALLERY

A ST

SUMMER ST

To World Trade Center and No-Name Restaurant

93

1

3

To Dorchester Heights

0 — 200 yds
0 — 200 m

To Logan Airport

MBTA STATION

© AVALON TRAVEL

the river to Cambridge, Boston's more bohemian "left bank." In addition to a more laid-back vibe, this sister city is home to Boston's most elite cultural institutions—Harvard University and the Massachusetts Institute of Technology.

ORIENTATION

Boston's quirky geography has caused more than a few headaches to visitors trying to keep its twisting roads straight. The bulk of the downtown still takes up the Shawmut Peninsula, with Boston Common as its beating green heart. The downtown neighborhoods are organized around the Common, with Beacon Hill and North End to the north, the Financial District and Downtown to the east, and the Back Bay and South End to the south. East Boston, along with Logan International Airport, is across Boston Harbor to the northeast, while South Boston and the new Seaport District form a peninsula to the southeast. Farther to the south are the city's ethnic residential communities, including Roxbury, Dorchester, and Jamaica Plain. Even farther south is the separate city of Quincy, while west of the Fenway is the chic Brookline, a

separate town despite being almost completely surrounded by Boston. Across the river to the north are intellectual Cambridge and hip Somerville.

SAFETY

Once upon a time it was foolhardy to walk around downtown Boston at night—especially in the blocks between Downtown Crossing and Chinatown colorfully known as the "Combat Zone." Now the Combat Zone is home to a luxury hotel, and with a little common sense it's safe to walk downtown at any hour. Keep in mind that because of Boston bars' early closing times of 1 or 2 A.M., the streets can seem somewhat empty during the early morning hours. It's probably a good idea to avoid crossing Boston Common after midnight. Most of the outlying neighborhoods are also safe to walk in at night, with the exception of parts of Roxbury and Dorchester, including Dudley Square, Grove Hall, Upham's Corner, and Franklin Park (though these areas are safe enough during the day). Most subway lines and stations are safe until closing at 12:30 A.M.; however, use caution for the stations on the Orange Line between Massachusetts Avenue and Forest Hills.

Sights

BEACON HILL

Victorian novelist Henry James and 1990's TV lawyer Ally McBeal felt equally at home on Beacon Hill, which rises steeply on the north side of Boston Common. This is the neighborhood that springs to most people's minds when they think "Boston": gas streetlamps lit 24 hours a day and cobblestone alleyways lined with brick Federal-style townhouses that are home to some of Boston's richest residents.

The most exclusive address on the hill is Louisburg Square, where wrought-iron railings surround a park of beech and alder trees, and wealthy Bostonians including Senator (and 2004 presidential contender) John Kerry make their homes. A block south of the square,

go ahead and snap a shot of the picturesque cobblestone alley of Acorn Street, supposedly the most photographed street in the world. At the bottom of the hill on the east is commercial Charles Street, where doyennes with small dogs shop in a profusion of antiques stores, and young lawyers in the mold of Ally take their laptops to cafés on weekends.

◖ Freedom Trail

It's easy now to look back on the Sons of Liberty as just a bunch of guys in funny hats and breeches, shooting off muskets and complaining about tea. But there is something undoubtedly stirring about visiting the graves of the early revolutionaries and sitting in the

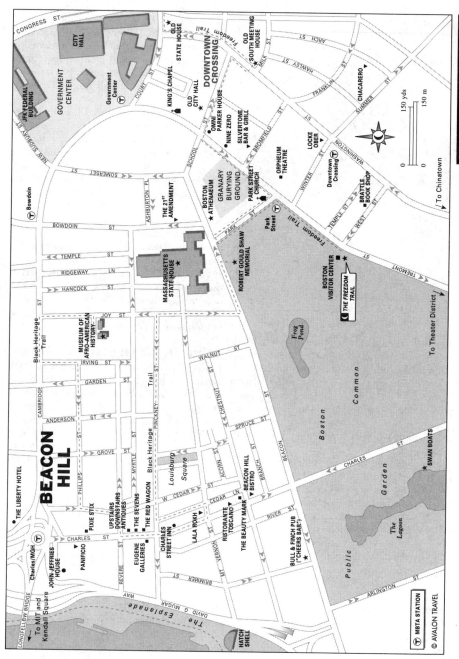

CONGRESS ST

CITY HALL

GOVERNMENT CENTER

Government Center Ⓣ

JFK FEDERAL BUILDING

NEW SUDBURY ST

OLD STATE HOUSE ★

Freedom Trail

DOWNTOWN CROSSING

OLD SOUTH MEETING HOUSE

ARCH ST

MILK ST

HAWLEY ST

FRANKLIN ST

CHACARERO ▶

SUMMER ST

KING'S CHAPEL ★ ■

COURT ST

OLD CITY HALL ★

OMNI PARKER HOUSE ■

NINE ZERO ▶

SILVERTONE BAR & GRILL ▶

BROMFIELD ST

LOCKE OBER ▶

150 yds

150 m

0

0

WASHINGTON ST

Ⓣ Bowdoin

SCHOOL ST

SOMERSET ST

ASHBURTON PL

THE 21ST AMENDMENT ▶

BOSTON ATHENAEUM ★

GRANARY BURYING GROUND

PARK STREET CHURCH ■

ORPHEUM THEATRE ■

WINTER ST

Downtown Crossing Ⓣ

BRATTLE BOOK SHOP ■

WEST ST

TEMPLE ST

To Chinatown

BOWDOIN ST

PARK ST

Park Street Ⓣ

Freedom Trail

TEMPLE ST

RIDGEWAY LN

HANCOCK ST

MASSACHUSETTS STATE HOUSE ★

ROBERT GOULD SHAW MEMORIAL ★

BOSTON VISITOR CENTER ■

★ THE FREEDOM TRAIL

TREMONT ST

To Theater District

JOY ST

Black Heritage Trail

MUSEUM OF AFRO-AMERICAN HISTORY ★

IRVING ST

GARDEN ST

CAMBRIDGE ST

ANDERSON ST

Trail

WALNUT ST

Frog Pond

CHESTNUT ST

Boston Common

THE LIBERTY HOTEL ●

BEACON HILL

GROVE ST

MYRTLE ST

Black Heritage Trail

Louisburg Square

PINCKNEY ST

SPRUCE ST

BEACON ST

CHARLES ST

Public Garden

SWAN BOATS ★

PHILLIPS ST

Charles/MGH Ⓣ

UPSTAIRS DOWNSTAIRS ANTIQUES ■

PIXIE STIX ●

THE SEVENS ■

THE RED WAGON ▶

W. CEDAR ST

CEDAR LN

LALA ROKH ▶

ACORN ST

BEACON HILL BISTRO ▶

RIVER ST

BRANCH ST

The Lagoon

JOHN JEFFRIES HOUSE ●

PANIFICIO ▶

CHARLES ST

EUGENE GALLERIES ●

CHARLES STREET INN ●

RISTORANTE TOSCANO ▶

THE BEAUTY MARK ●

BULL & FINCH PUB ('CHEERS BAR') ▶

ARLINGTON ST

LONGFELLOW BRIDGE

To MIT and Kendall Square

REVERE ST

MT. VERNON ST

BRIMMER ST

DAVID G MUGAR WAY

The Esplanade

HATCH SHELL

Ⓣ MBTA STATION

© AVALON TRAVEL

© TIM GRAFFT/MOTT

Acorn Street, Beacon Hill

11 A.M., noon, 1 P.M., 3:30 P.M., and 4:30 P.M. daily, $12 adults, $10 students and seniors, $6 children) that covers the first eleven sites along the route in the company of a costumed actor playing one of the lesser-known patriots such as William Dawes, Abigail Adams, or James Otis.

Perhaps the best way to take in the trail is to book the morning tour, then stop for lunch at the Quincy Market food court or a trattoria in the North End. After lunch, continue along by yourself to the sites in the North End and Charlestown, taking the ferry back to Boston; or return back along the way you came, taking more time to explore the inside of the Old State House, the Old South Meeting House, and the Massachusetts State House. The foundation also offers two-hour self-guided audio tours, with sound effects and voices of historians to bring the trail to life ($15). Since part of the fun of the trail is experiencing the contrast between Revolutionary Boston and the sights and sounds of the modern city, however, the headphone tours can be a bit insulating.

Boston National Historical Park

Seven of the sites along the Freedom Trail, along with the additional site of Dorchester Heights in South Boston, have also been incorporated into a national park (Charlestown Navy Yard, Charlestown, 617/242-5642 or 617/242-5601, www.nps.gov/bost). The park has visitors centers at the USS *Constitution,* Bunker Hill, and 15 State Street, across from the Old State House. From that site, rangers lead 90-minute tours (2 P.M. Mon.–Fri., 10 A.M., 2 P.M., and 3 P.M. Sat.–Sun. mid-Apr.–mid-June; 10 A.M., 2 P.M., and 3 P.M. daily mid-June–Aug.) that take in five sites along the Freedom Trail. The rangers are not quite as entertaining as the costumed actors from the Freedom Trail Foundation, but their tours have the additional appeal of being free.

Boston Common

The Common began its life as a sheep and cow pasture in 1634, just a few years after the city itself was founded. By Puritan law, it was

pews of the church where they first thundered their speeches that brings alive the true passion of the American Revolution. In fact, the days leading up to the War for Independence were less like a noble war for freedom and more like a running mob insurrection. The few passionate men and women who worked to rile up a reluctant populace are very accessible, and it's easy to get drawn into their stories—both those you know and those you don't.

In the 1960s, Boston made it easier to trace the history of the Revolution by connecting 16 historical attractions in downtown Boston with a red line, alternately painted on the sidewalk and embedded in it with a double line of brick. From Boston Common to the Bunker Hill Monument, the trail stretches for two and a half miles, with each site designated by a bronze medallion in the pavement. Visitors can walk the line themselves or hook up with a 90-minute guided tour offered by the **Freedom Trail Foundation** (Boston Common Visitor Information Center, 148 Tremont St., 617/357-8300, www.thefreedomtrail.org,

CHEERS!

© MICHAEL BLANDING

A familiar sign marks Cheers' Faneuil Hall location.

Beware the imposters found in corners all over town: There's only one Boston bar that inspired the hit sitcom **Cheers**, and it's located on Beacon Street (#84, 617/227-0150, www.cheersboston.com, 11 A.M.-10 P.M. or midnight depending on business). For years the bar/restaurant was called The Bull & Finch Pub (as it had been since it first opened), but recently changed its name to Cheers Beacon Hill – one presumes to establish itself as the undisputable, original basis for the show. While the exterior of the bar was used in the show's opening, the interior is almost completely different from the show's set. So while visitors shouldn't come expecting to see Sam or Woody mixing up martinis, they can fully expect to find "Sam's Starters" and "Woody's Garden Goodies" on the menu. That may not be quite as funny, but they certainly can be tasty – just ask the regulars on the other side of the bar. If it's the *feeling* of *Cheers* you're after, then line up with the rest of the nostalgia-seekers at the restaurant's newer Faneuil Hall location (Quincy Market, Southwest Cafe, 617/227-0150, 11:30 A.M.-10 P.M. or midnight depending on business, Mon.-Thu.; opens 11 A.M. Fri.-Sun.), which has been designed to look like an exact replica of the set – right down to the picture of Geronimo hanging on the wall.

legal for any resident of the city to graze their livestock on the common land. Alas, that law was repealed in 1833, so you'll have to leave your cows at home. Within the boundaries of the park, however, are 44 acres of gently hilly grassland, occupied on sunny days by residents lying on the grass or playing Frisbee.

Several monuments within the park are attractions in and of themselves. The stunning fountain located just a few steps down from Park Street towards Boylston is named Brewer Fountain, and is a bronze replica of a fountain exhibited at the Paris World's Fair of 1855. The objects on its base depict sea gods and goddesses

© MICHAEL BLANDING

Francis Parkman Bandstand in Boston Common

Neptune, Amphitrite, Acis, and Galatea. Near the intersection of Park and Beacon Streets, the Frog Pond becomes winter's prime location for ice skating in the center of the city. On the Tremont Street side, at the intersection with Boylston, the Francis Parkman Bandstand is used as the site for summer concerts, political rallies, and Shakespeare in the Park.

Massachusetts State House

On a sunny day, the shimmering gold dome of the state's capitol building can be seen from miles around. The brick building beneath it is a tidy Federal structure (617/727-3676, www.sec. state.ma.us/trs, 10 A.M.–3:30 P.M. daily, free) designed by prominent Boston architect Charles Bullfinch and built in 1798. At the time, fifteen white columns were pulled up Beacon Street in a procession of 15 white horses, one for each state. The wooden dome on top was gilded in copper by Revolutionary renaissance man Paul Revere in 1802, and re-covered with 23-karat gold leaf in 1948. Two marble wings were added at the turn of the 20th century.

An impressive selection of statutes graces the park side of the building. The equestrian statue in front of the main entrance depicts Joseph "Fighting Joe" Hooker, a Civil War general from Massachusetts who led the Army of the Potomac for all of six months. (There is no basis, however, to the urban myth that "hookers" are named after his troops, who were supposedly wont to visit brothels while on leave.) Other statues in front of the building are dedicated to 19th-century orator Daniel Webster and educator Horace Mann. In front of the wings are statues of two women martyrs: Anne Hutchinson, a freethinking Puritan who was banished to Rhode Island; and Mary Dyer, a prominent Quaker minister sadly hanged on Boston Common in 1660.

There isn't much to see inside the building, outside of more statues of various Massachusetts politicians. The most appealing item of interest is the "sacred Cod," a five-foot-long pinewood fish that hangs over the chamber of the state House of Representatives. Given to the state by a Boston merchant in 1784, it changes direction depending on which party is in control of the legislature. Free tours of the State House, lasting approximately 40 minutes, are offered daily; advanced reservations are required.

Robert Gould Shaw Memorial and the Black Heritage Trail

Across from the State House is the life-sized bronze bas-relief plaque of Colonel Robert Gould Shaw designed by New England sculptor Augustus Saint-Gaudens. Considered one of the best American sculptures of the 19th century, it depicts the commander of the first all-Black regiment to fight during the Civil War, marching out of Boston with his troops in March 1863. Two months later, Shaw and 271 of his men were killed during a suicide mission on Fort Wagner in South Carolina, galvanizing the country with the bravery of his Black soldiers. (Later, his story was immortalized in the Academy Award–winning 1989 film *Glory*.) The sculpture is a surprisingly realistic depiction of Shaw atop his horse, surrounded by soldiers carrying rifles, backpacks, and bedrolls. Above them is an angel with an olive branch, symbolizing peace, and poppies, symbolizing death.

The Shaw Memorial is the beginning of the Black Heritage Trail, a lesser-known path that traces the separate journey to freedom of Black Americans, nearly one hundred years after the first freedom trail. Plaques at historic houses en route detail the lives of abolitionists and orators who lived on the back side of Beacon Hill, where Boston's free Black community numbered more than a thousand by the turn of the 19th century. The trail ends at the African Meeting House, once headquarters of the New England Anti-Slavery Society and called the "Black Faneuil Hall" for the impassioned speeches by William Lloyd Garrison and other abolitionists heard within. The church now houses the **Museum of Afro-American History** (46 Joy Street, 617/720-2991 x14, www.afroammuseum.org, 10 A.M.–4 P.M. Mon.–Sat., $5 suggested donation), which has exhibits and films dedicated to the story of Boston's abolitionists. The trail is also part of the Boston **African-American National Historic Site** (617/742-5415, www.nps.gov/boaf), run by the National Park Service, which offers free tours on request.

Boston Athenaeum

The center of intellectual life during Boston's golden age in the early 19th century was this private library located near the State House, where scholars such as Ralph Waldo Emerson and Oliver Wendell Holmes gathered to debate the political and philosophical issues of the day. Today, docents offer tours of the renovated building (10 ½ Beacon St., 617/227-0270, www.bostonathenaeum.org, 8:30 A.M.–8 P.M. Mon. and Wed., 8:30 A.M.–5:30 P.M. Tues., Thu., and Fri. year-round; 9 A.M.–4 P.M. Sat. Sept. 12–May 22, free), including the study where Nathaniel Hawthorne reportedly saw the ghost of an old friend. Among the library's more unusual holdings is the private library of George Washington, and one of the world's largest collections of books about the Romany people (commonly known as gypsies). Tours are

offered at 3 P.M. on Tuesdays and Thursdays and require reservations.

Park Street Church

The landmark church at the corner of Park and Tremont Streets is one of the most recognizable meeting places downtown. Dating from 1809, the church (1 Park St., 617/523-3383, www.parkstreet.org) touts itself as the location of the first Sunday School and first place where the song *America (My Country'Tis of Thee)* was publicly sung. During the War of 1812, the church was known as "brimstone corner" for the gunpowder stored in the basement. Later, the brimstone came from the fiery speeches of its ministers, a tradition continued by its current evangelical congregation.

Granary Burying Ground

The bar across the street from this graveyard bills itself as the only place you can drink a Samuel Adams beer while looking out the window at the grave of Samuel Adams. Many of the leaders of the Sons of Liberty are buried in this prime piece of real estate amid the office buildings at Tremont and Park Streets. In addition to Adams, those with a final resting place here include Paul Revere, John Hancock, the victims of the Boston Massacre, and Ben Franklin's parents. (Despite the large Franklin monument, Ben's remains are in Philadelphia.) Also look out for the grave of the original nursery rhymer, Mary "Mother" Goose. The grave markers of the patriots all date from the 20th century—the originals were either stolen or "lost." However, many of the gravestones here date from the 17th century. Their weatherbeaten forms are in a classic "tombstone" shape, often with eerie winged death skulls at their tops.

King's Chapel

A smaller and more crowded burying ground is across the street next to Boston's original Anglican church (Tremont and School Streets, Boston, 617/523-1749 or 617/227-2155, www.kings-chapel.org, 1:30–4 P.M. Sun., 10 A.M.–4 P.M. Mon., Thurs., and Fri.–Sat.,

10 A.M.–11:15 A.M. and 1:30–4 P.M. Tues.–Wed. late May–early Sep.; 10 A.M.–4 P.M. Sat., 1:30–4 P.M. Sun. mid Sep.–late May, 10 A.M.–4 P.M. Fri. Sep. and May, $2 suggested donation), founded in 1686. (Needless to say, it wasn't a popular place in a community founded by Puritans who fled the Church of England.) The current stone church building was built in 1749 and features a bell cast by Paul Revere that is still rung before services. The adjoining graveyard is the oldest in Boston; as such, it contains the graves of some of the original colonists of Massachusetts, including governor John "City on A Hill" Winthrop, and Anne Prine, said to be the real Hester Prynne on whom Nathaniel Hawthorne based his book *The Scarlet Letter.* Along with them are several "B-list" patriots, such as William Dawes, the "other rider" who raised the alarm on the eve of the battles of Concord and Lexington.

DOWNTOWN CROSSING

Few places in Boston are more democratic than the neighborhood known as Downtown Crossing. Down Summer Street from the Park Street T stop, this is an almost entirely commercial district that has been mostly closed to car traffic. After school, teenagers congregate here to flirt and buy clothing and music at the many discount stores lining Washington Street. The bargains here aren't just for schoolkids, however. In-the-know Bostonians raid Filene's Basement, the original "bargain basement" clothing store, for last season's fashions at cut-rate prices.

Architecturally speaking, Downtown Crossing is strikingly uniform in its solid brick-and-granite office buildings, with lovingly detailed sculpted friezes, curlicued cornices, and grand engravings. That uniformity is due to the Great Fire of 1872, when a chance warehouse fire grew to a conflagration that leveled the neighborhood. Flush with money from the China trade, rich merchants rebuilt the neighborhood in a matter of only a few years. One of the buildings that survived the fire is the Old Corner Bookstore, at 3 School Street, which once hosted transcendentalist writers including

Ralph Waldo Emerson, Henry David Thoreau, and Bronson Alcott as regular guests.

Old City Hall

Before Boston City Hall was moved to its current location at Government Center, a succession of three different city halls occupied a site on School Street between Tremont and Washington. The last building (45 School Street, 617/523-8678, www.oldcityhall.com), built at the end of the Civil War, is a perfectly preserved example of Second Empire style, with a wedding-cake layer of columns beneath a sloping mansard roof. (It has long been adapted for use as an office building.) In the courtyard is a statue of Benjamin Franklin, looking as if he popped right out of a history book, along with two whimsical statues that represent the mascots of the two political parties—a donkey for Democrats and an elephant for Republicans.

On the sidewalk in front of the building, be sure to note the plaque that designates the original location of the Boston Latin School, the first public school in America, which gave its name to the street and still exists in a new location in the Fenway. Among its graduates are Samuel Adams, Ben Franklin, Ralph Waldo Emerson, and Leonard Bernstein. The plaque itself is in the form of a hopscotch board, surrounded by the letters of the alphabet designated by their appropriate objects (apple, bird, cat...). Particularly Bostonian is the grasshopper representing G, which is copied from the weathervane on top of Faneuil Hall.

Old South Meeting House

The Boston Tea Party may have ended in the harbor, but it started at this brick church building with a grey-shingled tower (310 Washington St., 617/482-6439, www.old-southmeetinghouse.org, 10 A.M.–4 P.M. daily Nov.–Mar., 9:30 A.M.–5 P.M. daily Apr.–Oct., $5 adults, $4 students and seniors, $1 children 6–18, free children under 6) dating from 1729. Led by Samuel Adams, some 6,000 patriots gathered here on the night of December 16, 1773, flooding out into the street. After fiery

© MICHAEL BLANDING
Old South Meeting House

who were all members of the Old South's congregation.

Old State House

Before construction of the new state house on Beacon Hill, British and American governors alike used this small brick building (206 Washington Street, 617/720-1713, www.bostonhistory.org, 9 A.M.–6 P.M. daily Jul.–Aug., 9 A.M.–4 P.M. daily Jan., 9 A.M.–5 P.M. daily Feb.–Jun., Sep.–Dec., $7 adults, $6 seniors and students, $3 children 6–18, free children under 6) as the headquarters for the Massachusetts government. Now dwarfed by the office towers around it, the cupola atop the center of the building used to be the highest point in Boston. On one side of the building are replicas of the standing lion and unicorn that signified the crown of England (the originals were torn down during the Revolution), while on the other is a gold-covered eagle signifying the new United States. On the second floor of the building is the headquarters for the Bostonian Society, which runs a small museum full of artifacts including tea from the Boston Tea Party, weapons from the Battle of Bunker Hill, and clothing worn by John Hancock. It also exhibits a Boston Massacre "sound and light show."

Boston Massacre Site

In front of the Old State House, on a traffic circle in the busy intersection of Congress and State Streets, an unadorned circle of grey bricks marks the site of the Boston Massacre, where five colonists were killed by a British soldier in 1770. (The actual site is in the middle of the intersection, but, as guides are wont to tell tourists, don't visit it unless you want to fall victim to "another Boston massacre.") The first victim of the Revolution was arguably Christopher Snider, a 12-year-old boy shot by a British loyalist after a protest over the trade acts. Two weeks later, on March 5, 1770, a mob protesting Snider's death converged on the Old State House, throwing snowballs laced with stones and oyster shells at the soldiers, and later returning with bats and sticks. Soldiers answered by firing their rifles into the crowd,

speeches, Adams spoke the code words, "This meeting can do no more to save our country." Those words were a signal to certain members of the audience to don face paint and feathers and head down to Griffin's Wharf, where three ships stood loaded down with bins of loose tea. In all, $33,000 of tea was thrown into the harbor, setting the stage for the battles that followed. (As a postscript, when Queen Elizabeth II visited Boston for the Bicentennial in 1976, the mayor of the city presented her with a check for $33,000 to cover the cost of the tea—not counting interest.)

The Old South still serves as a meeting place of sorts, offering lectures and classical music concerts of a less revolutionary nature. It is also home to a museum that traces the events surrounding the tea party through an "audio exhibit" that features actors reading the words of Sam Adams and the other patriots along with sound effects to re-create the time period. A separate multimedia exhibit dubbed "Voices of Protests" focuses on Adams, statesman Ben Franklin, and abolitionist Phyllis Wheatley,

© MICHAEL BLANDING

A circle of bricks in front of the Old State House marks the Boston Massacre site.

and when the smoke cleared, five colonists lay dead, including Crispus Attucks, a former slave and whaler of Black and Native American descent. The soldiers were later exonerated of the charges on the basis of self-defense. But the image of the "massacre" that stuck in the minds of the people was an engraving made by Paul Revere, which shows the soldiers firing unprovoked into a defenseless crowd.

GOVERNMENT CENTER

Further up Tremont Street, the neighborhood around Boston City Hall was once known as Scollay Square, an area synonymous with debauchery for its mix of bars and burlesque clubs that entertained soldiers returning from World War II. All good things come to an end, however, and Scollay Square met its end in the 1960s, when the entire area was razed for a massive urban redevelopment scheme to create a new center of city government. The result is generally agreed to be a disaster, a windswept plaza of concrete, with the hulking modernist form of Boston City Hall shipwrecked in the

center. In recent years, city planners have attempted to improve the area with the addition of a new T station and a covered arcade, but the area is what it is: ugly and depressing.

A considerably more pleasing example of urban renewal is down behind city hall in the bustling center of Quincy Marketplace. Once a derelict collection of old fish warehouses behind the historic Faneuil Hall, the area was transformed in the 1970s to become a pedestrian paradise along the lines of London's Covent Garden. The gamble was wildly successful, and the marketplace is still crowded at all times of the day and night with shoppers poking into the many upscale chains or watching the street performers who juggle and do magic tricks on the flagstone plaza in front of the main market building. That building is also home to an immense "food corridor" that seems to stretch forever with stalls on either side offering clam chowder, pizza, rotisserie chicken, and anything else your hunger pangs might ask for. Many of the stalls are branches of restaurants elsewhere in the city, making the quality of the offerings better than most food courts.

Faneuil Hall

Spelling the name of this landmark public building is a rite of passage for Boston schoolchildren. Named after one of the wealthiest of Boston's merchants, Peter Faneuil, the building (Congress St, 617/523-1300, www.cityofboston.gov/freedomtrail/faneuilhall.asp, 9 A.M.–5 P.M. daily, free) demonstrated Yankee thrift and mercantile ingenuity by serving two purposes. Downstairs was a public food market, full of stalls for meat, vegetables, milk, and cheese, while upstairs was a meeting hall for discussion of pressing local issues. When the hall was built in 1742, the most pressing issues were taxation on goods by the British government, and Faneuil Hall became the main meeting space for protests and discussions by the Sons of Liberty—earning it the nickname the "Cradle of Liberty." After it was expanded in size by architect Charles Bullfinch, the hall was also the main venue for talks by William

Lloyd Garrison, Frederick Douglass, and other anti-slavery activists. Public talks and citywide meetings are still held in the upstairs hall, lent more gravitas by the huge mural of Daniel Webster arguing against slavery that overlooks the stage. During the day, historic talks are given by National Park rangers every half hour. Downstairs, the stalls still exist, even though they have long since stopped selling food products; most are now the venue for souvenirs and other made-in-Boston goods.

NORTH END

The scent of marinara sauce wafts inescapably over the neighborhood that juts out into the harbor on the north side of the city. Congested and lively, the North End is Boston's answer to New York's Little Italy, with dozens of Italian restaurants, grocers, pastry shops, and small businesses such as tailors and cobblers lining every inch of storefront space. The area is the oldest part of the city, and claims as its own a number of Puritans and revolutionaries, including Paul Revere, whose house still stands.

At the turn of the 20th century, however, it became the firm territory of a new wave of Italian immigrants who made the neighborhood over in the image of Napoli. Even while it has slowly gentrified over the years, it has retained its ethnic identity, with third- and fourth-generation Italians choosing to age in place or returning on Italian Feast Days, which usually occur on Sundays during the summer and feature churches and community clubs attempting to outdo each other with lavish parades full of floats, bunting, and sizzling Italian sausage.

To the east of the North End proper is North Station, one of the main transit hubs of the city. Built partially over the station, the TD Banknorth Garden is the official home of the Boston Celtics and Bruins—though many still lament the passing of the original Boston Garden that was located next door, the site of the many championship banners that Boston brought home with the help of a few Larry Bird three-pointers.

Paul Revere House

Every town in New England, it seems, claims

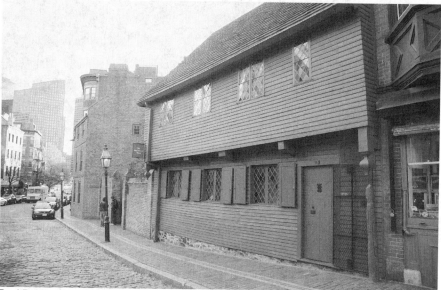

Paul Revere House

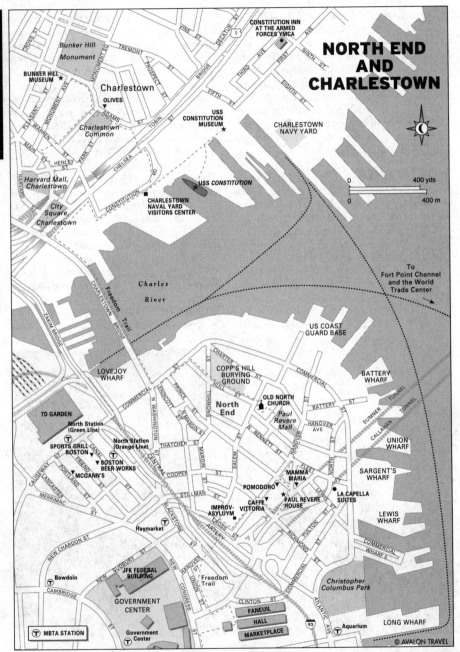

NORTH END AND CHARLESTOWN

CONSTITUTION INN AT THE ARMED FORCES YMCA

Bunker Hill Monument

BUNKER HILL MUSEUM ★

Charlestown

OLIVES ▼

Charlestown Common

USS CONSTITUTION MUSEUM ★

CHARLESTOWN NAVY YARD

Harvard Mall, Charlestown

City Square, Charlestown

CONSTITUTION RD

USS CONSTITUTION ✚

■ CHARLESTOWN NAVAL YARD VISITORS CENTER

Charles River

To Fort Point Channel and the World Trade Center

0   400 yds
0   400 m

US COAST GUARD BASE

Freedom Trail

ZAKIM BRIDGE

CHARLESTOWN BRIDGE

LOVEJOY WHARF

COMMERCIAL

COPP'S HILL BURYING GROUND

BATTERY WHARF

North End

OLD NORTH CHURCH ▲

Paul Revere Mall

SUMNER TUNNEL

CALLAHAN TUNNEL

UNION WHARF

TD GARDEN

North Station (Green Line) ⓣ

SPORTS GRILL BOSTON ▼

North Station (Orange Line) ⓣ

BOSTON BEER WORKS ▼

MCGANN'S ▼

HANOVER AVE

SARGENT'S WHARF

MAMMA MARIA ▼

POMODORO ▼

LA CAPELLA SUITES ●

LEWIS WHARF

IMPROV-ASYLUYM

CAFFÈ VITTORIA ▼

PAUL REVERE HOUSE ★

COMMERCIAL WHARF E

Haymarket ⓣ

Bowdoin ⓣ

JFK FEDERAL BUILDING

Freedom Trail

Christopher Columbus Park

GOVERNMENT CENTER

CAMBRIDGE

CLINTON

FANEUIL HALL MARKETPLACE

Aquarium ⓣ

LONG WHARF

ⓣ MBTA STATION

Government Center ⓣ

© AVALON TRAVEL

ZAKIM BRIDGE

Despite the construction debacle Boston's "Big Dig" has become, the project does have one soaring success story: the stunning double-wishbone towers of the Leonard P. Zakim Bunker Hill Bridge. Raised in 2002 to connect Boston to Charlestown, the bridge provides a beautiful backdrop to the North End, and serves as a bona fide engineering marvel as well. Building it in a tangle of highways that was notoriously difficult to bridge, engineers solved the conundrum by running eight lanes between the center of the wishbones, and cantilevering an extra two lanes on one side. The resulting asymmetrical design is the widest cable-stayed bridge in the world, and has quickly formed a stirring of attachment and pride akin to what San Franciscans feel for the Golden Gate. Its asymmetrical mouthful of a name, however, is a result of classic Boston infighting. Liberal Bostonians wanted to name the bridge after Jewish civil rights activist Lenny Zakim, while working-class conservatives from Charlestown felt strongly about honoring the nearby site of the Battle of Bunker Hill. In the end, lawmakers split the difference by combining the two monikers with the result that, depending on which side of the bridge you are standing on, you may hear it called by a different name. So much for bridging over divides!

© MICHAEL BLANDING

Zakim Bridge

to have a bell cast by Paul Revere in its belfry, if not a genuine piece of Revere silver in its historical museum. The patriot who made the famous midnight ride to warn the suburbs of the British march, however, was virtually unknown until before the Civil War, when Massachusetts poet Henry Wadsworth Longfellow made him the subject of a poem to stir up passion for the Union cause. Contrary to the poem (and many simplified history books), however, Revere never made it to Concord to warn the minutemen of the British approach; he was arrested by the British after warning John Hancock and Sam Adams in Lexington. Nor did he shout "The British Are Coming!" from his horse—probably a whisper of "The regulars are out tonight" was more like it. And he wasn't the only

rider out that night. At least two other riders, William Dawes and Dr. Samuel Prescott, were also out warning the colonists.

Whatever the details of Revere's famous night, however, he was by any measure a veritable Leonardo da Vinci of the colonial world, who won acclaim as a silversmith, coppersmith, bell ringer, dentist, and father of 16 children. Many of them were raised in the house that still bears his name (19 North Square, 617/523-2338, www.paulreverehouse.org, 9:30 A.M.–4:15 P.M. daily Nov.–mid-Apr., closed Mon. Jan.–Mar.; 9:30 A.M.–5:15 P.M. daily mid-Apr.–Oct., $3.50 adults, $3 seniors and students, $1 children 5–17, free children under 5), a typical example of 17th-century architecture and the oldest house still standing in the city.

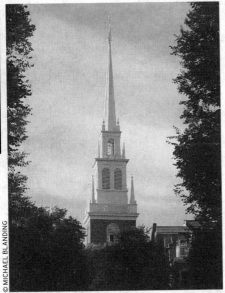

© MICHAEL BLANDING

"One if by land, two if by sea" was the signal that went out from the Old North Church.

If you are looking for an exhibit of Revere silver, you are better off going to the Museum of Fine Arts; the house has only a small collection of artifacts relating to the patriot, contained in a few poorly labeled cabinets (though a case full of Revere-inspired tchochkes, including a whisky bottle in the shape of the patriot on his horse, is amusing).

The house is more interesting as a window into the living quarters and implements of a typical family in colonial urban America. Interpretive guides are on hand to lead guests up creaking narrow staircases into the surprisingly snug quarters where Revere and his wife slept and entertained guests. On Saturday afternoons, artisans demonstrate such arts as silversmithing and gilding in the outdoor courtyards.

Old North Church
Situated right in the middle of the oldest neighborhood in town, the Old North Church was one of the most recognizable landmarks in colonial Boston. So it was the perfect vantage point if, say, one wanted to hang a lantern to warn that the British were on the march. As a pre-teen, Paul Revere was a bell ringer in the church. Thus, on the night of April 18, 1773, he was able to convince the church's sexton to climb into the belfry and hold two lanterns up for under a minute, a signal to the patriots that the British were moving by sea across to Charlestown, thence to march on to Concord and Lexington. The sexton, Robert Newman, was the unsung hero in the story—arrested by the British the following morning, he was held in prison until freed by General George Washington in an exchange. Inside the church, reproductions of colonial flags hang from the ceiling, and every half hour a guide tells Revere's story from the pulpit.

Between Old North and Hanover Street is the Paul Revere Mall, with a huge bronze statue of Revere upon his horse by local master sculptor Cyrus Dallin, usually lorded over by wizened Italian women feeding the pigeons. Look for the plaques along the wall that honor other patriots who grew up in the North End and reach back into history to tell the stories of some of the original Puritan settlers of the neighborhood, including theologians Cotton and Increase Mather, governor John Winthrop, and Ann Pollard, the first White woman to disembark onto Boston soil.

CHARLESTOWN
The original settlement of the Puritans was named after the king they left behind. A swampy mess of a place without much access to fresh water, Charlestown was eventually abandoned when John Winthrop and the gang were invited over to the Shawmut Peninsula to found Boston. Charlestown, which is incorporated as a neighborhood of Boston, grew to be an important port in the 18th century. Then tragedy struck during the Revolutionary War, when the British fired cannonballs filled with incendiary oil across the channel and burned the city to the ground as a retaliation for their losses at the Battle of Bunker Hill.

The city was rebuilt in the early 19th century, about the same time as the brick mansions and brownstones were going up on Beacon Hill, and it shares a similar colonial feel with that neighborhood. Gas lamps, black shutters, and window boxes give an antique feel to much of the neighborhood, especially in the area around Monument Square, at the top of the hill surrounding the Bunker Hill Monument. In the 20th century, the area became home to an Irish working-class community known by the rest of the city as "townies." They still come out to celebrate on Bunker Hill Day, a special neighborhood holiday to commemorate the battle. Charlestown has changed in recent decades, as young professionals priced out of Beacon Hill and the Back Bay in the 1980s descended upon its quaint streets and carved its townhouses into thousands of luxury condos. Boutiques and gourmet restaurants sprang up to serve the new crowd, giving the neighborhood a feel similar to Georgetown in Washington, D.C. The isolation of the enclave gives its residents, whether recent arrivals or townies, a sense of community few other neighborhoods match.

Bunker Hill Monument

High on the top of Breed's Hill stands a 221-foot granite obelisk (Monument Square, Charlestown, 617/242-5641, www.nps.gov/bost/historyculture/bhm.htm, exhibit: 9 A.M.–5 P.M. daily, monument: 9 A.M.–4:30 P.M. daily, free) to mark the misnamed first major battle of the Revolutionary War. In it, the patriots—while defeated—inflicted such high casualties upon the British Army that thousands rushed to the colonist cause to begin a protracted siege of Boston. The monument itself has some 300 steps inside that lead up to one of the best views of the Boston Harbor and the city skyline.

Across the street, the impressive new **Bunker Hill Museum** (43 Monument Square, 9 A.M.–5 P.M. daily, free) opened in 2007 with two floors of exhibits about the battle. In addition to artifacts such as a British cannonball, the museum features two dioramas with miniature figurines that perpetually fight the battle over again with the help of a sound and light display. The highlight, however, is the beautifully painted "cyclorama" on the second floor, depicting the battle in breathtaking 360 degrees.

USS Constitution

The oldest commissioned ship in the American Navy, the USS *Constitution* has earned many nicknames over the years, including "Old Ironsides" and the "Eagle of the Sea." Originally designated as simply "Frigate D," the frigate was built in Portsmouth Navy Yard in Maine, named by President Washington, and launched in 1798. In 17 years of active duty, it racked up a battle record as celebrated as any ship of its time, defeating the heavier British ships *Guerrière* and *Java* during the War of 1812, and leading a blockade of Tripoli during the War of the Barbary Coast.

The ship is now docked at Charlestown Navy Yard, where navy sailors wearing funny hats give tours every half hour. Fans of *Master and Commander* will be thrilled to stand behind a long gun cannon on the gun deck or sit at the gambrel table in the captain's quarters. Even casual visitors will snicker at the toilet seats located on the aptly named poop deck. Some of the stones in the bilge are the originals placed there for ballast more than 200 years ago. The last time the *Constitution* detached from a tugboat to sail freely under its own power was in 1997 during its 200th anniversary; the ship, however, is towed out into Boston Harbor and turned around with a 21-gun salute every year on July 4. (Members of the public can sign up on the ship's website for a lottery to board the ship for these cruises.)

To get to the ship, visitors first pass through the newly renovated **Charlestown Naval Yard Visitors Center** (Charlestown Navy Yard, Building 5, 617/242-5601, www.nps.gov/bost/historyculture/cny.htm, 9 A.M–5 P.M. daily), which features a 10-minute video on the history of the Yard, along with ropes, chains, uniforms, and other artifacts. Near the ship is a much-larger **USS Constitution Museum** (Charlestown Navy Yard, 617/426-1812, www.ussconstitutionmuseum.org, 10 A.M.–5 P.M.

daily Nov.–Apr., 9 A.M.–6 P.M. daily May–Oct., free) that displays swords, pistols, and cannonballs captured from the *Constitution*'s various engagements, along with a giant-sized model of the ship under full sail. Several short films give more information about the ship and its history. Kids love the upper floor of the museum, which features a cannon they can swab, wad, and "fire" against an enemy ship; and a rudimentary video game in which they can engage the HMS *Java* while learning the basic principles of battle under sail.

FINANCIAL DISTRICT

The financial engine of the city—and indeed the whole region of New England—can be found in a skyscraper forest that takes up just a few dozen blocks between downtown and the waterfront. While many of the banks and companies that once made their headquarters in Boston have left for other cities, the area is still anchored by the office buildings of powerhouses Fidelity Investments and State Street Bank. Most of the neighborhood's office towers were built during the second half of the 20th century, and reflect an eclectic (a better word might be random) mix of styles, some beautiful and some, well, not so much. The area is worth a ramble just to take in the variety—especially the older buildings sprinkled into the mix. The Richardson-Romanesque Flour & Grain Exchange Building at 177 Milk Street, for example, looks like the fanciful castle of a feudal lord, while the Batterymarch Building at 89 Broad Street employs 30 different colors of bricks in its art deco facade. At the center of the neighborhood is Post Office Square, an oasis of flowers and grass where businesspeople bring their bag lunches to enjoy a brief respite from the rat race.

Custom House Tower

Close to the waterfront is Boston's oldest "skyscraper," the 500-foot tall Custom House Tower (3 McKinley Square, 617/310-6300, www.marriott.com, 7 A.M.–11 P.M.). Built in 1915, the distinctive Beaux Arts tower features a 22-foot-wide clock, and a pair of peregrine

Custom House Tower

© MICHAEL BLANDING

falcons who nest at its top during the summer. You can try to catch a glimpse of them, along with knockout views of the harbor, on the 26th-floor observation platform (tours 10 A.M. and 4 P.M. Mon.–Thu., 4 P.M. Fri., year-round, free). Inside the tower is also a small museum with a few paintings and American historical artifacts on loan from the Peabody Essex Museum in Salem. The building was recently converted into one of Marriott's more interesting urban hotels.

◖ New England Aquarium

Fish have always loomed large in Boston, from their role as the foundation of the city's early maritime economy, to their position grilled or buttered at the top of most restaurant menus. So it is only fitting that the city should also have a world-class aquarium (Central Wharf, 617/973-5200, www.neaq.org, 9 A.M.–5 P.M. Mon.–Fri., 9 A.M.–6 P.M. Sat.–Sun., $21 adults, $13 children 3–11, free children under 3, IMAX: 9:30 A.M.–9:30 P.M. daily, $10 adults, $8 children 3–11, whale watch: $40 adults, $32 children 11 and under) that pays homage to the wonders of the sea.

The literal centerpiece of the massive waterfront museum is a 200,000-gallon tank full of sharks, sea turtles, and giant ocean fish that rises like a watery spinal column through the center of the building. A long walkway spirals around the tank, giving viewers a chance to see sealife on all levels of the ocean, from the toothy pikes that float on the surface to the 45-year-old sea turtle, Myrtle, who often sleeps on the floor. Other crowd-pleasers are the harbor seals in the courtyard and the enormous open-air penguin pool, filled with three dozen rockhopper, little blue, and African penguins who fill the building with their raucous cries.

The aquarium is not just a museum, but also a research-and-rescue organization that finds stranded seals, dolphins, and other animals and nurses them back to health. You can see the aquarium's latest convalescents in a hospital ward on the second floor. The aquarium also ventures out into the harbor itself for whale watch trips, seeking out the humpbacks and right whales that make their way into Massachusetts Bay. The aquarium's exterior was renovated in the late 1990s, and the IMAX theater opened in 2001 along with a revitalized series of special exhibits. There is also an interactive children's center, where you can drop off the tykes for sea-related projects.

CHINATOWN

Like most major U.S. cities, Boston has a bustling Chinatown, where Asian immigrants shop at crowded markets with the pungent smells of strange roots and dried fish, while restaurants with live-seafood tanks draw hungry tourists and residents from other neighborhoods. Also in the mix of a bewildering array of storefronts are shops selling discount cookware and electronic items, shiny red facades of Buddhist temples, and banks and businesses with Cantonese characters over the doorways. The main drag of the neighborhood is Beach Street, the site every February of a colorful and loud Chinese New Year parade. At the foot of the street, the Chinatown Gate signals the official entrance to passing motorists. In recent years, Southeast Asian immigrants—particularly those from Vietnam—have outnumbered the ethnic Chinese, so that the corner cafés are more likely to be serving *pho* than chow mein.

The neighborhood is also one of the few in the city that stays up into the early morning hours. Top-name chefs often meet over sushi or egg rolls at back-alley restaurants long after their own eateries have closed. Restaurants in Chinatown have long had the reputation for being the only place that you can still get served alcohol after 2 A.M., the ridiculously early closing time of most bars in Boston. Night owls in the know ask for "cold tea" to get a discreet mug of beer—though you didn't hear it from us. For years, the residents of Chinatown have also had to fight off the bad reputation of an encroaching red-light district once known as the Combat Zone. Nowadays, the "zone" has all but disappeared, with only a pair of strip clubs and a few tired-looking XXX bookstores remaining on Washington Street.

THEATER DISTRICT

Boston has always been a great town for theater. Back in the golden days of the Great White Way, shows would debut in Boston weeks before they went on to Broadway, often tweaking the performances based on the reviews of the literate local critics and audiences of the day. The tradition has been revived somewhat in the last decade, with many of the old classical theaters getting facelifts and new shows trying their luck in Beantown before retooling for New York. When they do, they come to one of the grand theaters in this neighborhood, an extension of Tremont Street sandwiched between the Back Bay and the South End. During the day, the area can be one of the seedier parts of town, where suspicious characters linger around the doorways of convenience stores and dive bars. Like much of downtown, however, the area has gotten spiffier in the last decade, especially since Emerson College moved some of its classrooms in to imbue it with a lively dose of student energy.

On weekend nights, however, all the glamour of the neighborhood's heyday returns, with the corner of Tremont and Stuart Streets becoming a morass of cabs and limousines disgorging young lovelies in strapless black dresses and men with camel-hair overcoats into the brightly lit mouths of the Wang, Colonial, Wilbur, and Schubert. After the performances let out, the restaurants and nightclubs along the street raise their own curtains to keep the show going.

BACK BAY

The most fashionable neighborhood of Boston, the Back Bay is also one of the most easily navigated. Grand boulevards in the style of Paris are lined with brownstones and large Victorian-style apartment buildings, linked by short side streets that are ordered alphabetically (Arlington, Berkeley, Clarendon…). Ironically, given how swanky the neighborhood has become, the area used to be one big disease-spreading swamp—it's no accident that

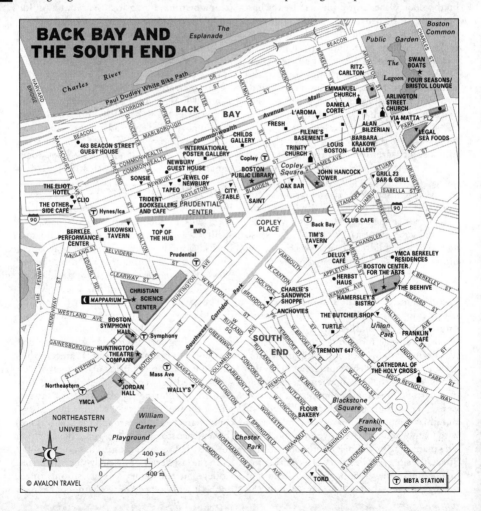

BACK BAY AND THE SOUTH END

© AVALON TRAVEL

Ⓣ MBTA STATION

the neighborhood's main drag, Boylston Street, is named after a doctor. In the days when Boston used to be a peninsula, the Back Bay was literally a bay in the Charles River, where refuse would wash up with the tides, and men and boys—including a young Ben Franklin—would fish from shore. As the city expanded in the 1800s, the earth from Beacon Hill and other high ground was used for landfill to fill up the bay, and a new neighborhood was born, quickly filling with larger and more impressive houses built for the glitterati of the day.

The heart of the neighborhood, if not the city, is Copley Square. The large plaza, which is half brick and half grassy lawn, is named after the Victorian-era painter John Singleton Copley, and is often the site of classical music concerts in the spring and summer. A statue of the painter, complete with pantaloons and artist's palette, stands at the southwest corner of the square. From Copley, each of the boulevards of the neighborhood has its own character. Boylston Street is the main commercial drag, lined with towering office buildings,

along with convenience stores and coffee shops. Newbury Street, by contrast, is the ritziest street in town, where you are more likely to hear Spanish or Italian than a Boston accent. Along the street are branches of national chains from Armani to Zegna, along with a few local clothing boutiques and jewelry designers.

Next in line, Commonwealth Avenue is a boulevard in grand Parisian style, with a large pedestrian mall lined with statues running down the center, and trees festooned with lights in the winter. Quaint Marlboro Street has a purely residential feel, enhanced by the legions of flowering dogwoods that spawn floating petals in the springtime. Lastly, Beacon Street lines the river with more giant brownstones, along with the parkland of the Esplanade.

Public Garden

In contrast to the Boston Common, which has an open, park-like feel, the Public Garden is an intimate outdoor space, full of leafy trees and flower beds. Built on landfill in the 19th century, the garden was America's first public

© MICHAEL BLANDING

Public Garden

botanical garden, envisioned by its creators as a respite from urban life. A stroll through the park at any hour makes an ordinary day instantly romantic, at no time more than sunset, when the trees cast mysterious shadows over the walkways. The centerpiece of the garden is a lagoon, which is crossed by a fairy-tale bridge and surrounded by willow trees that trail their branch tips in the water. Tracing lazy circles around the lagoon during the day are Boston's famous **swan boats** (617/522-1966, www. swanboats.com, 10 A.M.–4 P.M. Apr.–mid-Jun., 10 A.M.–5 P.M. late Jun.–Labor Day, 12–4 P.M. Mon.–Fri., 10 A.M.–4 P.M. Sat.–Sun. $2.75 adults, $2 seniors, $1.25 children 2–15), a flotilla of six large paddleboats with large white cygnets at the stern. The boats are a mandatory attraction if you are in Boston with children (even if you have to borrow some). Children are also big fans of the nearby bronze statues of Mrs. Mallard and her seven little ducklings. The statues pay homage to the children's book *Make Way for Ducklings,* which was partially set in the Public Garden.

Arlington Street Church

Located on the corner of Boylston and Arlington Streets, Arlington Street Church is where the sect of Christianity known as Unitarianism reached its full flower. (In fact, it was once known as the "Boston religion," based on its association with the social and political elite of the time.) Among other social causes, Unitarianism threw its weight early on behind the abolitionist movement, led by preachers Theodore Parker and William Ellery Channing, who has a statue dedicated to him across the street from the church. The sect, now known as Unitarian Universalism, still has its headquarters in Boston on Beacon Hill, and was recently one of the strongest religious voices supporting gay marriage. (Arlington Street Church itself has for a long time had an openly lesbian minister.)

Inside the church, the highlight is a collection of Tiffany stained-glass windows. Installed over thirty years at the beginning of the 20th century, the windows are subtly breathtaking, with light from outside filtering through multiple layers of opalescent glass and skin tones so real they might as well be warm to the touch.

Trinity Church

In the heart of Copley Square stands the undisputed masterpiece of architect H. H. Richardson, one of the most-photographed buildings in Boston. Richardson cultivated a bold style, which after his success with Trinity became all the rage in the 1870s and 1880s. Called "Richardson Romanesque" in honor of its creator, the style featured massive blocks of stone, often worked in a contrasting "checkerboard" pattern, along with sweeping Romanesque arches and towers. The inside of the Presbyterian church (206 Clarendon St., 617/536-0944, www.trinitychurchboston.org, 9 A.M.–6 P.M. Tues.–Sat., 7 A.M.–7 P.M. Sun., $6 for tours) is calculated to impress, with a vaulted ceiling and a huge carved wooden pulpit in front of the altar. Classical music concerts are regularly offered inside the church,

Trinity Church, reflected in the windows of the John Hancock Tower

especially around the holidays, and tours of the church are led several times a day from the bookshop inside.

John Hancock Tower

When it was first proposed in the 1970s, the 790-foot Hancock Tower was met with fierce resistance by residents who feared it would wreck the historic ambience of Copley Square. In a stroke of genius, architect I. M. Pei covered the outside of the building with reflective glass, thereby enhancing rather than overshadowing the architectural beauty of Trinity Church, the Boston Public Library, and other nearby buildings. Not everything ended happily, however—due to a design flaw, many of the 10,344 panes of glass began falling out and shattering on the sidewalk below before the building was completed. Pei later corrected the technique for hanging the glass (which he also used on the pyramid for the Louvre) and the building is now one of the most striking in the city skyline. The observation deck on the 60th floor was closed to the public due to security

concerns after 2001, and is only opened for special events.

Nearby, the much smaller "old" John Hancock building features a beacon on top that changes color depending on the weather forecast. Many older Bostonians can still recite the rhyme that cracks the code: "Steady blue, clear view / Flashing blue, clouds due / Steady red, rain ahead / Flashing red, snow instead." During summer and fall, flashing red means the Red Sox game is cancelled (though snow isn't out of the question at that time of year either).

Boston Public Library

Added to Boston's long list of firsts in 1848 was the nation's first municipal public library. The library (700 Boylston St., 617/536-5400, www.bpl.org, 9 A.M.–9 P.M. Mon.–Thurs., 9 A.M.–5 P.M. Fri.–Sat., closed Sun., free), which fills two city blocks on the south side of Copley Square, consists of two buildings. The original, designed by Charles McKim and opened in 1895, is now the research library,

Boston Public Library

with a more modern building next door holding the circulating collection. Aside from its collection of hundreds of thousands of books, magazines, and videos, the library is full of art and architectural flourishes that make the building as much of an attraction as its contents. The outside exterior is built on pleasing classical proportions and covered with names of great thinkers down through the ages; twin female statues of Art and Science keep guard outside. One of the best-kept secrets of the city is the library's central courtyard, an Italianate plaza accented by a fountain that makes a peaceful asylum from the busy streets around.

Inside the McKim Building, you can feel smarter just by stepping into the impressive Bates Reading Room, a 200-foot-long testament to scholarship, with a 50-foot-high barrel ceiling, high arched windows facing Copley Square, and long tables full of scholars sitting at green banker's lamps and thinking great thoughts. Those in need of further inspiration can step into the 80-foot-long Sargent Gallery, which features painter John Singer Sargent's fantastical mural sequence "Triumph of Religion," a sensual, often tempestuous journey through the gods, goddesses, and prophets of the ancient world. Other artistic works in the library are a mural sequence dedicated to the story of the search for the Holy Grail by American artist Edwin Austin Abbey, and a painting of George Washington at Dorchester Heights by Emanuel Gottlieb Leutze (who also did the famous painting of Washington crossing the Delaware). Free hour-long tours of the library's art and architecture are offered at various times daily; call for times.

SOUTH END

As the city of Boston expanded outwards from Beacon Hill and the North End, the next logical place to populate was the southern end of the Shawmut Peninsula. In the late 19th century, then, the South End quickly became *the* place to see and be seen, and rich merchants and ship captains built large brownstones on its waffle-iron layout of streets. Literally made of large brown stones, these homes were distinguished from the smaller brick buildings on Beacon Hill by their larger rooms and high ceilings, frequently with tall stairways leading up to the entrance door on the second floor (an assurance against flooding). Nearly as quickly as they colonized it, however, the fickle abandoned the South End in favor of the Back Bay, which was newly reclaimed from landfill in the river and built on an even grander scale than its neighbor.

For more than 100 years, the neighborhood was a melting pot of various immigrant groups who occupied the buildings left behind by the bourgeoisie, and it achieved a reputation for being a rough-and-tumble area. That reputation is hard to imagine now as the neighborhood reaches the height of a long, slow gentrification that began in the 1970s when it was rediscovered, primarily by artists and middle-class gay men and lesbian women. The neighborhood is still the center of Boston's GLBT population, and it's not unusual to see rainbow flags proudly fluttering from the upper stories of brownstones. The neighborhood also has a pleasing mix of residential and commercial uses, with the busiest streets of Tremont and Columbus lined with intimate (and expensive) neighborhood restaurants and storefronts occupied by boutiques selling $100 T-shirts and cutting-edge alternative fashion.

In the late 1990s, the South End expanded even farther southward past its historical boundary of Washington Street to create a brand-new neighborhood cheekily called SoWa (South of Washington). All of the available land in one of downtown's last frontiers has quickly been snatched up by modern loft apartment buildings that give the street an in-the-moment vibe. The area appeals to a certain intersection of art and commerce, with some of the city's edgier galleries cheek-by-jowl with its hotter new restaurants. Thus far, however, it has retained a certain grittiness that has forestalled its complete gentrification.

Boston Symphony Hall

The acoustics in this elegant concert hall are generally recognized as among the top three in the world (only Vienna and Amsterdam can compare). The home of both the Boston Symphony Orchestra and the Boston Pops, the hall (301 Massachusetts Ave., 617/638-9390, www.bostonsymphonyhall.org) was built in 1900 with a minimum of ornamentation. For many Bostonians, it's an annual holiday rite to see a performance of Handel's *Messiah* utilizing the impressive Aeolian Skinner organ behind the stage. Free tours of the hall, which include an explanation of its legendary acoustics, are offered every Wednesday at 4 P.M. and the second Saturday of the month at 2 P.M., from October to early December and early January to mid-June.

Christian Science Center

The towering dome of the "mother church" is the centerpiece of the sprawling headquarters for the worldwide religion of Christian Science. Founded in 1879 by Mary Baker Eddy, the religion is best known for its practice of "faith healing" that forbids its practitioners to take medicine for illnesses. Eddy, however, was once a larger-than-life figure in American culture who was a leader of the early women's movement and a pioneering publisher. Visitors can learn more about Eddy's life at the eclectic **Mary Baker Eddy Library** (200 Massachusetts Ave., 617/450-7000, www.marybakereddylibrary.org, 10 A.M.–4 P.M. Tues.–Sun., $6 adults, $4 seniors, students, and youth 6–17, free children under 6). A series of multimedia exhibits encourages visitors to develop their own life philosophies while at the same time tracing the evolution of its matriarch's ideas with refreshingly little proselytizing. Another exhibit within the museum literally provides a window into the newsroom of the *Christian Science Monitor,* which has its headquarters in the complex.

Mapparium

Within the Christian Science Center, one hidden gem deserves special mention. The Mapparium (200 Massachusetts Ave., 617/450-7000, www.marybakereddylibrary.org, 10 A.M.–4 P.M. Tues.–Sun., $6 adults, $4 seniors, students, and youth 6–17, free children under 6) is like nowhere else on the world—maybe because it's literally inside of it. Visitors are ushered along a bridge into a 30-foot-diameter globe with the countries of the world (circa 1935) displayed in vibrant stained glass around the walls. For map geeks, it would be possible to spend an hour tracing the outlines of countries and continents, reflecting on their changes over the years. Every twenty minutes, a seven-minute light show explores the spread of ideas around the globe through the voices of Nelson Mandela, Eleanor Roosevelt, and other seminal thinkers.

Cathedral of the Holy Cross

At the turn of the 19th century, the famine Irish spent nine years constructing New England's largest Catholic church. The cruciform neo-Gothic edifice (1400 Washington St., 617/542-5682, www.angelfire.com/ma4/cathedral/home.html) rivals the largest in Europe. The city's Yankee forefathers, of course, promptly hid it behind the screaming tracks of an elevated railway, which drowned out homilies for almost 90 years. Now not only are the tracks gone, but also lights have been added to illuminate the facade. The seat of the Archdiocese of Boston, the cathedral on Washington Street features rare Munich stained glass and a (supposed) relic of the true cross in the base of a crucifix. For years, eleven o'clock Sunday Mass was said by Bernard Cardinal Law, who stepped down in disgrace in 2003 after a prolonged scandal of molesting children that had been covered up for years. Now mass is said by the new archbishop, Sean O'Malley, a former Capuchin friar who has rehabilitated the church in the eyes of many Bostonians. Occasional organ concerts featuring the reconstructed Hook & Hastings are the closest thing to divine transport in Boston.

FENWAY

Upon first glance, the area of the city known as the Fenway doesn't seem to offer much. A gritty network of streets lined with pubs and discount stores, the neighborhood has traditionally been

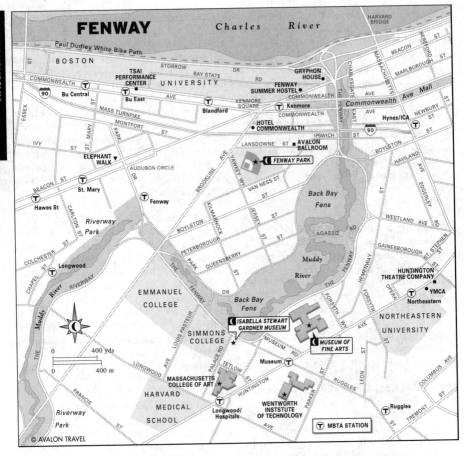

the stomping grounds for students of nearby Boston University. Scratch beneath the surface, however, and you'll find several of the city's premier cultural attractions, including the Museum of Fine Arts and the jewel box Isabella Stewart Gardner Museum. The neighborhood gets its name from the Back Bay Fens, a winding, swampy greensward that serves as the drainage channel for the city. Today, The Fens is a rambling parkland, lined with ball fields and community gardens, including the hidden Kelleher Rose Garden, a dreamy garden full of vine-covered trellises and over 100 varieties of roses. The center of the neighborhood

is Kenmore Square, a lively crossroads of student bars, discount stores, and burrito joints, just down the street from the historic home of the Boston Red Sox: Fenway Park. Behind the baseball stadium, Landsdowne Street is lined with the city's flashiest dance clubs, where international students shake their stuff after midnight.

◖ Fenway Park

A new banner was flapping in the breeze here after the Red Sox's come-from-behind race to win the 2004 World Series, after 86 years of trying. While the high of that victory has

© SARAH MUSUMECI/MOTT

historic Fenway Park

infused the park (4 Yawkey Way, 617/226-6666, www.redsox.com, $12 adults, $11 seniors, $10 children) with a new energy, Fenway has long been one of the most electric places to catch the national pastime. First opened in 1912, Fenway has a soul that none of the more modern parks can match. For the uninitiated, the geography of the park—with its Green Monster, Pesky's Pole, and Ted Williams' seat—can seem more complicated than many whole cities. Thankfully, true believers lead tours of the park daily from 9 A.M. to 4 P.M. (or until three hours before the game). As good as those tours may be, however, nothing quite beats taking a seat in the bleachers, grabbing a Budweiser, and waiting for the first crack of the bat.

◀ Museum of Fine Arts

Quite simply, behind the neoclassic marble facade of this grand art museum is one of the best and most beloved art collections in the country. The MFA, as it's known, is particularly noted for its collection of French Impressionist works—posters of which have been decorating college dorm rooms for decades. But it also has outstanding Asian and Egyptian collections, as well as many celebrated early American paintings and artifacts. The museum (465 Huntington Ave., 617/267-9300, www.mfa.org, 10 A.M.–4:45 P.M. Sat.–Tues., 10 A.M.–9:45 P.M. Wed.–Fri., $17 adults, $15 seniors and students, $6.50 youth 6–17 but free on weekends, holidays, and after 3 P.M. on weekdays, free children under 6) began its life as the painting collection of the Boston Athenaeum, the private library located on Beacon Hill. Over the years, it benefited from Brahmin patronage to amass a fine collection of both classical and modern art objects. Under its current leadership, the museum has taken some gambles to bring more modern viewers into the galleries, staging artistic exhibitions on guitars and racecars alongside show-stopping special exhibits on the likes of Monet, Van Gogh, and Gauguin. A new addition to the museum, currently being designed by internationally renowned architects Foster and Partners, will provide even more space for exhibition of the museum's 350,000 works of art. When completed in 2010 or 2011, the renovation will include an entire new wing for American art, glassed in over the current wing of the museum, as well as spiffed-up European galleries and more room for contemporary artwork.

At present, most visitors to the MFA make a beeline for the 2nd floor, which is home to several jaw-dropping rooms dedicated to works by French impressionists Monet, Manet, Renoir, Van Gogh, and others. Particular highlights are Renoir's *Dance at Bougival,* and Gauguin's *Where Do We Come From? What Are We? Where Are We Going?,* the centerpiece of a recent Gauguin exhibit that was one of the museum's most successful shows ever. Less trafficked but equally rewarding are the American galleries. On display is arguably the most famous American painting ever: Gilbert Stuart's original unfinished painting of George Washington, which was used as a model for more than 100 paintings of the first president, including the one that appears (in reverse) on the one dollar bill. The collection includes several paintings by John Singer Sargent, including the arresting *Daughters of Edward Darley Bolt,* as well as those by Boston's own adopted artist, John Singleton Copley, including his portrait of Paul Revere. Several examples of the patriot silversmith's work are on display in adjoining galleries of colonial artifacts and furniture.

John Singer Sargent is also the master behind the Sargent murals that cover the ceiling of the museum's grand rotunda with rich classical imagery. The murals, which Sargent considered the culmination of his life's work, have caused more than one visitor to develop a crick in the neck from looking up at them in amazement for so long. The rotunda marks the crossroads of culture, separating galleries dedicated to Egypt and Asia. The Egyptian galleries contain many items that were unearthed in a fruitful museum-sponsored exhibition at Giza that began in 1905; the towering statue of *Pharaoh Menkaure and his Queen* is one of the finest Egyptian pieces on display anywhere. The entire Asian collection meanwhile is hands down one of the best in the world. Many of its galleries were filled through the enterprising efforts of William Sturgis Bigelow and Ernest Fenollosa, who were known as the "Boston Buddhists" for their contribution in bringing Buddha into the West. Among the highlights of the collection is a "Japanese temple room" that features three exquisite life-size stone Buddhas, along with other Japanese sculpture contemplatively arranged in a dimly lit alcove.

Tours of various collections within the museum are offered free with admission throughout the day. Introductory tours to the entire museum run at 10:30 A.M. and 3 P.M. Monday through Friday, 6:15 P.M. on Wednesday, and 11 A.M., 12:30, and 3 P.M. during weekends. On the first Friday of every month, the museum also hosts a popular singles event where the artsy and amorous mingle over red wine and jazz while they ogle the art and each other.

◖ Isabella Stewart Gardner Museum

This small museum (280 The Fenway, 617/566-1401, www.gardnermuseum.org, 11 A.M.–5 P.M. Tues.–Sun., $12 adults, $10 seniors, $5 students, free youth and children under 18) is filled with priceless European and American paintings. The most cherished work of art, however, may be the building itself, which is constructed around a plant-filled Italianate courtyard that may be the most pleasing indoor space in the city. The namesake socialite who built the museum was known as something of a brilliant eccentric, who wore Red Sox caps with her ball gowns and scandalized polite society by posing for an eroticized portrait by John Singer Sargent. (On display in the museum, the portrait was exhibited only once in Gardner's lifetime due to the wishes of her husband.) The museum keeps alive Gardner's eccentric spirit by allowing any woman named Isabella free admission to the museum at all times. Other works of art in the collection include Titian's *Europa,* which may be the single most important work of art in Boston; Sargent's dynamic *El Jaleo;* Boticelli's *Virgin and Child with an Angel;* and an early Rembrandt self-portrait.

The building, which was also Gardner's residence, has four floors of artwork organized as a living house museum, with some of the original typed labels still in place. Gardner's will stipulated that nothing in the museum be moved, or else the entire collection would be sold and the proceeds donated to Harvard's art faculty. That requirement presented particular problems after the night of St. Patrick's Day, 1990, when two thieves broke into the museum and cut thirteen paintings out of their frames. Among the priceless works of art stolen were two rare Rembrandt paintings, including a later self-portrait, and one of only about 35 Vermeers in the world. The theft, which some have called the largest art heist in history, still remains unsolved despite a $5 million reward offered by the museum; the frames for the stolen paintings still hang in a room called the Dutch Room. Next door, a room called the Tapestry Room provides a beautiful background for periodic chamber music concerts. Ms. Gardner's collection isn't all that is on display at the museum; a small exhibition space hosts contemporary shows.

Not to be left behind in the Boston art museum renovation sweepstakes, the Gardner too plans a major expansion, which will include a new building adjacent to the museum designed by award-winning architect Renzo Piano, further increasing the space for contemporary work and traveling exhibitions. The renovation recently passed a major hurdle when the Massachusetts Supreme Judicial Court ruled that it was consistent with Gardner's will and could proceed.

SEAPORT DISTRICT

Located across Fort Point Channel from downtown, the South Boston waterfront district is a neighborhood in transition. For years, it has been home to New England's largest community of artists, who have taken advantage of the solid warehouses that once housed the stores for Boston's wool trade to build artist studios and performance spaces. The neighborhood itself is a visual artist's dream, with open spaces broken by iron girders and views of the harbor. As downtown has become built up however, the newly christened Seaport District is the next development frontier, with cranes and bulldozers furiously breaking ground on new hotels, condo buildings, and a gargantuan new convention center. After years of negotiating, the artists have been worked into the plan, and a new urban neighborhood is taking shape that retains its urban edge and allows conventioneers to walk to stores and galleries sprouting up in old buildings.

Boston Tea Party Ship and Museum

The original three British ships that provided the dance floor for the Boston Tea Party were moored at Griffin's Wharf, which was later buried in landfill during the expansion of the city. The best estimate of the location is near the present-day corner of Atlantic Avenue and Congress Street, near South Station. Not far from that spot, this newly renovated museum (Congress Street

BOSTON BY SEA

No matter how many tours visitors to Boston go on, many miss seeing the city from one very important angle: the ocean. Viewed from in and around the harbor, the city's skyline is not only immense, but astoundingly peaceful, and offers an entirely new perspective and sense of place. To that end, there are a number of ways of getting out on the harbor that don't require a private charter. One of the easiest means is the Lighthouse Cruises offered by **Boston Harbor Cruises** (departing from Long Wharf, 617/227-4321, www.bostonharborcruises.com). The voyages last five hours, are narrated by members of the American Lighthouse Foundation, and pass numerous lighthouses – including Boston Light, the oldest lighthouse station in America, and Thacher Island, the only operational twin lighthouses in the country. Rather do your wining and dining offshore? **Spirit of Boston dancing and dinner cruises** (departing from World Trade Center, 617/748-1450,www.spiritofboston.com) lays out candlelit tables, an enormous buffet, and live music on its enormous boat. Likewise, the huge dinner cruises offered by **Odyssey Cruises** (departing from Rowes Wharf, 866/307-2469, www.odysseycruises.com) play everything from live jazz to pop dance tunes while you dig into dinner and take in the ever-changing water view. On a more hands-on note, passengers are encouraged to participate in sailing when they cruise aboard the schooners **Liberty** or **Liberty Clipper** (depart Long Wharf, 617/742-1422,www.libertyfleet.com/) – replicas of early-1800s schooners used by New England fishermen.

Bridge, www.bostonteapartyship.com), scheduled to be opened in 2010, will feature replicas of the three original ships—the *Beaver,* the *Dartmouth,* and the *Eleanor*—along with other artifacts to bring alive the cold night of December 16, 1773, when 342 chests of British tea were broken open and hurled into the harbor, the tipping point for the American Revolution. Among the items on display is the so-called "Robinson Tea Chest," which was recovered by a participant the day after the event, and one of only two original tea chests known to survive.

Institute of Contemporary Art

Once upon a time, Boston's Institute of Contemporary Art (ICA) was viewed as being on par with New York's Museum of Modern Art (MoMA) on the vanguard of experimental modern art. While MoMA decided to collect the artists it exhibited, and now boasts the likes of Jackson Pollock and Jasper Johns, the ICA felt that it could better remain on the cutting-edge by continually exhibiting new work. Oops. Making up for lost time, however, in 2006 the ICA opened a new home on the waterfront (100 Northern Ave., 617/478-3100, www.icaboston.org, 10 A.M.–5 P.M. Tues.–Wed. and Sat.–Sun., 10 A.M.–9 P.M. Thurs. and Fri., $15 adults, $10 seniors and students, free children under 17, free to all Thurs. after 5 P.M.) in a space-age glass building that triples the size of the museum's old home in the Back Bay, and more importantly adds a permanent collection for the first time. In its old location, the museum garnered a reputation for staging explosive exhibitions such as the first U.S. exhibition of the photos of Robert Mapplethorpe in the 1980s; in recent years, however, its exhibits of contemporary multimedia installations and photography has had a more uneven reception. The new building, designed by edgy architectural firm Diller Scofidio + Renfro, has reinvigorated the museum, providing dramatic views of the waterfront from flexible gallery spaces, and adding a 325-seat performing arts theater overlooking the harbor. It has already set tongues wagging in the art world with its successful exhibition of pop graffiti artist Shepard Fairey, best known for the enigmatic Andre the Giant tags in cities all over the country, and more recently, for the iconic Barack Obama campaign poster that was ubiquitous during his presidential campaign. On his way to the opening exhibition, Fairey was arrested by Boston police for vandalism—only adding to the publicity of the show.

Boston Children's Museum

Back in the 1970s this waterfront museum (308 Congress St., 617/426-6500, www.bostonkids. org, 10 A.M.–5 P.M. Sat.–Thurs., 10 A.M.–9 P.M. Fri., $12 adults, $9 seniors and children 1–15, free children under 1) pioneered the kind of messy, hands-on learning that is now de rigueur in children's museums. In 2007, it underwent a renovation to update the exhibits to the 21st century. Budding construction workers can build skyscrapers and jackhammer them down in the Construction Zone; little monkeys can tackle a brightly colored maze of tunnels, towers, and walkways called the Climb; and the nautically inclined can float their boats in a 28-foot-long model of the Fort Point Channel (visible outside the museum's walls) called Boats Afloat. Word to the wise: get there early or come late on weekends to avoid playing referee to dozens of kiddie skirmishes that break out when the exhibits reach capacity. Better yet, come mid-week when you and the kids will have the best exhibits to yourself!

Boston Fire Museum

Boston has always has had a tempestuous relationship with fire—from the great fire of 1872 to the infamous 1942 Cocoanut Grove conflagration (a fiery tragedy that killed almost 500 people in a crowded nightclub and led to important changes in the fire code). This small museum in a historic old firehouse (344 Congress St., 617/482-1344, www.bostonfiremuseum.com, 11 A.M.–4 P.M. Thurs., 11 A.M.–9 P.M. Fri., 11 A.M.–3 P.M. Sat., free) is calculated to thrill the under four-foot-high set with displays of shiny antique fire engines and memorabilia from Boston's fiery history, including items from the Cocoanut Grove itself. The museum is run by the Boston Sparks Association, a group of several hundred fire fanatics who still listen to scanners late at night and show up at fire scenes to watch the jakes do their thing.

OTHER NEIGHBORHOODS
East Boston

To most Bostonians, the peninsula known as East Boston is synonymous with Logan Airport. Alongside the planes, however, is a residential community that has changed its ethnic makeup over the years. The spaghetti restaurants and pizza joints of an old Italian neighborhood are still bustling, but they've been joined by taquerias and *pupuserias* of a vibrant new Central and South American population. More recently, developers have taken interest in the brick warehouse buildings on the harbor, transforming them into high-priced luxury condos that promise (or threaten) to remake the neighborhood. If you take some time to explore here, you'll note that the streets are all named after battles in the Revolutionary War. The vantage point from the waterfront in front of Maverick Square is also one of the best views you could have of the city skyline without being on the water—especially during fireworks on New Year's Eve.

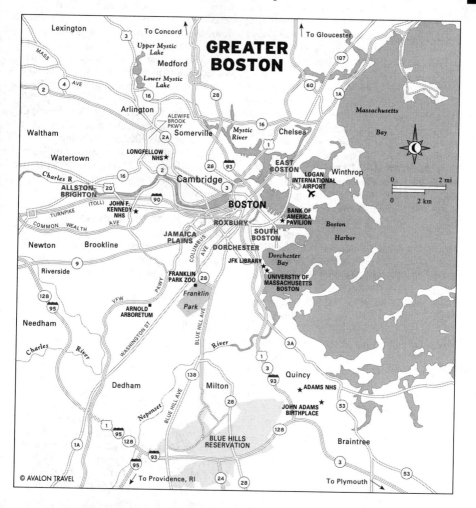

South Boston

Every year, the sidewalks of Broadway are lined with spectators for the annual St. Patrick's Day parade, the annual outpouring of pride in this heavily Irish enclave. Set apart on a peninsula, South Boston—or "Southie" as it's called by residents—has always been a tight-knit, insulated community that has kept to a code of family and neighborhood alliances. Much of the life of the community still tran-spires in the pubs that line the streets, includ-ing the famous L Street Tavern, which served as Robin Williams's neighborhood bar in the movie *Good Will Hunting*. (The movie's Oscar-winning screenwriters, Matt Damon and Ben Affleck, grew up across the river in Cambridge, a neighborhood that South Boston residents love to deride.) The best way to really get the flavor of the community is to pop into one of these throwbacks to Boston's Irish past, order a Guinness and fish-and-chips, and talk to the guy next to you at the bar.

Dorchester Heights

South Boston is also home to this little-vis-ited historic site (G St., S. Boston, www.nps.gov/bost/historyculture/dohe.htm Sat–Sun noon–6 P.M., free), where in 1776 the siege of Boston was finally lifted. Despite the bat-tles of Concord and Bunker Hill, the British and Americans were in a long stalemate, with the colonists controlling the west bank of the Charles, and the British blockading the harbor. During the winter of 1775, Bostonian General Henry Knox braved snow and cold in an epic 300-mile journey to drag the cannons of New York's Fort Ticonderoga to Boston. Wrapping their wheels in straw, colonists moved the can-nons up onto the high ground at Dorchester Heights during the night of March 4, 1776, when a British attack was thwarted by storms. With the cannon pointing down at them, the British position was untenable, and they deserted Boston under a gentleman's agree-ment with Washington a week later. While the heights have since been leveled for land-fill, the high ground is capped by a monument and offers an impressive and unusual vantage of Boston Harbor. Call ahead to determine opening hours for the monument, as they can be capricious due to recent National Park staff cuts. In one recent year, it was only open on weekend afternoons from June to Labor Day.

Roxbury and Dorchester

Roxbury was once its own town connected to Boston by a narrow isthmus. As the sea filled in, however, the boundary between it and Boston blurred until it was sucked up and an-nexed by its northern neighbor. In the 20th century, African Americans displaced from downtown settled around Dudley Square and on the heights of Fort Hill. The area is still the heart of Boston's Black community, where you can find African clothing stores and soul food along with Caribbean grocers. Between Roxbury and South Boston is the sprawl-ing plain of Dorchester, a true melting pot of African Americans, Asian Americans, and Irish, among other ethnicities. Upham's Corner is home to a vibrant community of immigrants from the African islands of Cape Verde, while Field's Corner is a little Saigon of Vietnamese restaurants and cafés.

John F. Kennedy Library

Located on the campus of University of Massachusetts–Boston, this underrated li-brary and museum (Columbia Point, Dorchester, 866/535-1960, www.jfklibrary.org, 9 A.M.–5 P.M. daily, $12 adults, $10 se-niors and students, $9 youth 13–17, free chil-dren under 13) is dedicated to Boston's modern political hero, with artifacts and exhibits that bring alive the 1960 Democratic National Convention in which Kennedy was nominated, his service during World War II, and other pe-riods of his life. The Kennedy Museum was also the site of a public viewing of the casket of JFK's brother and longtime Massachusetts Senator Ted Kennedy, who died in 2009. The museum plans to install a new exhibit relating to the life and accomplishments of the younger Kennedy in upcoming years.

In addition to the Kennedy paraphernalia, the museum is also the unlikely home to the

Hemingway Collection, the largest collection of Ernest Hemingway memorabilia located in one place. The bulk of the holdings are manuscripts, letters, and other papers available for research; however, the Hemingway Research Room also contains items belonging to the adventurous writer, including his hunting bag, shrapnel taken from his leg during World War I, and an impala shot by Mary Hemingway on safari in 1954. History buffs should also check out the **Commonwealth Museum** (220 Morrissey Blvd., Dorchester, 617/727-9268, www.sec.state.ma.us/mus/museum, 9 A.M.–5 P.M. Mon.–Fri., free) across the street, which contains archaeological items unearthed during the building of the Big Dig, including "America's oldest bowling ball."

Allston-Brighton

Sandwiched between Boston University and Boston College, the twin neighborhoods of Allston-Brighton have become the quintessential student ghetto. Run-down apartments are often filled over capacity by slumlords willing to look the other way. Along the main drags of Harvard and Brighton Avenues is a riot of student bars that feature live bands and lively flirtation. The number of struggling rock-band members who have lived in the neighborhood has given it the slightly tongue-in-cheek name of "Allston Rock City."

Jamaica Plain

One of the only Boston neighborhoods that is genuinely racially integrated, Jamaica Plain includes remnants of a sizeable "lace curtain" Irish population living side-by-side with a lesbian community and Boston's largest Latino enclave. Centre Street is one of the funkier shopping districts in town, with hipster clothing and record stores interspersed with coffee shops and bakeries. The neighborhood is also surrounded by green space, with the large Jamaica Pond on one side and gargantuan Franklin Park, designed by landscape architect Frederick Law Olmsted, on the other. On the southern rim of the neighborhood is the **Arnold Arboretum** (125 Arborway, Jamaica

© MICHAEL BLANDING
Samuel Adams Brewery in Jamaica Plain

Plain, 617/524-1718, www.arboretum.harvard.edu, sunrise–sunset daily, free), owned by Harvard University and containing more than 200 acres of rambling hillside covered with rhododendrons, lilacs, and other flowering plants and hardwood trees.

No one is quite sure how Jamaica Plain got its unusual name—some speculate it comes from the rum distillers who settled there during colonial times. The neighborhood certainly made its fortunes through alcohol, as German brewers set up shop along the fresh water of Stony Brook. One of their breweries is now occupied by **Boston Beer Company** (30 Germania St., Jamaica Plain, 617/368-5080, www.samueladams.com), the makers of **Samuel Adams** beer. Founded in 1984, the company began the revolution that turned American beer from watery pilsners to full-bodied microbrewed lagers and ale. The company offers tours (10 A.M.–3 P.M. Mon.–Thurs., 10 A.M.–5:30 P.M. Fri., 10 A.M.–3 P.M. Sat., year-round, $2 suggested donation) of the brewing process along with a historical presentation on the history of beer in Boston—including the early efforts by patriot Sam Adams himself.

CAMBRIDGE AND SOMERVILLE

Few places are defined as much by intellect as the city of Cambridge. To folks across the river, it's where the "smaht kids" are. To scholars around the world, it's equivalent to academic excellence. University culture permeates the axis of Massachusetts Avenue, which runs roughly from Harvard University to the Massachusetts Institute of Technology (universally referred to as MIT) and is awash in bookstores, pubs, and cafés. At even the grungiest bar you are apt to find earnest patrons debating Friedman and Keynes. Despite the high-powered intellectualism, however, the populace of Cambridge exudes a more relaxed vibe than the business chic of downtown Boston. Flannel and jeans outnumber suits, and even the fine-dining restaurants have a whimsical or downbeat feel.

Cambridge justly has a reputation as one

of the country's two "people's republics" (the other being its Californian soul sister, Berkeley), and the city has been a hotbed of student activism on issues from the Vietnam War to anti-globalization. As rents have risen over the years, however, many say that the real spirit of Cambridge has drifted north to the more proletarian Somerville, a working-class community that has picked up the slacker overflow, especially in the neighborhood of Davis Square.

Harvard Square

The geography of Cambridge is inexplicably organized into more than a dozen "squares," which are actually anything but. The heart of them all is Harvard Square, a spider web of streets outside the walls of the university that is crowded at all hours with students, parents, professors, and tourists. Gone are the days when the square was a downbeat mecca of bars and used record stores; the chain stores have long since swallowed up all but a few struggling independents. Still, there's something about strolling the brick sidewalks or people-watching from an outdoor table that is quintessential Cambridge. When the weather turns

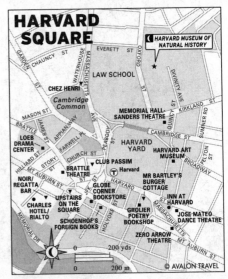

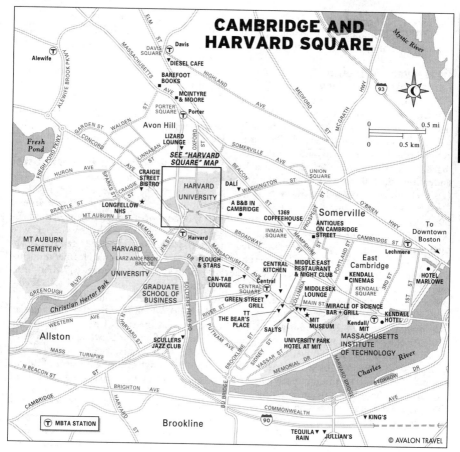

balmy, street performers flood nooks and crannies, offering everything from folk music sets to magic acts, and turning the area into a spontaneous carnival. Equally satisfying is a stroll down Brattle Street, the heart of Cambridge literati, where John Kenneth Galbraith, Robert Reich, and other leading political lights inhabit miniature colonial mansions.

Harvard University

Harvard is the kind of place people love to hate—most often out of jealousy. For some, it's synonymous with snobbery and effeteness; for others it represents the culmination of a

lifelong dream. Whatever your feelings, the campus itself doesn't disappoint. It is filled with important-looking brick buildings with actual ivy clinging romantically to their marble friezes. Most have stories, which the tour guides at the **Harvard Events & Information Center** (Holyoke Center Arcade, 1350 Massachusetts Ave., Cambridge, 617/495-1573, www.harvard.edu, 10 A.M. and 2 P.M. Mon.–Fri., 2 P.M. Sat., free) are happy to divulge. If you venture into Harvard Yard yourself, be sure to touch the foot of the statue of John Harvard for luck. It's known as the "statue of three lies" since it doesn't depict Harvard; wrongly calls him the founder; and gets the date of the founding wrong (it was 1636, not 1638). So much for the university's motto, *Veritas*—Latin for truth.

〖 Harvard Museum of Natural History

Before there was science, there was "natural history," and for decades Harvard sponsored naturalist exhibitions to catalog the animals, plants, and minerals of the world. The naturalists brought their booty back home, cataloged it, and ensconced it in one of the more endearing and eclectic museums in the area (26 Oxford St., Cambridge, 617/495-3045, www.hmnh.harvard.edu, 9 A.M.–5 P.M. daily, $9 adults, $7 students and seniors, $6 children 3–18) in the area. The bulk of the museum is taken up by gallery after gallery of real stuffed animals—taxidermy beasties of all shapes and sizes, from elephants to a pair of pheasants once owned by George Washington. Even more impressive is the rock-and-mineral collection, full of geodes, crystals, and precious stones the size of a small child. The pièce de résistance of the museum, however, is undoubtedly the glass flowers. Created by a father-and-son team from Germany, the flowers are meticulous representations of almost 900 species, made entirely from glass. The models are so exacting that they seem real, from the petals on a coneflower to the hairs on the leg of a tiny glass bee.

Harvard Art Museum

The paintings at Harvard's underrated art museum (485 Broadway, Cambridge, 617/495-9400, www.artmuseums.harvard. edu, 10 A.M.–5 P.M. Mon.–Sat., 1 P.M.–5 P.M. Sun., $9 adults, $7 seniors, $6 students, free Sat. before noon, every day after 4:30 P.M., and children 17 and under) were mostly acquired through random donations by rich alumni. Thus, it has pretty much one of everything, and everything is exceptional. Alas, much of it is also not available for viewing at present, since the museum is undergoing a major renovation that will combine Harvard's three disjointed art museums (the Fogg, Busch-Reisinger, and Sackler museums) into one glorious new space

designed by Renzo Piano, the busy beaver who is also designing the Isabella Stewart Gardner Museum addition across the stream. Until the new museum opens in 2013, visitors will have to content themselves with a rotating exhibition of the highlights of the museum—including a large number of Impressionist and post-Impressionist paintings, including a Van Gogh self-portrait, Degas' dancers, and several Picassos—that will be on view at the Sackler.

Longfellow National Historic Site

Today, Americans may not remember "The Song of Hiawatha" or the "Midnight Ride of Paul Revere," but back in the Victorian era, Henry Wadsworth Longfellow was the literary equivalent of George Clooney—a poet who transcended his art to become a genuine celebrity. Rangers lead tours of his former residence (105 Brattle St., Cambridge, 617/876-4491, www.nps.gov/long, 10:30 A.M.–4 P.M. Wed.–Sun. June–Oct., $3 adults, free children 15 and under), which features elegant Victorian furniture and the study where the poet composed many of his works. Other exhibits detail the home's earlier history as headquarters to George Washington during the siege of Boston in 1775–1776. Throughout the year, the site often offers performances of actors portraying other famous writers, including Walt Whitman and Louisa May Alcott. Longfellow devotees can see the poet's final resting place a short walk away at **Mount Auburn Cemetary** (580 Mt. Auburn St., Cambridge, 617/547-7105, www.mountauburn.org, 8 A.M.–5 P.M. daily Oct.–Apr., 8 A.M.–7 P.M. daily May–Aug., free), a grand Victorian burial ground that also holds the graves of other Victorian intellectuals, such as Mary Baker Eddy, Oliver Wendell Holmes, Buckminster Fuller, and "Battle Hymn of the Republic" composer Julia Ward Howe.

Central Square

As Harvard Square "jumped the shark," the alternative crowds moved to the next square down Massachusetts Avenue, which became the unwashed center for Boston's 1990s rock renaissance. Bands including the Lemonheads,

Morphine, Juliana Hatfield, and the Pixies all got their start at the legendary Middle East and other rock clubs in this stretch. Even as some chain stores have filled in the gaps (and The Gap), this section of Cambridge is still seen as more "real" by the tattooed and tongue-pierced crowd. Ethnic restaurants, art stores, and dance studios line the avenue, while the rock clubs still pack them in at night.

Massachusetts Institute of Technology

Cambridge's "other university" is, if anything, more acclaimed among the segment of society that wears pocket protectors and horn-rimmed glasses. The first computer was invented here in 1928, and the inventor of the World Wide Web is now a scientist-in-residence. The center of the school is known as the Infinite Corridor, a hallway that runs like a spine through the central buildings. If you are worried about inadvertently stepping into a particle reactor, you can join a free tour that leaves from Lobby 7 (77 Massachusetts Ave., Cambridge,

617/253-4795, www.mit.edu, 11 A.M. and 3 P.M. Mon.–Fri., free). Maps for self-guided tours are also available there. For the inner geek in all of us, the nearby **MIT Museum** (265 Massachusetts Ave., MIT Museum Bldg N51, Cambridge, 617/253-5927, web.mit.edu/museum, 10 A.M.–5 P.M. daily, $7.50 adults, $3 seniors, students, and youth 17 and under, free 10 A.M.–12 P.M. Sun.) has photographs and working specimens of everything from slide rules to robots. Holograms and kinetic sculptures explore the uneasy intersection of art and technology. The same could be said about one of MIT's newest and most striking buildings. The **Ray and Maria Stata Center** at 42 Vassar Street was designed by architect Frank Gehry, of Guggenheim Bilbao fame, and looks like a row of skyscrapers after getting a workout by Godzilla. Inside are unusually shaped communal spaces, designed to help scientists get out of their labs and actually talk to one another.

Davis Square

Once the subway was extended up to Somerville in the 1980s, Davis Square went through a dramatic transformation from forgotten gulch of dollar stores and newsstands to a funky hipster heaven. The neighborhood has no fewer than five cafés, and come Saturday afternoon all of them are overflowing with Tufts students or recent grads, with real or computerized notebooks propped open. True, the attempts by the Somerville Theater to brand the neighborhood the "Paris of the '90s" fizzled, but the theater still anchors a vibrant cultural scene, and bars along Elm Street keep the streets hopping after dark.

BROOKLINE

Despite being completely surrounded by Boston, the large town of Brookline maintains a clearly separate identity. As soon as you cross the town line, the streets get leafier and the houses get bigger. Brookline residents pride themselves on living a quasi-urban lifestyle while still enjoying the suburban benefits of good schools and green space. Sophisticated but proudly unhip, the neighborhood's

© TIM GRAFFT/MOTT

MIT's unmistakable Stata Center

crossroads of Coolidge Corner is like a more adult Harvard Square, where you are more apt to run into a professor than a student. The town is also home to one of the largest Jewish populations outside of Israel and Palm Beach—a fact evident from all of the kosher delis, temples, and Hebrew bookstores that line its streets.

John F. Kennedy National Historic Site

Just steps up from Coolidge Corner is the birthplace of the 35th president, where John F. Kennedy took his first steps and said his first words. The home (83 Beals St., Brookline, 617/566-7937, www.nps.gov/jofi, 10 A.M.–4:30 P.M. Wed.–Sun. mid-May–Sept., $3 adults, free children under 17) is now filled with furniture, photographs, and other memorabilia collected by Kennedy's mother, Rose, who also provided an audio tour describing life in Brookline in 1917. Rangers also occasionally lead tours to the Kennedys' second home up the street, as well as St. Aidan's, the Catholic church where JFK and his family worshipped.

QUINCY

South of Boston and accessible by the T, Quincy is actually the fourth-largest city in the state, and might be thriving if it were located anywhere else. As it is, the city tends to be overshadowed by its larger neighbor. Apart from an area of old historic homes, the city is mostly dilapidated and depressed. For a brief time in the 19th century, Quincy was the center for granite quarrying in the region, and many of the monuments in Boston were mined from quarries that still stand open (and are used by rock climbers). The city is better known, however, as the birthplace of two American presidents—John Adams and his son John Quincy Adams.

Adams National Historic Site

The second president of the United States always got short shrift—not as acclaimed as Washington (#1) or as controversial as Jefferson (#3). That all changed a few years ago when David McCullough published his blockbuster biography *John Adams*, and showed its title character to be a forthright scholar swept into greatness by the historic tides of war. Even after the Revolution, Adams was able to stay above the sectarian wrangling of his time to put the interests of the country foremost. Much of his moral center can be attributed to his wife, Abigail Adams, who was a brilliant thinker and early feminist in her own right. The family headquarters was in a palatial home called the "Old House," at 135 Adams Street, which was home to four generations of the Adams family. Two-hour guided trolley tours take visitors literally from cradle to grave, starting at the birthplaces of Adams and his son, proceeding to the Old House, and ending at the church where the two are buried along with their wives. Trolleys leave from the National Park Visitors Center (1250 Hancock Street, Quincy, 617/770-1175, www.nps.gov/adam, 9 A.M.–5 P.M. daily mid-Apr.–mid-Nov., 10 A.M.–4 P.M. Tues.–Fri. mid-Nov.–mid-Apr., $5 adults, free children under 17, $10 family pass). Alternately, you can walk to the Old House from Quincy Center and tour the home and the grounds, which still include some of Adams' beloved apple trees.

Entertainment and Events

As a city that has always prided itself on culture, Boston rarely lacks for interesting arts and entertainment offerings. Performances range from meticulous renderings of chamber music to off-beat theater productions in experimental studios. Both major papers, the *Boston Globe* and *Boston Herald,* run comprehensive arts listings on Thursdays and Fridays, while the *Globe* also provides a roundup of events in its daily "Go!" section. A more alternative take on the week's events, including previews for upcoming rock shows, can be found in the weekly newspapers *The Boston Phoenix* and *The Weekly Dig.* For tickets to theater performances, a great resource is **BosTix** (617/262-8632, www.bostix.org), which offers half-price tickets the day of the show. Booths are located in Quincy Marketplace (10 A.M.–6 P.M. Tues.–Sat., 11 A.M.–4 P.M. Sun.) and Copley Square (10 A.M.–6 P.M. Mon.–Sat., 11 A.M.–4 P.M. Sun.) and only accept cash.

CLASSICAL MUSIC

In addition to **Boston Symphony Hall** (301 Massachusetts Ave., 617/266-1492, www.bso. org), Boston has many excellent smaller halls that regularly offer classical concerts. These include: New England Conservatory's acoustically refined **Jordan Hall** (30 Gainsborough St., 617/585-1260, www.newenglandconservatory.edu/concerts); Boston University's **Tsai Performance Center** (685 Commonwealth Ave., 617/353-8725, www.bu.edu/tsai); and Harvard's intimate **Sanders Theatre** (45 Quincy St., Cambridge, 617/496-2222, www. fas.harvard.edu/tickets).

Boston Symphony Orchestra

Since its founding in 1881, the BSO (888/266-1200, www.bso.org) has been one of the country's premier classical orchestras. In 2006, classical aficionados were clapping vigorously (their version of cheering) when modern legend James Levine ascended to the BSO's podium as conductor of both Boston's orchestra and the New York Metropolitan Opera.

Boston Pops

From the very beginning of its existence, the BSO has interspersed classical music with lighter fare. In 1900, the latter became the specialty of Boston Pops, which reached national prominence under the baton of march-master Arthur Fiedler in the 1970s and further acclaim with movie-theme composer John Williams. The current manifestation of the Pops is under the direction of the boyishly exuberant Keith Lockhart, whose lineups might feature show tunes, movie themes, or vocal pop music. The orchestra performs in Symphony Hall in May and June, and then stages free outdoor concerts through July.

Handel and Haydn Society

Dedicated to the performances of choral works from the 19th century and earlier, H&H (617/262-1815, www.handelandhaydn.org) regularly performs at Symphony Hall, Jordan Hall, and the Sanders Theatre. The highlight of the year is its Christmastime performances of *Messiah,* a Boston tradition.

Boston Lyric Opera

In addition to classics by Rossini, Mozart, and other masters, the BLO (617/542-6772, www. blo.org) regularly stages modern works, such as a recent opera based on the children's book *The Little Prince.* Performances take place at the Shubert Theatre.

Chamber Music

The eight-person **Boston Chamber Music Society** (617/349-0086, www.bostonchambermusic.org) performs classics by Mozart, Beethoven, and other composers. The **Pro Arte Chamber Orchestra** (617/779-0900, www.proarte.org) is a co-op orchestra that presents relatively more daring fare.

Church Concerts

A little-known choral gem, **Emmanuel Music** (15 Newbury St., 617/536-3356, www.

emmanuelmusic.org) performs entire Bach masses on Sundays at Emmanuel Church. **Trinity Boston** (206 Clarendon St., 617/536-0944, www.trinitychurchboston.org) performs half-hour recitals on Fridays at noon, as well as occasional choral concerts in one of the most beautiful settings in Boston—Copley Square's Trinity Church.

ROCK AND POP CONCERTS

The biggest names in rock and pop come to the **TD Garden** (100 Legends Way, 617/624-1050, www.tdbanknorthgarden.com), which is converted to a concert auditorium when the Celtics and Bruins aren't in town. Acoustics are about what you'd expect from a sports arena. During the warmer months, a much nicer place to see a show is the **Bank of America Pavilion** (290 Northern Ave., 617/728-1600, www.livenation.com), an open-air auditorium in the Seaport District with the twinkling lights of the harbor as a backdrop to folk and pop performers. During the summer months, many area radio stations also sponsor shows with of-the-moment pop stars at the **Hatch Memorial Shell** (617/626-4970, www.mass.gov/dcr/hatch_events.htm) on the Charles River Esplanade.

The **Orpheum Theatre** (1 Hamilton Pl., 617/679-0810) is run-down, hot, and cramped, but still provides a sufficiently grungy venue for alternative-rock shows. A much more exciting place to see mid-size performers is the **House of Blues** (15 Lansdowne St., 888 /693-2583), which despite its name hosts mostly indie rock performers such as Regina Spektor and The Bravery in a huge amphitheatre with multiple balconies. Shows are general admission, so get there early to get close to the stage.

JAZZ CONCERTS

The "Harvard of jazz," Berklee School of Music sponsors performances of both modern legends and up-and-coming prodigies at its **Berklee Performance Center** (136 Massachusetts Ave., 617/747-2261, www.berkleebpc.com), which also occasionally has folk and pop acts.

THEATER
Citi Performing Arts Center

The most opulent performance space in Boston is the **Wang Theatre** (270 Tremont St., 617/482-9393, www.citicenter.org) in the Citi Performing Arts Center. It's a 3,000-seat theater in the European tradition, with a grand lobby, marble-column proscenium, and giant crystal chandelier. Most of the performances here are not terribly original, however, tending towards traveling Broadway musicals and spectaculars like Riverdance and the Ten Tenors. Recently, the Wang has experimented with rock acts, the likes of Death Cab for Cutie and The Pixies. Citi saves its (relatively) more artsy theater fare for its sister property, the 1,800-seat **Shubert Theatre** (265 Tremont St., 617/482-9393, www.citicenter.org).

Broadway Across America

Since coming to town a decade ago to revive Boston as a tryout town for New York, this organization (866/523-7469, www.broadwayacrossamerica.com) has breathed new life into the Theater District, staging plays that always garner buzz, even if they don't always deliver. Its flagship theater is the **Colonial Theatre** (106 Boylston St., 617/246-9366, www.bostoncolonialtheatre.com/), a restored space with colorful history that now stages exciting Broadway-bound productions.

In addition, the newly renovated **Opera House** (539 Washington St., 617/259-3400, www.bostonoperahouse.com/) is giving the Wang a run for its money with a 2,500-seat venue for mainstream musicals such as *The Lion King* and *The Phantom of the Opera*.

Theater Companies

For two decades, the **Huntington Theatre Company** (264 Huntington Ave., 617/266-0800, www.huntingtontheatre.org) has been regarded as Boston's top professional theater company. Under the tutelage of artistic director Nicholas Martin, several of its performances have recently gone on to Broadway. The company's works tend toward well-crafted dramas with emotional storylines. In addition to its main stage at the Boston University Theatre, it also performs at the BCA's Calderwood Pavilion.

Across the river in Cambridge, the **American Repertory Theatre** (617/547-8300, www.amrep.org) has earned an enthusiastic following for its more avant-garde performances that often feature elaborate post-modern stage design. In addition to two stages at Harvard's Loeb Drama Center (64 Brattle St., Cambridge), the company recently opened the Zero Arrow Theatre (2 Arrow St., Cambridge, 617/495-2668), which has a flexible stage for even more cutting-edge productions.

The multistage **Boston Center for the Arts** (539 Tremont St., 617/426-5000, www.bcaonline.org) is a South End complex that features several modern resident theater companies. In addition to the 360-seat Calderwood Pavilion, the complex has four smaller stages of varying sizes.

Affiliated with the Wang Center, the **Commonwealth Shakespeare Company** (617/426-0863, www.commshakes.org/) has been performing the Bard outdoors for the past decade. The free summertime performances take place in July and August at the Parkman Bandstand in Boston Common.

Last but not least, the **Charles Playhouse** (74 Warrenton St., www.charles-playhouse.com) is home to two long-running Boston favorites, the bizarrely comic Blue Man Group (800/982-2787, www.blueman.com) and the interactive whodunnit *Shear Madness* (617/426-5225, www.shearmadness.com), a cheesy Boston tradition for more than 25 years and 12,000 performances.

DANCE

Few ballet companies are as respected as the **Boston Ballet** (19 Clarendon St., 617/695-6950, www.bostonballet.org), which has been performing classic and modern interpretations of the form for 40 years. Its annual productions of *The Nutcracker,* performed at the Opera House, are internationally famous. A younger ballet company, which puts its emphasis on the dancing rather than costumes or sets, is the **Jose Mateo Dance Theatre** (400 Harvard St., Cambridge, 617/354-7467, www.balletheatre.org). It performs in the Sanctuary Theatre, a beautifully restored Gothic church in Cambridge.

FILM

The revivals of Humphrey Bogart classics during Harvard's exam period long ago put the **Brattle Theater** (40 Brattle St., Cambridge, 617/876-6837, www.brattlefilm.org) on the map. It sill runs Bogey marathons along with foreign films, New Wave cinema, and more recent independent fare in a delightfully shabby Harvard Square theater. Film directors regularly show up to introduce shows. Also in Cambridge, **Kendall Cinemas** (1 Kendall Sq., Cambridge, 617/499-1996, www.landmarktheatres.com) shows first-run art-house and foreign films in a well-appointed theater serving espresso at the candy counter.

The large, art deco **Coolidge Corner Theatre** (290 Harvard St., Brookline, 617/734-2500, www.coolidge.org) anchors its

Boston Center for the Arts

LECTURES AND READINGS

As befits an intellectual populace, Boston and Cambridge's many colleges and universities often open their doors to the public for lectures by speakers at the top of their academic games. The **Harvard University** *Gazette* (www.news.harvard.edu/gazette) publishes a full schedule of talks, as do the websites of **Boston University** (www.bu.edu/calendar) and **Massachusetts Institute of Technology** (http://events.mit.edu). Public lectures, often on topics relating to the city's history, geography, or various ethnic cultures, are also held periodically at **Boston Public Library** (700 Boylston St., 617/536-5400, www.bpl.org/news/comingevents.htm) and **Old South Meeting House** (310 Washington St., 617/482-6439, www.oldsouthmeetinghouse.org). Contemporary readings and talks by authors are held at several noteworthy bookstores, including **Harvard Bookstore** (1256 Massachusetts Ave., Cambridge, 800/542-7323, www.harvard.com) and **Brookline Booksmith** (279 Harvard St., Brookline, 617/566-6660, www.brooklinebooksmith.com), which for popular authors takes over the **Coolidge Corner Movie Theater** (290 Harvard St., Brookline, 617/734-2500, www.coolidge.org) across the street.

neighborhood with a gorgeous space for second-run and cult movies, as well as concerts and lectures by best-selling authors. It also has a smaller video screening room for DV (digital video) films and local work.

Free films, tending towards the classics, are shown in the Rabb Lecture Hall of the **Boston Public Library** (700 Boylston St., 617/536-5400, www.bpl.org), usually on Mondays. During the summer, **Free Friday Flicks** (617/787-7200, www.wbz1030.com) brings family-friendly blockbusters outdoors to the Hatch Shell on the Esplanade. The **Museum of Fine Arts** (465 Huntington Ave., 617/369-3306, www.mfa.org) also regularly screens contemporary foreign films and movies relating to current art exhibitions.

COMEDY

After years in a cramped spot in Quincy Market, the **Comedy Connection** (The Wilbur Theatre, 146 Tremont St., 800/745-3000, www.thewilburtheatre.com, $12–24) has hit the big time with a move into the Theater District. In addition to local up-and-comers, it routinely books the biggest names in yuks, recently including Bill Maher, Janeane Garofalo, and Mike Bribiglia. (The Wilbur Theatre also occasionally hosts rock acts such as Neko Case and Sonic Youth.) Quick-thinking young comics incorporate audience suggestions into improvisational sketches à la *Whose Line Is It Anyway?* at the North End's **ImprovAsylum** (216 Hanover St., 617/263-6887, www.improvasylum.com).

EVENTS

Boston's events calendar starts on New Year's Eve with **First Night,** a citywide celebration featuring concerts, kid's activities, and artistic events throughout the day of December 31. The night is capped off by two fireworks celebrations, one in the early evening and another at midnight. Just after the holiday bulge disappears, Bostonians fatten up again with the **Boston Cooks!** festival in late January and early February, during which celebrity chefs offer cut-rate meals with the proceeds donated to charity. Around the same time **Boston Wine Expo** takes over the World Trade Center for samplings of thousands of vintages from more than a dozen countries.

If that's not enough partying for you, **St. Patrick's Day** is right around the corner on March 17. The main event is a parade on the nearest Sunday through South Boston, whose streets are bedecked with green for the occasion. To work off all of the weight they've put on in the winter, residents turn out for the **Boston Marathon,** the oldest (and some say toughest) marathon in the United States. Spectators start lining the route to cheer along

Beacon and Boylston Streets, all the way to Copley Square. The race is held on the second Monday in April, which is also known in Massachusetts as **Patriot's Day** to celebrate the early victories of the Revolutionary War.

Patriotism continues when the neighborhood of Charlestown celebrates its own holiday, **Bunker Hill Day,** on June 17. The celebration features military demonstrations by colonial re-enactors, along with a parade and street vendors. Boston's patriotic triptych concludes with the gala celebrations on the **Fourth of July.** Residents wake up early to hear the reading of the Declaration of Independence from the balcony of the Old State House. The main event is the concert by the beloved Boston Pops on the Esplanade, which is televised nationally every year and draws hundreds of thousands to hear musical medleys accompanied by celebrity performers. Get there early if you have any hope of snagging a patch of grass.

The fall in Boston is dedicated to the arts, with theaters commencing their new seasons of plays, and neighborhoods including the South End, Cambridge, and Jamaica Plain holding annual **open studios** to showcase local artwork. The holidays officially begin with the **Holiday Tree Lighting** at the Prudential Center, which brings out politicians and celebrities along with the mayor to throw the switch.

Nightlife

After hours, Boston has a rambunctious mix of old-time Irish bars, dance clubs, and newer upscale lounges. As a remnant of the blue laws, "happy hour" drink specials are forbidden here—though many bars offer free food for the after-work crowd. Smoking is also illegal in all bars, though a few may quietly let you light up in back. Bars in Boston and Somerville generally close at 1 A.M. during the week and 2 A.M. on weekends. Cambridge bars close at 1 A.M. nightly.

BARS AND LOUNGES
Beacon Hill

Catch up on political gossip at **The 21st Amendment** (150 Bowdoin St., 617/227-7100, www.21stboston.com), a beat-up watering hole across from the State House. Named after the amendment that ended prohibition, it caters mostly to a draft-beer crowd. Down the hill, **The Sevens** (77 Charles St., 617/523-9074, 11 A.M.–11 P.M. Mon.–Sat.; 12 P.M.–11 P.M. Sun., www.sevensalehouse.com) is the closest thing Beacon Hill has to a neighborhood bar, where well-mannered brahmins and well-coifed business consultants share wooden booths and watch the flow of people on Charles Street.

Government Center and Faneuil Hall

The laid-back **Hennessy's** (25 Union St., 617/742-2121, 11 P.M.–1 A.M. Mon.–Sat.; 12 P.M.–12 A.M. Sun., www.somerspubs.com/) is carefully crafted to evoke a Victorian roadside tavern, with a selection of Irish whiskies and occasional Celtic music that draws an expat Irish crowd. A reliable pour of Guinness and raucous live fiddlers can be found at **The Black Rose** (160 State St., 617/742-2286, 12 P.M.–2 A.M. Mon.–Sat.; 12 P.M.–1 A.M. Sun., www.irish-connection.com/), an Irish pub near Faneuil Hall that is a favorite with tourists. Pictures of Hibernian writers line the walls, and hearty fare such as corned beef and fish-and-chips is served. Located inside the Omni Parker House, **The Last Hurrah** (60 School St., 617/725-1888, 10 A.M.–1 A.M. Mon.–Sat.; 1 P.M.–1 A.M. Sun., www.omnihotels.com) is named after a book about one of Boston's most notorious politicians, "Rascal King" James Michael Curley. Its elegant, plant-filled room is a hangout for City Hall types and Financial District suits, who trade favors and stock tips over martinis.

Downtown Crossing

Cops, reporters, businessmen, and hipsters

can all be spotted ordering boilermakers at **J. J. Foley's** (21 Kingston St., 617/695-2529, 4 P.M.–2 A.M. Mon.–Sat.; 3 P.M.–12 A.M. Sun.,), one of the last great downtown neighborhood bars. The lighting is dim, the jukebox exceptional, and the crowd usually quite thirsty.

North End

If you couldn't get into the game at the Garden, or if you're just a multitasker, you'll enjoy the **Sports Grille Boston** (132 Canal St., 617/367-9302, 5 P.M.–1 A.M. Mon.–Sat.; 4 P.M.–11 P.M. Sun.,), which has 140 TVs, all tuned to one thing: sports. The bar's mammoth interior has a bit of a soulless feeling, offset slightly by the authentic memorabilia of Boston sports legends on the walls. As an antidote to all those plastic Paddy pubs that serve beer green, the Irish pub **McGann's** (197 Portland St., 617/227-4059, 11 A.M.–1 A.M. daily) is the real thing, with a decor straight from County Clare, and the likes of Belhaven and Tetley's on tap. Sinead O'Connor once even played a (very) intimate show on stage here. The industrial decor and smell of roasted malts at **Boston Beer Works** (112 Canal St., 617/896-2337, 11 A.M.–1 A.M. Mon.–Sat.; 12 P.M.–11 P.M. Sun., www.beerworks.net) harken back to the days when brewpubs were king. If the fad has paled, the beer at least hasn't—brews like Boston Red and Back Bay IPA hit the spot, while TVs show all the action at the arena next door.

Financial District

Working stiffs clock out of their cubicles and become human again at **Market** (21 Broad St., 617/263-0037, 4 P.M.–2 A.M. Mon.–Sat.; 12 P.M.–11 P.M. Sun., www.mktboston.com) A round wooden bar and rough-hewn wooden pillars create a rustic vibe to chill out the after-work crowd, while crafted cocktails with lychee and blackberries help stir up a juicy singles scene.

Back Bay

There could be a raging nor'easter outside, but inside the legendary **Oak Bar** (138 St. James St., 617/267-5300, 11 A.M.–2 A.M. Mon.–Sat.; 11 A.M.–12 A.M. Sun., www.theoakroom.com) in the Fairmont Copley Plaza, it's always 70 degrees, with the sun just setting over the Indian Ocean, and the distant whack of a cricket bat audible over the veldt. The crisp service of the gold-vested bartenders bespeaks civilization, while the generous martinis whisper pure decadence. In the basement of the nearby Copley Square Hotel, **Saint** (90 Exeter St., 617/236-1134, 4:30 P.M.–2 A.M. Mon.–Sat.; 5 P.M.–1 A.M. Sun.,) is like a grown-up version of a "heaven and hell" party—cool and opalescent in one room and devilish red velvet in the other. Insouciant patrons spend their time sampling a fusion tapas menu, listening to cool techno, and making provocative glances across the room. On Newbury Street, the young and lovely hang out at **Sonsie** (327 Newbury St., 617/351-2500, 8 A.M.–1 A.M. Mon.–Sat.; 8:30 A.M.–12 A.M. Sun., www.sonsieboston. com), where French doors open up onto the street, the better to check out the handbags and clothing labels of passersby.

South End

The neighborhood living room for the South End's gay scene, the **Club Cafe Lounge & Video Bar** (209 Columbus Ave., 617/536-0966, 4 P.M.–2 A.M. Mon.–Thurs.; 12 P.M.–2 A.M. Thurs.–Fri.; 11 A.M.–1 A.M. Sun., www.clubcafe.com) is clean and well-lit, all the better to check out the attractive stranger at the next table. Groups of people play musical chairs while trading gossip before and after clubbing. Located on two levels beneath the Boston Center for the Arts, **The Beehive** (541 Tremont St., 617/423-0069, 5 P.M.–2 A.M. daily, www.beehiveboston.com) buzzes with a bohemian crowd who come for laid-back jazz and a potent drink list that tastes of blood orange and apricot nectar. The space itself is a knockout, designed within an inch of its life from an eclectic mix of influences ranging from Spanish bordello to New York pop art. Upstairs, tables serve a bistro menu of bouillabaisse and steak frites.

The hole-in-the-wall **Delux Cafe & Lounge** (100 Chandler St., 617/338-5258, 5 P.M.–1 A.M.

daily) is one of the most trippy bar scenes in the city, where a heterogeneous crowd downs pints beneath Christmas lights and Elvis album covers. Snack food includes the best grilled cheese sandwich in the city. **The Butcher Shop** (552 Tremont St., 617/423-4800, 11 A.M.–11 P.M. Sun.–Mon.; 11 A.M.–12 A.M. Tues.–Sat., www. thebutchershopboston.com) is only a meat market in the most literal sense. Butchers prepare cuts of meat during the day; at night, however, the giant butcher block table is taken over by the young and metrosexual, who toy with an extensive by-the-glass wine list and nosh on honey-soaked figs and panini sandwiches.

Other Neighborhoods

Boston's only drag-queen bar, **Jacque's Cabaret** (79 Broadway, 617/426-8902, 11 A.M.–12 A.M. Mon.–Sat.; 12 P.M.–12 A.M. Sun., www.jacquescabaret.com) is like a pomegranate: deliciously seedy. Anything goes and frequently does at shows in which female impersonators lip-synch for cat-calling audiences that usually include at least one bachelorette party. Located in the neighborhood of Bay Village, behind the Theater District, the bar has a small room downstairs that hosts indie bands and cabaret acts. The local hangout for Fort Point Channel's artists community, **Lucky's Lounge** (355 Congress St., South Boston, 617/357-5825, 11 A.M.–11 P.M. Mon.–Thurs.; 10 A.M.–11 P.M. Sat.–Sun., www.luckyslounge.com) rewards those who can find it. A basement door without a sign opens up onto a retro-cool cocktail lounge where kitschy landscapes line the walls and Frank Sinatra is in regular rotation.

A true Jamaica Plain institution, **Doyle's Cafe** (3484 Washington St., Jamaica Plain, 617/524-2345, 9 A.M.–11 P.M. Mon.–Sat.; 11 A.M.–9 P.M. Sun., www.doyles-cafe.com) is a temple to more than 100 years of city politics, with memorabilia on the wall dedicated to politicians from John F. Kennedy to John Kerry—and a new generation of politicos writing history over pints or single malts in the corner booths. Beer lovers make regular pilgrimages to Allston to sample the more

than 112 brews on tap at **Sunset Grill & Tap** (130 Brighton Ave., Allston, 617/254-1331, 4 P.M.–2 A.M. Mon.–Sat.; 11 A.M.–1 A.M. Sun., www.allstonsfinest.com). Another 400 are served in bottles; if you are really thirsty you can order it by the yard.

Cambridge

The black leather couches and velvet curtains of **Noir** (1 Bennett St., Cambridge, 617/661-8010, 4 P.M.–2 A.M. daily, www.noir-bar.com) could easily serve as the backdrop for an illicit affair. Located in Harvard Square's Charles Hotel, the lounge does its best to stir up intrigue with cocktails named for classic film noir movies. The more rambunctious **Grendel's Den** (89 Winthrop St., Cambridge, 617/491-1160, 11:30 A.M.–11 P.M. daily, www.grendelsden.com) is a subterranean lair where surly waitstaff serve pints and finger food to a heavily Harvard-saturated crowd.

In Central Square, the **Plough & Stars** (912 Massachusetts Ave., Cambridge, 617/576-0032, 11:30 A.M.–12 A.M. daily, www.ploughandstars.com) is an Irish bar with a working-class feel. It features an eclectic mix of live music and European soccer matches on the telly. The New York–cool **Middlesex Lounge** (315 Massachusetts Ave., Cambridge, 617/868-6739, 11:30 A.M.–1 A.M. Mon.–Wed.; 11:30 A.M.–2 A.M. Thurs.–Fri.; 5 P.M.–2 A.M. Sat., www.middlesexlounge.com) puts its couches on wheels, the better to convert from techno lounge to dance floor with the shake of a booty. The zen minimalist vibe attracts a cross-section of Cambridge pseudo-literati. At MIT's neighborhood bar, **Miracle of Science Bar + Grill** (321 Massachusetts Ave., Cambridge, 617/868-2866, 7 A.M.–1 A.M. Mon.–Fri.; 9 A.M.–1 A.M. Sat.–Sun.; www.miracleofscience.us), the menu is modeled after the Periodic Table of Elements. Amorous nerds use their laptops to send instant messages across the room.

Somerville

An Irish bar on steroids, **The Burren** (247 Elm St., Somerville, 617/776-6896,

11:30 A.M.–12 A.M. Mon.–Fri.; 11 A.M.–1 A.M. Sat.–Sun.; www.burren.com) nevertheless manages to keep it real with Irish *seisiuns* and step-dancing on a stage in the back room. On other nights, patrons drink their stout while listening to open-mic poetry.

Brookline
The **Coolidge Corner Clubhouse** (307A-309 Harvard St., Brookline, 617/566-4948, 4 P.M.–1 A.M. Mon.–Fri.; 11:30 A.M.–12:45 A.M. Sat.–Sun.; www.thecoolidgecornerclubhouse. com) is a curious hybrid of French brasserie and neighborhood sports bar. Its 22 TVs ensure that there is always a game on worth watching.

LIVE MUSIC
Rock
The center of Boston's rock scene is actually in Central Square in Cambridge. The legendary **Middle East Restaurant & Nightclub** (472–480 Massachusetts Ave., Cambridge, 617/864-3278, www.mideastclub.com) is a complex of three rooms with different styles. Larger bands play in the grungy basement downstairs, while local acts and indie bands play the cozier upstairs. Belly dancers and the occasional singer-songwriter take the stage in the Middle Eastern restaurant upstairs. Word to the wise: skip the food. Named 30 years ago for a pet hamster, **TT The Bear's Place** (10 Brookline Ave., Cambridge, 617/492-2327, www.ttthebears. com) is the hangout of choice for the city's own rock stars, groupies, and wannabes. Bookings tend heavily toward the local, but also include touring bands on their way up. Several rooms allow rockers to talk or shoot pool until their friend's band takes the stage.

U2 made their first legendary U.S. performances at **Paradise Rock Club** (967–969 Commonwealth Ave., 617/562-8800, www. thedise.com), a mid-sized club with good views from several tiers of balconies (each with its own bar). Next door, the Paradise Lounge is a smaller space decked out with modern art that stages everything from acoustic performances to erotic poetry. Outside of Harvard Square,

the **Lizard Lounge** (1667 Massachusetts Ave., Cambridge, 617/547-0759, www.lizardlounge-club.com) is the place to go for esoteric rock, neo-burlesque, or poetry readings in its small basement.

Jazz and Blues
The cream of the jazz and Latin crop come to the **Regattabar** (1 Bennett St., Cambridge, 617/395-7757, www.regattabarjazz.com), a 225-capacity room in Harvard Square. Tables are arranged around a stage floor in a simple space with no distractions from the music—which in the past has included the likes of Branford Marsalis and Joshua Redman. Booked by legendary jazz club promoter Fred Taylor, **Scullers Jazz Club** (Doubletree Guest Suites, 400 Soldiers Field Rd., 617/562-4111, www.scullersjazz.com) is impressive both for the quality of its talent and the expansiveness of its view of the Charles River. The 200-capacity room has hosted everyone from Lou Rawls to Chris Botti.

The South End's **Wally's** (427 Massachusetts Ave., 617/424-1408, www.wallyscafe.com) hosts jazz the way it was meant to be played, in a closet-sized room that heats up both on and off stage. It is one of the few places in Boston that brings people of all backgrounds together to worship at the altar of syncopation. Don't expect big names—just talented performers. The **Can-Tab Lounge** (738 Massachusetts Ave., Cambridge, 617/354-2685, www.cantab-lounge.com) is a joint in the classic sense of the word, where R&B and blues acts alternate nights with multi-ethnic poetry slams. Crooner and minor legend Little Joe Cook performs on weekends here, as he has for the past 25 years.

Folk
The intimate **Club Passim** (47 Palmer St., Cambridge, 617/492-7679, www.clubpassim. org) has a history many times its small size. Many great names have gotten their start in this Harvard Square folk institution, including Joan Baez, Suzanne Vega, and Shawn Colvin. Now, it has a talented group of regular performers who have developed a singer-songwriter style

known as the "Boston Sound" for its catchy harmonies and erudite lyrics. Every Memorial Day and Labor Day weekend, it stages a three-day marathon of music. No alcohol is served, but good vegetarian cuisine is.

DANCE CLUBS
Downtown

The beautiful people shake their thing at **Gypsy Bar** (116 Boylston St., 617/482-7799, www.gypsybarboston.com), a plush downtown dance club decked out in deep-brown leather, dark wood, and pulsing red lights. It draws an international crowd who mingle at the long wine bar before they take the plunge onto the dance floor to dance to house music as the night wears on. At the other end of the spectrum, the fraternity brothers who frequent **Liquor Store** (25 Boylston St., 617/357-6800, www.liquorstoreboston.com) are more randy than the mechanical bull featured in a bikini bull-riding competition every Friday night. The club does have some standards, however—no sneakers or shorts are allowed.

The Roxy (279 Tremont St., 617/338-7699, www.roxyplex.com) used to be a grand ballroom, and the opulent decor sets the stage for its air of modern decadence. High-energy and heavily European crowds come here to dance to hip-hop and '80s music. Occasionally the stage also hosts rock bands and Chippendale's male reviews.

Fenway

Behind Fenway Park, it's always Mardi Gras at **Tequila Rain** (3 Lansdowne St., 617/437-0300, www.tequilarainboston.com), a testosterone-filled dance club that features Top 40 music and periodic hormonal tomfoolery like wet T-shirt contests and dunk tanks. It caters to a post-game and suburban crowd.

Two different tastes can be found at the co-joined gay clubs **Ramrod/Machine** (1254 Boylston St., 617/266-2986; 1256 Boylston St., 617/536-1950; www.ramrod-boston.com, www.machine-boston.com). Ramrod is a cruisy leather bar with a back room open only to those wearing leather or not wearing a shirt. Next door, Machine is a more casual hangout with a large dance floor and a hot, hot Friday-night scene. The two mix over a pool table that connects the two spaces.

BILLIARDS AND BOWLING

Flat Top Johnny's (1 Kendall Square, Cambridge, 617/494-9565, www.flattop-johnnys.com) feels like a 1940s pool hall, updated with a punk-rock soundtrack and a Roy Lichtenstein–esque mural on one wall. The crowd consists of the hipper denizens of Cambridge, who seem like they've taken time off from their art or recording studio to rack a few.

The computerized scorekeepers at **Kings** (50 Dalton St., 617/266-2695, www.kingsbackbay.com) keep track of the pins so you don't have to. The self-consciously retro Back Bay bowling alley is a favorite with after-work leagues. The balls are the regular size—not the smaller candlepins common in New England. A small side room has eight vintage pool tables.

The Fenway area's **Jillian's** (145 Ipswich St., 617/437-0300, www.jilliansboston.com) is an homage to attention deficit disorder, with a 16-lane bowling alley and what seems like miles of the latest arcade games and pool tables on three different floors. If you can't have fun here, you probably don't know how.

MASSACHUSETTS

Shopping

Several shopping malls are connected in the center of the city, allowing shoppers to browse for a mile without suffering so much as a raindrop. Near Copley Square, the **Shops At Copley Place** (2 Copley Place, 617/369-5000, www.simon.com) include upscale clothing designers such as Neiman Marcus, Barneys New York, and Louis Vuitton, and jewelry stores Montblanc and Tiffany & Co. They are connected through a pedestrian walkway to the **Shops at Prudential Center** (800 Boylston St., 617/236-3100, www.prudentialcenter.com), which has a diverse selection of upscale and casual stores. In Cambridge, the two-story **Cambridgeside Galleria** is filled with books, music, and clothing stores. (100 Cambridgeside Place, Cambridge, 617/621-8666, www.cambridgesidegalleria.com).

ANTIQUES

Charles Street has some 40 antiques stores along its one-third-mile length. While pricey, they offer a selection you won't find anywhere else in the city. One of the best is **Upstairs Downstairs Antiques** (93 Charles St., 617/367-1950, 10 A.M.–6 P.M. daily) a warren of rooms stuffed with tableware, glassware, and other knickknacks from a dozen decades. Armchair historians and explorers alike thrill at the selection of antique maps and charts at **Eugene Galleries** (76 Charles St., 617/227-3062, 10 A.M.–5 P.M. Mon.–Sat.; 11 A.M.–5 P.M. Sun.), which cover Boston, New England, and the rest of the world. Worth making a trip out to Cambridge for the prices alone, **Antiques on Cambridge Street** (1076 Cambridge St., Cambridge, 617/234-0001,

© MICHAEL BLANDING

Quincy Market is a former fish warehouse turned upscale mall.

9:30 A.M.–5:30 P.M. daily) is filled with the wares of more than 100 sellers—furniture, artwork, vintage clothing, housewares, and more.

ART GALLERIES

The most prestigious art galleries are in the high-rent district of Newbury Street. The biggest name on the street is the **Barbara Krakow Gallery** (10 Newbury St., 617/262-4490, 10 A.M.–5 P.M. Mon.–Sat.; or call for an appointment, www.barbarakrakowgallery.com), which draws nationally known contemporary artists. More traditional paintings and prints are on display at the venerable **Childs Gallery** (169 Newbury St., 617/266-1108, 10 A.M.–5:30 P.M. Mon.–Fri; 11 A.M.–5 P.M. Sat.–Sun.), www.childsgallery.com), which focuses on pre-WWII American and European work. The **International Poster Gallery** (205 Newbury St., 617/375-0076, by appointment only, www.internationalposter.com) is a treasure trove of original French liquor prints and Russian propaganda posters.

Anchoring the cutting-edge SoWa arts district, the **Carroll and Sons Gallery** (450 Harrison Ave., 617/482-2477, 10 A.M.–5 P.M. Mon.–Fri; or by appointment, www.carrollandsons.net) is the place to spot new and often local talent. You can't get much closer to the source of creation than the **Fort Point Arts Community Gallery** (300 Summer St., 617/423-4299, 10 A.M.–7 P.M. Mon.–Fri; weekend hours vary), www.fortpointarts.org), which exhibits the work of New England's largest and oldest artists community in a building where many of them have their studios.

BATH AND BEAUTY

Boston is the original home of **Fresh** (121 Newbury St., 617/421-1212, 10 A.M.–7 P.M. Mon.–Fri.; 10 A.M.–6 P.M. Sat.; 11 A.M.–5 P.M. Sun., www.fresh.com), a luxury bath boutique that features milk, tea, and sake among its natural ingredients. Hard-to-find hair and makeup products line the shelves at **The Beauty Mark** (33 Charles St., 617/720-1555, 10:30 A.M.–6 P.M. Mon.–Fri.; 11 A.M.–5 P.M.

Sat., closed Sun.), www.thebeautymark.com), a tiny store with a cult following.

BOOKS
New

Professors and students alike shop at **Harvard Book Store** (1256 Massachusetts Ave., Cambridge, 617/661-1515, 9:30 A.M.–8 P.M. Mon.–Sat.; 10 A.M.–5 P.M. Sun., www.harvard.com), which has been named one of the best in the country for its combination of erudite bestsellers and brainy staff. **Brookline Booksmith** (279 Harvard St., Brookline, 617/566-6660, 10 A.M.–8:30 P.M. Mon.–Sat.; 10 A.M.–7 P.M. Sun., www.brooklinebooksmith.com) anchors the neighborhood of Coolidge Corner with an attractive bookstore well laid out for browsing. **Trident Booksellers and Cafe** (338 Newbury St., 617/267-8688, 8 A.M.–12 A.M., www.tridentbookscafe.com) has a good selection of magazines along with books focusing on philosophy and Eastern spirituality.

Used

The owner of the **Brattle Book Shop** (9 West St., 617/542-0210, 9 A.M.–5:30 P.M. daily, www.brattlebookshop.com), Ken Gloss, scours estate sales for rare and antique page-turners, then dusts them off for browsing. In Porter Square, the large and musty **McIntyre & Moore** (1971 Massachusetts Ave., Cambridge, 617/229-5641, 10 A.M.–8 P.M. Mon.–Wed.; 10 A.M.–10 P.M. Mon.–Wed.; 12 P.M.–8 P.M. Sun., www.mcintyreandmoore.com) has a great selection of literary criticism and cultural theory, along with shelves of fiction and nonfiction books.

Specialty

You've heard about Curious George and Snow White, but what about Herb the Vegetarian Dragon? A "thinking child's bookstore," **Barefoot Books** (1771 Massachusetts Ave., Cambridge, 617/349-1610, 10 A.M.–6 P.M. Mon.–Sat.; 12 P.M.–5 P.M. Sun., www.barefootbooks.com) offers decidedly imaginative titles. In Harvard Square, **Grolier Poetry Bookshop** (6 Plympton St., Cambridge,

MAP QUEST

Traveler, tourist, victim of wanderlust – whatever you call yourself, don't bypass the **Globe Corner Bookstore** (90 Mt. Auburn St., Cambridge, 617/497-6277, www.globecorner.com, 9:30 A.M.-9 A.M. Mon.-Sat., 11 A.M.-7 P.M. Sun.). With some 15 years amassing a dedicated following for its excellent stock of in-depth travel information (one of the largest in North America), it offers mesmerizing oversized atlases, an epic selection of travel guidebooks, regional cookbooks, nautical books, recreational guides, and a huge case of geographical survey maps of locales in New England. Even more books and maps are available on the website of the shop, which will place a special order for any item it doesn't have readily in stock.

617/547-4648, 10 A.M.–8 P.M. Mon.–Sat.; 11 P.M.–5 P.M. Sun., www.grolierpoetrybookshop.com) is one of only two bookstores in America devoted completely to poetry. Nearby, **Schoenhof's Foreign Books** (76A Mount Auburn St., Cambridge, 617/547-8855, 10 A.M.–8 P.M. Mon.–Fri.; 10 A.M.–7 P.M. Sat.; 10 A.M.–6 P.M. Sun., www.schoenhofs.com) offers the largest selection of foreign books in North America. Art scholars worldwide go to **Ars Libri** (500 Harrison St., 617/357-5212, 9 A.M.–6 P.M. Sat.–Fri.; 11 A.M.–5 P.M. Sat.; closed Sun.,www.arslibri.com), full of rare and out-of-print tomes on art and sculpture.

CLOTHING AND ACCESORIES

The place to shop for clothes is stylish **Newbury Street,** which carries outposts of international designers from Armani to Zegna, alongside local boutiques. Other neighborhoods have their own local clothing shops that range from style-conscious to bargain-conscious.

Unisex

A techno-powered emporium inside a classy old museum building, **Louis Boston** (234 Berkeley St., 617/262-6100, 11 A.M.–6 P.M. Mon.–Wed.; 11 A.M.–7 P.M. Thurs.–Sat.; closed Sun., www.louisboston.com) is where "proper Bostonians" shop for Loro Piano cashmere and clubbers stay abreast of the latest European fashions. The pages of *Vogue* and *GQ* leap into the retail world at **Alan Bilzerian** (34 Newbury St., 617/536-1001, 10 A.M.–7 P.M. Mon.–Sat.; 11 A.M.–6 P.M. Sun., www.alanbilzerian.com), Boston's supplier of the most of-the-moment labels.

The myth. The legend. The bahgains. Even if you don't find what you are looking for at **Filene's Basement** (497 Boylston St., 617/424-5520, 9 A.M.–9 P.M. Mon.–Sat.; 11 A.M.–7 P.M. Sun., www.filenesbasement.com), you'll find something irresistible at the original designer discount store.

Women's

Emerging urban designers spruce up the rack at **Turtle** (619 Tremont St., 617/266-2610, 11 A.M.–7 P.M. Tues.–Fri.; 10 A.M.–6 P.M. Sat., noon–5 P.M. Sun., closed Mon., www.turtle-boston.com), a boutique with all of the style at a fraction of the price. International flair and old-world elegance meet at **Daniela Corte** (91 Newbury St., 617/262-2100, www.danielacorte.com, by appointment only), an Argentine clothing designer who constructs one-of-a-kind designs.

Men's

The Ivy League clothier of choice for over 100 years, **J.Press** (82 Mt. Auburn St., 617/547-9886, 9 A.M.–5:30 P.M. Mon.–Sat.; www.jpressonline.com) will outfit you with argyle and herringbone worthy of Harvard Yard. The South End's **Market** (558 Tremont St., 617/338-4500, 9 A.M.–5:30 P.M. Mon.–Sat.) stocks the latest fashions from Dolce & Gabbana and Paul Smith.

Children's

High-powered moms shop for too-cute-for-words ensembles at **The Red Wagon** (69 Charles St., 617/523-9402, 10 A.M.–7 P.M. Mon.–Sat.; 11 A.M.–5 P.M. Sun., www.theredwagon.com), which carries both American and

European labels. Tween fashions fill **Pixie Stix** (131 Charles St., 617/523-3211, 10 A.M.–7 P.M. Mon.–Sat.; 11 A.M.–5 P.M. Sun., www.pixiestixboston.com), a pink-and-aqua emporium of designer jumpsuits, T-shirts, and skirts.

Vintage

Cowboy hats, cocktail dresses, or leather jackets, you'll find everything you need for Halloween—or just Saturday night—at the closet-sized vintage shop **Oona's** (1210 Massachusetts Ave., Cambridge, 10 A.M.–8 P.M. Mon.–Fri.; 10 A.M.–6 P.M. Sat., noon–5 P.M. Sun., 617/491-2654). The gargantuan **Garment District** (200 Broadway, Cambridge, 617/876-5230, 11 A.M.–midnight Sun.–Fri.; 9 A.M.–midnight Sat., www.garment-district.com) has threads for every style, whether it's the Mod Squad or the Jimi Hendrix Experience.

Jewelry

The **Jenny's Jewelry** (345 Washington St., 617/523-0610, 10 A.M.–9 A.M. Mon.–Fri.; 10 A.M.–7 A.M. Sat.; noon–5 P.M. Sun., www.jewelryexchange.com) is an emporium of gold, pearls, and gemstones, with dozens of discount jewelers vying for your hand. Modern jewelry as well as a wide selection of estate pieces can be found at **E. B. Horn** (429 Washington St., 617/542-3902, 9:30 A.M.–6 P.M. Tues., Wed. and Fri.; 9:30 A.M.–5:30 P.M. Mon. and Thurs.; closed Sun., www.ebhorn.com), a downtown jeweler with 165 years of history in the same location. State-of-the-art timepieces take center stage at **Ross-Simons** (800 Boylston St., 617/236-3100, www.ross-simons.com).

FOOD

Alligator, rattlesnake, or ostrich meat might not be what you had in mind for dinner, but they might tempt you at **Savenor's Market** (160 Charles St., 617/723-6328, 11 A.M.–8 P.M. Mon.–Fri.; 10 A.M.–8 P.M.Sat; midnight–7 P.M.Sun; www.savenorsmarket. com). Chefs themselves shop at this gourmet shop which also carries more pedestrian fare like *kobe* beef and truffle oil. **Cardullo's**

Gourmet Shoppe (6 Brattle St., Cambridge, 617/491-8888, 10 A.M.–9 P.M. Mon.–Sat.; 11 A.M.–7 P.M.Sun., www.cardullos.com) is a Harvard Square institution, stocked with international and New England foodstuffs. Take the North End home with you at **Salumeria Italiana** (151 Richmond St., 800/400-5916, 8 A.M.–6 P.M. Mon.–Sat.; www.salumeriaitaliana.com), an old-world storefront packed with fresh pasta, sauces, and oils.

HOME DECOR

Funky and functional touches for the hip homebody make **Bliss Home** (225 Newbury St., 617/421-5544, 10 A.M.–8 P.M. Mon.–Fri.; 10 A.M.–7 P.M.Sat., midnight–5 P.M.Sun., www.blisshome.com) one-stop gift shopping—for others or yourself. Inventory includes glasses, dinnerware, bar sets, and bath items. Dutch for "alluring," **Lekker** (1317 Washington St., 10 A.M.–7 P.M. Tues.–Sat.; noon–6 P.M.Sat., closed Sun., 617/542-6464, www.lekkerhome.com) sells a combination of clean and contemporary furniture from Germany and the Netherlands, antique armoires from Asia, and textiles and other unique home accessories. Plastic has been given a new life at **Kartell** (10 St. James Ave., 617/728-4442, 10 A.M.–7 P.M. Mon.–Sat.; noon–5 P.M.Sun.) an ultra-modern furniture store featuring European "it"-designers such as Phillipe Starck.

MUSIC

For more than 25 years, **Newbury Comics** (332 Newbury St., 617/236-4930; 36 JFK St., Cambridge, 617/491-0337; and other area locations; 10 A.M.–9 P.M. daily, www.newburycomics.com) has been the music store of choice for area aficionados, with a terrific selection by local artists, regular in-store appearances, and hard-to-find singles and imports. For used CDs, it's hard to beat the selection at **CD Spins** (324 Newbury St., 617/267-5955; 54 Church St., Cambridge, 617/497-7070; and other area locations; 10 A.M.–7 P.M. Mon.–Fri.; noon–5 P.M. Sat.–Sun., www.cdspins.com), a local chain with everything from punk rock to show tunes.

ODDITIES

Part one-of-a-kind shop, part museum of shipbuilding history, the **Lannan Ship Model Gallery** (99 High St., 617/451-2650, www.lannangallery.com) honors Boston's maritime past with more than 300 historical ship models and antique bells, and navigational devices. Coin and baseball card collectors, take note: It gets no better than at **Kenmore Collectibles** (466 Commonwealth Ave., 617/482-5705, 11 A.M.–6 P.M. Mon.–Fri.; 11 P.M.–4 P.M.Sat.; closed Sun., www.kenmorecollectibles.com), where every genre and era are amply represented. Pick up rare and vintage coins, alongside sports memorabilia you never thought you'd see again.

SOUVENIRS

Bostonians may know **Shreve, Crump & Low** (440 Boylston St., 617/267-9100, 10 A.M.–6 P.M. Mon., Wed., and Fri.; 10 A.M.–7 P.M.Thurs., noon–5 P.M.Sun., www.shrevecrumpandlow.com) as one of the city's luxury jewelers, but it also carries a classy line of made-in-Boston souvenirs, from swan-boat pins to ceramic cod pitchers. Cross off everyone on your list at once at the stalls at Faneuil Hall, which are filled with Boston mugs, magnets, keychains, and T-shirts. The **Bostonian Society Museum Shop** (Faneuil Hall, 617/720-3284, 10 A.M.–7 P.M. Mon.–Fri.; 11 A.M.–5 P.M.Sat., closed Sun.) carries colonial-style quilts and ties, and even tea that purports to be the kind thrown overboard at the Boston Tea Party. For sports lovers, **The Brearly Collection** (Faneuil Hall, 800/563-6544, 10 A.M.–8 P.M. Mon.–Sat.; 10 P.M.–6 P.M. Sun., www.brearley.com) offers framed and signed photos of great Boston sports moments. The perfect

birthday or anniversary gift: a framed copy of any day's paper from the **Boston Globe Store** (135 Morrissey Blvd., Boston, 617/929-3000, 9 A.M.–4 P.M. Mon.–Fri; closed Sat.–Sun). Known locally as "the Coop," **Harvard Cooperative Society** (1400 Massachusetts Ave., Cambridge, 617/499-2000, 9 A.M.–6:30 P.M. Mon.–Fri.; 10 A.M.–6 P.M. Sat.; closed Sun., www.thecoop.com) anchors Harvard Square with a bookstore and souvenir emporium filled with products emblazoned with the crimson *Veritas* logo. Finally, what's a more delicious souvenir of New England than its trademark delicacy—lobster? Before you board the plane at Logan, snag a few ice-packed crustaceans to go at the airport's branch of **Legal Sea Foods** (Logan International Airport Terminal B, 857/241-2000; Terminal C, 617/568-2800; 10 A.M.–11 P.M. daily, www.legalseafoods.com).

SPORTING GOODS

The city's recognized leader for everything outdoors, **City Sports** (480 Boylston St., 617/267-3900, 10 A.M.–7 P.M. Mon.–Sat.; noon–6 P.M. Sun., www.citysports.com) has active clothing and sports equipment. Straight from the four-time winner of the Boston Marathon, the **Bill Rodgers Running Center** (North Market Bldg., Quincy Marketplace, 617/723-5612, 10 A.M.–7 P.M. Mon.–Sat.; 10 A.M.–5 P.M. Sun., www.billrodgers.com) will suit you up in sweats, sneaks, and advice from its runners turned sales staff. Perfect for stocking up before venturing to Great North Woods, **Joe Jones Wilderness House** (1048 Commonwealth Ave., 617/277-5858, 11 A.M.–6 P.M. daily,) carries skis, fishing rods, tents, crampons, and anything else you could need to tackle the elements.

Sports and Recreation

SPECTATOR SPORTS

Red Sox

On October 27, 2004, sportswriters from around New England dusted off columns they had written long ago, but never thought they'd have a chance to use in their lifetimes. After 86 years, the Boston Red Sox had done the impossible and won the World Series. For most fans of the team (877/733-7699, www.redsox.com), their entire lives had been an exercise in frustration, blaming a supposed curse visited on their team when the Red Sox traded Babe Ruth to their archrivals, the New York Yankees, in 1918. Despite that, the team has some of the most rabid fans in baseball, who became if anything even more enthusiastic (and title-hungry) after breaking their long World Series drought. They were rewarded again in 2007 when the Sox bested the Colorado Rockies to once again win the Series and prove that lighting can strike twice.

Bruins

After the Red Sox, the Bruins come next in the hearts of most true Bostonians (though the Super Bowl–winning Patriots have supplanted them in some). Names like Ray Borque and Bobby Orr are still quick to the tongue of hockey fans, though the Stanley Cup has eluded the team (617/624-2327, www.bostonbruins.com) since 1972. (Few Bostonians begrudged Borque's decision to leave for Colorado, where he won the title in 1996.) When the rival Montreal Canadiens play in town, tickets can still be hard to come by.

Patriots

Though based 30 miles southeast in Foxboro, and officially belonging to the entire region, the New England Patriots are an honorary Boston sports team—and one the city is only too happy to claim. After decades of drought and heartbreaking games against rivals Miami Dolphins and New York Jets, the team (800/543-1776, www.patriots.com) hit upon a winning formula with quarterback Tom

Championship banners proudly hang outside Fenway Park.

Brady and a team-oriented style of play that earned it three Super Bowl titles in four years, from 2001–2005, and official bragging rights as a "dynasty."

Celtics

For most Bostonians, the heyday of the Celtics (866/423-5849, www.nba.com/celtics) will always be the 1980s, when players like Larry Bird, Kevin McHale, and Robert Parrish racked up title after title against their nemesis, the Los Angeles Lakers. The C's struggled throughout the 1990s under a string of coaching changes and player changes—but like their cousins the Sox and the Pats, they too finally hit pay dirt in 2008 when they hit upon a winning formula with veteran players Paul Pierce, Kevin Garnett, and Ray Allen schooling the leagues youngsters to grab the championship banner and make Boston once and for all the undisputed "winningest" city in the country.

College Sports

Perhaps because of the success of its pro teams, Boston has never seen itself as much of a college sports town. Several annual events are worth seeing however, including the **Head of the Charles Regatta** (617/868-6200, www.hocr.org), which fills the river near Harvard with hundreds of rowing sculls every October. Despite both Harvard and Yale generally fielding lackluster football teams, the annual match-up between them is internationally known as **The Game** (www.the-game.org) due to its fierce competition for Ivy League bragging rights. Now more than 125 years old, the Game is played at Harvard stadium in Allston on alternating years. Perhaps the most eagerly awaited college sporting event is the annual **Beanpot Tournament,** a hockey matchup between Harvard, Boston College, Boston University, and Northeastern University. These days, it's an upset when BU doesn't win.

FITNESS CLUBS

Fitness clubs in Boston range from old-school gyms to the most modern of yoga and Pilates studios. It's fun to work out at the **Central YMCA of Boston** (316 Huntington Ave., 617/536-7800, www.ymca.net, day pass $10), the most affordable place to shoot hoops, swim laps, or lift weights. The gargantuan **Boston Athletic Club** (653 Summer St., 617/269-4300, www.bostonathleticclub.com, day pass $25) has indoor basketball, racquetball, squash, and tennis courts, along with nautilus and weight-training equipment. It's located in the Seaport District. Hands down, the most flexible man in Boston is Baron Baptiste, whose **Baptiste Power Yoga** (25 Harvard St., Brookline, 617/232-9642; 2000 Massachusetts Ave., Cambridge, 617/661-9642; www.baronbaptiste.com, classes $14) incorporates meditation, breathing, and nutrition consults into an energetic style of yoga. Personal trainers are available for drop-in classes or longer regimens. Bodies are sculpted through a variety of methods at **Boston Body** (8 Newbury St., 617/262-3333, www.bostonbody.com, one-time visit $20), which offers classes in yoga and pilates, as well as Thai massage and acupuncture.

RUNNING AND BIKING

As befitting the town where a marathon is one of the year's most anticipated events, Boston is

WHAT A RUSH: THE BOSTON MARATHON

The world's oldest annual marathon and one of its most prestigious, the Boston Marathon nearly swallows the city whole year after year, drawing runners from all over the world and spectators from every corner of the region. The race, which starts in the suburb of Hopkinton and ends in Boston's Back Bay, happens every year on Patriot's Day (the third Monday in April), and is by far New England's most-watched sports event. The size of the race itself is noteworthy, too; it boasts an average of 20,000 official runners (many other participants, called "bandits," run unregistered) – remarkable since the race's qualification requirements are unusually high (simply qualifying has become a bragging point in its own right). The exacting standards for entrance aside, the marathon is also famous for its tough course – the difficulty of which literally peaks at Heartbreak Hill. One of a series of hills in Newton, Heartbreak is feared not so much for its height, but because runners reach it between the 20th and 21st miles of the race – a time when they're likely to be already low on energy. Challenging as running the race is, viewing it can be tricky, too, given the crowds of spectators that average 500,000 every year. Sidewalks outside the city tend to have more viewing space, but if you're determined to get as close to the finish line as possible, the best way is to go early in the day to one of the restaurants or bars close to the finish line in Copley Square. By late afternoon, they become loud, boisterous parties full of revelers. But then again, by the end of the race, so have all the blocks surrounding the finish line.

crazy about running. Numerous runners' shops and paths exist to accommodate them. Biking is another story. A few years back, Boston was declared the worst city in the country for biking by *Bicycling* magazine, and despite some stabs at creating a more cohesive network of bike paths, it has yet to live down the reputation.

Sailboats spice up the view along the **Charles River Esplanade** (www.mass.gov/dcr/parks/metroboston/charlesR.htm), the park of choice for runners, bikers, and inline skaters. A long strip of green along both sides of the river, the park runs 17 miles in a loop from the Charles River Dam to Watertown. More out of the way, but less traveled, is the **Southwest Corridor** (www.mass.gov/dcr/parks/metroboston/southwestCorr.htm), a five-mile bicycling and running path that starts in the South End. After crossing Massachusetts Avenue, the path provides a mostly uninterrupted stretch of parkland all the way down to Forest Hills and the Arnold Arboretum. Landscape designer Frederick Law Olmstead envisioned an **"Emerald Necklace"** (www.emeraldnecklace.org) of parks that would encircle Boston, beginning at the Back Bay Fens and including the Arnold Arboretum and Franklin Park. The bulk of the necklace is still intact, especially along the Fens, where running paths trace leafy brooks and brackish fens that seem like they have left the city far behind. For more hardcore cyclists, the **Minuteman Bikeway** (www.minutemanbikeway.org) offers 11 miles of graded terrain along an old rail bed, beginning behind Davis Square in Somerville, and running all the way out to the suburb of Bedford, passing historic Arlington and Lexington along the way. If you start early enough, you can stop to see the Revolutionary War sights and still be back in plenty of time for dinner.

HIKING AND CAMPING

Surprisingly, there are many places to camp within and around Boston—and we're not talking about pitching a tent on the Common.

Boston Harbor Islands

Cradled within the arms of Boston Harbor are dozens of islands, ranging from a little dollop of land barely big enough for a seagull to land to the 188-acre **Peddock's Island,** which has a network of roads and trails as well as a campsite for overnight stays. Other islands within the harbor that allow camping include **Grape Island,** with quiet wooded trails and wild blackberries; **Lovell's Island,** which has paths among the sand dunes and rocky tidal pools; and **Bumpkin Island,** with fields of wildflowers and the remains of an old stone farmhouse to explore. All of the islands offer an enviable solitude in full view of the twinkling lights of the city skyline. While camping is not allowed on **Georges Island,** the island has a Civil War-era fort with ranger-led tours, as well as plenty of hiking trails along the beaches. Ferries leave from Long Wharf to Georges Island, where boats are available to other islands. Campers must bring all water and other supplies with them to the islands (617/223-8666, www.bostonislands.org, June–Oct., ferry: $14 adults, $10 seniors, $8 children 3–11, free children under 3; camping reservations: 877/422-6762, www.reserveamerica.com, group sites $25, individual sites $8), which are jointly managed by the National Park Service and the State Department of Conservation and Recreation.

Blue Hills Reservation

On the southern edge of Boston, the protected green space of the Blue Hills rises 600 feet into the sky. The reservation, which is popular with families in the summer, offers a full slate of recreational activities year-round. For hikers, 125 miles of trails wind their way through bottomland forests, swamps, and meadows. If you are lucky, you might spot a coyote or turkey vulture along the way; you are sure to see the delicate lady slipper, a beautiful but endangered Massachusetts flower. Trail maps are available at **Blue Hills Reservation Headquarters** (695 Hillside St., Milton, 617/698-1802, www.mass.gov/dcr/parks/metroboston/blue.htm).

BOATING
Canoeing

There are few better ways to spend an afternoon

than canoeing the Charles River and taking in the waterside views of the State House and Back Bay brownstones. **Charles River Canoe & Kayak** (1071 Soldiers Field Rd., Allston, 617/462-2513, www.ski-paddle.com, 12–8 P.M. Fri. and 10 A.M.–6:30 P.M. Sat.–Sun. May–early Oct.; 12–8 P.M. Mon.–Thurs. June–Aug., Rentals $7–24/hour, $28–96/day) rents a range of canoes and kayaks from its boathouse in Allston. On Friday nights, the company also offers "BBQ Tours" ($63) that include kayak instruction and a post-paddling grill-out.

Sailing
The sailboats picturesquely dotting the Charles in all those postcards belong to **Community Boating** (21 Mugar Way, 617/523-1038, www.community-boating.org, 1 P.M.–sunset Mon.–Fri. and 9 A.M.–sunset Sat.–Sun. Apr.–Oct.), an institution on the Charles River Esplanade for 70 years. It offers unlimited sailing instruction and boat privileges for a $190 flat fee for the season, as well as two-day sailboat rentals for experienced mariners for $100. To ply the waves of the harbor, **Courageous Sailing Center** (1 First Ave., Charlestown Navy Yard, Charlestown, 617/268-7243, www.courageoussailing.org, noon–sunset Mon.–Fri., 10 A.M.–sunset Sat.–Sun. May–Oct.) offers a range of lessons (three beginner sessions $250, three advanced sessions $299, private lessons $95–150/hour).

ROCK CLIMBING
For the weekend warrior who just can't wait for the weekend, the **Granite Railway Quarry** (Ricciuti Dr., off Willard St., West Quincy, 617/727-4573 or 617/698-1802, www.mass.gov/dcr/parks/metroboston/quincyquarries.htm) has some precipices nearly as challenging as those found in the White Mountains.

Accommodations

As with most major cities, hotels in Boston aren't cheap. The amenities offered at the upper end, however, rival any city on the planet—especially after a recent spate of new luxury hotels. For the budget-conscious, however, there is no need to go the fleabag route. Bed-and-breakfasts and furnished apartments scattered throughout the city offer excellent value, especially if you plan on staying a week or longer. A good place to check for listings is the **Bay Colony Bed & Breakfast Associates** (888/486-6018, www.bnbboston.com). Additionally, several low-cost hostels offer clean and comfortable lodging right in the hottest neighborhoods downtown.

BEACON HILL/GOVERNMENT CENTER/NORTH END
$100-150
A quaint bed-and-breakfast on the back side of Beacon Hill, the ◖ **John Jeffries House** (14 Mugar Way, 617/367-1866, www.johnjeffrieshouse.com, $108–184) helps keep costs down further with kitchenettes in all of the rooms. Originally quarters for nurses at the nearby Massachusetts Eye & Ear Infirmary, the turn-of-the-century Victorian house has spartan but comfortable rooms.

Located in an addition built above a one-story chapel, **La Cappella Suites** (290 North St., 617/523-9020, www.lacappellasuites.com, $95–225) is the North End's only bed-and-breakfast. For an affordable rate, you get a balcony with a view of downtown Boston and complimentary Wi-Fi. Bathrooms are shared, and breakfast consists of frozen waffles, but who cares when you have the pastries of Hanover Street just three blocks away?

$150-250
Ho Chi Minh was a bellhop and Malcolm X a busboy at the historic **Omni Parker House** (60 School St., 617/227-8600, www.omnihotels.com, $159–239); still, the 150-year-old hotel is anything but revolutionary. It opts instead for polished, old-fashioned refinement in rooms

with upholstered couches and heirloom antiques. The hotel was recently refurbished to add high-speed Internet and other technological gadgetry to the rooms.

$250 and Up

Before the TV show, CSI: Boston stood for the **Charles Street Inn** (94 Charles St., 617/314-8900, www.charlesstreetinn.com, $250–550), a luxury bed-and-breakfast that is the ultimate honeymoon hotel. Nine sumptuous rooms overflow with Victorian-era antiques, each channeling the personality of a different 19th-century luminary. All rooms feature four-poster beds with high-thread-count sheets, original marble fireplaces, whirlpool tubs, and other amenities.

The sleek design of boutique hotel **(Nine Zero** (90 Tremont St., 617/772-5800, www.ninezero.com, $240–369) is as stylish and modern as its high-powered clientele. In-room features include high-speed Internet access, printer, and OnDemand games. The stylish eye of the city's newfound fashion and celebrity storm, the cool-but-laid-back **(Liberty Hotel** (215 Charles St., 617/224-4004, www.libertyhotel.com, $290–760) is a magnet for fashion shows, local luminary's hosting parties in the lobby, and A-listers looking to crash while filming movies in the city.

DOWNTOWN
$150-250

Oriental rugs and sleigh beds deck out every room of the **(Harborside Inn of Boston** (185 State St., 617/723-7500, www.harborsideinnboston.com, $119–169), a converted 19th-century mercantile building that is one of the most affordable hotels downtown. Exposed brick walls hung with reproductions from the Museum of Fine Arts give a unique Boston feel to large rooms that overlook a central sky-lit atrium.

Unlike most of the cookie-cutter Courtyard by Marriott hotels, the Theater District's **Courtyard Boston Tremont Hotel** (275 Tremont St., 617/426-1400, www.marriott.com, $149–269) is located within a historic

1925 brick building with thoughtful touches like granite countertops in the bathrooms.

$250 and Up

One of the most unique hotels in Boston is located in the landmark 500-foot-tall Custom House Building, which for decades was the highest point in Boston. **Marriott's Custom House** (3 McKinley Sq., 617/310-6300, www.marriott.com, $189–329) has guest rooms elegantly decorated in navy and taupe, as well as kitchenettes and drop-dead views of downtown and the North End.

Located right on the park, the **Ritz-Carlton Boston Common** (10 Avery St., 617/574-7100, www.ritzcarlton.com/en/Properties/BostonCommon/Default.htm, $395–645) eschews its chain's stuffy reputation in favor of a towering building of glass and steel, filled with contemporary art and a stylish ambience. All of the luxury you'd expect is still there, however, including overnight shoeshine and laundry service, and a "bath butler" who will draw you one of a selection of aromatic baths. Packages include access to the on-site Sports Club/LA.

BACK BAY AND SOUTH END
Under $100

The minimalist style sense of the **YWCA Berkeley Residences** (40 Berkeley St., 617/375-2524, www.ywcaboston.org/berkeley, single $65, double $80, triple $99) makes this hostel seem cool rather than spartan. Friendly staff and ideal location combine to create the best budget option in the city. (Men are welcome as well as women.)

A short walk from Newbury Street, the **463 Beacon Street Guest House** (463 Beacon St., 617/536-1302, www.463beacon.com, $79–169) offers a range of rooms in a restored Back Bay brownstone. While small, the rooms are cheerily decorated with an eye toward period detail. The house also has furnished apartments for longer stays.

$100-150

You can't find closer accommodations to Newbury Street shopping than the **Newbury**

Guest House (261 Newbury St., 617/670-6000, www.newburyguesthouse.com, $120–219), which offers simple rooms with white bedspreads and pastel walls, as well as a full breakfast with trademark freshly baked muffins.

$150-250

The South End has many charming bed-and-breakfasts in its historic district. One of the best, the **Herbst Haus** (Appleton St., 617/266-0235, www.herbsthaus.com, $150–225) is located in an 1870s townhouse with two simple but comfortable suites, a parlor with a marble fireplace, and a friendly hostess.

$250 and Up

You might be forgiven if you think for a moment you are in Paris during a stay at the **Eliot Hotel** (370 Commonwealth Ave., 617/267-1607, www.eliothotel.com, $195–335). Everything here is made to conjure up the Continent, including marble bathrooms, French doors in the rooms, plush linens, and a refined, multilingual staff. Even its location on the Commonwealth Mall seems a nod to the Champs Elysées.

When it comes to the **((Jewel of Newbury** (254 Newbury St., 617/536-5523, www.jewel-boston.com, $175–295), the name says it all. One-of-a-kind suites blend a personal collection of North African, Indian, and Western antiques to create a sophisticated guesthouse right out of the world of Phineas Fogg. The art deco bar area is a jewel within a jewel.

FENWAY
Under $100

One of Boston University's most modern dorms is converted during the summer into the **Fenway Summer Hostel** (610 Beacon St., 617/267-8599, www.bostonhostel.org, single $100, quad $34.45–45), one of the nicest hostels you're likely to find anywhere. Basic rooms each contain just three beds, as well as a writing desk.

$150-250

French wallpaper, tasseled lampshades, and marble mantels are just some of the details

that make **((Gryphon House** (9 Bay State Rd., 617/375-9003, www.gryphonhouseboston.com, $189–365) a favorite place for returning visitors. A Victorian townhouse tucked into the back of Kenmore Square, the hotel has eight rooms, each with a different personality, including the sunny garden room and neo-Gothic sanctuary.

CAMBRIDGE
$100-150

Located behind Harvard University, **((A Bed & Breakfast in Cambridge** (1657 Cambridge St., Cambridge, 617/868-7082, www.cambridgebnb.com, $95–200) has three rooms decked out with antique writing desks, canopy beds, and down comforters. The owners clearly delight in hospitality, with freshly baked breads and homemade jams served for breakfast, and a library of books on Boston and Cambridge for guests to peruse. The three guest rooms share a common bath.

$150-250

Jaws often drop when their owners pass beneath the unassuming brick facade of the **Inn at Harvard** (1201 Massachusetts Ave., Cambridge, 617/491-2222, www.theinnatharvard.com, $1950–1700) and enter the spectacular four-story Italianate courtyard inside. Merely ten years old, the inn has worked hard to create an atmosphere befitting its namesake 400-year-old university. Rooms are luxuriously appointed with plush bedding and sheer curtains. Perks for guests include free calls to the Harvard telephone system and passes to the Harvard Faculty Club.

Located within a renovated 1894 Queen Anne–style brick firehouse, the **Kendall Hotel** (350 Main St., Cambridge, 866/566-1300, www.kendallhotel.com, $130–240) bills itself as a "historic boutique hotel" within the MIT campus. Rooms have been lovingly constructed to evoke the era, with country quilts, reproduction furniture, and period antiques. Rates include a breakfast buffet served at an in-house restaurant.

The **((Hotel Marlowe** (25 Edwin Land

Blvd., Cambridge, 800/825-7140, www.ho-telmarlowe.com, $180–600) might not have the best location, situated above a mall in a no-man's-land between Boston and Cambridge. For style and ambience, however, there is no compe-tition on either side of the river. Every inch has been designed to evoke a mind-blowing pastiche of Buck Rogers and Alice in Wonderland. Bold colors and plush fabrics combine with techno-logical touches like in-room PlayStations and CD players to make this the boutique hotel of choice for the visiting urban sophisticate. Did we mention the complimentary evening wine hour and 24-hour room service?

$250 and Up

When the literati come to Cambridge, there is only place for them to stay. ((**The Charles Hotel** (1 Bennett St., Cambridge, 617/864-1200, www.charleshotel.com, $300–480) is filled with every modern luxury, including down comforters, handmade quilts, Bose Wave radios, and DVD players in every room. At the same time, the hotel is quintes-sentially Cambridge, with an in-house lend-ing library filled with autographed literary bestsellers and a health spa and restaurants frequented by resident academes and visiting celebrities alike.

Food

BEACON HILL AND GOVERNMENT CENTER
Classic New England

Daniel Webster used to polish off a glass of brandy with every dozen oysters he scarfed down at the raw bar of the **Union Oyster House** (41 Union St., 617/227-2750, 11 A.M.–9:30 P.M. Sun.–Thurs.; 11 A.M.–10 P.M. Fri.–Sat., www.unionoysterhouse. com, $22–34), the oldest operating restau-rant in the United States. Entrées includ-ing baked scrod and filet mignon are a bit overpriced, but worth it for the Olde New England ambience.

French

In stark contrast to many of Charles Street's stuffier addresses, **Beacon Hill Bistro** (25 Charles St., 617/723-7575, 7 A.M.–10 P.M. daily, www.beaconhillhotel.com/bistro, $24–29) is an easygoing (but still upscale, mind you) bistro serving French stalwarts like steak *frites* alongside creative constructions such as skate with spinach and sunchokes.

Italian

The owner of ((**Ristorante Toscano** (47 Charles St., 617/723-4090, 11:30 A.M.–10 P.M. Tues.–Fri.; 11:30 A.M.–11 P.M. Sat.–Sun., www.

toscanoboston.com, $13–36), Vinicio Paoli, is Tuscan to his core—and so is his eatery. No daredevil renderings here: The kitchen keeps it real with simple dishes of carpaccio and penne *arrabbiata*.

Middle Eastern

Who knew that one of New England's most Yankee neighborhoods was a prime place to experience the charms of Persian (that's Iranian to you) cuisine? Grab a table at refined, pretty **Lala Rokh** (97 Mt. Vernon St., 617/720-5511, 12 P.M.–3 P.M. daily; 5:30 P.M.–10 P.M. daily, www.lalarokh.com, $14–19) to dig into a menu loaded with rose petal–scented dishes, kabobs, and fruit-laden sauces. And don't miss the saf-fron ice cream.

Sandwiches

One of the area's most affordable lunches is found at **Panificio** (144 Charles St., 617/227-4340, 8 A.M.–10 P.M. daily., www.panificio-boston.com, $7–23), where you can snag an overstuffed sandwich—on, as the name suggests, great bread—and salad for under $15. At night, the bakery turns more posh: Candles are lit, prices go up, and dishes get more elaborate—à la lobster penne and gnoc-chi marinara.

DOWNTOWN AND CHINATOWN
American

Years before retro became so very this-minute, **(Silvertone Bar & Grill** (69 Bromfield St., 617/338-7887, 12 P.M.–1 A.M. daily, silvertone-downtown.com, $10–20) had a lock on hip, vaguely 1950s style with homey dishes (the mac 'n' cheese is out of this world) and oversized cocktails.

Reserve (far ahead) at the very upscale **(Radius** (8 High St., 617/426-1234, 11:30 A.M.–10 P.M. Mon.–Sat.; 11 A.M.–9 P.M. Sun., www.radiusrestaurant.com, $32–42) for a cutting-edge meal that might include tuna with radish and *yuzu*, for example. Not for nothing has chef Michael Schlow become the darling of rock stars and Hollywood bigwigs alike; his food is tremendous.

The North End may be Boston's Italian center, but **Teatro** (177 Tremont St., 617/778-6841, 5 P.M.–10:30 P.M. Fri.–Sat.; 4 P.M.–10 P.M. Sun.; closed Mon., www.teatroboston.com, $10–25) is a like-minded little enclave of its own. From the dramatic mosaic ceiling and blue lighting to the high-energy bar, the sleek trattoria hums with a well-heeled crowd eagerly digging into freshly made pastas.

Classic New England

Once upon a time, **Locke Ober** (3 Winter Pl., 617/542-1340, 5 P.M.–10 P.M. Mon.–Fri.; 5 P.M.–11 P.M.Sat.; closed Mon., www.locke-ober.com, $28–44) was literally the only place around for fine dining. Its venerable dark wood interior is still the place to come for lobster Savannah, *finnan haddie*, and other New England classics, updated by chef-owner Lydia Shire.

Chinese

Go with what the name suggests at **(Jumbo Seafood** (7 Hudson St., 617/542-2823, 11:30 A.M.–10 P.M. Mon.–Sat.; noon–9 P.M.Sun.,www.jumboseafoodrestaurant.com, $5–18), where the fish specials—served right from the tanks up front—are flapping-fresh. Plump, steamed oysters in black-bean sauce are a specialty, as is the whole steamed sea bass with ginger.

Dim sum is the name of the game at **Chow Chau City** (83 Essex St., 617/338-8158, 8 A.M.–1 A.M. Mon.–Sat.; 11 A.M.–11 P.M.Sun., $7–15), where it's served every day, 8 A.M. to 1 P.M. The emporium caters to big groups with dishes both staid (scallion pancakes) and daring (shark-fin dumplings).

French

Fresh from a multimillion-dollar renovation, The Four Season's tony **(Bristol Lounge** (Four Seasons Hotel, 200 Boylston St., 617/351-2037, 6:30 A.M.–2 A.M. Mon.–Sat.; 7 P.M.–midnight Sun., $35–45) has resumed its place among the city's most refined Big Deal restaurants. France rules the day here, from the china (Bernardaud) to the specialties (soufflés are a tradition)—-though the burgers are equally as popular.

Sandwiches

Line up with everyone else at **Chacarero** (101 Arch St., 617/542-0392, 11 A.M.–7 P.M. Mon.–Fri.; closed Sat.–Sun., www.chacarero.com, $2–8), a Chilean sandwich shop consisting of two windows serving piping-hot sandwiches. The secret ingredient: green beans.

Sushi

Not too many people head to Chinatown looking for good Japanese, but those who do are fed happily at **Ginza** (16 Hudson St., 617/338-2261, 11 A.M.–2 A.M. Mon.–Sat.; 11 A.M.–1 P.M.Sun., $11–46), the always-busy sushi spot. Easily one of the best sources for raw fish in town, it's home to creations such as Boston *maki* (lobster with roe and lettuce) plus good cooked Japanese staples.

NORTH END AND CHARLESTOWN
Italian

Reservations aren't accepted at the small, one-roomed **Pomodoro** (319 Hanover St., 617/367-4348, www.pomodoroboston.com, 11:45 A.M.–10 P.M. Mon.–Sat.; closed Sun.,

$15–24), but diners who arrive before the crowds are rewarded with a table immediately, and a much shorter wait for the fresh and authentic Italian specials. **Mamma Maria** (3 North Sq., 617/523-0077, 5 P.M.–11 P.M. Tues.–Sun.; closed Mon., www.mammamaria.com, $26–38) may sound like a cheap pizza joint, but it's in fact a refined spot full of tapestries and serving the likes of oysters Florentine with *prosecco zabaglione*. Before the North End became a Disneyland-style jumble of Italian-American ristorantes and caffes, there was the Old World likes of **Caffe Vittoria** (290-296 Hanover St., 617/227-7606, 7 A.M.–midnight daily, www.vittoriacaffe.com, $2–6). Lined with wooden pastry cases and filled with students and couples scarfing down everything from tiramisu to grappa, Vittoria could as easily be a neighborhood hangout in Milan. One of the first restaurants to put Boston on the national culinary map, **Olives** (10 City Sq., Charlestown, 617/242-1999, 5 P.M.–11 P.M. daily, www.toddenglish.com, $19–39)—the original prototype for celebrity chef Todd English's now national chain—is still going strong in historic Charlestown. The dramatic, loud dining room serves bold dishes like chargrilled squid with chickpeas and pistachio-crusted lamb loin.

BACK BAY AND SOUTH END
American
When celebration is in order (or money simply isn't an object), Bostonians reserve at ◖ **Clio** (370 Commonwealth Ave., 617/536-7200, 6:30 A.M.–10:30 A.M., 5:30 P.M.–10 P.M. Mon.–Sat.; 5:30 P.M.–10 P.M. Sun., www.cliorestaurant.com, $34–44). With one of the most elegant menus in town, chef Ken Oringer pulls out all the stops on both flavor (butter-basted Maine lobster and California squab with truffles) and adventure (red shrimp sashimi with caviar).

Grab a seat at cheeky ◖ **Delux Café** (100 Chandler St., 617/338-5258, 5 P.M.–1 A.M. daily, $7–13) and prepare for the unexpected. The clientele is a mix of seemingly every kind, as is the decor—which includes an Elvis shrine and a miniature Christmas tree that stays up all year. The menu makes the lowly grilled cheese sandwich into a work of art.

One of the first restaurants to help transform the South End into a restaurant mecca, **Hamersley's Bistro** (553 Tremont St., 617/423-2700, 5:30 P.M.–9:30 P.M. Mon.–Fri.; 5:30 P.M.–10 P.M. Sat.; 11 A.M.–2 P.M. and 5:30 P.M.–9:30 P.M. Sun., www.hamersleysbistro.com, $25–38) evokes a slice of French countryside. The buzzing, airy dining room fills with the smell of roasted chicken with garlic and the sound of conversation and food being enjoyed.

Ask most chefs where they go to unwind after hours and they'll tell you ◖ **Franklin Café** (278 Shawmut Ave., 617/350-0010, 5:30 P.M.–2 A.M. daily, www.franklincafe.com, $16–19). There they can slip into the wooden booths and sup on rosemary-grilled shrimp and just chill out.

Short of hang gliding, the best view of the city is from the windows of the **Top of the Hub** (800 Boylston St., 617/536-1775, 11:30 A.M.–1 A.M. Mon.–Sat.; 11 A.M.–midnight Sun, www.topofthehub.net, $27–48), on the top floor of the Prudential Center. Go for the vista rather than the victuals; dinners are mostly perfunctory continental cuisine.

Cafés
Bumped up against the upscale world of Newbury Street, **The Other Side Café** (407 Newbury St., 617/536-9477, 11:30 A.M.–1 A.M. Mon.–Wed.; 11:30 A.M.–2 A.M.; Thurs.–Fri.; 10 A.M.–2 A.M. Sat.; 10 A.M.–1 A.M. Sun., www.theothersidecafe.com, $6–10) is a refreshing enclave of funky, alternative café culture and cheap vegetarian sandwiches and salads.

Gelati, sandwiches, and pastries fly from the counter to tables at **L'Aroma** (85 Newbury St., 617/412-4001, 7 A.M.–7 P.M. Mon.–Fri.; 7:30 A.M.–7 P.M. Sat.; 8 A.M.–7 P.M. Sun., www.laromacafe.com, $6–7).

Italian
On the bang-for-your-buck front, don't miss the eclectically decorated **Anchovies** (433 Columbus Ave., 617/266-5088, 5 P.M.–11 P.M.

Mon.–Sat.; 5:30 P.M.–11 P.M. Sun., $7–14). None of the pasta prices rise much above $10, and pizzas start at $5.

Meaning "crazy way" in Italian, **Via Matta** (79 Park Plaza, 617/422-0008, 11:30 A.M.–1 A.M. Mon.–Sat.; 11 A.M.–midnight Sun., www.viamattarestaurant.com, $16–38) is one of the hottest restaurants in a culinary ghetto known as Park Square. The loud dining room jumps with a crew of regulars downing perfectly made pasta and simple Italian classics.

Seafood

One of the hottest new tables in Back Bay is **City Table** (61 Exeter St., 617/933-4800, 11:30 A.M.–1 A.M. Mon.–Sat.; 11 A.M.–midnight Sun., $24–34), the big-ticket seafood restaurant that takes the whole ocean as its inspiration. Chef Robert Fathman has concocted witty takes like "oysters in bondage" (that is, encrusted in smoked salmon and potato, and daubed with sour cream and caviar). Now a national chain found in eight states, **Legal Sea Foods** (26 Park Plaza and other area locations, 617/426-4444, 10:30 A.M.–midnight daily, www.legalseafoods.com, $16–37) still sets the standard for creamy New England clam chowder and other classics like steamed cod and boiled lobster. Its latest menu twist is "ayurvedic" cuisine loaded with fiery South Indian spices.

Steakhouse

In most cases, a steakhouse is a steakhouse. But **Grill 23 Bar & Grill** (161 Berkeley St., 617/542-2255, 11:30 A.M.–2 A.M. Mon.–Fri.; 11 A.M.–2 A.M. Sat.; 11 A.M.–midnight Sun., www.grill23.com, $27–49) moves beyond the usual formulaic clubby decor and menu to include big bouquets of flowers in its airy space and tilapia on its specialty board. The usual suspects (prime rib to lobster) are there, too— as are desserts like rhubarb cobbler and an epic wine list.

Sandwiches

A café with counter service, **Flour Bakery** (1595 Washington St., 617/267-4300, 7 A.M.–9 P.M. Mon.–Fri.; 8 A.M.–6 P.M. Sat.; 9 A.M.–5 P.M. Sun., www.flourbakery.com, $8–13) does a swift business in both take-out and eat-in. The biggest draw is the baked goods— fruit tarts, sandwiches, and cookies.

At ◖ **Charlie's Sandwich Shoppe** (429 Columbus Ave., 617/536-7669, noon–10 P.M. Mon.–Sat.; 5 P.M.–10 P.M. Sun., $4–9), you go for the excellent turkey hash and breakfast specials, and stay for the communal tables, loud diner atmosphere, and funny wait staff.

Odds are you won't find a juicier burger in town than those at **Tim's Tavern** (329 Columbus Ave., 617/437-6898, 11 A.M.–11 P.M. Mon.–Sat.; 5 P.M.–10 P.M. Sun., $7–14), and if you do, you certainly won't find one any cheaper. The people-watching, meanwhile, is equally good: Cops gab with artists, barflies drink with students, and everyone plays tunes on the jukebox.

Southern

The eclectic **Tremont 647** (647 Tremont St., 617/266-4600, 10:30 A.M.–2 P.M. and 5:30 P.M.–10:30 P.M. Sun.–Thurs.; 10:30 A.M.–3 P.M. and 5:30 P.M.–10:30 P.M. Fri.–Sat., www.tremont647.com, $13–25), with its lively staff and even livelier dining room, has one of the most loyal clienteles in town. They come back for fixings like lamb sirloin with pomegranate glaze and "two stinky cheeses" with black truffle honey.

Tapas

The multi-floored **Tapeo** (266 Newbury St., 617/267-4799, 5 P.M.–midnight Mon.–Sat.; noon–10 P.M. Sun., www.tapeo.com, $24–25) is as popular for its al fresco patio as for its tiny plates of tapas (the roast duck with blackberry sauce is a knockout) and citrusy pitchers of sangria.

Picture the quintessential tapas hangout in Spain, and you've got **Toro** (1704 Washington St., 617/536-4000, noon–midnight Mon.–Sat.; 10:30 A.M.–2 P.M. and 4:30 P.M.–midnight Sun., $4–15), a paragon of the genre.

FENWAY
Cambodian

One of the more elegant ethnic restaurants around Boston, **Elephant Walk** (900 Beacon St., Cambridge, 617/247-1500, 11 A.M.–10 P.M.Mon.–Sat.; 10 A.M.–9 P.M. Sun., www.elephantwalk.com, $14–20) feels like a night in a well-appointed Phnom Penh hotel, between the swaying palm fronds and dark woods. But the menu is more Cambodia-meets-Cannes, split between classic French dishes and Southeast Asian dishes like banana leaf–wrapped scallops in coconut milk.

SEAPORT
Seafood

Overlooking Fort Point Channel, **The Barking Crab** (88 Sleeper St., 617/426-2722, 11:30 A.M.–1 A.M. daily, www.barkingcrab.com, $9–25) serves seafood the way it was meant to be eaten, with the smell of sea air and cackling of gulls. Loaded with salty decor, the joint serves platters of fried clams at long picnic tables.

Since 1963, **Anthony's Pier 4** (140 Northern Ave., 617/482-6262, 11 A.M.–9 P.M. Sun.–Thurs.; 11 A.M.–11 P.M. Fri.–Sat., www.pier4.com, $19–36) has served the classic seafood you came to Boston for, and offered an impressive wine list and sea view to boot.

Cult seafood favorite and hole-in-the-wall 【 **No-Name Restaurant** (15 Fish Pier, Northern Ave., 617/338-7539, noon–7 P.M. Mon.–Sat.; closed Sun., $5–23) is acclaimed for its seafood literally right off the boat. The menu changes depending on what's in season, but always includes some variation on a tummy-warming fisherman's stew. Other entrées are simply fried or baked, offering unadulterated seafood at half the price of more celebrated restaurants.

CAMBRIDGE AND SOMERVILLE
American

Playing the part of both cozy neighborhood restaurant and urban sophisticate, 【 **Central Kitchen** (567 Massachusetts Ave., Cambridge, 617/491-5599, 5 P.M.–1 A.M.Tues.–Thurs.; 5 P.M.–2 A.M. Sat.; closed Sun. and Mon., www.enormous.tv/central/index1.html, $20–28) hosts a nightly scene of regulars in for squid salad and grilled flank steak.

Rialto (1 Bennett St., Cambridge, 617/661-5050, 5 P.M.–11:30 P.M. daily, www.rialto-restaurant.com, $27–39) chef-owner Jody Adams has rightfully earned a following for her Mediterranean-inspired cuisine. Her spring pea soup is electric with both color and flavor, and her gnocchi is a marvel.

Few restaurants could pull off being so unabashedly glamorous in fusty Harvard Square, but **Upstairs on the Square** (91 Winthrop St., Cambridge, 617/864-1933, 5 P.M.–11 P.M. daily, www.upstairsonthesquare.com, $13–34) does so with huge fireplaces and walls of gold leaf and animal prints. Don't miss the buttermilk panna cotta with basil.

Caribbean

The fun and boisterous **Green Street Grill** (280 Green St., Cambridge, 617/876-1655, 5 P.M.–1 A.M. Mon.–Sat; 5:30 P.M.–1 A.M. Sun., www.greenstreetgrill.com, $11–24) is as loved for its spicy tropical menu as it is the well-mixed and potent drinks.

France and Cuba may be far apart on a map, but at sultry 【 **Chez Henri** (1 Shepard St., Cambridge, 617/354-8980,6 P.M.–10:30 P.M. Mon.–Sat; 5:30 P.M.–9:30 P.M. Sun., www.chezhenri.com, $26–30) they mingle seamlessly. The steak tartar with cumin and chile-cocoa sauce shouldn't be missed; ditto on the Cuban sandwich.

Cafés

The living room of Davis Square's lesbian community, **Diesel Cafe** (257 Elm St., Somerville, 617/629-8717, 7 A.M.–8 P.M. daily, www.dieselcafe.com, $5–6) has crossover appeal for everyone, with a photo booth tucked by the pool table in the back, and a menu of creative coffee drinks and vegetarian sandwiches. High-octane coffee and a decidedly cool vibe are what have Central Square hipsters addicted to **1369 Coffeehouse** (1369 Cambridge St., Cambridge, 617/576-1369, www.1369coffeehouse.com,

6:30 A.M.–11 P.M. Mon.–Fri; 7 A.M.–11:30 P.M. Sat.; 7:30 A.M.–10 P.M. Sun., $3–6). The regulars come in as much to hang out as they do to nosh on freshly baked scones.

Eastern European
Good old-fashioned hospitality and simplicity of dining are in the spotlight at **Salts** (798 Main St., Cambridge, 617/876-8444, 5 P.M.–10 P.M. Tues.–Sun.; closed Mon., www.saltsrestaurant. com, $28–36). The humble bistro's homemade bread, lavender crème caramel, and thoughtful service are all reasons to keep coming back.

French
The spirit of simple French bistro cooking is found at **Ten Tables** (5 Craigie Circle, Cambridge, 617/576-5454, www.tentables.net, 5:30–10 P.M. Mon.–Thurs., 5:30–10:30 P.M. Fri.–Sat., 5–9 P.M., $19–25), an offshoot of the popular restaurant in Jamaica Plain. Chef David Punch assembles beautiful plates of locally sourced, intensely flavored, and always seasonal dishes—the likes of Atlantic cod with brussels sprouts in winter, garlicky roasted lamb in spring, and sumptuous freshly made tomato tarts in summer. Regulars come for the laid-back but romantic atmosphere as much as the food—and know to make reservations well ahead of time.

Sandwiches
It's hard to argue with a burger so big and juicy you can barely manage it with two hands. Said patty is the reason for the line outside **Mr. Bartley's Burger Cottage** (1246 Massachusetts Ave., Cambridge, 617/354-6559, 11 A.M.–9 P.M. Mon.–Sat; closed Sun., bartleysburgers.com, $10–13)—though accompaniments like sweet-potato fries and raspberry-lime rickeys have also earned fans.

Tapas
Surrealism meets romance—usually over sangria—at (**Dalí** (415 Washington St., Somerville, 617/661-3254, 11 A.M.–10 P.M. Tues.–Sat; closed Sun. and Mon., www.dalirestaurant.com, $6–16), the brightly tiled den serving excellent Spanish food with an emphasis on tapas. Share a few plates of potatoes, spicy baked cod, and a bottle of rioja in the dark bordello-like setting to experience the whole effect.

BROOKLINE
American
Those searching for a model of a modern New England restaurant should look no further than **The Fireplace** (1634 Beacon St., Brookline, 617/975-1900, 5 P.M.–10 P.M. Tues.–Sat.; 10 A.M.–10 P.M. Sun.; closed Mon., www.fireplacerest.com, $22–33), home to sublime dishes with fresh, local ingredients: maple-glazed pork ribs with green-apple slaw, for example. The restaurant itself is refined but comfy, full of linen-covered tables and (of course) a fireplace.

Kosher
Imagine your favorite Jewish deli. Now picture it with a pop-art makeover. That's **Zaftigs** (335 Harvard St., Brookline, 617/975-0775, 8 A.M.–10 P.M., www.zaftigs.com, $8–17), a longtime favorite for its killer potato pancakes, overstuffed corned-beef sandwiches, and rich kugel.

Thai
There's above-average Thai food to be found at (**Khao Sarn** (250 Harvard St., Brookline, 617/566-7200, 11:30 A.M.–11 P.M. daily, $11–21), starting with standards like pad thai and culminating with specials like sautéed lobster with mango. The attractive, streamlined dining room is blessed with Thai textiles on the walls, and a friendly staff happy to answer any questions about the menu.

Sushi
First-rate sushi can be tough to find in Boston, so it's often in droves that locals head to **Fugakyu** (1280 Beacon St., Brookline, 617/734-1268, 11:30 A.M.–1:30 A.M. Mon.–Sat.; noon–1:30 A.M. Sun., www.fugakyu.net, $19–54). Beyond the long lines, though, await platters of extremely fresh, high-quality raw fish artfully arranged to impressive effect. (There's high-quality cooked Japanese food as well.) The two-

floored room, with its blonde wood and running fountains, is equally appealing.

OTHER NEIGHBORHOODS
Cuban

Loved for its casual Cuban fare, **Miami Restaurant** (381 Centre St., Jamaica Plain, 617/522-4644, 11:30 A.M.–10:30 P.M. Mon.–Fri; 11 A.M.–9 P.M. Sun., $3–8) is worth a visit if only for its Cubano—a savory pressed sandwich filled with pork, ham, and pickles. The cheap, quick meals are served to customers in a handful of booths beneath news clips and posters about baseball and Cuba.

Tapas

For sumptuous and authentic Spanish, **Tasca** (1612 Commonwealth Ave., Brighton, 617/730-8002, 5 P.M.–10 P.M. Mon.–Fri; 5 P.M.–9 P.M. Sun., www.tascarestaurant.com, $14.95–19.95) shouldn't be missed. From the charming brick facade to the savory paella and pitchers of sweet sangria, the dark restaurant is as cushy a setting for dates as it is for groups.

Information and Services

INFORMATION

A good place to get oriented is the **Boston Common Visitor Information Center** (148 Tremont St., 888/733-2678, www.bostonusa.com, 8:30 A.M.–5 P.M. Mon.–Sat., 9 A.M.–5 P.M. Sun.), located in the park halfway between the Park Street and Boylston Street T stops. There you can pick up maps and guides, along with discount museum coupons and brochures for major attractions. It's also the starting place for the Freedom Trail and several trolley tours around the city. Another information center is the **Prudential Center Visitor Information Center** (Prudential Center, 9 A.M.–5 P.M. Mon.–Fri.; 10 A.M.–6 P.M. Sat.–Sun.), located inside the mall. The National Park Service runs its own **Downtown Visitor Center** (15 State St., 617/242-5642, www.nps.gov/bost, 9 A.M.–5 P.M. daily), which includes a good collection of books on Boston and Massachusetts. If you are planning ahead, you can contact the **Greater Boston Convention and Visitors Bureau** (800/733-2678, www.bostonusa.com) for additional publications with the latest tourist information.

SERVICES
Emergencies

For medical emergencies, call 911. Boston has many hospitals with 24-hour emergency rooms, including **Massachusetts General Hospital** (55 Fruit St., off Cambridge St., 617/726-2000, www.massgeneral.org) and **Beth Israel Deaconess Medical Center** (330 Brookline Ave. at Longwood Ave., 617/667-7000, www.bidmc.org).

Internet

If you brought your laptop, you can access free wireless Internet in the Bates Reading Room at the **Boston Public Library** (700 Boylston St., 617/536-5400, www.bpl.org, 9 A.M.–9 P.M. Mon.–Thurs.; 9 A.M.–5 P.M. Fri.–Sat.). A guest library pass is required. You can also access the Internet through **Newbury Open.Net** (252 Newbury St., www.techsuperpowers.com/newburyopen.net, 9 A.M.–8 P.M. Mon.–Fri.; noon–7 P.M. Sat.–Sun., $5/hr), which runs a cyber café and also provides free wireless to many cafés on Newbury Street.

Discounts

If you plan on seeing a lot of attractions while in town, the **Go Boston Card** (85 Merrimac St., 800/887-9103, www.gobostoncard.com) provides good value. Cards are sold in one-day ($54 adult, $38 children 3–12), two-day ($80/$50), three-day ($110/$66), five-day ($158/$98), and seven-day ($196/$120) increments, and offer free admission to most area attractions, including many in Concord, Salem,

TROLLEY TOURS

In 1898, Boston produced the first subway in America. Since then, the city's tourism industry has done seemingly everything in its power to twist that form of transportation into as many silly (albeit often quite fun) ways to see the town as possible. Here are the most popular:

- **Boston Upper Deck Trolley Tours:** If it looks like there's a party going on inside these trolleys as they roll down the street, it's probably because there is. They come equipped with everything from strobe lights and disco balls to plasma TVs, bubble machines, and wireless microphones (departing from Long Wharf, 617/742-1440, www.discoverbostontours.com).

- **Duck Tours:** A full fleet of authentic WWI amphibious vehicles have been converted into "ducks" that take passengers on a narrated tour of the city's streets and the Charles River, encouraging them to "quack" throughout the tour (departing from the Prudential Center and the Museum of Science, 617/267-3825, www.bostonducktours.com).

- **Beantown Trolley:** These trackless trolleys stop at upwards of 20 major Boston museums and attractions, and allow passengers to take as many round-trips in a day as they like (800/343-1328, www.brushhilltours.com/tours/beantown.html).

- **Silver Trolley Tours:** The one-hour, narrated tour aboard silver trolleys made in Maine come complete with DVD players, air-ride suspension for comfort, and free tickets to either the Sports Museum (year-round) or a Boston Harbor Cruise (in summer). Children under 12 ride free (departing from various locations, 617/363-7899, www.cityviewtrolleys.com).

and surrounding areas. In addition, many guesthouses and hotels have discount museum passes for guest use.

Guided Tours

Taking advantage of Boston's reputation as a "walking city," **Boston By Foot** (77 North Washington St., 617/367-2345 or 617/367-3766 for recorded information, www.bostonbyfoot.com, $12 adults, $8 children 6–12) offers architectural and history tours of several Boston neighborhoods, including Beacon Hill, the Back Bay, and the North End. The organization also offers tours of the Freedom Trail for children, and a unique Boston Underground tour that explores closed-off subway tunnels and the construction of the Big Dig.

Getting There and Around

GETTING THERE
By Air

Flights to Boston's **Logan International Airport** (www.massport.com/logan) are available from almost all major cities. From Logan, ground transportation can be arranged from the information desk at baggage claim. The most efficient way to get into the city is via taxi, though expect to pay a minimum of $25 for downtown locations. A cheaper option is to take shared van service, which runs to hotels downtown and in the Back Bay for $10–12 per person. Water taxis also cross Boston Harbor to downtown and Seaport District locations, as well as Quincy and Hull, year-round, for about $10 per person.

A much cheaper option is to take a $1.70 subway ride; the airport station is on the Blue

Line, and accessible by taking the #22 or #33 bus from any terminal. All told, expect it to take 30–45 minutes to get downtown. Even easier is the Silver Line, which runs express bus service to South Station and picks up directly in front of terminals A and E. It takes 15–30 minutes.

By Rail

From most destinations, **Amtrak** (South Station, Summer St. & Atlantic Ave., 800/872-7245, www.amtrak.com) runs service to both South Station and Back Bay Station. Trains from New York and Washington take about four and seven hours respectively. Note that Amtrak trains from all destinations in Maine run to North Station, not South. The **Massachusetts Bay Transportation Authority** (617/222-5000, www.mbta.com) also runs commuter rail service from locations in Greater Boston for fares of up to $6. Trains from the North Shore, Lowell, and Fitchburg arrive at North Station, while those coming from the South Shore, Providence, and Worcester arrive at South Station.

By Bus

Bus service arrives at South Station. Most U.S. destinations are served by **Greyhound** (800/231-2222, www.greyhound.com). However, smaller bus companies also run from various locations around the region.

GETTING AROUND

Boston drivers are justly famous for the temporary insanity they acquire when they get behind the wheel. Don't expect much help from street signs downtown either; they have a habit of jumping out right before a needed turn. Pay close attention to the lane you are in, lest you find yourself routed up onto the Expressway unawares.

A smart alternative to a car is taking the "T," which is short for MBTA, itself an acronym for the **Massachusetts Bay Transportation Authority** (617/222-5000, www.mbta.com). Subway fares are $2 with a ticket—or $1.70 with a reloadable Charlie Card you can pick up at major stations (definitely worth seeking out if you are going to be in town for more than a dayS). More out-of-the-way locations require taking one of the MBTA buses, which are often slow but give good coverage across the city. Fare is currently $1.50, or $1.25 with a Charlie Card. Often overlooked as a means of transportation are the ferries that ply Boston Harbor. A trip from Charlestown Navy Yard to Long Wharf (perfect after completing the Freedom Trail) costs $1.70.

Keep in mind that the MBTA doesn't run between 12:30 A.M. and 5:30 A.M. The only option at that time is to take a taxi cab, which isn't cheap. Fares start at $2.60 for the first one-seventh mile, and add 40 cents for each additional one-seventh mile, with $24 for each hour of waiting time. Got that? Flat rates to certain communities around Boston are also available at $3.20 per mile. Also note that trips to Logan are saddled with an additional $2.75 for tolls, while trips from Logan cost an extra $6. There is no charge, however, for baggage or extra passengers. In some areas—notably downtown and the Back Bay—bicycle-driven "pedi-cabs" are available (617/266-2005, www.bostonpedicab.com). You can't beat the price, which is an enigmatic "pay as you please."

EASTERN MASSACHUSETTS

Traveling through the towns surrounding Boston is like leafing through the different eras of a history book. The area is filled with legends of resolute minutemen, grizzled sea-captains, dour Pilgrims, and unfortunate "witches," all of whom have left their mark on the forests and fields of Eastern Massachusetts. History books, however, don't allow you to smell the musket smoke on Patriot's day or the scent of corn cakes smoldering on the fire of a Native American encampment. Simply put, folks here know their past, and specialize in bringing it alive for visitors better than anywhere.

The vast majority of the state's population lives within reach of I-495, which describes a lazy semicircle around Boston. Within that ring lie bedroom communities full of commuters to the city, crumbling old mill towns that once played a part in fomenting the Industrial Revolution, and small hamlets that have—so far—resisted the encroaching sprawl of the city. Recently, the Boston area was declared the most expensive place to live in the country, and it's easy to see why—there just simply isn't anywhere to put new housing. Where open space does exist, it is jealously guarded by those residents hoping to preserve the rural character that adds to the area's historic appeal.

For the most part, however, you won't see the density of the area manifest itself in strip malls or the runaway development that has ruined many an American city. Even though the residents here are computer engineers and office drones, you can still imagine that stern-faced minuteman emerging from their doorways.

© MICHAEL BLANDING

HIGHLIGHTS

◖ Witch Trials Sights: The original "witch city" is a fascinating journey back into a time of collective insanity (page 99).

◖ Hammond Castle: This authentic medieval castle has got to be one of the most elaborate wedding presents ever given (page 103).

◖ Minuteman National Historical Park: The larger-than-life events that shaped our nation are brought down to size at this park (page 112).

◖ Walden Pond State Reservation: Live deliberately (and take a dive) at the former home of America's first environmentalist (page 112).

◖ Worcester Art Museum: This little-visited gem specializes in genres missed by other art museums (page 118).

◖ Plimoth Plantation: It's virtually impossible to find a single anachronism at this meticulously re-created historic site (page 126).

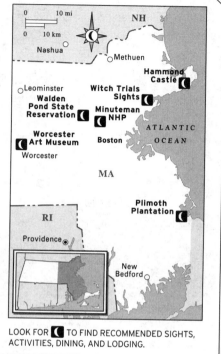

LOOK FOR ◖ TO FIND RECOMMENDED SIGHTS, ACTIVITIES, DINING, AND LODGING.

PLANNING YOUR TIME

If you only have a few days to explore this area, you have a tough choice in choosing a direction to set out in. Do you go north, to explore the fishing and shipbuilding villages in and around the rocky shores of Cape Ann? If so, a must-see is the cultural mecca of Salem, which offers the **witch trials sights** and so much more. Another highlight of the region is the gritty fishing port of Gloucester, with its straight-out-of-Camelot **Hammond Castle** overlooking the harbor. Or do you go west, into the heartland of Boston's Revolutionary history? Here, you'll find the perfectly preserved battlefields of **Minuteman National Historical Park** and the literary monuments of Concord, which pay homage to literary legends Ralph Waldo

Emerson, Nathaniel Hawthorne, Louisa May Alcott, and Henry David Thoreau (including Thoreau's former stomping grounds at **Walden Pond**). Lesser known but equally fascinating attractions are the industrial center of Lowell, and the re-created hamlet of Old Sturbridge Village. Or should you go all the way back, and head south? Here, you can step on the same ground that the pilgrims did with a visit to **Plimoth Plantation,** and the whaling port of New Bedford.

Whichever direction you choose, you'll need a minimum of two or three days to really do any one of these areas justice; unless you are really a history buff, you probably shouldn't pick more than two of these areas to explore in one trip. In the fall, the country lanes around

MASSACHUSETTS

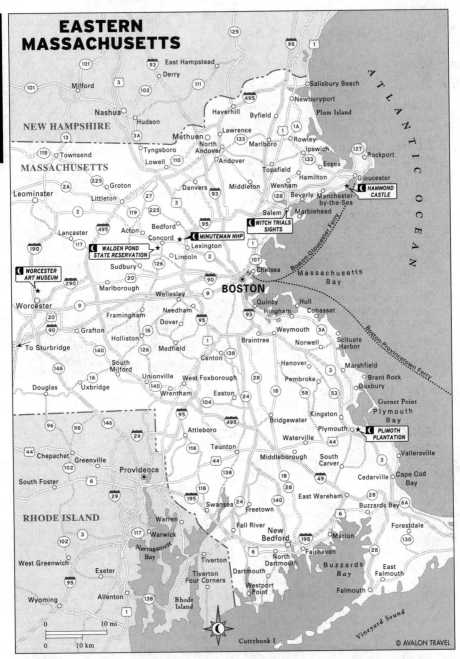

EASTERN MASSACHUSETTS

NEW HAMPSHIRE

MASSACHUSETTS

RHODE ISLAND

ATLANTIC OCEAN

Massachusetts Bay

Boston-Gloucester Ferry

Boston-Provincetown Ferry

Plymouth Bay

Cape Cod Bay

Buzzards Bay

Narragansett Bay

Vineyard Sound

Cuttyhunk I

BOSTON

WITCH TRIALS SIGHTS

MINUTEMAN NHP

WALDEN POND STATE RESERVATION

WORCESTER ART MUSEUM

HAMMOND CASTLE

PLIMOTH PLANTATION

To Sturbridge

0   10 mi
0   10 km

© AVALON TRAVEL

Concord and Lexington are bursting with fall foliage by October. At the same time, the cranberry bogs to the south are blooming with red berries. It goes without saying that if you are in the area in the weeks before Halloween, Salem is positively bewitching, while Plymouth pulls out all the stops in November leading up to Thanksgiving. During summertime, Bostonians here head to the shore. The coastlines both north and south of Boston have

devotees, and fistfights have broken out over whether Duxbury or Crane Beach is best. During wintertime, many of the attractions around Boston go into hibernation, but sitting by a roaring fire in a historic inn by the seacoast has its own charms to recommend. Even then, however, it pays to call ahead, as a handful of restaurants and hotels in the area are seasonal and either close or reduce their hours of operation in colder months.

The North Shore

The coastline north of Boston is smaller than the long curving seashore to the south. The ocean here, however, is arguably much more present in the towns that cling to the rocky coves and hidden beaches along the shoreline. The North Shore (that's "Noath Shoah" to locals) contains a mix of historic seaside villages like Essex and Ipswich; artists colonies like Rockport; and fishing communities like Gloucester. Newburyport's Plum Island and

Ipswich's Crane Beach are both known for bird-watching and sunbathing. The can't-miss destination of Salem is just as interesting for its museums and maritime history as for the witch trials that made it famous.

SALEM

On Valentine's Day, you go to Paris. For Mardi Gras, you head to New Orleans. For Halloween, there's only one place to go: 15

© MICHAEL BLANDING

the Witch House

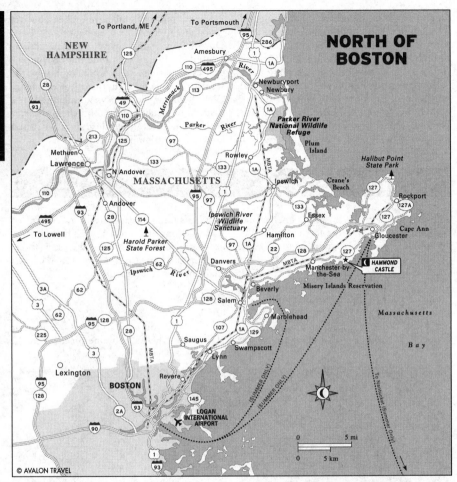

NORTH OF BOSTON

© AVALON TRAVEL

miles north of Boston to the original Witch City. Anyone who's seen or read Arthur Miller's *The Crucible* knows the story: In 1692, several young women took ill and cried out the names of alleged witches they claimed were causing their torments. The famous trials were convened, and from May to September of that year, 13 women and five men were tried, convicted, and hanged for vague crimes involving black magic.

Even now there's something about the historic seaport that curdles the blood after

sundown. The country nights are inky dark, and the proximity of the ocean wafts spooky mists and fogs around the Gothic Victorian homes downtown. Witchcraft isn't the only thing that Salem has going for it, however. Settled in 1629 at the mouth of the Naumkeag River, the town got involved in the cod and West Indies trades early. By the start of the 19th century, its merchants and sea captains had made it the richest town in the *country*, second only to Boston in importance in the region. Among those who grew up here during

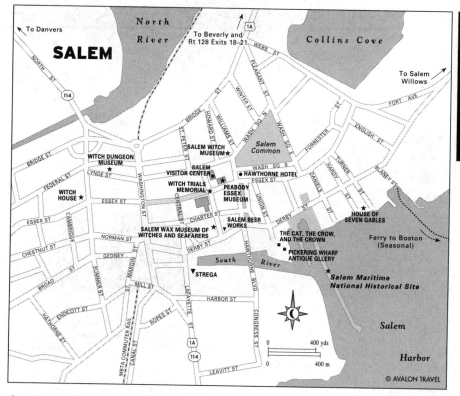

that time was Nathaniel Hawthorne, who was inspired by the town's history to weave some of the most haunting tales of American literature. Much of the history here is still very much in evidence, sharing cobblestone streets with cosmopolitan restaurants and occult bookshops.

Witch Trials Sights

Looking back today, it's difficult to understand the collective madness that overtook the town here, leaving 18 people dead and making "witch trials" synonymous with unjust accusations. Many sights around Salem do their best to shed light on the tragedy, with results ranging from sobering to cheesy. The most affecting is the simple **Salem Witch Trials Memorial** (Liberty St., www.salemweb.com/memorial), which displays the names of the victims on stone benches next to the central burying ground. Nearby, the **Witch House** (310½ Essex St., 978/744-8815, www.salem-web.com/witchhouse, 10 A.M.–5 P.M. May–early Nov., $8.25 adults, $6.25 seniors, $4.25 children 6–14, free children under 6) is the former home of magistrate Jonathan Corwin, who sentenced the guilty to death. Tours detail the restored interior, giving a sense of the time.

The most popular museum dedicated to the trials is the **Salem Witch Museum** (Washington Sq. North, 978/744-1692, www.salemwitchmuseum.com, 10 A.M.–5 P.M. daily Sept.–June, 10 A.M.–7 P.M. daily July–Aug., extended hours in Oct., $8 adults, $7 seniors, $5.50 children 6–14, free children under 6), which has an effective multimedia show that narrates the sequence of events in 1692. The museum also has an interesting exhibit about the perceptions of witches through the ages.

© TIM GRAFFT/MOTT

typical October visitors in Salem

A somewhat more hokey depiction of the trials is on display at the **Salem Wax Museum of Witches and Seafarers** (288 Derby St., 978/298-2929, www.salemwaxmuseum.com, 10 A.M.–6 P.M. daily Apr.–June, 10 A.M.–9 P.M. daily July–Aug., 10 A.M.–6 P.M. daily Sept., extended hours in Oct., 10 A.M.–5 P.M. Nov.–Dec., 11 A.M.–4 P.M. Jan.–Mar., $7 adults, $6 seniors, $5 children and students, free children under 5), which also purports to display the various pirates and rogue captains who colored the populace. A reenactment of the trials, using original transcripts, is performed at the **Witch Dungeon Museum** (16 Lynde St., 978/741-3570, www.witchdungeon.com, 10 A.M.–5 P.M. Apr.–Nov., extended hours in Oct., $8 adults, $7 seniors, $6 children 4–13), which has melodramatic exhibits on the affair.

Other Sights

With a collection originally culled from the private stores of merchant captains, the **Peabody Essex Museum** (East India Sq., 978/745-9500 or 866/745-1876, www.pem.org, 10 A.M.–5 P.M. Tue.–Sun., $15 adults, $13 seniors, $11 students, free youth 16 and under) should be on the short list of anyone visiting Salem. Exhibits include priceless antiques from Asia and Polynesia, as well as antique American furniture. The highlight is a 19th-century house imported post-and-beam from China. A new glass-enclosed wing provides even more space for top-notch temporary exhibitions. Exploring Salem's other claim to fame, the **Salem Maritime National Historical Park** (160 Derby St., 978/740-1650, www.nps.gov, 9 A.M.–5 P.M. daily, prices for tours vary), includes several authentic old sea-captain's homes, the Custom House featured in Hawthorne's *The Scarlet Letter,* and a replica of sloop from the Golden Age of Sail.

Speaking of Hawthorne, feel free to count the roofs at the **House of the Seven Gables** (115 Derby St., 978/744-0991, www.7gables.org, 10 A.M.–5 P.M. daily Nov.–June, 10 A.M.–7 P.M. daily July–Nov. 1, $12 adults, $11 seniors, $7.25 children 5–12, free children under 5)—they are all there. The 17th-century mansion is legendary for its role in the Nathaniel Hawthorne novel that probably tortured you in high school. Inside, costumed interpreters take guests through three centuries of Salem history, including the early years of its favorite native son.

Events
Three guesses for the biggest time of the year in Salem, and the first two don't count. Every October, **Haunted Happenings** (877/725-3662, www.hauntedhappenings.org) takes over the whole city with a month of spooktastic events. All of the historic sites get into the act with extended hours and special programs (such as the "Spirit of the Gables," when the Hawthorne house is open for tours by candle-light). The event culminates in a huge costume party on the Common that draws some 50,000 revelers from around the region to dance the monster mash until the wee hours.

Shopping
Unless you want to chance a hex, you'll visit Salem's "official" witchcraft shop, **The Cat, the Crow, and the Crown** (63R Wharf St., 978/744-6274, www.lauriecabot.com), where proprietrix Laurie Cabot hooks up amateur occultists with everything they need to cook up a spell. Showcasing the mercantile side of Salem, **Pickering Wharf Antique Gallery** (69 Wharf St., 978/741-3113) has 30 dealers with a range of American furniture and nautical souvenirs.

Food
More than a dozen hand-crafted brews are on tap at **Salem Beer Works** (278 Derby St., 978/745-2337, www.beerworks.net, 11 A.M.–10 P.M., Mon.–Sat.; 11 A.M.–8 P.M., Sun., $8–17), including the honey-scented Seven Gables Golden, the spicy Pumpkinhead Ale, and the hoppy Witch City Red. To pair with the suds is a creative menu of burgers, sandwiches, and bar food. Specials include New York strip streak or a full rack of ribs. Named after the Italian word for "witch," **Strega** (94 Lafayette St., 978/741-0004, www.stregasalem.com, 5 P.M.–10 P.M., Tues.–Sat.; closed Sun. and Mon., $17–20) goes beyond pasta to serve Italian-influenced meat and fish dishes. Befitting the

name, the dining room is decked out in over-the-top plush red fabrics and swooping blood-red curtains.

Information and Services
Information about all aspects of the town is available at the **National Park Visitor Center** (2 New Liberty St., 978/740-1650, www.nps.gov/sama).

MARBLEHEAD
Few towns in Massachusetts have as delightful a location as Marblehead. Situated on a rocky outcropping 17 miles north of Boston, the town is divided into two parts—the headland known as Marblehead Neck is populated with old-money mansions that are as stunning as the vantage they command; across the harbor, the town center is a pedestrian-friendly collection of old colonial homes and brick buildings shot through with clothing boutiques and eateries.

Like many towns on the North Shore, Marblehead earned its living early from the sea. Founded a year before Boston, it was recognized early as one of the best fishing harbors around. As the Revolution approached, it became a strategic location on the coast, and the British landed there in 1775 to capture ammunition, a year before a similar attempt at Concord (they were turned back without a battle). Residents also proudly proclaim the town the "birthplace of the American navy" for its role in outfitting and basing the small fleet of schooners that General Washington procured the same year to harass British shipping. The town is now better known as a yachting capital, with thick forest of white masts covering its sheltered harbor year-round.

Sights
The jaunty fife-and-drum squad depicted in the painting *The Spirit of '76* is one of the most iconic images in American history—so much so that you might expect it to be hanging in a museum in Washington. Actually, the massive 8-by-10-foot painting hangs on the wall of Marblehead's town hall, **Abbot Hall** (188 Washington St., 617/631-0000, 8 A.M.–5 P.M.

Mon., Tues., and Thurs.; 7:30 A.M.–7:30 P.M. Wed.; 8 A.M.–1 P.M. Fri., free). Painted in 1876 for the country's centennial by a native of the town (who used his father as one of the models), it was donated in honor of Marblehead's role in Revolutionary naval battles.

George Washington slept at the **Jeremiah Lee Mansion** (161 Washington St., 781/631-1768, www.marbleheadmuseum.org, 10 A.M.–4 P.M. Tues.–Sat., $5)—as did James Monroe, Andrew Jackson, and the Marquis de Lafayette. The three-story 1768 mansion was home to a shipping magnate who was once the wealthiest in Massachusetts. It is a rare New England example of Georgian architecture, with highlights including the only surviving example of hand-painted English wallpaper.

Entertainment and Events

The Tex-Mex **Rio Grande Cafe** (12 School St., 781/639-1828, 5:30 P.M.–10:30 P.M., Sun.–Wed.; 5:30 P.M.–12:30 A.M., Thurs.–Sat.) presents live blues and rock on the weekends.

The highlight of the social calendar, however, is **Race Week** (www.mheadrace.org, late July), when some 200 boats descend on the area for regattas in the harbor and parties on shore.

Shopping

The independent-minded **Spirit of '76 Bookstore** (107 Pleasant St., 781/631-7199, 10 A.M.–7 P.M., Mon.–Fri.; 10 A.M.–5 P.M. Sat.; 12 P.M.–5 P.M., Sun.; www.spiritof76bookstore. com) has been a mainstay of Marblehead for more than 40 years. In addition to the regular fiction and nonfiction selections, it boasts a strong section on sailing and nautical history. Try and resist uttering the words "Oh, how cute" when you enter **Lester Harry's** (140 Washington St., 781/631-4343, 10 A.M.–5 P.M., Mon.–Sat.; 12 P.M.–5 P.M. Sun., www.lesterharrys.com), a high-end baby and kid's clothing store chock-full of signature designs as well as to-die-for luxury American and European labels. In nearby Beverly Farms you'll find **Glee** (29 West St., Beverly Farms, 978/922-4777, www.glee. us), a favorite among the area's style-conscious

(though not overly trendy) females. Find embroidered coats by Biya, slouchy pants by Trina Turk, and unimaginably soft hand-knit sweater coats. Men needn't feel left out, either; there's plenty of high-quality haberdashery for them at **Giblees** (85 Andover St., Danvers, 978/774-4080, 10 A.M.–7:30 P.M., Mon.–Sat.; 12 P.M.–6 P.M., Sun., www.giblees.com), from Pelham slip-ons and button-down Oxfords to houndstooth Magli jackets and Nat Nast polos.

Food

A catering operation with an attached café, **Foodie's Feast** (114 Washington St., Marblehead, 781/639-1104, www.foodiesfeast. com, $3–7) is where the locals go for gourmet sandwiches (try the lavender-roasted chicken breast), soups, and salads. Located just a block from the harbor, the café is also acclaimed for its weekend brunch, which features eggs benedict, breakfast burritos, and super-addictive scones, served at *al fresco* tables with the smell of salt in the air. The views are as fine as the eating at **Red Rock Bistro** (141 Humphrey St., Swampscott, 781/595-1414, www.redrockbistro.com, $19–34), the little harborside boîte serving up seafood like pan-seared fluke with turnip mash, wood-grilled pizzas, and a brunch that has the whole of Swampscott addicted.

Information

In addition to providing a wealth of information about the town, the **Marblehead Chamber of Commerce** (62 Pleasant St., 781/631-2868, www.marbleheadchamber.org) sponsors historic walking tours of downtown.

CAPE ANN

Unlike the sandy barrier beach that makes up Cape Cod, its sister Cape Ann is a rocky headland jutting forcibly out into the rough waters of the Atlantic. Because of that, the cape has a dramatically different character than the rest of the Massachusetts coast, with rocky shores more reminiscent of Maine. The topography has drawn two very different types of people to the area—fishermen, who have used the vantage point for quick access to the prime

MOTIF NO. 1

If the little red fish shack perched on Rockport's Bradley Wharf looks familiar, that's because you've probably seen it in a painting somewhere. The picturesque shack was a favorite subject for the artists who came to Cape Ann every summer in the 1920s and '30s to paint the buildings and denizens of the harbor. One day after a student brought in yet another treatment of the building, Paris-trained illustrator and art teacher Lester Hornby is said to have shouted, "What, Motif Number One, again?" The name stuck, and to this day, "Motif No. 1" is known as one of the most frequently painted buildings in the world, turning up in paintings from South America to the Czech Republic. Rockport's "dirty little secret," however, is that the original building actually collapsed and washed out to sea during the swells of the great Blizzard of '78. Within a year, the town fathers had built and painted an exact replica to replace it. Perhaps it should be called "Motif No. 2"?

© TIM GRAFFT/MOTT

Rockport's Motif No. 1

fishing grounds of Georges Bank; and artists, who have delighted in the changing dance of sunlight and surf on the granite rock faces.

Roughly, the two groups are divided into the two towns that hug the point. On the north side, **Rockport** has been home to artists colonies for more than a century. A dry town until just a year ago, it has a quaint atmosphere full of art galleries and boutiques. By contrast, **Gloucester** is a rough-and-tumble fishing village. While it has gentrified somewhat over the years, the fishing tradition is very much alive in the working harbor and bars that line the waterfront. The town's 15 minutes of fame came a few years ago with the book and film *The Perfect Storm,* which told of the harrowing disaster of the fishing boat *Andrea Gail,* and gave what residents generally agree to be an accurate, if sentimentalized, view of their trade.

◀ Hammond Castle

No buts about it—Dr. John Hays Hammond Jr. was a singular individual. An energetic

psychologist who produced the patents for over 400 inventions (including the remote control and the stereo), Hammond was also a voracious collector of all things Roman, medieval, and Renaissance. In 1926, Hammond decided the perfect venue for displaying his treasures was a castle of his own, and over the next three years set about building an authentic medieval edifice on the shores of Gloucester harbor as a present for his wife, Irene. The two opened the castle (80 Hesperus Ave., Gloucester, 978/283-2080, www. hammondcastle.org, 10 A.M.–4 P.M. Sat.–Sun., $10 adults, $8 seniors, $6 children 4–12, free children under 4) as a museum in 1930, since which time it has left visitors agog at the rich collection of antiques. Highlights include the Gothic bedroom, Renaissance dining room, and the largest pipe organ in a private residence, a behemoth with 183 pipes. Every year at Halloween, ghosts and ghouls fill the halls for a scary hauntfest.

Other Sights

All aspects of the working waterfront are

covered at the **Gloucester Maritime Heritage Center** (23 Harbor Loop, Gloucester, 978/281-0470, www.gloucestermaritimecenter.org, 10 A.M.–5 P.M. daily late May–Oct.), which includes an ocean aquarium, boatbuilding demonstrations, and a flotilla of watercraft moored in the harbor, including working fishing boats and a replica of one of the Boston Tea Party ships. As might be expected with a rocky headland, Cape Ann has a half dozen lighthouses scattered around its rocky shores. Perhaps the most picturesque is **Annisquam Light** (Wigwam Point, Lighthouse Rd., Gloucester, www.lighthouse.cc), a 41-foot white tower ringed with a black railing, with a walkway over the rocks to the front door.

By far the most unusual sight in Gloucester is an abandoned village in the center of the peninsula. Once called the Commons Settlement, it was abandoned in the 1700s, when wild dogs took it over and it earned a new name: Dogtown. Now one of the country's oldest ghost towns, it comes alive again in **Walk the Words Tours** (978/546-8122, www.walkthewords.com, $15 adults, $7 children), guided hikes given by two local women who regale visitors with tales of some of its most colorful former residents. The highlight of the three mile hike is the Babson Word Rocks—23 huge boulders carved with motivational phrases commissioned to employ out-of-work Finnish stonecutters during the Great Depression. At the time, mottos like "Never Try, Never Win" and "Prosperity Follows Service" must have seemed inspirational, but now lost amidst the forest and cellar holes they seem downright ironic.

Entertainment

Made famous by *The Perfect Storm,* the **Crow's Nest** (334 Main St., Gloucester, 978/281-2965) is just as rough-and-tumble as you'd expect. Be forewarned, no one as cute as Mark Wahlberg or George Clooney warms the barstools.

Events

The highlight of the year in Gloucester is the **St. Peter's Fiesta** (www.stpetersfiesta.

org, late June), a five-day Italian festival that celebrates Gloucester's fishing community with boat races, the annual "blessing of the fleet," and the always-entertaining greasy pole contest.

Shopping

The art galleries in Rockport are concentrated in the area known as **Bearskin Neck,** an artists colony jutting out into the working harbor. Studios are clustered around the picturesque red fish shack known as "Motif No. 1"—held up alternately as the most painted and most photographed building in the country (see the sidebar *Motif No. 1*). A good place to start is the **Rockport Art Association** (12 Main St., Rockport, 978/546-6604, www.rockportartassn.org). Though not as large, Gloucester has an artists colony called **Rocky Neck,** which features galleries of its own.

Food

Grab a true taste of this seaside community—literally and otherwise—at **Portside Chowder House** (7 Tuna Wharf, Rockport, 978/546-7045, 11:30 A.M.–9:30 P.M., daily, $8–16), where diners nosh casual seafood on a porch overlooking the water. Don't come expecting four-star fare, however; meals here are as straightforward as fried fish sandwiches, lobster rolls, and salmon salad. By contrast, the urbane, sleekly designed **◖ Franklin Cafe** (118 Main St., Gloucester, 978/283-7888, www.franklincafe.com, 5 P.M.–10:30 P.M., Sun.–Thurs.; 5 P.M.–12 A.M., Fri.–Sat., $15–22) is an echo of its popular Boston sister restaurant, though with slightly lower prices and a menu sporting more seafood. The kitchen does right by its fresh catches, too, with dishes like split-grilled lobster with lemon sauce and garlic-grilled calamari with pesto and white beans.

Despite its Rocky Neck location, the intimate **Duckworth's Bistrot** (197 East Main St., Gloucester, 978/282-4426. www.duckworthsbistrot.com, 5 P.M.–10 P.M., Tues.–Sat.; 5 P.M.–9 P.M., Sun., $12–30) conspicuously lacks a harbor view. That's a clue to the emphasis of Boston expat chef Ken Duckworth, which is all on the food. His menu includes such lovelies as sautéed filet of sole with caramelized corn and lemon-parsley brown butter, and Muscovy duck breast over couscous with a plum and red-onion relish. All of the entrées are available as half-portions.

Information

Info on the area can be found at the **Cape Ann Chamber of Commerce** (33 Commercial St., Gloucester, 978/283-1601, www.capeannvacations.com).

NORTH OF CAPE ANN

Hugging a shallow bay in the lee of Cape Ann, the town of Essex was once renowned around the world for its shipbuilding prowess, having launched some 4,000 wooden ships into harbors all over the world. These days, however, it's more known as the birthplace of the fried clam. Bostonians still make pilgrimages to this part of the North Shore simply to taste the buttery goodness of fried food on a summer day. Two towns that share the stretch of waterfront above Essex each have their own unique charms—Ipswich has dozens of 17th-century homes and miles of beautiful conservation land framing its harbor; while the brick downtown of Newburyport has been renovated into a pedestrian paradise of restaurants, shops, and fine restaurants.

Sights

It's difficult to understate the impact that the little town of Essex had on establishing American commercial supremacy in the period after the Revolution. The **Essex Shipbuilding Museum** (66 Main St., Essex, 978/768-7541, www.essexshipbuildingmuseum.org, 10 A.M.–5 P.M. Wed.–Sun. June–Oct. and Sat.–Sun. Nov.–May, $7 adults, $6 seniors, $5 children 6 and over, free children under 6) traces almost 350 years of framing, rigging, and outfitting the craft that carried on our country's trade before the advent of the steam engine. Twenty models on loan from the Smithsonian present the range of wooden vessels built here. Kids love trying their own hands at boring holes and caulking seams.

Children of all ages are fascinated by the animals at **Wolf Hollow** (114 Essex Rd., Ipswich, 978/356-0216, www.wolfhollowipswich.com, tours at 1:30 Sat.–Sun., by appointment only Mon.–Fri., $7.50 adults, $5 seniors and children 3–17), a wildlife sanctuary where 10 British Colombian timber wolves wander around the grounds.

Decidedly more civilized, the 1926 manor known as the **Great House at Castle Hill** (290 Argilla Rd., 978/356-4351, www.thetrustees.org, tours 10 A.M.–3 P.M. Wed.–Thurs., 10 A.M.–1 P.M. Fri.–Sat. June–Oct., $10 adults, $5 children minimum age 8) is the centerpiece of the Crane Estate, a Victorian expanse of buildings and grounds located overlooking scenic Crane Beach. The home, which is full of period antiques, is open for tours in the summer.

Entertainment

Located in a former fire station, **Firehouse Center for the Arts** (1 Market Sq., Newburyport, 978/462-7336, www.firehousecenter.org) is one-stop shopping for culture. Among its offerings are theater productions, folk singers, indie films, and even step-dancing workshops. In the same complex, **The Grog** (13 Middle St., Newburyport, 978/465-8008, www.thegrog.com, 5 P.M.–11:30 P.M. daily) is a restaurant and bar that features live rock, folk, and jazz.

Shopping

Ipswich may have the historic homes, but Essex specializes in filling them. Known as the "antiques capital of the Northeast," the little town is acclaimed as much for the quality as the quantity of stores. Any antiquing trek starts at the **White Elephant Shop** (32 Main St., 978/768-6901, www.whiteelephantshop.com, 10 A.M.–5 P.M., Mon.–Fri.; 11 A.M.–5 P.M., Sat. and Sun.), where owners Rick and Jene Grobe scour attics and estate sales to find the finest pieces, along with art from local artists. Another good bet is **Americana Antiques** (48 Main St., 978/768-6006, www.americanaantiques.com, 10:30 A.M.–5 P.M. daily), which specializes in Victorian and early 20th-century furniture.

Food

This is where it all began, folks. One summer day in 1916 on Massachusetts' North Shore, Lawrence "Chubby" Woodman dunked a littleneck clam into the deep-frier he used to cook potato chips, and *voila!*—the fried clam was born. Many have imitated the recipe in the century since, but few with the same success. Now a dining-and-catering empire, **Woodman's of Essex** (Main St./Rte. 133, Essex, 978/768-2559, www.woodmans.com, 11:30 A.M.–9:30 P.M., Mon.–Sat.; 12 P.M.–8 P.M. Sun.; $9–25) can get chaotic on weekends—but in these parts, it still sets the standard. To skip the lines, head to **The Clam Box** (246 High St., Ipswich, 978/356-9707, www.ipswichma.com/clambox/index.htm, 11 A.M.–8 P.M., Mon.–Fri.; 11:30 P.M.–7 P.M., Sun., $7–23), a no less venerable institution that has been serving up fresh bivalves for 60 years. (The creation is even kicked up a notch here, with special homemade tartar sauce.)

Sample a creatively tweaked menu of New England staples at the brick-walled **Scandia** (37 Main St., Amesbury, 978/834-0444, 5:30 P.M.–10:30 P.M. daily;, $15–23), where the steamed mussels are tossed with andouille sausage and the crab cakes come daubed with aioli. A tad more casual, the sunny, lively dining room of **BluWater Cafe** (140 High St., Newburyport, 978/462-1088, www.thebluwatercafe.com, 12 P.M.–11 P.M., Tues.–Sat.; 12 P.M.–10 P.M., Sun.; closed Mon., $15–25) focuses on daily deliveries of locally caught fish, prepared simply (as is the blackened swordfish) or with flair (like the yellowfin tuna, served with sesame, sticky rice, wasabi, and ginger). If the weather's cooperating, there's no beating the al fresco eating at the friendly **Black Cow Tap & Grill** (54R Merrimac St., Newburyport, 978/499-8811, www.blackcowrestaurants.com, 11 A.M.–11:30 P.M., Mon.–Sat.; 10:30 A.M.–9:30 P.M. Sun., $15–32). Otherwise—or if the deck (which boasts a fantastic water view) is full—then grab a seat in the tavern indoors and dig into simple, unpretentious fare like pan-roasted halibut with braised fennel.

Information and Services

Brochures and information can be found at **Essex National Heritage Area Visitors Centers** (221 Essex St., Salem, 978/740-0444, www.essexheritage.org).

SPORTS AND RECREATION
Beaches

The North Shore abounds in gorgeous beachfront. One of the very best in New England is **Crane Beach** (Argilla Rd., Ipswich, 978/356-4354, www.thetrustees.org), a four-mile stretch of white sands and crashing white surf. The only time it isn't idyllic is the brief period of greenhead fly season (usually late July or early August—call ahead to check). The half-mile **Good Harbor Beach** (Thatcher Rd./Rte. 127A, Gloucester) offers a range of terrain, including sandy barrier beach, salt marsh, and rocky headland for tidepooling. The more secluded **Singing Beach** (Masconomo St., Manchester) is named for an interesting phenomenon wherein under certain conditions the sand seems to sing—or more accurately, squeak—when you walk on it.

Hiking and Biking

The wilderness jewel of the North Shore is Plum Island, a barrier island extending for 11 miles along the entrance of Newburyport Harbor. The bulk of the island is taken up by **Parker River National Wildlife Refuge** (6 Plum Island Tpke., 978/465-5753, www.fws.gov), a stopover for migratory birds on the Atlantic Flyway. A two-mile trail wends its way through sand dunes and swamps, providing excellent opportunities for bird sightings. It's also possible to surf-fish from the beach. The five-mile **Marblehead Rail Trail** offers beautiful vantages of the ocean and oceanfront mansions, with a two-mile spur into Salem. Rent bikes from **Marblehead Cycle** (25 Bessom St., 781/631-1570, www.marbleheadcycle.com).

Boating

Sea-kayak tours of the tidal estuaries in and around the Essex River are offered by **Essex River Basin Adventures** (1 Main St., Essex,

978/768-3722, www.erba.com), which boasts sightings of osprey, heron, and egrets.

Whale Watches

Cape Ann is ideally suited for access to the humpbacks and finbacks that patrol Stellwagen Bank. The oldest company in the business, **Cape Ann Whale Watch** (415 Main St., Gloucester, 800/877-5110, www.seethe-whales.com), boasts the speeds of its flagship *Hurricane,* which jets out to the fishing grounds at 30 knots.

ACCOMMODATIONS
Under $100

Located in a colonial home in the center of historic Marblehead, the 1721 **Brimblecomb Hill B&B** (33 Mechanic St., Marblehead, 781/631-3172 or 781/631-6366, www.brimblecomb.com, $95–125) was once owned by a close friend of Ben Franklin. The two less expensive rooms share a bath, while the pricier room has a private bath, four-poster queen-sized bed, and a wall full of books. Depending on the season, a continental breakfast is served by the fireplace or out in a small garden.

$100-150

Rockport abounds with bed-and-breakfasts situated in captain's houses and colonial homes. One of the most welcoming is ⟨ **Inn on Cove Hill** (37 Mount Pleasant St., Rockport, 978/546-2701, www.innoncovehill.com, $120–235), a lovingly restored Federal-style home crowded with antiques and original architectural flourishes. The rooms are named after members of the family of the original resident, Caleb Norwood, and feature a range of antique beds, including an iron trundle bed and Shaker low beds for children. The sense of humor of the current owner, Betsy Eck, is evidenced by her own line of "Inn Sane" clothing. Situated smack dab on Salem's common, the **Hawthorne Hotel** (18 Washington Square West, Salem, 978/744-4080, www.hawthornehotel.com, $114–315) is a miniature grand European hotel, with a marble lobby and ballroom. Rooms are individually furnished

with a rich, gender-neutral palette. Rates at Halloween include coveted tickets to the hotel's annual costume ball. You can't get any closer to the water than at the **Cape Ann Motor Inn** (33 Rockport Rd., Gloucester, 978/281-2900, www.capeannmotorinn.com, $80–275), a three-story family-style resort located right on the curving sands of Long Beach, on the Gloucester-Rockport line. All 31 rooms offer views of the water, and include mini-fridges and breakfast in the rates; kitchenettes are only slightly more expensive.

$150-250

Newburyport's premier lodging, the **Clark Currier Inn** (45 Green St., Newburyport, 978/465-8363, www.clarkcurrierinn.com, $125–195) is a grand Federal-style mansion once owned by a shipbuilder and silversmith. The eight rooms contain individual flourishes, including lace canopies, antique Victorian couches, and mahogany furniture. Several also offer separate entries for privacy. Offering a chance to stay on the historic Crane Estate, the **Inn at Castle Hill** (280 Argilla Rd., Ipswich, 978/412-2555, www.theinnatcastlehill.com, $115–385) brings alive the Victorian era with grand dimensions and a wraparound verandah. The overriding atmosphere, however, is one of pristine quiet, with elegant all-white and pastel furnishings, and an absence of televisions or radios on the grounds. Add a walk under the stars with the sound of the surf, and you could be miles from civilization.

GETTING THERE AND AROUND

From Boston, drive North on Route 1A to get to Marblehead (15 mi., 30 min.) or Salem (15 mi., 35 min.) For Cape Ann, take I-93 North to Route 128. Take exit 14 and head north on Route 133 for Essex (35 mi., 50 min.) and Ipswich (45 mi., 1 hr.). Follow 128 to the end for Gloucester (40 mi., 50 min.) and Rockport (45 mi., 1 hr.). The **Massachusetts Bay Transportation Authority** (617/222-3200, www.mbta.com) runs commuter trains to Salem, Manchester, Gloucester, Rockport,

Ipswich, and Newburyport. The MBTA also runs buses to Marblehead and Salem. The New Hampshire–based **Coach Company** (800/874-3377, www.coachco.com) runs daily buses to Newburyport. In addition, the **Cape Ann Transportation Authority** (800/874-3377, www.coachco.com) runs buses between Rockport and Gloucester.

West of Boston

It was an accident of geography that put Concord at the center of the American Revolution. The Sons of Liberty needed a place to store their guns and ammunition close enough to Boston to allow easy communication, but far enough away that the Minutemen would have time to rally in the event of attack. On the morning of April 19, 1775, the alarm was sounded that the British were marching to capture the weapons cache at Concord, and the rest, as they say, is history. Today, the twin towns of Concord and Lexington are among the wealthy suburbs west of Boston, where doctors, lawyers, and businessmen commute daily into the city, then return to bed down in old colonial homes. History is still very much in evidence in both towns, which have taken no small amount of pride in labeling themselves the birthplace of America. History isn't the *only* reason to visit, however. The cosmopolitan and educated populace of the area has built an infrastructure of fine restaurants, bookshops, and boutiques in and among the historic buildings.

A dozen miles north of Concord and Lexington, meanwhile, the old mill town of Lowell has a decidedly different feel, as poor as the other towns are rich, and as funky as they are patrician. Lowell, along with a dozen other cities in a ring of rivers around Boston, was instrumental in the Industrial Revolution that established New England as the nation's first manufacturing powerhouse. Now variously reincarnated as a home for artists and refugees from around the world, the city has done an excellent job of preserving the industrial past in a series of museums and exhibits.

LEXINGTON

Historians may debate where the famous "shot heard 'round the world" was actually fired, but there can be no doubt that the first armed combat of the Revolutionary War took place in the town of Lexington, 11 miles west of Boston. By all accounts, it was a tentative and slapdash affair, in stark contrast to the American victory at Concord Bridge that would take place a few hours later. Even so, it marks the first time that the rebellious colonists fired on their own country's troops, outnumbered and outgunned though they were. For that reason, the town now stands as monument to the patriot's courage.

Orientation

Because of the nature of the Battles of Lexington and Concord—which moved back and forth between the towns as the day went on—a visit here can be a confusing mishmash of history. The best way to tour them is to follow the chronology of the battle itself, starting at the visitors centers in Lexington and seeing the Battle Green and the historic sights there; then heading into Concord to see the Old North Bridge; and then retracing your steps by foot or car down the Battle Road to end up again in Lexington.

Historic Houses

Paul Revere arrived in Lexington on the night of April 18, 1775, on a mission—to get word to John Hancock and Samuel Adams. "The regulars are out," he told the two rebel leaders, who were staying as guests in a parsonage now known as the **Hancock-Clarke House** (35 Hancock St., 781/862-1703, 10 A.M.–4 P.M. Sat.–Sun. April to mid-June and daily mid-June–Oct., $6). Today, the home retains much of its original 18th-century character, as well as several artifacts from the day of the battle.

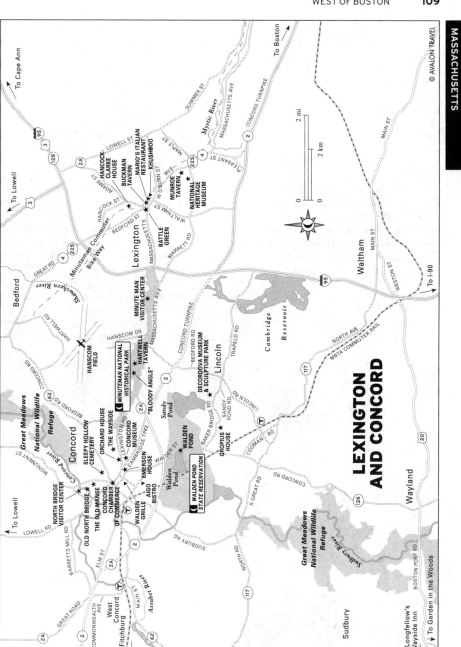

© AVALON TRAVEL

LEXINGTON AND CONCORD

After debating their course of action, Hancock and Adams decided to flee back to Boston to evade capture, while other rebels took up arms. During the long night, they gathered at **Buckman Tavern** (1 Bedford St., 781/862-5598, 10 A.M.–4 P.M. daily Apr.–Oct., $6) under the leadership of Captain Jonas Parker to steel themselves for the confrontation. The interior of the tavern has been meticulously restored to its original state, down to its old front door that still bears a bullet hole from a British musket ball.

Later in the afternoon of April 19, the retreating British again stopped in Lexington under much different circumstances to regroup and treat their wounded. They set up their headquarters at **Munroe Tavern** (1332 Massachusetts Ave., 781/674-9238, 12–4 P.M. Sat.–Sun. Apr.–mid-June and daily mid-June–Oct., $6), a 17th-century barroom where George Washington also later dined; the table where he sat is marked to prove it. All three of these historic homes are now owned by the **Lexington Historical Society** (www. lexingtonhistory.org), which offers regular guided tours of their interiors. A combination ticket for all three houses is $10.

Lexington Battle Green

By order of Congress, an American flag flies 24 hours a day on the green in the center of Lexington, marking the place where colonists first took up arms against the Redcoats. Unless you have the good fortune of arriving for Patriot's Day celebrations, you'll now have to imagine the fateful battle that kicked off the fight for Independence, which as battles go was somewhat anti-climatic. Captain Parker lined his 77 men in a ragtag formation behind a meeting house at the western side of the green. Outnumbered by the 300-some British who marched into town (with another 400 behind them), they were ordered by British Major John Pitcairn to disarm. Somewhere a shot rang out, and in the ensuing melee eight Americans were killed and 10 wounded before Parker beat a hasty retreat.

Several monuments on the green bear testimony to the fracas. At the eastern end, the

The Minuteman stands over Lexington Green.

© TIM GRAFFT/MOTT

callipygous statue of *The Minuteman,* which represents Parker, was placed there in 1900. A rock halfway down the green shows the location of the original battle line. At the far end, where the minutemen actually fell, is an older monument placed over their graves in 1799 with an inscription capturing the passion of the events only 20 years earlier.

Other Sights

If you haven't already had enough of the battles, you can drink your fill at the **National Heritage Museum** (33 Marrett Rd., 781/861-6559, www.monh.org, 10 A.M.–4:30 P.M. Tue.–Sat., 12–4:30 P.M. Sun.), a free museum with an ongoing exhibit on the Revolution as well as other aspects of American history.

Events

The events of the battle are commemorated on the third Monday of every April in a statewide Massachusetts holiday called **Patriot's Day,** when costumed interpreters reenact the events of that long-ago April morning. You'll have to get up pretty early to see them—the first shots on Lexington Green are fired, in keeping with history, at 6 in the morning, with events transpiring along the Battle Road for the rest of the day.

Shopping

Artisans around the world have found a home at **Muse's Window** (The Concord Depot, 84 Thoreau St., Concord, 978/287-5500, www.themuseswindow.com), an *Alice in Wonderland*–type shop featuring eclectic crafts in glass, wood, and more. More-traditional New England handicrafts and souvenirs can be found at the **Crafty Yankee** (1838 Massachusetts Ave., 781/863-1219, www.craftyyankee.com), which counts ties with a Minuteman motif among its offerings.

Food

In addition to the usual curries and Tandoori dishes, the fine Indian restaurant **Khushboo** (1709 Massachusetts Ave., 781/863-2900, www.khushboorestaurant.com, $13–16) has some more unusual offerings on the menu, including South Indian *dosas,* pan-roasted shrimp curry, and many vegetarian selections like Punjabi black lentils. Hearty (but not heavy) Italian takes center stage at **Mario's** (1733 Massachusetts Ave., 781/861-1182, $17–24), known most for its rich pastas and jovial atmosphere. Note: Arrive early at lunchtime—the place fills up quickly for its daily specials. Also in the successful Italian category is **Bertucci's** (1777 Massachusetts Ave., 781/860-9000, www.bertuccis.com, $15–21), a brick-oven-pizza joint that began in Massachusetts and can now be found around the country. Ask for extra rolls, you won't be sorry. Meanwhile, the menu at nearby **C Catch** (34 Church St., Winchester, 781/729-1040, www.catchrestaurant.com, $21–28) is far from "the usual." The cushy bistro wows diners nightly with presentation of salt-roasted Wellfleet clams and grilled lemon, scallops with celery root and roasted pineapple, and oysters with *yuzu* sauce.

Information and Services

Just off the Battle Green, the **Lexington Chamber of Commerce** (1875 Massachusetts Ave., 781/862-2480, www.lexingtonchamber.org) has an office with information and brochures, as well as patriot-themed gifts and an excellent diorama of the battle. Located within the national historic park it shares with Concord (see next section), the **Minute Man Visitor Center** (250 North Great Rd., 978/369-6993, www.nps.gov/mima) has exhibits detailing the events (Boston Tea Party, Paul Revere's Ride, etc.) leading up to the first battles; it also has a posted schedule of ranger-led talks and activities happening that day.

Most medical centers closest to Lexington are specialty clinics, so for general **emergency services,** it may be wisest to contact one of the excellent hospitals in Boston. For outpatient services, **Beth Israel Deaconness** does have a Lexington Center (482 Bedford St., Lexington, 781/672-2000) for adults and children. Fill prescriptions or satisfy other pharmacy needs at **CVS Pharmacy** (1735 Massachusetts Ave., Lexington, 781/862-4080).

Paid **wireless Internet** access is offered at Starbucks (1729 Massachusetts Ave., Lexington, 781/863-8485), and faxing and shipping services are available at **The UPS Store** (405 Waltham St., Lexington, 781/861-7770).

CONCORD

"I think I could write a poem to be called Concord," wrote writer and philosopher Henry David Thoreau. "For argument I should have the River, the Woods, the Ponds, the Hills, the Fields, the Swamps and Meadows, the Streets and Buildings, and the Villagers." The town has changed little since Thoreau's day, with the same distinguishing features surrounding a quaint downtown of shops and historic sights.

In addition to its role in the Revolution, Concord played another significant part in history some 60 years later, when it became the home base for a 19th-century literary and religious movement known as transcendentalism. Its proponents, among them Thoreau, Ralph Waldo Emerson, and Bronson Alcott, believed in a new philosophy inspired by nature, replacing the formalistic theology they'd inherited from Europe. Their writings helped inspire the flowering of a truly American form of literature, as well as the modern environmental movement.

◖ Minuteman National
   Historical Park

After their easy victory in Lexington, British soldiers marched on to Concord, where they found the pickings not quite so easy. There, about 500 minutemen from surrounding towns had converged by the Old North Bridge to protect the weapons cache beyond it. When a British soldier fired at them, the colonists fired volley after volley, scattering the regulars back to town. The **Old North Bridge** is now one of the highlights of the national historical park, which has kept alive much of the original infrastructure of the route the British took back to town. While the current bridge, built in 1969, is the fourth on the site, the location

gives a good idea of what the minutemen faced. A statue by Daniel Chester French depicts Captain Isaac Davis, head of the Acton militia, who was killed in the battle.

Located by the bridge, the **North Bridge Visitor Center** (174 Liberty St., 978/369-6993, www.nps.gov/mima) has an informative film and ranger talks as well as guides to the rest of the park. Although it's possible to drive along the highway or take a shuttle to major sites, try and walk some of the trail to really understand the claustrophobia felt by the panicked retreating British. Along the way, highlights include the **"bloody angle,"** where 30 British soldiers were ambushed and killed by colonists, and **Hartwell Tavern,** an authentic colonial public house that hosts military and domestic demonstrations daily.

◖ Walden Pond
   State Reservation

"I went to the woods because I wished to live deliberately…" As his famous words explain, Henry David Thoreau retired for two years to the shores of Walden Pond to seek a simpler mode of living closer to nature. The book he wrote about the experience, *Walden,* has since inspired generations of philosophers, environmentalists, and other readers, who now come regularly to pay homage to the site of **Thoreau's cabin** (915 Walden St., 978/369-3254, www.mass.gov). While the home itself is no longer there, the hearthstone from his chimney was uncovered years later. Nearby, a huge cairn of rocks grows yearly with the offerings of pilgrims. (If you'd like to add one, bring one with you, as the woods around the site have been picked clean.)

Sights

A wealth of artifacts bringing alive both the military and literary history of Concord are on display at the **Concord Museum** (200 Lexington Rd., 978/369-9763, www.concordmuseum.org, 11 a.m.–4 p.m. Mon.–Sat., 1–4 p.m. Sun. Jan.–Mar.; 9 a.m.–5 p.m. Mon.–Sat., 12–5 p.m. Sun. Apr.–Dec., $10 adults, $8 seniors and students, $5 children 6–17, free children under 6), a small museum with an enviable collection. Among the highlights are the simple bed, writing desk, and snowshoes that Thoreau used at Walden; the red-carpeted study of Ralph Waldo Emerson; and one of the two extant signal lanterns that warned Paul Revere of British attack—a simple iron lamp whose plainness belies its place in history. Unlike Thoreau, who died in poverty, his compatriot Ralph Waldo Emerson was recognized as the preeminent philosopher of his time, traveling around the world to deliver his essays. The **Emerson House** (28 Cambridge Turnpike, 978/369-2236, www.rwe.org/emersonhouse, 10 A.M.–4:30 P.M. Thurs.–Sat., 1–4:30 P.M. Sun. mid-Apr.–Oct., $7 adults, $5 seniors and students, free children under 7) remains furnished much as it was during his time—except for the furniture in his study (which is now in the museum across the street).

Other literary landmarks in the area include **Orchard House** (399 Lexington Rd., 978/369-4118, www.louisamayalcott.org, 10 A.M.–4:30 P.M. Mon.–Sat., 1–4:30 P.M. Sun. Apr.–Oct.; 11 A.M.–3 P.M. Mon.–Fri., 10 A.M.–4:30 P.M. Sat., 1–4:30 P.M. Sun. Nov.–Mar., $9 adults, $8 seniors and students, $5 children 6–17, free children under 6), where Louisa May Alcott penned *Little Women.* Fans of that book will swoon over the rooms, which contain original furniture owned by the family, including the writing desk made by Louisa's father, Bronson. Next door, **The Wayside** (455 Lexington Rd., 978/318-7826, www.nps.gov/archive/mima/wayside/index.htm) was Alcott's earlier home, where she and her sisters performed the childhood plays famously recreated in her book. It was also home in later years to novelist Nathaniel Hawthorne, whose study is largely intact. Several of the incestuous transcendentalists also inhabited **The Old Manse** (269 Monument St., 978/369-3909, www.thetrustees.org, 10 A.M.–5 P.M. Mon.–Fri., 12–5 P.M. Sun. mid-Apr.–Oct., 12–5 P.M. Sun. mid-Apr.–Oct., $8 adults, $7 seniors and students, $5 children 6–12, free children under 6), by the Old North Bridge. They include Emerson, Hawthorne, and Emerson's grandfather, Rev. William Emerson, who witnessed the battle there. The final resting place of many of the Concord authors can be found at **Sleepy Hollow Cemetery** (Bedford St., 978/318-3233, 7 A.M.–dusk daily), which contains the graves of Thoreau, Emerson, Hawthorne, and Alcott in an area poetically named Author's Ridge.

Tours
If you don't have a car of your own, a good way to see the sights in both Lexington and Concord is aboard the **Liberty Ride** (33 Marrett Rd., Lexington, 781/862-0500, www.libertyride.us, 10:30 A.M.–3 P.M. daily, $25 adults, $10 students 5–17, free children under 5), a shuttle that makes regular 90-minute trips from one end of the Battle Road to the other. You can get off and on as much as you'd like. In Concord proper, **Concord Guides** (48 Monument Sq., Concord, 978/287-0897, www.concordguides.com, 2–4 P.M. Sat.–Sun. Apr. 15–Nov. 1, $19 adults, $15 seniors and students, $12 youth 11–18, $7 children 6–10, free children under 6) offers two-hour walking tours with various themes, including history, literature, and architecture.

Entertainment and Events
In the center of Concord, the **Colonial Inn** (48 Monument Sq., 978/369-9200, www.concordscolonialinn.com, no cover) features nightly live music, including jazz, rock, and acoustic folk.

The **Festival of Authors** (late Oct.–early Nov.) keeps Concord's literary traditions alive with big-name authors in a two-week-long festival every year. In addition to book readings, the festival usually includes sessions on literary history and how-to advice for writers.

Shopping
The best independent bookstore in the area, **The Concord Bookshop** (65 Main St., 978/369-2405, 10 A.M.–5 P.M. Mon.–Fri.; 11 A.M.–5 P.M. Sat and Sun., www.concordbookshop.com) has an attractively arranged selection of bestsellers, books by all of the Concord authors,

and an extensive kids' section. Across from an old fishing spot, **Many Nations Trading Post** (19 Main St., 978/369-0668, 10 A.M.–5 P.M. Mon.–Sat.; closed Sun., www.manynation-stradingpost.com) has crafts made by local Native Americans, including peace pipes and turquoise jewelry, presented in an authentic setting. In addition to selling gourmet cheeses and foodstuffs from around the world, **The Cheese Shop** (29 Walden St., 978/369-5778, www.concordcheeseshop.com) regularly hosts events such as wine-and-cheese tastings and mozzarella-making demonstrations.

Food

A popular spot with locals, **Helen's** (17 Main St., 978/369-9885, $6–10) is a cute lunch spot with comfy booths and a retro feel. The menu contains 50 different kinds of burgers, sandwiches, and wraps for both meat-eaters and vegetarians alike, as well as a few dinner plates. Concord's old fire station has been re-incarnated as **Walden Grille** (24 Walden St., 978/371-2233, www.waldengrille.com, $14–23), a casual yet sophisticated eatery that draws a regular crowd of young professionals. The menu runs toward simply prepared comfort cuisine, such as hanger steak with rosemary parmesan polenta or steamed cod loin wrapped in a banana leaf. The homey, rich flavors of Southern France are the draw at **La Provence** (105 Thoreau St., Concord, 978/371-7428, www.laprovence.us), a sweet little spot with a welcoming staff and addictive menu. Specialties like coq au vin and bouillabaisse come out at dinnertime, while simple-but-delicious sandwiches filled with pate, cheese, and ham are the focus at lunchtime.

Information

The **Concord Chamber of Commerce** (15 Walden St., 978/369-3120, www.concord-chamberofcommerce.org) runs an informative visitors center.

LINCOLN AND SUDBURY

Just south of Lexington, the sleepy town of Lincoln is a mostly residential community home to some of the richest people in the state. While it lacks the history of its neighbors, however, it does have several sites worth visiting. Sudbury, meanwhile, is a rural town whose namesake river meanders through fields of grass and purple heather.

Sights

The best Boston-area museum consistently missed by visitors is the **DeCordova Museum** (51 Sandy Pond Rd., Lincoln, 781/259-8355, www.decordova.org, 10 A.M.–5 P.M. Tues.–Sun., $12 adults, $8 seniors, students, and children 6–18, free children under 6), a contemporary art museum and sculpture garden with a heavy emphasis on New England artists. Every spring, the museum highlights the best art of the area in its annual exhibition. The adjoining sculpture garden is a 35-acre preserve of walking trails interspersed with some 75 works that both harmonize and clash with the native environment. Another modern work situated in a natural environment is the **Gropius House** (68 Baker Bridge Rd., Lincoln, 781/259-8098, www.spnea.org, 11 A.M.–4 P.M. Wed.–Sun. June–Oct. 15 and Sat.–Sun. Oct. 16–May 31, $10), which was designed by architect Walter Gropius, founder of the Bauhaus movement. Daily tours show off the home's pleasing minimalist design.

It's difficult to get more "Ye Olde New Englande" than **Longfellow's Wayside Inn** (72 Wayside Inn Rd., Sudbury, 978/443-1776, www.wayside.org), a historic tavern mentioned in *Tales from a Wayside Inn* by Henry Wadsworth Longfellow. In 1923, the property was bought by auto-titan Henry Ford and restored into a historic tourist attraction, with an old grist mill, and even the schoolhouse to which Mary's little lamb allegedly followed her each day. A few miles away over the border in Framingham, the **Garden in the Woods** (180 Hemenway Rd., Framingham, 508/877-7630, www.newfs.org, 9 A.M.–5 P.M. Tues.–Wed. and Sun., 9 A.M.–7 P.M. Thu.–Fri. Apr. 15–July 3; 9 A.M.–5 P.M. Tues.–Sun. July 4–Oct. 31, $8 adults, $6 seniors and students, $4 children 6–18, free children under 6) is a must-visit for any plant- or flower-lover. The acres of trails are planted with some 1,600 different species, including such lovelies as Trout Lilies, Wood Phlox, and Calopogon orchids.

Food

While you are visiting the **Wayside Inn** (72 Wayside Inn Rd., Sudbury, 978/443-1776, www.wayside.org, 11:30 A.M.–9:30 P.M. Mon.–Sat.; 12 P.M.–8:30 P.M. Sun., $19–33), you can stop in for a bite. The inn specializes in hearty New England classics, from prime rib to lobster pie. As might be expected, the dining room is decorated with authentic colonial antiques, and attended by families and seniors who have been dining here for decades.

LOWELL

The Industrial Revolution wasn't invented in Lowell, but it was perhaps perfected here. No other city in the Northeast poured more of its heart into the project of industrial production. Blessed by the natural turbines of the Merrimack River, the city became the center of cloth and textile manufacturing in the region in the middle half of the 19th century. In fact, European visitors raved over the city as a miracle of modern ingenuity. As one Scottish visitor of the time said: "Niagara and Lowell are the two objects I will longest remember in my American journey—the one the glory of American scenery, the other of American industry."

Much of the success of the story, of course, was based on the exploitation of the workforce, mostly immigrant women from French Canada, Ireland, Italy, and other countries. Because of that, Lowell and the neighboring city of Lawrence could also be said to be the beginning of the modern labor movement, as these women risked their lives to strike for better working conditions. Lowell today is still a melting pot of immigrants from different countries, including a strong Cambodian community that settled here after the Vietnam War. Now that the mills have shut down, the city is one of the poorest in the state. It has seen new life in the past decade, however, as a haven for artists priced out of Boston, as well as a proud multicultural city—making it one of the most dynamic destinations in New England.

HEY, JACK KEROUAC

Beat Generation writer Jack Kerouac is most often associated with the frenetic city life of New York or San Francisco, but it's in the quiet backstreets of his native Lowell that you'll find the writer's soul. It's here that Kerouac grew up, and it's here he set much of his early fiction, including *Visions of Gerard, Doctor Sax, Maggie Cassidy, Vanity of Duluoz,* and his first published novel, *The Town and the City.* And it's also here that he came to die – when disillusioned with the acid tests and love-ins of the later beatniks, he returned to embrace his native Catholicism and live out his last years with his mother as a lonely alcoholic. Lowell honors its wayward son with the **Kerouac Commemorative** (Eastern Canal Park, Bridge St.), a series of stone monoliths inscribed with passages from his writings and arranged in a Buddhist mandala on the riverfront. Another popular pilgrimage site for beat-idolaters is his grave in Edson Cemetery (375 Gorham St.), where a simple headstone is engraved with a three-word epigraph chosen by his third wife: "He Honored Life." Like Jim Morrison's grave in Paris, it is often surrounded by flowers, scraps of poetry, and even bottles of cheap booze left by fans. For information on more sites where Kerouac hung out in Lowell, stop by the **Lowell National Historic Park Visitors Center** (246 Market St., 978/970-5000, www.nps.gov/lowe, 9 A.M.-5 P.M. daily, free parking available), which has a guided-tour pamphlet, as well as a short film about Kerouac's life shown daily at 4 P.M. Or visit during October, when latter-day beats fill the streets for **Lowell Celebrates Kerouac!** (877/537-6822, http://lckorg.tripod.com), an annual homage to the writer that includes readings of his works.

Sights

The industrial past of Lowell is celebrated at the **Lowell National Historical Park** (246 Market St., 978/970-5000, www.nps.gov/lowe, visitors center 9 A.M.–5:30 P.M. daily Aug. 24–Sep. 7; 9 A.M.–5 P.M. daily Sept. 8–Oct. 12), which centers around the most prosperous mills of the 19th century. The centerpiece of the park is the Bootts Cotton Mill Museum, which includes a working weave room of 88 power looms, along with the squalid boarding houses of the "mill girls." A more moving evocation of the lives of immigrant workers is displayed in the **Mill Girls and Immigrants Exhibit** (40 French St., 978/970-5000, www.nps.gov/lowe, 1–5 P.M. daily June 24–Sept. 7; 1:30–5 P.M. daily Sept. 8–Oct. 12, free), affiliated with the University of Massachusetts–Lowell, which explores the lives of immigrants over the years. Among the exhibits there, don't miss a small case that incongruously displays the backpack and typewriter of Beat writer Jack Kerouac, one of Lowell's native sons (see the sidebar *Hey, Jack Kerouac*).

Another native son, James McNeil Whistler, is honored by the **Whistler House Museum of Art** (243 Worthen St., 978/452-7641, www.whistlerhouse.org, 11 A.M.–4 P.M. Wed.–Sat., $5 adults, $4 seniors and students, free children). Located in the home where the painter was born, the collection does not, unfortunately, include the famous *Whistler's Mother* (which hangs in the Musee d'Orsay in Paris)—though it does contain a copy done by the artist's cousin. The galleries also contain etchings by Whistler, who was among the most celebrated American artists of the 19th century, alongside works of other artists of the period. The modern artistic community of Lowell can be found at the **Revolving Museum** (122 Western Ave., 978/937-2787, www.revolvingmuseum.org, 11 A.M.–4 P.M. Tues.–Sun., free), an art and performance space that relocated here from Boston several years ago. The city has actively encouraged the arts scene by helping build the **Ayer Lofts Art Gallery** (172 Middle St., 978/970-3556, www.ayerlofts.com), in a building inhabited by working artists.

Events

Celebrating the multicultural nature of the city, the **Lowell Folk Festival** (978/970-5200, www.lowellfolkfestival.org) is a cornucopia of culture, featuring hundreds of music and dance performers from around the world. In August, the **Lowell Southeast Asian Water Festival** (978/596-1013, www.lowellwaterfestival.org) celebrates Cambodian culture with traditional Khmer dance performances and the mesmerizing sight of hundreds of candles floating on the Merrimack River.

Food

Located in the center of town in a restored mill building, **Cobblestones** (91 Dutton St., 978/970-2282, www.cobblestonesoflowell.com, 11:30 A.M.–10 P.M. Mon.–Sat., closed Sun., $7–29) has something for everyone. A formal dining room serves grilled flatbreads, risotto, and fisherman's stew, while a casual bar area dishes out sandwiches, buffalo wings, and a variety of oysters on the half shell (including, we kid you not, Rocky Mountain oysters). The oldest Asian restaurant in Lowell, the **C Southeast Asian Restaurant** (343 Market St., 978/452-3182, www.foodventure.com, 11:30 A.M.–10 P.M. daily, $4–13) was started by an Italian man and his Laotian wife, who set about trying to re-create the food served in open-air stalls across the subcontinent. Twenty-five years later, it is still one of the most popular eateries in the city, serving a range of authentic Cambodian, Laotian, Vietnamese, Thai, and even Mongolian cuisine in a large and festive dining room.

Information

The **Greater Merrimack Valley Convention and Visitors Bureau** (40 French St., 978/459-6150, www.merrimackvalley.org) runs an office stocked with information about Lowell and the surrounding region.

SPORTS AND RECREATION

Beaches

In addition to the connection with Thoreau, **Walden Pond State Reservation** (915 Walden

St., Concord, 978/369-3254, www.mass.gov) draws hordes of summer visitors every year to swim in its deep, cool waters. Be forewarned that the only parking available is in the official lot, which fills up quickly on hot summer mornings.

Hiking

Situated along the banks of the Concord and Sudbury Rivers, the **Great Meadows National Wildlife Refuge** (73 Weir Hill Rd., Sudbury, 978/443-4661, www.fws.gov/northeast/great-meadows) contains almost 4,000 acres of meadow and marshland that teems with wildlife. Trails wind their way through both parts of the reservation, one located in Concord and the other in Sudbury. Among the wildlife that can be spotted are deer, red fox, and great blue herons.

Boating and Fishing

Before *Walden,* Thoreau wrote *A Week on the Concord and Merrimack Rivers.* You can follow in his paddle marks by renting a canoe at the **South Bridge Boathouse** (496 Main St., Concord, 978/369-9438, www.canoeconcord. com) for a trip down the heather-lined banks of the Concord River.

ACCOMMODATIONS
Under $100

A strange blend between a motel and a greenhouse, the **Battle Green Inn** (1720 Massachusetts Ave., Lexington, 781/862-6100, www.battlegreeninn.com, $89–109) has cute and affordable rooms arranged around a central indoor courtyard. Its location just steps from the Battle Green and other historic sites can't be beat. Your best bet for lodging in Lowell is the **Courtyard by Marriott** (30 Industrial Ave. East, Lowell, 978/458-7575, www.marriott.com, $74–174), which has pay-per-view movies and in-room coffee service.

$100-150

It may sound too cozy to be true, but **Fireside Bed and Breakfast** (24 Eldred St., Lexington, 781/862-2053, www.firesidebb.com, $90–140),

lives up to its name with modern bathrooms, beds laid with homemade quilts, and a location snug up against miles of conservation land. In colder seasons, the elaborate breakfasts are served in the formal dining room next to (where else?) the fireplace. Just off the highway on the north side of Lexington, the **Quality Inn & Suites** (440 Bedford St., Lexington, 781/861-0850, www.choicehotels.com, $70–120) offers complimentary Wi-Fi as well as sports-club passes, cable TV, and a free shuttle to nearby historic attractions.

$150-250

No lodging in Concord gets more into the spirit of the town than the ◖ **Hawthorne Inn** (462 Lexington Rd., Concord, 978/369-5610, www. concordmass.com, $125–325), which trumpets its location on land once owned by Emerson, Hawthorne, and the Alcotts, and challenges its guests to "think an original thought" while they stay. The seven guest rooms are decked out with original artwork and handmade quilts, as well as copies of poetry and novels written by the Concord authors to provide the proper inspiration while you are there.

While it's not quite within walking distance of the Old North Bridge, the **North Bridge Inn** (21 Monument St., Concord, 978/371-0014, www.northbridgeinn.com, $165–275) is as close as you are likely to get to Concord historic sites. The unpretentious guesthouse features all-suite accommodations, from a "studio suite" with microwave alcove to a larger suite with separate room and kitchenette. Lithographs of Revolutionary battles on the walls and toile bedspreads on the beds give the inn a colonial feel without going overboard. A full breakfast is served at a sunny breakfast nook downstairs.

GETTING THERE AND AROUND

To drive to Lexington from Boston, take Route 2 west to exit 55, then Route 4 north to Lexington center (15 mi., 30 min.). For Concord, take Route 2 west from Boston past I-95. When the road takes a sharp left, continue

MASSACHUSETTS

on straight down the Cambridge Turnpike to Concord Center (25 mi., 40 min.). From Lexington to Concord, take Route 2A west, parallel to the Battle Road (7 mi., 5 min.) To drive to Lowell from Boston, take I-93 north to I-95 south to US Route 3 north (30 mi., 40 min.).

The **Massachusetts Bay Transportation Authority** (MBTA, 617/222-3200, www.mbta.com) runs commuter trains to stations in Concord (90 Thoreau St.) and Lowell (Thorndike St.). Buses by **Yankee Line** (800/942-8890, www.yankeeline.us) run once daily from Boston to Concord, stopping at Concord Center.

It is difficult to get around Concord without the benefit of your own car, unless you plan on walking a lot around town. The major historical sites are all a mile's walk from the train station. In Lexington, a shuttle bus called **Lexpress** (781/861-1210, http://ci.lexington.ma.us) runs routes throughout the town. Lowell is also bus-rider friendly, with trips all over town run by the **Lowell Regional Transportation Authority** (978/452-6161, www.lrta.com).

Worcester and Vicinity

West of Concord, the area between I-495 and the Pioneer Valley is a transitional area of suburbs and farms, as the urban core of Boston gives way to the more rural western part of the state. Because of that, it's an area that is often passed over by travelers, on their way from one end of the state or the other. Those who stop, however, will find several attractions to catch their interest, including Worcester's underrated art museum and the historical village at Sturbridge.

WORCESTER

Though Worcester is the third-largest city in Massachusetts, it has had a troubled economic history. Named county seat in 1731, it suffered from lack of good transportation and waterpower, which prevented it from becoming an industrial powerhouse like other towns. Managing a good living as a manufacturing center instead, it drew waves of immigrants who flooded the city to produce tools and household items. Since the city's economy collapsed after World War II, however, it has yet to find a winning formula to rescue its downtown. On the upside, the city is notable for several fine museums and nine colleges and universities, including Clark and Holy Cross, which infuse a young energy into its nightlife.

◖ Worcester Art Museum

Given Worcester's reputation, many natives are surprised to discover the city even *has* an art museum, never mind that it's one of the very best in New England. Though it does have some paintings by top-name artists—such as Paul Gauguin's excellent *The Brooding Woman*—most of the collection (55 Salisbury St., 508/799-4406, www.worcesterart.org, 11 A.M.–5 P.M. Wed.–Fri., 11 A.M.–8 P.M. third Thurs. of every month, 10 A.M.–5 P.M. Sat., $10 adults, $8 seniors and students, free children under 18) focuses on areas rarely covered by other museums, making the halls of WAM (as it's known) a constant discovery. Among the museum's strengths are a wonderful collection of early American portraits, dozens of medieval paintings and sculptures, and a good cross-section of pre-Columbian Native American artwork. Weekly tours are given by docents on Saturday at 11 A.M. and Sunday at 1 P.M.

Other Sights

Founded by an eccentric millionaire with a taste for romantic sagas, the **Higgins Armory Museum** (100 Barber Ave., 508/853-6015, www.higgins.org, 10 A.M.–4 P.M. Tues.–Sat., 12–4 P.M. Sun., $10 adults, $7 seniors and children 4–16, free children under 4) draws fans of King Arthur to wow over a vast collection of weapons and armor. The museum has hundreds of suits of armor, including a rare Roman gladiator helmet, and features demonstrations on weapon-making and wielding. The Worcester Art Museum was founded by Stephen Salisbury, a leading industrialist whose home is now on display as **Salisbury Mansion** (40 Highland St., 508/753-8278, www.worcesterhistory.org, 1–4 P.M. Thurs.–Sat., $5 adults, free children under 18). Period 1830s furnishings and changing exhibits bring Worcester's manufacturing heyday to life. More than just a zoo, the **EcoTarium** (222 Harrington Way, 508/929-2700, www.ecotarium.org, 10 A.M.–5 P.M. Tues.–Sat., 12–5 P.M. Sun., $10 adults, $8 seniors and students, $8 children 3–18, free children under 3) bills itself as an indoor-outdoor nature center, with polar bears, foxes, and other wildlife on the grounds. Among its more unusual experiences is a tree-canopy walkway 40 feet above the ground.

Entertainment
The gorgeous 19th-century **Mechanics Hall** (321 Main St., 508/752-5608, www.mechanicshall.org) anchors the arts scene of the city with regular performances by classical orchestras from around the region. The young and the restless converge at **Palladium** (261 Main St., 508/797-9696, www.thepalladium.net), a dance club and concert hall that spotlights acts like The Mighty Mighty Bosstones and The Dropkick Murphys. Even bigger, national acts perform at the **DCU Center** (50 Foster St., 508/755-6800, www.centrumcentre.com), the largest concert hall in New England, which often draws performers that don't appear in Boston.

Shopping
Located at the Worcester Antiquarian Society, the **Ben Franklin Book Store** (21 Salem St., 508/753-8685, www.benfranklinbookstore.com) has dozens of cases full of rare, out-of-print, and first edition books. Among other subjects, the store specializes in history, music, and psychology. A browser's paradise of antiques and collectibles, the **Kelley Square Flea Market** (149 Washington St., 508/755-9040)

THE DINER CAPITAL OF THE WORLD

Worcester is virtually synonymous with diners. Tradition has it that the modern diner started out as a horse-drawn lunch carriage pioneered by Providence, Rhode Island, entrepreneur Walter Scott in 1872. But it was the commercial manufacturing of lunch wagons starting in Worcester in 1887 that ensured their popularity. Over the next few years, several companies set up shop in the city, but the most famous was the Worcester Lunch Car Company, which pioneered the railroad-diner-car look in the 1930s. The diner cars were designed for factory workers, who needed a good hearty meal served cheap and quickly, and frequently at odd hours to accommodate their schedules. Now genuine Worcester cars are prized by restaurant owners all over the Northeast. Of course, there are many fine examples of diners in the city that once created them. Known locally as "the Bully," the 24-hour **Boulevard Diner** (155 Shrewsbury St., 508/791-4535, $5-8) sets the mood with a neon exterior and dark wood interior. But it's the greasy-spoon menu of homemade meatloaf, leg of lamb, and chicken soup that really brings back yesteryear. Across from the former site of the Worcester Lunch Car Company itself, the **Miss Worcester Diner** (300 Southbridge St., 508/753-5600, 5 A.M.-2 P.M. Mon.-Fri., 6 A.M.-2 P.M. Sat.-Sun., $4-8) has been reopened after being shuttered for several years. Otherwise known as the "Miss Woo," it is located inside the original Worcester Lunch Car No. 812, which once served the factory workers who made the cars themselves; now it may be the only surviving Worcester car in the city that gave them their name.

is an indoor emporium with booths operated by some 150 members.

Food

An enthusiastic favorite among locals, **O'Connor's Restaurant & Bar** (1160 W. Boylston St., 508/853-0789, www.oconnorsrestaurant.com, 11:30 A.M.–11 P.M. Mon.–Sat.; 11:30 A.M.–10 P.M. Sun., $11–21) is a family-style Irish restaurant that draws a cross-section of city residents. The maze of dining rooms is covered floor-to-ceiling with Irish beer and liquor advertisements. The menu includes authentic Auld Sod dishes like shepherd's pie and bangers 'n' mash. The upper crust from around Central Massachusetts converges on **111 Chop House** (111 Shrewsbury St., 508/799-4111, www.111chophouse.com, 4 P.M.–10 P.M. Mon.–Thurs.; 4 P.M.–11 P.M. Fri.–Sat.; 4 P.M.–9:30 P.M. Sun., $19–36) for high-quality steaks and other meat dishes such as Dijon-encrusted rack of lamb. The swank dining room is a welcome change for Worcester; a cheaper tapas-and-pizza menu is served at the bar.

Information and Services

The **Central Massachusetts Convention and Visitors Bureau** (30 Elm St., 508/755-7400, www.worcester.org) runs a visitors center downtown with information on Worcester and the surrounding area.

The area's biggest hospital is **Umass Memorial Hospital** (119 Belmont St., Worcester, 508/334-1000, www.umassmemorial.org), which provides emergency and various other services. Chains such as **CVS Pharmacy** (283 Park Ave., Worcester, 508/792-3866, www.cvs.com) and **Walgreens** (320 Park Ave., Worcester, 508/767-1732, walgreens.com) fill prescriptions and sell other medicines.

Free **Internet access** on terminals is offered at **Worcester Public Library** (3 Salem Sq., Worcester, 508/799-1655, www.worcpublib.org) and free wireless access is offered (with purchase) at cafes such as **Java Hut Cafe** (1073-A Main St., Worcester, 508/752-1678). Faxing and printing services are available at **Staples** (541B Lincoln St., Worcester, 508/852-3771, www.staples.com).

STURBRIDGE

Arriving in the small town of Sturbridge expecting historic New England heaven, many visitors are surprised instead to find the worst kind of strip-mall purgatory. Push on past the town center, however, and you'll find what puts the town on all the tour-bus itineraries: Old Sturbridge Village, a living-history museum that completely immerses visitors in the spirit of the past.

Old Sturbridge Village

New England history is mostly associated with the Revolutionary War era, but it's the prosperous period just before the Industrial Revolution that most closely typifies the image of small-town life passed down to us from Burl Ives and Grandma Moses. That's the time period captured at this living-history museum (1 Old Sturbridge Village Rd., 508/347-3362, www.osv.org, 9:30 A.M.–5 P.M. daily Apr.–Oct. 23; 9:30 A.M.–4 P.M. Wed.–Sun. Oct. 24–Nov.; Thu.–Sun. Dec.–Mar., $20 adults, $18 seniors, $7 children 3–17, free children under 3), a reconstructed 1830s New England village. It dates back to the 1920s, when several local industrialists, overwhelmed with a fast-moving society of motion pictures, automobiles, and airplanes, set out to preserve a simpler past. They found buildings all over the region, moved them to the site of an old farm, and filled them with antiques gathered in decades of collecting.

The coup de grace—and what still makes the village so interesting today—was hiring dozens of costumed actors who assumed roles in the town and learned traditional country skills to demonstrate to visitors. Today, you can spend several hours going from building to building to see performers (who *never* break character) demonstrate blacksmithing, weaving, food storage, and animal husbandry. The museum has adjusted over the years to become a year-round destination, offering sleigh rides in the winter and old-time baseball games in summer. Whenever you visit, you'll leave more thankful for your dishwasher than ever.

Other Sights

Nurse Clara Barton is best known for founding the Red Cross in 1881. The Victorian Renaissance woman, however, was equally well known in her time as a suffragette and social reformer. Her accomplishments are on display at the **Clara Barton Birthplace Museum** (66 Clara Barton Rd., North Oxford, 508/987-2056, www.clarabartonbirthplace. org, 11 A.M.–5 P.M. Wed.–Sun. June–Aug.; 11 A.M.–5 P.M. Sat. Sept., $6 adults, $3 children 6–12, free children under 6), which contains exhibits on her life.

Events

The best-known antiques fair in the country, the **Brimfield Antique Show** (www.brimfieldshow.com), occurs yearly in Brimfield, the town next door to Sturbridge. Every September, the small town of 3,000 people explodes in population, as 30,000 visitors and 5,000 dealers descend upon it to barter over their wares.

Shopping

If you are intrigued by the craftsmen demonstrations at Old Sturbridge Village, you can pick up some of their handiwork at the **Shops at Old Sturbridge Village** (1 Old Sturbridge Village Rd., 508/347-0244, www.osv.org, 10 A.M.–5 P.M. daily), which features village-made tin and pottery items, along with heirloom seeds and books on New England history. A whirlwind of sampling and noshing, the snack emporium that is **Cracker Barrel Old Country Store** (215 Charlton Rd., 508/347-8925, 6 A.M.–10 P.M. Sun.–Thurs.; 6 A.M.–11 P.M. Fri.–Sat., www.crackerbarrel.com) peddles everything from candied popcorn tins and cheddar cheese to peanut brittle and relish. Many a holiday gift basket is born here—as are equally many "homemade" creations, by way of the shop's corn muffin mix and cherry cobbler filling.

Food

Sturbridge has two types of restaurants—fast food and colonial-style taverns. In the latter category, costumed interpreters provide music and circulate among diners at **Wight Tavern** (1 Old Sturbridge Village Road, 508/347-3362, 10 A.M.–5 P.M. daily, $9–14), a family-style tavern at the center of Old Sturbridge Village that serves up burgers, sandwiches, and affordable Yankee dinners. Four different rooms are each filled with antiques and exhibits drawn from the museum's collections. The best in the category is the **Whistling Swan** (502 Main St., 508/347-2321, www.thewhistlingswan.com, 11 A.M.–10 P.M. Sun.–Thurs.; 11 A.M.–11 P.M. Sat., $24–37), a formal dining room with quiet New England ambience that prides itself on the freshness of its ingredients. The menu includes hearty entrées of the likes of rack of lamb and lobster filet mignon. The less pretentious **Ugly Duckling Loft** ($14–37) offers up the same menu, along with lower-priced items, in a pub setting next door.

SPORTS AND RECREATION
Skiing and Hiking

Algonquin for "the great hill," **Wachusett Mountain Ski Area** (499 Mountain Rd., Princeton, 978/464-2300, www.wachusett. com, 9 A.M.–10 P.M. Mon.–Fri., 8 A.M.–10 P.M. Sat.–Sun., $29–54 adults, $20–40 seniors and children 6–12) is a magnet during winter months for skiers who can't make it up north to Vermont or New Hampshire. While the mountain can't compare, of course, to its northern cousins, its 22 trails provide enough terrain to occupy a range of skill levels, including some decent moguls and challenging vertical runs. In the summer months, the trails are open to hikers, who delight in the views from the highest mountain for miles around.

Camping

One of the prettiest campgrounds in the state, **Wells State Park** (Rte. 49, 508/347-9257, www.mass.gov) offers 60 sites in an attractive woodland setting within easy striking distance of Worcester and Sturbridge. A lake on the premises is for the exclusive use of campers.

MASSACHUSETTS

ACCOMMODATIONS
Under $100
Directly across from Old Sturbridge Village, **Motel 6** (408 Main St., Sturbridge, 508/347-7327, $50–70) offers bare-bones accommodations for the cheapest price around. Rooms are polyester-chic, but the motel does include cable TV and a large pool in back.

$100-150
Don't let the canopy beds and Victorian flourishes fool you; **The Inn at Restful Paws** (70 Allen Hill Rd., Holland, 413/245-7792, $120–160, www.restfulpaws.com) welcomes as many four-legged guests as it does two-legged. ("The place where pooches bring their people to relax" is their motto.) From bean bag beds and special towels for pets, the place bends over backwards to make pets comfy—and does the same for humans, with picturesque walking trails, not to mention healthy breakfasts and clothing steamers in rooms. The region also abounds with numerous chain hotels, including a **Hampton Inn** (800/426-7866, www.newenglandhampton-inns.com, $105–169) in both Worcester and Sturbridge.

$150-250
Catering to skiers at the nearby mountain, **Wachusett Village Inn** (9 Village Inn Rd., Westminster, 978/874-2000, www.wachu-settvillageinn.com, $109–189) is a full-service inn with simply designed rooms, but lots of perks. Some rooms have fireplaces, while the grounds have a pool, hot tub, and spa. Packages suited to families and couples also include vouchers for dinner and massage treatments. While Worcester and luxury aren't often included in the same sentence, the **Beechwood Hotel** (363 Plantation St., Worcester 508/754-5789, www.beechwoodhotel.com, $179–340) provides beautiful boutique accommodations in the center of the city. Despite its lackluster exterior, the hotel's interior features dark woods and plush furniture, along with all of the amenities—printer, high-speed Internet, Frette linens, fitness center—a business traveler could ask for.

More casual and catering to business travelers, **The Crowne Plaza Hotel** (10 Lincoln Sq., Worcester, 508/791-1600, www.ichotelsgroup.com, $152–309) is part of the national chain offering guests services from valet and newspapers to complimentary breakfast.

GETTING THERE AND AROUND
To drive to Worcester from Boston, take the Mass Pike (I-90) West (45 mi.,55 min.) Continue along the Pike another 15 mi. (20 min.) for Sturbridge.

The **Worcester Train Station** (2 Washington Sq.) is serviced by both AMTRAK (800/872-7245, www.amtrak.com) and the Massachusetts Bay Transportation Authority (617/222-3200, www.mbta.com) commuter trains from Boston. **Peter Pan Bus Lines** (800/343-9999, www.peterpanbus.com) runs buses to Worcester Bus Terminal (2 Washington Sq.).

Buses throughout Worcester are run by the **Worcester Regional Transit Authority** (508/791-9782, www.therta.com).

South of Boston

Follow Route 3A from Boston down toward Cape Cod and you'll find yourself on what many argue was the state's oldest public highway—once called the "Mattachusetts Payth." It ran between Boston and Plymouth, where the Pilgrims had made their fateful arrival on the Mayflower in 1620 and soon thereafter established the Plymouth Colony. Farther south lie the waters of Buzzard's Bay, a sheltered arc between Long Island and Nantucket Sounds that is home to two great port cities: the former whaling port and fishing community of New Bedford, and the textile center and immigrant gateway of Fall River.

THE SOUTH SHORE

While the Plymouth Pilgrims may have been the first settlers of the area, they were followed in no short order by countless other Brits, who set up fishing and trading posts that would later become the cities of Weymouth and Quincy. From there, small waves of Pilgrims—with last names like Alden, Bradford, Weston, and Winslow—were granted land and built houses in areas now called Duxbury, Marshfield, Kingston, and Pembroke.

Thanks to the efforts of extremely active local conservation groups, many of those homes are well preserved today—as is much of the shore's natural beauty. Many of the towns maintain strict zoning laws mandating only specific paint colors for homes and stone walls instead of Jersey barriers, and barring chain stores in certain areas of town.

Of course, commerce still reigns supreme in much of the region. Cities like Hanover, Weymouth, and Braintree are home to plenty of shopping malls and commercial centers. But oftentimes just down the road a few miles is a town like Cohasset, with its pristine harbor, or Duxbury, with its quietly conserved meadows, scarlet cranberry bogs, and picturesque beaches. And scattered throughout all of it are homes built by those who first came over on the Mayflower, maintained by dedicated residents and descendants.

Sights

The **John Alden House** (105 Alden St., Duxbury, 781/934-9092, www.alden.org, noon–4 P.M. mid-May–mid-Oct., $5 adults, $3 children under 18) is remarkable not only as a piece of 17th-century architecture built by one of America's original settlers but as a family heirloom; it is still owned today by the Alden Kindred of America, Inc. Likewise the **Maritime and Irish Mossing Museum** (301 Driftway, Scituate, 781/545-1083, www.scituatehistoricalsociety.org, 1–4 P.M. Sat.–Sun. July–Aug., $4 adults, $3 seniors, free children under 18), housed in the 1739 residence of Capt. Benjamin James. The museum spotlights the South Shore's place in history as a seafaring center through an epic collection of photos, a history of original families, and a dramatic "Shipwreck Room," which, true to its name, relays the stories of some of the area's most historic storms. Pity that some of those storms' victims didn't find themselves closer to the heroes featured in the **Hull Lifesaving Museum** (1117 Nantasket Ave., Hull, 781/925-5433, www.lifesavingmuseum.org, 10 A.M.–4 P.M. Sat.–Thurs.; 10 A.M.–1 P.M. Fri., year-round, $5 adults, $3 seniors, free children 18 and under). Here find all kinds of tributes—exhibits on lifebuoys, tours, and collections of gear—to the local maritime culture and, in particular, 19th-century coastal lifesavers.

In Hingham, the bucolic **World's End** (250 Martin's Ln., 781/740-6665, www.thetrustees.org, 8 A.M.–sunset daily year-round, $5 adults, free children 12 and under) makes for a magnificent walk—the 251-acre property designed by Frederick Law Olmsted overlooks Hull and Boston Harbors, and is particularly stunning in the fall. Trees, however, hardly have a lock on fall foliage.

Entertainment and Nightlife

As a primarily residential community, the South Shore has only a small handful of noteworthy nightlife destinations. For concerts of almost every stripe (from Julio Iglesias to Ani DiFranco), there's the **South Shore Music Center Circus** (130 Sohier St., Cohasset, 781/383-9850, www.themusiccircus.org, summer only). Year-round, **Eli's Pub in The Barker Tavern** (21 Barker Rd., Scituate, 781/545-6533, www.barkertavern.com, 4 P.M.–10 P.M., Tues.–Fri.; 5 P.M.–10 P.M. Sat.; 1 P.M.–10 P.M., $12–15) is a cozy and convivial spot for a drink on weeknights and weekends. The historic harborside watering hole is full of local couples, boat lovers, and chatty singles.

Events

Autumn brings the South Shore's cranberry bogs to a brilliant red hue, and aside from sampling the tart little treasures, there's but one way to celebrate: at October's **National Cranberry Festival** held at **Edaville Railroad** (7 Eda Ave., South Carver, 877/332-8455, www.edaville.com, $18, free children under 2), where you can ride an antique steam train through a working berry bog.

Shopping

Apart from Braintree and Hanover's goliath shopping malls filled with chain stores, you'll find plenty of independent (often quaint) shops in the South Shore's smaller towns. Case in point: **Olivia Rose** (1945 Ocean St., Marshfield, 781/834-8851, http://oliviarosechildrensboutique.com/, 10 A.M.–5 P.M. Mon.–Sat.; 12–4 P.M. Sun.) is far from your run-of-the-mill children's clothing shop. Score everything from Baby Lulu capris and Mulberribush pinafores to Mustela baby beauty products.

The selection of home accessories and furnishings—both new and antique—at **Octavia's** (35 Depot St., Duxbury, 781/934-9553, www.octaviashomedecor.com, 10 A.M.–5 P.M. Mon.–Sat.; noon–5 P.M. Sun.) is interwoven with handmade jewelry, fine art paintings, colorful pottery, and hand-painted lamps.

Some of the most meticulously tailored men's clothing around the Boston area can be found at **Natale's** (2001 Washington St.,

Hanover, 781/982-8080, natalesofhanover.com, 9 A.M.–9 P.M. Mon.–Fri.; 9 A.M.–5:30 P.M. Sat.; 12–5 P.M. Sun.)—whether you're in the market for bespoke suits or windbreakers.

One of New England's finest selections of hard-to-find beauty supplies is at **Zona** (65 South St., Hingham, 781/749-4500, 2–8 P.M. Mon.; 9 A.M.–8 P.M. Tues.–Thurs.; 9 A.M.–6 P.M. Fri.–Sat.)—everything from the chic Japanese line Shu Uemura and Kerastase to Kiehl's and Red Flower.

Adults and kids can get their literary fill at the quaint **Westwinds Bookshop** (45 Depot St., Duxbury, 781/934-2128, www.westwindsbookshop.com, 10 A.M.–5 P.M. Mon.–Fri.; closed Sun.), stocked with a slew of titles (covering everything from taxidermy to taxes), cards, toys, and gifts made around the area.

Food

Dining on the South Shore was once an unfortunate chore, with only baked-stuffed everything, a few inauthentic Italian joints, and poor-quality Chinese food as typical options. But the past decade has pushed the area to new heights, to a point where plenty of food lovers from all over New England—including Boston—are making the drive for a great meal. One major draw is (**Tosca** (14 North St., Hingham, 781/740-0080, 4 P.M.–10 P.M. Tues.–Sun.; closed Mon., www.eatwellinc.com, $23–30), named for Puccini's famed opera, and almost as dramatic. From the bustling open kitchen the staff serves authentic, creative Italian in the high-ceilinged, white-linen dining room—specialties like wild-boar Bolognese and lavender-brined pork chop. But enough with the turf; in an area with this many ties to the water, seafood's the thing. Find it in one of its freshest forms at **Jake's Seafood** (250 Nantasket Rd., Hull, 781/925-1024, www.jakesseafoods.com, 11:30 A.M.–9:30 P.M. Mon.–Sat.; 12 P.M.–9:30 P.M. Sun., $14–24), the quintessential fish shack perched between a little bay and Nantasket Beach. From the fine specimens of simple boiled lobster to fried clams and scallops and linguine, the casual atmosphere is a nice balance between formality and net-and-buoy kitsch. Equally delicious and fun is the brunch at the funky seaside **Arthur & Pat's** (239 Ocean St., Brant Rock, 781/834-9755, $6–12), which serves a killer lobster omelet, fried oyster roll, and fresh crab eggs Benedict. The morning lines (quelled by the complimentary mimosas passed out) can get long but are always worth the wait. Speaking of something worth waiting for, the Danish ice cream parlor **Farfar's** (272 Saint George St., Duxbury, 781/934-5152, 11 A.M.–6 P.M. daily) churns out cold stuff that's so rich and exquisite it's considered a local tourist attraction in its own right.

Information and Services

Because the South Shore is an expansive area of many towns of various sizes, the information and types of services offered from town to town varies widely. Start by gathering general information, maps, and brochures on the area at **Plymouth Convention & Visitors Bureau** (170 Water St., Suite 24, Plymouth, 508/747-0100, www.seeplymouth.com). The area's biggest full-service hospital is **South Shore Hospital** (55 Fogg Rd., South Weymouth, 781/624-8000, www.

sshosp.org). Fill prescription needs at the 24-hour branches of **CVS Pharmacy** (474 Washington St., Weymouth, 781/335-0404; 600 Southern Artery, Quincy, 617/472-7534; or 1880 Ocean St., Marshfield, 781/837-5381, www.cvs.com).

Free **Internet access** on terminals is offered at nearly every town library, as well as by payment at office centers such as **FedEx Office Print & Ship Center** (44 Granite St., Braintree, 781/849-7737, www.fedex.com) and **The UPS Store** (300 Grove St., Braintree, 781/356-8771, www.theupsstore.com). The latter also offers faxing and shipping services as well.

PLYMOUTH

Here it is, the place where this experiment in democracy we call America first started. Named after the Mayflower's port of embarkation in England, Plymouth was the first permanent settlement in New England. Fleeing what they viewed as the Church of England's incomplete work of the Reformation, the Pilgrims (mostly poor farmers) bid adieu to what they considered Britain's lax morality, endured a grueling transatlantic voyage, hit land, and

BERRY IMPRESSIVE

Cranberries are an enormous industry in Southeastern Massachusetts and Cape Cod, employing thousands of workers. They also do their part to beautify the region: Every September and October, the wetlands on which they're grown become crimson with their ripened bounty. (Known as bogs, the spongy, low-lying wetlands retain enough water to provide an ideal habitat for the berries.) The fruits are native to the region (early settlers called them "crane-berries" because their blossoms reminded them of the heads of cranes), but today they are grown commercially in man-made bogs, created by planting small vines in sandy plots. The state requires that each acre of planted cranberries be surrounded by at least four acres of wetlands. Most cranberry

harvests are done in the late fall by flooding the bogs and using a machine to gently dislodge the berries from the vines. Employees then use tubing to collect the berries onto a conveyer belt. Family farmers Jack and Dot Angley fill in the missing links between berries and juice with free daily tours of their **Flax Pond Farm** (1 Robbins Path, Carver, 508/866-3654, www.flaxpondfarms.com, 1–5 P.M. daily mid-Sept.–Oct.). Tours include a trip to the old "screening house" where kids can try their hand at sorting berries on antique equipment. Or view one from above by booking with **Ryan Rotors'** aerial tours via helicopter (Plymouth, 508/746-3111).

You'll never taste cranapple juice the same way again.

quickly set about founding Plymouth Colony in 1620.

It's here that you'll find the famed Plymouth Rock (kept protected under a stone, miniature Parthenon-like canopy these days)—not to mention hordes of tourists snapping pictures of it. But of course, the rock itself tells extraordinarily little about the Pilgrims' history or how they lived their lives in the area. For that, visitors turn to **Plimoth Plantation,** a historically accurate working replica of their settlement, complete with actors playing the parts of real Pilgrims. In the real world beyond the plantation's gates, Plymouth is a modern fishing center popular for its boating areas, beaches, and other tourist sites.

(Plimoth Plantation

A living-history museum, the plantation is best known for replicating a 17th-century colonial village from top to bottom (an enclave known as the "1627 Village"). Virtually everything here is now as it was then—from the foods grown and eaten to the chores and social structure.

the *Mayflower II* at Plymouth

But the plantation also encompasses a Native American camp (called **Hobbamock's Homesite**) that houses Wampanoags—not actors, but real native New Englanders whose people have lived in the area for more than 12,000 years—in their traditional homes. Thanks to the combination of perspectives experienced through these two camps, Plimoth Plantation may be one of the best ways to teach kids about America's humble beginnings, with a slew of hands-on educational programs that teach about this slice of life through the eyes of both the Pilgrims and the area's indigenous people.

There's also an exact replica of the vessel that bore the first settlers here—*Mayflower II*—which (again, courtesy of actors playing historic characters) sheds some light on what they endured and how they lived on their journey. Rounding out the experience are the **Carriage House Craft Center** (where you can quiz modern craftspeople about historic trades like weaving, basket-weaving, and glass-blowing)

and the **Nye Barn,** a major conservation effort full of rare and heritage breeds of livestock.

Other Sights

To many, the sight of the literal **Plymouth Rock** (Pilgrim Memorial Park, Water St., 508/747-5360) is fairly underwhelming. It is, after all, merely an oversized glacial boulder. But lest we forget, the fuss is really over the New World that it symbolizes, and the story of those who first sighted it. Our concepts of guts and glory these days tend to be laid at the feet of sports teams. But the Pilgrims lacked nothing in the bravery department themselves. In fact, they were what you might call the original nation builders (take that reference with whatever positive or negative connotations you like) who felt strongly enough about their religious beliefs that they were willing to risk everything they had in England—their lives included—to find a land in which to practice it.

Unfortunately, theirs was an intolerant and extremist creed, and still more unfortunately,

© KINDRA CLINEFF/MOTT

Wampanoags at Hobbamock's Homesite

high **National Monument to the Forefathers** (Allerton St., one block from Plymouth Rock), a solid-granite statue erected in 1889. Two abutting tablets list the names of each original Mayflower passenger.

Bearing little if any connection at all to Plymouth's legitimate historic sites, but entirely fun regardless, are the **Lobster Tales Pirate Cruises** (Town Wharf, 508/746-5342, www.lobstertalesinc.com, May–Oct., call for times, $18). On these cruises little buccaneers are offered face paint and pirate hats as the ship sets sail to do battle and reclaim a treasure chest in the harbor. Gimmicky? Of course. But when the kids have gotten antsy from an overload of education, it's the ideal fix.

Witness the way corn was ground during the time of the Pilgrims at the rebuilt **Jenney Grist Mill** (6 Spring Ln., Plymouth, 508/747-4544, www.jenneygristmill.com, 9:30 A.M.–5 P.M. Mon.–Sat., noon–5 P.M. Sun., Apr.–Nov.; closed Dec.–Mar., $6 adults, free youth under 17); the original, owned by Pilgrim John Jenney, was destroyed by a fire in 1847. Today the mill makes for a fun family outing, with tours, a spring herring run in the abutting pond, and a general store peddling freshly ground corn and penny candy.

Events

Autumn puts Plymouth in its element, with foliage hitting its colorful peak, cranberry bogs alight with crimson berries, and Thanksgiving bringing a spotlight to the area. **Halloween Lantern Tours** hit in late October at Plimouth Plantation, offering guided nighttime walking tours of the historic village by punched-tin lanterns. Come November, there are few more appropriate places to be than Plymouth, site of the first Thanksgiving. The town pulls out all the stops, throwing **America's Hometown Thanksgiving Celebration** (508/746-1818, www.usathanksgiving.com) with a giant parade, marching bands, and floats galore down its center street; the Plantation rolls out scores of 17th-century family activities—from games and hands-on crafts to a full Victorian Thanksgiving Dinner.

they ran roughshod over many of the peoples who had already existed on their newfound continent for thousands of years. (Plimoth Plantation is to be commended for acknowledging the reality of this fact.) But history is history, and in a nation that to this day admires pluck as much as anything, it makes sense to learn about our chutzpah-based roots, if not necessarily admire each and every last one of them.

To that end, a visit to the **Pilgrim Hall Museum** (75 Court St., 508/746-1620, www.pilgrimhall.org, 9:30 A.M.–4:30 P.M. daily Feb.–Dec., $7 adults, $6 seniors, $4 children 5–17, free children under 5) can be as educational as one to Plimouth Plantation, if a tad bit less fun. Exhibits include displays of artifacts and possessions of the Pilgrims (aka Separatists) from both England and Holland, explanations detailing their transatlantic sojourn, the first contact with the Wampanoags, and accounts of the first Thanksgiving. In honor of Miles Standish, William Bradford, and the rest of the gang, stands the 81-foot-

Shopping

You'll find the requisite seaside and colonial-themed tourist traps in the center of town, but also a number of unique shops like the pretty, old-fashioned **Lily's Apothecary** (6 Main St. Ext., 508/747-7546, www.lilysapothecary.com, 10 A.M.–5 P.M. Mon.–Fri., 10 A.M.–3 P.M. Sat.). Its shelves are lined with imported cosmetics, tony fragrances like Payot Paris, plus skin and hair products by Mario Badescu and Bumble & Bumble. Souvenirs of a more concrete (literally) nature are found at **Sparrow House Pottery** (42 Summer St., 508/747-1240, www.sparrowhouse.com, 10 A.M.–5 P.M. daily). Score plenty of stoneware and handmade porcelain pottery made by local artists, not to mention contemporary gemstone jewelry, sculpture, glass and hand-inlaid boxes. Right next to Plimoth Plantation is the quaint **Bramhall's Country Store** (2 Sandwich Rd., 508/746-1844, 10 A.M.–8 P.M. daily in summer), a great stop for fresh fruits, smoothies, sweets, and sandwiches best devoured at the outdoor picnic tables.

Food

Fresh bounty from the nearby sea is the catch at **Lobster Hut** (25 Town Wharf, 508/746-2270, 11 A.M.–9 P.M. Tues.–Sat.; 11 A.M.–8 P.M. Sun.; $3–18), the ultra-casual takeout joint. (In nice weather, hit the outdoor deck for a water view.) Kick things off smoothly with the rich lobster bisque, or just dive right into an all-meat lobster roll. Breakfast is served all day at the **All-American Diner** (60 Court St., 508/747-4763, allamericandiner.biz, 7 A.M.–3 P.M. daily, $3–8), a wise choice for cheap and hearty (borderline overwhelming, in fact) omelets and decent chili burgers, served at a classic retro diner counter. With a striking view of Plymouth Harbor, **Mamma Mia's** (122 Water St., 508/747-4670, http://mammamiaspizzas.com, 11 A.M.–10 P.M. daily, $11–15) is a key spot for families in search of simple pastas and pizzas. Meanwhile, Mexican and Southwestern fixings get the spotlight at **Sam Diego's** (51 Main St., 508/747-0048, www.samdiegos.com, 11:30 A.M.–9 P.M. daily, $3–12), though the kids' menu of burgers and other such simple noshes gets quite a workout, too. It's also a favorite for its setting—just a few minutes from Plymouth Rock in an old historic fire station. Meanwhile, no one seems to pay much attention to the setting of **Peaceful Meadows Ice Cream** (170 Water St., Village Landing, 508/746-2362, 10 A.M.–10 P.M. daily, www.peacefulmeadows.com)—for the record, a friendly little waterfront creamery—because they're far too preoccupied lapping up homemade ice cream and creating their own sundaes from goodies like crushed Oreos, peanut butter sauce, hot apples, and chocolate-covered almonds.

NEW BEDFORD

On the very same expedition on which British explorer Bartholomew Gosnold settled Cuttyhunk Island in 1602 (note to Mayflower descendants: that was a full 18 years before anyone landed on Plymouth Rock), he and his troupe also set up camp in what is now New Bedford. Had they not left that same year to return to Mother England, New Bedford might well have been what Plymouth is today.

Instead, New Bedford has enjoyed a very different kind of fame: In the early 19th century, it was second only to Nantucket as the world's major whaling center—by the middle of the century, it had surpassed it. Unlike Nantucket, however, New Bedford had other sources of revenue in place when whale oil was made obsolete by the discovery of petroleum in 1859—namely cotton goods manufacturing and fisheries, both of which were in full swing by the mid-19th century. The city is still a center for the New England fishing industry, though to a much lesser extent, since overfishing has greatly affected the area's fish population. The human population, meanwhile, has risen to 100,000, with a citizenry that reflects its globally recognized past. The Portuguese population is of particular influence in and around New Bedford, and it shows in its restaurants and festivals.

Sights

Dedicated to the history of humanity's interaction with the great mammals of the sea, the

New Bedford Whaling Museum (18 Johnny Cake Hill, 508/997-0046, www.whalingmuseum.org) also houses 150,000 whaling artifacts and whale-related art, including the world's largest ship model. Built between 1831 and 1832 as a memorial to whalers who had lost their lives at sea, the **Seamen's Bethel** (15 Johnny Cake Hill, 508/992-3295)—the same one in Melville's *Moby-Dick*—is today used to honor fisherman whose fate has been the same. Search the main wall for three cenotaphs; you'll find a list of all of their names. On a cheerier note, it's well worth the short drive to **Westport Rivers Winery** (417 Hixbridge Rd., Westport, 508/636-3423, www.westportrivers.com). The working vineyards, which produce excellent reds, whites, and a lovely bubbly, are reminiscent of Provence.

Events

Every July, the folk- and arts-centric **Greater New Bedford Summerfest** (New Bedford Whaling National Historic Park, 508/979-1568, www.newbedfordsummerfest.com) takes over the city with its whaleboat races, fireworks, performances, and plentiful seafood. And during the first weekend in August, upwards of a hundred thousand pour into New Bedford for the Portuguese **Annual Feast of the Blessed Sacrament** (at the junction of Achushnet Ave. and Earle St., 508/992-6911, www.portuguesefeast.com). The massive celebration dates back to 1915 and is a frenzy of live entertainment, Portuguese food, music, and dance.

Shopping

Play 19th-century shopper at the **Bedford Merchant** (28 William St., 508/997-9194, 10 A.M.–7 P.M. Mon.–Sat.; 12 P.M.–5 P.M. Sun.), stocked with reproductions of old clocks, ship models, and lots of cast iron—in the form of everything from bird feeders to garden finials. And what's a former whaling capital without a little scrimshaw? Duck into **Whale's Tale Scrimshanders** (42 North Water St., 508/997-4233, 10 A.M.–5 P.M. daily) and pick up an intricately carved jewelry box or lightship basket.

Food

In a town so filled with delicious Portuguese food, it's tempting to eat nothing but linguica all day long. But other options abound, too—like the casual but tasty menu at **Freestones City Grill** (41 William St., 508/993-7477, www.freestones.com, 4 P.M.–10 P.M. Mon.–Sat.; 4 P.M.–9 P.M. Sun., $8–19)—an assembly of classically prepared stuffed quahogs, reggae chicken jerk sandwiches, and grilled meatloaf. Or just skip the kid's stuff and go for some of the town's best eats at ◖ **Antonio's** (267 Coggeshall St., 508/990-3636, 5 P.M.–10 P.M. daily, $14–25, cash only), where classic Portuguese foods meet the incredibly fresh fish of New Bedford. Sample *bacalhau* (salt cod), grilled sardines, and superb seafood stew.

CUTTYHUNK ISLAND

You won't hear it mentioned alongside Nantucket's yacht-filled wharfs or Martha's Vineyard's sophisticated restaurants anytime soon, but that may be precisely what makes this New England island so inviting. With just a small handful of businesses and restaurants (including a pizza joint, a casual hotel serving weekend brunch, a gift shop, and a post office), little-known Cuttyhunk is where to come when you don't just want to get away from it all, you want to get away from it *all*. That includes cars, too; golf carts and bikes are the preferred method of transport all over the island. (And a word of warning: Hit the ATM before boarding the ferry, as there aren't any on-island, and credit cards are rarely accepted.)

But what the island lacks in luxury it makes up for in history and heart-stopping natural beauty. Situated in the far southwestern corner of the Elizabeth Islands, the two-mile-long Cuttyhunk was actually one of the first pieces of America spotted by British explorer Bartholomew Gosnold (all of the Elizabeth Islands together comprise the town of Gosnold). And not terribly much about the island has changed since then, thanks to enormous conservation efforts that have kept the epic marshes clean, the woods intact, and the water views unsullied by McMansions or huge hotels.

Sights

Much of Cuttyhunk's allure is its distinct lack of things to do and see—that is, other than watch the sunset over grassy cliffs, pick wildflowers, and slurp oysters on the dock. However, a few sites do deserve a visit: foremost the **Navy Lookout Bunker** (Tower Rd.) that sits at the island's highest point, boasting breathtaking views of nearly the entire island and its surrounding waters. Another worthy jaunt: through the **Nature Preserve/Cliff Walk** (follow the road past the Fishing Club) conservation lands, which stretch through winding trails in flower-filled woods and wind-swept marshes.

Entertainment

In lieu of any actual bars or clubs, Cuttyhunk has found its own form of evening entertainment: bonfires. In this weekend ritual, locals bring their own wood to the spit connecting the dock at Capasit Point, add it to the fire, tell stories, and let the giant orange flames lick the inky black sky.

Shopping

It isn't tough deciding where to spend your cash on Cuttyhunk; there simply aren't many options. The best bets for souvenirs of any kind are the **General Store** (Broadway and Post Office Way), one of the only spots in town to find a deli and snacks, and film and pottery; and the **Cuttyhunk Corner Store** (at the Four Corners, 508/984-7167, 10 A.M.–5 P.M. Mon.–Sat.; 12 P.M.–5 P.M. Sun.) for handmade jewelry, pottery, clothing, and beach bags. You may feel more inclined to look than buy at the contemporary **Pea in Your Pants Gallery** (Bayview Dr., 603/321-6326,hours vary; call ahead), but its makeshift gallery-in-a-barn is worth a look, for certain.

Food

A word to the wise: Plan your meals carefully. Wait just a little too long, and you'll find yourself fresh out of options, as the few eateries available here close quite early. The most reliable is **Soprano's Pizza** (Broadway, 508/992-7530, 11:30 A.M.–7 P.M. Mon.–Sat.; closed Sun., $10–19), which is essentially a pizzeria run out of a local's garage. At the **Fish Market** (Town Dock), you place your orders for fresh seafood—shucked oysters or cooked lobster—early in the day and pick them up at 6 P.M. sharp. Catch dessert a few doors (literally) down at **The Ice Cream Stall.**

FALL RIVER

This former textile epicenter is best known not for the clothing it once produced, or for the diversity of immigrants that industry has attracted over the years. In fact, its biggest draw is its most notorious (ex)citizen—one Lizzie Borden, who murdered both her parents in 1892. Balancing out that unfortunate karma is the modern-day hometown boy, celebrity TV chef Emeril (Bam!) Lagasse.

Sights

Step into the fleet of naval ships known as **Battleship Cove** (5 Water St., 508/678-1100, www.battleshipcove.org, 9 A.M.–5 P.M. daily summer; 9 A.M.–4:30 P.M. daily spring, $15 adults, $13 seniors, $9 children 6–12, free children under 6) and you'll have free reign of all of the vessels, including the 46,000-ton **USS Massachusetts.** What used to be the **Lizzie Borden House** (92 Second St., 508/675-7333, www.lizzie-borden.com, tours 11 A.M.–3 P.M., $12.50 adults, $10 seniors and students, $5 children 6–15, free children under 6) where the infamous murders took place is now a bed-and-breakfast and tourist site, restored to look almost exactly as it did—from the couches to the pear trees outside—on that fateful day.

Events

Every summer, everyone anywhere near Fall River flocks into town for **Fall River Celebrates America** (Battleship Cove at Fall River Heritage State Park, 508/676-8226, www.fallrivercelebrates.com, Aug.). The four-day waterfront fiesta includes music performances, food fiestas, parades, rides, and fireworks.

Shopping

With a past so tied to textile manufacturing, it's little surprise to find lots of locally made clothing in Fall River. Opened in 1911, **Northeast Knitting Mills** (657 Quarry St., 508/678-7553, www.neknitting.com, 10 A.M.–6 P.M. Mon.–Fri.; 10 A.M.–5 P.M. Sat.; closed Sun.) sells sweaters made by the fourth generation of the family that founded it. Pick up a souvenir or two at **Desro Gift Shops** (638 Quequechan St., 508/646-9096, 9 A.M.–5 P.M. daily), chock-full of handmade candles, dried wreaths, and home accessories.

Food

Provincetown has its lobsters, Boston has its cream pies, and Fall River has its hot dogs. In fact, Fall River has a *lot* of hot dogs. One of the best is at **Tabacaria Acoriana Restaurant** (408 S Main St., 508/673-5890, 11 A.M.–4 P.M. Mon.–Fri.; closed Sat. and Sun.), though the kitchen's marinated grilled chicken is also a favorite. Just as casual, but with a few more ties to the city, is the pork pie. **Hartley's Original Pork Pies** (1729 South Main St., 508/676-8605, 11:30 A.M.–7 P.M. daily) serves them up piping hot and made with the traditional recipe, the way they have been in Fall River for decades.

SPORTS AND RECREATION
Beaches

As a residential community, the South Shore tends to fill its wide, sandy beaches with locals rather than tourists. That means that each beach tends to take on many of the characteristics of its town. **Duxbury Beach** (Duxbury Beach Park by Gurnet Rd., 781/934-1108, www.town.duxbury.ma.us) is the very picture of quaint coastal living. With its long wooden bridge spanning the abutting bay, the beach attracts hordes of preppy families (mostly to the area near the main parking lot and bathhouse, though in-the-know locals make the trek all the way down toward the lighthouse, where there's notably more space to stretch out). Likewise, the clean, long shoreline of **Horseneck Beach**

(Rte. 88, Westport Point, 508/636-8816, www.mass.gov) is a magnet for day-trippers in search of an easy-to-access pristine natural setting—but things can get crowded, so it's best to arrive early to claim a spot. Trading bucolic for breezy, cheesy charm, **Nantasket Beach** (Rte. 3A, Hull, 617/727-5290, www.mass.gov) is swarmed during summer months with a jumble of sun worshippers, from the trendy to the tattooed. The beach's boardwalk stretches from end to end, sporting everything from bingo rooms and sports bars to clam shacks. The buzz continues into autumn, too; families and packs of teens line up to ride the historic wooden **Paragon Carousel** (205 Nantasket Ave., Hull, 781/925-0472, www.paragoncarousel.com), one of the few remaining vestiges left from Nantasket's heyday as a 19th-century seaside theme park and resort.

Hiking and Biking

A handful of excellent land reservations around the South Shore make for great walks—many blessed with spectacular views of the ocean. **World's End** (250 Martin's Ln., Hingham, 781/740-6665, year-round, 8 A.M.–sunset daily, $5 adults, free children), for example, is upwards of 250 acres of rolling hills, wooded paths, and groves—with glimpses of Hingham Harbor and the Boston skyline throughout. Leashed dogs and mountain biking are permitted. At the smaller **Ellisville Harbor State Park** (Route 3A, Plymouth, 508/866-2580, year-round) there are 100 acres of well-tended hiking, fishing, and cross-country ski trails. Small but charming, the **Two Mile Farm** (Union St., Marshfield, 781/784-0567, year-round) abuts the winding North River—which it has beautiful views of. The park, which allows pets but no bikes, is considered a local gem for bird-watchers.

Boating and Fishing

Many of the premiere boating clubs on the South Shore are private clubs, but there are also marinas like **Onset Bay** (RFD #3, Green St., Buzzards Bay, 508/295-0338, www.onsetbay.com), which repairs and stores boats, and

Borden Light Marina (1 Ferry St., Fall River, 508/678-7547, www.bordenlight.com), which provides fueling and docking services.

ACCOMMODATIONS
$100-150

The one, the only place to lay your head on Cuttyhunk is the **Cuttyhunk Fishing Club** (One, Road to the Landing, Cuttyhunk Island, 508/992-5585, www.cuttyhunkfishingclub.com, $164–185). Perched above the roaring ocean surf, the breezy building is much like the island itself: quiet, humble, and a little rough at the edges. Still, there's a musty library filled with hurricane lamps and board games, and the hotel serves an extremely popular brunch on weekends. Touristy Plymouth, meanwhile, has the lion's share of the South Shore's hotels and inns. Named after the long-necked flocks at the nearby beaches, the **White Swan B&B** (146 Manomet Point Rd., Plymouth, 508/224-3759, www.whiteswan.com, $120–175) is a simply decorated 1800s home with a surprising number of amenities, including wireless Internet, a whirlpool tub, hair dryers, and in-room fridges. Overlooking the spot where the Mayflower hit dry land, **The Governor Bradford Inn** (98 Water St., Plymouth, 508/746-6200, www.governorbradford.com, $79–129) is actually more of a hotel than inn—the rooms have all the personal charm of a Ramada—but for pure proximity to Plymouth Rock, it can't be beat. Small, friendly, and a stone's throw from working cranberry bogs, **Cranberry Cottage Bed & Breakfast** (10 Woodbine Dr., Plymouth, 508/747-1726) is home to four guest rooms (some with fireplaces), a pool, and outdoor games like horseshoes, badminton, and table tennis.

$150-250

More of a residential than resort community, Duxbury really has need for only one inn, but it's a lovely one. Surrounded by impeccably kept gardens, the **1803 Winsor House Inn** (390 Washington St., Duxbury, 781/934-0991, www.winsorhouseinn.com, $110–210) houses an English-style pub and rooms with antiques, canopy beds, and an impressive homemade breakfast.

GETTING THERE AND AROUND

To drive from Boston to the South Shore, take I-93 South to US Route 3 South. For Hingham, take exit 15 (25 mi., 40 min.), for Duxbury, exit 11 (35 mi., 45 min.), and for Plymouth, exit 6A (40 mi., 50 min.) To drive from Boston to New Bedford, take I-93 South to Route 24 to Route 140 (60 mi., 1 hr. 10 min.).

From Boston, you can access the South Shore easily by public transportation on the Massachusetts Bay Transportation Authority (MBTA, 617/222-5000, www.mbta.com); the subway's Red Line runs from numerous in-city stations, including South Station, to Quincy, Wollaston, and Braintree stations. From there, and between a number of key South Shore points, you can access MBTA buses that run throughout most of the area's towns. Check the website for individual schedules.

To get to Cuttyhunk, take the **Cuttyhunk Ferry Co.** (66B State Pier, South Bulkhead, New Bedford, 508/992-0200, www.cuttyhunkferryco.com, $25/40 adult, $20/30 children 12 and under).

With careful planning and a schedule from the **Plymouth & Brockton** (8 Industrial Park Rd., Plymouth, 508/746-0378, www.p-b.com) bus line, you can get nearly anywhere on the South Shore—even all the way to Provincetown on the tip of Cape Cod, if need be. Call for schedules and route information.

CAPE COD AND THE ISLANDS

As President, John F. Kennedy didn't only create the Peace Corps and stare down Fidel Castro. He also signed a sweeping law in 1961 that protected 27,000 acres of some of the most beautiful beachfront in America. The Cape Cod National Seashore is one of the conservation jewels not only of Massachusetts, but of the entire region, drawing generations of beachgoers to the miles of sandy beach fronting the Atlantic. Perhaps because it lacks the development of, say, the Jersey Shore, the Cape has always had an old-time feel, with ice cream parlors and clam shacks dotted among the distinctive shingled cottages that gave their name to a style of house architecture. Then there is the conservation land itself, an expanse of dunes, grasslands, and scrub-pine forests, cut through with biking trails and anchorages.

It's fitting that Kennedy should have signed the bill that preserved all of this beauty. After all, he and his family summered in Hyannisport in the compound that still bears the family name. Outside the summer capital of Hyannis, the Cape has a striking diversity of landscapes, from the acclaimed oceanographic institute of Woods Hole to the Ye Olde Yankee ambience of the bayshore towns, and from the pristine beauty of the Outer Cape beaches to the flamboyant gay mecca of Provincetown. Along the way, of course, are all the mini-golf courses and tacky souvenir shops you can ask for.

Cape Cod, as might be imagined, is named for the rich fisheries that lay just off the coast in an oceanic rise known as Georges Bank. The rich ecosystem there has supported generations

© HYANNIS AREA CHAMBER OF COMMERCE

of fishing fleets, which still leave from the towns of the Outer Cape. Though over-fished almost to the point of extinction 50 years ago, the fishery has made a comeback through delicate environmental management, and cod is once again a staple of New England restaurant menus.

The Cape itself, with its sideways-L topography, was formed by the moraine of the last continental ice sheet, which stopped here some 20,000 years ago. The same ice sheet had previously retreated from its last gasp to the south, where it formed Massachusetts' two major islands—resort communities with characters as different as old and new money. On buttoned-up Nantucket, whale belts and lightship baskets are always in fashion, while trousers-rolled Martha's Vineyard is where the rich and famous come to kick back by the surf.

ORIENTATION

Residents often speak of Cape geography as resembling an arm, held up at 90 degrees and curved towards the face. The Cape's de facto capital, Hyannis, is just about tricep level, Chatham is at the elbow, and Provincetown at the furthest tip of the fingers. The area is further divided into three different regions—the Upper Cape, which runs from the canal to the Barnstable line; the Mid-Cape, which takes in Barnstable and Hyannis through to Brewster and Harwich; and the Lower Cape, which encompasses the National Seashore from Monomoy Island to the Province Lands. To confuse matters more, locals sometimes refer to the area from Chatham to Orleans as the Lower Cape, while calling the area from Eastham to Provincetown the Outer Cape. A more practical division is between the bayshore, which is typified by tidal flats and warmer water, and the oceanside, home to the colder and wilder beaches.

PLANNING YOUR TIME

Summertime is, of course, when the Cape comes into its glory, but it can also mean roads clogged with traffic, and beaches, especially in the Mid-Cape, insufferably crowded. It makes sense to base yourself in one area, since traffic

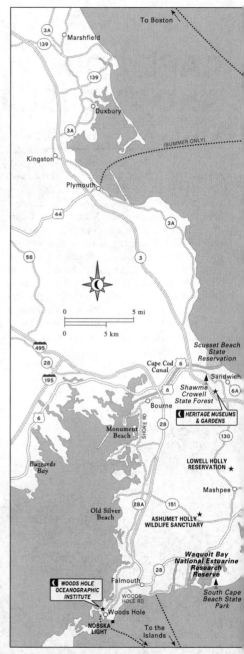

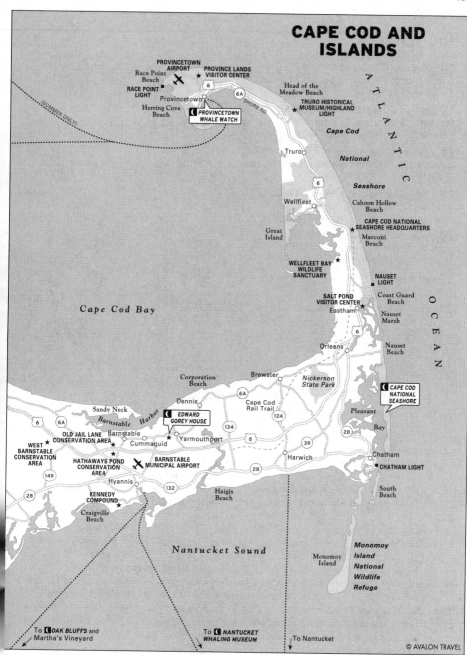

CAPE COD AND ISLANDS

ATLANTIC

Cape Cod

National

Seashore

OCEAN

PROVINCETOWN AIRPORT
PROVINCE LANDS VISITOR CENTER
Race Point Beach
RACE POINT LIGHT
Provincetown
Herring Cove Beach
PROVINCETOWN WHALE WATCH
(SUMMER ONLY)

Head of the Meadow Beach
TRURO HISTORICAL MUSEUM/HIGHLAND LIGHT
SHORE RD
6
6A

Truro

6

Wellfleet

Cahoon Hollow Beach
CAPE COD NATIONAL SEASHORE HEADQUARTERS
Marconi Beach

Great Island

WELLFLEET BAY WILDLIFE SANCTUARY

NAUSET LIGHT
Coast Guard Beach

Cape Cod Bay

SALT POND VISITOR CENTER
Eastham
Nauset Marsh

6

Orleans
Nauset Beach

Brewster
Nickerson State Park

Corporation Beach

CAPE COD NATIONAL SEASHORE

Dennis
6A

Sandy Neck
Barnstable
Harbor
EDWARD GOREY HOUSE
134
Cape Cod Rail Trail
124

Pleasant

Bay

6
6A
OLD JAIL LANE CONSERVATION AREA
Barnstable
Cummaquid
Yarmouthport
6

28

WEST BARNSTABLE CONSERVATION AREA
149
HATHAWAYS POND CONSERVATION AREA
BARNSTABLE MUNICIPAL AIRPORT
39

Harwich

Chatham
CHATHAM LIGHT

28
Hyannis
132
KENNEDY COMPOUND
Haigis Beach
28

Craigville Beach

South Beach

Nantucket Sound

Monomoy Island

Monomoy Island National Wildlife Refuge

To OAK BLUFFS and Martha's Vineyard

To NANTUCKET WHALING MUSEUM

To Nantucket

© AVALON TRAVEL

HIGHLIGHTS

(Heritage Museums & Gardens: Two centuries of Americana live on at this palatial garden estate (page 138).

(Woods Hole Oceanographic Institute: Deep-sea explorers reveal the mysteries of the real "final frontier" (page 138).

(Edward Gorey House: Stephen King, move over for the true "master of macabre" (page 140).

(Cape Cod National Seashore: Stroll miles of sandy beaches with nothing between you and Portugal but waves (page 146).

(Provincetown Whale Watch: Seeing these leviathans in their natural habitat is anything but a fluke (page 147).

(Oak Bluffs: This Vineyard town is on permanent vacation (page 154).

(Nantucket Whaling Museum: Scrimshaw, harpoons, and a giant skeleton bring *Moby-Dick* to life (page 164).

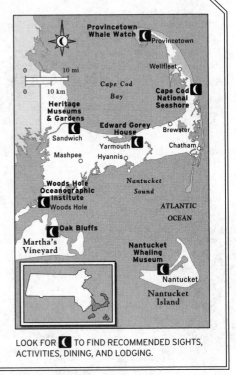

LOOK FOR (TO FIND RECOMMENDED SIGHTS, ACTIVITIES, DINING, AND LODGING.

can make driving difficult and quickly spoil a good vacation. The Upper Cape is the easiest to get to and least crowded. It's also home to several popular family attractions, including the eclectic **Heritage Museums & Gardens** and the educational **Woods Hole Oceanographic Institute.** The Mid-Cape is home to historic attractions and the best restaurants and nightlife. One can't-miss attraction in this area is Yarmouthport's **Edward Gorey House,** dedicated to the late great creepy kids' book author. The Lower Cape, meanwhile, is your destination for beaches and the natural beauty of **Cape Cod National Seashore.**

You can easily spend a week based in any one of these areas, relaxing at the beach and taking a few day trips to other attractions on the Cape. No

Cape vacation is complete, however, without at least a day trip to one of the islands of Nantucket or Martha's Vineyard. In fact, either one of these islands has plenty to offer for a longer visit of a few days to a week. (Though don't expect to beat the crowds by taking the ferry; half of Boston goes to the islands every summer weekend.) Choosing which island to visit is largely a matter of temperament: Nantucket is old New England, buttoned-down and traditional, with plenty of historical sites that pay homage to its one-time whaling industry (starting with the excellent and recently renovated **Nantucket Whaling Museum**). The Vineyard, meanwhile, is where the jet-set comes to play; the larger of the two islands, it also has more varied scenery and more secret hideaways to reward a longer visit.

Cape Cod has a year-round population of about 230,000, but every year between Memorial and Labor Days it groans under the weight of thousands upon thousands of tourists. Though summer is undoubtedly the warmest time of year to visit, its crowds can make true relaxation a challenge, which is why many opt instead to go during shoulder season (mid- to late spring and again in early to mid-fall). Hotel prices are lower, stores are still open, and the weather, while not sunbathing-friendly, is warm enough for beach visits and outdoor activities ranging from hiking to biking.

In the winter, many tourist-driven businesses close for the season, though a handful of hotels and shops in every town often do stay open. Restaurants tend to greatly reduce their hours of operation, and some even close completely. So be sure to call ahead. And these days, holiday events and festivities often attract enough visitors in December to keep them open as well. January through March is extremely chilly in Cape Cod—usually too cold for most outdoor activities or extended strolls—but early spring, while brisk, can also be surprisingly pleasant.

Upper and Mid-Cape

Summer tourists frequently rush past the first part of the Cape on their way to the outer beaches. Because of that, the Upper Cape is sleepier and more residential than the rest of the peninsula. It's worth visiting, however, for two very different towns—historic Sandwich and the bustling research center of Woods Hole. The Mid-Cape is traversed by three parallel highways. On the bayside, Route 6A is known as the Old King's Highway, and it retains the colonial feel of some of the oldest towns in the state, crawling with quiet bed-and-breakfasts and antiques stores. Along Nantucket Sound, meanwhile, Route 28 is the bustling beachfront terrain of mini-golf courses and sticky fried seafood, anchored by the relative metropolis of Hyannis. In between the two routes, US Route 6 is the featureless but efficient express route to the Lower Cape.

SANDWICH AND FALMOUTH

Though it has nothing to do with the famous lunch item, Sandwich *was* named after the same earl who invented it. Founded just 17 years after the Pilgrims landed, the village was a haven for Quakers and others who disagreed with the powers-that-be in Plymouth. Later, it became one of the first tourist communities for hunters and beachgoers from Boston. Both qualities are retained in a village that is one of the most quaint in Massachusetts.

Despite its location below where the Cape's proverbial arm attaches to the body, Falmouth

THE CAPE'S FORMATION

The existence of Cape Cod as we know it is owed largely to the advance and retreat of the most recent continental ice sheet that resulted in changes of sea level.

About 23,000 years ago, in the late Pleistocene geological era, the sheet reached its greatest southward extent, then eventually retreated back from the Cape. When it melted, it pushed the sea level to rise roughly 11 feet per millennium between 6,000 and 2,000 years ago, then slowed down to about three feet per millennium.

Eventually the sea level was high enough to start eroding the glacial deposits that the melted ice sheet had left behind, and carry them along the shoreline all the way out to the tip of the Cape. As a result, the Provincetown Spit today is made up primarily of marine deposits transported from farther up the shore.

is anything but the armpit of the Cape. Its downtown is pure Americana—befitting the town where Katherine Lee Bates first penned "America the Beautiful"—and its coastline is spotted with nature preserves and forested beaches. At the far end of Falmouth, Woods Hole has been a center of science since 1927, when the eponymous oceanographic center was founded. The town is now a delightful confluence of scientists, fishermen, and tourists passing through to the Vineyard.

(Heritage Museums & Gardens

When he was a child, pharmaceutical giant J. K. Lilly collected ticket stubs and coins; as he grew older, fascination became an addiction, leading to collections of classic cars and folk art. Now more than 200 years of American history are breathlessly encapsulated on Lilly's former 100-acre estate (67 Grove St., Sandwich, 508/888-3300, www.heritagemuseumsandgardens.org, 10 A.M.–5 P.M. daily Apr.–Oct, $12 adults, $11 seniors, $6 children 4–16, free children under 4). Various exhibits include an antique-car museum, a windmill, a carousel, and the Hall of Fame for the Cape Cod Baseball League. If that isn't enough, the grounds are filled with bed after bed of hybrid flowers created by the estate's previous owner.

(Woods Hole Oceanographic Institute

How many of us once harbored dreams of swimming with the dolphins? At WHOI (locally pronounced as "hooey"), visitors can fulfill their marine biology fantasies at the country's most prominent oceanographic research institution. The institute is home to the famous Alvin submersible, which famously discovered the wreck of the *Titanic,* as well as the new five-foot-long REMUS, which can explore 98 percent of the ocean floor. A good exhibit center (15 School St., 508/289-2663, www. whoi.edu, by appointment April; 10 A.M.–4:30 P.M. Mon.–Sat. May–Oct. and Tues.–Fri. Nov.–Dec., donation requested) details the institute's past, including an exhibit on the *Titanic* and a life-size replica of Alvin. During

the summer, scientists lead a more hands-on view of the facility with tours (10:30 A.M. and 1:30 P.M. Mon.–Fri. July–Aug., free) of the labs and docks.

Other Sights

In the 19th century, entrepreneur Deming Jarves opened a glass factory in Sandwich, importing sand from Florida when the local stuff wouldn't work. His output is on display at the **Sandwich Glass Museum** (129 Main St., Sandwich, 508/888-0251, www. sandwichglassmuseum.org, 9:30 A.M.–5 P.M. daily Apr.–Dec.; closed Jan.; 9:30 A.M.–4 P.M. Wed.–Sun. Feb.–Mar., $5 adults, $1.25 children 6–14, free children 6 and under), a fascinating tour through the history and techniques of the art, including glassblowing demonstrations using a 2,000-degree furnace. The modest **Woods Hole Science Aquarium** (166 Water St., Woods Hole, 508/495-2001, http:// aquarium.nefsc.noaa.gov, 11 A.M.–4 P.M. Tues.–Sat. June–Aug.; 11 A.M.–4 P.M. Mon.–Fri. Sept.–May, free) makes a good activity for kids and rainy days, complete with a seal pool and "touch tanks" where you can pick up crabs and other critters.

Shopping

The **Sandwich Antiques Center** (131 Route 6A, Sandwich, 508/833-3600, 10 A.M.–5 P.M. daily, www.sandwichantiquescenter.com) includes a good selection of Sandwich glass.

Food

There's nothing earth-shattering about the menu of steaks and seafood at (**The Captain Kidd** (77 Water St., Woods Hole, 508/548-8563, 5:30 P.M.–11 P.M. Mon.–Sat.; 5 P.M.–10 P.M. Sun., www.thecaptainkidd. com, $10–26), a cozy pub in the center of Woods Hole. The freshness of the ingredients and back patio overlooking Eel Pond, however, make it a favorite for both fishermen and scientists, who meet here nightly to talk over the day's catch. With cheeky menu divisions like "not so small" and "not small at all," **Roöbar** (285 Main St., Falmouth, 508/548-

8600, 5 P.M.–11 P.M. Tues.–Sat.; 5 P.M.–10 P.M. Sun.; closed Mon., www.theroobar.com, $18–33) adds a dash of high-spirited fun to the sometimes fusty Cape restaurant scene. High-concept dishes like Polynesian lobster spring rolls and wasabi oyster shooters introduce New England seafood to the world. Not to be confused with the foregoing, **The Raw Bar** (252 Shore Dr., Mashpee, 508/539-4858, www.therawbar.com, 11 A.M.–7 P.M. daily June–Oct.; 11 A.M.–5 P.M. daily Oct.–May, $4–23) has plenty of cheap eats like hot dogs—but why would you order them when the lobster rolls here are the best around? Atmosphere is somewhere between Spring Break and Mardi Gras.

Information
Information about Sandwich and surrounding towns is available at the **Sandwich Visitor Center** (Rte. 130, 508/833-1632, www.capecodcanalchamber.org). Info for Falmouth and Woods Hole is available from the **Falmouth Chamber of Commerce** (20 Academy Ln., 508/548-8500, www.falmouthchamber.com).

HYANNIS
Technically speaking, Hyannis is just one of the seven villages of the large town of Barnstable. Practically, it overshadows every other town on the cape as the hub of activity. The bars and restaurants are ground zero for the scores of teens and college students who descend upon the Cape each summer, while its streets throng with tourists awaiting the ferries or perusing souvenir shops for just one more Cape Cod sweatshirt.

Sights
Joseph P. Kennedy and his wife, Ethel, first rented a cottage on Marchant Avenue in Hyannisport in 1926. Three years later they bought it, ushering the lasting association with the Cape through their three children, John, Robert, and Ted. The so-called **Kennedy Compound** consists of six cottage-dotted acres behind a high fence, though only three of the houses within are owned by the Kennedys. It's

possible to do a quick drive-by in the off-season. During the summer, two police cars guard the turnoff onto the road (though rumor has it that the troopers in the front seat are just stuffed dummies).

In Hyannis proper, the modest and somewhat disappointing **John F. Kennedy Museum** (397 Main St., 508/775-2201, jfkhyannismuseum.org/, 9 A.M.–5 P.M. Mon.–Sat. and 12–5 P.M. Sun. late–May–mid-Oct.; 10 A.M.–4 P.M. Thurs.–Sat. and 12–4 P.M. Sun. mid-Oct.–Dec. and mid-Feb.–mid-May, $5 adults, $2.50 children 10–17, free children under 10) has a short video about the Kennedys' time here, along with a collection of black-and-white photographs of JFK sailing, playing ball, and relaxing with his family on the Cape.

Entertainment
Firmly planted on the Las Vegas circuit, the **Cape Cod Melody Tent** (21 W. Main St., 508/775-5630, www.melodytent.com) draws deathless crooners such as Tony Bennett and Engelbert Humperdinck, along with occasional more modern performers. Cheekily known as the BBC, the **British Beer Company** (412 Main St., 508/771-1776, www.britishbeer.com) draws a teen and twentysomething crowd for live rock, DJs, and karaoke.

Events
Calling chowder soup is like calling filet mignon steak. Lovers of New England's favorite appetizer flock to the **WCOD Chowder Festival** (Cape Cod Melody Tent, W. Main St., June) to sample the best offerings from local restaurants.

Shopping
The only shopping mall for miles, the **Cape Cod Mall** (Rte. 132, Hyannis, 508/771-0200, www.simon.com, 10 A.M.–9:30 P.M. Mon.–Sat.; 12 P.M.–7:30 P.M. Sun.) draws hordes of teens to shop at stores including Macy's, Sears, Best Buy, and Barnes & Noble. When you tire of the standard Cape Cod T-shirts, stop by **Vanilla & Chocolate** (497-503 Main St.,

508/778-4844, 10 A.M.–7:30 P.M. Mon.–Sat.; 12 P.M.–5 P.M. Sun.), which will put pop culture icons from Homer Simpson to Oscar the Grouch on your chest.

Food

Hyannis is one of the only options on the Cape for good ethnic cuisine. The hole-in-the-wall **Bangkok Thai Cuisine** (339 Barnstable Rd., 508/771-2333, entrées $9–19, 11 A.M.–9 P.M. Mon.–Sat.; closed Sun.) is a cut above most Thai places, with specials such as crispy duck with tamarind. Traditional *rodizio* is on the menu at **Brazilian Grill** (680 Main St., 508/771-0109, www.braziliangrill-capecod.com, 11:30 A.M.–9 P.M. Mon.–Thurs.; 11:30 A.M.–10 P.M. Fri and Sat; 5 P.M.–9 P.M. Sun., 13–26), where waiters carve skewer after skewer of beef, pork, and sausage at your table. One of the only places to check email on the Cape, the **Cape Cod Internet Cafe** (599 Main St. #13, 508/862-8025, $5 minimum for 30 min., 10 A.M.–8 P.M. daily) has Wi-Fi and printers, as well as pastries and cold bubble teas.

Information

The **Cape Cod Chamber of Commerce** (Rtes. 6 & 132, 508/362-3225, www.capecodchamber.org) runs a comprehensive center for the region. The **Hyannis Area Chamber of Commerce** (397 Main St., 508/775-2201, www.hyannis.com) focuses on the city.

The area's largest full-service hospital is **Cape Cod Hospital** (27 Park St., Hyannis, 508/771-1800, www.capecodhealth.org). Fill prescription needs at the 24-hour branches of **CVS Pharmacy** (176 North St., Hyannis, 508/775-8462 or 105 Davis Straights, Rte. 28, Falmouth, 508/540-4307, www.cvs.com). The commercial center of town is home to a handful of banks and ATMs.

Free **wireless Internet access** is offered to patrons with laptops at the **Hyannis Public Library** (401 Main St., Hyannis, 508/775-2280, www.hyannislibrary.org), and by payment on terminals at **FedEx Office Print & Ship Center** (297 North St., Hyannis,

508/778-9454, fedex.com/us/office). The latter also offers faxing and shipping services as well.

YARMOUTH TO BREWSTER
🅒 Edward Gorey House

The name might not be immediately recognizable, but Edward Gorey's not-quite-children's books have a way of drilling themselves into the subconscious. His best-known book, the *Ghastlycrumb Tinies* ("A is for Amy who fell down the stairs; B is for Basil, assaulted by bears") serves as inspiration for this delightfully macabre home (8 Strawberry Ln., Yarmouth Port, 508/362-3909, www.edwardgoreyhouse.org, 11 A.M.–4 P.M. Thurs.–Sat. and 12–4 P.M. Sun. mid-Apr.–June; 11 A.M.–4 P.M. Wed.–Sat. and 12–4 P.M. Sun. June–early Oct., $5 adults, $3 students and seniors, $2 children 6–12, free children under 6) where the author lived for 25 years. Many of the docents are the late Gorey's friends, who are if anything just as eccentric as he was, and regale even casual visitors with tales of the bearded author.

Other Sights

The sophisticated **Cape Cod Museum of Natural History** (869 Route 6A, Brewster, 508/896-3867, www.ccmnh.org, 11 A.M.–3 P.M. Thurs.–Sun. Feb.–Mar. and Wed.–Sun. Apr.–May and Oct.–Dec.; 9:30 A.M.–4 P.M. daily June–Sept., $8 adults, $7 seniors, $3.50 children 3–12, free children under 3) uses wave tanks and computer screens to trace the effects of Cape Cod geography and landscape on its native wildlife. Behind the museum, a trail leads to flats perfect for tidepooling.

Twenty-five years ago, Cape residents frustrated with the amount of local artwork leaving for Paris and Washington founded the **Cape Cod Museum of Art** (Rte. 6A, Dennis, 508/385-4477, www.ccmoa.org, 10 A.M.–5 P.M. Mon.–Sat., until 8 P.M. Thurs., 12–5 P.M. Sun. late May–mid-Oct., $8 adults, free children), which showcases consistently high-quality work in a restored Victorian barn.

MASSACHUSETTS

© HYANNIS AREA CHAMBER OF COMMERCE

Edward Gorey House

Shopping

An old-time country store modified for pre- or après-beach stop-offs, **The Brewster Store** (1935 Rte. 6A, Brewster, 508/896-3744, www. brewsterstore.com, 9:30 A.M.–6 P.M. daily May–Aug.; 10 A.M.–5 P.M. daily Sept.–April) is filled with penny candy, beach toys, housewares, and antiques. The mother of the Cape's independent bookstores, the **Parnassus Book Service** (220 Rte. 6A, Yarmouthport, 508/362-6420, www.parnassusbooks.com, 10 A.M.–5 P.M. daily June–Aug.; hours vary in winter) stocks thousands of used tomes, along with new books on the Cape and a complete catalog of Edward Gorey. An outdoor extension is open around the clock on the honor system.

Food

The best fried seafood on the Cape is doled out at **Kream N' Kone** (961 Rte. 28, W. Dennis, 508/394-0808, www.kreamnkone. com, 11 A.M.–10:30 P.M. daily July and August; 11 A.M.–9:30 P.M. Sept.–June, $11–19), a garish strip-mall shack known to spawn pilgrimages

from Boston—or farther—for its juicy fried clams and onion rings. Winner of countless chowder competitions, **Captain Parker's Pub** (668 Rte. 28, W. Yarmouth, 508/771-4266, www.captainparkers.com, 11 A.M.–10 P.M. daily July and August; 11 A.M.–9:30 P.M. Sept.–June, $12–27) is a family-style pub overlooking the scenic Parker's River that is a favored spot for locals. Fresh-cut flowers fill the manor house at **Chillingsworth** (2449 Rte. 6A, Brewster, 508/896-3640, www.chillingsworth. com, $60–70 prix fixe, $17–37 à la carte), the most romantic dining room on the Cape. The kitchen mixes the rich flavors of French truffles and foie gras with fresh local seafood for a gut-busting seven-course menu.

Another of those restaurants that is slowly dragging the Cape into the 21st century culinary light is **Gracie's Table** (800 Main St., Dennis, 508/385-5600, www.graciestablecapecod.com, 5:30 P.M.–9 P.M. Mon.–Sat.; 5 P.M.–9 P.M. Sun.; 5 P.M.–9:30 P.M. Wed.–Mon., May–Sept., call for hours in the off-season, $18–30), an authentic Spanish restaurant featuring tapas and "petite entrées" from the

Basque region of Northwestern Spain and Southwestern France. It features both traditional tapas items such as *patatas bravas* and *bacalao*, with more unexpected offerings—pork adobo and frog's legs Provençal. Situated in Dennis' arts complex, a stone's throw from the Cape Cod Playhouse (see below), Cape Cod Cinema, and Cape Cod Art Museum (see above), it's the perfect place to catch a bite and a glass of Rioja before or after the show.

Entertainment
Humphrey Bogart, Gregory Peck, and Lana Turner are among those who got their start at the **Cape Playhouse** (820 Rte. 6A, Dennis Village, 877/385-3911, www.capeplayhouse. com), the nation's oldest summer theater, which has been drawing crowds for musicals, comedies, and dramatic premieres for more than 80 years.

Information
Each of the Mid-Cape towns has its own information center, as follows: **Yarmouth** (424 Rte. 28, W. Yarmouth, 508/778-1008, www. yarmouthcapecod.com), **Dennis** (238 Swan River Rd., 508/398-3568, www.dennischamber.com), **Brewster** (2198 Rte. 6A, 508/896-3500, www.brewstercapecod.com), and **Harwich** (Intersection of Schoolhouse Rd. and Rte. 28, Harwich Port, 508/432-1600, www. harwichcc.com).

SPORTS AND RECREATION
Beaches
The warmest beaches on the Cape are on Buzzard's Bay. The popular **Old Silver Beach** (Quaker Rd., N. Falmouth) features soft sand, gentle surf, and a snack shack and other amenities, while **Chapoquoit Island** is rockier and more secluded. Tidepooling is popular on **Brewster Flats,** so-called because the beach along Cape Cod Bay stretches out for a mile at low tide. Eight beaches line 6A in Brewster. On Nantucket Sound, the under-21 set flocks to **Craigville Beach** (Craigville Rd., Barnstable) for cruising and ice cream, while **Red River Beach**

BEACH FACTS

Most Cape Cod beaches have parking lots that charge a daily fee (usually between $5 and $15) from Memorial Day until Labor Day. Many have public bathrooms and concession stands as well; when the latter is not available, local grocery stores often cater to beachgoers' picnic needs.

The beaches on Cape Cod's north and west shores face Cape Cod Bay, and have mile-wide tides and the least surf. Thus, they're often the best for toddlers and babies. The southside beaches face Nantucket Sound, and tend to have small waves, so they're also relatively safe for toddlers. More wave action – and undertow – happens on the east-facing beaches of the Atlantic Ocean.

(Uncle Venies Rd., Harwich) is a quiet stretch ready-made for sunbathing.

Biking
The only bike path on the Cape that runs along the seashore, the aptly named **Shining Sea Bikeway** is a four-mile paved ride along former Native American paths. The highly scenic route takes in scrub forest, hidden bays, and swampland along the Falmouth coastline, from Woods Hole to Pin Oak Way. Bikes can be rented at **Woods Hole Cycle** (6 Luscombe Ave., 508/540-7718). The longer and more varied **Cape Cod Rail Trail** starts in South Dennis, off of Route 134, and runs almost 30 miles through wooded conservation land along a former railroad right-of-way to the salt marshes of Orleans. Bikes are available at **Barbara's Bike Shop** (430 Rte. 134, S. Dennis, 508/760-4723, www.barbsbikeshop.com), at the trailhead.

Boating and Fishing
The best way to see the Kennedy Compound without risking arrest is to take a tour of Hyannis harbor with **Hy-Line Cruises** (220 Ocean St., Hyannis, 800/492-8082, www.hy-linecruises. com), which runs one-hour jaunts as well as jazz

and blues cruises. Harwichport is home to many deep-sea fishing boats, including the gargantuan **Yankee** (508/432-2520) and the more intimate **Tuna Eclipse** (508/737-0923, www.tunaeclipse.com). Romantic sails along the Falmouth coast and Vineyard Sound are offered on **The Liberté** (508/548-2626, www.theliberte.com) a 74-foot three-masted schooner. **Pirate Adventures** (Ocean St. Dock, Hyannis, 508/430-4693, www.pirateadventures.com) promises more spirited expeditions, complete with face paint, buried treasure, and sea shanties.

Camping

Situated among forested kettle hole ponds, **Nickerson State Park** (Rte. 6A, Brewster, 508/896-3491) has some 400 campsites, as well as eight miles of trails for hiking and mountain biking.

ACCOMMODATIONS
Under $100

Despite the high concentrations of tourists in the summer, the even higher concentrations of motels around Hyannis helps keep costs down. The **Seacoast Inn** (33 Ocean St., Hyannis, 508/775-3828, www.seacoastcapecod.com, $68–148) has the best rates downtown, along with free continental breakfast and microwaves in some rooms.

$100-150

Located within walking distance of downtown and beaches, **Woods Hole Passage** (186 Woods Hole Rd., 508/548-9575, www.woodsholepassage.com, $100–195) is a charming bed-and-breakfast in a renovated century-old carriage house. Rooms are decked out in bright colors and fish-themed artwork, with wireless Internet and private baths. Breakfast might include strawberry shortcake or crème brûlée French toast. Known as much for its excellent restaurant as for its accommodations, the **Bramble Inn** (Rte. 6A, Brewster, 508/896-7644, www.brambleinn.com, $140–170) offers small but cozy rooms featuring four-poster beds and skylights. Innkeeper Cliff Manchester is as free with local recommendations as his wife,

Ruth, is proficient in the kitchen. A path behind the bed-and-breakfast leads to the beaches of Brewster Flats.

$150-250

With that extra "e" on its name, you know that old-time ambience is key at the antiques-filled **Belfry Inne** (8 Jarves St., Sandwich, 508/888-8550, www.belfryinn.com, $149–315), a complex of four historical buildings in the heart of Sandwich. Stained-glass windows and other architectural details are preserved in the Abbey, while whirlpool tubs and DVD players seduce guests in the renovated 1638 Meetinghouse.

$250 and Up

The spirit of the Great Gatsby lives at the sprawling 400-acre **Ocean Edge Resort** (2907 Rte. 6A, Brewster, 508/896-9000, www.oceanedge.com, $99–325), the Mid-Cape's premier resort. At its center is an 1890s mansion with marble fireplaces, brass sconces, and a grand staircase leading to function rooms

room at the Belfry Inne

with sweeping views of the long forearm of the Cape. Guest rooms include kitchenette suites that range from large to humongous, along with beachside villas and family-friendly cottages. Other amenities include six pools, four restaurants, an 18-hole golf course, and front-lawn croquet.

GETTING THERE AND AROUND

Cape Air (800/352-0714, www.flycapeair.com) runs daily flights from Boston, Providence, and the Islands (Nantucket and Martha's Vineyard) to **Barnstable Municipal Airport** (480 Barnstable Rd., Hyannis, 508/775-2020, www.town.barnstable.ma.us). Buses by **Plymouth & Brockton Bus Lines** (508/746-0378, www.p-b.com) run from Boston and Plymouth to the **Hyannis Transportation Center** (215 Iyannough Rd., Hyannis, 508/775-8504).

The **Cape Cod Regional Transit Authority** (800/352-7155, www.capecodtransit.org) runs the Breeze shuttle throughout Hyannis and along Route 28 from Woods Hole to Orleans.

Lower Cape

The stable of seaside communities in this region prides itself on comprising the "less touristed" area of the Cape. With an increasing number discovering its pretty (and often public) beaches, that claim may become more and more dubious with the years. But for now, the little artists communities of Wellfleet, the year-round residents of Orleans, and the preservationists of Truro can be content in knowing that the area's biggest draw remains the beautiful Cape Cod National Seashore. When travelers envision the sandy shores and soft dunes of New England, that still-pristine park is where they'll find it—minus the crowds of other areas. At least, that is, for now.

CHATHAM TO ORLEANS

Relatively quiet compared with many of Cape Cod's larger and towns, this area has plenty of year-round residents who are deeply involved with its conservation and upkeep. A number of clean, well-kept public beaches are in the area, though be warned that even in the less tourist-swarmed areas parking in summertime can seem nearly impossible. Your best bet: Follow the beach-going rule of thumb and rise as early as you can to claim spots for both your car and your towel.

Food

Routinely named one of the best restaurants on Cape Cod by publications that tend to decide these things, ⟨ **Abba** (89 Old Colony Way, Orleans, 508/255-8144, www.abbarestaurant.com, 5 P.M.–10 P.M. Mon.–Sat.; 5 P.M.–9 P.M. Sun., 5–10 P.M. daily year-round, $18–35) dishes up an unusal combination of Thai and Mediterranean cuisines, with a bit of Moroccan décor and an Israeli chef thrown in for good measure. If the thought of grilled filet mignon with green curry pasta or grilled tuna in balsamic miso doesn't set your mouth watering, one bite will. On a more casual note there's **Sir Cricket's Fish & Chips** (Rte. 6A, Orleans, 508/255-4453, 11 A.M.–8 P.M. daily, $7–19)—also open year-round—for fried clams and oysters that are hot and tender inside, crispy out.

Information

Drop by the **Chatham Chamber of Commerce** (533 Main St., Chatham, 508/945-5199, www.chathamcapecod.org) for information on parking in the area, hotels with current vacancies, and beaches and boat landings. The **Orleans Chamber of Commerce** (44 Main St., Orleans, 508/255-1386, www.capecod-orleans.com) has notably less information to hand out, but offers several pamphlets on activities in the town; the staff can answer most questions off the tops of their heads.

EASTHAM TO TRURO

Provincetown might be the fat boy in the canoe—drawing much of the area's attention, day-trippers, and spending dollars—but for natural beauty alone, Eastham, Wellfleet, and Truro have their own spotlight. Wellfleet is home to arguably the best bivalves (clams and oysters in particular) in the nation. And Eastham, historically a farming community, provides easy access to the breathtaking National Seashore (plus several exceptional beaches that are open to non-residents).

Highland Light and the Highland House

Part museum, part working lighthouse, this 18th-century structure (27 Highland Rd., Truro, 508/487-1121, www.trurohistorical.org, 10 A.M.–5:30 P.M. mid-May–Oct., tours are $4 adults) is full of exhibits on sea memorabilia, with exhibits on shipwrecks, 17th-century weapons, and whaling gear. The observation deck of the adjoining lighthouse is one of the highest vantage points on all of Cape Cod. Children must be at least 51 inches tall to climb the lighthouse stairs.

Eastham Windmill

The oldest windmill on Cape Cod is Eastham Windmill (Rte. 6 and Samoset Rd., Eastham, 508/240-5900), built in the mid-17th century in Plymouth, moved to Provincetown in the latter part of that century, and finally moved to Eastham in 1793. Tours are offered in summertime.

Entertainment

Raw bar and oceanfront restaurant by day, music venue and bar by night, the **Beachcomber** (1120 Cahoon Hollow Rd., Wellfleet, 508/349-6055, www.thebeachcomber.com, Memorial Day–Labor Day) is a great spot for live rock, zydeco, and rockabilly bands. The small but daring **Wellfleet Harbor Actors Theatre** (Rte. 6, 508/349-6835, www.what.org) is a point of community pride for its original political satires, modern tragedies, and whodunnits for kids.

THE OUTERMOST HOUSE

A hundred years after Henry David Thoreau spent two years in the woods at Walden Pond, another Henry – writer-naturalist Henry Beston – pulled a similar retreat among the sand dunes of Cape Cod. There he catalogued the rhythms of the sea, the lashings of the storms, and the migrations of the shore birds in his classic *The Outermost House*, which still stands as one of the best natural-history books of all time. A burned-out magazine writer at the time, Beston originally only meant to spend two weeks at the home he had built about two miles from the Coast Guard Station in Eastham. But he became so enamored of the little home, named the Fo'castle after the spot on a sailing ship where the deck hands live, and the wildness of the environment that he stayed for a whole year. After the house was destroyed in a storm in 1978, a small plaque was placed in front of the Coast Guard Station to mark the spot. For more information, contact the **Henry Beston Society** at 508/246-7242 or www.henrybeston.org.

Shopping

Consignment shops don't get much better than **The Emperor's Old Clothes** (354 Main St., Wellfleet, 10 A.M.–6 P.M. Mon.–Sat.; 11 A.M.–5 P.M.Sun., 508/349-1893), stocked with a mix of elegant kimonos, brocade bags, and plush hand-knit sweaters. For far above-average gifts and furnishings, pay a visit to **Whitman House Gift Shop** (Rte. 6 at Great Hollow Rd., North Truro, 508/487-1704, www.whitmanhouse.com, 10 A.M.–6 P.M. Mon.–Sat.; 11 A.M.–5 P.M.Sun.) and find handmade Amish quilts, dining tables, and painstakingly constructed chairs.

Food

Fresher-than-fresh seafood can be found at the deceptively humble-looking **Finely JP's**

MASSACHUSETTS

(554 Rte. 6, 508/349-7500, 11 A.M.–9:30 P.M. daily, $17–29). Don't miss excellently prepared dishes like garlicky calamari and scallop fettucine. Outside of Provincetown, **(The Wicked Oyster** (50 Main St., Wellfleet, 508/349-3455, 5 P.M.–10:30 P.M. Tues.–Sat.; 5 P.M.–9 P.M.Sun.–Mon., $10–30) is about as cool as Cape Cod gets. The casual spot jumps with young well-dressed patrons supping on fennel-infused oyster stew and spinach-and-scallop salads. For plain ol' simple-but-scrumptious fried fish, get on line at **Mac's Seafood Market** (Wellfleet Town Pier, Wellfleet, 508/349-0404, www.macsseafood. com, 8 A.M.–9:30 P.M. daily June–Oct., $4–40). Order up a plate of steamers (or an entire lobster clambake) and head out back to one of the umbrella-covered picnic tables overlooking the bay.

Information

The **Eastham Tourist Information Booth** (1700 Rte. 6 at Governor Prence Rd., 508/255-3444, www.easthamchamber.com) doles out information on local businesses, maps, and local tides. Find out about local events, new restaurants, and boating and fishing information at **Wellfleet Chamber of Commerce** (1410 Rte. 6, Wellfleet, 508/349-2510, www.wellfleetchamber.com). The **Truro Information Booth** (Rte. 6 at Head of the Meadow Rd., North Truro, 508/487-1288, www.trurochamberofcommerce.com) has free booklets on the town and its hotels and restaurants, plus maps and recreational information.

(CAPE COD NATIONAL SEASHORE

Unquestionably one of the Cape's greatest treasures, the National Seashore is an overwhelmingly beautiful utopian swath of coast, encompassing countless warm-weather activities—from camping and swimming to hiking, bike riding, off-roading, and sunset-supervising. Start your expedition of the park's 43,000 acres at the **Salt Pond Visitor Center** (Rte. 6 at Nauset Rd., 508/255-3421, www.nps.gov/caco, 9 A.M.–4:30 P.M. daily, extended hours

in summer) to stock up on maps and information on where to find the best bike trails, lighthouses, and picnic areas.

SPORTS AND RECREATION

Home to bike paths, nature trails, beautiful lakes, and the **Highland Golf Links** (Lighthouse Rd., North Truro, 508/487-9201), the Cape's oldest golf course, lower Cape Cod has no shortage of ways to keep visitors active.

Beaches

Known around town as an excellent family spot, the clean and well-maintained **Corn Hill Beach** (Castle Rd., off Rte. 6, Truro, 508/349-3635, non-resident parking $10 per day)—named such because it was where Pilgrims had once found corn gathered by Native Americans—has easy parking, views of Provincetown, and a warm bay for swimming. The sandy ocean beach of **Cahoon Hollow** (Cahoon Hollow Rd., Rte. 6, Wellfleet, 508/349-9818, parking $15 per day), meanwhile, gets considerably more crowded, but can be counted on by parents to usually have a lifeguard on duty, by surfers to have decent waves, and by seafood lovers to have fresh specimens at its restaurant, the Beachcomber (1120 Cahoon Hollow Rd., Wellfleet, 508/349-6055, www.thebeachcomber.com, Memorial Day–Labor Day). A veritable magnet for kids in the on-season, **Oyster Pond** (1233 Main St., Chatham, 508/945-5180, free parking) also boasts waters warm enough to stay welcoming in the shoulder season, when things calm down and the sheltered pond regains some serenity.

Boating

Whether you're heading to one of the area's many lakes and rivers or straight to the ocean, almost all of the outfitting you'll need is at **Jack's Boat Rentals** (Rte. 6 at Cahoon Hollow Rd. and at Gull Pond, Wellfleet; Nickerson State Park, Brewster, 508/349-9808, www.jacksboatrental.com). In addition to small boats like kayaks and sunfish, they also offer sailing lessons and guided tours by the hour.

ACCOMMODATIONS
$100-150

With its well-maintained gardens and homey rooms, the **Nantucket House of Chatham** (2647 Main St., Chatham, 508/432-5641, $130–185), an old white Greek Revival house within easy distance to downtown Chatham and the beach, is a veritable bargain for the area.

$150-250

Nestled on the stunning marsh of a private Wellfleet beach, **Aunt Sukie's Bed and Breakfast** (525 Chequesset Neck Rd., Wellfleet, 508/349-2804, www.auntsukies.com, $195–270) is a peaceful and friendly place to stay with antiques-filled rooms (some with fireplaces and water views) and first-rate homemade continental breakfasts every morning.

$250 and Up

Arguably the premiere resort on all of Cape Cod, (**Chatham Bars Inn** (297 Shore Rd., Chatham, 508/945-0096, www.chathambars-inn.com, $299–685) pulls out all the stops on subdued luxury. It's one of the area's most lauded—and with a full-service spa, a restaurant serving food that's nothing short of impeccable, and a breezy spot on gorgeous Pleasant Bay, it's easy to see why.

GETTING THERE

The **Plymouth & Brockton** (8 Industrial Park Rd., Plymouth, 508/746-0378, www.p-b.com) bus line hits every major—and just about every minor—Cape Cod town, from the tip of Provincetown all the way to Boston. Fares vary; call for schedules.

Provincetown

Jutting into the cold waters of the Atlantic, the little village of Provincetown is perched both literally and figuratively on the edge. Literally, because the tip of Long Point is the farthest fingertip of Cape Cod. Figuratively, because like many remote peninsulas, the colorful town has been a magnet over the years for visionaries, artists, and eccentrics. The town is also well known for its active gay and lesbian community, and since Massachusetts legalized gay marriage in 2004, its main drag has been alive with wedding processions. The history of the town, however, is much more complex. A heavy Portuguese influence lingers from when it was predominantly a fishing village, and the "blessing of the fleet" is still an event. Apart from that, P-Town (as it's known) is home to the oldest artists colony in the country. Painters like Charles Hawthorne and poets and playwrights like Eugene O'Neill and Tennessee Williams once painted and wrote masterpieces in shacks among the dunes. Since then, the community has resisted the "resort-ification" that has subsumed other artists colonies, giving the town a living air of creativity and anything-goes spontaneity. If P-Town is a state of mind, it is one that is open to anything—exactly the attitude you should bring to a visit here.

SIGHTS
(Provincetown Whale Watch

Just north of the tip of P-Town is a sand-and-gravel rise in the ocean named Stellwagen Bank. Nineteen miles long and six miles wide, the bank causes an upwelling of nutrient-rich currents on either side that supports an aquarium of ocean life. Among the sealife present are dolphins, sea turtles, and, of course, whales. There's nothing quite like being in the middle of the ocean and seeing the giant fluke of a leviathan crest above the blue waves—or if you are lucky, seeing a humpback or right whale breach before your eyes.

The two fleets that leave from Macmillan Wharf both guarantee sightings of these magnificent creatures. **Portuguese Princess Excursions** (800/826-9300, www.province-townwhalewatch.com, Apr.–Oct.) bills itself as an ecofriendly whale watch, with naturalists who collect data and provide an environmental

MASSACHUSETTS

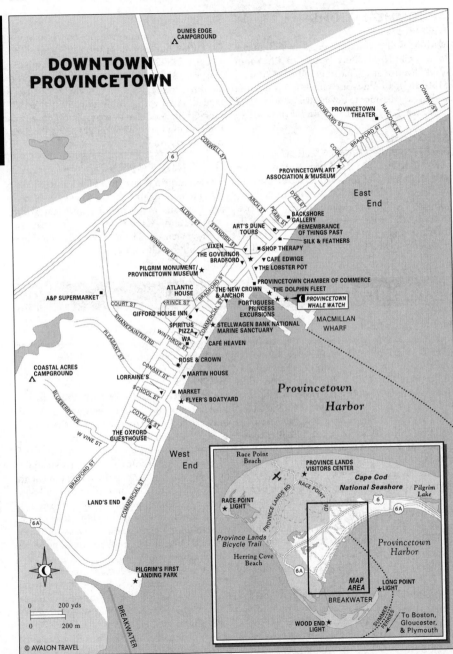

DOWNTOWN PROVINCETOWN

DUNES EDGE CAMPGROUND

CONWAY ST

HOWLAND ST

PROVINCETOWN THEATER

BRADFORD ST

HANCOCK ST

COOK ST

CONWELL ST

6

ALDEN ST

STANDISH ST

WINSLOW ST

ARCH ST

PEARL ST

DYER ST

PROVINCETOWN ART ASSOCIATION & MUSEUM

East End

BACKSHORE GALLERY
REMEMBRANCE OF THINGS PAST
SILK & FEATHERS

ART'S DUNE TOURS

SHOP THERAPY

VIXEN
THE GOVERNOR BRADFORD

CAFÉ EDWIGE
THE LOBSTER POT

PILGRIM MONUMENT/ PROVINCETOWN MUSEUM

BRADFORD ST

PROVINCETOWN CHAMBER OF COMMERCE
THE DOLPHIN FLEET

ATLANTIC HOUSE

A&P SUPERMARKET

COURT ST

PRINCE ST

THE NEW CROWN & ANCHOR

COMMERCIAL ST

PORTUGUESE PRINCESS EXCURSIONS

PROVINCETOWN WHALE WATCH

GIFFORD HOUSE INN

SHANKPAINTER RD

SPIRITUS PIZZA
WA

WINTHROP ST

STELLWAGEN BANK NATIONAL MARINE SANCTUARY

MACMILLAN WHARF

CAFÉ HEAVEN

PLEASANT ST

COASTAL ACRES CAMPGROUND

CONANT ST

ROSE & CROWN

MARTIN HOUSE

LORRAINE'S

SCHOOL ST

Provincetown Harbor

MARKET
FLYER'S BOATYARD

BLUEBERRY AVE

COTTAGE ST

W VINE ST

THE OXFORD GUESTHOUSE

West End

BRADFORD ST

COMMERCIAL ST

LAND'S END

6A

PILGRIM'S FIRST LANDING PARK

0   200 yds
0   200 m

BREAKWATER

© AVALON TRAVEL

Inset map

Race Point Beach

PROVINCE LANDS VISITORS CENTER

PROVINCE LANDS RD

RACE POINT RD

RACE POINT LIGHT

Cape Cod National Seashore

6

Pilgrim Lake

6A

Province Lands Bicycle Trail

Herring Cove Beach

6A

Provincetown Harbor

MAP AREA

LONG POINT LIGHT

BREAKWATER

WOOD END LIGHT

SUMMER FERRIES

To Boston, Gloucester, & Plymouth

commentary. **The Dolphin Fleet** (Macmillan Wharf, 800/826-9300, www.whalewatch.com, Apr.–Oct.) is the older and more experienced outfit, touting itself as being especially child-friendly. The two companies recently merged in 2009, ensuring consistency in prices, which are $39 for adults and $31 for children 5–12. Both have regular trips in the morning, afternoon, and at sunset.

Pilgrim Monument

Before the Pilgrims touched down at Plymouth Rock, they spent five weeks in Provincetown, where they nailed down the definitive version of the Mayflower Contract and made their first "encounters" with Native Americans. Memorializing the pilgrims' stay here is a monument (High Pole Hill Rd., 508/487-1310, www.pilgrim-monument.org, 9 A.M.–5 P.M. daily Apr.–May and mid-Sept.–Nov.; 9 A.M.–7 P.M. daily June–mid-Sept., $7 adults, $5 seniors and students, $3.50 children 4–14, free children under 4) that has become a symbol of Provincetown for generations of

© HYANNIS AREA CHAMBER OF COMMERCE

Pilgrim Monument

visitors. Looking at it, you'd think the Pilgrims had come from Italy, not England, since the tower is a copy of a *torre* from Sienna, complete with crenellated top and gargoyles perched on the sides. The walk to the top utilizes 60 ramps and 116 steps. Short of a plane, it's virtually the only way to behold the geography of the Cape in its glory. On a clear day, you can see Boston. At the base of the monument is the **Provincetown Museum,** which details the Pilgrims' brief stay here as only kitschy dioramas can.

Lighthouses

Provincetown has an embarrassment of riches when it comes to lighthouses, with three real lookers. Only **Race Point Light** (Race Point Beach, Rte. 6, 508/487-9930, www.racepoint-lighthouse.net) is easily accessible. The 45-foot tower was built in 1876 and is open for tours on some Saturdays from 10 A.M. to 2 P.M. The adjoining keeper's house is also a summer bed-and-breakfast ($145–185) with the most dramatic location on the Cape. The other two beacons—Wood End Light and Long Point Light—stand sentinel on the bay side of Provincetown's curving claw. You can hike to Wood End across the breakwater at the west end of town, and from there walk the coast to Long Point. For an easier trip, take a shuttle from **Flyer's Boatyard** (131A Commercial St., 508/487-0898, www.flyersrentals.com, 10 A.M.–6 P.M. daily, $8 one-way, $12 round-trip), which also runs a pink party boat for sunset cruises.

Other Sights

It isn't everywhere you can visit and view dozens of artistic renderings of the places you've just seen. Since the 1920s, the **Provincetown Art Association and Museum** (460 Commercial St., 508/487-1750, www.paam.org) has been offering instruction to artists young and old at its P-Town campus. Over the years, it has collected thousands of paintings from artists like Charles Hawthorne and Ross Moffet, who have gone on to achieve some measure of fame. The collection, along changing exhibitions on Cape Cod themes,

Provincetown Art Association and Museum

is displayed in a new waterfront museum. To learn more about **Stellwagen Bank National Marine Sanctuary** visit the free exhibit center (205-209 Commercial St., 781/545-8026, www.stellwagen.noaa.gov, 11 A.M.–6 P.M. daily July–Aug., plus Fri.–Sat. June and Sept., free), which explains the unique habitat with touch-screen computer exhibits and other displays. Step on the same ground that the pilgrims did at **Pilgrim's First Landing Park** at the west end of Commercial Street. A plaque there memorializes the Pilgrims' touch-down on November 21, 1620.

ENTERTAINMENT

Local thespians date the beginning of American drama to 1916, when the first Eugene O'Neill play was performed on P-Town's Lewis Wharf. The theater community was reborn in 2001 with the construction of the beautiful 200-seat **Provincetown Theater** (238 Bradford St., 508/487-7487, www.provincetowntheater.org, $20–75), which stages everything from campy musicals to heart-wrenching original dramas. On Friday nights, the shirts come off at **The Atlantic House** (4–6 Masonic Pl., 508/487-3821, www.ahouse.com), P-Town's premier gay nightclub for two decades, with a main club and smaller "macho room" for fans of leather and Levis.

No matter what you're looking for, you'll find it (and maybe more than you bargained for) at **The New Crown & Anchor** (247 Commercial St., 508/487-1430, www.onlyatthecrown.com), an entertainment complex with a high-energy dance club, "video bar," leather bar, and cabaret that caters to a mix of queer and straight clientele. Across the street, **The Governor Bradford** (312 Commercial St., 508/487-2781) draws a mix of tourists and locals for weekend karaoke led by a caustic drag queen. Meanwhile, lesbian women and their friends head to **Vixen** (336 Commercial St., 508/487-6424) for dancing, pool, and sometimes cabaret and folk music performances.

EVENTS

Filmmaker John Waters is a regular at the **Provincetown International Film Festival** (508/487-3456, www.P-Townfilmfest.org, mid-June, $35–2000), which showcases truly independent films. The town's thriving fishing community celebrates its heritage during the weekend-long **Provincetown Portuguese**

Festival (508/487-0086, www.provincetown-portuguesefestival.com, late June, free) that culminates with the annual "Blessing of the Fleet." The **Fourth of July Celebration** (508/487-7000, www.P-Townchamber.com, July 4, free) has the best beachside fireworks on the Cape. Last but not least, **Carnival Week** (508/487-2313, www.P-Town.org, late Aug., $5–125) is a seven-day Mardi Gras that features a parade, elaborate dance parties, and performances by internationally renowned drag queens.

SHOPPING

Patchouli wafts from **Shop Therapy** (346 Commercial St., 508/487-8970, www.shoptherapy.com), a tie-dyed emporium with everything you need for the next Grateful Dead reunion. Women's clothing shop **Silk & Feathers** (377 Commercial St., 508/487-2057, www.silkandfeathers.com, 10 A.M.–7 P.M. daily May–Sept.; closed Oct.–Apr.) sells a well-edited selection of cutting-edge designs and hip, high-end dresses. Upscale **Market** (145 Commercial St., 508/487-1772, 10 A.M.–5:30 P.M. Mon.–Sat. June–Oct.; closed mid-Oct.–May) features designer men's clothing from the likes of Versace and Paul Smith. More than an antiques store, **Remembrance of Things Past** (376 Commercial St., 508/487-9443, www.things-past.com, 10 A.M.–5 P.M. daily) peddles collectibles including Betty Boop lamps and tickets to the 1940 World's Fair. **Wa** (184 Commercial St., 508/487-6355, www.waharmony.com) carries bamboo wind chimes, Tibetan altar tables, and real-life South American bugs. **Backshore Gallery** (394 Commercial St., 508/487-6870, 12 P.M.–5 P.M. daily, or by appointment), www.backshoregallery.com) sells art inspired by—and created in—the dune shacks.

SPORTS AND RECREATION
Beaches

The most stunning beach on the Cape is **Race Point Beach,** an eight-mile stretch of sand with crashing waves and sport fishing in the breakers, dominated by its eponymous lighthouse. More sheltered is **Herring Cove Beach,** a peaceful swath on the bay side

separated into straight, lesbian, and gay areas. The beach was once the province of nude sunbathers; however rangers have since quashed the practice, so disrobe at your own risk. Both beaches are accessible by public bus. Shuttles leave Macmillan Wharf for Race Point every 40 minutes 7 A.M.–8 P.M. and for Herring Cove every 20 minutes 9 A.M.–a half-hour before sunset. To get to Race Point by bike, head down Conwell Street to Race Point Road, where a bike path parallels the roadway. For Herring Cove, cyclists have two options: they can fight the traffic along Route 6, or take the longer but nicer ride along the bike path through the Province Lands. Pick up the trail at the Beech Forest Parking Area off of Race Point Road.

Province Lands

Provincetown is named for the Province Lands, a seemingly desolate area of dunes and beach grass that teems with its own unique ecosystem. Heavily forested when the Pilgrims first landed, the area was later clear cut, and erosion worked its magic to expose sand along the back side of the town. Eventually it became home to isolated dune shacks where artists and playwrights created with only the waves and wind for inspiration. **Province Lands Visitors Center** (Race Point Rd., 508/487-1256, www.nps.gov/caco, 9 A.M.–5 P.M. May–Oct.) has good exhibits on the flora and fauna, as well as guided nature walks in the area, which is now part of the Cape Cod National Seashore.

Perhaps the best way to explore the dunes is through **Art's Dune Tours** (4 Standish St., 508/487-1950, www.artsdunetours.com, $25 adults, $17 children 6–11, free children under 6), which has operated tours in 4x4 vehicles for 60 years. Now run by Art's son Rob, the tours take in a sandy moonscape where hawks ride wind currents in search of field mice and magenta petals of the *rosa rogosa* light up the beach grass. Along the way are the beach shacks, austere in their crumbling grey-shingled solitude. If you'd rather see the dunes under your own power, the paved

Province Lands Bike Trail meanders for five miles in and out of the dunes. Bikes can be rented from **P-Town Bikes** (42 Bradford St., 508/487-8735, www.P-Townbikes.com). You can also walk into the heart of the dunes along the Snail Trail, which begins on Route 6 just before the water tower. The 3.5-mile path leads to Race Point Beach. Save strength for the hike back, however, as tired legs make for slow going over sand.

Boating and Fishing

The largest selection of boats for rent on Cape Cod is at **Flyer's Boat Rentals** (131A Commercial St., 508/487-0898, www.flyersrentals.com), which has both motor boats and sailboats. If you are a lubber, lessons by expert sailors start at $80 for two hours. The 73-foot gaff-rigged schooner *Bay Lady II* (20 Berry Ln., 508/487-9308, www.sailcapecod.com, $20–25 adults, $12 children) sails several times daily for the Corn Hill bluffs and Long Point Light. Sportfishing boats lining Macmillan Wharf include the *Ginny G* (508/246-3656, www.ginnygcapecodcharters.com), which goes in search of bluefish, bass, cod, and tuna. **Venture Athletics Kayak Shop** (237 Commercial St., 508/487-9442) rents sea kayaks and leads guided tours to Wood End Light.

Camping

Located at the gateway to town, **Dune's Edge Campground** (386 Rte. 6, 508/487-9815, www.dunes-edge.com, $30–40 for basic sites) has 85 tent sites in a wooded area with hot showers and laundry.

ACCOMMODATIONS
Under $100

A painted figurehead greets guests arriving at **The Rose & Crown** (158 Commercial St., 508/487-3332, www.provincetown.com/rosecrown, $55–285), a unique guesthouse located in the center of town. Rooms are small but imaginatively designed; one is decked out with purple fabrics and Victorian antiques, another features exposed beams and a stately

brass bed. Three less-expensive rooms upstairs share a bath.

$100-150

Once the last stop for the stagecoach from Boston, **Gifford House Inn** (9 Carver St., 508/487-0688, www.giffordhouse.com, $65–282) has hosted Ulysses S. Grant and Theodore Roosevelt. The airy guesthouse features spacious guest rooms and cocktails served nightly on a wraparound front porch.

$150-250

English elegance is just the first of many contradictions at (**The Oxford Guesthouse** (8 Cottage St., 508/487-9103, www.oxfordguesthouse.com, $119–329), an oasis of tranquility just steps from the hubbub of Commercial Street. The expat British owners are both hyper-attentive and delightfully deferential, and room decor is both masculine and chic, with rich colors and welcome amenities such as fireplaces and 500-count sheets.

$250 and Up

For a truly over-the-top experience, check into **Land's End** (22 Commercial St., 508/487-0706, www.landsendinn.com, $145–570), a secluded inn complete with a tower overlooking the ocean. Inside, the owner's exceptional collection of art nouveau antiques fills every conceivable nook of the common areas. Guest rooms feature skylights, interior balconies, and domed ceilings and decor from Victorian to Moroccan.

FOOD

The best brunch in town can be found at **Cafe Heaven** (199 Commercial St., 508/487-9639, $7–16), a cozy storefront with big, bold art splattered on the walls; it also serves affordable sandwiches and homemade breads and soups. At the end of a hard night of clubbing, the entire town meets at the legendary **Spiritus Pizza** (190 Commercial St., 508/487-2808, www.spirituspizza.com, 11:30 A.M.–2 A.M. daily April–Oct.; closed Nov.–March, $18–27) to gorge on steaming-hot slices and recount the night's gossip. Imagine Mexican-Continental fusion, then imagine it being delicious. That's what you'll find at **Lorraine's Restaurant** (133 Commercial St., 508/487-6074, 11:30 A.M.–10 P.M. Mon.–Sat., 5:30 P.M.–10 P.M. Sun. June–Sept.; hours vary Oct.–May., $16–26), which goes beyond burritos to offer items such as rack of lamb with roasted garlic chipotle and cognac demi-glacé. The dark-wood barroom also features 100 different sipping tequilas.

For the freshest seafood and a view of the harbor, local families crowd **The Lobster Pot** (321 Commercial St., 508/487-0842, www.P-Townlobsterpot.com, 10 A.M.–11 P.M. daily May–Oct.; 12 P.M.–9 P.M. daily Nov–April; closed Jan., $16–27), which serves fried clams, boiled lobster, and Portuguese specialties. The highly formal **Martin House** (157 Commercial St., 508/487-1327, 12 P.M.–10 P.M. Mon.–Fri.; 10 A.M.–10 P.M. Sat.–Sun. June–Sept.; 5:30 P.M.–10 P.M. Tues.–Sat. Oct.–May, $16–33) seems out of place in Provincetown, but its location in an old captain's house with a fireplace and bay view proves there is something to be said for old-fashioned romance. If popularity is any measure, P-Town's best breakfast is at **Café Edwige** (333 Commercial St., 2nd floor, 508/487-2008, 8 A.M.–9 P.M. Mon.–Fri., 5 P.M.–10 P.M. Sat.–Sun. April.–Oct; 12 P.M.–9 P.M. Mon.–Sat., 5 P.M.–10 P.M. Sun. Nov.–March, $19–29). Given the food-savvy palates in this town, acclaim like this is no small thing. Among the touches that explain the approving chorus are a choice of tabouli or home fries with the big fluffy omelets, pots of honey for tea drinkers, broiled flounder among the usual pancake and egg options, and fresh flowers on each table. Though it's only seasonal, if you miss a table for breakfast, you can try again at dinner Thursday–Sunday. (Ask for a window table—it's one of the best people-watching seats in town.)

INFORMATION

The **Provincetown Chamber of Commerce** (307 Commercial St. at Lopes Sq., 508/487-3424, www.P-Townchamber.com) runs a visitors center just off the ferry landing. **Provincetown Trolley** (508/487-9483) offers 40-minute sightseeing tours leaving from town hall every half hour.

GETTING THERE AND AROUND

The easiest way to P-Town is by ferry. **Bay State Cruise Company** (World Trade Center, 200 Seaport Blvd., Boston, 877/783-3779, www.baystatecruises.com, mid-May–mid-Oct) runs both a 90-minute fast ferry ($49 one-way/$79 round-trip adults, $44/$69 seniors, $32/$58 children) and a three-hour slow boat ($22/$44 adults, free children). **Cape Air** (800/352-0714, www.flycapeair.com) runs daily flights from Boston. Buses by **Plymouth & Brockton** (508/746-0378, www.p-b.com) stop at the Chamber of Commerce building.

The **Cape Cod Transit Authority** runs the Breeze shuttle (800/352-7155, www.thebreeze.info), which provides transport to the airport, beaches, and town center. Travel in style with **Mercedes Cab** (508/487-3333), an actual vintage Mercedes.

Martha's Vineyard

Unlike the Hamptons or Aspen—where the beautiful people compete to see who can look more beautiful—the island of Martha's Vineyard is where the rich and the famous like to let their hair down. Titans of Wall Street walk around Edgartown with sand in their rolled-up Dockers, while Hollywood actresses don sandals and leave (most of) their makeup at home. The island really was covered with wild grape vines when explorer Benjamin Gosnold first happened upon it in 1602 and named it for either his daughter or mother-in-law (you be the judge). Many years later, the scenic island 25 miles off the Upper Cape developed a reputation as a retreat for writers and artists. Celebrities followed, and residents got used to seeing the likes of Billy Joel and Michael J. Fox at the corner market.

All that ratcheted up a notch in the 1990s, when president Bill Clinton made the Vineyard his "summer White House," and an A-list of Hollywood liberals such as Sharon Stone and Sean Penn descended on the beaches. While the celebrity wattage has dimmed since then, the island still exists somewhere between the planes of it-island and laid-back retreat. The landscape of the Vineyard is the star attraction, with endless beach roads and peaceful salt-water ponds, often lit by the stunning golden light that drew the artists here in the first place.

ORIENTATION

Residents divide the island into down-island (east) and up-island (west). The former is home to the island's three main population centers: touristy Vineyard Haven, chic Edgartown, and charming Oak Bluffs. Up-island is more rural, with the cow pastures of West Tisbury and Chilmark sharing space with the scenic fishing village of Menemsha and the cliffs of Aquinnah.

DOWN-ISLAND SIGHTS
◖ Oak Bluffs

Nowhere else in the world looks quite like the seaside village of Oak Bluffs, which grew from a Methodist revival camp into an African American summer enclave. In the 19th century, minister Thomas Mayhew founded a summer camp for Methodists. As pilgrims flocked here to hear religious speakers, many of them turned their tents into more permanent structures. Now the town common overlooking the beach is surrounded by literally hundreds of **gingerbread cottages**—miniature Victorians hung with decorative woodwork icing and capped with towers and turrets. Every night during the summer months, romantics bring their beach blankets and white wine to sit around the gazebo and watch the sun douse itself in the harbor.

Oak Bluffs has always had a more festive attitude than the rest of the island, dating back from the amusements and theaters founded to entertain revivalists. The **Flying Horses Carousel** (Oak Bluffs Ave., Oak Bluffs, 508/693-9481, 10 A.M.–10 P.M. Sat.–Sun. Easter–early May; 10 A.M.–10 P.M. daily early May–mid-Oct., $1.50) is still the oldest operating carousel in the United States. During summer months, throngs of children wait to ride one of 20 carved wooden horses and take turns grabbing for the brass ring. The town is also refreshingly multicultural compared to the rest of Martha's Vineyard and is home to a large African American community, particularly during the summer months when wealthy vacationers descend on the island. Many well-known African American celebrities have made their summer homes here, including Vernon Jordan and Spike Lee.

Edgartown and Vineyard Haven

The town of Edgartown has the oldest architecture on the island, including many examples of Federal-style homes built by whaling captains in the 18th century, complete with white clapboard facades and widow's walks. While the Vineyard never achieved the same prominence in whaling as New Bedford or

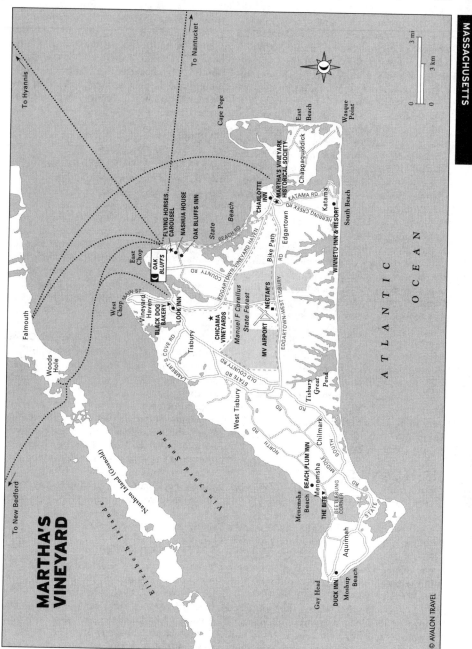

MARTHA'S VINEYARD

To Hyannis

To Nantucket

To New Bedford

Falmouth

Woods Hole

Elizabeth Islands

Naushon Island (Gosnold)

Cape Poge

East Beach

Waque Point

Chappaquiddick

MARTHA'S VINEYARD HISTORICAL SOCIETY

Katama

South Beach

CHARLOTTE INN

KATAMA RD

Edgartown

FLYING HORSES CAROUSEL
NASHUA HOUSE
OAK BLUFFS INN

WINNETU INN & RESORT

HERRING CREEK RD

Beach

State

BEACH RD

East Chop

OAK BLUFFS

EDGARTOWN-VINEYARD HAVEN

COUNTY RD

Bike Path

EDGARTOWN-WEST TISBURY RD

West Chop

Vineyard Haven

MAIN ST

BLACK DOG BAKERY
LOOK INN

Tisbury

Manuel F Correllus State Forest

NECTAR'S

MV AIRPORT

CHICAMA VINEYARDS

LAMBERT'S COVE RD

STATE RD

OLD COUNTY RD

West Tisbury

Vineyard Sound

Tisbury Great Pond

NORTH RD

ATLANTIC OCEAN

BEACH PLUM INN

Menemsha Beach

Menemsha

Chilmark

THE BITE

MIDDLE RD

BEETLEBUNG CORNER

SOUTH RD

STATE RD

Guy Head

DUCK INN

Moshup Beach

Aquinnah

3 mi

3 km

© AVALON TRAVEL

Nantucket, you can learn more about the history at the **Martha's Vineyard Historical Society** (59 School St., Edgartown, 508/627-4441, www.marthasvineyardhistory.org, 10 A.M.–5 P.M. Mon.–Sat. mid-June–mid-Oct.; 10 A.M.–4 P.M. Mon.–Sat. mid-Oct.–mid-June, $6–7 adults, $4 children 6–15, free children under 6), a complex of buildings filled with more than enough old artifacts to while away a rainy day. Exhibits include scrimshaw whale's teeth, Wampanoag arrowheads, models of whaling ships, and diaries of early settlers. The centerpiece of the compound, literally, is the huge Fresnel prismatic lens that used to shine from atop the Gay Head lighthouse.

The town of Vineyard Haven has its own collection of old captain's houses, though not as impressive as those in Edgartown. It is also known as the main center for the island's artists community, with galleries sprinkled throughout town. Near the ferry landing is the **Black Dog Bakery** (11 Water St., Vineyard Haven, 508/693-4786, www.theblackdog.com, $7), which has grown from a small sandwich shop supplying hungry vacationers boarding the ferry to a veritable symbol of the island. A complex of buildings now sells T-shirts, hats, beach bags, tennis balls, and every other imaginable object emblazoned with the eatery's trademark black Labrador. The symbol has long since gone from cachet to cliché, especially after Bill Clinton gave a Black Dog cap to intern-turned-mistress Monica Lewinksy.

UP-ISLAND SIGHTS

Driving through the long stretches of pastures and fields south and west of Vineyard Haven, you can quickly forget that you are on an island. The western side of the island is more "real" than the glitzy towns to the east, with sleepy corner stores and cattle barns. In the center of the Vineyard is, fittingly, **Chicama Vineyards** (Stoney Hill Rd., off State Rd., West Tisbury, 508/693-0309), the first winery in Massachusetts, which offers tours and samples of its wines, mustards, and vinegars. Nowhere is more of a throwback to the early days of the island than the pristinely crumbling

fishing village of **Menemsha,** a smattering of grey-shingled shacks and beach houses beside a small harbor of fishing trawlers and lobster boats. On the far western end of the island, Aquinnah is home to both a Wampanoag community and the breathtaking clay cliffs of **Gay Head,** which glow with orange and purple hues in the afternoon sun.

EVENTS

Summer on the Vineyard officially kicks off with the **Oak Bluffs Harbor Festival** (Oak Bluffs, mid-June, www.oakbluffsmv.com), a carnival full of live music, craft vendors, and food booths along the waterfront. Competition is fierce for the annual chalk-art contest. Every Sunday during the warmer months, local artists and craftsmen display their wares at the **Vineyard Artisans Fair** (Grange Hall, West Tisbury, 508/693-8989, www.vineyardartisans.com, 10 A.M.–2 P.M. Sun. June–Sept.; 10 A.M.–2 P.M. Thurs. July–Aug.). There is always a good selection of watercolors and photography of island scenes. One of the most anticipated nights of the summer is the **Grand Illumination** (Campground, Oak Bluffs, 508/693-0525, mid-Aug.), when the gingerbread cottages of the Oak Bluffs revival camp are all lit up with thousands of paper lanterns. Depending on your frame of mind, the effect is romantic or intensely spiritual. The week following the illumination is the annual **Martha's Vineyard Agricultural Society Livestock Show and Fair** (West Tisbury, 508/693-4343, www.mvas.vineyard.net), which for almost 150 years has celebrated the farming history of the island. Displays include sheep and cow pens, wood-chopping competitions, country bands, fireworks, and, of course, a Ferris wheel.

ENTERTAINMENT

The island's biggest nightclub, **Nectar's** (17 Airport Rd., Edgartown, 508/693-1137, www.nectarsmv.com), draws bands from throughout the northeast to its secluded up-island location. A satellite location of the Burlington nightclub that launched cult band Phish, its offerings tend towards funk and reggae. Several bars in Oak

CELEBRITY-SPOTTING

For decades, Martha's Vineyard had been the unofficial playground of everyone from legends like Jacqueline Kennedy Onassis and Walter Cronkite to singers like Carly Simon and Billy Joel. Then, in the summer of 1993, along came President Bill Clinton and family, who made the island their vacationing ground for years running, and drew the national spotlight to the resort community. In their wake came waves of Hollywood celebrities and Wall Street moguls alike: Sharon Stone reportedly bought a secluded multimillion-dollar property up-island, Mick Jagger made visits, landing on his helipad just off the beaches of Edgartown, and drew the late Princess Diana came to sail in its salty waters. That trend has continued – swelled, even – ever since the mid-1990s, to a point where celebrity spotting has become as much a favorite island recreation as fishing, sunbathing, and biking. Is that Ted Danson over there at the bar? Did anyone see Spike Lee eating at the Black Dog last night? Diane Sawyer was at the farmers market this morning! The island has become such a scene that it was only natural that Barack Obama would vacation on the island after becoming president in 2009 – taking at least one well-marked bike ride along Shore Rd. with a small army of secret security agents. True or not (and often they are), rumors of star sightings rumble through the island all summer long – usually spread by giddy summer and weekend visitors, while the year-round residents, by now jaded to the influx of glitz, tend to greet the gossip with nonchalant shrugs.

Bluffs also feature live music at night, including **Offshore Brewing Company** (Kennebec Ave., Oak Bluffs, 508/693-2626, www.offshoreale.com), and **The Lampost** (111 Circuit Ave., 508/693-4032), which also sports a sweaty dance floor catering to the under-30 set.

SHOPPING
Oak Bluffs
The colorful jumble of odds and ends spread throughout **Craftworks** (42 Circuit Ave., Oak Bluffs, 508/693-7463, www.craftworksgallery.com) is actually a dream team of artwork, all handmade by contemporary American artists. The highlights include nearly life-size papier-mâché cows, funky butterfly garden benches, and exquisitely carved and painted wooden plaques. Located a short drive north of town, the **Book Den East** (71 New York Ave., Oak Bluffs, 508/693-3946, www.bookden.com) is a musty old barn filled to the eaves with secondhand books; check out their collection of vintage postcards.

Vineyard Haven
Owner Carly Simon (who's also been known to sing a tune from time to time) sees to it that **Midnight Farm** (18 Water-Cromwell Ln., Vineyard Haven, 508/693-1997, www.midnightfarm.net) is stocked with a smorgasbord of high-end, quasi-bohemian wares: beaded moccasins and sequined dresses, handmade honey and soaps, etched antique cocktail glasses, and shabby-chic furniture. Opposite the Black Dog Tavern, on the dead-end lane headed toward the harbor, is **stina sayre design** (13 Beach St. Extension, 508/560-1011, www.stinasayre.com, year-round by appointment or chance), a small atelier of women's couture. If you're on the island around Thanksgiving you can catch Sayre's annual fashion show at the Mansion House, but she welcomes drop-ins, too, as she enjoys meeting potential clients in person. The very presence of **The Devil's Dictionary** (9 Main St., 508/693-0372, 10 A.M.–10 P.M. Mon.–Sat., noon–7 P.M. Sun. mid-June–mid-Sept.; off-season hours vary; closed Feb.–Mar.) on Main Street is one of those defiant gestures proving that the Vineyard is not just your parent's family resort. If you must have something emblazoned with a Black Dog, **B.D. Gear** (11B Water St., Vineyard Haven, 508/693-7381, www.theblackdog.com, 10 A.M.–5 P.M.

daily April–Dec.; 12 P.M.–5 P.M. daily March–April; closed Jan.–Feb.) sells T-shirts, mugs, backpacks, and tennis balls that sport the Labrador profile.

Edgartown

Awash in Edgartown's pink-and-green sea of preppy boutiques, **The Great Put On** (Dock St., Edgartown, 508/627-5495, 10 A.M.–6 P.M. Mon.–Sat.; 11 A.M.–5 P.M. Sun. May–Oct.; 12 P.M.–5 P.M. Mon.–Sat.; closed Sun. Nov.–April; hours vary in Jan.) is a refreshing blast of innovative women's clothing from designers like Moschino and Vivienne Tam.

Up-Island

The bluefish icon of casual clothing store **Menemsha Blues** (Basin Rd., Menemsha, 508/693-9599, www.menemshablues.com, 10 A.M.–5 P.M. daily in summer; closed Nov.–May) has replaced the black dog as the island symbol of choice. The shop also has branches in Vineyard Haven (36 Water St.), Edgartown (Dock St.), and Oak Bluffs (15 Circuit Ave.).

SPORTS AND RECREATION
Beaches

The most accessible beach on the island is **Owen Park Beach,** off Main Street in Vineyard Haven. The strip of sand at the bottom of a grassy hill affords a view of the sailboats in the harbor. Despite the two miles of pristine sand and gentle surf, you may feel nervous getting in the water at **Joseph Sylvia State Beach** along Beach Road between Oak Bluffs and Edgartown. After all, it was along this stretch that much of the movie *Jaws* was filmed. A more dramatic landscape is **Katama Beach,** a narrow barrier beach near Edgartown, with surf crashing on one side and a warm salt-water lagoon on the other. **Lobsterville Beach,** near Aquinnah, is a favorite for beachcombing, with plenty of shells and sea glass that wash up on the shore. Bring your bike, however, as there is no parking along the road.

Biking

A bike path runs alongside Beach Road from Oak Bluffs to Edgartown, so you can focus on the beautiful view, not oncoming traffic. Winds off of the waves can sometimes make for slow going, however. An easier ride is to take the ferry from Edgartown to the small island of Chappaquiddick, and bike the two miles through pitch pines and protected dunes to **Wasque Reservation.** The beach at the end is ideal for sunbathing. More challenging is the backcountry route from Vineyard Haven to Aquinnah. The hilly 20-mile round-trip offers good exercise and amazingly varied scenery. After lunch in Menemsha, you can cheat the last two miles with a bike ferry to Aquinnah.

Nature Walks

Martha's Vineyard abounds with bird life, and you can spot wood ducks, ospreys, and even nesting barn owls at the **Felix Neck Wildlife Sanctuary** (off Edgartown-Vineyard Haven Rd., Edgartown, 508/627-4850, www.mas-saudubon.org), a rambling preserve of salt marsh and beach meadow. If you prefer flora to fauna, island naturalist Polly Hill gathered nearly 1,000 different species of plants at the **Polly Hill Arboretum** (809 State Rd., West Tisbury, 508/693-9426, www.pollyhillarbo-retum.org, sunrise–sunset daily, $5 requested donation for adults), which has miles of paths through wildflower meadows and woodland of dogwood and magnolia.

Boating and Fishing

The tide ponds and lagoons around the island are perfect for maneuvering in and out of by kayak. **Island Spirit Kayak** (Oak Bluffs, 508/693-9727, www.islandspiritkayak.com) leads paddling tours that emphasize island geology and wildlife, and also rents boats ($35 for a half-day single kayak to $250 for weeklong double sea kayak), delivered to the beach or pond of your choice.

For anglers, the *Skipper* (Oak Bluffs Harbor, 508/693-1238, www.mvskipper.com, half-day trips $50 adults, $40 children 12 and under) bills itself as a "party fishing boat," which takes family-friendly trips in search of sea-bass and fluke. Serious fishermen can ride along with

Surf Master Charter Fishing (6 Mariners Circle, 508/400-9208, surfmastercharters@ hotmail.com, trips are 7–11:30 A.M. and 1–5:30 P.M., $100 deposit), which goes after bluefish, tuna, and—for *Jaws* fans—shark.

Flying

Strap on leather goggles and get a bird's-eye view of the island with a ride in a 60-year-old cherry-red biplane. **Classic Aviators** (Katama Airfield, Edgartown, 508/627-7677, www.bi-planemv.com) runs sightseeing trips that range from 15 minutes to one hour, buzzing over the island's beaches and towns in the company of an experienced guide.

ACCOMMODATIONS
Under $100

The rooms at **The Nashua House** (30 Kennebec Ave., Oak Bluffs, 508/693-0043, www.nashua-house.com, $69–219) are a bit musty, but you can't beat the view of the ocean from rooms with pastel walls and battered antiques.

$100–150

A laid-back and centrally located bed-and-breakfast, the **Look Inn** (13 Look St., Vineyard Haven, 508/693-6893, $125) has a hot tub in the backyard and friendly innkeepers who give free personalized tours of the island.

$150–250

A pink wedding cake of a house at the top of Oak Bluffs' main drag, the **Oak Bluffs Inn** (64 Circuit Ave., Oak Bluffs, 800/955-6235, www.oakbluffsinn.com, Apr.–Oct., $140–300) is appointed with a tasteful mix of modern country furniture and old English antiques. It has an informal, lived-in air that makes staying there feel like bunking at Grandma's. Up-island, the secluded **(Duck Inn** (10 Duck Pond Way, Aquinnah, 508/645-9018, www.gayheadrealty. com, $135–195) is located in an 18th-century home with bohemian furnishings and a knock-out ocean view. One room has a bathtub in the middle; another is swept at night with the beam from Gay Head Light. The personable owner is

© MICHAEL BLANDING

oversize diversions at the Winnetu Inn & Resort

a 30-year island resident who gives therapeutic massages and makes killer organic breakfasts.

$250 and Up

Located by the beach outside of Edgartown, the **❰ Winnetu Inn & Resort** (31 Dunes Rd., Edgartown, 508/627-4747, www.winnetu.com, $195–890) offers luxury without pretension. The managers pride themselves on being both kid-friendly (witness the giant-sized chessboard in the courtyard) and relaxing (a strictly enforced "quiet time" begins at 9 P.M.). All-suite kitchenettes are beach-house minimalist, many with views of the surf. Activities include oceanside tennis courts and yoga.

Your fantasies of living as a sea captain can be fulfilled at the over-the-top romantic **Charlotte Inn** (27 S. Summer St., Edgartown, 508/627-4151, charlotte@relaischateaux.com, www.relaischateaux.com, $325–795), where a personal touch is evident in every detail of plush, individually decorated rooms. The innkeepers use a collection of hand-chosen antiques to make you feel at home, for example putting an old top hat on your bed or antique looking-glass on your desk when you return at night. Behind the house, gardens are filled with a fantasia of flowers and sitting areas, and the dining room has glass walls. On the other side of the island, the **Beach Plum Inn** (50 Beach Plum Ln., Menemsha, 508/645-9454, info@innatmenemsha.com, www.beachpluminn.com, $225–450) is a secluded retreat, with six acres of hilltop property overlooking Vineyard Sound and the Elizabeth Islands. Rates include a full breakfast and a coveted pass to the residents-only Lucy Vincent Beach, one of the most beautiful on the island.

FOOD

Like everything else on the island, food on the Vineyard isn't cheap, but it does include restaurants to rival any on the mainland.

Edgartown

Taken as either verb or noun, **Lure Grill** (The Winnetu Resort, 31 Dunes Rd., 508/627-3663, 8 A.M.–10 P.M. daily May–Oct.; 9 A.M.–9 P.M.

daily Nov.–April., www.winnetu.com/dining.htm, $18–29) lives up to its name. The elegant modern nautical setting tempts diners with an equally elegant and seaworthy cuisine—whether its briny local oysters on ice dressed with pink peppercorn and pineapple, butter-poached lobster, or a simple classic grilled tuna filet. Historic sea captain's houses may be a dime a dozen in Edgartown, but you won't find many serving food like that whipped up at **❰ Atria** (137 Main St., 508/627-5850, www.atriamv.com, 5 P.M.–11 P.M. daily May–Oct.; 5 P.M.–9 P.M. Nov.–April; hours vary in Jan., $30–42). The globally inspired menu revolves around dishes like foie gras with vanilla French toast, prosciutto-wrapped island cod, and duck confit with spicy plum sauce. The intimate brick cellar bar is a quiet spot for dessert, a nightcap, or post-prandial flirtation.

Vineyard Haven

Reasonable prices, unpretentious but pretty decor, and the très authentic hand of a Lyon-trained French chef have kept **Le Grenier** (96 Main St., 508/693-4906, www.legrenierrestaurant.com, 5 P.M.–10:30 P.M. daily April–Nov.; 5 P.M.–9 P.M. daily Dec.–March, $23–34) going strong for more than two decades. Well-executed warhorses like *duck à l'orange*, frogs legs Provençal—not to mention a killer crème caramel—make no mystery of the spot's success. BYOB. Easily the most famous Vineyard restaurant is **The Black Dog Tavern** (21 Beach St. Extension, 508/693-9223, www.theblackdog.com, 7 A.M.–11 A.M., noon–4 A.M., 5 P.M.–10 P.M. daily June–Sept.; call for off-season hours, $14–31), next to the ferry staging area in Vineyard Haven, behind the Black Dog bakery-cum-clothing store full of Black Dog brand wearables. The T-shirts have been sighted from Patagonia to Nepal, and if you're grabbing a snack at the bakery counter, you may marvel that global fame hasn't brought about tremendous price hikes. The tavern's prices, on the other hand, are more typical of the island's best dining spots, although it isn't one of them—not for dinner, at any rate. Better to come for breakfast, when you can enjoy the harbor view and nautical mementos without breaking the bank. It's absolutely mobbed in summers; no reservations accepted.

Oak Bluffs

Crushed peanut shells litter the floor at **Offshore Ale Co.** (Kennebec Ave., 508/693-2626, 11 A.M.–12:30 A.M., Tues.–Sat., 12 P.M.–11 A.M., Sun.–Mon. June–Sept.; hours vary Oct.–May, www.offshoreale.com, $11–32), a warehouse turned brewpub in Oak Bluffs with a nautical decor and friendly atmosphere. Brick-oven pizzas and hamburgers join more substantial fare like fisherman's stew and porterhouse steak. Small and crammed with tiny tables and big baskets of wildflowers, **Slice of Life** (50 Circuit Ave., 508/693-3838, www.sliceoflifemv.com, 8:30 A.M.–8 P.M. daily, $10–22) is where tourists convene to kick back over quiche Florentine and thin-crusted pizzas, and where locals pick up takeout (pan-roasted salmon, bagels, and the day's paper) before heading to the beach.

Whatever you decide to eat for dinner, do as the locals do and skip dessert. Instead, head for one of the island's many ice cream shops or candy stores. Martha's Vineyard has more fudge and ice cream shops than you could shake a waffle cone at, but **Ben & Bill's Chocolate Emporium** (20 Circuit Ave., Oak Bluffs, 508/696-0008, 11 A.M.–6 P.M., Mon.–Sat., March–April; 10 A.M.–9 P.M. daily May–Dec.; www.benandbills.com) has some of the largest selection and richest character. Drop into the dark-walled interior for a handful of candy from the old-fashioned bins (gummy sharks, perhaps, or cashew brittle, or any of the 20-plus flavors of salt water taffy), or just grab some of the cold stuff (in flavors from chai tea to peanut butter).

Up-Island

Beach Plum Inn (50 Beach Plum Ln., Menemsha, 508/645-9454, www.beachpluminn.com, 5:30 P.M.–10 P.M. Mon.–Sat.; closed Sun.; call for off-season hours, $30–42, three-course prix fixe $50) has earned a permanent space among the island's most *amour*-inducing spots. That's largely thanks to the intoxicating sunsets seen over the abutting harbor, but

also to dishes like hazelnut-crusted halibut and wild salmon napoleon with ginger-cashew glaze. BYOB. On the opposite end of the amenities spectrum sits **The Bite** (29 Basin Rd., Menemsha, 508/645-9239, www.thebitemenemsha.com, 11 A.M.–6 P.M. Mon.–Sat., closed Sun. June–Sept.; closed off-season, $5–30), doling out what may just be the island's best fried fish from what could only be described as a hut. Fried clams are succulent and greaseless; the fish-and-chips is flaky, juicy, and featherlight. Order at the door and stake your seat at the picnic tables next door.

INFORMATION AND SERVICES

Find all the maps and information you need to get around the island—plus advice on accommodations and dining—at **Martha's Vineyard Chamber of Commerce** (Beach Rd., Vineyard Haven, 508/693-0085, www.mvy.com).

The island's full-service hospital is **Martha's Vineyard Hospital** (One Hospital Rd., Oak Bluffs, 508/693-0410, www.mvhospital.com), with emergency services offered 24 hours a day. Fill prescription needs at **Leslie's Drug Store** (65 Main St., Vineyard Haven, 508/693-1010). The commercial centers of Edgartown and Vineyard Haven are home to several banks. Each also has an ATM—which are also scattered around the streets of those towns, as well as in Oak Bluffs.

Major cell phone networks function within the main towns, but can be undependable in the island's less-crowded areas. Free **Internet access** and terminals is offered at the **Vineyard Haven Public Library** (200 Main St., Vineyard Haven, 508/696-4211, www.vhlibrary.org), and **Edgartown Free Public Library** (58 North Water St., Edgartown, 508/627-4221, www.edgartownlibrary.org).

GETTING THERE

Ferries leave for the Vineyard from a variety of locations. From Woods Hole to Vineyard Haven or Oak Bluffs, take the **Steamship Authority** (508/477-8600, www.steamshipauthority.com, year-round). From Falmouth to Edgartown, take **Falmouth Ferry Service** (508/548-9400, www.falmouthferry.com, late May–early Sept.). From Hyannis to Oak Bluffs, take **Hy-Line Cruises** (800/492-8082, www.hy-linecruises. com, late May–mid-Oct.). Hy-Line also runs boats from Nantucket to Oak Bluffs (late June–early Sept.). From New Bedford to Vineyard Haven, take **Martha's Vineyard Express Ferry** (866/683-3779, www.mvexpressferry. com). During the summer, several flights a day are offered by **Cape Air** (508/771-6944, www. flycapeair.com) from Boston, New Bedford, Hyannis, and Nantucket.

GETTING AROUND

Unless you are going to be spending a lot of time up-island, a car is by no means essential.

The **Martha's Vineyard Regional Transit Authority** (508/693-9440, www.vine-yardtransit.com) runs buses between all of the towns. If you must have your own wheels, **AAA Island Auto Rentals** (196 Main St., Edgartown; Five Corners, Vineyard Haven; 800/627-6333 www.aaaislandautorentals.com) offers free pick-up in Edgartown, Oak Bluffs, and Vineyard Haven. A less expensive—and more fun—option is to rent a moped from one of several dealers around the island. Try **Adventure Rentals** (19 Beach Rd., Vineyard Haven, 508/693-1959, www.islandadventuresmv.com) or **Ride-On Mopeds and Bikes** (9 Oak Bluffs Ave., Oak Bluffs, 508/693-2076, www.mvmoped.com).

Nantucket

Life doesn't get much more idyllic—or frankly, more preppy—than it is in the cobblestoned main streets, salt-box homes, and creaking docks of this community, renowned for its past life as the whaling capital of the world. It was that status—enjoyed from about 1800 to 1840—that brought great wealth to the community, which is to this day studded with the immense captain's homes of yore. That wealth is still readily apparent today in the form of new gargantuan mansions (sometimes complete with a helipad or two in the backyard), and boutique shopping that puts the "up" in upscale.

Not for nothing was Herman Melville's *Moby-Dick* set partially on Nantucket: This little spit of land was a major international player—in fact, *the* source of the world's whale oil—for nearly the first half of the 19th century. Nantucket was settled in 1658 by a small band of Massachusetts colonists who had their fill of the Puritans' intolerance and were looking for a solid place to raise some sheep. When the first sperm whale washed up on the beach in 1712, however, it sparked a gold rush of whaling vessels that increased Nantucket's reputation and its coffers as they sailed around the world.

By 1850, however, the whaling era was over; whales had been overhunted, and new forms of fuel were replacing whale oil. Nantucket's economy took a dive, and it wasn't until the island discovered and slowly capitalized on the appeal of its historic charm as a resort that the money started flowing back in.

As recently as two decades ago, the island was still a sleepy summer haven for bluebloods, full of family cottages, fusty country shops, and few tourist attractions. But the world has since discovered its charm, and Nantucket Town is now packed with luxury inns, high-end restaurants and stores, and bed-and-breakfasts that are as pretty as they are pricey. Its waters still teem with boats, to be sure, but nowadays they're more apt to be cruise ship–sized yachts than humble little schooners.

Outside of the main town sit two outlying communities known as **Siasconset** (or simply "'Sconset," if you summer or live here) and **Surfside**. Both are blink-and-you-miss-it small, with just one or two eateries and stores to mark them as quasi-towns. The rest of the island, meanwhile, is dotted with homes both new and historic (more than 800 houses here were built before or during the Civil War)

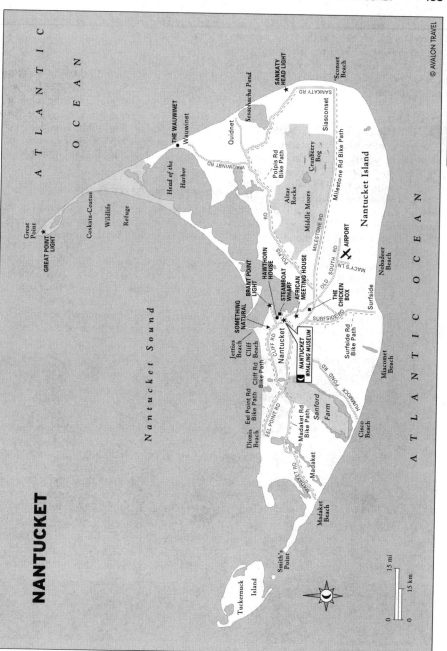

NANTUCKET

A T L A N T I C   O C E A N

Great Point

GREAT POINT LIGHT

Coskata-Coatue Wildlife Refuge

Nantucket Sound

Head of the Harbor

THE WAUWINET
Wauwinet

Quidnet

Sesachacha Pond

SANKATY HEAD LIGHT

'Sconset Beach

Siasconset

Nantucket Island

Polpis Rd Bike Path

Cranberry Bog

Altar Rocks

Middle Moors

Milestone Rd Bike Path

MILESTONE RD

SANKATY RD

WAUWINET RD

RD

BRANT POINT LIGHT

HAWTHORN HOUSE

STEAMBOAT WHARF

SOMETHING NATURAL

AFRICAN MEETING HOUSE

POLPIS RD

OLD SOUTH RD

MILESTONE RD

MACY'S LN.

AIRPORT

THE CHICKEN BOX

SURFSIDE RD

Surfside

Nobadeer Beach

A T L A N T I C   O C E A N

Jetties Beach

Cliff Rd Beach

Cliff Rd Bike Path

CLIFF RD

Nantucket

NANTUCKET WHALING MUSEUM

Surfside Rd Bike Path

Miacomet Beach

HUMMOCK POND RD

Eel Point Rd Bike Path

EEL POINT RD

Dionis Beach

Madaket Rd Bike Path

Sanford Farm

Cisco Beach

MADAKET RD

Madaket

Madaket Beach

Smith's Point

Tuckernuck Island

15 mi

15 km

0

0

© AVALON TRAVEL

around its beaches and large swaths of untouched land. Much of it, thanks in no small part to the ongoing efforts of the island's conservationists, is as similar to what it was in the island's yesteryear as Nantucket Town itself is now different.

SIGHTS
◖ Nantucket Whaling Museum

The history of whaling comes alive at this museum (15 Broad St., 508/228-1894, www.nha. org, 10 A.M.–5 P.M. daily mid-Sept.–Oct; call for off-season hours, $15 adults, $12 seniors $8 children 6 and over, free children under 6), which recently underwent a multimillion-dollar renovation. Peruse halls detailing the first whale killing off of Nantucket, firsthand descriptions of life on whaling boats, explanations of how the industry worked, and breakdowns of everything that the parts of whales were once used for. The new space accommodates an enormous life-size whale skeleton that hovers above visitors' heads, and a gallery of whaling artifacts—from harpoons to scrimshaw. A

movie and regularly scheduled live talks round out the experience.

Other Sights

Also recently restored, the **African Meeting House** (29 York St., 508/228-9833, www. afroammuseum.org/afmnantucket.htm, 11 A.M.–3 P.M. Mon.–Fri., 11 A.M.–1 P.M. Sat., and 1–3 P.M. Sun. June–Oct., free, donations accepted) dates to 1827, when it was used as a meeting place and schoolhouse for the island's African residents.

ENTERTAINMENT

The city that never sleeps it's not, but for a town that until only a decade ago was always shuttered by early evening, Nantucket has a respectable number of nightlife options. **The Chicken Box** (16 Dave St., 508/228-9717, www.thechickenbox.com)—named such because it's housed in what was once a fried-chicken stand—is the area nightclub, with cover and tribute bands and DJs several nights a week. Standouts among the town's cluster of

Brant Point Lighthouse at the entrance to Nantucket Harbor

bars and pubs are **The Ropewalk** (1 Straight Wharf, 508/228-8886, www.theropewalk.com), which has a salty-aired, wharfside setting to recommend it; **The Boarding House** (12 Federal St., 508/228-9622, www.boardinghouse-pearl.com), an upscale magnet for the perkiest bar-hoppers in the area; and **Cambridge Street Victuals** (12 Cambridge St., 508/228-7109, www.cambridgestreet-nantucket.com), probably the coolest spot for a cocktail in town, and usually the least crowded.

EVENTS

Outside of the summer season, there are plenty of reasons to visit the island—not the least of which is an absence of on-season visitors. But the **Christmas Stroll Weekend** (508/228-1700, www.nantucketchamber.org/visitor/events.html) is a bona fide lure in its own right—an early December festival that sees the town's Christmas trees lit up, theater performances, concerts, and the requisite Santa arrival. Once the weather warms up, there's the **Daffodil Festival** (508/228-1700, www.nantucketchamber.org) in April, which takes over with parades of blossom-festooned antique cars and a tailgating picnic.

SHOPPING

With its crush of cute retail stores—from antiques and jam stores to art galleries and clothiers—Nantucket has made shopping a major local sport. There are the old standbys such as **Murrays Toggery** (62 Main St., 508/228-0437, www.nantucketreds.com, 10 A.M.–7 P.M. Mon.–Sat., 11 A.M.–5 P.M. Sun. June–Oct.; 10 A.M.–5 P.M. daily Nov.–May), a local institution that has been selling fragrances, shoes, and sporty duds (including the iconic "Nantucket Reds"—the faded twills synonymous with the island) for men and women since 1945. Then there are the cutting-edge ready-to-wear shops, represented on the high-fashion end by **Gypsy** (20 Federal St., 508/228-4404, www.gypsyusa.com, 10 A.M.–6 P.M. daily June–Dec.; call for off-season hours), with its beautiful big-ticket women's clothing with labels like Catherine Malandrino, True Religion, and Chloe. Francophiles find bliss among the shelves of **L'Ile de France** (8 India St., 508/228-3686, 10 A.M.–6 P.M. daily June–Dec.; closed Jan.–March, www.frenchgeneralstore.com). The friendly French owner imports an impressive sweep of items, including authentic nautical sweaters, Provençal paintings, and weekly deliveries of the beloved Poilane bread.

SPORTS AND RECREATION

Pretty as Nantucket Town may be, it's nothing compared with the rest of the island's natural splendor. And the best way to experience it is up close and personal on a bike, by foot, or by boat.

Beaches

The first beach seen by most visitors to the island is **Brant Point Lighthouse Beach** (on Brant Point, at the tip of Easton St.), which is poised at the mouth of Nantucket Harbor and is passed by all the steamships that dock in town. It's a quiet and very small beach, about a 15-minute walk from town. As it has no facilities or lifeguard, it's frequented mostly by those looking for a brief stroll or a view of the lighthouse or town. A quick five-minute walk from town, just around the bend in the harbor toward Brant Point, is **Children's Beach** (www.nantucketchamber.org). With very few waves, a small park, a lifeguard on-duty, and restrooms, it's a perfect spot to take the tykes. On the outskirts of town, equipped with lifeguards and restrooms, is **Jetties** (508/228-5358, www.nantucketchamber.org). There's also a playground; a concession stand selling burgers, ice cream, and such; and boat rentals. Meanwhile, at the end of Surfside Road, is the extremely popular **Surfside** (www.nantucketchamber.org), named for its notoriously heavy surf.

Biking

Rent bikes or scooters (the latter, it must be noted, are frowned upon by locals) at **Nantucket Bike Shop** (with two locations on Steamboat Wharf and Straight Wharf,

508/228-1999, www.nantucketbikeshop.com). Or, if you'd rather have the wheels come to you, give **Easy Riders** (508/325-2722, www.easyridersbikerentals.com) a call. The warehouse-based operation has reasonable rates, all kinds of bikes, and free delivery to wherever you like around the island.

Boating and Fishing

One of the most peaceful ways to see the island is from the water; **Brant Point Marine** (32 Washington St., 508/228-6244, www.brant-pointmarine.com), rents kayaks, canoes, and other boats as well as fishing gear, trailers, and anything else you need to get on the water. If you'd rather let someone else do all the legwork for you, find a spot on **The Christina** (Straight Wharf, Slip 1019, 508/325-4000, $25 per person), a mahogany catboat that sails regularly out of Nantucket Harbor. (The longest of the cruises, the 90-minute sunset cruise, is the best bang for your buck. For added romantic value, bring a bottle of champagne for the ride.)

ACCOMMODATIONS
$100-250

Whether your preference is toward the historic or the hip, Nantucket has a solid selection of each these days—particularly the former. Case in point: **The Ships Inn** (13 Fair S., 508/228-0040, www.shipsinnnantucket.com, $100–275), built in 1831 by local sea captain Obed Starbuck, the house was later the birthplace of Lucretia Mott. The ten sunny rooms are decorated individually in floral wallpapers, cushy duvets, and fridges. A two-minute walk from the center of town, the inn also has a commendable restaurant and a continental breakfast that includes a dynamite home-made granola.

One of the better values in town is the ◖ **Hawthorn House** (2 Chestnut St., 508/228-1468, www.hawthornhouse.com, year-round). Doubles, all with private bath, run $170–255 mid-June–mid-September (there's also a two-room suite for $275), the low end of that range representing selected rooms outside of July and August. In the shoulder season before

Memorial Day and after Labor Day rates drop up to $75. A $9 coupon is given to each guest for breakfast at either of a couple of nearby local eateries—enough to get you a hot entrée, not just muffins and juice. The premises are enlivened by an extensive collection of fine art and unique crafts, including his wife's beautiful needlepoint pillows, his own art glass lamps, and his dad's hooked rugs. The wide-ranging aesthetic brightens the 1849 house at least as much as the sunlight that so many of the rooms enjoy. The absence of phones in the individual rooms mirrors the tranquility of this little downtown block, so near to shops yet off the main path of traffic. In sum, this is an attractive and comfortable oasis.

$250 and Up

Nine miles outside of town sits ◖ **The Wauwinet** (120 Wauwinet Road, 508/228-0145, www.wauwinet.com, $380–800) designated by the prestigious Relais & Chateaux group as one of its member properties. The gray-shingled building gazes across a perfectly manicured bloom-filled lawn facing a private bay. Sound nice? That's just the beginning, from the property's luxury-laden rooms to Toppers, its world-class restaurant with the million-dollar sunset view. (Don't miss the chance to sample the house's rare wine list.)

The impeccably kept **White Elephant** (50 Easton St., 508/228-2500, www.whiteelephanthotel.com, $300–1,250) is perched directly on Nantucket Harbor. Rooms come complete with exquisite linens, high-speed Internet, CD players, personal patios, and plush bathrobes and beach towels. Many have fireplaces as well. The hotel's suite-style freestanding garden cabins are ideal for families.

FOOD

While seafood clearly tops the wish list of many Nantucket visitors, the island has also developed a healthy stable of other cuisines as well, from Italian and New American to Japanese and fusion fare. Of course, wherever seafood plays a major role in those cuisines here, it's bound to be excellent. Global-meets-coastal cuisine can be found at **The Pearl** (12 Federal St., 508/228-9701, 5 P.M.–11 P.M. Tues.–Sat., closed Sun. May–Oct.; 5 P.M.–9 P.M. Tues.–Sat., closed Sun. Nov.–April; www.boarding-house-pearl.com, $35–44), a blue-cast room as luminous as its name. Dress your snazziest and come to dig into grilled whitefish tacos with spicy mayo, salt-and-pepper wok-fried lobster, and sea scallops with buckwheat risotto.

True food lovers—that is to say, those who relish eating the dishes rather than being seen in the right place eating them—make a bee-line for ◖ **Black Eyed Susan's** (10 India St., 508/325-0308, www.black-eyedsusans.com, 5:30 P.M.–10 P.M. Tues.–Fri.; 10 A.M.–3 P.M. and 5 A.M.–9 P.M. Sat.–Sun.; call for off-season hours; $18–29). From the counter (the chandelier-topped eatery's set in a former dining car) flames jump and skillets sizzle as chefs expertly whip up sophisticated, simply scrumptious dishes like chile-revved tuna tartare and, at brunch, sourdough French toast with orange Jack Daniels butter. No reservations are taken, but you can arrive early and put your name on a list to come back later in the evening.

If **Something Natural** (50 Cliff Rd., 508/228-0504, www.somethingnatural.com, 10 A.M.–5 P.M. daily April–Oct.; closed Nov.–May, $4–7) were based in a city business district, it would have made a mint and spawned thirteen offspring by now. But as it is, the country-style bakery/store serves locals and biking visitors quietly on the outskirts of town. The draw? Homemade sandwiches like chicken salad with extraordinary chutney on thick-sliced still-warm oatmeal bread.

INFORMATION AND SERVICES

Get the lowdown on where to stay, where to eat, and how to get there from the centrally located **Nantucket Chamber of Commerce** (0 Main St., Nantucket, 508/228-3643, www.nantucketchamber.org).

The island's only emergency medical facility is **Nantucket Cottage Hospital** (57 Prospect St., Nantucket, 508/825-8100, www.nantuckethospital.org), which offers 24-hour care. Fill

prescription needs at **Pharmacy-Valu-Rite** (122 Pleasant St., Nantucket, 508/228-6400, islandrx.com).

Nantucket Town's Main Street is home to two banks, **Nantucket Bank** (104 Pleasant St.; 2 Orange St., Nantucket, 508/228-0580, www.nantucketbank.com) and **Pacific National Bank** (61 Main St., Nantucket, 508/228-1917). Both have ATMs—as does the nearby **A & P** (Straight Wharf, Nantucket, 508/228-1700) grocery store. Be aware each charges a fee of $2–3 if you are not on their network.

Major cell phone networks function within town, but can be spotty beyond. Paid **wireless Internet access** is offered to patrons with laptops at the **Even Keel Cafe** (40 Main St., Nantucket, 508/228-1979) and to guests at numerous hotels on the island. Faxing and shipping services can be found at **The UPS Store** (2 Windy Way, Nantucket, 508/325-8884, www.theupsstore.com).

GETTING THERE

Ferries leave for Nantucket Town from Hyannis on both the **Steamship Authority** (508/477-8600, www.steamshipauthority.com) and the **Steamship Authority Fast Ferry.** Also leaving from Hyannis: **Hy-Line Cruises High Speed Ferry** (508/778-2600, www.hylinecruises.com). You can also get to Nantucket from Oak Bluffs on Martha's Vineyard (late June–early Sept.).

During the summer, several flights a day are offered by **Cape Air** (508/771-6944, www.flycapeair.com) from Boston, Hyannis, and Martha's Vineyard.

GETTING AROUND

Several of the usual national agencies rent vehicles from Nantucket Airport, but unless you're visiting in winter, a car isn't really necessary, given the close proximity of everything in town and the excellent bike paths running over the island. The **Nantucket Regional Transit Authority** (508/228-7025, www.shuttlenantucket.com) does continuous loops between Straight Wharf in Nantucket Town and Madaket, Surfside, Siasconset, and the airport.

WESTERN MASSACHUSETTS

In both topography and attitude, Western Massachusetts has a dramatically different character than the eastern part of the state. If the area around Boston looks toward the ocean, then Western Mass. is all about the mountains. The Berkshire range defines the region, with blue-tinted hills rising out of river valleys, and highways snaking through gorges capped with brilliant foliage in the fall. At the same time, the flat valley area along the Connecticut River has the area's richest farmland—with its loamy topsoil supporting a diverse range of crops in contrast to the hardscrabble glacial soil of much of New England.

Historically, the western part of the state has always had somewhat of a pioneer mentality, thumbing its nose at the effete ways of the city in favor of more honest pursuits of farming and manufacturing. A trace of that remains in the political independence of the people here, who skew wildly between college-town liberals and flinty hill-town conservatives, united in the common belief that the state government is unduly tilted towards Boston. This is, after all, the area of Shays' Rebellion—the last hiccup of the American Revolution, in which farmer Daniel Shays led a misguided revolt against the new federal government, only to be put down months later by Washington's army.

As the cities of New York and Boston grew in industrial might, however, they looked to the hills of Western Mass. as both a sobering refuge for their children and a summer playground for socialites. As a result, the area nowadays is known especially for its colleges and artistic attractions. In the summer, especially,

© KINDRA CLINEFF/MOTT

HIGHLIGHTS

◖ **Naismith Memorial Basketball Hall of Fame:** Chamberlain, Bird, and Jordan all get their due at this temple of ball (page 171).

◖ **Emily Dickinson Homestead:** The poet's former home is a mandatory pilgrimage spot for her devotees (page 175).

◖ **Shelburne Falls:** The Bridge of Flowers is just the beginning in a delightful town frozen in time (page 179).

◖ **Massachusetts Museum of Contemporary Art (MassMoCA):** The former mill buildings this museum inhabits are just as impressive as the modern art within them (page 184).

◖ **The Sterling and Francine Clark Art Institute:** One of the best small museums in the country specializes in Monet and Renoir (page 185).

◖ **Berkshire Athenaeum:** The Melville Room is chock-full of artifacts of the *Moby-Dick* author (page 187).

◖ **Tanglewood:** The summer home of the Boston Symphony Orchestra is the region's premier attraction (page 190).

◖ **Norman Rockwell Museum:** The man who immortalized small-town America is himself immortalized in a small town (page 192).

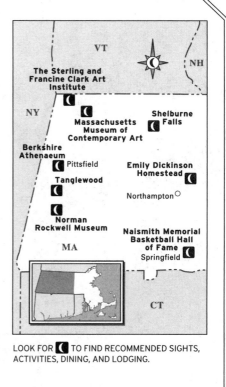

LOOK FOR ◖ TO FIND RECOMMENDED SIGHTS, ACTIVITIES, DINING, AND LODGING.

the hills are alive with the sounds of music (and art and dance), while fall signals the annual influx of youth.

PLANNING YOUR TIME

For most visitors, Western Mass. means the Berkshires, where most of the region's cultural attractions can be found. The southern Berkshires are focused more on performances and shopping, while the northern mountains have art museums and outdoor pursuits. If you have more than a few days to spend, it's well worth spending time in the Pioneer Valley as well, where the college towns of Amherst and Northampton perfectly blend big-city culture with small-town charm.

Ideally, a visit to this area in its entirety would last about a week. That kind of time provides two to three days to explore the antiques stores, theater, and arts of the Southern towns; approximately three days to take in art exhibits, galleries, and to hike several of the trails in the mountains; and two more days to soak up the funky culture of the Pioneer Valley's coffee houses and shops around campuses like Smith and Amherst Colleges. The best time to see the entire region is in autumn, so that you can take in brilliant foliage at nearly every turn. If you visit during the summer, however, plan to spend at least an extra day or two in the Berkshires, where the ongoing outdoor

MASSACHUSETTS

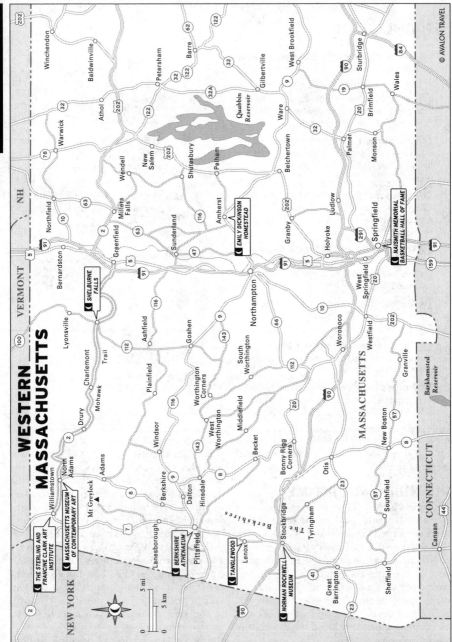

WESTERN MASSACHUSETTS

© AVALON TRAVEL

VERMONT

NH

NEW YORK

CONNECTICUT

MASSACHUSETTS

The Berkshires

THE STERLING AND FRANCINE CLARK ART INSTITUTE

MASSACHUSETTS MUSEUM OF CONTEMPORARY ART

BERKSHIRE ATHENAEUM

TANGLEWOOD

NORMAN ROCKWELL MUSEUM

SHELBURNE FALLS

EMILY DICKINSON HOMESTEAD

NAISMITH MEMORIAL BASKETBALL HALL OF FAME

Winchendon
Baldwinville
Barre
West Brookfield
Petersham
Sturbridge
Wales
Brimfield
Monson
West Springfield
Springfield
Gilbertville
Ware
Belchertown
Palmer
Ludlow
Holyoke
Granby
Quabbin Reservoir
Athol
Warwick
New Salem
Shutesbury
Pelham
Amherst
Millers Falls
Northfield
Bernardston
Greenfield
Sunderland
Northampton
Westfield
Granville
Barkhamsted Reservoir
Lyonsville
Ashfield
Goshen
South Worthington
Woronoco
New Boston
Worthington Corners
Plainfield
Windsor
West Worthington
Middlefield
Becket
Bonny Rigg Corners
Otis
Southfield
Drury
Charlemont
Mohawk Trail
Adams
Berkshire
Dalton
Hinsdale
Pittsfield
Lanesborough
Mt Greylock
North Adams
Williamstown
Stockbridge
Lenox
Tyringham
Great Barrington
Sheffield
Canaan
Wendell
Monson
Winchendon

NEW YORK

5 mi
5 km
0

concerts at Tanglewood and summer theater festivals could keep you happily busy for weeks.

The area is a year-round destination, with hotels, restaurants, and attractions staying open throughout the seasons. Note, though, that many restaurants do not offer all meals; many higher-end spots serve lunch and dinner (and sometimes dinner) only. Always call ahead to be safe.

Pioneer Valley

The Connecticut River cuts a swath through the middle of Massachusetts, drawing a line between the gentle hills of the east and the rising Berkshire Mountains to the west. In between is a fertile bread basket of vegetable and livestock farms that seems more like the Midwest than the Northeast. Adding to the surrealism are acres of tobacco plants, which are dried in barns by the roadside. In the midst of the farmland is the mini-metropolis of Springfield, along with the vaunted "five colleges": the University of Massachusetts–Amherst, Smith, Amherst, Hampshire, and Mount Holyoke.

SPRINGFIELD

Even though it is the second-largest city in Massachusetts, Springfield has nowhere near the appeal of Boston. The city grew up as a manufacturing town, in a broad valley straddling the banks of the mighty Connecticut River, a location that gave it enviable access to natural resources and the means to get them to rich ports in Connecticut and New York. (A macho town to be sure, guns and motorcycles were its two main exports.) As the city entered the 20th century, however, the frontier moved further west, leaving it a backwater that declined slowly, but surely, into decay.

The architecture downtown still gives a nod to the city's manufacturing heyday. Most of the city, however, is abjectly poor. In recent years, migrant workers from Mexico and Puerto Rico who work the nearby tobacco fields have been settling here, adding a touch of salsa music and Latin food to the neighborhood of West Springfield. Despite a general air of depression, however, Springfield has quite a few attractions worth visiting, including the national shrine to

basketball, which was invented here by schoolteacher James Naismith in 1891; and a memorial to children's author Dr. Seuss.

C Naismith Memorial Basketball Hall of Fame

Whether you are a fan of the game or not, it's impossible not to get caught up in the high-energy excitement of this museum (1000 W. Columbus Ave., 413/781-6500, www.hoophall.com, 10 A.M.–4 P.M. Sun.–Thurs.; 10 A.M.–5 P.M. Fri.–Sat., $17 adults, $14 seniors, $12 youth 5–15, free children under 5), which was completely redesigned in 2000 to provide even more interactive exhibits on the sport. In addition to the predictable cases of players' uniforms and really big shoes, the hall has a circular gallery with the names and faces of all its members, and a large central court where you can practice your own ball-handling skills.

Other Sights

One of two national munition factories created after the Revolutionary War, the **Springfield Armory National Historic Site** (1 Armory Sq., 413/734-8551, www.nps.gov/spar, 9 A.M.–5 P.M. daily, free) churned out muskets, rifles, pistols, and even machine guns for almost 200 years. Unless you are a gun nut, the rows of rifles on display here are apt to look quite monotonous; there are, however, some unusual exhibits—such as one that shows what happens to guns when they are struck by lightning or gnawed by porcupines.

Before there was Harley, Ducati, or anything else, there was Indian, the original motorcycle, which dominated the industry from 1901 until

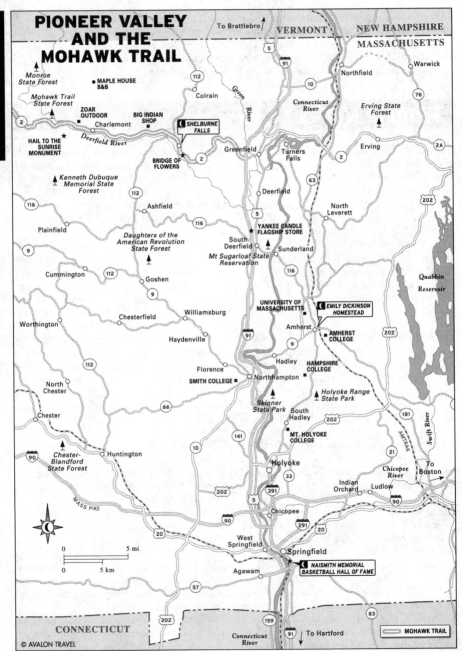

PIONEER VALLEY AND THE MOHAWK TRAIL

To Brattlebro

VERMONT   NEW HAMPSHIRE

MASSACHUSETTS

Monroe State Forest

● MAPLE HOUSE B&B

Warwick

Colrain

Mohawk Trail State Forest

ZOAR OUTDOOR

Charlemont

BIG INDIAN SHOP

Northfield

Green River

Connecticut River

Erving State Forest

☾ SHELBURNE FALLS

HAIL TO THE SUNRISE MONUMENT ★

Deerfield River

BRIDGE OF FLOWERS

Greenfield

Turners Falls

Erving

▲ Kenneth Dubuque Memorial State Forest

Deerfield

North Leverett

Ashfield

YANKEE CANDLE FLAGSHIP STORE

Plainfield

Daughters of the American Revolution State Forest

South Deerfield

Sunderland

Mt Sugarloaf State Reservation

Quabbin Reservoir

Cummington

Goshen

Chesterfield

Williamsburg

Worthington

UNIVERSITY OF MASSACHUSETTS

☾ EMILY DICKINSON HOMESTEAD

Amherst

■ AMHERST COLLEGE

Haydenville

Florence

Hadley

HAMPSHIRE COLLEGE

North Chester

SMITH COLLEGE ■

Northampton

Skinner State Park

Holyoke Range State Park

Chester

South Hadley

MT. HOLYOKE COLLEGE

Chester-Blandford State Forest

Huntington

AMTRAK

Swift River

Holyoke

Chicopee River

To Boston

Indian Orchard

Ludlow

MASS PIKE

Chicopee

West Springfield

Springfield

Agawam

☾ NAISMITH MEMORIAL BASKETBALL HALL OF FAME

CONNECTICUT

Connecticut River

To Hartford

□ MOHAWK TRAIL

© AVALON TRAVEL

0   5 mi

0   5 km

DR. SEUSS NATIONAL MEMORIAL SCULPTURE GARDEN

From there to here, from here to there, funny things are everywhere! That's certainly true of Springfield, where you can find some of the most beloved children's characters – the Lorax, Horton, and of course the Cat in the Hat – immortalized in bronze on the grassy lawn of Springfield's **Museum "Quadrangle"** (21 Edwards Street, Springfield, 413/263-6800, www.catinthehat.org, 9 A.M.–8 P.M. daily Apr.-mid-Oct., 9 A.M.-5 P.M. daily mid-Oct.-Mar.). Sitting in the center at his drawing board is their creator, "Dr. Seuss" himself, whose alter ego Theodor Seuss Geisel was born in Springfield in 1904 and lived here until he was a teenager. The author actually incorporated many of Springfield's sights and architecture into his fanciful kids' books. There actually is a Mulberry Street that served as inspiration for *And To Think That I Saw It On Mulberry Street* (though don't expect to find an elephant pulling a brass band there). Seuss also grew up only a few blocks from the Forest Park Zoo, where his father was keeper for a time, giving *If I Ran the Zoo* an interesting Oedipal twist. Inside the park is a monument with three stories of twisting stairs similar to those that find their way into the architecture of many of Seuss's books. An exhibit nearby at the **Connecticut Valley History Museum** (11 A.M.-4 P.M. Tues.–Sun., $10 adults, $7 seniors and college students, $5 children 3-17, free children under 3) shows how other landmarks around Springfield made it into his books. It also has an eclectic collection of Seuss ephemera, including the illustrator's Boy Scout badges and banjo.

the company's implosion half a century later. The **Indian Motorcycle Museum** (21 Edwards St., 413/263-6800, www.springfieldmuseums.org, 11 A.M.–4 P.M. Tues.–Sun., $12.50 adults, $9 seniors and students, $6.50 children 3–17, free children 2 and under) contains dozens of exhibits in leather and chrome, including the first motorcycle made of wood and a 1940 Indian Junior Scout owned by famous trick-rider Louise Sherbyn.

Landlocked Springfield might seem an unusual place to pay homage to the greatest oceangoing disaster in history. However, the **Titanic Museum** (208 Main St., Indian Orchard, 413/543-4770, www.titanichistoricalsociety.org, 10 A.M.–4 P.M. Mon.–Fri.; 10 A.M.–3 P.M. Sat., $4 adults, $2.50 children under 12, free children under 6), however, boasts the world's largest collection of memorabilia from the HMS *Titanic,* bringing alive the fateful night of April 14, 1912, better than a Leonardo DiCaprio movie ever could.

Events

Known as the "Big E," the **Eastern States Exhibition** (1305 Memorial Ave./Rte. 147, W. Springfield, 413/737-2443, www.thebige.com, mid-Sept.–early Oct.) brings farmers, breeders, and trainers from around New England for the region's largest agricultural fair. When the fair isn't in town, events are often held at the fairgrounds on weekends.

Food

If your idea of culinary heaven involves lederhosen, then you'll find nirvana at **The Fort** (8 Fort St., 413/788-6628, www.studentprince.com, 11 A.M.–9 P.M. Mon.–Wed.; 11 A.M.–10 P.M. Thu.–Sat.; noon–8 P.M. Sun., $10–23), a Springfield institution that has been serving bratwurst, schnitzel, and sauerbraten for more than 70 years. Its dining room, on the original 1660 site of Fort Springfield, is decorated with stained-glass windows and hundreds of beer steins.

Italian pride is on the menu at **Mom & Rico's Specialty Market** (899 Main St., 413/732-8941, 8:30 A.M.–5 P.M. Mon.–Sat., $5–10), a lunch counter that serves sandwiches with imported cold cuts and pastas with sauces made on the premises. The owner, Rico Daniele, is also president of the Wonderful World of Bocce Foundation, and literally wrote the book on the lawn bowling sport.

For special occasions, Springfielders spring for **Lido's Ristorante** (555 Washington St., Springfield, 413/736-9433, 11 A.M.–11 P.M. daily, $9–23), a stylish Italian-American spot with down-home but lovingly created pasta dishes and an Italian stone-lined dining room tended by ultra-friendly servers.

Information
Springfield has a large and helpful **Visitor Information Center** (1441 Main St., 413/787-1548, 9 A.M.–5 P.M. Mon.–Fri., www.valleyvisitor.com), which offers information on not only the city but also the surrounding Pioneer Valley and Berkshires regions.

NORTHHAMPTON
The brick downtown of Noho, as it's called, is an urban oasis for hipsters lost in the country. Goth kids roam the streets with brightly painted hair, while students from the all-women's Smith College pore over books in the many bars and cafés lining Main Street. The town has a progressive and active lesbian community that adds to the diverse culture of the area.

Sights
The 150-acre campus of **Smith College** (413/584-2700, www.smith.edu) is a particularly beautiful place for a stroll, incorporating botanical gardens with over 10,000 plants. Many of them are grown in the **Lyman Conservatory** (College Lane, behind Admissions Office, 413/585-2740, 8:30 A.M.–4 P.M. daily, free), the campus's star attraction. The glass-covered hothouses of the conservatory showcase plants from all over the world, from Asian bamboo to African coffee.

Entertainment
Ultracool cocktail lounge 🄲 **Tunnel Bar** (125A Pleasant St., 413/586-5366, www.unionstationrestaurant.com) is literally located in a 100-foot-long tunnel that once connected the train station to nearby streets. At the opposite end of the spectrum, **Ye Ol' Watering Hole** (287 Pleasant St., 413/585-0990, www.yeolwateringhole.com) boasts a "beer can museum" of hundreds of rusting cans hanging over grungy pool tables. Music lovers have an embarrassment of options. The **Iron Horse Music Hall** (20 Center St., 413/586-8686, $8–55) has two levels of tables arranged around a stage. Acts run to national indie rock and folk performers. More formal is the **Calvin Theater** (19 King St., 413/586-8686, $21–85), a restored grand movie theater that books big names in jazz and folk such as Bela Fleck and Joan Baez. Local rock bands take the stage at the intimate **Pearl Street Nightclub** (10 Pearl St., 413/586-8686, $8–35). For all three venues, check out the website for the Iron Horse Entertainment Group (www.iheg.com).

Events
Each Memorial Day and Columbus Day weekend, the country's top artisans and craftspeople descend on Northampton for the **Paradise City Arts Festival** (Three-County Fairgrounds, Route 9 and Old Ferry Rd., 800/511-9725, www.paradisecityarts.com, 10 A.M.–6 P.M. Sat.–Sun., 10 A.M.–4 P.M. Mon., $12 adults, $10 seniors, $8 students, free children under 12) to hawk and gawk over Shaker furniture, art nouveau pottery, and funky glass jewelry.

Shopping
Northampton is heaven to thrift store fans. The proprietor of **Sasha's Psychedelic Clothing and Ethnic Bling** (Mill River Marketplace, 375 South St./Rte. 10, www.gypsyheartboutique.com, Sun. 8 A.M.–3 P.M. or by appointment), Sasha Berman, describes her clothes as "funky-sexy-psychedelic," meaning paisley dresses and burlesque bikini tops. Would-be punks make the pilgrimage to **Sid Vintage** (18 Crafts Ave., 413/582-9880, www.sid-vintage.com, noon–6 P.M. Mon.–Thu.; noon–7 P.M. Fri.; 11 A.M.–7 P.M. Sat.; noon–5 P.M. Sun.) sells a bewildering assortment of counterculture T-shirts.

Food

Befitting its urban ambience, Northampton has a wide range of food options. Brightly painted Mexican art fills the walls at **La Veracruzana** (31 Main St., 413/586-7181, www.laveracruzana. com, 11 A.M.–10 P.M. Mon.–Sat.; noon–8 P.M. Sun., $4–18), a taqueria that offers authentic south Mexican dishes and Berkshire Brewing Company beers on tap. Vegetarians fill the tables at **The Haymarket Cafe** (185 Main St., 413/586-9969, www.haymarketcafe.com, 7 A.M.–9:30 P.M. Mon.–Thu.; 7 A.M.–11 P.M. Fri.–Sat.; 8 A.M.–9:30 P.M. Sun., $5–7), which serves pan-fried tofu sandwiches and cheap rice dishes in an ambience best described as the Italian Renaissance on an acid trip. On Smith's parents weekend, its near-impossible to score a table at **Spoleto** (50 Main St., 413/586-6313, www. spoletorestaurants.com/spoleto_northampton. html, 5 P.M.–9:30 P.M. Mon.–Thu.; 5 P.M.– 11 P.M. Fri.–Sat.; 10 A.M.–9 P.M. Sun., $15–26), an upscale Italian restaurant with regional dishes spiced with the surprising tastes of ginger, cardamom, and even jalapeños. Speaking of spicy, the raw fish creations at **Osaka** (7 Old South St., 413/587-9548, www.osakanorthampton.con, 5 P.M.–10 P.M. Mon.–Sat.; 5 P.M.–9 P.M. Sun., $12–22) are the perfect foils for the house-made wasabi-lined sauces.

Information

The **Northampton Chamber of Commerce** (99 Pleasant St., 413/584-1900, www.explorenorthampton.com) runs a visitors center downtown.

AMHERST

The quintessential college town of Amherst is always finding its way onto those "best small town" lists—and with good reason. The immaculate town center overflows with colonial architecture around a town common that melds with the campus of its namesake Amherst College, where poet Robert Frost once taught. The town also has a vibrant commercial center that circles around its *other* institution of higher learning—the gargantuan University of Massachusetts–Amherst.

◖ Emily Dickinson Homestead

The Belle of Amherst spent her fifty-some years in or around the homestead where she was born (280 Main St., 413/542-8161, www.emilydickinsonmuseum.org, 11 A.M.–4 P.M. Wed.–Sat. Mar.–Dec., $10 adults, $9 seniors and students, $5 youth 6–17, free children under 6). The perception that she was a recluse who never showed her poems, however, is a myth. The newly opened Evergreens, the mansion of her sister and brother-in-law, gives a more accurate portrayal of the drawing-room society that Dickinson moved in during her life. For many devotees, however, the prime attraction is still Emily's simple bedroom, where she composed her work and where a "certain shaft of light" still inspires pilgrims to her chamber.

Other Sights

For such a small museum, Amherst College's **Mead Art Museum** (Amherst College, 413/542-2335, www.amherst.edu, 9 A.M.–midnight Tues.–Thurs. and Sun. and 9 A.M.–5 P.M. Fri.–Sat. Sept.–May; 9 A.M.–5 P.M. Tues.–Sun. June–July, free) has a first-rate collection of American and European art. A more unusual museum is the **Eric Carle Museum of Picture Book Art** (125 West Bay Rd., 413/658-1100, www.picturebookart.org, 10 A.M.–4 P.M. Tues.–Fri.; 10 A.M.–5 P.M. Sat.; 12–5 P.M. Sun., $9 adults, $6 seniors, students, youth under 18), which features work by the local creator of *The Very Hungry Caterpillar* and other beloved children's books. On the nearby campus of Hampshire College, the **Yiddish Book Center** (1021 West St., 413/256-4900, www. yiddishbookcenter.org, 10 A.M.–4 P.M. Mon.– Fri.; 11 A.M.–4 P.M. Sun., free) tells the history of this little-known subculture.

Shopping

Grab both a sense of the town's history and its academic tradition at **A.J. Hastings, Inc.** (45 South Pleasant St., 413/253-2840, www. ajhastings.com, 7 A.M.–8 P.M. Mon.–Sat.; 6 A.M–5 P.M. Mon.; closed Sun.), which got its start by providing school supplies to the local college market way back when. These days it peddles a slew of Amherst College and UMass-decorated items, alongside clever stationery, calendars, and anything else required to keep your life well documented.

Atkins Farms Country Market (1150 West St., 413/253-9528, www.atkinsfarms.com, 7 A.M.–8 P.M. daily Apr.–Aug.; 7 A.M.–7 P.M. daily Sept.–Mar.) offers up the region's agricultural bounty with gift assortments of apples, jellies, and bakery items.

Food
On the lighter side, **The Black Sheep** (79 Main St., 413/253-3442, www.blacksheepdeli.com, $2–8) is a country deli that serves New York–quality foodstuffs and sandwiches that cry out to be taken for a picnic. The Northampton burrito joint **La Veracruzana** (63 S. Pleasant St., 413/253-6900, www.laveracruzana.com, 11 A.M.–10 P.M. Mon.–Sat.; noon–8 P.M. Sun. $4–18) also has a branch here.

Information
The **Amherst Area Chamber of Commerce** (28 Amity St., 413/253-0700, www.amherstarea.com) runs an information booth on the common, as well as a larger office down the street from the Dickinson Museum.

DEERFIELD AND GREENFIELD
The small town of Deerfield has a split personality, with one of the area's most prestigious historical attractions and some of its schlockiest tourist traps. To call the gritty crossroads of Greenfield the gateway to the Berkshires is perhaps giving it too much credit. Located at the intersection of Route 2 and I-91, it is nevertheless a good place to stock up on gas and sundries before heading up the Mohawk Trail.

Historic Deerfield
When Henry Flynt took his son to Deerfield Academy in the 1930s, he was amazed to see how well-preserved the center of the town of Deerfield was. Over the years, he set about buying and restoring the old homes and putting them into a trust. The result today is an

Historic Deerfield

© TIM GRAFFT/MOTT

open-air museum (84B Old Main St., 413/774-5581, www.historic-deerfield.org, 9:30 A.M.–4:30 P.M. daily Apr.–Nov., $12 adults, $5 youth 6–17, free children under 6) that provides one of the best introductions to early New England history. Thirteen houses built between 1730 and 1850 contain 25,000 antique items from around New England, while museum exhibits tell the story of the early settlers of the area. Innovative hands-on history classes allow you to learn skills from sheep-shearing to open-hearth cooking.

Other Sights

Like the world's largest ball of twine, the **Yankee Candle Flagship Store** (25 Greenfield Rd., S. Deerfield, 877/636-7707, www.yankeecandle.com, 9:30 A.M.–6 P.M. daily Jan.–Jul; free) grew from humble beginnings into a tourist trap of epic proportions. At its center is a warehouse-sized candle store, an alphabetized assault on the nostrils from apple cider to white zinfandel. That is just the beginning, however, of a complex that includes countless home-goods stores, a candle-making museum, and even a Bavarian Christmas village complete with model trains and gondolas. Even on the coldest days, the **Magic Wings Butterfly Conservatory** (281 Greenfield Rd., S. Deerfield, 413/665-2805, www.magicwings.com, 9 A.M.–6 P.M. Memorial Day–Labor Day; 9 A.M.–5 P.M. Sept.–May, $12 adults, $10 seniors, $8 children 3–17, free children under 3) is a doorway into a tropical vacation, with walkways through lush vegetation and 3,000 butterflies of all shapes and colors flitting past. "Flight attendants" are available to help identify species.

Shopping

Dinosaurs leap from the brush behind **The Rock Fossil and Dinosaur Shop** (213 Greenfield Rd., Rtes. 5 & 10, S. Deerfield, 413/665-7625, www.georgesrocks.com), a deliciously cheesy gem and fossil store that features its own mini–Jurassic Park and "mines" where kids can go spelunking.

Food

Why should meat-eaters get all the beer? **The People's Pint** (24 Federal St., Greenfield, 413/773-0333, www.thepeoplespint.com, 4 P.M.–midnight Mon.–Fri.; noon–midnight Sat.–Sun., $6–16) melds a vegetarian ethos with finely crafted drafts. Meals of blackened veggie burgers and cheese plates are apt to please vegetarians and carnivores alike; the restaurant offers discounts for bike riders.

With food so beautifully plated you almost don't want to eat it, **Sienna** (6-B Elm St., S. Deerfield, 413/665-0215, www.siennarestaurant.com, 11 A.M.–2 P.M. and 5–10 P.M. Mon.–Sat., 11 A.M.–2 P.M. and 5–9 P.M. Sun.; $17–20) is a culinary gem that could hold its own anywhere in the world. Eat it you should, because the delicate flavors of chef Richard Labonte's roast duck breast and pan-seared beef tenderloin virtually melt on the tongue. The decor of bamboo stalks and burnt-sienna walls strives to be as elegant as the food.

Information

The **Upper Pioneer Valley Visitors Center** (18 Miner St., I-91, Exit 26, 413/773-9393) has information about Deerfield, Greenfield, and the Mohawk Trail.

SPORTS AND RECREATION
Six Flags New England

New England's premier amusement park (Rte. 159/1623 Main St., Agawam, 413/786-9300, www.sixflags.com, hours vary Apr.–Oct., $42 adults, $31 youth under 5'3", free children under 3) has more than 100 rides and thrills, including the must-ride Bizarro roller coaster and a gargantuan water park with a "rocket-propelled" water coaster. Be forewarned, however, that the park can get both pricey and crowded. The best strategy is to pick either the theme park or the water park, and invest in the quick pass that helps you beat the lines.

Walking and Hiking

The 157-acre **Look Park** (Northampton, 413/584-5457, www.lookpark.org) is a beautifully sculpted Victorian park that really does have something for everyone. In addition to walking trails, paddle boats, and picnic shelters, it has a small zoo, train ride, and mini-golf course.

A few miles west of Northampton is the trailhead for **Chesterfield Gorge** (River Rd., W. Chesterfield, 413/532-1631, www.thetrustees.org), a half-mile trail that traces the seventy-foot-high cliff walls of a chasm over the Westfield River. The gorge is the entrance to an expansive recreation area that features catch-and-release fly-fishing for trout.

Biking

The 10-mile **Norwottuck Rail Trail** (Damon Rd., Northampton, 413/586-8706, ext. 12) provides a pleasant afternoon ride along the Connecticut River between Northampton and Amherst. The trail offers diverse scenery of farmland, tobacco barns, and swampy conservation area frequented by birds, turtles, and other critters. Bicycles can be rented at the Damon Road entrance in Northampton, and at **Laughing Dog Bicycles** (63 S. Pleasant St., Amherst, 413/253-7722, www.laughingdogbicycles.com).

Camping and Canoeing

You can rent canoes and kayaks at **Barton Cove** (Rte. 2, Gill, 413/863-9300, late May-early Sept., boat rentals: $25 up to 2 hours, $40/day, tents: $22/night), a campground on a bend in the Connecticut River within easy paddling distance of the scenic French King Gorge. The camp also provides a shuttle for longer river trips.

Cross-Country Skiing

The **Northfield Mountain Cross Country Ski Area** (Rte. 63, Northfield, 800/859-2960, $12 adults, $11 seniors, $6 children 8–14, free children under 8, rentals: $14 adults, $9 children under 14) provides 25 miles of groomed and sculpted trails including backwoods jaunts and grueling mountain climbs.

ACCOMMODATIONS
Under $100

West Springfield has many budget hotels, including an **Econo Lodge** (1553 Elm St., W.

Springfield, 413/734-8278, www.econolodge.com, $65–109). The **Five College Bed & Breakfast Association** (www.fivecollegebb.com) lists many small bed-and-breakfasts in the area. One of the most popular is the **Lupine House** (185 N. Main St., Florence, 413/586-9766 or 800/890-9766, www.lupinehouse.com, $80–90), where hosts Evelyn and Gil Billings go out of their way to make guests feel at home. In addition to a fireplace, VCR, and computer access, the house provides convenient access to the bike path.

$100-150

For a touch of the old grandeur of Springfield, check into the **Lathrop House B&B** (188 Summer Ave., Springfield, 413/736-6414, www.lathrophousebandb.com, $100–175), an 1899 columned mansion that had previous lives as both a Jewish temple and an art school. The multilingual innkeeper tends a rose garden and outdoor swing, and cooks breakfast in a kosher kitchen. Looking like the gingerbread house right out of the Brothers Grimm, the surprisingly affordable **C Allen House Inn** (599 Main St., Amherst, 413/253-5000, www.allenhouse.com, $75–195) sports art, antiques, and wall coverings meticulously chosen to evoke Emily Dickinson's day. A five-course breakfast is included.

Black walnut trees dot the acre of grounds at the **Black Walnut Inn** (1184 N. Pleasant St., Amherst, 413/549-5649, www.blackwalnutinn.com, $120–170), a luxurious Federal-style brick mansion. The rooms are individually decorated with sleigh beds and lace and organza canopy beds; the largest has a gas fireplace and whirlpool tub. Children are welcome—and will appreciate the hot apple pie served with breakfast.

$150-250

The grand brick **Hotel Northampton** (36 King St., Northampton, 413/584-3100 or 800/547-3529, www.hotelnorthampton.com, $205–270) is a 1927 colonial revival building overlooking a park downtown. Rooms are filled with floral prints and include wireless Internet,

HBO, and continental breakfast. You can't get much closer to history than the **Deerfield Inn** (81 Main St., Deerfield, 413/774-5587, www.deerfieldinn.com, $150–260), located within the heart of Historic Deerfield. The rooms include four-poster beds, plush mattresses, and plaques telling the story of historic town residents. In one room, a ghost named Herschel is known to throw magazines around when peeved.

INFORMATION AND SERVICES

For hospital and emergency services, turn to **Baystate Medical Center** (759 Chestnut St., Springfield, 413/794-0000, www.baystatehealth.com), and for pharmacy needs, to chains such as **Rite Aid** (198 Pine St., Florence, 413/584-0182, www.riteaid.com). Banks are found all over the area (particularly in Springfield), and ATMs are easy to find all over Springfield and Northampton at bus stations, in and around hotels, in convenience stores, and, of course, at banks.

Free **Internet access** is offered at **Springfield City Library** (220 State St., Springfield, 413/263-6828, www.springfieldlibrary.org) and on the campuses of the area's colleges. Find faxing and shipping services at **The UPS Store** (340 Cooley St., Springfield, 413/782-2277, theupsstore.com).

GETTING THERE AND AROUND

I-91 runs like a spine down the Pioneer Valley, connecting the Mass Pike (I-90) to the south and Route 2 to the north. Shuttles to the valley are available from **Bradley International Airport** (11 Schoephoester Rd., I-91, exit 40, Windsor Locks, www.bradleyairport.com), just south of Springfield over the Connecticut border. All of the major car rental companies are available at the airport. Several shuttle companies offer transport from Bradley Airport, including **Valley Transporter** (413/253-1350, www.valleytransporter.com) and **Michael's Limousine & Airport Service** (800/555-5593, www.michaelslimo.com). Shuttles to Springfield take about 15 minutes and cost around $40.

Springfield is the headquarters for **Peter Pan Bus Lines** (1776 Main St., 800/343-9999, www.peterpanbus.com), which has routes from the airport and all over Western Massachusetts, including to stations in Northampton (1 Roundhouse Plaza) and Amherst (8 Main St., 893 West St., University of Massachusetts). Trains arrive at the **Springfield Amtrak Station** (66 Lyman St., 800/872-7245, www.amtrak.com).

Buses to all locations within the valley are run by the **Pioneer Valley Transportation Authority** (413/781-7882, www.pvta.com).

The Mohawk Trail

Souvenir dinner plates and sepia picture postcards come to mind along the Mohawk Trail, which seems perpetually stuck in an era of early-twentieth-century auto-touring. The route was established as a scenic byway in 1914, and still has a retro feel, with motor-lodges, cottages, Native American trading posts, and scenic overlooks lining the roller coaster ride through the mountains.

Historically speaking, the Mohawk really did use the stretch of what is now Route 2 that bears their name. The Mohawk hiked from New York through the mountains to find prime fishing spots and, on more than one occasion, to attack enemies—including the infamous French-Indian raid on Deerfield in 1704. Nowadays the biggest threat is the lack of amenities between Greenfield and North Adams. Make sure your gas tank is full and brakes and coolant are in prime condition before tackling the scenic stretch.

◖ SHELBURNE FALLS

A short detour off the Trail, this delightful village feels stranded in time. Actually the meeting place of two towns—Shelburne and Buckland—the town is a curious blend of old-time Americana and enlightened headquarters for artisans and craftspeople. Its main street is lined with owner-occupied shops and diners, and crawling with teenagers who, aside from the Slipknot T-shirts and low-rise shorts, might have stepped out of an Archie comic.

Sights

The main attraction in town is the so-called **Bridge of Flowers,** a once-blighted trolley bridge that was transformed by the local women's club in 1928. Now the 400-foot span is a linear garden full of more than 300 varieties of flowering plants, with some trees a dozen feet high. The town's other main attraction is a natural one—underneath Salmon Falls the **"glacial potholes"** are a lunar landscape of holes up to 40 feet wide, formed by the swirling action of little stones during the last ice age. While not open for swimming, they make for picturesque viewing.

Shopping

Modern arts and crafts can be found at the many artisan shops in Shelburne Falls. At **Young Constantin & Associates Glass** (4 Deerfield Ave., 866/625-6422, http://yandc-glass.com/), you can watch artisans blow and shape stained-glass vases and ornaments in a blast furnace before purchasing them next door. By the glacial potholes, **Mole Hollow Candles** (3 Deerfield Ave., 877/226-3537, www.molehollowcandles.com) sells foot-long tapers and votive candles, as it has for more than 30 years.

Food

Bridge Street Cafe (65 Bridge St., 413/625-6345, $5–9) offers home-style cooking in a cute country kitchen, with vinyl floral tablecloths and black-and-white photos on the wall. Slightly more formal, **The Shire Restaurant** (2 State St., 413/625-2727, $13–19) serves blackened chicken sandwiches and portabella parmigiana on an outdoor deck overlooking the Bridge of Flowers. Sure, there are snacks, but

Shelburne's Bridge of Flowers

© KINDRA CLINEFF/MOTT

go for the beer (and more beer) at **Moan and Dove** (460 West St., 413/256-1710, Mon.–Fri. 3 P.M.–1 A.M. Mon.–Fri.; 1 P.M.–1 A.M. Sat.–Sun., $9–21), home of more on-tap selections than you can shake a bottle at. Meanwhile, those who proudly claim membership to the cult of the popover will find utter bliss at **Judie's Restaurant** (51 North Pleasant St., 413/253-3491, 11:30 A.M.–10 P.M. Sun.–Fri., 11:30 A.M.–11 P.M. Sat., $14–22, www.judiesrestaurant.com). The funky, centrally located spot (overlooking downtown square) serves sandwiches, light daily specials, homemade soups, and (of course) killer popovers at hand-painted tables—and on the way out, sells apple butter and poppy seed salad dressings, to boot.

Information

The **Village Information Center** (75 Bridge St., 413/625-2526, www.shelburnefalls.com) has information about the town and the rest of the Mohawk Trail.

CHARLEMONT TO NORTH ADAMS

As the Mohawk Trail continues, it quickly becomes one of the most scenic drives in all of New England, playing tag with the Deerfield and Cold Rivers and opening up on stunning vistas of the surrounding hills.

Sights

The most recognizable symbol along the trail is the **"Hail to the Sunrise" Memorial,** a half-ton bronze statue of a praying Mohawk man erected near the highway at the crossroads town of Charlemont to pay homage to the Mohawk Indians. A short detour up Route 8A is the **Bissell Covered Bridge,** a 120-foot-long span over the Deerfield River. The best panoramic view is at **Whitcomb Summit,** the highest point of the trail at 2,200 feet.

Events

The acoustics in the Federated Church in Charlemont are near-perfect, making it a beautiful setting for the **Mohawk Trail Concerts**

THE HOOSAC TUNNEL

Before there was the "Big Dig," there was the Hoosac Tunnel, a massive project during the 19th century that became the construction boondoggle of its day. During 20 years of construction, workers learned the hard way how to use nitroglyceride – claiming the lives of 195 men in the process – and Massachusetts was driven into debt for a tunnel made obsolete almost as soon as it was completed due to the building of the Erie Canal. Even so, those who worked on it could take pride in the fact that a 4¾-mile tunnel met in the middle of the range within 1/16 of an inch. You can view the eastern portal of the tunnel, which still carries train traffic, by taking the long winding Whitcomb Hill Road (just east of the Whitcomb Summit) down from Route 2 to the Deerfield River. Turn left on River Road and drive until you hit the train tracks. The entrance is a short walk down the tracks to the left. In addition, North Adams' **Western Gateway Heritage State Park Visitors Center** (115 State St., Bldg. 4, 413/663-6312, www.mass.gov, 10 A.M.–5 P.M. daily, free) has a film and exhibits about the construction of the tunnel, which still stands as the longest railroad tunnel in North America.

(75 Bridge St., 413/625-9511 or 888/MTC-MUSE, www.mohawktrailconcerts.org, Fri.–Sat. in late June–July, $15–20), a series that brings internationally renowned musicians to play chamber music.

Shopping

If you've ever hankered after moccasins, dream-catchers, or spirit animals enameled on jewelry boxes, you've come to the right place. Several Native American emporiums line the trail, including **Big Indian Shop** (2183 Mohawk Trail, between Shelburne Falls and Charlemont, 413/625-6817, 9 A.M.–5 P.M. daily), which boasts a 20-foot-tall statue of a

Native American man and includes a petting zoo, and the **Wigwam and Western Summit Gift Shop** (2350 Mohawk Trail/Rte. 2, North Adams, 413/663-3205, www.thewigwam.net), which offers a stunning view from coin-operated binoculars.

SPORTS AND RECREATION
Boating
The white water of the Deerfield River provides the best terrain for kayaking and rafting in southern New England. Two companies have mastered the river. The original pioneer of the Deerfield is **Zoar Outdoor** (7 Main St., Charlemont, 800/532-7483, www.zoaroutdoor.com, Apr.–Oct., rafting $78–95/day), which runs a popular 10-mile rafting trip through the raging Zoar Gap, along with other weekend and day trips on the river. It also leads canoeing, kayaking, rock climbing, and biking trips. The Maine-based **Crab Apple White Water** (2056 Mohawk Trail/Rte. 2, Charlemont, 800/553-7238, www.crabapplewhitewater.com, Apr.–Oct., rafting $40–107/day) also offers half- and full-day rafting and inflatable kayak trips on the Deerfield, as well as other rivers throughout New England. It prides itself on its riverside cooking.

Hiking
Several trailheads leave from in and around Shelburne Falls, including an easy walk to the scenic High Ledges picnic area, and a more rugged five-mile riverside footpath along the Mahican-Mohawk Trail. Maps are available at the town information center.

ACCOMMODATIONS
Under $100
This region abounds in cheap lodging, from roadside motels to family-owned bed-and-breakfasts. One of the best is **Maple House B&B** (51 Middletown Hill Rd., Rowe, 413/339-0107, www.maplehousebb.com, $60–100), an 18th-century farmhouse situated on acres of scenic grounds with a beautiful view of the mountains. Friendly hosts Rebecca and Michael Bradley provide five rooms filled with homemade quilts and wall-hangings, as well as a full breakfast. Not to be confused with Maple House, **Six Maple Street B&B** (6 Maple St., Shelburne Falls, 413/625-6807, www.sixmaplestreet.com, Fri.–Sun. May–Nov. only, $90–100) is in a colonial home built by one of the original settlers of Shelburne Falls, and one of the only places to stay within walking distance of town. The low-ceilinged rooms are filled with antique bottles, clocks, and books. Baths are shared and children are not allowed.

$100-150
Set up on a hill overlooking the trail, ◖ **The Warfield House Inn** (200 Warfield Rd., Charlemont, 413/339-6600 or 888/339-8439, www.warfieldhouseinn.com, $100–125) is the area's most unique place to stay. Part working family farm, part country resort, the bed-and-breakfast offers a chance to meet cows, llamas, and emus. Rooms in the two converted farmhouses are simply decorated, but include access to common fireplaces and hot tubs.

Northern Berkshires

The towering peak of Mount Greylock dominates the skyline from many a backcountry road here. The highest peak in Massachusetts, it is capped by a war memorial that enables viewers to pick it out from a distance, and sets the wild tone for the area's mountainous terrain. This corner of the state has always been its most remote, a fact that has led at times to economic stagnation. The combination of cosmopolitan Williamstown and the spreading influence of summer folk in the southern Berkshires, however, has given the area a new lease on life as a cultural destination, anchored by a pair of art museums worth the trip from anywhere in New England.

MASSACHUSETTS

NORTHERN BERKSHIRES

To Greenfield

VERMONT
MASSACHUSETTS

NORTH ADAMS DETAIL

Natural Bridge State Park ★
CENTER FOR ROBOTIC ARTS ★
MASSACHUSETTS MUSEUM OF CONTEMPORARY ART

THE PORCHES INN ★
★ WESTERN HERITAGE STATE PARK

MOHAWK TRAIL

To Northampton

Deerfield River

Monroe

Monroe State Forest

HOOSAC TUNNEL EAST ENTRANCE

Cold River

Florida

Tannery Falls

Tower Brook

Gulf Brook

Savoy Mountain State Forest

Windsor State Forest

Notchview Reservation (TTOR)

Windsor

WHITCOMB HILL RD

North Branch Hoosic River

Clarksburg State Park

Clarksburg

SEE NORTH ADAMS DETAIL

CENTRAL SHAFT RD

HOOSAC TUNNEL

Spruce Hill

North Pond
South Pond

Adams

North Adams

SEE WILLIAMSTOWN DETAIL

NOTCH RD

HOT TOMATOES

Williamstown

To Bennington

Hoosic River

Taconic Trail State Park

South Williamstown

GUEST HOUSE AT FIELD FARM

GREYLOCK MOUNTAIN RD (CLOSED IN WINTER)

BERKSHIRES VISITORS BUREAU
STONE SOUP CAFE/TOPIA ARTS CENTER

Mt Greylock ▲

BASCOM LODGE

Mount Greylock State Reservation

ROCKWELL RD (CLOSED IN WINTER)

Cheshire

Appalachian Trail

BERKSHIRE ATHENAEUM and Pittsfield

New Ashford

Lanesborough

Hancock

NEW YORK
MASSACHUSETTS

3 mi
3 km

WILLIAMSTOWN DETAIL

Hoosic River

MEZZE BAR & BISTRO

CHAPIN LIBRARY

WILLIAMS COLLEGE MUSEUM OF ART

GOLD-BERRY'S B&B

★ THE STERLING AND FRANCINE CLARK ART INSTITUTE

© AVALON TRAVEL

NORTH ADAMS

It'd be hard to find a more stirring urban renewal story than North Adams, a depressed mill town that hit rock bottom in the 1990s when its main employer, Sprague Electric, took its marbles and went home. Back then, someone had the hare-brained idea to create a modern art museum in some of the old mill buildings. Fast forward a decade, and not only is the Massachusetts Museum of Contemporary Art a wild success, but its opening started a chain reaction leading to dozens of art studios, fine restaurants, and even a boutique hotel that has made this once-downtrodden town the hippest place in 100 miles. Despite its success, the town hasn't given up its working-class roots, making it a fascinating combination of opposites, with lunch-pail conservatives and blue-haired hipsters doing a daily dance of discovery with one another.

◖ Massachusetts Museum of Contemporary Art (MassMoCA)

Just the size of this museum (1040 Mass MoCA Way, 413/662-2111, www.mass-moca.org, 11 A.M.–5 P.M. Wed.–Mon. mid-Sept.–late June; 10 A.M.–6 P.M. daily late June–early Sept., $15 adults, $10 students, $5 children 6–16, free children under 6) is cause for oohs and ahs. Composed of 27 red-brick former factory buildings and connected by an interlocking network of bridges, walkways, and courtyards, the galleries are of a vast size that allows artwork of an unusually epic scale—whether it's cars suspended with glowing fiber-optic cables, or a pyramid of action figures constructed by Norman Rockwell's grandson. Indeed, some say that the building is often more impressive than the artwork inside. But whatever its quality, the art is presented with a lack of pretension and an almost infectious delight in the creative process that makes the museum quite unlike any other.

Other Sights

The brainchild of local artist Eric Rudd, the

Center for Robotic Arts (Historic Beaver Mill, 189 Beaver St., 413/664-9550, www.darkrideproject.org, 11 A.M.–5 P.M. Wed.–Sun. summer–fall, $10 adults, $7.50 seniors and students, children under 6 free) consists of a 15,000-square-foot immersive environment filled with robotic art creatures and moving sculptures for visitors to interact with. Rudd has also constructed **A Chapel for Humanity,** an overwhelming, gigantic tableau of 54 ceiling panels and 150 life-sized figures in the tradition of Rodin's *Gates of Hell,* installed in a former Baptist church at 82 Summer Street. In addition to the Beaver Mill, where the Dark Ride is located, the **Eclipse Mill** (243 Union St., 413/664-9109, www.eclipsemill.com) has also been converted into artists space, with 60 artists inhabiting 40 lofts, and eight galleries open to the public.

For a trip back in time, the **North Adams Museum of History and Science** (115 State St., Bldg. 5A, 413/664-4700, www.geocities.com/northadamshistory, 10 A.M.–4 P.M. Sat. and 1–4 P.M. Sun. Nov.–Apr.; 10 A.M.–4 P.M. Thurs.–Sat. and 1–4 P.M. Sun. May–Oct., free) is a wonderful evocation of small-town Americana, made more precious by the amateur quality of its exhibits. Three floors of old photos, clothing, Native American artifacts, and kitschy dioramas tell the story of the town from its founding.

Entertainment

In addition to its art exhibits, **MassMoCA** (Fri.–Sat. year-round, free–$30) serves as the cultural center of the community, staging silent movies accompanied by a string quartet, cutting-edge dance performances, and avant-garde musical performances by the likes of Yo La Tengo and Laurie Anderson.

Nightlife

In the nearby town of Adams, a Greek musician and a New York choreographer recently opened **Stone Soup Cafe** (27A Park St., 413/743-9600, www.topiaarts.org, 11 A.M.–2 P.M., Tue.–Sun., 6–11 P.M. Fri.–Sat.), an "art bar" with graceful nudes painted on the walls and wine tastings, music, and "aerial dance" on the schedule. The owners' eventual plan is to renovate a dormant 80,000-square-foot theater space behind the bar to offer concerts and avant-garde theater performances.

Shopping

The owner of **Persnickety Toys** (13 Eagle St., 413/662-2990, 10 A.M.–8 P.M. Thu., 10 A.M.–6 P.M. Fri.–Wed.) got so sick of driving to specialty stores for non-mass-produced toys that she opened her own shop. The one-of-a-kind folk-art objects at **Widgitz** (16 Eagle St., no phone) include country scenes painted on saw blades by a local barber. Tucked into an unassuming storefront, **Tangiers** (45 Main St., 413/664-4444, tangiersnorthadams.blogspot.com, 10 A.M.–6 P.M. Mon.–Fri.; 10 A.M.–4 P.M. Sat.) is a treasure trove of post-ironic gifts, along with a massage parlor and tanning salon.

Food

The cheapest meal in town is **Jack's Hot Dogs** (12 Eagle St., 413/664-9006, www.jackshotdogstand.com, 10 A.M.–7 P.M. Mon.–Fri.; 10 A.M.–4 P.M. Sat., $1–3), an authentic lunch counter dishing out dogs and burgers to blue-collar types who line the counter two deep at lunch time. If you are *really* hungry, you can enter the ongoing hot dog–eating competition—the record at press time was 30. Though it serves creative New American cuisine, ◖ **Gramercy Bistro** (24 Marshall St., 413/663-5300, www.gramercybistro.com, 5–10 P.M. Wed.–Mon., $18–26) lives up to the "bistro" concept, with excellent food, reasonably priced.

Information

The **North Adams Office of Tourism** (6 W. Main St., 413/664-6180, tourist@northadams-ma.gov) runs an information office in town. In Adams, the **Berkshire Visitors Bureau** (3 Hoosac St., Adams, 413/743-4500, www.berkshires.org) runs a mammoth visitors center providing information on the entire Berkshire region.

WILLIAMSTOWN

A sign at the crossroads of Williamstown's small town center proclaims the town "the village beautiful"—and so it is. Completely ringed by mountains, the town is dominated by Williams College, whose green lawns and eclectic architecture makes every street corner a Kodak moment. The college is actually one of the oldest in the country, founded in 1791 through the will of Colonel Ephraim Williams, who was killed during the French and Indian Wars, but provided money for the establishment of a "free school" in the town of West Hoosac, provided it change its name to Williamstown. Just 30 years after its founding, the president and half the student body left to found Amherst College in the southeast, thus ensuring a rivalry that continues in sports to the present day. Today, the town is well known for its art museums and theater festival, which brings theatergoers from New York and Boston every summer.

◖ The Sterling and Francine Clark Art Institute

Visitors to this small mountainside museum (225 South St., 413/458-2303, www.clarkart.edu, 10 A.M.–5 P.M. daily July–Aug.; 10 A.M.–5 P.M. Tues.–Sun. Sept.–June; $12.50 adults, free students and children under 18 June–Oct.; free to all Nov.–May) are often agog that so much high-quality art is contained in a relatively obscure location. The Clark is simply one of the best small museums in the country, with a collection full of gems picked by the unerring eyes of its founders. Works by Renoir, Monet, Degas, Copley, Remington, and other well-known artists each seem hand-picked for their individual beauty or interest, often even surprising visitors familiar with a particular artist with unusual works.

Other Sights

For such a small college, Williams has an excellent art-history program, and many curators of art museums around the country are graduates of the school. That tradition is felt at the **Williams College Museum of Art** (15

Lawrence Hall Dr., 413/597-2429, www.wcma. org, 10 A.M.–5 P.M. Tues.–Sat.; 1–5 P.M. Sun., free), which has an excellent collection of 20th-century art along with a collection of underrated American Impressionist Maurice Prendergast. Williams is also the only institution outside the National Archives to have an original copy of each of the four founding documents of the United States (the *Declaration of Independence,* the *Constitution,* the *Bill of Rights,* and the *Articles of Confederation*) on view at the **Chapin Library** (temporarily located at Southworth Schoolhouse, 96 School St., 413/597-2462, www.williams.edu, 10–noon and 1–5 P.M. Mon.–Fri., free).

Events
For more than 50 years, some of the biggest names of Hollywood have descended upon the **Williamstown Theatre Festival** (413/458-3200, www.wtfestival.org, July–Aug., $15 for rush tickets, $20 for musical productions) to try out their acting chops on the stage. The festival stages a range of productions, from gala premieres to intimate play readings, allowing theatergoers a chance to see a different side of Ethan Hawke, Gwyneth Paltrow, Marisa Tomei, and dozens of other acclaimed actors.

Shopping
The main drag of Spring Street is full of art galleries and antiques shops. Owned by two Williams alumni (including a former overseer of Boston's Isabella Stewart Gardner Museum), the **Harrison Gallery** (39 Spring St., 413/458-1700, www.theharrisongallery.com, 10 A.M.–5:30 P.M. Mon.–Sat.; 11 A.M.–4 P.M. Sun.) displays artists of national standing. **LiAsia Gallery** (31 Spring St., 413/458-1600, 11 A.M.–5 P.M. Mon.–Fri.; 10 A.M.–5 P.M. Sat.; noon–5 P.M. Sun.) specializes in antique Chinese altar tables and architectural items. The overwhelming **Library Antiques** (70 Spring St., 413/458-3436, www.libraryantiques.com) has everything from Victorian-era books to mahogany beds from India.

Food
Many of the actors who have performed at the Williamstown Theatre Festival over the years are enshrined in sandwich form at **Pappa Charlie's Deli** (28 Spring St., 413/458-5969, 8 A.M.–8 P.M. daily), from Richard Chamberlain (turkey, swiss, and cranberry sauce) to Gwyneth Paltrow (eggplant parmesan). The popular student hangout has many vegetarian options. A wide variety of homemade cookies and pastries is available at **Tunnel City Coffee** (100 Spring St., 413/458-5010, 6:30 A.M.–6:30 P.M., daily), which serves coffee roasted in North Adams and abounds in comfortable couches and armchairs. Gourmet takeout-pizza joint **Hot Tomatoes** (100 Water St., 413/458-2722, http://hottomatoespizza. com, 11 A.M.–10 P.M. daily) has mastered the art of Neapolitan pizza, with cracker-thin crust and fresh, chunky tomato sauce. If the weather's nice, the adjoining park is a nice place for a picnic and a stroll. The village's culinary jewel is **(Mezze Bistro + Bar** (16 Water St., 413/458-0123, www.mezzerestaurant.com, 5–9 P.M. Sun.–Thu.; 5–10 P.M. Fri.–Sat.), which blends equal parts Manhattan (leather banquettes, soft lighting, stiff martinis) and the Berkshires (birch-tree columns). A rotating menu includes such specialties as roasted skate with chanterelles.

Information
The **Williamstown Chamber of Commerce** (413/458-9077, www.williamstownchamber. com) runs a small information booth at the corner of Routes 2 and 7.

PITTSFIELD
The image of this economically depressed little city is not improved by its unfortunate-sounding name (a nod to English prime minister William Pitt, who was a sympathizer with the American colonists). In the early 20th century, the city was home to the Stanley Electric Manufacturing Company, a predecessor to electronics giant General Electric, which has long since left for greener pastures. Despite its gritty appearance, the area is now notable for several fine museums in and around the city, including two dedicated to Herman Melville,

who made his unlikely home in the landlocked community from 1850 to 1863. Recently, the city has been coming back to life with the renovation of its gorgeous 1903 Colonial Theatre and the opening of several new restaurants downtown.

◖ Berkshire Athenaeum

The grand-sounding name of Pittsfield's public library (1 Wendell Ave., 413/499-9480, www. berkshire.net/PittsfieldLibrary, 9 A.M.–5 P.M. Mon. and Fri., 9 A.M.–9 P.M. Tues.–Thurs., 10 A.M.–5 P.M. Sat. Sept.–June; 9 A.M.–5 P.M. Mon., Wed., and Fri., 9 A.M.–9 P.M. Tues. and Thurs., 10 A.M.–5 P.M. Sat. July–Aug., free) doesn't quite seem to fit its blocky, concrete appearance. Inside, however, the **Herman Melville Memorial Room** is one of the region's hidden gems—a room with hundreds of artifacts from the life and travels of the author of *Moby-Dick.* The wealth of riches inside includes a case of family photos and daguerreotypes, ceremonial paddles Melville brought back from the South Seas, the desk where he wrote *Billy Budd Sailor,* and the holy of holies—a case full of quill pens and other items that were on his desk when he died.

Other Sights

After coming so close to the ephemera of the author, also visit his old home on the south side of town, **Arrowhead** (780 Holmes Rd., 413/442-1793, www.mobydick.org, 9:30 A.M.–4 P.M. with tours hourly 10 A.M.–3 P.M. daily late May–mid-Oct.; tours by appointment only mid-Oct.–late May, $12 adults, $5 students, $3 children 6–14, free children under 6), where Melville actually wrote *Moby-Dick.* Fans will appreciate the view from the room where he completed his masterpiece about the white whale, from which the ridge of Mount Greylock looks uncannily like the back of a sperm whale.

One of the most curious religious subcultures in America, the Shakers are known for their excellent furniture, their habit of shaking themselves into trances, and their strict separation of men and women, which probably led to their demise as a culture. The **Hancock Shaker Village** (1843 W. Housatonic St., Rtes. 20 & 41, 413/443-0188, www.hancockshakervillage.org, 10 A.M.–5 P.M. daily Apr.–mid-Oct., $16.50 adults, $8 children 13–17, free children under 13) provides an eye into their lifestyle in an authentic village preserved from the mid-19th century.

Chances are you have Crane paper in your pocket. The official suppliers of paper for American currency reveals the secrets of its craft at the **Crane Museum of Papermaking** (30 South St., Dalton, 800/268-2281, www. crane.com, 1–5 P.M. Mon.–Fri. June–mid-Oct., free), located in a historic old stone mill.

A great rainy-day destination for families, the **Berkshire Museum** (39 South St., 413/443-7171, www.berkshiremuseum.org, 10 A.M.–5 P.M. Mon.–Sat.; 12–5 P.M. Sun., $11 adults, $6 children 3–18, free children under 3) has a mummy, aquarium tanks, and children's toys created by modern artist Alexander Calder.

Information

The **Pittsfield Visitors Center** (111 South St., 413/4443-9186, www.pittsfield-ma.org/ tourism.asp) provides information on the town and surrounding area.

SPORTS AND RECREATION
Mount Greylock
State Reservation

The 3,491-foot summit (Rockwell Rd., Lanesborough, 413/499-4262, www.mass. gov) of the highest peak in Massachusetts is a favorite for both challenging overnight hikes and scenic afternoon drives. Several trails lead to the summit—from Pattison Road in North Adams, the 6.7-mile trail offers terrific views from the summits of Mount Prospect, Mount Williams, and Mount Fitch, before the strenuous climb on the Appalachian Trail to the summit. From the Hopper Road in Williamstown, the challenging 4.1-mile Hopper Trail climbs along brooks and rocky rises in a steep climb to the top, with a campsite halfway. The (slightly) easier 6.9-mile Appalachian Trail up Saddle

MASSACHUSETTS

cabin atop Mount Greylock

Ball Mountain begins at Outlook Avenue in Cheshire and ends with the steep Misery Hill pitch up to the summit. For gain without the pain, a scenic auto-road (May–Oct.) climbs from Notch Road in North Adams to the summit, from which you can climb to the top of a 100-foot-high war memorial for fantastic views of virtually all of the Berkshires (and some of New York besides). Also at the top is a snack bar and visitors center with information on short hikes and nature activities, as well as accommodations in **Bascom Lodge** (413/743-1591, bascomlodge.net, May–Nov., bunks $35, private rooms $100–125).

Hiking

The region abounds with shorter hikes. A favorite of Williams students is **Pine Cobble Trail** (413/458-2494, www.wrlf.org), a 2.1-mile all-season climb beginning on North Hoosac Road and rising 2,000 feet to a quartzite outcropping with fantastic views of the valley. In North Adams, **Natural Bridge State Park** (413/663-6392 or 413/663-8469), at the intersection of Routes 2 and 8, has a short hike from a rock quarry to a pint-sized natural bridge.

Biking

Running 11 miles from Adams to Lanesboro, the **Ashuwillticook Rail Trail** (413/442-8928, www.mass.gov) offers up excellent scenery of Mount Greylock and the Hoosac Range, as well as the salt marsh habitat of the Hoosic River. The trail starts at the Adams visitors center and ends at the Berkshire Mall. Bicycles can be rented at **Berkshire Outfitters** (169 Grove St., 413/743-5900, www.berkshireoutfitters.com, $21/day).

Sculling

If you've ever envied those collegiate rowers skimming the water in their sculls, take a lesson from the **Berkshire Rowing and Sculling Society** (43 Roselyn Dr., Burbank Park, Pittsfield, 413/496-9160, www.berkshiresculling.com, May–Oct., lessons $50/hr, rentals $25/hr), which rents boats on the beautiful mountain-ringed Onota Lake.

Skiing

While just a molehill compared to the big mountains in New Hampshire and Vermont, the best small-mountain skiing in the area can be found at **Jiminy Peak** (Hancock, 413/738-5500, www.jiminypeak.com, $54–64 adults, $46–57 teens 13 to 19, $40–47 seniors and children 12 and under, $19 children 6 and under), which has a good set of steep summit trails and a half pipe for snowboarders.

ACCOMMODATIONS
Under $100
The cheapest accommodations are at once the most scenic and least convenient. Overlooking North Adams, the **Wigwam and Western Summit Cottages** (2350 Mohawk Trail/Rte. 2, 413/663-3205, www.thewigwam.net, $70) offer bare-bones cottages from May to October.

$100-150
Named after a character in Tolkien's *Lord of the Rings,* **Goldberry's Bed & Breakfast** (39 Cold Spring Rd., Williamstown, 413/458-3935, www.goldberrys.tripod.com, $80–125) aspires to be a place of refuge for "weary hobbits." Genial host Mary Terio provides high-speed Internet and homemade breads and muffins in a homey Greek Revival house a short walk from Williamstown's center. Located at the crossroads of North Adams, the **Holiday Inn Berkshires** (40 Main St., North Adams, 413/663-6500, www.ichotelsgroup.com, $91–180) offers reasonable accommodations along with inoffensive art and polyester bedspreads.

$150-250
The tiered, cubist exterior, painted in hues of teal and mauve, is your first sign that the **Guest House at Field Farm** (554 Sloan Rd., Williamstown, 413/458-3135, http://guesthouseatfieldfarm.thetrustees.org, $150–295) is not your ordinary bed-and-breakfast. A Bauhaus-inspired modernist masterpiece, the home is full of modern art and design-conscious period furniture. A heated outdoor pool, private decks, and terry-cloth robes create a sense of peaceful refuge that melds with the natural setting of 300 protected acres that surrounds the house.

In a world of techno-and-neon boutique hotels, **The Porches Inn** (231 River St., North Adams, 413/664-0400, www.porches.com, $130–335) stands out for channeling the spirit of North Adams—both old and new. Workmen's rowhouses from the 1890s have been transformed into luxury guest rooms, with DVD players and ultra-soft sheets. The design sensibility, however, comes right out of blue-collar Americana, with paint-by-numbers paintings, vintage lamps scrounged through eBay, and breakfast delivered in steel lunch pails.

GETTING THERE AND AROUND
The closest airport to the region is **Albany International Airport** (737 Albany Shaker Rd., Albany, NY, 518/242-2200, www.albanyairport.com). Taxi service from the airport is available from a variety of limousine services, including **Advantage Transportation Services** (518/433-0100, www.albanycarservice.com), which charges $75 to Williamstown and $80 to North Adams. Buses to Williamstown are run by **Peter Pan Bonanza** (www.peterpanbus.com) and stop in front of the Williams Inn at the corner of Routes 2 and 7. The company also runs buses to **Pittsfield Bus Terminal** (1 Columbus Ave., Pittsfield, 413/442-7465).

Buses throughout the region are run by the **Berkshire Regional Transit Authority** (413/449-2782 or 800/292-BRTA).

Southern Berkshires

Compared to the northern Berkshires, the towns along the southern half of the mountain chain have a more sophisticated feel. The mountains themselves are smaller and have a smoother, gentler appearance than their northern neighbors, and the area has long been a country-getaway destination for wealthy urbanites from New York and Boston. Starting in the late 1900s, robber barons and socialites established summer "cottages" in the area, ranging from stone Victorian homes to sprawling manor houses with acres of grounds. Many of these homes have found a second life as spa resorts or hotels, adding grandeur to the season of art and music that fills the hills each summer.

LENOX

During the so-called Gilded Age, Lenox was ground zero for the barons of industry who made their homes here. Much of the character of the time is preserved in the green sculpted lawns and mammoth trees overhanging the roads, with an occasional mansion poking out of the greenery. The Boston Symphony Orchestra's summer presence at Tanglewood has spawned a cottage industry of other arts series and diversions, including a vibrant (if

overpriced) gallery scene, and spas where the rich and famous come for respite from the spotlight.

(Tanglewood

Music lovers head west from Boston every summer to the warm-weather home of the Boston Symphony Orchestra (297 West St., 413/637-1600, www.bso.org, late June–early Sept.). The tradition dates back to the 1930s, when a classical music–crazy Berkshire family offered their 200-acre estate to the BSO as a gift, and legendary conductor Serge Koussevitzky gave his first all-Beethoven concert outdoors. The close feeling of nature and the outdoors imparts a languid feel to the music, often accentuated by visitors who bring picnic blankets and thermoses full of white wine. In addition to the full orchestra, the program features smaller chamber music concerts and an annual performance by singer-songwriter James Taylor.

Jacob's Pillow Dance Festival

Stars of the dance world invigorate the tiny town of Becket every summer with this internationally renowned festival (358 George Carter Rd., Becket, 413/243-0745, www.jacobspillow.org, mid-June–Aug., free–$55) founded

THE LAWN AND THE SHORT OF IT

Believe it or not, the first-rate musical performances are only part of the allure of Tanglewood, the Boston Symphony Orchestra's outdoor summer home. The other draw? The lavish picnics that concertgoers bring with them to devour on the perfectly manicured lawn during shows. These are no mere paper-bag affairs: Visitors are known to go to great lengths to outdo one another's fixings with intricate, gourmet spreads of multiple courses, wine, real glasses, and fine china and flatware. Many even tote along elaborate lawn furniture and canopies, though those outfits are relegated to the sidelines, so as not to block other guests' views of the stage. For your own picnic supplies, try **Loeb's Foodtown of Lenox** (42 Main St., Lenox, 413/637-0270, www.loebsfoodtown.com, 7 A.M.-6 P.M. Mon.-Thu. and Sat., 7 A.M.-7 P.M. Fri., 7 A.M.-4 P.M. Sun.) or better yet stop by **Nejaime's Wine Cellars** (60 Main St., 413/637-2221, www.nejaimeswine.com, 9 A.M.-9 P.M. Mon.-Sat.), which offers picnics packed and ready to go.

© TIM GRAFFT/MOTT

Edith Wharton's former mansion, The Mount

by modern-dance pioneer Ted Shawn. Every style from hip hop to ballet gets its time in the spotlight during the two-month celebration, which includes dozens of free performances and gallery talks. The main draw, however, is the showcases of artists from around the world, featuring both established companies such as Mark Morris and Alvin Ailey and emerging choreographers like Aszure & Artists.

Other Sights

You can practically hear the gossip whispering through the corridors of **The Mount Estate & Gardens** (2 Plunkett St., 413/551-5100, www.edithwharton.org, 10 A.M.–5 P.M. daily May–Oct., $16 adults, $13 students, free children under 12), *House of Mirth* author Edith Wharton's palatial home. Though much of the author's furniture was spirited to Europe following her husband's descent into mental illness, top designers have re-created the feel of the estate with antique furniture and artwork. The highlight for most visitors, however, is a stroll along the magnificent gardens, which have been meticulously sculpted with 3,000

flowers to re-create the vision of Wharton—who once famously contended she was "a better landscape gardener than novelist."

Part of the movie *Cider House Rules* was filmed at **The Museum of the Gilded Age at Ventford Hall** (104 Walker St., 413/637-3206, www.gildedage.org, 10 A.M.–3 P.M. daily, tours hourly, $12 adults, $5 children), a celebration of all things Victorian. The restored mansion was once owned by J. P. Morgan's sister, and tours bring alive the 1890s, when the Berkshires was the playground of the super-rich.

Events

Some of the best summer Shakespeare in the country is performed by **Shakespeare & Company** (70 Kemble St., 413/637-1199, www.shakespeare.org, free–$60), which performs in an air-conditioned scaffold-and-canvas theater. In addition to plays by the Bard, the company also stages premieres by area playwrights and special events, such as one-acts by Edith Wharton or interpretations of Edgar Allen Poe stories by actor F. Murray Abraham. The company is in the process of an ambitious plan to build a replica of the 1587 Rose Playhouse, surrounded by a mock-Elizabethan village.

Shopping

The main street of Lenox features many high-class boutiques and art galleries to occupy the rich during their idle time. One of the least pretentious is the **Wit Gallery** (27 Church St., 413/637-8808, www.thewitgallery.com), which features whimsical sculptures and surrealistic paintings that pop from the frames. Meanwhile, one of the most unabashedly fun is **The Gifted Child** (72 Church St., 413/637-1191, 10 A.M.–6 P.M. Mon.–Sat.; closed Sun.), a mishmash of games and books for toddlers, kids, preteens, and teens, plus cooler-than-cool clothing for all of the above ages. In nearby Lee, **Prime Outlets** (50 Water St., Rte. 20, Lee, 413/243-8186, www.primeoutlets.com, 10 A.M.–9 P.M. Mon.–Sat.; 10 A.M.–7 P.M. Sun.) features discounted clothing and housewares from dozens of name brands, including Bass, Coach, and Liz Claiborne.

Food

It's always summer at **Betty's Pizza Shack** (26 Housatonic St., 413/637-8171, http://bettyspizza.com, 11:30 A.M.–9:30 P.M. daily, $6–20), a tin-roof eatery with surfboards hung from the ceiling and some of the only cheap eats in town. A teenage and twentysomething crowd is drawn to the unlikely combination of burritos, pizza, and sandwiches.

A yellow-and-white striped awning overhangs the coveted outdoor patio at **Café Lucia** (80 Church St., 413/637-2640, www.cafelucialenox.com, 5:30 P.M.–10 P.M. Tue.–Sat., open Sun. during summer, $18–39), a bright and sophisticated Italian restaurant serving classics such as osso buco con risotto and veal parmigiana. The food is consistently good, and the wine list first-rate. **C Bistro Zinc** (56 Church St., 413/637-8800, www.bistrozinc.com, 11 A.M.–1 A.M. daily, $18–30) has earned a sterling reputation for unerring renditions of French bistro food, subtly tweaked for the modern palette by chef Michael Stahler. Expect dishes like organic chicken breast with crispy prosciutto or lobster with herb gnocchi and Pernod sauce, served in a dining room of blonde wood and circular marble tables.

Information

The **Lenox Chamber of Commerce** (12 Housatonic St., 413/637-3646, www.lenox.org) runs a visitors center in town.

STOCKBRIDGE

The quaint little town of Stockbridge doesn't just feel like a Norman Rockwell painting—it is one, as you can see from the ubiquitous reproductions of *Main Street, Stockbridge,* the artist's rendition of his adopted hometown. Rockwell painted here for the last 25 years of his life in a 19th-century carriage–barn-turned-studio behind Stockbridge center, and the museum dedicated to the master of small-town Americana is one of the region's most popular attractions. The town has gone to great lengths to preserve its Rockwellian character, with white picket fences shining in the sun and few visible relics of life after 1950 on Main Street. Of course, the tiny Main Street is just about all there is to the town, making it a quick study to say the least. But the busloads of senior citizens and tourists who book themselves in at the Red Lion Inn looking for a slice of nostalgia like it that way just fine.

C Norman Rockwell Museum

For such a supposedly vanilla artist, Norman Rockwell elicits strong reactions from viewers, who swoon at his vision of small-town life that never was, or hold their nose at his saccharine depictions of school kids in ponytails, stern but grandfatherly cops, and ubiquitous soda fountains. This large and comprehensive museum (9 Rte. 183, 413/298-4100, www.nrm.org, 10 A.M.–5 P.M. daily May–Oct.; 10 A.M.–4 P.M. Mon.–Fri. and 10 A.M.–5 P.M. Sat.–Sun. Nov.–Apr., $15 adults, $13.50 seniors, $10 students, free children under 19), however, may surprise viewers who think they know the artist from his *Life* magazine covers. Among the many paintings on exhibit is the serious series that Rockwell did on civil rights, including a haunting depiction of the three civil rights workers killed in Mississippi. Behind the museum is the artist's barn studio (open May–Oct.), preserved almost identically to the time when Rockwell painted here, and containing the artists' chair, brushes, and palette, along with his humorous collection of old military rifles and helmets.

Other Sights

Sculptor Daniel Chester French called his Berkshire home **Chesterwood** (4 Williamsville Rd., 413/298-3579, www.chesterwood.org, 10 A.M.–5 P.M. May–Oct., $15 adults, free children) his "heaven." The creator of the seated Lincoln Memorial in Washington, D.C., was one of the leading sculptors of an art period called the American Renaissance, during which a growing concentration of wealth found its outlet in patronage of parks, museums, and monuments. Tours take visitors through his elegantly appointed house, intimate studio, and 122 acres of grounds designed by the artist.

The first resident of Stockbridge, Rev. John Sergeant, came as a missionary to convert the native Mahican Indians in 1739. His home is preserved as **The Mission House** (19 Main St., 413/298-3239, www.thetrustees.org, 10 A.M.–5 P.M. late May–early Oct., $6 adults, $3 children 6–12, free children under 6), now a museum furnished with period items and containing exhibits on early colonial and Native American life.

Entertainment

At the Red Lion Inn, **The Lion's Den** (30 Main St., 413/298-5545, www.redlioninn.com) has live music nightly, ranging from Celtic to jazz to rock, along with pub grub.

Shopping

True to its name, **Country Curtains** (Red Lion Inn, 30 Main St., 800/937-1237, www.countrycurtains.com, 9:30 A.M.–8 P.M. Thu., 9:30 A.M.–6 P.M. Fri.–Wed.) carries a full selection of floral and checkerboard patterns, along with bedding, pillows, and everything else you need to turn your home into Avonlea. The trip

to West Stockbridge is worth making just to visit **Charles H. Baldwin & Sons** (1 Center St., W. Stockbridge, 413/232-7785, www.baldwinextracts.com, 9 A.M.–5 P.M. Mon.–Sat.; 11 A.M.–3 P.M. Sun.), a family-owned country store that dispenses homemade syrups and extracts, including the best vanilla extract you're ever likely to taste.

Food

An intimate bistro located on Main Street, **Once Upon A Table** (36 Main St., 413/298-3870, www.onceuponatablebistro.com, 11 A.M.–3 P.M. and 5–8:30 P.M. daily, $18–27) puts a creative American twist on continental cuisine—potpie of escargot, anyone? The chef-owned restaurant has an unpretentious but romantic atmosphere.

A rarity in the country, authentic Vietnamese cuisine is served up at **Truc Orient Express** (3 Harris St., W. Stockbridge, 413/232-4204, 11 A.M.–10 P.M. daily, $11–19), a white-tablecloth eatery originally started by two Vietnamese refugees in the 1970s. The *pho* is particularly good, as are salads, spring rolls, and seafood dishes.

Meat and potatoes figure heavily on the menu at **The Red Lion Inn** (30 Main St., 413/298-5545, 7:30 A.M.–9:30 P.M. daily, $23–34), which caters to leaf-peepers and bus tours with a heavy menu of New England classics served in a formal dining room.

Information

The **Stockbridge Chamber of Commerce** (413/298-5200, www.stockbridgechamber.org) has a small visitors booth on Main Street.

GREAT BARRINGTON

As soon as you cross the border into Great Barrington, the landscape changes, with trees and picket fences giving way to mill buildings along the Housatonic River and rusting trains on disused railroad tracks. The influx of summer guests to the Berkshires has put a new shine on a delightful downtown, making it reminiscent of what downtowns used to look like before Wal-Mart and shopping malls forced mom-and-pop stores out of business. Upscale restaurants and shops cater to the symphony and theater crowds.

Entertainment

Pronounced muh-HAY-wee, **The Mahaiwe Performing Arts Center** (14 Castle St., 413/528-0100, www.mahaiwe.org) is located in a restored 100-year-old theater and presents a first-rate, if eclectic, line-up of music, spoken-word, and theater performances. The 2005 season included a tribute to W. E. B. Dubois' "Souls of Black Folk," Cuban jazz pianist Omar Sosa, and a play reading with actress Marisa Tomei.

Events

What Tanglewood is to symphony music, the **Aston Magna Festival** (Daniel Arts Center, Alford Rd., 413/528-3595, www.astonmagna.org, $35 per concert) is to chamber music. During weekends in July and early August, both vocal and instrumental masters of the form perform at Simon's Rock College.

Shopping

A number of boutiques makes Great Barrington a great place to while away a few hours of shopping. Wistful Italian linens, robes, and hand towels are on sale at **La Pace** (313 Main St., 413/528-1888, www.lapaceinc.com, 10:30 A.M.–5:30 P.M. Mon.–Sat.; 11 A.M.–4 P.M. Sun.). Top-name women's clothing as well as spangly Indian kurta-style dresses and embroidered tapestry coats perfect for Tanglewood are on sale at **Gatsby's** (25 Railroad St., 413/528-9455). **Rubiner's Cheesemongers & Grocers** (264 Main St., 413/528-0488, 10 A.M.–6 P.M. Mon.–Sat.; 10 A.M.–4 P.M. Sun.) is Zabar's in the Berkshires, with imported cheeses from English cheddars to Italian gorgonzola. **Yellow House Books** (252 Main St., 413/528-8227, 10:30 A.M.–5:30 P.M. Mon–Sat; noon–5 P.M. Sun.) is a rambling farmhouse full of used and rare books, with a particularly good children's section. Outside of Great Barrington, the stretch of Route 7 down to Sheffield is known as **antiques alley** for its many fine antiques stores.

FROM GREAT BARRINGTON TO THE GROUP W BENCH

Every Thanksgiving, radio stations around the country play "Alice's Restaurant," an 18-minute-and-20-second talking blues satirical tour de force by folk singer Arlo Guthrie, about, among other things, his arrest for illegally dumping garbage and his subsequent rejection for service in Vietnam because of it. In fact, there actually was an Alice and she did actually own a restaurant. But at the time the song was written in 1967 she served her famous Thanksgiving dinners at the former church in Great Barrington where she lived and where much of the drama of the song takes place. Years later, in 1991, Guthrie purchased the very same church to create the **Guthrie Center** (4 Van Deusenville Rd., 413/528-1955, www.guthriecenter.org), a performance space that draws folkies from far and away for appearances by Arlo Guthrie himself as well as regular open-mic "hootenannies." The lobby of the center has photos and paintings of three generations of musical Guthries – Woody, Arlo, and Arlo's daughter Sarah Lee. Incidentally, the "Group W Bench" where Guthrie said he was banished with the other criminals and disqualified from service actually never existed. Guthrie was declared fit to serve in Vietnam, but escaped the draft because his lottery number wasn't called, not because he was arrested for illegally dumping garbage. But *that* song wouldn't have been nearly as long – or as funny!

One particularly worth a stop is **The Painted Porch** (102 So. Main St., Sheffield, 413/229-2700, www.paintedporch.com, 10 A.M.–5 P.M. daily Jun.–Dec.; 10 A.M.–5 P.M. Thu.–Mon. Jan.–May), whose owners scour the English and French countrysides for rare furniture.

Food

You can smell the garlic from the street outside

of **Baba Louie's** (286 Main St., 413/528-8100, www.babalouiessourdoughpizzacompany.com, 11 A.M.–3 P.M. and 5–9:30 P.M., $10–18) half Indian *dhaba,* half pizza cave that makes the best pizza around. The casual eatery uses a special recipe for its sourdough crusts, then piles on gourmet toppings including roasted red pepper, portabella, and chevre. A dark barroom with exposed brick walls and wooden booths, **20 Railroad Street** (413/528-9345, 11:30 A.M.–midnight or 1 A.M. daily, $8–10) serves buffalo and ostrich burgers in addition to sandwiches and pub fare. Meanwhile, bistro gets done right at **Once Upon a Table** (34 Main St., 413/298-3870, 12 P.M.–9:30 P.M. Mon.–Thurs.; 11 A.M.–10 P.M. Sat.; 11 A.M.–9 P.M. Sun., www.onceuponatable.com, $22–28). Berkshire regulars are understandably addicted to the Alaskan salmon burger with guacamole, as well as the gnocchi with roasted red pepper.

Summer reservations are made in the spring for the acclaimed **Verdura Cucina Rustica** (44 Railroad St., 413/528-8969, 5–9 P.M. Thu. and Sun.; 5–10 P.M. Fri.–Sat., $22–28), which uses the finest imported ingredients for "rustic" Tuscan cuisine of meat and seafood dishes. A happening bar menu ($7–10) at the *enoteca* next door includes a signature aged-balsamic martini.

Information

The **Southern Berkshires Chamber of Commerce** (362 Main St., 413/528-1510, www.greatbarrington.org) runs a visitors center with information on the town as well as the rest of the region.

SPORTS AND RECREATION
Spas

When the beautiful people find life too hard to bear, they book themselves in at **Canyon Ranch** (165 Kemble St., Lenox, 800/742-9000, www.canyonranch.com, 3-night packages start at $1,690), an offshoot of the original Arizona spa that takes a holistic approach to health, including exercise, bodywork, nutrition, and even lab work to get your chakras humming again.

Less intense but more relaxing, the **Cranwell Resort** (55 Lee Rd., Lenox, 413/637-1364, www.cranwell.com, 3-night packages start at $615) puts its world-class golf course front and center, along with a full range of beauty treatments, body wraps, and massages. East meets Western Mass. at the **Kripalu Center for Yoga & Health** (297 West St., Lenox, 413/448-3152, www.kripalu.org, 2-night packages start at $328), recognized as the best "yoga spa" in the country. For the rest of us, inexpensive à la carte massages and spa services are available at **Lenox Fitness Center** (90 Pittsfield Rd., Lenox, 413/637-9893, www.lenoxfitnesscenter.com), which charges $65 for a one-hour massage, and also offers reflexology, hot-stone massages, and yoga classes.

Hiking

Named by Herman Melville, October Mountain is particularly noted for its brilliant fall foliage. **October Mountain State Forest** (256 Woodland Rd., Lee, 413/243-1778, www.mass.gov) is the largest in Massachusetts, offering miles of backwoods trails and 46 campsites on a sun-drenched hillside. In the far southwestern corner of Massachusetts is one of the state's best hikes—the 20-minute ramble up to Bish Bash Falls. The waterfall tumbles through a mountain gorge down 80 feet to a sparkling pool. The hike is within **Mount Washington State Forest** (3 East St., Mt. Washington, 413/528-0330, www.mass.gov), which has more than 30 miles of trails through mountainous terrain.

Fishing

The **Berkshire Fishing Club** (Becket, 413/243-5761, www.berkshirefishing.com) runs fishing trips aboard a 16-foot bass-fishing boat on a private 125-acre lake.

ACCOMMODATIONS
Under $100

The stretch of Route 7 between Lenox and Pittsfield has many low-priced motels. The **Wagon Wheel Motel** (Rtes. 7 & 20, Lenox, 413/445-4532, www.bestberkshirehotel.com,

$45–195) is both cheery and cheesy—some of the rooms actually have heart-shaped whirlpool tubs. In Great Barrington, **The Lantern House Motel** (256 Stockbridge Rd., Rte. 7, Great Barrington, 413/528-2350, www.thelanternhousemotel.com, $45–200) has a heated outdoor swimming pool and rustic rooms set back from the road.

$100-150
The hills around Stockbridge and Great Barrington are alive with small bed-and-breakfasts. For listings, contact the **Berkshire Lodgings Association** (888/298-4760, www.berkshirelodgings.com). The ◖ **Arbor Rose B&B** (8 Yale Hill, Stockbridge, 413/298-4744, $115–185) actually has a rose arbor on the front path that blooms in mid-June. Proprietor Christina Alsop is as laid-back and unfussy as the rooms are overflowing in rich details, including four-poster beds and dramatic window treatments. Full breakfasts include Alsop's "famous" homemade muffins. A Federal-style country inn located on ten acres, **Windflower Inn** (684 S. Egremont Rd., Great Barrington, 413/528-2720, www.windflowerinn.com, $100–225) is one of those special properties where every detail feels plucked from a romance novel. Fires blaze in a stone fireplace in one room, while perennial gardens surround an outdoor swimming pool.

$150-250
The closest you'll get to a Norman Rockwell painting is a stay in the **Red Lion Inn** (30 Main St., Stockbridge, www.redlioninn.com, $95–490), an "olde New England" inn featured in Rockwell's famous painting of Stockbridge.

A wrap-around verandah with rocking chairs provides the perfect setting for an afternoon of reverie, while rooms are simply decorated in period style. For more privacy, the inn owns several detached houses in the block behind. (Pass up the "cat suite," however, as Wilbur can be a bit temperamental.)

$250 and Up
To capture the luxury of the Gilded Age, book yourself at the **Blantyre** (16 Blantyre Rd., 413/637-3556, www.blantyre.com, $675–1,300), a Tudor-style manor modeled after a Scottish castle. Living rooms are decked out with brocade chairs, dark woods, and fireplaces, while guest rooms feature four-poster beds and sweeping views of the 100-acre grounds. The crisp staff seems to anticipate guests' needs.

GETTING THERE AND AROUND
The Southern Berkshires are easily accessible from the Mass Pike (I-90) and Route 7. **Bonanza Bus Lines** (888/751-8800, www.peterpanbus.com) runs buses to the region. In Lenox, they stop at Village Pharmacy (5 Walker St.); in Stockbridge, at the visitor booth on Main Street, and in Great Barrington, at the visitors center at 362 Main Street. **Peter Pan Bus Lines** (800/343-9999, www.peterpanbus.com) also runs buses to the Village Pharmacy in Lenox.

Buses throughout the region are run by the **Berkshire Regional Transit Authority** (413/449-2782 or 800/292-2782, www.berkshirerta.com).

RHODE ISLAND

GREATER PROVIDENCE

Providence has turned what was once its black eye into a selling point: Now that the mafia that centered here has largely disappeared, the city basks in its romantically corrupt image, bolstered by its ex-mayor turned felon Buddy Cianci. Tales of the Providence Renaissance, however, are not exaggerated. Few cities in the country can claim either the kind of history-steeped beginning or modern revitalization that Rhode Island's capital has seen.

In addition to being one of the nation's oldest towns (it was founded in 1680 by Roger Williams, who was seeking refuge from the religious intolerance of Puritanical Boston), it's also one of its most forward-thinking. The population, currently about 175,000, is a mix of everyone from Portuguese immigrants and third-generation Italian families to bluebloods and international students. And when Providence celebrates its newfound renaissance—with a regular event called Waterfire that turns its two rivers into the center of a blazing (literally) party of art and music—everyone is invited.

The rest of the time, the city's thriving creative culture is thanks in large part to its partnerships with the three exceptional universities that call it home: the Ivy League powerhouse Brown, a liberal arts university; Rhode Island School of Design (RISD), an art and architecture school with graduate and undergraduate programs; and Johnson & Wales culinary school. Each of the three is considered among the very best in its field, and each continues to partner with the city on a multitude of projects—from restaurant openings and galleries

HIGHLIGHTS

◖ Providence Performing Arts Center: The ornate stage at this stunning theater is host to national shows and musicals (page 201).

◖ Brown University: Among the nation's preeminent universities, Brown is the proverbial black sheep of the Ivy League (page 203).

◖ Roger Williams Park Zoo: One of New England's finest zoos; its seven habitats house everything from armadillos to zebras (page 204).

◖ Waterfire: Providence's rivers are filled with fire and its streets filled with music during this citywide celebration (page 205).

◖ Slater Mill: This historic mill is arguably nothing less than the birthplace of the American Industrial Revolution (page 210).

◖ Herreshoff Marine Museum: You can practically feel the bracing wind and smell the salt air at this homage to everything yachting (page 214).

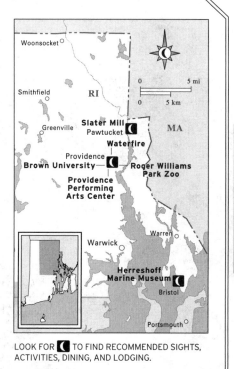

LOOK FOR ◖ TO FIND RECOMMENDED SIGHTS, ACTIVITIES, DINING, AND LODGING.

RHODE ISLAND

to public art displays—that add to the city's creative element.

That effort is intertwined with the restoration that the city and its architecture (one of the country's biggest and best shows of colonial structures) have undergone in the last several decades. In some cases that has meant simple investment and cleanup efforts. In others, it has meant enticing new blood and energy into the neighborhoods—in one such example, artists and performers were given tax breaks to live in renovated downtown buildings. The result brought new life to the historic entertainment district near the renowned Trinity Repertory Theatre and the Providence Performing Arts Center.

Many residents also credit Buddy Cianci himself. During his five terms (when he wasn't being investigated or charged by the police for assaults or mafia ties) Cianci oversaw the plan to uncover the city's two rivers, build elegant bridges around them, and otherwise beautify the downtown area. For this, the citizens of Providence were duly grateful; even while under indictment, Cianci's approval rating never dropped below 60 percent.

PLANNING YOUR TIME

With its concentrated layout, Providence is an easily walkable city, with only a handful of sites falling outside the Downtown, College Hill, and Federal Hill areas. Even on foot, it's easy to walk through each of these areas in one day, though to enjoy them more extensively, you

RHODE ISLAND

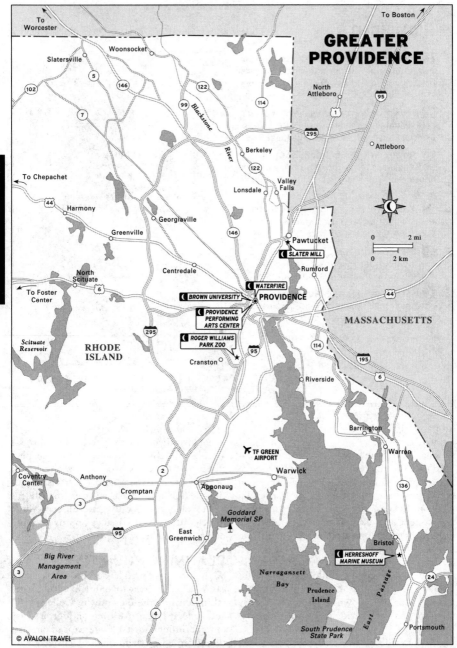

GREATER PROVIDENCE

To Worcester
To Boston

Slatersville

Woonsocket

North Attleboro

Attleboro

Blackstone River

Berkeley

Valley Falls

Lonsdale

To Chepachet

Harmony

Georgiaville

Greenville

Pawtucket

SLATER MILL

Centredale

Rumford

North Scituate

To Foster Center

WATERFIRE

BROWN UNIVERSITY

PROVIDENCE

Scituate Reservoir

RHODE ISLAND

PROVIDENCE PERFORMING ARTS CENTER

ROGER WILLIAMS PARK ZOO

MASSACHUSETTS

Cranston

Riverside

Barrington

Warren

TF GREEN AIRPORT

Warwick

Coventry Center

Anthony

Cromptan

Apponaug

Big River Management Area

East Greenwich

Goddard Memorial SP

Bristol

HERRESHOFF MARINE MUSEUM

Narragansett Bay

Prudence Island

East Passage

Portsmouth

South Prudence State Park

© AVALON TRAVEL

0   2 mi
0   2 km

may want to consider dedicating a day to each one. For example, history buffs may want to spend an entire day admiring the architecture on College Hill's Benefit Street and nearby **Brown University,** whereas those of a mind to shop may appreciate an entire day to peruse Thayer Street's shops.

In the summer, try and plan your visit to coincide with **Waterfire,** the city's inimitable artistic spectacle. Regardless of when you come, no visit to the city should be without at least one dinner at one of the restaurants on Federal Hill, the city's Little Italy, which is known as much for its delicious meals as for its equally delicious people-watching. After dinner take in a show at one of Providence's many theaters, such as **Providence Performing Arts Center** or the Tony-winning Trinity Rep.

If you have an extra day, it's well worth it to drive to the southern part of the city to spend a few hours at the excellent **Roger Williams Park Zoo,** and perhaps stroll the park or rent paddleboats to round out the day. While you can experience most of Providence's attractions in two days, those staying longer should take the third day to venture north to the Blackstone Valley, where the sites dedicated to the Industrial Revolution, such as **Slater Mill,** make for impressive viewing. Alternatively, on your way down to Newport, stop for an overnight in all-American Bristol, where you can see the America's Cup Hall of Fame at the delightful **Herreshoff Marine Museum.**

Providence

From its beginning, Providence has been a fiercely independent city. Roger Williams got the title to its land (the first populated area was on the river's east side, along the base of what is now College Hill) from Narragansett chiefs in 1636, after being exiled from puritanical Massachusetts for his religious beliefs. He then promptly founded Rhode Island's first Colonial settlement here, in the name of religious and political freedom. It wasn't long before the city was a thriving farming area and, with its active port, a player in foreign trade. Nor was it long before the city showed the spirit of defiance on which it was founded: In 1776, Providence became the very first colony to declare independence from England.

Once the war was over, the city lost no time becoming a center for—arguably even the cradle of—the Industrial Revolution. It was here that the country's jewelry industry was started by Seril and Nehemiah Dodge. And in 1793, down the road in Pawtucket, Samuel Slater built a water-powered cotton mill; as word of its success spread, other cities followed suit.

The area continued to be known for its industrialization in the 19th century. Three brothers—Nicholas, Moses, and John Brown—had a huge impact on the town's success, starting, among other industries, the area's textile trade. (And, it has been well documented, the rum and slave trades.) Immigrants from Europe and Canada, looking for manufacturing jobs, began making their way to Providence, adding to the cultural diversity that defines the city today.

After years of renovation, the ever-evolving city centers around the State House, with its marble dome and abutting green park in the Downtown neighborhood. The most sight-packed areas are concentrated around it—in the entertainment district, along the riverfront, up College Hill where Brown and RISD lie, and on the hill's other side on funky Thayer Street, with its eclectic shops and restaurants. (Most of the city's bistros and trattorias don't serve breakfast—only lunch and dinner, and sometimes only dinner. Call ahead to be certain, and rely instead on the area's abundance of cafes, diners, and hotel restaurants for earlier meals.)

SIGHTS
◖ Providence Performing Arts Center

The rejuvenation of downtown Providence's entertainment area has meant major renovations

RHODE ISLAND

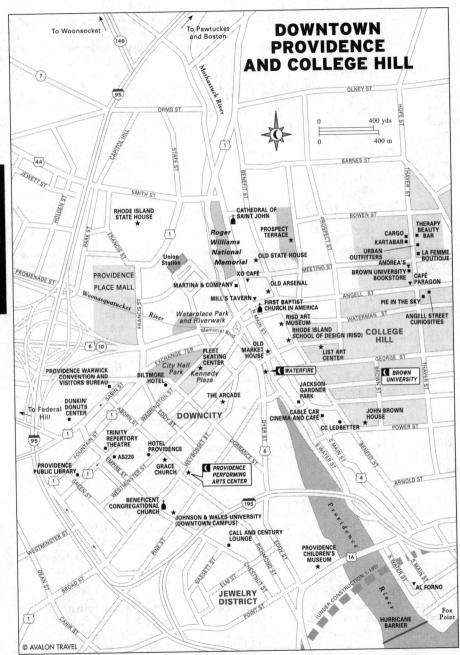

DOWNTOWN PROVIDENCE AND COLLEGE HILL

To Woonsocket

To Pawtucket and Boston

146

7

95

ORMS ST

CAPITOL HILL

STATE ST

Moshassuck River

OLNEY ST

HOPE ST

400 yds

400 m

BARNES ST

44

JEWETT ST

HOLDEN ST

PARK ST

FRANCIS ST

SMITH ST

RHODE ISLAND STATE HOUSE ★

THAYER ST

BENEFIT ST

BOWEN ST

CATHEDRAL OF SAINT JOHN

PROSPECT TERRACE ★

Roger Williams National Memorial

PROSPECT ST

CARGO ■
KARTABAR ■

THERAPY BEAUTY BAR ■

URBAN OUTFITTERS ■

LA FEMME BOUTIQUE

PROMENADE ST

PROVIDENCE PLACE MALL

Union Station

OLD STATE HOUSE ★

ANDREA'S ■

XO CAFÉ ▼

MEETING ST

BROWN UNIVERSITY BOOKSTORE ■

CAFÉ PARAGON

Woonasquatucket River

FRANCIS ST

MARTINA & COMPANY ■

MILL'S TAVERN ▼

OLD ARSENAL

FIRST BAPTIST CHURCH IN AMERICA ★

ANGELL ST

PIE IN THE SKY ■

N MAIN ST

RISD ART MUSEUM

WATERMAN ST

ANGELL STREET CURIOSITIES

Waterplace Park and Riverwalk

Memorial Blvd

RHODE ISLAND SCHOOL OF DESIGN (RISD) ★

COLLEGE HILL

6 10

EXCHANGE TER

City Hall Park

FLEET SKATING CENTER

OLD MARKET HOUSE ★

LIST ART CENTER

GEORGE ST

BROWN ST

PROVIDENCE WARWICK CONVENTION AND VISITORS BUREAU

BILTMORE HOTEL

Kennedy Plaza

WATERFIRE ◄

BROWN UNIVERSITY

THAYER ST

To Federal Hill

DUNKIN' DONUTS CENTER

SABIN ST

ABORN ST

WASHINGTON ST

EDDY ST

THE ARCADE ★

DOWNCITY

JACKSON-GARDNER PARK

DYER ST

CABLE CAR CINEMA AND CAFÉ ●

JOHN BROWN HOUSE ★

95

1

FOUNTAIN ST

TRINITY REPERTORY THEATRE

● AS220

HOTEL PROVIDENCE

WEYBOSSET ST

DORRANCE ST

6

CC LEDBETTER ■

S WATER ST

BENEFIT ST

POWER ST

PROVIDENCE PUBLIC LIBRARY

EMPIRE ST

GRACE CHURCH ★

☾ PROVIDENCE PERFORMING ARTS CENTER

4

ARNOLD ST

GREEN ST

WESTMINSTER ST

BENEFICENT CONGREGATIONAL CHURCH ★

JOHNSON & WALES UNIVERSITY (DOWNTOWN CAMPUS)

195

Providence

WESTMINSTER ST

PINE ST

BASSET ST

CALL AND CENTURY LOUNGE ■

RICHMOND ST

EDDY ST

PROVIDENCE CHILDREN'S MUSEUM ★

1A

S WATER ST

S MAIN ST

DEAN ST

BROAD ST

CAHIR ST

1

JEWELRY DISTRICT

ELM ST

CHESTNUT ST

POINT ST

(UNDER CONSTRUCTION I-195)

River

HURRICANE BARRIER

AL FORNO ▼

Fox Point

© AVALON TRAVEL

THE LEGEND OF BUDDY CIANCI

As infamous as he is famous, Providence legend Buddy Cianci was one of the longest-serving mayors of a major U.S. city (and the first Italian-American mayor of Providence). He's also one of the country's most controversial (and yet popular) political figures, inspiring everything from outrage to fascination – and even a high-profile documentary film about his life, released in 2006.

Mayor of Providence from 1974 to 1984 and again from 1991 to 2002, he was a Republican who unseated a Democrat stronghold of more than thirty years, was the chief orchestrator of Providence's renaissance, and a man who came back again and again after a multitude of political skirmishes, personal scandals, and criminal indictments. Case in point: After resigning from office for the first time in 1984 (pleading no contest to assaulting a man with a lit cigarette and a fireplace log), he spent the next few years as a Providence radio talk show host. Six years later, he managed to get himself reelected.

Never one to shy away from the spotlight, Cianci continued his media appearances on radio and TV (including the network show *Providence*), and even produced and sold his own line of marinara sauce under the label "Mayor's Own," which sported his picture. Then, in 2001, Cianci was indicted on federal criminal charges of racketeering, conspiracy, extortion, and mail fraud, and later sentenced to five years in prison for conspiracy.

Released in 2007, he promptly returned to the airwaves, with both a radio show and a job as special commentator on WLNE channel 6, where he can be seen every weekday at 4 P.M. in a segment named, what else, "Buddy TV." He was later named chief political analyst for the station, disproving F. Scott Fitzgerald's famous maxim that there are "no second acts in American lives."

for spots like this beautiful theater (240 Weybosset St., 401/421-2997, www.ppacri.org, box office 10 A.M.–5 P.M.), referred to locally as PPAC. A former Loews movie theater built in the 1920s, the gilded interior sports intricate plasterwork, marble columns, and huge crystal chandeliers. The current state-of-the-art sound system is perfect for blasting the music of the Broadway shows that are hosted here, from *My Fair Lady* and *The Lion King* to *The Nutcracker*.

Downtown

The downtown neighborhood swirls around the **State House** (Francis St., 401/222-2357), worth a look for its freestanding enormous dome—one of the largest of its kind in the world. Follow your nose a few blocks behind that to **Johnson & Wales University** (8 Abbott Park Pl., 401/598-1000, www.jwu.edu). One of the most respected culinary and hospitality programs in America, Johnson & Wales is the source of many of Providence's—and the nation's—best-known chefs and restaurateurs.

You can make like you're in Venice courtesy of **LaGondola, Inc.** (WaterPlace Park, 401/421-8877, www.gondolari.com, 5–11 P.M. Sun.–Thurs.; 4 P.M.–midnight Fri.–Sat., closed on Tues., May–Oct., $79 for first two people, $15 for each additional person). Ride in the company's (authentically Italian) brass-trimmed boats to tour the city's rivers—complete with serenade.

You can't be a graphic artist or interior designer these days without having at least heard of, if not attended, **Rhode Island School of Design** (Office of Admissions, 62 Prospect St., 401/454-6140, www.risd.edu). The campus proper runs from Benefit to Waterman Streets. For more than a century, the **Providence Art Club** (11 Thomas St., 401/331-1114, www.providenceartclub.org, 12–3 P.M. Mon.–Fri.) has met in its two 18th-century brick homes, displaying ever-changing works by the Club's members.

Brown University

One of the most competitive members of the Ivy League, Brown is known for its rigorous but non-traditional approach to liberal arts education. Translation: encouragement of interdisciplinary research and, among other things, allowing courses to be taken as a pass/fail option rather than a standard letter grading system. The tradition of exceptional faculty is mirrored by the school's other resources, including four libraries—one of which holds the world's preeminent collection of Americana from before 1825. Apart from that, the leafy hillside campus (Admission Office, 45 Prospect St., 401/863-1000, www.brown.edu) makes for an enjoyable stroll, especially during the early fall when students lounge in the quads as if posing for a calendar of brilliant minds at work.

College Hill

For a peek into the daily life of John Brown, who gave his name to the local university, pop into the **John Brown House** (52 Power St., 401/331-8575, www.rihs.org, 10:30 A.M.–4:30 P.M. Tues.–Sat. Apr.–Dec., 10:30 A.M.–4:30 P.M. Fri.–Sat. Jan.–Apr., $8 adults, $6 seniors and students, $4 children 7 and over, free children under 7). Meticulously restored, the grand Georgian mansion, built in 1786, is chock-full of excellent-quality period antiques and local art.

◖ Roger Williams Park Zoo

Several miles outside the city sits this justifiably popular zoo (1000 Elmwood Ave., 401/785-3510, www.rwpzoo.org, 9 A.M.–4 P.M. daily, $12 adults, $8 seniors, $6 children 3–12, free children under 3), considered one of the best in the region. Situated in the enormous 430-acre park, the zoo is home to more than 800 animals, plus numerous education and conservation programs. Among the highlights is an exhibit on the animals of the ancient Silk Road, including cuddly moon bears and three jaw-droppingly beautiful snow leopards, which are among the rarest creatures on earth. Another pavilion re-creates a South American rainforest, with monkeys without a net (or cage) leaping and cavorting above the heads of visitors.

Other Neighborhoods

A short drive from J&W's downtown campus sits a food fanatic's dream: the University's **Culinary Archives and Museum** (315 Harborside Blvd., 401/598-2805, www.culinary.org, 10 A.M.–5 P.M. Tues.–Sun., $7 adults, $6 seniors, $3 students, $2 children 5–18, free children under 5), a treasure trove of cookbook, menu, and cooking-equipment collections. It's considered the Smithsonian of the food world.

ENTERTAINMENT
Film

On the celluloid end of the entertainment spectrum sits the very quirky, quaint **Cable Car Cinema and Café** (204 S. Main St., 401/272-3970, www.cablecarcinema.com, afternoon and evening shows). It's where the city's hipper citizens congregate on the funky couches to take in art films, munch vegan snacks, and schmooze.

Music

Catch everything from poetry slams and improv to rock shows and comedy at **AS220** (115 Empire St., 401/831-9327, 10 A.M.–6 P.M. www.as220.org), a space dedicated to all things creative and entertaining. There's also a café-cum-bar (and a printshop for local artists). Much bigger national shows can be found at the **Dunkin' Donuts Center** (1 LaSalle Sq., 401/331-6700, www.dunkindonutscenter.com), whereas more alternative rock and blues acts tend to hit the **Call and Century Lounge** (150 Chestnut St., 401/751-2255, www.centurylounge.com). Though it bills itself as much a restaurant as a bar or club, **Kartabar** (284 Thayer St., 401/331-8111, www.kartabar.com, 6 P.M.–2 A.M.) sees the majority of its business at night, when the international students move in to soak up electronica and monopolize the place. Sleek and trendy, outfitted in shots of red and lounge-y banquettes, it's one of the most hopping (and loud) places to grab a martini in the area.

Theater

One of the most respected regional theaters in

the country, **Trinity Repertory Theatre** (201 Washington St., 401/351-4242, www.trinityrep.com, 12 P.M.–8 P.M. Tues.–Sun.) performs everything from Tennessee Williams to Shakespeare, quite often to rave review.

EVENTS

Summertime each year sees Roger Williams Park's **Hear in Rhode Island Festival** (401/949-0757, http://users.ids.net/~hearinri)—a mishmash of live music, crafts, food, and performance art. One of the most impressive festivals all year is September's **Convergence** (WaterPlace Park and India Point, 401/621-1992). The weeks-long event pulls a dizzying number of artists, dancers, filmmakers and musicians from all over Rhode Island. Boat fanatics shouldn't miss the **Providence Boat Show** (Rhode Island Convention Center, 401/458-6000, www.providenceboatshow.com) in January, every winter.

☾ Waterfire

In 1994, dozens of wood-filled braziers in the river were set alight for the city's annual New Year's Eve celebration in a massive art installation. That one-time display has now become a tradition (401/272-3111, www.waterfire.org), carried on during weekends throughout the summer. Starting at sunset, music is piped in on giant speakers, street performers and food stalls are set up on the river banks, and the city becomes one big open-air carnival, made romantic by the smell of smoke and the sight and sounds of crackling flames.

SHOPPING
College Hill

Known less as a shopping destination than a place to people watch, eat, and browse, Thayer Street has nonetheless seen an influx of young, hip new shops recently. One of the best is **Therapy Beauty Bar** (297 Thayer St., 401/331-4777, 10 A.M.–5 P.M.). Bright limeade-hued walls electrify this sunny, friendly beauty studio, where you'll find cult beauty collections like the entire line of Fresh products, plus hard-

to-find lines like T. LeClerc, Skinceuticals, and Red Flower. Services are also on offer: facials, waxing, and excellent manicures and pedicures in the upstairs loft. Down the street is **Pie in the Sky** (225 Thayer St., 401/861-3954, piegirl225@verizon.net, 11 A.M.–5 P.M.), a gift shop peddling everything from pig-shaped toasters and Lucite jewelry to Shakespeare action figures. The selection of women's clothing and accessories may not be epic at **La Femme Boutique.** (297 Thayer St., 401/270-7016, femme_boutique@yahoo.com, 10 A.M.–6 P.M.), but what's there is worth a gander. A nice selection of denim labels—Blue Cult and True Religion, for starters—plus racks of cardigans, dresses, and skirts. Women and men can bone up on the latest fads at **Urban Outfitters** (285 Thayer St., 401/351-4080, www.urbanoutfitters.com, 10 A.M.–9 P.M.); this branch of the national chain is here largely for the local college crowd, as witnessed by the extensive selections of dorm-room gadgets and accessories, trendy clothes, and CDs. Typifying Thayer Street's eclectic sensibility, **Angell Street Curiosities** (183 Angell St., 401/455-0450, www.angellstcuriosities.com, 10 A.M.–4 P.M.) overflows with vintage clothing, jewelry, postcards, and old photographs, amusingly labeled by the owner. Catering to the trust-fund backpacker, **Cargo** (294 Thayer St., 401/831-1500) clearly believe in traveling in style, with discounts on outdoor clothes from Patagonia and North Face, and hip labels like True Religion, Water Girl, and Ben Sherman.

Downtown

Off of College Hill sits **Comina** (201 Wayland Ave., 401/273-4522, comina.com, 10 A.M.–5:30 P.M.), a jumble of pretty home accessories and European furnishings—both new and antique. Strictly contemporary treasures are found at **Martina & Company** (120 N. Main St., 401/351-0968, www.martina-company.com, 11 A.M.–6 P.M. Tue.–Wed. and Fri.; 11 A.M.–7 P.M. Thu.; 10 A.M.–5 P.M. Sat.), a gallery space exhibiting the city's premiere collection of jewelry. Keep an eye out for cutting-edge pieces (silver industrial chokers and

RHODE ISLAND

wire-wrapped diamond bracelets) as well as more traditional (elegant engagement rings and delicate semiprecious earrings).

With the addition of **Providence Place Mall** (71 Providence Pl.,) 10 A.M.–9 P.M. Mon.–Sat.; 12 P.M.–6 P.M. Sun.) in the last few years, Downtown Providence now has an easy-to-access downtown mall full of national high-end chains. Of particular note is **Nordstrom** (6 Providence Place, 401/621-3111, www.nordstrom.com), one of the only in New England. The national luxury department store stocks clothes by designers like Trina Turk and Ralph Lauren, Dooney & Burke, and Marc Jacobs.

Brush up on quantum mechanics or Derrida at **Symposium Books** (240 Westminster St., 401/273-7900, www.symposiumbooks.com, 10 A.M.–6 P.M. Mon.–Wed.; 10 A.M.–8 P.M. Thu.–Sat.; 10 A.M.–5 P.M. Sun.), a huge bookstore opened by expat Manhattanites and catering to the city's collegiate crowd. Contrary to expectations, **Cellar Stories** (111 Mathewson St., 401/521-2665, www.cellarstories.com) occupies the upper floor of a Downcity warehouse with the largest selection of used books

in Rhode Island—including a good selection of rare books and first editions.

Federal Hill

The delectable truffles, caramels, and turtles made at **Ocean State Chocolate and Confectioners** (294 Atwells Ave., 401/273-2022, www.oceanstatechocolates.com, 10 A.M.–4 P.M.) incorporate surprising filings, including wine from nearby Sakonnet Vineyards. Feel like a million dollars as you puff away at **Catanzaro's Fine Cigars** (372 Atwells Ave., 401/455-0100, 10 A.M.–5 P.M.), a stogie store that includes leather chairs where you can sample the merchandise. Imported Italian groceries line the shelves at **Tony's Colonial Food Store** (311 Atwells Ave., 401/621-8675, www.tonyscolonial.com, 10 A.M.–4 P.M.) which has been selling olive oils and handmade pasta for more than 50 years.

SPORTS AND RECREATION
Hiking and Biking

Most Providence residents tend to head outside the city for their exercise, thanks to the multitude of parks within an easy drive or bus ride. Even so, runners find plenty to enjoy in jogs along the riverfront or down the very pretty and well-kept **Blackstone Boulevard**—also a favorite of bikers. You can rent bikes nearby at **Esta's** (257 Thayer St., 401/831-2651, 10 A.M.–5 P.M.).

Skating

Summer inline skaters and winter ice skaters alike flock to the outdoor **Fleet Skating Center** (Kennedy Plaza, 401/331-5544, Oct.–Mar.). On some summer nights, the rink is turned into a giant stage for salsa dancing.

Boating

Boaters who find themselves peering longingly at Narragansett Bay should head to **Baer's River Workshop** (222 S. Water St., 401/453-1633, 9 A.M.–4 P.M.) for canoe and kayak rentals.

Spas

If you could use a little decompression

MODERN IMMIGRANTS

Much of Rhode Island's ethnic history has long been identified with the influences of its Italian and Portuguese immigrants. But between 1990 and 2000 alone, the foreign-born population of Rhode Island increased by no less than 25 percent, adding 24,000 immigrants to the state (and continued to grow by an estimated 14,000 more between 2000 and 2007). This influx has both stabilized the local population numbers (which had previously been waning) and continued to add new diversity to its cities – providing a surge in immigrants from Latin America to the mix (mirroring national statistics) as well as a great number of Liberians, who began settling in the state in the early 1990s, when their home country fell into civil war.

after all your shopping, head to the serene **Spadyssy** (75 Dorrance St., 401/273-9777, 10 A.M.–8 P.M. Mon.–Fri.; 9 A.M.–6 P.M. Sat.; 12–6 P.M. Sun.) for a Swedish massage, a little yoga, or a facial employing the *gogi* berry. Or book an appointment at **Chestnut Salon** (10 Davol Sq., 401/351-5250, 9 A.M.–7 P.M. Tues.–Thurs.; 9 A.M.–6 P.M. Fri.; 8 A.M.–5 P.M. Sat.), where you can grab a Hungarian herbal mud body treatment as easily as you can microdermabrasion or a hot-oil manicure.

ACCOMMODATIONS
Under $100
The personal vibe at **CC Ledbetter** (326 Benefit St., 401/351-4699, www.ccledbetter.com, $95–115), located not far from the John Brown House and a block away from Brown University, lends a calming element to any stay. With just five bedrooms—complete with handmade quilts, antiques, paintings, and lithographs—the small 1768 house offers breakfast (included in the rates) in the living room near the fireplace.

$100-150
Historic inns abound in the city, making it possible to base your stay in something remarkably close to a miniature museum. One case in point is the **Edgewood Manor** (232 Norwood Ave., 401/781-0099, www.providence-lodging.com, $120–300). Merchant Samuel Priest had the out-of-the-way Greek Revival mansion built in 1905, and today it sports whirlpool tubs, fire places, and stained-glass windows in its three elegant floors. Don't miss the afternoon tea in the Louis XIV–style library.

$150-250
The historic 290-room **Biltmore** (11 Dorrance St., 401/421-0700, www.providencebiltmore.com, $140–210) boasts 18 suites (and, after a $10 million renovation in the last three years, wireless Internet access and voicemail). Meanwhile, the newly opened **C Hotel Providence** (311 Westminster St., 401/861-8000, www.thehotelprovidence.com, $160–180) is equally posh, what with its rich

tapestried furniture, down comforters, marble bathrooms, and Bulgari soaps. Just as charming are the pieces of local art—from city scenes to ceramic fish sculptures—that are found in every room.

FOOD
American
The airy, large dining room of **C Mill's Tavern** (101 N. Main St., 401/272-3331, www.millstavernrestaurant.com, 5–10 P.M. Mon.–Thu.; 5–11 P.M. Fri.–Sat.; 4–9 P.M. Sun., $18–31) opened in 2003 and quickly became a local favorite for big plates of icy oysters and *pappardelle* with rabbit stew. The trendy **XO Café** (125 N. Main St., 401/273-9090, www.xocafe.com, 12 P.M.–10 P.M., $26–32) oozes sleek urbanity with its red walls and epic cocktail list. The dessert list tops the menu (along with the instruction: "Life is short. Order dessert first"). But some of the entrées are just as rich—like the foie gras dumplings with champagne ponzu sauce, or the prosciutto mac 'n' cheese with truffle essence. The original outpost of the successful steakhouse chain **Capital Grille** (1 Union Station, 401/521-5600, www.thecapitalgrille.com, 11:30 A.M.–3 P.M. Mon.–Fri.; 5–10 P.M. Mon.–Thu.; 5 P.M.–11 P.M. Fri.–Sat.; 4 P.M.–9 P.M. Sun., $26–35) is a clubby, masculine house of sirloin and seafood. It's also a magnet for bigwigs and politicos, in for the dry-aged porterhouses, double-cut lamb chops, classic caviar presentations, and hefty wine list.

Very popular for pre- and post-theater dining, **Gracies** (194 Washington St., 401/272-7811, www.graciesprov.com, 4 P.M.–11 P.M., $19–24) is a refreshing combination of refinement and relaxation. The professional but friendly staff whizzes about the red-walled room, serving excellent artisanal cheese platters, and entrées like duck breast with braised apples, cranberry corn bread, and foie gras butter.

Italian
An institution on Federal Hill, **Angelo's Civita Farnese** (141 Atwells Ave., 401/621-8171,

www.angelosonthehill.com, 11:30 A.M.–9 P.M. Mon.–Thu.; 11:30 A.M.–10 P.M., Fri.–Sat.; noon–9 P.M. Sun., $3–12) has been feeding hungry crowds in a family-style atmosphere for more than 80 years. Thankfully, they haven't changed their prices much in the meantime—heaping portions of pasta and Italian meat dishes are rarely more than 10 dollars. If that's too rich for your blood, the restaurant also offers rock-bottom daily specials. Sauce and dough made daily makes **Federal Hill Pizza** (200 Atwells Ave., 401/273-7452, www.federalhillpizza.com, 11 A.M.–9P.M., $4–20) popular among pizza-lovers. Gourmet Italian toppings include kalamata olives, roasted peppers, and goat cheese; depending on your mood, you can choose outdoor seating or the dark-tinted interior, which includes a full bar and cigar humidor. Italian for "bread and wine," **Pane e Vino** (365 Atwells Ave., 401/223-2230, www.panevino.net, 11 A.M.–10 P.M., $11–31) is too modest a description for the excellent rustic fare at this romantic, candlelit *ristorante*. The emphasis is on brushed-up versions of Neapolitan cuisine, such as veal *scaloppini* with prosciutto and Madeira tomato sauce and rigatoni giganti—that is, large tube pasta with a pink cream sauce. Not that the bread (made locally at Olga's Cup and Saucer) or the wine (with two dozen Italian varieties by the glass) are anything to complain about either. At **Raphael's Bar Risto** (1 Union Station, 401/421-4646, www.raphaelbarristo.com, noon–11 P.M. daily, $18–29), bright paintings compete with clients' bright jewelry; the bar is filled with twentysomethings dressed to the nines and men in designer suits. Just as impressive are the pastas—particularly unusual creations like *trenette* with rich cheese and dried strawberries. The fried zucchini flower stuffed with ricotta is also memorable. *Sex and the City* meets *The Sopranos* at **Mediterraneo** (134 Atwells Ave., 401/331-7760, www.mediterraneocaffe.com, 12 P.M.–10 P.M., $18–34), a modern Italian eatery taking up prime real estate at the gate to Federal Hill. The city's bigwigs come here as much for the atmosphere as for the food; the French doors opening out onto the street make for exceptional people-watching. The menu is well-prepared but standard upscale fare: filet mignon, pork tenderloin, and surf 'n' turf. Restaurateurs George Germon and Johanne Killeen started the culinary fire in Providence years ago with C **Al Forno** (577 S. Main St., Fox Point, 401/273-9760, alforno@aol.com, 11 A.M.–9 P.M., $28–34), a Northern Italian spot serving everything from mouthwatering thin-crust pizza and roasted clams in spicy sausage to freshly made raspberry tart.

PROVIDENCE'S LITTLE ITALY

One of the country's most vibrant (and least touristy) Italian enclaves, the Little Italy on Federal Hill abounds with authentic trattorias boasting pretty al fresco seating, inexpensive pizzerias, *gelaterias*, and *salumerias* (grocery stores peddling imported meats, cheeses, and other specialties). The area makes for an excellent evening out; it isn't too large to explore by foot, but holds enough attractions that most visitors leave hoping for a return trip (usually for another dinner).

You'll know you've reached the neighborhood once you spot the red, white, and green stripe down Atwells Avenue and the huge pinecone (Italian symbol of abundance and quality) hanging above the street. Just past that, pick any of the reasonably priced, family-owned institutions – Angelo's Civita Farnese is a good bet – and dig into the basic but flavorful pastas. Among the stable of sit-down eateries you'll find scores of boutiques, *gelaterias*, and Italian bakeries (Scialo Bros. Bakery is a local favorite for cheesecake). Then simply walk it all off exploring the courtyards, complete with water fountains and street music, that continue down the street.

Greek

The venerable Greek tavern **Andrea's** (268 Thayer St., 401/331-7879, 11 A.M.–10 P.M.) is an institution among Brown students who

FEEDING FRENZY

None too surprisingly, seafood looms large among the finest foods found in the Ocean State. Local clams (medium-sized, hard-shell bivalves known as quahogs) are extremely popular, and show up on menus stuffed, in fried clam cakes (aka fritters), or in the state's version of clam chowder – a clear broth (minus the cream or tomato base of other renditions) full of briny clam juice.

But many local menus eschew seafood altogether, focusing instead on hearty (and calorie-rich) state specialties like johnnycakes, the staple of nearly every breakfast platter around. Essentially pancakes loaded up with stone-ground cornmeal, they're both soft and slightly crunchy, and usually come served with maple syrup and/or fruit.

On the beverage front, one of the most widely devoured treats is coffee milk, made with a simple mixture of coffee syrup and milk. Order it in almost any casual restaurant, or make it yourself. (You can buy coffee syrup in most grocery stores around the state.) But the coup de grace of local coffee concoctions is the coffee frappe, made most famously by Newport Creamery (which, despite the name, is found throughout the state rather than only in Newport). The fast-food restaurant's version is coined Awful-Awful (as in, awful thick, awful good), and is made with an extra dose of ice milk, rendering it far creamier than most milkshakes.

return again and again for the house's cheap kebabs, generously poured drinks, and terrific people-watching from its sidewalk tables.

Korean

It only sounds like an Italian restaurant—**Cafe Angelrose** (262 Atwells Ave., 11 A.M.–10 P.M., $4–7) is actually a Korean hole-in-the-wall famed for Korean BBQ and *bibimbop*, along with bagels and sandwiches.

Snacks and Sandwiches

With an utter lack of formality, **Spike's Junkyard Dog** (485 Branch Ave., 401/861-6888, 11 A.M.–11 P.M. Mon.–Thu.; 11 A.M.–1:30 A.M. Fri.–Sat.; noon–10 P.M. Sun., www.spikesjunkyarddogs.com, $1.50–4.75) is a funky, junky temple to the hot dog—from "Samurai Dogs" (with teriyaki sauce) to tofu wieners. Chomp into the best burgers in the city at **Café Paragon** (234 Thayer St., 401/331-6200, www.paragonandviva.com, 11 A.M.–1 A.M. Mon.–Thu.; 11 A.M.–2 A.M. Fri.–Sat.; 10 A.M.–1 A.M. Sun., $6–20) a stylish eatery on Thayer Street near Brown University that serves up gourmet black angus beef patties topped with Cajun onion strips, blue cheese-and-bacon and other mouthwatering combinations. The restaurant also has a full menu of entrées, pizza, tapas, and sushi—but for the prices, none of it holds up to the quality of the burgers. Next door, Viva lounge serves stiff cocktails with DJ music at night.

INFORMATION AND SERVICES

For maps, updates on the city's events, and any other tourist information, call or stop by the **Providence Warwick Convention and Visitors Bureau** (1 W. Exchange St., 401/274-1636, www.pwcvb.com).

The city's major hospitals are **Miriam Hospital** (164 Summit Ave., Providence, 401/793-2500, www.lifespan.org/partners/tmh) and **Roger Williams Medical Center** (825 Chalkstone Ave., Providence, 401/456-2000, www.rwmc.com). There are a number of pharmacies open 24 hours, as well, including **East Providence CVS** (640 Warren Ave., East Providence, 401/438-2256) and **North Providence CVS** (1919 Mineral Springs Ave., North Providence, 401/353-0580).

Banks are found all over the downtown area and in the college and touristed neighborhoods, and ATMs are scattered throughout the city.

Internet is available for free in libraries and for a small fee (usually a few dollars per hour) in cafés and at **FedEx Office** (160 Westminster

St., Providence, 401/331-8200), which also provides faxing and shipping services. Free Wi-Fi is offered at **Coffee Connection** (207 Wickenden St.), Cuban Revolution (50 Aborn St.), and other locations around town.

GETTING THERE
By Air
The state's airport is **T. F. Green** (2000 Post Rd., Warwick, 401/737-8222, www.pvd-ri.com), an international, clean, and efficient facility with plenty of parking. About a 30-minute drive from downtown Providence, the airport is also easily accessed by buses run by **Rhode Island Transportation Authority** (RIPTA, 401/781-9400, www.ripta.com). Many Providence hotels also offer free shuttle service.

By Train
The commuter line that runs frequently every day between Boston and Providence is operated by the **Massachusetts Bay Transportation Authority** (617/222-3200, www.mbta.com). Also, **Amtrak** (800/872-7245, www.amtrak.com) runs regular service between Providence and Washington, D.C., stopping in Boston and New York, among other towns, along the way.

By Bus
Peter Pan Bus Lines (401/331-7500, www.peterpanbus.com) operates several routes in and out of Providence from key cities—including runs to Boston, New York City, Newport, Cape Cod, and others.

GETTING AROUND
Providence is a remarkably walkable city—indeed, that may be the very best way to admire its historic nooks and crannies, monuments, great homes, and university campuses. But when foot transport isn't an option, turn to the affordable bus system, well-run by **RIPTA** (Rhode Island Transportation Authority, 401/781-9400, www.ripta.com). All bus routes start at Kennedy Plaza (in front of the State House) and cover the city for the usual fare of $1.75. Buses run from 6 A.M. to 7 P.M. There's also an eco-friendly trolley system (running on compressed natural gas), known as the **LINK** (401/781-9400, www.ripta.com). It runs two lines from Federal Hill to Fox Point and from the State House to the Southside. At a cost of $1.75 per ride, it runs every day until about 6:30 P.M.—except for the trolley between Fox Point and Federal Hill, which runs until 10 P.M. on weekdays and 11 P.M. on weekends.

Around Providence

Providence's early prosperity may have started with the role its wharf played in the slave and rum trades, but it was secured a few miles northeast in Pawtucket and Woonsocket, by the success of the industrial forerunners who founded the area's mill communities around the Blackstone River's rushing waters.

PAWTUCKET
Rhode Island's fourth-largest city, Pawtucket is an easygoing mix of historic awareness and present-day pleasures. Most of the town's sights and festivals center on its past—much effort is made by local historic groups to educate both visitors and younger generations

about the town's place in industrial history. But it isn't all just a long look backward; from the Paw Sox and Convergence Festival to eateries like the aptly named Modern Diner, there are plenty of modern diversions to enjoy here, too.

◖ Slater Mill
Arguably the starting point for the Industrial Revolution in America, this interactive museum (67 Roosevelt Ave., 401/725-8638, www.slatermill.org, 10 A.M.–4 P.M. Tue.–Sun. May–Oct., $9 adults, $8 seniors, $7 children 6–12, free children under 6) is housed in original 18th- and 19th-century buildings. Costumed

interpreters at the colonial-era Sylvanus Brown House demonstrate the enormous amount of work it took to produce clothing and food by hand—contrasted with the hulking Old Slater Mill, its industrial counterpart, which demonstrates how clothing and tool production became increasingly mechanized. You'll leave treating your cotton shirt with newfound respect.

Events

Considered a more keep-it-real alternative to the Boston Red Sox, a **Pawtucket Red Sox** game is fun and relatively inexpensive. They play at McCoy Stadium (1 Ben Mondor Way, 401/724-7300, www.pawsox.com). Pawtucket's **Convergence Pawtucket Festival** (401/724-2200, www.pawtucketartsfestival.org) is a smaller version of Providence's larger annual celebration. Held each September, it draws the area's artists, craftspeople, and musicians around the historic Slater Mill. The holiday season sees **Winter Wonderland at Slater Park** (Armistice Blvd., 401/728-0500, www.pawtucketri.com), a small and festive village erected around a carousel, with live entertainment and plenty of food.

Shopping

Ship a little slice of the Rhode Island coast home through **Clambakes to Travel** (560 York Ave.,800/722-2526, www.clambakeco.com). The company will send a full clambake—lobster, corn, clams, potatoes, and all—straight to your address. And given Pawtucket's claim to textile fame, it's no shock to find an inordinately extensive selection of fabrics at **Lorraine Mills Fabrics** (593 Mineral Springs Ave., 401/722-9500, 10 A.M.–6 P.M. Mon.–Sat.; noon–5 P.M. Sun.). While you shop, get a bonus history lesson: The store is housed in an original mill.

Information

There are plenty of brochures and other pieces of tourist information at the **Blackstone Valley Tourism Council** (171 Main St., 401/724-2200, www.tourblackstone.com).

WOONSOCKET

Nestled in among a handful of quieter suburbs, this well-groomed town of roughly 50,000 centers around the Blackstone River. Its water power was the source of Woonsocket's place as an industrial forerunner starting in 1810, when its first textile mill was built. Three decades later, there were upwards of 20 mills operating in the area, and French-Canadian immigrants began arriving to help run them. Today, many of those mills can still be walked through, and French-Canadians are still the town's biggest ethnic group.

Sights

The town's history as a center for wool manufacturing is evident at **The Rhode Island Historical Society Museum of Work and Culture** (42 S. Main St., 401/769-9675, www.woonsocket.org, 9:30 A.M.–4 P.M. Tues.–Fri.; 10 A.M.–5 P.M. Sat.–Sun.; closed Mondays, $7 adults, $5 seniors and students, free children under 10) which offers excellent exhibits on the town's history and culture, religion, and industry. That sense of history continues outside the museum, in abutting Market Square. Here you'll find a handful of historic yarn mills, a hydroelectric power plant, and the river that feeds them both.

Entertainment and Events

Every spring, Woonsocket's River Island Park hosts the **Blackstone River Watershed Association Canoe/Kayak Race** (401/762-0440, www.thebrwa.org), which starts in the park and ends about four miles later in Mannville. By the end of May, it's time for the **Jubilee Franco-American Weekend** (401/765-6141), which is celebrated throughout Woonsocket in riverboat tours, concert halls, galleries, and restaurants. All of the festival's celebrations are meant to illuminate the cultural assets that immigrants from French Canada have brought to Woonsocket over the years.

Nightlife

Jazz aficionados won't be disappointed by the

excellent acts brought in by **Chan's** (267 Main St., 401/765-1900, www.chanseggrollsandjazz.com, 11:30 A.M.–10 P.M. Mon.–Thurs.; 11:30 A.M.–12:30 A.M. Fri.–Sat., $5–15). The funky eatery/club stages performers from far and wide three nights a week.

Shopping
Relive your sweet youth at **Pearl's Candy and Nuts** (4 Eddie Dowling Hwy., 401/769-1166, 11:30 A.M.–5 P.M. Tues.–Fri); the place is stocked from end to end with every kind of sugary treat—some hard-to-find these days—from licorice whips and Dots to peanut brittle and homemade fudge.

SPORTS AND RECREATION
Hiking and Biking
It's hard to imagine a more bucolic trail than **Blackstone River Bike Trail** (accessed most easily in Blackstone State Park); the 15-mile-plus ride follows the Blackstone River past historic mills, pristine fields, and fresh-smelling woods. Also popular for walking and biking is the **Arboretum at Riverside** (724 Pleasant St., 401/724-8733), 80 acres of riverside forest wooded with rare cedars and aspens.

Boating
Even experienced boaters can find the rushing waters of the Blackstone River a challenge. Lessons, maps, excursions, guided trips, and advice are all offered through the kayaking and canoeing experts at **Blackstone Valley Paddle Club** (401/762-0250, http://ricka-flatwater.org, weekend trips).

ACCOMMODATIONS
Under $100
Even if Woonsocket had no other attractions, it's almost worth a visit to stay in the very reasonably priced, extremely charming **Pillsbury House B&B** (341 Prospect St., Woonsocket, 401/766-7983, www.pillsburyhouse.com, $95–135). The 19th-century house, situated close to the downtown area's shops and restaurants, is an elegant ode to the town's history, with its period antiques, tasteful rooms, and hospitable service.

$100-150
True river rats don't have to leave the water at day's end—at least not if they opt to sleep in the **Samuel Slater Canal Boat B&B** (175 Main St., Pawtucket, 401/724-2200, www.bedandbreakfastblackstone.com, $130–180). An authentic British canal boat, its accommodations include phone, television, and pastries or a full English breakfast.

FOOD
A stone's throw from Slater Mill, the steel railroad car **Modern Diner** (364 East Ave., Pawtucket, 401/726-8390, 6 A.M.–3 P.M. Mon.–Sat.; 7 A.M.–2 P.M. Sun., $5–7) serves huge plates of fluffy pancakes, burgers, and homemade blueberry pie. The bounty of the nearby ocean makes it no surprise to find such fresh dishes at **Horton's Seafood** (809 Broadway, E. Providence, 401/434-3115, 11 A.M.–9 P.M., $5–12). Make sure to order the fish-and-chips. The local Portuguese community has yielded a gem in **Madeira** (288 Warren Ave., E. Providence, 401/431-1322, www.madeirarestaurant.com, 11:30 A.M.–10 P.M. Mon.–Thu.; 11:30 A.M.–11 P.M. Fri.–Sat.; noon–10 P.M. Sun., $12–20), known for authentic dishes of paella, grilled linguica, and kale soup.

Ye Olde English Fish and Chips (25 S. Main St., Woonsocket, 401/762-3637, 12 P.M.–10 P.M., $3–8) may sound ominous (unless the idea of old fish appeals to you), but the fare is in fact quite fresh. Order up a plate of rich stuffed quahogs or a bowl of chowder and savor it outside, with a front-seat view of the Blackstone River. The casual, bustling **Mezza Luna** (4077 Mendon St., Cumberland, 401/658-0449, 1 P.M.–11 P.M., $8–15) is extremely popular locally for its spinach-and-sausage pizzas. A little more daring but just as delicious, the specialties at **Thai Garden** (280 Main St., Woonsocket, 401/765-7010, $15–30) include platters of spicy lemongrass mussels, crispy shrimp pad thai, and green-tea ice cream.

East Bay

In their rush to get from Providence to Newport, most travelers simply bypass the east side of Narragansett Bay, pausing just to notice the stunning views from the series of bridges between East Providence and Portsmouth. The area, however, is a destination in its own right for anyone who prizes small-town life. The two port cities of Warren and Bristol are both known for their attractive main streets and summer boating communities. Bristol is also the unofficial headquarters for the America's Cup Yachting Race, and maintains a museum inspired by the competition.

WARREN

Somewhat overshadowed by its charismatic cousin Bristol, Warren has been fast becoming a destination itself, with the same concentration of colonial homes and historic waterfront, but more ethnic diversity and a less precious feel. Founded on land once held by the Wampanoags, the city was a center of shipbuilding and whaling after the Revolution. In the 1800s, it also became home to many textile mills, which brought an influx of French-Canadians, Portuguese, Italians, and Irish who each brought their own cultural heritage to the mix.

Throughout the 20th century, Warren was also known as the "oyster capital of the world" due to the famed Warren Oyster Company, which closed its doors after the Rhode Island oyster trade dried up in the 1950s. Now it is better known for its antiques, with more than a dozen shops along the Main Street historic district.

Sights

A plaque on Baker Street marks the site of **Massasoit Spring,** where the great Womponoag sachem Massasoit ruled over his people and kept peace with the Englishmen for 40 years. Exhibits on Native American life as well as 18th-century colonial customs are displayed at the brick **Maxwell House** (corner of Church and Water Sts., 401/245-0392, www.massasoithistorical.org, 10 A.M.–2 P.M. Sat., free), run by the Massasoit Historical Association.

Events

Rhode Island's favorite bivalve is feted at the **Warren Quahog Festival** (Burrs' Hill Park, S. Water St., 401/410-0045, www.warrenbartingtonrotary.org, mid-July), which features chowders, cakes, and stuffies, as well as displays by the many artists who have taken up residence in town.

Shopping

Downtown Warren is honeycombed with antiques stores catering to every possible taste. One of the more unique is **Water Street Antiques** (147-149 Water St., 401/245-6440, 12 P.M.–4 P.M.), which specializes in kitsch and retro lamps, along with furniture that would seem at home in Josie & the Pussycats' pad. More elegant is **Wren & Thistle Antiques** (19 Market St., 401/247-0631, http://wrenandthistlebandb.com, 11 A.M.–5 P.M. Mon.–Sat.; noon–4 P.M. Sun.), which scours estate sales for the finest old linens, china, and silver. For your period colonial, **The Meeting House** (47 Water St., 401/247-7043) has historic reproductions, old-fashioned candles, and light fixtures.

Food

Channeling a Florentine trattoria, **Tuscan Tavern** (632 Metacom Ave., 401/247-9200, www.tuscantavern.net, noon–9 P.M., $6–25) serves Italian comfort food in a cozy ambience. Some of the many pasta dishes have a New England spin—such as lobster ravioli with vodka cream sauce. A large brick oven churns out wood-grilled calzones. The East Bay branch of the lauded Providence restaurant, (**India** (520 Main St., 401/245-4500, www.indiarestaurant.com, 11 P.M.–5 P.M., $8–15) is one of the best Indian restaurants in New

RHODE ISLAND

England. The menu specializes in fiery curries of both meat and vegetarian varieties, as well as char-grilled kabobs. Fresh cilantro perks up the masala sauce. For years, the Nathaniel Porter Inn, the 200-year-old home of a whaling captain, was a stuffy Warren warhorse. In 2004, new owners scrapped the inn and christened the **Nat Porter Restaurant** (125 Water St., 401/289-0373, www.natporter.com, 11 A.M.–10 P.M. daily, $8–24), keeping the original mahogany and teak parquet flooring and adding modern light fixtures reminiscent of a ship's lantern. Despite the historic ambience, the food is modern, chef-driven cuisine, such as spicy lamb sirloin with red-pepper polenta and muscat grapes; and a pan-seared tofu and portabello Napoleon.

Information

Tourist information is available from the **East Bay Chamber of Commerce** (654 Metacom Ave., 401/245-0750 or 800/556-2484, www.eastbaychamberri.org).

BRISTOL

If there was a run-off for all-American town, Bristol would be a finalist. The main street is festooned with flags left waving after the city's annual Fourth of July parade, the oldest in the country. The street itself is a vibrant vision of what main streets once looked like before malls, with boutique stores and storefront cafés interspersed with solid granite buildings and picturesque colonial homes.

From the beginning, Bristol has had a contentious history. It was founded after King Philip's War on land near the site of King Philip's camp, and soon became an important seaport, active in the triangle trade that imported countless slaves from Africa. Because of its strategic importance and Revolutionary sympathies, the town was repeatedly bombarded by British cannons during the Revolutionary War. Along with neighboring Warren, Bristol was partially burned in 1778 by a party of 600 British soldiers and Hessian mercenaries in the lead-up to the Battle of Rhode Island.

While never as well-to-do as Newport,

Bristol's heyday as a shipping center after the Revolution led to many fine Victorian mansions and gardens being built on the outskirts of town. After the slave trade was made illegal in the early 1800s, Bristol's main source of income was cut off and the town went into temporary decline. It was rescued by a rubber refinery that made boots and clothing, as well as a boatbuilding industry that made both steamboats and yachts. The latter was compliments of the Herreshoff brothers, famous for creating the racing ships that helped the United States win the America's Cup sailing race year after year.

⬤ Herreshoff Marine Museum

Nat and J. B. Herreshoff created their famous manufacturing company in 1878, beginning with navy torpedo boats before settling into the form they were born to create—sailing yachts. Starting in 1893 with the *Vigilance,* their ships would repeatedly win the international sailing competition known as the America's Cup, run for decades in neighboring Newport. Situated on the harbor, the huge plate glass–sided museum (1 Burnside St., 401/253-5000, www.herreshoff.org, 10 A.M.–5 P.M. daily May–mid-Oct.; 10 A.M.–5 P.M. Wed.–Sun. mid-Oct.–Dec., $8 adults, $7 seniors, $4 students and children 11–17, free children under 10) holds dozens of sweeping ships' hulls, along with explanations of what makes them so damn fast. An America's Cup Hall of Fame pays respects to the winners of more than 150 years of competition.

Other Sights

The blinding-white facade of **Linden Place** (400 Hope St., 401/253-0390, www.lindenplace.org, tours by appointment, 10 A.M.–4 P.M., Thu.–Sat. and occasionally Sun. May–early Oct., $5 adults, $2.50 children under 12) wows even the most jaded of historical-home aficionados. The Federal-style mansion was once owned by US Rubber president Samuel Colt, and was featured in the film version of *The Great Gatsby.* Tours take in the opulent ballroom, bedrooms, and sculpture-filled gardens.

A grand mansion in the English Country style, **Blithewold Mansion, Garden & Arboretum** (101 Ferry Road/Rte. 114, 401/253-2707, www.blithewold.org, 10 A.M.–4 P.M. Wed.–Sat.; 10 A.M.–3 P.M. Sun. mid-Apr.–mid-Oct; gardens only 10 A.M.–5 P.M. mid-Oct.–mid-Apr., $10 adults, $8 seniors and students, $2 children 6–17, free children 5 and under) is filled with original furniture dating from the 17th century, as well as fine china and Baccarat crystal. Just as impressive are the 33 acres of sculpted oceanside grounds.

One of the country's best museums of indigenous cultures, Brown University's **Haffenreffer Museum of Anthropology** (300 Tower St., 401/253-8388, www.brown.edu, call for hours and prices) is located on the grounds of Metacomet/King Philip's camp at Mt. Hope Farm. Begun by beer magnate Rudolph Haffenreffer, who had a hobby of collecting local Native American artifacts, the museum's collection goes way beyond New England's natives to encompass the entire range of the world's indigenous cultures, from Thai paintings to Aleut canoes. Exhibits are meticulously researched and presented in a sensitive style that is a refreshing change from many "natural history" museums. (Note: The museum closed in 2008 to bring its buildings in line with Rhode Island's fire safety codes. It plans to reopen exhibits by the summer of 2010. Call ahead for the latest updates.)

Entertainment

Bristol's waterfront has a good bar scene, especially in the summer. **Gillary's** (198 Thames St., 401/253-2012, www.gillarys.com, noon–1 A.M.) features grungy rock bands and karaoke, along with pool and air hockey tables and an outdoor patio. **Jersey Lillie's** (1 State St., 401/253-7526, noon–11 P.M.) draws a college crowd for imported British drafts served at an authentic Victorian-era bar. The town of Bristol sponsors **Concerts on the Common** with classical performers on summer Thursdays from July to Labor Day.

Events

Established just 12 years after Independence,

Bristol's annual **Fourth of July Celebration** (www.july4thbristolri.com) brings revelers from around the country for a grand parade and bugle corps competition. Other highlights include a grand ball, teenage beauty pageant, old-time "orange crate derby" race, and—of course—fireworks on the harbor.

Shopping

Hope Street is lined with many cute boutiques and craft stores. **Green River Silver** (297 Hope St., 401/253-5005, www.greenriversilver.com, 10 A.M.–6 P.M.) has literally hundreds of different styles of sterling silver jewelry. **Boo Bracken & Co's Montage** (361 Hope St., 401/253-8614, noon–11 P.M.) is a fabulous shop bursting with Victorian-style hats and eclectic crafts. **Kate & Co.** (301 Hope St., 401/253-3117) 10 A.M.–4 P.M.) is a too-cute-for-words shop for women's clothing, bath products, and gourmet foodstuffs.

Food

A small storefront selling wraps with exotic fillings, **Papa Joe's Wrap Shack** (567 Hope St., 401/253-9911, www.papajoeswrapshack.com,, 12 P.M.–9 P.M., $5–10) features varieties from Mongolian beef to triple mushroom. For a plate as pleasing to the eye as to the stomach, stop into **Persimmon** (31 State St., Bristol, 401/254-7474, 5–9 P.M. Sun.–Tue., 5–10 P.M. Fri.–Sat., Jul.–Dec.; closed Sun. Jan.–Jun., $20–28), where attention to detail shows in both the flawless presentation and the artful combination of flavors. The restaurant strives to cook in harmony with the seasons, changing the menu four times a year to highlight farm- and boat-fresh ingredients. Summer might feature Massachusetts striped bass with squash-and-chanterelle ragout or Long Island crispy duck breast served with duck confit and a rosemary reduction.

Chef-owned by two Roberts, neither of which is demonstrably Italian, **Roberto's** (301 Hope St., 401/254-9732, www.robertosonline.com, 11 A.M.–9 P.M., $14–25) is romantic with white tablecloths and candles. Aside from pasta and seafood dishes, most of the menu consists of just two items—veal and chicken—done in any one of 12 regional Italian styles. Bristol's oldest and best-known restaurant, ❰ **The Lobster Pot** (119 Hope St., 401/253-9100, 12 P.M.–8 P.M., $25–35), proves that despite the fads, traditional New England seafood dishes are often still best. The seventeen lobster entrées on the menu include split-grilled, steamed, broiled, and—so-bad-it's-good deep-fried, all served with a gorgeous view of Narragansett Bay.

Information
The town of Bristol runs a volunteer-staffed information center at **Bristol Town Hall** (400 Hope St., 401/253-7000, ext. 150, www.destinationbristol.com).

SPORTS AND RECREATION
Beaches
Located in the sprawling Colt State Park, **Bristol Town Beach** (401/253-7482, www.riparks.com) is the most accessible beach in the East Bay, but tends to be somewhat rocky and crowded in the summer.

Hiking and Biking
The **Audubon Society of Rhode Island** (1401 Hope St./Rte. 114, Bristol, 401/245-7500, www.asri.org) runs an excellent environmental center and wildlife preserve on the bay coast. Along with nature exhibits (including a 33-foot-long whale model), it maintains boardwalks and paths to nearby marshes. The 15-mile **East Bay Bike Path** (www.riparks.com) offers beautiful views of the bay as it meanders from East Providence to Bristol. Bikes can be rented from **Your Bike Shop** (51 Cole St., Warren, 401/245-9755).

Sailing and Boating
Cygnus Sailing Adventures (401/413-8109, www.sailcygnus.com) offers narrated sails in Bristol harbor on the gaff-rigged sloop *Cygnus.* The **East Bay Sailing Foundation** (Bristol Yacht Club, Poppasquash Rd., Bristol, 401/253-0775, www.bristolyc.com) offers sailing instruction in 15-foot Mercurys. **Bay Queen**

Cruises (461 Water St., Bristol, 401/245-1350, www.bayqueen.com) provides narrated tours of the bay on a 114-foot cruise boat. **Ocean State Adventures** (99 Poppasquash Rd., Bristol, 401/254-4000, www.kayakri.com) rents out sea kayaks as well as leading nature tours and moonlight paddles in the bay.

ACCOMMODATIONS
$100-150
Run by an affable husband-and-wife team and their cats, **Candlewick Inn** (775 Main St., Warren, 401/247-2425, www.candlewickinn.net, $90–140) is a pretty and relaxed spot to spend a few nights. Family heirlooms, antiques, and handmade quilts fill the four guest rooms; gardens surround the property, and the complimentary, delicious breakfast is of epic proportions.

Small touches make the **William Grant Inn** (154 High St., Bristol, 401/253-4222, www.wmgrantinn.com, $140–160), located a block from Bristol's main street, a first-rate place to stay. The bed-and-breakfast's innkeepers fill guest rooms with fresh-cut flowers and bake cookies in the afternoons. Rooms are decorated with antiques and oriental art; a piano and back porch are also available for use of guests.

$150-250
You can't get closer to the water than the ❰ **Bristol Harbor Inn** (259 Thames St., Bristol, 401/254-1444, www.bristolharborinn.com, $155–255), a former bank and rum distillery renovated into a boutique hotel right on the harbor. Rooms are simply decorated with understated nautical decor—but who needs wallpaper when you have the view of the harbor outside your window? Continental breakfast is served in the room where rum casks were once filled; wireless Internet is available throughout the hotel.

You can imagine yourself as a manor lord at the **Governor Bradford House** (250 Metacom Ave./Rte. 136, Bristol, 401/254-9300, www.mounthopefarm.com, $175–250). Situated on Mount Hope Farm, a 200-acre preserve of fields, ponds, and woodlands, the house was once owned by one of the first governors of Rhode Island and later by Rudolph Haffenreffer of Narragansett beer fame. And, of course, Washington stayed here, when he was an old man in 1793. Rooms are decorated with a designers' eye, with canary or lime-green walls, grand four-poster beds, and some with working fireplaces.

GETTING THERE AND AROUND

Driving from Providence, it's a quick shot down I-95 and Route 114 to Warren (12 mi., 20 min.) and Bristol (18 mi., 25 min.). The **Rhode Island Public Transportation Authority** (RIPTA, 401/781-9400, www. ripta.com) stops at all of the East Bay towns on its Providence–Newport route (Rte. 60). Buses from Providence to Warren take approximately 20 minutes, and stop at Main and Joyce streets. Buses from Providence to Bristol take a half hour, stopping at Hope and State streets. Fares are a reasonable $1.75, regardless of distance.

NEWPORT AND SOUTH COUNTY

Despite its latter-day glory as a summer playground for the wealthy during the 19th century, these days Newport finds itself relatively democratic. Sure, it's still scattered with seaside mansions once owned by eminent families bearing names like Duke and Astor, and certainly it still draws plenty of the modern-day equivalent: celebrities, CEOs, and astoundingly preppy families (many of whom purchase summer property to be near the thriving yacht culture).

But it also welcomes a salad of others: artists (who build their galleries along the cobblestoned Thames—pronounce the "th" and so it rhymes with James—Street); college students (who tend to share summer homes by the group outside of downtown); mansion gawkers; and bona fide sailors (who come for the big boat shows and top-notch sailing resources).

The bustling yacht-filled harbor contrasts sharply with the rest of the area around Narragansett Bay, which takes a bite out of the eastern shore of the state. East of the bay, the small farming communities might seem more at home in the Midwest, if it weren't for the frequent glimpses of the sea shining between their stone walls and grey-shingled barns. The long south coast of Rhode Island, meanwhile, may be the best-kept summertime secret in New England. Home to many old resorts and summer "cottages" in the late 1900s, the area fell out of favor as the crowds moved to Newport and Cape Cod. As a result, the thirty miles of seacoast are filled with deserted beaches, quaint little towns, and conservation areas that define "getting away from it all."

That goes double for the little pork chop of

HIGHLIGHTS

◖ **Newport's Mansions:** In contemporary times, we like to say our home is our castle. In the Gilded Age of Newport, it really was (page 221).

◖ **Cliff Walk:** Enjoy a genuinely breathtaking seaside walk – the pathway is sandwiched between a row of Newport's grand mansions and the rocky, misty ocean's edge (page 224).

◖ **Sakonnet Vineyards:** The location of this winery on Sakonnet Point is as spectacular as the wine it produces (page 228).

◖ **Fantastic Umbrella Factory:** This fanciful, fantastical shop is filled with all manner of flowers, gifts, and live fowl (page 237).

◖ **Watch Hill:** Ride the country's oldest carousel in this quaint resort community (page 239).

◖ **Southeast Lighthouse:** Perched on the cliffs of Block Island, the lighthouse offers a magnificent view (page 244).

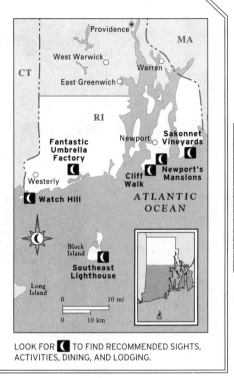

LOOK FOR ◖ TO FIND RECOMMENDED SIGHTS, ACTIVITIES, DINING, AND LODGING.

an island known as Block Island, a dozen miles off Rhode Island's south coast. For years one of the last undiscovered quiet places on the New England coast, the island has recently been targeted by the summer tides of tourists. At least thus far, however, they haven't broken the isle's spirit of laid-back relaxation and pristine wilderness that make it one of the best summertime destinations anywhere.

PLANNING YOUR TIME

Lives have been spent studying the history of **Newport's mansions** and the families that owned them. For most people, a day or two is sufficient. Tours through the homes usually last about an hour, and it's recommended that visitors leave time in their schedules before and

after to stroll the grounds, and walk the famous **Cliff Walk.** That said, it isn't advisable to try and see more than one or two mansions in one day—that much grandeur alone may leave your head spinning. There's more than enough shopping to be done on Thames Street for an entire day as well, and of course, the beaches and sailing could take up any water baby's entire vacation. (Note that in the less-touristy off-season, restaurants in Newport—and particularly in the neighboring towns and on Block Island—greatly reduce their hours. Call ahead to check meals offered.) If all four activities are tempting, your best bet may be to break each day into halves, dedicating the first to one activity and the second to another.

If you've only got two or three days in

RHODE ISLAND

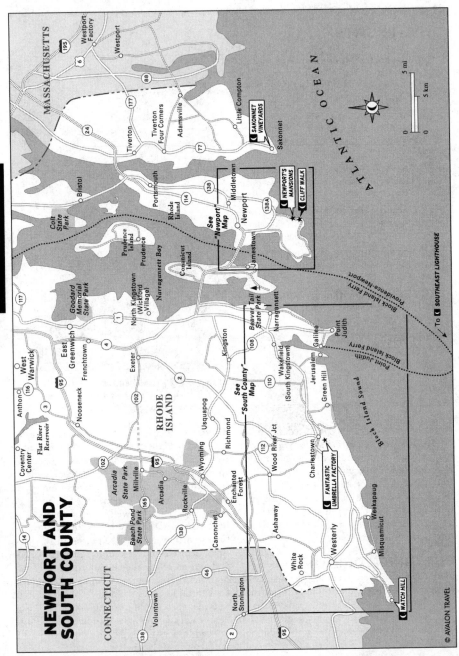

© AVALON TRAVEL

the area, Newport will probably be all that you can handle. On the third day, however, you might consider taking a pleasant detour over one of the bridges to the quaint town of Wickford, the old resort community of Narragansett, or the quiet Sakonnet Peninsula, where **Sakonnet Vineyards** makes a convenient (and delicious) stopping place. Drive to the end of the state to shop at the funky **Fantastic Umbrella Factory** (hint: they don't make umbrellas) and take a ride on the carousel at **Watch Hill.**

It's definitely possible to take a day trip to Block Island, but to really experience what makes the island so special, you're teasing yourself if you don't stay over for one or two nights. A day or two is plenty to see the island's major sights, including stunning **Southeast Lighthouse.** Another day for lying on the beach is mandatory.

Newport and Vicinity

Settled in 1639, Newport first became prominent as a prosperous international seaport (and a player in the rum and slave trades) until the British occupation in 1776. Once the Revolutionary War ended, it soon began its life as America's first resort—drawing artists and writers first, followed by the country's captains of industry.

By the middle of the 19th century, almost any family with a big name (from Edith Wharton to the Vanderbilts) and an even bigger trust had a summer "cottage" (read: mansion) on Ocean Drive or Bellevue Avenue. And those who didn't had friends to visit here, and were thus still a part of the town's culture. (One prime example: Poet Henry Wadsworth Longfellow, whose visits to see friend Samuel Ward—brother of Julia Ward Howe—in Newport inspired his works *The Skeleton in Armor* and *The Jewish Cemetery*.) Since then, everyone from President Kennedy to Billy Joel has had homes here.

NEWPORT
The town itself is spread out from Bellevue Avenue (which meets First Beach and the mansions along it at one end) all the way to the tip of Thames Street, where the main drag's commercial shops drop off. Most of Newport's galleries, commercial wharfs, restaurants, retail shops (both independent boutiques and chain stores) are found on Thames. Over on Bellevue and Ocean Avenues, you'll find the majority of mansions, beaches, historic homes, and inns.

◖ Newport's Mansions
The mansions of Newport are numerous, and each is an undeniably overwhelming display of wealth, beauty, and design. But even among such over-the-top grandeur, certain structures cast taller shadows than others. Considered the most lavish of them all is **The Breakers** (44 Ochre Point Ave., 401/847-1000, www.newportmansions.org, 10 A.M.–5 P.M. daily Jan.–early Apr.; 9 A.M.–6 P.M. daily mid-Apr.–early Oct.; 9 A.M.–5 P.M. daily mid-Oct.–Dec., $18 adults, $4.50 children 6–17, free children under 6), built in 1893 as the summer home of steamship and railroad giant Commodore Cornelius Vanderbilt II. Designed by an international dream team of architects, the palazzo holds no less than 70 rooms, and is a dead ringer for Italy's most opulent 16th-century palazzos. Another modest little Vanderbilt home is **Marble House** (596 Bellevue Ave., 401/847-1000, www.newportmansions.org, 10 A.M.–6 P.M. daily early Apr.–early Oct.; 10 A.M.–5 P.M. daily mid-Oct.–Dec., $12 adults, $4.50 children 6–17, free children under 6), this time finished in 1892 for Cornelius's grandson once removed, William K. Vanderbilt. Inspired by parts of Versailles, the home is filled with nearly a half million cubic feet of marble, and includes on its grounds a Chinese teahouse built by William's wife, Alva. Versailles' influence once again rears its head down the street at **Rosecliff** (548 Bellevue Ave., 401/847-1000, www.newportmansions.org, 9 A.M.–6 P.M.

RHODE ISLAND

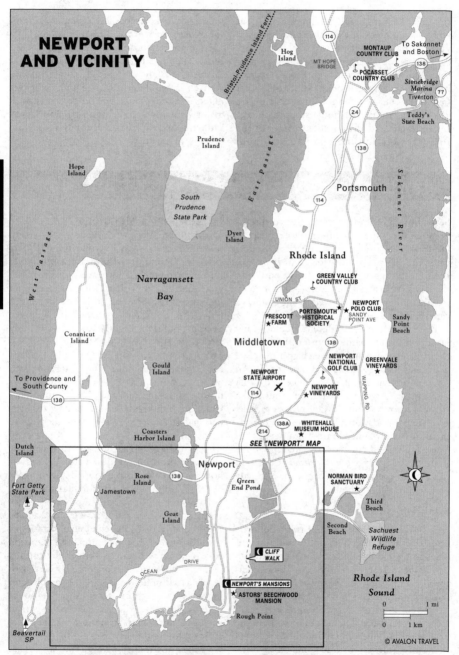

NEWPORT AND VICINITY

Bristol-Prudence Island Ferry

Hog Island

114

MT HOPE BRIDGE

MONTAUP COUNTRY CLUB

To Sakonnet and Boston

138

POCASSET COUNTRY CLUB

Stonebridge Marina Tiverton

77

24

Teddy's State Beach

138

Sakonnet River

Prudence Island

114

Portsmouth

East Passage

West Passage

Hope Island

South Prudence State Park

Dyer Island

Rhode Island

GREEN VALLEY COUNTRY CLUB

Narragansett Bay

UNION ST

PORTSMOUTH HISTORICAL SOCIETY

NEWPORT POLO CLUB

SANDY POINT AVE

Sandy Point Beach

PRESCOTT FARM

Conanicut Island

Middletown

138

NEWPORT NATIONAL GOLF CLUB

GREENVALE VINEYARDS

Gould Island

NEWPORT STATE AIRPORT

114

NEWPORT VINEYARDS

WAPPING RD

To Providence and South County

138

WHITEHALL MUSEUM HOUSE

Coasters Harbor Island

214

138A

SEE "NEWPORT" MAP

Dutch Island

Newport

Rose Island

138

Green End Pond

NORMAN BIRD SANCTUARY

Fort Getty State Park

Jamestown

Goat Island

Third Beach

Second Beach

Sachuest Wildlife Refuge

CLIFF WALK

OCEAN DRIVE

NEWPORT'S MANSIONS

ASTORS' BEECHWOOD MANSION

Rhode Island Sound

Rough Point

Beavertail SP

0   1 mi

0   1 km

© AVALON TRAVEL

TOURING THE MANSIONS

© RHODE ISLAND TOURISM

Rosecliff's opulent interior

Boasting over 15 historic properties and 80 acres of gardens and parks, Newport's collection of sprawling mansions can seem an overwhelming tour indeed. If you're intent on seeing as much of them as possible, it's best to plan with the following tips in mind.

Buy tickets ahead of time. The crowds in high season can be crushing, so take advantage of some of the online packages available through the Preservation Society of Newport County (http://tickets.newportmansions.org).

Tours are offered quite regularly at the largest mansions (approximately every 15 minutes during high season and every 30 minutes in spring). Times vary at many of the smaller mansions, but generally the wait time is no longer than 30 minutes. And because most tours are finished in under an hour and the mansions are within easy walking distance of one another (and transportation is provided in the form of natural-gas trolleys between the houses), it is quite reasonable to plan three mansion tours in one day. Some ambitious visitors opt to do four or five, though it should be noted that there are only so many gilded ceilings and marble hallways the human eye can gaze upon before they all start to blend together. To fully appreciate the level of grandeur and detail, it may be wisest to take in three tours per day, leaving time for a change of scenery – à la Newport's beaches, downtown, or parks.

The mansions are wheelchair accessible; however, baby strollers are not allowed.

RHODE ISLAND

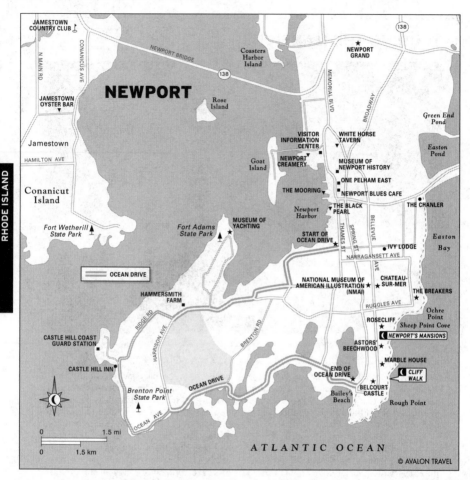

Sat.–Sun. Jan.–early Apr.; 10 A.M.–6 P.M. daily mid-Apr.–early Oct.; 10 A.M.–5 P.M. daily mid-Oct.–mid-Nov., $12 adults, $4.50 children 6–17, free children under 6), built in 1902 and inspired by the Grand Trianon section of the French castle. It was originally commissioned by Theresa and Hermann Oelrichs, and has been featured in a handful of movies, including *The Great Gatsby* and *Amistad*. While none of the bigger and best-known mansions in the area are still owned by their original families, one would almost seem to be: **Astors' Beechwood** (580 Bellevue Ave., 401/846-3772, www.

astorsbeechwood.com, 10 A.M.–4 P.M. Wed.–Sun. late Jan.–mid-May and mid-Nov.–mid-Dec.; Sun.–Fri. mid-May–mid-Nov.; Sat. hours vary, $15 adults, $6 children 6–17, free children under 6). The mansion is home to the Beechwood Theatre Company, which on every tour portrays the Astors, their friends, and staff at the height of the Victorian era.

Cliff Walk

The two finest things Newport has to offer—its natural seaside beauty and the architectural relics of its Gilded Age—collide along the seaside

Cliff Walk (www.cliffwalk.com), arguably one of the country's grandest strolls. Beginning at the western end of First Beach (a.k.a. Easton's Beach), the 3.5-mile path runs between the rocky beach and many of the town's most impressive mansions—designated a National Historic District. It was also deemed a National Recreational Trail in 1975, thus making the walk a double-whammy of natural and manmade glory. Along its path, strollers pass such palatial marvels as Marble House, Beechwood, The Breakers, and Rosecliff Mansions, plus the French Gothic chateaux (complete with high roofs, turrets, and gargoyles) belonging to Salve Regina University.

Other Sights

Before setting foot in any of the area's mansions, culture and history buffs should take a detour to **Museum of Newport History** (82 Touro St., 401/846-0813, www.newporthistorical.org, 10 A.M.–5 P.M. daily, $4 adults, $2 children), a well-laid-out mix of pieces of the town's past (with an emphasis on the 18th century): paintings, ship models, textiles, and antique furniture. The museum also offers walking tours of town.

Entertainment

Jazz lovers who couldn't be in town for the Newport Jazz Festival (or just want a second show) will find proper consolation at the **Newport Blues Cafe** (286 Thames St., 401/841-5510, www.newportblues.com). The restaurant-cum-lounge showcases live music from acclaimed artists seven nights a week. And progressive rock fans can catch indie acts—some big names, but mostly local—at **One Pelham East** (270 Thames St., 401/847-9460, www.thepelham.com). Usually packed on summer nights, it can be a great, comfortable spot to catch fall and winter acts.

Events

In 1854, Newport Commodore Matthew Perry sailed to Japan and opened trade with

RHODE ISLAND

NEWPORT JAZZ FESTIVAL

Every August, Newport's already impressive number of summer visitors swells by leaps and bounds thanks to one thing: the global draw of the renowned Newport Jazz Festival. Founded as the first outdoor jazz music festival by pianist George Wein and several Newport socialites in 1954, the festival is now a magnet for jazz fans drawn to its mix of well-known legends and up-and-coming musicians. Over the decades, everyone from Miles Davis and Duke Ellington to Billie Holiday and Frank Sinatra has graced its stages.

Usually a three-day series of concerts and events, the festival packs in hundreds of performances, from organ trios and vocalists to Brazilian duos and big-band productions, all divided between three primary stages. Performance schedules are always available ahead of time (either by calling the main office at 401/847-3700 or online at www.jazzfestival55. com). Tickets are plentiful and can be bought both prior to the event and by showing up in person any time during the event. Regulars strongly recommend booking a hotel ahead of time, as the more desired properties book up months in advance. There is also camping offered nearby in Melville Ponds Campground in Portsmouth (401/682-2424).

Most of the festival's action takes place in Fort Adams State Park on Harrison Avenue, which has strict rules about what attendees may bring. When packing, bear in mind that they allow only one small handheld cooler per person; individual blankets must measure less than 8 by 10 feet; and only low-backed chairs (under 30 inches) are allowed, to ensure good viewing for those around you. No glass containers, alcohol, pets, bikes, or beach umbrellas are permitted. Children are welcome – and there are plenty of inexpensive kids' meals sold among the concession stands.

the country. Now, every July, Newport takes on a citywide celebration of that trip, and of Japanese culture, with the **Black Ships Festival** (401/847-7666, www.blackshipsfestival.com). August sees the hugely popular **Newport Jazz Festival** (401/848-5055, www.jazzfestival55.com), which takes place in the sprawling, well-kept Fort Adams State Park. Big international acts congregate here alongside promising up-and-comers to entertain jazz enthusiasts. (See the sidebar *Touring the Mansions* for more information.)

Meanwhile, the holiday season sees the town's mansions decked out even more elaborately than usual; heavyweights such as Marble House and the Breakers are festively dressed in a slew of white lights and Christmas decorations for **Christmas at the Newport Mansions** (401/847-1000, www.newportmansions.org, late Nov.–early Jan., prices vary for different mansions). And come spring, every boat lover in New England heads for the **Spring Boat Show** (401/846-1115, www.newportspringboatshow.com, late May, $5 adults and children, free children under 12), the region's largest. They come to ogle the new and used vessels, of course, but also to haggle at the stalls of the show's flea market, which hawks everything from fishing line to used kayak paddles.

Shopping

Shops in and around Newport cover the spectrum of quality and uniqueness; you'll find everything here from upscale, independent clothing boutiques and supply stores for serious sailors to Banana Republic and Helly Hansen. Some of the most unique souvenirs you'll find are, unsurprisingly, nautical in nature—from artwork and crafts to clothing and the yachts themselves, sold during the town's many boat shows. From lithographs of J-class sloops to oil paintings of Newport beaches, **Arnold Art** (210 Thames St., 800/352-2234, www.arnoldart.com) brings together marine artists like Keith Reynolds and Helena Sturtevant—some of the area's most respected. Before hitting the surf, hit the shelves and racks of **Helly Hansen**

(154 Thames St., 877/666-8742, www.helly-england.com, 9 A.M.–9 P.M. daily). The boating gear selection ranges from base layers to keep you warm on windy sails to fully waterproof parkas and snuggly soft shell jackets. Home to an excellent selection of stained-glass artwork, **Aardvark Antiques** (9 JT Connell Hwy., 401/849-7233, www.aardvarkantiques.com, 9 A.M.–5 P.M. Mon.–Sat., by appt. Sun.) is also where you'll find garden statues and fountains like nowhere else outside a Roman square: Giant gargoyles and ceramic fish squat next to structures festooned with mermaids and gods. Artwork on the opposite end of the size scale is found at **Newport Scrimshanders** (14 Bowen's Wharf, 401/849-5680, www.scrimshanders.com, 10 A.M.–10 P.M. daily summer; 10 A.M.–6 P.M. daily winter), where artist and owner Brian Kiracofe creates and peddles carved whale ivory (acquiring ivory from whales is illegal these days; Kiracofe gets all of his from estate sales and auctions).

Not quite as rare, but arguably just as pretty, are the blown-glass gifts at **Thames Glass** (688 Thames St., 401/846-0576, www.thamesglass.com, 10 A.M.–6 P.M. Mon.–Sat.; noon–5 P.M. Sun.). Stop in and watch as the vases, glasses, paperweights, and fish bowls are created. Many of the town's high-end clothing stores are either slavishly nautical in theme or more Palm Beach prepfest than fashion-forward. The exception is **Mandarine** (16 Bannister's Wharf, 401/848-9360, www.shopmandarine.com, 10 A.M.–6 P.M. Mon.–Thu.; 10 A.M.–9 P.M. Fri.–Sat.; 11 A.M.–6 P.M. Sun.). Full of young, chic pieces by the international likes of Catherine Malandrino and Rozae Nichols, the shop also spotlights a solid selection of accessories—lingerie by FleurT, jewelry by Lanula, and handwoven shawls by Pret a Porter.

Food

Even hard-core vegetarians have a hard time leaving Newport without craving seafood, what with shellfish and lobster shacks at almost every turn. Those who heed the call will fare quite nicely at **The Mooring** (Sayer's Wharf, 401/846-2260, www.mooringrestaurant.com,

11:30 A.M.–9 P.M. Sun.–Thu;, 11:30 A.M.–10 P.M. Fri.–Sat., $12–44), particularly if they're able to nab a table with a view of the harbor and sunset. No one's breaking the culinary sound barrier in the kitchen, but it's a great place to dig into a plate of fresh fried clams or seafood pie—or sample the impressively lengthy wine list.

Bar culture had to begin somewhere in this country, and **The White Horse Tavern** (26 Marlborough St., 401/849-3600, www.whitehorsetavern.us, 11:30 A.M.–2:30 P.M. Mon.–Sat., noon–3 P.M. Sun.; 5:30 P.M.–10 P.M. Mon.–Sun., $29–48) may just be where. Opened in 1687 by the father of a pirate, the tavern features clapboard walls and huge ceiling beams typical of original 17th-century architecture—but its menu (from grilled bruschetta to maple-glazed salmon) is surprisingly here-and-now. The globally inspired, luxury-laden New England dishes that fly from the kitchen at **The Spiced Pear** (in the Chanler Hotel, 117 Memorial Blvd., 401/847-2244, www.spicedpear.com, 7:30–10:30 A.M. and 11:30–2:30 P.M. daily; 6–9 P.M. Sun–Thu.; 6–9:30 P.M. Fri.–Sat., $27–43) make such an impression, you could hear a fork drop throughout the elegant dining room as they're served. The butter-poached lobster with Israeli couscous is a must-try, and the fondue for two (with melted white chocolate and Godiva liqueur) is alone worth the hefty bill.

Loud and jovial, the candlelit tavern area's the place to be in **The Black Pearl** (Bannisters Wharf, 401/846-5264, www.blackpearlnewport.com, lunch and dinner daily, $8–30)—the abutting more formal dining room is notoriously overpriced for similar fare. Here's the spot to order up a bowl of the killer chowder (loaded with dill) and get your lobster fix; the two and a half pounders come boiled and unadorned except by butter and a lemon wedge. An institution in the region, the **Newport Creamery** (Newport Mall, 181 Bellevue Ave., 401/846-6332, www.newportcreamery.com, 7 A.M.–9 P.M. Sun.–Thu.; 7 A.M.–10 P.M. Fri.–Sat., $4–10) chain manages to capture the hearts of even staunchly anti-fast-food diners.

The burgers and fries are decent enough, but it's the super-thick frappe (the New England version of a shake)—in flavors like mocha and Oreo—that have kept this ice cream joint on the map.

Information

Stock up on brochures, maps, and any other kind of information on the area at the centrally located **Newport County Convention & Visitors Bureau** (23 America's Cup Ave., 401/845-9123, www.gonewport.com, 9 A.M.–5 P.M. daily)—you'll find it right next to the town's main bus terminal.

JAMESTOWN

In the bay between Newport and South County is Jamestown, which is actually an island called Conanicut. The downtown area is close to a ferry landing that brings visitors to and from Newport in the spring, summer, and fall, and it claims several worthwhile eateries and places to stay.

Sights

More rugged travelers bypass the main drag and head straight for the island's 150-acre **Beavertail State Park** (401/423-9941, www.riparks.com/beavertal.htm, sunrise–sunset daily, free). Blessed with beautiful views of coastline and a picturesque lighthouse, the park is a favorite destination for hikers and picnickers.

Food

Oyster lovers find bliss at the friendly and bare-bones **Jamestown Oyster Bar** (22 Narragansett Ave., 401/423-3380, 11:30 A.M.–9:30 P.M. Sun.–Thu.; 11:30 A.M.–10 P.M. Fri.–Sat., $7–18). The pub-meets-bistro ambience makes it the perfect place to slurp bivalves fresh from local waters.

MIDDLETOWN

Originally part of Newport until 1743, Middletown is a relatively sleepy town, home to about 17,000 people. But in contrast to Newport, there isn't a lot to do here except relax and admire the area's pristine beaches, historic homes, and natural scenery. If that's your idea of an ideal sojourn, you've come to the right place. Most visitors make their way here from Newport for the day, for either one of the beaches or the area's excellent bird-watching at the local bird sanctuary.

Sights

If you've got kids in tow, there's a miniature aquatic petting zoo awaiting them at **Save the Bay Exploration Center** (175 Memorial Blvd., 401/324-6020, www.savebay.org, 10 A.M.–4 P.M. daily late May–early Sept., $5 adults and children, free children under 3). The educational facility is filled with tanks of local marine life and, while not big enough to offer an entire day's worth of activity, makes for a fun stop on the way to or from abutting Easton's Beach.

Food

There's above average sushi to be found at **Sea Shai** (747 Aquidneck Ave., Middletown, 401/849-5180, and Long Wharf Mall, Newport, 401/841-0051, www.seashai.com, 11:30 A.M.–2:30 P.M. and 5–10 P.M. daily, $8–22), known for feather-light tempura, fresh sashimi, and decent Korean dishes such as classic *bulgogi* (sliced barbecue beef).

PORTSMOUTH

Located at the tip of the island known as Rhode Island, Portsmouth claims to be none other than the "birthplace of American democracy." The claim is a strong one; founded in 1638 by religious heretics banished from Massachusetts Bay, the town was the first to be ruled by its own members instead of the crown of England—at least until Rhode Island colony was consolidated under royal charter. A bronze tablet erected on a pudding stone rock at Founders Brook memorializes the so-called Portsmouth Compact that founded the independent community.

Sights

A peaceful coexistence between the worlds of humanity and shrubbery is on display at **Green Animals Topiary Gardens** (380 Cory's Lane, off Rtes. 114 & 24, 401/847-1000, www.newportmansions.org, 10 A.M.–6 P.M. daily Apr.–mid-Oct., $12 adults, $4.50 children 6–17), a menagerie of some 80 shrubs and trees sculpted into whimsical shapes, some of which have been intriguing visitors for almost a century. Among them are teddy bears, a giraffe, a unicorn, and an elephant.

SAKONNET PENINSULA

Surrounded on one side by Massachusetts, and on the other by the ocean, the Sakonnet peninsula is the quiet corner of Rhode Island. The two towns of Tiverton and Little Compton are typified by acres of flat farmland, surrounded by trim stone walls and grey-shingled farmhouses that look as if they were airlifted from Nantucket. At the end of the scenic drive, Sakonnet Point is home to a pretty fishing village and marina, along with some of the most secluded beaches in the state.

Sakonnet Vineyards

Back when wine was a solely West Coast phenomenon, one enterprising winemaker rolled the dice in Rhode Island, where he surmised the cool microclimate could support vines similar to those in France's Loire Valley. Founded in 1975, the vineyard (162 W. Main Rd., 800/919-4637, www.sakonnetwine.com, 10 A.M.–6 P.M. daily late May–mid-Oct.; 11 A.M.–5 P.M. daily mid-Oct.–Dec. and Apr.–late May and Thurs.–Sun. Jan.–Mar., tours year-round at noon and 3 P.M.) has since been a smashing success—one of the first in New England, and still among the best. Acres of grapevines produce several wines from the winery's signature *vidal blanc* grape, a French-American hybrid with floral aromas and fresh acidity. Also notable is the aromatic gewürztraminer. The winery features tours, tastings, and an outdoor café with a menu specially created for pairings.

Other Sights

At the historic crossroads of a 17th-century village, **Tiverton Four Corners** (www.

tivertonfourcorners.com) is a cutesy collection of restored houses and mercantile buildings, many now housing shops and art galleries. Nearby, the 1788 **Gray's Store** (4 Main St., Adamsville, 401/635-4566, 6:30 A.M.–8 P.M. daily) is reputedly the oldest continuously operating store in America. It retains the original soda fountain and penny candy case, along with a mini-museum of historical ephemera. Further down the peninsula, the **Little Compton Commons** is as idyllic a town green as you are ever likely to find, with a Congregational church, general store, and library fronting an old graveyard and green space. If you can withstand more quaint scenery, at the far end of the peninsula on Sakonnet Point is a collection of pleasingly ramshackle fishing villages with a strand of sandy beach. Some 600 yards offshore on an iron pier, **Sakonnet Point Light** (www.lighthouse.cc/sakonnet) is a majestic 66-foot-tall cylindrical tower still lit at night.

Shopping

Among the many boutiques worth poking around in at Tiverton Four Corners, **The Metal Works** (3940 Main Rd., Tiverton, 401/624-4400) is both shop and studio producing unique copper lanterns, weathervanes, and garden statuary. Tucked into a backside of the Little Compton Commons, the **Commons Cottage Gallery** (7 South of Commons) has high-quality local art at reasonable prices. **Wilbur's General Store** (50 The Commons, Little Compton, 401/635-2356, 7:30 A.M.–7 P.M. Tues.–Sun., closed Sun.) is a reminder of life before Home Depot and Wal-Mart, a small shop stuffed with groceries, housewares, beach pails, hardware, and a deli counter with gourmet foodstuffs.

Food

A gourmet food shop with creative sandwiches (and even more creative names), **Provender** (3883 Main Rd., Tiverton, 401/624-8084, $3.75–6.75) is a mandatory stop for many Sakonnet beachgoers. Vegetarians will appreciate offerings such as the Great Garbanzo, with spicy orange hummus and mango

chutney. Next door, **Gray's Ice Cream** (16 East Rd., Tiverton, 401/624-4500, www.graysicecream.com, 6:30 A.M.–8 P.M. daily) has developed a near-maniacal following for its homemade ice cream, which features heavy amounts of butterfat and distinctive flavors like peach brandy and grapenut. Overlooking a small marina underneath the bridge to Newport, **Evelyn's Drive-In** (2335 Main Rd., Tiverton, 401/624-3100, www.evelynsdrivein.com, 11:30 A.M.–8:30 P.M. Mon.–Thu.; 11:30 A.M.–9 P.M. Fri.–Sun., $3–17) is a clam shack reduced to its bare essentials—a weather-beaten hut, and an outdoor patio where diners dive into deep-fried clam cakes, Rhode Island stuffed quahogs and a heart-warming Grape-Nuts pudding. A favorite among locals, **Four Corners Grille** (3841 Main Rd., Tiverton, 401/624-1510, 11 A.M.–7:30 P.M. Mon–Thu.; 11:30 A.M.–9 P.M. Fri.; 7 A.M.–9 P.M. Sat.; 7 A.M.–8 P.M. Sun., $9–20) serves inspired seafood dishes in simple yet cozy surroundings. Favorites include Creole crab cakes and shrimp Mozambique—a Portuguese specialty featuring shrimp and pasta with a spicy pepper sauce.

PRUDENCE ISLAND

Located in the center of Narragansett Bay, this large and lonely island is a nature-lover's dream. Farmed until the 1900s, the island has slowly reverted back to a habitat of forest and salt-marsh home to the densest white-tailed deer herd in New England, as well as wading birds including great blue herons. Much of the island is part of the **Narragansett Bay National Estuarine Research Reserve** (401/683-6780, www.nbnerr.org), which is full of hiking trails and beaches perfect for combing. A mile's walk from the boat docks is the 25-foot-high **Prudence Island Light** (www.lighthouse.cc/prudence), which stands sentinel on the island's east side. Transportation to the island is through the **Prudence Ferry Company** (Church Street Wharf, 401/253-9808), which runs several boats between sunrise and sunset. Unfortunately, camping is not permitted.

RHODE ISLAND

SPORTS AND RECREATION
Beaches
Though hardly deserted, Newport's beaches are rocky, salty wonders. The majority are public and well-kept, and small to medium in size. **King Park** (Wellington Ave., 401/846-1398, free) is the easiest to access off of Thames Street; it attracts swimmers, sunbathers, and picnickers alike. A short stroll from the main entrance to the Cliff Walk is larger Easton's Beach, a magnet for surfers and sunbathers. You'll find little peace and quiet here, but it offers convenient parking, food, and a fun carousel nearby.

Just off of Ocean Drive and on the edge of Newport Harbor lies **Fort Adams State Park** (Harrison Ave., off Rte. 138, 401/847-2400, www.riparks.com/fortadams.htm, sunrise–sunset daily, free), 100-plus acres of manicured lawns, picnic spots, beaches, soccer fields, and boating and camping areas. Each year it's home to the area's folk and jazz festivals, as well as a plenitude of private clambakes.

The Sakonnet Peninsula also has a number of attractive beaches with considerably smaller crowds. **Grinnell's Beach** (Main Rd. at Old Stone Bridge) is a sandy crescent at the head of the Sakonnet River, popular with surf fishers; it has a lifeguard and changing rooms. On the southeast tip of the peninsula, **Goosewing Beach Preserve** (off S. Shore Rd., Little Compton, 401/331-7110, www.nature.org) is a spectacular expanse of sandy barrier beach that narrowly divides the sea from a series of pristine coastal ponds.

Hiking
Just north of Newport, bird-watchers flock to **Norman Bird Sanctuary** (583 Third Beach Rd., Middletown, 401/846-2577, www.normanbirdsanctuary.org, 9 A.M.–5 P.M. daily, $5 adults, $2 children 4–13, free children under 4). Its 450 acres encompass plenty of forest and farmlands, and offer great views of several nearby beaches. On the Sakonnet Peninsula, the **Emilie Ruecker Wildlife Refuge** (Seapowet Ave., Tiverton, 401/949-5454, www.asri.org) has some 50 acres of marsh environment

crisscrossed by trails. Bird-watching blinds offer a chance to see snowy egrets, glossy ibis, and a breeding pair of ospreys.

Sailing and Boating
No town can call itself a seaside resort without a plethora of ways to get in, at, and near the ocean, and Newport doesn't disappoint. Foremost, however, the town is a center for boating, and that's evident in its many marinas and wharfs. Charter a tiny sailboat or a gargantuan yacht through the **Newport Yacht Charter Association** (401/841-8686, www.newportcharters.com, $25–75 for a 2-hour sail), or strike out in solitary style, renting from the **Newport Kayak Company** (18 Elm St., 401/849-7404).

ACCOMMODATIONS
$100-150
Comfortable and centrally located, the **Chestnut Inn** (99 Third St., Newport, 401/847-6949, www.newportchestnutinn.com, $125–175) is a year-round Victorian bed-and-breakfast with several air-conditioned double rooms. The front porch makes a relaxing spot for breakfast before a day of sightseeing, boating, or mansion-touring in Newport.

Once the summer home of a well-to-do Boston doctor, **The Ivy Lodge** (12 Clay St., Newport, 401/849-6865, www.ivylodge.com, $119–319) near Bellevue Avenue is a charming and refined stay at rates that (for the amenities offered) can be quite good value. Dominated by a 33-foot gothic entryway, the house is filled with antiques—and many rooms come with fireplaces, DVD players, and whirlpool tubs. Daily teatime and breakfast are included. (And if the savory bread pudding is on offer, don't refuse.) Several small bed-and-breakfasts offer lodging in Little Compton. One dependable option is **Harmony Home Farm Inn** (465 Long Hwy., Little Compton, 401/635-2283, www.harmonyhomefarm.com, $130–175), where the rooms and cottages either have their own entrances and private porches or come with fully equipped kitchens.

$150-250

Perched on Narragansett Bay, the **Bay Voyage Inn** (150 Conanicus Ave., Jamestown, 401/423-2100, www.bayvoyageinn.com, $103–191) is more resort than inn. With 32 suites (including kitchenettes and parlor areas), the Victorian-style building is also home to a pool, indoor whirlpools, a fitness center, and a recreation director to help arrange any sailing, fishing, or biking excursions in the area.

On the grounds of the winery, **The Roost at Sakonnet Vineyards** (162 W. Main St., Little Compton, 401/635-8486,www.sakonnetwine.com, $130–190) makes the perfect landing spot after an afternoon of tastings. The original vineyard farmhouse has three renovated rooms, as well as a porch out back for sunning.

$250 and Up

The ne plus ultra of small luxury hotels, ❰ **The Chanler** (117 Memorial Blvd., Newport, 401/847-1300, www.thechanler.com, $309–1,399) feels a lot like sleeping in your own private mansion—except, of course, for the other guests. Not that you'll really notice them; you'll be too busy taking in the sumptuous decor (each room sports a different theme, from English Tudor to Martha's Vineyard), lounging in your private whirlpool tub, and gazing at the views of the ocean. Don't miss the "beach butler" service, wherein a tuxedoed staff member drives you to and from a semi-private beach, and sets you up with chairs, an umbrella, a customized beach picnic, and reading materials.

INFORMATION AND SERVICES

The area's major hospital is **Newport Hospital** (11 Friendship St., Newport, 401/846-6400,

www.lifespan.org/newport). Local pharmacies include **Rite Aid** (268 Bellevue Ave., Newport, 401/846-1631, www.riteaid.com) and **CVS** (181 Bellevue Ave, Newport, 401/846-7800, www.cvs.com). A handful of banks are found on Thames Street, and several ATMs are located on Thames Street and on Bellevue Avenue, as well as at the bus station and in convenience stores. Free **Internet access** is available in several local cafés, including **Jack and Josies** (111 Broadway St., Newport, 401/851-6900, www.jackandjosies.com), and at the majority of hotels (offered to guests only) in town. Faxing and shipping services are offered at **The UPS Store** (270 Bellevue Ave., Newport, 401/848-7600, www.theupsstore.com).

GETTING THERE

Newport is an easy drive from Boston (approximately an hour and a half), New York City (about three hours), or Providence (about one hour). It's also a fairly quick bus ride from Providence; **Rhode Island Transportation Authority** (RIPTA, 401/781-9400, www.ripta.com) runs from both downtown Providence and the airport. From Boston, **Peter Pan Bus** (888/751-8800, www.peterpanbus.com) offers service to and from Newport a few times each day.

GETTING AROUND

RIPTA buses run all over the major attraction areas of Newport, including Thames Street, Bellevue Avenue, and right to the Cliff Walk. One-way fare is $1.50. There are also several taxi companies, the most dependable of which is **Cozy Cab** (401/846-2500, www.cozytrans.com). RIPTA also stops at towns along the Sakonnet Peninsula. To really do the area justice, however, you'll want a car to explore the back roads.

RHODE ISLAND

South County

This is where Rhode Island's nickname, the Ocean State, really earns its keep. Clam shacks and chowder houses dot a 30-mile-long coastline, much of it covered with sandy barrier beaches. Even in summer, when Newport and Cape Cod are packed to the gills with tourists, much of South County retains a rural feel. The quaint hamlet of Wickford could sit in the dictionary next to the entry for "small-town New England." The appeal of backcountry

Charlestown, meanwhile, is to nature-lovers, who thrill at its miles and miles of untrammeled costal nature preserves. Not all of the area is so quiet, of course. Several beachfront communities draw teenagers from Providence and college students from the nearby University of Rhode Island, who do their best to imitate spring break on summer weekends. Other spots appeal to families, who stroll the resort areas of Watch Hill and Narragansett with kids and

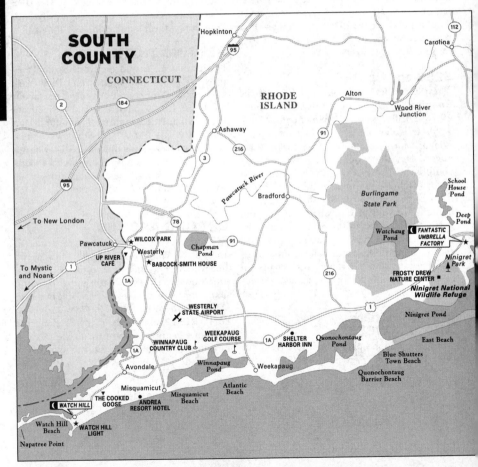

baby strollers in tow—or drop the kids off at the seemingly ubiquitous water parks and mini-golf courses, while they peruse upscale galleries dotted along the coast.

NORTH KINGSTOWN

Founded as Kingstown in 1641, North Kingstown was once home to many thriving farms and plantations, several of which are still in operation or have now become museums. The town, however, has long since been overshadowed by its own village of Wickford, one of the most delightful you are ever likely to meet.

Wickford Village

New England is crawling with historic homes, but in few towns are they as tightly packed and picturesque as in Wickford, a former shipbuilding center after the Revolutionary War. Perhaps that's why author John Updike chose the village to represent the quintessential New England town for his novel *The Witches of Eastwick*. The village center is barely a crossroads, but it is overflowing with brick and clapboard buildings from the 18th and 19th centuries, all pleasantly weathered and peeling. Making them more attractive are the many

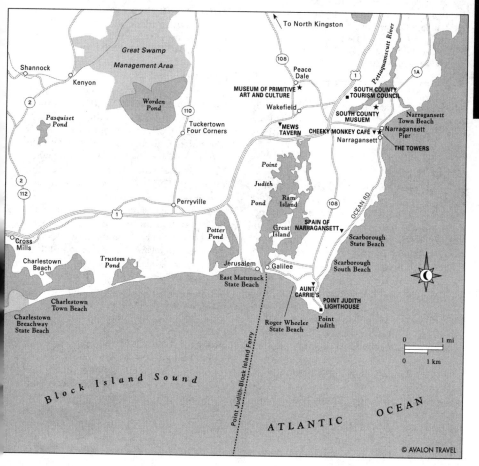

© AVALON TRAVEL

SOUTH COUNTY VILLAGES

To an out-of-towner, it may seem like South County delights in confusing travelers, as each of the major towns is divided into several villages with obscure Native American names or maddeningly similar sobriquets. As a quick guide, then: **North Kingstown** contains the villages of Quonset Point, Saunderstown, and Wickford; **Narragansett** includes Galilee and Point Judith; **South Kingstown** encompasses Jerusalem, Kenyon, Kingston, Matunuck, Peace Dale, Wakefield, and West Kingston; **Charlestown** includes Cross Mills and Quonochontaug; and **Westerly** contains Avondale, Misquamicut, Watch Hill, and Weekapaug. All straight now?

boutiques and galleries that have taken root among them—making this the perfect place to forget about the modern world for an afternoon or a weekend.

Other Sights

Open up your wallet, and chances are you'll find an example of the work of Gilbert Stuart, best known for his portrait of George Washington that graces the one-dollar bill. Stuart's life and work are encapsulated at the **Gilbert Stuart Birthplace & Museum** (815 Gilbert Stuart Rd., Saunderstown, 401/294-3001, www.gilbertstuartmuseum.com, 11 A.M.–4 P.M. Thurs.–Sat. and Mon. and 12–4 P.M. Sun. early May–Sept.; limited hours Oct., $6 adults, $3 children 6–12, free children under 6), which also includes a grist mill that once produced Rhode Island johnnycakes, and a serene pond with rowboat rentals. Don't expect to see battlements at **Smith's Castle** (55 Richard Smith Dr., Wickford, 401/294-3521, www.smithscastle.org, Thurs.–Sun. June–Aug.; Fri.–Sun. May and Sept.–Oct.; open for tours only at 1, 2 and 3 P.M., $5 adults, $1 children 6–12, free children under 6); the 200-year-old mansion, however, does provide

a fascinating glimpse into little-known New England history. Tours take in the history of the site, from its beginnings as an Native American trading post to its 19th-century heyday as a horse and dairy plantation, complete with indentured servants and slaves.

Events

Every Summer, Wickford Village comes alive with the much-anticipated **Wickford Art Festival** (401/294-6840, www.wickfordart. org, July), when hundreds of artists set up booths in the town center. Rhode Island's favorite bivalve takes center stage during the **International Quahog Festival** (235 Tower Hill Rd., Wickford, Aug.), which includes clambakes, shucking contests, and Native American jewelry displays.

Shopping

For modern nautical accoutrements, stop by **Nautical Impressions** (16 W. Main St., North Kingstown, 401/295-5303, 10 A.M.–7 P.M. Mon.–Sat.; 10 A.M.–5 P.M. Sun.), which sells all the books and gear you need to set sail. Chances are something will be chiming when you walk in **The Hour Glass** (15 W. Main St., Wickford, 401/295-8724, www.the-hourglass. com, noon–5 P.M. Sun.–Mon.; 10 A.M.–6 P.M. Tue.–Sat.), a clock store with everything from antique grandfathers to splashy modern wall clocks. For a preview of the annual art festival, stop by the **Wickford Art Association Gallery** (36 Beach St., North Kingstown, 401/294-6840, www.wickfordart.org, 11 A.M.–3 P.M. Tue.–Sat.; noon–4 P.M. Sun.; closed Jan.), which showcases work of local artists.

Food

A pint-sized diner car in the center of town, **Wickford Diner** (64 Brown St., Wickford, 401/295-5477, www.quahog.com/diner.html, 7 A.M.–2 P.M. daily, $2–15) has a cheery staff and nautical decor. In the mornings, it serves cheap but good breakfasts; afternoons, it adds quahog chowder, fish-and-chips, and lobster rolls to the menu. Diners breathe in the smell of the sea with every bite at **Tavern**

By the Sea (16 W. Main St., Wickford, 401/294-5771, www.tavernbytheseari.com, 11:30 A.M.–5 P.M. Mon.; 11:30 A.M.–9 P.M. Tue.–Thu.; 11:30 A.M.–10 P.M. Fri.–Sat.; 11:30 A.M.–8 P.M. Sun., $15–19), which has an outdoor patio overlooking Wickford Creek and a comprehensive, if uninspired, menu of burgers, steaks, pizza, and seafood.

Information

Info is available from **North Kingstown Chamber of Commerce** (8045 Post Rd., North Kingstown, 401/295-5566, www.north-kingstown.com).

NARRAGANSETT

Better known as a bay, beer, and Native American tribe, Narragansett was once America's first seaside resort, drawing Gilded Age tourists to frolic 'til dawn at its swanky beachfront casino. After the casino burned down in 1900, the community underwent a slow decline that left it overshadowed by neighboring Newport. (In an odd twist of fate, the Narragansett tribe is currently lobbying to open a new casino.) The town still draws scads of tourists for its beaches and restaurants, but apart from the obvious draw of the Towers and picturesque Point Judith, it's hard to avoid feeling that its best days are behind it.

Sights

Though its neighboring casino burned down, the majestic arch of the **Towers** (35 Ocean Rd., 401/782-2597, www.thetowersri.com, free) survived in all of its turn-of-the-century elegance. The 1886 building was designed by Boston architects McKim, Mead & White, and is famous as the location where "clams casino" was invented. Now the building hosts a small museum with old photographs as well as lectures, dances, and musical performances. One of the most picturesque lighthouses for miles, **Point Judith Lighthouse** (401/780-0444, www.lighthouse.cc/pointjudith) is a 51-foot octagonal tower protecting a particularly treacherous rocky point. Located on the estate of a former state governor, the **South County**

© MICHAEL BLANDING

the Towers

© MICHAEL BLANDING

Point Judith Lighthouse pierces the fog.

Museum (Strathmore St., 401/789-5400, www.southcountymuseum.org, 10 A.M.–4 P.M. Fri.–Sat., 12–4 P.M. Sun. May–June and Sept.; 10 A.M.–4 P.M. Wed.–Sat., 12–4 P.M. Sun. July–Aug., $5 adults, $4 seniors, $2 children 6–12, free children under 6) has displays of antique furniture and clothing, as well as demonstrations of blacksmithing and carpentry.

Food

Locals are crazy about **Crazy Burger Cafe & Juice Bar** (144 Boon St., 401/783-1810, www.crazyburger.com, 8 A.M.–8 P.M. Sun.–Thu.; 8 A.M.–9 P.M. Fri.–Sat., $4–11), a hoppin' joint serving pancakes and "breakfast pizzas" for pennies, as well as uniformly high-quality meat and veggie burgers. Flavors include "quirky Cajun" and *hummabouli*. Lace curtains on the windows are the only decoration at ◖ **Aunt Carrie's** (1240 Ocean Rd., Pt. Judith, 401/783-7930, www.auntcarriesri.com, Wed.–Mon., late May–early Sept., noon–8 P.M. Fri.–Sat., Apr.–May and Sept., $12–24), a clam shack extraordinaire run by the third generation of a family that started out selling

lemonade and chowder to fishermen. The fried clams are lightly fried—to highlight the taste of the bellies, not the breading—and stuffed quahogs are served with a cocktail sauce that could stand in the Seafood Hall of Fame. Leave room for homemade pies made from original recipes by Aunt Carrie herself (yes, there really was one). The restaurant is BYOB.

Slightly more adventurous specials are served up at the nearby ◖ **Cheeky Monkey Cafe** (21 Pier Marketplace, 401/788-3111, www.cheeky-monkeycafe.com, 5:30–10 P.M. Wed.–Sun., $18–32). True to its name, the spot is filled with cheeky appointments (like the faux leopard-skin carpeting) and monkey motifs. The menu runs the gamut, from delicious calamari with spicy prosciutto and pepper sauce to sesame-seared tuna with lemongrass.

A stone structure beneath the eaves of the Towers, **Coast Guard House** (40 Ocean Rd., 401/789-0700, www.thecoastguardhouse. com, 11 A.M.–9 P.M. Mon.–Sat.; 10 A.M.–2 P.M. Sun., $7–24) features an oceanside deck with an après-beach raw bar, burgers, and grilled sandwiches. The main dining room serves

RHODE ISLAND

New American cuisine, including lobster ravioli and signature crab cakes. Go beyond tapas at the romantic **Spain of Narragansett** (1144 Ocean Rd., 401/783-9770, www.spainri.com, 4–10 P.M. Tue.–Thu.; 4–11 P.M. Fri.–Sat.; 1–9 P.M. Sun., $14–33), a lush dining room conjuring an Iberian courtyard with potted plants, waterfall, and candlelit tables. Affordable entrées include traditional shrimp paella and a delectable Andalusian chicken stuffed with *manchego* cheese, smoked ham, and pine nuts.

Information
Located in the Towers, the **Narragansett Chamber of Commerce** (36 Ocean Rd., 401/783-7121, www.narragansettri.com/chamber) provides information as well as sporadic historic trolley tours.

SOUTH KINGSTOWN TO CHARLESTOWN
The bulk of South County is taken up by the township of South Kingstown, home to a bewildering fourteen villages. Among them are the bustling (for Rhode Island) urban center of Wakefield, an architectural gem featuring many 19th-century buildings converted to restaurants and boutiques; and Kingston, known as the home of the University of Rhode Island. By contrast, the town of Charlestown is the most rural of South County towns, with more than half of its area taken up by nature preserves and farm stands selling vegetables by the side of the road. Its seven miles of sandy beaches are among the state's most treasured possessions.

◖ Fantastic Umbrella Factory
When the back-to-the-land movement was in full swing during the 1960s, a pocket of hippies took up residence in the backwoods of Charlestown. There they created a curiosity shop and flower nursery that has grown over the years into a veritable Wonka-esque fantasyland (4820 Old Post Rd./Rte. 1A, Charlestown, 401/364-6616). Guinea fowl and emu prowl the grounds among shops selling African

© MICHAEL BLANDING

RHODE ISLAND

A sign points the way to the Fantastic Umbrella Company.

masks and rain sticks, while a greenhouse full of Technicolor perennials dazzles the eye.

Other Sights
If you like your brawn with brains, you'll appreciate the **International Scholar-Athlete Hall of Fame** (3045 Kingstown Rd., Kingston, 401/874-2375, www.internationalsport.com/sa_hof, 10 A.M.–5 P.M. Mon.–Fri.; Sat. and Sun. by appointment, free), a quirky museum on the URI campus that honors those who "exemplify the scholar-athlete ideal." Its egalitarian list of honorees includes Jackie Robinson, George H. W. Bush, and Plato.

Entertainment
URI's spanking-new **Thomas M. Ryan Center** (1 Lincoln Almond Plz., Kingston, 401/788-3200, www.theryancenter.com) hosts national performers like Bob Dylan and John Mayer in an 8,000-seat auditorium. Inside a Romanesque granite building, the **Courthouse Center for the Arts** (3481 Kingstown Rd., W. Kingston, 401/782-1018, www.courthousearts.org) features

indie films and community theater. A ramshackle seaside roadhouse, **Ocean Mist Beach Bar** (895A Matunuck Beach Rd., Matunuck, 401/782-3740, www.oceanmist.net) fills with sandal-wearing patrons getting down to rock and tribute bands.

Events
The salty air fills with the aroma of fried clams and melted butter in early August for the **Charlestown Seafood Festival** (Ninigret Park, Charlestown, 401/364-4031, www.charlestownrichamber.com), a self-proclaimed "gastronomic extravaganza" that combines musical performances with all the lobster and chowder you can eat. Two dozen brightly colored hot-air balloons take to the sky every July for the **South County Hot Air Balloon Festival** (URI Athletic Fields, Rte. 138, Kingston, 401/783-1770, www.wakefieldrotary.com), sponsored by the Wakefield Rotary Club.

Shopping
Located in a former art deco gas station,

COURTESY OF KINDRA CLINEFF/RHODE ISLAND TOURISM

South County beach

Glass Station (318 Main St., Wakefield, 401/788-2500, www.ebenhortonglass.com, 10 A.M.–5 P.M. Tue.–Sat.)—get it?—is now the studio-gallery of glassblower Eben Horton, who creates vases inspired by ocean waves and whimsical glass fish. Inside an old diner car, **Kiddie Closet** (329 Main St., Wakefield, 401/783-8680, 10 A.M.–5 P.M. daily, is heaven to cash-strapped parents (as if there were any other kind) with rack after rack of sporting clothing, strollers, books, and more. In the 19th-century historic home of a blacksmith, **Fayerweather House** (1859 Mooresfield Rd./Rte. 138, South Kingstown, 401/789-9072, www.fayerweatherhouse.8m.net, 10 A.M.–4 P.M. Tue.–Sat. mid-May–Dec.) is now a craft center selling hooked rugs, woven baskets, and other handmade items. A team of five artists throws the clay at **Peter Pots Pottery** (494 Glen Rock Rd, W. Kingston, 401/783-2350, www.peterpotspottery.com, 10 A.M.–4 P.M. Mon.–Sat.; 1–4 P.M. Sun.), which has been producing distinctive stoneware for over 50 years.

Food
Meat lovers won't be disappointed by a night at **Crave Steakhouse** (333 Main St., Wakefield, 401/789-0914, www.craveseafoodsteak.com, 5–9 P.M. Wed.–Thu., 5–10 P.M. Fri.–Sat., 4–9 P.M. Sun.; $14–31); the kitchen grills and churns out admirable specimens of beef, lamb, and pork. Seafood is less spectacular, but the pasta dishes more than make up for it. Excess is the name of the game at **Mew's Tavern** (456 Main St., Wakefield, 401/783-9370, www.mewstavern.com, 11 A.M.–1 A.M. daily, $10–18), which boasts 69 beers on tap and 200 single-malt scotches—and that's just for starters. The comprehensive menu runs from steak to seafood to pizza, served up in a faux log cabin ski lodge.

Information
Info about the entire region is available from the **South County Tourism Council** (4808 Tower Hill Rd., Wakefield, 800/548-4662, www.southcountyri.com). For local

TO THE LIGHTHOUSE

Some of New England's prettiest and most historic lighthouses are found on coastal Rhode Island. Most are closed to the public, but allow visitors on the grounds.

- **Beavertail Light** (1749), Conanicut Island/Narragansett Bay, Jamestown

- **Block Island** (North) **Light** (1829), Sandy Point/North End Block Island

- **Block Island** (Southeast) **Light** (1875), Mohegan Bluffs

- **Bristol Ferry Light** (1846), Strait between Mount Hope and Narragansett Bays

- **Castle Hill Light** (1890), Narragansett Bay East Passage, Newport

- **Conanicut Island Light** (1886), north end of Conanicut Island, Jamestown

- **Conimicut Shoal Light** (1868), Providence River Mouth/Narragansett Bay, Warwick

- **Dutch Island Light** (1826), Dutch Island/Narragansett Bay, Jamestown

- **Hog Island Shoal Light** (1886), East Passage Narragansett Bay, Portsmouth

- **Ida Lewis Rock Light** (1854), Inner Newport Harbor, Newport

- **Nayatt Point Light** (1828), Nayatt Point/Providence River Mouth, Barrington

- **Newport Harbor Light** (1824), Goat Island/Newport Harbor entrance, Newport

- **Plum Beach Light** (1897), West Passage/Narragansett Bay, North Kingstown

- **Point Judith Light** (1810), west side of Narragansett Bay

- **Pomham Rocks Light** (1871), Providence River, East Providence

- **Poplar Point Light** (1831), Wickford Harbor, North Kingstown

- **Prudence Island (Sandy Point) Light** (1852), east side Sandy Point/Narragansett Bay, Portsmouth

- **Rose Island Light** (1870), north of Newport Harbor, Newport

- **Sabin Point** (1872), Providence River, Providence

- **Sakonnet Light** (1884), Little Cormorant Rock/Sakonnet River, Little Compton

- **Warwick Light** (1827), Warwick Neck/Narragansett Bay, Warwick

- **Watch Hill Light** (1808), Fishers Island Sound, East Approach, Watch Hill

information, visit the **South Kingstown Chamber of Commerce** (230 Old Tower Hill Rd., Wakefield, 401/783-2801, www.sk-chamber.com) and **Charlestown Chamber of Commerce** (4945 Old Post Rd., 401/364-3878, www.charlestownrichamber.com).

WESTERLY

Named for its location on the far end of the Rhode Island coast, Westerly is one of those rare towns where the past and the present seem in perfect harmony. The downtown area is as picturesque as they come, with solid granite buildings from the 19th and early 20th centuries built with stones from nearby granite quarries. The granite made the little town rich, and its residents gained a rich appreciation for the arts, a tradition that carries on to the present day. Several downtown theaters and contemporary galleries still give the town a charming, sophisticated feel.

◖ Watch Hill

Rhode Islanders call the rocky point at the south end of Westerly one of the best-kept secrets in the state. And no wonder. The village of Watch Hill—so called because it was once used as a Revolutionary War lookout—is a quaint resort community welcoming to families and couples alike. At the turn of the 20th century, an enterprising local rented out rooms on the lighthouse at the top of the hill; grand old hotels followed, and high society including Clark Gable, Douglas Fairbanks, and Henry Ford came to cool their heels by the sea. The beachfront resort has an intimate feel, fronted by boutiques and restaurants and home to the country's oldest carousel, the **Flying Horse Carousel** (Bay St., 401/348-6007, 11 A.M.–9 P.M. Mon.–Fri.; 10 A.M.–9 P.M. Sat.–Sun., $1). Up the hill, surrounded by mansions of the summer folk, **Watch Hill Lighthouse** (Lighthouse Rd., www.lighthouse.cc/watchhill) still sends forth its beacon. Built in 1856, the granite tower isn't the prettiest lighthouse in the world, but its vantage on the top of the hill is spectacular.

Entertainment

The crowd-pleasing **Granite Theatre** (1 Granite St., 401/596-2341, www.granitetheatre.com) showcases Broadway musicals and children's plays in a beautifully converted Greek Revival church. Somewhat more artistic fare is performed at the **Colonial Theatre** (Granite St., 401/596-7909, www.thecolonialtheater.org), which stages dramas and comedies as well as the annual summer Shakespeare in Wilcox Park. Misquamicut Beach comes alive with a twentysomething crowd that comes to party. One of the most popular spots is **Paddy's Beach Restaurant** (159 Atlantic Ave., Westerly, 401/596-2610, www.paddysbeach.com), which serves up potent cocktails with obvious names like Shark Attack and Hurricane.

Events

Westerly has many events throughout the year. Strangely one of the most popular is **Guy Fawkes Bonfire Night** (Misquamicut Beach, early Oct., www.guyfawkesusa.com), celebrating the obscure British holiday with an effigy burned in a raucous beachside bonfire. Each

spring, the arts are celebrated with the **Virtu Art Festival** (Wilcox Park, 401/596-7761), which features artists and musicians from all over the world. Smaller gallery nights are held the first Wednesday of every month.

Shopping

A treasure trove of used books facing Watch Hill Beach, the **Book & Tackle Shop** (124 Bay St., 401/556-6905, www.bookandtackle.com, 10 A.M.–4 P.M. May–Oct.) stocks many books on old New England history, along with a whole section on the Kennedys. (The same store also has a year-round location in Westerly at 166 Main St., 401/315-2424.) Near the carousel, **Comina** (117 Bay St., Watch Hill, 401/596-3218, www.comina.com, 8 A.M.–5:30 P.M. Mon.–Sat., 11 A.M.–5 P.M. Sun., May–mid-Oct.) sells unique contemporary housewares, including leather club chairs and distinctive aluminum dishware.

Food

A favorite among locals and beachgoers alike, **The Cooked Goose** (92 Watch Hill Rd., 401/348-9888, www.thecookedgoose.com, 7 A.M.–3 P.M. daily, $6–13) serves prepared gourmet lunches and creative sandwiches to go. Breakfast includes such unusual fare as baked eggs with fontina cheese and truffle oil. The menu at **Olympia Tea Room** (74 Bay St., 401/348-8211, www.olympiatearoom. com, 11 A.M.–10 P.M. daily Jun.–Sept.; limited hours Apr.–May and early–mid-Oct., $12–26) is standard New England (baked scrod, bacon-wrapped scallops), but the setting of the 100-year-old eatery is alone worth a visit. The decor evokes the Victorian era with black-and-white tiled floors and high-backed wooden booths, while outdoor tables fronting the beach make a perfect setting for cocktails and people-watching. Serving excellent food without the pretense, **Up River Cafe** (37 Main St., 401/348-9700, www.theuprivercafe. net, 5–9 P.M. Tue.–Thu.; 5–10 P.M. Fri.–Sat., lounge open 4 P.M.–late, $11–26) wows with its location in a refurbished mill overlooking the Pawcatuck River. Similarly, the San

Francisco–trained owners provide updated riffs on old classics, such as a Parisian-style Delmonico steak with potatoes au gratin, and seared local scallops with lobster home fries. Save room for dessert, which includes nostalgia-heavy items such as root beer floats, ice cream sundaes, and a butterscotch pudding to die for.

Information
Info is available from the **Greater Westerly-Pawcatuck Chamber of Commerce** (1 Chamber Way, 401/496-7761 or 800/732-7636, www.westerlychamber.org), which runs a comprehensive visitors center off of Route 1.

SPORTS AND RECREATION
Beaches
The most popular beaches on the South Coast are **Narragansett Town Beach** (Ocean Ave., Narragansett), known for its surfing and summer crowds, and **Misquamicut Beach** (257 Atlantic Ave., Misquamicut, 401/596-9097, www.misquamicut.org), which attracts a Baywatch-like beach scene of randy college students. Quieter **Charlestown Town Beach** (557 Charlestown Beach Rd., Charlestown, 401/364-1208) has a wide swath of yellow sand and crashing surf, while **Roger Wheeler State Beach** (Rte. 108, Narragansett, 401/789-3563), overlooking the fishing boat traffic around Point Judith, is one of the prettiest spots of sand in the state. Family-friendly **Watch Hill Beach** (Bay St., Watch Hill, 401/348-6007) includes restrooms and changing facilities; from there, it is also possible to walk out to **Napatree Point,** known for its quiet seclusion and bird-watching.

Ninigret National Wildlife Refuge
The wilderness jewel of the south coast, this reserve occupies the former home of a naval base (Charlestown, 401/364-9124, www.fws.gov) with more than 3,000 acres of unspoiled tidal bays full of shore birds and bioluminescent sea organisms behind a protective barrier beach. Next door, the town-owned Ninigret Park is home to the **Frosty Drew Nature Center**

and Observatory (61 Park Ln., Charlestown, 401/364-9508, www.frostydrew.org), which provides nightly displays of some of the darkest skies in Southern New England.

Hiking
A linear trail running the length of western Rhode Island, the unimaginatively named **North-South Trail** (www.rigreenways.org) takes in 75 miles of streambeds, rocky hillsides, and abandoned foundations of 17th- and 18th-century homes. The trail starts at Ninigret Pond; maps are available from the Greenways Alliance of Rhode Island or the state department of transportation (Two Capitol Hill, Providence, 401/222-2450, www.dot.state.ri.us).

Boating and Fishing
The **Kayak Center of Rhode Island** (9 Phillips St., Wickford, 401/295-4400, www.kayakcentre.com) runs kayak rentals and tours into Narragansett Bay from its waterfront location in Wickford; it also has an outlet in Charlestown (562 Charlestown Beach Rd., 401/364-8000). For deep-sea fishing, the **Frances Fleet** (401/783-4988, www.frances-fleet.com) runs boats out of Galilee. Anglers engage in surf-fishing right off of Charlestown Beachway State Beach; stop by **Breachway Bait & Tackle** (166 Charlestown Beach Rd., Charlestown, 401/364-6407) for supplies.

Camping
More than 750 campsites are available at **Burlingame State Park** (Rte. 1, Charlestown, 401/322-7994, www.riparks.com/burlgm-camp.htm), which also has five cabins and a yurt, and facilities for boating and swimming on Watchaug Pond.

ACCOMMODATIONS
$100-150
Convenient to downtown Westerly, the **Blue Star Motor Inn** (110 Post Rd., Westerly, 401/596-2891, $119–139) is a trim motel along Route 1 with an outdoor pool and continental breakfast. A rambling 1906 Victorian

RHODE ISLAND

RHODE ISLAND

just over the bridge from Wickford Village, **℃ Haddie Pierce House** (146 Boston Neck Rd., Wickford, 401/294-7674, www.haddiepierce.com, $130–150) features a supercutesy decor of lace, dolls, and teddy bears. Each of five rooms has its own bath, though some are located in the hall; the largest has a whirlpool tub. For breakfast, friendly innkeepers John and Darya Pressl have been known to whip up baked apple-stuffed French toast. A Narragansett bed-and-breakfast, the **1900 House** (59 Kingstown Rd., Narragansett, 401/789-7971, www.1900houseri.com, $85–150) re-creates the resort's heyday with old wooden boxes full of antiques, a genuine stereoscope, and two hat boxes stuffed with old postcards. After the block-and-a-half walk back from the beach, guests can "shower under the stars" in an enclosed outdoor shower (rooms also have private baths).

$150-250

A rambling white building smack dab on Misquamicut Beach, the **Andrea Resort Hotel** (89 Atlantic Ave., Misquamicut, 888/318-5707, www.andreahotel.com, $110–265) is legendary for its friendly service and beach-bum atmosphere. If you are looking for quiet, keep looking; if you are looking for a short stumble home from the bonfire, this is the place. Some rooms include porches overlooking the action. At the opposite extreme, even the name of the **Shelter Harbor Inn** (10 Wagner Rd., Westerly, 401/322-8883, www.shelterharborinn.com, $125–200) suggests romantic seclusion. A converted farmhouse near the sleepy village of Weekapaug, the 24-room inn features rooms with wood fireplaces, exposed beams, and four-poster beds. The inn's 200 acres of grounds include a hot tub, croquet course, and putting greens, just a short drive from pristine barrier beaches.

GETTING THERE AND AROUND

Amtrak (800/872-7245, www.amtrak.com) runs trains to stations located in Westerly (14 Railroad Ave.) and West Kingston (1 Railroad Ave.). Buses run by the **Rhode Island Public Transit Authority** (RIPTA, 401/781-9400, www.ripta.com) stop in Narragansett, North and South Kingstown, and Westerly.

Block Island

The grey cliffs that rise from the waves of Block Island's north shore are conspicuously naked. If this were another island within such easy grasp of both Boston and New York, they would be capped with sprawling homes of moneyed summer folk. But only the green fringe of conservation land tops the cliffs of Clay Head, the first sight that you are likely to see of the island coming over on the ferry from Point Judith. It's a fitting introduction to an island that counts conservation land as almost half of its land area, the result of a dogged campaign by island residents eager to preserve Block Island's sense of tranquility.

Since the secret got out a few years ago, Block Island has been reluctantly colonized by the overflow of tourists from the Vineyard and the Hamptons, and the main drag of Old Harbor can get crowded in summer. Especially during the shoulder season, however, you can still find deserted beaches, country roads scenically bordered by stone walls, and dramatic vistas of clay and limestone that plummet 250 feet down to the waves below.

The heart of Block Island is Old Harbor, which has a population of just 800 in the winter but swells with as many as 10,000 seasonal visitors. On the fringes of nearby Great Salt Pond, New Harbor is a bit more upscale, with anchorages for pleasure craft gracing the waterfront. Even so, the overriding attitude of the entire island is unpretentious and even a bit funky, the legacy of the island's agrarian past and perhaps too of the hardships it has faced over the years.

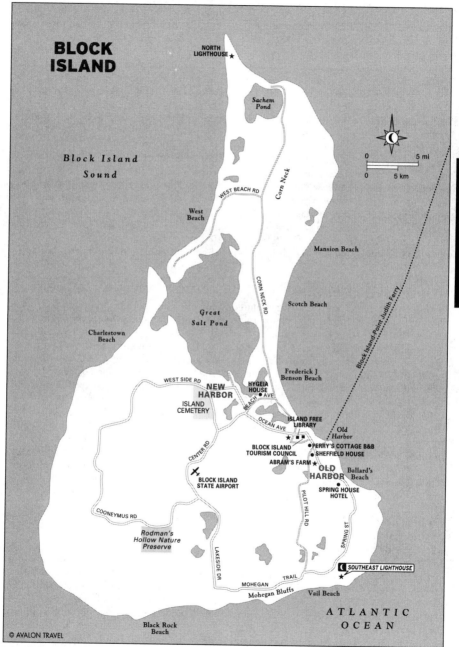

BLOCK ISLAND

NORTH LIGHTHOUSE ★

Sachem Pond

Block Island Sound

Corn Neck

0   5 mi
0   5 km

WEST BEACH RD

West Beach

Mansion Beach

CORN NECK RD

Scotch Beach

Great Salt Pond

Charlestown Beach

Frederick J Benson Beach

Block Island-Point Judith Ferry

WEST SIDE RD   **NEW HARBOR**   HYGEIA HOUSE

ISLAND CEMETERY

BEACH AVE

OCEAN AVE   ISLAND FREE LIBRARY

Old Harbor

CENTER RD   BLOCK ISLAND TOURISM COUNCIL   PERRY'S COTTAGE B&B
SHEFFIELD HOUSE

ABRAM'S FARM ★

OLD HARBOR   Ballard's Beach

✈ BLOCK ISLAND STATE AIRPORT

SPRING HOUSE HOTEL

COONEYMUS RD

PILOT HILL RD

Rodman's Hollow Nature Preserve

LAKESIDE DR

SPRING ST

☾ SOUTHEAST LIGHTHOUSE
★

MOHEGAN   TRAIL
Mohegan Bluffs   Vail Beach

Black Rock Beach

ATLANTIC OCEAN

© AVALON TRAVEL

Stuck out all alone in its eponymous sound, Block Island has always been easy pickings for invaders, including pirates and French privateers who were constantly sacking the island's early settlements. (It's rumored still that no less a seadog than Captain Kidd buried treasure on the north shore.) The early settlers made their livings through agriculture, and stone walls and sheep herds are still to be found within its shores. In the second half of the 19th century, it enjoyed a brief time as a tourist destination, when its fame as "Bermuda of the North" sprouted leviathan grand hotels of the period. These days, however, the joy of visiting for many summertime guests is rambling among unspoiled trails and grassland, biking the roads with the wind and sea spray in their faces, and topping their days off with long afternoons sunbathing beneath the cliffs.

SIGHTS
◖ Southeast Lighthouse

Perched way up on the cliffs of Mohegan Bluffs, this lighthouse is the highest and most visible on the New England coast, with a beam that can be seen 35 miles out to sea. And for good reason—it's been estimated that of all the shipwrecks in New England, half have occurred off the treacherous shores of Block Island. The lighthouse itself (122 Mohegan Tr., 401/466-5009, www.lighthouse.cc/blockisoutheast, 10 A.M.–4 P.M. daily late June–early Sept.; 10 A.M.–4 P.M. Sat.–Sun. late May–late June and early Sept.–early Oct., free) looks more like a Gothic mansion than the traditional black-and-white tower. The brick keeper's house is attached to the structure, making the 52-foot lighthouse itself seem like a turret.

Part of the lighthouse's appeal for visitors is its history of migration. While the lighthouse was originally built 300 feet from the bluffs in 1878, erosion over time narrowed that gap to just 35 feet. In 1993, the Southeast Lighthouse Foundation spent more than $2 million to lift the entire structure up on beams lubricated with Ivory soap and slide it back to its original distance from the edge. Inside, a small museum details the history of the structure and the

move, supplemented by tours ($10 adults, $5 seniors and children 6–17, free children under 6) every hour on the half-hour. Currently, the interior of the structure is being restored, and plans are to soon open a larger museum inside with more old photos and reconstructed keepers' quarters. At the rate the cliffs are receding, no doubt the museum will one day include exhibits about the heroic move back from the edge in 2107.

Other Sights

For more about the history of the island, drop by the **Block Island Historical Society** (Old Town Rd., New Harbor, 401/466-2481, dgasner@ids.net, www.blockislandinfo.com, 10 A.M.–4 P.M. daily late June–early Sept.; 10 A.M.–4 P.M. Sat.–Sun. Sept.–June, free), which maintains a series of well-labeled exhibits on 16th- and 17th-century farming and household life, as well as several rooms set up in the style of the island's heyday of Victorian tourism. The island's agricultural past comes alive, sort of, at **Manisses Farm,** also known as Abrams' Farm (Spring and High Sts., 401/466-2421, www.blockislandresorts.com, daily dawn–dusk, free), an exotic animal farm at the Hotel Manisses with llamas, camels, Highland steers, and Zeke the zebu (a breed of cattle from India that is the oldest known). Though its location isn't as dramatic as its southern cousin, the 55-foot-tall granite **North Lighthouse** (Corn Neck Rd., 401/466-3200, www.lighthouse.cc/blockinorth, early July–early Sept., $2) is located on a rocky beach a half-mile's walk from the road. Inside, a small museum details the history of Block Island shipwrecks and rescues.

ENTERTAINMENT

The island's nightlife tends to center around the anchorages of New Harbor. The most popular dance club is **Captain Nick's** (Ocean Ave., 401/466-5670, www.captainnicks.com), a rollicking "rock 'n' roll bar" that imports live bands Tuesday through Sunday nights. In June, it hosts an annual music festival that brings in some 40 bands from out of town.

THE NAME GAME

The genesis of how and why Rhode Island acquired its official name – technically known as Rhode Island and Providence Plantations – has never been definitively nailed down. The region has no particular history tying it to the Greek island of Rhodes, and is quite clearly not an island of any kind. So how did it come to be known as Rhode Island?

The history is a jumble of vague associations and mistaken identities, but it's believed that the name Rhode was first put forth in describing Block Island, by 16th-century Italian explorer Giovanni da Verrazano, who wrote that it reminded him of the Greek island. In the next century, sailors passing by another small Narragansett Bay island – which is today known as Aquidneck – mistook it for the island Verrazano had identified, and started calling *that* Rhode Island. Later, as Providence developed, the entire region became known as Rhode Island and Providence Plantations.

Confused? No doubt the state's residents were, too, which may be why they later shortened the state's name to simply Rhode Island. Legally, however, it remains Rhode Island and Providence Plantations – the longest name in all the United States, ironically held by its smallest state.

DJs and reggae bands perform at **McGovern's Yellow Kittens Tavern** (Ocean Ave., 401/466-5855, www.yellowkittens.net), a dance club and Mexican restaurant that specializes in frozen margaritas. A more "alternative" crowd flocks to **Club Soda** (35 Connecticut Ave., 401/466-5397), a subterranean bar that features grungy rock bands, mudslides, and Philly cheesesteaks.

EVENTS

The most exciting time on the island is during **Block Island Race Week** (914/834-8857, www.blockislandraceweek.com), held in June

of odd-numbered years. Some 2,000 sailors and 200 boats from around the world vie for trophies during a week of regattas and onshore partying. An off-season highlight of the island calendar is the **Block Island Christmas Stroll** (800/383-2474, www.blockislandinfo.com, late Nov.), a post-Thanksgiving celebration that lights up the streets of Old Harbor with music and merriment.

SHOPPING

The funky attitude of the island extends to the shops lining the harbor. **Archipelago** (Water St., 401/466-8920, 10 A.M.–10 P.M. daily) features clothing and accessories from Southeast Asia, along with its own line of custom-designed sarongs and bikinis from Bali. High-quality men's clothes are on sale at **Mahoney's Clothier** (Water St., 401/466-8616 10 A.M.–5 P.M. Tues.–Fri.; 10 A.M.–3 P.M. Sat.; closed Mon. June–Oct.), which sells a popular line of polo shirts and silk ties with a Block Island logo. Sailors delight in **The Glass Onion** (Water St., 401/466-5161, 10 A.M.–6 P.M. Tues.–Sat., closed Mon. June–Oct.,), which features antique yachting books, nautical charts, and Victorian-era engravings. **Lazy Fish** (235 Dodge St., 401/466-2990, 11 A.M.–4 P.M. Mon.–Tue. and Thu.–Fri., 10 A.M.–5 P.M. Sat.–Sun., May–Oct.) sells affordable old furniture, attractively weathered by decades of salt and sun, as well as vintage children's toys. Making salt water taffy from scratch with a 1940s taffy-pulling machine, **Old Salt Taffy Co.** (Chapel St., 401/466-5005, 11 A.M.–7 P.M. Thurs.–Sun., 11 A.M.–5 P.M. Mon.–Wed., May–Oct.; 11 A.M.–5 P.M. Thurs.–Sun. Nov.–Apr.) is the closest you'll get to recapturing those youthful memories of the beach.

SPORTS AND RECREATION
Beaches

A short walk north from Old Harbor, **Crescent Beach** (Water St.) stretches two and a half miles in a wide sweeping curve of gorgeous yellow sand, making it a favorite for the hordes of summer tourists. In general, families crowd the southern portion, while teenagers and couples take over the less-crowded north side. Even on hot August days, the relative inaccessibility of **Vail Beach** (Payne Overlook, Mohegan Trail) leaves it spectacularly quiet. The beach is located down a 150-foot-high stairway climbing down Mohegan Bluff. A short walk from the bottom is one of the more curious structures on the island—a huge driftwood sea-fort built by a waitress in her off-hours several years ago, and now decorated with netting, buoys, shells, and business cards from landlubbers all over the world.

Hiking and Biking

The centerpiece of Block Island's conservation land is **Rodman's Hollow** (Cooneymus Rd.), a 230-acre basin scooped out by glaciers 10,000 years ago, and now filled with forested meadows and maritime shrubland. Among its trails you can find some 40 different endangered species (most of the insect variety) as well as migratory birds looking for a rest on the Atlantic Flyway. The Hollow is part of a larger network of some 25 miles worth of trails known as the **Greenway,** which stretches throughout much of the southwest corner of the island. On the north side of the island, stunning views grace the tops of **Clay Head,** where a series of intertwining paths known as "the maze" provides fodder for hours of wandering among shrub-forested heights. For maps and information on all of these properties, contact **The Nature Conservancy** (401/331-7110, www.nature.org). The gentle paved roads of the island are ideal for biking, with 40 miles of country lanes sweeping along the fields and shoreline and occasionally climbing to scenic vistas along the cliffs. (See *Getting Around* for information on bike rentals.)

Boating and Fishing

Affiliated with the acclaimed outdoor outfitter Orvis, **Oceans and Ponds** (Ocean and Connecticut Aves., New Harbor, 401/466-5131 or 800/678-4701) offers one-stop shopping for outdoor pursuits, including kayak and canoe rentals, guided surf-fishing trips, deep-sea fishing cruises, and sails aboard *Ruling Passion,* a 45-foot tri-catamaran. Sailboats

can be rented and chartered from the **Block Island Maritime Institute** (Smuggler's Cove Marina, New Harbor, 401/466-7938, www.blockislandmaritimeinstitute.org), a nonprofit organization that offers both group and private sailing lessons aboard 22-foot Pearson Ensigns or 15-foot Herreshoffs.

ACCOMMODATIONS
Under $100

Finding a place to stay on Block Island on a budget can be difficult, especially in the high season. One exception is the delightful **Perry Cottage B&B** (High St., 401/466-2342, www.biri.com/perrycottage, $45–95), a small guesthouse a few minutes' walk from town. Its three rooms are bare-bones and share a bath, but do include a continental breakfast in the rate.

$150–250

From the turret atop **C Sheffield House** (High St., 401/466-2494 or 866/466-2494, www.thesheffieldhouse.com, $125–225), you get a picture-perfect view of the ocean as well as the animals in Manisses Farm next door. Rooms have an understated flower decor with either shared or private baths and homey touches like the Victorian inn's own brand of glycerin soap. Friendly owners Diane and Ed Hayde cook up hearty breakfasts including baked apple French toast. A Third Empire inn lovingly restored by the great-grandson of its original owner, **Hygeia House** (Beach Ave., 401/466-9616, www.hygeiahouse.com, $65–315) offers views of New Harbor from the rocking chairs on its front porch. Rooms have not only been restored to their Victorian-era splendor, but include personal effects (such as letters and a doctor's bag) from some of the house's original occupants.

$250 and Up

While many of the Victorian grande dames on the island are still impressive on the outside, time has taken its toll on the interiors. Not so with the elegant **Spring House Hotel** (Spring St., 401/466-5844 or 800/234-9263, www.springhousehotel.com, $125–450), situated on

the verandah at Spring House Hotel

its own promontory with 15 acres of grounds, and recently renovated to luxurious effect. Rooms are tastefully decorated with pastels and floral bedspreads, some with private baths as big as the bedrooms. For the true spirit of the era, watch the sun glinting off the ocean from the wraparound verandah, or sip cognac and single malts in the sumptuous salon.

FOOD

Owned by Molly, Brigid, and Maria Price, **Three Sisters** (Old Town Rd., 401/466-9661, 11:30 A.M.–2 P.M. daily, $7–23) offers oversized sandwiches with funky names and hearty soups like sweet-potato apple. Out back, tanned college kids lounge on picnic tables and Adirondack chairs, or swing in the hammock for a little after-dinner digestion. For dinner, islanders congregate for BBQ ribs cooked on a smoker in the backyard and served with sweet potato, corn on the cob, and live music under the stars. It's not easy being all things to all people, but **Mohegan Cafe and Brewery** (Water St., 401/466-5911, 11:30 A.M.–9:30 P.M. Mon.–Thurs., 11:30 A.M.–10 P.M. Sat., 11:30 A.M.–9 P.M. Sun. May–Oct.; hours vary in

winter, $17.95–23.95) does a pretty good job at convening the whole island under one roof. Centrally located in the middle of Old Harbor, the restaurant serves everything from burgers to filet mignon, as well as reliable Asian and Southwestern fare, a range of hand-crafted beers, and an excellent wine list to boot. The setting is casual, with dark wood tables and picture windows perfect for watching people get off the ferry on the street below. The place to go for your classic boiled pound-and-a-half, **Finn's Seafood Restaurant** (Water St., 401/466-2473, 5 P.M.–9:30 P.M. daily June–Oct.; closed in winter, $2.50–34) is a no-frills seafood shack with both takeout and a table service on a deck overlooking the harbor. To see how fresh its ingredients are, peruse the offerings at the seafood market next door. Fine dining gets funky at **Eli's** (456 Chapel St., 401/466-5230, elisblockisland.com, 5:30 P.M.–10 P.M. Tues.–Sun.; closed Mon., June; hours vary in winter, $19–28)—starting with the name, an homage to the chef-owner's late black Labrador. Pictures of said canine are preserved beneath the glass of several of the tables, which are capped in summer with wildflowers in Mason jars. The eclectic American menu features several imaginative pastas in huge portions (there's an extra charge for splitting on two plates), as well as overachieving seafood dishes such as grilled mahimahi with roasted fennel and radicchio, white and wild rice and a honeydew macadamia sauce.

INFORMATION AND SERVICES

Brochures and advice are available from the **Block Island Chamber of Commerce** (Water St., 800/383-2474, www.blockislandchamber. com), which runs a visitors center at the ferry landing in Old Harbor.

There is no major hospital on the island, but **The Block Island Medical Center** (6 Payne Rd., Block Island, 401/466-2974) offers daily care and emergency services. Locals rely on **Block Island Pharmacy** (High St., Block Island, 401/466-5825) for prescription needs and **Washington Trust Company** (Ocean Ave., 401/466-7710, www.washtrust.com) for banking. ATMs aren't easy to find, though there are a couple near the ferry terminal, as well as at **Chamber Visitors Center** (Old Harbor, 800/383-2474, www.blockislandinfo.com), and **Winfields Restaurant** (214 Corn Neck Rd., 401/466-5856, mysite.verizon.net/restkino).

For **Internet services,** look to your hotel or visit the **Island Free Library** (Dodge St., 401/466-3233, www.islandfreelibrary.org), which offers free access.

GETTING THERE

The easiest way to get to the island is by ferry. **Block Island Ferry** (401/783-7996, www.blockislandferry.com) runs boats year-round from Point Judith (State Pier, Rte. 108, Galilee, 55 min.) and during the summer from Newport (Fort Adams State Park, July–early Sept., 2 hrs.). If you just have to get there, **Island Hi-Speed Ferry** (877/733-9425, www.islandhighspeedferry.com) runs a fast boat from Point Judith that gets there in half the time. From Connecticut, **Block Island Express** (860/444-4624 or 401/466-2212, www.longislandferry.com/bif/home. htm) runs a fast ferry from New London (2 Ferry St., 1.25 hrs.). Block Island also sees a limited amount of air traffic. **New England Airlines** (56 Airport Rd., Westerly, 800/243-2460, www.block-island.com/nea) has regular flights from Westerly Airport in South County, while **Action Airlines** (East Haddam, Conn., 800/243-8623, www.actionairlines.net) has flights from New London/Groton airport in Connecticut.

GETTING AROUND

Cars are not only unnecessary on Block Island, they are liable to be more hassle than they are worth. Instead, rent a bike or moped in town. Try **Old Harbor Bike Shop** (432 Water St., 401/466-2029) at the ferry landing, or the slightly less expensive **Island Moped and Aldo's Mopeds** (Weldon's Way, 401/466-5018). If you are just craving four wheels, the former also rents cars, though expect to pay dearly for the privilege. For the occasional auto trip, several taxis run service throughout the island, including **Monica's Taxi** (401/742-0000) and **Mig's Rig** (401/480-0493, www. migsrigtaxi.com).

CONNECTICUT

EASTERN CONNECTICUT

Of all the states in New England, Connecticut embodies the greatest contrasts, and nowhere is that more apparent than in the eastern part of the state, which is home to big cities, rural farm country, and the state's largest tourist attractions in Mystic Seaport and the Native American casinos of Foxwoods and Mohegan Sun. East of the Connecticut River, the state looks more toward New England than New York. Much of the land here is devoted to farming—or at least was at one point in time. The remnants of stone walls and foundations are still visible through the trees in land that has been slowly reclaimed by forest. The land is especially scenic in the northeastern corner, which has been dubbed the "Quiet Corner" for its lack of bustle, and is the absolute antithesis of the bedroom communities and Manhattanites

in the southwestern corner of the state. Indeed, driving its back roads, you might think for a moment that you've gone through a teleporter into the Northeast Kingdom of far northern Vermont. The fact that such a bucolic landscape is only an hour and a half from Boston is a secret jealously guarded by its residents.

The history of the region has been anything but quiet, however. This part of the state was very active in the maritime field, taking part in shipbuilding enterprises, naval battles, and the lucrative China trade throughout the 18th and 19th centuries. Like the Litchfield Hills in the west, areas of the state here were also heavily involved with the procurement of aid and supplies for soldiers in the Revolutionary War. In the 20th century, the urban centers of Hartford and New London suffered while many upper- and

© MYSTIC SEAPORT, MYSTIC, CT

HIGHLIGHTS

◖ **Mark Twain House & Museum:** America's most celebrated author wrote about rafting the Mississippi in a billiards room in Connecticut (page 254).

◖ **Wadsworth Atheneum:** The oldest public art museum in the country is particularly known for its collection of Hudson River School paintings (page 256).

◖ **Nathan Hale Homestead:** The only thing you'll "regret" is not visiting this loving homage to the Revolution's dashing secret agent (page 266).

◖ **Roseland Cottage/Bowen House:** A pink parfait of arches and rosettes is the quintessential example of Gothic Revival architecture (page 267).

◖ **Mashantucket Pequot Museum and Research Center:** Explore the recovered history of New England's first people with a life-sized re-creation of a Pequot tribal village (page 271).

◖ **Mohegan Sun Casino:** Even as you lose your twentieth hand of the night, the starry sky overhead makes you feel like you are enjoying the great outdoors (page 272).

◖ **Mystic Seaport:** Give it your best "arrgh!" as you take the wheel of an authentic whale ship, or board a replica of the infamous *Amistad* (page 277).

LOOK FOR ◖ TO FIND RECOMMENDED SIGHTS, ACTIVITIES, DINING, AND LODGING.

middle-class residents moved to the surrounding suburbs, leaving the cities somewhat stagnant and depressed. New London has slowly been clawing itself back by restoring the buildings on its historic waterfront, while Hartford still struggles from lack of investment. While it has gotten its crime problems under control, it still needs a visionary mayor with the solid backing of the rich suburbs around it in order to recover from its malaise.

PLANNING YOUR TIME

If you have just one day to spend in Eastern Connecticut, head straight to the historic shipbuilding center of Mystic. The reconstructed 19th-century community of **Mystic Seaport** is consistently rated as one of New England's top attractions, and one of the best maritime museums anywhere. Better yet, spend several days along the southeast coastline, exploring the salty city of New London and the historic village of Stonington.

By contrast, you won't want to spend more than a day or two in Hartford, which has just a few sights to recommend (and closes many of its restaurants and stores on weekends). Base yourself outside the city in one of the country towns to the north or south, and dip into the

CONNECTICUT

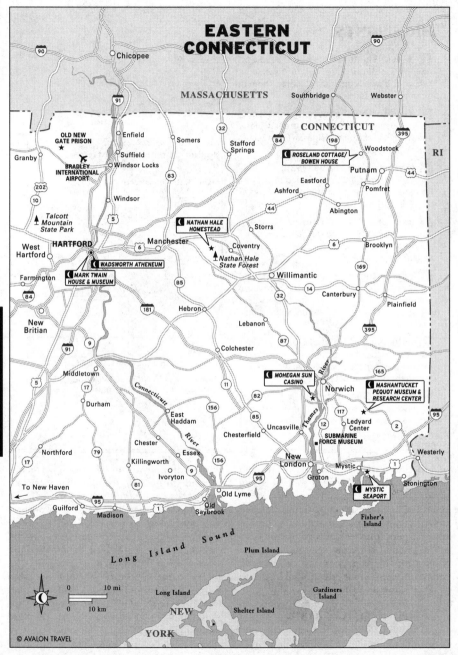

EASTERN CONNECTICUT

MASSACHUSETTS

CONNECTICUT

RI

Chicopee

Southbridge   Webster

Old New Gate Prison ★

Enfield   Somers   Stafford Springs   Woodstock

Granby   Suffield   Windsor Locks   Roseland Cottage/Bowen House   Putnam

Bradley International Airport   Eastford   Pomfret

Windsor   Ashford   Abington   Brooklyn

Talcott Mountain State Park   Storrs

Nathan Hale Homestead ★

Manchester   Coventry   Nathan Hale State Forest

Hartford   Wadsworth Atheneum   Willimantic   Canterbury

West Hartford   Mark Twain House & Museum   Plainfield

Farmington   Hebron

New Britian   Lebanon

Middletown   Colchester   Mohegan Sun Casino   Mashantucket Pequot Museum & Research Center

Durham   Norwich

Connecticut River   East Haddam   Chesterfield   Uncasville   Ledyard Center

Northford   Chester   Essex   Submarine Force Museum

Killingworth   New London   Westerly

Ivoryton   Groton   Mystic   Stonington

To New Haven   Old Lyme   Mystic Seaport

Guilford   Madison   Old Saybrook   Fisher's Island

Long Island Sound   Plum Island

0   10 mi
0   10 km

Long Island   Gardiners Island

NEW   Shelter Island

YORK

© AVALON TRAVEL

urban core to see attractions such as the **Mark Twain House & Museum** and the fine art collection at the **Wadsworth Atheneum.**

The northeastern Quiet Corner has even fewer formal attractions, but you can easily spend a week there relaxing with long looping bike rides through dairy farms and picking your own apples at wooded country orchards. This is also one of the more historic areas of the state, with a monument to Connecticut's state hero at the **Nathan Hale Homestead** and the amazing Gothic Revival house museum at the **Roseland Cottage/Bowen House.** While you are in the area, blow off some steam (and lighten your wallet) at the **Mohegan Sun Casino,** one of two casinos on Indian reservations that have made southeastern Connecticut a gaming destination throughout the East Coast.

Connecticut River Valley

Since the very earliest of geological times, the waters of New England have drained out through a central valley that would become the Connecticut River after the last ice age 11,000 years ago. The river actually has its source in tributaries reaching into far northern Vermont and New Hampshire, but it really gathers steam after flowing into the state that shares its name, where it grows to a width of more than 1,000 feet across. As the major artery of the region, the river was home to a thriving population of Native Americans before Europeans arrived. The river was "discovered" by Dutch captain Adrian Block in 1614, six years before the Pilgrims landed at Plymouth Rock. Early on, it was a major population center, spawning active trading posts between the Dutch and English New World settlements, and later serving as a conduit for raw materials and manufactured goods from

© MICHAEL BLANDING

downtown Hartford

northern New England. Today, many travelers zip right through the valley along I-91, stopping only to see the sights in the capital city of Hartford. Both north and south of the city, however, are a number of former farming and manufacturing centers with historic house museums and offbeat attractions.

HARTFORD

Smack dab in the middle of the state, the city of Hartford isn't the prettiest introduction to Connecticut. In the middle of the 20th century, the city suffered as much of the middle class moved to a ring of suburbs around the city, taking their wealth with them. While nearby cities like Providence were able to revitalize their cores with new restaurants and galleries in the 1990s, Hartford has so far stubbornly resisted gentrification. That's a shame, since its downtown is home to many fine attractions and magnificent architecture left over as a legacy of its one-time status as an important river shipping port.

Hartford was settled soon after Boston, when Thomas Hooker led an expedition of 130 souls to found a settlement just north of a Dutch trading port in 1637. For the next two hundred years it flourished as a port city, despite being more than 30 miles away from the nearest ocean. After trade declined in the mid-19th century, the city reinvented itself by selling insurance to protect ship's cargoes; from that seed the city grew into the so-called "insurance capital of the world." Even today, it is headquarters to many insurance companies, such as Travelers, which keep it bustling during the week. On weekends, however, it's a different story—and a different city—as white-collar workers go home to the suburbs and leave downtown a ghost town. Not that that means you should avoid the city at that time; the lack of crowds makes weekends the best time to check out its many museums and historic sights.

◖ Mark Twain House & Museum

Samuel Langhorne Clemens—the writer who become known to the world as Mark

Mark Twain House & Museum

© CT CULTURE & TOURISM

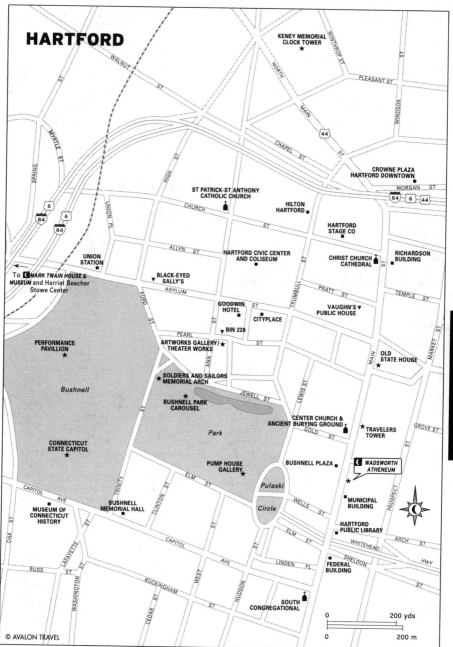

HARTFORD

KENEY MEMORIAL CLOCK TOWER ★

WINTHROP ST

WALNUT ST

ST

PLEASANT ST

NORTH MAIN ST

WINDSOR ST

44

CHAPEL ST

MYRTLE ST

SPRING ST

CROWNE PLAZA HARTFORD DOWNTOWN ■

84 6 44

MORGAN ST

6 84

84

ST PATRICK-ST ANTHONY CATHOLIC CHURCH ✝

HILTON HARTFORD ●

HARTFORD STAGE CO ■

RICHARDSON BUILDING ■

UNION PL

HIGH ST

CHURCH ST

ALLYN ST

HARTFORD CIVIC CENTER AND COLISEUM ■

CHRIST CHURCH CATHEDRAL ✝

TRUMBULL ST

UNION STATION ■

To ☾ MARK TWAIN HOUSE & MUSEUM and Harriet Beecher Stowe Center

BLACK-EYED SALLY'S ▼

ASYLUM ST

FORD ST

GOODWIN HOTEL ●

CITYPLACE ■

PRATT ST

VAUGHN'S ▼ PUBLIC HOUSE

TEMPLE ST

PEARL ST

BIN 228 ▼

ANN ST

ST

MARKET ST

PERFORMANCE PAVILLION ★

ARTWORKS GALLERY/ THEATER WORKS ▼★

MAIN ST

OLD STATE HOUSE ★

SOLDIERS AND SAILORS MEMORIAL ARCH ★

Bushnell

JEWELL ST

LEWIS ST

BUSHNELL PARK CAROUSEL ★

Park

CENTER CHURCH & ANCIENT BURYING GROUND ✝

TRAVELERS TOWER ★

GROVE ST

GOLD ST

CONNECTICUT STATE CAPITOL ★

PUMP HOUSE GALLERY ★

BUSHNELL PLAZA ■

WADSWORTH ATHENEUM ★

PROSPECT ST

Pulaski Circle

MUNICIPAL BUILDING ■

CAPITOL AVE

OAK ST

MUSEUM OF CONNECTICUT HISTORY ■

BUSHNELL MEMORIAL HALL ■

TRINITY ST

CLINTON ST

ELM ST

WELLS ST

ELM ST

HARTFORD PUBLIC LIBRARY ■

WHITEHEAD ST

ARCH ST

HWY

LAFAYETTE ST

RUSS ST

WASHINGTON ST

CEDAR ST

BUCKINGHAM ST

WEST ST

CAPITOL AVE

HUDSON ST

LINDEN PL

SHELDON ST

FEDERAL BUILDING ■

SOUTH CONGREGATIONAL ✝

ST

0   200 yds

0   200 m

© AVALON TRAVEL

Twain—is more often associated with the wide, muddy flow of the Mississippi River than with the relatively sedate surroundings of urban Connecticut. But many of his masterpieces, including *The Adventures of Huckleberry Finn* and *The Adventures of Tom Sawyer*, were penned in this Victorian Gothic manse (351 Farmington Ave., 860/247-0998, www.marktwainhouse.org, 9:30 A.M.–5:30 P.M. Mon.–Sat., noon–5:30 P.M. Sun., closed Tue. Jan.–Mar., $14 adults 17–64, $12 seniors, $8 children 6–16, free children under 6) just outside of downtown Hartford. Twain lived here for 16 years, between 1874 and 1891, at a time when he was achieving fame as a master—and as some would later say, the creator—of American literature. (Among those who credit Twain with being the first real American author are Ernest Hemingway and William Faulkner.) While he was here, he formed the nucleus of a literary group that included Harriet Beecher Stowe (author of

Uncle Tom's Cabin), Booker T. Washington, and other giants of the Gilded Age.

Twain's home has now been opened as a fine literary museum. Inside, docents give tours of the house, including the billiards room where Twain did most of his writing; the elaborate Middle Eastern–inspired decor by Louis Comfort Tiffany; and Twain's telephone, one of the first installed in a private residence. In 2003, a modern museum containing exhibits that tell of Twain's life and career was attached to the residence.

◖ Wadsworth Atheneum

This gargantuan art museum (600 Main St., 860/278-2670, www.wadsworthatheneum.org, 11 A.M.–5 P.M. Wed.–Sat.; 10 A.M.–5 P.M. Sun.; 11 P.M.–8 P.M. first Thu., $10 adults, $8 seniors, $5 students, free children 12 and under, $5 first Thu.) is not only America's oldest art museum, it's also one of its best. Founded in 1842 by arts patron Daniel Wadsworth, the

THE CHARTER OAK

When the explorers first arrived in Hartford, they noted the presence of a huge white oak tree, much larger than the others, growing at the top of what would later become Wyllys Hill. That tree was to play a significant role in the early history of Connecticut; in fact, if it weren't for it, Connecticut might not be an independent state today. The legend goes like this: In 1662, King Charles II granted a charter for the state of Connecticut to John Winthrop Jr. that was far more liberal than most colonial charters of the period. Charles's successor, King James II, however, decided to flex his muscle 25 years later by establishing the Dominion of New England, consolidating several colonies under the command of hated governor Edmund Andros. When the king's representative came to collect the charter, however, he met with spirited resistance. Supposedly, a heated argument ensued at a local tavern, at which the candles were suddenly extinguished while the charter sat on

the table. It ended up in the hands of Captain Joseph Wadsworth, who took the charter and secreted it inside the oak tree until the King's representatives left town. The Charter Oak, as it was called thereafter, grew for another 200 years, reaching a diameter of more than 10 feet across before it fell down during a severe storm in 1856. Now a plaque stands in Charter Oak Tree Park on Charter Oak Avenue a block east of Main Street. The old charter, with a miniature ink portrait of Charles II, is now on display at the **Museum of Connecticut History** (231 Capitol Ave., Hartford, 860/757-6535, www.cslib.org/museum. htm, 9 A.M.–4 P.M. Mon.-Fri.; 9 A.M.-3 P.M. Sat., free). The tree itself was cut up and made into various relics, such as the seat still used by the president of the Connecticut state senate. It's more likely to be found in your piggy bank, however: in 1999, Connecticut officially chose the tree as its symbol for a quarter honoring the state.

Atheneum holds all the requisite genres, including works by European masters such as Monet, Picasso, and Dali; a fantastic collection of Classical bronzes; and early American portraiture, including the oldest known portrait, *Elizabeth Eggington*. But what really separates the museum from the herd are two collections: the paintings of the Hudson River School, which formed the original basis of Wadsworth's collection and includes many fine works by Hartford native son Frederic Church; and the *Amistad* collection, which includes documents and relics related to the slave ship rebellion that achieved modern fame through the eponymous Steven Spielberg movie.

Harriet Beecher Stowe Center

Practically across the street from the home of her mentor and friend Mark Twain, Harriet Beecher Stowe lived in this Victorian "cottage" (77 Forest St., 860/522-9258, www.harrietbeecherstowecenter.org, 9:30 A.M.–4:30 P.M. Wed.–Sat., noon–4:30 P.M. Sun., plus 9:30 A.M.–4:30 P.M. Tue. June–mid-Oct.; closed Mon., $8 adults, $7 seniors, $4 children 5–12, free children under 5) from 1873 until 1891, the year of her death. Befitting the author's passion for social justice, her home has now been turned into a museum of social change, with as much emphasis on the great political movements of the 19th century—emancipation and women's rights—as on her biography. The center was started by Stowe's niece, Katharine S. Day, who bought a more luxuriously appointed home that is also open for tours.

Other Sights

The regal facade of the 1796 **Old State House** (800 Main St., 860/522-6766, www.ctosh.org, 10 A.M.–5 P.M. Tue.–Sat., $6 adults, $3 children 6–17, free children 5 and under, $3 students, $3 seniors, $5 groups over 15 people) dominates Hartford's downtown. The building was designed by Charles Bulfinch, the foremost architect of the Federal Period, who also designed the Massachusetts State House and redesigned the U.S. Capitol. Inside the state

house is an amusing "museum of curiosities," drawn from the private collection of a colonial portrait artist who had his studio in the building and collected, among other things, the horn of a unicorn and a two-headed calf. A bit more serious "Acoustiguide audio tour" takes visitors inside the events that took place in the building, including the trials of the *Amistad* slaves and abolitionist educator Prudence Crandall.

The modern replacement of the state house, the **Connecticut State Capitol** (210 Capitol Ave., 860/240-0222, www.cga.ct.gov, tours 9:15 A.M.2:15 P.M. Mon.–Fri. July–Aug.; 10:15 A.M.–2:15 P.M. Sat. Apr.–Oct., free) is a mishmash of architectural styles dominated by a soaring central tower capped by a 12-sided golden dome. Tours take in the building's ornate interior, as well as works of painting and sculpture important to the state.

Entertainment

Known locally as "The Bushnell," **Bushnell Memorial Hall** (166 Capitol Ave., 860/987-5900, www.bushnell.org) is the city's premier arts venue, with performances ranging from the Hartford Symphony Orchestra to *Spamalot*. Big rock concerts come to the gargantuan (if soulless) **XL Center** (1 Civic Center Plaza, 860/249-6333, www.xlcenter.com), which also hosts UConn basketball and American Hockey League's Hartford Wolf Pack.

Events

Hartford celebrates the start of summer with **Rose Weekend** (Prospect Ave. and Asylum Ave., 860/231-9443, www.elizabethpark.org/rose_weekend.htm, 11 A.M.–4 P.M. last weekend in June), an event in Elizabeth Park that features the blooming of 15,000 roses along with music, poetry, and storytelling. The cultural event of the year is **African American Parade Day** (860/524-0086, May), which includes a jazzy parade through downtown as well as a multicultural craft bazaar and lip-smacking BBQ-rib cook-off competition. From Thanksgiving until after Christmas, Hartford is brightened nightly by the **Festival of Light** (860/525-8629, www.letsgoarts.org, late

Nov.–early Jan.), during which a quarter of a million points of light transform Constitution Plaza into a starry fantasia.

Shopping

Almost all of the city's shopping lies outside the city itself, in suburbs like Farmington, West Hartford, and Avon. That said, there are some distinctive souvenirs to be found at the **Museum Store at the Old State House** (800 Main St., 860/522-6766, 10 A.M.–5 P.M. Tue.–Sat.)—namely a solid stash of books about Connecticut, distinctive jewelry, and games and toys. There's also **The CT Creative Store** (25 Stonington St., 860/297-0112, 10 A.M.–2 P.M. Wed.–Fri.; 10 A.M.–4 P.M. Sat.; hours may vary, call ahead), selling locally made products such as honey, jam, sauces, wool, and hand-crafted bowls. All proceeds go toward building a proposed Hartford Botanical Garden.

Food

They don't call it soul food for nothing; the comfort fixings at **(Black-Eyed Sally's** (350 Asylum St., 860/278-7427, www.blackeyedsallys.com, 11:30 A.M.–10 P.M. Mon.–Sat.; bar open until 11 P.M. Thurs–Sat., $9–12) are first-rate. Blackened catfish and jambalaya are house specialties, but the big don't-miss is the rib-and-sausage "piglet platter" (you'll understand the true meaning of that name after you eat the entire thing).

Can an Irish pub be romantic? If it's **Vaughan's Public House** (59 Pratt St., 860/882-1560, 11:30 A.M.–1 A.M. Sun.–Sat.; bar open until 2 A.M. Fri.–Sat., $10–16), the answer is affirmative. The place is literally furnished with love, in the form of hand-crafted Irish furniture, and the menu spotlights traditional Irish dinners—shepherd's pie with brown bread, feather-light fish-and-chips, and corned beef and cabbage. Wash it all down with homemade Irish cream, Irish coffees, or something from the top-notch single malt list.

Low-key but snazzy, **Bin 228** (228 Pearl St., 860/244-9463, 11:30 A.M.–10 P.M. Mon.–Wed.; 11:30 A.M.–11 P.M. Thurs; 11:30 A.M.–midnight Fri.; 4 P.M.–midnight Sat.; closed Sun, $3–8) is a vino-centric Italian spot decorated with bottles everywhere. The menu actually plays second fiddle to the wine, so order up some of the tapas-style light antipasti (cured olives, bruschetta, panini, and smoked meats) and focus on swirling and swilling.

An institution in the area, the New York–style **(Rein's Deli** (435 Hartford Turnpike, Vernon, 860/875-1344, www.reinsdeli.com, 7 A.M.–midnight daily, $6–14) is always abuzz with devotees downing delicious traditional Jewish delicacies from matzo ball soup and cheese blintzes to chopped liver and whitefish salad. On your way out the door, grab a few black-and-white cookies for the road.

Information and Services

Info on the region is available from the **Greater Hartford Tourism District** (860/728-6789 or 800/446-7811, www.enjoyhartford.com), which operates an information kiosk on the **Civic Center Mall** (Center Court, Trumbull and Asylum Sts., 860/275-6456).

The city's major hospital is **Hartford Hospital** (80 Seymour St., 860/545-5000, www.harthosp.org). Pharmacies are numerous in the city, though most are not open 24 hours. For a local pharmacy, contact **West Hartford CVS** (1099 New Britain Ave., West Hartford, 860/236-6181). Banks are found all over the downtown area.

Internet is available for free in libraries and for a small fee (usually a few dollars per hour) in cafés and at **FedEx Office** (544 Farmington Ave., 860/233-8245), which also provides faxing and shipping services.

TOBACCO COUNTRY

Contrary to what most people think, tobacco isn't just down south. The plant grew wild along the Connecticut River from pre-European times, when it was dried and smoked by Native Americans. Today, the upper valley north of Hartford is still active in growing so-called "shade tobacco," which is literally grown underneath huge shades covering the rows, dried, and used for the outer shell for cigars. While the industry isn't as vibrant as it once was, towns like Enfield and Windsor are still dotted with picturesque drying sheds filled with the large leaves left to dry in the sun. The area's other claim to fame is as a transportation hub; Bradley International Airport serves both Hartford and Springfield from its location in the small town of Windsor Locks.

New England Air Museum

This ambitious museum (36 Perimeter Rd., Windsor Locks, 860/623-3305, www.neam. org, 10 A.M.–5 P.M. daily, $10 adults, $6 children 4–11, $9 seniors, free children under 3) on the outskirts of Bradley International Airport sets out to do nothing less than tell the entire history of manmade flight—and largely succeeds. On display are more than 125 full-sized aircraft, restored and polished to perfection. The museum's two hangars are divided into civilian and military aircraft; the first has highlights including the impressive VS-44 Flying Boat and a vintage hot-air balloon; the second includes a shining B-29 bomber and enough Tomcats, Hellcats, and Panthers to thrill the most jaded five-year-old.

Other Sights

Founded originally as a copper mine in 1707, **Old New-Gate Prison and Copper Mine** (115 Newgate Rd., East Granby, 860/653-3563, www.chc.state.ct.us, 10 A.M.–4:00 P.M. Fri.–Sun. May 1–Oct. 31, $10 adults, $8 seniors, $6 children 6–17, free children 5 and under) found a novel solution to its worker shortage by imprisoning criminals in the mine shafts starting in 1773 and requiring them to mine during the day. After the mine closed, the prison stayed, incarcerating 800 criminals until it was closed in 1827. Luckily for them, the prison wasn't constructed very well; the current museum details some of the more exciting escapes.

The 1761 **Phelps-Hatheway House** (55 South Main St., Suffield, 860/668-0055, 1 P.M.–4 P.M. Sat.–Sun. mid-May–mid-Oct., donation) is one of the best-preserved house museums in New England. Once the home of wealthy land-speculator Oliver Phelps, the home was successively augmented with grander and grander side wings as Phelps grew in wealth and prominence. The interior contains original 18th-century hand-blocked French wallpaper.

The region's Native American history is preserved at **Wood Memorial Library** (783 Main St., S. Windsor, 860/289-1783, www.woodmemoriallibrary.org, 10 A.M.–8 P.M. Mon.–Thu., free), which has Native American arrowheads dating back 8,000 years, along with thousands of other artifacts collected on the South Windsor flood plain.

Events

Four of the region's agricultural villages have teamed up for the annual **Four Town Fair** (860/749-6527, www.fourtownfair.com, mid-Sept.), one of the state's largest harvest celebrations. In an apparent homage to Mark Twain, one of the highlights is the jumping frog competition.

Food

Subdued (read: not entirely authentic) but still entirely palatable Italian is all over the menu at **Figaro** (90 Elm St., Enfield, 860/745-2414, www.figaroenfield.com, 11:30 A.M.–10 P.M. Mon.–Sat.; noon–9 P.M.Sun., $13–20). Reasonable prices and fresh pastas (like the simple fettuccine pomodoro) keep it a popular spot. Things get spicier at **A Taste of India** (216 Broad St., Windsor, 860/688-8333, 11:30 A.M.–10:30 P.M. Mon.–Fri.; 11:30 A.M.–10 P.M. Sun., $10–13). The relaxed atmosphere and quick service make it a good place to sample authentic tandoori. The welcoming, fun **Beanery Bistro** (55 Palisado Ave., Windsor, 860/688-2224, www.thebeanerybistro.com, 7 A.M.–8 P.M. Mon.–Fri.; 8 A.M.–6 P.M. Sat.; 11 A.M.–3 P.M. Sun., $4.50–7) doles out more than just good food; it puts on regular book club meetings, entertainment, and weekly newsletters. That's all the more reason to linger over your cranberry-rum-laced turkey sandwich or your homemade macaroons and chai tea. Overlooking the Podunk River, **The Mill on the River** (989 Ellington Rd., S. Windsor,

860/289-7929, www.themillontheriver.com, 11:30 A.M.–10 P.M. Mon.–Fri; 5 A.M.–10 P.M. Sat.; 11 A.M.–8:30 P.M. Sun., $17–27) pairs a breathtaking setting with an ambitious menu. House standouts include eggplant timbale, fire-roasted tomato soup, and miso-glazed pork tenderloin.

Shopping
New England artists and their work are on display at **Bayberry Designs** (700 Poquonock Ave., Windsor, 860/285-0005, www.bayberrydesigns.com, 10 A.M.–5:30 P.M. Tue., Wed., and Fri.; 10 A.M.–7 P.M. Thu.; 10 A.M.–3 P.M. Sat., closed Sun. and Mon., $17–27), from etchings and watercolors to limited-edition prints. The establishment also provides framing services. Have you been very, very good lately? Treat yourself to custom trinkets and baubles sold at **Bill Selig Jewelers** (161 Broad St., Windsor, 860/688-3111, www.billseligjewelers.com), from diamond pendants to funky handmade necklaces.

WEST OF HARTFORD
As the middle class fled Hartford in the 1950s, much of it ended up in the city's western suburbs, where professional workers built trophy houses on the on cul-de-sacs and settled down to life in the much-vaunted Connecticut suburbs. Unlike many cities, however, these transplanted urbanites took the city's commercial base with them; today, the highways in towns like Avon, Farmington, and Simsbury are lined with Madison Avenue retailers and big-box department stores. Outside the immediate suburbs, the Farmington River Valley quickly becomes wooded, with a dozen historic villages scattered through the trees.

Noah Webster House
In these days of post-structuralism and deconstructionism, the very idea of setting out to codify our language is a task fraught with semiotic pitfalls. Thankfully, the dictionary's founding father Noah Webster didn't concern himself with such angst; he just systematically set down word after word. This house

museum (227 South Main St., W. Hartford, 860/521-5362, www.noahwebsterhouse.org, 1 P.M.–4 P.M. Thu.–Mon., $7 adults, $5 seniors, $4 students, free children under 5) explores Noah's obsession with language as well as his little-known political views; moreover, it re-creates the typical life of a colonial citizen with hands-on activities and demonstrations by costumed interpreters.

Other Sights
Self-taught architect Theodate Pope Riddle not only achieved success in a time when women were limited in their professional pursuits, she also created a real stunner in the 1901 colonial revival mansion known as **Hill-Stead** (35 Mountain Rd., Farmington, 860/677-4787, www.hillstead.org, tours 10 A.M.–5 P.M. Tue.–Sun. May–Oct.; 11 A.M.–3 P.M. Tue.–Sun. Nov.–Apr.; grounds open 7:30 A.M.–5:30 P.M. year-round, $10 adults, $9 seniors, $8 students, $5 children 6–12, free children under 6). The mansion still has several works by Monet and Degas hung among its original furnishings, as well as a sunken garden on 152 acres of grounds.

Events
Pies, parades, and face-painting usher in the harvest at the **Pumpkin Festival** (860/232-1134, mid-Oct.), a tradition in West Hartford for more than 30 years.

Shopping
Get your bling fix at **Lux Bond & Green** (46 LaSalle Rd., W. Hartford, 860/521-3015), 10 A.M.–6 P.M. Mon.–Fri; 9:30 A.M.–5:30 P.M. Sat.; closed Sun.), a graceful family-owned jewelry store offering one-of-a-kind pieces with price tags that run from bargain to no-holds-barred splurge.

Food
At **C Max's Oyster Bar** (964 Farmington Ave., W. Hartford, 860/236-6299, www.maxrestaurantgroup.com, 11:30 A.M.–11 P.M. Mon.–Fri.; 4 P.M.–11 P.M. Sat.; 11:30 A.M.–9 P.M. Sun.,, $25–30), interior

design bigwig Peter Niemitz has created a room in muted ruby tones that perfectly complements the creative seafood menu. Offerings include rock shrimp nori rolls, pan-roasted lobster with sweet chili and fennel, and char-grilled salmon with lavender. Arguably West Hartford's favorite Asian restaurant, **Butterfly** (831 Farmington Ave., W. Hartford, 860/236-2816, www.butterflyrestaurantct.com, 11:30 A.M.–10 P.M. Sun.–Thu.; open until 11 P.M. Fri.–Sat.) is a dimly-lit, comely spot with a menu of fresh Szechuan and Cantonese specialties. The high-energy **Prospect Cafe** (345 Prospect Ave., W. Hartford, 860/523-8069, www.theprospectcafe.com, 11 A.M.–11:30 P.M. Mon.–Sat., noon–10 P.M. Sun., $15–22) has been a fixture in West Hartford since it opened in the 1960s. The eclectic cuisine (heavily peppered with Italian specialties) is always a hit (the rich sausage carbonara is utterly addictive), as is the wide al fresco patio. The gleaming interior of ◖ **Grant's** (977 Farmington Ave., W. Hartford, 860/236-1930, www.billygrant. com, 11:30 A.M.–10 P.M. Mon.–Fri.; open until 11 P.M. weekends, $16–23) is filled with 1920s lamps and tiled floors, while the exterior has a nice enclave for outdoor dining. In both, diners can dig into a menu of American dishes met with Mediterranean influences, such as the crab cakes with rouille and pistachio-crusted trout.

Information

The **Greater Hartford Convention and Visitor's Bureau** (31 Pratt St., Hartford, 800/446-7811, www.enjoyhartford.com) also serves the city's western suburbs.

LOWER CONNECTICUT VALLEY

South of Hartford, the river is anchored by the former industrial town of Middletown, an all-American city reinvented as an academic hub in the 19th century with the founding of Wesleyan University. Farther downriver, the Connecticut does a dogleg to the east before flowing out in a broad estuary into Long Island

Sound. Along the way, the modern era seems to have left behind Chatam, Haddam, and Essex, which are a mix of old Victorian homes and family farms and orchards.

Wesleyan University

Connecticut's preeminent liberal arts institution (Wesleyan Station, Middletown, 860/685-2000, www.wesleyan.edu) got a late start as New England colleges go—it wasn't founded until 1848. But it has made up for lost time in the prestige department, measuring up now with the top schools around the country. The school was founded by John Wesley, who also founded the Methodist religion and envisioned the school as a place to instruct future religious leaders. The college quickly outgrew its original mission, however, to become a secular liberal arts school, one of the first to add modern science to the curriculum. It now has a reputation as being one of the most countercultural and politically active campuses anywhere. You can observe the vibrant student body on a free tour of the campus (9 A.M., noon, and 3 P.M. Mon.–Fri.; noon Sat.–Sun.; information sessions at 10:30 A.M. and 2 P.M.), which also takes in an eclectic mix of architectural styles.

Goodspeed Opera House

This wedding cake of an opera house (6 Main St., East Haddam, 860/873-8668, www. goodspeed.org, show times vary, box office: 10 A.M.–5 P.M., Mon.–Sat.; 10 A.M.2 P.M. Sun., $45–56.50) is known as one of the country's premier venues for new musicals, drawing theater critics from New York and Boston to the openings of top shows (seven of which have gone on to win Tonys on Broadway). The theater was originally built by shipping magnate William Goodspeed in 1876. Gradually, however, the building fell into misuse, serving as a barracks for soldiers in World War I and then as a general store. The building was restored to its former opulence in 1959. Docents now give backstage tours in the afternoons, regaling visitors with stories of what *really* happened in the dressing rooms of actors throughout the decades.

Other Sights

If you don't have a child under 8, grab one quick to check out the "wicked cool" exhibits at **Kidcity Children's Museum** (119 Washington St., Middletown, 860/347-0495, www.kidcitymuseum.com, 11 A.M.–5 P.M. Sun.–Tue.; 9 A.M.–5 P.M. Wed.–Sat., $7 adults and children, free children under 1). Just a decade old, the museum incorporates high-tech equipment into hands-on exhibits, including a theater where kids can use props to act out their own video fantasies.

The **Connecticut River Museum** (67 Main St., 860/767-8269, www.ctrivermuseum.org, 10 A.M.–5 P.M. Tue.–Sun., $8 adults, $7 seniors, $5 children 6–12) is literally *on* the Connecticut River, sitting on stilts overlooking the water. Inside, the museum explores the history of early America's most important waterways, including the shipbuilding history of the little town of Essex. A special exhibit on the "American Turtle" looks at one of the more fascinating experiments of the Revolutionary War, in which an underwater submarine nearly succeeded in planting a bomb to blow up a British ship.

Shopping

Unique hand-crafted gifts cram the shelves at **Connecticut River Artisans Cooperative** (5 W. Main St., Chester, 860/526-5575, www.ctartisans.com, noon–5 P.M. Sat.–Sun. Jan.–Mar., Wed.–Sun. April–June and Sept.–Oct.; noon–6 P.M. Mon.–Sun., July–Aug. and Nov.–Dec.). Take your pick from oil and watercolors, silk clothing, fused glass dishware, quilts, and loads more. The owners of **English Accents Antiques** (4 N. Main St., Essex, 860/767-0113, www.englishaccents-ct.com, 11 A.M.–5 P.M. Thu.–Sat.; noon opening Sun.) make frequent trips across the Big Pond to buy period pieces and collectibles from British country estate sales for their friendly showroom. There's no shortage of excellently kept silver, crystal, porcelain, art, and rugs. Let the friendly yellow awning over **Silkworm of Essex Village** (23 Main St., Essex, 860/767-1298, www.thesilkworm.com, 10:30 A.M.–5 P.M. Mon.–Sat.;

closed Tue.; noon–4 P.M. Sun.) be your first indication of the service you'll receive here. The extra-helpful staff assists patrons in finding the perfect fit from women's clothing designers such as Nicole Miller, Philippe Adec, and Theory. Ever-so-cutely retro, **Moxie Vintage** (466 Main St., Middletown, 860/638-0030) pulls its clothing and accessories from every decade of the last century—from semi-precious brooches and 1920s silk Chanel jackets to 1940s Gucci dresses and burnished leather totes. The antiques, artifacts, jewelry, and handmade carpets at **Little Tibet** (680 Main St., Middletown, 860/343-1975, www.littletibet.com, 10 A.M.–6 P.M. Tue.–Fri.; 11 A.M.–6 P.M. Sat.; 11 A.M.–5 P.M. Sun.) are first-quality and very well priced. Don't be surprised if you walk in looking for gifts and souvenirs and leave inspired to decorate your own home.

Food

A town gathering point as much as a sandwich and tea shop, **Essex Coffee & Tea Company** (51 Main St., Essex, 860/767-7804, 7 A.M.–5 P.M. Mon.–Sat.; 8 A.M.–5 P.M. Sun., $3–7), encourages hanging out with newspapers, very good breakfasts (the Essex Eggel sandwich is hearty and delicious), gourmet coffee and teas, and freshly made pastries. Sandwiches—clubs, grinders, and wraps—dominate the menu at the casual **Cypress Restaurant** (1265 S. Main St., Middletown, 860/346-3367, www.cypressgrill.com, 11 A.M.–9 P.M. Mon.–Thu.; 11 A.M.–10 P.M. Fri.–Sat., $5–11), making it one of the best bets for lunch in town. The Wesleyan University–owned **Red & Black Cafe** (45 Broad St., Middletown, 860/685-7333, 8 A.M.–8 P.M. Mon.–Fri.; 9 A.M.–5 P.M. Sat.–Sun., $6–9) functions as both eatery and bookstore, so diners can devour both the latest bestseller and their turkey panini. Don't leave without trying at least one of the homemade chocolate truffles.

Information

For more information on the area, contact the **Greater Hartford Tourism District** (860/244-8181 or 800/793-4480, www.enjoyhartford.com).

CONNECTICUT

SPORTS AND RECREATION
Hiking and Biking

Perched high up on the Metacomet Ridge west of Hartford, the 165-foot Heublein Tower makes a tantalizing goal for hikers in **Talcott Mountain State Park** (Rt. 185, Bloomfield, 860/242-1158, www.ct.gov.dep, noon–2 P.M. Thu.–Sun., free). Reached by a moderate 1.5-mile stretch of the Metacomet Trail, the tower is done in the Tyrolean style, and has a rich history including a visit by President Eisenhower. The Metacomet Trail stretches for 40 miles up the ridge and is also accessible from other parks in the region, including **Peak Mountain** in Granby. Another good spot for some outdoor exercise is the **Windsor Lock Canal** (Bridge St., Windsor Locks to Canal Street, Suffield, www.ct.gov/dot), which has five miles of level trails overlooking the river and its ingenious series of locks.

Boating

Mark Twain would surely approve of the relaxing river trips offered by **Huck Finn Adventures** (21 Waterville Rd., Collinsville, 860/693-0385, www.huckfinnadventures.com, $55 per canoe, launch times vary based on trip type), a canoe-and-kayak outfitter that leads trips on the Farmington River. Additionally, paddlers can strap on headlamps and enter the tunnels beneath the city of Hartford for eerie and historical "lost city tours."

ACCOMMODATIONS
$100-150

Plenty of tidy and modern rooms at modest rates are at **Crowne Plaza Hartford-Downtown** (50 Morgan St., Hartford, 860/549-2400, www. cphartford.com, $115–142). It isn't the most personal place to crash, but with an outdoor pool, breakfast included, and professional service, it's a terrific value.

Smack next to the state capital building, with easy access to the Hartford Civic Center, **Hilton Hartford** (315 Trumbull St., Hartford, 860/728-5151, www.hilton.com, $100–140) is a tightly run operation of about 400 rooms. Expect all the usual Hilton amenities (in-room coffeemakers and high-speed Internet access) plus an indoor pool, and fully outfitted fitness center.

$150-250

With its proximity to Wesleyan (it's literally a minute's walk away), the **Inn at Middletown** (70 Main St., Middletown, 860/854-6300, www.innatmiddletown.com, $149–199) is a good option for visitors to the university. Some of the decor comes off as a bit corporate, but it offers a number of amenities, including large beds, speakerphones, Internet access, coffeemakers, and two-room suites for families.

The Business District's **Goodwin Hotel** (1 Hayes St., Hartford, 860/246-7500, www. goodwinhotel.com, $139–189) is as well-situated as it is tastefully outfitted. Its comfy beds, fitness center, valet parking, and myriad business services (from data ports to faxing) have made it a popular choice among visiting professionals.

$250 and Up

Since it opened in the mid-18th century, the **C Griswold Inn** (36 Main St., Essex, 860/767-1776, www.griswoldinn.com, $100–370) has been hosting guests with meticulous, personal service. Rooms are laid out with Oriental carpets and carved wooden beds, fireplaces and fresh flowers. The inn also houses a tap room/piano bar, plus a fine-dining restaurant where dinners are borderline-gala affairs. Sundays see the epic and grand Hunt Breakfast (a tradition started at the hotel by the British, when they occupied it during the War of 1812). Picture an enormous spread of carved meats, cocktails, fresh-baked breads, game, and seafood—all served fireside. Beautiful fabrics and bold wallpapers define the tasteful guest rooms at the undeniably romantic **C Copper Beech Inn** (46 Main St., Ivoryton, 888/809-2056, www.copperbeechinn.com, $195–350), which come with luxuries from mahogany four-poster beds to massage tubs and heated marble floors. Breakfast is a sedate affair in the sun-filled atrium, while dinners—prepared by talented chef Henri Laaksonen—are more epic, and can include anything from five-spice duck to lamb in curry with chanterelles.

GETTING THERE AND AROUND

Bradley International Airport (I-91, exit 40, Windsor Locks, www.bradleyairport. com) serves both Hartford and Springfield, Massachusetts, from its location in Windsor Locks, halfway between the two cities. All of the major car rental companies are available at the airport. In addition, **CT Transit** (860/522-8101, www.cttransit.com) also operates bus routes to the city. Take the Bradley Flyer service (BDL), which runs express from the airport to downtown Hartford in about a half-hour. Fare is $1.25.

Amtrak (800/872-7245, www.amtrak.com) runs trains to Hartford's train station at One Union Place; as well as to Windsor (41 Central St.) and Windsor Locks (S. Main St. at Rte. 159). **Greyhound** (800/231-2222, www.greyhound.com) runs buses to many area locations,

including Enfield (Freshwater Blvd.), Farmington (12 Batterson Park Rd.), Hartford (1 Union Pl.), and Middletown (340 Main St.).

If you are driving from Boston, the quickest way to Hartford is to head west down I-90, take exit 9 at Sturbridge onto I-84, and follow that to the end (100 mi., 1 hr. 30 min.). Traveling from Providence, your best bet is to take U.S. Route 6 west, I-395 south, and then double back northwest on Route 2 (90 mi., 1 hr. 30 min.). From New Haven, Hartford is a straight shot down I-91 (40 mi., 45 min.).

CT Transit (860/522-8101, www.cttransit.com) also operates bus service throughout Hartford and the greater Connecticut River Valley. The E line runs from the corner of Main and Travelers Streets to West Hartford (15 min.) and Farmington (35 min.). The N line runs from the Old State House (800 Main St.) to Windsor center (45 min.), and the U line runs from the Old State House to Middletown (1 hour). All fares are $1.25. For taxi service, try **City Cab** (860/416-6587), or pick one up at the taxi stand in front of Union Station.

The Quiet Corner

A satellite photo of the eastern seaboard at night shows the entire coast from Washington, D.C., to Boston lit up like a Christmas tree—except one small portion, the northeastern corner of Connecticut. Tucked into a pocket between the big cities of Worcester, Hartford, and Providence, the upper right corner of the state has been called the "last green valley" for its miles of wooded back roads and scenically decaying farmhouses and stone walls. While that may be a bit of hyperbole, the area's other nickname, the "quiet corner," seems just about right. The pace of life *is* quieter here, with a country-store mentality that seems more like Vermont than Connecticut.

Not that the Quiet Corner was always so quiet; back at the turn of the 19th century, the area's swift-flowing rivers and proximity to the early mill industry of Rhode Island

meant that it was one of the first areas to industrialize. For decades, the Quinebaug River currents churned the wheels of textile mills of manufacturing centers like Putnam and Willimantic until they gradually fell into disuse in the 20th century. The area also has rich associations with colonial history, as it's home to two of Connecticut's most celebrated patriots: Johnathan Trumbull and Nathan Hale.

UCONN TERRITORY

Perhaps it's irony—or perhaps foresight—that located Connecticut's largest university in the region's most sedate territory. Founded as Storrs Agricultural College in 1893, the University of Connecticut now draws a population of more than 15,000 students annually. Thankfully Storrs is close enough to Hartford that many students go there for their fun; the

THE GREAT FROG BATTLE

© MICHAEL BLANDING

Windham town hall

During a steamy June night in 1754, the settlers of the village of Windham awoke to terrible screams. Thinking that they were being attacked by Native American tribes – or perhaps vengeful ghosts – they grabbed their muskets and waited anxiously for morning. At first light, a hardy group of villagers set out in the direction of the noise, where to their shock they found hundreds of dead and dying bullfrogs who had apparently fought in a midnight battle over a puddle at the bottom of the drought-ravaged pond. The event was so remarkable that versions of the story have been passed down ever since, and town fathers even put a frog on the town seal in honor of the fallen.

area around the university itself is mostly farmland ranged around the urban centers of former mill towns.

Willimantic

Of these old mill towns, the largest is Willimantic, which has earned not one but two nicknames: "Thread City" for the town's former most significant product; and "Frog City" for the momentous colonial-era amphibian battle that took place in the village of Windham. A typically depressed former mill town, Willimantic has bounced back with a surfeit of civic pride in recent years, thanks in part to the construction of **Thread City Crossing** (Rte. 661 at Main St.), a bridge built in 2000 that features 11-foot-tall bronze frogs sitting on giant spools of thread. The ultimate in roadside kitsch, the bridge has brought hundreds of tourists off the beaten track to view it, and even inspired a "Zippy the Pinhead" comic in 2002. That, in turn, has led to more public displays of art and an active cultural scene. On the southern edge of the Quiet Corner, the postcard-ready town of Lebanon is the center of the region's colonial history.

◖ Nathan Hale Homestead

If you know anything about Revolutionary War spy Nathan Hale, you know his famous last words: "I only regret that I have but one life to lose for my country." Of course, like most pithy words, Hale probably never said it; and if he did, he was merely quoting a play by British author Joseph Addison. No matter; there is enough engrossing material in Hale's biography no matter what he said before he was hanged by the British as a secret agent on September 21, 1776.

A dashing and charismatic 21-year-old, Hale was recruited into an elite Ranger force after General Washington's defeat at the Battle of Long Island, sent to find out when and where the British strike on Manhattan would come. He spent months behind enemy lines in the city performing secret operations before he was eventually betrayed by his first cousin, a loyalist who saw through his ruse.

The farmhouse in Coventry that now bears his name (2299 South St., 860/742-6917, www.ctlandmarks.org, 11 A.M.–4 P.M. Sat.–Sun. May and Sept.–Oct., Wed.–Sun., closed Thu. June–Aug., $5) was actually built in 1776, the same year he died. Hale *was* born on the site, however, in 1755, and later generations of Hale fans have collected many artifacts once owned by the captain. Tours of the homestead start in the barn behind the house and tell the story of Hale's life as well as the typical life of a colonial-era citizen; a restored kitchen serves as a site for hearth cooking and other educational programs.

Windham Textile Museum

The Quiet Corner might seem like bucolic farm country nowadays, but just over 100 years ago, it was the bustling center of one of the richest textile producing regions in the world. This engaging museum (411 Main St., Willimantic, 860/456-2178, www.millmuseum.org, 10 A.M.–4 P.M. Tue. and Fri.–Sun. summer, $5 adults, $4 seniors and students), located on the former headquarters of the American Thread Company, re-creates the lives of both textile barons and ordinary mill workers through a series of juxtaposed exhibit rooms. Tour guides also give spirited demonstrations of the old thread-spinning equipment, and even allow visitors to try their soft hands at carding wool and spinning thread (which is not as easy as it seems). Don't miss the gift shop full of frog- and thread-themed merchandise.

Governor Trumbull House and the Lebanon War Office

Make no mistake; the Revolutionary War was won just as much on beef and grain as on bullets and cannon fire. As the only colonial governor to side with the Rebels, Connecticut's Jonathan J. Trumbull was charged with a massive provisioning effort that sustained the Continental Army in its darkest moments—including the awful winter at Valley Forge. Trumbull commanded the effort from his modest Georgian home (169 West Town St., Lebanon, 860/642-7558, noon–4 P.M. Wed.–Sun. mid-May–mid-Oct., $3, free children under 6), which is now a house museum featuring period furniture and original intricate woodwork. A few doors down, a big red barn served as the official war office (149 W. Town St., Lebanon, 860/916-1804, noon–4 P.M. Sat.–Sun., donations); the building has been moved from its original site 100 feet south. The museum now houses arms and artifacts relating to the Revolution.

Other Sights

No one knows where the British buried Hale's remains after his hanging, but a tall cenotaph at **Nathan Hale Cemetery** (Lake St., Coventry) commemorates his service. One of UConn's quirkier attractions is the **Ballard Institute and Museum of Puppetry** (Weaver Rd. off Rte. 44, Storrs, 860/486-0339, www.sp.uconn.edu, noon–5 P.M. Fri.–Sun. May–Nov., $5 adults, $4 children, students and seniors), a museum that began two decades ago as a gallery displaying the unique puppets created by UConn theater professor Jack Ballard. Over the years, the collection has expanded into a tour through the international history of puppetry, including shadow puppets, hand puppets, and celebrity marionettes (including a credible Elvis).

Entertainment

For old-school entertainment, head to the **Mansfield Drive-In Theatre** (Rtes. 31 and 32, Mansfield, 860/423-4441, www.mansfielddrivein.com, box office 7:10 P.M., $9 adults 12+, $5 children 6–11, free children under 3), an authentic drive-in showing first-run movies alongside a playground and snack bar. UConn students congregate at **Huskies** (28 King Hill Rd., Storrs, 860/429-2333), a student-y dive with pool tables and drink specials.

Events

During the summer season, the main street of Willimantic is blocked off on the third Thursday of each month for the **Willimantic Street Fest** (Jillson Square to Walnut St., www.willimanticstreetfest.com, 6 P.M.–9 P.M. Oct–Apr.), which features music, craft vendors, and beer from the local brewing company. Willimantic's July Fourth **Boom Box Parade** (Jillson Square, 860/456-1111, www.wili-am.com, 11 A.M. July 4th) began 20 years ago with a local resident who, hearing that the parade was cancelled, convinced an AM radio station to broadcast marching music and took to the streets with her radio. Now hundreds of townsfolk turn out with their own boom boxes for the parade—which features more and more elaborate costumes each year. Fittingly for a town called Scotland, the **Highland Games** (Waldo Rd., Scotland, 860/423-9634, www.scotlandgames.org, 10 A.M.–5 P.M., early Oct. $12 adults, $10 seniors and students, $5 children 6–12, free children under 5) brings kilts, bagpipes, and caber tosses to the Quiet Corner.

Food

Cliff Claven would adore the **Willimantic Brewing Company** (967 Main St., Willimantic, 860/423-6777, www.willibrew.com, 11:30 A.M.–1 A.M. Tue.–Thu.; 11:30 A.M.–2 A.M. Fri.–Sat.; 11:30 A.M.–1 A.M. Sunday, $7–17); the brew house sits in a revitalized, beautified postal building. Patrons down beers and simple but flavorful dishes like chili and pizza beneath the pub's huge mural. Wing nuts shouldn't pass up a stop at **Blarneys Cafe**

(49 High St., Willimantic, 860/423-9496, 4 P.M.–1 A.M. Sun.–Thu.; 4 P.M.–2 A.M. Fri–Sat., $4–6). An otherwise nondescript Irish pub/sports bar, its kitchen makes its mark with a sub-menu (in its list of bar food) of buckets of inexpensive chicken wings with unusual flavors such as creamy garlic, sweet and sour, and rum and coconut.

Information

For more information on the region, contact the **Windham Region Chamber of Commerce** (1010 Main St., Willimantic, 860/423-6389). The **Lebanon Historical Society** (856 Trumbull Hwy., 860/642-6579, www.historyoflebanon.org/index.htm) also runs a museum and visitors center with more information on the area.

SCENIC ROUTE 169

It's easy to see why the federal government designated the Quiet Corner's Route 169 as one of New England's few "scenic byways." You won't see icy mountain peaks or crashing surf here, but the endless miles of rolling dairy farms, apple orchards, historic homes, and crumbling stone walls make for one of the most pleasant drives you are likely to have in the region.

The road begins near the former manufacturing center of **Putnam,** a hardscrabble mill town that has gone through decay and rebirth. In the 1950s, a massive flood destroyed the downtown commercial base. More recently, however, antiques dealers began gobbling up the dirt-cheap real estate downtown; now day-trippers drive from Boston and southern Connecticut to take advantage of the cheapest deals around. The other towns along the roadway are pure rural America. Wealthy **Woodstock** has a number of fine craft galleries; **Pomfret** has several exclusive private schools and restaurants and bed-and-breakfasts to serve them; **Canterbury** and **Brooklyn** are simply given over to the scenery.

◖ Roseland Cottage/ Bowen House

The first thing you notice about this quirky

Victorian (556 Rte. 169, Woodstock, 860/928-4074, www.historicnewengland.org, tours hourly 11 A.M.–4 P.M. Wed.–Sun. June–mid-Oct., $8) is the color: bright rose pink. In fact, that was the original shade that Henry Bowen painted the cottage, which he gave as a gift to his wife, a lover of roses. The building is now the country's best surviving model of the Gothic Revival architecture that was all the rage for a brief period of time in the mid-19th century. The exterior is all quatrefoils and balustrades, and the interior feels more like a cathedral, with high ceilings and stained glass in the parlors.

Bowen grew up in Woodstock, and later became a wealthy printer in New York; but he never forgot where he came from. He returned to this cottage every summer with his wife and ten children(!), and virtually built the town of Woodstock through his philanthropy. Among his efforts was a July Fourth celebration in the neighboring park that was renowned as the best in the country; several presidents, including Taft and Theodore Roosevelt, stayed at the cottage for the celebration. Today the home is owned by Historic New England, which has done a bang-up job of restoring the house, including an unusual embossed wallpaper known as lincrusta Walton, which a tour guide describes as "linoleum for your wall." Because the home was continuously in the hands of the family, all of the furniture and artwork is original to the house—a rarity in house museums. As a special treat, don't miss the 19th-century bowling alley, with wooden pins and balls, in a barn on the property.

Prudence Crandall Museum

An unsung pioneer of the abolitionist era, schoolteacher Prudence Crandall ran an academy in the town of Canterbury decades before the Civil War. When a Black girl asked for entrance, the White townspeople howled in protest. Crandall responded by sending the White girls home and opening the first all-Black girls' academy. This quaint museum (Rtes. 14 and 169, Canterbury, 860/546-7800, www.ct.gov/, 10 A.M.–4 P.M. Thu. May.–Oct., $6 adults, $4 seniors, students and children 6–17, free children under 5) does an excellent job of dramatizing the challenges Crandall faced in keeping the school open—her struggles make

Roseland Cottage

© CT CULTURE & TOURISM

Connecticut in the 1830s look worse than Mississippi in the 1960s. After a lawsuit and an attack by an angry mob, Crandall was forced to shut down the school after only eight months, but she spent the rest of her life fighting for the abolitionist cause.

Sharpe Hill Vineyard

With the profusion of local wineries in New England these days struggling at producing good product after trying winters, there is simply a lot of plonk out there in the tasting rooms. That's why this vineyard (108 Wade Rd., Pomfret, 860/974-3549, www.sharpehill. com, 11 A.M.–5 P.M. Fri.–Sun., free) is such a welcome gem. A labor of love by a pair of transplanted New Yorkers, the winery has won more than 60 medals for its signature semi-dry white called Ballet of Angels. (Better yet, B of A sells for only $12 at the retail store.) The vino is just the beginning at the winery, where attention to detail extends to a bathroom commode constructed of an antique European metal wine trug. On weekends, the winery sponsors exclusive lunches for 12 people, which might feature steak Delmonico or chicken with *herbes de provence*. Meals are preceded by a wine tasting, so you can pair just right.

Other Sights

Situated far off the beaten track, the wooded **Buell's Orchard** (108 Crystal Pond Rd., Eastford, 860/974-1150, www.buellsorchard. com, 8 A.M.–5 P.M., Mon.–Fri., 8 A.M.–3 P.M. Sat., closed Sun., mid-July–Aug.; 8 A.M.–5 P.M., Mon.–Sat., 1 P.M.–5 P.M. Sun., Sept.–Oct.; 8 A.M.–4 P.M. Mon.–Fri., 8 A.M.–3 P.M., Sat., closed Sunday, Nov.–Dec.; 8 A.M.–noon, Mon.–Sat, closed Sundays, June.)offers pick-your-owns starting in May with strawberries and continuing through apples in October. The *real* draw of this family-run orchard, however, is a rare automatic candy-apple factory, which dunks an apple a second in gooey caramel and peanuts, and it's open to visitors for tours (and samples). The apples are so fresh, they almost seem healthy.

Among the trivia on display at **Creamery**

Brook Bison Farm (19 Purvis Rd., Brooklyn, 860/779-0837, www.creamerybrookbison. ney, 2–6 P.M., Mon.–Fri. and 10 A.M.–2 P.M. Sat. Apr.–Oct.; 2 P.M.–6 P.M. Wed.–Fri. and 10 A.M.–2 P.M.Sat. Nov.–Mar.; and by appointment, group tours $90 minimum charge for 1–15 people, $6 adult, $5 child for 16th person and up) is the fact that buffalo can "easily" jump over a six-foot-tall fence. That's a bit nerve-wracking when you are staring down a beast on the other side of the boards; the owners of this bison-and-emu farm however stress that they only jump over fences when they are really angry. Visitors can keep the buffalo happy by purchasing food to hand-feed them; then they can purchase (cow's milk) ice cream to feed themselves.

Fishermen salivate when they look through the glass windows at **Quinebaug Valley Trout Hatchery** (Trout Hatchery Rd., Plainfield, 860/564-7542, www.ct.gov, 9:30 A.M.– 3:30 P.M. daily, free), which raises some 600,000 brown, brook, and rainbow trout annually. Released into the wild, the fish provide about three-quarters of all trout stocked in Connecticut rivers and lakes.

Entertainment

Despite its 90-person capacity, the 🄲 **Vanilla Bean Cafe** (corner of Rtes. 44, 169, and 97, Pomfret, 860/928-1562, www.vanillabeancafe. com, 7 A.M.–8 P.M., Wed.–Thu.; 7 A.M.–9 P.M. Fri.; 8 A.M.–9 P.M. Sat.; 8 A.M.–8 P.M. Sun.) plays host to nationally known folk acts such as Brooks Williams and Dar Williams, as well as up-and-comers from throughout New England. On Saturdays, an informal jam session follows the scheduled performer. A restored century-old vaudeville theater in the heart of Putnam's antiques district, **Bradley Playhouse** (30 Front St./Rte. 44, Putnam, 860/928-7887, www.bradleyplayhouse.org, shows $15 adults, $12 students and seniors, musicals $17 adults, $14 students and seniors) plays host to amateur drama and musicals.

Events

Historic New England throws open the

grounds of Roseland Cottage each October for its annual **Fine Arts and Craft Festival** (860/974-3020, 10 A.M.–4:30 P.M., mid-Oct.), which features original works by some 175 artisans. Many communities take pride in the age of their county fair, but the **Brooklyn Fair** (860/779-0012, www.brooklynfair.org, 4–11 P.M. Thu.; 8 A.M.–11 P.M. Fri.–Sat., late Aug., $10, free children under 13) is actually the oldest continuous agricultural fair in the country. The fair, which includes midway rides and livestock displays, has been active since 1809.

Shopping

A mind-boggling selection awaits at **Antiques Marketplace** (109 Main St., Putnam, 860/928-0442, 10 A.M.–5 P.M., Mon.–Sun.), the largest and most diverse antiques mall around. Pore over goods from more than 30 showcases, including collectibles from seemingly every time period and several continents. Those searching for furniture from the late 18th and 19th centuries will be happy to find **Antiques Unlimited**

© MICHAEL BLANDING

antiquing in Putnam

(91 Main St., Putnam, 860/963-2599). The selection also features lots of excellent sterling silver (both American and European). It's just too cute not to stop in at **Martha's Herbary** (589 Pomfret St., Pomfret, 860/928-0009, www.marthasherbary.com, 10 A.M.–5 P.M. Tue.–Sun.). It not only sells handmade knickknacks such as pottery, floral wreaths, and cashmere sweaters, the shop also grows its own herbs in the garden outside, and you'll find them in many of the products inside. Locally made vividly glazed bowls and platters line the shelves at **Sawmill Pottery** (112 Main St., #14, Putnam, 860/963-7807, www.sawmillpottery.com, 11 A.M.–5 P.M. Tue.–Thu. And Sat.; 11 A.M.–8 P.M. Fri.; or by appointment)—and prices are reasonable enough that you may want to pick up several.

Food

The murals overlooking the dining area of **Vanilla Bean Cafe** (corner of Rtes. 44, 169, and 97, Pomfret, 860/928-1562, www.thevanillabeancafe.com, 7 A.M.–3 P.M. Mon.–Wed.; 7 A.M.–8 P.M. Wed.–Thu.; 7 A.M.–9 P.M. Fri.; 8 A.M.–9 P.M. Sat., 8 A.M.–8 P.M. Sun, $12–15) are almost as colorful as the crowd. All Pomfret seems to file in and out of this cozy spot throughout the day, chatting over big bowls of homemade heirloom-tomato soup, golden-beet salad, still-warm muffins, and molasses-brined pork. And since it's as much a coffeehouse as café and art gallery, you can also catch regular live folk music every Saturday night. At first glance, the sight of a sushi bar plunk in the historic building belonging to **The Harvest** (37 Putnam Rd./ Rte. 44, Pomfret, 860/928-0008, www.harvestrestaurant.com, 11 A.M.–9 P.M. Tue.–Thu.; 11 A.M.–10 P.M. Fri.–Sat.; 11 A.M.–8:30 P.M. Sun., $14–35) seems odd. But put it in the context of the rest of the international menu (from seared Pacific tuna and bouillabaisse to steakhouse-style beef cuts), and it all makes sense. Service can be a bit on the slow side, but then again, odds are you didn't come to this romantic spot for a quick meal anyway. Part farm museum, part ultra-friendly eatery,

C Golden Lamb Buttery (499 Wolf Den Rd., Brooklyn, 860/774-4423, www.thegoldenlamb.com, lunch noon–2:30 P.M. Tue.–Sat., dinner 7–11 P.M. Fri.–Sat., prix fixe dinner $65, lunch $13–18) is as much a learning experience as it is a meal. Before every dinner, guests arrive for cocktails, walking past a flock of sheep, a barn full of antiques, and several horses to the back porch overlooking the property's pond. They're then treated to a hay ride before marching into the dining room for traditional dishes like chateaubriand and roast duck with orange sauce. There's as much style as there is taste at **Vine Bistro** (85 Main St., Putnam, 860/928-1660, $9–24), serving light fare such as portabellas sautéed with spinach and veal *piccata* in the simple but pretty dining room. If the pumpkin cheesecake is available, don't miss it. Everything you've heard is true: **C Pyzzz** (8 Harris Rd., Putnam, 860/928-7424, 11:30 A.M.–1 A.M. Mon.–Thu.; 11:30 A.M.–2:30 A.M. Fri.–Sat., $6–16) truly is some of (if not the) best pizza around. The thin-crusted wonders are served fast and to-order in a charming 19th-century building. For dessert, you don't know what good ice cream truly is until you've sampled a cone from **We-Lik-It Ice Cream** (Rich Rd., Abington, 860/974-1095, www.welikit.com, noon–7 P.M. Mon.–Sun. Apr.–Oct., $2–4), a working dairy farm that makes its deliciously fresh ice cream directly after milking.

Information

The Route 169 corridor is promoted by the nonprofit **The Last Green Valley** (107 Providence St., Putnam, 860/963-7226 or 866/363-7226, www.thelastgreenvalley.org), which runs a well-stocked information center in downtown Putnam.

CASINO COUNTRY

While not technically a part of the Quiet Corner, the twin cities of Norwich and Ledyard form a quasi-urban buffer between the farm country of northeast Connecticut and the maritime character of the southeast seacoast. The area was once known for the important city of Norwich, which was founded in 1659 and quickly took advantage of its position on the deep and wide Thames River to become a very wealthy trading port (second only to New Haven for the time). Later, the area emerged as an early resort destination, with steamers from New York unloading passengers into grand Victorian hotels.

Norwich declined quickly, however, when a bridge was finally constructed over the wide Thames, allowing coastal traffic to bypass the city. It went into a slow decline, losing both population and industry throughout the 20th century. That all reversed dramatically in 1992, when the Mashantucket Pequot tribe worked out a deal with the State of Connecticut to turn a bingo hall into Foxwoods gambling casino. In 1996, the neighboring Mohegan tribe got into the act as well, opening the smaller but more popular Mohegan Sun casino. Together, the resorts have grown to rival Atlantic City in the traffic they bring in from throughout the Northeast. While the resorts are mostly self-contained entities, Norwich and surrounding towns have also tried to capitalize on the influx with various revitalization schemes.

C Mashantucket Pequot Museum and Research Center

The gleaming glass facade of this modern museum (110 Pequot Tr., Mashantucket, 860/411-9671, www.pequotmuseum.org, 10 A.M.–4 P.M. Wed.–Sat., last admission at 3 P.M., $15 adults, $13 seniors, $10 children 6–15, free children under 6) doesn't seem to owe much to the spirit of the Native American tribes who used to inhabit the area of southeastern Connecticut and Rhode Island. Through the entrance and down the great escalator, however, visitors are transported back thousands of years into an immersive environment that convincingly brings alive the era before Christopher Columbus and John Winthrop. Told from the Natve Americans' perspective, the museum gives moral heft to the heartbreaking story of how European settlers decimated Native American tribes through disease and played tribes off of one another.

In fact, outside New York and Washington,

this may be the best Native American museum in the country. It ought to be—heavily funded by the lucre from the casinos next door, it employs interactive touch-screen exhibits and life-sized wax figures alongside hundreds of authentic artifacts. All of the glitz, however, is itself a facade over the center's primary mission of researching, collecting, and preserving Native American artifacts from southern New England; the center has a collection of some 150,000 books for research.

Mohegan Sun Casino

Foxwoods may have been first, but the casino resort (1 Mohegan Sun Blvd., exit 79A off I-395, Uncasville, 888/226-7711, www. mohegansun.com, 24 hours daily) built by the Mohegan Tribe in 1996 is by far the more atmospheric of the two resorts. The 300,000 square feet of gaming space is divided into two Native American–themed rooms, Earth and Sky, each with its own over-the-top decor. Earth is the more subdued of the two, with fake wolves, pines, and buffalo hides; the newer Sky, meanwhile, is dominated by a 55-foot waterfall and a 30-foot "crystal mountain" called Wombi Rock, along with a planetarium ceiling.

Together, the two casino rooms have some 6,000 slot machines and just under 300 table games. Of course, once you win your money, you'll need somewhere to spend it, and Mohegan Sun is happy to oblige with three soaring glass hotel towers for overnight stays, dozens of restaurants—including those by all-star New England chefs Todd English and Jasper White—and three entertainment venues that feature a crap-shoot of current and long-gone musical performers. Big shows (Eric Clapton, Black Eyed Peas) are reserved for the 10,000-seat arena, where the Boston Celtics also sometimes play exhibition games; more intimate performances take place in the smaller Wolf Den or Cabaret Theatre (remember Eddie Money?).

Foxwoods Resort and Casino

If bigger is better, then Foxwoods (39 Norwich-Westerly Rd., Ledyard, 800/369-9663, www. foxwoods.com) takes the prize. With more than 340,000 square feet of gaming space, 7,000 slot machines, and 350 table games, the gargantuan resort is the largest casino in the world. And it's about to get even bigger with a new expansion, set to be completed in 2008, which will create a new $700 million MGM Grand resort. For all its superlatives, however, Foxwoods is pretty standard in the decor department, looking like pretty much any other casino between here and Vegas. Like Mohegan Sun, the resort includes hundreds of hotel rooms, dozens of shops and restaurants (which tend on average to be slightly more expensive than Mohegan), and several entertainment venues.

Slater Memorial Museum

Okay, you could spend your life traveling the world in search of the finest specimens of classical Greek, Roman, Egyptian, and Italian Renaissance sculpture. Or you could just hoof it on over to this impressive museum (860/887-2506, 108 Crescent St., Norwich, www.norwichfreeacademy.com, 9 A.M.–4 P.M. Tue.–Fri.; 1–4 P.M. Sat.–Sun., $3 adults, $2 seniors, free children under 12), located on the campus of the Norwich Free Academy, and see all the same in one place. Well, almost the same anyway: Founded in 1887, the museum has some 150 plaster casts of all of the world's finest statuary. In recent years, the collection has expanded to include original artwork from around the globe.

Entertainment

In addition to the concerts at Foxwoods and Mohegan Sun, downtown Norwich has several bars and clubs that feature live music. The star attraction is **Club Ballaro** (276 Main St., Norwich, 860/889-9387), which has two floors of dancing and sometimes rock bands. Attached to an Italian restaurant, **Bella Notte** (543 W. Thames St., Norwich, 860/887-1944, 5 P.M.–1 A.M. Tue.–Fri.; 5 P.M.–2 A.M. Sat.–Sun.) hosts DJs and live music acts that cater to a local crowd.

Shopping

Handbag addicts, unite: **Satchels** (Foxwoods, 39 Norwich-Westerly Rd., Ledyard, 800/369-9663, 10 A.M.–9 P.M. Sun.; 11 A.M.–9 P.M. Mon.–Thu.; 11 A.M.–midnight Fri.; 10 A.M.–midnight Sat.) has what you crave. From Dooney & Bourke clutches to Donald Pliner totes, the designer specimens you're after are here. Want to look like a shark at the tables? Swing by **Jazz** (Mohegan Sun, 1 Mohegan Sun Blvd., Uncasville, 860/862-8270, 11 A.M.–10 P.M. Sun.–Thu.; 11 A.M.–midnight Fri.–Sat.) first; the boutique has a full stash of excellent-quality suits, shirts, and ties, from the well-respected men's designer Joseph Abboud. And if you do manage to hit it big, make your next stop the jewelry cases of **Lux, Bond & Green** (Mohegan Sun, 1 Mohegan Sun Blvd., Uncasville, 860/862-9900, 11 A.M.–10 P.M. Sun.–Thu.; 11 A.M.–midnight Fri.–Sat.); the high-end shop sells both internationally known and cutting-edge brands.

Food

It's seafood season all year long at **The Summer Shack** (Mohegan Sun, 1 Mohegan Sun Blvd., Uncasville, 860/862-9500, www.mohegansun.com/dining/summer_shack.jsp, 11 A.M.–11 P.M. Mon.–Wed. and Sun., 11:30 A.M.–1 A.M. Thu.–Sat., $13–24), the domain of New England star chef Jasper White. Designed after a classic colorful oceanside fish shanty, the restaurant offers far more than the usual shack fare: roasted lobster, for starters, plus specialties like corn and crab fritters, and grilled snapper. Another Boston-based celebrity chef, Todd English, shows his chops at **Todd English's Tuscany** (Mohegan Sun, 1 Mohegan Sun Blvd., Uncasville, 888/226-7711, 6 A.M.–10 P.M. Sun.–Thu.; 6 A.M.–11 P.M. Fri.–Sat., $15–40), where the kitchen whips up dishes veering from the simple (gnocchi Bolognese) to the elevated (lamb porterhouse with blue cheese popover). More hearty fare is on offer at **Cedars Steak House** (Foxwoods, 39 Norwich-Westerly Rd., Ledyard, 800/369-9663, 5–11 P.M. Sun.–Thu.; 5 P.M.–12 A.M. Fri.–Sat., $19–40), the leather booth–filled eatery that's home to more rib eyes, filets, and chops than you can shake a steak knife at. From dim sum to rice congee, the pan-Asian menu at **Golden Dragon** (Foxwoods, 39 Norwich-Westerly Rd., Ledyard, 800/369-9663, 11:30 A.M.–1 A.M. Sun.–Thu.; 11:30 A.M.–11 P.M. Tue.; 11:30 A.M.–3 A.M. Fri.–Sat., $7–15) is—if not exactly 100 percent authentic—fast, reasonably fresh, and tasty.

Information

The **Norwich Tourist Office** (69 Main St., 860/886-4683, www.norwichct.org) runs a helpful visitors center downtown.

SPORTS AND RECREATION
Hiking and Biking

The Quiet Corner abounds with hiking opportunities in many state-owned forest and conservation lands. One of the most secluded is **Bigelow Hollow State Park** (166 Chestnut Hill Rd., Stafford Springs, 860/424-3200, www.friendsctstateparks.org, $7 Conn.-registered vehicle, $10 out-of-state-registered vehicle), which has several miles of trails leading through dense forest to hidden fishing ponds. Tracing a 26-mile path from Putnam to Pomfret, the **Air Line Walking Trail** (860/928-6121) follows a former railroad bed through pretty farms and woodlands.

The roads in the region are also particularly good for cycling, with sparse traffic, gentle grades, and scenery with every mile. The brochure *Northeast Connecticut's Bike Guide* details 10 self-guided loops through the region. Bikes can be rented at **Scott's Cyclery** (1171 Main St., Willimantic, 860/423-8889, www.scottscyclery.com) and **Silver Bike Shop** (6 Livery St., www.thesilverbikeco.com, Putnam, 860/928-7370).

Boating and Fishing

Self-proclaimed "water rat" Ian MacRea leads guided canoeing tours of the Quinebag River through his outfit **Cider Rides** (241-G Church St., Putnam, 860/928-5040, www.ciderrides.com). Post-paddling cider is included.

ACCOMMODATIONS
$100-150

Set among gloriously kept gardens, the three rooms offered at **Fitch House** (563 Storrs Rd., Mansfield Center, 860/456-0922, www.fitchhouse.com, $110–125) are set with reproduction wallpapers, antique beds, and vintage prints. There's also a full breakfast, nightly turndown service, and wireless Internet access. One of the best bargains around is **Elias Child House** (50 Perrin Rd., Woodstock, 860/974-9836, www.eliaschildhouse.com, $120–150), filled as it is with canopy beds, fireplaces, and romantic vistas of the surrounding horse-dotted fields.

$150-250

Idyllic inside and out, the (**Inn at Fox Hill Farm** (760 Pomfret St., Pomfret, 860/928-5240, www.innatfoxhillfarm.com, $185) is an uber-cozy little cottage sitting on 75 acres of scenic byway and overlooking a lake. And it's perfect for privacy seekers, since it actually has only one bedroom (and hosts one set of guests at a time). Those guests, however, have nearly the run of the place, with full access to its kitchen/dining area, private patio and deck, and living room.

The (**Inn at Woodstock Hill** (94 Plaine Hill Rd., Woodstock, 860/928-0528, www.woodstockhill.net/, $130–200) isn't quite so secluded, but it hardly lacks for serenity. The 19th-century manse's 18 luxury rooms all have private baths, wireless Internet, and many offer fireplaces and four-poster beds.

GETTING THERE

To get to the Quiet Corner by car, take I-395 south from Worcester (30 mi., 40 min. to Putnam); U.S. Route 6 west from Hartford (30 mi., 40 min. to Willimantic); or U.S. Route 6 east from Providence (30 mi., 50 min. to Brooklyn). To get to Casino Country, take I-395 south from Worcester to exit 85 for Foxwoods (60 mi., 70 min.) or 79A for Mohegan Sun (65 mi., 70 min.). From Hartford, take Route 2 until it merges with I-395. Then head north on I-395 to exit 85 for Foxwoods (50 mi., 1 hour total); or south on I-395 to exit 79A for Mohegan Sun (45 mi., 50 min. total).

Greyhound (800/231-2222, www.greyhound.com) offers limited service to the University of Connecticut in Storrs, as well as regular bus routes to Willimantic from Hartford, stopping at several locations on Main Street (stopping at the Rte. 66 Quick Mart, 790 Main St.), Foxwoods, and Mohegan Sun. **Peter Pan Arrow** (860/289-1531, www.arrowline.com) also has bus routes to Willimantic. **Amtrak** (800/872-7245, www.amtrak.com) also runs shuttle service to Foxwoods from New London.

GETTING AROUND

Windham Region Transit District (860/456-2223, www.wrtd.net) operates several bus routes along Route 195 between Willimantic, Mansfield, and Storrs, also making connections to Norwich and the casinos along Route 32. **Southeast Area Transit** (SEAT, 860/886-2631, www.seatbus.com) runs buses connecting Norwich and Ledyard to the southeast coast. Buses start at the Norwich Transportation Center (Rte. 12) and operate on a "flag-down" system, meaning they will stop anywhere along their routes.

Mystic and the Southeast Coast

The little town of Mystic made its fortunes in shipbuilding; now the town and neighboring communities earn their keep by bringing alive the romance of the sea for tourists. You won't find a saltier part of New England anywhere. Each of the towns along the southeastern coast celebrates the sea in its own way, from the fishing port of Stonington to the industrial port of New London.

STONINGTON

You won't find much to do in the quaint fishing village of Stonington, and that's just the point. Folded into the southeastern corner of the state, the port is home to Connecticut's last working fishing fleet, which drags for bottom fish, clams, and scallops in surrounding waters. Previously, the town was an important shipbuilding and trading port, and the collection of historic buildings downtown is one of the finest anywhere. Stonington achieved brief fame during the War of 1812, when its two 18-pound cannons repelled an attack by five British warships. Nothing quite as exciting as that has happened to the town since; its main trade now is the yachtsmen and tourists who poke around its antiques shops and take advantage of the scenic views along the waterfront.

Sights

Of all the continents, Antarctica was (understandably) the last to be discovered. It wasn't until 1821 that Captain Nathaniel Palmer, known as "Captain Nat," happened upon a strange bit of land in a search for seal rookeries in the South Atlantic that turned out to literally be the tip of the iceberg. Memorabilia from the captain's career commanding clipper ships and packet boats is on view at the **Nathaniel B. Palmer House** (40 Palmer St., 860/535-8445, www.stoningtonhistory.org, tours hourly 1–5 P.M. Wed.–Sun. May–Oct., $8 adults, $5 children), a stately Greek Revival home with a distinctive octagonal cupola run by the Stonington Historical Society. The society

LET THERE BE LIGHT

The shores of Connecticut are home to some 20 lighthouses – most are closed to the public, but many are either open or easily accessible for up-close-and-personal viewing. At the 19th-century 97-foot-tall **New Haven Harbor Light** (Washington St. & N. Water St., 203/838-9444), for example, visitors can wander its four levels and 10 rooms. Nearly as tall at 70 feet high, Lynde Point Light, built in 1839, isn't open to the public, but you can admire its octagon tower from below. You'll need to take a cruise to get that close to the historic **Sheffield Island Light** (I-95, exits 14N/15S, Norwalk), built in 1868, but once there you can stop off on the island for a few hours, stroll its pretty paths, and have a picnic. In New London, there's Ledge Light, plunk in the middle of the Thames River and the entrance to New London Harbor; tours (or just cruise-bys) can be arranged through Project Oceanology (www.cr.nps.gov/maritime). You can climb straight up to the top of **Stonington Lighthouse Museum** (7 Water St., Stonington, 860/535-1440), which has exhibits on maritime artifacts and historic local battles, and even a children's room.

also operates the **Old Lighthouse Museum** (7 Water St., 860/535-1440, 10 A.M.–5 P.M. daily May–Oct., $8 adults, $5 children), featuring six rooms of paintings and artifacts located inside a historic 30-foot stone lighthouse tower.

For a taste of California in Connecticut, stop by the **Jonathan Edwards Winery** (74 Chester Maine Rd., N. Stonington, 860/535-0202, www.jedwardswinery.com, 11 A.M.–5 P.M. Wed.–Sun.; 3 P.M. weekday tours), a hilltop vineyard in North Stonington that imports grapes from Napa Valley to age in its oak barrels. Even the tasting rooms (which

CONNECTICUT

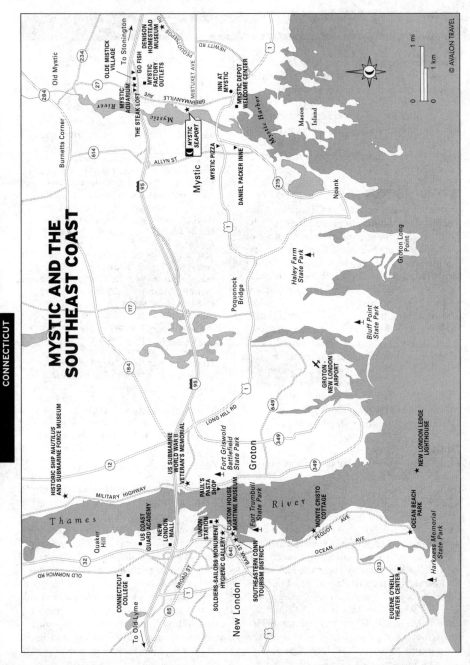

MYSTIC AND THE SOUTHEAST COAST

© AVALON TRAVEL

Old Mystic

To Stonington

OLDE MISTICK VILLAGE

GO FISH

DENISON HOMESTEAD MUSEUM

MYSTIC FACTORY OUTLETS

MYSTIC AQUARIUM

THE STEAK LOFT

INN AT MYSTIC

MYSTIC DEPOT WELCOME CENTER

MYSTIC SEAPORT

MYSTIC PIZZA

DANIEL PACKER INNE

Mystic

ALLYN ST

Mystic River

GREENMANVILLE AVE

MISTUXET AVE

HEWITT RD

PEQUOTEPOS RD

Mystic Harbor

Mason Island

Noank

Groton Long Point

Burnetts Corner

Haley Farm State Park

Paquonock Bridge

Bluff Point State Park

GROTON-NEW LONDON AIRPORT

HISTORIC SHIP *NAUTILUS* AND SUBMARINE FORCE MUSEUM

US SUBMARINE WORLD WAR II VETERAN'S MEMORIAL

MILITARY HIGHWAY

LONG HILL RD

Fort Griswold Battlefield State Park

Groton

NEW LONDON LEDGE LIGHTHOUSE

PAUL'S PASTA SHOP

CUSTOM HOUSE MARITIME MUSEUM

Fort Trumbull State Park

Thames River

MONTE CRISTO COTTAGE

OCEAN BEACH PARK

US COAST GUARD ACADEMY

NEW LONDON MALL

UNION STATION

SOLDIERS-SAILORS MONUMENT

HYGIENIC GALLERY

SOUTHEASTERN CONN TOURISM DISTRICT

PEQUOT AVE

OCEAN AVE

Harkness Memorial State Park

Quaker Hill

CONNECTICUT COLLEGE

New London

BROAD ST

BANK ST

EUGENE O'NEILL THEATER CENTER

OLD NORWICH RD

To Old Lyme

0   1 mi

0   1 km

charge a steep $6 a flight) are laid out to resemble a Western-style ranch. Whites, however, are home-grown; they include a popular gewürztraminer that routinely gets snapped up early upon its release.

Events

Marching bands, floats, and even Miss Connecticut turn out for the annual **Blessing of the Fleet** (Stonington Fishermen's Dock, 1 High St., Stonington, late July, free), which begins with a parade through downtown and culminates with a clambake on the waterfront and boats moored in the harbor. A Catholic priest is on hand to ensure a safe and successful fishing season.

Food

Serious dining in a candlelit little bistro is the name of the game at **Boom** (194 Water St., 860/535-2588, 11:30 A.M.–3 P.M. Tue.–Sat., 10 A.M.–3 P.M. Sun.; 5:30–9 P.M. Tue.–Sun, $13–25). Dinners can be as simple as a duck quesadilla, or as constructed as pan-roasted halibut with roasted tomato-leek tarragon broth. Sitting on 600 square feet of dock space, **Skipper's Dock** (66 Water St., 860/535-0111, www.skippersdock.com, 11 A.M.–10 P.M. Mon.–Sun.; closed Tue. during winter,, $8–26) gives its patrons ample opportunity to gaze out at passing boats and nearby Fisher's Island. This is what coastal dining should be: simple seafood at moderate prices, with amiable service and a setting that makes you feel as close to the ocean as possible (without getting wet, that is). The prompt service deserves its raves at **Noah's Restaurant** (113 Water St., 860/535-3925, noahsfinefood.com/new/, 7:45 A.M.–9 P.M. Tue.–Thu.; 7:45 A.M.–9:30 P.M. Fri.–Sat.; 7:45 A.M.–9 P.M. Sun., $14–21), the small, tin-ceilinged spot where locals bounce between the cherry booths and bar. Opt for the seafood—dishes of tender swordfish or the superb lobster roll—and you won't be sorry.

Shopping

Pick up some clever home accessories (from handmade mirrors to umbrella stands) or invest in a more substantial piece of furniture at **Rue Auber Antiques** (135 Water St., 860/535-3070, 10 A.M.–5:30 P.M. daily), a café-cum-shop selling creative and classic herbal mixes.

Information

For more information on Stonington, contact **Stonington Town Hall** (152 Elm St., 860/535-5000, www.stonington-ct.gov) or the **Greater Mystic Chamber of Commerce** (860/572-1102, www.mysticchamber.org).

MYSTIC

Yes, there really is a Mystic Pizza, and yes, the cult movie starring Julia Roberts really was filmed on location in this small seaside town. More significantly, however, Mystic achieved fame in the colonial era as one of New England's primary centers of shipbuilding, buoyed by the deep but sheltered estuary of the Mystic River, which was ideal for launching craft into the ocean. Starting in the late 1700s, more than 600 ships were eventually constructed here, including whale ships, clipper ships, and steamships. By the dawn of the 20th century, however, manufacturing had long ago overtaken shipbuilding as Mystic's main industry. With a nostalgia for the Golden Age of Sail, three citizens decided to transform the old shipyard into a living history museum, dubbed Mystic Seaport, that in 75 years has become America's preeminent museum celebrating the country's shipbuilding past. In addition to the seaport, Mystic's downtown has an attractive collection of shops on both sides of the river—including not one but two branches of the famous pizza parlor.

◖ Mystic Seaport

Situated a mile upriver from downtown, the seaport now has a collection of more than 500 vessels contained in a miniature city (Rte. 27, exit 90 off I-95, 860/572-5315, www.mysticseaport.org, 9 A.M.–5 P.M. daily Apr.–Oct.; 10 A.M.–4 P.M. daily Nov.–Mar.; $24 adults, $22 seniors and students, $15 children 6–17, free children under 5) drawn up to look and feel like a bustling 19th-century seaport.

© MYSTIC SEAPORT, MYSTIC, CT

sails aloft at Mystic Seaport

Educational exhibits are seamlessly integrated into pubs, outfitters, and dry-goods stores. By far the most engaging attractions, however, are the village folk and old salts, who regale visitors with tales of the sea. On the water, the prime attraction is the *Charles W. Morgan,* America's last surviving whale ship, which was launched in New Bedford in 1841. Interpreters detail how the tryworks dissembled all that whale blubber, and also lead parties in hoisting sails, complete with authentic sea shanties. The seaport's newest exhibit, the *Amistad* is a fully-functioning re-creation of the famous 1830s slave ship with exhibits onboard tracing the roots of the uprising. Taken together, the seaport is a little too much to take on in a single day; strategize carefully or buy a multi-day pass to make a weekend of it.

Mystic Aquarium & Institute for Exploration

Emphasis is on interaction at this aquarium (55 Coogan Blvd., 860/572-5955, www.mysticaquarium.org, 9 A.M.–5 P.M. daily Mar.–Oct. 31; 9 A.M.–4 P.M. daily Nov.; 10 A.M.–4 P.M.

daily Dec.–Feb., $26 adult, $23 seniors, $19 children 3–17, free children under 2), which affords visitors several opportunities to get up close to aquatic animals. At a "ray touch pool," visitors can handle the creepy but gentle shark-relatives, while a wading pool lets you hang out with Beluga whales. New exhibits include an interactive game about dinosaur extinction, and an exhibit on the *Titanic* discovery that features an incredible 18-foot model of the doomed ocean liner.

Other Sights

In the center of Mystic, the **Bascule Bridge** drawbridge crosses Route 1 with picturesque views of the river. Along the bridge is a pedestrian walkway where you can take in the view. Six generations of Denisons inhabited the 1717 house once known as Pequotsepos Manor. The sight is now the **Denison Homestead Museum** (120 Pequotsepos Rd., 860/536-9248, www.denisonsociety.org, noon–4 P.M. Thu.–Sun., 1–5 P.M. Mon. and Fri.–Sat. mid-June–mid-Oct., $5 adults, $4 seniors and students, $2 children under 12, free children under 2), an

Mystic Harbor

innovative museum that has restored each room in the home to a different time period, incorporating family heirlooms and authentic furnishings.

Events

You won't find many lobsters this far south along the New England coast, but that doesn't stop Mystic Seaport from celebrating the crustaceans with its annual **Lobsterfest** (888/973-2767, www.mysticseaport.org, May); the celebration includes a lobster bake and music performances under the open-air boat shed. More than 250 visual artists compete each year in the juried **Mystic Outdoor Art Festival** (860/572-5098, www.mysticchamber.org, mid-Aug.), which also features food and craft vendors ranged along Main Street.

Food

The legend is real: ◖ **Mystic Pizza** (56 W Main St., 860/536-3700, 10 A.M.–10 P.M. daily, $8–14), the real-life pizza shop that served as the inspiration for Julia Roberts's late-'80s film of the same name, is still churning out pies every night. Tables can get crowded for dinner, so be prepared to wait. (Don't worry: your fire-roasted veggie or seafood delight pizza will most certainly be worth it.) The barn setting may not be entirely congruent with modern steakhouse style, but the menu at **The Steak Loft** (Olde Mistick Village, 860/536-2661, www.steakloftct.com, 11:30 A.M.–10:30 P.M. Mon.–Sun., $15–29) is the very model of it. Choose from big cuts of good-quality beef, seafood like the Maryland-style crab cakes, or tasty foul like apricot-glazed duck. Owned by the same company and also part of Mystic Seaport, **Go Fish** (Olde Mistick Village, 860/536-2662, www.gofishct.com, 11:30 A.M.–9:30 P.M. Mon.–Sun., $17–27) sports a surprisingly daring menu of seafood. Think yellowfin tuna with tapenade, pastrami-style smoked salmon plates, and a sizeable raw bar to top it all off. Fans of traditional New England dining will enjoy a meal at **Daniel Packer Inne** (32 Water St., 860/536-3555, www.danielpacker.com, 11 A.M.–10 P.M. daily, $16–24), a 1756 downtown establishment housing both pub and restaurant. In the latter, take a seat near the fireplace and sup on lemon-peppered chicken and baked scallops from nearby Stonington.

Shopping

The re-created **Olde Mistick Village** (at exit 90 off I-95, 860/536-4941, www.oldemystickvillage.com, 10 A.M.–6 P.M. Mon.–Sat.; 11 A.M.–5 P.M. Sun.; extended hours in summer) is more Disneyland fantasy than actual history, but it serves to get visitors into the spirit of the Seaport. Stroll past clusters of touristy shops selling souvenirs, plus some filled with genuinely unique crafts (hand-knit scarves, painted furnishings, and the like). With several decent restaurants and pretty gardens, the center makes for a full afternoon for families (of which there are loads here). If you're feeling inspired by the water's proximity, you're not alone. So are the owners of **Cutwater Gallery** (14 Holmes, 860/572-1576, 12 P.M.–5 P.M. Wed.–Sat., or by appointment),

CONNECTICUT

© CT CULTURE & TOURISM

CONNECTICUT

© MYSTIC SEAPORT, MYSTIC, CT

Mystic Seaport is home to hundreds of historic vessels, including the *Charles W. Morgan*.

a space dedicated entirely to art (fine and otherwise) and gifts that depict fishing and/or nautical life.

Information

You'll find no lack of information on the Mystic area. The Greater Mystic Chamber of Commerce runs the comprehensive **Mystic Depot Welcome Center** (2 Roosevelt Ave., 860/572-1102, www.mysticchamber.org) right before the bridge. In addition, it's worth stopping at Olde Mistick Village to check out the **Mystic & Shoreline Visitor Information Center** (Coogan Blvd., 860/536-1641), which has maps, menus, brochures, and discount tickets to area attractions.

NEW LONDON AND VICINITY

The gritty city of New London has an edge of reality that is lacking in most of the Connecticut coast. The predominantly blue-collar city once had a seedy reputation, with an active drug trade on its waterfront promenade, Bank Street. In the past decade, however, the city has cleaned up its act and gained new confidence through resurgence in the artistic community led by several new galleries and coffee shops that have opened downtown. While Bank Street has an unmistakably urban feel, that is mitigated somewhat by the many historic captain's houses and heavy stone warehouses that pay due to the town's rich maritime history.

New London was actually one of the first cities founded in Connecticut, settled by a party led by John Winthrop Jr.—son of the founder of Boston—in 1646. Perhaps it was a bit of an Oedipal rivalry that led Winthrop to one-up his dad by taking on the name of England's capital city. After a promising beginning, however, New London suffered a devastating setback during the Revolutionary War, when the infamous traitor Benedict Arnold attacked the city, burning it to the ground. The city regained its footing in the next century as a whaling port, behind only New Bedford and Nantucket in prominence—and opened up the Antarctic seal fishery as well.

© MICHAEL BLANDING

the historic side of New London

Across the Thames River, the smaller town of Groton draws its identity from the presence of its submarine base, the birthplace of the U.S. Navy's submarine force, which still employs 6,500 sailors in charge of 18 nuclear submarines.

Custom House Maritime Museum

As you enter this operating custom house and museum (150 Bank St., 860/447-2501, www.nl-maritimesociety.org, 1–5 P.M. Tue. and Thurs–Sat. Jan.–Mar.; 1–5 P.M. Tue.–Sun. Apr.–Dec., free, donations accepted), be sure to notice its front doors, which are fashioned from planks of "Old Ironsides"—the USS *Constitution*. The museum's exhibits, drawn from the collections of the New London Maritime Society, include ship models, *Amistad* memorabilia, and other items relating to Connecticut's seafaring past.

Historic Ship Nautilus and Submarine Force Museum

Tours of the world's first nuclear-powered submarine form the nucleus of this museum (1 Crystal Lake Rd., Groton, 860/694-3558 or 800/343-0079, www.ussnautilus.org, 9 A.M.–4 P.M. Wed.–Mon. Nov.–May; 9 A.M.–5 P.M. Wed.–Mon. mid-May–Oct., closed Tues.; free), which traces the history of the United States "silent force." Other exhibits include models of every submarine ever built by the U.S. Navy, and a re-creation of a WWII submarine attack center.

Fort Griswold Battlefield State Park

After Benedict Arnold turned his coat red, he proved his worth to the British by launching a devastating attack against the city of Groton, which served as home port for many colonial privateers who were harassing the British navy and guarded the rich port of New London. Arnold launched his 1781 attack against this fort (57 Fort St., Groton, 860/449-6877, www.dep.state.ct.us, 10 A.M.–5 P.M. daily Memorial Day–Labor Day; 10 A.M.–5 P.M. Sat.–Sun. Labor Day–Columbus Day; grounds open 8 A.M.–sunset year-round, free) on the mouth of the Thames River. After easily defeating those inside, Arnold purportedly led a

CONNECTICUT

massacre, killing half of the 160 defenders as they tried to surrender. In addition to a monument commemorating the battle, a house on the grounds where the wounded were tended has been turned into a small museum of the engagement.

Monte Cristo Cottage

Playwright Eugene O'Neill grew up in this home (325 Pequot Ave., 860/443-0051, www.oneilltheatercenter.org, noon–4 P.M. Thu.–Sat., 1–3 P.M. Sun. late May–early Sept.; group tours available by appointment Labor Day–Memorial Day, $7 adults, $5 students and seniors), which was named in honor of O'Neill's father, an actor famous for his role in the play *The Count of Monte Cristo*. It was in this home that O'Neill set his most famous play, the semi-autobiographical *A Long Day's Journey Into Night*. In 2005, the house was completely renovated using O'Neill's stage directions to re-create the setting for the play. Other rooms in the house display objects owned by the poet and period posters advertising his plays.

Other Sights

Across the river from Fort Griswold on the New London side, **Fort Trumbull State Park** (90 Walbach St., 860/444-7591, http://dep.state.ct.us/stateparks/parks/fort_trumbull.htm, 9 A.M.–4 P.M. Wed.–Sun. mid-May–Columbus Day; grounds open 8 A.M.–sunset daily year-round, $12 adults, $5 children 6–17, free children under 5) is the site of a later fort built after the War of 1812 to help defend the U.S. Coastline. Tours explore the interior, which incorporates unique Egyptian Revival features into its design. At the center of New London's artistic community is the **Hygienic Gallery** (83 Bank St., 860/443-8001, www.hygienicart.com), a cooperatively owned gallery that frequently pushes the bounds of what could be considered art. The gallery was started as an art show in the 24-hour Hygienic Restaurant in 1979. Though the restaurant eventually died, the art didn't, and the co-op took over the space, a stunning 1919 diner with checkerboard floors, in 1985. During its renovations,

the co-op also installed a sculpture gallery in a next-door vacant lot, where it sponsors a zany "bacchanalia" fundraiser each spring.

Entertainment

For more than 40 years, the **Eugene O'Neill Theater Center** (305 Great Neck Rd., Waterford, 860/443-5378, www.oneilltheatercenter.org) has been a top incubator of dramatic talent. In addition to staged readings of new American plays, the theater sponsors a summer cabaret series with musicians, magicians, and dancers.

The friendly bartendresses are half the draw at the **Bank Street Roadhouse** (36 Bank St., 860/443-8280, www.crosbyrestaurantgroup.com), a rowdy bar that books blues and roots bands during the weekends. Down the street, **Bank Street Cafe** (639 Bank St., 860/444/1444, www.bankstreetcafe.com) combines eight dart boards, three pool tables, and karaoke under one roof. On weekends, local rock and blues acts perform there.

Events

As long as Groton's sub base remains open, the sailors there will invite the public for **Subfest** (860/694-3559 or 800/343-0079, www.ussnautilus.org, early July), a celebration of all things deep and torpedo-filled on the Fourth of July. Not to be outdone, New London breaks the surface with **Sailfest** (860/440-1879, www.sailfest.org, early July), a downtown celebration at the same time with fireworks, a road race, a car show, and dance parties celebrating the city's Irish and Latino populations.

Shopping

Beyond the national chain stores that line **Crystal Mall** (850 Hartford Tnpk, Waterford, 860/442-8500, 10 A.M.–9 P.M. Mon–Sat.; 10 A.M.–6 P.M. Sun.), the area has few shopping spots. That said, it's worth a swing by **Hannoush Jewelers** (850 Hartford Tnpk, Waterford, 860/447-1922, www.hannoush.com, 9 A.M.–4:30 P.M. daily) for impressively crafted (and fairly priced) trinkets ranging from costume-level jewelry to fine pieces.

Information

The **Southeastern Connecticut Tourism District** (470 Bank St., 860/444-2206, www.mysticmore.com) runs a well-appointed visitors center downtown, as well as a staffed information booth at the corner of Golden Street and Eugene O'Neill Drive.

OLD LYME

To those outside Connecticut, the little town of Lyme is best known for the tick-borne disease that shares its name (and was first recognized here in 1977). For generations, however, the portside village of Old Lyme was better known as a center of an art colony that cemented the movement of American Impressionism. The colony began with an artist named Henry Ward Ranger, who arrived there in 1899 and took up quarters in a home owned by Florence Griswold. Other artists followed, and the community officially became a colony in 1903 with the arrival of Childe Hassam, who was already famous for employing the Impressionist techniques he had learned from study in France.

Griswold was the fairy godmother of the group, adding on rooms to her home and renovating other structures on her sprawling estate to accommodate artists. The home itself was the primary gallery of the artists, who began hanging works on palettes in the dining room, after a similar practice at the artists colony in Giverny, France. The home, now a museum, is located in the center of Old Lyme, which is now a center for art galleries and antiques.

Florence Griswold Museum

Located in the home of the art colony where "Miss Florence" welcomed her boarders, this giant columned museum (96 Lyme St., 860/434-5542, www.flogris.org, Krieble Gallery and Griswold House 10 A.M.–5 P.M. Tue.–Sat. and 1 A.M.–5 P.M. Sun.; Chadwick Studio mid-May–Oct., $9 adults, $8 seniors, $7students, free children 12 and under) displays three centuries worth of American art. Its main focus, however, is the American Impressionist movement, with major works by Childe Hassam, John Henry Twachtman,

and especially Willard Metcalf. Among the paintings are many that incorporate the Griswold house and surrounding countryside. The museum also features changing exhibits that often feature artists and movements with Connecticut associations.

Other Sights

The artistic traditions of Lyme are carried on by the **Lyme Academy College of Fine Arts** (84 Lyme St., 860/434-5232, www.lymeacademy.edu), which frequently holds gallery shows of student work. Professional artists exhibit through the **Lyme Art Association** (90 Lyme St., 860/434-7802, www.lymeartassociation.org), which has a gallery sandwiched between the museum and the school.

Events

Old Lyme's **Midsummer Festival** (860/434-5542, www.flogris.org, late July) evokes the feel of a European country fair with art exhibits and fresh country products. A highlight is the En Plein Aire market on the grounds of the Griswold Museum.

Shopping

There's a little bit of everything for self-pampering at **The Bowerbird** (46 Halls Rd., 860/434-3562, www.thebowerbird.com, 10 A.M.–5:30 P.M. Mon.–Sat.;11 A.M.–4 P.M. Sun.), with nearly 5,000 square feet of things for the home, for the kids, and for you. There are books (cookbooks to fiction to atlases), body creams, bath salts, embroidered pajamas, fancy clocks, kitchen gadgets, and adorable wooden toys for toddlers. The specialists who run **Oriental Rugs Limited** (23 Lyme St., 860/434-1167, www.orientalrugsltd.com, 10–4 P.M. Mon.–Sat.) have picked out such a beautiful stock of antique carpets (from locally woven to Oriental), their wares may just have you on the floor—literally.

Food

The wine list alone has earned a notable reputation for the dining at **Old Lyme Inn Grill** (Lyme St., 860/434-5352, www.oldlymeinn.

com, 11:30 A.M.–9 P.M. daily, $24–34), but go for the food, too. Anchored by a century-old oak bar, the restaurant sports no less than three fireplaces and a menu of steaks, oysters Rockefeller, and tandoori swordfish.

SPORTS AND RECREATION
Beaches
There's not a rock in sight at **Rocky Neck State Park** (244 W. Main St., 860/739-5471, http://dep.state.ct.us/stateparks/parks/rockyneck.htm, $9 in-state-registered vehicle or $14 out-of-state-registered vehicle weekends, $7 in-state or $10 out-of-state weekdays) outside of Old Lyme—just miles of white sand beach fronting Long Island Sound. The beach is a popular one with families. Other good swimming spots in the area include **Esker Point State Park** (Eastern Point Beach, Groton, 860/536-5680, $10 weekday parking, $20 weekend parking), a 600-foot stretch of sand with picnic facilities and snack bar; and the picturesque **DuBois Beach** (Water St., Stonington, 877/286-9784), which offers nice views of Stonington Harbor and shallow depths for swimming. The latter fills up quickly, so arrive early to snag a day-use permit.

Hiking and Biking
Behind the Denison Homestead Museum, the **Denison Pequotsepos Nature Center** (109 Pequotsepos Rd., 860/536-1216, www.dpnc.org, 9 A.M.–5 P.M. Mon.–Sat. and 10 A.M.–4 P.M. Sun. year-round, $6 adults, $4 seniors and children under 12) offers eight miles of gentle trails in its 300-acre nature preserve. Several species of hawks and owls hang out in flight enclosures on the grounds.

Boating and Fishing
Located just outside New London, the **Sunbeam Fleet** (15 First St., Waterford, 860/437-3699, www.sunbeamfleet.com, $40 adults, $37 seniors, $25 children under 12, plus $5 pole rental) has three boats of various sizes for deep-sea fishing charters. Two-to-three-day trips go out in search of tuna, shark, marlin, and swordfish. The fleet also runs lighthouse

cruises and seal-spotting expeditions. The 1967 windjammer **Mystic Whaler** (860/535-1556, www.mysticwhalercruises.com) sails from her home port of Mystic for multi-day cruises in search of whales, lighthouses, and moonlit nights. Ports of call include Block Island, Newport, Shelter Island, and New York City. The ship is also available for day sails on select dates.

ACCOMMODATIONS
Under $100
Acres of quiet woods surround the cozy **Fox Trail Lodge** (682 Norwich Westerly Rd., N. Stonington, 860/535-2721, www.foxtraillodge.com, $59–99), but while it may feel out of the way, it's actually a short drive to all the action in Mystic and the casinos. Simple early-American decor reigns here; think antique hutches and tables, fireplaces, and plush settees. All rooms have private baths.

$100-150
Owned and run by a family of ex-Manhattanites, **Old Lyme Inn** (85 Lyme St., Old Lyme, 860/434-2600, www.oldlymeinn.com, $135–175) is a perfect balance of sophistication and relaxation. Rooms all have queen or king canopy beds, pretty views, and include an excellent (and filling) continental breakfast.

Close to both Mystic Seaport and the Foxwoods and Mohegan Sun Casinos, **Groton Inn** (99 Gold Star Hwy., 860/445-9784, www.grotoninn.com, $80–173) is ideal for families, thanks to its plentiful, inexpensive suites with kitchenettes and microwaves.

$150-250
Its majestic views overlook Mystic Harbor and Long Island Sound, but that's just part of what makes **◖ The Inn at Mystic** (Rtes. 1 and 27, Mystic, 860/536-9604, www.innatmystic.com, $95–325) so darn pretty. Between the beautifully manicured flower gardens, the rooms outfitted in designer fabrics and massive beds (some with fireplaces, whirlpools, and patios), and the charming mansion itself, it's hard to decide where to look next. With

three rooms to let and a host of antiques to sell, **Antiques & Accommodations** (32 Main St., N. Stonington, 800/5547829, www.antiquesandaccommodations.com, $110–229) lives exactly up to its name. The two restored Victorian carriage houses have incredibly homey chambers with four-poster beds, and one with a fireplace. Meanwhile, breakfasts are no mere danish: the kitchen rolls out treats like cantaloupe mint soup, crab soufflés, and fresh-baked lemon-blueberry bread.

All ten rooms at the **Steamboat Inn** (73 Steamboat Wharf, 860/536-8300, www.steamboatinnmystic.com, $150–275) overlook the Mystic River, are a stone's throw from the sights of the Seaport, and come stashed with perks like DVD players and whirlpool baths. Complimentary tea, hot chocolate and coffee are offered all day long in the common rooms downstairs, as are sherry and cookies in the evening.

$250 and Up

All the major travel magazines have raved about **❇ Inn at Stonington** (60 Water St., Stonington, 860/535-2000, www.innatstonington.com, $160–440) at one point or another, and with excellent reason. The superbly run, impeccably kept spot offers personal (but never intrusive) service. The 18 rooms all look as though Martha Stewart herself decorated them; each comes with fireplaces and oversized bathrooms, and most have whirlpool tubs and modem ports, to boot. There's also a home-made continental breakfast, free bike loans, and use of the exercise room.

GETTING THERE

Amtrak (800/872-7245, www.amtrak.com) runs trains to stations in Mystic (Rte. 1), New London (27 Water St.), and Old Saybrook (455 Boston Post Rd.). **Greyhound** (800/231-2222, www.greyhound.com) operates bus service to New London (45 Water St.). New London is also a major hub for ferries crossing Long Island Sound, including the **Cross Sound Ferry** (2 Ferry St., 860/443-5281, www.longislandferry.com) to Orient Point, the **Viking Fleet** (631/668-5700, www.vikingfleet.com) to Montauk Point, and the **Block Island Ferry** (401/783-7996, www.blockislandferry.com) to Block Island.

GETTING AROUND

Bus company **Southeast Area Transit** (SEAT, 860/886-2631, www.seatbus.com) operates routes through area towns including New London, Groton, East Lyme, and Stonington. In addition, the **Discover New London Shuttle** (Eugene O'Neill Dr. at Golden St., 860/443-1209, www.newlondonhistory.org) makes loops around the city's major historic sights, bus and train stations, and ferry terminal.

WESTERN CONNECTICUT

The most common images of Connecticut come to us through the many movies and TV shows that depict the state as an idyllic—or sinister—land of wealthy suburbia, where attitudes are sophisticated and urbane. Sitcoms like *Bewitched, I Love Lucy, Who's the Boss?,* and *Gilmore Girls* were all filmed or took place here, while books and films such as *The Ice Storm* and *The Stepford Wives* skewered the pretensions of those who live here. Even the queen of suburban bliss, Martha Stewart, made her home in Connecticut for more than 25 years. All of those depictions hail from the western half of the state, which often seems more like one giant suburb of New York than an independent commonwealth. The richest zip code in the country is in Greenwich (06830), which anchors the far end of the so-called Gold Coast, the southwestern coastline that is filled with the mansions of one fabulous commuter town after another.

But that image is just one side of the story of western Connecticut, which encompasses a wide variety of landscapes. After all, just up the coast from Greenwich is one of the country's *poorest* zip codes, in the depressed city of Bridgeport. The western side of the state was once a strong industrial area, where cities each specialized in a different product. But during the 1950s, so-called white flight hit Connecticut harder than any other state, with wealthy and middle-class residents fleeing for the manicured cul-de-sacs of the suburbs and the cities left to fend for themselves. Some, like New Haven and Danbury, have since been gloriously reborn

© MICHAEL BLANDING

HIGHLIGHTS

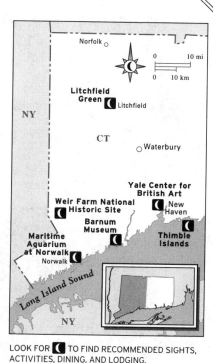

◖ **Yale Center for British Art:** Thousands of paintings, prints, and sculptures comprise the best collection of British art west of Land's End (page 289).

◖ **Thimble Islands:** This confetti of islands on Long Island sound is best explored at water-level, by kayak (page 296).

◖ **Barnum Museum:** The ringmaster turned mayor is front and center at this museum of art and oddities (page 298).

◖ **Maritime Aquarium at Norwalk:** Sharks, sea turtles, and Spongebob Squarepants await at this excellent marine aquarium (page 301).

◖ **Weir Farm National Historic Site:** The beauty of the estate that inspired three generations of artists never ceases to impress (page 306).

◖ **Litchfield Green:** Arguably the most attractive village green in New England, Litchfield's is ringed with historical buildings, restaurants, and boutiques (page 312).

LOOK FOR ◖ TO FIND RECOMMENDED SIGHTS, ACTIVITIES, DINING, AND LODGING.

into thriving urban centers. Others, like Bridgeport, Hartford, and Waterbury, continue to stagnate, looking for the right formula for a renaissance.

Outside of the city and the suburbs, however, the little-visited northwest corner of the state is as rural as rural can be. Known as the Litchfield Hills, the area is more Martha Washington than Martha Stewart, boasting rich associations with colonial history, scenic drives through gently rolling Berkshire foothills, and one immaculate village green after another. Unlike the hills in the eastern part of the state, however, the Litchfield area has benefited from traffic from New York, lending it a sophistication and culture that belies its seemingly sedate character.

PLANNING YOUR TIME

The must-visit destination in this corner of New England is the revitalized university city of New Haven, home to Yale and its many fine museums. The jewel in its crown is the highly acclaimed **Yale Center for British Art.** After a day or two in New Haven, give yourself another two or three days to drive down the coast. Along the way, take in several other fine museums, including the Big Top extravaganza of the **Barnum Museum** in Bridgeport, and the **Maritime Aquarium at Norwalk.** Alternatively, drive the other way, up the coast from New Haven to the sleepy town of Stony Creek, where you can tour the magical **Thimble Islands** by kayak or cruise ship.

The Gold Coast was also once home to the

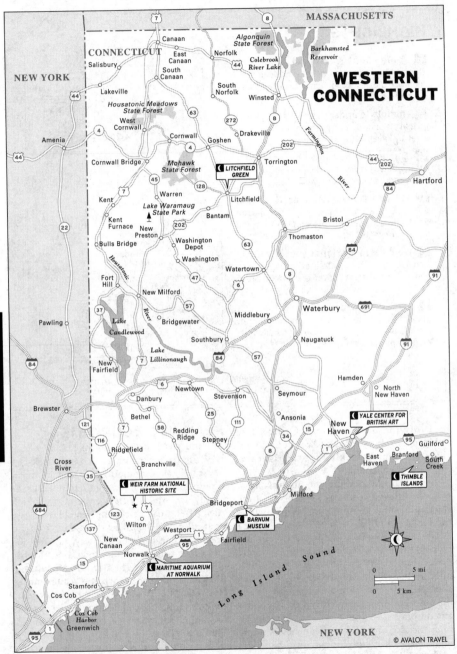

CONNECTICUT

artists of the American Impressionist movement. Several sights chronicle their time here, including the beautiful **Weir Farm National Historic Site.** In the northwestern part of the state, the Litchfield Hills are lacking in formal attractions, but that shouldn't stop you from spending several days driving up and down the hilly back roads, especially if it's foliage season. A good place to start your trip is **Litchfield Green,** a quaint country green surrounded by many historic buildings.

Greater New Haven

The city of New Haven is surrounded by a thriving area of quiet bedroom communities proud of their history and culture. This was one of the first areas of Connecticut to be settled, and residents have taken pride in retaining and restoring its many historic buildings. The presence of New Haven and Yale adds to the sophistication of the area, with many fine restaurants and boutiques nestled in the salt marshes.

NEW HAVEN

The shadow of Yale University looms large over this sprawled-out city perched on Long Island Sound. But said shadow is a benevolent one, and in most ways has become happily integral to the flavor of the city with its young, educated population, lively arts culture, and diverse restaurant scene. Truth be told, however, Yale is hardly New Haven's sole educational resource. They may not have quite the brand recognition, but other institutes of higher learning include the University of New Haven, Albertus Magnus College, and Quinnipiac and Southern Connecticut State Universities—each of which has contributed to the city's cultural life from their start.

The city itself—one of the country's oldest—was settled by Puritans in 1638, primarily along its harbor, which was used for shipping, commerce, and, of all things, oystering. (Still today, upwards of 30 percent of the state's oysters come from New Haven.) After thriving as an active port for three centuries, New Haven fell under the malaise that struck many other Connecticut cities in the mid-20th century, effectively making Yale an island in a city with a reputation for drugs and violence. More than any other city in the state, however, New Haven has experienced a miraculous rebirth in the last decade—led by an active decision by the university to invest in the city's infrastructure and improve its image. Nowadays, the city is known around the state as a funky and educated oasis. The liveliest areas tend be around the tree-lined green of Wooster Square and the College-Chapel Street districts.

◖ Yale Center for British Art

While Yale has many attractions worth visiting, this center (1080 Chapel St., 203/432-2800, http://ycba.yale.edu, 10 A.M.–5 P.M. Tues.–Sat.; noon–5 P.M. Sun., free) is particularly worth singling out. British art is frequently overshadowed by its more showy European neighbors from Italy and the Netherlands. But the United Kingdom has a style and artistic history all its own, and this museum is the largest and most comprehensive collection outside of the British Isles themselves. Highlights of the museums include the psychedelic drawings of poet-artist William Blake, the luminous seascapes of J. W. Turner, and the bucolic landscapes of Thomas Gainsborough and John Constable. The building itself is no slouch either; designed by Louis Kahn, it is a modernist grey cube confronting the adjoining plaza.

Yale University

Founded in 1701, Yale was the third college in the United States, and quickly established itself as a rival to its more venerable northern neighbor Harvard, a tradition of one-upsmanship that continues to this day. Unlike Harvard's redbrick, however, many of Yale's buildings are done in a striking Gothic style, making

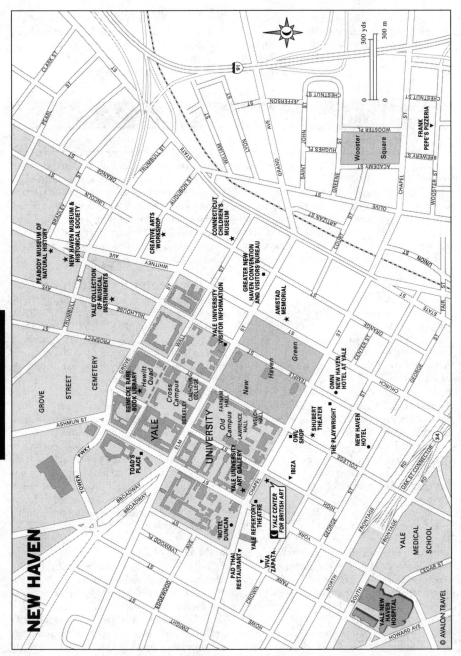

CONNECTICUT

NEW HAVEN

PEABODY MUSEUM OF NATURAL HISTORY
NEW HAVEN MUSEUM & HISTORICAL SOCIETY
YALE COLLECTION OF MUSICAL INSTRUMENTS
CREATIVE ARTS WORKSHOP
CONNECTICUT CHILDREN'S MUSEUM
GREATER NEW HAVEN CONVENTION AND VISITORS BUREAU
YALE UNIVERSITY VISITOR INFORMATION
AMISTAD MEMORIAL
BEINECKE RARE BOOK LIBRARY
Hewitt Quad
Cross Campus
Old Campus
Calhoun College
Farnam Hall
Lawrence Hall
Welch Hall
New Haven Green
OMNI NEW HAVEN HOTEL AT YALE
SHUBERT THEATER
THE PLAYWRIGHT
NEW HAVEN HOTEL
TOAD'S PLACE
OWL SHOP
IBIZA
YALE UNIVERSITY ART GALLERY
YALE CENTER FOR BRITISH ART
HOTEL DURAN
YALE REPERTORY THEATRE
PAD THAI RESTAURANT
VIVA ZAPATA
YALE MEDICAL SCHOOL
YALE NEW HAVEN HOSPITAL
FRANK PEPE'S PIZZERIA
Wooster Square

YALE UNIVERSITY

CEMETERY
STREET
GROVE

91

300 yds
300 m

© AVALON TRAVEL

THE *AMISTAD* AFFAIR

Most people had never heard of the slave ship *Amistad* until Steven Spielberg made a movie about it in 1997. But more than 150 years before the film hit theaters, the ship was a cause célèbre that galvanized the abolitionist movement and became a contributing factor to the Civil War. The *Amistad* was a Spanish vessel that in June 1839 was carrying slaves who had been bought in Africa and smuggled to Cuba in contravention of a treaty between Spain and Great Britain. In Cuban waters, a heroic slave named Cinque led his fellow captives in a rebellion, managing to kill the captain and commandeer the crew. Due to trickery by the sailmaster, however, the ship sailed not to Africa, but to Long Island, where it was seized by the Coast Guard and towed to New London, Connecticut. The 39 Africans – or Amistads, as they were called – were thrown into jail in New Haven to await judgment by the courts. During their time in New Haven, the Amistads exercised on the town green and charmed visitors with their attempts to communicate. They were caught, however, between the competing agendas of President Martin Van Buren, who was eager to return the Amistads to the jurisdiction of Spain, and the New England abolitionists led by Lewis Tappan, who mounted a defense based on the fact that the "slaves" were illegally captured in the first place. After a dramatic trial in Hartford, the Amistads prevailed, winning their freedom to stay in the United States. The government appealed the case twice, however, all the way to the Supreme Court, which was dominated by Southern slave owners. Fearing defeat, the abolitionists prevailed upon former president John Quincy Adams to argue the case. In an eloquent speech, Adams, then 79, made a referendum on slavery, saying, "The moment you come to the Declaration of Independence, that every man has a right to life and liberty, an inalienable right, this case is decided." In March 1941, the Supreme Court announced its decision: the Amistads were illegally kidnapped Africans and could be immediately freed to return to their homeland. Since the movie came out, the state of Connecticut has savvily capitalized on its role as the setting for the dramatic events. At visitors centers, the state offers a brochure titled the **Connecticut Freedom Trail** (www.ctfreedomtrail.ct.gov), which includes a list of sites associated with the case, including those in New Haven, Hartford, and Farmington. In addition, the New Haven Historical Society, the Wadsworth Atheneum in Hartford, and the Custom House Maritime Museum in New London all have artifacts relating to the case. Finally, a nonprofit called **Amistad America** (203/495-1839, www.amistadamerica.org) even built a fully functioning re-creation of the ship, with exhibits onboard tracing the roots of the uprising. Based in New Haven, the ship makes trips around the eastern United States and is often berthed for extended periods at Mystic Seaport.

CONNECTICUT

a tour of the campus a genuine visual treat. Tours start at the **Mead Visitor Center** (149 Elm St., 203/432-2300, www.yale.edu/visitor, 10:30 A.M. and 2 P.M. Mon.–Fri.; 1:30 P.M. Sat., free) and include visits to several of Yale's libraries, including the rare book library, which holds a copy of the Gutenberg Bible.

In addition to its collection of British art, Yale also has several other outstanding museums. The **Yale University Art Gallery** (1111 Chapel St., 203/432.0600, http://artgallery.yale.edu, 10 A.M.–5 P.M. Tues.–Sat., open until 8 P.M. Thurs., closed Sept.–June, free) holds art from all over the world, with a strong collection of Medieval European paintings and several fine canvases by American modernist Edward Hopper. The **Yale Collection of Musical Instruments** (15 Hillhouse Ave., 203/432-0822, www.yale.edu/musicalinstruments, 1–4 P.M. Tues.–Fri., 1–5 P.M. Sun., Sept.–June, free) includes instruments from all over the globe, starting with a 1,000-year-old Incan conch trumpet. A "sound gallery" plays highlights from Yale concerts. The **Peabody Museum of Natural History** (170 Whitney Ave., 203/432-5050 or 203/432-8987, www.yale.edu/peabody,

10 A.M.–5 P.M. Mon.–Sat.; noon–5 P.M. Sun., $7 adults, $6 seniors, $5 students and children 3–18, free to all 2–5 P.M. Thurs.) has exhibits drawn from Yale expeditions, including a fascinating study of the history of evolution. The centerpiece, however, remains the famous dinosaur skeletons—stegosaurus, triceratops, and brontosaurus—collected by C.O. Marsh, the museum's first director and one of the founding fathers of paleontology.

Other Sights
The **New Haven Museum & Historical Society** (114 Whitney Ave., 203/562-4183, www.newhavenmuseum.org, 10 A.M.–5 P.M. Tues.–Fri.; noon–5 P.M. Sat., $4 adults, $3 seniors, $2 students and children, free children under 6) contains a mishmash of 350 years of history, ranging from Quinnipiac artifacts to mementoes of New Haven's role in the China trade. The museum also has a collection of artifacts relating to the *Amistad* affair, including a striking portrait of the leader of the Africans, Joseph Cinque (also known as Sengbe Pieh), on trial. New Haven also pays homage to those brave Africans with its *Amistad* **Memorial** (165 Church St.), a 14-foot bronze relief sculpture that depicts their capture, trial, and return home. The monument was sculpted in 1992 and placed on the former site of the New Haven jail, where the crew was imprisoned in 1839 while they awaited trial.

Entertainment
A nationally known music hall, **Toad's Place** (300 York St., 203/624-8623, www.toadsplace.com) attracts names that range from unheard-of to huge (the Rolling Stones kicked off their tour on its stage in 1989). An ever-rotating roster of music (from reggae and pop to techno DJs and blues) keeps the scene fresh. With three bars (one juice-only) and an enormous waterfall near the dance floor, it's little wonder **Alchemy Nightclub** (223 College St., 203/777-9400) is packed nearly every night it's open. Undergrads, grad students, and twenty-something yups come to dance, flirt, or play pool in three separate rooms: a hip-hop room,

a house dance floor (complete with 30-foot wide waterfall) and a more chilled-out lounge room. Even more sedate schmoozing is the name of the game at **The Playwright** (144 Temple St., 203/752-0450, www.playwrightirishpub.com), a downtown Irish pub lined with gleaming woods and a wide, friendly bar filled with young professionals, construction workers, and (depending on the night) everyone in between.

Events
Every year, tennis's top names come to New Haven to compete in the **Pilot Pen Tennis Women's and Men's Championships** (203/776-7331 or 888/997-4568, www.pilotpentennis.com, mid-Aug.). Local residents join the celebration with jazz concerts and activities for kids. Just in time for the holidays, New Haven launches a **Celebration of American Crafts** (203/562-4927, www.creativeartsworkshop.org/html/exhibitions/cac.html, Nov.–Dec.), a juried craft show exhibition featuring jewelry, ceramics, and other items from hundreds of artisans from all over the country.

Shopping
What began as a bookstore in the 1940s has since morphed into **Owl Shop** (268 College St., 203/624-3250, www.owlshopcigars.com, 4 P.M.–1 A.M. Mon.; 10 A.M.–1 A.M. Tue.–Thu.; 10 A.M.–2 A.M. Fri.–Sat., noon–1 A.M. Sun.), one of the oldest cigar and tobacco shops in the country. Behind the kitschy-retro facade, you'll come upon imported pipes and endless glass cases filled with smoking accessories. If you're dying to partake, take a seat in the adjoining brick-walled café, have a drink, and puff away. Step inside **Casablanca Boutique** (1146 Chapel St., 203/562-7700, 10:30 A.M.–6:30 P.M. Mon.–Sat.) to Arabic music and a collection of African masks, chunky bright gold jewelry, and belly-dancer costumes (on which alterations are offered for a small fee). The New Haven outpost of **Ten Thousand Villages** (1054 Chapel St., 203/776-0854, http://newhaven.tenthousandvillages.com, 10 A.M.–6 P.M. Mon.–Wed.; 10 A.M.–8 P.M.

Thu.–Sat.; 1 P.M.–6 P.M. Sun.) is chock-full of fairly traded crafts from all over the planet. Pick up a hand-carved giraffe for the living room, a chunky necklace made of semiprecious beads, or hand-woven table linens.

Food
The pizza was reportedly introduced to America in New Haven, so it's only natural that the city's pizzerias would be its pride. Exhibit A is (**Frank Pepe's Pizzeria** (157 Wooster St., 203/865-5762, www.pepespizzeria.com, 11:30 A.M.–10 P.M. Mon.–Sat.; noon–10 P.M. Sun., $8–14). The simple interior lets the pies take center stage, with toppings from mozzarella and bacon to mushrooms and fresh clams. Pull up a chair at one of the wide, burnished-wood tables of **Viva Zapata** (161 Park St., 203/562-2499, 11:30 A.M.–4 P.M. daily; 4 P.M.–midnight Sun.–Thu., 4 P.M.–1 A.M. Fri.–Sat., $6–16) and brace your taste buds for some simple-but-good Mexican food. Staples like tostadas and fajitas are always available, as are seafood chimichangas and *filet con queso* (butterflied filet mignon stuffed with jack cheese and jalapenos). Italy meets Spain in a quirky-but-happy collision at **Ahimsa** (1227 Chapel St., 203/786-4774, 4:30 P.M.–10 P.M. Mon.–Sat.; 5 P.M.–9 P.M. Sun., $12–20). Here find healthy tapas (read: tasty vegan snacks) in the adjoining room, and heftier (but still vegan) entrées of squash fettucine in nut cheese Alfredo sauce, stuffed beets, and lasagna of zucchini, marinara, and freshly made pesto. The reign in Spain starts at (**Ibiza** (39 High St., 203/865-1933, www.ibizanewhaven.com, noon–2:30 P.M. Fri.; 5–9 P.M. Mon.–Thu.; 5–10 P.M. Fri.–Sat., $25–29), an excellent place to sample grilled sea scallops in Catalan squid ink pasta or steamed octopus with potato emulsion. For dessert, don't bypass the flans—particularly the sweet-sour green-apple version. The name of **Pad Thai Restaurant** (170 Chapel St., 203/562-0322, 11:30 A.M.–10 P.M. Sun.; 11:30 A.M.–3:30 P.M. and 5–10 P.M. Mon.–Thu.; 11:30 A.M.–3:30 P.M. and 5–10:30 P.M. Fri.; 11:30 A.M.–10:30 P.M. Sat., $6–16) may be a little on the pedestrian side, but the food is anything but. Authentic Thai is all over the menu here—from the spicy *chaiya* noodles (with seafood and basil in red curry) to the whole fried fish with coriander.

Information
New Haven is served by the **Greater New Haven Convention and Visitors Bureau** (169 Orange St., New Haven, 203/777-8550, www.newhavencvb.com). For maps, brochures, and reservations, stop by **INFO New Haven** (1000 Chapel St., 203/773-9494, www.infonewhaven.com), which runs an information center downtown.

AROUND NEW HAVEN
With New Haven as the big draw for visitors, the outlying areas of the city are generally content to serve as quiet suburbs. As the sixth-oldest town in the state (founded in 1639), the small but squeaky-clean Milford abuts a pretty harbor fed by Long Island Sound. The town green, complete with gardens, a gazebo, and several monuments, is the pride of the community. Just north of New Haven, the cultural mecca of Hamden sits in the shadow of an unusually shaped mountain known as the "sleeping giant" for its similarity to a reclining man. In addition to acres of hiking and biking trails, the town was once home to inventor Eli Whitney.

Up the coast to the east, meanwhile, the pretty seaside towns of Brandon and Guilford compete in the beauty contest with their own meticulous town greens. Brandon is known for its quirky museums and revitalized downtown, as well as its ready access to the beautiful Thimble Islands. Guilford sports several historic house museums as well as miles of trails along picturesque coastal wetlands.

Eli Whitney Museum
Until the light bulb, no invention in American history was as momentous as that of the cotton gin, an innovative machine that separated out the sticky green seeds from cotton bales grown on Southern plantations, allowing cotton growers to actually turn a profit

CONNECTICUT

in the enterprise. The machine was invented by Eli Whitney, a Yale graduate working as a tutor in Georgia at the time. This museum (915 Whitney Ave., Hamden, 203/777-1833, www.eliwhitney.org, noon–4 P.M. daily summer; noon–5 P.M. Wed.–Fri., 10 A.M.–3 P.M. Sat., noon–5 P.M. Sun. winter; rates vary by exhibit, call for specifics), which fills the house where he lived in later years, details the invention of the machine as well as how it changed the course of American history. Because of Whitney's invention, cotton profits doubled each decade after 1800, fueling the industrialization of New England through its textile mills and, as an unfortunate side effect, the slave trade.

As for Whitney, he didn't do as well as his invention. Forced into costly lawsuits to protect his patent, he eventually left the South virtually penniless and headed back to New Haven. Even in later life, however, his mind was forever curious—in New Haven he invented a manufacturing technique for rifles that was a precursor to the modern assembly line, eventually revolutionizing factories even though he didn't live to see it. The museum carries on his spirit with interactive activities for kids to assemble simple machines designed by museum staff.

Shore Line Trolley Museum

Once upon a time, every major American city had at least one trolley line, and most of them had a dozen. With the coming of the automobile, the tracks were ripped up one by one and the trains put out to pasture. Many of them have found their way to this wonderful little museum (17 River St., East Haven, 203/467-6927, www.bera.org, 10 A.M.–5 P.M. Sat.–Sun. Apr.–late May and mid-Sept.–mid-Nov., daily late May–mid-Sept, $8 adults, $6 seniors and students, $4 children 2–15, children under 2 free), which has 100 antique trolley cars and operates a 3-mile train ride along the tracks. The museum is open daily from Memorial Day to Labor Day and on weekends during the spring and fall. It is closed January through March.

Puppet Show Theater

Erase all images of socks and paper bags… The puppets at this marionette theater (128 Thimble Island Rd., Stony Creek, 203/488-5752, www.puppethouse.org, shows 7–11 P.M.; doors open at 5:30, tickets $10 unless otherwise noted) are elaborate works of art from turn-of-the-century Sicily. Collected by a local puppet aficionado, the 300-some puppets are made of steel-reinforced hardwood, complete with silk robes and brass body armor, each weighing up to 80 pounds. Known as the Stony Creek Puppets, they perform regularly in scripts drawn from Medieval European poetry. When they are not on stage, they display their finery in the lobby.

Other Sights

The tiny town of Milford has a great collection of houses dating from the 17th and 18th centuries around its town green. Three of them, including the oldest in town, have combined to serve as the setting for the **Milford Historical Society** (34 High St., 208/874-2664, www.geocities.com/siliconvalley/park/3831, Sun. 1–4 P.M. late May–mid-Oct., free). The rooms inside have been restored to their colonial-era time period and include a collection of Native American artifacts and a mock-up of a general store. On the other side of New Haven, Guilford has an even older home in the 1639 **Henry Whitfield Museum** (248 Old Whitfield St., Guilford, 203/453-2457, www.whitfieldmuseum.org, 10 A.M.–4:30 P.M. Wed.–Sun. Apr.–mid-Dec., $4 adults, $3 seniors and students, $2.50 children 6–17, free children under 6). The all-stone home has the feel of an old English manor house; among the exhibits here are several Revolutionary-era muskets.

Entertainment and Events

Live blues, comedy shows, retro dance parties, and open mic nights are held every night of the week at loud but fun **Daniel Street** (21 Daniel St., Milford, 203/877-4446, www.danielstreetclub.com).

Dads have a reason to celebrate during the

Branford Festival (www.branfordfestival.com, June), a three-day celebration filled with music, food, and a road race every Father's Day weekend. During the holidays, Milford ups the cuteness quotient with **Christmas Candlelight House Tours** (Wharf Ln., Milford, 203/874-2664, early Dec.) of the village's historic homes, which are decked out for the season. Expect carols and hot drinks.

Food

Filling and oozing with cheese, the pies at **Bella Napoli Pizza** (864 Boston Post Rd., Milford, 203/877-1102, www.bellanapolionline.com, 11 A.M.–11 P.M. Mon.–Thu.; 11 A.M.–midnight Fri.–Sat.; 11 A.M.–10 P.M. Sun., $6–19) are said to feed half of Milford on weekend nights. Specialty pizzas include creations like clams casino, three cheese, and the Philly Cheesesteak. With its wide windows and simple interior, **Café Atlantique** (33 River St., Milford, 203/882-1602, www.cafeatlantique.us, 8 A.M.–7 P.M. Mon.–Tue.; 8 A.M.–10 P.M. Wed.–Sat.; 8 A.M.–6 P.M. Sun., $5–9) is an ideal spot for quick-but-tasty (and inexpensive) lunches. Order up a pesto-chicken panini and smoothie, or opt for the crepes, which are the stars of the show. There are savory renditions (try the goat cheese, olives, and almonds) as well as sweet (banana and Nutella).

The easygoing pace at **Gusto Trattoria** (255 Boston Post Rd., Milford, 203/876-7464, www.gustotrattoria.com, 11:30 A.M.–10 P.M. Mon.–Fri.; 4–10 P.M. Sat.; 4–8:30 P.M. Sun., $9–26) won't have you out the door in a hurry, but it will guarantee you a meal of fresh northern Italian flavors. The pastas—and gnocchi in particular—are excellent.

Popular with Quinnipiac students for its cheap, filling pizza, **Si Mangia** (3825 Whitney Rd., Hamden, 203/230-8610, www.simangia.com, 11 A.M.–9 P.M. Sun.–Wed.; 11 A.M.–10 P.M. Thu.–Sat., $6–15) is where to grab a quick slice on the way in or out of town. Both student- and family-friendly, **Aunt Chilada's** (3931 Whitney Rd., Hamden, 203/230-4640, http://auntchilada.com, 11 A.M.–1 A.M. Sun.–Thurs.; 11 A.M.–2 A.M. Fri. and Sat., $6–16)

has regular taco nights, happy hours, and kids-eat-free nights (Sun. 4–8 P.M.).

The chef-owner of **Le Petit Cafe** (225 Montowese St., Branford, 203/483-9791, www.lepetitcafe.net, 6–9 P.M., Wed.–Sun., $50 prix fixe for four courses) may be originally from Hong Kong, but the restaurant itself is a perfect evocation of a French bistro. Four-course prix fixe dinners are served in a dining room that feels formal without feeling pretentious. The menu includes bistro standards like cassoulet and *moules frites*, expertly prepared by chef Roy Ip, who was trained in Paris. As a nod to his homeland, however, a couple of Asian-inspired dishes have sneaked their way onto the menu.

One of the best places in New England to sample native seafood is also one of the simplest. The red-and-white outdoor canopy sits right along the highway of Route 1 at ◖ **The Place** (901 Boston Post Rd./Rte. 1, Guilford, 203/453-9276, 5–10 P.M. Mon.–Fri., 1–10 P.M. Sat., noon–10 P.M. Sun. late Apr.–mid-Oct., $9–25), where all manner of seafood is cooked on a huge outdoor grill. "Guests" sit down on stumps along large picnic tables to dig into fire-roasted lobster, clams, and, if they are lucky, melt-in-your-mouth filets of smoky fresh bluefish.

Shopping

Tasteful souvenirs abound at **The Canvas Patch** (5 River St., Milford, 203/878-7505, www.downtownmilfordct.com, 10:30 A.M.–5 P.M. Mon.–Sat.; noon–4 P.M. Sun.), which mixes imports from Germany and Russian nesting dolls with locally made totes, scrimshaw, and garden sculptures. Colorful works by local painters sit next to intricate blown glass and jewelry (some tame, some outlandish) in the eclectic **Gilded Lily Gallery** (101 Rover St., Milford, 203/878-7007, www.gildedlilygallery.com, 10 A.M.–6 P.M. Tue.–Sat., 10 A.M.–4 P.M. Sun.).

If it's funky, metal, and wearable, you'll probably find it at **Given to Gauche** (4 Daniel St., Milford, 203/878-2625, www.giventogauche.com, 10 A.M.–6 P.M. Mon.–Sat.), a cheeky little studio for artist Susan Ashelford. Her expressive and colorful pieces range from wire-wrapped shell necklaces to postmodern pearl-strung bracelets.

As the name suggests, **Basic Black** (3540 Whitney Ave., Hamden, 203/407-7722, www.basic-blacketc.com, 10:30–5 P.M. Tue.–Sat., open until 6 P.M. Thu.) is a retail ode to the color's essential place in every woman's wardrobe. Its racks are full of black pantsuits, black skirts, black button-downs, and—you guessed it—little black dresses. Vintage fiends find bliss at **Dava** (2100 Dixwell Ave., Hamden, 203/230-0039, www.shopdava.com, 10 A.M.–6 P.M. Mon.–Tue. And Fri.–Sat.; 10 A.M.–7 P.M. Wed.–Thu.; noon–5 P.M. Sun), a boutique specializing in women's shirts and dresses, plus musical instruments, books, and body products like soaps, oils, and aromatherapy candles.

Information

Information on the region is available from the **Greater New Haven Convention & Visitors Bureau** (59 Elm St., New Haven, 203/777-8550, www.newhavencvb.org).

◖ THIMBLE ISLANDS

The scattered archipelago off the coast of Branford is named after the thimbleberry, a cousin to the raspberry that grows wild on the islands. They could just as well be named for their diminutive size, however; in addition to 24 populated islands, literally hundreds of pink granite outcroppings poke their peaks out of the waves. The islands are home to a variety of critters, including a winter population of seals—and a summer influx of rich people from New York, who have built elaborate mansions, tiny cottages, and even little gazebos on the rocks.

In addition to being unlike anything else on the Connecticut (or for that matter New England) coast, the islands have spawned dozens of legends, such as an enduring myth that the pirate Captain Kidd buried treasure on so-called Money Island. The best way to take in the islands is at sea level, from the vantage of

your very own sea kayak. Owner Christopher Hauge leads expeditions out to the Thimbles with **Connecticut Coastal Kayaking** (Stony Creek, 860/391-3837, www.ctcoastalkayaking.com, May–Oct., $80–100/2.5 hour tour), giving impromptu seminars on sealife and history with each stroke of the paddle. If you'd rather let someone else do the paddling, sign up for a cruise with "Captain Mike," who grew up among the Thimbles and now leads tours aboard the *Sea Mist* (Thimble Island Rd., Stony Creek, May–Oct., $10 adults, $9 seniors, $5 children under 12).

SPORTS AND RECREATION
Hiking and Biking

Along the Milford coast, the **Connecticut Audubon Coastal Center** (1 Milford Point Rd., Milford, 203/878-7440, www.ctaudubon.org, 10 A.M.–4 P.M. Tues.–Sat.; noon–4 P.M. Sun.) is located on a protected tidal estuary that's home to a rich variety of bird species. An elevated boardwalk along the marsh leads to a 70-foot observation platform with expansive views of the shoreline. On the northern edge of New Haven proper, **East Rock Park** (Cold Spring and Orange Sts., 203/946-6086, www.cityofnewhaven.com) has a dozen hiking trails through its wooded hills. A monument to soldiers and sailors caps the crest of East Rock, which offers views down to Long Island Sound. A nature center on the property also teaches about local flora and fauna. You can say you bested a giant at **Sleeping Giant State Park** (200 Mt. Carmel Rd., Hamden, 203/789-7498, www.ct.gov), which offers 32 miles of moderate hiking trails, including a popular climb up to a stone observation tower on the giant's left hip.

Sailing

The 91-foot gaff-rigged schooner *Quinnipiack* is known as the flagship of New Haven. Through the nonprofit **Schooner, Inc.** (60 South Water St., New Haven, 203/865-1737, www.schoonerinc.org, 6–9 P.M. Wed. and Fri.; 1–4 P.M. and 5–8 P.M. Sun., $25 adults, $10 children 12 and under), it makes trips out into the sound for history and natural-history tours.

ACCOMMODATIONS
Under $100
Vintage couches and a marble lobby belie the low nightly price tag of **Hotel Duncan** (1151 Chapel St., New Haven, 203/787-1273, www.hotelduncan.com, $78–109), located a block away from Yale. It's the oldest hotel in the city—a fact that can occasionally show in small details—but overall adds an authentic charm to the place. Rooms on the top floor have outstanding views.

$100-150
Located smack downtown and close to just about everything, **New Haven Hotel** (229 George St., New Haven, 203/498-3100, www.newhavenhotel.com, $100–140) is both convenient and quiet. Rooms offer good perks (from data ports to free newspapers), and the property's health club includes a pool.

A Touch of Ireland Guest House (670 Whitney Ave., New Haven, 203/787-7997, www.touchofirelandguesthouse.com, $130–150) sits just on the cusp of Yale's campus—and that's hardly its only convenience. The rooms come with fireplaces and a full gourmet breakfast; the inn houses a lovely sun room and offers fax and Internet service.

$150-200
A quick drive to the Connecticut Wine Trail, **The Inn & Vineyard at Chester** (318 West Main St., Chester, 860/526-9541, www.innatchester.com, $135–190) sits on 20 acres of quiet rolling lawn, and houses 44 immaculate rooms furnished with canopied pencil post beds, orthopedic mattresses, and several with fireplaces. The rooms are part colonial-era cuteness, part modern-era comforts at **Farnam**

Guest House (616 Prospect St., New Haven, 203/562-2843, www.farnamguesthouse.com, $99–225). A glance around includes restored armoires and writing desks in sunny, pretty rooms, whereas a night's stay also includes an enormous breakfast your appetite won't soon let you forget.

Built with Ivy League bigwig visitors in mind, the ◖ **Omni New Haven Hotel at Yale** (155 Temple St., New Haven, 203/772-6664, www.omnihotels.com, $180–220) is the luxury choice for its health club, rooftop restaurant, function space, and scads of business services (including a business center).

GETTING THERE AND AROUND
A half dozen daily flights from Philadelphia arrive at **Tweed New Haven Regional Airport** (155 Burr St., New Haven, 203/466-8833, www.flytweed.com), which also offers seasonal flights to Orlando, Florida. Both **Amtrak** (800/872-7245, www.amtrak.com) and **Metro North** (800/638-7646, www.mta.nyc.ny.us) run trains to and from Union Station (50 Union Ave.); **Greyhound** (203/772-2470, www.greyhound.com) and **Peter Pan Bus Lines** (800/343-9999, www.peterpanbus.com) provide bus routes to the same location.

The New Haven regional service of **CT Transit** (203/624-0151, www.cttransit.com) operates buses around the city and immediate suburbs. **Milford Transit** (203/874-4507, www.ci.milford.ct.us) runs shuttle buses around the town of Milford. The **Shore Line East** (800/255-7433, www.shorelineeast.com) commuter rail service runs trains to Guilford, Brandon, and other eastern suburbs, continuing on to New London.

CONNECTICUT

Fairfield County

The closest swath of New England to New York, the coastal stretch between Greenwich and Fairfield is considered but a suburb of Manhattan to many of those who live here. Over the years, these urban refugees have plowed their Wall Street or Madison Avenue wealth into terrific seaside mansions and expansive country retreats, earning the area the not-ironic nickname "the Gold Coast." In the midst of them, the mid-sized city of Norwalk has struggled back from depression with the revitalization of its beautiful waterfront area. While on the far side to the east, the big and brash Bridgeport is off-putting in its sprawl but holds its own charms with several small museums such as the wonderfully quirky Barnum Museum.

BRIDGEPORT AND FAIRFIELD

Bridgeport owes its status as Connecticut's largest city primarily to its river and harbor access, which propelled its industry starting in the early 19th century. Alas, in the latter half of the 20th century it fell on hard times, becoming one of the poorest cities in America, and attempts at urban renewal have resulted in waves of unfortunate architecture in place of historic buildings. Only now does the city seem to be coming around, with corruption finally cleaned up and a new waterfront development seemingly leading the city on the right track. True revival, however, still seems some ways off.

On the flip side is relatively sleepy Fairfield, next door. It never hit the big time that Bridgeport did, which may have ultimately been its saving grace. One of the state's oldest settlements, it was originally named Fairfield because the farmers who moved there found its marshland ideal for raising cattle. And because it has always depended largely on farming, the town has stayed unusually scenic and industry-free. Add to all that the serenity of Fairfield's lakes and beaches, and it's little wonder so many city residents make the pretty town a weekend destination.

◖ Barnum Museum

It may be true that "there's a sucker born every minute," but if you believe that P. T. Barnum originally said that, you might be one yourself. The colorful Big Top ringmaster almost certainly never said the famous phrase, which was attributed to him by a vengeful newspaper columnist. And that's only the beginning of the revelations at this fun and quirky museum (820 Main St., Bridgeport, 203/331-1104, www.barnum-museum.org, 10 A.M.–4:30 P.M. Tues.–Sat.; noon–4:30 P.M. Sun., $7 adults, $5 students and seniors, $4 children 4–17, free for members and children under 4) celebrating the life of one of the most out-sized characters of the 19th century. Phineas Taylor Barnum wasn't only a circus master—in his long and varied career, he was a journalist, museum owner, and even mayor of Bridgeport.

This Romanesque castle-like building now holds the collection of Victorian historical and scientific items that Barnum helped collect when he bequeathed funds to the city in 1891. The most interesting exhibits, of course, are those relating to Barnum and his Big Top career, including a scale model of his famous "Three-Ring Circus," a 700-pound stuffed elephant, and displays relating to circus performers like Tom Thumb and Jenny Lind, the "Swedish Nightingale." It may just be the "Greatest Show on Earth," and if you believe that…well, you know.

Beardsley Zoological Gardens

Barnum used to take his circus animals for a stroll in Bridgeport's Beardsley Park. That fact inspired the city to create this wildlife park (1875 Noble Ave., Bridgeport, 203/394-6565, www.beardsleyzoo.org, 9 A.M.–4 P.M. daily, $11 adults, $9 seniors and children 3–11, free for children under 3 and Connecticut Zoological Society members), which has more than 300 animals. The grounds were designed by renowned landscape architect Frederick Law Olmsted and make a pleasing walk in any type

CONNECTICUT FOR KIDS

Just when you start to think Connecticut is all stores filled with fragile antiques and quiet inns, suddenly you bump right into one of the state's many kid-friendly spots. In fact, there's loads of hands-on fun for the wee ones in these parts, starting with the **Beardsley Zoo,** the state's only zoo, where you can see plenty of species (some endangered) in well-kept environments. There's a tropical rainforest full of exotic birds, a carousel, restaurant, and picnic areas. At the **Peabody Museum of Natural History** you'll find live animals alongside brontosaurus and stegosaurus skeletons and exhibits on evolution and Ancient Egypt, plus rocks, minerals, and meteorites. **The Essex Steam Train & Riverboat Ride** (1 Railroad Ave., Essex, 860/767-0103, www.essexsteamtrain.com, daily late Jun.-early Sept.; weekends May-Jun. and Sept.-Oct.) lets families cruise a riverboat down the Connecticut River, then hop on board an authentic steam locomotive. Meanwhile, the **Children's Museum of South-**

eastern Connecticut (409 Main St., Niantic, 860/691-1111, www.childrensmuseumsect.org, 9:30 A.M.-5 P.M. Tue.-Sat.; noon-5 P.M. Sun. year-round) offers rotating indoor and outdoor exhibits that literally let kids get their hands on subjects like sciences, literacy, culture, and world geography. It's all fun and games at **Quassy Amusement Park** (Rte. 64, Middlebury, 203/758-2913, www.quassy.com, daily Jun.-Aug.; weekends Apr.-May and Sept.-Oct.), the 20-acre family playground on Lake Quassapaug with interactive water attractions, swimming, boat rides, and live entertainment. Still more water fun happens at **Mystic Aquarium & Institute for Exploration,** home to Amazon and African penguin exhibits, plus sea lion shows and live marine animals. Or, head straight into the state's historic relationship with the sea at **Mystic Seaport.** Sure, it's crowded, but for good reason: Kids love exploring the wooden whalers, historic tall ships, the planetarium, and working shipyard.

of weather. Highlights of the exhibits include an indoor rainforest, an energetic troupe of monkeys, and the éminence grise, a Siberian tiger named Robeki.

Housatonic Museum of Art

Ordinarily, community colleges aren't ones to harbor significant art collections. But this museum (900 Lafayette Blvd., Bridgeport, 203/332-5052, www.hcc.commnet.edu/artmuseum, 8:30 A.M.–5:30 P.M. Mon.–Fri., Thurs. until 7 P.M., 9 A.M.–3 P.M. Sat., noon–4 P.M. Sun. Sept.–May; closed weekends June–Aug., free) on the grounds of Housatonic Community-Technical College is the exception to the rule. Among the 4,000 objects in the museum's collection are modern-art originals by Rodin, Picasso, Matisse, Miro, and Chagall.

Other Sights

Kids can plan their very own space shuttle mission to Mars at the **Discovery Museum** (4450 Park Ave., Bridgeport, 203/372-3521, www.discoverymuseum.org, hours scheduled weekly, $8.50 adults, $7 seniors, students and children 5–17, free for children under 5), a children's museum full of interactive exhibits that teach about science and teamwork. The museum also includes art exhibits for both adults and kids and a planetarium with two shows daily.

More animals are on display at the **Connecticut Audubon Birdcraft Museum** (314 Unquowa Rd., Fairfield, 203/259-0416, www.ctaudubon.org/visit/birdcraft.htm, 9 A.M.–1 P.M. Tues.–Fri year-round, $2 adults, $1 children under 14), the country's first nature center, established in 1914. The dioramas and dinosaur footprints inside the small museum are showing their age a bit, but still make an engaging trip into the way Nutmeggers saw their wildlife 100 years ago. The museum sits on six acres of sanctuary teeming with avian species.

Fairfield's namesake liberal arts college,

Fairfield University (1073 North Benson Rd., Fairfield, 203/254-4000, www.fairfield. edu) doesn't have much in the way of formal attractions, but the gorgeous tree-lined campus will have you sighing for the days when you could spread out on the quad with a good book. While you are there, sit awhile in the peaceful Japanese Garden, or check out the small but significant **Kress Foundation Collection** (DiMenna-Nyselius Library, Room 302, Fairfield University, Fairfield, 203/254-4000, ext. 2215, www.fairfield.edu/arts/art_kress.html, by appt., restricted hours, call for information) of paintings by Old Masters from Italy.

Entertainment
Popular for its monthly Poetry & Beer series, the lovably scruffy **Acoustic Cafe** (2926 Fairfield Ave., Bridgeport, 203/335-3655, www.acousticcafe.com) is also a venue for live folk, blues, jazz, and bluegrass, plus the occasional rock show. The **Downtown Cabaret Theatre** (263 Golden Hill, Bridgeport, 203/576-1636, www.dtcab.com) stages musical productions from *Hair* to *Heidi*. Or grab a nightcap at **Southport Brewing Company** (2600 Post Rd., Fairfield, 203/256-2337), a mellow brewpub in which homemade beer takes center stage.

Events
Barnum would be proud of the celebration launched in his honor every June. The **Barnum Festival** (203/367-8495 or 866/867-8495, www.barnumfestival.com, July) fills downtown Bridgeport with fireworks, parades, and circus performers. A long-running church festival takes advantage of Fairfield's leafy goodness with the annual **Dogwood Festival** (203/259-5596, http://web.me.com/greenfieldhillchurch, mid-May), which includes a bake-off and craft tables.

Shopping
Grab a well-priced bottle of wine for the picnic at **Harry's Wine and Liquor** (2094 Post Rd., Fairfield, 203/259-4692, www.harryswine.

com, 8 A.M.–8 P.M. Mon.–Thu.; 8 A.M.–9 P.M. Fri.–Sat.), stocked with more than 4,000 labels. The highly knowledgeable staff will be more than happy to help you find just the right vintage. Gather the victuals to go with it at **The Pantry** (1580 Post Rd., Fairfield, 203/259-0400, www.thepantry.net, 7 A.M.–7 P.M. Mon.–Sat.), a gourmet grocery shop with fresh-baked pastries, prepared delicacies, and an on-site butcher. High-quality, upscale men's clothing (from shoes and shirts to tuxes)—much of it imported from Italy and hand-tailored—is for sale at **Fairfield Clothiers** (1551 Post Rd., Fairfield, 203/255-8889, www.suityourself.com, 11 A.M.–7 P.M. Mon.–Fri.; 10 A.M.–6 P.M. Sat.; by appt. Sun.). Incessant travelers (armchair and otherwise) will fall in love with **Where in the World** (27 Unquowa Rd., Fairfield, 203/254-2627, 10 A.M.–6 P.M. Mon.–Thu.; 10 A.M.–5 P.M. Fri.–Sat.), which has everything your wanderlust requires: maps, atlases, plus luggage, and guides.

Food
Vegetarians gasp with happiness at the sight of the menus at **Bloodroot Restaurant** (85 Ferris St., Bridgeport, 203/576-9168, www.bloodroot.com, 11:30 A.M.–2:30 P.M. Tue. and Thu.–Sun; 6–9 P.M. Tue.–Thu.; 6–10 P.M. Fri.–Sat., $8–14), housed in a funky feminist bookstore. The lengthy roster of options includes dishes like penne in slow-roasted tomato sauce, tempeh-stuffed eggplant, and *spanikopita*. Don't show up at **Taco Loco** (3170 Fairfield Ave., Bridgeport, 203/335-8228, www.tacoloco.com, 11:30 A.M.–10 P.M. Mon.–Thu.; 11:30 A.M.–10:30 P.M. Fri.–Sat.; 11:30 A.M.–9:30 P.M. Sun., $8–14) expecting burrito-stand staples. Everything here is homemade, from the mahimahi with cilantro to the shrimp and scallop enchiladas. Delectable Spanish and Argentine tapas and entrées fly from the kitchen at the loud-and-happening ◖ **Barcelona Wine Bar** (4180 Black Rock Turnpike, Fairfield, 203/255-0800, $9–14 for small plates). Dishes are just as lively as the room, too—specialties like pan-seared grouper with grilled fennel and skirt steak with deep-

green *chimichurri* sauce. Named after one of the oldest cities in South India, **Tanjore** (222C Post Rd., Fairfield, 203/255-1970, http://tanjorect.com, $8–12) serves excellent North and South Indian dishes in a pastel-purple dining room.

Information
For more information on Bridgeport and Fairfield, contact the **Coastal Fairfield County Convention & Visitors Bureau** (203/853-7770, www.coastalct.com).

WESTPORT TO STAMFORD
This area is the heart of Connecticut's so-called "Gold Coast," a name that presumably refers to more than just the color of the leaves in fall. Westport is the community that Ricky and Lucy moved to in *I Love Lucy* and where Martha Stewart lived for 25 years. It's a largely residential community of quiet cul-de-sacs and giant trophy houses. Next up, the maritime city of Norwalk is still very much tied to its past. Its long history is best embodied along the Norwalk River in the redeveloped and trendy South Norwalk neighborhood (which has been cheekily rebranded SoNo). That's the place for shopping excursions, excellent dinners, and late-night dancing.

By contrast, Stamford is all business—large corporations are headquartered here, and have modernized seemingly every inch of the metropolis. Most of the tourist attractions lie in the northern area of the city, where the bulk of shops, restaurants, museums, and entertainment can be found.

◖ Maritime Aquarium at Norwalk
Rivaling the New England Aquarium in Boston, this aquatic wonderland (10 North Water St., Norwalk, 203/852-0700, www.maritimeaquarium.org, 10 A.M.–6 P.M. daily July–Aug.; 10 A.M.–5 P.M. daily Sept.–June, $12–24 adults, $11–21 seniors, $10–19 children 2–12) also happens to be a model of how to do redevelopment right. When the aquarium opened inside a dramatic 19th-century brick ironworks factory in 1986, it spurred the revitalization of the entire SoNo area. Now half a million visitors annually pass through its doors to commune with sharks, river otters, sea turtles, and 1,000 other animals in two sprawling floors of exhibits. Of course there are plenty of interactive areas where kids can get nice and wet while handling ocean rays and fishing around for crabs and starfish in mock tidal pools (parents, pack a change of clothes).

The museum isn't just about the natural history of the harbor—a two-story Boat Hall pays homage to the region's maritime history with hands-on demonstrations in boatbuilding. In 2006, the aquarium bowed to commercialism with a new Spongebob Squarepants "4-D Adventure Ride," in which riders follow Bob and Patrick on an educational trip through Bikini Bottom. (If you're wondering what the fourth dimension is, the aquarium somewhat strangely claims it's "bubbles.") Other draws include an IMAX theater and nature cruises in the harbor.

Stamford Museum & Nature Center
Given the fast pace of Stamford's frenetic downtown, this nature center (39 Scofieldtown Rd., Stamford, 203/322-1646, www.stamfordmuseum.org, 9 A.M.–5 P.M. Mon.–Sat.; 11 A.M.–5 P.M. Sun.; some exhibit hours vary, $8 adults, $6 seniors, $6 students over 17, $4 children 4–17, free members and children under 3) in North Stamford is a welcome relief. The sprawling preserve contains over 100 acres with woodland honeycombed with quiet creeks and ponds, as well as a tidal river with a boardwalk nature trail. Animals such as red foxes, raccoons, woodchucks, and otters are commonly spotted on the trails. Not that everything here is wild—the center was once an elegant estate, and a stone mansion full of museum exhibits and a working farm still grace the grounds. Behind the farm, an observatory invites you to look past the bright lights of Fairfield County to glimpse some more impressive celestial bodies. It's open to the public on Fridays from 8–10 P.M. ($3 adults, $2 children).

Other Sights

Leaving from a dock by the Maritime Aquarium, ferries take trips during the summer to **Sheffield Island Lighthouse** (Seaport Dock, Norwalk, 203/838-9444, www.seaport.org, May–Sept., in Norwalk, schedules set annually, $20 adults, $$12 children 4–12, $5 children 3 and under), a handsome stone beacon that was built in 1868. Now retired, the house harbors a lighthouse museum; nature trails loop around the three-acre island. On the other side of the highway ("NoNo?"), the **Lockwood-Mathews Mansion Museum** (295 West Ave., Norwalk, 203/838-9799, www.lockwoodmathewsmansion.org, tours hourly, noon–4 P.M. Wed.–Sun., free) is located in a Second Empire château-like home owned by wealthy merchant Charles D. Mathews. The entire home is filled with knock-your-socks-off furniture and artwork, including an impressive painted ceiling.

Entertainment

Calling itself the biggest little bar in town, **Blackrock & Blue** (3488 Fairfield Ave., Bridgeport, 203/384-1167) is actually more rock club than bar. There is a bar, of course, which fills up every weekend with patrons hoping to hear some of the best local bands around. The local laugh factory is **Harborsideb** (946 Ferry Blvd., Stratford, 203/375-3037, www.harborsidebargrill.com, 11:30 A.M.–10 P.M. Sun.–Thurs; 11:30 A.M.–10:30 P.M. Fri.), where local comedians line up to spill their guts, and split everyone else's sides.

Events

Slurping down bivalves is just the beginning of the fun at the **Norwalk Oyster Festival** (203/838-9444, www.seaport.org, early Sept.), which the city proudly proclaims is the "best shuckin' festival anywhere." The festival has been growing for the past 30 years, and now features three days of arts and crafts, harbor tours, and entertainment by once-big-name stars (Asia, Big Bad Voodoo Daddy). If the name is any indication, you *can* find a kitchen sink at the **Minks to Sinks Sale** (203/762-0032, early Oct.) held every year in the posh suburb of Wilton. The Columbus Day weekend tent sale includes jewelry, tableware, and whatever other goodies Fairfield County residents have cleaned out of their attics.

Shopping

Office-appropriate meets street-casual in the oh-so versatile stock at **Vide de Luxe** (73 North Main St., Norwalk, 203/354-5835, 10 A.M.–6 P.M. Mon.–Sat.; 10 A.M.–5 P.M. Sun.). Racks here brim with lovely suits, separates, and extremely pretty evening dresses. More artistic endeavors grace the shelves of **Perry-Matto Gallery** (68A Washington St., Norwalk, 203/866-9119, 10 A.M.–5 P.M. daily), full of hand-blown crystal vases, oil lamps, perfume bottles, and Balinese puppets.

Food

Watch the sailboats bob along the harbor from your table at the aptly named **Paradise Bar & Grille** (78 Southfield Ave., Bldg. 5, Stamford Landing, Stamford, 203/323-1116, noon–9 P.M. Mon.–Sat.; 11:30 A.M.–9 P.M. Sun., $12–35). Dinners are less utopian than the setting, but are perfectly fine plates of fried cod, broiled chicken, and wrap sandwiches. Carnivores and business travelers alike flock to the Stamford branch of **Morton's of Chicago** (377 N. State St., Stamford, 203/324-3939, www.mortons.com, 5–10 P.M. Mon.–Thu.; 5–11 P.M. Fri.–Sat.; 5–10 P.M. Sun., $25–54). The clubby, upscale dining room brings out high-quality steakhouse staples such as double-cut filet mignon with béarnaise sauce, shrimp Alexander, and huge pieces of chocolate velvet cake. In the happening South Norwalk area, (**Match** (98 Washington St., Norwalk, 203/852-1088, www.matchsono.com, 5–10 P.M. Sun.–Thu.; 5–11 P.M. Fri.–Sat., $22–38) is a favorite for dinner and drinks. A steel bar spans the room's entrance, and seems always full of twenty- and thirtysomethings swilling martinis and digging into menu offerings like wasabi-and-sesame-rubbed tuna.

Information

The **Coastal Fairfield County Convention**

& **Visitors Bureau** (297 West Ave., Norwalk, 203/853-7770, www.coastalct.com) runs a welcome center in Norwalk with information on the entire Fairfield County area.

GREENWICH

More than for any official attractions, Greenwich is famous for its wealth. Here, Manhattan finance wizards and other high-earning professionals build McMansions galore in the leafy streets and raise children, many of whom attend the area's bountiful private prep schools (of which there are nearly as many as public schools).

All which leaves the question: What is there to actually do in Greenwich? Shop, for starters. In an area with this much surplus cash hanging around, it's no shock that the stores would rise to the occasion. Likewise, the high-end restaurants, of which there are many. Mostly, however, visitors come to admire the picture-perfect downtown area, gawk at the homes, and engage in some good old-fashioned American envy.

Bruce Museum of Arts and Science

For such a small museum, this jewel box (1 Museum Dr., 203/869-0376, www.brucemuseum.org, 10 A.M.–5 P.M. Tues.–Sat.; 1–5 P.M. Sun., $7 adults, $6 seniors and students, free children under 5) has a stellar permanent collection. You might not recognize all the names of the artists on display here, but you'll be wowed by the consistently high quality of their work—and perhaps inspired to add some new favorites to your own list. Highlights include *Girl Feeding Pigeons* by Venetian-style painter Alessandro Milesi and *The Broken Flower Pot,* a cheeky morality tale by Belgian painter Jan Verhas. The museum also has a significant collection of "Cos Cob Impressionists," including Childe Hassam, Emil Carlsen and Leonard and Mina Fonda Ochtman, who painted their works only a few miles up the shore.

Bush-Holley Historic Site

This fascinating site (39 Strickland Rd., Cos Cob, 203/869-6899, www.hstg.org/index.

cgi/632, noon–4 P.M. Wed.–Sun. Mar.–Dec.; noon–4 P.M. Fri.–Sun. Jan.–Feb., $10 adults, $8 seniors and students, free children under 7) explores two eras simultaneously. The heart of the site is the Bush-Holley House, a combination of two homes that date from the early 18th century and are filled with period furnishings and antiques. In its later life, however, the homes were purchased by the Holley family, who set up a boarding house for writers and painters in the 1880s that became Connecticut's first art colony.

The colony took off when New York painter John Henry Twachtman set up shop in the complex to teach students in the hot Parisian style of Impressionism. They found ideal subjects in the surrounding orchards and salt marshes on Long Island Sound. As the colony gained fame, Twachtman was joined by other European-trained Impressionists such as Childe Hassam and Leonard Ochtman and his wife, Mina. The free-spirited atmosphere at the house was looked upon with raised eyebrows by the genteel residents of nearby Greenwich. As the community gradually lost its rural character, the artists moved on in 1914, many up the coast to the Griswold house in Old Lyme. Some of their work, however, remains on-site at a small museum.

Entertainment

The town singles scene happens at **Boxing Cat Grille** (1392 E. Putnam Ave., 203/698-1995). Well-heeled thirty- and fortysomethings congregate at its bar to meet, greet, eat (there's a tasty bar menu served), and drink up while listening to the live music (Thurs.–Sat.). The vibe is Scottish to its core at **MacDuff's Public House** (99 Railroad Ave., 203/422-0563, www.macduffspub.com), where you can down a pint of ale, chase it with some bangers 'n' mash, and cheer for your favorite soccer team alongside other avid fans.

Events

While many New England communities hold craft fairs, few sport the quality of work of the Bruce Museum's **Outdoor Arts Festival**

CONNECTICUT

FOR YOUR HEALTH

Thanks in large part to their function as weekend getaway spots for Manhattanites, many of Connecticut's rural and suburban towns have become centers of world-class spas. Case in point: **Water's Edge Resort & Spa** (1525 Boston Post Rd., Westbrook, 860/399-5901, www.watersedge-resort.com), a full-service resort with luxury treatment rooms overlooking the water, where guests receive hot-stone massages, caviar moisturizing facials, and sea mud wraps. Step into **The Spa at Norwich Inn** (607 W. Thames St., Norwich, 860/886-2401, www.thespaatnorwichinn.com), a turn-of-the-century country inn renovated to include an ultramodern spa, and find a full-service salon, plus thirty-plus treatment rooms ready to administer body waxes, hydrotherapy, aromatherapy facials, and microdermabrasion. Less extravagant but every bit as relaxing are the massages at **Hands On Massage Therapy and Wellness Center** (282 Railroad Ave., Greenwich, 203/531-7929, www.handsonwellnesscenter.com), a cozy enclave dedicated to all forms of massage – lymphatic and Yoga Su to myofascial and Reiki. At **Lavender Fields Day Spa** (1842 Meriden-Waterbury Turnpike, Southington, 860/276-9958), couples can receive tandem massage and individuals can undergo facials, manicures and pedicures, or microdermabrasion (among other things) before enjoying the European steam shower.

(203/869-0376 or 203/869-6786, ext. 336, www.brucemuseum.org, Oct.); the yearly festival is strictly juried, with exhibitors limited to 80 of the finest visual artists and photographers from around the country. The museum also holds a crafts festival every May featuring ceramics, jewelry, and metalwork.

Shopping

Socialite-gone-designer **Tory Burch** (255 Greenwich Ave., 203/622-5023, www.toryburch.com, 10 A.M.–6 P.M. Mon.–Sat.; noon–5 P.M. Sun.) peddles her chic women's collection—from skinny jeans to leopard-print dusters—in this namesake boutique. Author events are a regular occurrence (thanks in part to the town's connections) at **Just Books** (28 Arcadia Rd., Old Greenwich, 203/637-0707, www.justbooks.com, 9 A.M.–5 P.M. Mon.–Sat.; noon–4 P.M. Sun.), a well-stocked bookstore overseen by the house cat, Stella. The appropriately named **Splurge** (19 E. Putnam Ave., 203/869-7600, 10 A.M.–6 P.M. daily) helps local and visiting gift-givers find the perfect gift (via a fairly sophisticated registry list from all over). Everything from classics and mysteries to kids' books are sold. Need something to wear on that upcoming duck hunt? **Eurochasse** (398 Greenwich Ave., 203/625-9501, www.eurochasse.com, 10 A.M.–6 P.M. Mon.–Fri.; 10 A.M.–5:30 P.M. Sat.) sells classic country and hunting clothes (from suede jackets to tartan wellies), so no one has to get their city silks dirty.

Food

Dinner at ◖ **Jean Louis Restaurant** (61 Lewis St., 203/622-8450, www.restaurantjeanlouis.com, noon–2 P.M. Mon.–Fri.; 5:45–10 P.M. Mon.–Sat., $21–39, prix fixe: $59–69) is no mere dinner; it's an event. Renowned and award-winning chef Jean-Louis Gerin masterminds delectables like rabbit with mild gingerbread spices, baked in a *tagine*—and a simply sumptuous boneless quail with potatoes, mushrooms, Armagnac, and bacon. Dress to impress. The bustling, chandelier-studded dining room of **L'Escale Restaurant** (500 Steamboat Rd., 203/661-9800, www.lescalerestaurant.com, 7–10 A.M. and 11:30 A.M.–2 P.M. Mon.–Sat.; 11:30 A.M.–3 P.M. Sun.; 5–10 P.M. Sun.–Thu.; 5–11 P.M. Fri.–Sat., $22–34) is a beautiful setting for magnificent French dishes such as skate with white bean ragu and duck with foie gras medallions. Lighter fare and cocktails are offered in the lounge (11:30 A.M.–11 P.M. daily), and the al fresco dining overlooks the harbor. Live music and DJs on weekends keeps things cool rather than stuffy. Chef William Kulhanek oversees the kitchen at the seafood-centric (**Elm Street Oyster House** (11 W. Elm St., 203/629-5795, www.elmstreetoysterhouse.com, 11:30 A.M.–10 P.M. Mon.–Thu.; 11:30 A.M.–11 P.M. Fri.–Sat.; 11:30 A.M.–9 P.M. Sat., $26–32). The white-walled dining room jumps with colorful paintings and reproductions, and plates arrive heaped with hickory-fried calamari, swordfish with tapenade, and lobster paella.

Information

For more information on Bridgeport and Fairfield, contact the **Coastal Fairfield County Convention & Visitors Bureau** (203/853-7770, www.coastalct.com).

DANBURY

Located inland from the Fairfield County coast, the industrious city of Danbury avoids the extremes of other nearby communities with a good mix of culture and industry, and a thriving multi-ethnic population with a strong sense of community. At one time—the late 19th century, to be exact—Danbury was the hat-making capital of the world. Today, that title (and most of the industry behind it) has faded, and the town has gracefully settled into the world's post-hat-wearing modern era.

You might say the area has something of a split personality: suburban in most outlying areas, but semi-cosmopolitan in its rapidly re-developing city center. Thus residents enjoy the best of both worlds, with easy access to business and events but peace and quiet whenever they want it. Visitors can easily enjoy the same mixture of environments, from the center's museums to nature preserves of greater Danbury.

Danbury Museum and Historical Society

During the Revolutionary War, Connecticut's role as the "Provision State" meant that its vast storehouses were under constant threat of attack. One of the most devastating raids occurred at Danbury in April 1777, when 2,000 British soldiers ranged themselves on the town green and burned down every building in sight, destroying thousands of dollars worth of army stores. Because of that, the two buildings making up this historical museum (43 Main St., 203/743-5200, www.danburymuseum.org, hours and rates vary seasonally) are some of the oldest surviving structures in Danbury, even they were only built in 1785 and 1790. Inside, the museum contains exhibits and relics from the Danbury Raid. In addition, one of the buildings used to be the factory of John Dodd Hat Shop, and now contains exhibits showing how straw, silk, and wool were turned into headgear for almost 200 years.

Danbury Railway Museum

Danbury's old train station is so picturesque, it was used by Alfred Hitchcock as a setting in his movie *Strangers on a Train*. The building (120 White St., 203/778-8337, www.danbury.org/drm, 10 A.M.–4 P.M. Wed.–Sat., noon–4 P.M. Sun. early Sept.–late May.; 10 A.M.–5 P.M. Mon.–Sat. and noon–5 P.M. Sun. late May–early Sept., $6 adults, $5 seniors, $4 children 3–12, free children under 3, additional charge for train ride) is now filled with collections of model trains and railroad memorabilia from all over Connecticut. Out back the rail yard is a wonderland for youngsters, chock-full of locomotives, box cars, and cabooses in an ever-expanding collection of over 60 railroad cars.

Keeler Tavern Museum

You'll know when you've come across this museum south of Danbury (45 Main St., Ridgefield, 203/438-5485, www.keelertavernmuseum.org, 1–4 P.M. Wed. and Sat.–Sun. Feb.–Dec., $5 adults, $3 seniors and students, $2 children under 12, free for members): It's the one with the cannonball stuck in the corner. Redcoats fired at the building during the Battle of Ridgefield, the only Revolutionary War battle fought in Connecticut. Four years before he turned traitor, the ubiquitous Benedict Arnold led a heroic band of Connecticut militiamen in an attempt to stop the British from retreating after the Danbury Raid. Eight militiamen were killed in the battle, including Connecticut militia captain David Wooster. Arnold himself had his horse shot out from under him in the battle but refused to surrender, displaying the bravery for which he was known in the early days of the war. A plaque on Main Street marks the site of the battle; the tavern museum has artifacts about the engagement, including a 1780 engraving.

C Weir Farm
National Historic Site

In 1877, American Impressionist painter Julian Alden Weir traded a still-life painting he had bought in Paris for $650 for this sprawling farm (735 Nod Hill Rd., Wilton, 203/761-9945, www.nps.gov/wefa, 9 A.M.–5 P.M. Wed.–Sun. May–Oct.; 10 A.M.–4 P.M. Thurs.–Sun. Nov.–Apr., free) in Branchville in the heart of Fairfield County. Weir, who signed his paintings J. Alden Weir, was one of the fathers of the American Impressionist movement, teaching classes alongside John Twachtman at the Cos Cob Colony for a time. While he spent most of the years in New York, every summer he'd come back to the farm to commune with nature and wander the grounds with his easel. The site is now Connecticut's only National Historic Site and sports a museum showcasing much of Weir's artistic output, along with the works of later artists who owned the farm. The on-site Art Farm Center (203/761-9945) now encourages visitors to bring their own easels to paint on the grounds; with brushes or without, you can wander through acres of woodland paths and wetlands.

Other Sights

History Channel buffs will want to stop by the **Military Museum of Southern New England** (125 Park Ave., 203/790-9277, www.usmilitarymuseum.org, 10 A.M.–5 P.M. Tues.–Sat. and noon–5 P.M. Sun. Apr.–Nov.; 10 A.M.–5 P.M. Fri.–Sat. and 1–5 P.M. Sun. Dec.–Mar., $6 adults, $4 seniors and youth 5–18, free children under 5), which was founded to honor the tank brigades of World War II. Out front are three dozen armored battle vehicles; in the museum itself, dioramas and films detail famous

tank battles. The **Aldrich Contemporary Art Museum** (258 Main St., Ridgefield, 203/438-4519, www.aldrichart.org, noon–5 P.M. Tues.–Sun., $7 adults, $4 seniors and college students, free for teachers and children 18 and under) has a strong history of rotating contemporary art exhibits, some with interesting themes such as "Native Americans in Contemporary Art." The museum is particularly known for its outdoor sculpture garden.

Entertainment

Classical music performances—orchestral to vocal—are held regularly at the **Danbury Music Centre** (256 Main St., 203/748-1716, www.danbury.org/musicctr). Part of Western Connecticut State University, **Berkshire Theatre** (Osborne St., 203/837-8732) puts on dramatic productions by students. Afterward, grab a nightcap or dessert at **Hat City Ale House** (253 Main St., 203/790-4287), which also hosts a mishmash of live music by local performers.

Events

Danbury's various ethnic communities outdo each other every year with elaborate cultural festivals. The season starts with *souvlaki* and ouzo at **Greek Experience** (203/748-2992, early June), moves to macaroni and grappa at the **Italian Festival** (early Aug.), and concludes with fish-and-chips and Guinness at the **Danbury Irish Festival** (203/730-8211, early Sept.). Lovers of food from all over the world converge on **A Taste of Greater Danbury** (203/792-1711, www.citycenterdanbury.com, mid-Sept.), which features food stalls from the area's gourmet restaurants lining the green alongside children's activities and craft vendors.

Shopping

Far more than your average hardware store, **Meeker's Hardware** (90 White St., 203/748-8017) is a creaky museum-like shop opened in 1883, full of the tools (and in some cases, the prices) of yore. The handmade furniture at **Jefferson Pine & Oak** (132 Danbury Rd.,

New Milford, 860/350-5900, www.jefferson-pineandoak.com, 10 A.M.–6 P.M. Tue.–Wed. and Fri.; 10 A.M.–8 P.M. Thu., 10 A.M.–5 P.M. Sat.; noon–4 P.M. Sun.) is excellent quality, though you can also expect to find pieces made from other fine woods—cherry, ash, and the like. Got an extra hour or two? Sneak into **Derm Essentials Day Spa** (22 Shelter Rock Ln., 203/748-3806, www.dermessentials. net, 10 A.M.–6 P.M. Mon.–Sat.; 10 A.M.–5 P.M. Sun.) for a facial or body treatment, or to pick up something from international beauty lines like Yonka Paris and Jane Iredale.

Food
Overlooking the Richter Park Golf Course, **Café on the Green** (100 Aunt Hack Rd., 203/791-0369, www.cafeonthegreenrestaurant. com, 11:30 A.M.–10 P.M. daily, $22–29) sets the scene—and the table—for fine dining. A Northern Italian menu specializes in meats and pastas such as fettucine with crabmeat cream sauce and filet mignon with gorgonzola-brandy sauce. Simpler fare comes out of the kitchen at **Molly Darcy's** (34A Mill Plain Rd., 203/794-0449, www.mollydarcy.com, 11:30 A.M.–1 A.M. Mon.–Thu.; 11:30 A.M.–2 A.M. Fri.–Sat.; 11 A.M.–3 P.M. Sun., $10–24), a traditional Irish pub inside and a pretty al fresco dining scene out. The corned beef Reuben is loaded with melted Swiss cheese.

Information
For information on downtown Danbury, visit **City Center Danbury** (186 Main St., 203/792-1711, www.citycenterdanbury.com). Other towns in the area are served by the **Northwest Connecticut Convention & Visitors Bureau** (860/567-4506, www.litchfieldhills.com).

SPORTS AND RECREATION
Beaches
Much of the beachfront in this part of the state is privately owned, which provides no end of controversy among less affluent residents. Among public beaches, **Calf Pasture Beach** (Calf Pasture Beach Rd., Norwalk, 203/854-7806, www.lisrc.uconn.edu/coastalaccess, late

Aug.–Sept., $15/car) is the largest, with 33 acres of sand and grass and various activities including mini-golf, windsurf and kayak rentals, and volleyball courts. One of the most beautiful is **Sherwood Island State Park** (Westport, 203/226-6983, http://dep.state.ct.us), with a big open stretch of sand fronting Long Island Sound and picnic tables and food vendors for snacks.

Hiking and Biking
In addition to the various parks and nature preserves around the area, there are several more strenuous hikes around Danbury. **Squantz Pond State Park** (178 Shortwoods Rd., New Fairfield, 203/797-4165, http://dep.state.ct.us) has several moderate trails along the hills surrounding the pond. In the summer, the pond is a popular site for swimming.

Boating
Get out on the water with a sail aboard **SoundWaters** (1281 Cove Rd., Stamford, 203/323-1978, www.soundwaters.org, $25pp), an 80-foot replica of a 19th-century schooner run by a nonprofit involved in natural preservation efforts on the coastline. Educational sails on the weekends include narration on the sealife and environmental issues; the ship is also available for private charters. **Captain's Cove Seaport** (1 Bostwick Ave., Bridgeport, 203/335-1433, www.captainscoveseaport.com, May–Sept.) offers tours of Black Rock Harbor aboard the 40-foot Navy launch *Chief;* the hour-long cruises take in three lighthouses, including one that is supposed to be haunted.

ACCOMMODATIONS
Under $100
It's nothing fancy—your basic motel, really. But the **Merritt Parkway Motor Inn** (4180 Black Rock Turnpike, Fairfield, 203/259-5264, $50–75) includes comfortable rooms and a continental breakfast.

$100-150
Close to Fairfield beach, the rooms at **The Inn at Fairfield Beach** (1160 Reef Rd., Fairfield,

CONNECTICUT

203/255-6808, $135–165) come with queen beds and galley kitchens. Decorations are simple and lovely, in pristine colors and fabrics; a number of rooms have cathedral ceilings, fireplaces, skylights, and balconies.

$150-250

The spacious and neutral-colored rooms at **Ethan Allen Hotel** (21 Lake Ave., Danbury, 203/744-1776, www.ethanallenhotel.com, $155–200) come with customized oversized armoires, high-speed Internet service, and robes and slippers. The property also has two dining rooms and full room service. The 23 individually decorated rooms at **(Stanton House Inn** (76 Maple Ave., Greenwich, 203/869-2110, www.shinngreenwich.com, $160–200) are steps away from Greenwich's shopping and restaurants, and are furnished with fireplaces, colonial beds, and soft florals.

$250 and Up

A little slice of wonder and ever-tasteful fantasy, **(The Homestead Inn** (420 Field Point Rd., Greenwich, 203/869-7500, www.homesteadinn.com, $250–400) takes pride and care in every little detail of their guests' stays. The 18 suites and deluxe rooms come appointed with gleaming, perfectly kept rare antique beds, Frette linens, Bulgari bathroom amenities, and ultra-plush robes. Restaurant Thomas Henkelmann, the inn's restaurant, is the ultimate in country refinement. With all this, it's little wonder the inn has received the prestigious Relais & Chateaux designation.

GETTING THERE AND AROUND

The towns and cities of Fairfield County are strung like pearls along the strand of I-95. Bridgeport is located about 25 miles from New Haven (20 min.), and 60 miles from Hartford (1 hour). The distance from Bridgeport to Greenwich is another 25 miles (25 min.).

Amtrak (800/872-7245, www.amtrak.com) runs trains from New York and Boston to stations in Bridgeport (525 Water St.) and Stamford (Washington Blvd and S. State St.). In addition, trains from New York run by **Metro North** (800/638-7646, www.mta.nyc.ny.us) stop in virtually every town up the Connecticut coastline. Another spur heads north to Danbury (1 Patriot Dr.). Also, **Greyhound** (203/772-2470, www.greyhound.com) and **Peter Pan Bus Lines** (800/343-9999, www.peterpanbus.com) operate bus routes to Bridgeport (35 John St.), Stamford (30 Station Pl.), and Danbury (48 Elm St.).

In addition to access via Metro North trains, Fairfield County's coastal towns are linked by bus via the Stamford branch of **CT Transit** (203/327-7433, www.cttransit.com).

Litchfield Hills

Tucked into the northwestern corner of the state, the countryside of Litchfield Hills is much less developed than the majority of the state. The relatively rural area is studded with lush hills, farms, and small villages. This is prime leaf-peeping territory come autumn, and come weekends, it's also prime getting-away-from-it-all territory for New York city-dwellers. That reliable stream of visitors has ensured a high level of culinary and retail panache that sets the area apart from other rural areas of New England.

WATERBURY AND BRISTOL

On the southeastern verge of the Litchfield Hills, the Naugatuck Valley was traditionally a major manufacturing center. Each of the small cities ranged along the river had their own specialty; the largest, Waterbury, established itself early in the 19th century as a major producer of brass, using know-how and even engineers imported from England. For a time, the city was known as "Brass City" for its prodigious output of buttons, buckles, and bullets. Another of the city's claims to fame was as a manufacturer of pocket watches. Alas, the Great Flood of 1955 that ravaged many Connecticut cities hit Waterbury particularly hard, destroying much of its downtown industrial district. Since then the fourth-largest city in the state has struggled, ruddlerless, to come up with a new identity. The promotion of the city's brass museum and opening of a new high-class mall have been a good start.

Up the valley from Waterbury, Bristol surpassed the larger city in the manufacture of clocks and watches, eventually becoming known as—say it with us—"Clock City." Despite being Connecticut's 11th-largest city, Bristol has retained an attractive character, the legacy of many parks donated by the rich industrialists. The city is also known as "Mum City" for its prominence in chrysanthemum production; it's also headquarters to the cable sports network ESPN, which occupies a huge campus on the edge of town that almost seems like a city unto itself.

Mattatuck Museum

Located on Waterbury's city green, this museum (144 West Main St., Waterbury, 203/753-0381, www.mattatuckmuseum.org, 10 A.M.–5 P.M. Tues.–Sat.; noon–5 P.M. Sun.,

THE CONNECTICUT WINE TRAIL

It may not be Napa Valley, but the Connecticut Wine Trail (www.ctwine.com) rarely disappoints those who come to explore, charmed by the region's small, well-run wine producers, as well as by the scenic meadows, seaport villages, and historic towns they pass along the way. The area is home to fifteen vineyards, joined by the eastern and western branches of the trail. (There are easy-to-spot blue signs all along the trail so visitors don't get lost.) The western trail runs through the Connecticut Highlands, connecting seven wineries: **Jones Winery** (606 Walnut Tree Hill Rd., Shelton, 203/929-8425), which offers tastings in its historic barn and sells crops of berries, pumpkins, and Christmas trees; **McLaughlin Vineyard** (Albert's Hill Rd., Sandy Hook, 866/599-9463), a 160-acre farm that also makes and sells its own maple products; **Digrazia Vineyard** (131 Tower Rd., Brookfield, 203/775-1616), grower of premium French hybrid grape varieties exclusively; **White Silo Winery** (32 Rte. 37 East, Sherman, 860/355-0271), specializing in dry and semisweet fruit wines (raspberry, blackberry, rhubarb, and sour cherry) and housing an art gallery as well as a patio/bar; **Hopkins Vineyard** (25 Hopkins Rd., New Preston, 860/868-7954), with its hayloft café in a 19th-century barn; **Haight Vineyard** (Chestnut Hill, Litchfield, 860/567-4045); and **Jerram Winery** (535 Town Hill Rd., New Hartford, 860/379-8749), which offers an art gallery year-round and a summer wine bar.

The eastern trail, meanwhile, is a bit more spread out, and usually requires several days to visit all the wineries. They include: **Gouveia Vineyards** (1339 Whirlwind Hill Rd., Wallingford, 203/265-5526), owned by a Portuguese family that welcomes picnickers; **Bishop's Orchards Winery** (1355 Boston Post Rd., U.S. Rte. 1, Guilford, 203/453-2338), which produces primarily fruit-based wines; **Chamard** (115 Cow Hill Rd., Clinton, 860/664-0299), specializing in Chardonnay; **Stonington Vineyards** (523 Taugwonk Rd., Stonington, 860/535-1222); **Jonathan Edwards** (74 Chester Maine Rd., N. Stonington, 860/535-0202), where you can swirl and taste at a custom-built wine bar next to the fireplace on 50 acres overlooking the shoreline; **Heritage Trail Vineyards** (291 N. Burnham Hwy., Lisbon, 860/376-0659), where the tasting room is housed in an 18th-century farmhouse complete with wide board floors, antique beams, and a fireplace; **Priam Vineyards** (11 Shailor Hill Rd., Colchester, 860/267-8520), which offers excellent picnic spots with 35-mile views of the area; and **Sharpe Hill** (108 Wade Rd., Pomfret, 860/974-3549), which also has its own restaurant offering dinners every Friday evening and lunches Friday through Sunday.

CONNECTICUT

$5 adults, $4 seniors, free children under 16) could define the word "eclectic." Yes, it's a mishmash of absolutely everything, including machine tools from Waterbury's brass industry, oil paintings from the Hudson River School and American Impressionists, ancient Babylonian and Assyrian artifacts, and—we kid you not—an exhibit of 10,000 different kinds of buttons. But the feeling that you never know what you are going to run into next is part of the charm. You could easily spend half a day here, your thoughts ricocheting from one thing to the next, then finish things off with a cup of coffee or a sandwich from the museum's elegant café.

Other Sights

Though the carousel was originally invented in the Byzantine Empire in 500 A.D., it reached the heights of its artistic expression in the northeastern United States in the early 20th century. The **New England Carousel Museum** (95 Riverside Ave./Rte. 72, Bristol, 860/585-5411, www.thecarouselmuseum.org, 10 A.M.–5 P.M. Mon.–Sat.; noon–5 P.M. Sun., $5 adults, $4.50 seniors, $2.50 children 4–14, free for children under 4) has systematically gathered one of the largest collections of carousel pieces in the country, arranging them in an exhibit on the history of the rotating amusement. Over the past 15 years, the museum has expanded into a campus of attractions including several art galleries, a Museum of Fire History, and a new Museum of Greek Art and History.

The person whose job it is to wind the displays at the **American Clock & Watch Museum** (100 Maple St., Bristol, 860/583-6070, www.clockmuseum.org, 10 A.M.–5 P.M. daily Apr.–Nov. 30; 10 A.M.–5 P.M. Fri.–Sat. and 1–5 P.M. Sun. Dec., $5 adults, $4 seniors and AAA members, $2 children 8–15) must have a busy job. The museum, which was started by the forefathers of the little town of Bristol a half-century ago to celebrate the region's clock-making history, now contains more than 1,500 timepieces. Grandfather clocks, punch-clocks, even blinking-eye clocks—if it ticks, it's here. And if all that's too high-tech

for you, the museum even has a sundial out front.

Food

Believe it or not, the beautiful shining wooden interior of **Dreschers Restaurant** (25 Leavenworth St., Waterbury, 203/573-1743, www.dreschers.com, 11:30 A.M.–2 P.M. Mon.–Fri.; 5–9 P.M. Mon.–Wed.; 5–10 P.M. Thu.–Sat., $16–20) isn't its main draw. In truth, it's the food: rich German comfort food like Wiener schnitzel, sauerbraten (German pot roast), and veal in mushroom-shallot sauce. Juicy Angus steaks and Maine lobsters may be standard steakhouse fare, but they're well above standard at **Carmen Anthony Steakhouse** (496 Chase Ave., Waterbury, 203/757-3040, www.carmenanthony.com, $20–40). Order your beef with classic bordelaise sauce or under a mushroom demi-glacé, and enjoy it with a bottle from the thoughtfully constructed wine list. You don't have to be rich to enjoy the rich menu, however; a three-course prix fixe menu featuring prime rib or filet mignon is just $30/person.

Shopping

Talk about local pride: **The Connecticut Store** (116 Bank St., Waterbury, 800/474-6728, 10 A.M.–3 P.M. Tue.–Fri.) is dedicated to every kind of product made in the state. That means clothing, puzzles, clocks, foods, home decor, wood carvings, and just about anything else you can think of.

Information

For more information on Waterbury and Bristol, contact the **Northwest Connecticut Convention & Visitors Bureau** (860/567-4506, www.litchfieldhills.com).

LITCHFIELD AND TORRINGTON

Litchfield was settled in 1721, and looks very much the part of the quaint colonial town. It still boasts the 18th-century architecture of its beginnings, and the town center's green is more pristine than ever. Surrounding it are

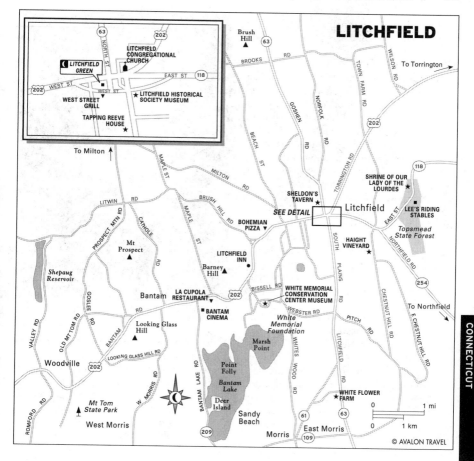

streets full of tony and stylish boutiques and restaurants, which then lead out to wide avenues lined with historic homes. Despite its remoteness, Litchfield played a big part during the Revolutionary War era, since it was a hotbed of Revolutionary sentiment that sired many famous figures from the age, including Vermont's militia captain Ethan Allen, future vice president Aaron Burr, and several signers of the Declaration of Independence.

Because of that tradition—not to mention its almost impregnable position deep in the hills—Litchfield served as a command center and storehouse during the war. General

George Washington passed through four times during 1780 and 1781, and Litchfield and its surrounding communities have painstakingly marked his steps and noted every place he laid his head at night. A few miles away, Torrington, the largest city in Litchfield County, has been the industrial and commercial hub of northwestern Connecticut for more than a century now. Fringing its center are picturesque hills and valleys, while in its downtown area sits a sizeable stable of art deco architecture, an area deemed a national historic district in 1988. Despite the fine architecture, however, Torrington is now mainly a

CONNECTICUT

working-class city routinely overshadowed by its much cuter neighbors.

◖ Litchfield Green

A story in the *Litchfield Monitor* in 1803 reported that this wide oval expanse in the center of town was filled with broken fences, woodpiles, and overgrown shrubbery, with hogs, not to mention truants, wandering around at will. Such an image today is all but inconceivable. Litchfield scores top honors in the New England town green department—a contest not without some stiff competition. The reasons are many—first, there's its size, which stretches as much as a football field from end to end. Then there is the pleasing collection of clustered trees and monuments that breaks up the space into a highly strollable area. Finally there are the shops and restaurants that line one side, all trying to outdo each other to exude a combination of colonial forthrightness and upscale panache.

Finally, there is Litchfield's 1828 **Congregational Church,** itself one of the most pleasing-to-the-eye New England churches you could ever hope to find (and reputedly the most photographed). Just looking up at its white clapboard facade, tapering into a perfect white steeple, is enough to transport you back into the era of tri-corner hats, musketry, petticoats, and breeches. It's interesting to know, then, that the church wasn't on the green more than 50 years before it was moved to make room for a more "fashionable" Gothic church. The original meetinghouse was used as an armory, dance hall, and even a skating rink before a colonial revival effort in the 20th century restored it to its righteous place on the green.

Litchfield Historical Society and Museum

Though all of Litchfield might be considered an open-air history museum, this peerless historical collection (7 South St., Litchfield, 860/567-4501, www.litchfieldhistorical-society.org, 11 A.M.–5 P.M. Tues.–Sat. and 1 P.M.–5 P.M. Sun. mid-Apr.–Nov., $5 adults,

© MICHAEL BLANDING

Litchfield's Congregational Church

$3 seniors and students, free for children under 14, and law students) is worth a stop to see the artifacts from the colonial, Federal, and Victorian periods. Among the items on display are period furniture, clothing, accessories, pewter, tavern signs, manuscripts...and the list goes on. The Historical Society also gives tours of the **Tapping Reeve House** (82 South St., Litchfield, 11 A.M.–5 P.M. Tues.–Sat. and 1–5 P.M. Sun. mid-Apr.–Nov., $5 adults, $3 seniors and students, free for members, children under 14, and law students), a colonial home that once housed a law school run by future Supreme Court Justice Tapping Reeve at the turn of the 19th century. More than 1,000 students were educated there, including 130 future U.S. senators and congressmen, and such luminaries as Horace Man, Noah Webster, and John C. Calhoun.

Other Historic Homes

Throw a stone and you'll probably hit a home that figured somehow into the early history of Connecticut, if not the country.

In his many travels through Connecticut, General Washington once passed the night at **Sheldon's Tavern** (73 North St.), a picturesque square house with a mansard roof. The home is now a private residence. Also private is the oldest house in Litchfield, the Oliver Wolcott House (South St.), which was named after a Revolutionary War general, signer of the Declaration of Independence, and later state governor who was instrumental in supplying the troops during the war. Wolcott is famous for leading the effort to melt down a lead statue of King George III and turn it into bullets to use against the king's own troops. The act took place on the back lawn of this five-bay Georgian house (look for the bullet molds on display at the historical society). And yes, Washington slept here—passing through with Marquis de Lafayette in 1780 on their way to West Point, where Washington would learn of Benedict Arnold's defection to the enemy.

White Memorial Conservation Center Museum

One of New England's best natural-history centers (80 Whitehall Rd., off Rte. 202, Litchfield, 860/567-0857, www.whitememorialcc.org, 9 A.M.–5 P.M. Mon.–Sat.; noon–5 P.M. Sun., $5 adults, $2.50 children 6–12), this 4,000-acre preserve educates visitors through exhibits in an impressive museum before sending them out on 35 miles of trails to look for wildlife. The museum is full of high-quality dioramas and interactive exhibits that introduce visitors to all of the characters in the New England forest—bobcats, foxes, deer, birds, and more. A special exhibit explains the secrets of taxidermy, or how animals are stuffed and mounted. If you prefer to see animals alive and running around, take to the trails, a mix of paths for cycling, waking, and horseback riding. Along the way, some 30 observation platforms have been set up to afford visitors a hidden vantage from which to view birds and other wildlife.

Other Sights

There's not much to see in downtown Torrington, but if you are in the neighborhood,

THROUGH THE LOOKING GLASS

The collection of cottages that has sprouted over **Winvian** (155 Alain White Rd., Morris, 860/567-9600, www.winvian. com, $750-2,300) resort is like a window into the id: a a treehouse that sways slightly in the breezes; a beaver lodge with birch trees for bed posts; a 7.5-ton Sikorsky helicopter dropped into the middle of a living room. Each was designed by a different architect who was given the once-in-a-lifetime opportunity to design without restriction. As whimsical as the cottages are, however, they are just the beginning of what makes this resort unique in New England. At dinner, semi-private tables in a warren of rooms in the main house receive a procession of sea urchin, foie gras, rack of lamb, and other imaginings of chef Chris Eddy, who was trained by Alain Ducasse and Daneil Boulud. A 5,000-square foot spa pampers guests with four-handed massages and Eve Lom facials – a multi-step deep-cleansing ordeal offered to American travelers only here and at one other spa in New York. And the setting in the Litchfield Hills fronting 4,000 acres of conservation land is nothing short of magical. The experience isn't cheap (cottages range from $1,250 "a la carte" to $2,300 per night – which includes food and booze), but it's not one you are likely to have anywhere else.

pop into the **Hotchkiss-Fyler House** (192 Main St., Torrington, 860/482-8260, www. torringtonhistoricalsociety.org, noon–4 P.M. Tues.–Sat., mid-Apr.–Oct., $5 adults, free for children under 12), home to the Torrington Historical Society, and a top-notch house museum in its own right. The 1900 turreted Queen Anne is filled with Victorian-era furniture and artwork.

Entertainment

Torrington's downtown center is home to two of the town's biggest attractions. For theatrical, music, and dance productions, there's the spectacular **Warner Theatre** (68 Main St., Torrington, 860/489-7180, www.warnertheatre.org). It's as entertaining offstage as on, painted with murals of Litchfield Hills and hung with an enormous chandelier. Then there's the **Nutmeg Conservatory for the Arts** (58 Main St., Torrington, 860/482-4413, www.nutmegconservatory.org), which houses its own ballet and dance school and stages everything from *The Nutcracker* to *Cinderella*.

Events

Litchfield's **Annual Gallery on the Green** (860/567-8298, www.jwclitchfieldhills.org, Jun.) isn't a permanent gallery, but a yearly installment of more than 100 artists and artisans who set up shop to exhibit original watercolors, oil paintings, jewelry, and other crafts. The **Litchfield Jazz Festival** (Goshen County Fairgrounds, 116 Old Middle Rd./Rte. 63, Goshen, 860/567-4162, www.litchfieldjazzfest.com, Aug.) is only a dozen years old—even so, it has drawn an impressive roster of jazz greats for music under the stars.

Shopping

The area is home to a bevy of excellent antiques shops, and one of the best is **Toll House Antiques** (38 Old Turnpike Rd., Bantam, 860/567-3130, www.litchfieldct.com/ant/tollhse/tollhse.html, noon–5 P.M. Sat.–Sun.; call for hours Mon.–Fri.). The freestanding red barn is packed with excellent examples of American furniture from several periods, stoneware, old clocks, handmade wooden bowls, and intricate quilts. What to get for the woman who has everything? Search us, but you can probably find it at **Flora & Fauna of Litchfield** (10 South St., 860/567-2754, 10 A.M.–5:30 P.M. Mon.–Fri.; 10 A.M.–6 P.M. Sat.; noon–5 P.M. Sun.), an anything-but-cookie cutter gift shop with affordable lovelies including jewelry, soaps, loose-leaf teas, and candles—each with it's own little twist to make it fun and unique. Relax after all that shopping in one of the plush treatment rooms at **The Spa at Litchfield Hills** (407 Bantam Rd., Litchfield, 860/567-8575,

www.litchfield-spa.com, 9 A.M.–6 P.M. Mon.–Tue. and Fri.–Sat.; 9 A.M.–9 P.M. Wed.–Thu.; by appt. Sun.). There, the detoxifying Moor mud bath or the one-hour whirlpool pedicure will restore all your energies for the next shopping trip. The name **Hayseed** (On the Green, 860/567-8775, 10 A.M.–6 P.M. Mon.–Sat.; noon–6 P.M. Sun.) is strictly tongue-in-cheek, as this "country couture" clothing store stocks the latest high-fashion items no self-respecting woman with a second home in the Litchfield Hills would be without. Think Ralph Lauren and then some.

Food

Highly acclaimed and for good reason, **West Street Grill** (38 West St., Litchfield, 860/567-3885, 11:30 A.M.–2:30 P.M. and 5:30–9 P.M., $21–38) is a little bit of big city in the country—a contemporary, buzzing bistro on Litchfield Green, with the requisite exposed brick and distressed wooden floors. Global flavors are the kitchen's focus, which translates to specialties such as pan-seared scallops with celery root and fire-roasted salmon with heirloom tomatoes. A top-notch wine list is also offered. Check ahead to find out the schedule for popular "bistro nights," with an affordable prix fixe menu and wine specials. The ever-excellent **La Cupola Ristorante** (637 Bantam Rd., Litchfield, 860/567-3326, noon–3 P.M. and 4–9 P.M. daily, $16–30) is known far and wide for its authentic Italian specialties. Be sure not to pass up any of the gnocchi specials, should they be on the menu.

There are fish specials aplenty on the menu at the casual and seafood-centric **Central Galapagos** (281 Winsted Rd., Torrington, 860/459-7259, www.northerngalapagosrestaurant.com, 5–9:30 P.M. Tue.–Sat., 7 A.M.–2 P.M. Sat.–Sun., $10–21). The grill figures heavily in the fresh, flavor-packed dishes, and the swift service is knowledgeable and friendly. For budget-conscious diners, the restaurant offers several prix fixe options for $20–25.

Calling itself the "weirdest restaurant in Litchfield County and quite possibly the world," **Bohemian Pizza** (342 Bantam Rd.,

860/567-3980, 11:30 A.M.–9 P.M. Mon.–Thu.; 11:30 A.M.–10 P.M. Fri.–Sat.; 11:30 A.M.–8 P.M. Sun., $8–19) tries hard to live up to the name, with an energetic young vibe and décor ranging from a canoe to Holstein-patterned seats. The little restaurant is serious about its pizza, however, turning out awesomely good pies topped with everything from sun-dried tomatoes to andouille sausage, alongside a full menu of pastas, meal salads, and other simple-but-tasty entrées.

Information
The **Northwest Connecticut Convention & Visitors Bureau** (860/567-4506, www.litchfieldhills.com) runs an information booth on the village green, open May through October.

WASHINGTON
Incorporated during the Revolutionary War, in 1777, the picturesque little town of Washington made the ultimate gesture of loyalty by naming itself after the Continental Army's General-in-Chief. (The town was originally called Judea.) Like the towns around it, Washington has its share of restored colonial houses—however, nature here tends to outshine anything man has done. The town has garnered a reputation for putting on one of the best foliage displays every year, with sugar maple, scarlet oak, beech, and honey locust trees each contributing their unique colors to the pallet. Washington Village is ranged around an attractive green with its own picturesque clapboard church and country inn; for activity, however, chug on down the hill to Washington Depot, the commercial center of the town, which has developed a strong collection of quaint shops and galleries.

Sights
The highlight of the **Institute for American Indian Studies** (38 Curtis Rd., 860/868-0518, www.birdstone.org, 10 A.M.–5 P.M. Mon.–Sat.; noon–5 P.M. Sun., $5 adults, $4.50 seniors, $3 children) is a life-sized Algonkian village, complete with three wigwams, a long house, and

© MICHAEL BLANDING

The Institute for American Indian Studies features a life-sized Algonkian village.

a native plant garden. Staff on hand at this research and education center demonstrate how Native Americans grew and processed food; equally interesting are exhibits and demonstrations into the field of archaeology, showing how sites are excavated without damaging their artifacts.

In nearby Washington Depot, the **Washington Art Association** (4 Bryan Hill Plz., Washington Depot, 860/868-2878, www.washingtonart.org, 10 A.M.–5 P.M. Tues.–Sat.; noon–5 P.M. Sun., free) is a top-notch exhibitor of local artwork. The association holds regular gallery openings, as well as art classes and a popular holiday sale.

Food

The **Mayflower Inn** (118 Woodbury Rd./Rte. 47, 860/868-9466, www.mayflowerinn.com,, noon–2 P.M. and 6–9 P.M. daily, $20–30) might sound like the epitome of old-school New England cuisine, but the chef mixes it up a bit with inventive cuisine spiced with unusual flavors. Dine on dishes like Hawaiian swordfish, flown in fresh and marinated with orange peel and coriander, in a white-tablecloth atmosphere. A similar blend of country charm and urban sophistication, **Marty's Café** (6 Green Hill Rd./Rte. 47, Washington Depot, 860/868-1700, www.seeyouatmartys.com, 7:30 A.M.–6 P.M. Mon.–Sat.; 7:30 A.M.–5 P.M. Sun.) is a Greenwich-style espresso bar with enough rustic touches to remind you that you are in the sticks. In addition to wireless Internet and racks full of newspapers, it offers up creative sandwiches—try the trio of sliders with pulled pork; Portobello and goat cheese; and turkey club with bacon.

George Washington never slept at **G. W. Tavern** (20 Bee Brook Rd., Washington Depot, 860/868-6633, www.gwtavern.com, 11:30 A.M.–10 P.M. Mon.–Thu.; 11:30 A.M.–11 P.M. Fri.–Sat.; 11:30 A.M.–9:30 P.M. Sun., $11–35), but the casual pub and eatery does everything it can to honor him, with a framed picture of you-know-who over the fireplace and a bust overlooking the light and airy dining room. After a full day of leaf-peeping, a piping-hot crock of French onion soup topped with gooey gruyere cheese is just the ticket. Entrées like ground-pork meatloaf and chicken pot pie are similarly comfort-food oriented. Specials are updated nightly online.

Shopping

The quaint commercial center of Washington Depot makes for a delightful afternoon of browsing. Start at the **Hickory Stick Bookshop** (2 Green Hill Rd., Washington Depot, 860/868-0525, www.hickorystickbookshop.com, 9 A.M.–5:30 P.M. Mon.–Sat.; 11 A.M.–5 P.M. Sun.), the area's cultural hub with well-stocked shelves of contemporary fiction and nonfiction books. The shop also hosts numerous local-author readings. Authors with Litchfield Hills homes who have read here in the past include Arthur Miller, Madeleine L'Engle, and William Styron. If the hills makes you feel far from home, stop by the nearby **Archway News** (64 Bank St., New Milford, 860/355-1557, 6 A.M.–7:30 P.M. Mon.–Fri.; 6 A.M.–6 P.M. Sat.; 6 A.M.–3 P.M. Sun.), a luxury tobacco and cigar shop that stocks more than 2,000 periodicals from around the world, including magazines from Russia, Italy, Spain, Germany, and even Korea and Japan.

Information

For more information, contact the **Northwest Connecticut Convention & Visitors Bureau** (860/567-4506, www.litchfieldhills.com).

KENT AND CORNWALL

Kent might be the quintessential New England town—nestled among hills that don't so much roll as tumble alongside the Housatonic River. They surround a downtown that bustles with art galleries, outdoor sculptures, and eclectic shops. The foliage here is as good as it is anywhere, and the town makes it easy to appreciate it, with several outdoor parks and preserves to amble out among the leaves.

A few miles north up Route 7, you'd never know the Cornwall countryside—which includes Cornwall Bridge, Cornwall Plains, North Cornwall, West Cornwall, and East

Cornwall—is a countrified version of the Hamptons, with homes here owned by Michael J. Fox, Whoopi Goldberg, Sam Waterston, and other big-name celebrities. Here, however, the idea is really to get away from it all. Old-time residents barely bat an eye when they see an actor at the general store or antiques shop, and that seems to be how everybody likes it.

Once upon a time, this area was heavily industrialized, taking advantage of the swift-flowing rivers and quantities of ore found in the hills to produce many manufactured metal goods. Those days are long gone, however. Now the unspoiled countryside seems tailor-made for leisurely afternoon drives or walks, with covered bridges and trickling streams flowing down from the hills.

Salisbury Cannon Museum

Before he won fame as the leader of Vermont's Green Mountain Boys, native Nutmegger Ethan Allen started a blast furnace in the Litchfield Hills. The site is now memorialized as the **Salisbury Cannon Museum** (860/435-0566, www.salisburycannonmuseum.org, call for hours), which explores the history of the enterprise. Allen and his partners used a rich lode of nearly pure iron ore in Salisbury to fuel the blast furnace, which became the primary producer of cannons for the Colonies during the American Revolution (churning out more than 800 in total.) Recently a hunk of pig iron produced by Allen in 1764 was dug out of the surrounding countryside; it is now on display at the museum.

Covered Bridges

The Cornwall area is home to two of the three covered bridges left in the state (and the only two that are still operating). One of the most-celebrated covered bridges in all of New England, the **West Cornwall Covered Bridge** carries Route 7 across the Housatonic Bridge. At 172 feet, it's one of the longer bridges in the region—and also one of the prettiest, painted barn-red and supported by a stone center post over the powerful, rushing waters of the Housatonic. The smaller **Bull's Bridge** crosses

Kent Falls

© MICHAEL BLANDING

the Housatonic at Bull's Bridge Road, named for a pair of brothers who once had an iron-works here. The 110-foot span has a weathered wood exterior.

Other Sights

The industrial history of the area is also celebrated at the **Sloane-Stanley Museum and Kent Furnace** (31 Kent-Cornwall Rd./Rte. 7, Kent, 860/927-3849, www.chc.state.ct.us/sloanestanleymuseum.htm, 10 A.M.–4 P.M. Wed.–Sun. mid-May–Oct., $8 adults, $6 seniors, $5 youth 6–17), free children under 6, a dream museum for any professional or amateur mechanic. On display are several hundred years of tools and manufacturing equipment, as well as informative exhibits on how they were used in early America. Nearby is the now-dormant Kent Furnace, which spat out pig iron for almost 70 years in the 19th century. The furnace's heavy granite blocks and Gothic arch make for an impressive picnic spot. Speaking of picnics, families from around the area bring their baskets and blankets to **Kent Falls State**

Park (Rte. 7, 5 mi. north of Kent, 860/927-3238, Sat.–Sun May–Oct., $20), a wide grassy area whose main attraction sluices down from the hills in a series of pitches some 250 feet long in all. A trail, complete with wooden steps and viewing platforms traces the side of the waterfall, allowing excellent views and photo opportunities of its various cataracts and pools. Swimming, sadly, is prohibited.

A welcome new addition to the area is the **Land of Nod Winery** (99 Lower Rd., East Canaan, 860/824-5225, www.landofnodwinery.com, 11 A.M.–5 P.M. Fri.–Sun. Apr.–Oct., tastings and tours free). The winery is still relatively young as New England wineries go, but it has already won acclaim for its pinot noirs and raspberry fruit wines. The family operation also runs a maple syrup house on-site—no word yet on whether they plan to produce a maple wine.

Food
Start the day right with one of the breakfasts served at the **Wandering Moose Café** (West Cornwall, 860/672-0178, www.thewanderingmoosecafe.com, breakfast & lunch Tue.–Sun.; dinner Wed.–Sun., $9–25), situated right next to the town's idyllic covered bridge. The banana-and-chocolate-chip pancakes and cinnamon toast are terrific—or come back at dinner for chestnut-stuffed chicken and salmon in lemon-leek sauce.

Shopping
At a time when it seems like you can buy just about anything from a catalog, **Foreign Cargo** (17 North Main St./Rte. 7, Kent, 10 A.M.–5:30 P.M. Mon.–Sat.; noon–5 P.M. Sun.) lets you do the same thing in person. Peruse one-of-a-kind jewelry, elegant women's clothing, international artwork, and home furnishings and accessories. Started 38 years ago by a family who has lived and worked around the world in foreign aid, the store is a delight to anyone who appreciates lacquered wooden Buddhas, African masks, yak-wool sweaters, and literally hundreds of other unique antique and hand-crafted items from around the world.

For something originating a bit closer to home, **Ballyhack Antiques** (16 Furnace Brook Rd., West Cornwall, 860/672-6751, www.ballyhackantiques.com) features American paintings, folk art, and 18th- and 19th-century furniture. The pretty, deep-red interior of **The Wish House** (413 Main St., West Cornwall, 860/672-2969, 11 A.M.–6 P.M. Wed.–Mon.) is stuffed with all manner of lovingly made gifts—handmade candles and throws, cashmere hoodies for women, and handwoven ties for men.

Information
For more information, contact the **Northwest Connecticut Convention & Visitors Bureau** (860/567-4506, www.litchfieldhills.com).

SPORTS AND RECREATION
Hiking
While Connecticut is not thought of as mountain-climbing country, a portion of the Appalachian Trail passes through Litchfield County, offering many nice (and some demanding) hikes along the ridges of the Southern Berkshires. The most popular hike is **Bear Mountain** in Salisbury, which at 2,316 feet is the highest peak in Connecticut (though it's not the highest point—that honor belongs to the south slope of Mount Frisell, whose peak is in Massachusetts). The summit ridge is rocky and open, giving great views of the hills all around. On the summit itself, an eight-foot observation platform gives even better views. For more information, contact the **Appalachian Mountain Club Connecticut Chapter** (www.ct-amc.org).

Another good bet for some outdoor exercise is the Nature Conservancy's **Sunny Valley Preserve** (Sunny Valley Rd., New Milton, 860/355-3716, www.nature.org, free) in New Milton. The site encompasses some 2,000 acres of rolling farmland and forest, with some 13 miles of trails taking in a diverse array of scenery. The Nature Conservancy also manages the **Cathedral Pines Preserve** (Essex Hill Rd., Cornwall, www.nature.org, free), one of southern New England's last stands of old-growth white pine and hemlock. The stand was devastated by a hurricane in 1989 and many trees fell; the remaining portion feels more like a hike in the redwoods of California than a hike in the Connecticut woods.

Biking

The Litchfield Hills area is a fantasyland for bikers, where hilly climbs and long, winding back roads are rewarded with plenty of white-steepled churches and country stores. The **Bicycle Tour Company** (9 Bridge St., Kent, 888/711-KENT, www.bicycletours.com) offers guided tours of the northwestern corner of the state, including both of Connecticut's covered bridges.

Boating and Fishing

You can see the West Cornwall Covered Bridge from underneath with canoeing tours offered by **Clarke Outdoors** (163 Rte. 7, West Cornwall, 860/672-6365, www.clarkeoutdoors.com), which leads a 10-mile easygoing canoe trip down the Housatonic (4 hrs., $55 weekends, $50 weekdays for two people, additional $85 for guided tour). In the spring, the outfitter also leads more adventurous whitewater rafting trips down the treacherous Bull's Bridge Gorge in Kent, which has Class IV and Class V rapids.

The Housatonic is also known as a great river for landing trout. Fly-fishing trips are led by **Housatonic Anglers** (26 Bolton Hill Rd., Cornwall, 860/672-4457 or 860/387-3300, www.housatonicanglers.com, $150–350), which leads both wading and drift-boat excursions.

Skiing

For Connecticut anyway, the **Mohawk Ski Area** (46 Great Hollow Rd., Cornwall, 860/672-6100 or 800/895-5222, www.mohawkmtn.com, $50 adult, $42 youth 5–15, $15 children under 5) offers a chance for some decent downhill skiing, created by the same visionary who created Vermont's Mount Snow. The mountain has two dozen groomed ski trails, including a handful of expert runs.

Cross-country enthusiasts can venture into the adjoining **Mohawk State Forest** (20 Mohawk Mountain Rd., Cornwall/Goshen, 860/491-3620, http://dep.state.ct.us), which has miles of trails along the slopes of the mountain.

Camping and Swimming

An S-curved lake smack dab between Litchfield, Washington, and Kent, **Lake Waramaug State Park** (30 Lake Waramaug Rd., New Preston, 860/868-0220, $13/site) makes a good home base for exploring the area. The park has some 80 wooded tent sites fronting one of the most gorgeous lakes in Connecticut. Swimming is also allowed at a small beach on the lakeshore.

ACCOMMODATIONS
Under $100

To say you'll sleep like a king at the **Royal Inn** (19 Nathaniel St., Torrington, 860/489-4400, www.torringtonroyalinn.com, $65–150) is probably pushing it, but you will find the cheapest accommodations for miles around, with rooms under $100 even during summer weekends. Each room includes a microwave and refrigerator to help stretch your restaurant dollar a little further as well.

$100-150

There are 60 guest rooms and two suites at **[Yankee Pedlar Inn** (93 Main St., Torrington, 860/489-9226, www.pedlarinn.com, $80–130), each with hand-stenciled walls and canopy beds, plus plenty of modern amenities like Internet and fax services available upon request. The inn's restaurant serves traditional steaks and seafood in a handsome room complete with rough-hewn beams and a frequently lit fireplace.

The colonial-style **Litchfield Inn** (432 Bantam Rd./US 202, Litchfield, 860/567-4503, www.litchfieldinnct.com, $150S) is actually a recently built hotel with modern amenities (and a few older-style ones, like the fireplaces found in some of the rooms). The on-site restaurant, Bistro East, serves quite good modern American fare.

$150-250

The thirteen brightly decorated guest rooms at (**Cornwall Inn** (270 Kent Rd., Cornwall, 860/672-6884, www.cornwallinn.com, $170–240) are filled with cozy bathrobes, cable TVs, wireless Internet, and feather beds. The meticulously kept gardens around the inn include an outdoor pool, and the restaurant features fireside meals in a tastefully restored dining room.

GETTING THERE AND AROUND

The Litchfield Hills are located about 30 miles west of Hartford; the most direct route is along U.S. Route 44 (45 min. to Torrington). From the south, the quickest (though not most scenic) route to Torrington is along Route 8, a multilane divided highway from Bridgeport (50 mi., 55 minutes). From New Haven, take Route 34 west to pick up Route 8 in Shelton (50 mi., 1 hour to Torrington). From the Berkshires, take the winding Route 7 from Stockbridge to Cornwall (35 mi., 1 hour).

Metro North (800/638-7646, www.mta.nyc.ny.us) runs trains to Waterbury Travel Center (188 Bank St.). **Greyhound** (203/772-2470, www.greyhound.com) and **Peter Pan Bus Lines** (800/343-9999, www.peterpanbus.com) also operate bus routes to Waterbury (188 Bank St.) and Torrington (429 Winsted Rd.). **CT Transit** (www.cttransit.com) runs local bus service within Waterbury (203/753-2538) and Bristol (203/327-7433). In the Litchfield Hills, your own car is almost essential. However, **Kelly Transit** (53 John St., Torrington, 717/292-4531 or 800/256-8163, www.kelly-transit.com) offers commuter shuttle service between Litchfield and Torrington, as well as car service for hire.

VERMONT

SOUTHERN VERMONT

The easy access to the southern part of Vermont means that license plates from New York and Massachusetts often outnumber the green-and-white plates of the locals. The winding roads of the Green Mountain foothills can get especially crowded on weekends around foliage season (mid-Sept.–mid-Oct.) and during school vacations in ski season. Why go farther north, skiers ask, when mountains like Stratton, Mount Snow, and Okemo offer challenging trails just a couple hours' drive from Boston?

The three major towns of southern Vermont each have their own distinctive personalities. Brattleboro exudes an artsy, crunchy-granola vibe that wafts from galleries and shops ready-made for browsing. Bennington is a working-class town living off its history as the site of a major battle during the Revolutionary War.

Manchester, on the other hand, is anything but struggling. Buoyed by its designer clothing outlets and luxury spas, this is where the New York set comes to get away and play.

In between these relative metropolises are the storybook villages that epitomize New England in the minds of many people. One of the best ways to see this part of the state is just to get in the car and drive. You are sure to come across that perfect gazebo on the town green; that country store packed with home-made fudge and handicrafts; or that maple syrup farm offering tours with the purchase of a jug.

North of Manchester, Route 4 cuts across the center of the state like a belt tied tight around its waist, serving as a physical and mental dividing line between northern and southern

HIGHLIGHTS

(Gallery Walk: If you aren't lucky enough to live in an artists colony, visiting this monthly festival in Brattleboro is the next best thing (page 325).

(Grafton Village Cheese Company: "You cheddar stop" here for demonstrations of Vermont's best cheese-making (page 330).

(Bennington Battle Monument: The first American victory on the battlefield is celebrated at this Revolutionary War landmark (page 337).

(The Vermont Country Store: Quaint it ain't, but this gargantuan store does provide one-stop shopping to authentic Vermont (page 341).

(Vermont Institute of Natural Science: Get sized up by eagle eyes at this raptor and nature center (page 348).

(Killington Resort: Love it or hate it, the six mountains of Killington provide the biggest and baddest skiing around (page 354).

(New England Maple Museum: The "sappiest" museum in the world offers a fresh taste of the sweet stuff whether it's syrup season or not (page 357).

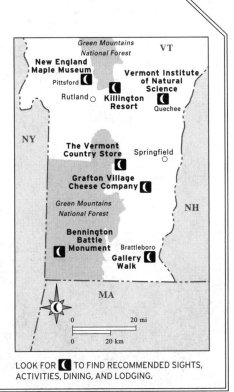

LOOK FOR (TO FIND RECOMMENDED SIGHTS, ACTIVITIES, DINING, AND LODGING.

Vermont and connecting some of the state's prime attractions, including the sophisticated little village of Woodstock, the skiers mecca of Killington and riot of restaurants and motels climbing up to the peak, and Rutland, which used to be one of Vermont's most populous city in the 19th century, but has since seen better days. Scratch beneath the rust, however, and you'll find a gorgeous Victorian downtown, surrounded by several stop-worthy tourist attractions in the surrounding valley.

PLANNING YOUR TIME

You could easily breeze through southern Vermont in a couple of days, but to really appreciate the area, a leisurely week of cruising the back roads or the ski slopes is more like it.

Unlike in the more northerly parts of the state, lodgings and restaurants in this area tend to stay open year-round, making it a nice place to visit in the winter (though be warned that the whole area shuts down during the month of March, otherwise known in these parts as "mud season"). Of course, the region really comes into its own in fall, when the foliage does its annual color dance on the back roads, and country inns often jack up their prices as well.

You're best off basing yourself in Brattleboro, the pint-sized cultural mecca that beguiles tourists. Try to time your trip to take in the monthly **Gallery Walk** on the first Friday of the month, when the town really displays its artistic talents. While in Brattleboro, you can

VERMONT

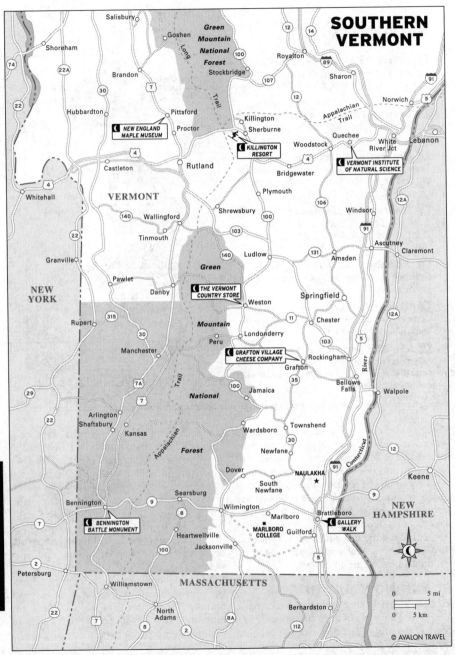

SOUTHERN VERMONT

© AVALON TRAVEL

take a few leisurely days to explore the nearby maple syrup farms, the cheesemaking operation at **Grafton Village Cheese Company,** and the quintessentially Vermont **Vermont Country Store.** Unlike Brattleboro, there's not much to see in downbeat Bennington, but it's worth making a daytrip to the city to see the Revolutionary War–era **Bennington Battle Monument** and its accompanying museum. For many shopaholic weekend visitors, a trip to the region begins, stays, and ends in Manchester. Full days of shopping at deeply discounted designer outlets and luxury inns have made the place a destination that can easily fill an enthusiast's vacation.

North of the Green Mountain National Forest, you could easily spend another couple of days along Route 4, starting in Woodstock. Nearby, plan to stop by the underrated **Vermont Institute of Natural Science** for a bit of a walk on the wild side. Farther west, **Killington Resort,** the biggest, baddest mountain in New England and a must-ski for any serious enthusiast, and the city of Rutland is worth a detour for its many covered bridges and the irresistible lure of the **New England Maple Museum.**

Brattleboro and Vicinity

The southeastern corner of Vermont is characterized by the gentle foothills of the Green Mountains as they descend in wave upon wave down to the Connecticut River Valley. Starting in 1724, this was the first part of Vermont to be founded—late compared to the rest of New England. The first permanent settlement in the state was at Fort Dummer, an outpost for protecting the fertile Connecticut River Valley from Native American raiders from the north. The fort grew steadily from a vibrant trading post to a solid base of manufacturing, eventually becoming the city of Brattleboro. In the mid-19th century, it became known as a therapeutic center, famed for a "water cure" that drew some of the country's most prominent citizens for plunges in its ice-cold springs. Later, it became the "organ capital of the country" for its Estey Organ Company. North of Brattleboro, smaller dairying communities sprang up in the surrounding hills, including the cheese-making center of Grafton. West of town, the so-called Molly Stark Trail, otherwise known as Route 9, climbs into the Greens.

BRATTLEBORO

Few places make art as much a part of daily life as Brattleboro, a former industrial hub that has reinvented itself in past years as a mecca for painters and artisans. During its monthly

Gallery Walk, shops and restaurants showcase local work, which is then left on the walls to inspire patrons in following weeks. (Don't be surprised if after dinner you find yourself asking for a painting with your doggie bag.) The artistic sensibility of the town extends to its politics, earning it a reputation as one of the most progressive towns in Vermont. This is the kind of place where shops advertise "Breastfed Babies Welcome" on their windows, and sell organic hemp clothing inside. Instead of a supermarket, it has a food co-op, where you can choose from 300 kinds of cheese and sign a petition against genetically modified foods on your way out the door. The town's mercantile past has even given its brick downtown a quasi-urban feel that harmonizes with its cosmopolitan leanings.

◖ Gallery Walk

Snow or shine, crowds throng the center of town on the first Friday of every month for the Gallery Walk (802/257-2616, www.gallerywalk. org, 5:30–8:30 P.M., free), Brattleboro's signature social event. Try to time your visit to coincide with Gallery Walk, as no other experience will give you a better feel for the spirit of the town. The streets take on a festival atmosphere as neighbors catch up on news and pore over the latest creations of their friends while noshing

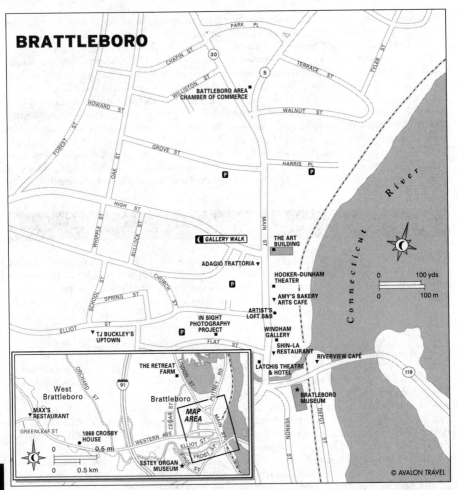

BRATTLEBORO

on vittles and red wine. A free map and guide, available online, will help you plan your attack on the fifty-some venues, which are mostly concentrated on Elliot and Main Streets.

Be sure to check out William Hays's landscapes and portraits (both human and canine) at the **Artist's Loft Gallery** (103 Main St., 802/257-5181, www.theartistsloft.com, mid-Sept.–mid-May). The best one-stop shopping is the **River Gallery School of Art** (32 Main St., 802/257-1577, www.rivergalleryschool.org/, 9:30 A.M.–5 P.M. daily, and nights and weekends when classes are in session), which usually features many different artists, along with refreshments, in its large and well-lighted space. Another sure bet is the **In-Sight Photography Project** (45 Flat St., 802/251-9960, www.in-sight-photography.org, 9:30 A.M.–5:30 P.M. Mon.–Fri.), which gets cameras into the hands of local youth, often with arresting results. Also worth checking out, the **Windham Art Gallery** (69 Main St., 802/257-1881, www.windhamartgallery.com, noon–5 P.M. Thurs.–Sun.) has a prominent location on Main Street.

Downtown Sights

In 2004, an exhibit of never-before-seen Andy Warhol paintings put the **Brattleboro Museum & Art Center** (10 Vernon St., 802/257-0124, www.brattleboromuseum.org, 11 A.M.–5 P.M. Wed.–Mon. May–Feb., $4 adults, $3 seniors, $2 students, free children under 6) on the art map. Its shows are rarely so impressive; but the center is worth a look for its unusual location in a renovated train depot, as well as for its provocative exhibitions of contemporary American art, often featuring leading artists from around New England. Harkening back to the past, **Estey Organ Museum** (108 Birge St., Brattleboro, 802/246-8366, www.esteyorganmuseum.org, noon–4 P.M. Sat.–Sun. June 13–Columbus Day, $3), which celebrates Brattleboro's century-long history as home to the largest organ-making factory in the world. The Estey Organ Company once employed more than 500 people and produced half a million organs; its former engine house now displays reed, pipe, and electronic versions along with exhibits on the history of the craft.

Outside Downtown

In 1892, Brattleboro gained a brief fame as the home of writer Rudyard Kipling, whose new bride was a native of the area. The author wrote *Captains Courageous* and the *Jungle Books* at his palatial home, **Naulakha** (Hindi for "jewel beyond price"), and may have lived there longer if it hadn't been for a feud with his neighbor and brother-in-law Beatty Balestier. Eventually the tiff grew so heated that Balestier forced Kipling's bicycle off the road with his carriage, instigating one of the country's first celebrity trials. Embarrassed by the publicity, Kipling escaped back to England instead of showing up in court. Kipling's former home is not open to the general public, but can be rented out for groups up to eight through the United Kingdom's **Landmark Trust** (707 Kipling Rd., Dummerston 802/254-6868, www.landmarktrustusa.com, $325–425 per night, 3-night minimum). The home still contains the author's original furniture, down to the billiard table in the attic.

The Retreat Farm

© WINDHAM FOUNDATION

Also on the outskirts of town, **The Retreat Farm** (350 Linden St., Brattleboro, 802/257-2240, www.theretreatfarm.com, 10 A.M.–4 P.M., Wed.–Sat., noon–4 P.M. Sun. late May–mid-Oct., $6 adults, $5 children under 12) has a family-friendly petting zoo showcasing dozens more animals, both familiar (rabbits, goats) and exotic (emus, llamas). It's a cut above ordinary petting zoos, in both mission and execution, since the 475-acre plot is still a working farm, owned by The Windham Foundation, a private foundation dedicated to preserving Vermont's rural traditions. Perhaps because of that, the big barn housing the animals is particularly interactive for children, providing not only food to feed the animals, but also brushes and scratchers to help care for them. Another section with farm implements allows budding farmers to play at being farmer for a day. For kids and grown-ups alike, the foundation recently revitalized a network of hiking trails accessible year-round from behind the farm as well as from other points of entry around town; and also opened

VERMONT

a satellite outlet of the popular Grafton Village Cheese Company (also owned by the foundation) next to the farm.

Entertainment

The landmark art deco building that houses the **Latchis Theatre** (50 Main St., 802/254-6300, www.latchis.com, $7.50 adults, $5.50 children and seniors, $5.50 matinees) is as much a part of the show as anything on the screen. Its 750-seat main theater has an iridescent mural of the zodiac on the ceiling and frolicking Greeks along the walls. Three movie theaters show a mix of first-run and independent films. The 1938 building is also a hotel. On the other end of the spectrum, patrons of the **Hooker-Dunham Theater & Gallery** (139 Main St., 802/254-9276, www.hookerdunham.org, 8:30 A.M.–4 P.M. Mon.–Fri., events $$5–20, gallery admission free) will be forgiven for thinking they've been buried alive in a funky crypt-like performance space that showcases art-house films, folk and chamber music, and avant-garde theater.

Nightlife

Singer-songwriters and experimental bands perform at **Mole's Eye Cafe** (4 High St., 802/257-0771, www.moleseyecafe.com, 3 P.M.–midnight, Mon. and Tues.; 11:30 A.M.–2 A.M. Wed.–Sat.; noon–5 P.M. Sun.), a lively subterranean spot that is your best bet for discovering local music. The first Thursday of every month is open mic night. Brattleboro's other local music showcase, **WeatherVane Gallery & Club** (19 Elliot St., 802/258-6529, www.theweathervanemusichall.com, 5 P.M.–2 A.M. nightly) is the quintessential Vermont coffeehouse, and has a relaxed vibe for conversation, with used books and games piled on the tables and live performances nightly.

Events

Each June, the cows take over for the **Strolling of the Heifers** (www.strollingoftheheifers.org, early June), a festival to celebrate the area's agrarian history and draw attention to the challenges faced by local farmers. In an opening parade, the pride of the pastures saunter down the street, followed by cow floats and kids in cow costumes. During the day, a Dairy Fest scoops out free ice cream, cheese tasting, and a "celebrity" milking contest, along with a include a "Green Expo" showcasing environmentally sustainable products and lifestyles. At a community contra dance in the evening, attendees party until the you-know-whats come home.

Shopping

Part of the pleasure of visiting Brattleboro is strolling along its main streets and poking around the eclectic mix of shops, which are anything but cookie-cutter. Stock up on your agitprop at **Save the Corporations from Themselves** (169 Main St., 802/254-4847, www.savethecorporations.com, 10 A.M.–6 P.M. Mon.–Fri., 11 A.M.–5 P.M. Sun.), an unabashedly left-of-center clothing and bookstore. For your budding revolutionary, it stocks a line of organic cotton onesies. Books tower from floor to ceiling at **Brattleboro Books** (34–36 Elliot St., 802/257-7777, Mon.–Sun.), an independent store with the best selection in town.

"Country cute" is the tone at **Dragonfly Dry Goods** (136 Main St., 866/927-0099, www.dragonflydrygoods.com, 9 A.M.–6 P.M. Mon.–Wed. and Sat.; 9 A.M.–7 P.M. Thurs.; 9 A.M.–9.P.M. Fri.; 10 A.M.–6 P.M. Sun.), a lavender-scented shop selling unique handcrafted housewares. You can find more one-of-a-kind gifts at **Vermont Artisan Designs & Gallery** (106 Main St., 802/257-7044, www.vtartisans.com, open daily), which features pottery, furniture, and other crafts made by artisans from across the state.

Do well while doing good at **Experienced Goods Thrift Shop** (77 Flat St., 802/254-5200, www.brattleborohospice.org, 10 A.M.–5:30 P.M. Mon.–Sat.; 10 A.M.–7 P.M. Fri.), two rooms of used clothing, books, and bric-a-brac at rock-bottom prices; proceeds from sales support the Brattleboro hospice. **A Candle in the Night** (181 Main St., 802/257-0471, www.acandleinthenight.com, 10 A.M.–6 P.M. Mon.–Sat.; noon–5 P.M. Sun.) is the kind of store that dreams are made of; in addition to a huge selection of Oriental rugs, it carries imported antique furniture pieces from India, many of which are on a truly mammoth scale.

Food

The town's unofficial meeting hall is **Amy's Bakery Arts Cafe** (113 Main St., 802/251-1071, 8 a.m.–6 p.m. Mon.–Sat.; 8 a.m.–5 p.m. Sun., $6.50–10), where locals catch up over fresh-baked bread, pastries, and coffee at tables overlooking the Connecticut River. A closer eye on the water can be had at the **Riverview Café** (36 Bridge St., 802/254-9841, www.riverview-cafe.com, 7:30 a.m.–9 p.m. daily in spring, summer, and fall; in winter open 7:30 a.m.–9 p.m. Sat. and Sun., 7:30 a.m.–3 p.m. Mon.–Fri., $15–20), where kayakers and blue herons sometimes join diners at river-level. The menu of sandwiches, pasta, and grilled entrées emphasizes fresh ingredients from local farms.

The best meal in town—and one of the best in Vermont—can be found at 🄲 **T. J. Buckley's Uptown** (132 Elliot St., 802/257-4922, 6 p.m.–9 p.m. Wed.–Sun., $30–35, cash or check only), a renovated 1927 Worcester diner car with an open kitchen and just five tables. Chef-owner Michael Fuller prepares a handful of options in a small open kitchen each night. All of them feature bold flavor combinations, such as venison with eggplant caponata, truffle oil, and fresh currants; and melt-in-your-mouth quail with duck leg confit and root vegetables.

Another great bet is **Adagio Trattoria** (123 Main St., Brattleboro, 802/254-6046, www.adagiotrattoria.com, 5 p.m.–10 p.m. Mon.–Wed.; 11:30 a.m.–3 p.m. and 5 p.m.–10 p.m. Sun.; 11:30 a.m.–3 p.m. and 5 p.m.–10 p.m. Thurs.–Sun., $21–30) whose fans regard Chef Eric Craw as a quasi-rock star for his creamy pastas (the Bolognese is a standout), and fresh and creative antipasti and salads. His "deconstructed tiramisu" is a sight-and-taste-to behold.

Information

The **Brattleboro Area Chamber of Commerce** (180 Main St., 802/254-4565, www.brattleborochamber.org) runs a visitors center downtown.

The area's premiere hospital is **Brattleboro Memorial Hospital** (17 Belmont Ave., Brattleboro, 802/257-0341). For pharmacy needs, there's **Rite-Aid Pharmacy** (499 Canal St., Brattleboro, 802/257-4204), which also offers faxing services, and **Walgreens** (467 Canal St., Brattleboro, 802/254-5327). Banks are found all over the downtown area, particularly on Main Street, and ATMs are plentiful around the retail stores as well as in and around hotels and in convenience stores.

Free Internet access is offered at **Twilight Tea Lounge** (51 Main St., Brattleboro, 802/254-

---

VERMONT

THE VERMONT FRESH NETWORK

It's unavoidable; you sit down at nearly any restaurant in Vermont these days, and there it is, looking back at you from the menu: "We are a proud member of the Vermont Fresh Network." But what does that mean, exactly? In essence, only good things – especially for someone about to eat a meal reaped from its benefits. The Vermont Fresh Network is a statewide group dedicated to encouraging farmers, food producers, and chefs to work more closely together, to build partnerships to support one another, and, essentially, to shorten the time from the moment an ingredient was made to the moment it hits your plate. The network, for its part, helps to promote and publicize those Vermont chefs and restaurants that use Vermont-grown and -produced foods. They also help educate the public about the nutritional upsides – not to mention the freshness – of eating locally grown foods, as well as the economic impact of supporting local farmers (www.vermontfresh.net, 802/434-2000).

8887, www.twilighttealounge.com/, 2 P.M.–10 P.M. Tues.–Sat.; noon–8 P.M. Sun.).

GRAFTON AND VICINITY

The gentle foothills of the Green Mountains hold a half dozen small villages tucked into their forested valleys. Red barns and trim white houses line the winding roads, often with brooks tracing alongside their paths. The heart of this area is the village of Grafton, painstakingly preserved by a private foundation that owns much of the town. A walking tour of the village is a nice way to slow up an afternoon; guides can be picked up at the Old Tavern. Grafton is also renowned for its cheese-making company, which, along with Cabot and Sugarbush farther north, has given the state its reputation for sharp and creamy cheddars. The surrounding towns, meanwhile, have their own attractions: the immaculate town green in Newfane, a basketmaker and music festival in Putney, and the historic downtown of Bellows Falls.

◖ Grafton Village Cheese Company

No trip to Vermont is complete without sampling the state's justly famous cheddar cheeses. Better yet, see how the stuff is made at this co-operative company (Townshend Rd., Grafton, 802/843-2221, www.graftonvillagecheese. com, 10 A.M.–5 P.M. daily) that revives more than a century of cheese-making in the village. Through a viewing window, visitors can see workers literally "cheddaring," or turning, blocks of soft curd. Each day the factory churns out more than 5,000 pounds of cheddar, made from the milk of Jersey cows on surrounding farms. A small store allows you to buy samples aged up to six years—unless you like your cheese crumbly and acidic, three or four years is usually ideal.

Bellows Falls Historic District

Bellows Falls is unique in having examples of homes of just about every architectural style in New England—including Federal, Greek Revival, Gothic Revival, Italianate, Second Empire, Stick, Shingle, Queen Anne, Colonial Revival, Dutch Colonial Revival—and pretty stellar examples at that. The town produces a self-guided walking tour to the Bellows Falls Historic District (802/463-3964, www.rockbf. org). Highlights include the Second Empire **Wyman & Almira Flint House Masonic Temple** (61 Westminster St.) and the curious Greek Revival/Queen Anne-hybrid **Babbitt Tenement House** (11 South St.). Homes are private and not open for tours, but a walking tour of their exteriors is a more than pleasant way to pass an afternoon.

Other Sights

Vermont's other famous foodstuff can be found down the road apiece at **Plummer's Sugar House** (Townshend Rd., Grafton, 802/843-2207, www.plummerssugarhouse.com), where sugar from 10,000 trees is turned into maple syrup every February and March. The proprietors, John and Debe Plummer, are happy to give tours of the syrup-making process in exchange for a purchase. Grafton is also home to a small **Nature Museum** (186 Townshend Rd., Grafton, 802/843-2111, www.nature-museum.org, 10 A.M.–4 P.M. Sat.–Sun.), which is filled with dioramas and stuffed examples of the local fauna. While some of the exhibits are a bit mangy, the museum is worth a look for its impressive catamount, the name for now-extinct mountain lions in these parts.

Stuffed animals of a different sort can be viewed at **Mary Meyer Museum of Stuffed Toys** (Rte. 30, 2 mi. north of Rte. 25, Townshend, 802/365-4160 or 888/758-2327, www.bigblackbear.com, 10 A.M.–5 P.M.Mon. and Tues.; 10 A.M.–2:30 P.M. Wed.; 10 A.M.–5 P.M. Thurs.–Sat.; 11 A.M.–5 P.M. Sun., free), a fun and informative museum at the site of a toy company that dates back to the 1930s. Kids will enjoy learning how their stuffed animals are made; parents should be warned, however, that they are unlikely to escape without a new addition to the menagerie. Also in the area is the **Scott Covered Bridge** (Rte. 30, west of Townshend), which at 166 feet is the longest in Vermont (though not open

CHEDDARING

© MICHAEL BLANDING

a covered bridge behind Grafton Village Cheese Company

It's been said that cheddar isn't merely a noun or an adjective, but also a verb. At least, that is, it's considered to be such in England and Vermont. Cheddaring began in Vermont in the 1800s as a way for dairy farmers to use up extra milk. Today, it's more of a craft, practiced among small dairy farms as a labor of love (as well as, of course, a way to make a living). Vermont cheddar houses take enormous pride in their product, proclaiming it by far America's finest sharp cheese. And they take great pain to live up to that claim. Cheddaring starts with adding rennet to warm milk to curdle it into a custard-like consistency. They then cut it with mesh wires and allow the curd to drain off all the whey before it is milled, salted, pressed, and aged. And that last stage is where the majority of the flavor and refinement come in. The most sharp-flavored (and most expensive) cheddars are those that have been aged the longest. There are scant few makers of authentic Vermont cheddar left these days, but most can be visited and are happy to offer tastings and sell their handcrafted delicacy. Following is a list of some of those cheese-makers; note that it's always wise to call ahead and make sure they will be making cheese during the time of your visit.

- **Grafton Village Cheese Company** (533 Townshend Rd., Grafton, 800/472-3866, www.graftonvillagecheese.com)

- **Cabot Cooperative Creamery** (1 Home Farm Way, Montpelier, 888/792-2268, www.cabotcheee.com)

- **Shelburne Farms** (1611 Harbor Rd., Shelburne, 802/985-8686, www.shelburne-farms.org)

- **Crowley Cheese** (Healdville Rd./Rte. 103, 2 mi. W of Rte. 100, Healdville, 802/259-2340, www.crowleycheese-vermont.com)

- **Plymouth Cheese Corporation** (106 Messer Hill Rd., Plymouth Notch, 802/672-3650, www.frogcitycheese.com)

- **Sugarbush Farm** (591 Sugarbush Farm Rd., Woodstock, 800/281-1757, www.sugarbush-farm.com)

VERMONT

to vehicle traffic). In all, seven covered bridges are scattered throughout this region, including the oldest bridge in the state—the 118-foot-long **Williamsburg Bridge** (Dover Rd., South Newfane).

Events
Every summer, 40 top chamber-music students gather at a yellow barn in the small town of Putney to study and perform with acclaimed instructors at the appropriately named **Yellow Barn Chamber Music School and Festival** (Putney, 802/387-6637, www.yellowbarn.org, late June–early Aug.). The sound of violin and piano filling up the eaves of the rustic old barn makes for a magical five weeks of music.

Shopping
Picnic baskets, step baskets, Shaker reproduction baskets, Nantucket lightship baskets, and every other conceivable form of wicker carrying apparatus can be found at the somewhat overblown **Basketville** (8 Bellows Falls Rd., Putney, 802/387-5509, www.basketville.com, 9 A.M.–8 P.M. daily) in "downtown" Putney. What started here as a family business more than 100 years ago has grown into a giant emporium, usually crowded with tourists. Less known but no less impressive,, **Vermont Botanical** (1126 South Valley Rd., Putney, 802/387-2474, www.vermontbotanical.com) is a labor of love of artist Maggie Lake, who takes Vermont wildflowers, Jack-in-the-pulpits, and fiddlehead ferns and presses them in frames of bird's-eye maple. Also taking Vermont's natural rhythms as its inspiration, **Grafton Seasons** (217 Main St., Grafton, 802/843-2499, www.graftonseasons.com, 9:30 A.M.–5:30 P.M., daily) fills its shelves with gifts and keepsakes that nod to each time of year. That means hand-blown glass candleholders by Simon Pearce sit next to Irish pottery, lots of clothing and toys, and of course, maple syrup.

Food
A blue school bus and a few scattered picnic tables is all that you'll find at the outdoor **Curtis's BBQ** (40 Old Depot Rd., Putney, 802/387-5474, www.curtisbbqvt.com, 10 A.M.–dusk Wed.–Sun. Apr.–Oct., $7–25, $5–15), which bills itself as the "ninth wonder of the world" and rarely disappoints. Run by transplanted Georgian Curtis Tuffs, this is where to get your fix of Southern-style pork ribs and grilled chicken, slathered with a tangy special sauce. (Just don't tell Curtis's pet Vietnamese potbellied pig what you are eating.)

Most of the best restaurants in these parts double as country inns. The menu at the **Old Tavern** (Grafton, 800/843-1801, www.old-tavern.com, 6–9 P.M. daily, $22–34) is creative continental, emphasis on creative. The menu usually features at least one dish utilizing cheddar from the Grafton Village Cheese Company next door. The **Four Columns Inn** (on the green, Newfane, 800/787-6633, www.fourcolumnsinn.com, 5:30–8 P.M. daily with reservation, $25–38) is arguably better known for its four-star dining room than for its bedrooms. Celeb chef Greg Parks has been blending Asian, French, and New American cuisine for three decades. Among those who have enjoyed his fare are Mick Jagger, Tom Cruise, and Paul Newman.

Information
The **Great Falls Region Chamber of Commerce** (17 Depot St., Bellows Falls, 802/463-4280, www.gfrcc.org) operates a visitors center stocked with brochures, educational exhibits, and enthusiastic staff. It's adjacent to the railway station. For more information on Historic Grafton, contact **The Windham Foundation** (802/843-2211, www.windham-foundation.org), which owns and operates many of the towns' attractions, including Grafton Village Cheese.

MARLBORO AND WILMINGTON
West of Brattleboro, Route 9 winds like a salamander through the southernmost peaks of the Green Mountains, dipping into creek beds forested with birch, beech, and sugar maple, and rising for stunning views of the surrounding hills. (The summit of Hogback Mountain

is particularly worth pulling over for.) The small college town of Marlboro is little more than a blip on the map, consisting of a few old farmhouses gathered around an old town hall. That changes every summer, however, when it becomes home to a renowned classical music festival.

Halfway between Brattleboro and Bennington, the unpretentious town of Wilmington has more worth stopping for. Unlike the ultra-quaint villages and overdeveloped ski resorts that surround it, Wilmington feels like the real deal, owing its atmosphere more to a 1950s-era vision of main street than the backwoods colonialism that pervades the rest of the region. Along the trail, an overflow of artists and craftspeople from Brattleboro fill the hills with galleries and scattered studios.

Sights

Step into your very own Christmas card with a sleigh ride at **Adams Farm** (15 Highley Hill Rd., Wilmington, 802/464-3762, www.adams-familyfarm.com, 11:30 A.M.–9 P.M. Tues.–Sun.

mid-Dec.–mid-Mar., $20 adults, $10 children 4–12, free children under 4). Drawn by Belgian draft horses, the sleighs travel through maple woods to a log cabin, where guest sip hot chocolate and listen to tunes from an old-fashioned player piano. In the summer,(10 A.M.–5 P.M. Wed.–Sun., day pass $15 adults, $13 children 2–12, children under 2 free)., fifth-generation hard-rock farmer Bill Adams exchanges horses for a sputtering 1959 John Deere for his entertaining tours of the farm, which has produced timber, maple syrup, sheep, and milk depending on Vermont's economic circumstances. The farm's latest economic driver is agritourism, with a full complement of livestock to instantly turn visiting kids into walking renditions of Old MacDonald (a "baa baa" here, a "neigh neigh" there), and evening hay rides bringing guests to a bonfire pit for s'mores under the stars and the smoky blues vocals of Bill's daughter, sixth-generation farmer Jill.

Events

Founded by two Austrian musicians who

© ALEXANDRA HALL

a resident at Adams Farm

VERMONT

WHO IS MOLLY STARK?

Route 9 between Brattleboro and Bennington is known universally as the Molly Stark Trail, after the wife of Revolutionary War general John Stark, hero of the Battle of Bennington. Stark is said to have marched along this route from New Hampshire across the state to the battlefield. Once there, he famously said: "We beat them today, or Molly Stark sleeps a widow tonight" (or something like that – the exact words are lost to history and faulty memory). Though Molly never even set foot on the trail herself, the name stuck, giving her imprimatur to schools, hospitals, parks, and lodgings along the way.

relocated to Vermont more than 50 years ago, the **Marlboro Music Festival** (Marlboro College, Marlboro, 802/254-2394, www.marlboromusic.org, Sat.–Sun. mid-July–mid-Aug., $5–30) has since become the country's preeminent festival of chamber music. Masters and students play music together on the hilltop campus of tiny Marlboro College.

Food

For a quick meal, the heart of Wilmington both physically and spiritually is **Dot's Restaurant** (3 W. Main St., Wilmington, 802/464-7284, www.dotsofvermont.com, 5:30 A.M.–8 P.M. Sun.–Thurs.; 5:30 A.M.–9 P.M. Fri. and Sat., $12–17), a wood-paneled diner with historical photos lining the walls and local characters lining the barstools. Townies line up at 5 A.M. beneath the neon sign of this greasy spoon for healthy helpings of gossip along with their "Berry Berry Pancakes," a molten mess of blueberries, raspberries, and blackberries. Lunch and dinner runs to tasty comfort food like chili, mac 'n' cheese, and burgers.

Despite the name, the taps at **Maple Leaf Brewery** (3 N. Main St., 802/464-9900, 12 P.M.–10 P.M. Sun.–Thurs.; 12 P.M.–10:30 P.M. Fri. and Sat., $9–19) go beyond

Molson to serve an ever-changing variety of microbrews. The pub also serves burgers and other entrées.

Tucked into a friendly inn looking out to the looming Mount Snow and warmed by brick fireplaces, **West Dover Inn** (108 Route 100, West Dover, 802/464-5207, 5–9 P.M. Thurs.–Tues., prix fixe menu $75) charms with handmade ravioli and breads, fresh local ingredients, and an intimate little tavern next door.

Shopping

The best of Wilmington's galleries is the **Young & Constantin Gallery** (10 S. Main St., Wilmington, 802/464-2515, www.ycgallery.com, noon–5:30 P.M., Fri–Sat., 2–5 P.M., Mon.-Thu.), a sun-splashed former church building filled with the elegant colored glass vases and molten glass sculptures of artist Kathleen Young. Its most unique, however, has to be the **Art of Humor Gallery** (30 Not A Road, Wilmington, 802/464-5523, www.theartofhumor.com, 10 A.M.–5 P.M. Sat.–Sun.; or by appointment), located on a back, back road in Wilmington. The gallery showcases the outlandish dogs, cats, cows, and plumber's cracks of pop cartoonist Skip Morrow.

Tucked into the hills along Route 100 north of West Dover are a number of artist studios. One of the most unique is **Hot Glass Works** (23 Goldman Ln., Jamaica, 802/874-4436, www.hotglassworks.net, 10 A.M.–5 P.M. daily): All items in this studio showroom are stamped "HOT"—meaning "Hank or Toby," the quirky husband-and-wife team who pour their creative spirits into colored glass coins, bowls, hummingbird feeders, and a whatever else strikes their fancy.

For the purist, **Hundredth Monkey Holistic Store** (17 W. Main St., Wilmington, 802/464-4640, 9 A.M.–6 P.M. daily) carries not only organic foods, herbs, and astrology books, but that most quintessential of Vermont foodstuffs: organic maple syrup.

Information

The **Mount Snow Chamber of Commerce** (21 W. Main St., 877/887-6884, www.

visitvermont.com, 10 A.M.–5 P.M. daily) operates an information center in Wilmington on Route 9 just west of the traffic light. www.visitvermont.com) operates an information center on Route 9 just west of the traffic light.

SPORTS AND RECREATION
Hiking and Camping
The actual grounds of Fort Dummer are now underwater, flooded when a dam was built along the Connecticut River. The area around it, however, has been preserved as **Fort Dummer State Park** (517 Old Guilford Rd., 802/254-2610, www.vtstateparks.com/htm/fortdummer.cfm, mid-May–Labor Day, campsites $14–21), a 217-acre retreat that contains a mile and a half of gentle hiking trails through a densely wooded oak forest. The campground has 50 wooded tent sites, as well as 10 more secluded lean-tos to accommodate overnight camping.

Hikers and campers will also find plenty of trails at **Ascutney State Park** (1826 Back Mountain Rd., Windsor, 802/674-2060, www.vtstateparks.com/htm/ascutney.cfm, late May–mid-Oct., 49 campsites, $14–21 nightly). The park is known for its hawks and hang-gliders, both of which soar from the granite ledges of Mount Ascutney.

Boating
Canoes and kayaks can be rented from the **Vermont Canoe Touring Center** (451 Putney Rd., 802/257-5008, $10/hour), located at the intersection of the Connecticut and West Rivers. Both rivers are peaceful paddles, though the West River can also offer class II and III whitewater after snowmelt.

Skiing
The 2000-foot tall **Stratton Mountain** (5 Village Lodge Rd., Stratton Mountain 800/787-2886, www.stratton.com, $72–79 adult, $63–69 youth, $56–59 children) signals the beginning of big-mountain skiing, just a two-and-a-half-hour drive from Boston. Accessibility doesn't come cheap, however—weekend lift ticket prices are among the highest in New England. For snowboarders, at least, it's worth the price. The sport was invented by a Stratton bartender in the 1980s, and five terrain parks and the annual US Open Snowboarding Championships continue to keep boarders busy. The smaller and cheaper **Ascutney Mountain Resort** (Rte. 44, Brownsville, 800/243-0011, www.ascutney.com, $55 weekend/$52 weekday adults; $40/$37 students and seniors, free children under 7), bills itself as a "family" skiing resort. It offers a range of programs to keep tykes busy while you tackle the diamonds.

An object lesson in capitalism run amok can be found at **Mount Snow Resort** (39 Mount Snow Rd., West Dover, 800/245-7669, www.mountsnow.com, 9 A.M.–4 P.M. Mon.–Fri., 8 A.M.–4 P.M. Sat. and Sun., $69–75 adults, $56–64 young adults 13–18, $45–52 seniors and students 6–12), which is chaotic, expensive, and often overcrowded. The resort's proximity to New York (a three- or four-hour drive depending on traffic) has given it a reputation for being favored by rowdy out-of-towners. If you enjoy skiing in a party atmosphere, however, the mountain's four faces will give you plenty to tackle, especially for intermediate skiers. The best bet is to get away from the main lodge as quickly as possible and head for the more out-of-the-way chairlifts, such as the steeper North Face.

Cross-country skiers will find plenty of well-groomed terrain at the **Grafton Ponds** (802/843-2400, www.graftonponds.com, 9 A.M.–4 P.M. daily, $12–18 adults, $10–14 seniors, $4 youth/student, children under 5 free), a skiing center featuring snowmaking over 2,000 acres of rolling fields and woodlands. The park converts to a biking center during the warmer months, when it rents mountain bikes (half days $20–30 adults, $20 children; whole days $30–40 adults, $25 children).

ACCOMMODATIONS
Under $100
The smell of buttered popcorn fills the lobby of the **Latchis Hotel** (50 Main St., Brattleboro, 802/254-6300, www.latchis.com, $80–180),

VERMONT

an unusual art deco theater-hotel. Period details like terrazzo floors and chrome fixtures transport guests back to the 1930s. The rooms themselves are a bit run-down, but an ongoing renovation has been spiffing them up of late, and the central location and historic-cool ambience more than make up the difference.

Named after the wife of the Revolutionary War general, the friendly **Molly Stark Motel** (Rte. 9, W. Brattleboro, 802/254-2440, $45–75) has basic rooms on the road towards Marlboro and Mount Snow, and is pet-friendly.

If you plan on skiing at Mount Snow but don't want to stay at the resort, you can get package rates on lift tickets along with lodging at the historic **Old Red Mill Inn** (Rte. 100, Wilmington, 802/464-3700 or 877/732-6455, www.oldredmill.com, $60–90). Cheap doesn't mean chintzy at this authentic ski-lodge style B&B with warm, friendly staff and a wrap-around fireplace in the lobby. Located in the center of Wilmington in a real converted old lumber mill, the country inn also offers a tavern menu of New England cuisine.

$100-150

Reasonably priced accommodations north of Brattleboro can be found at the **Putney Inn** (I-91, exit 4, Putney, www.putneyinn.com, $98–188). It has clean, basic rooms with quilts and flowered wallpaper, and includes a Vermont country breakfast in the rates. There is no easier way for an outsider to feel part of the community than to stay at (**The Artist's Loft B&B and Gallery** (103 Main St., Brattleboro, 802/257-5181,www.artistsloft. com, $138–178), located among the galleries along Main Street. Artists Patricia Long and William Hays rent out a suite with an inspirational view of the river; guests are invited to observe the artists at work and shoot the breeze in the adjoining studio and gallery.

Cinnamon-baked apples and ice cream with breakfast are just the start of the Vermont hospitality at (**Baked Apples at Shearer Hill Farm** (802/464-3253 or 800/437-3104, www.shearerhillfarm.com, $115), where

gregarious innkeepers Patty and Bill Pusey have taken a former farm and car junkyard and transformed it into a quiet retreat several miles back from the highway. The bed-and-breakfast features plush king-sized beds along with fields of Hereford cows, potatoes, and wildflowers.

Romance practically runs from the faucets at the **Crosby House 1868** (175 Western Ave., Brattleboro, 802/257-4914 or 800/528-1868, www.crosbyhouse.com, $140–165), a bed-and-breakfast on the west side of Brattleboro. Three individual rooms each have queen-sized beds and fireplaces; the largest has a double-whirlpool bath. Fans of Merchant/Ivory films will love the afternoon tea, at which the innkeepers lay out a selection of gloves and hats for guests, along with feathers and other accessories for "decorating."

$150-250

On a sunny day, one might be blinded by all of the white clapboard that surrounds the town common in Newfane. Several of the buildings there are part of the (**Four Columns Inn** (on the green, Newfane, 802/254-2352, www.fourcolumnsinn.com, $175–400), an upscale bed-and-breakfast with 15 rooms. In some, the bathrooms are nearly as big as the bedrooms, complete with whirlpool tubs and gas fireplaces.

A bit stuffier, but no less luxurious, is Grafton's historic **Old Tavern** (Grafton, 800/843-1801, www.old-tavern.com, $160–420), which enjoyed a reputation after the Civil War as a hangout for literary types, including Rudyard Kipling, Daniel Webster, Ralph Waldo Emerson, and Oliver Wendell Holmes. History practically speaks from the walls, along with oil portraits of presidents, four-poster beds, and period furniture.

You can't get much more elegant than the **White House** (178 Rte. 9 East, Wilmington, 802/464-2135 or 866/774-2135, www.whitehouseinn.com, 125–295), a hilltop Victorian mansion with enough terraces, fireplaces, and whirlpools to melt the most obstinate honeymooner.

GETTING THERE AND AROUND

To get to Brattleboro from Boston (115 mi., 2 hrs. 15 min.), take Route 2 west to Greenfield, then I-91 north to exit 1. From Hartford (85 mi., 1 hr. 30 min.) and Springfield (60 mi., 1 hr.), Brattleboro is a straight shot north up I-91 to exit 1. From Manchester, New Hampshire (80 mi., 1 hr. 40 min.), take I-93 andI-89 to exit 5, then head west along Route 9 to the Vermont border.

Amtrak (800/872-7245, www.amtrak.com) trains stop at **Brattleboro Train Station** (10 Vernon Rd.) once daily. Buses with **Greyhound Bus Lines** (800/642-3133, www.greyhound. com) run to Brattleboro from Boston and New York, stopping at the **Vermont Transit Terminal** (Rtes. 5 & 9, 802/254-6066).

Brattleboro's municipal bus service, the **Bee Line** (802/254-4541), offers routes throughout downtown and outlying areas. The **Deerfield Valley Transit Association** (802/464-8487, www.moover.com) operates the MOOver!, a Holstein-patterned bus offering free rides between Wilmington, West Dover, Brattleboro, Mt. Snow, and other nearby locations.

Southern Green Mountains

The Green Mountain National Forest is divided into two parts by a valley in the middle of Vermont where Route 4 cuts across the state. The southern branch of the forest is the larger of the two sections, but that is mitigated by the fact that the peaks here are smaller and the valleys more populated. The backbone of southern Vermont is Route 7, which runs from the historic (if run-down) town of Bennington up along the mountain ridges to the posh community of Manchester, which seems to get another big designer outlet store every time you turn around. Halfway between Brattleboro and Bennington, Route 100 is an alternate route northward (all the way to Canada if you choose). The twisting highway is on the short list of one of the most scenic in New England; if you drive on it a little, you'll quickly see why. In addition to stunning mountain scenery, the route is also home to the little fairy-tale village of Weston, with its picturesque town common and landmark Country Store.

BENNINGTON

In the southeastern corner of the state, the large town of Bennington is perhaps best known for the Revolutionary War battle that shares its name. Ironic, then, that the actual battle took place eight miles farther west over the New York border. (The clash is named for the storehouses in Bennington that were the object of the British troops.) In more recent years, Bennington has become better known for the small liberal arts college that is one of the artsiest (and most expensive) colleges in the country.

Despite these promising attributes, the town declined in recent decades due to a lack of industry, and the old brick downtown became depressed and uninviting. It's only in the past few years that Bennington has been looking up, taking a page from nearby Vermont towns to accentuate the art and culture generated by the college. That's a good thing, since both the town and in the surrounding villages have a number of attractions worth a visit, including those paying homage to famous Vermonters Robert Frost and Grandma Moses.

◀ Bennington Battle Monument

It's hard to miss the 300-foot-tall limestone obelisk (15 Monument Cir., 802/447-0550, www. historicvermont.org/bennington, 9 A.M.–5 P.M. mid-Apr.–Oct., $2 adults, $1 children) that towers over the town like a smaller version of the Washington Monument. Inside is a diorama of the second engagement of the Battle of Bennington, along with an elevator that takes visitors two-thirds of the way up for a knockout view of the Green

Mountains, the Berkshires, and the Taconic Range (in Vermont, Massachusetts, and New York respectively). Appropriately heroic statues of the battle's heroes, colonels John Stark and Seth Warner, stand on the monument grounds, along with a gift shop located on the actual site of the storehouse the British hoped to capture.

Other Sights

If you haven't had enough of the battle, you can learn even more at the underrated **Bennington Museum** (75 Main St., 802/447-1571, www. benningtonmuseum.org, 10 A.M.–5 P.M. Sun.–Tues. Sept. and Oct., and Thurs.–Sat. Nov.–Aug., $9 adults, $8 students and seniors, free for youth under 18), which has a room explaining troop movements and displaying rifles and other Revolutionary War paraphernalia. The museum's other big draw is the Grandma Moses gallery, which includes two dozen framed paintings by the famous New England folk artist, along with her painting desk (itself painted on) and chair. Anna Mary Robertson Moses lived in Bennington for eight years, from 1927 to 1935, and developed a simple (some might say simplistic) style that captured the past times of rural America—harvests, mills, sleigh rides, and ice skating—during a time when the United States was undergoing rapid industrialization. The museum also has several worthwhile galleries of 18th- and 19th-century furniture, pottery, and portrait paintings.

The first pottery in Bennington was made by a Revolutionary War veteran in 1793. Since then, the town has become famous for its earthenware, a tradition that is carried on at **Bennington Potters** (324 County St., 802/447-7531 or 800/205-8033, www.benningtonpotters.com, 9:30 A.M.–6 P.M. Mon.–Sat., 10 A.M.–5 P.M. Sun.), which is equal parts outlet store and museum. You can browse several rooms of mugs, bowls, and plates made in the company's distinctive "speckleware" patterns then watch craftsmen at work, spinning clay in the potters' yard.

Robert Frost once wrote, "One could do worse than be a swinger of birches." It's fitting that his final resting place should be under a small grove of birches behind Bennington's **Old First Church** (1 Monument Cir., 802/447-1223, www.oldfirstchurchbenn.org, 10 A.M.–noon and 1–4 P.M. Sat., 1–4 P.M. Sun. late May–Jun.; 10 A.M.–noon and 1–4 P.M., Mon.–Sat., 1–4 P.M. Sun July–mid-Oct., donations welcomed). In addition to Frost's grave, the cemetery also contains those of American, British, and Hessian soldiers killed at the Battle of Bennington. Robert Frost's trail can be followed north of town to the **Robert Frost Stone House Museum** (121 Rte. 7A, Shaftsbury, 802/447-6200, www.frostfriends. org, 10 A.M.–5 P.M. Tues.–Sun. May–Dec., $5 adults, $2.50 students under 18), where the poet lived for several years. Inside are changing exhibits dedicated to exploring Frost's life, along with a permanent exhibit dedicated to the poem "Stopping by the Woods on a Snowy Evening," which he wrote at the dining room table here "on a hot June morning in 1922." On the grounds, you can amble among the stone walls and some of Frost's original apple trees.

It was only a matter of time before someone decided to dedicate an entire museum to that cult tourist phenom, the covered bridge. Enter, the **Covered Bridge Museum** (Rte. 9 at Gypsy Lane, 802/442-7158, www.benningtoncenterforthearts.org/CBMHome.htm, 10 A.M.–5 P.M. Wed.–Mon., $9 adults, $8 students and seniors, children under 12 free), which includes exhibits on bridge design and tools along with a light-up map showing the locations of all 100-some Vermont examples. No less than five are within a few minutes' drive of Bennington, including the dramatic **Chiselville Bridge** (East Arlington Rd., off Rte. 7A, Sunderland), which spans a gorge over the Roaring Branch Brook. The museum is located in the **Bennington Center for the Arts** (44 Gypsy Lane, 802/442-7158, www.benningtoncenterforthearts.org, 10 A.M.–5 P.M. Wed.–Mon., $9 adults, $8 students and seniors, children under 12 free), a large complex with mediocre displays of New England paintings and Native American arts.

VERMONT

One of the most impressive Victorians in New England is the **Park-McCullough House** (1 Park St., 802/442-5441, www.parkmccullough. org, 10 A.M.–4 P.M. daily mid-May–mid-Oct., tours on the hour, $10 adults, $9 seniors, $7 students, children under 12 free), a Second Empire mansion filled with lavish antiques and period furniture. A separate carriage barn contains carriages, sleighs, and fire-fighting equipment.

Entertainment and Events

On August 16, Vermont celebrates its very own holiday of **Bennington Battle Day** (802/447-3311 or 800/229-0252, www.bennington. com), during which the town holds an annual parade along with battle reenactments on the monument grounds.

Shopping

Every once in awhile you stumble across a store so unique, you have no idea how to categorize it. Such a place is **Fiddlehead at Four Corners** (338 Main St., 802/447-1000, 10 A.M.–5 P.M. Mon.–Sat.; noon–5 P.M. Sun.), a browser's dream of crafts and oddities in a huge old bank building. Recent finds here include limited-edition Dr. Seuss lithographs, framed animation cells from *The Simpsons,* and a "brew vault" full of antique light-up beer signs from the last 40 years.

More crafts can be found at the **Hawkins House Craftsmarket** (262 North St., 802/447-0488, www. hawkinshouse.net, 10 A.M.–6 P.M. Mon.–Sat.; 11 A.M.–5:30 P.M. Sun.), including hooked rugs, blown glass, and jewelry from some 400 artisans. Stock up for your expedition to the Green Mountains at **Nature's Closet** (400 Main St., 802/442-0476, www. naturescloset.net), an outdoor-clothing store with an environmental ethos, right down to the recycled carpet and "natural" bathroom tile. You can smell the dust at **Now and Then Books** (439 Main St., 2nd Fl., 802/442-5566, www.nowandthenbooksvt.com, noon–5 P.M. Sun.–Mon.; 11:30 A.M.–5:30 P.M. Wed.–Sat.; seasonal hours may vary), a warren of rooms piled eight feet high with books on every subject.

Food

If you don't know what to order at **Sonny's Blue Benn Diner** (314 North St./Rte. 7, 802/442-5140, 6 A.M.–5 P.M. Mon. and Tues.; 6 A.M.–8 P.M. Wed.–Fri.; 6 A.M.–4 P.M. Sat.; 7 A.M.–4 P.M. Sun., $3–11), just look up. Every inch of wall space in this prefab 1940s diner car is covered with specials. Especially to-die-for are the waffles and French toast, topped with every imaginable combination of syrups, fruits, and nuts.

Located in the center of town in a historic hotel building, **Izabella's Eatery** (351 West Main St., 802/447-4949, www.izabellaseatery.com, 7:30 A.M.–4 P.M. Tues.–Fri.; 8:30 A.M.–4 P.M. Sat.; seasonal hours may vary, $4–8) is a brightly painted "urban style café" that serves all-day breakfasts and over-stuffed sandwiches with ingredients from local farms. The convivial **Madison Brewing Company** (428 Main St., 802/442-7397, 11:30 A.M.–9:30 P.M. Sun–Thurs; 11:30 A.M.–10:30 P.M. Fri. and Sat., $8–15) serves hand-crafted beers with names like Old 76 Strong Ale and Suckerpond Blonde along with pub grub, steaks, and pasta.

Information and Services

The **Bennington Area Chamber of Commerce** (100 Veterans Memorial Dr., 802/447-3311, www.bennington.com) runs a visitors center in town. Emergency medical services are handled by **Southwestern Vermont Medical Center** (100 Hospital Dr., East Bennington, 802/442-6361, www.svhealthcare.org). For medications, **Extended Care Pharmacy** is located in the center of town 207 North St., 802/442-4600), along with chain pharmacy **Rite-Aid** (194 North St., 802/442-2240). For non-medical emergencies, contact Bennington Police Department (118 South St, 802/442-1030).

MANCHESTER

If you've had your fill of maple syrup and cheddar cheese and could go for a hot latte and the *New York Times* crossword puzzle, then Manchester is your place. Vermont's Madison

Avenue in the Mountains, the winding path of Route 7 is lined with outlet shops bearing the names of top designers such as Coach, Escada, and Ralph Lauren. There's more to the town than shopping, however. Its location between the Taconic Range and Green Mountains makes it the perfect jumping-off point for outdoor pursuits.

Manchester began taking shape as a resort community in the 1850s, when Franklin Orvis began touting the Equinox House as one of the most fashionable hotels in Vermont. Located at the base of Mount Equinox, the highest peak in the Taconics, the hotel and the town drew moneyed guests from New York and Massachusetts to hike, ski, and fly-fish for trout in the Batten Kill River. Thanks to Franklin's brother Charles, the Orvis name is synonymous with fly-fishing, which is still avidly practiced in the area.

Sights

Among those who once made Manchester their summer home was Abraham Lincoln's son, Robert Todd Lincoln, who entertained guests at **Hildene** (1005 Hildene Rd., 802/362-1788, www.hildene.org, 9:30 A.M.–4:30 P.M. daily, $12.50 adults, $5 children 6–14, children under 6 free), a Georgian Revival mansion with grounds overlooking the Batten Kill River. Musical performances and craft fairs frequently take place on the grounds. See how the masters cast and tied at the **American Museum of Fly Fishing** (4070 Main St./Rte 7A, 802/362-3300, www.amff.com, 10 A.M.–4 P.M. Tue.–Sat., $5 adults, $3 children 5–14, donations). The quaint museum showcases flies tied by Mary Orvis Marbury and other originators of the sport, along with rods owned by such celebrities as Ernest Hemingway, Babe Ruth, and George H. W. Bush.

Few art museums are as beautifully situated as the **Southern Vermont Art Center** (West Rd., 802/362-1405, www.svac.org, 10 A.M.–5 P.M. Tues.–Sat.; noon–5 P.M. Sun., admission donations $8 adults, $3 students, children under 13 free), which has its wooded grounds on the flank of Mount Equinox.

Inside, the center plays host to traveling art exhibitions, jazz and classical music concerts, and author readings.

For a closer look at the mountain (and a more distant view of the valley), take the **Mount Equinox Skyline Drive** (off Rte. 7A, 802/362-1115, www.equinoxmountain.com/skylinedrive/, $12 car and driver, $2 per passenger, children under 12 free). The winding toll road climbs 3,800 feet to the summit for an unparalleled view of the surrounding peaks and sometimes sightings of eagles and peregrine falcons.

Shopping

If you could afford it, you could spend a week shopping at all of the **Manchester Designer Outlets** (97 Depot Street, 802/362-3736, www.manchesterdesigneroutlets.com, hours vary by store), which has some 30 factory outlet stores, including such top names as Giorgio Armani, Brooks Brothers, and Coach. The best stores are along Routes 11 and 30 (take a right after you hit the town center), conveniently grouped in several strip malls.

Peruse copper weathervanes and whimsical wooden animals at **Flying Cow Signs** (5073 Main St., 802/362-4927, www.flyingcowsigns.com, 10 A.M.–5 P.M. Mon.–Sat.; closed Sun), which will also make you a customized sign for your house starting at $65 and $9–11 per letter.

Finally, when you get hungry after all of the shopping, replenish your sugars at **Mother Myrick's Confectionary** (Rte. 7A, 888/669-7425, www.mothermyricks.com, 9 A.M.–6 P.M. daily), an old-fashioned candy shop carrying such mouthwatering classics as buttercrunch, truffles, and linzer torte, along with New England–specific recipes like maple-blueberry cheesecake.

Food

Vintage French posters fill the wall space of the large but intimate ◖ **Bistro Henry** (1942 Rte. 11/30, 802/362-4982, www.bistrohenry.com, 5–9 P.M. Mon.–Fri., noon–4 P.M. and 5–9 P.M. Sat.–Sun., $25–32)founded by two transplanted

Manhattan chefs. As the name suggests, the restaurant serves heavily Americanized bistro food, like grilled venison with lingonberry sauce and fettuccine with rabbit ("We only use the ugly ones, not the cute ones," says Chef Henry). Henry's wife, Dina, makes desserts, including a Grand Marnier crème brûlée. The food may be fancy, but the atmosphere isn't at **The Perfect Wife** (2594 Depot St./Rte. 11/30, 802/362-2817, www.perfectwife.com, 5–10 P.M. Mon.–Sat.; seasonal hours may vary, $19–28), which feels more like a dinner party than a restaurant. Whether you have a perfect wife at home or not, you'll appreciate chef and "aspiring perfect wife" Amy Chamberlain's seared yellowfin tuna, pecan pork tenderloin, coq au vin, and "howling wolf" vegetarian special.

You might not expect to find good Mexican food this far up in Vermont, but **Candelero's** (5103 Main St., 802/362-0836, www.candeleros.net, 4–9 P.M. daily, $15–23) does a great job with creative Southwestern cuisine, served in a brick Victorian house.

If the rooster motif at **Up For Breakfast** (4935 Main St./Rte. 7A, 802/362-4204, 7 A.M.–12:30 P.M. Mon.–Fri.; 7 A.M.–1 P.M. Sat. and Sun., $8–12) doesn't open your eyes, the hearty meals here will. It's located on the second floor overlooking Main Street. The "red flannel hash" and sourdough *batard* French toast are perfect for bulking up on carbs before hitting the hills or the slopes.

Information and Services
The **Manchester and the Mountains Chamber of Commerce** (5080 Main St., 802/362-2100 or 800/362-4144, www.manchestervermont.com) runs a small information booth on the town green on Route 7A. Manchester has several pharmacies in the town center, including **Rite-Aid Pharmacy** (4993 Main St., Manchester Ctr, 802/362-2230).

Free Wi-Fi is available at Spiral Press Cafe (15 Bonnet St., 802/362-9944), right at the corner of Rtes. 15 and 30, attached to Northshire Bookstore. For emergencies, contact **Manchester Police Department** (6041 Main St., 802/362-2121).

OKEMO VALLEY
West of Manchester, Route 100 really takes flight through the heart of the Green Mountains, tracing ridges with panoramic views of the valleys below. Tucked into one of them, the tiny village of Weston might be the most scenic in all of Vermont, with a collection of lost-in-time houses and shops surrounding a perfect town green. In fact, the entire town is on the National Register of Historic Places. Despite its beauty, however, Weston might just be a quaint hamlet if not for the presence of the mother of all country stores, the Vermont Country Store, which draws tourists in fistfuls. Heading northward, scenic Route 100 skirts around the base of Mount Okemo on its way through hills sprinkled with secluded mountain resorts.

◖ The Vermont Country Store
Back in the day, when roads between villages were long and the snows would block mountain passes for months, the country store had to be all things to all people, packing foodstuffs, medicines, clothes, hardware, and everything else the family needed to prosper. Over time, stores specialized, and the country store literally fell by the wayside. That is, until it was revived by Vrest Orton, who opened the original restored country store (657 Main St., Weston, 802/824-3184, www.vermontcountrystore.com, 9 A.M.–5:30 P.M. daily, year-round) on Weston Common in 1949. The shop was so successful that it has spawned countless imitators and expanded many times over in the past decades. Now the store is a Vermont vision of a country mall, with wood floorboards and rafters going back as long as a football field, and shelves packed with state-made products.

If you haven't yet found that perfect block of cheddar cheese or a tin of maple syrup, you'll find it here. But this is not just another tacky souvenir shop; the proprietors—still members of the Orton family—have gone out of their way to closely evoke the old-time rural character of the state, taking requests from customers to stock hard-to-find beauty products, medicinal balms, and rugged clothing items they

VERMONT

© MICHAEL BLANDING

The Vermont Country Store

remembered from yesteryear but despaired of ever finding again. Especially poignant for some customers are the children's toys and candy thought to have vanished long ago. For the true spirit of old-time Vermont, this is one-stop shopping.

Other Sights
Situated on the town common in Weston, the F-style **Farrar-Mansur House Museum** (Rte. 100, Weston, 802/824-8190, 1–5 P.M. daily late May–early Oct., suggested donation $2) was originally built as a tavern at the turn of the 19th century. It is now filled with early American furnishings and portraits. Paintings in the parlor by Roy William, a student of John Singer Sargent, depict life in the town circa 1830. Also run by the Weston Historical Society, the **Old Mill Museum** (Rte. 100, Weston, 802/824-8190, 10 A.M.–4 P.M. daily late May–early Oct., suggested donation $2) displays proof that not everything in the town was always so cute. Room after room is filled with rough-hewn farming and logging implements with which village folk carved out their lives. The building itself is an old sawmill, rebuilt after being burned in 1900.

A few miles north of Weston in the town of Plymouth is one of the best presidential historical sites in the country. The **President Calvin Coolidge State Historic Site** (Rte. 100A, Plymouth Notch, 802/672-3773, www.historicvermont.org/coolidge, 9:30 A.M.–5 P.M. daily late May–mid-Oct.; office exhibits only Mon.–Fri. mid-Oct.–May, $7.50 adults, $2 children 6–14, children under 6 free) is situated on the grounds of the 30th president's boyhood home, a sprawling collection of houses, barns, and factories nobly situated in a mountain-ringed valley. The exhibits inside give a rarely intimate look into the upbringing of the president known as "Silent Cal" for his lack of emotion, but who restored the dignity of the office during a time of widespread scandal.

Entertainment and Events
Party like it's 1499 at **Weston Priory** (58 Priory Hill Rd., Weston, 802/824-5409, www.westonpriory.com), where Benedictine monks sing plainsong several times a day during

prayers, which the public is invited to attend. The **Weston Playhouse Theatre Company** (on the green, Weston, 802/824-5288, www.westonplayhouse.org, late June–early Sept., $28–48) has been performing above-average community theater for 70 years. In addition to Broadway musicals and stage classics, the company performs a cabaret-style review nightly after each main performance.

The **Weston Antiques Show** (802/824-5307, www.westonantiquesshow.org) has been recognized as one of the best in New England. It takes place every year in the beginning of October, when the foliage is at its height.

Food

Next door to the Vermont Country Store, the spirit of Victorian New England is kept alive at the **Bryant House Restaurant** (Rte. 100, Weston, 802/824-6287, www.vermontcountrystore.com, 11 A.M.–3:30 P.M. Sun.–Thurs,.; 11 A.M.–8 P.M. Fri.–Sat., $13–20). The bright red house is filled with antique lighting fixtures and furniture that surrounds diners as they savor gourmet salads and sandwiches. An adjoining barroom, adorned with mahogany wall paneling, serves key lime margaritas and apricot sours. Be forewarned, however, that on busy days at the store you can expect a wait of over an hour; a loudspeaker system next door ensures that you can shop while you wait. If you aren't careful, you may live up to the name of the **Pot Belly Pub & Restaurant** (130 Main St., Ludlow, 802/228-8989, 11 A.M.–8 P.M. daily, $7–27)a convivial bar located at the foot of Mount Okemo that serves oversized burgers and hearty portions of BBQ ribs. When the skiers leave the slopes, a somewhat raucous bar scene ensues, often featuring live jazz or R&B.

A private ski club has the best dining in Okemo Valley. You'll find it at **Bear Creek Mountain Club** (Route 100, Plymouth, 802/672-4242, www.bearcreekclub.com, 11 A.M.–6 P.M. daily, $18–32). Head in for the likes of lobster-stuffed ravioli and free-range chicken *piccata*. On weekends, live local bluegrass bands keep the vibe as good as the food.

Information

For more information on the Okemo area, contact **Okemo Valley Regional Chamber of Commerce** (Ludlow, 802/228-5830, www.okemovalleyvt.org) which runs information booths at the clock tower in Ludlow.

SPORTS AND RECREATION
Hiking

Near Bennington is the start of the Long Trail, Vermont's predecessor to the Appalachian Trail, which wends its way along the spine of the Green Mountains from Massachusetts to the Canadian border. You can find information about day hikes along the trail as well as other hiking paths from the **Green Mountain Club** (802/244-7037, www.greenmountainclub.org). Guided trips near Bennington are offered by the **Bennington Chapter** (802/442-3469, www.bennington.com/outingclub) of the club. For the more adventurous, the Green Mountain Club maintains some 70 campsites along the Long Trail from Bennington to the Canadian border. Hikers interested in venturing forth on the Trail would do well to pick up a copy of the *Long Trail Guide*, available in any bookshop or outdoor store in the area (and often at pharmacies and convenience stores as well), or through the GMC's website.

For day-hikers, the hills around Manchester and Bennington are filled with many more hiking trails, which start from several of the most popular sights. The **Manchester Ranger Station** (2538 Depot St./Rte. 11/30, Manchester, 802/362-2307) offers a free (if rudimentary) trail map of day hikes within Green Mountain National Forest that range from easy to difficult, with distances up to 11 miles. You can find a trail map for **Mount Equinox** at the tollhouse for the skyline drive. Trails on the mountain vary from a short hike to a panoramic view at Lookout Rock, to a strenuous four-mile hike to the summit. A system of more gentle trails is located at the **Equinox Preservation,** behind the Equinox Resort (see *Accommodations* later in this chapter). Park in the hotel parking lot and ask for a map at the concierge desk.

VERMONT

Skiing

In the winter months, Manchester becomes a playground for cross-country skiers, who have several trail systems to choose from. Several miles of groomed and tracked trails can be found at the **Hildene Touring Center** (Rte. 7A, Manchester, 802/362-1788, www.hildene.org, 9:30 A.M.–4 P.M. Dec.–mid-Mar., trail pass $12.50 adults, $6 youth; rental $15; lessons $30), where the estate's carriage barn is turned into a warming hut and rental shop. The sound of your own breathing will be all you hear at **Merck Forest** (Rte. 315, Rupert Mountain, 802/394-7836, www.merckforest.com, daily year-round, $25 camping, $45–80 cabins), a backcountry family farm and trail system on a remote stretch of the New York border.

The south-facing slopes of **Bromley Mountain** (3984 Rte. 11, Peru, 802/824-5522, www.bromley.com, $63 weekend/$39 midweek adults, $55/$39 youth 13–17, $39/$39 youth 6–12, children under 6 free) make it one of Vermont's sunniest for downhill skiers. While not as challenging as some of the bigger mountains nearby, at least Bromley lets you get a tan while you ski. It's also known for family programs, including a kids' ski school with animal friends Alex the Alligator and Clyde Catamount.

The slopes at **Okemo Mountain Resort** (77 Okemo Ridge Rd., Ludlow, 800/786-5366, www.okemo.com, $49–77 adults, $42–65 youth 13–18 and seniors 65–69, $32–50 children 7–12 and seniors 70 and over, children under 7 free) provide the perfect balance for families who want fun and accessible programs for the kids but still want reasonably challenging runs for mom and dad. The mountain has won a cult following for its refreshingly no-frills atmosphere and emphasis on customer service, which has gotten even better with the addition of a new attractive slope-side village and base lodge. In recent years, however, the mountain has become overcrowded during peak periods. Also, diehards will be disappointed by its lack of really advanced terrain.

Snowmobiling

West of Manchester, **Equinox Snow Tours** (junction of Rte. 11 and Rte. 30, Winhall, 802/824-6628, www.vermontsnowmobile.com, $40–203 per person) offers tours through the national forest.

Fishing

The Equinox Resort & Spa is also home to the **Orvis Fly Fishing School** (800/362-4747, $470 for two-day course), which carries on the tradition of Frank Orvis by offering close instruction on snaring brook trout on the Batten Kill.

For a more flexible itinerary, contact **The Young Outdoor Company** (673 Crow Hill Rd., Arlington, 802/375-9313, bobyoung@together.net), whose proprietor, Bob Young, is a veteran instructor for the Orvis School and will instruct you in your choice of fly or spin fishing, with or without a boat.

Chartered bass fishing on nearby lakes is offered by **Green Mountain Fishing Guide Service** (593 Rte. 140, Tinmouth, 802/446-3375), whose bass master, Rod Start, has 25 years of experience on the fishing-tournament circuit.

Boating

If your vision of enjoying the river doesn't include a fishing rod, **BattenKill Canoe** (6328 Rte. 7A, Arlington, 802/362-2800, www.battenkill.com) rents canoes and leads package canoe tours with stays in country inns along the rivers.

Horseback Riding

A few miles up Route 7, the **Chipman Stables** (Danby Four Corners, 802/293-5242, www.chipmanstables.com) takes out guided horseback rides ($35/hr., $125/day), as well as hayrides and sleigh rides depending on the season.

Other Sports

The **Equinox Resort** (802/362-7873) also offers several "upscale" outdoor activities,. Perhaps the most impressive is the **British School of Falconry** (from $110 per person for a 45-minute lesson to around $1,800 for a four-day course), which if you have the money to spend will teach you how to hunt quail, pheasants, and other game birds with your very own Harris hawk. The school also offers archery and crossbow lessons ($185 per person for a 90 minute lesson) and year-round off-road driving on an 80-acre course ($225 per hour) through its affiliated **Land Rover Experience Driving School.** If you harbor images of chewing up mud and rock while you whiz around curves in your Land Rover, however, be forewarned that the driving school is more of an exercise in technology than skill—the truck does most of the work through its impressive array of dashboard settings that can take on snow, sand, mud, or any other terrain. Your job is to mostly keep your hands on the wheel and try not to scratch the paint job as you slowly maneuver through the course. If you are a gearhead, you'll love it; if not, you might find yourself wishing for a bit more control.

ACCOMMODATIONS
Under $100

Just down the hill from the Bennington Battle Monument, the **Knotty Pine Motel** (130 Northside Dr., Bennington, 802/442-5487, www.knottypinemotel.com, $63–77) offers exceptional value for a motel, with refrigerators, coffee-makers and cable television in each of its spotless rooms.

Located in Manchester Center, the **Four Winds Country Motel** (7379 Rte. 7A, Manchester, 802/362-1105, www.fourwindscountrymotel.com, $66–120) is a cut above the usual motel, with country furniture and antiques in the rooms.

The **Colonial House Inn & Motel** (287 Rte. 100, Weston, 802/824-6286 or 800/639-5033, www.cohoinn.com, $70–175) combines the hospitality of a bed-and-breakfast with the prices of a motel. A rustic living room has a warm stove and plenty of comfy chairs, along with wireless Internet access for your laptop. The proprietors' baked pies were so popular that they created a separate business; pies are available for takeaway with advance notice.

$100-150

Four chimneys really do project from the roof of **The Four Chimneys Inn** (21 West Rd./Rte. 9, Bennington, 802/447-3500, www.fourchimneys.com, rooms $125–295, entrées $19–36), a sprawling Revolutionary-era parsonage that has been converted to an upscale bed-and-breakfast. As might be expected, many of the rooms have fireplaces, including one with a real wood-burning hearth. The white-cloth dining room has French doors looking out on the grounds and serves a menu of refined New England cuisine, with specialties such as grilled apple cider salmon and mushroom and leek risotto.

The current owner of the **Barnstead Inn** (Bonnet St., Manchester, 800/331-1619, www.barnsteadinn.com, $85–300) used to sled down the hill beside the hay barn that has been converted into a bed-and-breakfast. The 14 individual rooms feature romantic touches like exposed beams and original antiques.

For a great deal, head into the **Salt Ash Inn** (4758 Rte. 100A/Jct. Rte. 100, Plymouth, 800/725-8274, www.saltashinn.com, $130–210), Just up from Calvin Coolidge's birthplace, new owners Karla and Naz Jenulevich have renovated this budget B&B with gas fireplaces and four-poster beds. The pair serve up local travel tips at an on-site bar.

$150-250

Manchester's most romantic B&B, ◖ **The Reluctant Panther Inn & Resturant** (17–39 West Rd., Manchester, 802/362-2568, www.reluctantpanther.com, $179–759), was gutted by fire several years back. Owners Liz and Jerry Lavalley took the occasion to renovate with even more upscale amenities. Each room in the antique-filled home now has at least one fireplace (some have two) and a Jacuzzi-style tub (most large enough to fit two people). In addition, a carriage house and a pair of older buildings on the grounds feature wood-burning fireplaces and private porches. Despite the heavy emphasis on couples, some rooms do allow small dogs or small children. A restaurant on premises offers a mix of upscale continental and American regional cuisine with a view of Mount Equinox. Panther or no, you'll be reluctant to leave.

Right on the Weston town green, the **Inn at Weston** (620 Rte. 100, Weston, 802/824-6789, www.innweston.com, rooms $185–325, entrées $26–34) offers romance in the form of queen featherbeds covered in country quilts, two-person whirlpool tubs, and in-room woodstoves. The innkeeper tends orchids in a greenhouse open for tours. The inn also features a dining room serving unusual contemporary cuisine such as seared diver scallops with vanilla infused butternut squash sauce and warm terrine of roasted eggplant, with chai crème brûlée for dessert.

$250 and Up

Much has changed at the **Equinox Resort & Spa** (3567 Main St./Rte. 7A, Manchester, 800/362-4747 www.equinoxresort.com, $239–439) since Orvis's day. What hasn't changed is that this is still where those with money to burn receive the ultimate in luxury. The sprawling resort contains almost 200 rooms outfitted with plush furnishings, along with wooded grounds that stretch for 1300 acres and include a luxury spa, a golf course, and a falconry school.

More intimate, but no less luxurious, is **The Inn at Ormsby Hill** (1842 Main St./Rte. 7A, Manchester, 802/362-1163, www.ormsbyhill.com, $205–535), a Revolutionary-era mansion named after a captain of the Green Mountain Boys. The inn, which underwent a renovation in 2008, prides itself on individual attention to guests and a lavish decor calling to mind an English drawing room (complete with carved mantelpieces and wood-beaded ceilings). Innkeeper Chris Sprague is an imaginative breakfast cook, along the lines of bacon-and-egg risotto and eggs Benedict bread pudding.

GETTING THERE AND AROUND

To get to Bennington, drive west along Route 9 from Brattleboro (40 mi., 1 hr.). Drive north up Route 7 from Bennington for Shaftsbury (10 mi., 15 min.), Arlington (15 mi., 25 min.), Manchester (25 mi., 40 min.), Dorset (30 mi., 45 min.), or Danby (35 mi., 50 min.).

Buses run by **Greyhound Bus Lines** (800/231-2222, www.greyhound.com) stop at **Bennington Bus Station** (126 Washington Ave., 802/442-4808). No buses or trains run to the Manchester area; the closest transit hub is Rutland, from which it's possible to take a free bus to Manchester with **Green Mountain Express** (802/447-0477), which also runs bus service within Manchester and to Bennington and other nearby locations.

Woodstock Area

Nestled onto Route 4 the dividing line between northern and southern Vermont, is Woodstock, a historic town that very well defines country chic. Here, the restaurants all sport linen (or adorably retro marble tables), the inns all have bath amenities worth snagging, and the artists all have city agents. Even the year-round residents in Woodstock are usually ex-Manhattan performance artists or creative types who've come to live their lifelong dream of opening a patisserie, antiques shop, or country B&B.

But let there be no doubt: This is Vermont you came here to see—ridiculously perfect white-steepled churches, farmhouses with cows grazing outside, and of course antiques stores and crafts shops as far as your wallet can take you. A must-stop site is Queeche Gorge, where trails plummet from the road hundreds of feet down to a rushing white-water river. This is prime ski country, with the granddaddy of all New England ski resorts, Killington, stretching its grooming equipment over six whole mountains.

WHITE RIVER JUNCTION

Despite it prominent location at the crossroads of the Connecticut River and two of northern New England's main thoroughfares—I-89 and I-91—White River Junction is a locale that most visitors to the state journey through, not to. After the decline of the railway, "WRJ" grew into an ugly industrial sprawl that doesn't provide the most inviting introduction to the state. Recently, however, the city's downtown has started to come back to life as artists seeking cheap rents have created lofts and studios, forming a residential community. That has given the town a funky vibe in some parts, which together with its inexpensive lodgings makes it a convenient stopover on your way to or from nearby Killington.

Sights

Located at the Amtrak passenger station in town, the **New England Transportation Museum** (100 Railroad Row, 802/291-9838, www.newenglandtransportationmuseum.org, 10 A.M.–5 P.M. Tues.–Sun. late May–early Sept., 9 A.M.–1 P.M. Tues. and Fri. Jan.–May, donations accepted) displays exhibits relating to White River Junction's history as a railroad hub. Highlights are the "Old 494," a meticulously restored gleaming old steam engine, and an intricate model railroad that speeds by a Vermont scene complete with pine trees and moose. It's not especially riveting for adults, but it's guaranteed to be among any child's vacation highlights. A dozen miles south along I-91 is the home of what is arguably the best beer made in New England. The **Harpoon Brewery** (336 Ruth Carney Dr., Windsor, 888/427-7666, www.harpoonbrewery.com, 10 A.M.–6 P.M. Sun.–Wed. and 10 A.M.–9 P.M. Thurs.–Sat. May–Oct.; 10 A.M.–6 P.M. Sun., Tues., and Wed., 10 A.M.–9 P.M. Thurs.–Sat. Nov.–Apr.) has won special acclaim for its India Pale Ale, giving Harpoon IPA a regular place on tap at most bars in New England. Just about everything the brewery makes, however, is a master in its class; other favorites are the Octoberfest and Munich Type Dark. The brewery is a bit stingy in its tastings, limiting visitors to four two-ounce samples per person. If you'd like more (and you will), you'll have to take a seat at the brewery's "beer garden," which serves sandwiches along with freshly poured pints.

VERMONT

"old 494" at the New England Transportation Museum

The other way on the highway, a few miles north from WRJ is the large **Montshire Museum of Science** (1 Montshire Rd./I-91 exit 13, Norwich, 802/649-2200, www.montshire. org, 10 A.M.–5 P.M. daily, $10 adults, $8 children 2–17, children under 2 free) is an ambitious local enterprise with exhibits on wildlife, astronomy, and physics. Highlights include a leaf-cutter ant colony and a 250-foot watercourse. Outdoors is a scale model of the solar system, along with several easy-grade nature trails.

Events

Especially good times to visit the Harpoon Brewery (888/427-7666, www.harpoonbrewery.com) are during the **Harpoon Championships of New England Barbecue** in late July—where you can discover how very well ale goes with ribs and grilled chicken—and **Harpoon Octoberfest** in early October, when the eponymous beer is released.

Food

Laid-back and high-energy at once, **Tip Top Cafe** (85 N. Main St., 802/295-3312, www. tiptopcafevermont.com, 11:30 A.M.–2 P.M. and–9 P.M. Tues.–Sat., $7–20) is a great blend of bistro and coffeehouse. At lunchtime, the sunny spot serves sandwiches and soups, and at night it brings the candlelight out, alongside entrées like the house specialty, pork and ginger meatloaf.

For a dash of nightlife mixed into your supper, grab one of the coveted tables at **Elixir Restaurant and Lounge** (188 S. Main St., 802/281-7009, www.elixirrestaurant.com, 4–10 P.M. Tues.–Wed., 4 P.M.–midnight Thurs.–Sat.; winter hours 6:30–9:30 pm Fri., 7–10 pm Sat., $7–14). Along with its groovy vibe, the local hot spot doles out tasty and cleverly named bites like potato gnocchi with rock shrimp and ham ("Pillows of Love"), and steak quesadilla with lime cream and blue cheese ("Blue Your Socks Off").

Information and Services

For more information about White River Junction and the surrounding area, contact the **Upper Valley Chamber of Commerce** (802/295-6200, www.uppervalleychamber. com), which staffs an information booth (100 Railroad Row) at the railroad station in downtown White River Junction.

QUECHEE

As Route 4 winds its way along the Ottauquechee River into the heart of the state, it passes through a region beset by contrasts. On one hand is the natural beauty of the river, which reaches its peak at the stunning Quechee Gorge. On the other is the runaway development of condos and schlocky tourist shops of Quechee, which somewhat mars the tranquility. Even so, there is something endearing even about all the schlock, which seems more beholden to a retro era of car-touring and motor lodges than modern strip-mall development.

◖ Vermont Institute of Natural Science (VINS)

This museum (Rte. 4 just west of Quechee Gorge, 802/359-5000, www.vinsnaturecenter.org, 10 A.M.–5 P.M. daily May–Oct.; call for winter hours, $9 adults, $8 seniors, $7 children 3–16, children 2 and under free) is simple in its concept—an outdoor semicircle of cages underneath a large awning. But to call the feathery raptors inside the cages "birds" is like calling John Lennon "a musician." Over the years, VINS has made it its mission to rescue and rehabilitate birds of prey, including hawks, owls, and eagles, and display them for the education of visitors. Watching the raptors watch you is an unforgettable experience; behind their hooked beaks, these birds hold the deadly eyes of a killer. They become more accessible with the expert interpretation of the center's trained staff, who know the habits and quirks of the birds inside and out.

Try to time your visit with a raptor educational program, at 11 A.M. and 3:30 P.M. daily (additional program at 1:30 P.M., Fri.–Sun.), during which you can see these predators take flight. Of course, the other prime time to visit is during feedings, just before dusk. In addition to the raptor exhibits, VINS also has an hour-long interpretive nature trail and offers guided hikes into nearby Quechee Gorge.

Other Sights

It's not quite Vermont's answer to the Grand Canyon, no matter what some might say. And yet there's no denying that **Quechee Gorge** (802/295-2990) is a breathtaking natural wonder. Part of the appeal of the narrow, rocky canyon is the way it comes across Route 4 so suddenly, plunging 165 feet down into the Ottauquechee River racing below. The gorge was formed some 13,000 years ago, when waters from a glacial lake cut inch by inch through tough bedrock schist. While the view from the railroad bridge on the highway is spectacular, a more rewarding view can be had by taking a short hike down to the river.

Just as impressive as the gorge next door, albeit in a completely different way is the **Vermont Toy & Train Museum** (Quechee Gorge Village, Rte. 4, 802/295-1550, 10 A.M.–5 P.M. daily July–Oct.; noon–5 P.M. Sat.–Sun. Nov.–June, $3 adults and children 3 and up), which has three complete model railroads and vintage toy train displays catering to the four-year-old in all of us. That's not the half of it, however. The real draw of this mini-museum is encapsulated in its slogan: "I had one of those!" Display after display exhibits vintage lunchboxes, dolls, robots, stuffed animals, and action figures from *Star Wars, Star Trek, Lost in Space, My Little Pony, Strawberry Shortcake,* and a dozen other galaxies you haven't inhabited in years. There's guaranteed to be at least one toy that sends you into spasms of reverie, if not a full-fledged nostalgia-fueled time warp back to an earlier simpler time when a couple hunks of plastic and your imagination were all you needed for a great afternoon.

Town and Country readers from all over the East Coast make special trips just to buy glassware and pottery at **Simon Pearce** (1760 Main St., the Mill at Quechee, 802/295-2711, www.simonpearce. com, 10 A.M.–9 P.M. daily), which has crafted exquisite specimens of both for more than three decades. Located in an old mill building completely run by hydroelectric power, the studio is open to the public for demonstrations. In the downstairs area, potters spin Pearce's distinctive shapes, while glassblowers blow bubbles into glowing orange balls of 2,400-degree silica (the glassblowing room is a particularly popular place to spend time in winter). Also on display are pictures from the excavation of the mill pond and installation of a turbine brought from Nova Scotia in 1983. And then, of course, there are several levels where you can buy Pearce's designs yourself, including a healthy sampling of cut-rate "seconds" with minor imperfections. To find the Mill at Quechee (coming from I-89), cross Quechee Gorge and take a right at the first blinking light.

Events

Colored canvas lights up the sky above Quechee Gorge at the annual **Quechee Hot Air Balloon, Fine Arts, Craft & Music Festival** (802/295-7900, www.quecheeballoonfestival.com, June), a tradition for more than 25 years. The event features musical performances, kids' games, and—of course—rides "up, up, and away" in more than two dozen brightly colored balloons.

Shopping

Quechee's mix of high-end artisanal wares (such as Simon Pearce) and unabashedly kitschy shops (one gargantuan hall is dedicated entirely to Christmas) is an exercise in eclecticism. Stop into the **Quechee Gorge Village** (5573 Woodstock Rd., on Rte. 4, 802/295-1550, www.quecheegorge.com, 9 A.M.–5 P.M. daily) to find wall after wall of vintage glass, Civil War–era coins, and estate jewelry in the Vermont Antique Mall.

Highland charm pervades at **Scotland by the Yard** (Rte. 4, 800/295-5351, www.scotlandbytheyard.com, 9 A.M.–5 P.M. daily), where high-quality kilts of genuine Scottish worsted wool tartans (plus sporrans and vests to match) can be bought premade or custom-ordered. (Kilts are also sold for women and children, too.) Or pick up a few non-wearable Scottish accessories such as crests or pewter.

Beatles fans may enter **Fool on the Hill** (8 Wood Rd., 802/457-3641) hoping for nostalgia, but they stay to peruse the charming jumble of wooden cows and sheep, rustic baskets, hand-painted wooden chairs, and blocks of maple-smoked cheddar. Both Scotland by the Yard and Fool on the Hill are easily spotted from the main road.

Food

Dining options run as high and low (casual to quite spiffy) as the landscape around Quechee.

Built in 1846, the Worcester "semi-stream-line" diner car that houses **(The Farmers Diner** (5573 Woodstock Rd., on Rte. 4, Quechee, 802/295-4600, www.farmersdiner. com, 7 A.M.–3 P.M. daily, $6–11) doesn't serve up your average train fare: The much-lauded restaurant has taken the use of completely local ingredients and products as its mission. Using produce from the closest farms and purveyors possible, the diner serves reasonably priced, traditional, and mostly organic specials ranging from crispy hush puppies to a melt-in-your-mouth bacon cheeseburger.

Truly memorable meals can be found at **Simon Pearce Restaurant** (1760 Main St., 802/295-1470, www.simonpearce.com, 11:30 A.M.–2:45 P.M. and 6–9 P.M. daily, $10–24). Settle into the elegant and sunny room overlooking the rushing Ottauquechee River and its dam, and dig into plates of horserad-ish-crusted cod, crisp confit duck with orange sauce, and beef and Guinness stew with pa-prika potatoes. As part of the Simon Pearce building, the kitchen serves everything on pot-tery and glassware literally made downstairs.

Fans of **Firestone's** (Rte. 4 and Waterman Hill Rd., 802/295-1600, www.firestonesrestau-rant.net, 11:30 A.M.–9 P.M. daily, $9–22) drive all the way from Boston to enjoy the kitchen's flatbread pizzas (cooked in a Canadian-style stone oven), unusually friendly atmosphere, and affable staff.

Information

The racks at Quechee Gorge Village (Rte. 4, 802/295-1550, www.quecheegorge.com) are stuffed with brochures on the town and

surrounding area. For more information contact the **Hartford Area Chamber of Commerce** (802/295-7900, www.hartfordvtchamber.com).

WOODSTOCK

Right off the bat, Woodstock looks different from most of the quaint villages in southern Vermont. The scale is grander, the houses more stately, and the downtown buildings more self-important. That's partly because shortly after the town was founded in 1765, it became the shire town for the county surrounding it, drawing a professional class of lawyers, doc-tors, teachers, and businesspeople who brought wealth and culture with them. Today, the town embodies both country-cute and upscale re-finement, with an unparalleled village green surrounded by Victorian homes and a collec-tion of upscale shops and galleries.

Almost from its beginnings the town has been a favorite tourist destination with visi-tors from Massachusetts and Connecticut. In 1793, Captain Israel Richardson built a tavern on the town green to serve the traffic from the stagecoach that passed through from Boston to Canada. That site is now occupied by the Woodstock Inn, which was founded in the 19th century to serve the growing tourist traf-fic from the railroad. In 1934, the first rope tow was installed on a pasture at the north end of town, ushering in a new era of winter sports for the moneyed set. That area survives as the modest ski area Suicide Six. Woodstock is also a good place to get in touch with Vermont's agricultural side, with a farm museum and cheese-maker in town.

Sights

Woodstock's most successful native son was Frederick Billings, a Vermonter who made it big as a lawyer in San Francisco during the Gold Rush. In the 1870s he returned to Woodstock determined to save the town's dying industry of dairy farming, and established a farm with cattle imported from the British isle of Jersey, putting into practice the most scientific prac-tices of land management. Today, **Billings Farm and Museum** (53 Elm St., 802/457-

2355, www.billingsfarm.org, 10 A.M.–5 P.M. daily May–Oct.; 10 A.M.–3:30 P.M. Sat.–Sun. Nov.–Feb., $11 adults, $10 seniors, $6 children 5–15, $3 children 3–4,, children under 3 free) afford visitors a chance to meet the descendants of those Jersey cows, who still produce milk in a working dairy farm. Exhibits and demonstrations explore typical Vermont farm life, in cooperation with **Marsh-Billings-Rockefeller National Historical Park** next door. The park (54 Elm St., 802/457-3368, www.nps.gov/mabi, late May–Oct.) is home to the mansion built by natural philosopher Charles Marsh in 1805–1807 and bought by Billings in 1861. The mansion, open for tours by advance reservation, has a Tiffany stained-glass window and an extensive collection of American landscape paintings. In 1934, Billings's granddaughter married Laurance Rockefeller and eventually donated the land to the National Park Service.

More cows and other farm animals can be found at **Sugarbush Farm** (591 Sugarbush Farm Rd., 802/457-1757, www.sugarbushfarm. com, 8 A.M.–5 P.M. Mon.–Fri.; 9 A.M.–5 P.M. Sat.–Sun.), which produces some of the best cheddar cheeses in Vermont. Set atop a scenic hilltop, the farm also produces maple syrup, mustards, and jams—all of which are free to sample. (Take a right across the covered bridge at the small village of Taftsville, and follow the signs to the farm—call ahead for road conditions in winter and early spring.)

Events

Billings Farm sponsors many special events throughout the summer, including **Cow Appreciation Day** every July, which includes judging of the Jerseys, ice cream and butter making, and (always gripping) dairy trivia; and a Harvest celebration in October with husking competitions and cider-pressing. In August, the oh-so-modestly-named **World's Greatest Book Sale and International Food Fair** (802/457-2557) brings rare and first-edition books alongside worldwide cuisine to the green.

Shopping

Billing itself as Vermont's oldest general store, the 1886 **F. H. Gillingham & Sons** (16 Elm St., 802/457-2100, www.gillinghams.com, 8:30 A.M.–6:30 P.M. Mon.–Sat.; 10 A.M.–4 P.M. Sun.; seasonal hours may vary) certainly looks the part, packed with locally made syrups, cheeses, and pottery, alongside more conventional grocery items. The eclectic **Unicorn** (15 Central St., 802/457-2480) specializes in bizarre and unusual gifts, from wooden kinetic sculptures to remote-controlled whoopee cushions.

Not your average vintage store, **Who Is Sylvia?** (26 Central St., 802/457-1110) stocks flapper dresses, pillbox hats, brocade jackets, and other hard-to-find items dating back more than a century. First among Woodstock's many galleries, the **Gallery on the Green** (1 The Green, 802/457-4956, www.galleryonthegreen. com, 10 A.M.–5 P.M. Mon.–Sat., 10 A.M.–4 P.M. Sun.) showcases paintings and sculptures of local and visiting artists.

On Route 4 between Woodstock and Killington is Vermont's version of a shopping mall. Don't expect to find Sears or Old Navy here—the three-story woolen mill, which opened in 1973, is filled with studio space for artisans and craftspeople. For example, a distant relation of Antarctic explorer Ernest Shackleton, **Charles Shackleton** (802/672-5175, www. shackletonthomas.com, 10 A.M.–5 P.M. Sun.–Thurs., 11 A.M.–5 P.M. Mon.–Thu., 10 A.M.–5:30 P.M. Fri. and Sat.), crafts simple but elegant Shaker and modern-style furniture. President Clinton once commissioned him to fashion a "peace bowl" to present to the pope. Shackleton's partner, **Miranda Thomas,** complements his work with fired pottery lamps and bowls hand-carved with animal designs.

Food

The food may be fresh, but the ambience at **Bentley's Restaurant** (3 Elm St., 802/457-3232, www.bentleysrestaurant.com, 11:30 A.M.–9:30 P.M. daily, $10–27) is charmingly (and authentically) old. The casual gleaming bar brims with tassled lamps, velvet couches, palm fronds, and brocade bar stools, while the kitchen churns out hearty comfort foods like maple mustard chicken and linguine with seafood.

VERMONT

Sedate and sophisticated, **Prince & The Pauper** (24 Elm St., 802/457-1818, www.princeandpauper.com, 6 A.M.–9 P.M. daily, $18–48) serves high-concept cosmopolitan dishes (don't miss the restaurant's signature Carre d'Agneau Royale) in a candlelit country setting—think high-backed wooden booths, exposed beams, and local art for sale on the wall. It's an ideal date setting, though it also successfully caters to families and groups. Meanwhile, a bit of sophisticated city comes to the country at the beautifully designed **Red Rooster** (14 The Green, Woodstock, 802/457-1100 or 800/448-7900, www.woodstockinn.com, 12 P.M.–10 P.M. daily). A new addition to The Woodstock Inn, the high-energy but comfortable space centers on a pretty water pool, around which couples and families alike dig into a New American menu of oysters on the half shell to coq au vin and braised short ribs.

Break out the dry cleaning for breakfast and lunch at **The Main Dining Room** (14 The Green, 800/448-7900, www.woodstockinn.com, $24–35) at the Woodstock Inn. The subtly grand space is where to find lovelies such as scallops with truffle vinaigrette followed by Grand Marnier soufflé glacé—not to mention a flat-out scrumptious (and epic) Sunday brunch.

Information and Services

The **Woodstock Area Chamber of Commerce** (29 Central St., 888/469-6378, www.woodstockvt.com) runs a welcome center (3 Mechanic St.) and an information booth (on the green). The well-stocked, independent **Woodstock Pharmacy** (19 Central St., 802/457-1306) is conveniently located in the center of town. The **Woodbridge Coffeehouse** (531 US Route 4, 802/332-6075) offers free Wi-Fi along with a selection of baked goods, sandwiches, and espresso drinks. **Woodstock Police** can be contacted at 454 Route 4, 802/457-2337.

SPORTS AND RECREATION

Hiking

In addition to the exhibits at **Marsh-Billings-Rockefeller National Historical Park** (54 Elm St., 802/457-3368, www.nps.gov/mabi, late May–Oct.), the preserve has 20 miles of carriage roads for walking. accessible from the park entrance on Route 12 and a parking lot on Prosper Road. The roads circle around the slopes of Mount Tom, which is forested with old-growth hemlock, beech, and sugar maples. Popular hikes include the loop around the mountain pond called the Pogue and the climb up the summit of Mount Tom, which lords over Woodstock and the river below. No mountain bicycles are allowed on the trails; in the winter, they are groomed for cross-country skiing.

Skiing

While it will never be confused with Vermont's larger ski resorts, **Suicide Six Ski Area** (802/457-6661, www.suicide6.com) has two dozen or so trails ranging from beginner to double diamond. Now owned and operated by the Woodstock Inn, the resort has a double-chair lift and a beginners area with a J-bar lift. Also affiliated with the inn, the **Woodstock Inn & Resort's Nordic Center** (Rte. 106/Cross St., 802/457-6674, www.woodstockinn.com, $16 adult, $12 child) has one of the best networks of cross-country-skiing trails in Vermont. More than 30 miles of trails marked easy, intermediate, and advanced weave up and around Woodstock's two mountains, Mount Tom and Mount Peg. The center also grooms trails for snowshoeing and winter hiking, and has skis and snowshoes for rent ($20 adult, $14 child per day).

Camping

The **Quechee Recreation Area** (Rte. 4, Quechee, 802/295-2990, www.vtstateparks.com/htm/quechee.cfm, late May–mid Oct., $14–16) has some 50 campsites for overnight stays on the banks of the Ottauquechee River.

ACCOMMODATIONS

With the ambient cuteness quotient as high as it is in these parts, it should come as no shock to find so many well-kept inns and bed-and-breakfasts operating here. Prices tend to be a bit higher than in other areas, but then again, so do the service and settings.

Under $100

Bonus points for correctly spelling the **Ottauquechee Motor Lodge** (529 Rte. 4, 802/672-3404, www.ottauquechee.com, $59–160), which offers motel accommodations on a quiet stretch of Route 4 between Woodstock and Bridgewater. The lodge is a cut above most motor lodges, with king-size beds and in-room refrigerators. And there's an added draw: the views of the surrounding mountains to the south.

$100-150

An 1830s farmhouse listed on the National Register, **The 1830 Shire Town Inn** (31 South St., Woodstock, 802/457-1830, www.1830shiretowninn.com, $85–160) offers an arguably perfect location for exploring Woodstock; the town's green is but a stone's throw from its white-picket-fenced facade, yet it's nestled on a quiet side street away from the bustle. Inside, the simple but well-kept rooms sport beamed ceilings and colorful quilts, and some have private porches. Breakfasts are individually prepared, homemade, and extra large.

$150-250

The present building of the **Woodstock Inn & Resort** (14 The Green, Woodstock, 802/457-1100 or 800/448-7900, www.woodstockinn.com, $235–395) dates from only 1892, but since 1793 the site it inhabits has been catering to tourists, who come as much for the recreational offerings as its 142 luxurious rooms. In summer, the property offers golf and tennis, while winter brings downhill and cross-country skiing. (And year-round, there's always the sparkling new 41,000-square-foot health and fitness center, complete with indoor pool, sauna, yoga room, and squash courts.) Recuperate afterward next to the fireplace in your room (many, though not all, have them) or over afternoon tea in the alcove. Meals (particularly brunch) in the refined Main Dining Room are an epic and memorable affair.

$250 and Up

Ten miles outside of Woodstock, **Twin Farms** (Off Stage Rd., Barnard, 800/894-6327, www.twinfarms.com, $1,300–3,000) is an exquisite and ultra-romantic resort filled with seemingly every luxury you could ever need—and the individually outfitted rooms (with four-poster beds and fireplaces, whirlpool tubs, rare woods, museum art, and pastoral views) are just the beginning. The property caters to your every whim throughout the day, with everything from fresh-squeezed juices and on-property fly-fishing to salt body scrubs and a 26,000-bottle wine cellar. Note that the inn does not welcome children.

GETTING THERE

To get to Woodstock from Boston, take I-93 to Concord (70 mi., 1 hr. 15 min.), then I-89 to White River Junction (70 mi., 1 hr. 15 min.), before exiting onto Route 4 west for another 10 miles (20 min.). The total trip from Boston to Woodstock is about 140 miles (2 hrs. 45 min.).

The Red Rooster bar at the Woodstock Inn

Killington to Rutland

As Route 4 heads west, it climbs out of the Outtaquechee Valley and into the Green Mountains, where it skirts some of the highest peaks in the state—notably the downhill skiing empire known as Killington Resort. On the other side of the mountains, Rutland was once a major city based on its trade in marble, though it has now fallen on hard times. Around it are several unique attractions worth a visit, including the informative Vermont Maple Museum.

KILLINGTON

For most visitors, Killington is synonymous with skiing. Long the most popular ski resort in the East, the mountain has more than enough terrain to challenge most skiers for a week. The peak of Mount Killington has always fascinated people. In 1763, Reverend Samuel Peters climbed to its summit and christened the area around it Verde-Mont after the lush green mountains all around. Its history as a resort, however, starts in the 1950s, when 25-year-old entrepreneur Preston Lee Smith identified the mountain's location and amazing views (which reach to Maine on a clear day) as the perfect spot to realize his dream for a skiing empire. Opening Killington in 1958, Smith expanded ambitiously, opening lift after lift on neighboring peaks and making it one of the first mountains to install snow-making equipment to extend the season. (It's still known as the first resort to open and last to close each year.)

In subsequent years, Killington became a leader in the conglomeration that consumed many of the resorts in New England. The mountain's size and popularity led to runaway development on its flank—with the long, twisting Killington Road now a very un-Vermont stretch of hotels, restaurants, and nightclubs extending up to the summit. For some, it's a welcome bit of civilization (and fun) in the midst of the too-cutesy towns around it; for others it's a garish display better off in New Hampshire (which might explain why some Killington residents actually voted to secede from Vermont a few years ago and join its neighboring state to the east). In recent years, Killington has become more and more crowded, giving it the nickname in some circles of "Beast of the East." For the sheer difficulty and exhilaration of its terrain, however, it is without equal east of the Rockies, leading skiers to return year after year to test themselves on its slopes.

◖ Killington Resort

The mountain that gives Killington its name is only one of six peaks that make up this massive ski resort (4763 Killington Rd., 800/621-6867, www.killington.com, $77–82 adults, $61–65 youth 12–18, $53–55 seniors and youth 6–12), which together boast more than 200 trails. The main event is still Killington Peak, where most of the toughest trails start their descent. The peak is accessible from the express gondola from the K-1 Lodge at the top of Killington Road.

AND EVERYTHING NICE . . .

Breakfast fiends come from all over to dig into the groaning platters of truly excellent pancakes cooked up at **Sugar and Spice** (Rte. 4 at Meadow Lake Dr., 3 mi. E of Rutland, Mendon, 802/773-7832, www. vtsugarandspice.com, 7 A.M.-2 P.M. daily, $6-11), a working sugar shack turned restaurant. Feather-light and studded with juicy blueberries, the specialties are a thing worthy of addiction – especially under a pour of the house-made maple syrup. In fact, during sugar season, upon request waitstaff will draw off hot syrup right from the evaporation tank and bring it directly to your table. And this may be the only breakfast spot where artificial syrup costs extra.

COURTESY OF KILLINGTON SKI RESORT

skiing beneath the gondola on Killington

Quicker and more comfortable is the heated Skyeship gondola that leaves from a base on Route 4 and whisks skiers up to the top of Skye Peak in 12 minutes. While that peak doesn't have the challenges of the main peak, it gives a longer ride down to the base. Popular with expert skiers, Bear Mountain is a steep peak loaded with double diamonds, including several tough glade-skiing trails.

Physically separate from Killington, the co-owned **Pico Mountain** (Rte. 4, 2 mi. west of Killington Rd., 866/667-7426, www.pico-mountain.com, $52 adults, seniors, and teens 13–18, $32 youth 6–12) is a quieter and less-crowded mountain with 50-some trails and a family-friendly reputation. On a busy weekend, however, both Killington and Pico get swamped—expect long waits in the lift lines and cattle herds in the cafeterias.

As might be expected, skiing is only the beginning of offerings at the resort, which stays open for outdoor recreation year-round. **Killington Snowmobile Tours** (802/422-2121, www.snowmobilevermont.com) offers one-hour gentle rides along groomed ski trails ($94

single/$119 double), as well as a more challenging two-hour backcountry ride through Calvin Coolidge State Forest ($144/$189). **Killington Snowshoe Tours** (800/767-7031, www.customtoursinc.com/killingtonsnowshoetours.htm) leads custom-designed backcountry tours for both beginners and advanced snowshoers.

In the summer months, Killington is famed for mountain biking on trails served by the same lifts that carry skiers in the winter. In fact, the resort produces a mountain biking map for its 45 miles of trails. Trail access is $15 for adults; a $64 pass is good for two days of trail access and unlimited rides on the lifts. The resort also rents bikes for use on its trails ($50 adult/day, $30 child/day).

Entertainment
There's plenty to do around the slopes after the sun sets—provided your idea of fun revolves primarily around bars and clubs. One such example is **Outback Pizza/Tabu Nightclub** (2841 Killington Rd., 802/422-9885, www.tkillingtonsbestrestaurants.com, pizza $13–19), a convivial multilevel complex that's a bit

VERMONT

like spring break in the mountains. Live bands play from a stage in back, while guests crowd the tiny dance floor up front.

Meanwhile, twentysomethings looking to party, families, and snowboarders alike crowd **Pickle Barrel Night Club** (1741 Killington Rd., 802/422-3035, www.picklebarrelnightclub.com) for live concerts put on by bands from near and far, pub grub, and high-octane cocktails.

Events

Every summer, the hills are alive with the sounds of you-know-what, when the **Killington Music Festival** (802/773-4003, www.killingtonmusicfestival.org) stages its "Music in the Mountain" chamber-music concerts. During the weekend after Labor Day, 1,000 motorcyclists invade town for the **Killington Classic Motorcycle Touring Rally** (877/245-3976, www.killingtonclassic.com). Events include a cycle rodeo and bike judging.

Shopping

This is ski country, say most visitors, not shopping country. And to that end, most of the retail you'll find is geared toward just that—gear. Ski shops are found at the base of every resort, but one of the best off-mountain is **Northern Ski Works** (Killington Rd., next to the Wobbly Barn, 802/422-9675, www.northernski.com, open Sept.–May). It's where to head for all manner of equipment, from snowshoes and helmets to boards and, of course, skis.

Pick up crafty gifts, foods like jams, and moccasins at **Bill's Country Store** (2319 Rte. 4, 802/773-9313, www.billscountrystore.com). One of the only stores worth stopping in town, **The Boutique at Killington** (2025 Rte. 4, 802/773-5770) is filled with handmade pottery, glasses, and gourmet cookware that will improve the kitchen of any chef.

Food

Most Killington eateries are about fast food—not junk food, mind you, but rather turning tables over as fast as possible to accommodate the hordes that fill their doorways every night.

During ski season, go early or prepare yourself for a long wait for a table. Such is the case at **The Garlic** (1724 Killington Rd., 802/422-5055, www.thegarlicinkillington.com, 3 P.M.–midnight daily, $16–28), where you can literally smell the namesake ingredient before you even open the door. Cozy with dim lighting, the dining room is filled with the comforting scent of marinara sauce—not surprising, as freshly made pastas are a specialty. (Also don't miss the osso buco and saltimbocca.)

For hearty après-ski comfort foods, make your way to **The Grist Mill** (Killington Rd., just off the road from Summit Pond, 802/422-3970, www.gristmillkillington.com, 11:30 A.M.–9:30 P.M. Mon.–Thurs.; 11:30 A.M.–10 P.M. Fri.–Sat.; 11:30 A.M.–9:30 P.M. Sun., $8–20), where house specialties like deep bowls of French onion soup and country turkey dinners fly from kitchen to table.

The pace slows notably at the quiet, sophisticated likes of **Hemingway's** (4988 Rte. 4, 802/422-3886, www.hemingwaysrestaurant.com, 6–10 P.M. Wed.–Sun., $25–38). Here's where to treat yourself to an elegant meal—Continental cuisine like lobster risotto and Niman Ranch pork loin expertly prepared and served with military precision—in several rooms as eclectic as Hemingway himself. (There's a Key West garden room, plus a Ritz room with boldly hued walls and crystal chandeliers.)

Information

The **Killington Chamber of Commerce** (2026 Rte. 4, 802/773-4181, www.killingtonchamber.com) operates a visitor information center at the intersection of Route 4 and Killington Road.

RUTLAND

Vermont's second-largest city is tucked into the valley between the Green Mountains and the Taconic Range, gracing it with a scenic horizon of purple peaks in whichever direction you look. Unfortunately, Rutland's downtown isn't quite so scenic. The city's brief Golden Age occurred in the mid-19th century with the exploitation of the milky-white marble deposits found along the Taconics from Manchester to Middlebury. The marble, in demand in civic buildings in New York, Washington, and other cities around the world, quickly made Rutland very rich indeed. Its downtown known as Merchant's Row became one of the busiest commercial streets in the country, and Victorian houses of the marble barons sprang up on the hills around town. Rutland also became an early example of multiculturalism, as Italian, Irish, and French-Canadian workers poured into the region to work in the quarries. The city slowly declined after the Civil War and other sources of marble became available; the last quarries closed sadly in the mid-1990s, costing the city many jobs. Since then, it has struggled to reinvent itself as a tourist destination, touting the nearby ski resorts, the grand historic buildings downtown area (many of them, not surprisingly, built with native marble), and a number of tourist attractions scattered throughout the valley.

New England Maple Museum

Vermont produces an estimated 500 million gallons of maple syrup each year—accounting for more than a third of the production of the entire country. And each one of those gallons of golden goodness takes 40 gallons of sugar sap to produce. If you are beginning to doubt there are enough trees in the state to make that possible, check out this museum (Rte. 7, just north of Pittsford, 802/483-9414, www.maplemuseum.com, 10 A.M.–4 P.M. daily mid-Mar.–late May; 8:30 A.M.–5:30 P.M. daily late May–Oct.; 10 A.M.–4 P.M. daily Nov.–late Dec., closed Jan.–Feb., $2.50 adults, $0.75 children) on the outskirts of Rutland. It takes visitors inside the history and art of sugar maple sap. One hundred feet of murals depict the history of syrup-making, from the Native Americans who heated sugar maple logs over the fire to the smokestacks of modern syruping outfits. These are complemented by black-and-white photographs, antique taps and other sugaring artifacts, and an evaporation tank that runs all year long, or as the museum puts it, "even

when the sap isn't." And of course, there's the gift shop, which provides free samples of different grades of syrup—though unfortunately no flapjacks to go with them.

Other Sights

Located on the grounds of an abandoned quarry, **The Vermont Marble Museum** (52 Main St., Proctor, 800/427-1396, www.vermont-marble.com, 9 A.M.–5:30 P.M. daily mid-May–Oct., $7 adults, $5 seniors, $4 teens, free for children) is filled with exhibits and photographs that tell the story of the Rutland marble industry and the thousands of immigrants who once labored in the quarries. A grand gallery contains marble bas-reliefs of all of the nation's presidents, along with other marble statuary carved over the years. Modern-day marble carver Allen Dwight, the museum's artist-in-residence, gives demonstrations on the craft.

Nearby is **Wilson Castle** (West Proctor Rd., Proctor, 802/773-3284, www.wilsoncastle.com, 9 A.M.–6 P.M. daily late May–mid-Oct., $9.50 adults, $5.50 children 6–12, children under 6 free), built in the late 19th century by a doctor with a taste for extravagance. The five-story mansion is a mishmash of European styles, with 19 proscenium arches, a turret, parapet, and balcony. Inside, the building is filled with antiques from around the world, including Chinese scrolls, Tiffany chandeliers, and a Louis XVI crown jewel case. Guided tours lasting 45 minutes are given throughout the day. (Last tour leaves at 5 P.M.) If you can, time your visit for a Sunday morning, when an electronic organ fills the art gallery with church music. Combination tickets for the maple museum, marble museum, and castle give a discount on admission.

More humble than royal, pop artist Norman Rockwell lived and painted in nearby Arlington for 15 years. On the eastern outskirts of Rutland, the small **Norman Rockwell Museum** (654 Rte. 4, 802/773-6095, www.normanrockwellvt.com, 9 A.M.–4 P.M. daily, $5.50 adults, $5 seniors, $2.50 8–17, children under 8 free), located just across the Rutland city line on Route 4, doesn't contain any original

VERMONT

work by the artist. It does, however, present an impressive overview of his career with several thousand original magazine covers, books, and reproductions—from Rockwell's beginnings in the 1910s as art editor of *Boys' Life* magazine to the illustration of Johnny Carson he made for *TV Guide* shortly before his death in 1978. A sizable gift shop has both original covers and reproduction posters.

For your own fix of Rockwellian America, take a driving tour around the towns of Pittsford and Proctor north of the city, where no fewer than four **covered bridges** crisscross the creeks. They include the 145-foot-long span that takes Kendall Hill Road over Otter Creek, which was dislodged during a 1927 flood and—remarkably undamaged—towed a mile back upriver to be put back in place.

Entertainment
Once upon a time, the **Paramount Theatre** (30 Center St., 802/775-0570, www.paramountvt.org, ticket prices vary) drew top names such as Harry Houdini, Groucho Marx, and Sarah Bernhardt. Recently restored to its 19th-century splendor, the theater now hosts musical performers such as Branford Marsalis, as well as classical music concerts and youth theater performances.

Events
For 10 days every September, the **Vermont State Fair** (175 S. Main St., 802/775-5200, www.vermontstatefair.net, $6–10 adults, $5 seniors, $3–4 children 6–12, children under 6 free) lights up the Vermont sky with a Ferris wheel and other nausea-inducing midway rides, along with the state's premier agricultural competitions. One recent fair included the state championship demolition derby, equestrian harness races, and musical performances by country legends Randy Travis and Charlie Daniels. Throughout the year, the fairgrounds play host to other agricultural and musical events.

Shopping
Get your country store fix along Route 4 and in Rutland Center, where a number of stores peddling handmade crafts, toys, and memorabilia are clustered. Start at **Rocking Horse Country Store** (Rte. 4 E., 802/773-7882), which is chock-full of the state's requisite cheese and maple products, plus T-shirts, postcards, and Vermont cookbooks and other books on Vermont culture. Speaking of rocking horses, Santa's workshop has nothing on **Michael's Toy Company** (64 Merchants Row, 802/773-3765, www.michaelstoys.com), a trip back to the Norman Rockwell era with wooden rocking horses (and rocking cows) and other decidedly non-plastic toys. The proprietor also makes custom-carved signs, and even serves ice cream for the kids.

Stock up for all seasons at **Mr. Twitters Garden and Gift Emporium** (24 McKinley Ave., 800/924-8948, www.mrtwitters.com, 9:30 A.M.–5:30 P.M. Mon.–Fri.; 9 A.M.–4 P.M. Sat., 9 A.M.–3 P.M. Sun.), a hodgepodge of hand-painted birdhouses, wind chimes, garden statues, homemade potpourri, seeds, bulbs, and garden implements to tend your own plot.

Food
Casual choices for a quick, inexpensive meal abound in Rutland Center. For wrap sandwiches or light entrées, such as chili, hearty soups, and chef's salads, hit **Clem's Cafe** (101 Merchants Row, 802/775-3337, 7 A.M.–5 P.M. Mon.–Fri. and 7 A.M.–1 P.M. Sat.–Sun.; open until 8 P.M. Thu.–Sat. during summer, $4–8). Plunked on a main intersection of town, its brightly painted interior is a cheery place to relax over a hot drink or salad and the day's newspaper. The owner keeps it local as much as possible, with a changing selection of photographs and paintings from local artists on the walls (including some *really* local photographs by the morning barista, and CDs from local artists for sale on the counter.

Heartier fare served with a tad more ceremony is what you can expect at **Three Tomatoes Trattoria** (88 Merchants Row, 802/747-7747, www.threetomatoestrattoria.com, 5 P.M.–9 P.M. Sun.–Thurs.; 5 P.M.–10 P.M. Fri and Sat., $12–18). The stylish spot's open kitchen churns out gourmet pizzas from a wood-fired oven, alongside pastas and seafood dishes. Diners, meanwhile, can relax at their white-linen table among miniature topiary.

If "meat and potatoes" is more your speed, head toward **Sirloin Saloon** (200 S. Main St., 802/773-7900, www.steakseafood.com/ss/, 11 A.M.–9 P.M. daily, $14–27). The family-friendly national chain isn't breaking any culinary barriers, but it serves dependable T-bones and sides at reasonable prices.

Information and Services
Rutland Region Chamber of Commerce (802/773-2747, www.rutlandvermont.com) runs a seasonal visitors center at the junction of Routes 4 and 7.

Emergency services are centered in Rutland—including Vermont's second-largest hospital. **Rutland Regional Medical Center** (160 Allen St., 802/775-7111) offers a full range of services, inpatient and outpatient. Several pharmacies are in the area, though none operate all night. Most central are **Walgreens** (10 Woodstock Ave., 802/773-6980) and **CVS** (31 N. Main St., 802/775-6736). **Rutland Free Library** (10 Court Street, 802/773-1860) provides free Wi-Fi to patrons.

State troopers can be found at **Vermont State Police** (124 State Place, 802/773-9101), and local authorities are at **Rutland Police** (108 Wales St., 802/773-1816).

SPORTS AND RECREATION
Hiking and Camping
In addition to the hiking trails at Killington, a popular short trek is the one up to the scenic overlook on Deer Leap Mountain, located in **Gifford Woods State Park** (34 Gifford Woods, Killington, 802/775-5354, www.vtstateparks.com/htm/gifford.cfm). The trail starts behind the Inn at Long Trail on Route 4 and is two miles round-trip to fantastic views of Pico Peak and Killington Mountain. Alternatively, you can hike the four-mile round trip from the state park campground, which also has 4 cabins, 22 tent sites, and 20 lean-tos for overnights. The northern tent loop is

much more secluded than the southern. Several "prime" lean-tos are especially secluded in a hardwood old-growth forest of giant sugar maple, white ash, and beech trees. The best old-growth stand, however is across the street from the campground. Between the entrance and the northern tent loop, a short interpretive trail leads hikers among the giants and explains the natural and human history of the area.

Rock Climbing
An 8,000-square-foot gym with dozens of rope stations on 25-foot climbing walls is just the beginning at the **Green Mountain Rock Climbing Center** (223 Woodstock Ave., Rutland, 802/773-3343, www.vermontclimbing.com). Owner Steve Lulek, who once served as head instructor at the military's Mountaineering School, also leads a full range of mountaineering classes and guided tours of Deer's Leap and other nearby cliff faces through his companion outfit, **Vermont Adventure Tours** (www.vermontadventuretours.com).

ACCOMMODATIONS
Sleeping comfortably without breaking the bank isn't always easy during ski season; in general, the closer you get to Rutland, the better value you get. Killington teems with less-expensive motels tailor-built to keep rowdy skiers happy, as well as larger resorts close to the slopes that can run into the hundreds of dollars per night. As with most ski areas, prices drop considerably in the off-season.

Under $100
Perfunctory but utterly sufficient for a stay is the **Rodeway Inn** (138 N. Main St., Rutland, 802/775-2575, www.choicehotels.com, $50–80). The staff is extremely helpful, and rooms are small but clean. Best of all, it's a quick hop to the slopes. Offering an outdoor pool, indoor hot tub, and mountain views, the **Edelweiss Inn** (119 Rte. 4, 802/775-5577, www.killington-lodge.com, $60–100) is close to both Killington and Pico Mountains, and offers an excellent price for its amenities.

VERMONT

$100-150

Several generations of Saint Bernards have greeted guests at the **Summit Lodge** (200 Summit Path, off Killington Rd., 800/635-6343, www.summitlodgevermont.com, $80–250), which is as famous for its canine companions as it is for its friendly staff. Even though the lodge is only a few minutes away from Killington Resort, its position at the top of a steep hill makes it feel secluded. Rooms are nothing fancy but are quiet and clean, with friendly service. (There's also a pool and reading room for extra relaxation.) One caveat—rates here vary dramatically throughout the season. The same room can be $80 in summer, $150 in foliage season, and $250 in the height of ski season. Study the website carefully to get the best deal.

$150-250

Once the home of a feed and grain merchant, the 1889 **(** **Inn at Rutland** (70 N. Main St., Rutland, 802/773-0575, www.innatrutland.com, $120–230) is a time-warp into the opulence of the city's Victorian era. Common rooms are filled with period details like parquet floors, tooled-leather wainscoting, and a grand oak staircase that takes guests to eight upstairs bedrooms with cable TV and whirlpool tubs. Hosts Leslie and Steven Brenner prepare a three-course breakfast every morning with treats like crème brûlée French toast and gingerbread blueberry pancakes; a wraparound front porch offers views of the Green Mountains and the city below.

If you're searching for a romantic spot seconds away from the base lodge, **Inn of the Six Mountains** (2617 Killington Rd., 802/422-4302, www.sixmountains.com, $159–239) is a good compromise. Still more convenient, the property offers ski lockers outside to keep all your gear perfectly safe.

$250 and Up

Eleven miles north of Killington, **The** **Mountain Top Inn & Resort** (195 Mountain Top Rd., Chittenden, 802/483-2311 or 800/445-2100, www.mountaintopinn.com, $160–580) sits in what was once the barn for a historic turnip farm. Since then, it has been renovated many times over as an inn (it played host to President Eisenhower in the 1950s). A year-round destination resort, Mountain Top offers everything from horseback riding and hiking trails to rustic-but-refined rooms with private balconies, vaulted ceilings, and fireplaces. Among the top amenities, however, has to be a meal in the inn's Dining Room, which is dedicated to serving local ingredients and supporting local farms.

GETTING THERE AND AROUND

Killington is a 20-mile (30-min.) drive down Route 4 from Woodstock. For such a popular destination, public transport options are limited. It's possible to schedule pickup service with **Killington Transportation** (802/770-3977) from Rutland or White River Junction. Within Killington, the resort offers shuttle bus service between the various base lodges and nearby lodging.

Rutland is 15 miles (20 min.) west of Killington on Route 4 and 35 miles (45 min.) north of Manchester or 15 miles (20 min.) south of Brandon on Route 7. In terms of public transportation, Rutland is a major transportation hub. Continental's CommutAir flies routes from Boston to **Rutland Airport** (802/747-9963, www.flyrutlandvt.com) for just $99 each way. **Amtrak** (800/872-7245, www.amtrak.com) runs trains to Rutland with its Ethan Allen service from New York City, stopping at the Rutland Depot behind Wal-Mart. **Vermont Transit Lines** (800/642-3133, www.vermonttransit.com) runs buses to the local bus station (102 West St., 802/773-2774).

Marble Valley Regional Transit (802/773-3244) runs bus routes throughout the Rutland area.

CHAMPLAIN VALLEY

Lake Champlain is New England's Great Lake, an inland sea of expansive views and rich history. Twenty thousand years ago, the entire valley between Vermont's Green Mountains and New York's Taconic Range was under more than 400 feet of water, the remnants of glacial meltwater called Lake Vermont. After a few millennia, the Atlantic Ocean backed up the St. Lawrence River valley, filling the lake with seawater. Geologists still find whale fossils along the shoreline. As the sea level fell, the lake gradually dried up, leaving a giant sliver 100 miles long and up to 20 miles wide at its widest points.

Driving northward on Route 7 toward Burlington, you can still feel the presence of the ancient lakebed. The sky opens up and the land flattens, giving the area an almost Midwestern appearance, if it weren't for the spruce trees among the farms and mountains on the horizon. Despite the remoteness of this area today, it was actually one of the first areas of New England to be settled. Two hundred years ago, rivers were the equivalent of roads, and the St. Lawrence was a mighty river that gave French fur-trappers access to the interior. Eventually, settlers from New Hampshire and Massachusetts came up to cut down the trees and build farms to take advantage of the moderate temperatures (for Vermont!) and the fertile clay soil left behind by the glacial lake, settling around the thriving city of Burlington. Now with 100,000 people in its metropolitan area, the city is the largest in the state.

Among the early settlers was Vermonter Ethan Allen, who along with the Green

COURTESY OF STATE OF VERMONT

HIGHLIGHTS

☾ **ECHO Lake Aquarium and Science Center:** Here the kids will be delighted by interactive exhibits, live animals, and a sea monster named Champ (page 366).

☾ **Ethan Allen Homestead:** The Robin Hood of Vermont comes alive in all of his complexities (page 366).

☾ **Royal Lipizzaner Stallions:** Olympic gymnastics have nothing on these majestic performing horses (page 370).

☾ **St. Anne's Shrine:** Contemplation is the order of the day at this Catholic shrine and historic site (page 371).

☾ **Shelburne Museum:** A miniature city of art, artifacts, and buildings from all over the 376).

☾ **Lake Champlain Maritime Museum:** Benedict Arnold's flagship is the centerpiece of this fascinating lakeside history museum (page 379).

☾ **Robert Frost Interpretive Trail:** The beloved poet often walked some of the same trails that are now lined with his poetry (page 388).

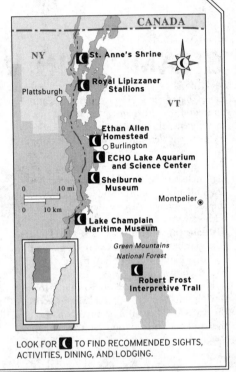

LOOK FOR ☾ TO FIND RECOMMENDED SIGHTS, ACTIVITIES, DINING, AND LODGING.

Mountain Boys helped foment resistance to encroachment from New York flatlanders. Ironically, today the region looks toward New York more than to Massachusetts or New Hampshire. It's still easier to cross the lake than to cross the Green Mountains, which rise much higher here than they do down south. It's perfectly reasonable to include a jaunt to the historical sites on the lake's western shore, or a hike in the Adirondacks along with a tour of Vermont's Champlain Valley. Meanwhile, in terms of demographics, this is not a region of country bumpkins. Vermont's two elite universities, Middlebury College and the University of Vermont in Burlington, span the valley like intellectual goalposts, giving their respective cities an energetic student atmosphere.

PLANNING YOUR TIME

Plan to spend at least a day or two in Burlington; the city's isolation on Lake Champlain, together with its vibrant student population, has given it a quirky character unlike any other city in New England. Historically, it was home to Vermont's very own Robin Hood; the **Ethan Allen Homestead** is open for tours. Another prime attraction in the city is the **ECHO Lake Aquarium and Science Center,** which details the lake's unique natural history, including the story of the sea monster purported to be plumbing its depths. If you are trained in scuba diving, you can't miss the chance to check out Lake Champlain's collection of well-preserved shipwrecks, managed through the Burlington branch of the Lake

VERMONT

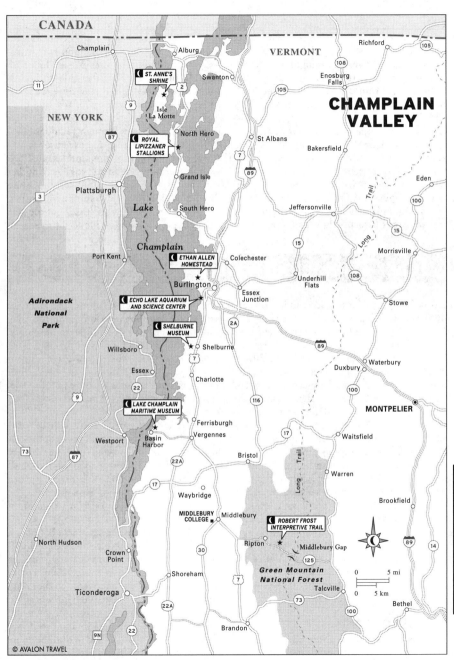

CANADA

Champlain   Alburg   **VERMONT**   Richford   105

☾ *ST. ANNE'S SHRINE*   Swanton   Enosburg Falls   108

NEW YORK   11   2   105

9   Isle La Motte   St Albans   Bakersfield

☾ *ROYAL LIPIZZANER STALLIONS*   North Hero   7   Eden

87   Grand Isle   89   100

3   Plattsburgh   **CHAMPLAIN VALLEY**

Lake   South Hero   Jeffersonville   Long Trail   15

Champlain   15   Morrisville

Port Kent   ☾ *ETHAN ALLEN HOMESTEAD*   Colechester   108

Burlington   Essex Junction   Underhill Flats   Stowe

☾ *ECHO LAKE AQUARIUM AND SCIENCE CENTER*   2A

Adirondack National Park   ☾ *SHELBURNE MUSEUM*

Willsboro   Shelburne   89   Waterbury

Essex   7   Charlotte   Duxbury

22   9   116   100   **MONTPELIER**

☾ *LAKE CHAMPLAIN MARITIME MUSEUM*   17

Westport   Ferrisburgh   Waitsfield

Basin Harbor   Vergennes   Long Trail

73   87   22A   Bristol   Warren

17   Brookfield

Waybridge   89   14

MIDDLEBURY COLLEGE ■   Middlebury   ☾ *ROBERT FROST INTERPRETIVE TRAIL*

North Hudson   30   Ripton   Middlebury Gap

Crown Point   125   *Green Mountain National Forest*

Shoreham   7   0   5 mi

Ticonderoga   Talcville   0   5 km   Bethel

22A   100   73

9N   22   Brandon

© AVALON TRAVEL

VERMONT

Champlain Maritime Museum. If you have another day or two, escape to the windswept Lake Champlain islands, which are filled with small farms and forested campgrounds. While you are there, catch the amazing leaping **Royal Lipizzaner Stallions,** or bask in the quiet tranquility of **St. Anne's Shrine.** (Note: By and large, restaurants in the cities and the islands alike stay open with regular hours year-round, but many don't serve all meals. Call ahead when planning.) In the lower valley, base yourself in the delightful college town of Middlebury, which in addition to restaurants and museums provides prime access to the hiking trails of the Green Mountains. The **Robert Frost Interpretive Trail** is one of the most moving tributes to the poet, who used to summer in the area. For a different view of the mountains, a hot-air-balloon ride is unforgettable, especially when foliage lights up the hills in fall. On the other side of the valley, the **Lake Champlain Maritime Museum** gathers together the history of the lake from Native American to modern times. Farther north, Route 7 passes through a schlocky area of family vacationland; the exception is the **Shelburne Museum,** a miniature village filled with fine art and historical artifacts. Another sure bet is the main branch of the **Lake Champlain Maritime Museum** in Vergennes, which gathers together the history of the lake from Native American to modern times.

Upper Champlain Valley

Lake Champlain is at its widest in its northern third, with wide blue vistas across a span of up to 12 miles in width. After the Great Lakes, Lake Champlain is the sixth-largest body of freshwater in the country. In fact, it was briefly declared to be a Great Lake for all of three months in 1997, due to a rider in a bill for lake research inserted by Vermont Senator Pat Leahy. After an uproar, the designation (along with funds for research) was rescinded, leaving Champlain a Great Lake in character if not in name. While not nearly as large as the Great Lakes, Champlain is unnaturally deep, reaching 400 feet deep in some areas (twice as deep as Lake Erie). That fact has helped to perpetuate the myth of a giant sea monster named Champ that inhabits the lake's depths, and occasionally surfaces for sightings by pleasure-boaters and kayakers. The lake is a popular destination for water-borne recreation, with dozens of state parks scattered around its north end. Not that this area is wilderness by any means—with 100,000 people in its metropolitan area, the university city of Burlington is the largest in the state.

BURLINGTON

Vermont's largest city is a surprisingly harmonious mixture of cultures: Start with a base of alternative undergrad culture, add plenty of wholesome families vacationing on the lake, and top that with a booming retail industry, and you've got Burlington in a nutshell. This is the kind of place where the average resident stays up late into the night to sip organic beer and hoot at the latest folk band at a local café, only to wake up early to don a fleece vest for a kayak trip in the bay.

Not that Burlington today will be confused with more cosmopolitan second-cities like Portsmouth or Portland. After all, the city proper only has 30,000 residents—10,000 of which are students—and the surrounding area is still relatively depressed economically. The outskirts of town are an unsightly blemish of strip malls, and even the downtown area has more chain stores than independent boutiques. But Burlington has two big things going for it: the university and the lake. The waterfront area has been spruced up in recent years into a park, with frequent concerts and events on the grassy area along the water. The waterfront is still a working one, with ships carrying cargo up and down the lake to New York State. But nowadays, most of the boats docked in the marina are pleasure crafts dedicated to exploring the lake.

VERMONT

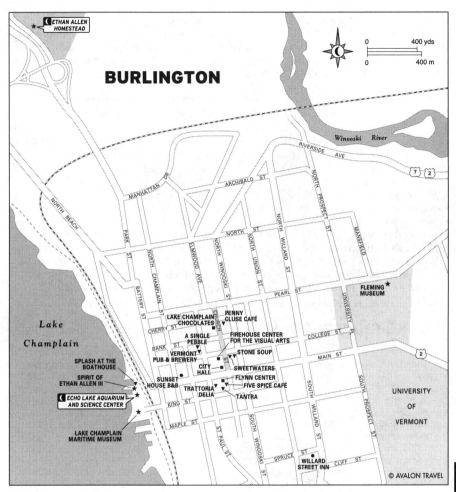

Across town, it's hard to tell where the University of Vermont, with its reputation for crunchiness and funkiness, ends, and the rest of the city begins. The university was founded in 1791 by Ira Allen, the wealthy landowner who, with his brother Ethan, dominates early history in these parts. Later, Burlington established itself as the major mercantile and trading port in the region, exploiting the vast reserves of timber and stone in the area, which could be easily carted down the lake to New York. All over

town, monuments to the city's wealth remain, from the imposing Unitarian Church that lords over Church Street to the monumental granite government buildings that ring the city's heart at City Hall Park.

Between the college and the waterfront, the main drag of Church Street combines the two into a pedestrian arcade of atmospheric, student-geared eateries that define the term "culinary ghetto," combined with lovely views of the waterway below.

◖ ECHO Lake Aquarium and Science Center

With ancient coral reefs, whale skeletons, and a supposed sea monster in its depths, Lake Champlain is one of the most distinctive bodies of freshwater in the world. The scientists behind this small aquarium (1 College St., 802/864-1848, www.echovermont.org, 10 A.M.–5 P.M. daily, $9.50 adults, $8 seniors and students, $7 children 3–17, children under 3 free) have done a bang-up job of making the geology and fauna of the lake accessible and family-friendly. "Hands-on" is the watchword here, with plenty of interactive exhibits to get kids good and wet while they learn about river currents or pull critters out of lake pools. That's not to say there isn't a lot here for adults, too—in the form of a film and exhibit exploring the enduring myth of Champ, the plesiosaur supposedly stranded in the lake millions of years ago, and plenty of aquarium tanks full of the fish, turtles, snakes, and frogs you may encounter on trips out on the lake. The latest addition to the aquarium's permanent exhibits is a display that tells the history of the Abenaki people who lived (and live) around the lake.

◖ Ethan Allen Homestead

Today, Ethan Allen is better known as the name of a furniture company. But he remains one of the most colorful—and enigmatic—figures of early Vermont history. The modest Cape Cod–style home (1 Ethan Allen Homestead Way, 802/865-4556, www.ethanallenhomestead.org, 10 A.M.–4 P.M. Thurs.–Sat.; 1–4 P.M. Sun., $7, $5 seniors, children 6 and under free) has been restored to the period, though only his kitchen table and a few other small Allen artifacts survive. Visits to the homestead include a low-budget film exploring the conflicting accounts of the man himself as well as a guided tour of the house.

LAKE CHAMPLAIN SHIPWRECKS

On a dark night in December 1876, the canal schooner *General Butler* lost its steering and crashed headlong into the Burlington Harbor, sinking just as the crew jumped to safety. The *Butler* is now one of hundreds of ships that line the bottom of the lake, one of the best surviving collections of shipwrecks in the world. Many of them are remnants of the 3,000 schooners built to haul timber, iron ore, and coal across the lake in the active shipping trade of the 19th century. Currently, nine vessels are open to those with scuba gear and the wherewithal to explore this unique state park. In addition to the *Butler*, which rests under 40 feet of water in the harbor, other ships include a canal boat loaded down with granite blocks, a rare horse-powered ferry boat, and two long side-wheel steamboats.

For underwater tours and equipment rentals, visit **Waterfront Diving Center** (214 Battery St., 802/865-2771 or 800/283-7282, www.waterfrontdiving.com). Basic scuba classes are $295, while two- and three-day summer trips are around $300 per person.

The shop also works with a local charter company for day trips at $40 a head. All divers are required to register with a dive shop or the Burlington Community Boat House (College St., Burlington, 802/865-3777).

You don't have to be a diver to experience the wrecks, however. A few years ago, sailing instructors (and husband and wife) Rachael Miller and James Line began offering dry-foot tours of the deep through their operation, **Lake Champlain Shipwrecks** (802/578-6120, www.shipwrecktour.com, 1 hour tours daily Jun.-Oct., $18 per person). The tour uses an ROV (remotely operated vehicle) equipped with a camera to view the *Butler* and other wrecks virtually on a video screen mounted on-board. Not only is the experience the next-best thing to viewing them through a diving mask, but Miller is also a master storyteller, brining alive the final hours of each wreck in lurid detail.

For more information on the wrecks, contact the Lake Champlain Maritime Museum (802/475-2022, www.lcmm.org).

ETHAN ALLEN

Colonial mountain man Ethan Allen looms large over the history of Vermont. Depending on which account you believe, he was an American Robin Hood, a war hero, a traitor, or a drunk. Born in Litchfield, Connecticut; Allen came to Vermont before the Revolutionary War with his brother Ira to start a farm near Bennington on a land grant received from New Hampshire Governor Benning Wentworth. When King George found out that Wentworth was giving out grants under his nose (without paying duties to the crown), he declared them void and gave the governor of New York rights to the same land. Caught in the middle, Allen and other landowners weren't about to give up without a fight. They defied the courts with a hastily arranged militia called the Green Mountain Boys, which helped enforce the New Hampshire grants by persuasion, threat, and force, and eventually led to the founding of Vermont as a separate state.

The Boys achieved legitimacy through valiant fighting in the Revolution, where they played key roles in the battles of Hubbardton and Bennington. Allen himself, however, took little part, since he was captured by the British in an ill-planned raid on Montreal the previous year, and lived out the war as a prisoner in England and New York. After the war, he was briefly named the General of the Army of Vermont, and then became fabulously wealthy through the Onion River Land Company, a holding company that bought up and distributed much of the land in Vermont. Though his brother entered into politics, Ethan Allen preferred to influence government behind the scenes – such as his controversial role in the ill-fated attempt to return Vermont to the British in 1782. By the time he built the homestead on the Onion River near Burlington in 1787, he was spending most of his time walking his land with surveyors' tools and a hip flask. He only lived in the home for two years, before he was killed in a freak sledding accident on Lake Champlain (the hip flask was no doubt involved). Almost as soon as he died, the arguments began about the role he played in early Vermont history. Only one thing is for sure: If it weren't for him, Vermont probably wouldn't exist as a state today.

While the exhibits relating to Allen may leave a bit to be desired, the tour guides are spirited in their evocation of Vermont's larger-than-life founding father, espousing opinions about his legacy that make him seem like a politician from the 20th century, not the 18th. And Allen aside, the home is an excellently restored lesson in how early Americans lived. (On our tour, we learned the origins of the phrases "Pop goes the weasel" and "Sleep tight, don't let the bedbugs bite." Trust us, you're glad you didn't live in the days of straw mattresses.)

Other Sights

The Burlington branch of **Lake Champlain Maritime Museum** (The Lyman Building at Perkins Pier, 802/475-2022, www.lcmm. org, May–Oct., 10 A.M.–6 P.M. Wed.–Sun., free), has a small exhibit on the history of the Burlington waterfront that includes some artifacts of the shipwrecks in the lake. It also serves as home base for the *Lois McLure,* an 88-foot, painstakingly reconstructed replica of an 1862-class canal schooner open for free tours. (Call ahead to find out whether the craft will be docked in Burlington or at the LCMM's main museum in Basin Harbor.)

To get out on the water, board the *Spirit of Ethan Allen III* (Burlington Boathouse, College St., 802/862-8300, www.soea.com, 10 A.M., noon, 2 P.M., and 4 P.M. daily May–Oct., $14–99 adults, $5–86 children 3–11), a 141-foot luxury cruise ship that conducts narrated cruises of the lake during the day as well as dinner and sunset cruises in the evenings.

On the east side of town, the **University of Vermont** (194 S. Prospect St., 802/656-3131, www.uvm.edu) educates some 10,000 students on a campus overlooking the lake. Chartered in 1791 by a group of Vermonters including

Ira Allen, it was the fifth college in the country (after Harvard, Yale, Dartmouth, and Brown). For visitors, its prized attraction is the **Robert Hull Fleming Museum** (University of Vermont, 61 Colchester Ave., 802/656-0750, www.uvm.edu/~fleming/, noon–4 P.M. Tues.–Fri. and 1–5 P.M. Sat.–Sun. May–early Sept.; 9 A.M.–4 P.M. Tues.–Fri. and 1–5 P.M. Sat.–Sun. early Sept.–Apr., $5 adults, $3 students and seniors, $10 family, children 6 and under free), an art and archaeology museum with mummies, Buddhas, Mesoamerican pottery, and other artifacts from all the world's great civilizations, presented in an up-to-date style that avoids the paternalism of many archaeology museums. It also has a small collection of American and European paintings.

Contemporary art with a Vermont theme is the purview of the **Firehouse Gallery at the Firehouse Center for the Visual Arts** (135 Church St., 802/865-7166, www.burlingtoncityarts.com/fcva, noon–5 P.M. Sun., Tues., and Wed., noon–8 P.M. Thurs.–Sat. in summer; 9 A.M.–5 P.M. Mon.–Fri., noon–5 P.M. Sun. in winter, free), which pushes the envelope with multimedia and interactive exhibitions in oversized gallery spaces. Some of its shows are more successful than others; all are provocative. A recent exhibit, for example, looked at perspectives from Iraq–vets-turned-artists working in media including U.S. currency and flags and their own uniforms to come to grips with their experiences in war.

There's no pretension at **Magic Hat Brewing Company** (5 Bartlett Bay Rd., South Burlington, 802/658-2739, www.magichat.net, tours 3:30–5:30 P.M. Thurs.–Fri. and noon–4 P.M. Sat. late Jan.–late May, 3–6 P.M. Wed.–Fri. and noon–4 Sat. Jun.–Dec.), just good beer. The brewery is justly famed for its No. 9, a subtly fruity ale found on tap all over New England.

If you've ever dreamed of getting a golden ticket to Willy Wonka's, stop in at **Lake Champlain Chocolates Factory Store and Café** (750 Pine St., 802/864-1807, www.lakechamplainchocolates.com, tours hourly 9 A.M.–2 P.M. Mon.–Thurs.; free chocolate tasting hourly 9 A.M.–2 P.M. Fri.; store/café hours 9 A.M.–6 P.M. Mon.–Sat. and noon–5 P.M. Sun.), where tours of the chocolate-making operation are enough to send any chocoholic into a swoon. The company has been producing gourmet chocolates for more than two decades, incorporating sweet cream from Vermont cows and other local ingredients such as honey and maple syrup. Tours take in huge chocolate-filled melting tanks, a chocolate bar assembly line, and the chocolate waterfall that douses hand-fashioned truffles in velvety goodness. Free samples, of course, are available.

Entertainment and Nightlife

A former vaudeville house, the **Flynn Center for the Performing Arts** (153 Main St., 802/863-5966, www.flynncenter.org) was restored to its art deco grandeur in 2000. It now serves as the cultural hub of the city, with musicals, dance performances, and shows by mainstream jazz and country acts from Diana Krall to Pink Martini. Grab a homemade beer and some local color at the state's first brewpub, the comfortable **Vermont Pub & Brewery** (144 College St., 802/865-0500, www.vermontbrewery.com). The pub pours all-natural brews like its award-winning Burley Irish Ale and Handsome Mike's Smoked Stout that are unfiltered, unpasteurized, and—many Burlingtonites claim—unparalleled. Their latest experiment: Flower beers, such as Blue Nile, a rye beer brewed with Egyptian blue lotus flowers. Occasional live entertainment—usually rock or folk—and pub noshes are also on offer. And speaking of music, **Nectar's** (188 Main St., Burlington, 802/658-4771) has made its name on it, primarily as the spot that gave the band Phish its first following. Just as it did back then, the pub-cum-club spotlights nightly live music, weekly pool tournaments, lots of bar food, and has earned the love of local regulars for all of it.

Events

Burlington is home base each summer for the **Mozart Festival** (802/262-7352 or 800/639-

3443, www.vtmozart.com, July–Aug.), a classical music festival that brings Amadeus outdoors to various locations in the valley. If you notice people stumbling down the streets, it's probably just the weekend of the **Vermont Brewers Festival** (802/244-6828, www.vermontbrewers.com, $5–125, July), a waterfront boozefest featuring Long Trail, Otter Creek, Magic Hat, Harpoon, and two dozen other beermeisters from around New England. Burlington's biggest festival, the **Champlain Valley Fair** (105 Pearl St./Rte. 15, Essex Junction, 802/878-5545, www.cvfair.com, late Aug.–early Sept.) has been bringing amusement rides and agricultural exhibits to the area for more than 80 years.

Shopping

With its deluge of national chain stores, it can be hard to tell Burlington's stores from those of any other mall in America. At least, that is, until you look a little harder. Tucked in among the Banana Republics and the Gaps, the town's outdoor pedestrian promenade does indeed host a handful of distinctive and local shops. Representing Burlington's large lefty element in fine style is **The Peace & Justice Store** (21 Church St., 802/863-2345, www.pjcvt.org, 10 A.M.–6 P.M. Mon.–Thurs.; 10 A.M.–7 P.M. Fri.–Sat.; noon–5 P.M. Sun.), a nonprofit shop dedicated to educating on everything from globalization and civil rights to healthy eating.

Looking to stock your kitchen right? Look to the selection of high-end cutlery and cookware at **Kiss the Cook** (72 Church St., 802/863-4226, www.kissthecook.net, 9:30 A.M.–6 P.M. Mon.–Thurs.; 9:30 A.M.–9 P.M. Fri.–Sat.; noon–5 P.M. Sun.). The locally owned business stocks Fiestaware, bakeware, and pots and pans by names like Emile Henry, Braun, and Viking.

An unusually good (and well-priced) selection of used books can be found at **North Country Books** (2 Church St., 802/862-6413). Stacked to its ceiling with literature, sci-fi, cookbooks, poetry, and children's tales, the shop prides itself on encouraging browsing and keeping prices low. It also sells prints, vintage posters and maps, and cards.

Food

Every town has its favorite flavors, and the tastes of Burlington's residents, it turns out, run spicy—with one Asian eatery after another offering up some of New England's best of the genre. The top-notch Southeast Asian organic eats at **Tantra** (169 Lower Church St., 802/651-9660, 5–10 P.M. daily, $14–21) are a citywide hit—in particular the Thai specialties such as green curry and spicy beef, and the exotic martini menu.

Forget Americanized Chinese food. The immensely popular **A Single Pebble** (133-35 Bank St., 802/865-5200, www.asinglepebble.com, 11:30 A.M.–1:45 P.M. Mon.–Fri.; 5 P.M.–10 P.M. nightly, $9–20) cooks authentic Szechuan fare like "Ants Climbing a Tree" (a traditional pork and cellophane noodle dish) and Red Chili Shrimp, served family-style. If you can't choose a country, the top-notch pan-Asian fixings at **Five Spice Café** (175 Church St., 802/864-4045, www.fivespicecafe.com, $14–20) have all Burlington raving. The menu draws from Vietnam, Thailand, Nepal, Indonesia, and China to cook up dishes like Burmese chicken with peppers and Hunan noodles. On Sundays, the place gets packed for dim sum.

Of course, Asian isn't all you'll find on the menu in Burlington—there's plenty of Italian (inexpensive and otherwise), American, pub grub, barbecue, and seafood—and all in relatively close proximity to one another. So if you're a fan of all of the above cuisines, the best way to decide your culinary fate on any given evening is to simply follow your nose. Wind up at **Sweetwaters** (120 Church St. 802/864-9800, www.sweetwatervt.com, 11:30 A.M.–midnight Mon.–Sat. and 11:30 A.M.–11 P.M. Sun., $16–24) and you won't be disappointed. Part pub, part bistro, with lovely al fresco dining in warm weather, it offers a slightly trendy but solid menu of dishes like a *kobe* beef burger with bacon and cheese.

On any pleasant-weather day, the place to be is **Splash at the Boathouse** (College St., 802/651-1081, 8 A.M.–9:30 P.M. daily, $6–12), housed on the floating boathouse at the end of

VERMONT

College Street. The ultra-casual setting (looking out to the lake's waters) matches the casual menu—the likes of Asian tuna sandwiches and fish tacos. Seafood lovers shouldn't pass up a chance to eat dinner at **Perry's Fish House** (1080 Shelburne Rd., South Burlington, 802/862-1300, 4–9 P.M. daily, $12–20), which has been voted best seafood in town for 10 years straight. The casual spot steams gargantuan lobsters and also serves straightforward dishes like steamed clams and fried flounder.

Serious Italian takes center stage at **Trattoria Delia** (152 Saint Paul St., 802/864-5253, www.trattoriadelia.com, 5–10 P.M. daily, $18–24), with an excellent wine list and an emphasis on freshly made pastas and authentically cooked high-quality meats.

Hipster vegetarians aren't the only ones crowding **Stone Soup** (211 College St., 802/862-7616, 7 A.M.–7 P.M. Mon.; 7 A.M.–9 P.M. Tues.–Fri.; 9 A.M.–7 P.M. Sat.). The hearty breads, soups, and sandwiches and incredible chocolate chip cookies have a fan base that reaches far beyond veganism.

The food is as whimsical as the hosts at **Penny Cluse Café** (169 Cherry St., 802/651-8834, www.pennycluse.com, 6:45 A.M.–3 P.M. weekdays and 8 A.M.–3 P.M. weekends, $4–9), named for the hipster owner's childhood dog and decked out with an ever-rotating collection of posters and local art. Dig into gingerbread pancakes at breakfast, or hang out till lunch and order up Baja fish tacos and a Bloody Mary.

Information and Services

The **Greater Burlington Chamber of Commerce** (877/686-5253,, www.vermont.org) runs an information booth on Church Street. Also look for a copy of the **Blue Map** (www.bluemap.com), a detailed tourist map of downtown and the Greater Burlington Area.

For emergency and hospital services, head to **Fletcher Allen Hospital** (Colchester Ave., Burlington, 802/847-0000), while **Vermont Children's Hospital** (111 Colchester Ave., Burlington, 802/847-5437) is equipped to handle younger patients' needs. Fill prescriptions at either location of **Rite-Aid** (158 Cherry St., Burlington, 802/862-1562 or 1024 North Ave., Burlington, 802/865-7822), which also offers faxing services.

Internet access is offered at **Speeder & Earl's Coffee** (412 Pine St., Burlington, 800/849-6041) and **FedEx Office** (199 Main St., Burlington, 802/658-2561), which also offers fax services and shipping services.

LAKE CHAMPLAIN ISLANDS

With more shoreline than any other part of Vermont, this cluster of five quiet islands feels entirely separate from the rest of the state—if not the world. Water seems to be everywhere, as do farms, humble homes, and friendly residents who all seem to be on a first-name basis with each other.

Discovered approximately 400 years ago by Samuel de Champlain, the islands are good for those seeking history as well as for a little R&R. They're home to New England's oldest log cabin (on Grand Isle), and each island's individual historical societies showcase artifacts from the islands' early settlers. All that said, besides a handful of other sights of note there isn't much else to do here—which is precisely how many visitors would have it.

Royal Lipizzaner Stallions

"Horse of Battle, Horse of Ballet," reads the motto for the milk-white stallions (407/366-0366, www.lipizzaner.com) who summer on Lake Champlain each year. The Lippazan breed supposedly dates back 2,000 years to Carthage, crossing over with the Moorish occupation of Spain in 700 A.D. Later bred by the King of Austria, the commanding stallions became the horses of the Austrian royal guard. More than 30 years ago, a producer by the name of Gary Lashinsky brought the horses to the United States to perform in musical dressage performances with leaps and gallops that mirror the equestrian maneuvers of the army. The current show is as much Vegas as Vienna—but there is something undeniably visually arresting about seeing the stallions standing upright

COURTESY OF STATE OF VERMONT

a rocky beach on North Hero Island

on powerful haunches, and soaring through the air with the lake as a backdrop. The stallions perform throughout the summer, from mid-July to Labor Day, at Knight Point State Park on North Hero Island.

◖ St. Anne's Shrine

Situated at the far northern end of Lake Champlain, the Isle La Motte is a haunting terrain of sparse forest and windswept solitude. It must have seemed all the more desolate in 1666, when the first settlement in Vermont, Fort St. Anne, was built by French explorers under command of Pierre de St. Paul, Sieur La Motte. They took solace in a shrine built to St. Anne, staffed by Jesuit priests who accompanied the expedition. Four hundred years later, the shrine (Isle La Motte, 802/928-3362, www.saintannesshrine.org, 9 A.M.–7 P.M. daily mid-May–mid-Oct., tours every half hour, $2 adults) still exists as a Catholic pilgrimage site, though the current building dates only from the late 19th century. In addition to the main building, where mass is still said regularly in

season, the picturesque lakeshore is dotted by various grottoes filled with religious statues, including a 15-foot gold-leaf statue of the Virgin Mary rescued from a Burlington cathedral. Up the hill, a rectory and cafeteria has a small museum full of relics dating back to the French occupation in the 17th century. The lake itself is fittingly graced by a statue of the man who discovered it in 1609, explorer Samuel de Champlain, sculpted by F. L. Weber for the Montreal Expo in 1967.

Other Sights

The best place to get in touch with the agricultural ambience of the islands is **Allenholm Farm** (150 South St., South Hero, 802/372-5566, www.allenholm.com), which has a petting paddock full of animals, including two donkeys, a Scotch Highland Cow, and a fat ewe with a taste for peppermints. A farm stand sells apples and farm-made apple pies. The legacy of Lake Champlain's prehistoric sojourn in the tropics is on view at the **Fisk Quarry** (The Main Road, Isle La Motte, 802/862-4150, www.lcltorg/guidefiskquarry.htm). Poking out of the quarry walls is the fossilized remains of the 480-million-year-old Chazy Coral Reef, the oldest known coral reef in the world.

Entertainment and Events

All of Lake Champlain becomes a stage each summer, when the **Vermont Shakespeare Company** (North Hero, 917/539-3181, www.vermontshakespeare.org) performs outdoors at Knight Point State Park. A celebration as American as you-know-what, **Apple Fest** (South St., South Hero, 802/372-8400, Oct.) celebrates the yearly harvest with pies, cider, auctions, and a craft show.

A celebration as American as you-know-what, **Apple Fest** (South St., South Hero, 800/262-5226, Oct.) celebrates the yearly harvest with pies, cider, auctions, and a craft show.

Shopping

Retail is sparse among the islands; most folks

here seem more interested in forgetting the rest of the world than buying something from it. There are, however, a few shops such as **Hero's Welcome** (Rte. 2, North Hero, 802/372-4121, www.heroswelcome.com), a general store stocked with Adirondack chairs, books on and maps of the area, squall jackets, and assorted gadgets. And if you didn't find what you were looking for there, odds are it's on the shelves—along with seemingly every other object on the planet—at **New England Via Vermont** (4 Milk St., Alburgh, 802/796-3665, www.new-englandviavermont.com). No one disputes that the place is a souvenir shop, but the question, souvenirs of what?, has not yet been settled. Civil War buffs will find plenty to buy among the antique-bullet selection and book section dedicated to the war. Those hoping to take a piece of Vermont home will do well to pick up any of the maple or cheese products or videos and books on the state; natural-science lovers, meanwhile, thrill to the fossilized shark teeth and rocks.

Food

Eat like the locals do (not that you'll have much of a choice; restaurants are few and far between on most islands) and you won't go wrong. Start at the **Blue Paddle Bistro** (316 Rte. 2, South Hero, 802/372-4814, www.bluepaddlebistro.com, 5:30–8:30 P.M. daily, $9–16) for friendly service, town gossip, and terrific gorgonzola-stuffed meatloaf. The bar is crowned with a full-sized canoe. For memorable views of the lake and mountains, grab a table at **Links on the Lake** (230 Rte. 129, Alburg, 802/796-3586, www.alburggolflinks.com, 5–8 P.M. Tues.–Sun., $11–15) in Alburg Golf Links public golf course. The casual restaurant is open May through October and serves staples like clam chowder, scampi, and fish-and-chips.

Information

The **Lake Champlain Islands Chamber** (802/372-8400, www.champlainislands.com) has information at its office on North Hero Island.

ST. ALBANS

Situated north of Burlington on the east shore of the lake, St. Albans was one of the first towns to fight and win against the incursion of Wal-Mart in the 1990s. Its main street is still a thriving center of mom-and-pop stores, set down from a town green half the size of a football field. The town's claim to fame is as the unlikely site of a Civil War "battle," the so-called Saint Albans Raid, which occurred in 1863. Following the war, St. Albans

THE ST. ALBANS RAID

Of all the quirky schemes dreamed up in wartime, the raid organized by Lieutenant Bennett Young takes the cake. A Kentucky calvary officer during the Civil War, Bennett received a commission from the Confederacy to stage raids from Canada to rob Union banks to line the South's coffers. His one and only action was the successful raid of St. Albans, in which he and 20 other cavalrymen galloped the 15 miles from the Canadian border and took over the town on October 19, 1864, herding the panicked townsfolk onto the village green and simultaneously robbing three banks. The soldiers made off with some $200,000, though their celebration was cut short when they were captured in Montreal a few weeks later and forced to give back some $90,000 they still had on them. Despite the best efforts of the United States, however, neutral Canada refused to extradite the soldiers, saying they were acting under official orders, and Young and his confederates were never tried for their offenses. As a postscript, the incident was made into a mildly successful movie, *The Raid*, in 1954, in which the Bennett Young character played by Van Heflin comes to St. Albans weeks before the raid and falls in love with a pretty townswoman played by Anne Bancroft. Needless to say, that part is heavily fictionalized.

© MICHAEL BLANDING

a farm near St. Albans

became a headquarters of the Central Vermont Railroad, which passed through here on its way to Montreal and Quebec. In its heyday, the town was known as "Railroad City," with some 1,500 workers employed in the town and great wealth from the railroad being invested in the Victorian homes that grace the top of the hill.

Sights

Situated on the east side of the green, the three-story **St. Albans Historical Society Museum** (Church St., 802/527-7933, www.vmga.org/franklin/st.albanshs.html, 1–4 P.M. Mon.–Fri. mid-June–early Oct., $3 adults, free children 14 and under) is chock-full of historical artifacts, including relics from the Civil War raid, a 3-D re-creation of Norman Rockwell's painting *The Doctors Office,* and railroad memorabilia. Its pièce de résistance is a new 18-foot-long LED-festooned diorama of the Lake Champlain region.

North of St. Albans, the **Chester A. Arthur Historical Site** (off Rte. 36 or 108, Fairfield, 802/828-3051, 11 A.M.–5 P.M. Sat.–Sun. July–mid-Oct., donations accepted) honors the nation's 21st president, best known for reigning in the worst of the Gilded Age excess with rigorous

prosecution of fraud and the establishment of the modern civil service. The site displays a pictorial history of Chas's life in a reconstruction of the home where Arthur was purportedly born (though modern research shows he actually moved to the house when he was one year old). To get to the site, head north from the small village of Fairfield and bear right after one mile. Continue for five miles along the road, which eventually turns to gravel.

Nearby, Swanton is also the tribal headquarters for the **Abenaki Nation** (100 Grand Ave., Swanton, 802/868-2559, www.abenakination. org), the western branch of the "People of the Dawn," the Native Americans who inhabited most of northern Vermont, New Hampshire, and Maine for thousands of years before the coming of European settlers. The Nation runs a museum with exhibits including headdresses, masks, and an authentic birch-bark canoe.

Entertainment and Events

The recently renovated **Opera House at Enosburg Falls** (123 Depot St., Enosburg Falls, 802/933-6171) hosts community theater and musical performances.

St. Albans' big annual event is the **Vermont**

VERMONT

Maple Festival (802/524-5800, www.vtmaple-festival.org, late Apr., free admission for most events and activities), which has grown from a humble celebration of the state's vaunted syrup into a grand festival that draws thousands each year from all over Vermont and beyond. The fair includes carnival rides, a craft show, a fiddling competition, a pancake breakfast (with maple syrup of course!), and the crowning of the Maple King and Queen, who "have the responsibility and FUN of representing the Green Mountain State's signature product during their reigning year." Marching bands from around the state parade in honor of Vermont's favorite animal at the **Vermont Dairy Festival** (802/933-9691, www.vermontdairyfestival. com, over the first Saturday in June), held each year in the hamlet of Enosburg Falls. The highlight of the festival is the annual "cow plop" contest, in which a grass-fed beast is let loose on a grid of numbered squares.

Shopping

Under an inviting pink-and-white striped awning, **Sweet Nothings** (94 N. Main St., 802/527-5118) sells the kind of candy you just never see anymore—wax bottles, licorice whips, and rock candy—from big glass jars. It also operates an old-fashioned ice cream parlor, doling out banana splits and ice cream sodas. The colorful exterior of **The Garden Patch** (69 N. Main St., 802/527-9680, www.countryhomevermont.com) hints at the charming merchandise they sell for your home's interior: framed prints and country signs, handmade candles, bird-shaped cast-iron napkin rings, green-tea lotions, and herb boxes.

Food

The straightforward specials at **The Abbey Restaurant** (6212 Rte. 105, Enosburg Falls, 800/696-4748, www.abbeygroup.net/restaurant.htm, 5 P.M.–9 P.M. Fri.–Sat.; 10:30 A.M.–12:30 P.M. Sun., $16–22) have earned a local following—as has the convivial atmosphere in the establishment's tavern. Depending on what's available daily, you'll sup on prime rib, fresh scrod, and grilled pork or chicken. **Chow!**

Bella (28 N. Main St., St. Albans, 802/524-1405, www.chowbella.us, 10:30 A.M.–2 P.M. Sun;, 4–9:30 P.M. Mon.–Tues.; 11:30 A.M.–9:30 P.M. Wed.–Sat., $12–21) may just be the best choice in town for curious palates. The cozy brick-walled restaurant emphasizes seasonal foods in a rotating menu—the likes of crabmeat-stuffed chicken breast and salmon in cider cream sauce. The list of wines by the glass is refreshingly long, and thoughtfully chosen.

Information and Services

For more information about St. Albans, contact the office of **St. Albans for the Future** (100 N. Main St., 802/524-1500, www.stalbansvt. info), located at City Hall. The only hospital north of Burlington is the **Northwestern Medical Center** (133 Fairfield St., 802/524-5911, www.northwesternmedicalcenter.org). For non-emergency medical needs, there's a **Rite-Aid** downtown (153 N. Main St, 802/524-2141), as well as the independent **Jack Rixon's Pharmacy** (40 N. Main St, 802/524-2020).

SPORTS AND RECREATION
Missisquoi National Wildlife Refuge

Bird-watchers flock to this refuge (29 Tabor Rd., Swanton, 802/868-4781, www.fws.gov, dawn–dusk daily) for a glimpse of ducks, grebes, and mergansers that make this 6,000-plus-acre preserve their temporary home during migrations to and from Canada. Several interpretive trails take in a mile and a half of wooded wetlands, which are also inhabited by beavers and other small mammals. The refuge can attract up to 20,000 waterfowl during the autumn migration. On-site, Shad Island is the state's largest great blue heron rookery. Trails are also open to snowshoeing and cross-country skiing in the winter months.

Biking

Champlain's flat terrain and lack of traffic make them ideal for two-wheeled touring. **Lake Champlain Bikeways** (1 Steele St. #103, 802/652-2453, www.champlainbikeways.org) runs a clearinghouse in Burlington with trail maps and information on the 1,300 miles of bikeways around the lake. Closer to home, the city has recently constructed the excellent **Burlington Bike Path** (Burlington Parks and Recreation, 802/864-0123, www.enjoyburlington.com), an eight-mile path that runs along the river and connects several parks perfect for picnicking. A spur leads off the Ethan Allen Homestead. Located on the bike path, nonprofit **Local Motion** (1 Steele St., 802/652-2453, www.localmotion.org) rents out bikes and provides a map to other bike paths in the city.

Boating

The sheer size of Lake Champlain makes venturing out in a kayak an unforgettable experience. The lake's famous changeability, however, requires paddlers to stay on their toes; be sure not to get too far out from shore lest a sudden squall leave you stranded. The **Lake Champlain Committee** (802/658-1414, www.lakechamplaincommittee.org) has established the Lake Champlain Paddlers Trail, with suggested routes for paddling. **True North Kayak Tours** (25 Nash Pl., 802/860-1910, www.vermontkayak.com) rents boats and sponsors tours of the lake around Kingsland Bay and Button Bay State Parks south of Burlington, secluded Isle La Motte, and other locations.

If paddling into the lake seems too daunting, sit back on the decks of *Friend Ship,* the flagship of **Whistling Man Schooner Co.** (1 College St., 802/598-6504, www.whistlingman.com, three tours daily noon, mid-afternoon, and early evening; hours vary slightly by season, $35 adults, $20 children under 12). Based on the Burlington waterfront, the boat takes intimate three-hour sails around the harbor with a maximum of 12 people on board.

Hiking and Camping

Runners, beachgoers, birdwatchers, fishermen, and hikers find plenty of activity and wildlife at **North Hero State Park** (3803 Lakeview Dr., North Hero, 802/372-8727, www.vtstateparks.com/htm/northhero.cfm, late May–early Sept.), a picturesque playground on a quiet peninsula sticking out onto the lake.

Several of Lake Champlain's smaller islands, however, offer a unique opportunity to really "get away from it all." Case in point: the former agricultural island that is now **Burton Island State Park** (St. Albans Bay, 802/524-6353, www.vtstateparks.com/htm/burton.cfm, late May–early Sept., $16–18 nightly base rate). Take a ferry to enjoy its campground, which has 17 tent sites and 26 lean-tos along with its swimming and recreation area; a resident naturalist gives deer-spotting tours. Ferry service is available several times a day from Kill Kare State Park, southwest of St. Albans center.

If even that's too much civilization for you, take a rented boat to **Woods Island** (St. Albans Bay, 802/524-6353, www.vtstateparks.com/htm/woodsisland.cfm, late May–early Sept., $14) with five carry-in/carry-out campsites along the beach each with only a simple fire-ring and basic latrine. Permits are available through Burton Island State park.

ACCOMMODATIONS
Under $100

The friendly and homey **Terry Inn** (2925 West Shore Rd., Isle La Motte, 802/928-3264, $79–99) feels a world away from everything, tucked into a shoreside corner of sleepy Isle La Motte. Rooms are humbly decorated, but all have private baths, and the inn has a private beach.

$100-150

If convenience and simple comfort are your priorities, reserve one of the four guest rooms at **Sunset House** (78 Main St., 802/864-3790, www.sunsethousebb.com, $99–149). Rooms are outfitted with quilts, queen or twin beds, and old photos (the home was built in 1908), and it's a close walk to downtown Burlington.

$150-250

The Willard Street Inn (349 S. Willard St., Burlington, 802/651-8712 ($125–225) is as beautiful inside the rooms as it is out; the sprawling Victorian manse lays claim to impeccably decorated rooms. Each is filled with thoughtful details—a hand-carved antique chest here, a gas fireplace with antique mosaic tile there. Terry bathrobes, wireless Internet access, and a full breakfast served in the marble-floored solarium come with every stay. Children under 12 are not welcome.

Arguably the most gentrified spot in the Lake Champlain Islands, **(The North Hero House** (3643 Rte. 2, North Hero, 802/372-4732, www.northherohouse.com, $125–350) is poised on the banks of the lake in one of the islands' more central areas. The colonial-style inn houses 26 lovely individually decorated rooms, most with antique beds (four-poster to wrought-iron), floral linens, and some with a private balcony. The semiformal on-site restaurant overlooks the water and serves an excellent menu of ambitious dishes (the shrimp and scallop *tian* is a favorite).

GETTING THERE AND AROUND

The easiest driving route to Burlington is I-89 across Vermont, a two-hour trip (90 mi.) from White River Junction. The more scenic route is to take winding Route 7 up from Rutland along the foothills of the Greens (65 mi., 1.75 hr.).

Flights from many major cities land at **Burlington International Airport** (BTV, 1200 Airport Dr., S. Burlington, 802/863-1889, www.btv.aero), which is served by half a dozen airlines. Reservation desks for half a dozen major rental car companies are available at the airport.

Amtrak (800/872-7245, www.amtrak.com) runs trains to Burlington (29 Railroad Ave., Essex Jct.), and **Greyhound Bus Lines** (800/231-2222, www.greyhound.com) runs buses to Burlington Bus Station (345 Pine St., 802/864-6811).

Chittenden County Transit Authority (802/864-2282, www.cctaride.org) has bus routes throughout Burlington and the surrounding area, including buses downtown from the airport and train station. To get to and from the airport, take bus route 1, which takes approximately 25 minutes to travel between BIA and downtown's Cherry Street station. From the train station, take bus route 2, which takes approximately 40 minutes to make the trip between Essex Junction and Cherry Street. Bus fare is $1.25. Taxi stands are also available at the airport and the train station; to call a cab from other locations, contact **Burlington Taxi** (905/333-3333, www.burlingtontaxi.com).

Lower Champlain Valley

Is it just your imagination, or does every bit of this area seem (and smell) like cow country? Actually, you're right on the nose: The Champlain Valley is currently home to most of the state's dairy farms, though a good number of fruit farms are also mixed in there. This means plenty of places to stop and sample ice cream and cheese (or apples) as you drive along the wooded stretches of Lake Champlain's banks—and plenty of scenic vistas of working farmhouses framed by mountains and calm waters.

SHELBURNE

Blessed with plenty of scenic roads and pastoral mountain views, Shelburne has always been a community based primarily on farming, and it shows, with farmland seemingly everywhere you look. Lacking the active downtown center that anchors so many other country towns, Shelburne is more a spread-out collection of various tourist magnets—the most impressive of which is the Shelburne Museum, one of Vermont's premier attractions.

(Shelburne Museum

If your jaw doesn't drop when you step onto the grounds of this 45-acre museum campus (5555 Shelburne Rd., 802/985-3346, www.shelburnemuseum.org, 10 A.M.–5 P.M. daily May–Oct., $20 adults, $10 children 4–18, children under 4 free, $50 family day pass), you might want to check your pulse. "Museum" might

the Round Barn at the Shelburne Museum

COURTESY OF THE SHELBURNE MUSEUM

be too small a word for 38 buildings displaying hundreds of thousands of items, including a full-size Lake Champlain steamship, a 1920s carousel, a fine horse-drawn vehicle collection, and galleries of American folk art and French Impressionist paintings. The museum is the work of art collector Electra Havemeyer Webb, who relocated buildings from across the country to display her collection, opening the museum in 1947.

After her death, Webb's children brought her own home to the museum, and it is still set up with the art and furniture in the exact locations Webb intended them, providing an intimate window into the private life of a wealthy collector. Hanging in the rooms of the Greek Revival mansion are many first-rate paintings by Cassatt, Degas, Monet, Corot, and Manet, including the first Impressionist painting brought to America, a Monet painting of a drawbridge, which was purchased by Webb in Paris for $20. Webb and her parents were also important contributors to the Metropolitan Museum of Art in New York; because of that association, the Shelburne Museum is able to snag world-class traveling exhibitions; recent shows featured a retrospective of Georgia O'Keeffe's paintings, including some of her best-known flower canvases; and an exhibit of never-before-seen furniture and glasswork by art-nouveau master craftsman Louis Comfort Tiffany.

Other Sights

The Webb family certainly thinks big. In addition to the Shelburne Museum, they are the benefactors behind **Shelburne Farms** (1611 Harbor Rd., 802/985-8686, www.shelburnefarms.org, 10 A.M.–4 P.M. daily mid May–Oct., $8 adults, $6 seniors, $5 children 3–17, children under 3 free), a sprawling agricultural estate perched literally on the shores of the lake. Attractions include a petting barn where kids can milk a cow or brush a donkey, a cheese-making operation, and eight miles of walking trails through achingly bucolic meadows and woodland. The farm also lets out rooms in its baronial estate.

From real animals to fake: Everyone knows the teddy bear was named after American

VERMONT

president Theodore Roosevelt. But in 1981, John Sortino was shocked to find out that that American invention was made exclusively overseas. He started making his own teddy bears, selling them from a pushcart in Burlington in 1983. From those humble beginnings, the cotton-stuffed empire of the **Vermont Teddy Bear Company** (6655 Shelburne Rd./Rte. 7, 802/985-3001, www.vermontteddybear. com, 9 A.M.–6 P.M. daily early June–Oct.; 9 A.M.–5 P.M. daily Nov.–May, $2 adults, children 12 and under free) was born. Now the company's flagship store is always packed with groups touring the operation and picking out their own fabric and stuffing to make their own creation. The factory and gift shop (if anything, bigger than the factory) retain enough home-grown charm to avoid seeming like a complete tourist trap.

Events
Past performers at the **Concerts on the Green** (5555 Shelburne Rd., 802/985-3346, www. shelburnemuseum.org) music series include Willie Nelson, Emmylou Harris, and Crosby, Stills, and Nash. Musicians play on select summer weekends on the grounds of the Shelburne Museum.

Shopping
The best bargains in town can be found among the crowded shelves at **Champlain Valley Antique Center** (4067 Shelburne Rd., 802/985-8116), a conglomeration of collectibles and furnishings from more than 25 local antiques dealers. Pick through the offerings to find fine china, vintage posters, folk art, and handmade armoires.

Food
A little slice of French country resides at **Café Shelburne** (5573 Shelburne Rd., 802/985-3939, www.cafeshelburne.com, 5:30–9 P.M. Tues.–Sat. Nov.–Aug.; also Sun. and Mon. Sept.–Oct.; $19–26), a lovely but low-key eatery with soft lighting, a well-chosen wine list, and an affable staff. Settle in for dinner and dig in to the Gallic menu, with specials such as

Vermont Teddy Bear Company

delicately flavored quail salad and escargot with prosciutto and almonds. Also French-leaning, also subtly romantic, is the **🄲 Bearded Frog** (5247 Shelburne Rd., 802/985-9877, www. thebeardedfrog.com, 5–9 P.M. daily, $6–25), a restaurant named for owner Michel Mahe's facial hair and French heritage. The spot has been a hit since it opened in spring of 2006, mostly thanks to Mahe's eclectic menu—a pastiche of international flavors, such as mussels with chipotle, served to an enthusiastic crowd in the large, polished room against oversized windows and elegant palms.

Information

The Shelburne Museum (5555 Shelburne Rd., 802/985-3346, www.shelburnemuseum.org, 10 A.M.–5 P.M. daily May–Oct.) has a visitors information center stocked with maps and brochures; no admission required.

A **Rite-Aid** (30 Shelburne Shopping Park, 802/985-2610) pharmacy is located in the center of downtown. Free Wi-Fi is available at **Bruegger's Bagel Bakery** (2989 Shelburne Rd, 802/985-3183). **Shelburne Police** are at 5420 Shelburne Rd., 802/985-8051.

VERGENNES

The little settlement on the banks of Otter Creek was the first city in Vermont, and one of the first in America. No, that's not a typo—though it may be a bit of an exaggeration. Until the late 1700s, most settlements in New England were known as "towns." When the mill center of Vergennes was formed out of bits of land from neighboring towns, it was so bully on its prospects that it took the grandiose name of "city." Now with a population of 2,800, Vergennes is dwarfish, even by Vermont standards, but it has risen up to its name with a citified atmosphere of fine restaurants and upscale shops. During the War of 1812, it was the home base for a shipyard along Otter Creek that heroically built a fleet to defeat the British on the lake—one of the few bright spots in a disastrous war.

A few miles east of town, on the part of Lake Champlain known as "the Narrows," the port of Basin Harbor makes a good base from which to venture out onto the water. Nearby Ferrisburgh is the most northern town in the county, and with its lively, picturesque town center and handful of shops and sights, it's certainly worth an afternoon or day trip.

🄲 Lake Champlain Maritime Museum

It's tempting to forget about Lake Champlain when contemplating New England's maritime history—focusing instead on the clipper ships and schooners that plied the Atlantic. But the lake was once the lifeblood of the country's interior, before the cutting of the Erie Canal and settlement of Ohio territory moved the frontier farther to the west. Champlain's history dates back even before the Pilgrims landed at Plymouth Rock, when Native Americans traversed its shores in birch-bark canoes and French trappers established camps on its islands.

This museum, just a few miles from the lakeshore (4472 Basin Harbor Rd., 802/475-2022, www.lcmm.org, 10 A.M.–5 P.M. daily late May–mid-Oct., $10 adults, $9 seniors, $6 students 5–17, children under 5 free, admission good for two consecutive days), does an exceptional job of bringing alive the scope of the lake's domestic and military history, with a hands-on boat-building workshop, an exhibit on the more than 200 shipwrecks that line the lake bottom, and an interactive display on the lake's importance in the Revolutionary War.

Perhaps the biggest surprise is the story of patriot-turned-traitor Benedict Arnold, who led a heroic defense of the lake in the early years of the war. Arnold commissioned a fleet of gunships to be built at the lake's southern end in Skenesborough and fought a hopeless battle with the British off the shore of Valcour Island, a few miles up from Basin Harbor. The engagement scuttled British plans for invasion in 1776, leaving another year for the Americans to plan their defenses. In 1997, the museum undertook the mammoth task of rebuilding one of Arnold's gunboats, the *Philadelphia II,* which now floats in the harbor.

VERMONT

Other Sights

The imposing Greek Revival facade of **Bixby Memorial Library** (258 Main St., 802/877-2211, www.bixbylibrary.org, 12:30–8 P.M. Mon.; 12:30–5 P.M. Tues. and Fri.; 10 A.M.–5 P.M. Wed. and Thurs., free) is only the beginning of its charms. Inside, the library has one of the largest collections of artifacts in the state, with exhibits of Native American arrowheads, antique maps, stamps, and documents relating to the early history of the region, including the Revolutionary and Civil Wars.

By the time escaped slaves arrived in Ferrisburgh, just north of Vergennes, they must have been able to taste the freedom of Canada on their tongue. The **Rokeby Museum** (4334 Rte. 7, Ferrisburgh, 802/877-3406, www.rokeby.org, tours 11 A.M., 12:30 P.M., and 2 P.M. Thurs.–Sun., $6 adults, $4 seniors and students, $2 children under 13) preserves the time when Quakers Rowland Thomas and Rachel Gilpin helped countless slaves escape on the Underground Railroad, hiding them and providing them employment on their sheep farm. In addition to being one of the best-documented Underground Railroad sites in the country, the museum contains artifacts relating to 200 years of Vermont history.

Entertainment and Events

In its 100-year history, the **Vergennes Opera House** (120 Main St., 802/877-6737, www.vergennesoperahouse.org) has seen many changes, from a grand classical music hall to a moving-picture theater to a condemned old building. In 1997, the town raised money to restore the hall to its Victorian splendor, and it now serves as the town cultural hub with an impressive array of entertainment offerings. Recent shows ranged from a 12-part a cappella jazz group to "Metal Fest," featuring bands with names like Blinded by Rage, Seething, and Black Out Frenzy.

The entire *city* comes out to celebrate **Vergennes Day** (802/388-8066, www.midvermont.com/events/vergennesday) every year at the end of the summer. Amusement rides, historical tours, and a 5K road race add to the fun.

Shopping

It just doesn't make sense to leave Vergennes without stocking up on the area's delicacies. Start at the craft- and treat-lover's jackpot that is **Kennedy Bros. Factory Marketplace** (10 Main St., 802/877-2975, www.kennedybrothers.com, 9:30 A.M.–5:30 P.M. daily), a huge selection of antiques, artisanal maple sugars and fudges, and wood-ware.

Grab imported specialty sauces, freshly made pastas, organic herbs, and locally made gelato at **Fat Hen Market** (10 Green St., 802/877-2923). Or wander through the aisles of **Second Star Toys & Gifts** (7 Green St., 802/877-9259) and find adorable baby, toddler, and children's clothing and handmade wooden toys.

Food

Small-town sophistication is exemplified in a handful of eateries, primarily centered along Main Street. For a solid dose, settle in at a table at the modern country deli ◖ **Three Squares** (221 Main St., 802/877-2772, www.3squarescafe.com, 8 A.M.–8 P.M. Mon.–Sat.; 8 A.M.–7 P.M. Sun., $5–8) and tuck into one of the house's panini of teriyaki flank steak with red onion and garlic mayonnaise.

For a pull-out-all-the-stops meal, turn to **Christophe's on the Green** (5 N. Green St., 802/877-3413, www.christophesonthegreen.com, 5:30–9:30 P.M. Tues.–Sat., $28), a chic but simple dining room filled with crisp linens and Villeroy & Boch china. Dinners here tend toward the romantic and creative—French classics like mushroom tart tweaked with comté cheese.

Originally a cider press, the setting for **Starry Night Cafe** (5371 Rte. 7, Ferrisburgh, 802/877-6316 www.starrynightcafe.com, 5:30–9 P.M. Wed.–Sun., $17–26) is a historic complex that includes a covered bridge. The dining room itself is blessed with an antique bar, chairs custom-made by local artists, and hand-blown glassware. Nor is the menu lacking for creativity; it's found in plates of steak tartar with chipotle aioli, *tagine* with tilapia and fennel, and duck with sour cherry-wine sauce.

There's a little slice of Paris to be found at a great price at **⟨ Black Sheep Bistro** (253 Main St., 802/877-9991, 5–8:30 P.M. daily, $14–19), where high-quality dishes like black sesame–crusted salmon with ginger beurre blanc make up the specials.

Information and Services

For more information on Vergennes, contact or visit the **Addison County Chamber of Commerce** (2 Court St., Middlebury, 802/388-7951, www.addisoncounty.com). Pharmacy needs can be taken care of downtown at **Marble Works Pharmacy** (187 Main St, 802/877-1190). Emergencies, contact **Vergennes Police** (120 Main St., 802 877-2201) or dial 911.

BRISTOL

While little Bristol has few bona fide sights, it makes up for that with a kind of "frozen in time" atmosphere that many towns boast and few deliver on. Cradled in the crook of Dearleap Mountain, the village is a welcoming sight for drivers who have just braved the pass over the Green Mountains from the Mad River Valley; it's also a last chance to fuel up for those venturing up into the peaks. The town's all-American downtown recalls the one Marty McFly stumbled upon in *Back to the Future,* with solid brick rows of storefronts strung with red, white, and blue bunting and filled with neighbors chatting at the bakery or launderette. If you are looking for a place to turn off your cell phone for a while, it might be just the ticket.

Sights

Don't get the wrong idea when you come into town and see **Lord's Prayer Rock,** a giant boulder with the "Our Father" carved into its face. No, you haven't entered a religious enclave. The rock dates back to the 19th century, when a local boy was tasked with bringing logs down the roller-coaster road from the mountaintop, and breathed a prayer whenever he made it down to see the boulder at the end of the road. A few decades later, after the boy had become a wealthy physician in New York, he returned to Bristol and had the prayer carved into the rock, hoping it would bring similar comfort to other travelers over the mountain.

THE LEGEND OF CHAMP

Hang around Lake Champlain long enough and you are bound to hear about Champ. Like the Loch Ness in Scotland, the lake is supposed to be the abode of a modern-day sea monster that has been "sighted" many times over the past 400 years. In fact, Samuel de Champlain himself supposedly spotted a "20 foot serpent thick as a barrel and [with] a head like a horse" when he discovered the lake in 1609. Since then, the legend has only grown over the last four centuries. In 1873, circus impresario P. T. Barnum offered $50,000 as a reward for its skin; subsequently both Vermont and New York have passed laws against harming the (supposed) creature. The most conclusive evidence of the monster is a photo taken in 1977 by vacationer Sandra Mansi that clearly shows a curved neck and head poking out of the lake.

When Champ fans try to explain what the "monster" is, however, they begin running into problems. Most theories hold that the creature is related to a dinosaur called a plesiosaur that got trapped in the lake back when Champlain used to be an arm of the ocean. However, the lake is only 10,000 years old, while plesiosaurs are thought to have been extinct for 65 million years. So in order to have a dinosaur in the lake, you'd need to have one plesiosaur that had been alive 65 million years – or 500 plesiosaurs to make a viable breeding population over the last 10,000 years. Whatever the truth, Champ has been embraced as a symbol by locals who have put his moniker on everything from Champ's Potato Chips to Burlington's Lake Monsters, a minor league baseball team.

Events

The biggest event of the year is Bristol's annual **Fourth of July** (802/453-2486, www.bristol4th.com), a 150-year-old celebration of national pride that features a footrace, parade, live band music, and of course fireworks. In past years, Miss Vermont National Teenager has put in an appearance. Bristol also holds a **Harvest Festival** (802/388-7951, www.bristolrec.org) each year at the end of September. In addition to the usual craft vendors and agricultural competitions, the event includes an antique car rally, with trophies given in more than 20 different categories.

Shopping

Pick up local artwork at **Art on Main** (25 Main St., 802/453-4032, www.artonmain.net, 10 A.M.–6 P.M. Mon.–Sat.; noon–4 P.M. Sun.), a cooperative community art center brimming with watercolors, oils, and acrylics, plus hand-carved walking sticks, quilts, and stained-glass kaleidoscopes. Potter Robert Compton and wife Christine are the forces behind **Robert Compton Pottery** (2662 N. Rte. 116, Bristol, 802/453-3778, www.robertcomptonpottery.com, 10 A.M.–6 P.M. daily, closed Wed., mid-May–mid-Oct.), a showroom and studio filled with pieces the artist has created with a salt glaze—a special process that introduces salt into the kiln at extremely high temperatures.

Food

The best of local fare tends to be tied to the area's farms—á la the fresh produce and goods at **Almost Home Market** (28 North St., 802/453-5775, www.almosthomemarket.net, 10 A.M.–7 P.M. daily, $6–15). Half country store, half café, it whips up fresh-baked breads and pastries, plus sandwiches and snazzy meals like lavender-roasted chicken with lemon and garlic or salmon teriyaki.

Even closer to the source is **C Mary's Restaurant** (1868 N. Rte. 116, 888/424-2432, www.innatbaldwincreek.com/marys, 5:30–9 P.M. Wed.–Sun.; 8:30–10:30 A.M. Sun. breakfast, $18–28), located at the Inn at Bald Creek, where much of the menu comes straight from the property's farm and other area farms. (Don't miss the cream of garlic soup.) And don't forget to reserve at the English-style **Bobcat Café** (5 Main St., 802/453-3311, www.bobcatcafe.com, 5–9 P.M. Mon.–Thurs.; 5–9:30 P.M. Sat.–Sun., $9–16), which gets packed with regulars in for burgers made from locally raised beef and sweet-potato fries.

Information

The **Bristol Parks, Arts & Recreation Department** (1 South St., 802/453-5885, www.bristolrec.org) runs an information center during the summer at the Howden Hall Community Center (19 West St.). For more information on Bristol, contact or visit the **Addison County Chamber of Commerce** (2 Court St., Middlebury, 802/388-7951, www.addisoncounty.com).

SPORTS AND RECREATION
Hiking and Camping

A favorite place for a stroll along Lake Champlain is **Button Bay State Park** (5 Button Bay Rd., Ferrisburgh, 802/475-2377, www.vtstateparks.com/htm/buttonbay.cfm, $3 adults, $2 children 4–13, free for children under 3), about four miles west of Vergennes. Located on the site of a tropical coral reef that remains from the time when Lake Champlain was attached to the ocean, the 1.5-mile walk passes by limestone deposits embedded with sea snail fossils. The bay gets its name from the "buttons" or smooth clay deposits strewn around the beaches. The park also has a campground, with more than 70 tent and lean-to sites ($16–25 nightly base rate) on a grassy area overlooking the lake.

Biking

The Lake Champlain area is a cyclist's dream, with miles of flat terrain studded with farm stands, country stores, and stunning views of the lake and Adirondack Mountains on the western shore. The **Lake Champlain Bikeways** (802/652-2453, www.champlainbikeways.org) trail system stretches for 1,300 miles on both

VERMONT

sides of the lake. Wind from the wider sections of the lake can make for tough going at points, but the ride is worth it for the sparkling views of the water. The Rebel's Retreat Trail is a 42-mile loop through the rolling farmlands around Vergennes. Parking is available at the trail's start downtown. Another trail starting from the same point, called Otter Creek Wandering, follows the river along mostly flat terrain for the 30 miles between Vergennes and Middlebury.

ACCOMMODATIONS

Some days, it seems harder to find an inn or bed-and-breakfast in Shelburne that is *not* historic. Fortunately, that proliferation tends to keep prices moderate and standards high.

$100-150

It may have just three rooms, but **Crystal Palace Victorian Bed & Breakfast** (48 North St., Bristol, 802/453-7609, www.crystalpalacebb.com, $90–135) welcomes guests with the fanfare of a major resort. Rooms are replete with stained-glass windows, poster beds, fireplaces, and whirlpool or claw-foot tubs. Meanwhile, the Victorian home's common spaces are refinished with white and red cherry, butternut, ash, and quarter oak. At breakfast, don't pass up the graham-cracker French toast.

$150-250

Simple and romantic, the **Inn at Baldwin Creek** (1868 N. Rte. 116, 888/424-2432, www.innatbaldwincreek.com, $95–215) appoints its spacious rooms with four-poster queen beds, gas-fired woodstoves, and TV/VCRs. Most overlook the property's gardens, and all come with free wireless Internet access, CD players, and fluffy bathrobes—not to mention a three-course breakfast and afternoon snacks (think chocolate chip cookies, blackberry scones, or apple and cheddar cheese fondue). One suite has trundle beds, ideal for families, and there's an outdoor heated swimming pool. The on-site restaurant, Mary's, is renowned for its dinners of local farm specialties.

$250 and Up

An old-fashioned family resort set on a 700-acre wooded cove of Lake Champlain, **Basin Harbor Club** (4800 Basin Harbor Rd., Vergennes, 802/475-2311, www.basinharbor.com, May–Oct., $150–550) has been owned and hosted by the same family for four generations. From May through October, it swarms with families (who can stay in either individual rooms or cabins) who thrill to the property's long roster of activities—from water skiing and tennis to hiking, pilates, bonfires, and fishing. Children's programs are available with a similar richness of offerings, including capture-the-flag games, digital scrapbooking, a ropes course and more (the teen program even has its own Facebook page). There are also a number of restaurants—the tavern-style Red Mill, the more formal Main Dining Room (with a classic menu and deep wine list), and al fresco buffets on the North Dock. Pets are welcome for a $10 surcharge.

◖ Shelburne Farms Inn (1611 Harbor Rd., Shelburne, 802/985-8498, www.shelburnefarms.org, $150–450) sits on a 1,400-acre working farm dedicated to conservation. (Regular classes and tours are offered, and you can buy any of the products made here—all humanely—at the retail store.) The inn, meanwhile, offers 24 tidy and sunny rooms (some with shared bath, some with private) and cottages decked out with country decor—soft handmade quilts, antique beds (many original to the home), and lake or garden views.

GETTING THERE AND AROUND

Shelburne is a short drive south down Route 7 from Burlington (7 mi., 15 min.). From Shelburne, Vergennes is another 15 miles down the road (25 min.). Alternatively, you can reach Shelburne by driving north on Route 7 from Middlebury (10 mi., 15 min.). From Vergennes, drive east on Route 17 to reach Bristol (15 mi., 20 min.). Or, to drive to Bristol from the highway, leave I-89 at exit 9, take Route 100B and then Route 100 south through Waitsfield, then head west along Route 17 through the

VERMONT

breathtaking Appalachian Gap (95 mi., 2 hr. 30 min. from White River Junction).

Addison County Transit Resources (802/388-1946, www.actr-vt.org) runs buses between Middlebury (Exchange St. or Merchants Row), Bristol (Shaw's Plaza), and Vergennes (Main St. and Green St.). The **Chittenden County Transit Authority** (802/864-2282, www.cctaride.org) runs buses from Vergennes (Main St. and Green St.) to Burlington.

Middlebury Area

As it slices through the lower Champlain Valley, Route 7 plays leapfrog with Otter Creek, Vermont's longest river, which tumbles down from the Green Mountain foothills into the southern end of Lake Champlain. For its southernmost 50 miles, the lake is extremely narrow, at points only a few miles across. That made it prime defensive ground for generations of French, British, and Americans soldiers who protected the waterway from attack at Fort Ticonderoga and Mount Independence. Farther inland, along the mountains, the region was rare in Vermont for making its money from mills and industry rather than farming. The concentration of wealth in Middlebury led to the founding of Vermont's most prestigious college, which still gives the town and surrounding communities an air of cultural refinement.

MIDDLEBURY

Competing theories exist about how the college town of Middlebury got its name. Some theorize that it was named for its location halfway between the Massachusetts and Canadian borders; others surmise it was named as the midpoint between two neighboring towns that were settled the same day in 1761. Whatever the origin, Middlebury has grown over the years into the cultural hub of the Champlain Valley, in large part to its eponymous liberal arts school, Middlebury College.

The college was founded in 1800 by Gamaliel Painter, one of the town's first settlers and a profoundly religious man who wanted to safeguard the spiritual education of local farmers' sons against the savage secularism of the nascent University of Vermont in Burlington. Buoyed by the college and a variety of industries including grist and woolen mills and marble quarrying, Middlebury became the largest community west of the Green Mountains by the mid-19th century, surpassing Bennington, Manchester, Rutland, and even Burlington. Since then, its population has leveled off at a modest 8,000 souls, who enjoy an energetic downtown full of upscale shops and restaurants. In town are several high-quality museums associated with the college; many students come here equally for the college's enviable access to the outdoors in the form of the Green Mountain National Forest, just a few miles east.

Middlebury College

Few college campuses are as visually harmonious as Middlebury's (802/443-5000, www.middlebury.edu), consisting of a collection of granite and marble academic halls, capped with white spires and cupolas and arranged around a wide central quad. For a stroll around campus, park in the visitors' lot behind the admissions office on South Main Street. Better yet, sign up for a student-led tour (10 A.M. and 2 P.M. Mon.–Fri. year-round; 10 A.M. Sat. Aug.–mid-Nov.). A campus highlight, the **Middlebury College Museum of Art** (S. Main St./Rte. 30, 802/443-5007, www.middlebury.edu/arts/museum, 10 A.M.–5 P.M. Tues.–Fri.; noon–5 P.M. Sat.–Sun., free) is a Met in miniature, with terra-cotta Greek urns, Roman marble reliefs, Chinese ceramics, Japanese woodcuts, and European paintings—many of which are used in the college's various art classes. Upstairs, a large open gallery displays changing exhibits of modern art and photography.

VERMONT

VERMONT BATTLEFIELDS

In addition to the war memorial in Bennington, two additional sites pay homage to Vermont's role in the Revolution, including one where actual fighting took place on Vermont soil. When colonial militias took over Fort Ticonderoga on the New York side of Lake Champlain early in the Revolutionary War, they encountered a problem, since the fort had been built to fend off invasions from the south, and would be of little use in countering the anticipated British thrust from Canada. They solved the problem by building a massive fortification on the Vermont side of the lake to defend against the northern attack. Named after the newly signed Declaration of Independence, they survive today as the **Mount Independence State Historic Site** (497 Mount Independence Rd., Orwell, 802/759-2412 or 802/948-2000, www.historicvermont.org/mountindependence, 9:30 A.M.-5 P.M. daily late May-mid-Oct., $5 adults, free children under 15).

In the summer of 1776, more than 12,000 defenders lived here, making it the largest military city in the New World at the time. By the time of the British attack the following summer, however, they numbered less than 3,000, not enough to adequately defend both sides of the lake. The British surprised the Americans by scaling the heights of Mount Defiance on the New York side to command an invincible position over Fort Ti. Rather than face death or surrender, General Arthur St. Clair made the savvy decision to retreat to Mount Independence across a giant floating bridge in the dead of night on July 4, 1777, thereby saving the army to fight another day.

Today, a visitors center has exceptional exhibits of the life of the average colonial soldier during the Revolution, made up in part of artifacts found in archaeological digs on the site. Remains of some of the cannon batteries, blockhouses, barracks, and the hospital have survived, making Mount Independence one of the best-preserved Revolutionary sites in the country. Pick up a trail map at the visitors center. The longest route, the orange trail, takes about an hour round-trip.

Though the floating bridge connecting Mount Independence is long gone, you can still take the nearby **Ticonderoga Ferry** (4675 Rte. 74, Shoreham, 802/897-7999, 8 A.M.-6 P.M. May-late June and early Sept.-Oct.; 8 A.M.-8 P.M. late June-early Sept., $8 cars, $1 pedestrians) across to New York to view Fort Ticonderoga and hike to the cannon placements at the top of Mount Defiance.

The final Revolutionary site in the area is the **Hubbardton Battlefield State Historic Site** (5696 Monument Rd., 802/759-2412 or 802/273-2282, www.historicvermont.org/hubbardton, 9:30 A.M.-5 P.M. Thu.-Sun. late May-mid-Oct., $2 adults, free children under 15), which memorializes the field where the British, under General "Gentleman Johnnie" Burgoyne, caught up with St. Clair's troops after they fled Mount Independence. Near the tiny hamlet of Hubbardton, a rear guard of more than 1,000 troops led by the Green Mountain Boys' Colonel Seth Warner stayed back to delay the Redcoats, setting up defenses on a hilltop and repulsing repeated attacks. The action, one of the most successful rear guard actions in history, headed off the British advance, as Burgoyne stayed behind for several days to bury dead and rest his troops, allowing St. Clair to escape with his men and eventually return victorious at the Battle of Saratoga. Today, the site includes a visitors center with relics of the battle, along with a three-dimensional map with fiber-optic lighting that takes visitors inside the heat of the engagement.

Other Sights

The culture and history of all of Vermont is on display at the **Henry Sheldon Museum of Vermont History** (1 Park St., 802/388-2117, www.henrysheldonmuseum.org, 10 A.M.-5 P.M. Mon.-Sat. and 1-5 P.M. Sun. June-Aug.; 10 A.M.-5 P.M. Tues.-Sat. Sept.-May, $5 adult, $4.50 senior, $3 youth 6-18, children under 6 free, $12 family), which has a rich collection of furniture and portraits stretching back more than 100 years. Rather than concern itself with battles and politicians, the museum sets out to demonstrate how the common people lived; one of its most affecting exhibits, "A Glimpse of Christmas Past," displays antique decorations and toys for each year during the holidays.

The common people also get their fanfare at the **Vermont Folklife Center** (88 Main St., 802/388-4964, www.vermontfolklifecenter. org, 10 A.M.–5 P.M. Tues.–Sat., free), whose mission is to preserve the voices and cultural traditions of Vermont's people. The centerpiece is a collection of 4,000 living-history recordings, preserved by field anthropologists who have scoured the state for local characters. The small museum also stages changing exhibits on the traditions of Native Americans, farmers, woodsmen, and quarrymen from all corners of the state.

When George Custer was defeated at the Battle of Little Bighorn, the only survivor was a Morgan horse named Comanche. Praised for their strength, versatility, and athleticism, the Morgan breed has long been associated with Vermont, where it has been bred since the late 1700s. That tradition continues at the **UVM Morgan Horse Farm** (74 Battell Dr., Weybridge, 802/388-2011, www.uvm.edu/ morgan, 9 A.M.–4 P.M. daily May–Oct., $5 adults, $4 youth 12–18, $2 children 5–12, free under 12), which is recognized as having one of the best bloodlines for breeding and competition. A video about the breed and tours of the barn are given every hour.

If all the history is making you thirsty, recoup at **Otter Creek Brewing Company** (793 Exchange St., 800/473-0727, www.ottercreek-brewing.com, 10 A.M.–6 P.M. Mon.–Sat.), which makes one of the better craft beers in New England. Tours of the brewing process, given daily at 1, 3, and 5 P.M., include samples of its signature Copper Ale and other varieties. (And if you want to skip the tour, free samples are given out all day to visitors.)

Not quite as fun, but just as impressive craftwise, **Vermont Soapworks** (616 Exchange St., 866/762-7482, www.vermontsoap.com) gives explanations of its product-making process, which uses all-natural ingredients to make the world's first truly organic soaps. A small "soap museum" has antique bars from over the ages.

Otter Creek is crossed by just one covered bridge, but it's a unique one. On the northwest side of town on Seymour Street, the **Pulp Mill Covered Bridge** is not only the oldest in Vermont, dating from 1820, but it is also one of six in the country that have two lanes, each with its own separate covered arcade.

Entertainment and Nightlife

Most of the nighttime action in Middlebury takes place on campus, leaving scant choices for the un-matriculated. There are, however, a few attractive bar options, including the casual watering hole **Two Brothers Tavern** (86 Main St., 802/388-0002, www.twobrotherstavern. com, 11:30 A.M.–10 P.M. Mon.–Fri.; 11 A.M.–10 P.M. Sat.–Sun., $6–12). It's the kind of place every college town should have. Students pour into its pub area to down tapas and cold beers within its brick walls, under photos of the historic town. (The noshing is as good as the imbibing, too: Dishes are a step above the average pub fare, with entrées such as Black Angus meatloaf and garlic roast chicken.) The college's various musical and theater groups perform at the **Middlebury College Center for the Arts** (S. Main St./Rte. 30, 802/443-3168, www.middlebury.edu/arts), a 100,000-square-foot facility housing an intimate black-box theater, a dance studio, and large recital hall.

Shopping

Housed in a stylishly converted old mill building and perched over the waters of Otter Creek Falls, **Frog Hollow Craft Gallery** (1 Mill St., 802/388-3177, www.froghollow.org, 10 A.M.–5:30 P.M. Mon.–Sat.; noon–5 P.M. Sun.) has made a profitable business of gathering arts and fine crafts from all over the region. Pick up delicate gourds-turned-holiday decorations, earthenware, hooked rugs, wood carvings, semi-precious jewelry, hand-carved furniture, and Vermont-made bath oils and hand creams.

If paying homage to the state's favorite animal seems in order, do so at **Holy Cow** (44

Main St., 802/388-6737, www.woodyjacksonart.com), an art gallery dedicated entirely to said bovines. There, artist Woody Jackson sells his creative odes to livestock—in the form of cow glassware, mugs, notecards, and limited-reproduction prints of iconographic Holsteins, swimming in fields of fluorescent grass.

Only a college town would name a trendy clothing store after a Hermann Hesse novel; the **Glass Bead Game** (66 Main St., 802/388-6380) sells au courant designer denim (Sevens to Citizens of Humanity), plus shoes, tops, and jewelry. Martha Stewart herself would feel right at home at **Sweet Cecily** (42 Main St., 802/388-3353), a collection of country knick-knacks, bright hand-woven socks, Provençal-esque decor, and ceramics. No less quaint is the **Ben Franklin Store** (63 Main St., 802/388-2101, www.benfranklinstores.com), a retro variety and toy store stashed with penny candy and aisles of educational playthings and crafts for kiddies.

Grooviness reigns at the hippie emporium that is **Wild Mountain Thyme** (48 Main St., 802/388-2580), where patchouli fills the nostrils and rack after rack of tie-dyed, flowing garments greets you.

Food

As much museum as it is restaurant, every inch of the upscale (but family-friendly) ◖ **Fire and Ice** (26 Seymour St., 802/388-7166, www.fireandicerestaurant.com, 5–9 P.M. Mon.–Thurs.; noon–9 P.M. Fri.–Sat.; 1–9 P.M. Sun., $12–28) is covered with old photographs, books, Victorian lamps, and map covers. A warren of interlocking rooms, the friendly, dimly lighted establishment focuses on classic American dishes—the likes of hand-cut steaks, boiled lobster, and broiled salmon. The homemade carrot cake is a local legend.

Nestled up against Otter Creek, **Tully & Marie's** (7 Bakery Ln., 802/388-4182, www.tullyandmaries.com, 11:30 A.M.–3 P.M. and 5–9 P.M. daily, $10–23) is a bold (but fun) mixture of cultural influences. For starters, there's the decor—seemingly inspired by a 1920s-style diner reimagined as a steamship.

Then there's the eclectic menu—a hodgepodge of Thai (basil shrimp), health foods (the salads are all organic), Italian (pastas are extremely popular here), and a little Mexican (chile-lime fajitas) thrown in. Somehow, it all works. The undisputed best spot in town for a burger is **A&W Drive-In** (Rte. 7, across from Middlebury transit, 802/388-2876, 11:30 A.M.–8 P.M. daily, $3–6), a classic bit of Americana that's been around for more than 40 years. Park your car near the window, and carhops on rollerblades will fetch you old-fashioned root beer floats in real glass A&W mugs, plus cooked-to-order sandwiches and falafel.

Gourmets and bohemians alike flock to ◖ **American Flatbread Restaurant** (137 Maples St., 802/388-3300, www.americanflatbread.com, 5–9 P.M. Fri.–Sat., $16–19), a funky and artsy wholesale bakery by weekday, an informal restaurant on Friday and Saturday nights. Hand-formed, wood-fired pizzas using all-organic ingredients are the mainstay of the menu; the locally made maple-fennel-sausage pizza with caramelized onions and Vermont mozzarella is alone worth the trip.

Information

For more information on Middlebury and the surrounding area, contact the regional tourism office, **Addison County Chamber of Commerce** (2 Court St., Middlebury, 802/388-7951, www.addisoncounty.com), which runs a visitors center across from the Vermont Folklife Center. For Middlebury proper, you can also contact the **Middlebury Business Association** (www.middbiz.org), which produces a helpful map of town.

Middlebury is the regional hub with hospital services at **Porter Medical Center** (115 Porter Dr., 802/388-4701, www.portermedical.org). Several pharmacies are located along Route 7, including **Kinney's Drugs** (38 Court St., 802/388-0973) in the center of town. Free wifi can be found at **Ilsley Public Library** (75 Main St., 802/388-4095) and **Two Brothers Tavern** (86 Main St., 802/388-0002). **Middlebury Police** is at 1 Lucius Shaw Ln., 802/388-3191.

VERMONT

MIDDLEBURY GAP

The only pass across the Green Mountains for 25 miles, Middlebury Gap was designated as a scenic byway by the state of Vermont as early as 1897. Route 125, which climbs steeply up from Middlebury before plunging just as precipitously down the other side, is lined with a dense forest of maple and birch mixed in with boreal spruce and fir. The route is best driven during the fall, when the foliage puts a lie to the mountains' name with a brilliant symphony of red and yellow leaves.

◖ Robert Frost Interpretive Trail

One thing is for sure—New England's preeminent 20th-century poet got around. Sites where he lived in New Hampshire, Massachusetts, and Vermont can all lay claim to significant chunks of his life. But perhaps none of them quite capture the spirit of his poetry more than this 1.2-mile walking trail located just past Ripton, near where Frost spent each of his last 22 summers.

As the path wends its way through a gentle terrain of forest and meadow, it is studded with plaques containing some of his poems set at contemplative spots along the way. The placement of the poems, which include "The Last Mowing" and "Stopping by Woods on a Snowy Evening," has an uncanny way of teasing out more meaning from the lines with the smell of pine boughs or the chirping of a lonely bird above. In fact, the trail was developed by Middlebury professor Reginald Cook, a friend of Frost's who used to hike with him in these very woods. The only poem that falls a bit flat is the "Road Not Taken," situated at an intersection in the path with an arrow pointing out the right direction—which is clearly the road far more often taken.

Events

When Frost summered in Middlebury, he was here for the **Breadloaf Writers' Conference** (1192 Rte. 125, Ripton, 802/443-5286, www.middlebury.edu/academics/blwc, Aug.), one of the first retreats to bring working and aspiring writers together each summer for inspiration.

The conference has grown in stature for more than 80 years; in addition to Frost, guests have included John Irving, Toni Morrison, and Norman Mailer. Now it lasts for 10 days in August, taking place in the little town of Ripton in the mountains 10 miles east of Middlebury; many of the readings by distinguished writers are open to the public.

BRANDON

Situated about halfway between Rutland and Middlebury, the delightful little village of Brandon makes a good lunch stop or home base for exploring the northern branch of Green Mountain National Forest. The town was founded in 1761 and quickly became an important mill town, with both sawmills and gristmills situated at strategic points on Otter Creek. Supplies of iron ore nearby later led the town to become an important manufacturing center, constructing iron stoves and railroad cars in the 19th century. More recently, Brandon has been reborn as a center for art galleries, which inhabit the brick storefronts of its downtown mill area and attract teary-eyed parents on their way up from New York to drop their kids off at college in Middlebury.

Sights

Take a time-out to saunter around Brandon's quaint brick downtown, which is listed on the National Register of Historic Places. At the lower end of town, **Lower Falls** is an impressive urban waterfall that once powered the town's mills. On the other side of town, the **Stephen A. Douglas House** (Grove St. at Champlain and Pearl Sts., 802/247-6401, www.brandon.org, open by appointment) is the birthplace of the politician who challenged Abraham Lincoln in a famous series of debates on slavery to decide the 1860 presidential race. Brandon is in the process of turning the home into a visitors center and historical museum.

Entertainment

Upstairs from Briggs Carriage Bookstore, the **Ball and Chain Cafe** (16 Park St., 802/247-0050, www.briggscarriage.com, 10 A.M.–6 P.M.

Mon.–Wed.; 10 A.M.–9 P.M. Thurs.–Fri.; 9 A.M.–9 P.M. Sat.; 11 A.M.–5 P.M. Sun.) is Brandon's one-stop cultural hub. Regular events include author readings; folk, jazz, and classical music performances; and a weekly knitting circle. During the day, the café serves up espresso drinks, pastries, and free wireless Internet.

Shopping

More than 35 artists have banded together to form the **Brandon Artists Guild** (7 Center St., 802/247-4956, www.brandonartistsguild.org), a gallery showcasing modern and whimsical takes on typical Vermont scenes. Works for sale include jewelry, hooked rugs, and modern folk art paintings. Brandon's most famous folk artist, Warren Kimble, sells his distressed wood paintings at **Liza Myers Gallery & Studio** (22 Center St., 866/442-8680, www.lizamyers.com), which also features Myers's arresting acrylics of birds and other animals from around the world.

Food

Owned and run by a French couple, **Café Provence** (11 Center St., 802/247-9997, www.cafeprovencevt.com, 11 A.M.–4:30 P.M. and 5 P.M.–9 P.M. Tues.–Fri.; 9 A.M.–4:30 P.M. and 5 P.M.–9 P.M.Sat.–Sun.,, $17–21) successfully evokes south-of-France charm with both its yellow walls and its flavor-rich seafood stew. The bustling open kitchen adds to the energy of the handsome room at dinnertime; if you can work it into your weekend itinerary, the brunch is terrific and filling.

Information and Services

On the town green is a well-stocked information booth run by the **Brandon Area Chamber of Commerce** (802/247-6401, www.brandon.org), with gobs of brochures and a map for walking tours of town. Brandon has a pair of downtown pharmacists: **Brooks Pharmacy** (1 Carver St., 802/247-8050) and **Brown's Pharmacy** (10 Park St., 802/247-4902). Wi-Fi is available with ice cream at **The Inside Scoop** (22 Park St., 802/257-6600). **Brandon Police** is located at 1 W. Seminary St. (802/247-0222).

SPORTS AND RECREATION
Moosalamoo Recreation Area

Those who have discovered this 20,000-acre wilderness reserve in the heart of the Green Mountain National Forest are not eager to let the word out. For now at least, Moosalamoo is a pristine area with more than 70 miles of quiet hiking trails leading to waterfalls, lakes, and striking views of Lake Champlain and the Adirondacks. From Route 125, a popular hike is to take the Oak Ridge and Moosalamoo Trails eight miles into the forest to end up at **Moosalamoo Campground** (tent sites $10/person). For those planning an overnight stay, the campground has 19 wooded sites, along with toilets, trash facilities, a grassy field, and self-guided nature trail. It's accessible by car from Goshen-Ripton Road, off Route 125 a little south of Ripton center.

A shorter but equally amazing hike begins at the roaring Falls of Lana, from whence you can hike up the Rattlesnake Cliff Trail for amazing views of the mountains and Lake Dummore below. The best time to climb is just before sunset; bring a flashlight for the descent. Another trail, popular with bird-watchers, is the Bluebird Trail, which takes hikers through meadows stocked with 40 houses that serving as habitat for cavity-nesting birds. In the winter, many of the trails are groomed for snowshoeing and cross-country skiing. And if you don't feel like getting your boots muddy, the area also advertises a loop trail that's a sure bet for seeing moose in the spring. For more information, contact the nonprofit **Moosalamoo Association** (802/747-7900, www.moosalamoo.org).

Hiking

In addition to Moosalamoo, a popular hike is the nature trail at **Texas Falls Recreation Area,** which overlooks a series of waterfalls through a gorge formed by glacial meltwater. For more information on this and other hikes in the Green Mountain National Forest, contact the **Middlebury Ranger Station** (1007 Rte. 7, 802/388-4362).

Skiing

Middlebury has a long history of fielding

VERMONT

champion ski teams in the Northeast College Athletic Conference. The team practices at the **Middlebury College Snow Bowl** (6886 Rte. 125, 802/388-4356, www.middleburysnowbowl.com, $22–42 adults, $20–30 students and seniors, $8 children under 6), which dates back to 1934, making it the third-oldest ski area in Vermont. While the dozen or so trails won't win any awards for difficulty, they are no cakewalk either, with several expert trails careening down from the 2,650-foot main peak. More to the point, in an area full of ski resorts, the Snow Bowl is often deserted on weekdays, allowing skiers to take a half dozen runs in the time it takes to get up and down Killington once. Throw in cheap prices and an atmospheric base lodge, and the bowl is a good bet for an afternoon of fun.

A mile and a half away at the Breadloaf campus, the **Rikert Ski Touring Center** (Rte. 125, 12 mi. west of Middlebury in Ripton, 802/443-2744, www.middlebury.edu/campuslife/facilities/rstc, 9 A.M.–4 P.M. daily, $15 adults, $6 Middlebury students, free seniors) has more than 25 miles of trails open to the public, skirting through the wilderness of Green Mountain National Forest. The base lodge has rentals ($12 adults, $6 students, $3 children under 5) and a warm woodstove in winter.

ACCOMMODATIONS
Under $100
Plunked right between Rutland and Middlebury sits the modest, affordable **Brandon Motor Lodge** (2095 Franklin St., Rte. 7, Brandon, 800/675-7614, www.brandonmotorlodge.com, $69–139). Rooms have standard motel decor but are well-kept, and all have access to a communal hot tub and pool. Well-behaved pets are welcome (with a $15 surcharge), and continental breakfast is included May through October.

$100-150
Name any creature comfort, and odds are you'll find it in spades at (**Middlebury Inn** (14 Court Sq., 802/388-4961, www.middleburyinn.com, $98–285). From free access to

the fitness center and extra-deep tubs with original fixtures, elegant breakfasts to afternoon tea, the 180-year-old spacious inn leaves guests wanting for very little indeed. Suites are also available.

$150-250
An 1814–home-turned-inn (once belonging to Vermont judge and governor John Stewart), (**Swift House Inn** (25 Stewart Ln., Middlebury, 866/388-9925, www.swifthouseinn.com, $110–265) is actually three buildings, each renovated and appointed with ornate stained glass and luxury furnishings. Pristine and individually decorated rooms, many outfitted in subtle florals, come with claw-foot tubs, quilt-covered wood or iron-wrought beds, and/or working fireplaces.

If you're looking for the Vermont of entertainment-world dreams, look no further than **Waybury Inn** (457 E. Main St., East Middlebury, 802/388-4015, www.wayburyinn.com, $100–250): The exterior was used at the beginning of the Bob Newhart show, *Newhart,* which ran from 1982 to 1990. The interior is just as picturesque; guests lounge in suites enjoying views to the lush lawns and mountains. Some rooms have four-poster beds and whirlpool tubs. Several rooms are located in private cabins. A quiet, elegant restaurant is on-site, as are beautifully kept gardens.

The Federal-style **Inn on the Green** (71 S. Pleasant St., 802/388-7512, www.innonthegreen.com, $119–189) overlooks the Middlebury town green; with a handful of suites, plus rooms with twins and queen beds, it's perfect for families (or couples looking to relax; the kitchen serves breakfast in bed). Rooms are cheerfully decorated with bright color, bay windows, and high-quality country wooden furniture—some antiques.

GETTING THERE AND AROUND
There's no easy way to get to Middlebury from the highway—whatever route you take involves a long (though beautiful) drive across the Green Mountains. Probably the

best option from I-89 is to take exit 3 south to Route 107, then head west on Route 125 and cross the mountains at Middlebury Gap (70 mi., 2 hr. from White River Junction). To drive to Middlebury from Rutland, take Route 7 north (35 mi., 1 hr.).

Run by the Chittenden County Transportation Authority, the **Middlebury LINK** (802/864-2282, www.cctaride.org) provides regular bus service every day but Sunday between Middlebury (Exchange St. or Merchants Row) and Burlington.

Addison County Transit Resources (802/388-1946, www.actr-vt.org) runs bus routes throughout the town of Middlebury.

Addision County Transit Resources (802/388-1946, www.actr-vt.org) runs bus routes throughout the town of Middlebury.

VERMONT

NORTHEAST VERMONT

As the mountains climb northward, they get higher and wilder than their southern cousins. At the same time, the largely unspoiled northern parts of Vermont get far less traffic than the southern parts of the state. What does that mean for the visitor? For starters, stunning views nearly every way you turn: dramatic mountain sunrises, pristine church steeples rising from verdant valleys, cute-as-can-be hilltop farms, and serene lakes. Of course, all of those picture-perfect mountains also tend to render cell phones useless, the drive between towns can be long and winding, and the people in those towns tend to live life as the rest of the country did four or five decades ago. But if it's quaintness you're after, you'll find plenty of it here.

Visitors come to this region just for the food: maple syrup harvested fresh from the trees; sharply aged cheddar cheeses from the famous Cabot Creamery; and of course, the sweet enticements of the Ben & Jerry's factory, the number-one tourist destination in Vermont. Another big draw is Stowe Mountain, which has resisted the overdevelopment of other ski resorts, to give visitors both a lovely little New England village and killer ski trails. Not all of the northern part of the state feels like the boondocks, however. The capital city of Montpelier may be the smallest state capital in the nation, but it still provides enough big-city culture and (with the New England Culinary Institute within its borders) culinary sophistication to satisfy urban travelers. At the opposite end of the spectrum, the Northeast Kingdom is pure farm country: rural, remote, and, compared to the rest of the state, virtually untouristed.

COURTESY OF STATE OF VERMONT

HIGHLIGHTS

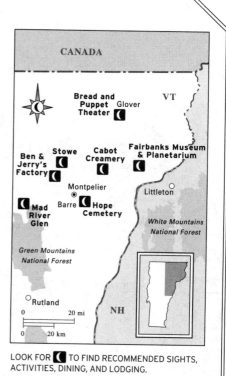

◖ **Hope Cemetery:** The final resting place of granite stonecutters is as much sculpture garden as graveyard (page 399).

◖ **Mad River Glen:** Leave your designer sunglasses and spa packages at home and come tackle a righteous ski mountain on its own terms (page 401).

◖ **Ben & Jerry's Factory:** This is the birthplace of Chunky Monkey, Cherry Garcia, and Chocolate Chip Cookie Dough. Two words: free samples (page 406).

◖ **Stowe:** The Alps or the Green Mountains? At this quaint European-style ski village, you can barely tell the difference (page 408).

◖ **Cabot Creamery:** Cheddar cheese from this famous farmers co-op has single-handedly kept Vermont dairy farming alive and mooing (page 415).

◖ **Fairbanks Museum & Planetarium:** A trip around the world, a trip to the stars, and a trip back in time all in one place (page 416).

◖ **Bread and Puppet Theater:** The legendary abode of papier-mâché giants and goddesses is a dairy barn in the Northeast Kingdom (page 418).

LOOK FOR ◖ TO FIND RECOMMENDED SIGHTS, ACTIVITIES, DINING, AND LODGING.

PLANNING YOUR TIME

Many visitors to Vermont make a beeline straight to the **Ben & Jerry's Factory** in Waterbury before discovering what other charms the region has on offer. A trip to the ice cream factory can be combined with a stay of several days in the mock-Tyrolean **Stowe** village, with its eponymous ski resort and village full of restaurants and outdoor activities. (Like other towns in the area, some Stowe restaurants serve only dinner in the less-touristed summer season. In all cases, it pays to call ahead in planning.) Alternatively, stay in the magical Mad River Valley, which boasts its own ski area, **Mad River Glen,** which has righteously earned a fanatic following for its challenging trails and uncompromising

attitude. The capital city of Montpelier has grown into a delightful city full of art galleries and independent businesses; next door the city of Barre is a living legacy to the granite industry, with working quarries and the work of the master carvers on display in **Hope Cemetery.**

In the far corner of the state, a minimum of three days is necessary to explore the vast Northeast Kingdom, a state within a state. On the way into the area, plan a stop at the **Cabot Creamery** to view its award-winning cheddaring operation. Also worth an afternoon is downtown St. Johnsbury, a tribute to the Victorian Age with an art gallery and an outstanding natural-history collection at the wonderfully eclectic **Fairbanks Museum.**

VERMONT

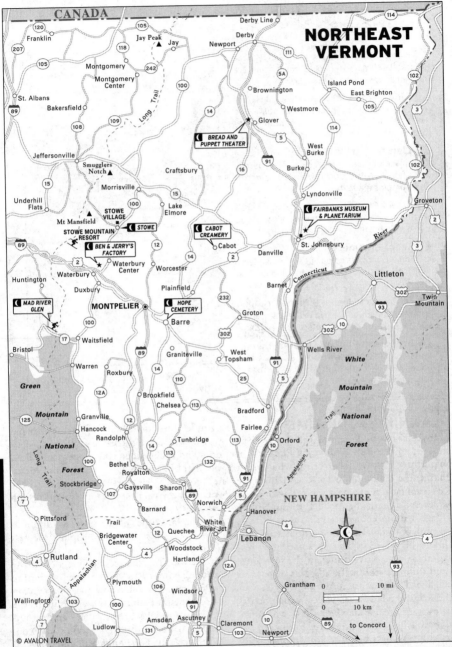

Capital Region

With only 15,000 people between them, it's probably a bit overstated to call the sister cities of Barre and Montpelier a metropolitan area. This will just have to do for Vermont, however, with the majority of the businesses between Brattleboro and Burlington clustered in the area. As you'll no doubt hear countless times, Montpelier takes pride in being the smallest state capital in the country. With a charming downtown honeycombed with art galleries, it feels more like a quaint county seat than headquarters for an entire state. Just a few miles down the road, Barre has a grittier, more working-class feel, accentuated by the still-active granite quarries that give the town its claim to fame. Situated a mountain range over to the west, the Mad River Valley is the recreation center for the area, a hidden glen of ski trails and paddling streams anchored by a quartet of scenic hamlets.

MONTPELIER

Vermont's state capital was founded in the last days of the Revolutionary War, at a time when the intercession of the French Navy in the war effort was creating a rage for all things French. (Neighboring Calais, founded the same day, was similarly given a Francophone name.) The fact it became the capital of the state in 1804 was probably more an accident of geography than anything else. The big cities of Bennington, Burlington, Rutland, and the like were all vying for the brass ring themselves; each eventually agreed it was better to give the government to a town in the center of the state than let any of its rivals get it.

From such tenuous beginnings, Montpelier thrived during the 19th century, mostly on the strength of the granite trade. Its downtown today is a uniform district of brick Federal-style mansions and gingerbread Victorians clustered around the shining gold dome of the Vermont State House.

Vermont's independent streak is on full display here—with dozens of locally owned businesses and nary a McDonald's in sight. The city's natural beauty and educated populace

Montpelier

VERMONT

THEY'RE NOT LOVIN' IT

An old trivia question asks, What is the only U.S. state capital without a McDonald's? The answer: Montpelier. The fast-food chain has tried many times to make inroads into the little city; the latest attempt was in 1996 when the company planned to occupy a historic building in Montpelier's downtown. That effort was bitterly fought by residents, who packed zoning hearings and made impassioned arguments against the restaurant, citing everything from the chain's destruction of local businesses to its destruction of rainforest in South America. The zoning commission voted 4-3 to turn it down, retaining Montpelier's Ronald-less status. If you just have to have a Big Mac, however, don't fret: there are two McDonald's just down the road in Barre.

have led to a creative renaissance in recent years, with art galleries and artsy cafés moving into the downtown historical area. Despite such "urban sophistication," however, ski runs and sugarhouses are still just a few minutes away.

Sights

For such a small capital, Montpelier has an impressive **State House** (115 State St., 802/828-2228, www.leg.state.vt.us, tours every half hour 10 A.M.–3:30 P.M. Mon.–Fri. and 11 A.M.–2:30 P.M. Sat. July–mid-Oct.; 9 A.M.–3 P.M. Mon.–Fri. mid-Oct.–July), with a 57-foot golden dome capping a columned Renaissance Revival building. (Try for a moment to imagine the dome painted dark red, as it was between 1857 and 1907.)

Fittingly for the state, the dome is topped by a wooden statue of Ceres, the goddess of agriculture. Facing the building, look for a **statue of Ethan Allen** in the Greek Revival front portico, a remnant of an earlier state house on the site. Tours of the building's interior take

in statues and paintings of Vermont politicians who figured in state and national history, including presidents Calvin Coolidge and Chester A. Arthur.

Next door, the **Vermont Historical Society Museum** 109 State St., 802/828-2291, www.vermonthistory.org, 10 A.M.–4 P.M. Tues.–Sat. and noon–4 P.M. Sun. May–Oct, 10 A.M.–4 P.M. P.M. Tues.–Fri., Oct.–May., $5 adults, $3 students and seniors, free for children under 6, $12 families) takes in the grand scope of state history, from reconstructions of an Abenaki dwelling and the Revolutionary-era Catamount Tavern to exhibits on Vermont's contribution to the Civil War and World War II. A whole room is dedicated to Vermont-born president Calvin Coolidge, and there's even a collection on the early history of skiing. The gift shop has an extensive selection of books on Vermont history and culture.

In Vermont, you are never far from a sugar house. On the edge of the city, seventh-generation mapler Burr Morse has turned his farm into one of the premier maple syrup producers in the state. **Morse Farm Maple Sugarworks** (1168 County Rd., 802/223-2740 or 800/242-2740, www.morsefarm.com, 8 A.M.–8 P.M. daily May–Oct.; 9 A.M.–5 P.M. daily Nov.–Apr., donations accepted) is a virtual museum of the industry, with old photographs and a "split-log" movie theater that shows a film of the sugaring process. A cavernous gift shop sells maple kettle corn and that most Vermont of treats, maple *creemees* (aka soft-serve maple ice cream cones).

In the age of iPods and mp3s, it may be difficult to conceive of a time when the only home entertainment system a family had was a music box as big as a mini-fridge. A few miles south down I-89 in the village of Randolph, the **Porter Music Box Museum** (Rte. 66, Randolph, 802/728-9694, www.portermusic-box.com, 9:30 A.M.–5 P.M. daily May–Oct., $6.50 adults, $4.50 children 3–12, free children under 3) takes visitors back to those days, with dozens of inlaid cherrywood automata and spool-fed music boxes. Tours include songs played on some of the models on display. The museum is on the site of the Porter Music Box Company, which is still making them today.

Art Galleries

One of the best of Montpelier's galleries is also the oldest. The **T.W. Wood Gallery & Arts Center** (36 College St., 802/828-8743, www.twwoodgallery.org, noon–4 P.M. Tues.–Sun.) has been showcasing the work of Vermont artists for more than 100 years, with a permanent collection of modern art and rotating shows by local contemporary artists.

Mary Stone's hand-sculpted clay animal whistles are just one of the unique crafts on display at the **Artisans Hand Craft Gallery** (89 Main St., 802/229-9492, www.artisanshand.com, 10 A.M.–6 P.M. Mon.–Sat.; 10 A.M.–8 P.M. Fri.; noon–4 P.M. Sun.), a hub for jewelry, pottery, woodwork, and metalwork from Vermont artisans.

A refreshing antidote to all those overly pretentious galleries, the **Lazy Pear Gallery** (154 Main St., 802/223-7680, www.lazypear.com, 11 A.M.–6 P.M. daily; closed Mon. in winter) specializes in art that is "playful, quirky, and fun," much of it sporting bright colors and whimsical animals. Located in a prominent yellow Victorian, the gallery not only showcases local artists, it also has a community art board for residents to contribute their own dabbling.

Entertainment

Montpelier's professional theater company, **Lost Nation Theater** (39 Main St., 802/229-0492, www.lostnationtheater.org) performs an eclectic mix of musicals, contemporary drama, and an annual fall Shakespeare production. The **Savoy Theater** (26 Main St., 802/229-0509, www.savoytheater.com) screens first-run and classic art films.

A collective community space and bar, the **Langdon Street Cafe** (4 Langdon St., 802/223-8667, www.langdonstreetcafe.com) epitomizes the spirit of modern Vermont. Blues jams, earnest singer-songwriter types, and spoken-word performers light up the stage, while patrons sample local beers on tap. Monday is open mike night.

Upscale pizzeria **Positive Pie** (69 Main St., Plainfield, 802/454-0133, www.positivepie.com) might have anything from reggae to belly-dancing in its music lounge Thursday through Saturday. The entire third floor of the **Black Door Bar and Bistro** (44 Main St., 802/223-7070, www.blackdoorvt.com) is given over to live music on the weekends. Offerings might include funk, bluegrass, or old-school soul.

Events

A raging bonfire takes off some of the winter chill at **Ice on Fire** (802/223-7335, Jan.), Montpelier's annual winter carnival. Activities include storytelling, games, and old-fashioned sled pulls.

Seems like every city of consequence has a film festival these days, and Montpelier is no exception. The **Green Mountain Film Festival** (26 Main St., 802/229-0598, www.savoytheater.com, Mar.) focuses on international films in two dozen screenings at the Savoy Theater.

Shopping

Get the pick of the local crops (for a hiking picnic, an edible souvenir, or just as a snack) at **Hunger Mountain Co-op** (623 Stone Cutters Way, 802/223-8000, www.hungermountain.com, 8 A.M.–8 P.M. daily), a bounty of locally grown organic produce, gourmet cheeses, and vitamins.

Readers searching beyond the bestseller lists can rely on the shelves of **Rivendell Books** (100 Main St., 802/223-3928, www.rivendellbooksvt.com, 9 A.M.–7 P.M. Mon.–Thurs., 9 A.M.–8 P.M. Fri.–Sat., 10 A.M.–6 P.M. Sun.; winter hours: 9 A.M.–6 P.M. P.M. Mon.–Thurs., 9 A.M.–7 P.M. Fri.–Sat., 11 A.M.–5 P.M. Sun.) for rare, antique, and otherwise collectible books. Or read what all the state's local authors have to say; **Bear Pond Books** (77 Main St., 802/229-0774, www.bearpondbooks.com, 9 A.M.–6 P.M. Mon.–Thurs. and Sat.; 9 A.M.–9 P.M. Fri.; 10 A.M.–6 P.M. Sun.) sells a roster of Vermont's best fiction and nonfiction—plus sponsors regular readings.

Fetch urban clothing in a country setting

at the chic **Salaam Boutique** (40 Main St., 802/223-4300, www.central-vt.com/web/salaam, 10 A.M.–6 P.M. Mon.–Wed.; 10 A.M.–7 P.M. Fri.–Sat.; 12–4 P.M. Sun.), the walls of which are neatly hung with jackets by An Ren, Twill 22, Tulle, and Velvet.

For the most expansive stock of outdoor gear around, step into **Onion River Sports** (20 Langdon St., 802/229-9409, www.onionriver-sportsonionriver.com, 9:30 A.M.–6 P.M. Mon.–Thurs.; 9:30 A.M.–8 P.M. Fri.; 9:30 A.M.–5 P.M. Sat.; 11 A.M.–4 P.M. Sun.). The selection of bicycles, cross-country skis, snowshoes, and camping and hiking gear (plus the footwear and clothes appropriate for all of it) is indeed impressive—as is the knowledgeable staff selling it.

Food

As much a local gathering spot as a place to find something to eat, **Capitol Grounds** (27 State St., 802/223-7800, www.capitolgrounds.com, 6:30 A.M.–6 P.M. Mon.–Wed., 6:30 A.M.–9 P.M. Thurs.–Fri., 7 A.M.–9 P.M. Sat.; 8 A.M.–5 P.M. Sun.; closes daily at 5 P.M. in winter, $6–10) whips up made-to-order sandwiches, offers free wireless Internet service, and froths fair-trade cappuccinos all day long.

Healthy eaters rejoice to find **Rhapsody** (28 Main St., 802/229-6112, 11:30 A.M.–7 P.M. Mon.–Fri. and 11:30 A.M.–8 P.M. Mon.–Sat., $8–13), which offers an organic and all-natural menu full of sushi, vegetarian pastas, and maple syrup–sweetened desserts.

The New England Culinary Institute runs a small handful of esteemed restaurants in the area, all of which are worth a visit—particularly **(La Brioche Bakery** (89 Main St., 802/229-0443, www.necidining.com, 6:30 A.M.–5 P.M. Mon.–Fri., 7 A.M.–4 P.M. Sat., 8 A.M.–2 P.M. Sun., $9–16), a European-style café that bakes up scrumptious pastries and beautiful rustic breads and churns out a daily spread of creative sandwiches on them all. Another don't-miss is the school's **Main Street Grill** (118 Main St., 802/223-3188, www.necidining.com, 11:30 A.M.–5 P.M. Tues.–Sat.; 10 A.M.–5:30 P.M. Sun.; 5:30 P.M.–10 P.M. Tue.–Sun.,

$12–19), a swanky and professionally run place that's as likely to feed you a pulled-pork sandwich as it is a plate of carrot, hazelnut, and tofu sausage.

One part music lounge to two parts hipster pizza joint, **Positive Pie** (22 State St., 802/229-0453, www.positivepie.com, 11:30 A.M.–9 P.M. Sun.–Thurs. and 11:30–10 P.M. Sat.–Sun., $9–12) is a great place to hang out for the night over homemade pastas (like the fettuccine with broccoli and ricotta) and a beer.

An emphasis of purity of flavor and easygoing fare pervades at **Ariel's Riverside Café & Bar** (168 River St., Montpelier, 802/229-2295, www.arielsriverside.com, 11 A.M.–10 P.M. Tues.–Sat., $6–9). The friendly eatery spotlights ethnic specialties like Moroccan chicken with almonds and apricots, moussaka, falafel, and great, big salads, complemented by an impressive wine list.

Information

The **State of Vermont** (800/837-6668, www.1-800-vermont.com) runs a comprehensive information center across from the State House at 134 State Street. A small, unstaffed information booth is located at 64 State Street. Free Wi-Fi is available at many spots downtown, including **Capitol Grounds** (45 State Street, 802/223-7800) Montpelier, and **Langdon Street Café** (4 Langdon Street, 802/223-8667).

Pharmacy needs can be taken care of at several locations as well, including the independent **Montpelier Pharmacy** (69 Main St., 802/223-4633). Both Vermont State and Montpelier City police are located at One Pitkin Ct., 802/223-3445.

BARRE

You may not have seen Barre, but you've definitely seen Barre Gray, the most highly prized grade of granite for government buildings and monuments. Local residents of Barre (pronounced "berry") first discovered the predominance of stone in their hills shortly after the War of 1812; but the industry didn't take off until Montpelier wanted to build a new

State House in 1836 and ordered up a load of granite from its sister city for the task. The high quality of the stone's texture led to orders by other cities down the Eastern Seaboard, and almost overnight, the town mushroomed into a city.

Many of the workers who performed the arduous task of cutting the stone blocks out of the quarries were immigrants, first from Scotland, then, after the turn of the 20th century, from Italy. The city still has one of the most ethnically diverse populations in Vermont. While the granite trade is still a flourishing industry (mostly for cemetery headstones), the city has gone through hard times in the 20th and 21st centuries as other industries dried up. The downtown now has a depressed feel that stands in contrast to the glory of the granite monuments that grace its parks and street corners.

◖ Hope Cemetery

The immigrants who worked in the quarries were given One unusual perk: each of them received one block of granite for their very own. Many chose to work on their own tombstones, creating a lasting tribute to the handiwork of men who mostly toiled and died for monuments to others. The enormous Hope Cemetery (224 E. Montpelier Rd., 802/476-6245, www.ci.barre.vt.us, dawn–dusk, tours available upon request, $5 adults, $3 seniors) is now a giant open-air sculpture gallery, with more than 10,000 gray granite headstones carved with art deco lettering and intricate representations of flowers, ships, and religious symbols. The town still administers burials here—with the only stipulation being that the headstones must be made of Barre Gray.

In modern times, residents have pre-ordered more and more fanciful markers, such as a granite soccer ball, a granite armchair, and an actual-size granite race car. Some stones even contain life-sized figures, such as the touching carving of a man and woman in adjoining beds reaching out to clasp hands for eternity. It's impossible to walk among them without contemplating a sculpture for your own plot.

Other Sights

The granite industry isn't just a thing of Barre's past. **Rock of Ages Corporation** (560 Graniteville Rd., Graniteville, 802/476-3119, www.rockofages.com) still cuts stone out of the same deep holes it has mined for more than 100 years. The company now gives narrated tours (9:15 A.M.–3:35 P.M. Mon.–Sat., late May–mid-Oct., $5 adults, $4.50 seniors, $2.50 children 6–12) of its main quarry, where a platform looks out on massive machines cutting blocks of granite more than 600 feet below. Guides explain the meticulous methods for cutting the ginormous blocks, which include boring dozens of small holes beneath the blocks and then blasting them free with dynamite.

Recently, the company inaugurated a visitors center (9 A.M.–5 P.M. Mon.–Sat. May–Oct., free) that includes historical memorabilia about the granite trade as well as a "cut stone activity center" where you can try your hand at sandblasting and other activities. And if you are *really* thinking ahead, you can order your own headstone from a showroom on the premises.

Separately, a volunteer group is working on transforming a former 30,000-square-foot granite shed right off Route 302 into an even more elaborate **Vermont Granite Museum** (7 Jones Bros. Way, 802/476-4605, www.granitemuseum.org). For now, the volunteers run a more modest visitors center (Pinsly Depot, 9 A.M.–2 P.M. Wed.–Fri.) with historical memorabilia.

Granite Monuments

Evidence of the granite trade remains all over town in the form of monuments erected by master carvers who worked in the quarries. At the turn of the 20th century, Scottish immigrant stone cutters banded together to produce a statue of **Robert Burns** on an enormous base on Washington Street. The memorial, considered one of the best granite sculptures in the world, was unveiled in 1899 on the occasion of the 100th anniversary of Burns's death. (As a point of national pride, the actual carving was done by Italian sculptors working on models by the Scots.)

The massive art deco warrior depicted in the 1924 **Soldiers and Sailors Memorial** on North Main Street is reminiscent of the figures at Rockefeller Center in New York. The statue, also known as *Young Triumphant*, was adopted as Barre's city seal.

A more recent memorial at last gives the generations of Italian stonecutters their due; erected in 1985, the **Italian-American Monument** on North Main Street depicts a 23-foot-high apron-clad figure heroically grasping a hammer and chisel. The monument is dedicated to Italian sculptor Carlo Abate, who established the first school for stone carving in Barre in the early 20th century.

Entertainment and Events

The 1899 **Barre Opera House** (6 N. Main St., 802/476-0292, www.barreoperahouse.org) was recently renovated into a community theater space that hosts local and national musical performances.

You knew it was coming. The **Barre Vermont Granite Festival** (802/476-4605, www.granitemuseum.org, early Sept.) celebrates all things gray and stony, with stonecutting and etching demonstrations on the future grounds of the granite museum, guided tours of Hope Cemetery, and games and family-friendly activities.

Shopping

A bit like Vermont itself, the wares at **Linda B. Pottery** (576 Higuera Rd., 802/476-4143, www.lindabpottery.com, by appointment) are equal parts rustic and pretty. The potter specializes in boldly glazed cappuccino mugs, oil lamps, bowls, and vases—each of which is individually handcrafted and unique in its color and design

Food

Spotlighting traditional, down-home neighborhood dishes from all over America, **Sean & Nora's** (276 N. Main St., 802/476-7326, www.seanandnoras.com, 11:30 A.M.–2 P.M. Mon.–Fri., 4:30–8 P.M. Mon.–Thurs. and 4:30–9 P.M. Fri.–Sat., May–Dec., $6–12) is

pure comfort food through and through. Dig into the Bronxville burger or a platter of New England beer-battered fish-and-chips while you surf the Web (free Internet access is offered) and take in the laid-back crowd.

Call ahead for breakfasts and lunches on the go to **Bag Ladies Express** (47 Patterson St., 802/479-7961, 10 A.M.–2 P.M. Mon.–Fri., $3–11). The creative wraps and overstuffed panini fly out the door, while others choose to sit and read the paper over the soups and salads.

Information

For more info on the area, contact the **Central Vermont Chamber of Commerce** (802/229-5711, www.central-vt.com/chamber) or stop by the visitors center in the old Pinsly Depot (62 Depot Sq., 9 A.M.–2 P.M. Wed.–Fri.). Free Wi-Fi is available at **Espresso Bueno** (136 N. Main St., 802/479-0896), a new coffee shop downtown. You can fill prescriptions and fulfill other medical needs at **Brooks Pharmacy** (215 N. Main St., 802/476-3491). For more serious medical care, the area's foremost hospital is **Central Vermont Medical Center** (130 Fisher Rd., 802/371-4100, www.cvmc.org). Contact **City of Barre Police Department** at 15 4th St, 802/476-6613.

MAD RIVER VALLEY

Tucked between the Green Mountains and a spur called the Worcester Range, the Mad River Valley is Vermont's own Shangri-La, a magical valley of white steeples and red barns against a backdrop of omnipresent peaks. The river is named for the fact that, unlike most rivers in North America, it flows south to north and is therefore crazy or "mad." The sobriquet extends to the character of the surrounding community, a quirky mix of farmers, artists, and ex-urbanites that calls to mind the live-and-let-live attitude of an episode of *Northern Exposure*.

The valley is anchored by two villages, Waitsfield and Warren, which both date back to Revolutionary times and together boast a formidable collection of historic buildings. But the area isn't a set-piece. Its two world-class

VERMONT

ski resorts, Mad River Glen and Sugarbush, are only the beginning of an absurd number of outdoor activities pursued with vigor by the townsfolk all year round.

Mad River Glen

In an era of ski-resort consolidation, rising lift-ticket prices, and runaway base-lodge development, Mad River Glen (MRG, Rte. 17, 5 mi. west of Waitsfield, 802/496-3551, www. madriverglen.com, $39–54 adults, $39–5140 seniors and youth ages 6–18) stands alone in stubbornly resisting the winds of "progress." Its trails are ungroomed, teeth-grittingly narrow, and chock-full of trees, moguls, and any other impediment the mountain can throw in your way. In fact, almost half of the trails on the mountain are for experts—an unheard-of marketing suicide for which MRG is unapologetic. Its motto, "Ski It If You Can," is more than just hype; the mountain has earned a stiff allegiance from diamond dogs who come to ski, not to boast or model the latest sunglasses.

In fact, the mountain was sold in 1995 to a cooperative of skiers who pledged to keep the spirit of the resort alive. They've remained true to the promise, continuing to run one of the few ski resorts in the country that ban snowboarding (the boards have a tendency to derail the 1950s-era single chairlifts anyway) and leaving the trails in their natural, unadulterated state. You can get a little bit of an idea of the mentality from the run named Paradise, a precipitous tumble down exposed ledges, rocky moguls, and a frozen waterfall to get to the bottom. If that doesn't seem like paradise to you, don't even bother.

Other Sights

The historic downtown of Waitsfield is anchored by the **Great Eddy Bridge,** the oldest operating covered bridge in the state, which crosses the Mad River at the intersection of Route 100 and Bridge Street. (Only the non-operating Pulp Mill Covered Bridge in Middlebury is older.) On the corner of the same intersection, the **Bridge Street Marketplace** was once an inn and tavern for wayfarers; following a devastating flood in 1998, it was restored into a country version of Covent Garden, with craft shops and eateries spread out between five different buildings.

Lest you think "Jingle Bells" made up all that "one-horse open sleigh" stuff, climb aboard one at **Mountain Valley Farm** (1719 Common Rd., Waitsfield, 802/496-9255, www.mountainvalleyfarm.com) for an impossibly quaint horse-and-carriage ride through the mountain landscape. Other times of year, sleighs are replaced with hay rides and carriages. Kids will love seeing the animals as well, and participating in farm activities like collecting goose eggs.

Not to be outdone, Warren has its own covered bridge, the 55-foot-long **Warren Bridge,** which sports an unusual asymmetrical design. (The angles on the eastern and western sides are slightly different.) The bridge is off Route 100, just below downtown. On the outskirts of the village, **Three Shepherds Cheese** (42108 Roxbury Mountain Rd., 802/496-45593998, www.rootswork.orgthreeshepherdscheese.com, 11:30 A.M.–6:30 P.M. Mon., Tues., and Thurs.; 8 A.M.–8 P.M. Fri. and Sat.; 8 A.M.–6:30 P.M. Sun.) is a father-daughter cheese-making operation that goes beyond cheddar to craft its own artisanal raw-milk sheep cheese varieties. The farm runs an organic food shop in an 1897 old schoolhouse. Out back you can see the cheeses being shaped through a small viewing window. Currently there aren't any sheep on the farm, as the family's flock was slaughtered by the U.S. government over the mad cow disease scare a few years back—an incident dramatically recounted by scientist-turned-shepherdess Linda Faillace in her book *Mad Sheep.* If you feel inspired (or outraged) you can sign up for one- or three-day cheese-making classes offered by the family to get started on your own varieties.

Entertainment

The **Purple Moon Pub** (Rte. 100 and Rte. 17, Waitsfield, 802/496-3422, www.purplemoonpub.com) is a big part of the reason for the area's nickname, the "Bad Liver Valley." It has plenty of comfy couches for resting sore

VERMONT

muscles après-ski or canoe—to say nothing of the specialty list of martinis and a host of other potent libations. It also offers live jazz and folk music throughout the week.

The sophisticated, artsy vibe at **Big Picture Theater and Cafe** (4648 Carroll Rd., off Rte. 100, 802/496-8948994, www.bigpicturetheater.info, 7 A.M.–10 P.M. Wed.–Sun.) makes for one-stop evening fun—cutting-edge movies, film series, and a dinner that happens one hour before your show. (Reservations are recommended.)

Events

To call the weekly music festival/craft fair/gossip session the **Mad River Green Farmers' Market** (9 A.M.–1 P.M. Sat. May–Oct.) is giving it short shrift indeed. For many residents, it's an event to look forward to all week; for visitors, there is perhaps no better way to clue into the communal spirit of the valley than the boisterous event full of craft booths, organic produce from local farms, and stagefuls of folk, Latin, and Celtic musical performers.

Shopping

Some places are more hangout than store, and **The Warren Store** (284 Main St., Warren, 802/496-3864, www.warrenstore.com, 8 A.M.–7 P.M. Mon.–Sat., 8 A.M.–6 P.M. Sun.) counts itself among them. Everyone seems to be on a first-name basis at this eclectic provisions shop, full of Vermont-made odds and ends (from pillows to salad bowls). They churn out excellent creative sandwiches from the deli—all on bread baked on-site—and have a nice selection of unusual wines for sale.

Find a trove of folk art and crafts, plus handmade furnishings from Vermont artists, at **Bradley House** (266 Main St., Warren, 802/496-9714, 10 A.M.–5 P.M. Mon.–Sat., 11 A.M.–4 P.M. Sun.). The gallery sprawls in a Greek Revival cottage, which allows plenty of space for the creative merchandise. A definite do-not-miss: the **Granville Bowl Mill** (45 Mill Rd., Granville, 800/828-1005, www.bowlmill.com, 9 A.M.–5 P.M., Mon.–Sat., 11 A.M.–4 P.M. Sun.), a venerable factory

and showroom originally founded in 1857 that which makes wooden bowls and cutting boards from Vermont wood the old-fashioned way—on 19th-century equipment, then perfected with 20th-century sanding techniques on the same equipment its been using for over 100 years. While not cheap, the one-of-a-kind bowls come in a multiplicity of shapes, sizes, and woods, including cherry, yellow birch, and sugar maple (some with the hole from the sugar tap still in the wood.)

Step into the **Artisan's' Gallery** (20 Bridge St., Waitsfield, 802/496-6256, www.vtartisansgallery.com, 10 A.M.–5 P.M. daily) in the Old Village area of Waitsfield, and prepare to feel bewildered by the enormous selection. Upwards of 175 local craftspeople sell their goods here, which means you'll have no problem finding jewelry, wood-block prints, hand-painted wooden bowls, jewelry, and stoneware.

The most respected outdoors outfitter in the area, **Clearwater Sports** (4147 Main St., Waitsfield, 802/496-2708, www.clearwatersports.com, 10 A.M.–6 P.M. Mon.–Fri.; 9 A.M.–6 P.M. Sat.; 10 A.M.–5 P.M. Sun.), offers scads of gear and all the equipment rentals and guided tours you need to put it to proper use.

Food

Looking for lively food and a livelier atmosphere? The **Purple Moon Pub** (Rte. 100 and Rte. 17, Waitsfield, 802/496-3422, www.purplemoonpub.com/food.html, 4–11 P.M. Mon.–Sat. and 4–9 P.M. Sun., $6–15) also serves a tasty pub menu of crispy fish wraps, Vermont-goat-cheese fondues, and maple flan.

When you feel the need to get down to business with a seriously sophisticated meal in a romantic setting, head to **Restaurant at 1824 House Inn** (2150 Main St., Waitsfield, 802/496-7555, www.1824house.com, 5:30–8 P.M. Thurs.–Mon., $23–31). The dinner menu changes regularly but may include the likes of phyllo-wrapped salmon with roasted-tomato coulis.

Arguably the Ben & Jerry's of the pizza world, ◖ **American Flatbread** (48 Lareau Rd., Waitsfield, 802/496-8856, www.

al fresco dining, Vermont style, at American Flatbread

americanflatbread.com, 5–9 P.M. Fri.–Sat., $7–16) just about has its own cult, and deservedly so. Every Friday and Saturday night, the unassuming farmhouse setting turns into a party, swarmed by lovers of the organic menu of wholesome and gourmet pies, salads, and desserts made entirely of sustainable, farm-fresh Vermont ingredients. Reservations aren't accepted, but do as the locals do and show up at 5 P.M. to put your name on the waitlist. You can request a specific time to come back, or just wait by the bonfire with a pint until your name is called.

Upscale and meticulously run, the restaurant at ❰ **The Dining Room at The Pitcher Inn** (275 Main St., Warren, 802/496-6350, www.pitcherinn.com, 5–10 P.M. Wed.–Sun., $28–35) boasts a superlative and hefty international wine list, and an impressive menu to match. Global in its influences but local in most of its ingredients, the kitchen emphasizes organic seasonal produce and fresh game such as grilled Vermont-raised lamb. Want to raise the romance bar even further? Reserve for a private dinner for two in the restaurant's

wine cellar. Find everything from cornmeal-crusted salmon with braised leeks to simple crab cakes on the menu at the relaxed and comfy **The Common Man** (3209 German Flats Rd., Warren, 802/583-2800, www.commonmanrestaurant.com, 4:30–9 P.M. Tues.–Sat., $16–29). The restaurant's airy building is 150 years old and outfitted with crystal chandeliers, candlelight, and a gargantuan fireplace.

Information and Services

The **Mad River Valley Chamber of Commerce** (800/828-4748, www.madrivervalley.com) runs a visitors center in the historic General Wait House on Route 100 in Waitsfield. Log onto the Internet through Wi-Fi hotspots at **Three Mountain Café** (107 Mad River Green, 802/496-5470) or **Big Picture Café** (48 Carroll Rd., 802/496-8994).

SPORTS AND RECREATION

The Mad River Valley abounds with recreational activities. In addition to the suggestions below, the Mad River Glen ski area runs the **Mad River Glen Naturalist Program**

VERMONT

(802/496-3351, www.madriverglen.com/naturalist) with guided tours that range from moonlit snowshoeing expeditions to wildlife-tracking trips to rock climbing.

Hiking and Biking

Three out of five of the 4,000-foot or higher peaks in Vermont rise from the Mad River Valley. While not the highest mountain in Vermont, the distinctly shaped **Camel's Hump** might be the best loved by state residents. Its shape is identifiable for miles around, and its summit remains completely undeveloped and pristine. The most popular ascent is up the 7-mile Monroe Trail, a rock-hopping ascent from a birch-and-beech forest up to the unique alpine vegetation zone of its undeveloped summit. The parking area for the trail is at the end of Camel's Hump Rd. in Duxbury; the direct way to the summit is up the Monroe Trail to the Long Trail, a distance of about seven miles. Two more demanding peaks, **Mount Ellen** and **Mount Abraham,** can be hiked singly or together, taking in the 4,000-foot ridge between them. For information on all of these hikes, contact the **Green Mountain Club** (802/244-7037, www.greenmountainclub.org), or pick up a copy of the club's indispensible *Long Trail Guide*, available in most bookstores and outdoors stores in Vermont.

If the mountains seem too daunting, the **Mad River Path Association** (802/496-78777284, www.madriverpath.com) manages several walking and biking trails that weave in and out of the villages of the valley, taking in farms, woodland, and bridges along the way. Bicycles can be rented from the **Inverness Ski Shop** (5274 Main St./Rte. 100, Waitsfield, 802/496-3343, www.iskishop.com).

Boating

With a quick flow and a few spots of good white water, the Mad River is ideal for canoeing and kayaking. **Clearwater Sports** (4147 Main St., Waitsfield, 802/496-2708, www.clearwatersports.com) leads affordable all-day tours on the Mad and Winooski Rivers ($6880 per person), as well as moonlight paddles.

Skiing

Once known as "Mascara Mountain" for its tendency to draw a jet-setting, zinc oxide–sporting population of skiers more into modeling their latest parka than tackling the slopes, **Sugarbush** (1840 Sugarbush Access Rd., Warren, 800/537-8427, www.sugarbush.com, $49 adults, $39 seniors and youth 7–18) has come a long way to rightly earn its place as Vermont's Second Slope, often favorably described as a more welcoming "alternative" to Killington. It's second to the Beast in the number and difficulty of the slopes it offers, with 111 trails descending from two peaks, Lincoln Peak and Mount Ellen. And it may have the most difficult trail in the East: the rock-and-glade ride known as the Rumble. Sugarbush is also prized for the high amount of natural snow it gets each year, as storms from Lake Champlain unload their cargo after passing over the mountains. Not that it needs it—the Bush has one of the most sophisticated snow-making systems in the East. As a bonus, Sugarbush and Mad River Glen have worked out lift packages that include both mountains—so you can experience big-mountain skiing on the Bush and still not lose out on the intimacy of the smaller mountain down the valley.

In the shadow of Sugarbush and the surrounding mountains, **Ole's Cross Country Center** (Airport Rd., Warren, 802/496-3430, www.olesxc.com) has 45 kilometers of trails through deep woods and farm country. In Montpelier, maple syrup producer Burr Morse also runs a cross-country ski touring center in the winter. **Morse Farm Ski Touring Center** (1168 County Rd., Montpelier, 802/223-2740 or 800/242-2740, www.morsefarm.com) has 25 kilometers of trails through light woods and meadows, designed by two-time Olympian skier John Morton. After skiing the trails, you can warm up by the fire with a cup of cider or chill out with a maple syrup snow cone.

Ice Skating

Waitsfield's outdoor skating rink, the **Skatium** (Village Sq., Waitsfield, 802/496-8909) is a community gathering place in winter. The rink has skate rentals during public skating hours, generally all day on Saturday and Sunday from early December as long as the ice lasts, as well as other hours during the week that vary by season. During the winter, call the rink directly for a full schedule.

Horseback Riding

Icelandic horses are genetically programmed to traverse the snowy landscape. The **Vermont Icelandic Horse Farm** (3061 N. Fayston Rd., Waitsfield, 802/496-7141, www.icelandic-horses.com) breeds well-mannered purebreds for half- and full-day trips ($80/$190) and longer overnight trail rides all year-round.

ACCOMMODATIONS
Under $100

Under the same ownership as the lovably bohemian American Flatbread, the hub of which is based on the property, **Lareau Farm Inn** (48 Lareau Rd., Waitsfield, 802/496-4949, www.lareaufarminn.com, $85–135) names its rooms after principles its management holds dear—love, patience, and respect among them. A copy of Dr. Seuss's *The Lorax* is found in every room, and of course, children are welcome. In fact, guests of every age are made to feel like part of the family. With delicious breakfasts and free wireless Internet included—not to mention the attention of a genuinely warm staff—Lareau couldn't offer better value.

Looking for cheap but clean? The **Pierre Motel** (362 N. Main St., Barre, 802/476-3188, www.vtpierremotel.com, $55–99), with 20 rooms with cable and fridges, is your answer. If that and the conveniently close location to downtown Barre don't convince you, the complimentary continental breakfasts and the outdoor pool will.

$100-150

Two gracious Federal-style buildings (filled with no fewer than 10 fireplaces) comprise the ◖ **Inn at Montpelier** (147 Main St., Montpelier, 802/223-2727, www.innatmontpelier.com, $132–229). The antiques-filled common areas lead into 19 neat rooms, with canopy beds, colonial-style bureaus, and walls ranging from tomato-red to bold floral.

$150-250

Exquisitely decorated, the Relais & Chateaux–designated ◖ **Pitcher Inn** (275 Main St., Warren, 802/496-6350, www.pitcherinn.com, $425–800) houses 11 rooms and suites—each individually decorated in a Vermont theme and with Wi-Fi, CD players, TVs, whirlpool tubs, and radiant floor heating; a few have wood-burning fireplaces. There's also a stand-alone spa on the property, offering everything from hair care and pedicures to facials.

Romance, thy name is the **Round Barn Farm** (1661 E. Warren Rd., Waitsfield, 802/496-2276, www.theroundbarn.com, $165–285). Most rooms in the 19th-century farmhouse have skylights, king-size canopy beds, whirlpool tubs, gas fireplaces, wireless Internet access, and jaw-dropping mountain views. In the wintertime, guests can take advantage of miles of snowshoeing trails, on trips guided by the resident Chocolate Lab, Cooper.

GETTING THERE AND AROUND

For the Mad River Valley, take exit 9 to Route 100B and then Route 100 south to Waitsfield. The distance from Montpelier is 20 miles (30 min.) The **Mad Bus** (802/496-7433, www.madbus.org) shuttle stops at various locations in Waitsfield and Warren, along with routes to Sugarbush, Mad River Glen, and Montpelier.

VERMONT

North Central Vermont

The Green Mountains begin to taper off as they climb northward into Canada, but not before one last peak performance by Mount Mansfield, the highest in the state. Along its southern slopes, the ski village of Stowe is the main attraction in this area—rightfully bustling with tourists three seasons out of the year (only during the "mud season" of spring do the chalets close up shop). Around Stowe, the Lamoille Valley provides a taste of rural northern Vermont sliced up nicely in two by the scenic byway of Route 100. Along the way, the town of Waterbury would be a blip on the map if it weren't for the two guys who decided to open up an ice cream factory in town.

FLAVA GRAVE

On your way out of the Ben & Jerry's factory, take a short walk up to the hill by the playground where you can find the "Flavor Graveyard," with 30 tombstones marked with flavors that didn't make it. Among them, you'll find Honey, I'm Home, a honey-vanilla ice cream with chocolate-covered honeycomb pieces; Lemon Peppermint Carob Chip, which just speaks for itself; and the ill-fated Sugar Plum, a plum ice cream with caramel swirl which was the worst-selling flavor in B&J history. In three weeks on the market, it sold exactly one pint.

WATERBURY

For all the hype surrounding Ben & Jerry's operation, the rest of the small city of Waterbury could only be something of a disappointment. North of the highway, Route 100 is a long touristy stretch of gift shops and inns. South of I-89, a small downtown area has a few shops and historic buildings without much character. But does that really matter? Everyone knows why you came here—so grab a cone of cookie dough and indulge.

◖ Ben & Jerry's Factory

After a five-dollar correspondence course in ice cream making from Penn State, Ben Cohen and Jerry Greenfield opened their first shop in Burlington in 1978. From that small seed grew a company that revolutionized the American ice cream market, proving that Häagen-Dazs didn't have a lock on thick and creamy. Though most of it is made in a second factory in St. Albans, the company still makes ice cream in its flagship Waterbury factory (1401 Rte. 100, 866/258-6877, www.benjerrys.com, 10 A.M.–6 P.M. daily mid-Oct.–May; 9 A.M.–6 P.M. daily June; 9 A.M.–9 P.M. daily July–mid-Aug.; 9 A.M.–7 P.M. daily mid-Aug.–mid-Oct., $3 adults, $2 seniors, children 12 and under free). A cowbell signals the start of tours, which take in a self-congratulating biopic about the duo, as well as a look from the mezzanine onto the factory floor—where ice cream is mixed, flavored, frozen, and packed into pints.

The secret to the ice cream's richness, as tour guides will tell you, isn't more butter or heavier cream—it's less air stirred into the mix. Of course the best part of the tour is saved for the end: the Flavoroom, where guests can taste free samples of whatever is coming off the floor, oftentimes a new or experimental flavor. While you are downing the cold stuff, you can fantasize about the fact that B&J employees are each allowed to take home 15 pints a week of factory seconds.

Other Sights

Forget the cider; those in the know really come to Cold Hollow Cider Mill (3600 Rte. 100, Waterbury Center, 800/327-7537, www.coldhollow.com, 8 A.M.–7 P.M. daily July–Oct.; 8 A.M.–6 P.M. Nov.–June) for the donuts, homemade gooey O's that blow Krispy Kreme out of the water. Of course, you'll need something to wash them down with, and that's where the cider comes in. Cold Hollow is one

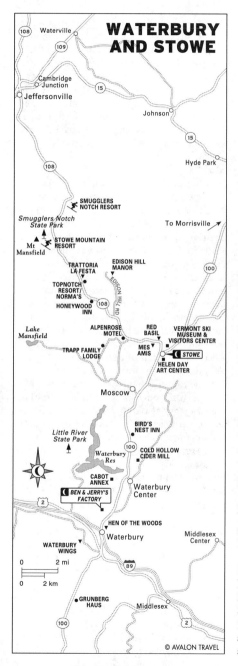

WATERBURY AND STOVE

of the leading producers of apple cider, which submits apples to a souring process to make a drink much tarter than just ordinary juice. Cold Hollow gives free samples of its cider, which is still made on an old-fashioned hydraulic cider press from the 1920s.

Nightlife

Serious beer lovers (or, serious drinkers masquerading as serious beer lovers) congregate nightly at **The Alchemist Pub** (23 S. Main St., 802/244-4120, www.alchemistbeer.com), a cozy brewpub that takes handcrafted beer as its raison d'etre. With seven barrels brewing in the basement, the house pours a number of rotating seasonal beers, plus a handful of static favorites.

Shopping

Need proof that tea isn't just for drinking? Get it at **Vermont Liberty Tea Company** (1 Derby Ln., 802/244-6102, www.vermontlibertytea. com, 10 A.M.–5 P.M. Mon.–Sat.), a panoply of exotic herbal infusions all under one roof. Find catnip toys, accessories like tea strainers and caddies, plus teas you actually do drink—rare black tea blends and chamomiles, and fruit teas from apple to blackberry.

Nestled among patches of wildflowers, **Cabot Annex** (26532657 Rte. 100, 802/244-6334, www.cabotcheese.com/annex.html, 9 A.M.–6 P.M. daily) is as cute as cheddar houses come. Stop in to sample Cabot cheeses and pick up a hunk of cheddar for the road. The shop also sells local crafts, microbrews, and wines. Watch the goods get made right before your eyes at **Ziemke Glassblowing Studio** (3033 Waterbury-Stowe Rd., 802/244-6126, www. zglassblowing.com, 10 A.M.–6 P.M. daily), then buy the cups, vases, and jewelry that result.

Food

Named for the rare mushroom that grows wild in the forests, **Hen of the Woods** (92 Stowe St., 802/244-7300, www.henofthewood.com, 5–9 P.M. Mon.–Sat., $16–28) is dedicated to seasonal cuisine fresh from local farms. Wine-soaked cherries that burst on the tongue;

VERMONT

roasted chicken as soft and sweet as butter; heirloom tomatoes coaxed out by a pinch of salt—each bite here threatens to short-circuit the brain and reawake the sheer pleasure of just eating. The 19th-century mill building-turned-dining room features an ample North American wine list and an ever-changing artisan-cheese list. In nice weather, outdoor patio seating overlooks the rushing Thatcher Brook.

Wing lovers rejoice at the sight of the menu at **Waterbury Wings** (1 S. Main St., 802/244-7827, www.waterburywings.com, 11 A.M.–midnight Mon.–Sat. and 11 A.M.–11 P.M. Sun., $5–14), filled with the classic bar food doused in sauces like wasabi-teriyaki and spicy horseradish. Not surprisingly, the vibe here is ultra-casual, with live bands every Saturday night, pool tables, and plenty of napkins passed around.

Information

The **Waterbury Tourism Council** (www.waterbury.org) runs an information booth on Route 100 just north of the highway exit. Wireless Internet is available at the **Waterbury Public Library** (28 N. Main St., 802/244-7036).

◖ STOWE

Look up "cute" in the dictionary, and it wouldn't be too surprising to see a photo of Stowe—not, at least, after you've visited the adorable resort village. A bit like Aspen without the attitude, this is mountain living gone upscale: world-class shopping, eating, and resorts with lots of crisp, fresh air; views of lush green Mount Mansfield in the summer, mind-blowing foliage in the fall, and excellent skiing in the winter.

Founded in 1763, Stowe earned its early living from sawmills and gristmills. But its beautiful setting and alpine climate started drawing tourists during the summer after the Civil War. Three Swedish families first aroused interest in skiing in 1913. A year later, a librarian from Dartmouth College was the first to ski down the sides of Mount Mansfield and tourists began coming during the winter as well. By 1937, ski pioneer Charlie Lord had installed the first ski lift on the mountain, and the modern ski resort was born. Despite Stowe's popularity, however, the resort has eschewed the modern trend of building up the base lodge with condos and restaurants, preferring to work with independent businesses in the community instead. For that reason, Stowe still feels like a real community that happens to have a ski resort, rather than the other way around.

Sights

So, what made those first alpine pioneers decide it was a good idea to strap two boards to their feet and hurl themselves down a mountainside? You might not find the answer to that question at the **Vermont Ski Museum** (1 S. Main St., 802/253-9911, www.vermontskimuseum.org, noon–5 P.M. Wed.–Mon., donations accepted), but you will gain a greater appreciation for the lunacy of the early practitioners of the sport, as well as an appreciation for modern equipment, lifts, and clothing. Located in Stowe's former town hall, the museum has several rooms of exhibits, a plasma screen with ski videos, and a Hall of Fame of great names in Vermont skiing history.

What happens after "happily ever after?" Well, you start a ski lodge in Vermont. At least, that's the trajectory of Baron and Maria von Trapp, whose story, as depicted in the musical *The Sound of Music,* has made generations swoon. After escaping the Nazis, the von Trapps came to Stowe to re-create the quintessential ski chalet as the **Trapp Family Lodge** (700 Trapp Hill Rd., 802/253-8511 or 800/826-7000, www.trappfamily.com), which has grown over the years to a skiers' resort complex complete with spa and slope-side villas. The lodge is a bit worse for wear now, but visiting for a linzer torte at the over-the-top Austrian Tea Room and a family sing-a-long around the bonfire at night is a requirement for any serious Rodgers and Hammerstein fan. The lodge also shows a documentary about the family three times a day (10 A.M., 4:30 P.M., and 7 P.M.) in St. George's Hall. And of course there's the obligatory showing of *The Sound of Music* every Thursday night at 8 P.M.

ARTISAN TRADITIONS

Vermont is justifiably proud – and notably supportive – of its artistic community. The state has the highest concentration of writers and visual artists in the country, plus upwards of 1,500 professional craftspeople, including quilt-makers, printmakers, potters, metalworkers, weavers, painters, glassblowers, and any other kind of artisan you can dream up. One of the state's biggest artistic resources (and one of the largest in the country, in fact) is the **Vermont Studio Center** (90 Pearl St., Johnson, 802/635-2727, www.vermontstudiocenter.org), which offers residency programs to artists and writers from around the globe on its campus outside of Stowe. Meanwhile,

the **Vermont Crafts Council** (Montpelier, 802/223-3380, www.vermontcrafts.com), with more than 300 members, helps organize open studios and crafts fairs for artists around the state, and helps visitors find the artists and galleries closest to them (with a full list of galleries and studios, organized by category, on its website). The council publishes a map of artisan studios in the state to coincide with the annual statewide Open Studios weekend in May. Or for one-stop shopping, try **Frog Hollow** (www.froghollow.org), an organization that sells work from over 250 artisans in its juried gallery in Burlington (85 Church St., 802/863-6458), as well as an "online gallery" on its website.

The Abenaki called the highest peak in Vermont Moze-o-de-be-Wadso or "Mountain with a Head Like a Moose." The 4,393-foot mountain has come down to us as the more prosaic Mount Mansfield. In the summer, Stowe Mountain Resort operates an eight-person high-speed **gondola ride** (Mountain Rd./ Rte. 108, 800/247-8693, www.stowe.com, 10:30 A.M.–4:30 P.M. late June–mid-Oct., $23 adults, $19 seniors, $15 youth 6–12, $53 families) up to the summit that takes in views of the village and surrounding mountains on the way up. The community-supported **Helen Day Art Center** (5 School St. at Pond St., 802/253-8358, www.helenday.com, noon–5 P.M. Tues.–Sat. year-round, $5 adults, $3 students and seniors, free for children under 12) has been dedicated to showcasing local art for more than 25 years. It inhabits the second floor of a Greek Revival building in the center of town, with a sculpture garden out back.

Entertainment

The **Stowe Theatre Guild** (Rte. 100 and Rte. 108, 67 Main St., 802/253-3961, www.stowetheatre.com) presents crowd-pleasing musicals throughout the year at the Stowe Town Hall Theatre.

The village abounds with bars for après-ski

libations. The **Rusty Nail** (1190 Mountain Rd., 802/253-6245, www.rustynailbar.com) is classier than its name might imply, with a martini menu and DJ dancing on weekends. The **Matterhorn** (4969 Mountain Rd., 802/253-8198, www.matterhornbar.com) has comedy nights and cover-band performances along with pool tables and sushi.

Events

The von Trapp Family continues its musical legacy with **Music in the Meadow** (802/863-5966, www.stowearts.com), a summer concert series of classical and popular music held in the meadow behind the lodge.

For more than 20 years, the Stoweflake Resort has literally been full of hot air. The annual **Stoweflake Hot Air Balloon Festival** (802/253-7355 or 800/253-2232, www.stoweflake.com, mid-July) offers opportunities for $10 tethered balloon rides, along with longer flights for those paying $500 for a package stay at the resort.

Stowe becomes the Austrian village it has always wanted to be each fall during **Stowe Oktoberfest** (802/253-7321853-2506, www.stoweoktoberfest.com, late Sept.), a two-day crush of oompah bands, schnitzel, beer, and more beer. Miss Vermont even makes a showing. Ski-jumping and ice-sculpture carving shake Stowe out of the winter doldrums during the **Stowe Winter Carnival** (www.stowecarnival.com, late Jan.). A highlight is the village-block-party night that fills the streets with bulky parkas and merriment.

Shopping

Designer and furniture maker John Lomas makes all of the high-quality furniture at **Cotswold Furniture Makers** (132 Mountain Rd., 888/253-3738, www.cotswoldfurniture. com, 10 A.M.–6 P.M. daily; seasonal hours may vary) in his local workshop. By turns contemporary and traditional, the pieces are paired in the showroom with lighting, pottery, and glassware by other Vermont artists, plus Tibetan rugs—all of which is for sale. Meanwhile, artist Susan Bayer Fishman owns and runs **Stowe Craft Gallery** (55 Mountain Rd., 802/253-4693, www.stowecraft.com, 10 A.M.–6 P.M. daily; extended holiday season hours 10 A.M.–7 P.M. daily; extended summer hours 10 A.M.–8 P.M. Thurs.–Sat.), an epic collection of many other artists' works—knick-knacks like pewter measuring cups, glazed vases, and hand-carved backgammon sets.

Food

The bustling low-ceilinged **[** **Trattoria La Festa** (4080 Upper Mountain Rd., 802/253-8480, www.stowetrattorialafesta.com, 4:30–9 P.M. Tues.–Sat., $16–22) is owned by Italian brothers Antonio and Giancarlo DeVito, who greet everyone at the bar by the door. The place is a paragon of the trattoria genre: casual and family-style, but serving sophisticated dishes—solidly prepared pastas like spaghetti with tender baby shrimp in garlic white-wine sauce, or yellowfin tuna with white puttanesca sauce. The tiramisu is to die for.

Dig into the Eastern end of the eating spectrum at **The Red Basil** (294 Mountain Rd., 802/253-4478, www.theredbasil.com, 11:30 A.M.–3 P.M. and 4:30–9:30 P.M. Mon.–Thurs.; till 10:30 P.M. Fri.; 2–10:30 P.M. Sat.; 2–9:30 P.M. Sun., $15–21), a bar-cum-restaurant that mixes up strong martinis and

creates specialties like scallops with ginger sauce and Japanese fixings such as salmon teriyaki and sushi ranging from octopus to eel with avocado. Rather opt for European flavors? The hearty, stick-to-your ribs breakfasts at **Dutch Pancake Café** (at Grey Fox Inn, 990 Mountain Rd., Stowe, 802/253-8921, www.greyfoxinn.com, 7:30 A.M.–12:30 P.M. daily in winter; 8 A.M.–12:30 P.M. daily in summer; $6–13) are just the (lift) ticket for carbo-loading before outdoor activities. Start with any of the 80 kinds of Dutch pancakes (which are thinner and more crepe-like than regular pancakes). The casual, noisy spot does an admirable job keeping big groups and kids happy. It's tough to beat the setting at **[** **Norma's** (4000 Mountain Rd., www.topnotchresort.com, 800/451-8686, 7 A.M.–9:30 P.M. daily, $14–49), the glass-enclosed dining room at Topnotch Resort. Looking out to a poster-worthy view of the mountains and a wide stretch of sky, the spot highlights chef Brian Tomlinson's organic ingredients in classic dishes like grilled tenderloin and creative turns like coffee-cured duck breast. There's also a well-edited wine list and a gorgeous outdoor terrace—the better to take in sunsets in warm weather.

Information

The **Stowe Area Association** (51 Main St., 877/467-8669, www.gostowe.com) runs a welcome center at the crossroads of Main Street and Mountain Road. Wi-Fi Internet can be accessed around the corner at **Stowe Coffee House** (57B Mountain Rd., 802/253-2189) or at **Stowe Free Library** (90 Pond St., 802/253-6145). Medical needs can be filled at **Heritage Drugs** (1878 Mountain Rd., 802/253-2544). **Stowe Police Department** is at 350 S Main St, 802/253-7126.

LAMOILLE VALLEY

North of Stowe, small-town relaxation meets big-time outdoor adventure in the sleepy little Lamoille Valley, with the towns of Jeffersonville and Morrisville as the highlights. It's as pretty a drive as any along Route 100, which cuts through villages full of clean white church steeples, neat-as-a-pin farmhouses, brick-sidewalked main streets, and covered bridges. Along the way, you'll find plenty of arts and crafts to pore over, as well as kid-friendly eateries and hotels. On the other side of Mount Mansfield from Stowe, Smugglers' Notch was named for its reputation as a favorite passage for bootleggers from Canada to evade the law during prohibition. Now the mountain pass is home to a family-friendly ski resort that is anything but shady.

Sights

On the east side of Morrisville is a rare covered railroad bridge. The 109-foot **Fisher Bridge** (Rte. 15, 11 miles south of Rte. 100) once served to carry the St. Johnsbury and Lamoille Country Railroad trains over the Lamoille River. It was built double-high to let the trains through, with a vented cupola (which now serves as a giant birdhouse for local tweeters) to allow the steam to escape.

Entertainment

Relax with a pint of microbrew at the convivial **Village Tavern** at Smugglers Notch Inn (55 Church St., Jeffersonville,, 802/644-6607, www.smuggsinn.com). The handsome-but-casual pub is a favorite for locals and visitors looking for a place to kick back and unwind at the end of a day.

Shopping

Jeffersonville is home to several fine galleries worth taking a peek at. Chief among them, the **Bryan Memorial Gallery** (180 Main St., Jeffersonville, 802/644-5100, www.bryangallery.com) is known as one of Vermont's premier showcases for local landscape artists, many of whom have drawn their inspiration from the countryside but a scant few miles away. If you haven't sated your sweet tooth by now, stop in at the **Vermont Maple Outlet** (3929 Rte. 15, Jeffersonville, 800/858-3121, www.vermontmapleoutlet.com), which produces maple candy and maple cream in addition to all grades of syrup.

Food

The café-cum-playroom that is **The Bee's Knees** (82 Lower Main St., Morristown, 802/888-7889, www.thebeesknees-vt.com, 7:30 A.M.–10 P.M. Tues.–Sun., $7–12) might just be the perfect place to take kids. Lovably crunchy in decor and attitude (nearly everything on the menu is organic, vegetarian options loom large, and live music plays regularly), it offers a wall of toys to borrow and healthy plates like mac 'n' cheese (with locally made cheddar). Yet more locally grown goods take center stage at **158 Main** (158 Main St., Jeffersonville, 802/644-8100, www.158main.com, 7:30 A.M.–3 P.M. and 5–9 P.M. Wed.–Sat., 8 A.M.–2 P.M. Sun., $9–30), which is perpetually crowded by addicted locals. The draw? Generous portions of home fries and pancakes, huge salads, and creative dinners like almond-seared salmon.

Information

The **Smugglers' Notch Area Chamber of Commerce** (802/644-8232, www.smugnotch.com) stocks an unstaffed information booth at the corner of Routes 15 and 108 in Jeffersonville. The **Lamoille Valley Chamber of Commerce** (43 Portland St., Morrisville, 802/888-7607, www.stowesmugglers.org) also has information on the surrounding area. Regional hospital services are available at **Copley Hospital** (Washington Hwy., Morrisville, 802/888-888).

SPORTS AND RECREATION

Hiking

Vermont's highest peak, **Mount Mansfield** is a tough slog; but the panoramic view of three states is well worth it. The trailhead starts north of Stowe on Route 108, and climbs four miles up steep terrain to the peak. Save some energy for the last third of a mile, "the Chin." (The parts of the mountain are named for the parts of a reclining person's profile, which it resembles.) The near-vertical slope is the toughest part of the climb—and is even more treacherous on the descent. A longer but slightly easier climb to the summit

VERMONT

COURTESY OF STATE OF VERMONT

canoeing in the Lamoille Valley

approaches from the west along the six-mile Sunset Ridge Trail. To get a bird's-eye view of Mount Mansfield itself, take the trail up to the **The Pinnacle,** the 2,740-foot peak on the east side of town. The trail rises gradually from Stowe Hollow for about a mile and a half, with a short rocky scramble at the top. For more information on these and other climbs, contact the **Green Mountain Club** (802/244-7037, www.greenmountainclub.org) or pick up a copy of the *Long Trail Guide.*

Biking

The impossibly quaint scenery of the Lamoille Valley makes it a favorite for cyclists. You can rent your steed at **AJ's Ski and Sports** (350 Mountain Rd., Stowe, 800/226-6257, www.ajsportinggoods.com) and pedal up to Morristown yourself. Or leave the arrangements to the reassuringly named **Peace of Mind Guaranteed Bike Tours** (888/635-2453, www.pomgbike.com), which offers two-day bike tours starting from the Smugglers Notch Inn in Jeffersonville.

Boating and Fishing

It doesn't get much better than a paddle down the Lamoille River, a country landscape of mountain-framed farms. **Umiak Outdoor Outfitters** (849 S. Main St., Stowe, 802/253-2317, www.umiak.com) rents kayaks and canoes and leads guided trips down the Lamoille and Winooksi Rivers.

Skiing

Stowe Mountain Resort (5781 Mountain Rd./Rte. 108, 800/253-4754, www.stowe.com, $89 adults, $74 seniors, $64 children 6–12, free for children under 6) is about half the size of neighboring Sugarbush and Killington, but the challenges posed by its famous "Front Four" trails are as heady as any on the East Coast. Most difficult of all is the Goat trail, a 36-degree ice chute through moguls, ledges, and boulders that will test the skill of any snow dog. Not all of Stowe's terrain is so difficult; the mountain presents some of the best skiing around for intermediate skiers, with two separate peaks devoted almost entirely to blue-square and single-diamond trails. On the other side of the mountain pass, **Smugglers' Notch** (4323 Rte. 108, Smugglers' Notch, 800/419-4615, www.smuggs.com, $62 adults, $46 seniors and youth 6–18, free for children under 6 and seniors over 69) has positioned itself as the ideal family resort. In addition to three peaks (roughly broken down into beginner, intermediate, and expert), the resort has a half-pipe for snowboarders and an indoor FunZone complete with inflatable slides and mini-golf.

Other Winter Sports

Behind the Trapp Family Lodge, the **Trapp Family Lodge Touring Center** (700 Trapp Hill Rd., 802/253-8511 or 800/826-7000, www.trappfamily.com) has some 100 kilometers of cross-country ski trails, through both groomed and ungroomed forest and meadowland.

Across town, **Edson Hill Manor** (1500 Edson Hill Rd., 802/253-7371 or 800/621-0284, www.edsonhillmanor.com) offers 25 kilometers of groomed trails for cross-country skiing and snowshoeing, along with lessons and guided midnight snowshoeing tours. For the long-distance skier, the trails connect to the Catamount Trail, which runs 300 kilometers down the length of Vermont.

Right in the center of the village, **Jackson Arena** (Park St., 802/253-6137) offers indoor ice skating during the winter months. At $3 admission and $3.50 skate rentals, you can't beat the price. Rides with **Stowe Snomobile Tours** (802/253-6221, www.stowesnowmobiletours.com) allow you to explore the woods in comfort, with fast-paced tours on top-of-the-line Polaris machines with heated handlebars.

Horseback Riding

A quiet country resort on the edge of Stowe, **Edson Hill Manor** (1500 Edson Hill Rd., Stowe, 802/253-7371, www.edsonhillmanor.com) has riding stables with horses and ponies available for backcountry trots. The resort also offers sleigh rides through the surrounding woodland—including romantic sleigh-and-dine packages.

Camping

On the flanks of Mount Mansfield just before the Stowe Mountain Resort, the small **Smuggler's Notch State Park** (6443 Mountain Rd., Stowe, 802/253-4014, www.vtstateparks.com/htm/smugglers.cfm) offers some 20 tent sites and 14 roomy lean-tos for overnight camping. The sites are quite close together, though several "prime sites" offer more privacy and nice views from the cliffs flanking Mountain Road. The campsite has a restroom employing alternative energy, as well as a hot showers and a trash station.

ACCOMMODATIONS
Under $100

Easy access to the Stowe Recreation Path isn't the only reason to stay at **Alpenrose Motel** (2619 Mountain Rd., 802/253-7277, www.gostowe.com/alpenrose, $70); the rooms are moderately priced and come with private baths, coffeemakers, and kitchenettes. The property also has a swimming pool and pleasant gardens and a patio for outdoor lounging.

$100–150

Handmade quilts and snowshoes decorate the compact but tidy rooms at the Austrian-style chalet **Grunberg Haus** (94 Pine St., Waterbury, 800/800-7760, www.grunberghaus.com, $120–160), tucked into a maple forest. Each room comes with large en suite bathrooms, private balconies, gas-fired woodstoves, fridges, and microwaves. Cabins are also available, and all rooms come with a full home-cooked breakfast. Another Austrian-style inn with slightly cutesy rooms (lots of pink and blue pastels), **Honeywood Inn** (4527 Mountain Rd., 800/659-6289, www.honeywoodinn.com, $119–269) offers significant perks and convenient services: babysitting and child care, business services, fireplaces, kitchenettes in some suites, and a pool. Pets are welcome.

$150–250

Not nearly as outdoorsy as its name suggests, the **Bird's Nest Inn** (5088 Stowe Rd., Waterbury Center, 802/244-7490, www.birdsnestinn.com,

VERMONT

$135–195) is actually a haven of creature comforts, starting with the three-course candlelight breakfast (yes, breakfast) and the hammocks for lazing in the outdoor garden and ending with guest rooms boasting cushy comforters, delicate floral walls, and custom bathrobes. Uniquely appointed rooms—many with working fireplaces, canopy four poster beds, and mountain views—make **Edson Hill Manor** (1500 Edson Hill Rd., Stowe, 802/621-0284, www.edson-hillmanor.com, $179–289) a worthy spot to rest your head. There's also complimentary afternoon tea, a library for relaxed reading, and a country breakfast served in the lovely dining room every morning.

$250 and Up

With loads of pampering and fantastic recreation for adults and kids, **Ⓒ Topnotch Resort** (4000 Mountain Rd., Stowe, 800/451-8686, www.topnotchresort.com, $385–535) wins the luxury-for-families award, hands-down. Grownups can chill out on the slopes, at either of the beautifully kept mountainside pools (one indoor, one out), or in the glorious new spa's treatment rooms. Meanwhile, the children's activity program is extensive and extremely well organized, so both they and mom and dad feel entertained by the day's end. Not for families only, the resort also manages to make couples feel catered to, with romantic dining at Norma's, sumptuously decorated suites with oversized tubs, and couples' massages.

Even better than visiting the **Trapp Family Lodge** (700 Trapp Hill Rd., 802/253-8511 or 800/826-7000, www.trappfamily.com, $245–375) for serious *Sound of Music* fans is staying there overnight. The lodge definitely stresses the "family" part of the name, with comfortable accommodations and staff who are especially patient with children. Once a bit worse for wear, the lodge has been slowly renovated over the past few years in a more modern, up-to-date style.

It was inevitable: After years of resisting the kind of big-lodge accommodations of other ski mountains in New England, Stowe has finally succumbed with the opening of the new **Stowe Mountain Lodge** (7412 Mountain Rd., 888/478-6938, www.stowemountainlodge.com, $400–850), located at the base of Spruce Peak. What's surprising, however, is how well the lodge has retained the "real Vermont" character of Stowe. From the birch trees and the Lake Champlain granite (with fossils of trilobites stuck inside) in the lobby to the Simon Pearce and Miranda Thomas pottery in the guest rooms, the lodge has gone out of its way to include, not ignore, its surroundings. Of course, the lodge also has every luxury you can imagine—goose-down pillows, flat-screens, iPod hookups, etc.—and every room is a suite with kitchenette and laundry to make travelling with the family easy. Finally, those two words that are music to every skiers ears: ski valet.

GETTING THERE AND AROUND

From Stowe, head up Route 100 for 8 miles (15 min.) to Morristown. For Jeffersonville and Smugglers' Notch, take Route 108 north from Stowe up and down the precipitous sides of Mount Mansfield for 10 miles (20 min.). Note, however, that the road is often closed because of snow from November to April. During those months, you'll need to take the long way around to Jeffersonville from Morristown along Routes 100 and 15 west (16 mi., 30 min.). The **Green Mountain Transit Agency** (802/223-7287, www.gmtaride.org) also operates routes to Morristown from Waterbury and Stowe, with transfers from Montpelier. There is no public transportation to Smugglers' Notch; however, the resort offers van service from Burlington's airport and train station (802/644-8851, ext. 1389) for a $45 charge each way (one child free per paying adult, additional children are $35 each).

VERMONT

Northeast Kingdom

A triangular chunk carved out of the upper-right part of the state, the so-called "Northeast Kingdom" is a world unto itself. Its name stems from a memorable utterance of U.S. Senator George Aiken, who said in 1949 that the area "is such beautiful country up here—it should be called the Northeast Kingdom." Something about the name stuck, and residents began proudly thinking of themselves as belonging to a somewhat mythical principality, with brilliant red foliage for raiment and golden maple syrup stored up for treasure. Those who live here love it for its sense of isolation from the madding crowds, its independent spirit, and its quirky population—which can include anyone from political artists and dropout lawyers to fourth-generation farmers.

As for the visitors, they similarly come to experience Vermont the way it used to be, but they also come to get out into nature. Blessed with some of the finest mountain biking trails on the planet and upwards of 200 secluded and unspoiled lakes and ponds, the Kingdom is known as a haven for outdoor adventure-seekers.

CABOT

There's not much to see in Cabot—just a collection of modest white clapboard houses arranged around a general store, library, and a couple of gas pumps. If it weren't for the presence of Vermont's most famous cheese-maker, this is the kind of town you might drive right though without giving a second glance. But the fact that Cabot is home to Cabot Cheese makes it an instant stop on the tourist itinerary.

◖ Cabot Creamery

To quote Monty Python, "Blessed are the Cheese-makers." Vermont might be a different place today had it not been for the industry spawned by some ambitious dairy farmers a century or so ago. From a simple farmer's cooperative started in a farmhouse 100 years ago, Cabot Cheese has grown to become Vermont's best-known (if not best) producer of cheddar cheese. Though the company now makes 15 million pounds of cheese annually, it is still run as a farmers cooperative (with now more than 2,000 farm families) and still operates on the same land where it began.

Enormous white silos loom over the factory campus (2878 Main St./Rte. 15, Cabot Village, 800/837-4261, www.cabotcheese. com, 9 A.M.–5 P.M. daily June–Oct.; 9 A.M.–4 P.M. Mon.–Sat. Nov.–Dec. and Feb.–May; 10 A.M.–4 P.M. Mon.–Sat. Jan., $2 adults and youth 13 and up), where tours are given every half hour down the Cheddar Hall to see the cheese-making process. Giant steel machines looking like something out of *War of the Worlds* have taken the place of hand churning, but in some ways, the cheese is still made the old-fashioned way, without the introduction of enzymes to speed the process. Along the way, tour guides present the opportunity to try different types of cheddar. Lately, the company has been experimenting with all kinds of additions to the cheese, including horseradish, jalapenos, and chipotle peppers. For our money, the three-year Private Reserve is still the best bet. A gift shop sells wax-wrapped blocks at a steep discount, along with other made-in-Vermont foodstuffs and gifts.

Other Sights

Nestled among the hills, **Goodrich's Maple Farm** (2427 Rte. 2, 800/639-1854, www.goodrichmaplefarm.com, 9 A.M.–5 P.M. Mon.–Sat.) is one of Vermont's largest maple syrup producers. Proprietors Glenn and Ruth Goodrich are always happy to take time out of evaporating sap to explain the syrup-making process. But they really shine during the farm's semiannual maple seminars, where they explain how to install and repair the plastic tubes for the sap, as well as how to boil it down efficiently. For $20 a person, the Goodriches teach custom seminars on topics such as cooking with maple.

THE MAKING OF A CLASSIC: MAPLE SYRUP

Many a pancake lover has silently thanked the state of Vermont for producing what is arguably its most glorious food product (referred to as "liquid gold" by many an addict), and Vermont has always been happy to oblige by producing more. After all, the process of making the stuff – known as "sugaring" – requires weather conditions that Vermont tends to get in spades: repeated alternating freezing and thawing in very early spring, so that the tree sap will start to flow. Once that happens (usually in March, while snow is still on the ground), the sap is then collected from the maple trees by drilling small tap holes into each tree, fixed with either tubing or a bucket. When a freeze hits, it acts as a suction to draw the sap out, which is then released during the next thaw. It's collected, then boiled to remove all of its water content, concentrating it into a rich syrup.

Events

The Northeast Kingdom's annual **Fall Foliage Festival** (802/748-3678, www.nekchamber.com/foliage/index.html, early Oct.) is a sort of "progressive dinner" of barbecues, bazaars, and kids' games that starts in Walden (near Cabot) and then moves through different area towns before ending with a fair in St. Johnsbury a week later.

ST. JOHNSBURY

The capital of the Kingdom, St. Johnsbury (or "St. J" to residents) is the largest town in the area, with a whopping 7,500 people. Its entire downtown is a monument to the Victorian era, during which St. Johnsbury saw its fortunes made thanks to the ingenuity of Thaddeus Fairbanks and his family. Since ancient times, weight had been measured by the cumbersome balance scale. Fairbanks invented the modern platform scale, with sliding weights on an arm above a spring-loaded platform. Construction of the scales instantly made Fairbanks—and the town—rich. His brother Erastus was later responsible for bringing the railroad to town in 1850, and later he twice became the governor of Vermont.

The Fairbanks family never forgot where they came from, and generations of the family invested heavily in the town, building an academy, natural-history museum, and art gallery, all of which they hoped would educate their fellow citizens. Today, St. J's train station has been turned into a visitors center, and the town has turned into more of a country backwater than sophisticated center of industry. But it's worth a stop for the Fairbanks legacy and the access to recreational offerings of the Kingdom.

🄲 Fairbanks Museum & Planetarium

Back in the days before Google and Wikipedia, if you wanted to find out something about your world, you went to the local natural history museum, where explorers from around the world displayed random oddities in glass cases. This museum (1302 Main St., 802/748-2372, www.fairbanksmuseum.org, 9 A.M.–5 P.M. Mon.–Sat. and 1–5 P.M. Sun. Apr.–Oct.; closed Mon. Nov.–Mar.; planetarium shows 11 A.M. Mon.–Fri. and 1:30 P.M. daily July–Aug., 1:30 P.M. Sat.–Sun. Sept.–June) is a delicious throwback to that era, with a menagerie of colorful stuffed parrots, menacing polar bears, Egyptian mummies, and Japanese fans displayed in crowded glass cases in a turreted Victorian exhibition hall.

The museum was founded in 1891 by Franklin Fairbanks, a philanthropist who himself made careful daily observations of weather and atmospheric conditions. The museum now carries on his work with a weather gallery, home to the public radio program "Eye on the Sky," which broadcasts weather information and lore to over 10 million listeners daily. Then there is the planetarium, one of only a few in New England, whose regular tours of the heavens have been eliciting gasps from crane-necked visitors for decades.

Other Sights

St. J's library, **The St. Johnsbury Athenaeum** (1171 Main St., 802/748-8291, www.stjathenaeum.org, 10 A.M.–5:30 P.M. Mon.–Fri.; 9:30 A.M.–5:00 P.M. Sat., free) is just as much an art museum, with dozens of fine canvases by American landscape and portrait painters. Highlights include the overpowering *Domes of the Yosemite,* by Albert Bierstadt, and the enigmatic *Raspberry Girl,* by Victorian-era realist Adolphe William Bouguereau. The museum has been left in its original Victorian state, with black-walnut floors and walls.

For a very different take on the landscape, venture into the rows at the **Great Vermont Corn Maze** (1404 Wheelock Rd., Danville, 802/748-1399, www.vermontcornmaze.com, 10 A.M.–4 P.M. daily, Aug.–Sept.; 10 A.M.–3 P.M. daily Oct., $9 adults, $7 seniors and children 4–14, children under 4 free), more than two miles of twisting confusion carved each year amidst 12-foot-tall corn stalks. Owners Mike and Dayna Boudreau have been constructing the maze for better than five years, getting progressively trickier with each course. Participants quest for the elusive "bell of success" in the center of the maze, which can take anywhere from one to four hours. If that sounds too tough, the complex has a smaller corn maze for kids, along with a barnyard mini-golf course among the animal paddocks. To relive *Children of the Corn,* come in October when the farm is transformed into "Dead North: Farmland of Terror" just in time for Halloween.

D-O-G and G-O-D are so close in spelling, it was only a matter of time before someone combined the two. Enter the cuddly-children's-book author and illustrator Stephen Huneck, whose **Dog Chapel** (143 Parks Rd., 802/748-2700, www.dogmt.com, 10 A.M.–5 P.M. Mon.–Sat.; 11 A.M.–4 P.M. Sun.) was truly a labor of love. After emerging from a life-threatening coma, Huneck was inspired to create a church celebrating the spiritual bonds we have with man's best friend. The church he built is a typical New England meetinghouse set high on a hill above St. Johnsbury. Only instead of saints, the stained-glass windows depict canines; instead of holy water, the church offers actual water and treats for four-legged visitors. Huneck encourages guests to bring their dogs for a walk through the hiking paths around the chapel. A gift shop sells the artist's trademark wood-block prints of retrievers.

Calling itself the "maple center of the world," **Maple Grove Farms** (1052 Portland St., 802/748-5141, www.maplegrove.com, 8 A.M.–5 P.M., tours until 2 P.M., Mon.–Fri. mid-May.–Dec.) has expanded beyond syrup to produce its own line of salad dressings and marinades. But the heart of the factory is still the sugarhouse, which has been producing maple syrup for more than 80 years. The farm boasts the world's largest maple candy factory as well; tours include demonstrations of how syrup is set in tanks to crystallize.

Shopping

Indulge your parental instincts at **Frogs & Lily Pads** (443 Railroad St., 802/748-2975, 9:30 A.M.–5:30 P.M., Mon.–Sat., 1 P.M.–4 P.M. Sun.), dedicated to creative and educational toys, impeccable children's clothing, and stylish maternity clothes. Another must-stop for families (not to mention bookworms) is **Boxcar & Caboose Bookstore** (394 Railroad St., 802/748-3551, www.boxcarandcaboose.com, 7 A.M.–7 P.M. Mon.–Fri.; 9 A.M.–7 P.M. Sat.; 9 A.M.–5 P.M. Sun.), a combination bookstore, café, and kids playroom complete with comfy leather chairs, espresso drinks, and a train table.

Score heirloom-quality carved wooden chairs, luminous glass bowls, and hand-woven scarves at **Northeast Kingdom Artisans Guild** (430 Railroad St., 802/748-0158, www.nekartisansguild.com, 10:30 A.M.–5:30 P.M. Mon.–Sat.), a collective of more than 100 craftspeople.

Food

Some of Vermont's freshest takes on classic

VERMONT

comfort food come off the stoves at **Elements Food & Spirit** (98 Mill St., 802/748-8400, www.elementsfood.com, 5–9 P.M. Tues.–Thurs.; 5–9:30 P.M. Fri. and Sat., $15–21). The blue-plate specials are always a hit (most diners just order those), but the kitchen also takes pride in dishes like smoked trout and apple cakes. There's a lengthy list of reasonably priced wines and Vermont-brewed beers.

Standard burgers, sandwiches, and nightly specials are the all-American fare at family-friendly **Mooselook Restaurant** (1058 Main St., Concord, 802/695-2950, 6 A.M.–7:30 P.M. Mon.–Thurs. and Sun.; 6 A.M.–8 P.M. Fri., $7–14).

Information and Services
The **Northeast Kingdom Chamber** (51 Depot Sq., 802/748-3678 or 800/639-6379, www.nekchamber.com) runs a well-staffed welcome center in the ground floor of the former train station.

State authorities in the area can be found at **Vermont State Police** (1068 U.S. Route 5, Suite #1., St. Johnsbury, 802/748-3111). Two full-service hospitals serve the area: **Northeastern Vermont Regional Hospital** (1315 Hospital Dr., St. Johnsbury, 802/748-8141) and **North Country Hospital** (189 Prouty Dr., Newport, 802/334-7331). Get prescriptions filled at **Barton's Pharmacy** (P.O. Box 578, Barton, 802/525-4098). Free public Wi-Fi is available at the **St. Johnsbury Athenaeum** (1171 Main St., 802/748-8291), **Boxcar & Caboose Bookstore** (394 Railroad St., 802/748-3551), and **Elements Food & Spirit** (98 Mill St., 802/748-8400).

HEART OF THE KINGDOM
Beautiful rolling meadows surrounded by hills treasured by cross-country skiers, the central area of the Northeast Kingdom encompasses the towns of Lyndonville, Craftsbury, Burke, and Glover. You'll find an unusual number of covered bridges in the historic area, not to mention neatly manicured common greens in every town. This is quiet living at its most content, with backcountry roads that just cry out for a long, relaxed road trip to the middle of nowhere.

◖ Bread and Puppet Theater
"Art is for Kitchens!" proudly trumpets one poster for sale at the barn-cum-museum of Bread & Puppet Theater performing puppet troupe (753 Heights Rd., Glover, 802/525-3031, www.breadandpuppet.org, 10 A.M.–4 P.M. daily June–Oct., free). With its mission that art should be accessible to the masses, B&P began more than 40 years ago with counterculture hand- and rod-puppet performances on New York's Lower East Side. Founder Peter Schumann moved back to the land in the 1970s, taking over an old farm in the middle of the Kingdom and presenting bigger and more elaborate political puppet festivals every summer. Along the way, the troupe virtually invented a new art form, pioneering the construction of larger-than-life papier-mâché puppets of gods and goddesses and other

---

ALL WET?

Called dowsing or "water-witching," the practice of using a brass rod or Y-shaped twig to find metals, gems, or water buried in the ground, goes back to the Middle Ages. Those who still swear by the ancient art come together at the **American Society of Dowsers Headquarters and Bookstore** (184 Brainerd St., Danville, 802/684-3874, www.dowsers.org, 8:30 A.M.–5 P.M. Wed.–Fri.; 9 A.M.–4 P.M. Sat.), which has a full selection of books and divining rods for purchase. While you are there, walk the labyrinth, a magical maze purported to bring wholeness and healing to those who walk it (to say nothing of dizziness). Undaunted by countless scientific studies that have declared the art so much as bunk, a hundred-some dowsers come together each June to share stories and techniques at the **American Society of Dowsers Conference** (802/684-3417, www.dowsers.org).

figures that now regularly spice up the atmosphere at left-of-center political protests around the world.

The troupe still performs on its original farm stage in Glover throughout the summer, before taking performances on tour in the fall. On the grounds, the old barn has been transformed into a "museum" filled with 10-foot-tall characters from past plays, along with photographs and descriptions of the political context of the times. A smaller school bus has been converted into a "cheap art" museum, where you can buy original works for $5 or less—and even hang them in your kitchen.

Other Sights

Lyndonville is the self-dubbed "covered bridge capital of the Northeast Kingdom," having no less than five examples scattered around town. The **Miller's Run Bridge** on Route 114 was rebuilt in 1995 using the original 19th-century trusses. The 117-foot-long **Sanborn Bridge** uses the distinctive X-shaped Paddleford trusses. It was moved several years ago onto dry land behind the LynBurke Motel at the intersection of Routes 5 and 114.

Entertainment and Events

The renowned **Craftsbury Chamber Players** (800/639-3443, www.craftsburychamberplayers.org) perform classical music throughout the region in July and August.

Tractor pulls, pig races, and alpaca shearing all delight the masses at the **Caledonia County Fair** (802/626-5538, www.vtfair.com, late Aug.), which has taken place in Lyndonville for more than 150 years.

Shopping

Invented in 1899 for use on farm animals, the now-famous **Bag Balm** (91 Williams St., 800/232-3610, www.bagbalm.com) product is these days used by people—to soothe cuts, scratches, skin irritations, and abrasions. It's made right in Lyndonville at the Dairy Association Co., where you can swing by for a visit and pick up a canister for the winter.

Browsing is encouraged at **Green Mountain**

Books & Prints (1055 Broad St., 802/626-5051, 9 A.M.–5 P.M. Mon.–Sat.), a quiet shop stocked to its gills with used and rare books and old maps and prints. Need to gear up before hitting the slopes? Do it at **East Burke Sports** (Rte. 114, East Burke, 802/626-3215, www.eastburkesports.com). The shop sells whatever you need for cycling, skiing, hiking, camping, or snowboarding, and has a well-trained staff happy to help with the selection process.

Food

Tuck into wholesome dishes in the **River Garden Cafe** (Rte. 114, East Burke, 802/626-3514, www.rivergardencafe.com, 11:30 A.M.–2 P.M. and 5–9 P.M. Wed.–Sun.; 11 A.M.–2 P.M. Sun., $6–14 lunch, $18–25 dinner) and look out to the restaurant's lovingly tended gardens. Owners Bobby Baker and David Thomas started this relaxing spot in the early 1990s, and since then it's become locally loved for specials like pepper-crusted lamb loin, fried ravioli, and warm artichoke dip.

Housed in the Wildflower Inn, the casual, crimson-walled **Juniper's Restaurant** (2059 Darling Hill Rd., 800/627-8310, www.wildflowerinn.com, 5:30 P.M.–9 P.M. Mon.–Sat.; seasonal hours may vary, $9–24) uses all-natural ingredients (many from nearby farms and purveyors), including everything from hormone-free dairy products and free-range turkey to organic wines. There's a full roster of Vermont-brewed beers, too.

The conversation's as good as the eating and drinking at **Trout River Brewing Company** (Rte. 5, 1 mi. north of I-91, 802/626-9396, www.troutriverbrewing.com, 4–9 P.M.Fri.-Sat., $6–14). During the week, the microbrewery churns out ales and stouts, but on Friday and Saturday nights it opens its pub, where seemingly the entire town gathers to eat hand-tossed, gourmet pizzas, drink good ales, and gossip.

Information

Located on I-91 South, the State of Vermont's **Lyndonville Information Center** (802/626-9669, www.vacationvermont.org) has information on the entire Northeast Kingdom. The **Lyndon Area Chamber of Commerce** (802/626-9696, www.lyndonvermont.com) also runs an information booth on Memorial Drive in downtown Lyndonville. The **Burke Area Chamber of Commerce** (802/626-4124, www.burkevermont.com) runs an information kiosk at the corner of Route 5 and Route 5A. Wi-Fi is available at **Bailey's and Burke Country Store** (466 Rte. 114, East Burke, 802/626-9250).

BORDER COUNTRY

The farthest north corner of Vermont and arguably the most quiet, the towns of Derby, Newport, and Jay look more towards Montreal than to Boston or Burlington. Don't be surprised to hear French spoken in the streets, or even to see it on street signs. Truth be told, however, this area is far from *any* urban center. Not that there isn't plenty to do: Cyclists, hikers, and skiers alike find thrills galore on the trails of Jay Peak, windsurfers and swimmers swear by the serene waters of the bi-national Lake Memphremagog, and leaf-peepers come to, well, just kick back and watch everything turn gold.

Haskell Free Library & Opera House

You can find a book in Vermont and check it out in Quebec at this Victorian library and performance center (93 Caswell Ave., Derby Line, 802/873-3022, www.haskellopera.org, 10 A.M.–5 P.M. Tues.–Wed.; 10 A.M.–8 P.M. Thurs.; 10 A.M.–5 P.M. Fri.–Sat., $2 suggested donation), the only cultural institution in the world that sits astride an international border. (Look for the thin, black line that runs down the middle of the reading room, separating the United States from Canada.) Built in 1901 for use by citizens of both countries, the building was gut-rehabbed a few years ago to revive musical performances in the Opera House upstairs. The turreted neoclassical building is unique in having a first floor of granite capped with a second story of yellow brick.

Other Sights

Literally constructed of heavy stone granite blocks, the **Old Stone House Museum** (109 Old Stone House Rd., Brownington, 802/754-2022, www.oldstonehousemuseum.org, 11 A.M.–5 P.M. Wed.–Sun. mid-May–mid-Oct., $5 adults, $2 students) once served as a boys' dormitory and school. It now houses the collection of the Orleans Historical Society, including Victorian-era furniture and cooking implements and some of the original schoolbooks from the academy library. Behind the museum is a wooden observation platform on Prospect Hill that commands the surrounding farm country.

Once native to Vermont, the mighty American elk was extinct for decades before it was reintroduced at the **Cowtown Elk Ranch** (Main St., Derby, 802/766-4724, www.derbycowpalace.com), in 1992. The herd of more than 350 animals is cultivated for big-game hunting in a preserve down the road in Irasburg. During daylight hours, the elk are available for viewing in the pasture; best time to see them is in the late afternoon when they are brought into the front pasture for feeding. Speaking of which, the ranch also serves lean venison steaks at its adjoining restaurant, the **Cow Palace** (11 A.M.–5 P.M. Tues.–Sun.). The little town of Montgomery has no fewer than seven covered bridges, all built with the same design between 1863 and 1890 by brothers Sheldon and Savannah Jewett. The Inn on Trout River has a map with the locations of all the bridges, and will even share some "covered bridgepoetry" if asked.

Entertainment and Events

The **Haskell Opera House** (802/873-3022, www.haskellopera.org) presents old-time entertainment, including fiddlers, blues, and classical concerts.

A "grand cavalcade" of livestock and farm machinery kicks off the annual **Orleans County Fair** (Barton, 802/525-1137, www.orleanscountyfair.org, mid-Aug.), which features a demolition derby and country music performances among its attractions.

Shopping

Picture the quintessential country store, and you've got **Derby Village Store** (483 Main St., Derby, 802/766-2215), a hodgepodge of natural foods and gourmet provisions (including locally made yogurts and butters). An even bigger selection lies at **Trout River Traders** (91 Main St., Montgomery, 802/326-3058, www.troutrivertraders.com), which is part store, part café (with wireless Internet access, comfy chairs, and a vintage soda fountain). Close to Jay Peak, it's a natural stop for a bite (fresh-roasted turkey sandwiches and chili—or brunch on Sunday). Or simply run in for souvenirs—various antiques, local art and photography, candles, and pottery.

Food

Simple Italian-inspired dishes using locally grown ingredients are the mainstay at **Lake Salem Inn** (1273 Rte. 105, Derby, 802/766-5560, www.lakesaleminn.com, 5–9 P.M. daily, $25–35). The farm-raised venison, vegetarian specials, and desserts are particularly popular options. There's plenty more pasta where that came from at **Lago Trattoria** (95 Main St., Newport, 802/334-8222, www.lagotrattoria.com, 5–9 P.M. daily, $9–19), which serves carb-centric Italian specials (with several meat dishes thrown in for good measure) in a casual dining room. It may look like your average red barn from the outside, but inside, **The Belfry Restaurant and Pub** (Rte. 242, Montgomery, 802/326-4400, $7–13) is more like a town meeting hall. The joint teems with families and pasta dishes on Italian night every Wednesday, and with the scent of fresh cod at the fish fries that take place every Friday.

Information

The **Jay Peak Area Association** (802/988-2259, www.jaypeakvermont.org) staffs an information center in Jay.

SPORTS AND RECREATION
Kingdom Trails Network

Biking in the country doesn't get any better than this 100-plus-mile network (Kingdom Trail Association, P.O. Box 204, East Burke, 802/626-0737, www.kingdomtrails.org) of old carriage paths, railroad right-of-ways, and forest trails that have been stitched together for two-wheeled pleasure. There may be no better way to really gain an appreciation for the size and beauty of the Northeast Kingdom. The Trails have something for every difficulty, from the precipitous Freeride Trail that carves its way down the side of Burke Mountain to the gentler curves of Darling Hill, where you'll have plenty of farmhouses and cows for company. The best part: no cars in sight. The trails leave from the village area in East Burke, just behind Burke General Store.

Hiking

The **Hazen's Notch Association** (Montgomery Center, 802/326-4799, www.hazensnotch.org) maintains 15 miles of hiking trails in forested conservation land. High Ponds Farm is a restored organic farm at the base of Burnt Mountain with walking trails among the orchards and woodland speckled with beaver ponds. More rigorous trails lead up to the summit of Burnt Mountain, a 3,100-foot peak with views of the notch below. All of these trails leave from the High Ponds Farm parking area, some two miles east of Montgomery Center. Directions and a trail map are available on the association's website.

Swimming and Boating

Split between Canada and the United States, **Lake Memphremagog** is more than just a mouthful—it also has a nice sandy beach for swimming (though be careful not to disturb Memphre, a sea serpent who reputedly lives in the lake). The lake is also a good place for an afternoon of flatwater canoeing. **Up the Creek Paddle Sports** (802/334-7350) leads tours of the lake's bays and inlets.

Skiing

Situated almost on the border with Canada, **Jay Peak Resort** (4850 Rte. 242, Jay, 802/988-2611, www.jaypeakresort.com, $65 adults, $21 seniors, $45 youth 6–18, $10 children 5 and

VERMONT

COURTESY OF JAY PEAK

powder skiing on Jay Peak

under) is known for two things: lots of snow and no crowds. The mountain gets hands-down more natural snow than any other peak in the Northeast—yet it takes a determined skier to drive the five hours up from Boston to take advantage of it (especially when there are so many other enticing mountains along the way). Skiers who make the trek are rewarded with 60 runs of mixed difficulty spread out on two peaks. Unique among area mountains, Jay also offers wide swaths of backcountry glade skiing, leaving skiers the freedom to carve their own paths among the trees.

A favorite among cross-country skiers in New England, the **Craftsbury Nordic Center** (535 Lost Nation Rd., Craftsbury Common, 802/586-7767, www.craftsbury.com) spans more than 300 acres of quiet farmland, lakes, and village centers with groomed cross-country trails. Centered on Craftsbury Common, the outdoor center offers rentals ($15 adults, $10 students and seniors) as well as day passes ($10 adults, $5 students and seniors, free children under 7) for use of the trails.

Camping

In the remote eastern section of the Kingdom, **Brighton State Park** (102 State Park Rd., Island Pond, 802/723-4360) has 5 cabins, 23 lean-tos and some 60 tent sites tucked into a stand of white birch on the pristine shores of Spectacle Pond. It's not uncommon to see moose on the park's nature trails. Just a short walk from the campground, campers have use of a sandy beach with boat rentals, play area, and a small nature museum.

ACCOMMODATIONS
Under $100

A newly opened B&B in the heart of St. Johnsbury, **Eastabrook House** (1596 Main St., St Johnsbury, 802/751-8261, www.eastabrookhouse.com, $90–105) is an 1896 Victorian home that has been lovingly renovated by a Massachusetts transplant who moved to St. J after falling in love with the area more than a decade ago. Listed on the National Register of Historic Places, the home features four individually decorated rooms crawling with antiques, and a shared bathroom with a claw-foot soaker tub. The parkside location is almost as attractive as the reasonable price tag.

$100-150

The 10 individually decorated rooms at the **Craftsbury Inn** (107 S. Craftsbury Rd., Craftsbury, 802/586-2848, www.craftsbury-inn.com, $60–130) are all in keeping with the style of the rest of the mid-19th-century Greek Revival mansion. Each sports quilts and goose-down comforters and period antiques. There's also a small pub, a refined but cozy French restaurant, and a wool shop on the premise.

Open year-round, **Labour of Love** (9 Sargent Ln., Glover, 802/525-6695, $99–110) offers one of the state's more unusual "farm-stays" with a few rooms in a restored 1800s Greek Revival farmhouse with an adjoining flower nursery. Its surrounding display gardens of local and exotic perennials are spectacular, while guestrooms are filled with antiques and botanical garden–sized tropical plants selected by cheerful proprietrix Kate Butler. As a bonus,

VERMONT

all of the plants on display are available for sale from bulb or seed.

$150-250

Simple decor marks the guest rooms at **Jay Village Inn** (1078 Rte. 242, Jay, 802/988-2306, www.stayatjay.com, $75–199). Visitors sleep easy under the colorful quilts, in sleigh or canopied beds. Rooms at **Inn at Mountain View Farm** (Darling Hill Rd., 802/626-9924, East Burke, www.innmtnview.com, $175–275) run from doubles to luxury suites, but all have an air of elegance about them. Filled with armoires, antique poster beds, floral wallpaper, and tasteful down comforters, they're a cosseting place to rest after a day on the slopes. Rates include country breakfast and afternoon tea.

$250 and Up

Lavishly decorated and tranquil to its core, **⟨ Rabbit Hill Inn** (48 Lower Waterford Rd., Lower Waterford, 802/748-5168, www.rabbithillinn.com, $199–359) fills rooms with such amenities as fluffy robes, private porches, and fireplaces, just for starters. But you may be tempted to leave your room once you hear about the perks in the rest of the property—afternoon tea and pastries, apple cheddar crepes at breakfast, and candlelight dinners prepared by Matthew Secich.

GETTING THERE AND AROUND

The remoteness of the Northeast Kingdom virtually demands you bring your own transportation. To drive to St. Johnsbury from the south, take I-93 north (100 mi., 2 hrs.) from Concord, New Hampshire, or I-91 north (60 mi., 1 hr.) from White River Junction. From Montpelier, you are better off leaving the interstate highways and cutting across the Kingdom on U.S. Route 2 to Cabot (20 mi., 40 min.) and St. Johnsbury (35 mi., 1 hr.). From St. Johnsbury, much of the rest of the Kingdom is accessible from I-91. For Lyndonville, take exit 23 (8 mi., 10 min.), for Glover, exit 25 (30 mi., 30 min.), for Newport, exit 27 (45 mi., 40 min.), and for Derby Line, exit 29 (50 mi., 1 hr.). To travel to Jay, take I-89 to exit 26, then north along U.S. Route 5, and state routes 14, 100, 101, and 242 (55 mi., 1 hr. 10 min.) from St. Johnsbury. From Central Vermont, Jay is also accessible along Route 100 north (40 mi., 1 hr. 15 min.) from Stowe.

If you need to rely on public transportation, **Rural Community Transportation** (802/748-8170, www.riderct.org) runs limited shuttle bus service on two routes, one between St. Johnsbury and Lyndonville (leaving from the Vermont Welcome Center) and the other between Newport and Derby Line.

NEW HAMPSHIRE

SOUTH AND SEACOAST

Many vacationers to New Hampshire race past the southern part of the state on their way to the lakes and the mountains farther north. But the southern hills and the valleys of the Piscataqua, Merrimack, and Contoocook Rivers are where the state was first settled, where most of the population still resides, and where its cultural heart still beats. What's that—New Hampshire, culture? You bet. The state might have a reputation for rugged individualism, but it also has a softer side, apparent in dozens of art and cultural museums big and small that dot this part of the state.

This is where New Hampshire concentrates its population in cities that once made their fortunes on shipbuilding and mills, and at least one—Portsmouth—is on the short list of the best in New England for travelers, offering a tantalizing mix of cultural attractions and history. Even outside the cities, this area proudly holds onto its past, with dozens of historic homes and buildings that date back to the earliest days of the country. And because New Hampshire has avoided the sprawl of states to the south, many of them are preserved in frozen-in-time villages that epitomize the best of small-town New England.

PLANNING YOUR TIME

Southern New Hampshire is comprised of several distinct regions, and traveling between them isn't always easy. You're best off concentrating on one part of the area depending on your interests. The delightful city of Portsmouth has more than enough attractions to occupy a serious history buff for several days,

© NHDTTD/DAVE SHAFER

HIGHLIGHTS

◖ **Strawbery Banke:** One of the oldest neighborhoods in New England is also one of its earliest examples of historic preservation (page 431).

◖ **Isles of Shoals:** The mist-enshrouded islands off Portsmouth Harbor keep the secrets of a notorious murder (page 433).

◖ **Hampton Beach:** Find honky-tonk heaven on New Hampshire's spot of seashore (page 436).

◖ **Frost Farm:** The first farm owned by Robert Frost was the inspiration for some of his very best-known poems (page 442).

◖ **Canterbury Shaker Village:** One of the most fascinating religious subcultures in America is known for its unparalleled degree of craftsmanship (page 447).

◖ **Mount Monadnock:** New England's favorite day hike is literally miles away from the rest (page 450).

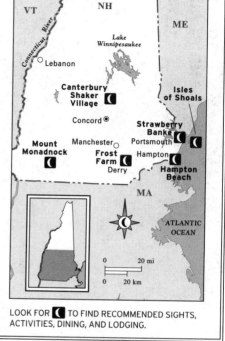

LOOK FOR ◖ TO FIND RECOMMENDED SIGHTS, ACTIVITIES, DINING, AND LODGING.

including the preserved urban colonial neighborhood of **Strawbery Banke** and a boat-trip to the beguiling **Isles of Shoals.** In the summertime, no trip to the area is complete without taking in the cocoa butter and fried dough of **Hampton Beach,** one of New England's most popular family destinations.

The Merrimack Valley, by contrast, is gritty and industrial, cut through by I-93 on its way northward. For those willing to take the time, however, the valley holds several first-rate cultural attractions that will well reward a day or three spent in the region. Among them are Robert Frost's former homestead of **Frost Farm,** probably the best site dedicated to the poet in New England; the New England–centric collections at the Currier Museum of Art in Manchester; and the fascinating former religious retreat of **Canterbury Shaker Village** outside Concord. If it's the outdoors you are looking for, however, head to the southwest corner of the state, where **Mount Monadnock** beckons with what may be the world's most perfect day hike. Base yourself at the mountain, but linger in the area for another day or two to drive around the rural environs of Hillsborough and Peterborough, New Hampshire's most charming region for its many covered bridges and small-town artisans.

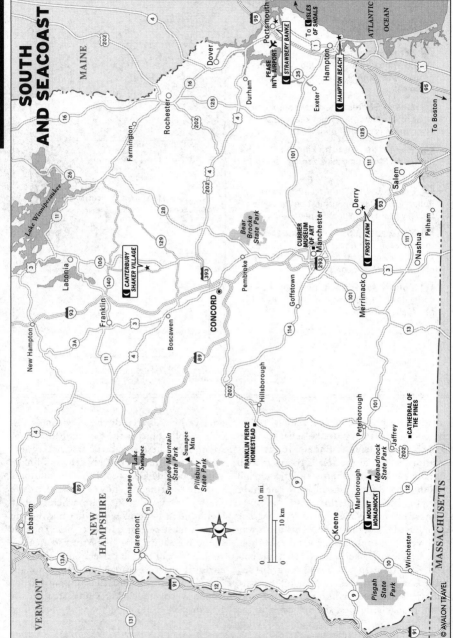

The Seacoast

New Hampshire has only a slim sliver of coastline compared to most New England states. But it makes the most of it, with an almost unbroken string of beaches leading up to the thriving city of Portsmouth. With history going back almost as far as the Pilgrims, this area has for centuries made its living on shipping and industry. After that slowed in the 20th century, the Portsmouth area reinvented itself as a knowledge center—wooing dot-com and computer companies and dubbing itself the "e-Coast." After the dot-com bust, many tech workers have remained in the city, giving it a young, artsy vibe.

Outside of the city itself, the beaches around Hampton have long been a family vacationland of cotton candy and arcades by the seashore; farther inland, the city of Exeter is one of the oldest in the state, and is known for its large number of historic buildings and its prestigious prep school.

PORTSMOUTH

Few cities in New England are more pleasant to visit than Portsmouth, New Hampshire's maritime center at the mouth of the Piscataqua River. The downtown area is a giant playground of old brick warehouses reinvented as trendy boutiques and artsy cafés that cater to a youthful crowd. Just as much a draw, however, is the city's history, which is as rich as any in New England.

Portsmouth was home to a settlement named Strawbery Banke, which was settled in 1630, just a decade after the pilgrims landed in Plymouth, and the same year the Puritans landed in Boston. Unlike those groups, however, the settlers were on a commercial, not religious, mission: to exploit the natural resources of the New World. Unfortunately they failed in their mission, going bankrupt just eight years later, and Strawbery Banke became part of Massachusetts Bay Colony.

Under the guidance of the Puritans, Portsmouth grew into an important trading

charming Portsmouth

© MICHAEL BLANDING

port, rivaling Boston and Salem in the early days of the country. In 1800, the creation of the Portsmouth Navy Yard established it as a shipbuilding center as well, churning out military vessels as well as the sleek clipper ships that were the Maseratis of their day (one Portsmouth clipper made the Liverpool run in just 13 days, an unheard of feat at the time). As the 20th century dawned, however, Portsmouth was caught flat-footed when fortunes shifted from sea trade to the industrial might of the textile mills, and began to decline in importance.

What turned Portsmouth around wasn't industry, but tourism. Bucking the prominent trend of "urban renewal" in the 1950s, Portsmouth decided not to demolish its many remaining colonial homes, but restore them. Over the next few decades, it established the colonial village of Strawbery Banke way ahead of a trend toward historic preservation in other

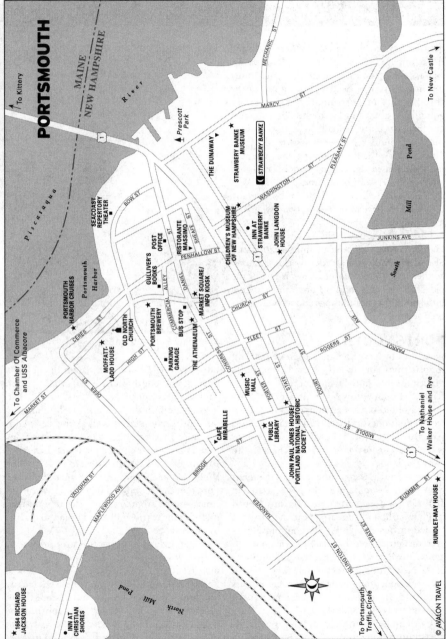

PORTSMOUTH

MAINE
NEW HAMPSHIRE

To Kittery

Piscataqua

River

Prescott Park

THE DUNAWAY

STRAWBERY BANKE MUSEUM

STRAWBERY BANKE

To New Castle

MECHANIC ST

MARCY ST

MARCY ST

SEACOAST REPERTORY THEATER

BOW ST

PORTSMOUTH HARBOR CRUISES

Portsmouth Harbor

POST OFFICE

GULLIVER'S BOOKS

RISTORANTE MASSIMO

PENHALLOW ST

SHEAFE ST

CHILDREN'S MUSEUM OF NEW HAMPSHIRE

INN AT STRAWBERRY BANKE

JOHN LANGDON HOUSE

WASHINGTON ST

PLEASANT ST

JUNKINS AVE

South

Mill Pond

CERES ST

PORTSMOUTH BREWERY

COMMERCIAL ALLEY

DANIEL ST

MARKET SQUARE/ INFO KIOSK

BUS STOP

CHURCH ST

CONGRESS ST

OLD NORTH CHURCH

HIGH ST

FLEET ST

PENHALLOW ST

STATE ST

ROGERS ST

PARROT AVE

MOFFATT-LADD HOUSE

PARKING GARAGE

THE ATHENAEUM

MUSIC HALL

PORTER ST

COURT ST

To Chamber Of Commerce and USS *Albacore*

MARKET ST

DEER ST

CAFÉ MIRABELLE

PUBLIC LIBRARY

JOHN PAUL JONES HOUSE/ PORTLAND NATIONAL HISTORIC SOCIETY

MIDDLE ST

To Nathaniel Walker House and Rye

VAUGHAN ST

MAPLEWOOD AVE

BRIDGE ST

HANOVER ST

STATE ST

SUMMER ST

ISINGTON ST

RUNDLET-MAY HOUSE

1664 RICHARD JACKSON HOUSE

INN AT CHRISTIAN SHORES

North Mill Pond

To Portsmouth Traffic Circle

© AVALON TRAVEL

PORTSMOUTH PEACE TREATY TRAIL

Portsmouth's modern claim to fame, as you'll learn if you spend more than five minutes in the city, is its role in the signing of the peace treaty that ended the bloody Russo-Japanese war between Russia and Japan. The way the city promotes the event, you'd think that it happened in 2005, not 1905. But the treaty-signing is a fascinating look into international diplomacy, and worth taking an afternoon to explore. In addition to ending the first war fought with modern weapons like machine guns and armored battleships, the treaty is also the first example of modern multi-party diplomacy. Russian and Japanese delegates stayed in Portsmouth for several months as city fathers pulled out all the stops to entertain them with social events, keeping them busy even after formal negotiations broke down. Meanwhile, back-channel negotiations all over the city helped bring about peace, which was formally signed on September 5, 1905. The event was so significant that President Theodore Roosevelt earned the Nobel Peace Prize for the effort. Today, dozens of sites around the city celebrate their role in the signing. The John Paul Jones House has a good overview exhibit with historic memorabilia from the delegates' time in Portsmouth. There, you can pick up a self-guided tour map to see the major sites along the tour (also available from the website of the **Portsmouth Peace Treaty Trail** (603/436-1118, www.portsmouthpeacetreaty.org). During summer, the **Greater Portsmouth Chamber of Commerce** (603/610-5510, www.portsmouth-chamber.org) also offers guided walking tours of the major sites upon request($10 adults, $8 students and seniors, $5 children 5-14, free children under 8).

parts of the country, and put itself on the map as a living-history museum. Now the colonial infrastructure of the city and the colorful energy of its hip population meld seamlessly to make it like nowhere else in New Hampshire. Indeed, many residents south of the border declare Portsmouth to be an unofficial part of Massachusetts. But that's just jealousy talking; Granite Staters proudly embrace the city as its cherished cultural jewel.

◀ Strawbery Banke

There are many historical re-creation villages around the United States, but this cluster of historic homes (14 Hancock St., 603/433-1100, www.strawberybanke.org, 10 A.M.–5 P.M. daily May–Oct., $15 adults, $10 children 5–17, free children under 4) from the 17th, 18th, and 19th centuries is the only one embedded inside a major city. By the time the city decided to preserve the neighborhood, there were more than 40 historic homes still standing. They are now arranged in a fenced-off city block honeycombed with streets and alleys around a waterway known as Puddle Dock. Part of the pleasure of visiting is the self-guided aspect

of the museum; in the summer you're invited to wander around, poke into houses, talk to costumed interpreters, and generally just explore colonial history for yourself. Don't be shy about talking with the "inhabitants" of the homes, who are happy to demonstrate how they cooked, cleaned, and performed other daily tasks.

Among the museum's many highlights is the Wheelwright House, home to an 18th-century ship captain active in the East Indies trade. His simple Georgian home is filled with furniture and ceramics from the period. Another must-see is the Daniel Webster House, which includes exhibits from the time that the great 19th-century statesmen spent in Portsmouth in the early part of his career. Another home is dedicated to Thomas Bailey Aldrich, the founder of the *Atlantic Monthly;* after his death, the home was purchased by friends and turned into a memorial. And if you are interested in seeing the actual items unearthed in the restoration of all of the homes in the museum, stop by the Jones Center, which displays the take from archaeological work on the neighborhood.

downtown Portsmouth

© NHDTTD/DAVE SHAFER

Portsmouth Harbor Trail

Strawbery Banke is just the beginning of historic properties on view in the city; if house museums are your thing, you could easily spend a week marveling at the variety and quality of those preserved here. The **Greater Portsmouth Chamber of Commerce** (500 Market St., 603/436-3988, www.portsmouthchamber.org) has made it easy by creating an informative walking tour arranged in three easy loops leaving from Market Square downtown. Guides to the route can be purchased from the information booth in the square for $3.

Several of the buildings on the tour route offer guided tours of their interiors. **The Athenaeum** (9 Market Sq., 603/431-2538, www.portsmouthathenaeum.org, 1–4 P.M. Tues., Thurs., and Sat., free) has housed a private library since 1823, making it one of the oldest in the country. It inhabits a beautiful Federal-style building right on the square. The **Moffat-Ladd House** (154 Market St., 603/436-8221, www.moffattladd.org, 11 A.M.–5 P.M. Mon.–Sat. and 1–5 P.M. Sun. mid-June–mid-Oct., $6 adults, $2.50 children) was home to a wealthy merchant in colonial times, and is filled with 150 years of artifacts owned by him and his descendants.

The elaborate **Governor John Langdon House and Garden** (143 Pleasant St., 603/436-3205, www.historicnewengland.org, 11 A.M.–4 P.M. Fri.–Sun. June–mid-Oct., $6) was owned by a signer of the Constitution and three-term governor of New Hampshire. Now maintained by Historic New England, it has been transformed into a museum exploring the lives of wealthy Portsmouth merchants. Historic New England also manages the oldest home in New Hampshire, the 1664 **Richard Jackson House** (76 Northwest St., 603/436-3205, www.historicnewengland.org, 11 A.M.–4 P.M. first Sat. of the month June–Oct., $5), a simple plank-frame building that stands in marked contrast to its more ostentatious neighbors.

If you only have time to visit one historic house in the city, however, make it the **John Paul Jones House** (43 Middle St., 603/436-8420, www.portsmouthhistory.org, 11 A.M.–5 P.M. daily June–mid-Oct., $6 adults, free children 12 and under), the 1758 Georgian home where the famous Revolutionary-era privateer John Paul Jones boarded during his time in the city while he waited for his ship of battle to be completed. In addition to exhibits about the famous seaman, the home is headquarters for the Portsmouth Historical Society, and includes exhibits and artifacts relating to the entire history of the city.

◖ Isles of Shoals

The nine rocky islands scattered just off of Portsmouth Harbor have long fascinated and beguiled residents. In fact, they were used for fishing grounds by European explorers for years before the Pilgrims landed in 1620. The name "shoals" doesn't refer to shallow water, but the "schools" of fish that would congregate here around upwellings of nutrients from the islands' unusually deep waters. Over the years the islands were home to a thriving community of fishermen and merchants. They achieved wider fame, however, when two grand hotels were built on Star and Appledore Islands to receive the rich and powerful of Boston society. The daughter of one of the hotel owners, poetess Celia Thaxter, added to the islands' allure with a bestselling 1873 book called *Among the Isles of Shoals,* which was filled with tales of ghosts, shipwrecks, and legends of Blackbeard's buried treasure.

Not that she had to make much up—the islands' most famous incident came that same year, in 1873, when two sisters were brutally murdered by an axe-wielding itinerant fisherman on the island of Smuttynose. A third woman managed to elude the killer and bring him to justice, but the story continues to haunt the area, with the most recent adaptation being Anita Shreve's novel *The Weight of Water,* later made into a film with Sean Penn and Elizabeth Hurley.

Tours of the islands with the **Isles of Shoals Steamship Company** (315 Market St., Portsmouth, 603/431-5500 or 800/441-4620, www.islesofshoals.com, 8 A.M.–7 P.M. mid-June–Labor Day; 9 A.M.–4 P.M. fall and spring; 10 A.M.–2 P.M. winter, several tours daily, prices vary) take advantage of all of the mist-enshrouded legends in guided cruises laden with history and lore. Perhaps just as satisfying, however, is to explore the islands yourself, taking a ferry with **Island Cruises** (Rye Harbor State Marina, Rte. 1A, Rye, 603/964-6446, www.uncleoscar.com) to Star Island to visit the grand Star Hotel and hike the surf-sprayed trails and ledges. That company also offers tours of the island that are a bit more

Candy apples are a local treat.

© NHDTTD/TARA LENHARTH

intimate than the Steamship Company, which fosters a reputation as a "party boat."

Other Sights

A precursor to modern nuclear submarines, the **USS *Albacore*** (600 Market St., 603/436-3680, www.ussalbacore.org, 9:30 A.M.–5 P.M. daily late May–mid-Oct.; 9:30 A.M.–4:30 P.M. Mon.–Thurs. Columbus Day–Memorial Day, $5 adults, $3 children 7–17, free children under 7, $4 military, $10 family) looks like a beached whale at its site on dry land on the outskirts of downtown. Inside the sub, a museum tells the story of the ship's construction at Portsmouth Navy Yard, as well as tales of other submarines in the nuclear sub fleet. North of Portsmouth, in the historic town of Dover, the **Woodman Institute Museum** (182 Central Ave., Dover, 603/742-1038, www.seacoastnh.com/woodman, 12:30 P.M.–4:30 P.M. Wed.–Sun.; Sat.–Sun. only Dec.–Jan.; closed Feb.–Mar., $5 adults, $4 students and seniors, $2 teens 14–16, free children under 13) is a little-known natural-history museum in the Victorian style, located in a historic brick mansion. Inside is a fascinating hodgepodge of rocks and minerals, taxidermed animals, and military artifacts. Among the items on display is a Civil War cannon and a saddle President Lincoln rode on soon before he was to be assassinated.

After filling their heads with knowledge, let the kids blow off steam at the **Children's Museum of New Hampshire** (6 Washington St., Dover, 603/742-2002, www.childrensmuseum.org, 10 A.M.–5 P.M. Tues.–Sat., noon–5 P.M. Sun. June–March; 10 A.M.–5 P.M. Wed.–Sat., noon–5 P.M. Sun. April–May, $8 adults and children, $7 seniors, free children under 1), also located in Dover, which includes interactive exhibits on dinosaurs, submarines, and musical instruments calculated to thrill those under four feet tall.

Entertainment

Despite the name, it isn't all just music at **The Music Hall** (28 Chestnut St., 603/436-2400, www.themusichall.org). The velvet-curtained 900-seat historic theater screens movies, kids' shows, and comedy performances. And yes, music too—jazz trios and vocal gigs to blues singers. Catch theater performances—musical and otherwise—by the **Seacoast Repertory Theater** (125 Bow St., 603/433-4472, www.seacoastrep.org) in the brewery turned performance center that is Bow Street Theatre. Come summertime, the company puts on a music series. With plenty of space—and still plenty more beer—**Portsmouth Brewery** (56 Market St., 603/431-1115, www.portsmouthbrewery.com) is an easy place to relax. Claiming to be New Hampshire's original brewpub, the place churns out award-winning brewed-on-the-premises lagers and ales. In good weather there's al fresco seating, and a lounge downstairs. Grab a game of pool with your pint at the noisy, fun **Legends Billiards & Tavern** (80 Hanover St., 603/433-1154). It also stages live music shows on weekends.

Events

On the first Friday of every month, the local art association sponsors a **Gallery Walk** (603/431-4230, www.artaroundtown.org), in which galleries around downtown break out wine and cheese for simultaneous openings. Portsmouth's annual summer celebration is **Market Square Day** (603/433-4398, www.proportsmouth.org, June), which features food and fun downtown and a 10K Road Race through the city. Additionally, Strawbery Banke sponsors several different theme weekends throughout the year, including a summer Maritime Weekend, Halloween ghost tours, and the popular **Candlelight Stroll** (603/433-1100, www.strawberybanke.org, Dec.) in which the streets of the museum are filled with hundreds of lit candles, and interpreters lead visitors in traditional holiday festivities.

Shopping

Kitchen accessories from the world over reside on shelves at **Attrezzi** (78 Market St., 603/427-1667, www.attrezzinh.com, 10 A.M.–5:30 P.M. Mon.–Sat.; 11:30 A.M.–5 P.M. Sun.)—meaning both the inedible (French pottery, Irish linens, and delicate tableware) and edible (excellent specialty foods and cheeses). The shop shows off its wine collection with regular in-store tastings. Bespoke men's suits, tailored pants, and casual-but-elegant shirts fill **Cavanaugh & Company** (57 Bow St., 603/430-3722, 10 A.M.–6 P.M. Mon.–Thurs., 10 A.M.–7 P.M. Fri.–Sat.; 11 A.M.–5 P.M. Sun.); the meticulously kept shop feels remarkably like a European men's shop, and has the high-quality duds to match. Stylish-to-its-core **Nahcotta** (110 Congress St., 603/433-1705, www.nahcotta.com, 10 A.M.–6 P.M. Mon.–Thu.; 10 A.M.–7 P.M. Fri. and Sat.; 11 A.M.–5 P.M. Sun.), a home and gift shop, operates with a gallery-like ethos: Showcase your best pieces as you would great pieces of art. To that end, you'll find glass lamps by Simon Pearce, luxurious shag rugs, downright adorable tea sets, and yes, original artwork too. There's more where that came from at **Worldly Goods** (37 Congress St., 603/436-9311, www.worldlygoodsnh.com, 10 A.M.–6 P.M. Mon.–Sat.; 11 A.M.–5 P.M. Sun.), an impressive collection of hand-crafted works by more than 200 artists. Think funky stained-glass-fish drink coasters, bowls carved from recovered timber, and contemporary glazed dishes.

Food

Thanks to the culinary handiwork of chef Mary Dumont, ◖ **The Dunaway** (66 Marcy St., 603/373-6112, www.dunawayrestaurant.com, 11:30 a.m.–2:30 p.m. and 5:30–9:30 p.m. Tue.–Sat., $22–30) has become one of the state's premiere dining destinations. Tucked in on the banks of the Piscataqua River, within the Strawbery Banke historical district, the dining room full of exposed beams and candlelight is a showcase for Dumont's superb regionally sourced cuisine. You'll be torn between specialties like grilled rib eye and tartar with orange and tarragon, stunningly rich plates of artisanal cheeses, and foie gras with pistachio and grapes.

If you've got Italian on the brain, look no further than **Ristorante Massimo** (59 Penhallow St., 603/436-4000, www.ristorantemassimo.com, 5 a.m.–2:30 p.m. and 5:30–9:30 p.m. Tue.–Sat., $21–33). There, authentic, rich dishes (such as the *tagliatelle* pasta with crispy prosciutto, peas, and shaved black truffles) are marched out to tables in the elegant stone-walled dining room. All March through November, dine on the decks of **BG's Boat House** (191 Wentworth Rd., 603/431-1074, 11 a.m.–10 p.m. Mar.–Nov.; closed Tues.–Wed. Mar.–mid-May and early Sept.–Nov., $13–23), a laid-back marina eatery on Portsmouth's Sagamore Creek. The kitchen cooks up simple but first-rate seafood: boiled lobster, fried clams and scallops, stuffed haddock, and broiled shrimp. The Paris-born chef and owner of ◖ **Café Mirabelle** (64 Bridge St., 603/430-9301, www.cafemirabelle.com, 5:15–10 p.m. Wed.–Sun., $19–28) takes the stuffiness out of French fare with a relaxed but creative menu of specials like salmon in shallot-champagne sauce or duck with mushrooms and sun-dried tomatoes—all served in an unpretentious bistro.

Information

For more information on the city, contact the **Greater Portsmouth Chamber of Commerce** (500 Market St., 603/436-1118, www.portsmouthchamber.org), which runs an information booth on the main corner of Market Square. Another good resource is **SeacoastNH.com** (www.seacoastnh.com), an exhaustive guide written and updated by prolific local author J. Dennis Robinson, who has written several books and more than 1,000 articles about the area.

The area's biggest hospital is **Portsmouth Regional Hospital** (333 Borthwick Ave., #100, Portsmouth, 603/436-5110, www.portsmouthhospital.com). Fill prescriptions at **CVS** (674 Islington St., Portsmouth, 603/431-0234) and **Rite Aid Pharmacy** (800 Islington Rd., 603/436-2214, 1500 Lafayette Rd., Portsmouth, 603/430-7595 and 1303 Woodbury Ave., 603/431-1580).

In keeping with its reputation as a plugged-in city, Portsmouth offers free Wi-Fi Internet access throughout the downtown Market Square area.

HAMPTON AND VICINITY

New Hampshire's most popular (and virtually only) beachfront community has infused generations of New Englanders with loving memories of cotton candy and fried clams, penny arcade games, and sunburns on the sand. Sure it's cheesy—but that's part of its allure. There's virtually no end to the people-watching on a 90-degree August day, and no end to the crowds either.

If you prefer a more picturesque seaside experience, the little town of Rye is your ticket. In fact, Rye more closely resembles the Hamptons of Long Island, with seaside mansions and inns facing the waves and a picturesque downtown that is one of the oldest in New Hampshire. An excellent state park offers a quieter beach.

On the other side of Hampton, Seabrook has the dubious distinction of being home to a nuclear power plant that spurred widespread opposition by the Clamshell Alliance, starting the No Nukes movement in the 1980s. The plant is still open (and open for tours), but the protest led to a nuclear freeze on future plants in the United States. If you mention the name, be prepared for controversy, as the nuclear issue is still a divisive one for many in the area.

◖ Hampton Beach

The first hotels opened in Hampton in the middle of the 19th century, but the place didn't really get hopping until the end of the century, when a trolley and casino opened up to lure new generations of vacationers. Since then, it's been a nonstop slide to honky-tonk heaven, with loads of sticky seafood shacks and tacky souvenir shops lining the main boardwalk. Hampton Beach is actually Hampton Beaches, with several separate stretches along the several miles of oceanfront. What people usually mean by the term, however, is the main beach along Route 1A, also known as The Strip. In the heart of the madness sits the **Hampton Seashell** (Rte. 1A, 603/926-8717, www.hamptonbeach.org), an open-air amphitheater that plays host to annual events such as the Miss Hampton Pageant and Hampton Idol competition and also has restrooms and first aid for beachgoers.

Across from the bandstand is the **Hampton Beach Casino Ballroom** (169 Ocean Blvd., 603/929-4100, www.casinoballroom.com), a historic building that was opened by a Boston businessman in 1899 in an effort to draw more tourists to the area, and continues to draw pop and rock performers for summer concerts. (The building does not, nor did it ever, contain a gambling casino. At the time it was built, the word was an exotic Italian sobriquet for a "social gathering place.") In both directions along the strip, the arcades and souvenir shops beckon with dubious charms. Despite its somewhat seedy appearance, the area is actually quite safe, with parents routinely dropping off their children for hours with a pocketful of quarters while they relax on the beach.

The Seacoast Science Center

Located on the quiet shores of Rye, this nature center (570 Ocean Blvd., Rye, 603/436-8043, www.seacoastsciencecenter.org, 10 A.M.–5 P.M., Sat.–Mon and school vacation days only, Nov.–Mar., $5 adults, $2 children 3–12, free children under 3) emphasizes hands-on learning, with an indoor tide pool filled with crabs, starfish, and other sealife, as well as guided trips

fun on a New Hampshire beach

to explore the tidal pools in the surrounding coastline. Maritime history exhibits also explore the laying of the transatlantic cable not far from here, and the disruption of this part of the coast during World War II, when government promptly evicted wealthy landowners to set up a network of bunkers and defenses to protect the coast from German U-Boats.

That property, known as Fort Dearborn, was closed after only 20 years, and sold to the state to create the 330-acre **Odiorne State Park** (Rte. 1A, Rye, 603/436-7406, www.nhstateparks.com/odiorne.html, year-round, $3, free children 12 and under), a truly special seaside preserve with a variety of environments. On several miles of hiking and biking trails, you can pass through sand dunes, pebble beach, freshwater marsh, and rocky shoreline. Also be sure to visit the "sunken forest," the fossil remnants of an underwater forest that is still visible at low tide.

Other Sights

In an effort to improve its public image, the Seabrook Nuclear Power Plant opened its own **Science & Nature Center** (Off Rte. 1, Seabrook, 603/773-7219, www.fpl.com, 10 A.M.–3 P.M. Mon.–Thu., free) in 1978, soon after the controversy that almost shut down the plant. The center includes a marine touch pool as well as a boardwalk nature trail, not to mention many exhibits extolling the environmental virtues of nuclear power…To get to the center, take exit 1 off I-95, cross Route 1 and proceed through the security checkpoint.

Entertainment

Back in the 1930s, the historic **Hampton Beach Casino Ballroom** (169 Ocean Blvd., Hampton Beach, 603/929-4100, www.hamptonbeachcasino.com) featured big-band headliners from Count Basie to Duke Ellington. Nowadays, it's more like Meatloaf and Hootie and the Blowfish. The current management, however, has been working hard to get hipper acts such as the Strokes. Any way you cut it, the historic 2,000-seat ballroom is a great place to see a show. Less-exalted names (usually local bands) play live at **Wally's Pub** (144 Ashworth Ave., Hampton Beach, 603/926-6954, www.wallyspubnh.com), where you'll never have difficulty securing a seat or a cold beer. Some nights can get a little raucous (as on pig roast nights, for example).

Events

The Strip is home to countless events over the course of the summer. Perhaps the most eagerly anticipated is the **Master Sand Sculpting Competition** (603/929-6301, www.greggrady.com, late June), in which 250 tons of sand are delivered to the beach for sculptors to turn into castles, mermaids, and whatever pop culture stars are hot at the moment. The **Miss Hampton Beach Pageant** (603/512-5257, late July) has been crowning young lovelies for more than 60 years. Needless to say, a swimsuit competition is part of the contest. A relatively newer event is the **Hampton Beach Idol Competition** (978/458-0919, www.hamptonbeach.org, late Aug.), a three-day event at the end of the summer in which audience members vote for their favorite amateur crooner. As a last gasp of the summer, Ocean Drive closes to traffic every Labor Day weekend for the **Hampton Beach Seafood Festival** (603/926-8718, www.hamptonbeachseafoodfestival.com), a mammoth event that brings more than 100,000 people to sample the fruits of the sea—as if Hampton Beach wasn't a giant seafood festival year-round anyway.

Shopping

Most shopping around the Hampton area is confined to shopping malls and several national chain outlets, but a small handful of independent specialty stores are found around the beach area. To wit: **Sanborn's Candies** (293 Lafayette Rd./Rte. 1, Hampton, 603/926-5061, www.sanbornscandies.com, 10 A.M.–6 P.M. Sun.–Thu.; 10 A.M.–8 P.M., Wed.–Sat.) sells a huge lot of handmade chocolates (creamy fudge in an array of flavors, chocolate casino coins) plus custom-made chocolate molds, sugar-free chocolates, and loads of saltwater taffy. It's a great souvenir—if you can stop yourself from eating it on the way home. Rifle through the bins of lizards and snakes, spend an hour at the wooden train set, or spring for one of the science kits at **Funny Bones Toys** (441 Lafayette Rd./Rte. 1, Hampton, 603/929-3555, 10 A.M.–5 P.M. Mon.–Sat.; 11 A.M.–5 P.M. Sun.). Sure it's supposed to all be for kids, but it's just as easy for adults to get drawn into the store's mix of learning and fun. More grown-up knickknacks constitute the wares at **Barrymore Designs** (61 Lafayette Rd./Rte. 1, North Hampton, 603/964-7337, www.barrymoredesigns.com, 10 A.M.–6 P.M. Wed., Fri., and Sat.; 10 A.M.–7 P.M. Thu.; noon–5 P.M. Sun.). The crafty gift shop sells everything from jewelry and photo frames to candlesticks, note cards, and dried flower wreaths.

Food

Hampton is home to more than its fair share of chain restaurants; if it's greasy and fast, odds are good you'll find it on the strip. But there are exceptions: For starters, there's the comfy street-level patio dining area at **Grille 139 at The Boardwalk Cafe** (139 Ocean Blvd., Hampton Beach, 603/929-7400, www.grille139.com, lunch and dinner daily, year-round, $10–19). The pub-restaurant cooks up basics like chicken fingers, ribs, and broiled scallops. You don't go to **Happy Clam Bar & Grille** (20 L St., Hampton Beach, 603/929-1536, lunch and dinner daily, year-round, $6–20) for fine dining; you go for fun. And that's what you'll get in this Caribbean-bar knock-off—well, that and big orders of fried clams, fish, and steak tips, and (go figure) excellent breakfast wraps full of eggs, bacon, and lots of cheese. Thursday night is Ladies Night. A bit more sedate, **Sea Ketch** (127 Ocean Blvd., Hampton, 603/926-0324, www.seaketch.com, breakfast, lunch, and dinner daily, late June–mid-Sept., limited hours spring and fall, closed mid-Oct.–mid-Apr., $11–25) serves classic surf 'n' turf dinners and straight-from-the-market seafood. There's nothing fancy about the place, but in good weather, the outdoor deck opens up with live music and remarkable water views. It's the handmade, fresh pastas that draw the crowds from all over Rye to **Carriage House Restaurant** (2263 Ocean Blvd., Rye, 603/964-8251, www.carriagehouserye.com, dinner nightly, year-round, $18–28), where they come with divergent influences from Italian (linguine with scampi) to Thai (spicy beef and shrimp) and French (chicken with Dijon). For meat-lovers, there's also a separate menu of all-natural, hormone-free beef cuts.

Information

The **Hampton Area Chamber of Commerce** (603/926-8717, www.hamptonchamber.com) runs a Visitor Information Center located at the Seashell (180 Ocean Blvd.,). More information is available from the **Hampton Village District** (22 C St., 603/926-8717, www.hamptonbeach.org).

EXETER

For a brief period between 1775 and 1789, the attractive historical town of Exeter was the capital of New Hampshire. To this day, the town celebrates its historical connections to the colonial period, when it was a bustling trade center and hotbed of Revolutionary sentiment. Nowadays, the town is best known as the site of Phillips Exeter Academy, one of the best private high schools in the country and the model of the typical New England preparatory school. Inland from the coast on the banks of the Squamscott River, the small town center is full of fancy shops and pricey restaurants where parents treat their kids when they are in town.

Phillips Exeter Academy

It's difficult to tell where the town ends and this prestigious prep school (20 Main St., 603/772-4311, www.exeter.edu) begins. The academy was founded in 1781 by local doctor and Harvard graduate John Phillips, under the sound principle, "Goodness without knowledge is weak and feeble, yet knowledge without goodness is dangerous." The academy hopes to address both with a unique teaching style that keeps classes limited to 12 students, sitting around an oval table for intensive study and discussion. With a campus more impressive than many small colleges, the school is a mix of Georgian colonial buildings and more modern structures radiating out in waves from downtown Exeter. Of particular note is Phillips Church, a Gothic stone structure purchased by the academy in 1922.

American Independence Museum

This smart little historic museum (1 Governors Ln., 603/772-2622, www.independencemuseum.org, 10 A.M.–4 P.M. Wed.–Sat. mid-May–early Nov., $5 adults, $3 students, free children under 6) seeks nothing less than to bring alive the passion of America's fight for independence. It includes two historic properties: the home of one of Exeter's rebel families, and the tavern where many political theories were hashed out at the time. Inside are interactive exhibits exploring the causes and characters of the Revolution. Exhibits include rare early drafts of the Constitution as well as early American furniture, silver, and military artifacts.

Entertainment

The low-key 〖 **Tavern at Rivers Edge** (163 Water St., 603/772-7393, www.tavernatriversedge.com, 3–10 P.M. Mon.–Sat.) was recently deemed the number-one bar in New Hampshire by popular vote. With an understated décor of dark wood and brick and a walloping martini menu, it is the perfect casual-but-lively place to relax over a nightcap.

Events

George Washington addresses the crowds at the annual **American Independence Festival** (603/772-2622, www.independencemuseum.org, mid-July), which takes place on the grounds of the American Independence Museum. Other costumed interpreters also circulate through the event, which features helicopter rides, fireworks, and craft vendors.

Shopping

Feast your eyes (or your stomach) on the goods at **Chocolatier** (27 Water St., 603/772-5253,

www.the-chocolatier.com, 10 A.M.–5 P.M. Mon.–Fri.; 10 A.M.–7 P.M. Sat.; 12 P.M.–5 P.M. Sun.), purveyor of good-quality chocolates and assorted other sweets. You'll find box after box of cutely molded white, milk, and dark chocolates (fish, turtles, and even gardening tools), plus cookies, salted and unsalted nuts, and chocolate popcorn mixtures. There are gifts galore at **Coventry Cottage** (85 Water St., 603/772-4543, http://coventrycottagenh.blogspot.com), an old-fashioned shop brimming with scented candles, rustic pottery, and other accoutrements of country life. An excellent selection of locally made art, pottery, weaving, and jewelry is for sale at **Exeter Fine Crafts** (61 Water St., 603/778-8282, www.exeterfinecrafts.com, 10 A.M.–5 P.M. Mon.–Sat.; closed Sun.). Many of the pieces—particularly the artists' prints, jewelry, and pottery—are heirloom quality. Pick up some good-quality sleepwear, lingerie, and accessories (from handbags to jewelry) from the welcoming **Top Drawer** (147 Water St., 603/778-2211, www.topdrawerboutique.com, 10 A.M.–5:30 P.M. Mon.–Wed. and Fri.; 10 A.M.–7 P.M. Thu.; 10 A.M.–5 P.M. Sat.; noon–4 P.M. Sun.). The selection is tasteful and comfortable, with subtle hints of sassy.

Food

Inexpensive and ultra-casual, the riverside café of **The Loaf and Ladle** (9 Water St., 603/778-8955, www.theloafandladle.com, 8:30 A.M.–8 P.M. Mon.–Sat.; 8 A.M.–8 P.M. Sun., $5–8) does, as the name would suggest, concentrate on soups and breads. But it's all remarkably filling—not to mention delicious. Everything is made from scratch, and the breads are as fresh as the soups are creative (potato pesto, anyone?). Don't get too used to any one item, however; the entire menu changes daily. A local favorite in a rural neighborhood, **The Townlyne Grill** (52 Hampton Rd., 603/772-3200, 5:30 P.M.–9 P.M. Mon.–Sat.; 11 A.M.–2 P.M. and 5 P.M.–8:30 P.M. Sun., $10–25) serves trumped-up classics (the steak topped with baby buffalo shrimp and blue cheese is a recurring special) in a jazzy room filled with pop-art posters. It isn't hard to guess that the focus at **The Green Bean** (33 Water St., 603/778-7585, 11 A.M.–3 P.M. Mon.–Sat., $5–8) is fresh produce, and you'd be correct: The cheery spot serves freshly made simple and wholesome salads, sandwiches, and homemade soups to an enthusiastic crowd. There are also fresh-baked pastries (like the incredible chocolate chip–oatmeal cookies) and daily breakfasts. Delicious food is served without ceremony or pretense at **Tavern at Rivers Edge** (163 Water St., 603/772-7393, 3–10 P.M. Mon.–Sat., $16–26), a handsome but casual dining room serving specialties like New Zealand rack of lamb, filet mignon, and rare seared tuna. The restaurant also has an extensive selection of appetizers and bar food if you'd just like to nosh over drinks.

Information
The **Exeter Area Chamber of Commerce** (10 Front St., 603/772-2411, www.exeterarea.org) stocks a map and brochures on area attractions in the basement of Exeter Town Hall.

SPORTS AND RECREATION
Harbor Cruises
Several companies lead guided tours of Portsmouth Harbor, taking in the islands, lighthouses, and scenic waterfront. The most intimate is the *Tug Alley Too* (47 Bow St., 603/430-9556 or 800/884-2553, www.tugboatalley.com, May–Oct., $49 adults, $29 children under 12), a tugboat that once carried lobsters to islands on the Maine coast. Now owners Bob and Natalie Hassold take her out for one-and-a-half-hour spins around the harbor, with a maximum of six passengers on board. A cheaper but more crowded tour is offered by **Portsmouth Harbor Cruises** (64 Ceres St., Portsmouth, 603/436-8084, www.portsmouthharbor.com, $16 adults, $14 seniors, $11 children), with several different routes aboard the M/V *Heritage.*

Kayaking
You can get out on the water in decidedly smaller craft through **Portsmouth Kayak**

Adventures (185 Wentworth Rd., Portsmouth, 603/559-1000, www.portsmouthkayak.com), which leads guided trips around the Piscataqua River estuaries as well as out on the open ocean of Portsmouth Harbor. A two-and-a-half-hour trip is $59. Full-day rentals are available for the same price.

ACCOMMODATIONS
Under $100
A giant fireplace-anchored common room greets you as you enter **The Old Salt & Lamie's Inn & Tavern** (490 Lafayette Rd., Hampton, 603/926-0330, www.oldsaltnh.com, $89–105), where its 32 brick-walled guest rooms have canopied king, queen, or double beds. The house's cocktail lounge and restaurant, The Old Salt, is open daily and offers room service and Sunday brunch.

$100-150
Furnished with an international collection of antiques and artifacts, the 19th-century **Inn at Christian Shore** (335 Maplewood Ave., Portsmouth, 603/431-6770, www.innatchristianshore.com, $135–155) has original fireplaces and hand-hewn beams. The five rooms have quilts and crocheted blankets, fireplaces, and hand-stocked bookshelves.

$150-250
The former home of New Hampshire Governor Charles Dale, the stately Georgian 🌙 **Governor's House** (32 Miller Ave., Portsmouth, 603/427-5140, www.governorshouse.com, $180–250) is a mix of history and modernity. Chambers come with luxuries such as Frette linens, wireless Internet access, Bose wave radios, fridges, mahogany sleigh beds, and coffeemakers. There's also wine and cheese offered every evening, and complimentary bikes—though it's just a ten-minute walk to downtown Portsmouth. There are seven cozy guest rooms in quiet, colonial 🌙 **Inn at Strawbery Banke** (314 Court St., Portsmouth, 603/436-7242, www.innatstrawberybanke.com, $160–170). Breakfasts are always memorable (especially if it happens to be the house's

sourdough-and-blueberry pancakes), and are served in the sunny breakfast room overlooking a strawberry patch.

The butter-yellow, 1809 building belonging to **Inn By The Bandstand** (4 Front St., Exeter, 603/772-6352, www.innbytheband-stand.com, $150–190) sits two blocks from Phillips Exeter Academy. Rooms come loaded with frills both literal (think lots of toile and garden patterned–linens) and otherwise (amenities like free wireless Internet, CD players, and goose-down comforters). The inn offers airport pickup in a hybrid vehicle for $75 from Manchester and $85 from Boston (available to non-guests for $10 more).

GETTING THERE AND AROUND

To drive to the Seacoast region from Boston, take I-93 north to I-95 north across the New Hampshire border. For Hampton Beach, take exit 2 to Route 101 east (45 mi., 50 min.). For Exeter, take exit 2 to Route 101 west (52 mi., 1 hr.). For Portsmouth, take exit 5 off I-95 and follow signs for downtown (56 mi., 1 hr.). For Rye, take U.S. Route 1 north for 8 miles from Hampton (12 min.). To drive from Manchester to the Seacoast, take 101 east to Exeter (30 mi., 40 min.) or Hampton (35 mi., 45 min.).

Amtrak (800/872-7245, www.amtrak. com) offers train service to Exeter, Durham, and Dover through its Downeaster service (www.thedowneaster.com). **C&J Trailways** (185 Grafton Dr., Portsmouth, 603/430-1100, www.ridecj.com) runs bus service between Dover and Boston's South Station, stopping in Portsmouth along the way. **Greyhound** (800/231-2222, www.greyhound.com) also runs bus service to Portsmouth, stopping at 22 Ladd Street in Market Square.

The local bus company, **COAST** (603/743-5777, www.coastbus.org), serves towns throughout the Seacoast area. In addition, the **Portsmouth Trolley** (603/743-5777, www.cityofportsmouth.com) and **Hampton Beach Trolley** (603/926-5789, www.hamp-tonbeach.org) make loops around their respective locales.

Merrimack Valley

With all the action on the Seacoast, the interior of southern New Hampshire was neglected for much of the early days of the country. That changed at the turn of the 19th century, when industrialization hit and the textile mills began to pop up practically overnight all over New England. Of all the rivers in the region, the Merrimack was hands-down the best location for the cotton and textile mills that drove the region's economy. Not only did it have a fast-running current with lots of waterfalls, but it had lots of trees to drive the furnaces and proximity to Boston and Portsmouth for transport of goods. It's no surprise the Merrimack took off as an industrial powerhouse in the 1800s.

Today, those formerly bustling mill towns are ranged up and down the valley, focused around Manchester—the largest city in New Hampshire and one of the largest in New England. The legacy of the Victorian era survives in the cities' imposing downtown architecture, even as each of them has struggled to find its groove in the modern era, with varying results.

NASHUA AREA

Nashua sits astride the border with Massachusetts, and often seems more like an exurb of Boston than the second-largest city in its titular state. In fact, it is probably best known to Bay Staters as a shopping mecca where they can avoid paying sales tax. The endless procession of malls and strip malls that line the highways are not the best introduction to the state. There's more to Nashua than initially meets the eye, however. Like surrounding cities, Nashua hit a boom in the 19th century when the Nashua Manufacturing

WHAT'S IN A MOTTO: LIVE FREE OR DIE

You'll see it adorning license plates across the state's highways: "Live Free or Die," New Hampshire's aggressively independent motto, first adopted in 1945. It's a highly recognized credo, originally part of a reunion party toast (given in absentia, by letter) in 1809 by Revolutionary War General John Stark. The full passage reads: "Live free or die: Death is not the worst of evils." It may sound like cowboy philosophy in the extreme to some, but to New Hampshire citizens, the phrase refers to (and some say drives) all areas of how life is lived here; it's come to embody everything from how the state regulates gun ownership (with a light hand) to how it taxes citizens (relatively little). Controversy and irony both surfaced around the motto in a 1977 Supreme Court case, Wooley v. Maynard: After the phrase had been mandated by the state legislature to appear on all non-commercial license plates in 1971, one motorist removed the "or die" portion of the motto for religious reasons. He was prosecuted, and the case went before the Supreme Court, which ruled in the motorist's favor, stating that it wasn't the state's right to require citizens to "use their private property as a 'mobile billboard' for the State's ideological message." Needless to say, more than a few cracks were made around the country concerning the state's attempts to take away a citizen's right to free speech by forcing him to carry out a message of freedom.

Company built three cotton mills in town that together produced nearly 10 million yards of cloth a year. Unlike some of its neighbors, however, Nashua came alive again in the late 20th century, when its mix of low taxes and proximity to Boston made it an attractive location for high-tech companies such as Digital Equipment Corporation.

The bustling economy led to a revitalization of the city's Victorian downtown, which is populated with thriving mom-and-pop stores patronized by locals, in contrast to the commercial congestion on the highways. The mix of good jobs and quality of life has made Nashua the only city named twice as the number-one best place to live in America by *Money* magazine (though on first glance, you might scratch your head to figure out how it was named *once!*). Around Nashua, the smaller cities of Merrimack and Derry are primarily bedroom communities for the larger cities in the area, while Salem has virtually become the tax-free commercial district for the Massachusetts city of Lawrence.

◖ Frost Farm

Poet Robert Frost lived in many places—and on many farms—throughout New England during his long life. But perhaps none inspired him—and his poetry—more than this 30-acre farm (122 Rockingham Rd./Rte. 28, Derry, 603/432-3091, www.robertfrostfarm.org, grounds open year-round; farmhouse and barn open 10 A.M.–5 P.M. daily late June–August, Wed.–Sun. only early May–late June and Sept.–mid-Oct., $7 adults and non–New Hampshire seniors, $3 children 6–17, free children 5 and under and all New Hampshire residents) on the outskirts of Derry. Frost moved here with his wife and two children when he was first starting out as a poet, hoping to make a living as a poultry farmer to support his family and his writing habit. While he failed miserably as a farmer, he did settle into the quiet life of the New England countryside, talked with his neighbors, and found a poetic voice unique in American literature. Several of his most famous poems were written or inspired by his time here, including "Mending Wall" and "Hyla Brook."

The farm became a historic site in 1965 when it was purchased by the State of New Hampshire; currently it is embroiled in a nasty (for New Hampshire) zoning fight that threatens to build a strip mall near the home. So far, however, the bucolic character has survived.

© MICHAEL BLANDING

Mending Wall, Frost Farm

but the archaeological digs here have turned up some interesting and mysterious artifacts. Several stone structures on the site were most likely used by early Native Americans as dwelling places and a place for ritual animal sacrifices. Exhibits explain how the site was laid out, like Stonehenge, as an accurate astronomical calendar. The site gets particularly crowded on the equinoxes and solstices, especially the Summer Solstice, which features a celebration each year.(Note: if you have Internet access, log on to the website for a dollar-off coupon on up to four tickets.)

Canobie Lake Park

The rides at this amusement park (85 North Policy St., Salem, 603/893-3506, www.canobie.com, hours vary, $25 adults, $14 children under 48" and seniors, free children 3 and under, $17 night-pass) might not be able to hold up to the Great Americas and Six Flags of today, but back at the turn of the 20th century, genteel visitors flocked there to ride on the steam train and carousels. The park retains some of that old-time charm, even as it has added all of the stomach-wrenching modern rides a 12-year-old could ever ask for.

Other Sights

The **Anheuser-Busch Brewery** (221 Daniel Webster Hwy., Merrimack, 603/595-1202, www.budweisertours.com, 10 A.M.–4 P.M. Thurs.–Mon. Jan.–Apr.; 10 A.M.–4 P.M. daily May and Sept.–Dec.; 9:30 A.M.–5 P.M. daily June–Aug., free) in Merrimack is the smallest of the beer conglomerate's five national breweries. In addition to demonstrations of the brewing process (with free samples!), the brewery has a faux-Bavarian hamlet that serves as a paddock for some of Budweiser's famous Clydesdale horses.

Nashua's history as a mill town is on display at the **Abbot-Spalding House Museum** (1 Nashville St., Nashua, 603/883-0015, www.nashuahistoricalsociety.org, 10 A.M.–4 P.M. Tues.–Thurs. Mar.–late Nov., free), an 1860 Federal Revival mansion once owned by prosperous cotton-mill owner Daniel Abbot, who

The restoration was aided by Frost's daughter, Lesley Frost Ballantine, who helped return the home to exactly how it looked when the Frosts lived there in 1900–1911, right down to the very same wallpaper patterns. Tours of the house include several items owned by the Frosts, including their fine china set and a soapstone sink that still has nicks from where Frost used to sharpen his knife. Arguably more inspirational than the house is the Hyla Brook Trail, a nature trail that wanders for a mile through the meadows, woods, and apple trees around the farm where Frost used to walk. A self-guided walking tour includes a brochure with anecdotes from the family's time here, as well as relevant snippets of poetry.

America's Stonehenge

This 4,000-year-old historic site (105 Haverhill Rd., Salem, 603/893-8300, www.stonehenge-usa.com, 9 A.M.–5 P.M. daily year-round, $9.50 adults, $8.50 seniors, $6.50 children 6–12, free children under 6) isn't nearly as impressive as the giant stone tables of England's Stonehenge, is known as the "father of Nashua." The house is full of antiques and household furnishings from the Victorian era to the present. To see a modern mill up close, visit **Frye's Measure Mill** (12 Frye Mill Rd., Wilton, 603/654-6581, www.fryesmeasuremill.com, 10 A.M.–5 P.M. Tues.–Sat.; noon–5 P.M. Sun.; until 4 P.M. Tues.–Sun. in winter, contact office for tour schedule, free), which has been churning out wooden "measures" (measuring cups) and Shaker boxes for more than 100 years. Tours are given of the manufacturing process, which is run entirely on water power.

Entertainment
Lively rock shows, blues and jazz, and comedy shows happen on the stage at the **Pub Grainery** (36 Otterson St., Nashua, 603/889-9524, www.pubgrainery.com), which, even when shows aren't happening, is also just a mellow place for a drink, with a pleasant vibe.

Events
An achingly charming small-town affair, the **Hollis Town Band Strawberry Festival** (603/883-2448, www.hollistownband.org, June) celebrates the fruit crop each summer with marches played by the town brass band as well as strawberry shortcake and jams made by the Hollis Woman's Club.

Shopping
Mall rats, unite: Nashua and its vicinity are home to a number of gigantic, chain store–filled malls—namely **Pheasant Lane Mall** (310 Daniel Webster Hwy., Nashua, 603/888-0005). For all things vintage (read: anywhere from valuable to questionable), turn toward the **Hollis Flea Market** (Rte. 122, 603/465-7677). It's filled with everything from old rocking chairs and antique rugs to homemade fudge and cosmetics.

Food
Housed in Nashua's oldest building, **Fody's Great American Tavern** (9 Clinton St., Nashua, 603/577-9015, www.fodystavern.com, 4:30–10 P.M. daily, $18–26) is as warm an atmosphere as they come, with exposed brick and an often-lit fireplace. It's all complemented by fare like grilled littlenecks with prosciutto and garlic, bacon-wrapped tuna, and mascarpone cheesecake. The tavern features live music or comedy most nights; if you don't like karaoke, don't come on Tuesdays.

Don't let the silly name fool you: Food at the family-owned **Ya Mamma's** (75 Daniel Webster Hwy., Merrimack, 603/578-9201, $16–18) is serious business. The Italian-American menu is full of filling, flavorful entrées like baked lasagna, fettuccini primavera, and juicy chicken *picatta*.

Information
For more information on towns around Nashua, visit the **Greater Nashua Chamber of Commerce** (151 Main St., Nashua, 603/881-8333, www.nashuachamber.org), the **Greater Derry Chamber of Commerce** (29 W. Broadway, Derry, 603/432-8205, www.derrychamber.org), the **Greater Salem Chamber of Commerce** (224 N. Broadway, Salem, 603/893-3177, www.salemnhchamber.org), or the **Merrimack Chamber of Commerce** (301 Daniel Webster Hwy., Merrimack, 603/424-3669, www.merrimackchamber.org).

MANCHESTER
Like the English city for which it is named, Manchester is a bustling industrial city that has been through various periods of boom and bust over its 150-year history. The city is young by New England standards, incorporated in 1846 to take advantage of the rushing Amoskeag Falls. They served as the powerhouse driving the Amoskeag Manufacturing Company, a collection of three cotton mills that were once the largest in the world. Manchester's downtown is still lined with the huge brick structures of former mill buildings, some of which have been converted into condominiums or headquarters for high-tech companies—but many of which sadly lie vacant.

Called the "Queen City" (for its status as the largest city in New Hampshire without being the capital), Manchester has its posh neighborhoods, but mostly exudes a working-class quality with a downtown of diners and cafés. Every four years, it gets its place in the sun when Presidential candidates swoop down on the city to chat up the common man in advance of the first-in-the-nation primary. (Though that practice is now in doubt given rumblings in Nevada.) More recently, the city has begun to latch onto the art boom that has revitalized other second cities in the region, playing off its strong collection of museums and instituting gallery walks and a popular annual art festival in its gorgeous Victorian-era park.

Currier Museum of Art

New Hampshire is known more for its outdoor pursuits than its fine art. Perhaps that's why philanthropist Moody Currier left money in his will for an endowment "to elevate the quality of life in New Hampshire." Built on the site of Currier's Victorian house, this fantastic art museum (150 Ash St., 603/669-6144, www.currier.org, 11 A.M.–5 P.M. Sun., Mon., Wed.–Fri.; 10 A.M.–5 P.M. Sat.; closed Tue., $10 adults, $9 seniors, $8 students, free children under 18 and to all Sat. 10 A.M.–noon) is now the foremost museum in northern New England. The focus of the museum is on American and New England artists, with paintings by the likes of Frank Benson, Andrew Wyeth, Childe Hassam, Fitz Hugh Lane, and John Singer Sargeant. But the collection also includes a fine gallery of European paintings and galleries with decorative furniture and photographs.

The museum also owns the **Zimmerman House** (tours 2 P.M. Mon. Thu., and Fri.; 10:30 A.M., 12:30 P.M., and 3 P.M. Sat.; 11:30 A.M. and 1:30 P.M. Sun., $18 adults, $17 seniors, $16 students, $8 children 7–17, children under 7 not allowed; rates include museum admission), the only house by famed architect Frank Lloyd Wright in New England open for tours. A shuttle bus departs the Currier for the home several times a day for short or in-depth narrated walkthroughs. Wright's attention to detail in the home is astounding. From the gardens to the built-in furniture to the mailbox, everything in the home seems designed in a single stylish vision.

Other Sights

On the site of Manchester's historic mill yard, the **Millyard Museum** (200 Bedford St., 603/622-7531, www.manchesterhistoric. org, 10 A.M.–4 P.M. Wed.–Sat., $6 adults, $5 students, $2 children 6–18, free children under 6) takes visitors through 11,000 years of Manchester history, starting with the Native Americans who camped at Amoskeag Falls, and continuing through the heyday of Manchester's industrial age. A highlight is a life-sized re-creation of Manchester's main street in the Victorian era. In the same building, the **SEE Science Center** (200 Bedford Street, Manchester, 603/669-0400, www.see-sciencecenter.org, 10 A.M.–4 P.M. Mon.–Fri.; 10 A.M.–5 P.M. Sat.–Sun., $6) is geared for kids with a simulated moonwalk, electrical Van de Graaf generator, and reptile exhibits. The highlight of the museum, however, is a scale model of Manchester Millyard created from LEGO blocks—some 3 million of them in all, making the model the largest permanent LEGO structure in the world.

Among the buildings on display in the model is **Manchester City Hall,** an impressive Gothic cathedral–like structure built in 1845. You can see the real thing (1 City Hall Plz., 603/624-6500, www.manchesternh.gov, 8 A.M.–5 P.M. Mon.–Fri., free) a few blocks away. Inside is a small museum dedicated to New Hampshire's traditional status as the nation's first presidential primary.

Entertainment

Originally built in 1914 as a stage for vaudeville acts, the **Palace Theatre** (80 Hanover St., 603/668-5588, www.palacetheatre.org) later became a movie theater, and now hosts performances of every stripe—from professional Broadway hits to local youth productions and classical concerts.

The most addictive thing at **Black Brimmer American Bar & Grill** (1087 Elm

St., 603/669-5523, www.blackbrimmer.com, 5–10 P.M. Tue.–Sat.) is neither the shepherd's pie nor the fish and chips (though both hit the spot): It's the fun music performed almost every night by local bands.

Rack 'em up and watch a live band or two over beer at **Jillian's** (50 Phillippe Cote St., 603/626-7636, http://manchester.jilliansbilliards.com), which has ten pool tables and serves a late-night menu of pizza and snacks.

Events

The historic Palace Theater hosts the **Manchester Jazz & Blues Festival** (Hanover St., 603/668-5588, www.palacetheatre.org, June), featuring performers on an outdoor stage downtown. For more than 130 years, the little town of Deerfield has staged the **Deerfield Fair** (603/463-7421, www.deerfieldfair.com, late Sept.), a classic New England agricultural fair with animal and exhibits and harvest competitions.

Shopping

Much like Nashua, Manchester is more about mall shopping these days than any other kind. The major centers are the **Bedford Mall** (Rte. 3, 603/668-0670, www.bedfordmall.net), which was torn down in 2009 and scheduled to be rebuilt as a big-box shopping center, and **The Mall of New Hampshire** (1500 South Willow St., www.simon.com). Got a hankering for some playtime outside? Hit **All Outdoors** (321 Elm St., 603/624-1468, 10 A.M.–5 P.M. Mon–Sat.; 11 A.M.–5 P.M., Sun.) first; the helpful staff can get you geared up for most any activity.

Food

Simple, wholesome foods are the kitchen's focus at **Puritan Back Room** (245 Hooksett Rd., 603/669-6890, www.puritanbackroom.com, 11 A.M.–11 P.M. Sun.–Thu.; open until midnight Fri.–Sat., $6–23), a family-friendly spot that caters to groups and makes most of its menu items from scratch. In a modest-but-soothing bistro setting, **Richard's Bistro** (36 Lowell St., 603/644-1180, www.richardsbistro.

com, lunch and dinner daily, brunch Sun., $15–23) offers diners excellent pastas, soups, and mouthwatering fresh-baked breads. And lovers of diner culture find bliss in the booths of **Red Arrow Diner** (61 Lowell Ave., 603/626-1118, www.redarrowdiner.com, open 24 hours, $6–11), a local institution serving hot burgers, fries, club sandwiches, and thick slices of apple pie to patrons all night long. Part of a small New Hampshire chain, **Fratello's Ristorante** (155 Dow St., 603/624-2022, 11:30 A.M.–10 P.M., $9–23) serves generous portions of Italian stalwarts like angel-hair *fra diavolo*, chicken and eggplant parmesan, and chicken carbonara. The often-loud dining room fills up with families and big groups of regulars for the hearty fare.

Information

For more information, stop by the welcome center run by the **Greater Manchester Chamber of Commerce** (Veterans Park, Elm & Merrimac Sts., 603/666-6600, www.manchester-chamber.org), in the center of town across from the Radisson Hotel.

CONCORD

Walking the tightly compressed downtown of New Hampshire's capital, you might be tempted to ask where the city is. With only 30,000 people, Concord is dwarfed by its more prosperous neighbors on the Merrimack. In fact, even though it is located on the river, it never made its fortune as a mill town. Instead, Concord began its life as a trading center and railroad depot named Rumford, back when the state capital was on the Seacoast. As the Merrimack River gained importance to the region, a compromise was reached to move the capital here, hence the name of the city. Today, Concord is a pleasant enough collection of government buildings, many made of granite from nearby quarries, surrounded by green parks and a ring of high-tech and health-care companies along the highway. All things considered, its central location makes a good base for exploring both southern New Hampshire and the Lakes Region.

C Canterbury Shaker Village

The religious sect known as the Shakers was formed in England in the 17th century but reached its peak in the United States, where the Shakers settled self-contained villages along the Eastern Seaboard. Followers of a prophet called Mother Ann Lee, they pursued an austere lifestyle of hard work and deprivation. Hardly hermits, however, the Shakers were thrifty and industrious, and became known for the superior quality of their crafts, including boxes, baskets, and furniture. Alas, one of the requirements of the religion was a strict separation of men and women—at all times. So once new recruits stopped entering the religion, it slowly died out. The last three remaining Shakers now live in seclusion in Maine.

At one time, however, the village within the town of Canterbury once held more than 300 Shakers employed in various businesses. Now the site is a museum (288 Shaker Rd., Canterbury, 603/783-9511, www.shakers.org, 10 A.M.–5 P.M. daily mid-May–Oct., $17 adults, $8 children 6–17, free children 5 and under, $42 family) showcasing 200 years of life in the village through guided and self-guided building tours and demonstrations of Shakers at work. To learn the secrets of their craftsmanship yourself, sign up for a day-long class in basketmaking, woodworking, or other traditional trades.

Christa McAuliffe Planetarium

The tragic explosion of the space shuttle *Challenger* in 1986 is still a wound on our national psyche—more so because it wasn't just astronauts who pledged their lives to the dangers of space who were killed in the tragedy. Also on board was a New Hampshire high school science teacher named Christa McAuliffe, who had promised to speak to her students from space. Even though she didn't live to do that, her spirit still speaks to generations of school children at this planetarium (2 Institute Dr., 603/271-7827, www.starhop.com, 10 A.M.–5 P.M. daily; open Fri. until 9 P.M., $9 adults, $8 students and seniors, $6 children 3–12, free children under 3) established in her name. One of the most modern planetariums in the country, the center features a 40-foot dome with shows of the night sky, as well as interactive exhibits such as a rocket-making workshop and a space shuttle flight simulator.

Other Sights

The gold-domed **New Hampshire State House** (Room 119, State House, 107 N. Main St., 603/271-2154, www.gencourt.state.nh.us, 8 A.M.–4 P.M. Mon.–Fri., free) is the oldest state house in the country where the legislature still meets in the original rooms. A visitors center in the building coordinates tours—call or email ahead to book a time. Outside of the state house, note the statue of New Hampshire's Revolutionary War hero, John Stark, who defeated the British at the Battle of Bennington and went on to fight at Trenton and other battles as well. Take in the Granite State in one fell swoop with a visit to the **Museum of New Hampshire History** (6 Eagle Square, 603/228-6688, www.nhhistory.org, 9:30 A.M.–5 P.M. Tues.–Sat. and noon–5 P.M. Sun. year-round, plus 9:30 A.M.–5 P.M. Mon. July–mid-Oct. and Dec., $5.50 adults, $4.50 seniors, $3 children 6–18, free children under 6, family $17), a (what else?) granite block building full of historical artifacts and exhibits on the state's political and natural history. Important New Hampshire figures General John Stark, Daniel Webster, and President Franklin Pierce are featured. An attached gift shop sells products made in New Hampshire.

For fresher home-grown produce, visit nearby **Hackleboro Orchards** (Orchard Rd., Canterbury, www.hackleboroorchards.com, 9 A.M.–6 P.M. daily in-season), a working family farm with 7 different varieties of pick-your-own apples in the fall, and blueberries, strawberries, and other fruit throughout the rest of the year. (Check the orchard's website to see what is currently in-season.). In addition to beautiful views of the surrounding hills, the orchard has goats, rabbits, and other animals to entertain the kiddies.

Entertainment and Events

A mix of shows and performances, folk and comedy sketches, dance, children's productions, and movies are put on at the beautifully restored **Capitol Center for the Arts** (44 South Main St., 603/225-1111, www.ccanh. com). On a much more casual level, local singers—blues and folk to rock—make a showing on the stage at **Penuche's Ale House** (16 Bicentennial Square, 603/228-9833).

On the last Saturday in July, the **Canterbury Country Fair** (www.canterburyfair.com) takes over Canterbury town center with crafts shows, road races, music performances, and barbecues.

Shopping

Masterpieces by the state's most talented craftspeople are for sale at **League of New Hampshire Craftsmen** (36 North Main St., 603/228-8171, www.nhcrafts.org, 9:30 A.M.–5:30 P.M. Mon.–Fri.; 9 A.M.–5 P.M. Sat.). The gallery features intricate jewelry, elegant glazed pottery, and handmade lighting. Take a trip around Peru, Argentina, and South Africa via the exotic imports at **Gondwana Imports** (13 N. Main St., 603/228-1101, 10 A.M.–6 P.M. Mon.–Wed. and Sat.; 10 A.M.–7 P.M. Thurs.–Fri.; 11:30 A.M.–5 P.M. Sun). Pick up hand-woven clothing, scarves, carved sculptures, and jewelry.

Food

True to its name, **The Moxy Grill** (6 Pleasant St., 603/229-0072, 11 A.M.–9 P.M. Mon.–Thurs. and Sun.; 11 A.M.–1 P.M. Fri.–Sat., $7–18) serves a tasty menu with a dash of chutzpah—think New England classics tweaked with Asian flavors. The pork loin comes glazed with apple-pepper sauce; the bouillabaisse is full of local seafood and spiked with ginger-carrot essence. The room sports a little bit of attitude as well, with bright art splashed on the walls and a genuinely charming waitstaff. No-frills but quite good Thai is whipped up in the kitchen at **Siam Orchid** (158 N. Main St., 603/228-1529 or 603/228-3633, www.siamorchid.net, $8–16), where you can sample light-as-a-feather fried squid rings in sesame sauce and shrimp with mango curry. The erstwhile town police station is the setting for quirky Mexican dinners at **Margaritas** (1 Bicentennial Sq., 603/224-2821, www.margs. com/concord, 4 P.M.–midnight; open until 1 A.M. Wed.–Sat., $7–12), one in a chain of New England Mexican eateries. Between the al fresco dining out back and the converted prison cells inside (that now double as dining areas), the place is a kick.

Information

For more information, contact the **Greater Concord Chamber of Commerce** (40 Commercial St., 603/224-2508, www.concordnhchamber.com).

SPORTS AND RECREATION
Bear Brook State Park

Located a few miles east of Concord and Manchester, New Hampshire's largest state park (157 Deerfield Rd./Rte. 28, Allenstown, 603/485-9869, www.nhstateparks.org/bearbrook.html, $4 adults, $2 children 6–12, free children under 6) has a little something for everyone—hiking and biking trails, a fitness path, boat rentals, swimming, and fly-fishing. If it sounds crowded, don't worry—with 10,000 acres, there's plenty of room for everyone. The park also has nearly 100 campsites ($23/day) on the wooded shores of Beaver Pond; a swimming beach is set aside exclusively for campers' use.

Biking

The **Nashua River Rail Trail** (Ayer, Groton, Pepperell, Dunstable, 978/597-8802, www.mass.gov/dcr/parks/northeast/nash.htm, free) connects Massachusetts and New Hampshire with a 12-mile biking trail on a former railroad right-of-way along the banks of the river.

Canoeing

Three seasons of the year, the **Merrimack River Watershed Council** (600 Suffolk St., Lowell, 978/275-0120, www.merrimack. org, free) leads guided canoe trips down the

Merrimack and Pemigewasset Rivers nearly every weekend from April to October. Trips range from easy to moderate; best of all, they are free.

Auto Racing

NASCAR action comes to New Hampshire several times a year at the **New Hampshire MOtor Speedway** (1122 Rte. 106, Loudon, 603/783-4744, www.nhms.com). The main event is the Sylvania 300 every September.

ACCOMMODATIONS
Under $100

There are only three rooms at **Derryfield B&B** (1081 Bridge St., Manchester, 603/627-2082, $70–95), but they're an absolute bargain: simple but neatly kept for singles or couples, and the property has an outdoor pool and serves a big breakfast. Close to downtown Concord but with plenty of privacy, **Olde Concorde Bed & Breakfast** (231 N. Main St., Concord, 603/228-3356, $85–95) lets recently renovated, clean rooms and serves a full breakfast.

$100-150

The national chain operated by **Crowne Plaza** (2 Somerset Pkwy, Nashua, 603/886-1200, $80–145) has standard through deluxe rooms (with coffeemakers and kitchenettes), plus perks like an indoor pool and sauna.

The decor can be a bit cookie-cutter in some areas, but the English Country style of the **Highlander Inn** (2 Highlander Way, Manchester, 603/625-6426, www.highlander-inn.com, $120–170) is certainly comfortable enough. Rooms come with lots of little perks (high-speed Internet access, coffeemakers, and some suites with whirlpool tubs), and the property has a fitness center, outdoor pool, hot tub, and video library.

$150-250

The carefully restored 19th-century **Centennial Inn** (96 Pleasant St., Concord, 603/225-7102, $150–170) is like sleeping in a little museum—the common areas and rooms are filled with mint-condition Victorian antiques and fixtures.

The most luxurious rooms are in the building's twin turrets, some of which come with whirlpool tubs and private verandas. There is a game room and fireplace dining in the downstairs bistro.

GETTING THERE

Driving to the Merrimack Valley from Boston, take I-93 north to exit 44, then I-495 south to exit 35, and finally U.S. Route 3 north across the border. For downtown Nashua, take exit 5 off U.S. Route 3 (50 mi., 1 hr.). For Manchester, take U.S. Route 3 north from Nashua to I-293 and take exit 5 for downtown (20 mi., 25 min.). For Concord, take I-293 north form Manchester to I-93, then take exit 14 (20 mi, 20 min.). From the Seacoast area, take Route 101 west from Hampton to Manchester (35 mi., 45 min.).

The city of Manchester serves as a secondary air gateway to New England, with flights from many national carriers, as well as Air Canada, arriving at **Manchester Boston Regional Airport** (603/624-6556, www.flymanchester. com). The airport is located six miles south of downtown Manchester. All major car rental companies have desks on the first floor near Baggage Claim B. The **Manchester Transit Authority** (603/623-8801, www.mtabus.org) runs buses from the airport to the Canal Street Transportation center downtown throughout the morning and afternoon for a fare of $1, taking approximately a half hour one-way. Alternately, you can hail a cab at the airport for a 15-minute ride downtown—fare is about $15.

Amtrak (800/872-7245, www.amtrak.com) makes stops in Manchester (119 Canal St.) and Concord (30 Stickney St.).

Greyhound (800/231-2222, www.greyhound. com) runs buses to Manchester (119 Canal St.) and Concord (30 Stickney St.) from around New England. Greyhound also stops in Nashua (30 Elm St.). Local carrier **Concord Coach Lines** (603/639-3317, www.concordtrailways.com) operates a commuter bus down the Merrimack Valley to Boston. Additionally, for passengers with a same-day ticket for Manchester airport, the **Manchester Shuttle** (603/624-6539, ext. 324) offers a free shuttle bus from Boston. The shuttle operates daily, 24 hours a day, leaving every other hour from MBTA Sullivan Station on the Orange Line. The trip takes approximately 1 hour and 15 minutes.

The **Manchester Transit Authority** (603/623-8801, www.mtabus.org) also runs routes within the city, and a shuttle to Hampton Beach. The **Nashua Transit System** (603/880-0100 x203, www.gonashua.com) runs shuttle buses around Nashua. **Concord Area Transit** (603/225-1989, www.bm-cap.org) has stops throughout Concord.

Monadnock Area

The southwest corner of New Hampshire is the sleepy part of the state, bypassed by most tourists and residents alike in favor of the big cities and the mountains. The exception is the region's own stand-out mountain, Mount Monadnock, a tough hunk of granite that resisted the bulldozer of the glaciers that moved through these parts 11,000 years ago. In fact, the word "monadnock" is a Native American term for a solitary mountain rising over a plain—and this is the model of the genre. It is now striking for being the only peak for miles around, drawing endless parades of hikers with the promise of 100-mile views from Connecticut to Maine.

The small villages around the base of the mountain reward those travelers who take the time to visit them by proudly fulfilling their stereotypes of what a New England village should be. There's a reason that *Yankee* magazine has its headquarters in these parts. The pace of life is slow, the churches and colonial buildings inordinately picturesque, and residents just as flinty as you could hope for.

◖ MOUNT MONADNOCK

Mount Monadnock might be the best day hike ever created. Its 3,165-foot peak is the perfect size to satisfy those looking for a challenge, while not overtaxing those looking simply for a view. And the fact that no other nearby mountain comes close in height draws hikers from all around southern New Hampshire and eastern Massachusetts to scale its sides. (It's claimed that Monadnock is the second-most-climbed mountain in the world after Mount Fuji.) The mountain is within the borders of **Mount Monadnock State Park** (Rte. 124, Jaffrey, 603/532-8862, www.nhstateparks.org/monadnock.html, office hours 8 A.M.–4 P.M. daily Nov.–May; 8 A.M.–6 P.M. daily May–Oct., $4 adults, $2 children 6–11, free children under 6 and seniors); the state produces a good trail map showing the various approaches to the summit.

Adding to the appeal of the climb, several grades of trail offer challenges for hikers of any skill level. The two most popular approaches to the summit are the **White Dot** and **White Cross Trails;** both leave from the ranger's station at the main parking lot and offer a moderate climb up through forested mountainside before ending up with a short steep climb up the ridge to Monadnock's exposed quartz and schist summit. In fact, for variety, many hikers choose to go up one trail and down the other. An easier, but more roundabout, route to the summit is the **Red Dot Trail,** which wends its way through a less-steep grade on the southeast side of the mountain.

By far the most difficult trail is the **Spellman Trail,** a breathtakingly steep climb to the summit that should only be attempted by experienced hikers. Lastly, several trails also climb to the peak from alternate locations, offering an escape from the crowds that mob the mountain, especially in July and August. For example, the **Marlboro Trail** climbs the west side of the mountain from its trailhead on Shaker Hill Road off Route 124. In difficulty, it's slightly harder than the White Dot Trail.

For hikers looking to nurse their blisters

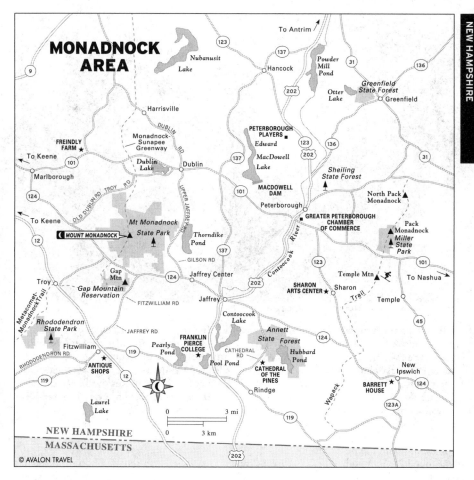

after a hike up and down the mountain, the state park has a small camping area at the base, with 21 tent sites open the public—half are by reservation only, the rest are first-come, first served. (Despite the popularity of the mountain as a day hike, the campsites are surprisingly often free.)

PETERBOROUGH AREA

When Thornton Wilder was looking for a model for the quintessential New England village for his now-classic play *Our Town,* he looked no farther than Peterborough, an achingly charming old town in the shadow of the mountain. Reinvented as "Grover's Corners," or so the story goes, the town still lives up to its image—up to a point. But this is no Hicksville in the middle of nowhere; in the past hundred years, Peterborough has grown to be a cultured and urbane oasis showcasing musical performances and visual art in its many galleries and performance spaces.

There was a reason that Wilder was in Peterborough, after all; he was attending the MacDowell Colony, the country's oldest artists colony, which still awards much-coveted

town common near Mount Monadnock

fellowships for writers to come to the quiet back roads of New Hampshire to finish their novels, poems, or musical scores. In addition to Wilder, past alumni of the tight-knit artists group include Leonard Bernstein, Willa Cather, Studs Turkel, James Baldwin, and Aaron Copeland. Under the influence of so many artists traveling in and out of town, it was only natural that some of the creative inspiration should rub off on the town itself.

Around Peterborough, other small towns are equally *Our Town*–ish, with small communities ranged around manicured town greens. Of these, Jaffrey has one of the best greens in the state; its proximity to Monadnock makes it a good base for exploring the mountain.

Cathedral of the Pines

A strange, yet strangely affecting, tribute to American war dead in the middle of the New Hampshire countryside, this "cathedral" (10 Hale Hill Rd., Rindge, 603/899-3300, www. cathedralofthepines.org, 9 A.M.–5 P.M. daily May–Oct., free) has pine trees for walls and the open sky for a ceiling. Around the grove of soaring trees are various altars and structures that pay homage to fallen soldiers, including a tall bell tower that honors women who have died in war (on its sides are several bas-reliefs designed by Norman Rockwell). Another altar has stones contributed by every U.S. president since Harry Truman.

Other Sights

As wedding presents go, the wedding-cake mansion given to Charles Barrett by his father is a pretty good one. Now known as the **Barrett House** (79 Main St., New Ipswich, 860/928-4074, www.historicnewengland.org, 11 A.M.–4 P.M. second and fourth Sat. of the month June–mid-Oct., $5), the home was furnished as opulently on the inside as it looks on the outside. It was recently snatched up by Historic New England and opened for tours. The glorified petting zoo **Friendly Farm** (Rte. 101, Dublin, 603/563-8444, www.friendly-farm.com, 10 A.M.–5 P.M. daily late May–early Sept., $6.75 adults, $6 children under 1–12) lives up to its name by giving visitors free reign to wander the grounds and feed

TO MARKET, TO MARKET

With the popularity of local and organic foods increasing country-wide, farmers markets have started popping up across New Hampshire like so many wild berry patches. Now, instead of getting the goods second-hand at grocery stores, you can get it straight from the source – apples sold by the people who grew and picked them, milk and cheeses from the dairy farmers who cared for the cows, and maple syrup from the very guy who tapped the trees. Here are some of the biggest and best markets around the state:

· **Amherst Farmers Market** (Amherst Village Green, 603/249-9809, Thurs. afternoon May-Oct.). Find organic produce, cut flowers, wine, seafood, milk, cheese, baked goods, preserves, and soaps.

· **Bedford Farmers Market** (Rte. 101, Wallace Rd. to Benedictine Park, 603/749-6410, Tues. afternoon, June-Oct.). Stock up on organic fruits (the berry selection is epic) and vegetables, wine, venison, baked goods, and cheese.

· **Claremont Farmers Market** (Broad Street Park, 603/542-4321, Thurs. late afternoon June-Sept.). Along with plenty of children's activities (from face painting to live entertainment), the market offers produce, fresh bread, baked goods, eggs, flowers, fudge, honey, jams, maple syrup, meats, seed, soaps, plus hand-crafted clothing and quilts.

· **Franklin Community Farmers Market** (206 Central St., 603/648-6586, Tues. afternoon late July-Sept.). Find produce, naturally raised meats, honey, maple syrup, jellies, ice cream, and baked goods.

· **Laconia Farmers Market** (Beacon Street East, upper parking lot, 603/267-6522, Sat. morning late June-Oct.). Farmers and their families sell fresh fruits and vegetables, baked goods, flowers, crafts, maple syrup, honey, goat cheese, milk, and eggs.

· **Lancaster Farmers Market** (Centennial Park, 603/788-3391, Sat. morning June-Oct.). Find a wide range of goat cheeses, eggs, and pies, plus homemade pestos, jams, maple syrup, free-range chickens, honey, and cider.

· **Peterborough Farmers Market** (Depot Square Park, 603/878-6124, Wed. afternoon May-Oct.). Choose from bushels of produce, bouquets, eggs, lamb, tarts and cakes, pickles, preserves, honey, maple syrup, goat cheese, jewelry, soap, candles, hand-knit clothing, and poultry (including goose and duck).

For more information on these and other farmers markets, contact the **New Hampshire Farmers' Market Association** (603/673-5792, www.nhfma.org).

and hug animals at will. The farm has dozens of "friendly" animals, including goats, pigs, cows, and a donkey named Jack. To find it, travel west on Route 101 for a half-mile after Dublin Lake.

Entertainment and Events

Every summer, the **Peterborough Players** (End of Hadley Rd., Peterborough, 603/924-7585, www.peterboroughplayers.com) put on comedies and dramas to the town's delight (tickets can be hard to come by for the more popular performances). Musicians from in and out of town (including some big names) make appearances at **Peterborough Town House** (1 Grove St., Peterborough, 603/924-7610), staging everything from theater, music, and dance productions to art and photography.

Shopping

Peruse the best of local artwork at **Sharon Arts Center** (20–40 Depot Square, Peterborough, 603/924-7256, www.sharonarts. org, 10 A.M.–5 P.M. Mon.–Thu., 10 A.M.–6 P.M. Fri.–Sat., 11 A.M.–4 P.M. Sun.), where a fine arts gallery flanks a craft store filled with elegant silver jewelry, oversized vases, woven blankets, and etchings. Organic produce comes straight from the on-site fields of **Rosaly's Garden** (Rte. 101, Peterborough, 603/924-7774, www.rosalysgarden.com, 9 A.M.–6 P.M., mid-May–mid-Oct.), where farmer Rosaly has been using non-chemical growing methods for years before it became trendy. Don't leave town without a trip to **Bacon's** (72 Dublin Rd., Jaffrey, 603/532-8836, 10 A.M.–5 P.M. Mon.–Sat.; call ahead for Sun. hours) sugar house, one of the oldest maple syrup makers around. Taste the house's just-made golden syrups, then buy some for the road.

Food

With first-rate views of the river, tables at **Intermezzo** (6 School St., Peterborough, 603/924-5000, 11 A.M.–2 P.M. and 5 P.M.–9 P.M. Tues.–Sat.; 11 A.M.–2 P.M. Sun., www.ragattos.com, $15–22) are the place to tuck into the solid menu of filling bacon-wrapped chicken, pork tenderloin with sweet and sour cabbage, or daily permutations of pasta. All Peterborough seems to clamor over **Peterborough Diner** (10 Depot St., Peterborough, 603/924-6202, www.peterboroughdiner.com, 6 A.M.–7 P.M. daily, $9–14) at lunchtime. The local institution is pure and genuine retro: an old green dining car with counter seats, where diners sup on made-from-scratch soups, hot turkey with cranberry sauce, grinders, and sundaes.

Information

The **Greater Peterborough Chamber of Commerce** (10 Wilton Rd., Peterborough, 603/924-7234, www.peterboroughchamber.com) runs a friendly visitors center downtown.

KEENE

The largest town in southwest New Hampshire, Keene's identity suffers from its location smack dab between the more established cities of Nashua and Manchester and Brattleboro, Vermont. Burned to the ground during the French and Indian Wars, the town reinvented itself as a railroad hub and manufacturing center of furniture, flannel, and pottery in the 19th century. Since then, it has become better known as the site of Keene State College, with a small student population that keeps the town lively.

Sights

The quirky scion of a prosperous mill baron, Horatio Colony turned his grandfather's sheep farm into a nature preserve and writing sanctuary. **The Horatio Colony House Museum** (199 Main St., 603/352-0460, www.horatiocolonymuseum.org, 11 A.M.–4 P.M. Wed.–Sun. May–mid-Oct., free) now contains a collection of antiques and curiosities purchased during his travels around the world. Keene's Revolutionary history is on display at **Wyman Tavern** (339 Main St., 603/357-3855, www.hsccnh.org, 11 A.M.–4 P.M. Thurs.–Sat. June–early Sept.; by appointment May–mid-Nov., $3), a 1762 alehouse where New Hampshire militiamen met before deciding (probably after a few too many) to march to Massachusetts and help their brethren after the Battles of Concord and Lexington. In later years, the tavern became a schoolhouse that educated many famous Granite Staters, including future Supreme Court Chief Justice Salmon P. Chase.

Covered Bridges

The "Covered Bridge Capital of New Hampshire" is the little town of Swanzey, just south of Keene. The town boasts five bridges over the twisting Ashuelot River. The 136-foot West Swanzey Bridge (Main St. and Rte. 10) is a brick-red beauty, with an attached pedestrian walkway on one side. The 158-foot Cresson Bridge (Sawyers Crossing Rd.), which is still open to traffic, is known for the intricate latticework on its inside. You can visit all of the bridges on a covered bridge biking or driving tour; inquire at the local Chamber of Commerce.

Entertainment

Live music on weekends and a lively crowd on

weeknights make **Elm City Brew Pub** (222 West St., 603/355-3335) the place to be. The homemade brews are an added attraction. During the school year, the **Redfern Arts Center** at Keene State College (229 Main St., 603/358-2168) puts on dramatic and comedic productions.

Events
Started in 1991, the **Keene Pumpkin Festival** (603/358-5344, www.pumpkinfestival.com, late Oct.) set the world record in number of lit jack-o'-lanterns, displaying 1,628 its first year. Every year since, the town has tried to beat the record, with the current record standing at close to 30,000 in 2003. (That record stood as Guinness's greatest until 2006, when Boston spoiled the fun with a one-off show of one-upsmanship by lighting 30,100 pumpkins on Boston Common.) Needless to say, the sight of so many carved and glowing gourds is quite a thing to behold.

Shopping
Keene likes its one-stop shopping, so those looking to buy head to the **Colony Mill Marketplace** (222 West St., 603/357-1240, www.colonymill.com, 10 A.M.–9 P.M. Mon.–Sat.; 11 A.M.–6 P.M. Sun.), a converted 19th-century wool mill now composed of 30-plus merchants. Find basketmakers, antiques dealers, bath products, candy, and kitchen supplies all in one spot. Sate your curiosity about all things nature and science with the toys, kits, games, and discovery sets at **Earth Treasures** (12 Main St., 603/352-7192 or 800/550-7192, www.earthtreasuresmall.com, 10 A.M.–9 P.M. Mon.–Sat., closed Sun.).

Food
Dine on fresh Mexican specialties, from enchiladas to burritos, at the family-friendly **Margaritas** (81 Main St., 603/357-4492, www.margs.com, 4 P.M.–11 P.M. daily; opens at noon Sat.–Sun.; open until 1 A.M. Wed.–Sat., $7–12), where service is generally fast. There's a sizeable vegetarian menu available. Still more veggie-only specialties compose the lunch-only menu at **Country Life** (15 Roxbury St., 603/357-3975, 11:30 A.M.–3 P.M. Mon.–Fri.; 10 A.M.–3 P.M. Sun., $4–7), a small and inexpensive spot popular with students. Choose from all-natural homemade soups and made-to-order sandwiches. Close-to-authentic Italian is what pulls the crowds into the handsome dining room of **Tony Clamato's** (15 Court St., 603/357-4345, www.tonyclamatos.com, 4 P.M.–1 A.M. Tue.–Sat.; 5 P.M.–8:30 P.M. Sun., $14–22). Dishes include fried calamari, fettuccine Alfredo, and shrimp with polenta. When you're ready for an Italian meal you'll be remembering years from now, make a reservation at **Nicola's Trattoria** (35 Central Square, 603/355-5242, 5 P.M.–9 P.M. Tue.–Thu.; 5 P.M.–9:30 P.M. Fri.; 5 P.M.–10 P.M. Sat., $22–30). The romantic, refined room bustles with staff feeding enthusiastic diners plates of seared duck breast in red-wine reduction sauce, sautéed shrimp, and generously sauced fresh-made fettuccine.

Information
The **Greater Keene Chamber of Commerce** (48 Central Sq., 603/352-1303, www.keenechamber.com) runs a well-stocked visitors center downtown.

HILLSBOROUGH AREA
Few towns in New England can match the picturesque beauty of Hillsborough, a self-contained village of colonial homes, many of them still owned by the descendents of the people who built them. The village has been invigorated by various artisans who have set up shop downtown, including the acclaimed Gibson's Pewter, one of the top pewter producers still in existence. Its downtown area, known as "Hillsborough Bridge," is also known for its small population of residents descended from German settlers; a delicious German bakery and annual Schnitzelfest attest to their ongoing influence. The area around Hillsborough is mainly farmland, dotted with equally picturesque villages and forested hillsides that light up with colorful foliage in autumn.

Franklin Pierce Homestead

The home where the 14th president of the United States spent his childhood (off Rte. 31, 603/478-3165, www.nhstateparks.org/franklin. html, 10 A.M.–4 P.M. Sat., 1–4 P.M. Sun. late May–early Oct.; 10 A.M.–4 P.M. Mon.–Sat., 1–4 P.M. Sun. Jul–Aug.; open by appointment Apr.–May and mid–late Oct., $7 adults, $3 children 6–11, free children under 6) is as opulent as any home in Hillsborough in the early 1800s. Pierce's father, General Benjamin Pierce, was a hero of the Revolutionary War, and decorated the home with the finest French wallpaper, furniture, and porcelain. Growing up, Pierce was exposed to many famous politicians and intellectuals, including Daniel Webster, the negotiator of the Great Compromise of 1850 that put off the Civil War for a decade by allowing slavery to continue in the South. Franklin Pierce himself became a war hero in the Mexican War, and he was put forth as a compromise candidate for president in 1852, winning a narrow victory due to his support of the Fugitive Slave Law that mollified Southern voters.

Personal and national tragedy, however, would mar his time in office. On the way to Washington, his son was killed in a train accident, sending Pierce into a downward spiral of grief. At the same time, violence erupted in Kansas between slave owners and Free Soilers who wanted to keep the new state free. Unable to successfully intervene, Pierce was blamed for the conflict, and spent his last few years in office as a pariah. In retrospect, perhaps, he is merely a scapegoat for a conflict that could only end in blood, but his reputation as one of the country's most unpopular presidents persists despite every attempt to rehabilitate his image. Some of Pierce's personal possessions are on display in tours of his boyhood home, arranged to re-create the opulence of the home as it was when he lived there.

Stone Arch Bridges

In an area that was prone to flooding, wood-beam bridges built over the Contoocook were constantly washing away. However, the limestone traditionally used as mortar for stone bridges wasn't strong enough to support the wide arches across the river. Plucky Scottish masons solved the conundrum by pioneering a form of "dry masonry" in which stones were painstakingly fit together without any mortar at all. Once there were a dozen of these beautiful stone bridges around the community. Five still remain, including a particularly handsome double-arch bridge at the intersection of Route 202 and West Main Street. Stop by the chamber of commerce office for a map of the rest.

Events

The highlight of Hillsborough's social calendar is the **Hillsborough Balloon Festival** (603/464-0377, www.balloonfestival.org, mid-July), a combination hot-air-balloon rally and country fair with horse pull, pie-eating contest, and, of course, rides in hot-air balloons ($175/person). If you'd rather admire them from afar, check out the "night glow" event, in which 10 balloons are inflated with a special white flame that makes them glow eerily in the dark. The town celebrates its German heritage with an annual **Schnitzelfest** (603/464-5858, www. schnitzelfest.com, late Sept.), a traditional Oktoberfest celebration complete with beer, sausage, and lederhosen.

Shopping

Since the 1960s, the Gibson family has been passing down the tradition of fine pewter-making (several of their productions have been accepted into the permanent collection of the Museum of Fine Arts in Boston) and selling their wares at **Gibson's Pewter** (18 E. Washington Rd., 603/464-3410, www.gibson-pewter.com, 10 A.M.–4 P.M. Mon.–Sat.; "by chance" Sun.). The store sells bowls, ornaments, mugs, key chains, and children's items like tiny mugs and spoons. Fans of the local foods wave (and otherwise) will find plenty to stock up on at **The Corner Store** (281 2nd New Hampshire Turnpike., 603/478-3335, 9 A.M.–6 P.M. Mon.–Sat.; 10 A.M.–5 P.M. Sun.)—a trove of products made from ingredients grown literally just down the street (including a killer wildberry jam). Dress yourself and find a loving companion—in one fell swoop—at **Feathers & Threads** (3 Depot Main St., 603/464-6141, 10 A.M.–5 P.M. Mon.–Sat.; closed Sun.), a two-for-one business that combines a pet shop and consignment shop under one roof. Both sides have some surprisingly tempting deals.

Food

Marked on the outside with two pretzels, **German John's Bakery** (5 W. Main St., 603/464-5079, www.germanjohnsbakery.com, 9:30 A.M.–5 P.M. Tue.–Sat., 11 A.M.–3:30 P.M. Sun. Jun.–Dec.; closed Tue. & Sun. Jan.–May, $2–4) $2–7) is a haven of fresh-baked and authentic baked goods—deliciously crusty sourdoughs, cinnamon-raisin *schnecken,* braided almond breads, and loads of cookies. Other German products (from liverwurst and mustards to sausage) are also for sale. Scoops of old-fashioned cold stuff await at **Central Square Ice Cream Shoppe** (5 W. Main St., 603/464-3881, www.centralsquareicecream.com, noon–9 P.M. daily Jun.–Aug.; Fri.–Sun. only Sept.–May, $2–4). The always-crowded shop and soda fountain sports big hand-painted murals and serves a long roster of delicious flavors and sundaes. It's little more than a shack, but the food at **Diamond Acres Seafood** (737 W. Main St., 603/478-3121, 11 A.M.–10 P.M. Mon.–Sat.; 11 A.M.–9 P.M. Sun., $5–10) is cooked-to-order and super-fresh.

Information

For more information on the village, stop by the **Hillsborough Chamber of Commerce** (25 School St., 603/464-5858, www.hillsborough-nhchamber.com).

SPORTS AND RECREATION
Hiking

Despite its draw, Monadnock isn't the only peak worth climbing in the area. The **Metacomet Trail** climbs from the town of Fitzwilliam to the top of the 1,833-foot Little Monadnock, which offers views of its big sister to the east. The **Monadnock-Sunapee Trail** snakes its way up and down the ridges of western New Hampshire between the area's two highest and best-known peaks—Mount Monadnock and Mount Sunapee. The 50-mile trail has five campsites along its length and takes between three and four days to traverse from peak to peak. For more information, contact the Monadnock Sunapee Greenway Trail Club (www.msgtc.org) or look for a copy of the *Monadnock-Sunapee Greenway Trail Guide* in local bookstores and outdoor stores.

Farther north, more than 20 miles of trails criss-cross **Fox State Forest** (Center Rd., Hillsborough, 603/464-3453, www.dred.state.nh.us) on the outskirts of Hillsborough. Trails for both hikers and mountain bikers skirt a landscape of mile-high pines and glacial kettle holes.

Boating

The high volume and fast flows of the Contoocook make it an ideal river for kayaking and canoeing (to say nothing of the pristine scenery of farmland and village church spires). The place to contact is family-run **Contoocook River Canoe Company** (9 Horse Hill Rd., Concord, 603/753-9804, www.contoocook-canoe.com/contoocook.html, $3–34), which hooks up rentals, tours, and shuttle service from its home base in Concord.

Camping

In the shadow of Mount Monadnock, **Greenfield State Park** (Forest Rd., off Route 136, Greenfield, 603/547-3497, www.nhstateparks.org, $4 adults, $2 children 6–11, free children under 6 and seniors) makes an ideal home base for climbers. Its 200-some campsites ensure that there is almost always availability, while the park's trails along Otter Lake allow the opportunity for solitude. Campsites are $24 per night. The park also has a small beach and canoe rentals.

ACCOMMODATIONS
Under $100

Tiny Fitzwilliam is home to the historic and charming **Fitzwilliam Inn** (Rte. 119, Fitzwilliam,

603/585-9000, www.historicfitzwilliaminn.com, $60–80), which has been around since 1796 and recently reopened in all of its historic splendor. Rooms are nothing fancy, but all have cozy beds and most have private bathrooms. The tavern downstairs acts as a popular gathering spot for locals. There are four simple guest rooms at the welcoming **Carriage Barn Bed & Breakfast** (358 Main St., Keene, 603/357-3812, www.carriagebarn.com, $90–100). Each is decorated in florals, with queen or twin beds, bathrobes, and complimentary coffee.

$100-150

A creaky-but-cute renovated old farmhouse sets the scene at the family-owned **Benjamin Prescott Inn** (433 Turnpike Rd./Rte. 124, Jaffrey, 603/532-6637, www.benjaminprescottinn.com, $95–160), which offers views of the property's farm from nearly every direction. Rooms are downright homey, with colorful quilts, family pictures, brass beds, and some with private sitting areas. Six lovely rooms—with private baths, phones, antiques, and some with fireplaces—are on offer at **Wright Mansion Inn** (695 Court St., Keene, 603/355-2288, $80–160), a huge 1860s Georgian Revival building. The kindly staff cooks up a full breakfast every morning.

$150-250

One of New England's oldest inns, **◖ The Hancock Inn** (33 Main St., Hancock, www.hancockinn.com, $105–260) makes for a great romantic getaway, with its rooms appointed with fireplaces, antiques, and hand-painted murals. Meals are also excellent here, starting with the delicious full breakfasts (of homemade granola, cooked-to-order omelets, and such) and ending with white-linen dinners of beautifully presented (and tasting) dishes of duck confit with apple slaw and balsamic-glazed chicken with goat cheese farfalle.

GETTING THERE AND AROUND

To get to the Monadnock region from Manchester, take the winding Route 101 west to Peterborough (35 mi., 1 hr.) or Keene (60 mi., 1 hr. 30 min.). To climb the mountain, take U.S. Route 202 south from Peterborough to Jaffrey (8 mi., 12 min.), then Route 124 west. After a few miles, take a right on Dublin Road, then a left on Poole Road to get to Monadnock State Park (4 mi., 6 min.).For Hillsborough, take Route 9 east from Keene (30 mi., 45 min.), U.S. Route 202 north from Peterborough (20 mi., 30 min.), or Route 9/U.S. Route 202 west from Concord (25 mi., 40 min.).

Greyhound (800/231-2222, www.greyhound.com) runs buses to Keene, stopping outside Corner News (67 Main St., 603/357-4696).

Local bus provider **City Express** (603/352-8494, www.hcsservices.org) makes stops at several locations throughout Keene.

LAKES REGION

Riverboats and speedboats alike ply the waves of New England's favorite freshwater vacation destination. But Winnipesaukee (extra points for spelling it right on the first try) is just one of the many—and be warned, one of the most crowded—lakes that offer recreational opportunities in this area. As a whole, the region focuses on fun more than relaxation, with water- and jet-skiers noisily cruising the bigger puddles. The sheer number of lakes in the region (more than 200 at last count, with 283 miles of shoreline and 274 habitable islands), however, ensures a range of accommodation from action-packed to tranquil.

In fact, the Lakes Region is made up of more than forty towns (some of which are so small, you don't know you've been in them until you pass a sign saying you've left). Laconia is the biggest city, but the quieter charms of many of the smaller towns—the country stores of Holderness, the neat lines of white houses lining the streets of Wolfeboro, and the bustling town green of Meredith—perhaps best represent what the region has to offer: uncrowded, natural beauty met with stress-free living.

PLANNING YOUR TIME

Visting the Lakes Region isn't about bagging sites per se; it's more about getting out on the water—whether that means by inner tube, a canoe, a speed boat, or a cruise ship. As far as that goes, you can't go wrong with the **M/S *Mount Washington*,** the queen of Winnipesaukee and the best way to get a feel for the history of the lake. If you want to experience all the bustle and excitement of Lake

© DEB SQUIRES, SUNBEAM IMAGES

HIGHLIGHTS

(Mount Washington Cruises: The queen of Lake Winni is this 230-foot floating tour (page 463).

(Squam Lakes Natural Science Center: The last known mountain lion in New England is just one draw of this compassionate ecology center (page 467).

(Mt. Kearsarge Indian Museum: More than a museum, this living Native American culture center holds a July powwow and grows traditional plants on-site (page 475).

(Saint-Gaudens National Historic Site: Creativity was the only agenda at this artists colony for leading lights of the Victorian Age (page 478).

(Hood Museum of Art: This is quite simply one of the best small college art museums in the country (page 480).

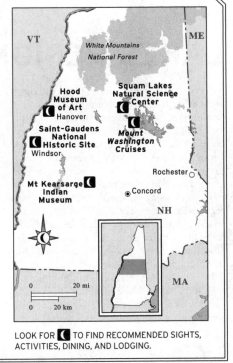

LOOK FOR (TO FIND RECOMMENDED SIGHTS, ACTIVITIES, DINING, AND LODGING.

Winni, base yourself in the quaint town of Meredith, which is close enough to the action of Weirs Beach without being *too* close. If it's solitude you're after, beat the crowds with a stay on Squam Lake—and while you are there, take in the excellent live animal displays and nature cruises offered by the **Squam Lakes Natural Science Center.**

A good compromise between action and quiet is Lake Sunapee, off by itself in western New Hampshire. Its slow pace and old-school harbor evoke the feel of a 1950s lakeside resort, however, there is still plenty to keep you busy in the area, including some great summer stock theater and the Native American artifacts and nature trails at the **Mt. Kearsarge Indian Museum.**

Along the Connecticut River, the presence of Dartmouth College kicks the culture up a notch with its impressive architecture and around-the-world art collection at the **Hood Museum of Art.** Anyone with even a passing interest in fine art and sculpture should also consider a detour down the Connecticut to Cornish, where the **Saint-Gaudens National Historic Site** evokes a bohemian colony of artists and writers who sought inspiration in the New Hampshire landscape.

NEW HAMPSHIRE

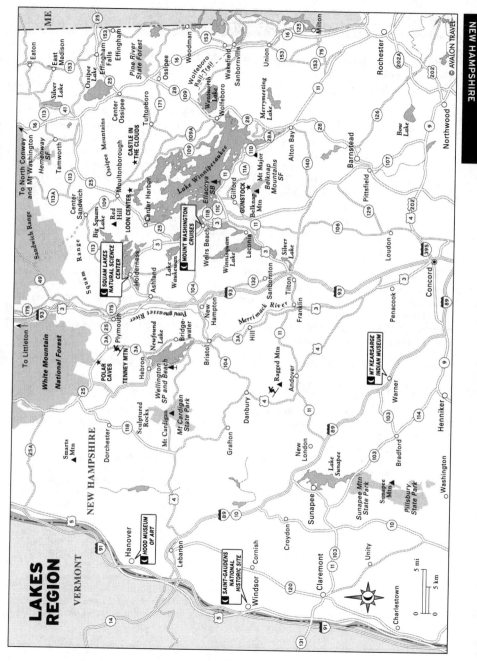

LAKES REGION

© AVALON TRAVEL

Lake Winnipesaukee

Four-season, water-bound activities are everywhere you look around Winnipesaukee, the largest lake in New Hampshire and the third-largest in New England (after Champlain and Moosehead). Known universally to residents as Lake Winni, the lake is a full 72 square miles of spring-fed water with upwards of 200 miles of shoreline. Come summer, tourists descend on the lake from all over New England for boating, swimming, and cruises. During the winter, they keep coming for ice skating, ice fishing, and snowmobiling.

Visitors seem to spend more time exploring the lake by boat than by car, but the villages surrounding it warrant some exploring, too. If kitschy fun is on your agenda, the boardwalks of Weirs Beach have more than their fair share of waterslides, public beaches, arcades, and pizza shacks. Meanwhile, spots like Meredith and Wolfeboro are more quiet, less crowded places, excellent for antiquing, searching out art and crafts galleries, and simply enjoying the scenery.

LACONIA AND MEREDITH

Laconia may be the biggest city on the western shore of Lake Winni (with a population of 27,800) and Meredith may be its most gentrified, with its handful of upscale resorts and spas. But Weirs Beach (named for the fishing baskets that early Native Americans once used on its shores) is the most notorious—if even just for the throngs that gather on its beach and boardwalk every summer. It's been that way since about 1848, when the railroad running from Boston to Montreal reached Weirs Beach (which is technically part of Laconia, but thought of as its own entity). The town quickly became an incredibly popular tourist destination. By the turn of the 19th century, four express trains left Boston's Union Station each day for Weirs Beach. The train service ended in 1960, but the annual migration did not: Each year, thousands of tourists still make their way here to ride the lake steamship, eat junk food, and get a tan or tattoo.

X MARKS THE SPA

For many, no getaway can be truly relaxing without a visit to a health resort or spa. New Hampshire has a handful of excellent health resorts, all designed with your rejuvenation in mind. For starters, there's the elegant day spa for men and women at **Cascade Spa** (The Inn & Spa at Mills Falls, 312 Daniel Webster Hwy./Rte. 3, Meredith, 800/622-6455, www.millfalls.com), a lakeside enclave offering massage, body treatments, facials, nail care, steam rooms, and both indoor and outdoor pools. Massages and hydrotherapy come from on high – literally – at the **Mountain View Grand Resort & Spa** (120 Mountain View Rd., Whitefield, 866/484-3843, www.mountainviewgrand.com). Treatment rooms at this resort sit at its very top – culminating with the Japanese-style hot tub, which combines aromatherapy with stellar views of the surrounding mountains from the Ofuro Tower. Catch a dose of exfoliation from the salt glow body treatments of **Adagio Spa Salon & Wellness Center** (320 Calef Hwy./Rte. 125, Barrington, 603/664-6000, www.adagiospa.com), the region's only spa-cum-restaurant. (So you can chase your steam bath with a steaming bowl of fettuccine at the adjoining Dante's Pasta & Vino.) Massage is the thing to go for at **Innovations Day Spa & Wellness Center** (228 Naticook Rd., Merrimack, 603/880-7499, www.innovationsnh.com), where the experts run the gamut in specialties, from Swedish and neuromuscular to hydrotherm, hot stone, and reflexology. Or stay awhile and relax at the aptly named **Tranquility Springs Wellness Spa** (23 Sheep Davis Rd., Pembroke, 603/226-2047). Settle into one of the treatment rooms and indulge in seaweed body masks, mud masks, Reiki, or reflexology.

◀ *Mount Washington* Cruises

The feeling strikes almost as soon as you catch a glimpse of Lake Winni's vast, folded shoreline—you've got to get *out* there! Thankfully, you don't need your own motor boat or personal watercraft to ply the waves. There are several boat-rental marinas and cruise companies that are more than willing to let you climb aboard, the same way that tourists to this region have been doing for the past 100 years. The grande dame of the lake is the **M/S Mount Washington** (211 Lakeside Ave., Weirs Beach, 603/366-5531 or 888/843-6686, www.cruisenh.com, May–Oct., $25–49 adults, $12–37 children 4–12, free children under 4), so named—the tour guides will tell you—because when the sky is clear you can see New Hampshire's tallest peak from the deck (M/S stands for motor ship). The current cruise ship is actually the second *Mount Washington* to cruise the lake. The first ship, built in 1872, was destroyed by a fire in 1939. Her replacement is an 1888 steamship that was completely overhauled and rebuilt in 1940. The ship is a whopping 230 feet long, and re-creates the era of the old paddlewheel steamships, even though she is now propelled by twin diesel engines.

The *Mount Washington* leaves from Weirs Beach as well as other locations around the lake, making a variety of cruises. The most popular are the 2.5-hour narrated sightseeing cruises, which give passengers a feel for the history of the lake. These are particularly breathtaking in foliage season in early October. "The Mount" also makes dinner cruises in the evening with entertainment that might charitably be called "campy." The same company also has two smaller boats in its fleet that are ideal for those wanting to avoid crowds or poke into some of the smaller bays the Mount can't get into. The M/S *Sophie C.* ($22 adults, $11 children) is the only U.S. Mail Boat on an inland waterway; it allows passengers to hitch a ride along its delivery route to the lake's various islands. The M/S *Doris E.* ($15–22 adults, $7–11 children) leaves Meredith for one- and two-hour guided cruises around Meredith Bay and its surrounding islands.

© MICHAEL BLANDING

The M/S *Mount Washington*

NEW HAMPSHIRE

© DEB SQUIRES, SUNBEAM IMAGES

sails on Lake Winni

Other Sights

Part of the original Boston & Maine Railroad that used to bring tourists to the region has been preserved and turned into the **Winnipesaukee Scenic Railroad** (603/745-2135, www.hoborr. com, 10:30 A.M.–4:30 P.M. daily mid-June–Aug.; weekends only late May–mid-June and Sept.–mid-Oct., $14 adults, $11 children 3–11, free children under 3). It now runs one-and two-hour rides along the shore between Meredith and Weirs Beach, including a bridge over a slice of the lake itself. There's a $2 surcharge to ride in Leo's Party Caboose. If you're at a loss for how to entertain the whole family, **Funspot** (Rte. 3, Weirs Beach, 603/366-4377, www.funspotnh.com, 9 A.M.–11 P.M. Sun.–Fri., 9 A.M.–midnight Sat., mid-June–early Sept.; 10 A.M.–10 P.M. Sun.–Thurs. and 10 A.M.–11 P.M. Fri., 9 A.M.–midnight Sat. early Sept.–mid-June) will probably do the trick. Proudly proclaiming itself the "second-largest arcade in the country," it includes thousands of square feet of arcade games, bowling, mini-golf, and even bingo.

It wouldn't be New Hampshire without motorcycles—and the king of the hog dealers is **Laconia Harley-Davidson** (239 Daniel Webster Hwy., Meredith, 603/279-4526, www.meredith-hd.com, 9 A.M.–6 P.M. Mon. and Thu.; 9 A.M.–7 P.M. Fri.; 9 A.M.–5 P.M. Sat.; 10 A.M.–4 P.M. Sun.; closed Tue. & Wed.), a giant showroom for Harley and Buell bikes, and the center of the action during Laconia's annual Motorcycle Week.

Nightlife

New Hampshire is no stranger to bikers, and neither will you be after a visit to **Broken Spoke Saloon** (1072 Waston Rd., Laconia, 603/366-5511, www.brokenspokesaloon.com, 11 A.M.–1 A.M. Wed.–Sat., 11 A.M.–10 P.M. Sun. Jun.–Oct.). Sure it's more of a joint than a relaxing bar, but there's no arguing the flavor's anything but genuine. Rather hit someplace a little more lighthearted? There's always **Forever Young** (10 Downtown Mall, Laconia, 603/524-9317, 11 A.M.–2: P.M. Fri.–Sat. May–March), a dance club that plays primarily DJ-spun pop and caters to single twenty- and thirtysomethings with a cushy lounge. Rather hear some live music? Make **Paradise Beach Club** (322 Lakeside Ave., Laconia, 603/366-2665, www.paradisebc.com,

© MICHAEL BLANDING

This way to honkytonk fun.

8 P.M.–1 A.M. Thurs.–Sat. May–Oct.) your next stop. Every weekend the bar-restaurant hosts performances by local rock bands.

Events

The **World Championship Sled Dog Races** (603/524-4314, www.lrsdc.org, mid-Feb.) live up to their name with competitors from Canada, Germany, Finland, and Norway joining home-grown canine talent every year in the snowy streets of Laconia. The event, which dates to 1929, also includes a "mutt derby" of junior mushers with their one- or two-dog teams.

The cultural event of the season is the **Winni Derby** (603/253-8689, www.winniderby.com, mid-May), a down-and-dirty fishing festival with honors going to anglers pulling in the largest landlocked salmon and lake trout. This is no idle competition—first prize in each category wins a fully equipped speedboat. When the fish are fried, however, in a sense everyone wins.

Shopping

The Bavarian setting may be faux, but the chocolates at **Kellerhaus** (259 Endicott St., Weirs Beach, 603/366-4466, www.kellerhaus.com,

10 A.M.–6 P.M. Wed.–Mon.; closed Tues.) are certainly not. Swing by to get your sugar fix, à la maple candies, fudges, peanut brittle, and pecan bark. There's no guarantee you'll be as emphatic about **Yikes! Gallery** (23 Main St., Center Harbor, 603/253-4966, www. yikesgallery.com, 10 A.M.–6 P.M. Mon.–Sat.; 10 A.M.–5 P.M. Sun.) as the store's name seems to be about itself, but odds are good you'll still find something worth taking home. Between the all-natural transparent soaps (all handmade), the cat-shaped blown glass, and the cases of funky silver jewelry, it's a complete selection. Stock up on annuals, perennials, and maybe a bouquet of hand-cut flowers while you're at it at **Petal Pushers Farm** (2635 Parade Rd., Laconia, 603/524-7253, www.petalpushersnh. com). Prices are good, the blooms are well cared for, and you can reward yourself for your smart purchase with an ice cream cone from the concession stand on your way out the door.

Food

Make a stop at **Awakenings Espresso Café** (62 Canal St., Laconia, 603/524-1201, www. awakeningsespressocafe.com, 7 A.M.–4 P.M.

REV IT UP

It might be something about the wide-open curves and scenic country roads – or maybe it's New Hampshire's "Live Free or Die" mentality that eschews such sissy rules like helmet laws. But New Hampshire is definitely motorcycle country. As soon as you cross the border, you notice the predominance of two-wheeled traffic on the highways. And every major town worth its pistons has at least one motorcycle shop. The main event of the motorcycle social calendar, however, is **Laconia Motorcycle Week** (603/366-2000, www.laconiamcweek.com, early June), New Hampshire's annual rally for iron horses. Only Sturgis in South Dakota has more cachet in biker circles than Laconia. Then again, maybe "cachet" isn't quite the right word; expect vintage motorcycle races, group tours of the surrounding area, and lots of late-night shenanigans in the biker bars of Weirs Beach.

Mon.–Fri.; 8:30 A.M.–12:30 P.M. Sat.; closed Sun., $2–7) first thing in the morning for snazzy signature coffee drinks alongside fresh-baked streusel cakes, or at lunch for freshly made sandwiches. No matter what time you go, there's free wireless Internet access and genuinely charming service. Tuck into some genuine home-style cooking at ◖ **Hart's Turkey Farm Restaurant** (233 Daniel Webster Hwy., Jct. Rtes. 3 & 104, Meredith, 603/279-6212, www.hartsturkeyfarm.com, lunch and dinner daily, year-round, $10–28), owned by the same family since it opened in 1954. True to its name, fresh turkey is one of the smartest things to order, but there's also prime rib, seafood, and perfectly al dente pastas. Don't pass up the ice creams, either: They're all homemade and deliciously creamy. Every Friday, seemingly all Laconia turns up at **Water Street Cafe** (141 Water St., Laconia, 603/524-4144, www.water-street-cafe.com, breakfast from 5:30 A.M., lunch, and dinner, daily year-round, $3–9) for all-you-can-eat fresh haddock. It's a great

deal—as are the homemade seafood chowders and farm-fresh egg omelets at breakfast. Just across the street from the frenzy of Weirs Beach, **Weirs Beach Smokehouse Restaurant** (38 Endicott St., Weirs Beach, 603/366-2400, 12 P.M.–9 P.M. Mon.–Fri.; 11 A.M.–11:30 P.M. Sat.; 11 A.M.–9 P.M. Sun., $9–23) doles out good ol' classic Southern specialties: smoked ribs, steak, and grilled chicken. Grab a seat in the Lakeview room, if you can, for a terrific view of the action.

Information and Services

For more information about the entire Lakes Region, visit the office of the **Greater Laconia/ Weirs Beach Chamber of Commerce** (383 S. Main St., Laconia, 603/524-5531, www.laconia-weirs.org), which also runs a seasonal information booth open on weekends in Weirs Beach (513 Weirs Beach Boulevard, 603/366-4770, Jun.–Oct.). Meredith also has a visitors center on Route 3 run by the **Meredith Area Chamber of Commerce** (272 Daniel Webster Hwy., 603/279-6121, www.meredithcc.org).

The area's primary hospital is **Lakes Region General Hospital** (80 Highland St., Laconia, 603/524-3211, www.lrgh.org), and prescriptions can be filled at **CVS Pharmacy** (96 Daniel Webster Hwy., Belmont, 603/528-1113) (note that it isn't open 24 hours).

Internet access is available in Laconia at **Awakenings Espresso Café** (62 Canal St., Laconia, 603/524-1201, www.awakeningsespressocafe.com) and in Meredith at the **Meredith Public Library** (91 Main St., Meredith, 603/279-4303, www.meredithnh.org/lib.php).

SQUAM LAKES

The natural, quiet beauty of the tiny towns surrounding Big Squam Lake ooze with such quintessential New England cuteness that Hollywood decided they were the perfect place to film *On Golden Pond* back in 1981. Visitors to the area feel that same sense of serenity, and often come back year after year to towns like Ashland, Holderness, and Moultonborough—each blessed with all the recreation of Winnipesaukee, but none of the noise or crowds.

Squam is actually two spring-fed lakes connected by a channel in Holderness: Little Squam is only two miles long to Big Squam's six. Between the two of them, they're home to 67 islands, not to mention miles of beaches and unspoiled forest.

€ Squam Lakes Natural Science Center

Mountain lions have long been extinct from New England, but you can still see a live one at this excellent nature center (23 Science Center Rd./Rte. 113, Holderness, 603/968-7194, www.nhnature.org, 9:30 A.M.–4:30 P.M. daily May–Oct., $13 adults, $11 seniors, $9 youth 3–15, free children under 3) that is hands-down the best in New England. The center has dozens of local animals, including a bobcat, several black bears, otters, and flying raptors arranged in spacious enclosures along a 0.75-mile wooded nature trail. (Most of the animals were injured and unable to survive in the wild.)

Where it really excels, though, is in the interactive exhibits that accompany each animal—they're imaginative and educational for kids and adults alike. (Case in point is the "long jump" that compares your personal best with the mountain lion's; let's just say you'll be glad she's behind a fence.) The center also has an informative exhibit on the star of the northern lakes: the common loon. If you'd like to see one up close, it also has a lakeside branch which offers 90-minute lake tours of Big Squam ($22 adults, $20 seniors, $18 youth, free children 3 and under) that explain the geography of the lakes as well as the ways loons communicate to avoid predators.

Castle in the Clouds

A few miles east of Squam Lake, this stone arts and crafts cottage (455 Old Mountain Rd./Rte. 171, Moultonborough, 603/476-5900, www.castleintheclouds.org, 10 A.M.–4:30 P.M. late May–mid-Oct., $12 adults, $9 seniors, $5 youth 7–14, free children 6 and under) is perched romantically above the surrounding lakes atop the Ossipee Mountain Range. Named Lucknow when it was built in 1914, the castle was the brainchild of Thomas Plant, an eccentric shoe company magnate with a love for the outdoors. Tours of the home include the brilliant art deco furnishings as well as the outdoor gardens. If you'd rather just admire the view, you can take a scenic drive around the property and enjoy the grounds for $5 a person.

Other Sights

The smart-looking brick home known as the **Whipple House Museum** (14 Pleasant St./Rte. 3, Ashland, 603/968-7716, www.oldashlandnh.org, 1–4 P.M. Wed. and Fri. July–Aug., free) was given to the town of Ashland for use as a historical museum by Nobel Prize–winning medical doctor George Whipple. On the grounds of the historical museum is also the **Glidden Toy Museum** (49 Main St., 603/968-7289, 1–4 P.M. Wed.–Fri. Jul.–Aug., $1 adults and youth over 12), a delightful trip down memory lane to the time when toys didn't have to have a million lights and buzzers to grab a kid's attention. The exhaustive collection of toys goes back to 1850, and includes doll houses, children's books, trucks and trains, and Raggedy Andy and Shirley Temple dolls. Ashland's newest historical museum is equally appealing to kids: the **Ashland Railroad Station Museum** (69 Depot St./Route. 132, 1–4 P.M. Sat. Jul.–Aug.) is one of the best preserved 19th century depots in New England. It's now chock-full of train photos and artifacts from the old Boston & Maine and Concord & Montreal Railroad companies.

If hanging out on the lakes for awhile makes you suddenly crazy for loons, learn more about the water bird with the eerie call at the **Loon Center** (183 Lee's Mill Rd./off Rte. 25, Moultonborough, 603/476-5666, www.loon.org, 9 A.M.–5 P.M. Mon.–Sat. year-round, plus 9 A.M.–5 P.M. Sat.–Sun. July–mid-Oct., free). This home-grown museum explains such mysteries as why loons' eyes are red, why chicks ride on their parents' backs, and what that ghostly cry actually means. A nature trail along the shores of Moultonborough Bay, a branch of Lake Winni, takes in coves where loons are known to nest in spring.

Shopping

Country store meets organic farm stand at **Longhaul Farm Country Store & Garden Centre** (Rte. 113, Holderness, 603/968-9333, www.longhaulfarm.com, 9 A.M.–4 P.M. daily., or call ahead, May–Oct.). In addition to all kinds of produce and New England specialty products (from homemade jams to organic stone-ground flour), the shop stocks fresh-baked pastries and hand-cut steaks. Stop by on a Friday night between 5 and 7 P.M. for free wine tastings. (To find the farm, drive on Route 113 a mile west of Holderness center.) If the country store has a sophisticated, modern-day equivalent, it's probably best embodied by **Holderness General Store** (863 Rte. 3, 603/968-3446, www.holdernessgeneralstore. net, 8:30 A.M.–7 P.M. Mon.–Fri.; 9 A.M.–6 P.M. Sat.–Sun.). Adorable inside and out, the bright, airy aisles are lined with imported French napkins, imported bath products, and designer picture frames. In back, a deli doles out *caprese* salads and Cubano sandwiches, while the grocery aisles sport gourmet coffees, organic apples, and locally made cheeses. A cooperatively owned, nonprofit **Village Artists & Gallery** (51 Main St., Ashland, 603/968-4445, www.villageartistsandgallery.org, noon–5 P.M. daily June–March; call for hours in spring) is nirvana for the gift-giver: ceramics and glass made by New Hampshire craftsmen, jewelry and small wooden furnishings, quilts, embroidered shirts, paintings, and original-artwork cards.

Food

Want to get up close and personal with the lake during dinner? The only waterfront dining on Squam is at **Walter's Basin** (Rte. 3, Holderness, 603/968-4412, www.waltersbasin.com, $7–18), a restaurant and pub serving a mishmash of Cajun specialties (turkey gumbo, crawdad beignets) and comfort foods

(meatloaf, burgers, and stuffed haddock). The dining room inside is open year-round, whereas outdoor seating runs May through October, and is as apt to see guests arrive by boat as by foot. Equally built for relaxation is the dining room at **The Common Man** (60 Main St., Ashland, 603/968-7030, www.thecman. com, 11:30 A.M.–11 P.M. daily, $13–20). The Ashland outpost of this friendly, quality New Hampshire chain sports a wood-burning stove surrounded by couches and plenty of board games. The food, meanwhile, is just as simple and comforting: New England baked scrod, cashew-crusted chicken, and country meatloaf. Kick the formality up a notch at **◖ The Manor on Golden Pond** (Rte. 3, Holderness, 603/968-3348, www.manorongoldenpond. com, breakfast and dinner, $28–41), an elegant estate house that's both inn and restaurant. The latter serves grand classics (flavor-rich plates of chateaubriand for two, seared foie gras with maple syrup reduction, and crab-stuffed lobster) in the white linen–filled Van Horn room. The house also offers a superb wine list and a special vegan menu. Humbler but equally enticing are the surroundings at **The Woodshed Restaurant** (128 Lee Rd., Moultonborough, 603/476-2311, www.thewoodshedrestaurant. com, 5:00 A.M.–10 P.M. Tues.–Sun.; closed Mon. $16–33), a rustic and rambling 19th-century barn-gone-restaurant, surrounded by wildflower gardens and filled to its rafters (literally) with antiques. Dinners range from hefty (big cuts of prime rib) to delicate (roast duck), and end sweetly with homemade cheesecakes.

Information

For more information on the area, contact the **Squam Lakes Area Chamber of Commerce** (603/968-4494, www.visitsquam.com).

WOLFEBORO AND VICINITY

In contrast to the motorboats and mini-golf of the western shore, the eastern side of Lake Winni is known as the quiet side. That reputation is bolstered by the quaint town of Wolfeboro, which is home to a whopping 5,500 people—most of whom came (and stayed) for its peaceful vibe and

© NHDTTD/ROBERT GRASSI

sunrise at a Wolfeboro beach

relaxed pace. They refer to their town as "the oldest summer resort in America"—a true, if somewhat vague, claim, based on the New Englanders who built homes here two centuries ago, after colonial governor John Wentworth built a summer home on what is now Lake Wentworth. Wolfeboro today is as all-American as you can get, with flags waving on tree-lined streets and a plethora of historic homes harkening back with a sigh to a simpler time.

Nearby Ossipee and Alton are equally sedate. The former stands at the crossroads of the Lakes Region and White Mountains in the shadow of one of New Hampshire's most dramatic peaks, Mount Chocorua. Alton firmly anchors the southern end of Lake Winni with a blink-and-you'll-miss-it town center and a gazeboed common overlooking Alton Bay. Much of the local action is found on the lake and the Merrymeeting River, as well as Mount Major and Straightback Mountain, which are both magnets for hikers.

Wright Museum of American Enterprise

The World War II–era tank bursting out of the brick facade of this ambitious museum (77 Center St., 603/569-1212, www.wright-museum.org, 10 A.M.–4 P.M. Mon.–Sat. and noon–4 P.M. Sun. May–Oct.; noon–4 P.M. Sun. and by appointment Feb.–Apr., $6 adults, $5 seniors and veterans, $3 students, free children under 8) offers a clue about what's inside: exhibits relating to each and every aspect of the years from 1939 to 1945, coeval with the war. In addition to military history, the museum looks at the amazing innovations in technology on the home front.

New Hampshire Boat Museum

There could be no more fitting place for a celebration of wooden boats than the shores of Lake Winnipesaukee, which has seen more than its fair share between its shores. This museum (395 Center St./Rte. 28, Wolfeboro Falls, 603/569-4554, www.nhbm.org, 10 A.M.–4 P.M. Mon.–Sat. and noon–4 P.M. Sun. late May–mid-Oct., $5 adults, $4 seniors, $3 students, children under 13 free) takes visitors from the time when boats were literally powered by horses to the modern era of 225-horsepower motor boats.

Other Sights

A quirky natural history museum built from the collection of an early 20th century doctor, the **Libby Museum** (Rte. 109, 603/569-1035, www.wolfeboronh.us/Libby Museum, 10 A.M.–4 P.M. Tues.–Sat. and noon–4 P.M. Sun. June–mid-Sept., $2 adults, $1 children 6–12, free children under 6) has a fascinating rainy-day collection of stuffed animals and Native American artifacts. The little town of Madison is home to the **Madison Boulder,** the largest glacial erratic in New England, which was washed from more than 12 miles away by a huge flow of glacial meltwater. Made of superheated feldspar and quartz, the hulking giant is 83 feet long, 23 feet high, and 37 feet wide, and weighs in at more than 5,000 tons (that's 10 million pounds, folks). The boulder, which has been designated a National Historic Site, is located in a state park on the north end of town (Rte. 113, Madison, 603/823-7722, ext. 757, www.nhstateparks.org).

Entertainment

Nighttime entertainment can be tough to come by in these quiet parts, but there's usually a good crowd at **Wolfe's Tavern** (90 N. Main St., 603/569-3016, www.wolfeboroinn.com, breakfast, lunch, and dinner) at the Wolfeboro Inn. The authentic New England–style pub (with several fireplaces and pewter beer mugs strewn across the ceiling) serves food, but later in the evening, it's all about the beer—more than seventy kinds. If you drink all 70 (no more than 2 a visit, alas), you'll get to kiss the moose head and hang your own mug on the ceiling.

Events

The active community of Wolfeboro is home to dozens of events throughout the year. The **Great Waters Music Festival** (80 Academy Dr., 603/569-7710, www.greatwaters.org, July–Sept.) draws top performers from nearly every genre, including classical, jazz (Branford Marsalis, Dave Brubeck), folk (Judy Collins, Natalie MacMaster), and Broadway (Linda Eder). Aerodynamic and not-so-aerodynamic crafts alike race in the **Vintage Race Boat Regatta** (603/569-4554, www.nhbm.org, Sept.), which takes place alternating years under the auspices of the local boat museum.

Shopping

Watch the goods getting made as you tour the facilities at **Hampshire Pewter** (43 Mill St., 603/569-4944, www.hampshirepewter.com, 9 A.M.–5 P.M. Mon.–Sat.; tours on the hour 10 A.M.–3 P.M. Mon.–Fri.), then afterward pore over the selection of candlesticks, baby spoons and cups, serving pieces, and Christmas ornaments. Engraving services are also offered. Anyone hungering for both a good book and a good meal at once should head toward **Camelot Books and Gifts** (40 N. Main St., Wolfeboro, 603/569-1771, www.wolfeborocamelot.com, 8 A.M.–5 P.M. daily) The butter-yellow storefront sells both adult and children's books, plus a hefty supply of house-made products such as cheddar-cheese spreads and hot pepper jellies. Outdoor enthusiasts can stock up on gear before hitting the slopes or trails at **The Nordic Skier** (47 N. Main St., 603/569-3151, www.nordicskiersports.com, 9 A.M.–5:30 P.M. Mon.–Sat.). The well-equipped shop has everything for mountain biking, cross-country skiing, and ice skating—including lessons.

Food

It's all ice cream, all the time (or, at least all summertime) at **Bailey's Bubble** (Railroad Ave., 603/569-3612, www.baileysbubble.com, 6 A.M.–8 P.M. Sun.–Wed.; 6 A.M.–9 P.M. Thurs.; 6 A.M.–10 P.M. Fri.–Sat., $2–4). Open May–September, the locally loved stand scoops up banana splits, brownie sundaes, and flavors like maple walnut and cherry chip, plus homemade hot fudge. For going on 40 years, **East of Suez** (775 S. Main St., 603/569-1648, www.eastofsuez.com, 5 P.M.–10 P.M. daily, summer only, $14–17) has been one of the most exotic places to eat in the area. Named for the term for Asia given in Rudyard Kipling's "The Road to Mandalay," the restaurant cooks up pan-Asian cuisine like Philippine adobo, Thai *satay*, Korean barbecue, and sushi. The setting at **Shibley's at the Pier** (Rte. 11, Alton Bay, 603/875-3636, www.shibleysatthepier.com, 11 A.M.–9 P.M. Sun.–Thu., 11 A.M.–10 P.M. Fri.–Sat. Feb.–Oct., $12–18) could be called downright basic if it weren't plunked directly on the shores of Winnipesaukee. Part dock, part restaurant, Shibley's often has a wait for tables (at which point the perfunctory lounge comes in handy). But the view is worth it, and the food is substantial, if unspectacular, with dishes such as broiled shrimp, prime rib, and chicken penne.

Information
The **Wolfeboro Area Chamber of Commerce** (32 Central Ave., 603/569-2200, www.wolfeboro.com) runs a comprehensive information center in the town's historic old train station.

SPORTS AND RECREATION
Beaches
There are of course dozens of beaches, large and small, in the Lakes Region. On Winni, the most popular (and crowded) is **Weirs Beach** (Rte. 3, 603/524-5046, www.city.laconia.nh.us), which has the advantage of being easily accessible and close to the action. A more pleasant and secluded bask in the sun can be found at **Alton Small Swimming Beach** (Rte. 28A, 603/875-0109, www.altonparksandrecreation.com) on Alton Bay. On the eastern side of the lake, avoid Winni entirely in favor of **Wentworth State Beach** (Rte. 109, Wolfeboro, 603/569-3699, www.nhstateparks.com/wentworthbeach.html, $4 adults, $2 children ages 6–11, free children under 5) on the site of colonial Governor Wentworth's former estate on Wentworth Lake. The lake has a bathhouse and picnic area.

Hiking
Several small mountains overlooking Winnipesaukee make for good vantages to take in the enormity of the lake. The highest peak in the region, the 2,384-foot **Belknap Mountain** is one of the most-climbed mountains in southern New Hampshire. Though steep in places, the trail to the summit is fairly moderate, the view of Winni and the Ossipee Mountain Range beyond is nothing short of spectacular. Though shorter than Belknap, the 1,780-foot **Mount Major** is actually a tougher climb with a higher increase in elevation and some steep ridges near the summit. The lack of tree cover at the top, however, makes for an excellent panoramic view.

Between Squam and Winni, the hike up to the 2,029-foot **Red Hill** starts virtually at the shores of Big Squam and climbs strenuously up a near-vertical pitch to the top of the Eagle Ledge. From there, it's a more gentle trail up to the summit of the hill, where a fire tower enhances the view. The total climb rises some 1,650 feet in elevation.

On the shores of Ossipee Lake, **Heath Pond Bog** (Off Rte. 25 near Pine River, 603/539-6323, www.ossipeelake.org) is one of the more unusual natural habitats in the area. The wetland seems almost prehistoric with its wild fauna of orchids, pitcher plants, and Venus flytraps. Part of the bog has actually grown over the pond to create an undulating "quaking bog." Mind the marked paths so as not to disturb the fragile environment here; and keep your eyes out for beavers, fisher cats, and porcupines.

Boating and Fishing
For flatwater canoeing and kayaking directly on Lake Winnipesaukee, visit **Wild Meadow Canoe & Kayak** (Rte. 25, "at the lights," Center Harbor, 603/253-7536, www.wildmeadowcanoes.com), which has several hundred boats for rent ($45/day) in the island-dotted bay of Center Harbor. For something with a little more "oomph," **Meredith Marina** (2 Bayshore Dr., Meredith, 603/279-7921, www.meredithmarina.com) rents Stingray 175s ($295/day) to cruise on your own around the lake. It offers discounts with advanced bookings.

On Squam Lake, **Squam Lakes Resort** (1002 Rte. 3, Holderness, 603/968-7227, www.squamlakesresort.com) has a marina that rents canoes ($49/day), power boats ($119–159/day), and pontoon boats ($189–279/day) for all your loon-spotting needs.

For more than 25 years, registered guide Curt "Gadabout" Golder has been fishing Winni and surrounding lakes for salmon, pickerel, perch, and largemouth bass. His outfit, **Angling Adventures** (Wolfeboro, 603/569-6426, www.fishingnewhampshire.com) offers four-hour fishing excursions ($260 for one person, $300 for two) on the lake complete with all the equipment you need to land your own big one.

Skiing

If you've just *got* to go skiing in the area, give **Gunstock Mountain** (Rte. 11A, Gilford, 800/486-7862, www.gunstock.com, $54 adults, $42 teens age 13–17, $29 seniors or children age 6–12) a try. The mountain's lack of variety and really challenging terrain, however, make it not one of New Hampshire's best. You are better off driving a couple of hours north to Cannon or Loon—or just an hour west to Mount Sunapee.

Camping

The family-run campground at **Bethel Woods** (245 Rte. 3, Holderness, 603/279-6266, www.bethelwoods.com) will get you within a few hundred yards of Squam Lake—close enough to hear the loons cackling at night. The campground has a mix of active and secluded tent sites, and family programs such as a Friday night barbecue and bonfire.

ACCOMMODATIONS
Under $100

The family-owned **1848 Inn and Motor Resort** (258 Endicott St., North Weirs Beach, 603/366-4714, Apr–Nov., $80–110) has clean rooms as well as cottages with kitchens and an outdoor swimming pool, game room, and picnic area. It's located within walking distance to Weirs Beach.

$100-150

Open year-round and located five minutes away from Weirs Beach, the **Lighthouse Inn** (913 Scenic Dr., Laconia, 603/366-5432, www.lighthouseinnbb.com, $90–180) sits on five nicely maintained acres. Rooms are equipped with fireplaces (and one has a whirlpool tub) and private patios. There are also four newly renovated one- and two- bedroom cottages directly on Weirs Beach. The full breakfast comes with very good homemade pastries—as does afternoon tea. Also near Weirs: spacious, comfy rooms are available in and around **Grand View Motel & Cottages** (291 Endicott St., North Weirs Beach, 603/366-4973, www.grandviewmotel-nh.com, Apr–Oct., $123–150), which also offers neatly kept cottages with views of the lake.

It won't win any design awards (at least not for the rooms' wall-to-wall carpeting), but the setting of Squam Lake's **Boulders Motel** (981 Rte. 3, Holderness, 603/968-3600, www.bouldersmotel.com, $115–145) is hard to beat. Private porches are attached to each room, where guests can relax, listen to the loons cry across the lake, and watch the sunset. The property's cottages, meanwhile, come with kitchens, living rooms, and porches. Open June to August only.

$150-250

Decorated with grandfather clocks, maple wood floors, and tufted sofas, **Cozy Inn-Lakeview House** (12 Maple St., Weirs Beach, 603/366-4310, www.cozyinn-nh.com, $65–210) offers 16 cottages (either poolside or with lake views) and rooms in two separate buildings. Rooms in the main houses are simple but functional enough, and are outfitted with quilts and futon seating. You'll find eight very pretty guest rooms (each with lake-themed decor) at **Squam lake Inn** (Rte. 3 & Shepard Hill Rd., Holderness, 603/968-4417, www.squamlakeinn.com, $160–180). The century-old Victorian farmhouse building outfits each chamber with exceptional linens and Wi-Fi, and offers a full breakfast (from four-grain blueberry pancakes to eggs Benedict). Common areas include a charmingly decorated library and a lovely wraparound porch.

$250 and Up

If there's such a thing as sleek country, it's

found at **The Inn & Spa at Mill Falls** (312 Daniel Webster Hwy./Rte. 3, Meredith, 800/622-6455, $129–279), offering the ultimate in comfort and relaxation. Three lovely distinctive inns each offer spectacular lake views, private balconies, in-room fireplaces, black wood furniture, sumptuous tapestries, fireplaces, and fresh flowers. Five wonderful restaurants are also on-site. The lakeside spa is phenomenal, with deluxe, world-class treatment rooms, indoor and outdoor pools, and steam rooms. There's also a first-rate (and enormous) buffet brunch.

GETTING THERE AND AROUND

Gone are the days when the railroad brought passengers from Boston up to Lake Winnipesaukee. These days, your best bet for transport to the region is to rent your own car (or better yet, motorcycle). To drive to the Lakes Region from Concord, take I-93 north to Tilton (20 mi., 20 min.), then take exit 20 to U.S. Route 3 north to Laconia (10 mi., 15 min.). Continue up U.S. Route 3 north to Weirs Beach and Meredith (10 mi., 20 min.). Alternately, to get to Meredith straight from Concord, take exit 23 off I-93, then Route 104 east (40 mi., 50 min.). For Squam Lake, take exit 24 off I-93, then U.S. Route 3 east to Holderness (40 mi., 55 min. from Concord). To get to Winni's eastern shore from Concord, take U.S. Route 202 east to Route 28 north to Wolfeboro (40 mi., 1 hr.).

Concord Coach Lines (603/228-3300 or 800/639-3317, www.concordtrailways.com) provides regional bus service to Meredith, Center Harbor, Moultonborough, and West Ossipee.

The **Greater Laconia Transit Agency** (603/528-2496 or 800/294-2496) runs routes around Laconia, including Weirs Beach.

Western Lakes

As much as it dominates the middle of the state, Lake Winnipesaukee is hardly the only lake around. More than 200 other bodies of water are scattered around the area west of Lake Winni, many of them offering a much quieter and more secluded vacation experience. Even the next biggest lake in New Hampshire, Sunapee Lake, is like a trip back to a bygone era, abounding with quiet coves and relaxing beaches and campgrounds. Even farther west, the area along the Connecticut River is dominated by the cultural mecca of Hanover, home to Dartmouth College and several fine museums.

NEWFOUND LAKE

Located in the no-man's-land between Winni and Sunapee, the hilly shores of Newfound Lake may not draw much attention to themselves, but the residents and kayaking, fishing, and hiking enthusiasts who frequent it wouldn't have it any other way. Surrounded by mountains on all sides, the seven-mile spring-fed lake is unusually pure and pristine, with nary an outboard to mar its surface. The area around it encompasses little communities like Alexandria, Bristol, Bridgewater, and Hebron, where shops tend to close for long lunches, artists sell their creations in a small handful of galleries, and, off-putting as it can be for visitors from the big city, it's perfectly common to have people on the street great you with a smile.

Sights

One of the more unusual terrain features in New Hampshire, the twisted moonscape known as the **Sculptured Rocks** (between Rtes. 3A & 118, Groton, 603/271-3556, www.nhstateparks.org) resulted at the end of the last ice age when rushing ice water whipped tiny grains of sand through a bedrock canyon to drill curious rounded shapes into the rock. Now situated on state park land, the natural

PRIMARY COLORS

Every four years, New Hampshire's residents prepare for an onslaught of glad-handing and baby-kissing when Presidential hopefuls set up shop in Manchester and go out campaigning. By state law, New Hampshire holds its primary at least a week ahead of any other state. Its small land area and population make the state perfect for the kind of retail politics that Americans love: chatting tax policy over diner pie, addressing Lions Clubs and senior centers, swinging an axe at the county fair. The notoriously fickle attitudes of New Hampshire voters have led to many an upset in past years. In 1968, liberal Democrat Eugene McCarthy's strong showing caused Lyndon Johnson to decide not to seek re-election. In 1992, Bill Clinton's upset loss to Paul Tsongas in New Hampshire led to his reputation as the "comeback kid" when he later won the party's nomination and then the national election, the first president to be elected without first winning the Granite State primary. Since then, however, two more presidents have joined that club: George W. Bush, who lost out to Senator John McCain in New Hampshire in 2000, and Barack Obama, who was bested by Hilary Clinton in the 2008 primary. In more recent years, rumblings from Democratic Party members who consider New Hampshire too conservative have led to calls to end the state's favored role. In 2008, Florida and Michigan both moved their primaries into January – but were punished by party officials with a loss of delegates to the convention. So far, the state's primary has survived.

baths make popular swimming holes. Known for the fine quality of its sand, the little town of Bristol was once a major manufacturing center for brick and pottery. Its downtown now makes for a scenic stroll. Of particular note is the Gothic brick **Minot-Sleeper Library** (35 Pleasant St., Bristol, 603/744-3352, www.townofbristolnh.org). Behind the library is a butterfly garden with contemplative benches and succulent flowers calculated to tempt butterflies looking for a snack.

Entertainment
Friendly and full of local characters (including its charismatic hostess/owner), **Kathleen's Cottage** (11 Hobart Rd, Bristol, 603/744-6336) sits on a lakeside spot, serving a late-night menu of traditional, made-from-scratch Irish dishes, lots of beer, and even more whiskey. Live Irish music is staged regularly.

Events
The various towns in this area each hold its own **Old Home Day,** a uniquely New Hampshire tradition begun in the 19th century to revive pride in the state's farming heritage. Alexandria, Bridgewater, Bristol, and Hebron each have their own day in August where they pull out the stops with parades, agricultural competitions, crafts shows, and the like. To find which Old Home Days are happening when, consult www.nhlibertycalendar.org.

Shopping
Under the same ownership and joined with **Earthly Treasures Home & Garden Accessories** gift store, the **Iron Horse Metal Works** (150 Lake St., Bristol, 603/744-5331, www.earthlytreas.com, 10 A.M.–5:30 P.M. Mon.–Fri.; 10 A.M.–5 P.M. Sat.; 11 A.M.–4 P.M. Sun.) is a busy studio that produces wrought-iron sconces, lamps, tables, and planters. Visit the Metal Works to watch them being made, then purchase them in the abutting store, along with hand-crafted cedar furniture, fine art, pottery, art glass, and candles. In the market for a seaworthy work of art? **Newfound Woodworks, Inc.** (67 Danforth Brook Rd., Bristol, 603/744-6872, www.newfound.com, 10 A.M.–5 P.M. Mon.–Wed.; 10 A.M.–5 P.M. Sat.; closed Thurs. and Sun.) is as much museum as it is boatmaker; stop by and admire (or buy) the small company's beautiful cedar canoes, kayaks, and row boats.

Food

Take your pick among three rooms (or a lounge) at **The Homestead Restaurant** (1567 Summer St./Rte. 104, Bristol, 603/744-2022, www.homesteadnh.com, 4:30 P.M.–10 P.M. nightly except Mon. from mid-Oct.–late May; 10 A.M.–2 P.M. Sun., $16–24), a casual and kid-friendly eatery in a country setting. Opt for the huge baked-potato skins, seafood fettuccine, or bourbon-laced tenderloin tips. On Sundays, come for the live jazz brunch. Wednesdays through Sundays, the riverside **Presidential Grille** (26 Central Sq., Bristol, 603/744-6363, $12–20) serves classic surf 'n' turf dishes—clam chowder, baby back ribs, and fried scallops. Be sure to save room for the caramel pecan pie. The food's all well and good at **Wild Hare Tavern** (1030 Mayhew Turnpike, Bridgewater, 603/744-9111, www.newfound-lake.com, $13–25)—the likes of seared day boat scallops and grilled rosemary chicken, but it's the view that takes the cake: Incredible sunsets take place over the lake next door, and the tavern's dining room and outdoor verandah offer front-and-center vantage points.

Information

The **Newfound Region Chamber of Commerce** (603/744-2150, www.newfound-chamber.com) runs a seasonal information booth in downtown Bristol.

SUNAPEE LAKE

Walking into the little town of Sunapee Harbor is like entering into one of those commercials for Pepperidge Farm or Country Time Lemonade. A perfectly manicured town common, complete with white gazebo, overlooks the sailboats bobbing in the bay. Children run free on the lawn outside a quaint country store, while their parents breathe deep in the knowledge they have nothing to do but relax. When the towns around Sunapee Lake (Sunapee to the west, Newbury to the southeast, and New London to the east) were first founded, they were agriculture-based, then manufacturing-based communities. Today, however, they survive by tourism and recreation alone. That isn't to say its shores are overcrowded with tourists; but the town of Sunapee in particular has evolved to please its visitors with a recently created Riverwalk, with live music on weekends, several charming shops, narrated boat tours, kayak rentals, and a town boat launch.

◖ Mt. Kearsarge Indian Museum

This tribute to Native Americans in New England and beyond began humbly enough, from a visit from a Connecticut Grand Chief Sachem Silverstar to the second-grade class of founder Bud Thompson. From that spark began a lifelong interest in Native American culture, as Thompson dutifully collected artifacts and information about the different tribes in the region. Just 15 years ago, he opened this museum (18 Highlawn Rd., Warner, 603/456-3244, www.indianmuseum.org, 10 A.M.–5 P.M. Mon.–Sat. and noon–5 P.M. Sun. May–Oct.; weekends and by appointment Nov.–Dec., $8.50 adults, $7.50 seniors and students, $6.50 children ages 6–12, free children under 6 and Native Americans) in the little town of Warner

country store in Sunapee Harbor

© MICHAEL BLANDING

NEW HAMPSHIRE

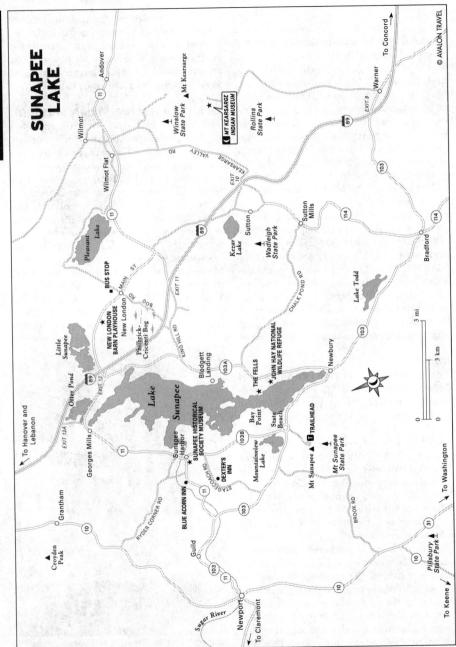

SUNAPEE LAKE

© AVALON TRAVEL

southeast of Sunapee Lake, stocking an exhibit hall with some 1,000 Native American artifacts including a birch-bark canoe and Hopi pottery. This isn't just a stale museum, however; Thompson sees his mission as preserving the living traditions of the country's original inhabitants. A nature trail behind the museum in the so-called Medicine Woods includes signposts explaining how Native Americans would use different plants for medicinal purposes. A garden on the grounds has been grown with the descendants of 2,000-year-old Indian corn plants. And each year in July, the museum sponsors a powwow that brings tribes from all over the country for traditional dancing and craft sharing.

Lake Cruises
There are plenty of ways to get out onto the lake. **Sunapee Cruises** (Sunapee Harbor, 603/938-6465, www.sunapeecruises.com, 2 P.M. daily July–Aug.; weekends only June and Sept.–mid-Oct., $18 adults, $10 children, free children under 4) offers narrated cruises in the afternoon aboard the M/V *Sunapee II.* On the other side of the dock in Sunapee Harbor, the **M/V *Kearsarge* Restaurant Ship** (Sunapee Harbor, 603/938-6465, www.mvkearsarge.com, 6:30 P.M. Tues.–Sun. May–Oct., $36 per person, children's price of $26 available only Tues., Wed., and Thurs. nights) departs for nightly narrated sunset cruises featuring a roast-beef buffet and full bar.

The Fells
The inside of this colonial revival summer cottage on the shores of Sunapee Lake might be impressive, but it's the outside that really shines. The former residence of Secretary of State John Hay, this mansion (456 Rte. 103A, Newbury, 603/763-4789, www.thefells.org, house tours 10 A.M.–4 P.M. Wed.–Sun. late June–early Sept.; weekends only late May–late June and early Sept.–mid-Oct., $6 adults, $2 children 6–15, free children under 6) is surrounded by acres of terraced gardens that include a 100-foot row of perennials, a rock garden of rare alpine plants, and a Japanese lily

pool. The owners took particular care to meld the landscaping with the natural environment of the lake. In addition, a mile-long nature trail ambles through the property.

Other Sights
Located in a former carriage stable right in Sunapee Harbor, the **Sunapee Historical Society Museum** (74 Main St., Sunapee Harbor, 603/763-9872, 1–4 P.M. Tues.–Sun., 7–8 P.M. Wed. Jun.–Aug.; 1–4 P.M. Sat.–Sun. Sept.–mid-Oct., free) is a paragon of the genre. Inside are exhibits telling the fascinating story of the area from its origins as a logging and manufacturing center to the grand hotels that once graced its banks. Highlights include old ship engines and a library of several thousand antique stereoscopic slides (the Viewfinders of their day).

Entertainment
A mainstay on the summer stock circuit since 1933, the **New London Barn Playhouse** (84 Main St./Rte. 114, New London, 603/526-6710, www.nlbarn.org) presents feel-good musicals and children's plays in a converted barn. Past graduates of the theater's apprentice program include Hollywood actors Laura Linney and Taye Diggs.

Events
The Fells' natural beauty is augmented by man-made creativity at the annual **Artists Weekend at the Fells** (603/763-4789, www.thefells.org, July), a juried art show featuring regional artists painting the historic gardens; Celtic musicians and a "wet paint" sale add to the mix. Sunapee takes center stage at the **Love Your Lakes Day** (603/763-2210, www.lakesunapee.org, Aug.), which features a parade and boat show in Sunapee Harbor. There might not be too many clams in the lake, but that doesn't stop area residents from celebrating **Chowderfest** (877/526-6575, www.lakesunapeenh.org, Oct.), a high-stakes chowder competition and music fest. Guests are invited to try samples and vote for their own favorite.

Shopping

Stock up on pottery, locally made soaps, and penny candy at **Wild Goose Country Store** (77 Main St., Sunapee, 603/763-5516, 8:30 A.M.–6 P.M. daily June–Feb.; call for winter and spring hours), the friendly little stop with scuffed wood floors, a helpful staff, and plenty to browse. Out front, an old checker board on a pedestal invites passersby to stop and jump a few kings. If you're on the lookout for incredibly well-priced heirloom-quality home furnishings, head straight for **Rosewood Barn and Country Store** (1386 Rte. 103, Newbury, www.rosewoodgallery.net, 603/763-2882, 10 A.M.–5 P.M. daily). The three-story red barn is brimming with the excellent-quality pieces that they import directly from the Himalayas. They also sell well-priced prayer rugs, plus marble vases, lamps, and chess sets. Everything you need to accessorize your home (particularly your lake home) can be found at **Deck Dock Home & Garden** (81 Edgemont Rd./Rte. 103B, Sunapee, 603/763-3266, www.deckdock.com, 9:30 A.M.–5 P.M. daily May–Sept.; 10 A.M.–5 P.M. Thurs.–Sun. Oct.–April). Browse shelf after shelf of blown-glass ornaments, birdhouses, carved wood sculptures, and model ships. And if you don't own a lake home? This place may just inspire you to get one.

Food

From May through October, Sunapee Lake visitors can grab dinner on a narrated cruise with **M/V Kearsarge Restaurant Ship** (Sunapee Harbor, 603/938-6465, www.mvkearsarge.com, 6:30 P.M. Tues.–Sun., $36 adults, $26 children). The dinner itself may not be terribly varied (it's a roast beef buffet nightly), but how else can you catch a bite while you catch a breath? The fresh pastas, thin-crust pizza, and panini at **Bellissima Brick Oven Trattoria** (Newbury Harbor, Newbury, 603/763-3290, www.bellissima-trattoria.com, $17–19) make for a satisfying end to any day's hiking or boating. The family restaurant also has an ice cream stand open in the summer.

Information

The **Sunapee Lake Area Chamber of Commerce** (603/526-6575, www.sunapeelakenh.org) runs an information booth by the docks in Sunapee Harbor.

CLAREMONT AREA

A small industrial city of just under 14,000 residents, Claremont has lots to offer the leaf-peeper and outdoor adventure-seeker alike. Its natural resources provide easy access to fishing and mountain biking and hiking trails. Meanwhile, its downtown Main Street, though hampered in the retail area by the presence of a Wal-Mart nearby, has undergone a recent revitalization effort that's made a farmers market and concerts fun weekly occurrences all summer long.

◖ Saint-Gaudens National Historic Site

The beauty of the country landscape of southwestern New Hampshire could inspire anyone to turn out great works of art. Imagine, then, what it did for a great artist like Augustus Saint-Gaudens, the master sculptor of the American Renaissance at the turn of the 20th century. Best known for the Robert Gould Shaw Memorial in Boston and the statue of William Tecumseh Sherman in New York's Central Park, Saint-Gaudens established his summer studio in the town of Cornish in 1885. At the height of his powers in 1900, he was struck with colon cancer while living in Paris, and returned to live in the area year-round, continuing to turn out great work and teach students in the art of sculpture.

Named Aspet after his father's hometown in France, the site (139 Saint-Gaudens Rd., Cornish, 603/675-2175, www.sgnhs.org, 9 A.M.–4:30 P.M. late May–Oct.; grounds only Nov.–late May, $5 adults, free youth and children under 16) is now a wild fantasia of gardens, terraces, barns, and pergolas in the middle of the New Hampshire countryside. The sculptor drew a colony of artists to him on the site, including writer Willa Cather, fellow sculptor Daniel Chester French, and painter

Maxfield Parrish (who, it's said, was inspired by the brilliant vistas in Cornish to create the famous cerulean blue "Parrish sky"). For nearly a decade, the artists lived a Bohemian lifestyle of mutual inspiration. Tours of the site take in six buildings, including the artist's studio and a carriage house with antique carriages, as well as terraced perennial gardens studded with fine sculpture and artwork.

The Fort at No. 4 Living Museum

Before the Revolutionary War, there was the French and Indian War, a kind of dry run for the colonists in which the British and French contested one another for control of disputed land from Quebec to Ohio. Back in 1759, this corner of New Hampshire was actually the northwestern frontier of the English colonies and bore the brunt of much of the fighting at a nameless colonial fort simply called "No. 4." Though it fell into disrepair over the course of 200 years, it has since been rebuilt into a living-history museum (267 Springfield Rd./Rte. 11, Charlestown, 603/826-5700, www.fortat4.org, 10 A.M.–4:30 P.M. Wed.–Sun. June–Oct., $8 adults, $6 seniors, $5 youth 6–12, free children under 6) stocked by costumed interpreters, some of whom live at the fort year-round. Visitors can participate with soldiers in churning butter, shooting muskets, and passing the time with 18th-century games. The fort also sponsors various historical reenactments over the course of the year.

Covered Bridges

The Cornish area is home to no fewer than four covered bridges, including the defiantly named **Blow-Me-Down Bridge** (Mill Rd., off Rte. 12A), an 86-footer over a deep gorge. The prime attraction, however, is the **Cornish-Windsor Bridge** (Rte. 12A), a 450-foot bridge in two spans over the Connecticut River that is the longest covered bridge in the United States. Built in 1866 on heavy spruce timber reinforced with steel plates, the bridge is still open to traffic, and remains a testament to 19th-century engineering.

COVERED BRIDGE CAPITAL OF NEW ENGLAND

Bridges were covered to protect the roadway and supports from the ravages of New England weather. The covers were relatively easy to replace compared with the supports driven into the river bottoms. Originally, there were hundreds more covered bridges in New England; but with modern road-building techniques, the covers became superfluous, and many were never replaced when they became damaged or rotted. Those that remain have largely been kept up for sentimental or aesthetic reasons, not to mention the economic benefits of drawing tourism to the area. Vermont and New Hampshire have long fought over which of the states can lay claim to being the "covered bridge capital of New England." Actually, Vermont blows New Hampshire out of the water, with 102 surviving historic bridges to the Granite State's 54. If it's any consolation, however, New Hampshire can lay claim to having the longest covered bridge, the 450-foot Cornish-Windsor Bridge over the Connecticut River. Because the official boundary between the states is the west bank of the river, nearly the entire bridge is firmly within New Hampshire state territory.

Entertainment

In Claremont, catching a game at **Mcgee's Sports Bar & Grill** (129 Broad St., Claremont, 603/542-0926) is considered second only to the real thing. The lively crowd packs the bar three bodies deep on big game nights, and still keeps the place jumping most other evenings, as well. The Italian Renaissance Revival building belonging to the **Claremont Opera House** (130 Broad St., Claremont, 603/542-4443, www.claremontoperahouse.com) actually shares space with the Claremont Town Hall. But there's nothing municipal about the upstairs space used by the Opera: The frescoed ceiling and frieze-covered walls are perfect foil for performances ranging from *The Nutcracker Suite* and *Peter Pan* to comedy shows and classical concerts.

Events

Claremont's annual **Fall Festival** (603/543-1296, www.claremontnhchamber.org, early Oct.) features a chili cook-off, apple-pie contest, and 5K road race. **Claremont Winterfest** (603/542-7019, www.claremontnh.com, late Feb.–early Mar.) is a weeklong festival of skiing, tubing, fireworks, and other events to warm the spirit. A few days before the festival, in nearby Unity, snowmobilers gather for the annual **Crescent Lake Snowmobile Ride In** (www.clrsr.com, Feb.), in which riders are clocked as they blast down a 1,000-foot-long icy chute on the lake to see who can go the fastest. Hot cider is provided to spectators.

Food

A true greasy spoon if there ever was one, **Daddypops Tumble Inn Diner** (1 Main St., Claremont, 603/542-0074, 6 A.M.–2 P.M. daily year-round, $4–9) has a near-cult following for its no-frills, authentic diner atmosphere. The huge plates of hash browns, burgers, and omelets may not be miraculous, but they come fast and at a good price. Even more retro than all that, **Jean Marie's Candy Works** (16 Opera House Sq., Claremont, 603/542-2229, 10 A.M.–5 P.M. Tues.–Sat.; 11 A.M.–5 P.M. Sun.; closed Mon., $2–6) operates as an old-fashioned soda fountain. Step up to one of the booths and take your pick between milkshakes, sundaes, and cones. Yet more comfort food is on the menu at **Martini Bar at Hullabaloo** (32 Pleasant St., Claremont, 603/542-5747, 5 P.M.–11 P.M. Mon.–Sat.; 3 P.M.–9 P.M. Sun, $6–13), a coffee shop that recently reinvented itself as a martini bar. In between swigs, nosh on homemade soups, salads, and wraps, and kick back to the nightly live music.

Information

For more information on the area, visit the **Greater Claremont Chamber of Commerce** (24 Opera House Sq., Claremont, 603/543-1296, www.claremontnhchamber.org).

LEBANON AND HANOVER

The first permanent settlers arrived in Hanover in 1765, four years before Dartmouth College was established. Today, it's difficult to separate the two; the college is the town's main source for economy and attention, and the town is considered by the college to practically be an extension of its campus and an invaluable resource for its students (perhaps because it provides students something to do besides cow-tipping).

And indeed, there is plenty to do and see around town, from shopping to loafing around in the cafés on Main Street. That's equally true of nearby Lebanon: Even with about 13,000 residents and a regional airport, the town's covered bridges and back roads still give it an air of village-meets-urban life.

Hood Museum of Art

The collection at this excellent college art museum (Dartmouth College, Hanover, 603/646-2808, http://hoodmuseum.dartmouth.edu, 10 A.M.–5 P.M. Tues. and Thurs.–Sat.; 10 A.M.–9 P.M. Wed.; noon–5 P.M. Sun., free) begins with the building itself—an award-winning postmodern design by architects Charles Moore and Chad Floyd. The collection inside is like a survey course of the world's art, presenting European and American painting, sure, but also holding a particularly strong collection of less familiar areas like the Near East and Africa. Among the highlights are a spectacular 9th-century bas-relief from an Assyrian palace, and a collection of art from Indonesia and the South Pacific that is among the most important in the country.

Situated on the main campus green, the museum is attached to the **Hopkins Center** (603/646-2422, http://hop.dartmouth.edu), a gargantuan performing arts center that is the cultural lynchpin of western New Hampshire and eastern Vermont. Any day of the week, the center might present circus performers, contemporary Latin dance, Japanese No theater, the swing revival rhythms of Big Bad Voodoo Daddy, or the sidesplitting rants of comedienne Margaret Cho. If you can't be entertained here, you probably don't know how.

Dartmouth College

Of all the elite Ivy League colleges in New England, Dartmouth (603/646-1110, www. dartmouth.edu) is the only one not situated in a city. Founded by Puritan minister Eleazar Wheelock under a royal charter in 1769, it is one of nine colleges in the country founded before the revolution. Its obscure location for the time stems from the fact that it was originally hatched by English clergy members as a college to educate Native American youth. That dream was scuttled almost from the very beginning, however, when Wheelock steered the college towards educating the descendents of Englishmen. The college has graduated a slew of notable alums over the years, from Daniel Webster to Dr. Seuss. Unlike most liberal arts colleges, however, Dartmouth distinguishes itself by a hard lean to the right politically—a source of tension at times with the surrounding community.

The college campus is beautiful, with many Georgian and Federal-style buildings situated around a vast green known as The Green. The information booth there distributes brochures with a self-guided walking tour to the area. Among the highlights are the 1782 Dartmouth Hall, the 200-foot bell tower of Baker Library, and the Romanesque Rollins Chapel. More formal student-led tours leave from the **Admissions Office** (McNutt, 603/646-2875, tours 11:15 A.M. Mon.–Thurs., 11:15 A.M. and 3 P.M. Fri., 10 A.M. and noon Sat., Sept.–May; call for summer hours).

Other Sights

Calling the shores of Mascoma Lake their "chosen vale," three families of the religious sect known as the Shakers settled near the town of Enfield in the 19th century. They lived there for more than 130 years, pursuing a simple life of farming and manufacturing, with 200 buildings at their height. Now the site is

the **Enfield Shaker Museum** (447 Route 4A, Enfield, 603/632-4346, www.shakermuseum. org, 10 A.M.–5 P.M. Mon.–Sat.; noon–5 P.M. Sun., $7.50 adults, $6.50 seniors, $5 students and youth 10–17, free children under 10), which interprets their beliefs and demonstrates traditional Shaker craftwork. For 30 years, the **AVA Alliance for the Arts** (11 Bank St., Lebanon, 603/448-3117, www.avagallery.org, 11 A.M.–5 P.M. Tues.–Sat., free) has been showcasing the best visual artists of the region, as well as providing art classes to nurture the creativity of future artists.

Entertainment

Serious beer drinkers frequent the bar stools at **Seven Barrel Brewery Pub** (North Country Plaza, Rte. 12A, W. Lebanon, 603/298-5566), where pints of home-brewed specialties like Seasonal Maple Ale, Cream Ale, and Cask-Conditioned Red Ale go down fast and smooth. On campus, the **Spaulding Auditorium** (Dartmouth College, Hanover, 603/646-2422, http://hop.dartmouth.edu) at the Hopkins Center for the Arts is where to catch plays, concerts, and dance shows put on by visiting artists as well as students.

Events

Dartmouth's biggest event each year is **Winter Carnival** (603/646-2466, www.dartmouth. edu, early Feb.), a four-day celebration of the season with athletic (and not-so-athletic) competitions, giant snow sculptures, and hot chocolate–induced merriment. Incidentally, the carnival served as the setting for a 1939 movie starring Ann Sheridan called, what else? *Winter Carnival.*

Shopping

Go green—quite literally—with a little help from the stock at **Dartmouth Co-op** (21 S. Main St., Hanover, 603/643-3100, www.dartmouthcoop.com, 9 A.M.–5:30 P.M. Mon.–Fri.; 10 A.M.–5 P.M. Sat.–Sun.). Here, everything from golf hats and tote bags to sweatshirts and sleepwear comes emblazoned with the school's logo. All royalties from the store go directly to the college. Stylish denim and various designer pants and frocks hang on the racks of **Campion's Women's Shop** (44 S. Main St., Hanover, 603/643-1700, 10 A.M.–5:30 P.M. daily), where you'll also find a solid selection of upscale cosmetics and beauty products. Indulge the pickiest sweet tooth at **Chocolate Now** (3 Lebanon St., Hanover, 603/643-9031, www. chocolatenow.com, 10 A.M.–6 P.M. Mon.–Sat.), stocked with specialty and artisan chocolates, imported and locally made alike. Pick up everything you need to revamp your home—including design advice and services—at **C. Beston & Co.** (1 South St., Hanover, 603/653-0123, www.cbeston.com, 9:30 A.M.–5:30 P.M. Mon.–Fri., 9 A.M.–5 P.M. Sat.). Mostly, however, they spotlight furnishings and accessories, from overstuffed chairs and painted benches to carved clocks and funky vases. One could spend hours rifling through the aisles of **Left Bank Books** (9 S. Main St, Hanover, 603/643-4479, 10:00 A.M.–5:30 P.M. Mon.–Fri., 10 A.M.–5 P.M. Sat.–Sun.), which carries loads of fiction (classic and contemporary), poetry, how-tos, and kids' books. Stock up on everything you need—except, perhaps, the time to read them all.

Food

Late-night cramming takes on new meaning at **Ramunto's Brick 'N Brew Pizzeria** (9 South St., Hanover, 603/643-9500, www.bricknbrew. com, 11 A.M.–midnight Mon.–Sat.; noon–midnight Sun., $6–8), home to extra-greasy, thin-crusted pies served on red-checked tablecloths. The garlic and cinnamon knots are a snack beloved by students. Snug in the corner of the Dartmouth Green, the 99-seat Irish pub **Murphy's on the Green** (11 South Main St., Hanover, 603/643-4075, www.murphysonthegreen.com, 11:30 A.M.–10:30 P.M. Mon.–Thurs.; 11:30 A.M.–12:30 A.M. Sat.; 11:00 A.M.–9:00 P.M. Sun., $15–22) serves students and professors an inexpensive, better-than-average bar menu and lots of Irish-pub atmosphere, as well as a pricier menu of creative American entrées. Sit in the beautiful back room (full of detailed wood wainscoting

and 19th-century pews) and nosh on snacks like nachos and wings, or fill up on the very good Irish stew, fresh fish-and-chips, or more eclectic options like fajitas and cheese ravioli.

Calling all tandoori lovers: The fiery menu at **India Queen** (44 S. Main St., Hanover, 603/643-6900, www.indiaqueenrestaurant. com, 11:30 A.M.–10:30 P.M. Mon.–Fri. $7–13) requires your attention. Opt for the chicken skewers if you're looking for something sumptuous and skewered, or the mixed grill if you're truly famished. With its snazzy new bar added, ◖ **Three Tomatoes Trattoria** (1 Court St., Lebanon, 603/448-1711, www.threetomatoestrattoria.com, 11:30 A.M.–10 P.M. Mon.–Fri.; 5 P.M.–11 P.M. Sat.–Sun., $11–18) has gone from locally loved trattoria to evening destination. And to be sure, the place gets packed—mostly for the simply prepared, authentic Italian dishes that fly out of the wood-fired oven. That means thin-crust pizzas, pastas like the unforgettable seafood cannelloni, and lots of daily specials. The attractive, spotlit dining room of **Mai Thai Cuisine** (44 S. Main St., Hanover, 603/643-9980, www.maithaicuisine.com, 12 P.M.–9:30 P.M. Mon.–Sat.; 5 P.M.–9 P.M. Sun., $8–15) happily caters to both Thai-food neophytes (with well-known staples like pad thai and spring rolls) and more adventurous eaters (with plates of *pla douk pad ped,* or catfish in spicy-sour sauce).

Information

The **Hanover Area Chamber of Commerce** (603/643-3115, www.hanoverchamber.org) runs an information booth on The Green.

SPORTS AND RECREATION
Hiking and Biking

The Newfound Lake area is popular for hikers. The 3,121-foot granite peak of **Mount Cardigan** offers a dizzying view of the lake below. The glaciers aid in the climb, having smoothed out one side into a moderate ascent, while leaving the other side a steep cliff. A fire atop the peak cleared out vegetation 150 years ago, affording a clear view from the Green Mountains to the Whites. Located on a 73-acre wildlife sanctuary, the hike up **Bear Mountain** (West Shore Dr., Hebron, www.nhaudubon.org) is a two-mile hike through quiet spruce and balsam fir, with views of Newfound Lake and Mount Cardigan visible through the trees. The trailhead is on West Shore Dr., about 4/10ths of a mile from the center of Hebron. Park on Cross Street, another 1/10th of a mile up the road.

In the Sunapee region, **Mount Sunapee** is better known for its ski area, but the 2,743-foot peak and its attached state park is also a great summer hiking destination. While the summit is built up with buildings, the trails to it are quiet and scenic. A favorite is the Andrew Brook Trail, which starts on Mountain Road in Newbury, a mile south of Route 103, and passes by the shores of the aptly named Lake Solitude on its way up the mountain. The hike is steep and strenuous, but not challenging in terms of footing.

A favorite hike for Dartmouth students is **Moose Mountain.** The trail to the 2,300-foot peak is part of the Appalachian Trail. Views include the college far below. For an equally scenic, but less demanding, walk in the woods, try the **Sugar River Recreational Trail,** an eight-mile trail cut along the riverbank from Newport to Claremont. The trail passes by two long covered bridges as well as several smaller iron truss and girder bridges, along with lots of natural beauty. In addition to hikers, the trail is suitable for mountain bikers and cross-country skiers.

Beaches and Boating

On the shores of Newfound Lake, **Wellington State Park** (West Shore Rd., Bristol, 603/744-2197, www.nhstateparks.com/wellington.html, mid-May–Oct., $4 adults, $2 children 6–17, free children under 6) has a quarter-mile beach along with picnic area and hiking trails. **Mount Sunapee State Park** (Rte. 103, Newbury, 603/763-5561, www.nhstateparks.com/sunapee.html, Jun.–Sept., $4 adults, $2 children 6–17, free children under 6) has a wide, family-style beach on the south end of Sunapee Lake. The beach also has canoe and kayak

rentals for a spin around the pond. **Sargents Marina** (Rte. 11 & Cooper St., Georges Mills, 603/763-5036, www.sargentsmarina.com) offers pontoon, ski, and row boat rentals ($125–250/day) at the northern tip of the lake.

Skiing

Less than two hours from Boston, **Mount Sunapee** (Rte. 103, Newbury, 603/763-3500, www.mtsunapee.com, $64–68 adults, $48–56 seniors 65–69 and youth 13–18, $38–42 seniors 70+ and children 6–12, free children under 6) offers an excellent compromise between terrain, location, and value. While certainly not as challenging as any of the mountains in Vermont or the Whites, Sunapee is known for excellent grooming and a friendly style that caters especially to families. Be warned that due to its popularity, the lift lines can get long on winter weekends. More serious skiers should turn to **Ragged Mountain** (620 Ragged Mountain Rd., Danbury, 603/768-3971, www.raggedmountainresort.com, $49–59 adults, $38–48 youth 6–18, $28–38 seniors 65–74 and children 6–12, $18–28 seniors 75+, free children under 6), a two-peak ski resort that bills itself as an "anti-Killington" for its two simple chair lifts and no-frills base lodge. What isn't simple are the trails, a good mix of narrow chutes, wide cruisers, and challenging glades that will keep you on the tip of your skis. Despite its proximity to Boston, however, Ragged has somehow stayed below the radar of many skiers, leaving it uncrowded even on peak weekends.

ACCOMMODATIONS
$100-150

Grab a great night's sleep and peace and quiet to boot at **Blue Acorn Inn** (21 Sleeper Rd., Sunapee, 603/863-1144, www.blueacorninn.com, $100–140). The bed-and-breakfast, open year-round, sits on 22 acres of meadows and hills, and offers guests plenty of room to spread out—in its enormous great room (complete with roaring fireplace), the wide backyard and patio, or in any of the six carefully decorated guest rooms with poster beds and both private and shared bathrooms.

With a back yard overlooking the Connecticut River, the natural setting of **Chieftain Motor Inn** (84 Lyme Rd., Hanover, 603/643-2550, www.chieftaininn.com, $120–175) is tough to beat. Guest rooms are paneled in shining pine, are humbly but neatly decorated, and the property offers an outdoor pool, a sitting room full of games and movies, and a continental breakfast. The beautiful, sumptuously decorated rooms at 【 **Inn on Newfound Lake** (1030 Mayhew Turnpike, Bridgewater, 603/744-9111, www.newfoundlake.com, $135–165) pair intricate wallpapers and plush fabrics with four-poster beds, antiques, and oil paintings. The lakefront inn is open year-round, and houses a good restaurant and tavern for enjoying a pre- or post-dinner drink.

Ten distinctive, pretty, guest rooms sit in the main house of **Dexter's Inn** (258 Stagecoach Rd., Sunapee, 603/763-5572, www.dextersnh.com, $110–185), while seven additional chambers are in the inn's Annex. Outside your room are activities galore—three tennis courts, an in-ground pool, a kids' play room, and an adult game room for playing pool, table tennis, foosball, and darts.

$150–250

Reminiscent of a Provençal estate, 【 **Home Hill Inn** (703 River Rd., Plainfield, 603/675-6151, www.homehillinn.com, $160–200) is an exquisite and romantic escape with only twelve guest rooms. Each is outfitted with tile or marble washrooms, crisp Frette linens, and many have fireplaces and private terraces. Dining in the butter-yellow dining room is a luxury indeed—dishes can be perfectly prepared organic roasted chicken, lamb loin with ratatouille, and beautiful plates of rare French cheeses.

$250 and Up

Overlooking the Dartmouth College green, **The Hanover Inn** (Main St., Hanover, 603/643-4300, $225–275) is a study in country elegance: Guest rooms are furnished with handmade quilts and wingback chairs, the common areas are recently renovated, and there are two acclaimed restaurants, the Daniel Webster Room (a crystal-laden, fine dining room) and Zins (a warmly appointed, bustling wine bistro).

GETTING THERE AND AROUND

To drive to Sunapee Lake from Concord, take I-89 north to exit 12, then Route 103B south, and look for the sign for Sunapee Harbor (40 mi., 50 min.). For Lebanon, take I-89 north from Concord to exit 18, then take Route 120 south (55 mi., 1 hr.). For Hanover, take the same exit, but take Route 120 north (60 mi., 1 hr. 5 min.). To get to Claremont, take Route 103 west from Sunapee (15 mi., 25 min.) or Route 120 south from Lebanon (15 mi., 25 min.).

Concord Coach Lines (603/448-2800 or 800/637-0123, www.concordtrailways.com) runs the Dartmouth Coach shuttle service from Boston to Hanover (The Hanover Inn, Main St.), Lebanon (90 Etna Rd.), and New London (NH Park & Ride, exit 12 off I-89). For the Sunapee Region, contact **Sunapee Coach** (603/606-7258) for limousine service from Boston or Manchester airports.

Advance Transit (802/295-1824, www.advancetransit.com) runs bus routes around Lebanon and Hanover, connecting them with Norwich and White River Junction in Vermont.

WHITE MOUNTAINS

This is a part of New Hampshire guaranteed to take your breath away—even before you scale the impressive heights of Mount Washington, the highest point in the Northeast. Here, there are peaks piled upon peaks, creating both stunning views and an irresistible magnet for rock climbers and day hikers eager to bag the summits of the Whites. At the same time, those eager to instead bag great shopping deals revel in the nearby retail utopia that is North Conway, famed for miles of premium outlet stores.

With wilderness in every direction, you'd hardly expect something as banal as national politics to rear its head. And yet New Hampshire's North Country holds the distinction of being home to Dixville Notch, which casts the first votes for president every election and thus sees the candidates making

the rounds earlier (and with far more fanfare) than nearly anywhere else. Meanwhile, historical distinction can also be found in the spectacular resort hotels that hover in these hills, harkening back to the days when the wealthy came here to escape civilization (though not, of course, civility).

PLANNING YOUR TIME

The White Mountains are divided conveniently into two halves, corresponding to the two highways that cut through the peaks. On the west side, along I-93, is the Franconia Region. Here the peaks are smaller (though by no means unimpressive) and the highway is studded by family-style attractions and trailheads to day hikes in the excellent Franconia State Park. The prime attraction is the hike

HIGHLIGHTS

◖ The Flume Gorge: Walk the boardwalk along a glacier-carved wonderland (page 490).

◖ Cannon Aerial Tramway: The Old Man might be gone, but the mountains will always remain (page 491).

◖ Kancamagus Highway: Be warned: Driving it is even more difficult than pronouncing it (page 493).

◖ Mount Washington Auto Road: The express route to the top of New England is eight miles of twisting vistas (page 504).

◖ Mount Washington Cog Railway: The progeny of Old Peppersass make their ascent of the White's highest peak (page 505).

◖ Tuckerman Ravine: Landslides are just part of the fun at this daredevils' hike-and-ski bowl (page 506).

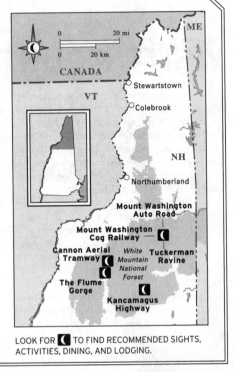

LOOK FOR ◖ TO FIND RECOMMENDED SIGHTS, ACTIVITIES, DINING, AND LODGING.

along the wooden boardwalk along the mossy cliffs of the **Flume Gorge.** In the same area, you can rise above the peaks with a ride up the spectacular **Cannon Aerial Tramway.**

In the eastern White Mountains, state Route 16 is bottlenecked by the retail paradise of the North Conway outlets. After that, it climbs high into the Presidential Range, named for the majesty of the peaks that seem to rise above mere mortal mounts. The star attraction, of course, is Mount Washington, the highest peak in northeastern United States. In addition to hiking to the summit, two unique routes rise to the occasion, the **Mount Washington Cog Railway** and the **Mount Washington Auto Road,** each with its own history and scenic thrills. Along the slopes of Mount Washington,

the bowl-shaped **Tuckerman Ravine** is a favorite destination for backpack powder skiing—just watch out for landslides.

Connecting the two sides of the region, the **Kancamagus Highway**—or as it's known, the "Kanc"—has to be driven to be believed. During foliage season, its vertiginous pitches and climbs defines the word scenic. North of the White Mountains, the Great North Woods stretch toward the Canadian border with endless landscape of mountains, hardwood forests, and wetlands.

Restaurants in the more touristed areas stay open year-round. Most keep regular hours; the majority serve just lunch and dinner. But keep in mind that hours can be more erratic in the outlying towns. If you're looking to plan a meal ahead, be sure to call and confirm first.

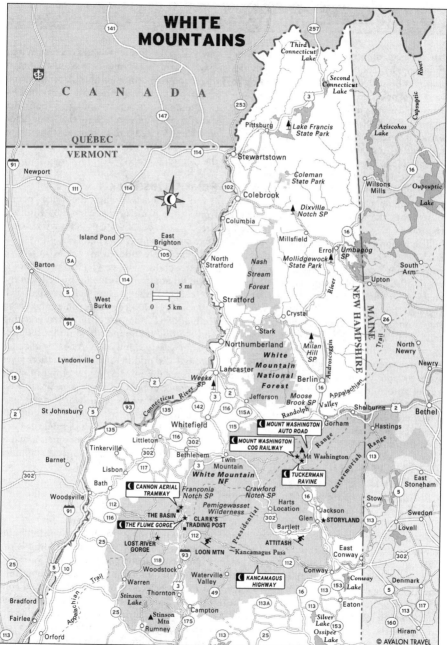

WHITE MOUNTAINS

CANADA

QUÉBEC
VERMONT

NEW HAMPSHIRE

MAINE

Third Connecticut Lake

Second Connecticut Lake

Pittsburg

Lake Francis State Park

Stewartstown

Coleman State Park

Colebrook

Dixville Notch SP

Columbia

Millsfield

East Brighton

Errol
Umbagog SP

Mollidgewock State Park

Wilsons Mills

Oupsuptic Lake

South Arm

Upton

North Stratford

Nash Stream Forest

Stratford

Crystal

Stark

Northumberland

White Mountain National Forest

Milan Hill SP

Lyndonville

Lancaster

Berlin

Moose Brook SP

North Newry

Newry

Weeks SP

Jefferson

Randolph

Gorham

Shelburne

Bethel

St Johnsbury

Whitefield

Valley

Hastings

Twin Mountain

White Mountain NF

Mount Washington Auto Road

Mount Washington Cog Railway

Mt Washington

Tuckerman Ravine

Littleton

Bethlehem

Franconia Notch SP

Crawford Notch SP

Harts Location

Cannon Aerial Tramway

Pemigewasset Wilderness

Presidential Range

Carter-Moriah Range

East Stoneham

Stow

Swedon

Lovell

Tinkerville

Lisbon

Bath

Woodsville

The Basin

The Flume Gorge

Clark's Trading Post

Glen

Jackson

Storyland

Barnet

Lost River Gorge

Loon Mtn

Bartlett

Attitash

East Conway

Woodstock

Kancamagus Pass

Kancamagus Highway

Conway

Denmark

Warren

Waterville Valley

Conway Lake

Bradford

Fairlee

Stinson Lake

Thornton

Campton

Eaton

Silver Lake

Ossipee Lake

Hiram

Orford

Stinson Mtn

Rumney

Appalachian Trail

Connecticut River

Androscoggin River

5 mi

5 km

© AVALON TRAVEL

Franconia Region

An unspoiled paradise for outdoorsmen, Franconia has abundant four-season activities that can be scaled up or down according to your level of expertise. In summer, the mountains yield excellent hiking and biking, and the rivers call fly fishermen and kayakers to their banks. Those same pursuits continue through fall, but against a backdrop of jaw-dropping foliage colors. Then comes winter, when many argue the area is at its best: That's when the slopes glisten with fresh powder, and ski resorts fling open their doors, drawing enthusiasts (both skiing and snowmobiling) by the thousands.

The region is named for Franconia Notch, the V-shaped cut carved out by the glaciers that runs through the mountains for eight miles north of the town of Lincoln. It was through that notch that the railroad was first run through the region in the 19th century, bringing lumbermen and sawmills into the mountains and the Great North Woods beyond. It wasn't long before the tourists followed; when the Interstate went through in the 1940s, the route became a prime attraction in the golden age of auto-touring, with family-friendly attractions popping up in Lincoln and around. Many of them still survive today, making the area a curious blend of natural beauty sprinkled with spots of garish commercialism.

PLYMOUTH AND WATERVILLE VALLEY

Considered the gateway to the White Mountains, the area from Plymouth to Thornton in best known for its alpine skiing, snowshoeing, and many miles of cross-country skiing trails. Spring through fall in the Waterville Valley brings biking, fishing, golf, and community picnics. It's all anchored by the Town Square of Waterville Valley Village, a picturesque pondside spot set against the rugged, looming mountains. Such scenery extends to Plymouth, a town also home to curiosities like the polar caves—glacial creations that you

can walk right through—and no less than four covered bridges. Plymouth was once a major manufacturing center in the 19th century, and still has a picturesque downtown framed by the mountains beyond. Among its industries was a baseball-glove company that once made gloves for the Red Sox; its most famous visitor was Babe Ruth, who posed for a photo-op at the factory.

Polar Caves Park

If you are wondering where the "polar" comes from in the name of this park (705 Rumney Rte. 25, Rumney, 603/536-1888, www.polar-caves.com, 9 A.M.–5 P.M. daily May–mid-Oct., $14 adults and children over 9, $10 children 4–9, free children under 4), it's courtesy of the glaciers that rammed through this valley in the last ice age. As the glaciers finally began to melt and recede 11,000 years ago, some gargantuan ice blocks fell from the cliffs above, cracking and eroding the granite here into a series of twisting passages and caves. A boardwalk built through the middle of the destruction gives visitors a close-up view of the power of water to conquer even solid rock. The site is a bit hokey with all of its polar bear imagery and efforts to appeal to the family demographic, but you really can't do much to spoil the force of Mother Nature. Also on the site is a maple syrup museum, a petting zoo, and a boulder maze for the kids to get lost in.

Sights

Before he became the 19th-century lion of the U.S. Senate, Daniel Webster made his very first pleas in a courthouse in Plymouth in 1806 (unfortunately, he lost). Now the building is the **Plymouth Historical Museum** (Court St., Plymouth, 603/536-2337, www.plymouthnh-historicalsociety.org, call for hours), and contains old photographs from the days when Plymouth was a major manufacturing center for sporting goods, and artifacts from the very first days of White Mountains tourism. On the campus of Plymouth State University, the **Karl Drerup Art Gallery** (Draper and Maynard Building, Main St., Plymouth, 603/535-2614, www.plymouth.edu/gallery, 10 A.M.–4 P.M. Mon.–Sat. and 4–8 P.M. Wed. Sept.–May, free) stages imaginative exhibitions of contemporary art from around the world. One of the newest covered bridges in New Hampshire, the 2001 **Smith Millennium Bridge** is also said to be the strongest. The 170-foot span crosses the Baker River at Smith Bridge Road.

Entertainment and Nightlife

In summer, **Shakespeare in the Valley** (Town Square, Waterville Valley, 603/726-0098, www.shakespeareinthevalley.com) bellies up to the bard at the Mary Devlin/Margaret Harmony "Women of Grace" Theatre Under the Stars in Town Square. With minimal sets and props, no sound amplification, and actors frequently performing in, with, or behind the audience, the troupe seeks to mirror Elizabethan performance traditions as closely as possible. The downstairs lounge of **Lucky Dog Tavern** (53 Main St., Plymouth, 603/536-2260, www.luckydogtavernandgrill.com, 4:30 P.M.–1 A.M. Mon.–Thu., 11:30 A.M.–1 A.M. Fri.–Sun.) operates as a music club and bar: Open mic nights are every Thursday, DJs come in every Saturday, and live bands play everything from jazz to '50s swing every other night. Can't stand to miss the game? Then don't. Watch it with scores of other dedicated fans at **Legends 1291 Sports Pub** (Town Square, Waterville Valley, 603/236-4678). The joint offers big-screen viewing, a nice outdoor deck, and plenty of pub grub for scarfing during the commercials. Dance performances, chamber music, and lectures and readings by big-name authors take place regularly at **Silver Center** (17 High St., Plymouth, 603/535-2787, www.plymouth.edu/silver), the performance venue for Plymouth State University.

Events

Every October, Waterville Valley Ski Resort celebrates the colors of the season with its **Fall Carnival** (603/236-8175, www.waterville.

com, early Oct.). Events include music, midway rides, and eating contests. The best entertainment, however, is provided by the foliage on the surrounding slopes.

Shopping

Health nuts and fans of good flavor alike make regular stops at **Peppercorn Natural Foods** (43 Main St., Plymouth, 603/536-3395, www.peppercornnaturalfoods.com, 9 A.M.–6 P.M. Mon.–Fri.; 9 A.M.–5 P.M. Sat.), where bins of bulk spices, fair-trade coffees, and organic produce share shelf space with gourmet teas and the house's own maple syrup. Both genders can freshen up their wardrobes at **Maurices** (389 Tenney Mountain Hwy., Plymouth, 603/536-9001, www.maurices.com, 9 A.M.–8 P.M. Mon.–Sat.; 10 A.M.–6 P.M. Sun.). The well-priced shop carries everything from tie-neck halter shirts and cropped cardigans for women to button-down shirts and lots of denim for men. Before you hit the hiking trails, stock up on foodstuffs at the old-fashioned **Jugtown Country Store** (Town Square, Waterville Valley, 603/236-8662, www.jugtowncountrystore.com, 8 A.M.–7 P.M. Mon.–Fri.; 8 A.M.–6 P.M. Sat.–Sun.): They have fresh-baked breads, pies, breakfast pastries, and delicious sandwiches.

If you need a trail map, a local guidebook, or just a good read for the afternoon, the shelves at **Bookmonger** (Town Square, Waterville Valley, 603/236-4544, 10 A.M.–5 P.M. Sun.–Thu.; 10 A.M.–6 P.M. Fri.–Sat.) can accommodate. The store also sells bestsellers, classic titles, magazines, and greeting cards. Buy or just rent what you need for conquering Mother Nature at **The Adventure Center at Waterville Valley** (Town Square, Waterville Valley, 603/236-4666, www.waterville.com, 9 A.M.–6 P.M. Mon.–Fri., 8 A.M.–6 P.M. Sat.–Sun. late Jun.–early Sept.; 9 A.M.–5 P.M. daily late May–Jun. and early Sept.–mid-Oct.), a full-service mountain biking and hiking center, selling bikes and accessories and cross-country skiing and snowshoe equipment. They'll even set you up with lessons and organize guided tours.

Food

Go, and go hungry to the **Lucky Dog Tavern** (53 Main St., Plymouth, 603/536-2260, www.luckydogtavernandgrill.com, 4:30–10 P.M. Mon.–Thu.; 11:30 A.M.–10 P.M. Fri.–Sun., $8–15); big portions, an all-you-can-eat salad bar, and generous portions of pork loin, fajitas, and eggplant casserole are the pride of the kitchen. Built from the reclaimed lumber of an old barn, the **Wild Coyote Grill** (Rte. 49, above White Mountain Athletic Club, Waterville Valley, 603/236-4919, www.wildcoyotegrill.com, 4 P.M.–9 P.M. daily, $15–22) boasts mind-blowing views of Mount Tecumseh, Mount Osceola, and Snow's Mountain. While you gaze, dig into grilled beef with butternut ravioli, almond-and-oatmeal-crusted chicken, and grilled venison steaks. Rather make the meal something quick and easy? ◖ **Bad Dawgs** (70 A Main St., Plymouth, 603/254-5640, www.baddawgs.com, 12 P.M.–8 P.M. Mon.–Sat.; 12 P.M.–6 P.M. Sun., $2–4), despite the name, serves hot dogs that are anything but bad; you might even call them gourmet.

Foster's Steakhouse (231 Main St., Plymouth, 603/536-2764, 4–10 P.M. Mon.–Fri.; noon–10 P.M. Sat.–Sun., $8–23) is owned by the Common Man group, a New Hampshire chain of good-quality and family-friendly eateries. This outpost is pure classic chop house—with a high-energy dining room and open kitchen. Specialties include steakhouse salad (iceberg lettuce, blue cheese dressing, bacon, and shaved red onion) and a monstrous 20-ounce cowboy steak served with steak *frites*. The newcomer in town is **Aglio** (6 Village Rd., Waterville Valley, 603/236-3676, $13–22), a family-friendly spot for good Italian (the pizza and pastas are the highlights). In good weather, be sure to ask for a table on the outdoor patio, which overlooks the rushing waters of Snow's Brook Waterfall.

Information

For more information about the area, stop by the **Plymouth Chamber of Commerce** (1 Foster St., Plymouth, 603/536-1001 or 800/386-3678, www.plymouthnh.org) right in front of the Common Man Inn. For activities in the Waterville Valley area, visit the **Waterville Valley Region Chamber of Commerce** (12 Vintinner Rd., Campton, 603/726-3804 or 800/237-2307, www.watervillevalleyregion.com), which runs an information center just off exit 28 on I-93. The **White Mountain National Forest** (603/447-5448, www.fs.fed.us/r9/forests/white_mountain) also runs a visitors center in Campton off the same exit (71 White Mountain Dr., Campton, 603/726-3804).

WOODSTOCK AND LINCOLN

Families are drawn to the area around Franconia Notch like Yogi Bear to a picnic basket—and for good reason. The area (encompassing the communities of Lincoln and North Woodstock, and Cannon and Loon Mountain) boasts a solid slew of outdoor attractions appropriate for all ages, from the Flume Gorge and Lost River to Clark's Trading Post and the aerial tramway. All of the above developed attractions make exploring the area's wilderness more convenient for groups and those with kids—so day trips and short hikes are relatively hassle-free.

◖ The Flume Gorge

The thrilling rush of river in this deep-sided gorge (I-93, exit 34A, Franconia Notch State Park, 603/745-8391, www.flumegorge.com, 9 A.M.–5 P.M. daily May–Oct.; until 5:30 P.M. July–Aug., $13 adults, $9 children 6–12, free children 5 and under) has been a tourist attraction since it was discovered in the 19th century. A wooden walkway suspended along the side of the cliff takes visitors alongside the rushing stream, past whirlpools and waterfalls and over two covered bridges before ending in a pleasant forest trail loop. If you've ever ridden a flume ride at an amusement park, you'll get the basic idea. A "flume" is a geological feature formed when a plug of basalt is worn away from between two walls of harder granite—the result is a torrent of water in a steep gorge. While *this* flume gorge isn't the only one in the region, it is notable for its size and ferocity, stretching almost three football fields in length, with 70- to 90-foot-high rock cliffs on either side.

◖ Cannon Aerial Tramway

There's no better way to see the White Mountains than to get on their level. And the quickest way to do that is this breathtaking gondola (I-93, exit 34B, Franconia Notch State Park, 603/823-8800, www.cannonmt. com, 9 A.M.–5 P.M. daily mid-May–mid-Oct., $13 adult, $10 children 6–12, free children under 6) that rises to the 4,180-foot summit of Cannon Mountain in just eight minutes. On that rhetorical "clear day," it's said you can see straight through to Canada and New York. You'll have enough work on your hands to gawk at the more immediate scenery, which includes the granite-capped peaks of the Franconia Range and the shimmering surface of Echo Lake far below.

The base camp for the tramway was once also the best viewing area for the White Mountain's most famous resident: The Old Man of the Mountain, a 40-foot-long stone visage in the rocks high atop Cannon Mountain that looked shockingly like the profile of a goateed old man. Alas, the rocks came down in a landslide in 2003, a tragedy from which the state (and its tourism base) is still reeling. You can relive the long life of the venerable symbol at the **Old Man of the Mountain Historic Site,** which features a small museum dedicated to the rock profile and the heroic efforts of the engineers who saved it from falling for more than 100 years.

Other Natural Wonders

The result of the glacial sculptors who worked over the mountains can be seen in several other places as well. Also located within Franconia Notch State Park, **The Basin** (I-93, exit 34A, 603/745-8391, www.nhstateparks.org) is a 20-foot-wide glacial pothole worn away by rocks and sand swirling in the Pemigewassett River 15,000 years ago. Located at the base of Cannon Mountain, the site includes a curious natural sculpture known as the "Old Man's Foot." A few miles west of North Woodstock, the **Lost River Gorge and Boulder Caves** (Rte. 112, Kinsman Notch, 603/745-8031, www.findlostriver.com, 9 A.M.–4 P.M. daily May–mid-Oct.; until 5 P.M. July–Aug., $14 adults, $10 children 4–12, free children under 4) is another glacier-formed gorge, with the notable distinction that the river here mostly flows underground. Boardwalks take visitors into the caves to see moss-covered chambers and underground waterfalls right out of an Indiana Jones movie.

New England Ski Museum

In these days of Gore-Tex and heated sky cars, it can be difficult to imagine the bravery and daring of the original pioneers who tackled the slopes with little more than a pair of wooden skis and a woolen hat. This museum (I-93, exit 34B, Franconia Notch State Park, 603/823-7177, 10 A.M.–5 P.M. daily late May–Mar., free) at the base of Cannon Mountain has an extensive collection of antique equipment and signage as well as biographical exhibits on some of the colorful men—and women—who

© NHDTTD/BRENDA RUDINSKY

Cannon Mountain gondola

brought the sport into the limelight. A special exhibit looks at the elite 10th Mountain Division of New England skiers who fought in World War II.

Clark's Trading Post

Capturing black bears and making them perform for tourists may seem just a bit, well, savage. But if you are into that kind of thing, check out the trained bear shows at this old-fashioned tourist trap (110 Daniel Webster Hwy./Rte. 3, Lincoln, 603/745-8913, www.clarkstradingpost.com, 9:30 A.M.–6 P.M. daily late June–early Sept.; open weekends mid-May–late Sept., $12 adults and children 6 and up, $6 children 3–5, free children under 3) along the lines of Wall Drug in South Dakota or South of the Border in South Carolina. Among the grab-bag of attractions here are a bumper-boat ride, an upside-down mansion, and a climbing wall designed as a scale model of the Old Man in the Mountains. Several retro museums cater to the eight-year-old in all of us with antique cars, firefighting equipment, and more.

Other Sights

The train that used to bring tourists to see the Old Man, the Flume, and other attractions of the Notch has now been pressed into service as the **Hobo Railroad** (64 Railroad St., Lincoln, 603/745-2135, www.hoborr.com, 11 A.M., 1 P.M., and 3 P.M. daily mid-June–Oct.; weekends only late May–mid-June and Dec., $13 adults, $10 children 3–11, free children under 3), a two-hour trip along the wooded banks of the Pemigewassett River in vintage cars. For the complete experience, get the Hobo Picnic Lunch, which comes free with your very own bindle staff.

Events

One of the more unusual events of the White Mountains, the **Rubber Ducky Regatta** (603/745-6621, www.lincolnwoodstock.com, early Sept.) allows kids (and grown-ups) to adopt a duck for five bucks, then throw it into the Pemigewassett to race against its yellow rubber brethren. Prizes in past years have included a kayak, a mountain bike, and $150 for the best duck name.

Sometimes the rugged peaks of the Whites resemble the Highlands of Scotland; at no time, in fact, more than during the **Highland Games** (Loon Mountain, 603/229-1975, www.nhscot.com, Sept.), in which kilted pipers and athletes from 60 different clans battle it out in games of skill. It's the largest annual Scottish gathering in the Northeast.

Shopping

You won't find the usual garden-variety antiques selection at **The Dreaming Pig** (141 Main St., Lincoln, 603/745-6900); the eclectic shop ferrets out animal-shaped glass sculpture, oversized hand-carved mirrors, rainbow-hued candles, and hand-stitched quilts. Before you head out on that expedition, explore the bookshelves of **The Mountain Wanderer** (57 Main St./Rte. 112, Lincoln, 800/745-2707 or 603/745-2594, www.mountainwanderer.com, 9 A.M.–6 P.M. Wed.–Mon.; closed Tue.). The selection of travel maps and outdoor guides is indispensable for paddling, hiking, biking, climbing, fishing, bird-watching, and anything else you can do in or to the outdoors.

Food

Housed in an original train depot built in the 1800s, the family-owned and -operated **Woodstock Station** (135 Main St./Rte. 3, North Woodstock, 800/321-3985, www.woodstockinnnh.com, 11:30 A.M.–10 P.M. daily; call for off-season hours, $9–23) camps it up for the kids (and, depending on how much you like trains, the adults) with a menu custom-built for young palates (à la dishes like the "artichoo-too" and "box car-o-shrimp"). Peter and Catherine Johnson, the couple behind **Gypsy Cafe** (117 Main St./Rte. 112, Lincoln, 603/745-4395, 11:30 A.M.–4 P.M. and 5–9:30 P.M. Fri.–Sat.; 5–9 P.M. only Sun., Wed., and Thu., $7–23), love to travel—and it shows in their menu combining Thai, Cuban, European, Latin, and American Southwest flavor influences. Dig into bowls of ale-cooked clams, Cuban pork, and barbecued chicken.

At the casual, buzzing **King's Corner Cafe** (264 Main St./Rte. 112, North Woodstock, 603/745-3802, www.kingscornercafe.com, 7 A.M.–2 P.M. Mon.–Sat.; 7 A.M.–1 P.M. Sun., $7–12), you can fill up on big country breakfasts, Caesar salads, and overstuffed sandwiches before or after perusing the adjoining gallery. An espresso bar and wireless Internet access are also offered.

Information

For more information on activities in the area, stop into the visitors center at **Franconia Notch State Park** (I-93, 603/745-8391, www.franconianotchstatepark.com) or the **Lincoln-Woodstock Chamber of Commerce** (Rte. 112, Lincoln, 603/745-6621, www.lincolnwoodstock.com). The **White Mountain National Forest** (603/447-5448, www.fs.fed.us/r9/forests/white_mountain) also maintains a new visitors center in Lincoln (I-93, exit 32, 603/528-8721).

◖ KANCAMAGUS HIGHWAY

It's difficult to find an *un*-scenic highway in the White Mountains. But some highways are just more scenic than others, and the Kancamagus (or the "Kanc") might just offer the best eye-candy in the entire Northeast. We're talking pinball-machine switchbacks, pitched dives through forested ledges, and narrow straightaways flanked by mountains on both sides that will leave you feeling alternately like a bird and an ant. The highway, also known as Route 112, begins in Lincoln, and ends 35 twisting miles away in Conway. Along the way it passes over the summit of Mount Kancamagus (the name means "The Fearless One," after a Penacook sachem in the early 1800s) and has several pull-offs for short hikes. Take the three-mile **Boulder Loop Trail** for views of the Passaconaway Valley far below. Of course, all of the scenery is enhanced tenfold during foliage season—then again, so is all the traffic, so you might be better off driving the Kanc in spring or summer instead. If you do venture out when the leaves are doing their thing, leave early in the morning. As a bonus, you might just disturb a moose or a black bear walking back across the road from an early breakfast.

FRANCONIA AND LITTLETON

Franconia's quietude is a bit surprising given that it has an entire area named after it; its biggest claim to fame is being the place where Robert Frost bought a farm. The rest of the town is undeveloped countryside and residential neighborhoods. The big town around is Littleton, which began as a small farming community along the fertile Connecticut River in the early 19th century. Then the Boston & Maine Railroad came through, and the community rapidly grew wealthy by crushing its corn and wheat into flour in grist mills and cutting the North Woods' abundant lumber in its sawmills. Today, Littleton's handsome downtown is filled with historic Victorian

THE OLD MAN OF THE MOUNTAIN

A moment of silence, please, for the craggy profile that once jutted out from Cannon Mountain in Franconia Notch State Park. Made of natural granite, the formation's grandfatherly resemblance lured thousands of visitors every year, and was said to symbolize the rugged spirit of New Hampshire's people. (Daniel Webster remarked about it: "Up in the Mountains of New Hampshire, God Almighty has hung out a sign to show that there He makes men.") Alas, the formation collapsed on May 3, 2003, and since then a public charitable trust fund and the Old Man of the Mountain Revitalization Task Force have combined to create an expanded museum at Cannon Mountain's base, which shows what the Old Man of the Mountain looked like before it fell. Exhibits include photos detailing the heroic efforts of Niels Nielson and his family to keep the rock from eroding, as well as pieces of the Old Man himself. Follow signs from exit 34B.

© NHDTTD/PETER SLATTERY

maple sugaring along the roadside

architecture and shops to poke around in, making for a pleasant afternoon outing.

Frost Place

This secluded farmstead where Robert Frost lived and worked with his family from 1915 to 1920 is hardly just a stale museum. Every year, the building's trustees sponsor a fellowship for a young poet to live in the house for several months and work on his or her own verses. Perhaps it's that living spirit of poetry that infuses this site (Ridge Rd., Franconia, 603/823-5510, www.frostplace.org, 1–5 P.M. Sat.–Sun. late May–June; 1–5 P.M. Wed.–Mon. July–early Oct., $5 adults, $4 seniors, $3 students 6–18, free children under 6) with such a contemplative feeling. This is the farm that Frost chose to buy after achieving some fame as a poet, and where he wrote some of his best verses, including "The Road Not Taken" and "Birches." The house is open for visitors to wander around the rooms where Frost commenced his "lovers quarrel with the world." Outside, a half-mile nature trail is lined with plaques with some of the poems from his Franconia years.

Other Sights

When you tire of the mountains, the picturesque downtown of Littleton makes for a charming return to civilization. Pick up a self-guided **walking tour** brochure at the local Chamber of Commerce office (111 Main St., 603/444-6561, www.littletonareachamber.com) with information on twentysome 19th-century buildings. Among them is the **Littleton Grist Mill** (18 Mill St., Littleton, 603/444-7478, www.littletongristmill.com, 10:30 A.M.–4 P.M. Wed.–Sat.; 10:30 A.M.–3 P.M. Sun., free), a 1798 waterpowered mill that once ground corn and flour and served as the economic powerhouse that built the community. The mill was meticulously restored to working order using authentic materials; however, current regulations on water releases from the dam upstream make it unable to operate. No matter, the mill is currently open for tours of the milling process, while another 19th-century mill does produce flour from organic grains on-site for purchase in the gift shop.

The prosperity of the booming mill town is

captured by the ebullient **Pollyana statue,** an homage to the goddess of optimism that stands outside the town library. You may wonder at the source of that bully outlook after viewing the hardships suffered by the original inhabitants of these rugged parts in the **Early Settlers Museum** (Rte. 117 & Sunset Hill Rd., Sugar Hill, 603/823-8478, www.sugarhillsampler. com, 9:30 A.M.–5 P.M. daily mid-May–Oct.; 9:30 A.M.–5 P.M. daily mid-Apr.–mid-May, 10 A.M.–4 P.M. daily Nov.–Dec., free). The collection of photographs and antiques offer an in-depth look at the founders of the little village of Sugar Hill, and is attached to a country store selling candles, candy, and other local products.

Entertainment

The musical productions just keep rolling out of **NCCA Papermill Theatre** (Papermill Dr., I-93, exit 32, Lincoln, 603/745-6032, www. papermilltheatre.org), where everything from *Evita* and *Cats* to *Chicago* and *Beauty and the Beast* have been staged over the past 20 years by the North Country Center for the Arts. The company also produces a children's theater. In nearby Whitefield, the nonprofit **Weathervane Repertory Theatre** (389 Lancaster Rd./Rte. 3, Whitefield, 603/838-6072, www.weathervanetheatre.org) puts on musicals and comedies (plus shows for young children) in a red-barn theater.

Events

The mountain meadows north of the notch are filled with violet blossoms every year in time for the **Lupine Festival** (603/823-8000, www. franconianotch.org, mid-June), a street festival and art show with events throughout the region. By governor's decree, each year in early July, Frost Place holds **Frost Day** (603/823-5510, www.frostplace.org, early July) with readings of poetry by the poet-in-residence and musical performances at the farmstead. Littleton rolls up a whole year of celebrations into its annual **Summer Fest** (www.summerfest03561.org, early June), which combines a typical New England county fair with

fireworks and a colorful New Orleans–style street parade.

Shopping

The coin-obsessed and curious alike will want to head for **Littleton Coin Company** (1309 Mt. Eustis Rd., Littleton, 800/645-3122, www.littletoncoin.com, 9 A.M.–4 P.M. Mon.–Fri., tours Wed. and Fri. 1:30 P.M. Jul.–early Sept.). A nationally recognized leader in collecting, the shop is like a miniature museum. Claiming to have the world's greatest cheddar cheese, **Harman's Cheese & Country Store** (1400 Rte. 117, Sugar Hill, 603/823-8000, www.harmanscheese.com, 9:30 A.M.–5 P.M. daily May–Oct.; 9:30 A.M.–4:30 P.M. Mon.–Sat. Nov.–Apr.) is most certainly worth a stop—even if its self-given title is debatable. Either way, the store is undeniably charming, housed in a red barn and stocked with homemade marmalades and jellies, crackers, maple sugar candy, and, of course, cheddar cheese. Individually crafted and full of intricate wooden detail, the tables, chests, chairs, and beds at **P. C. Anderson Handmade Furniture** (253 Center District Rd., Sugar Hill, 603/823-5209, www.andersonfurniture. com, 9 A.M.–5 P.M. daily.) are the kind of investment pieces that last a lifetime.

Food

Owned by a local family and run with everyone else's family in mind, **The Dutch Treat Bar & Grill** (317 Main St., Franconia, 603/823-8851, 11:30 A.M.–8:30 P.M. daily, $6–14) serves big breakfasts, lunches, and dinners at incredibly reasonable prices. After dinner, the pub area rolls out local live music until close. Load up on the maple syrup at ◖ **Polly's Pancake Parlor** (Hildex Maple Sugar Farm, Sugar Hill, 800/432-8972, www.pollyspancakeparlor. com, 7 A.M.–2 P.M. Mon.–Fri., 7 A.M.–3 P.M. Sat.–Sun. May–Oct., $4–7). The sugar house uses organically ground buckwheat, whole wheat, oatmeal-buttermilk, and cornmeal batters (using their own stone-ground corn) to make ethereal pancakes and waffles. Feeling decadent? Add in chocolate chips, walnuts, coconut, or blueberries at will. On your way out, purchase some pre-made mixes so you can re-create the magic at home.

Housed in a friendly bed and breakfast, **The Beale House Inn** (2 West Main St., Littleton, 603/444-2661, 5 P.M.–9:30 P.M. Mon.–Sat.; 5 P.M.–9 P.M. Sun., $17–21) is one of the area's most refined spots for dining. Come for the meticulously prepared entrées of grass-fed beef, free-range chicken dishes, and desserts made from as many local products as possible. Diner lovers will find bliss at **Littleton Diner** (145 Main St., Littleton, 603/444-3994, www.littletondiner.com, 6 A.M.–8 P.M. daily year-round, $4–9), a classic, authentic set-up serving big stacks of pancakes, thick sandwiches, and even thicker burgers. The riverside setting alone at **Miller's Cafe & Bakery** (16 Mill St., Littleton, 603/444-2146, www.millerscafeandbakery.com, 8:30 A.M.–2:30 P.M. Mon.–Sat., 10 A.M.–2 P.M. Sun. Jun.–late Oct.; 8:30 A.M.–2 P.M. Tue.–Sat. late Oct.–May, $4–8) is worth a visit. Fortunately, the food is just as alluring: Order homemade specials like roast beef on herbed focaccia with horseradish, spiced pumpkin soup, big salads, and fresh-baked cookies.

Information

The **Franconia Notch Chamber of Commerce** (603/823-8000, www.franconianotch.org) runs an information center stocked with brochures on I-93 just north of the notch. In downtown Littleton, stop by the information center run by the **Littleton Area Chamber of Commerce** (124 Main St., 603/444-0616, www.littletonareachamber.com) for a self-guided walking tour of town and information on other area businesses.

SPORTS AND RECREATION
Hiking

In addition to the Flume and the Basin, **Franconia Notch State Park** (603/745-8391, www.franconianotchstatepark.com) has many more challenging hikes into the surrounding mountains. You can earn your views from the top of Cannon Mountain by taking the **Kinsman Trail** from the base of the tramway up to the top of the peak, a grueling two-mile ascent that'll have you sounding a barbaric yawp by the end of it. If that's not enough mountain for you, the trail continues another 15 miles over the peak to Lost River Gorge. On the other side of the highway, the **Franconia Ridge** is a popular day hike, despite the difficulty of the gorgeous climb up above the tree line. The loop is a seven-mile passage over Mount Lafayette (5,240 ft.), Mount Lincoln (5,089 ft.), and Little Haystack Mountain (4,760 ft.), with many places to stop and admire the scenery. Keep on your toes for a particularly dangerous section known as the Knife's Edge (use your imagination). The hike takes about seven hours all told; start early during peak season to avoid the cattle herd.

For a fun family hike in the Waterville Valley region, head out on the **Cascade Trail**, a 3.6-mile walk to a picnic area by some impressive waterfalls. The trailhead starts on Route 49, eight miles east of I-93. From the same location also rises the much tougher **Sandwich Mountain Trail,** a little-known hike to one of the most gorgeous mountain views in the area. Since the peak is only 3,993 feet high, it resists the hordes of hikers obsessed with bagging all the 4,000-footers.

Biking

Despite the hills (or because of them) there are many fine routes here for bikers. **Beebe River Road** is an easy ride over a covered bridge and along a former railroad bed that traces the river; it starts at the Town Hall in Campton. Mountain bikers should head for the more challenging territory of the **Greeley Ponds Trail,** which climbs the flank of Mount Osceola and offers views of the Mad River and beaver ponds. Even more challenging is the **Timber Trail** that spurs off of the pond trail for a vertiginous climb rewarded with views of Mount Kancamagus, Mount Tripyramid, and the Painted Cliffs. Rent bikes at **Richelson's Feet First** (7 Town West Rd, Plymouth, 603/536-3338, www.myfeetfirst.com, 10 A.M.–6 P.M. daily) or **Rhino Bike Works** (1 Foster St./Rte.

3, Plymouth, 603/536-3919, www.rhinobike-worksnh.com, 10 A.M.–6 P.M. daily; closes at 5 P.M. on Sat. and Wed., 4 P.M. on Sun.).

Boating and Beaches
In the state park, **Echo Lake** has a small swimming beach and boat rentals.

Skiing
Arguably the best mountain for skiing in New Hampshire, **Cannon Mountain** (I-93, Franconia,603/823-8800, www.cannonmt. com, $64 adults, $46 teen 13–17, $36 youth 6–12 and seniors, free children under 6) has everything a serious skier could want—challenging runs, varied terrain, and a vaunted history that goes back to the beginnings of the sport. Just as refreshing, its location in the middle of a state park means that the base lodge hasn't been built up into a spa/resort/condo complex like some mountains we could name. The biggest downside is the lack of perfect grooming—not that there is much you could do with the sheets of ice that sometimes form on this side of the Whites.

Speaking of overly developed mountains, **Loon Mountain** (60 Loon Mountain Rd., Lincoln, 603/745-8111, www.loonmtn.com, $73 adult, $63 teen 13–18, $53 youth 6–12 and senior, free children under 6) gets hit hard by the crowds, especially on vacation weekends. Come during the week, however, and you'll find a cruiser's paradise, with 45 trails spread out between two lifts, with snowmaking covering almost every inch. A new sky gondola sticks it in Cannon's eye by proclaiming it the longest gondola in New Hampshire. As might be imagined, the view from the top is amazing, with jagged peaks in every direction you look.

Nestled in a valley with its own charming base village, **Waterville Valley** (1 Ski Area Rd., Waterville Valley, 800/468-2553, $67 adult, $57 teen 13–18, $43 youth 6–12 and seniors, free children under 6) doesn't offer the thrills of Cannon or Loon, but does offer excellent value for families, and a few expert runs so dad won't get bored while he's waiting for the

kids. The undiscovered gem of the area may be **Tenney Mountain** (151 Tenney Mountain Rd., Plymouth, 603/536-4125, www.tenneymtn. com, $40–49 adults, $30–39 youth 6–17 and seniors, free children under 6), a smaller mountain that nevertheless offers many exhilarating trails with lots of well-carved turns and glades. Many of the runs are left ungroomed for powder skiing. You won't find any real expert trails here, but you won't ever find any crowds either.

ACCOMMODATIONS
Under $100
At **Cobblestone Inn of Plymouth** (304 Main St., Plymouth, 603/536-2330, www.hotelnh. com, $70–100), the sunny, brightly colored rooms are no-frills, motel-style chambers. The property has an outdoor pool.

$100-150
You may not end up writing home about the accommodations at **Kancamangus Motor Lodge** (Rte. 122, Lincoln, www.kancmotor-lodge.com, $100–150), but for the price, you won't find much to complain about, either. In addition to the clean rooms (most with two double beds and steam bath showers, and some with private balconies), the lodge has an indoor pool. It's located on the Kanc, a mile and a half west of Lincoln center.

Convenient to Plymouth State University, the historic bed-and-breakfast 【 **Federal House Inn** (27 Rte. 25, Plymouth, 603/536-4644, www.federalhouseinnnh.com, $130–170) sits just at the base of Tenney Mountain and offers five guest rooms and suites. Rooms are unusually pretty, and come with amenities like claw-foot tubs, four-poster beds, fireplaces, and Bose alarm clock–radios. Twenty-one comfortable rooms grace the **Woodstock Inn** (135 Main St./Rte. 3, Main St., Woodstock, 603/745-3951, www.woodstockinnnh.com, $125–165), most with amenities like gas fireplaces and pedestal sinks, and some with whirlpool tubs and views of the river. All include coffeemakers, access to the inn's health club, and a full breakfast.

GETTING THERE AND AROUND

To drive to the Franconia area, take I-93 north from Concord to exit 26 for Plymouth (40 mi., 45 min.), exit 28 to Route 49 east to Waterville Valley (60 mi., 1 hr. 15 min.), exit 32 for Lincoln (65 mi., 1 hr. 15 min.), or exit 38 for Franconia (80 mi., 1 hr. 40 min.).

Concord Coach Lines (800/639-3317, www. concordtrailways.com) runs a daily bus from Boston to Plymouth (Chase Street Market, 83 Main St.), Lincoln (Munce's Konvenience, 36 Main St.), Franconia (Mac's Market, 347 Main St., I-93, exit 38), and Littleton (Irving Oil/Circle K, 366 Cottage St., I-93, exit 41). Greyhound Bus Lines (800/231-2222, www. greyhound.com) also runs buses to Lincoln (Munce's Konvenience), Franconia (Mac's Market), and Littleton (Irving Gas Station, 326 Cottage St.)

The Presidential Range

The crowning glory of the White Mountains, the Presidentials are spectacular natural monuments—rugged white granite cliffs, the most notable of which are named for past American presidents or prominent Americans of the 18th and 19th centuries. So while Mount Washington, the range's central summit (and, at 6,288 feet, the highest in the Northeast), may be its best-known and most touristed, there are certainly others well worth exploring—including Mount Webster (after Daniel Webster), Mount Eisenhower, Mount Franklin (after Benjamin), Mount Jefferson, Mount Samuel Adams, and Mount Madison.

Visiting the summit of Mount Washington has become a rite of passage for many New England families—thus the prevalence of bumper stickers stating "This Car Climbed Mount Washington," sold on the mountain. Indeed, the chilly peak is more like a touristy town than a barren wasteland: It's home to a restaurant, museum, souvenir shop, weather

HAIL TO THE PEAKS

Many of the White Mountains are named after our country's past leaders, but who gets top honors? Well, the first three highest peaks follow the order of the Presidents themselves, with Washington (6,288 ft.) at number one, followed by John Adams (5,798 ft.) and Thomas Jefferson (5,715 ft.). Riding on his father's coattails as a subsidiary peak, however, sixth president John Quincy Adams (5,410 ft.) edges out both fourth president James Madison (5,363 ft.) and fifth president James Monroe (5,372 ft.). They shouldn't feel bad; after that, the peaks skip ahead to honor 16th president Abraham Lincoln (5,088 ft.) and then leapfrog a century of presidents to give the nod to 34th president Dwight Eisenhower (4,760 ft.). Originally named Mount Pleasant, that peak was renamed to honor Ike after the president's death in 1969. Rounding out the list, 20th president James Garfield (4,500 ft.) was also honored posthumously after his assassination in 1881; controversial 14th president Franklin Pierce (4,312 ft.) was included no doubt because of his New Hampshire roots; and Grover Cleveland (2,397 ft.) was honored with a small peak as a nod to the fact that he summered in the nearby town of Tamworth. Then, of course, there are the peaks that seem to be named after presidents but aren't. Mount Jackson was named for New Hampshire state geologist Charles T. Jackson, not Andrew; Mount Hayes was named for local hotel owner Margaret Hayes, not Rutherford; and Mount Clinton was named for former state governor DeWitt Clinton, not Bill (or, for that matter, Hillary).

station, and even a train station. Not so the other mountains' summits, which remain un-developed (if not uncrowded in the peak tourist season). The mountains on the high ridge leading north from Mount Washington (Mounts Madison, Adams, and Jefferson) are considered some of the most excellent hikes and climbs in New England.

The lure of all this mountaineering has made the area around the mountains a bustle of ac-tivity—from serious climbers and explorers to cliff-gawkers, day-trippers, and vacationing families. Because this section of the Whites was developed earlier than the western peaks, however, it is scattered with mementoes of the golden age of railroad cars, steamer trunks, and grand hotels.

THE CONWAYS

What was once home to the Pequawket people and, by the 19th century, had become a log-ging and farming village, is now a year-round

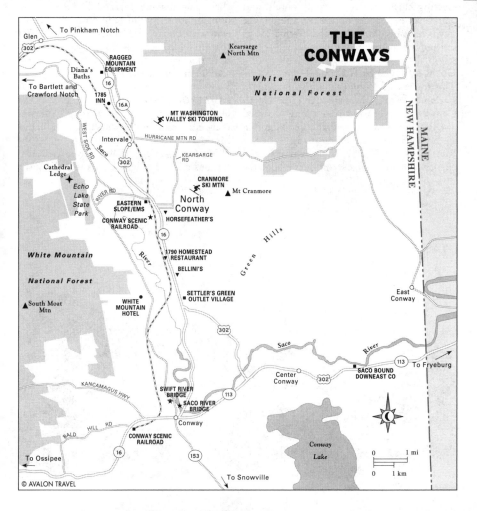

© AVALON TRAVEL

resort area. That's largely thanks to picturesque Conway's proximity to the recreational offerings of the White Mountains, Echo Lake State Park, and Conway's Cathedral Ledge, a favorite among rock climbers. Tourism started flooding into the area in earnest in the 1870s, when railroad service came through the town; by the 1930s, the trains were bringing skiers into the area by the hundreds. They came with plenty of dollars to spend, and one of Conway's villages, North Conway, answered that call by erecting clusters of restaurants, hotels, and brand-name shopping outlets. As a result, the towns have become as much a destination as the mountains themselves.

Conway Scenic Railroad

The towers of Conway's whimsical train station lord over the main street of North Conway like a beacon from a long-vanished age. Passengers can relive that era of Victorian splendor on this restored railroad (Main St./ Rte. 16, 603/356-5251, www.conwayscenic. com), which offers three scenic rides around the Mount Washington Valley on vintage trains. The Valley Train (mid-Apr.–mid-Oct., $22–36 adults, $15–28 children 4–12, free–$16 children under 4) takes in the scenery of the Presidential Range and Saco River with a two-hour trip to Bartlett. A Pullman observation car has original wicker chairs for rocking as you roll. The Notch Train (mid-June–mid-Oct., $40–65 adults, $30–40 children 4–12, $10–28 children under 4) drives straight up through the heart of Crawford Notch with a five-hour chug along dizzying cliffs and sky-high railroad bridges. For the ultimate in nostalgia, hitch a ride with Steam Locomotive #7470, a 1921 coal-fired locomotive that runs periodic short-haul trips between Conway and North Conway. Call for current schedule and rates.

Entertainment

Hear live music Thursday through Sundays year-round at **May Kelly's Pub** (3002 White Mountain Hwy., North Conway, 603/356-7005, 4 P.M.–11 P.M. daily)—from Irish jam sessions and U2 tribute bands to folk music.

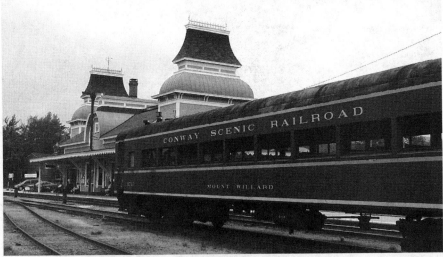

© MICHAEL BLANDING

Conway Scenic Railroad

Musicals and dramatic classics are offered in the summertime by **Mt. Washington Valley Theater Company** (Eastern Slope Playhouse, Main St., North Conway, 603/356-5776, www.mwvtheatre.org). Community Theater Productions are put on by **M&D Productions** (1857 White Mountain Hwy., North Conway, 603/662-7591). Pine-paneled and filled with moose antlers, the cozy **Muddy Moose Restaurant & Pub** (2344 White Mountain Hwy., 603/356-7696, www.muddymoose.com, 11:30 A.M.–9 P.M. daily) is a pleasant place to while away an evening over brews and good local company.

Events

Dirty-minded athletes throw on their jerseys for **Mud Bowl** (Hog Coliseum, 800/367-3364, early Sept.), billed as the World Championships of Mud Football. In addition to the main event, the games include synchronized mud swimming and cheerleader competitions. Even the outlet stores celebrate the foliage in these parts. Each October, the Settlers Green Outlet Village sponsors a **Fall Festival** (603/356-7031, www.settlersgreen.com, late Sept.) in North Conway with pumpkin-carving demonstrations, pumpkin pies, and hot apple cider to go around.

Shopping

To most shoppers anywhere near Conway, it's all about the bargains. Thus they head to **Settlers' Green Outlet Village** (2 Common Ct./Rte. 16, North Conway, 888/667-9636, www.settlersgreen.com, 9 A.M.–6 P.M. Mon.–Thu.; 9 A.M.–9 P.M. Fri.–Sat.; 10 A.M.–6 P.M. Sun.) for tax-free designer goods from stores such as Brooks Brothers, Eddie Bauer, Banana Republic, Coach, and scores of others. There are, however, also a few noteworthy independently owned shops with less-universal wares: For high-quality pottery, woven scarves and linens, and the like, step into **League of New Hampshire Craftsmen** (Rte. 16, North Conway, 603/356-2441, www.nhcrafts.org, 10 A.M.–5:30 P.M. Mon.–Fri., 9:30 A.M.–6 P.M. Sat., 9:30 A.M.–4:30 P.M. Sun.). For any

who came to Conway for both shopping and the great outdoors, the two dovetail at **Ragged Mountain Equipment** (Rte. 16/302, Intervale, 603/356-3042, www.raggedmt.com, 10 A.M.–6 P.M. Sun.–Fri.; 9 A.M.–6 P.M. Sat.). The store has a hefty selection of well-made (and well-priced) mountaineering and hiking equipment.

Food

There's no shortage of chains—from Friendly's to Applebee's—lining the roads in and around Conway and North Conway center. But there are also several good restaurants more unique to the area, such as **Bellini's Ristorante Italiano** (Willow Pl., North Conway, 603/356-7000, www.bellinis.com, 4–10 P.M. daily, $16–25), where Italian specialties (like fettuccine with peas, mushrooms, and ham) and other American staples (ribs, steaks, and burgers) roll out of the kitchen at breakneck pace. The fun, boisterous room centers on a busy martini bar. For more than three decades, **Horsefeathers** (2679 White Mountain Hwy., North Conway, 603/356-2687, www.horsefeathers.com, 7 A.M.–11 P.M. daily, $9–23) has been offering grazing that's as good as the hobnobbing: The watering hole-cum-restaurant serves great onion gratinée, black-pastrami sandwiches, and a filling traditional scallop pie. Some of the best and most original eating in the area is at ◖ **The 1785 Inn** (3582 White Mountain Hwy./Rte. 16, North Conway, 603/356-9025 or 800/421-1785, www.the1785inn.com, 5 P.M.–9 P.M. daily, $18–30), a dining room in a traditional New England bed-and-breakfast. The kitchen creates filling and flavorful dishes like lobster crepes and sherried rabbit, and rolls out an incredible list of homemade desserts (chocolate mousse and coffee buttercrunch pie to chocolate-strawberry cheesecake). The 19th-century farmhouse turned dining room of **1790 Homestead Restaurant** (1921 White Mountain Hwy./Rte. 16, Conway, 603/356-5900, www.homesteadrestaurant.com, 11:30 A.M.–3 P.M. and 4–10 P.M. daily, $12–24) is now a rustic spot serving turkey dinners, big plates of pastas in rich sauces, and grilled steaks.

Information

For more information on the entire Mount Washington Area, visit the **Mount Washington Valley Chamber of Commerce** (2617 White Mountain Hwy./Rte. 16, Village Square, North Conway 877/948-6867, www.mtwashingtonvalley.org), which has an electronic information kiosk at its visitors center. **Conway Village Area Chamber of Commerce** (250 Main St./Rte. 16, Conway, 603/447-2639, www.conwaychamber.com) operates an information booth at the junction of Route 16 and West Main Street.

JACKSON AND GLEN

A little storybook village chock-full of covered bridges and gabled buildings, Jackson fulfills the fantasies of Victoriana fans everywhere. Its village center is almost too cute to be believed, with steepled churches and stable of antiques and country stores. All that beauty drew a gaggle of artists during the mid-1800s, who arrived by rail to board with farmers and paint the mountains around them. Eventually, several grand hotels sprung up in the community, though none still survive. The most prominent landmark now is the covered bridge that was built in 1876 to cross the Ellis River at the entrance to the scenic loop around town. Called the "Honeymoon Bridge," it has long been a favorite spot for newly married couples to have their photographs taken.

Nearby Glen, while less historic, is certainly no less tourist-conscious; instead of attracting visitors with actual quaintness, it manufactures the charm with StoryLand, a sort of low-tech Disney where all the rides are based on nursery and fairy tales.

StoryLand

You've heard of Cinderella and Humpty Dumpty, but what about Professor Bigglestep and Doctor Geyser? You'll meet all of the above at this over-the-top amusement park (850 Rte. 16, Glen, 603/383-4186, www.storylandnh.com, 9 A.M.–5 P.M. daily May–Oct.; until 6 P.M. mid-June–early Sept., $25 per person, free children under 4) that tries to outdo Disney at its own game. The rides are tame, and the whole shebang is a bit overpriced for what you get—then again, it's a bargain compared to Disneyland, and if you have little ones in tow, the look on their faces will be worth every dime.

Entertainment

Every July and August, the **Jackson Gazebo Music Series** comes to the town's center. The free evening concerts range from jazz to orchestral. Everything you want from a sports bar and more is at **Red Fox Bar & Grille** (Rte. 16, Jackson, 603/383-4949, www.redfoxbarandgrille.com, 4 P.M.–10 P.M. nightly; open at noon Sat. and 7:30 A.M. Sun.): wide-screen plasma TVs, wood-fired pizzas, and a full bar. The restaurant is located on Route 16 a mile-and-a-half north of StoryLand. Meanwhile, everything you want from an Irish pub (namely, lots of beer, live music, and good conversation) is on tap at **Shannon Door Pub** (Rte. 16 & 16A North, Jackson, 603/383-4211, www.shannondoor.com, $9–16).

Events

Jackson has an active social calendar. One of the more entertaining events in the area is the **Pumpkin People Festival** (Oct.), in which area residents and businesses compete to create the best pumpkin-headed scarecrow. One of the prettiest road races in the world is the **Covered Bridge Footrace** (June), which takes a five-mile scenic loop around Jackson's "downtown." Expect lots of pretty scenes of mountains at the **White Mountains Art & Artisan Festival** (Aug.), an annual juried art show that takes place in Jackson Park along with music and crafts vendors. For all of these events, contact the **Jackson Area Chamber of Commerce** (603/383-9356, www.jacksonnh.com).

Shopping

Kids will hope to see Santa himself at **Kringle's Country Store** (Rte. 16, Glen, 603/383-6669, 6 A.M.–6 P.M. daily.), and they won't be far off—the old-fashioned store resembles Christmas morning, what with its shelves stocked heavily with treats like maple sugar candy, unusually flavored sodas, and oversized chocolate chip cookies. Sweet tooth still isn't sated? Make your next stop **Flossie's General Store** (Rte. 16A, Jackson, 603/383-6565, www.flossiesgeneralstore.com, 10 A.M.–5 P.M. Mon. and Thurs.–Sat.; 9:30 A.M.–4 P.M. Sun.; closed Tues.–Wed.), right next to the town's covered bridge. And in addition to the penny candy selection, you'll happen upon jewelry, handbags, and colorful puzzles made by local craftsmen. Speaking of which, puzzle lovers ought not miss **White Mountain Puzzles** (Rte. 16B, Jackson Falls Marketplace, Jackson, 603/383-4346, www.whitemountainpuzzles. com, 8:30 A.M.–4:30 P.M. Mon.–Fri.). While not a store per se, the company headquarters sells more than 150 designs of intricate puzzles created by big-name designers in the puzzle world. An ever-evolving collection of glassworks by local artists and hand-crafted gifts are for sale at **Ravenwood Curio Shoppe** (7 Main St., Jackson, 603/383-8026, 10 A.M.–5 P.M. Mon.–Sat.; closed Sun.).

Food

You needn't wait until yuletide to taste the New England fare served in the genteel, candlelit dining room of ◖ **Christmas Farm Inn** (Rte. 16B, Jackson, 603/383-4313, www.christmas-farminn.com, 5–9 P.M. Wed.–Sun., $25–31). The intimate restaurant serves an excellent wine list and specialties ranging from pork chops with orange ancho-chili sauce to potato-crusted salmon with balsamic reduction. Don't feel like getting dressed up? Relax and enjoy the casual bistro atmosphere of **Highfield's at Eagle Mountain House** (179 Carter Notch Rd., Jackson, 603/383-9111, www.eaglemt. com, 7:30–9:30 A.M. daily; 5:30–8 P.M. Sun.–Thu.; 5:30–9 P.M. Fri.–Sat., $8–27), where you can still order excellent specials like mac 'n' lobster and macadamia-crusted swordfish. Waking up is made a little bit easier if you have a stop at **A Fresh Start** (Rte. 302, Glen, 603/383-4517, 7 A.M.–2 P.M. Mon.–Fri.; 7 A.M.–3 P.M. Sat.–Sun., $4–8) on your morning's agenda. The friendly eatery doles out good coffee, fresh-baked muffins, and puffy omelets in the morning, plus fresh sandwiches and soups at lunch. Or, for a still stronger hit of caffeine, there's the high-octane espresso bar at **As You Like It Bakery & Cafe** (1 Black Mountain Rd./Rte. 16B, Jackson, 603/383-6425, www.asyoulikeit-bakery.net, 8 A.M.–3 P.M. daily, $4–8), which also happens to make fantastic egg sandwiches, creative deli sandwiches, and fresh-as-can-be salads. Take a seat under the exposed beams and near the roaring fireplace at ◖ **White Mountain Cider Company Restaurant** (Rte. 302, Glen, 603/383-9061, www.whitemountaincider.com, dinner nightly, 5–9 P.M. Sun.–Thurs.; 5–10 P.M. Fri.–Sat., $18–28). The renovated 19th-century farmhouse serves contemporary, excellent cuisine—including such lovelies as risotto with butternut squash and sage and roasted duck breast with a marjoram cherry glaze.

Information

For more information on the Jackson area, stop by the **Jackson Area Chamber of Commerce** (603/383-9356, www.jacksonnh.com), located at the Jackson Falls Marketplace next to the post office.

PINKHAM NOTCH

A mostly undeveloped stretch of the White Mountains lined by forests and a few ski areas, Pinkham sits at the base of the best hiking trails on Mount Washington, or as it's affectionately known by generations of hikers, "the Rockpile." The first recorded ascent of the peak goes back to 1642, when settler Darby Field made the ascent just two decades after the Pilgrims landed at Plymouth Rock. Since then literally thousands have followed him by foot, train, and car. The modern era of tourism started in 1819, when visionary Ethan Crawford blazed the first trail up to the peak (still in use today). It wasn't long before Victorian entrepreneurs began building hotels, including the now-ruined Tip Top House, at the summit for intrepid tourists. Given the legendary bad weather on top of the mountain, one can only imagine the average steamer-trunk tourist of the day braving the ascent for beef Wellington on the summit. In the 1920s, the Appalachian Mountain Club established a lodge in the Notch and began blazing the network of trails that climbers now use to reach the peak.

◖ Mount Washington Auto Road

You'll start seeing the bumper stickers as soon as you start driving around New England: "This Car Climbed Mount Washington." You can get your own (even if it's just for a rental) at this zig-zag highway (Rte. 16, Pinkham Notch, 603/466-3988, www.mountwashingtonautoroad.com, 7:30 A.M.–6 P.M. daily mid-Jun.–early Sept.; shorter hours starting in early May and until mid-Oct.) that climbs eight miles to the top of New England. The history of the road goes back to the mid-19th century, when laborers working 10 to 12 hours a day took seven years to cut a winding passage to the top of the peak. Back then, it was an all-day affair to climb the mountains in uncovered horse-drawn wagons, and could get quite wet if the weather didn't cooperate.

On that score, Mount Washington's weather has been called the "worst in the world," and even in a modern automobile, the drive to the top is always unpredictable (and exciting). But if the day is even partly clear, you are in for a treat, looking down the sheer sides of Tuckerman Ravine and above the heads of the mountains that you were looking up at just an hour before. Passengers up the road can choose to take a guided bus tour to the top ($29 adults, $25 seniors, $12 children 5–12, free children under 5), or drive themselves (and get their bumper stickers) with the help of a self-guided CD tour ($23/car and driver, $8 each additional adult, $6 children 5–12, free children under 5). At the bottom of the road, the free **Red Barn Museum** displays objects relating to the auto road's past, including antique cars and a carriage that used to climb the mountain.

Other Sights

With its frigid temperatures and relentless icy wind, the **Mount Washington Observatory**

(603/356-2137, www.mountwashington.org, mid-May–mid-Oct., free) has got to be the most exciting posting in the world for those who like the weather; either that or they're just crazy. Either way, the rest of us can vicariously experience the Rockpile's wild weather with a small museum at the summit dedicated to the climate and geology of the area.

Events

If your car had a tough time climbing the mountain, you'll be impressed by the performance of the vintage speedsters in the annual **Climb to the Clouds Auto Race** (603/466-3988, www.climbtotheclouds.com, July), a tradition on the mountain for more than 100 years. The record of 6 minutes, 42 seconds to the summit was set in 1998. (The race was not held in 2009 for economic reasons, but has plans to return.)

Shopping

None too surprisingly, there isn't much shopping to be done in this heavily forested area at the foot of the mountains. But you can grab last-minute hiking and camping supplies in the Pinkham Notch Visitors Center at **Joe Dodge Lodge** (Rte. 16, Gorham, 603/466-2725, www.outdoors.org, 6:30 A.M.–10 P.M. May–Oct.; 6:30 A.M.–9 P.M. Nov.–Apr.).

Food

Laid out with white linens and china and dotted with candlelight, the dining room at **Dana Place Inn** (Rte. 16, Pinkham Notch, 800/537-9276, www.danaplace.com,, 5 –9 P.M. daily, $21–27) sends out ambitious (and successful) dishes of rainbow trout and brandied apple chicken. Part of the Appalachian Mountain Club Visitors Center at the base of Mount Washington, the **Black Moose Deli** (Rte. 16, Pinkham Notch, 603/466-2725, www.outdoors.org, 9:30 A.M.–3:30 P.M.) serves up quick à la carte lunches including soups, salads, and sandwiches.

Information

For more information on the outdoor

opportunities in the area, visit the Pinkham Notch Visitors Center run by the **Appalachian Mountain Club** (603/466-2727, www.outdoors.org) at the base of the mountain. The center has a bunk lodge and restaurant for hikers in addition to educational displays about the flora and fauna of the region.

CRAWFORD NOTCH

Drive along U.S. 302 from Glen and you'll run straight into the heart of this 20-mile-wide valley, which is split in half by the Saco River. The area's state park draws hikers and fishermen as well as sightseers to its waterfalls and plethora of scenic overlooks. The notch was first settled in 1790 by rugged Abel Crawford and his family, who opened an inn called the Mount Crawford House and began guiding visitors up the peaks of the region. After Abel's son Ethan opened the Crawford Trail in Pinkham Notch, he blazed a shorter trail from the area of Bretton Woods on the side of the mountain in 1821. In the same location 40 years later, the area would make engineering history with the construction of a cog railway to bring groups of tourists up to the hotels at the summit.

With the waves of tourists, the age of grand Victorian hotels began in earnest. In 1902, one of the grandest hotels in the world, the Mount Washington Hotel, opened in the shadow of its namesake peak. In 1944, it grabbed a piece of the global spotlight when it was chosen as the site for 45 of the world's delegates to discuss the postwar recovery of Europe. Together they established the International Monetary Fund and the World Bank, the underpinnings of the world financial system. Today, VIPs still gather in and around the sprawling hotel, but primarily for more recreational pursuits—skiing, horseback riding, snowshoeing, and fine dining.

◀ Mount Washington Cog Railway

When Chicago meatpacking magnate Sylvester Marsh originally presented his idea for a railway to the top of the Rockpile, the state legislature told him that he might as well "build a railway to the moon." Sometimes it feels like you are climbing that high as you sit in the rickety vintage railway cars as they make their 30-degree ascent up to the top of the peak. The railway first opened in 1869, and it was the first in the world to employ toothed gears, or cogs, that meshed with a pinion on the track to prevent the train from slipping backward. When it opened, the railway immediately stole the thunder of the carriage road in Pinkham Notch. These days, the Auto Road is more popular, but the railway (Base Rd., off Rte. 302, Bretton Woods, 603/278-5404 or 800/922-8825, www.thecog.com, Jul.–Oct., $59 adults, $54 seniors, $39 children 4–12, free children under 4) is a more relaxing and romantic—as well as more expensive—way to climb to the top. The train runs year-round, with hourly trips during the summer and winter and a limited schedule in the spring and fall. Round-trip takes about three hours, and is accompanied by a guided narration that explains the natural features of the valley as well as the history and technology of the railway itself. A museum at the base station includes Old Peppersass, the first locomotive to make the climb.

Food

Fill up on German specialties in the warmly colored, relaxed dining room at **The Bernerhof** (Rte. 302, Crawford Notch, 603/383-9132, www.bernerhofinn.com, 8 A.M.–10 P.M. Mon.-Sat.; 8 A.M.–9 P.M. Sun., $19–26). The menu sways toward the truly traditional: Wiener schnitzel with eggs, homemade schnitzel, and soul-warming fondue. Jump on the hearty carb wagon at **Scarecrow Pub** (Rte. 16, Intervale, 603/356-2287, 3 P.M.–11 P.M. daily, $9–17)—the place to fuel up on pastas, nachos, and burgers before or after a chilly hike. Hit the ATM before you go; the pub is cash only.

Information

To better appreciate the area, stop by the Highland Center, a lodge and wilderness education center run by the **Appalachian Mountain Club** (Rte. 302, 603/278-4453, www.outdoors.org). The center has interactive exhibits on geology and wildlife along with a gift store and environmentally friendly composting toilets.

SPORTS AND RECREATION

Tuckerman Ravine

When the wild New Hampshire winds blow snow off the peaks, it collects in this deep bowl-shaped ravine (www.tuckerman.org) on the southeast side of Mount Washington. Like everything in these parts, Tuckerman was formed by the glaciers; it is a feature known as a glacial cirque, a large bowl formed by prolonged erosion at the leading edge of a glacier. Since the early 20th century, it's exuded a unique fascination for skiers, who see all that deep-packed powder and just can't wait to get up there. No lifts have been built on the feature, however, mostly because of the constant danger of landslides. Thousands every year brave the challenge, anyway, by hiking up to the top of the ridge in order to ski down 800 feet of powder.

If you want to join them, climb the Tuckerman Ravine Trail from Pinkham Notch straight up the bowl, a distance of about three miles (and an up to 3,000-foot rise in elevation). Generally, the trip takes about three hours, but can take longer in-season due to crowds. If you'd rather just sit and watch the skiers as they come down the bowl, bring a picnic on the hike out to the exposed Lunch Rocks, a cluster of rocks on the north side of the ravine that frequently take on a party-like atmosphere as spectators watch the daredevils descend the slopes. Even here, however, you'll have to be careful of avalanches. The official warning is to yell "Ice!" as loud as possible. If you hear someone yell it, stay alert and get behind a rock; it's also recommended to have an escape route planned beforehand.

Hiking Mount Washington

During the summer months, the **Tuckerman Ravine Trail** is also the most popular route to the summit of Mount Washington (that is, if you ignore all of those tenderfeet on the Cog Railway and the Auto Road). The trail rises for 4.1 strenuous miles from **Pinkham Notch Visitors Center** (Rte. 16), straight up the middle of the ravine. Two other trails, the **Boott Spur Trail** (5.4 miles) and **Lion Head Trail** (4.5 miles), also climb Tuckerman along the south and north sides of the ravine respectively. They are both longer, but also more moderate in incline. The most difficult trail of all is the **Huntington Ravine Trail,** which branches off from Tuckerman to ascend an even steeper cirque to the northeast. All of these trails meet at the top of the ravines along the Tuckerman Crossover Trail for the final steep climb to the summit.

There are also several approaches from Crawford Notch on the west face of the mountain. Just before the entrance to the Cog Railway is the trailhead for two routes, the **Ammonoosuc Ravine Trail,** a steep 3.9-mile scramble to the aptly named Lakes of the Clouds, where an **AMC hut** (603/466-2727, www.outdoors.org) base lodge allows hikers to rest their legs and admire the view before taking the more moderate Crawford Path to the peak. Plan ahead if you want to snag one of the 90 bunkroom accommodations in the hut for an unforgettable night in the sky. Also leaving from Crawford Notch, the **Jewell Trail** (4.6 miles) climbs to a ridge on the north side of the mountain, where it then parallels a 1,500-foot cliff on a ridgeline hike to the top.

Other Hikes

Mount Washington might be the biggest game in town, but it's not the only mountain around here worth climbing. Especially during the summer months you might be better off taking the Auto Road to the top of the big guy, and then hiking up a less crowded slope (then again, you won't find solitude on any of the 4,000-footers). Pick up a copy of the *White Mountain Guide,* published by AMC books, at the visitors center for detailed instructions on other hikes in the area. The two next-highest peaks are the 5,384-foot **Mount Monroe** and the 5,774-foot **Mount Adams**. The former is on the southwestern side of Washington near the Lakes of the Clouds hut, and makes a popular side trip while climbing the mountain or staying in the hut. Adams, on the other hand, is deep in the backcountry north of Washington, and is, if anything, a more difficult climb. The two most popular routes to the top are the **Valley Way** (4.7 miles) and **Airline Trail** (4.3 miles), both of which leave from a trailhead on Route 2, three miles west of Route 16. The **Randolph Mountain Club** (www.randolphmountainclub.org) maintains four year-round shelters and several campgrounds in the northern Presidentials for overnights.

Another popular but strenuous climb is the hike up to **Wildcat Mountain,** from which you can get a close-up view of Mount Washington. From the Pinkham Notch Visitors Center, the **Lost Pond Trail** climbs moderately for a mile up to the Wildcat Ridge Trail, which then rises steeply to several open ledges and Wildcat's two peaks, named Wildcat A and Wildcat D. The ridge is also accessible from the shorter but more difficult **Nineteen-Mile Brook** trail, which leaves from a trailhead four miles north of the visitors center and meets up with the Wildcat Ridge Trail on the other side of the summits. The AMC's self-service **Carter Notch Hut** (603/466-2727, www.outdoors.org) is located at the junction of the two trails, and is open year-round for overnight stays.

Hiking in this region is not all about bagging 4,000-foot peaks. There are plenty of shorter hikes to scenic views or secluded glens for day hikers. The popular **Glen Ellis Falls** is a 64-foot cascade on the Ellis River, accessible by a paved trail that begins a mile south of Pinkham Notch. An optional steep descent takes you to the base of the falls. From the visitors center, a short but steep climb leads to a rewarding view at **Square Ledge**, a good hike for small children and their parents. Even if you don't want to climb all the way up Tuckerman Ravine, another good day hike leads up the trail to **Cascade Ledge,** a half-mile hike that offers both a waterfall and an outstanding view of the ravine.

Rock Climbing

The Mount Washington area has the best climbing in the east, centered around **Cathedral and Whitehorse Ledges,** two sheer granite cliffs that face Route 16 just beyond North Conway. Together they present an amazing variety of climbs, as well as plenty of elbow room to do it in. Even if you've never seen a carabiner, the folks at **EMS Climbing School** (1498 White Mountain Hwy./Rte. 16, North Conway, 800/310-4504, www.emsclimb.com) will hook you up for a climb up Cathedral. The school is located in North Conway behind Walgreen's and next to the Eastern Mountain Sports store. It also runs trips up more secluded faces along the Kancamagus Highway and up the sides of Mount Washington for more experienced climbers.

Biking

There are plenty of opportunities for mountain biking in the **White Mountain National Forest** (603/447-5448, www.fs.fed.us/r9/forests/white_mountain). One of the best is the **Cherry Mountain Loop,** 25 miles of roller-coaster backwoods trails in the Crawford Notch area. The route takes in three waterfalls and heavily wooded paths crisscrossed with logging roads. The trailhead starts on Route 302, three miles east of Twin Mountain. (Note, however, that it's not actually a loop due to some impassable trails on Mount Mitten.) For family biking, check out the **Great Glen Outdoors Center** (Mt. Washington Auto Rd., Rte. 16, Pinkham Notch, 603/466-2333, www. greatglentrails.com) outside Pinkham Notch. This center makes the work easy by grooming the trails to within an inch of their lives—removing any debris or surface hazards that could catch up your wheels. For some that might mean no fun; for others, that's where the fun begins. In the winter, the center grooms its trails for cross-country skiing.

Beaches

The Saco River has several swimming holes for a quick dip. Check out the small beach at **Davis Park** (Eastside Rd., Conway), scenically situated just beneath a covered bridge. North Conway has its own Echo Lake in **Echo Lake**

State Park (off Rtes. 16/302, 603/356-2672, www.nhstateparks.com/echo.html, $4 adults, $2 children 6–11, free children under 6), which offers a beach, trails, and picnic area with a view of Cathedral Ledge above.

Boating

The Saco River might not be the fastest river in New England, but it's certainly the most popular due to its wide, gentle current and well-developed infrastructure of campgrounds. **Saco Bound Outdoors** (Rte. 302, Center Conway, 603/447-2177, www.sacobound.com) is the local expert in guided trips down the river; it also has canoe rentals and shuttle service for trips of any length.

Skiing

The king of the hill in New Hampshire is **Attitash New Hampshire** (Rte. 302, 3 mi. west of Rte. 16, Bartlett, 800/223-7669 or 603/374-2600, www.attitash.com, $62–69 adults, $48–54 youth 13–18, $39–48 seniors and youth 6–12, free children under 6), a monster ski resort with almost 300 rideable acres, 12 lifts, and 70 runs between two peaks: the more traditional New England trails at Attitash, and the wide-open cruisers of the newer Bear Mountain. Attitash is known for its grooming, and often has snow when other area mountains don't—and its relative inaccessibility makes the lift lines shorter than Loon or Waterville Valley. The only criticism is that by trying to be all things to all people, it doesn't have the really tough double-diamonds that more-advanced skiers crave.

The same can't be said of **Wildcat Ski Area** (Rte. 16, Pinkham Notch, halfway between Jackson and Gorham, 603/466-3326, www.skiwildcat.com, $65 adults, $55 youth 13–18, $39 seniors and youth 6–12), which is as close to the natural state of the mountain as you can get. This is a raw experience, with dizzying views of Mount Washington and Tuckerman Ravine, and no apologies for its difficult terrain or lack of grooming. Wildcat's exposed location means lots of fresh powder—but it also means lots of cold wind, so be sure to pile on

the layers. But for the sheer joy of skiing, you can't do much better in the east.

ACCOMMODATIONS
Under $100

In the **Oxen Yoke Motel** (170 Kearsarge St., North Conway, 800/862-1600, www.theoxenyoke.com, $69–109), pastel-colored rooms come with two queen or double beds each, coffeemakers, fridges, and microwaves. Located close to the top of Cranmore Notch, it has an outdoor pool open in the summer. The **Appalachian Mountain Club** (603/466-2727, www.outdoors.org/lodging, $45–145) offers inexpensive, friendly beds at both the Joe Dodge Lodge in Pinkham Notch and the Highland Center in Crawford Notch.

$100-150

The facilities also house restaurants and stores. The casual country guest rooms and suites at **Eagle Mountain House** (Carter Notch Rd., Jackson, 603/383-9111, www.eaglemt.com, $129–189) are decked out with solid four-poster beds and cushy down comforters, plus wireless Internet access. A full breakfast is also included. Say it five times fast, or just cut to the chase and reserve a room at **Ammonoosuc Inn** (641 Bishop Rd., Lisbon, 603/838-6118, www.ammonoosucinn.com, $130–180), where rooms come with CD players, wireless Internet, queen beds, claw-foot tubs, and full gourmet breakfasts.

$150-250

Surrounded by the mountainous skyline, the sky-blue **Darby Field Inn** (185 Chase Hill, Albany, 800/426-4147, www.darbyfield.com, $140–185) has pretty rooms with Victorian beds, fireplaces, VCRs, whirlpool tubs, and a full breakfast. Many of the rooms have beautiful views, and the property offers an outdoor pool in the summer and sleigh rides in winter. Little wonder the ◖ **White Mountain Hotel** (2560 West Side Rd., North Conway, 800/533-6301, www.whitemountainhotel.com, $109–229) is considered one of the top-notch spots to rest your head in these parts. The resort's recent renovation has it sparkling with amenities—à la the year-round heated outdoor pool and hot tub, an impressive golf course, fitness center, game room, tavern, and gourmet restaurant boasting tremendous mountain views. Then there are the rooms: full of tasteful and pristine country furnishings with free wireless Internet, 310-thread-count sheets, and luxury mattresses.

$250 and Up

Since 1902, there's been no grander place to stay in the White Mountains than ◖ **Omni Mount Washington Resort** (Rte. 302, Bretton Woods, 800/843-6664 or 603/278-1000, www.mountwashingtonresort.com, $179–469). The Joseph Stickney–designed building—a National Historic Landmark—is like a luxury-laden city unto itself, filled with an indoor pool, hot tubs, fireplaces galore, and perk-filled guest rooms and suites. With no less than eight venues for dining (some formal, some pubby) and/or entertainment, the property also offers a slew of activities—starting with golf and ending with a new zipline tour through the trees.

On a smaller—but still remarkably plush—scale is **Inn at Thorn Hill & Spa** (Thorn Hill Rd., Jackson, 603/383-4242, www.innatthornhill.com, $209–400), an intimate but stately 19th-century home turned exquisite inn. In guest rooms, you'll find fireplaces, whirlpool tubs, steam showers, wet bars, scads of antiques, and mountain views. Then there's the spa, which offers everything from massage and facials to body rubs and wraps. Thorn Hill also has three highly regarded dining rooms serving superb New England dinners and a top-notch wine list.

GETTING THERE AND AROUND

There is no direct way to the Presidential Range area from the center of the state. From Concord, your best bet is to take I-93 north to exit 23, then cut across Routes 104 and 113 west and Route 16 north to Conway (80 mi., 2 hrs.). You can also get to Conway from Portsmouth by taking Route 16 north the entire way (80 mi., 2 hr.). From Conway, continue

© MICHAEL BLANDING

the Omni Mount Washington Resort

up U.S. Route 302 north to North Conway, Glen, and Bretton Woods (35 mi., 1 hr.). **Concord Coach Lines** (800/639-3317, www.concordtrailways.com) runs a daily bus from Boston through the White Mountains, stopping at Conway (First Stop Market & Deli, 13 West Main St.), North Conway (Eastern Slope Inn, 2760 Main St./Rte. 16), Jackson (Covered Bridge, Rte. 16), and Pinkham Notch (AMC Visitors Center, Rte. 16, Gorham). Greyhound (800/231-2222, www.greyhound.com) also runs buses to Conway (First Stop Market & Deli, 13 Main St.), North Conway (Eastern Slope Inn, 2760 Main St./Rte. 16).

The Great North Woods

Only a small fraction of tourists to New Hampshire venture "north of the notches" to the northern third of the state. Those who do will find a backcountry nirvana replete with hiking, boating, camping, fishing, and seemingly dozens of other ways to get out into nature. This is the area where the Brake for Moose signs are ubiquitous on the highways—and not just for show. The king of New England quadrupeds is commonly sighted on the highways, to say nothing about the moose tours that take visitors back to secluded ponds and wetlands where the moose come for their breakfast and evening snacks. The human inhabitants of the region are true salt-of-the-earth Granite Staters, who wear flannel, drive pickups, and know their way around a duck blind or salmon run.

BERLIN/GORHAM AREA

North of Pinkham Notch, the territory of New Hampshire known as the Great North Woods has been prized for one thing: its trees. The "metropolis" in these parts is Berlin, a town of 10,000 that made its fortune on logging in the 19th century. Now it is the center for several paper companies who have unfortunately polluted the fast-running Androscoggin River.

In recent years, however, the river is running cleaner and the trees of the region are more prized left standing, as an overflow of hikers from the Whites have been venturing here to take advantage of less-populated peaks that evoke the spirit of the way the White Mountains *used* to be. Near Berlin, the smaller town and logging center of Gorham has done

a better job at keeping its Victorian downtown intact, making a pleasant enough place for a lunch stop. Farther west are the family-friendly town of Jefferson and the farming community of Lancaster. The latter is home to the grand estate of John Weeks, a descendent of one of the original settlers of the region who went on to become a U.S. Senator and Secretary of War.

Family Attractions

The northern frontier of New Hampshire has been transformed into the western frontier of the United States at **Six Gun City & Fort Splash** (1492 Rte. 2, Jefferson, 603/586-4592, www.sixguncity.com, 9:30 A.M.–6 P.M. daily July–Aug.; 10 A.M.–5 P.M. daily late May–June and late Aug.–early Sept., $2 adults and children 4 and up, $17 seniors, free children under 4), a family amusement park and waterpark centered around a Western-movie-set main street. Not sure the laser-tag arena is authentic to the period, but it's all great fun anyway. Also competing to reel in the family demographic is **Santa's Village** (528 Presidential Hwy./Rte. 2, Jefferson, 603/586-4445, www.santasvillage.com, 9:30 A.M.–6 P.M. daily late June–late Aug.; limited hours weekends late May–late June and late Aug.–Dec., $24 adults and children 4 and up, $22 seniors, free children under 4), a North Pole theme park complete with Yule Log flume ride, Rudolph Rollercoaster, and live reindeer petting zoo. Parents might have trouble explaining why Santa summers in New Hampshire, but the kids will be so psyched to see him outside the mall they won't care.

WILDLIFE PHOTOGRAPHY TIPS

© NHDTTD/DONNA BINGHAM

Make the most of photo ops like this one.

You know the feeling – you finally get that moose, black bear, or loon in your viewfinder and snap what you think is the perfect shot, only to get a picture back later of a far-off indistinct blob. Wildlife can be notoriously difficult to photograph well. Here are a few tips for your jaunts in the Great North Woods.

- A good zoom lens is essential for getting close to your subject. You'll need at least 300mm, if not 400mm. Alternatively, get a digital camera with at least 4.0 or 5.0 megapixels. That way, you can "zoom" in on the computer later and the image will hold its resolution.

- Pay attention to the background. Animals with dark bodies will look better against a light background, such as an overcast sky. Those with light bodies will look better against a dark background like water or a blue sky. Avoid backgrounds that are too busy, like a tree-filled forest or green field.

- Bright light isn't always the best for photography, since direct sun can wash out details or create too harsh a contrast. Take photos in the early morning or late afternoon, when soft, indirect light will flatter your subjects. Luckily, that's the time when most animals are most active anyway.

- Good hunters know to let their prey come to them, and photography is no different. Find a hidden spot upwind from a water source, assume a comfortable position, and wait. Once the animals feel the coast is clear, they will come out of hiding to give you a good shot.

Other Sights

An affectionate reconstruction of the early pioneer days of the area, the **Northern Forest Heritage Park** (961 Main St., Berlin, 603/752-7202, www.northernforestheritage. org, 10 A.M.–2 P.M. Tues.–Sat. May–Oct., $6 adults, $3 children 5–11, free children under 5) consists of an operating logging camp along the Androscoggin. On the grounds is a house museum, saw mill, and logging museum filled with old photographs of the rustic roots of the region. The park is also the site for lumberjack and blacksmith demonstrations as well as river tours and moose-spotting exhibitions.

Just as the farms were beginning to disappear at the start of the 20th century, a conservation movement was launched to preserve them. The most successful attempt was made by U.S. Senator John Wingate Weeks, who bought up a beautiful farm and estate atop Mount Prospect in Lancaster. The **John Wingate Weeks Estate** (off Rte. 3, Lancaster, 603/788-4004, www.nhstateparks.com/wingate.html, 10 A.M.–5 P.M. Wed.–Sun. late June–mid-Oct., $7 adults, $3 children 6–11, free children under 6) is now a park with an opulent country lodge (look for the moose head given to Weeks by Theodore Roosevelt) and 35 acres of grounds with views over the surrounding countryside. Even if you opt out of the house tour, be sure to admire the view from the 56-foot fieldstone observation tower out front.

Events

The largest county fair in the region is the **Lancaster Fair** (603/788-4531, www.lancasterfair.com, mid-Sept.), a six-day humdinger featuring oxen- and horse-pulls, sheep-dog competitions, and plenty of junk food and amusement rides. During the evenings, singing groups lead sing-alongs.

Food

Most of the area's eateries are in Gorham, which, while smaller than Berlin, is a bit more recreationally minded. At **J's Corner Restaurant & Lounge** (277 Main St.,

Gorham, 603/466-5132, www.jscornerrestaurantandlounge.com, 11 A.M.–9 P.M. Sun.–Thu.; 11 A.M.–10 P.M. Fri.–Sat., $14–24), surf 'n' turf is the house specialty—and the kitchen delivers. The popular, upbeat spot packs its attractive casual dining room with locals digging into steak with garlic-mushroom sauce, filet mignon, and jumbo shrimp loaded with buttery stuffing. Set in an old Victorian manor, the inviting interior of **Libby's Bistro** (111 Main St., Gorham, 603/466-5330, www.libbysbistro.net, 5:30–9 P.M. Wed.–Sat.; closed Sun.–Tues., $17–26) is a jumble of antiques and homey touches, and the food is a perfect match: Homemade pumpkin soup, seared tuna, and rack of lamb with fig are just a few of the enticing offerings. Friendly, fast service and fresh sushi are what keep **Yokohama Restaurant** (288 Main St., Gorham, 603/466-2501, 5–9 P.M. Tues.–Sat.; closed Sun., $8–17) a Gorham favorite. In addition to the list of basic sushi rolls and sashimi, there are cooked specials for the raw-adverse.

Shopping

Get good deals on new and used outdoor equipment at **Moriah Sports Bicycle Shop** (101 Main St., Gorham, 603/466-5050, www. moriahsports.com, 10 A.M.–6 P.M. Mon.–Fri.; 11 A.M.–5 P.M. Sat.–Sun.). The selection runs from bikes and shoes to tents and backpacks. The staff will also arrange guided tours and expeditions for you.

Entertainment

It's nothing fancy at all, but if you're up for a drink and some local color, make your way to **Fagin's Pub** (777 Main St., Berlin, 603/752-3074, 4:30 P.M.–12 A.M. Mon.–Sat.; 5 P.M.–11 P.M. Sun.), where drinks are strong and the pace is leisurely.

Information

The **Androscoggin Valley Chamber of Commerce** (603/752-6060 or 800/992-7480, www.androscogginvalleychamber.com) has an office in Berlin (961 Main St.) and an information booth on the town common in Gorham

(603/466-3103). For more information on Lancaster, contact the **Northern Gateway Chamber of Commerce** (877/788-2530 or 603/788-2530, www.northerngatewaychamber.org), which runs a seasonal information booth on Main Street.

NORTH COUNTRY

Sparsely populated and utterly remote, the lands between Dixville Notch and the Canadian border are known for their wild mountain scenery; for the grandeur of their lone luxury resort, the Balsams; and, every four years, for their votes. Traditionally, tiny Dixville Notch has been the first town to cast votes in the presidential primary, thus earning the town a momentary but recurring spot on the nation's political map.

Sights

The beauty of the natural environment here has inspired countless pilgrims, so it's not surprising that the Oblates of Mary Immaculate established a Catholic shrine here. The **Shrine of Our Lady Grace** (1992 Rte. 3, Colebrook, 603/237-5511, tours daily mid-May–mid-Oct.) has some 50 marble monuments in a tranquil spot on the banks of the Mohawk River. A short distance away, the **Columbia Covered Bridge** is your last chance to cross from New Hampshire to Vermont in style before Canada. The 145-foot-span over the Connecticut has an unusual half-sheathing that lets the light in on one side, while being fully sheathed on the other side. If you haven't yet bagged your moose, tote your camera along Route 3 north of Pittsburg to the Canadian border, known as **Moose Alley** for the frequency of the sightings here. Best times for sightings are in the early morning and at dusk.

Events

Only in New Hampshire could there be an event called the **Blessing of the Motorcycles** (http://nhblessingofthebikes.tripod.com, late June). Road warriors bring their steeds to the Shrine of Our Lady Grace and wait in a long line to have the demons exorcised from their tailshafts.

waterfall in the Nash Stream Forest

© NHDTTD/DALE LARY

Food

Restaurants are few and very, very far between in North Country. If you're famished, stop in at **Buck Rub Pub & Connecticut Lakes Lodge** (Rte. 3, Pittsburg, 603/538-6935, www.buckrubpub.com, $3–20), which is in the unenviable position of having been named for the process by which a male deer marks his territory during mating season. Fortunately, the only thing rubbed on at this lodge are spices—onto foods such as curly fries, fried mushrooms, BLTs, and fried chicken.

Information

For more information, contact the **North Country Chamber of Commerce** (603/237-8939, www.northcountrychamber.org). The chamber runs a seasonal information booth on Route 3 in Colebrook.

SPORTS AND RECREATION
Hiking

Compared to the White Mountains, the **Mahoosuc Range** outside of Berlin is a ghost-town—and that's just how hikers like it. You

THE INDIAN STREAM REPUBLIC

The remote northern tip of New Hampshire may seem like another country now. But for four years, between 1832 and 1836, it actually was an independent nation. Called the Indian Stream Republic, the land was subject to a border dispute between the United States and Canada following the American Revolution. The Treaty of Paris set the boundary between the two countries as the northernmost source of the Connecticut River. However, since three tributaries fed into the river, each of the countries set their own boundary at the one that gave them more territory. After 60 years of living in disputed lands, the 400 or so settlers declared themselves sovereign, drawing up a constitution and establishing their own system of courts. It wasn't long, however, before internal disputes began to break down the unity of the settlers, leading to violence, and the New Hampshire militia was called in to restore order. Great Britain finally relinquished its claims in January 1836, and the Indian Streamers themselves relented in May of that year, at which point the land was incorporated into the town of Pittsburg.

may not see a soul on a spring hike through the range along the Appalachian Trail. And unlike the rest of the range across the border in Maine, this section of the Mahoosucs is full of moderate stretches with flowered glades and paper birch stands below the tree line. You can enter the range from the **Success Trail,** a former logging road off of Route 16 a few miles north of Berlin.

New Hampshire's largest state forest isn't the White Mountains, it's the **Nash Stream Forest,** a vast wilderness of wetlands and wooded peaks that makes up the bulk of the Great North Woods. Cutting through the center of the forest, the **Cohos Trail** (www.cohostrail.org) offers 162 miles of virtually unbroken wilderness from the White Mountains to the Canadian border. The heart of the trail are hikes over **South Percy,** a gum drop of a mountain with some dramatic cliffs, and **North Percy,** a steep climb to a vast treeless summit with spectacular vistas over the forest.

Farther north, Dixville's namesake Notch is a tight and narrow cut through the mountains with cliffs on either side. You can look straight down onto it from a height of 1,000 feet at Table Rock in **Dixville Notch State Park** (Rte. 26, Dixville, 603/538-6707, www.nhstateparks.com/dixville.html). The half-mile climb up on all fours starts on Route 26 across from the entrance to the Balsams.

Boating

The area around Errol, north of Berlin, affords the opportunity for both flat-water and whitewater canoeing. Located on the Androscoggin River, **Northern Waters Canoe and Kayak** (Rte. 26, off Rte. 16, Errol, 603/482-3817, www.beoutside.com) rents boats to explore the moose- and waterfowl-infested **Umbagog National Wildlife Refuge** (Rte. 16, 5 miles north of Errol, 603/482-3415, http://lakeumbagog.fws.gov). It also leads kayak clinics down the New Hampshire stretch of the **Androscoggin River** (www.avcnet.org/arwc) on a stretch including Class II and III rapids. **Northwoods Rafting** (308 Milan Rd./Rte. 16, Milan, 603/449-2628, www.northwoodsrafting.com) also leads white-water rafting trips on the Androscoggin.

Skiing

The Balsams Resort (1000 Cold Spring Rd., Dixville Notch, 800/255-0600, www.thebalsams.com) offers some of the best crosscountry skiing in New England, with nearly 100 kilometers of tracked and groomed trails that plunge deep into the heart of the North Woods. With a four-star resort running heated shelters at regular intervals, however, you are never far from civilization. The Balsams also has a handful of alpine trails with a 1,000-foot vertical drop; it is particularly accommodating for telemark skiing.

For the ultimate in backcountry skiing, the **Phillips Brook Backcountry Recreation Area** (Gorham, 603/447-1786) offers an experience found nowhere else. A system of seven wilderness yurts are connected by trails on land owned by a paper company and leased to a nonprofit organization. What you'll get is a chance to lose yourself in the woods with only moose, spruce, and, if you are lucky, the sound of lightly falling snow for company. Rates per night are more than reasonable, at $34 for a bunk or $145 for a whole yurt, which sleeps six.

Camping

Situated right in the middle of the wildlife sanctuary, **Lake Umbagog State Park** (Rte. 26, Cambridge, 603/482-7795, www.nhstateparks.com/um.html, $4 adults, $2 children 6–11, free children under 6) is one of the newest parks in the state system. It includes 35 campsites and three cabins in a base camp on the lake, with 34 more sites around the lake in remote locations only accessible by boat. The park also has a beach for swimming and fishing, as well as canoes, kayaks, rowboats, and motor boats for rent. High up near the Canadian border, **Mountain View Cabins and Campground** (2787 N. Main St./Rte. 3, Pittsburg, 603/538-6305, www.mountain-viewcabinsandcampground.com) has a lakeside campground with 55 tent sites ($18/night) as well as a number of remote housekeeping cabins ($150–170/night) scattered around the back roads of Pittsburg. The main office is located at Happy Corner, five miles north of Pittsburg Village.

ACCOMMODATIONS
Under $100

Given the low price tag, you wouldn't expect to see so many amenities at **Town and Country Motor Inn** (Rte. 2, Shelburne, 800/325-4386, www.townandcountryinn.com, $80–105), but they're here: an indoor pool, steam room and hot tub, and complimentary wireless Internet. If you need something to do after dinner in the on-site restaurant (which, incidentally, serves basic fare such as pork chops, baked chicken, and pastas), the motel hosts DJs and rock bands on weekends. All rooms at the **Moose Brook Motel** (65 Lancaster Rd., Gorham, 603/466-5400, www.moosebrookmotel.com, $50–90) are well kept and have private baths, phones, and color TVs with cable. The motel also has an outdoor pool. Other than that, what you see is what you get.

$150-250

Plunk in the middle of the no-man's-land of the North Woods, ◖ **The Balsams** (Dixville Notch, 800/255-0600, www.thebalsams.com, $210–290) is an enclave of comfort and luxury. The all-inclusive, elaborate edifice of just over 200 rooms overlooks Lake Gloriette and includes golfing, tennis, live entertainment, and ski trails on its property.

GETTING THERE

Concord Coach Lines (800/639-3317, www.concordtrailways.com) runs a daily bus from Boston to Gorham (Irving Oil/Circle K, 350 Main St.) and Berlin (Irving Gas Station, 318 Glen Ave./Rte. 16). Greyhound (800/231-2222, www.greyhound.com) also runs buses to the same locations in both towns.

MAINE

THE SOUTH COAST AND PORTLAND

No matter where you are from, it's difficult to visit the city of Portland and its surrounding area without being tempted to move there. For starters, the city has all the sophistication of an urban center twice its size, with its performing arts centers and galleries, top-notch museums, and indisputably creative restaurants. But it also boasts all the benefits of a small town—residents are genuinely friendly, cafés are full of locals, streets are kept clean, and there is almost completely unfettered access to the area's many parks, beaches, and countryside.

Maine's largest city, Portland proper has a population of about 70,000, while its greater area is home to about a quarter of a million. With an impressive stable of cultural resources (from the renowned Impressionist collection at the Portland Art Museum down to small historic sites such as the Wadsworth-Longfellow House) and a citizenry that stays active in the community year-round, the city has long since transcended the summer-only appeal of many seaside cities.

Outside city borders, things quiet down dramatically in suburbs like Westbrook, Gorham, and Cumberland. Those pretty bedroom communities still have their own seasonal attractions, however: namely picturesque beaches, lighthouses, woodland parks, rivers seemingly built for white-water rafting, hiking and biking trails, and nature preserves.

It isn't far, either, to the rest of the South Coast—a collection of historic communities ranging from once-prosperous and now-touristy to once-prosperous and still-prosperous. Each has its own character and abundance of

HIGHLIGHTS

(Old York Historical Society: Tour any of the organization's beautiful old homes for an authentic taste of early Maine (page 522).

(Marginal Way: Ogunquit's mile-long seaside pathway gives ample views of sea crashing on the rocks below (page 524).

(Perkins Cove: A historic lobster fishing port turned shopping area is filled with crafts and character (page 524).

(Portland Head Light: Maine's oldest lighthouse, and arguably its most majestic sits on a dramatic rocky headland (page 534).

(Portland Museum of Art: From Homer to Renoir, the American and Impressionist works at this 19th-century museum are a collection not to be missed (page 537).

(L. L. Bean Factory Store: The famed outfitter's original (and discount) retail space is open 24 hours a day, 365 days a year (page 541).

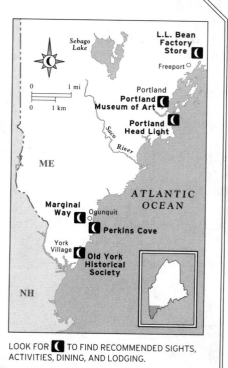

LOOK FOR (TO FIND RECOMMENDED SIGHTS, ACTIVITIES, DINING, AND LODGING.

coastal must-sees. In the historic Kennebunks, spruced-up sea captains' houses and Victorian mansions are as plentiful as tony inns and rocky beaches. Kittery and Freeport are a bargain-hunter's bliss, brimming with enough international designer outlets to fill a thousand wardrobes and years of holidays to come. (The more, shall we say, aggressive shoppers have been known to leave stocked up on Christmas gifts for the next decade.) The seaside community of Ogunquit is a magnet for urbanites looking to relax among, well, other relaxing urbanites—without sacrificing the sophisticated restaurants, high-quality boutiques, or maddening dearth of parking they've become accustomed to in the city. On the other end of the aesthetics spectrum sits Old Orchard

Beach, home to a kitschy-as-can-be old-school amusement park, complete with rickety roller coasters, arcades, cotton candy stands, and all the vibrant people-watching you can handle.

PLANNING YOUR TIME

Most of the region's attractions can be seen in clusters, with each group taking about a day to see. Spend the first day driving scenic Route 1, meandering past the antiques shops and other sights of York—including the impressive historic homes run by the **Old York Historical Society**—before visiting the **Cape Neddick Light** in late afternoon, when the light is most dramatic. Ogunquit's crowded streets are best seen via its trolley system, so take one to **Perkins Cove** and spend the

MAINE

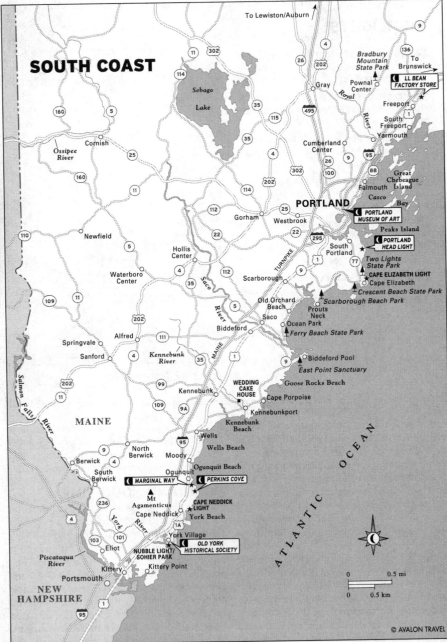

SOUTH COAST

To Lewiston/Auburn

To Brunswick

LL BEAN FACTORY STORE

Bradbury Mountain State Park

Pownal Center

Freeport

South Freeport

Yarmouth

Cumberland Center

Gray

Sebago Lake

Ossipee River

Cornish

Newfield

Waterboro Center

Springvale

Sanford

Alfred

Hollis Center

Gorham

Westbrook

PORTLAND

Falmouth

Casco

Great Chebeague Island

Casco Bay

PORTLAND MUSEUM OF ART

Peaks Island

South Portland

PORTLAND HEAD LIGHT

Two Lights State Park

CAPE ELIZABETH LIGHT

Cape Elizabeth

Crescent Beach State Park

Scarborough Beach Park

Prouts Neck

Ferry Beach State Park

Biddeford Pool

East Point Sanctuary

Goose Rocks Beach

Cape Porpoise

Kennebunkport

Kennebunk Beach

Scarborough

Old Orchard Beach

Ocean Park

Saco

Biddeford

Saco River

Kennebunk River

Kennebunk

WEDDING CAKE HOUSE

MAINE

TURNPIKE

Wells

Wells Beach

Moody

Ogunquit

Ogunquit Beach

MARGINAL WAY

PERKINS COVE

Mt Agamenticus

Cape Neddick

CAPE NEDDICK LIGHT

York Beach

York Village

NUBBLE LIGHT/ SOHIER PARK

OLD YORK HISTORICAL SOCIETY

North Berwick

Berwick

South Berwick

York River

Eliot

Piscataqua River

Kittery

Kittery Point

Portsmouth

NEW HAMPSHIRE

Salmon Falls River

MAINE

ATLANTIC OCEAN

0   0.5 mi

0   0.5 km

© AVALON TRAVEL

morning shopping and snacking there, then walk back to the town center along **Marginal Way.** (Note that a handful of restaurants in town shut down in the winter off-season.) In Portland, park your car and tour the **Portland Museum of Art** in morning, follow it with lunch and shopping in the city, and then a drive to the Cape Elizabeth Lighthouse by sunset. Freeport's **L. L. Bean Factory Store** could easily demand the better part of a serious shopper's day, but knock off by lunchtime, pick up some sandwiches, and put your newly bought hiking gear to the test on the trails of the Heath of Saco.

South Coast

A beach-lover's utopia, this region more than doubles its population in summer—and for good reason. Its shoreline is peppered with craggy beaches boasting soft sand and unforgettable sunsets, nature preserves, and bird and wildlife sanctuaries.

But there are plenty of manmade reasons to visit, too. The area was originally settled not two decades after *The Mayflower* hit Plymouth Rock, and that shows in its pervasive sense of history, from Kennebunkport's 17th-century homes to Kittery's old naval museums. More modern treasures are abundant, too, from Kennebunk's clam shacks to the antiques shops of Wells, cafés and top-notch restaurants of Ogunquit, and bargain outlets of Kittery. From June through October, the region's streets get congested with vacationing families and urbanites; the best times to soak up the area's pleasures are in early to mid-autumn.

KITTERY

A successful outlet town not far from the Massachusetts border, Kittery is a bargain-filled day trip for many Bostonians, or a week-long stay for shopaholics who also want close proximity to the area's woodland hikes, rivers, parks, and history (the town is Maine's oldest, settled in 1623).

But for most visitors, Kittery is all about getting a good buy—not a real challenge in a town where the average sale price is 40 percent off the original. Clotheshorses can stock up on labels ranging from high-end (Calvin Klein and Geoffrey Beene) to sporty (J. Crew and Eddie Bauer); home decor fanatics will find fancy goods (china at Villeroy & Boch, cookware at Le Creuset) and practicalities (gadgets at Brookstone). Sales are ongoing, but the best deals are generally to be found right after holidays and at summer's end.

Sights

Nautical buffs ought not miss the **Kittery Historical and Naval Museum** (200 Rogers Road Extension, 207/439-3080, www.kitterymuseum.com, 10 A.M.–4 P.M. June–Oct., $3 adults, $1.50 children 7–15, free children under 7), full of seafaring gear, loads of intricate scrimshaw, ship models, and a collection of painted seascapes.

Shopping

Over one mile of discount designer-brand stores—mostly in strip-mall form—await in the center of Kittery. From mainstream chains like **J. Crew, The Gap, Banana Republic,** and **Polo Ralph Lauren** to expensive companies like **Calvin Klein, Cole Haan, Le Creuset,** and **Wedgewood,** the big guns are all here. That said, there isn't much in the way of independent, local stores, unless you count the giant **Kittery Trading Post** (301 Rte. 1, Kittery, 207/587-6246, www.kitterytradingpost.com, 9 A.M.–9 P.M. Mon.–Sat.; 10 A.M.–6 P.M. Sun.), where you'll find an epic selection of gear for camping, fishing, hiking (and in the hunting section, the frankly off-putting sight of ten-year-old boys fondling rifle models set out in racks on the open floor). Grab a dose of lumberjack chic in the store's well-stocked plaid flannel section, or stock up for your next kayaking excursion in the boat section.

Food

Seafood quickly served in a casual setting. That's the dining genre that Kittery appears to have chosen as its culinary representation, and within those confines, it's done an admirable enough job. (The better to bring both shopping bags and the whole family.) At **Cap'n Simeon's Galley** (90 Pepperrell Rd./Rte. 103, Kittery Point, 207/439-3655, www.capnsimeons.com, 11:30 A.M.–10 P.M. daily; 10 A.M.–2 P.M. Sun., $7–28), platters of fisherman's specials (fried clams, cod, and scallops) and fried oysters are served up with an excellent view of the water. **Bob's Clam Hut** (315 Rte. 1, Kittery, 207/439-4233, www.bobsclamhut.com, 11 A.M.–8 P.M. Mon.–Thu.; 11 A.M.–8:30 P.M. Fri.–Sat.; 11 A.M.–7:30 P.M. Sun., $7–29) does its "fryolater" justice with fresh, hot, and crispy fried haddock, calamari, and, of course, clams. If you're headed to the beach or on a hike, grab picnic fixings at **Beach Pea Baking Co.** (53 Rte. 1, 207/439-3555, www.beachpeabaking.com, 7:30 A.M.–6 P.M. Mon.–Sat., $6–9), where all breads are fresh-baked and sandwiches are overstuffed and made-to-order.

Information

Get maps, directions, restaurant recommendations, and shopping outlet information at the **Kittery Visitor Information Center** (I-95 and Rte. 1, Kittery, 207/439-1319, www.mainetourism.com).

YORK

First settled by Colonists in 1624, York chugged along as a modest seaside town until the 19th century, when it earned a reputation as a posh coastal vacation spot. It isn't far from that today, with its pretty (though relatively modest, compared with some in nearby Kennebunkport) beach homes and sloop-filled harbors.

The entire town of York is made up of four small sections: York Village (where you'll find a cluster of beautifully restored homes), York Harbor, Cape Neddick (a residential suburb home to the well-known lighthouse of its namesake), and York Beach.

◖ Old York Historical Society

The small and meticulously kept York Village is a historian's jackpot, filled with colonial homes, a library and schoolhouse, and cemetery. Many of them are open for tours through this society (207 York St., York, 207/363-4974, www.oldyork.org, 10 A.M.–5 P.M. Mon.–Sat. in summer, $10 adults, $9 seniors, $5 children 6–16, free children under 6, $20 families); some are self guided, some are not. Check in at the **Jeffords' Tavern Visitor Center** (5 Lindsey Rd.) to find out which is which, and to purchase tickets and get a map.

Cape Neddick Light

Otherwise known locally as Nubble Light, this stark-white lighthouse (Nubble Rd., Rte. 1A, off of Short Sand Beach, York Beach, 207/363-1040, http://lighthouse.cc/capeneddick) and rocky grounds are so perfect-looking, they seem straight out a calendar. But it's the view it has as well as the one it creates that makes Nubble worth a visit—the breezy point looks out to mile upon mile of unfettered ocean. The lighthouse itself is on small rocky island some dozen yards off the coast-tantalizingly close, yet off-limits to the public. Viewers congregate on the grounds of Sohier Park (Nubble Rd., York) instead, snacking on ice cream, scrambling over the rocks, or just gazing past the lighthouse to the horizon.

Nightlife and Events

Without a local theater or bar scene, evenings in York are generally made for relaxing at home or the occasional beach party. One exception is **Talpey's Tavern** (Rte. 1, Cape Neddick, 207/351-1145), where locals hang out, share stories about the day, and otherwise kill time around the fireplace over brews.

Every October, York throws a month-long **Harvestfest** (207/363-4422, www.gatewaytomaine.org). For visitors that means lots of food festivals (including more than one taste-off), sidewalk sales, crafts fairs, and antique car shows.

Shopping

Sample your way through the delicious stock of award-winning and creatively flavored jams, barbecue sauces, salsas, salad dressings, ice cream sauces and more at the company store of **Stonewall Kitchen** (Stonewall Lane, Rte. 1 off exit 7, 207/351-2712, www.stonewallkitchen.com, 8 A.M.–7 P.M. Mon.–Sat.; 9 A.M.–6 P.M. Sun.). The gourmet retailer also houses a take-out café and bistro on the premises, serving fresh foods made with the label's signature condiments. The **York Village Marketplace** (26 Brickyard Ct., York, 207/363-4830, www.yorkvillage-marketplace.com, 10 A.M.–7 P.M. Mon.–Sat.; 10 A.M.–6 P.M. Sun.) is full of crafts by local artisans, from hand-knit shawls and blankets to bright-painted ceramics and woven placemats.

Food

No pilgrimage to Nubble Light is complete without a stop off at **C Brown's Old-Fashioned Ice Cream** (232 Nubble Rd., 207/363-1277, 10 A.M.–6 P.M. daily June–Sept.; 10 A.M.–5 P.M. Wed.–Sun. Oct.–Dec. and March–May; call for Jan.–Feb. hours) for a cone of deep chocolate. Whether you prefer to rusticate on the deck or eat inside by candlelight, the **Cape Neddick Lobster Pound** (60 Shore Rd., Cape Neddick, 207/363-5471, www.capeneddick.com, noon–10 P.M. Wed.–Sun., $17–30) can accommodate. Both share a view of Neddick River, plus an informal menu of everything from chicken fingers to baked stuffed lobster. Everything from vegetarian chili to brick oven–baked seafood pizzas can be found at **Ruby's Genuine Wood Grill** (433 Rte. 1, York, 207/363-7980, www.rubyswoodgrill.com, 11:30 A.M.–10 P.M. Sun.–Thu.; 11:30 A.M.–11 P.M. Fri.–Sat., $8–13)—good for its diverse menu and live rock shows on the occasional weekend night.

Information

The **Greater York Region Chamber of Commerce** (1 Stonewall Lane, York, 207/363-4422, www.gatewaytomaine.org, 9 A.M.–5 P.M. Mon.–Fri.; 9 A.M.–4 P.M. Sat.; 10 A.M.–3 P.M. Sun.) passes out local restaurant, shopping, and lodging information, plus beach times, maps, and the lowdown on any events or farmers markets happening in town.

OGUNQUIT

Until 1980, Ogunquit was part of neighboring Wells; a dispute over whether or not to put street lights up (followed by more arguments over shared taxes) led Ogunquit to effectively secede. It has since become one of Maine's most successful vacation destinations, thanks to its centrally located (and beautiful, white-sand) beach and plenitude of cosmopolitan boutiques, restaurants, and lodging.

It's all rendered the town a magnet for a diverse group of artists and city dwellers in the summer (the town has a history of welcoming gay and lesbian visitors, though plenty of straight vacationers make their way here as well), when crowds can border on

Ogunquit gazebo

COURTESY MAINE OFFICE OF TOURISM

MAINE

MAINE

© MICHAEL BLANDING

parking in Perkins Cove

claustrophobia-inducing. Things calm down nicely, however, later in the season and into the fall—and you won't miss much of the town's charm by missing the crowds; most shops and restaurants are open year-round.

Marginal Way

The mile-and-a-quarter paved walking path that skims Ogunquit's harbor was bequeathed to the town (it was then York) by York resident Josiah Chase in 1923. The path, which runs from Ogunquit beach to a rocky cove, sports the Atlantic's surf on one side and benches, assorted wild plants, trees, and brush on the other. The salty air, wide sky, crashing waves, and loud seagulls evoke nature's raw power, making the path a favorite subject of local artists and nature lovers alike, with an estimated 100,000 visitors every year. The walkway's craggy granite overhangs are crowned with trees and bittersweet, which create comfortable alcoves perfect for admiring the ocean's briny surf. Bayberry bushes and roses, in white and seemingly every shade of pink, perfume the path in summertime.

Perkins Cove

Known in its early days as Fish Cove, this stubby peninsula was once the focal point of the area's fishing and trade industry. (It still uses a historic manually drawn footbridge.) Today, it still is a focal point, just in a different form. With a cadre of art galleries, chowder houses, and unique gift shops, the Cove makes for a charming afternoon's stroll. Window shop at the handful of excellent artist studios, jewelry shops, pottery makers, and remarkably untacky souvenir shops. Leave plenty of time to gawk at the scenic water views, taking in the real working lobster boats and fishing boats that fill the area, and make stops for saltwater taffy and ice cream along the way. It can get very crowded in summertime, so plan to come toward the beginning or end of the day if you'd like some breathing room. Parking can be difficult in busy summer months; one popular option is to park downtown and take the local trolley to the Cove. Visit in the late summer or early fall, and you'll find that the weather is still agreeable but the foot traffic isn't quite so heavy.

Other Sights

Being the successful artist's resort that it has become, Ogunquit surprises no one by being home to the splendid **Ogunquit Museum of American Art** (542 Shore Rd., 207/646-4909, 10:30 A.M.–5 P.M. Mon.–Sat. July–Oct., $7 adults, $5 seniors, $4 students, free children under 12), a museum whose spectacular setting perched on a cliff above the ocean is outdone by the art contained inside. The excellent collection of American paintings includes watercolors, oils, sculpture, and drawings. Artists such as Eliot O'Hara, Henry Strater, and Isabella Howland might not be household names, but they are well-known and respected in the artists community. In addition to the art within the museum, the gift shop has a range of arts and crafts by local artists for purchase. Each year, the museum holds the Almost Labor Day Auction, a live auction of local artwork on the first weekend in September.

Entertainment and Events

All summer long catch dramatic productions (*Jesus Christ Superstar, Nunsense II,* and assorted other lighthearted family-friendly shows) compliments of **Booth Productions** (13 Beach St., 207/646-8142, www.boothproductions.com), which runs a community theater by the shore. The highly regarded **Ogunquit Playhouse** (10 Main St., 207/646-5511, www.ogunquit-playhouse.org, summer only) stages comedies, musicals, and other off-broadway productions throughout the season.

Ogunquit celebrates each fall with the aptly named **OgunquitFest** (late Oct., 207/646-2939, www.visitogunquit.org) a Halloweentime celebration featuring a road race, haunted house, craft sales, and ghost stories about forlorn pirates and sea captains. Holidays see the annual town-wide **Christmas by the Sea Festival** (mid-Dec., 207/646-2939, www.visitogunquit.org), an extravaganza of bonfires, caroling, parades, open houses, and a chowderfest.

Shopping

The work of two local craftsman is in the spotlight at **The Pottery Shop In Perkins Cove** (Perkins Cove, 207/646-7619, 10 A.M.–7 P.M. Sun.–Thurs., 10 A.M.–8 P.M. Fri.–Sat., Apr.–Jan.; call for winter hours). Stock up on handmade rustic pieces like candlesticks, big salad bowls, vases, and anything else ceramic. Gifts and home goods fill the shelves of **Spoiled Rotten** (27 Beach St., 207/641-8477, www.spoiledrottenogt.com, 10 A.M.–7 P.M. Sun.–Thurs.; 10 A.M.–9 P.M. Fri.–Sat.), the likes of garden furniture, tableware, and tea-scented candles. Don't miss the exquisite jewelry fashioned from sea glass and semiprecious materials at **Seaglass Jewelry Studio** (Perkins Cove, 207/646-3393, www.seaglassjewelrystudio.com, 10 A.M.–5 P.M. Mon.–Sat., 10 A.M.–4 P.M. Sun. June–Oct.; winter hours vary). Pieces run from pearl-stranded pendants and silver chokers to chunky silver

MAINE

QUEER-FRIENDLY OGUNQUIT

Like Provincetown on the tip of Cape Cod, Ogunquit has long been a welcoming place for gay and lesbian beachgoers. It's generally seen as a more relaxed alternative to the frenetic P-Town scene, but boasts plenty of nightlife as well. A gay and lesbian crowd tends to gather in the middle section of the beach, between the Main Beach and Footbridge Beach. At night, the living room of the community is the **Front Porch Piano Bar** (9 Shore Rd., Ogunquit, 207/646-4005, www.thefrontporch.net), a hopping live piano bar open Friday and Saturday nights to a friendly, boisterous crowd. Also lots of fun is **Oxygen Lounge** (237 Main St., Portland, 207/646-6655, www.oxygenbarogunquit.com), a newer cocktail lounge and wine bar with a sleek modern interior. Just down the street, **Maine Street Video Bar** (195 Main St., Ogunquit, 207/646-5101, www.mainestreetogunquit.com) is the center of gay nightlife in the town, with karaoke and DJ'd dance nights, as well as an outdoor patio and monthly women-only dances.

MAINE

rings. Swing into **Bread & Roses Bakery** (246 Main St., 207/646-4227, www.breadandroses-bakery.com, 7 A.M.–7 P.M. daily) for a gourmet snack; the pear tarts and fresh-baked boules are terrific.

Food

Ogunquit's dining scene is simply excellent. With new restaurants popping up all the time, you can dine any given night on anything from boiled lobster to Thai food to French cuisine.

For more than a decade, (**98 Provence** (262 Shore Rd., 207/646-9898, www.98 provence.com, 5:30–9 P.M. Wed.–Mon. Apr.–mid-Dec., $23–31) has been serving country-style French dishes in a clean, serene dining room. Dig into plates of duck confit with prunes and grilled rabbit with goat cheese. Simple flavors meet sophisticated palates at (**Arrows** (41 Berwick Rd., Cape Neddick, 207/361-1100, www.arrowsrestaurant.com, 6–9 P.M. Wed.–Sun. Jun.–early Sept.; Thu.–Sun., Apr–May and mid-Oct.–Dec., $41–44), the big-ticket restaurant housed in an 18th-century farmhouse. Almost all of the produce here comes straight from the garden—and gets made into lovelies such as English pea soup with prosciutto, crispy mushroom salad with kafir lime and green peppercorns, and ravioli with parsley and saffron paprika oil. It ain't cheap, but there are few places better in Northern New England for special occasion dinners. Reservations are essential in the formal, antique-appointed dining room.

Lobster shacks don't get much more fun than (**Barnacle Billy's** (Perkins Cove, 207/646-5575, www.barnbilly.com, 11 A.M.–10 P.M. daily mid-Jun.–Oct., $4–20). The loud, gray-shingled harborside eatery's tables fill up nightly for boiled lobsters, clam chowder, and cocktails on the deck. Next door, **Billy's Etc.** offers a more varied menu that includes fish filet, broiled scallops, and other seafood favorites as well as grilled chicken and steaks. Locals and vacationers alike look forward to dinner at **Gypsy Sweethearts** (Shore Rd., 206/646-7021, www.gypsysweethearts. com, 5:30–10 P.M. Tue.–Sun., summer only,

$18–29), which serves up solid entrées (like almond-crusted haddock or the spectacular cranberry-marinated pork tenderloin) and an epic wine list. The restaurant is located on Shore Road, on the right just after the turn off Main St. For breakfasts that will keep you full straight through to lunch, set your sights on **The Egg & I** (501 Main St., 207/646-8777, www.eggandibreakfast.com, 6 A.M.–2 P.M. daily, $7–14) and dig into the hearty omelets and scrambles.

Information

Head toward the **Ogunquit Chamber of Commerce** (Rte. 1, Ogunquit, 207/646-2939, www.visitogunquit.org) to collect a bevy of advice on local dining sites, museums, and where and when to hop on the local trolley.

WELLS

This family-friendly beach resort sports a slightly different character than neighbors like Ogunquit and the Kennebunks. While respectably old (it was founded in 1640), it lacks the historic emphasis of Kennebunkport. And while full of retailers and eateries, it lacks the sophisticated tastes of Ogunquit's galleries and high-end restaurants. What it boasts over both of them, however, is pure beach and nature access. The town encompasses Moody Beach, Wells Beach, and Drakes Beach, three unspoiled slices of the shore that keep people coming back summer after summer. For crowdless access to nature, Wells also has several excellent nature preserves that are paradise for bird-watchers, hikers, and cross-country skiers. Finally, the Route 1 stretch of Wells is one of the antiquing centers of New England—problem is, with fame has come high prices, so caveat emptor.

Events

In mid-September, a mega-crafts fair is put on by **Wells National Estuarine Research Reserve.** Go for the nature walks, the food, and (of course) the competition.

Shopping

Buying well in Wells means buying antiques.

Route 1, running through the heart of town, passes myriad houses peddling vintage wares—the good, the bad, and the overpriced. One promising cooperatively run destination is **Wells Union Antiques** (1755 Post Rd./Rte. 1, 207/646-6612, 10 A.M.–5 P.M. Mon.–Sat., 10:30 A.M.–5 P.M. Sun. daily), with nine dealers in one locale selling everything from vintage children's books and paintings by 1920s American artists to Depression glass and old records. Feel like your home is missing something? Could that something be a sleigh? Look no further than **Elaine's Sleighs & Buggies** (1318 Post Rd., 207/646-7267, call for hours). The selection ranges from vintage wooden farm carts to fancy and elegant painted little trolleys. Formal and country antiques at fair prices are on display at **R. Jorgensen Antiques** (502 Post Rd., Rte. 1, 207/646-9444, www.rjogensen. com, 10 A.M.–5 P.M. Mon.–Sat.; noon–5 P.M. Sun.). Antiques fanatics and bibliophiles alike delight in the selection at **East Coast Books** (Depot Rd. & Rte. 109, 207/646-0416, 11 A.M.–6 P.M. daily Apr.–mid-Oct.), a jumble of rare and historical publications and artwork. Not to be missed by nautical enthusiasts is **The Lighthouse Depot** (Rte. 1, 207/646-0608, www.lighthousedepot.com, 9 A.M.–6 P.M. Mon.–Sat., 10 A.M.–5 P.M. Sun. late May–mid-Oct.; limited off-season hours), purportedly the globe's largest gift store dedicated exclusively to lighthouse-centric items. Pick up a lighthouse calendar, a lighthouse magnet collection, or crystal lighthouse-shaped salt and pepper shaker sets. Whether you're buying or not, the comprehensive stock's worth a peek.

Food

Wells visitors, frequently with children in tow, generally want it fast and inexpensive—and within those parameters, Wells does well. Case in point is **Jake's Seafood** (139 Post Rd./Rte. 1, 207/646-6771, 11:30 A.M.–7 P.M. Mon.–Sat.; 11:30 A.M.–6 P.M. Sun., $11–26), which serves paper buckets of fried clams, fries, and coleslaw from its takeout windows (there's both inside and outside seating on the premises). The lines may be out the door at **The Maine Diner**

(2265 Post Rd./Rte. 1, www.mainediner.com, 7 A.M.–8:30 P.M., $6–18), but for good reason: The seafood salad is full of meaty, sweet lobster and shrimp; the turkey is house-roasted, and the chili, meatloaf, and mac 'n' cheese are freshly homemade.

There's good Thai food to be had at **Mekhong Thai** (162 Post Rd., 207/641-8805, www.mekongthai.com, 11 A.M.–9:30 P.M. Mon.–Fri.; noon–9:30 P.M. Sat., $8–14), where spicy & sour shrimp and chili paste chicken are specialties. Meet local policemen (or local anyone, for that matter) at **Congdon's Doughnuts** (207/646-4219, www.congdons. com, 6 A.M.–1 P.M.). The fast-paced counter service doles out fresh pastries and muffins (the blueberry sports tiny, sweet Maine blueberries) and, of course, doughnuts. On a hurry to the beach? Catch one on your way through the drive-thru.

Information

The **Wells Information Center** (Rte. 1 and Kimball's Lane, at the Moody traffic light, 207/646-2451, www.wellschamber.org) doles out pamphlets on town history, restaurants, beach information, and parking, and gives you the layout of the local antiques stores.

SPORTS AND RECREATION
Beaches

Each town on the South Coast believes without a doubt that its beaches are the finest. And to be fair, comparing the area's bounty is rather like comparing Olympic medalists. Even so, some are less crowded and sport better dunes than others. **Footbridge Beach** (Ocean Ave., Ogunquit, 207/646-2939, www.visitogunquit.org) sees far less hordes of sunbathers and swimmers than the town's Main Beach, and is easily accessible. In Wells, **Crescent Beach** (Webhannet Dr., 207/646-2451, www.wellschamber.org) is small and without facilities, but a day spent in its soft sands and quietude feels like your own personal Eden.

Hiking and Biking

Recreationally speaking, you can't do much

MAINE

better than the 1,600 acres of the **Wells National Estuarine Research Reserve at Laudholm Farm** (342 Laudholm Farm Rd., Wells, 207/646-1555, www.wellsreserve.org, 7 A.M.–sunset daily year-round; visitors center 10 A.M.–4 P.M. Mon.–Sat., noon–4 P.M. Sun. late May–mid-Oct.; closed Sat.–Sun. mid-Oct.–late May, $2 adults, $1 children). Full of wetlands, beach dunes, and show-stopping sunsets, the reserve contains a network of trails perfect for hiking, bird-watching, and cross-country skiing. Hikers in search of something other than sand to cross are well-served by turning their sights to **Mount Agamenticus** (186 York St., York, 207/361-1102, www.agamenticus.org). Kilimanjaro it's not—standing at just below 700 feet, it's an easy afternoon climb. But with beautiful views of the area's beaches and towns, plus mountain biking and sledding areas, it's well worth a day trip.

Boating and Fishing

Take a boat tour with **Captain & Patty's Piscataqua River Tours** (Pepperrell Rd., Kittery Point, 207/439-8976, www.capandpatty.com, Tue.–Sun. Jun.–mid-Oct., adults $12, children $10) and spot various local lighthouses, forts, shipyards, and other historic sights on the guided one-hour tour. Or, if you'd rather go marine biology route, see firsthand how to fish for lobster with **Captain Tom Farnon** (Town Dock #2, Harris Island Road, York Harbor, 207/363-3234, every hour 10 A.M.–2 P.M. weekdays in summer, $8 per person), who runs clear-bottom-boat excursions, and has plenty of knowledge about the crustacean to relay.

ACCOMMODATIONS
$100-150

Filled with art and antiques, **The Beach Farm Inn** (97 Eldridge Rd., Wells, 207/646-8493, www.beachfarminn.com, $100–135) offers garden cottages, a pool, and chic country decor throughout. A 1727 farmhouse converted to a quiet guest house, **The Apple Blossom B&B** (25 Brixham Rd., York, 207/351-1727, www.appleblossombandb.com, $120–130) has six guest rooms with private baths, cable, and air conditioning, several with queen sleigh beds, canopies, and a few with double beds. Almost all have pretty views of the 11 acres of lawn around the house.

$150-250

Seemingly built for families with lots of beach-loving kids, **The Seafarer Motel** (Rte. 1, across from Ogunquit Playhouse, Ogunquit, 207/646-4040, www.seafarermotel.com, $140–200) offers two pools, laundry machines on the premises, and a score of rooms with twin double beds. Rates decline considerably—to less than $100/night—in the off-season. A boutique bed-and-breakfast operation, the personal feel of **The Inn at Tanglewood Hall** (611 York St., York Harbor, 207/351-1075, www.tanglewood-hall.com, $155–225) is balanced by a respect for privacy (as in, yours). Lots of thoughtful extras make the price absolutely right: Relax in the meditation room, watch passersby from the porch, or simply curl up with a book in your suite. The riverside **Portsmouth Harbor Inn and Spa** (6 Water St., Kittery, 207/439-4040, www.innatportsmouth.com, $160–190) sports a handful of handsome rooms decorated in a style every bit as Victorian as the rest of the 19th-century house. The property also houses a spa, with facials and massages on offer at varying prices. (A first-rate breakfast and bikes and beach necessities are complimentary.)

$250 and Up

Set on its own isolated peninsula, the modern **Stage Neck Inn** (Rte. 1A, York Harbor, 207/363-3850, www.stageneck.com, $285–405), is steps from the beach, with swimming pools, in-room spa services, and tennis courts, to boot. Rooms have fireplaces and many have water views. With spectacular ocean views and a full-service spa (including sauna, whirlpool, and pool), it isn't hard to feel cosseted at **The Cliff House Resort** (Shore Rd., Ogunquit, 207/361-1000, www.cliffhousemaine.com, $265–310), the choice of moneyed visitors to Ogunquit since 1872. It's been renovated and added-onto many times since, with the latest addition being a new spa and outdoor terrace overlooking the Atlantic. Between dining on a full clambake in the dining room and golfing, de-stress with a wild-Maine-rose body wrap.

GETTING THERE AND AROUND

To drive to Maine's south coast from Boston, take I-93 to I-95 north. The Maine border at Kittery is 60 miles (1 hr. from Boston). Continue north along I-95 to exit 7 for York (10 mi., 15 min.) or exit 19 for Wells (20 mi., 25 min.). Ogunquit is located on Route 1 halfway between York and Wells; you can use either exit from the highway.

The Amtrak train **The Downeaster** (800/872-7245, www.thedowneaster.com) stops a handful of times every day in Wells on its route between Portland and Boston. Most towns have local trolley service (usually costing several dollars each way) to the major tourist points. In York, **The New England Trolley Company** (207/363-9600, www.yorktrolley.com) runs sightseeing buses on a continuous loop every day in summer and fall. Stops are made at Nubble Light and Long Sands Bath House, among others. Trolleys also run throughout summer days in Ogunquit, from Main Beach to Perkins Cove, and many stops in between.

MAINE

Kennebunkport to Cape Elizabeth

A shipbuilding center beginning in the 17th century, the Kennebunks (the official name for the towns of Kennebunkport, Cape Porpoise, Goose Rocks Beach, and Kennebunk) have since enjoyed an affair with prosperity that has hardly diminished. The area's reputation as a summer playground for well-to-do sailing fiends and families is not undeserved, as any stroll to the beach or wharf will prove. But the towns are also home to a dedicated population of year-round residents—collectively a population of about 14,000—who make sure the historic homes and sights of the area are kept in excellent shape, and keep the communities themselves a vital place to be any month of the year.

KENNEBUNKPORT

Every summer, bluebloods and preppies flock to Kennebunk and Kennebunkport's shores—including the Bush family, which keeps its summer compound on Ocean Avenue. (Rest assured, you're bound to feel comfortable in these parts whatever your political leanings; the 2004 election saw just as many Kerry/Edwards as Bush/Cheney bumper stickers around town.)

Politics plays even less a part in Kennebunkport's most sought-after pursuits—namely shopping, dining, and sailing. The

RUSTIC CHIC

The concepts of "Maine" and "luxury resort" are so antithetical, the words themselves practically tear each other apart. But surprisingly, the new **Hidden Pond** (354 Goose Rocks Rd., 888/967-9050, www.hiddenpondmaine.com, $400-700) perfectly titrates the rustic feel of the state with a breezy modern style high on concept and design. The resort features 14 cabins, each one individually designed by a local interior designer in a different hybrid style. One features bright tropical colors and dragonfly and butterfly motifs alongside a fieldstone fireplace and wicker porch furniture; another a zebra pattern rug with a lobster sculpture on the wall. Somehow it all works. In addition, the resort offers other nice Maine touches such as an on-site organic garden where guests are invited to pick their own produce to cook in the cottage kitchens, and a nightly bonfire complete with s'mores – and cocktails.

MAINE

© MICHAEL BLANDING

Kennebunkport cottage

town's centrally located Dock Square is filled with crafts and clothing boutiques, cafés and al fresco patios. Burn off the calories at any of the town's lovely parks and beaches, golf courses and boat outings. And there are plenty of places to witness the town's history in architectural form: old homes—from colonial and Federal to Greek Revival and Italianate in style—all overseen by the very active Kennebunkport Historical Society.

Sights

You won't find the usual local historic paraphernalia at **The Brick Store Museum** (117 Main St., Kennebunk, 207/985-4802, www. brickstoremuseum.org, 10 A.M.–4:30 P.M. Tues.–Fri. and 10 A.M.–1 P.M. Sat. year-round, $5 suggested donation). Instead, the staff gets curatorially creative with exhibits such as "The Kennebunks During the Civil War," and "Kennebunks A–Z." The museum also runs an architectural walking tour ($5 per person) every Tuesday, Wednesday, and Friday at 10 A.M. throughout summer. If you'd rather guide yourself, you can also tour one of the sea captains'

homes run by the museum. Vehicular history comes alive at the **Seashore Trolley Museum** (195 Log Cabin Rd., Kennebunkport, 207/967-2800, www.trolleymuseum.org, 10 A.M.–5 P.M. in summer; weekends only May and Oct.; closed Nov.–Apr. except during Christmas Prelude, $8 adults, $6 seniors, $5.50 children 6–16, free children under 6). With a collection of more than 200 trolleys (some of which you can ride through nearby woods from the museum), plus a gift shop dedicated entirely to streetcars, the operation has no shortage of specialization. The 1826 **Wedding Cake House** (104 Summer St., Kennebunkport) is an essential stop for most tourists, though they can only enjoy its beauty from the exterior. (The home, originally a gift from George Bourne to his wife, is still owned by the Bourne family.) But the outside—an elaborate Federal-style facade—is stunning enough to warrant a look.

Entertainment

Catch live folk, blues, karaoke, and rock on weekends at **Federal Jack's Pub** (8 Western Ave., Kennebunkport, 207/967-4322, www.

HONEYMOON SWEET?

COURTESY MAINE OFFICE OF TOURISM

Wedding Cake House

Shipbuilder George Washington Bourne bought the brick Federal home that would become known as the **Wedding Cake House** (104 Summer St., Kennebunkport) in 1826, soon after marrying his bride, Jane. Retired and bored a few decades later, he began hand-carving decorations for the home modeled after the Gothic cathedrals he admired in Europe. One thing led to another, and before long, he had created a towered frosting of ornamentation that put the best dessert platters to shame. Dubbed the "Wedding Cake House" after his death, the home has been an essential stop for tourists to Kennebunk for more than 100 years. The beauty of the house is ordinarily only viewable from the exterior. (You'll have to park down the street in the designated lot and walk half a block for the photo-op.) For two weeks in 2005, however, the owner, Jimmy Barker, opened the house for an unprecedented benefit for hurricane victims, bringing inquisitive guests inside for the first time. Visitors ooh'd and ah'd at crystal chandeliers and impeccable trompe l'oeil paintings. If this happens again, don't wait to snatch up a ticket.

MAINE

federaljacks.com). Throughout the year, **River Tree Arts** (35 Western Ave., Kennebunkport, 207/967-9120, www.rivertreearts.org) organizes concerts and other shows. Call for the latest schedule.

Events

There's no shortage of cheer in town during **Christmas Prelude,** the two-week holiday carnival that brings out carolers, tree lightings, visits from Santa on a boat, and literally tons of decorations on the area's most historic homes. Not long after, the **Winter Carnival** starts up. The early February festivities are a weekend full of tobogganing and sleigh riding, ice skating, and other competitions.

Shopping

With a wealth of adorable, tasteful gift shops, Kennebunkport's **Dock Square** is easily a day's worth of window shopping. Duck into **Carrots & Company** (19 Ocean Ave., Kennebunkport, 207/967-5300, www.carrotsandcompany.com, 10 A.M.–6 P.M. Sun.–Thurs., 10 A.M.–8 P.M. Fri.–Sat., June–Sept., 10 A.M.–5:pm Oct.–Dec., call for spring hours); past the huge green Volkswagen bug, find hand-printed stationery, shell-handled servingware, patterned garden gloves, and Angela Adams bags. Find anything and everything you need for a picnic at **H. B. Provisions General Store** (15 Western Ave., Kennebunkport, 207/967-5762, www.hbprovisions.com, 6 A.M.–10 P.M. May–Oct., 6 A.M.–9 P.M. Oct.–May). Pick up locally made apricot preserves, pickled garlic, canned wild Maine blueberries, and an oyster-shucking kit. The beautiful stoneware at **The Good Earth** (7 Ocean Ave., Kennebunkport, 207/967-4635, 10 A.M.–5 P.M. daily Apr.–Dec.) comes in unique shapes—wide mugs, skinny platters, and square plates adorned with nature patterns like leaves, ferns, and acorns. Those

with the holidays on the brain year-round will delight in **Christmas Presence** (1 Dock Square, Kennebunkport, 207/967-5049) a panoply of every kind of ornament imaginable—from dancing hand-painted elves and lobster claws to entire North Pole villages.

Food

Funky and off-handedly cool, the high-ceilinged and airy **(Bandaloop** (2 Dock Square, Kennebunkport, 207/967-4994, www.bandaloop.biz, 5–11 P.M. Sun.–Thu.; 5–midnight Fri.–Sat., $17–29) is an energetic place to catch dinner made from organic, all-natural, and local foods served by a young, hip waitstaff. Creations include the likes of tomato-and-fresh-corn chowder, garlic mussels, and Chai tea crème brûlée. Dig into more traditional Maine fare at **The Landing** (192 Ocean Ave., Kennebunkport, 207/967-4221, www.landingintheport.com, 11:30 A.M.–11 P.M., $22–32), where deep-fried seafood and lobster pie fly out of the kitchen next to baked-stuffed scallops. The al fresco patio overlooking

The Clam Shack has some of the best fried clams anywhere.

the harbor makes for prime seagull-watching. Seating isn't quite as lovely (patrons make do by plunking themselves on benches in an abutting parking lot) at ◖ **The Clam Shack** (2 Western Ave., Kennebunkport, 207/967-2560, www.theclamshack.net, 11 A.M.–9 P.M. daily May–Sept.; 5 P.M.–9 P.M. Oct.–Dec.; call for winter hours), but the food is well worth the inconvenience. Clams are fresh (whole or strips) and fried on the premise; lobster rolls are full of huge chunks of tail and claw meat—some of the best of its kind anywhere. On the other end of formality sits ◖ **The White Barn Inn** (37 Beach Ave., Kennebunkport, 207/967-2321, www.whitebarninn.com, four-course prix fixe $95, wine-pairing $48–85), a justifiably revered restaurant (housed in an 1860s barn) that has received seemingly every award and honor a restaurant can win in America. You may want to give it one of your own, after tasting lobster with homemade fettuccine, snow peas, ginger, and cognac-coral butter sauce. The wine list is equally exquisite. If you're not stuffed to the brim by the end of your stay in town, swing by **Aunt Marie's** (10 Ocean Ave., Kennebunkport, 207/967-0711) for an ice-cold taste of Maine: homemade ice cream flavors like wild berry, cashew turtle, and "wicked good" chocolate.

Information

Hotel, dining, maps, and recreation pamphlets plus area business listings are available at the **Chamber of Commerce,** which in summer is located in the Brick Store Museum (117 Main St., Kennebunk, 207/985-4802, www.brickstoremuseum.org, 10 A.M.–4:30 P.M. Tues.–Fri. and 10 A.M.–1 P.M. Sat. year-round). Outside of high season, the office moves to **The Yellow House** (17 Western Ave., Kennebunkport, 207/967-0857, www.visitthekennebunks.com).

OLD ORCHARD BEACH

Picture the archetypical seaside amusement park of yesteryear—boardwalk vendors, tented arcades, wooden rides—and you've got Old Orchard Beach. Of course, plenty of modern (not to mention cheesy) elements have found their way here, too: tattoo parlors and bikers sit beside kids lapping ice cream and scantily bathing-suited senior couples holding hands. Forget the amusement rides; the march of humanity doesn't get more entertaining than this.

Also worth a detour for nature lovers: the nearby small town of Saco. Once a well-to-do mill town, it's still blessed with plenty of large, pretty homes and a bustling downtown—particularly these days on its island (plunk in the middle of Saco River), home to an increasing number of charming retailers. But largely, it's the undeveloped areas of Saco that visitors are after: the gushing waters of the Saco River, and the well-kept trails of its parks, which provide year-round activities.

Sights

Little-known but highly regarded among the antiquities community, the **Saco Museum** (371 Main St., Saco, 207/283-0684, noon–4 P.M. Tues.–Thu., 12–8 P.M. Fri., 10 A.M.–4 P.M. Sat. year-round; noon–4 P.M. Sun. Jun.–Dec., $4 adults, $3 seniors, $2 students and children 7–18, free children under 6, free Fri. 4–8 P.M.) houses a treasure trove of historic American paintings, hand-crafted furniture, and old tools of the 18th through the mid-19th century.

Events

Mondays and Tuesdays at 7 P.M. during summer, there are free live concerts and comedy acts at Old Orchard's **Seaside Pavilion,** followed by fireworks every Thursday at 9:30 P.M. And every August, the **Beach Olympics** come to town, filling the streets with music, games, and crafts exhibits.

Shopping

The Pier (1 Old Orchard St., 207/934-2001) on Old Orchard Beach is a boardwalk-cum-arcade that stretches out across the water and peddles every kind of kitschy junk: blow-up Bart Simpson dolls, pennies stamped into pendants, and photos of you posed in front of a fake wave. On the more elegant end of retail, Saco has handmade crafts made by a collective of upwards of 50 local artists at **Stone Soup Artisans** (232 Main St., Saco, 207/283-4715,

MAINE

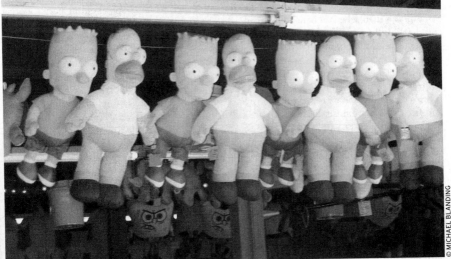

© MICHAEL BLANDING

prizes at Old Orchard Beach

10 A.M.–5:30 P.M. Mon.–Sat. Memorial Day to New Year's).

Food

Food at this fair is exactly what you'd expect: fried, fried, and fried some more. You'll find a (relative) break from all the junk food at **Lisa's Pizza** (17 Old Orchard St., 207/934-7655), though it's hardly health food. It's hardly worth complaining, however; what else is a carnival for?

Information

In Saco, direct yourself to the **Biddeford-Saco Chamber of Commerce** (138 Main St., Saco, 207/282-1567, www.biddebordsacochamber.org, 8:30 A.M.–4:30 P.M. Mon.–Thurs., 8:30 A.M.–4 P.M. Fri.) and get maps and restaurant and lodging information. For Old Orchard Beach, contact the **Old Orchard Beach Chamber of Commerce** (207/934-2500, www.oldorchardbeachmaine.com).

CAPE ELIZABETH

Thrust out into the Atlantic like a fist of granite, the rocky headland of Cape Elizabeth is one of the most romantic locations in all of New England. It was here that artist Winslow Homer chose to spend his summer capturing the dynamic interplay of rock and wave in his many celebrated seascapes, and it was here that President George Washington chose to site one of America's first lighthouses-the eminently photogenic Portland Head. Now Routes 207 and 77 make a nice scenic detour around the Cape between Old Orchard Beach and Portland.

◖ Portland Head Light

Tapering gracefully from the granite headland of Cape Elizabeth, the whitewashed conical tower of Portland Head Light is Maine's oldest lighthouse and arguably its most picturesque (only Pemaquid Point, farther up the coast, can rival it). Commissioned by George Washington in 1787 and completed in 1791, the rubblestone tower is one of four colonial-era lighthouses that has never been rebuilt. The tower has been in continuous operation ever since, literally rising and falling in prominence depending on the times (at one point in the late 1800s, it was shortened 20 feet, only to be

COURTESY MAINE OFFICE OF TOURISM

Portland Head Light

his moody oil paintings that frequently chose their subjects from the surrounding drama of water and wave. The house was acquired by the Portland Museum of Art in 2006, and the institution has been promising to restore it for visitors for years. Currently, however, the project remains on hold; check back with the museum (207/775-6148, www.portlandmuseum.org) for updates. Until then, guests will have to content themselves with ambling around the Neck by themselves, painting pictures in their own minds. Park at Scarborough Beach (Black Point Rd.) or stay at the Black Point Inn (below).

Food

For flavors and sauces that take you straight back to Italy (even if you've never been there), take a tour through **Anjon's** (521 US Route 1., Scarborough, 207/883-9562, 11:30:am–9 P.M. daily year-round). Low-key, it's not-with wine cork-covered walls and a bar fresco of Venice— but thankfully then again, neither is the food. Take your choice of sausage gnocchi, veal *piccata,* or the homemade tiramisu, and you won't be disappointed.

raised again shortly thereafter). Now a remotely operated second-order Fresnel lens still guides shipping traffic into Portland. Visitors can learn more about the light and see artifacts relating to its storied history at a small museum in the keeper's house (1000 Shore Rd., 207/799-2661, www.portlandheadlight.com, 10 A.M.–4 P.M. daily late May–Oct.; weekends only mid-Apr.– late May and mid-Oct.–late Dec.,$2 adults, $1 children 6–18, free children under 6). The lighthouse is located on the grounds of Fort William Park, home to a former military fort (since decommissioned), and now home to 90 acres of grassy fields and beachfront, with several tennis courts and playing fields.

Other Sights

South of Portland Head, the delicate Prout's Neck trails into the sea in a jumble of rocks and surf, home to a hundred or so homes of sturdy Mainers. One of those homes was once the **Winslow Homer Studio,** the home where one of New England's most famous artists lived off and on for 25 years. Homer is famed for

SPORTS AND RECREATION
Beaches

Clean and filled with beach plum bushes at its edges, **Goose Rocks Beach** (King's Hwy., off Rte. 9, Kennebunkport, no parking, catch the trolley from downtown) is one of the area's loveliest and least mobbed. For kids, there's the well-kept **Mother's Beach** (Beach Ave., off Rte. 9, Kennebunkport, no parking, catch the trolley from downtown), which has a jungle gym and swings. In Saco, **Ferry Beach State Park** (Bay View Rd., off Rte. 9, Saco, 207/283-0067, year-round, adults $2, children $1) is a stunning natural setting: On top of the beach, there are woodland trails and marshes.

Hiking and Biking

Abundant wildlife, extensive hiking and snow-shoeing trails, and seemingly untouched woodlands are what make **The Heath** (Rte. 112, Buxton Rd., Saco, 207/729-5181, www.nature.org, sunrise–sunset year-round) a favorite destination among nature lovers. Much of the park's 870 acres are filled with foliage, deer, and a breathtaking bog created by the accumulation of layer upon layer of peat. One of the finest walks in the Kennebunk area is in **Emmons Preserve** (Gravelly Brook Rd., off of Beachwood Ave., Kennebunkport, www.thekennebunkportconservationtrust.org, year-round), managed by the Kennebunkport Conservation Trust. Its nearly 150 bird-filled acres contain two walking trails—each of which can be walked in less than two hours—and offer views of picturesque Gravelly Brook.

Boating and Fishing

Get out and sailing local waters in half-day trips aboard *Bellatrix* (95 Ocean Ave., Kennebunkport, 207/590-1125, www.sailing-trips.com, $300 for 1–6 people), a sleek 37-foot yacht. One of the best whale-watching excursions around is operated by **Nautilus Whale Watch** (67 Ocean Ave., Kennebunkport, 207/967-0707, 10 A.M. daily plus additional times in summer, adults $30, seniors $25, children $15). It offers plenty of commentary, lots of deck viewing, and a full galley for snacking.

ACCOMMODATIONS
Under $100

The centrally located 🄲 **Crown 'n' Anchor Inn** (121 North St., Saco, 207/282-3829, $75–110, no children under 12) is an exquisite Greek Revival mansion with six fireplace- and antiques-blessed suites and a formal and filling breakfast.

$150–250

Casually and simply decorated, the waterfront **Green Heron Inn** (126 Ocean Ave., Kennebunkport, 207/967-3315, www.greenheroninn.com, $160–190) includes ten charming rooms (some with fireplaces), and a big breakfast of pancakes, bacon, and whatever else the chef feels compelled to cook up. The recently renovated **Old Orchard Beach Inn** (6 Portland Ave., Old Orchard Beach, 207/934-5834, www.oldorchardbeachinn.

com, $135–200) sports tasteful rooms and a quite-good breakfast. In Kennebunkport, the centrally located **Captain Fairfield Inn** (8 Pleasant St., Kennebunkport, 800/322-1928, www.captainfairfield.com, $150–380) is a worthy splurge. The 19th-century house has rooms with fireplaces, a pleasant garden, afternoon tea, and a dynamite full breakfast.

$250 and Up

A 19th-century butter-yellow Victorian on manicured, flowered grounds, 🄲 **The Beach House** (211 Beach Ave., Kennebunk Beach, 207/967-3850, www.beachhseinn.com, $190–390) faces the rolling Atlantic with guest rooms full of down comforters, chic decor, complimentary port and brandy in the fireplaced living room, and Molton Brown amenities. In addition to its ideal beachside location, the property serves a first-rate continental breakfast. The surf-splashed **Black Point Inn** (510 Black Point Rd., 207/883-2500, www.blackpointinn.com, $220–420) has remained authentic to its 130-year history, with its gracious guest rooms and grand dining room overlooking the ocean. Several years ago, however, a group of nearby residents purchased and punched it up to the modern era, decreasing the number of rooms from 84 to 25, adding plush new linens and décor, and opening a new bar onto an outdoor patio readymade for cocktails at sunset.

GETTING THERE AND AROUND

For Kennebunkport, take exit 25 off I-95 and drive east on Route 9A (10 mi., 15 min. from Wells). For Old Orchard Beach take exit 36 to I-195 east (25 mi., 30 min. from Wells). For Saco, also take exit 36 to I-195 east but then take exit 2A to Route 1 south (20 mi., 25 min. from Wells).

Amtrak's **Downeaster** (800/872-7245, www.thedowneaster.com) train makes stops several times a day in Old Orchard Beach and Saco on its way between Boston and Portland.

The Kennebunks operate trolleys through

Intown Trolley (207/967-3638, www.intown-trolley.com, $15 adult, $5 children 3–17, free children under 3, $25 couples) all around Kennebunk and Kennebunkport and their beaches, on a narrated 50-minute loop; fares are good for one whole day, making this a useful option if you plan on doing a lot of sightseeing. **Shuttle-Bus** (207/282-5408, www.shuttlebus-zoom.com) operates buses between and around Saco and Old Orchard Beach, among other points on the Southern Coast. Fares and schedules vary.

Portland

MAINE

Bumped up against breezy Casco Bay, Portland is one of the last working waterfronts in the country. Founded in 1632, it soon prospered as the primary point of trade between Canada and Europe. Today it still serves as New England's second-largest fishing and oil port and its largest port for tonnage.

All of which could have made Portland into an unattractive, polluted, industrial-looking town. But nothing could be further from the truth. Anchored by its Old Port district, the city is filled with art galleries, pubs, museums, chic bistros, and independent boutiques. Its cobblestone streets and squares are serenaded by the cries of seagulls and foghorns, and its high-rise buildings (Portland is a regional center for banking and import/export) are met with the historic charm of revitalized brick warehouses now used for retail, offices, and artsy movie houses.

The proliferation of those warehouses is actually the result of the city's greatest tragedy; in 1866 a fire swept through almost all of the neighborhoods, destroying most of the previous architecture. The brick warehouses were built in its place, giving a pleasing uniform look to the waterfront area of the city

Its outlying towns—South Portland, Scarborough, Cape Elizabeth, Cumberland, Falmouth, and the Casco Bay Islands—are primarily bedroom communities. But in them you'll find excellent historic inns, world-famous lighthouses, and pristine beaches.

SIGHTS

To orient yourself in Portland, find its two major thoroughfares. Commercial Street connects the Old Port and the waterfront, which together comprise the bulk of downtown. The Arts District centers around Congress Street, and is a collection of fine art galleries, studios, and the excellent Portland Museum of Art. Meanwhile, to the west, up-and-coming areas Munjoy Hill and West Bayside are primarily residential, with a handful of art galleries and cafés.

© MICHAEL BLANDING

Portland has its own charm.

◖ Portland Museum of Art

The highly regarded I. M. Pei–designed Portland Museum of Art (7 Congress Sq.,

MAINE

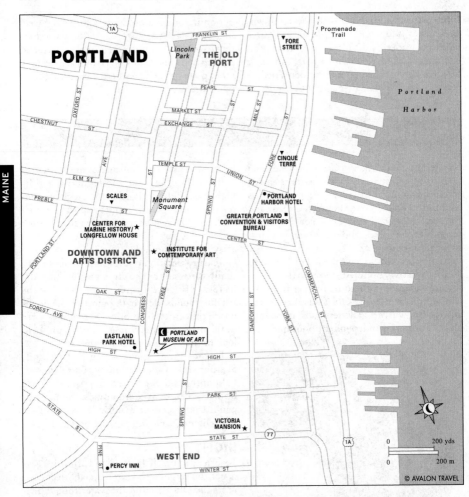

207/775-6148, www.portlandmuseum.org, 10 A.M.–5 P.M. Tues.–Thurs. and Sat.–Sun., 10 A.M.–9 P.M. Fri. year-round; 10 A.M.–5 P.M. Mon. late May–mid-Oct., $10 adults, $8 seniors and students, $4 youth 6–17, free children under 6 and free to all 5–9 P.M. Fri.) is a world-class collection of Impressionist and American pieces. You won't find any earth-shattering masterpieces here, but what you will find is uniformly excellent.

A highlight is the paintings of Maine artist Winslow Homer, who made a genre out of

the powerful depiction of sea breaking against ledges of the coast. The paintings are made even more dramatic by the fact that the subject of the paintings is only a few miles away, at the artist's studio on Prout's Neck. The artist's portraits and domestic scenes are less well known, but just as masterfully done.

The museum also contains fine Impressionist work by Monet, Renoir, and Pisarro, along with their American cousins, including the underrated Maine artist Rockwell Kent, many of whose mythic landscapes and woodcuts were made on the nearby Maine island of Monhegan.

Other Sights

For a more modern slice of the art scene, check out the **Institute of Contemporary Art at the Maine College of Art** (522 Congress St. or 87 Free St., 207/879-5742 or 207/669-5029, www.meca.edu, 11 A.M.–5 P.M. Wed.–Sun.; 11 A.M.–7 P.M. Thu.; 11 A.M.–8 P.M. first Fri. of the month, tours 12:15 P.M. on Wed., free). The school's galleries draw cutting-edge installations from local and global artists, both established and aspiring. Hit the mother lode of Maine lore at **Center for Maine History** (489 Congress St., 207/774-1822, www.mainehistory.org, 10 A.M.–5 P.M. Mon.–Sat.; noon–5 P.M. Sun., $5 adults, $4 seniors and students, $2 children), which illustrates (often with real innovation) the state's past through collections, exhibits, and lectures. Particularly riveting are the exhibits pertaining to the shelling that Portland received at the hands of the British during the Revolutionary War, when the port, then known as Falmouth, was literally burned to the ground in October 1775. The British captain offered mercy if the townspeople would swear allegiance to King George. No oath came, and the city was destroyed-only to be rebuilt over the next two decades through the hardwork of its populace and rechristened Portland. Next door, the **Wadsworth-Longfellow House** (487 Congress St., 207/774-1822, www.mainehistory.org, tours on the hour, 10:30 A.M.–4 P.M. Mon.–Sat., noon–4 P.M. Sun. May–Oct.; open Dec. for holiday tours; call for hours) was built in 1786, and achieved fame as the childhood home of poet Henry Wadsworth Longfellow. The home has been restored to the time of the early 1800s, around the time when Longfellow lived there. Tours take in the life of the poet-a Renaissance man of his time—as well as other members of the Longfellow family, such as Revolutionary war general Peleg Wadsworth.

Built in 1807, Munjoy Hill's **Portland Observatory** (138 Congress St., 207/774-5561, www.portlandlandmarks.org, tours 10 A.M.–4:30 P.M. daily late May–mid-Oct.; sunset tours Thu. 5 P.M.–8 P.M. late July–early Sept., $7 adults, $4 children 6–16, free children under 6) has heart-stopping views of Portland, Casco Bay, and beyond. If you are visiting during the late summer, try and time your visit for a Thursday evening sunset tour, where the golden rays lighting up the waterfront and islands beyond are nothing short of magical.

Fans of Italianate architecture (or anyone who likes a pretty building, for that matter) should be sure to swing by the **Victoria Mansion** (109 Danforth St., 207/772-4841, www.victoriamansion.org, tours 10 A.M.–4 P.M. Mon.–Sat., 1–5 P.M. Sun. May–Oct.; 11 A.M.–5 P.M. Tue.–Sun. late Nov.–early Jan., $15 adults, $13.50 seniors, $5 students 6–17, free children under 6, $35 family), considered a paragon of the style. Built by a hotel magnate between 1858 and 1860, the mansion is quite simply the greatest surviving example of pre–Civil War architecture in the country. Ahead of its time, it employed central heating, running water, and gas lighting in an era when they were virtually unknown luxuries. These days, the house is particularly impressive at Christmastime, when it is decorated from baseboards to ceilings with ornaments and wreaths.

Entertainment

A loyal local following pours into **Brian Boru Public House** (57 Center St., 207/780-1506, www.brianboruportland.com) for its cheap pints of Guinness, views of Casco Bay, and free live Irish music. Come Sunday afternoons for a traditional Irish session Big-deal, national musicians take the stage at **Port City Music Hall** (504 Congress St., 207/899-4990, www.portcitymusichall.com), from rap and soul artists to blues and alterna-jazz artists.

Events

With such a deluge of art venues, it's no surprise that Portland offers a slew of art performances, concerts, openings, and other events over the course of every year. One of the most regular—and festive—is **First Friday Art Walk** (www.firstfridayartwalk.com, 5–8 P.M. on the first Friday of every month). All Portland turns out to stroll the city's streets for free self-guided tours of its art galleries, performance art, and sidewalk concerts. Come holiday time, a sure bet is the month-long **Light Up Your Holidays** festival (207/772-6828, www.portlandmaine. com). Kicked off by a tree-lighting ceremony in early November, the celebration continues with free horse and wagon rides, late shopping hours, and Santa visits.

Shopping

In this day and age of mass chain stores, Portland has a refreshingly high ratio of independent, cleverly stocked shops. Odds and ends made by craftspeople both local and global cram the shelves at **Abacus American Craft Gallery** (44 Exchange St., 207/772-4880, www.abacusgallery.com, 10 A.M.–7 P.M. Mon.–Thu.; 10 A.M.–8 P.M. Fri.–Sat.; 11 A.M.–6 P.M. Sun.). Keep an eye out for the beautiful handmade jewelry and whimsical ceramic seagulls made nearby. If you're planning to picnic in the area (or just want a top-notch snack), head to **Browne Trading Market** (262 Commercial St., 207/775-7560, www.browne-trading.com, 10 A.M.–6:30 P.M. Mon.–Sat., noon–5 P.M. Sun. during summer only) for specialty noshes like imported cheeses, caviar, and smoked seafood.

Score tunes by everyone from Beethoven to Billy Idol at **Bull Moose Music** (151 Middle St., 207/780-6424, www.bullmoose.com, 10 A.M.–11 P.M. daily), as much a hangout as it is CD and movie store. Small but cleverly stocked, the women-owned and -operated **Condom Sense** (424 Fore St., 207/871-0356, www.qualitycondoms.com, 10 A.M.–6 P.M. Mon.–Wed.; 10 A.M.–8 P.M. Thu.; 10 A.M.–10 P.M. Fri.–Sat.; 10 A.M.–6 P.M. Sun.) peddles everything from the obvious (condoms) to the surprising (political magnets).

There's an impressive selection of reading material—from used religious autobiography to poetry and new crossword-puzzle journals—at **Cunningham Books** (188 State St., 207/775-2246, 10 A.M.–5:30 P.M. Mon.–Sat.).

THE BIG FRAME-UP

With so many artists living within the city limits, it only makes sense that Portland should be home to an impressive stable of galleries. What's surprising, however, is the variety of art condensed in such a relatively small city – everything from Impressionism and antique seascapes to contemporary oils and modern photography. Some of the most reputable and distinctive spaces include:

· **Aucocisco Galleries** (89 Exchange St., 207/775-2222, www.aucocisco.com); fine and antique art, focusing on Maine artists.

· **Calitano Gallery** (29 Forest Ave., 207/774-1205); contemporary paintings and sculpture.

· **Domaine Gallery** (223 Commercial St., 207/772-2270); photography from Maine.

· **Du'e** (81 Market St., 207/879-1869, www.duegallery.com); abstract oils and watercolors by local artists.

· **Greenhut Galleries** (146 Middle St., 207/772-2693, www.greenhutgalleries. com); contemporary art and sculpture by Maine artists.

· **Jameson Estate Collection, LLC** (377 Cumberland Ave., 207/772-5522, www. jamesongallery.com); 19th- and 20th-century fine art.

· **R. N. Cohen / Exchange Street Gallery** (425 Fore St., 207/772-0633, www.rn-cohen.com); limited-edition works depicting Portland and coastal Maine.

· **SPACE** (538 Congress St., 207/828-5600, www.space538.org); contemporary and emerging art forms.

Famous for flannel plaid overshirts and preppy sporting gear, **The L. L. Bean Factory Store** (542 Congress St., 207/772-5100, www.llbean. com, 9 A.M.–7 P.M. Mon.–Sat.; 10 A.M.–6 P.M. Sun.) makes it all available at a heavily discounted price. Buy some of the state's true treasures at **Maine Potters Market** (376 Fore St., 207/774-1633, www.mainepottersmarket. com, 10 A.M.–9 P.M. Mon.–Sat., 10 A.M.–6 P.M. Sun.), a cooperative owned and operated by 13 Maine potters.

Food

There aren't many cities of Portland's size that can compete with its culinary punch. It's home to internationally respected heavyweight chefs and their multi-starred eateries as well as family operations, ethnic bistros, and humble, candlelit boîtes.

Arguably single-handedly responsible for first putting Portland on the international foodie map, **Fore Street Restaurant** (288 Fore St., 207/775-2717, www.forestreet. biz, 5:30–10 P.M. Sun.–Thu.; 5:30–10:30 P.M. Fri.–Sat.; bar open at 5 P.M. daily, $14–29) is a knowing ode to simplicity. Everything— from the burnished copper-topped tables and the water view to the epic wood-fired oven— speaks of sophisticated rustication, and the food is no exception. (For proof, try the apple-wood-roasted chicken with a side of heirloom tomatoes.) There's excellent, impressively authentic Thai food (much of it made with local seafood) to be found at **Siam City Cafe** (339 Fore St., 207/773-8389, 5 P.M.–10:30 P.M. daily, $10–16).

Speaking of seafood, some of the freshest catch is at **Scales** (25 Preble St., 207/228-2008, $5–13), a cushy take on the classic seafood shack. (Instead of sawdust on the floor, you'll find slate counters and pine.) But the value and freshness are as genuine as can be: Grab a table on the outdoor deck and dig into one of the best lobster rolls around. A dose of turf to that surf is the perfectly grilled lamb at **Cinque Terre** (36 Wharf St., 207/347-6154, www.cinqueterremaine.com, 5–11 P.M. nightly, $18–21). With a menu that's pure

Northern Italian, the trattoria serves lots of sharp-flavored grilled items with a wine list that follows suit.

Information

The **Greater Portland Convention & Visitors Bureau** (245 Commercial St., 207/772-5800, www.visitportland.com) can make dinner and tour reservations, help plan itineraries, and offers free maps and brochures. It runs information centers on the waterfront at 14 Ocean Gateway Pier (207/772-5800, Mar.–Dec.), in Deering Oaks Park just off I-295 (207/828-0149), and in the Jetport Terminal next to baggage claim (207/775-5809).

You can also arm yourself with brochures of local businesses and maps of the entire Portland area at the **Portland Regional Chamber of Commerce** (60 Pearl St., 207/772-2811, www. portlandregion.com).

FREEPORT

A mere 20-minute jaunt from Portland and a one-hour drive from Boston, Freeport is a magnet for those with one thing on the mind: shopping. The coastal outlet town is lined with upwards of 170 outlets for international designer brands mixed with local mom-and-pop shops. That said, it also makes for a decent base for exploring the area's nearby parks and waterways (between shopping trips, of course).

L. L. Bean Factory Store

Here it is: the original outlet that started it all, launching myriad retail outlets across the nation, millions of catalogs, and God only knows how many hiking and fishing obsessions. Open since 1917, the three Freeport outlets of L. L. Bean (95 Main St., 877/755-2326, www.ll-bean.com)—the flagship store, the Hunting & Fishing store, and the Bike & Boat store— are open 24 hours a day, 365 days a year, making them a favorite midnight–shopping road trip for college students all over New England. In fact, more than three million people visit the Freeport stores each year. At the flagship, everything from camping and hiking to home furnishings and outdoor clothing for

MAINE

MAINE

© MICHAEL BLANDING

L.L. Bean's factory store

grown-ups and kids are under one roof—not to mention in-store archery clinics, clay shooting demonstrations, and lectures on training pointers and learning duck calls. The Hunting & Fishing Store is full of fly- and spin-fishing equipment, hunting bows and firearms, and every kind of jacket you could possibly wear while angling for critters. Meanwhile, the Bike & Boat store stocks goods like cycling helmets, clothing, and kiddie seats; kayaks and canoes (plus accessories like paddles and flotation devices); and, in winter, skis and snowshoes.

Other Sights
Swing by **Pettengill Farm** (Pettengill Rd., 207/865-3170, www.freeporthistoricalsociety. org) for a glimpse of what 19th-century saltwater farm life was like, from its saltbox house to its extensive apple orchards on an estuary of the Harraseeket River.

Shopping
It would take days to shop your way through all of Freeport's outlet stores properly. The highlights, however, include: The international

home of the infamous plaid, **Burberry** (42 Main St., 207/865-4400, www.burberry.com, 9:30 A.M.–8 P.M. Mon.–Sat.; 10 A.M.–6 P.M. Sun.), which stocks the upscale label's outerwear, plus skirts, dresses, sweaters, and suits at up to 50 percent off. Snag leather bags, wallets, belts, and hats that are slightly irregular at as much as 60 percent off at the **Coach Factory** (48 West St., 207/865-1772, 9 A.M.–9 P.M. Mon.–Sat.; 10 A.M.–6 P.M. Sun.). Stock up on unusual strategy and board games for the wee ones at **Puzzles & Games** (58 Main St., 207/865-4185). Find beautiful handmade beds, tables, armchairs, and media cases at **Thom. Moser Cabinetmakers** (149 Main St., 800/708-9041). Those that are slightly imperfect can be had at almost 40 percent off.

Food
Chowder (haddock, clam, seafood, or corn) is the main meal at **Morrison's Maine Chowderhouse** (4 Mechanic St., 207/865-3404, www.morrisonsmaine.com, 11:30 A.M.–7 P.M. daily June–Oct.; call for hours in winter, $4–12). Get it fast and eat

it casually out of the take-out stand's paper bowls. Hungrier souls can wander to **◖ Azure Cafe** (123 Main St., 207/865-1237, www.azurecafe.com, 11:30 A.M.–3 P.M., 5–9 P.M. daily; open until 10 P.M. Fri.–Sat., $12–32) for hearty bowls of cioppino and lobster fettuccini Alfredo, best eaten on the pretty outdoor stone courtyard. For a dash of history with your risotto, duck into **Jameson Tavern** (115 Main St., 207/865-4196, www.jamesontavern.com, 11:30 A.M.–9 P.M. Sun.–Thu.; 11:30 A.M.–10 P.M. Fri.–Sat., $16–26), which purports to be where Maine's statehood documents were signed in 1820. It seems a credible enough claim, if the eatery's 18th-century trappings are any indication. The food, however, is notably more up-to-date: Look for specials like pumpkin bisque alongside staples of grilled hanger steak and seafood salad.

Information

Grab shopping information for the Freeport outlets at the **Freeport Merchants Association Information Center** (23 Depot St., 207/865-1212, www.freeportusa.com, 9 A.M.–9 P.M. Mon.–Sat., 10 A.M.–6 P.M. Sun. in summer; 10 A.M.–6 P.M. daily in winter).

SPORTS AND RECREATION
Beaches

Monuments, cliffs, easy boating access, walking and biking paths—not to mention unforgettable sea views—are what call so many to Portland's **Eastern Promenade** (East Portland Harbor, 207/874-8793, 6:30 A.M.–10 P.M. daily).

Hiking and Biking

Hikers find bliss in **Wolfe's Neck Woods State Park** (Wolfe's Neck Rd., Freeport, 207/865-4465, www.state.me.us/doc/parks, Apr.–Oct.), a network of nature trails and bird-watching, with plenty of spots for picnicking. For a bit more quietude, head toward **Bradbury Mountain State Park** (528 Hallowell Rd., Pownal, 207/688-4712, www.state.me.us/doc/parks), which has a respectable number of trails in almost 600 acres of

woods, ball fields, and meadows; but sees far fewer visitors. Camping, biking, and horseback riding are permitted. Snowshoe rentals are available. The easy terrain of **Hedgehog Mountain** (Landfill Road, Pownal) makes for good mountain biking. In the winter, it's also a favorite trekking ground for cross-country skiers.

Boating and Fishing

Sit back and let someone else do the sailing around Casco Bay once you board *Bagheera* or the *Wendameen*, the 72-foot and 88-foot schooners operated by **Portland Schooner Co.** (Maine State Pier, 56 Commercial St., Portland, 207/766-2500, www.portlandschooner.com, $35 adults, $10 children). If you're in the market to rent kayaks, buy a canoe, or grab some sailboat riggings, your best bet is **Ring's Marine Service** (Smelt Brook Rd., South Freeport, 207/865-6143, www.ringsmarineservice.com, 8 A.M.–5 P.M. Mon.–Fri., $38/day kayaks, $27.50/day canoes), which also offers mooring services and boat transporting.

ACCOMMODATIONS
$150-250

In Freeport, just steps away from L. L. Bean, **Brewster House Bed & Breakfast** (180 Main St., Freeport, 207/865-4121, www.brewsterhouse.com, $150–190) is replete with Oriental carpets, antiques, and paintings of seascapes. Owners Lester and Nikki Evans cook up a full breakfast every morning. (Note to any who aren't at their most social or chipper in the morning: It's served at individual tables, so you can slurp your coffee and wake up in peace.)

The Percy Inn (15 Pine St., Portland, 207/871-7638, www.percyinn.com, $130–210) takes a renovated 1830s Federal-style brick house as its setting, and makes the ten suites cozy with queen beds, private baths, and wet bars. Snuggle up with a book in the library near the fireplace or a hot chocolate in the 3rd-floor common room, known as Poet's Corner. Designed to evoke a Spanish patio, **The Eastland Park Hotel** (157 High St., Portland, 207/775-5411, www.eastlandparkhotel.com,

MAINE

$190–210) is a chic enough spot to lay your head. The hotel's rooftop lounge is a swanky hangout, and rooms are stocked with plush bathrobes, hair dryers, free wireless Internet, and ironing boards. Meanwhile, poster beds, velvet chairs, and leather couches keep things cozy.

Over $250

Old Port's grandest stay is the sunny (**Portland Harbor Hotel** (468 Fore St., Portland, 207/775-9090, www.portlandharborhotel.com, $260–320). Complete with views of the city and bay, soaking tubs, bathroom sound systems, down pillows, and luxury linens, the rooms leave little to be desired. There's also a garden-cum-restaurant for lunch and dinner and a sleek fitness center. Freeport's (**Harraseeket Inn** (162 Main St., Freeport, 207/865-9377, $185–295) rolls out the luxury wagon in its 84 rooms, with whirlpool tubs, fireplaces, and an indoor pool. It's also easy walking distance (just a few blocks) to the most popular outlets.

INFORMATION AND SERVICES

The city's major hospital is also the state's largest: **Maine Medical Center** (22 Bramhall St., Portland, 207/662-0111, www.mmc.org). Pharmacies are numerous in the city, though most are not open 24 hours. Several **Rite Aid** (290 Congress St., Portland, 207/774-0344 and 713 Congress Street, West Portland, 207/774-8456) branches are open until 8 or 9 P.M. Internet is available for free at **Portland Public Library** (5 Monument Sq., 207/871-1700) and for a small fee (usually a few dollars per hour) in restaurants such as **Bull Feeney's Restaurant** (375 Fore St., 207/773-7210) and at **FedEx Office** (50 Monument Sq., 207/773-3177).

GETTING THERE

Portland is serviced by **Portland International Jetport** (1001 Westbrook St., 207/774-7301, www.portlandjetport.org), from which United, Delta, Continental, Northwest, and USAir all fly. There you'll find national car rental agencies Alamo, Avis, Budget, Hertz, and National. By train, the Amtrak **Downeaster** (800/872-7245, www.thedowneaster.com) arrives at the **Portland Transportation Center** (100 Thompson's Point Rd.) four times daily from Boston. Buses are operated from Boston through **Concord Coach Lines** (100 Thompson's Point Rd., Portland, 800/639-3317, www.concordtrailways.com) and to the rest of New England through **Greyhound** (950 Congress St., Portland, 207/772-6587, www.greyhound.com).

GETTING AROUND

To drive to Portland, take I-95 to exit 44, then I-295 into the city. The drive is approximately 110 miles from Boston (1 hr. 50 min.) and 50 miles from Kittery (50 min.). For Freeport, continue north from Portland on I-295 to exit 15A (15 mi., 20 min.).

If you're visiting sans vehicle, Portland's local bus company is **Metro** (114 Valley St., Portland, 207/774-0351, www.gpmetrobus.com, $1.25 adults, $1 students, free children under 5), which runs out of its downtown station to points that include the airport. Compared to most capital cities, Portland has a decent amount of metered street parking, which doesn't guarantee you'll find any right away (particularly in the summer), but the odds are good. That said, the city has pay lots and garages located every few blocks. Local taxis to call are **ABC Taxi** (207/772-8685) and **Town Taxi** (207/773-1711). In Freeport call **Yarmouth Taxi** (207/846-9336).

MIDCOAST

North of Freeport, the Maine coast starts to look like a jagged sawblade, with crannied bays carved out of the coast, and long points jutting out into the Atlantic. For many people, this is quintessential Maine, washed clean of the honky-tonk beaches of the South Coast and teeming with panoramic vistas wherever the eye lands. In fact, it may be where you spend the bulk of your time in the state, driving slowly down one peninsula after another and pausing to eat lobster-in-the-rough at the end of a dock, watch fishing boats stream into harbor, or climb to the top of one of the area's many lighthouses.

The area is far from homogenous, however. Each town along the coast has established a distinctive character. The military base near Bowdoin College makes Brunswick a college town with a difference, while nearby Bath is acclaimed both as a shipbuilding center and artists community. Wiscasset is a picture-postcard village that might have been dropped here from Vermont. Boothbay Harbor might be its foil—a cotton-candy and T-shirt-shop tourist destination that teems with families in the summer months.

Heading further north, Penobscot Bay is the heart of the region, a wide crinkly bay scattered with dozens of small islands and anchored by two very different towns. Camden has been a yachting capital for decades and is filled with ritzy shops and eateries, while the working lobstering town of Rockland has woken from a long slumber to provide a good mix of industry and tourism. The latter is also home base for several ferries that provide access to

MAINE

HIGHLIGHTS

🌙 **Maine Maritime Museum:** Maine's love affair with the sea is a long and rocky romance (page 548).

🌙 **Pemaquid Point Light:** You won't find an angle that hasn't already been photographed – but that doesn't stop countless visitors from trying (page 555).

🌙 **Maine Lobster Festival:** The state's premier homage to the crustacean features the annual crowning of the Sea Goddess (page 558).

🌙 **Farnsworth Art Museum:** Maine's favorite artistic family, the Wyeths, anchor an exceptional collection of Maine-based art (page 558).

🌙 **Maine Windjammer Cruises:** The most thrilling way to explore the coast, these picturesque sailboats have been a Maine tradition for more than 100 years (page 561).

🌙 **Monhegan:** Bring your paintbrushes to this rustic island, which has long beguiled artists with its beauty (page 566).

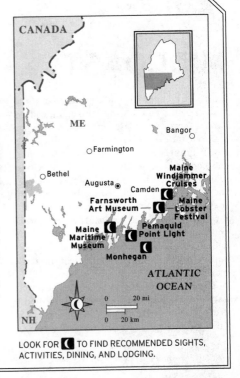

LOOK FOR 🌙 TO FIND RECOMMENDED SIGHTS, ACTIVITIES, DINING, AND LODGING.

the islands in the neighboring bay, which each have their own charms—the fishing village of Vinalhaven, the long flat Islesboro (a bicyclist's dream), and the artists' magnet of Monhegan.

PLANNING YOUR TIME

You'd need a month to really explore all of the nooks and crannies of this area—some Mainers take their whole lives to really do it justice. If you only have a few days, you'll have to strategize to hit the highlights. If you've come for lobsters and lighthouses, then Rockland provides a good home base, as it's home to the annual **Maine Lobster Festival,** as well as the Maine Lighthouse Museum. It also teems with seafood restaurants, most of which are open

year-round, although hours vary with the season. Rockland provides a good introduction to artists' long relationship with the coast through the works exhibited at the **Farnsworth Art Museum.** From here it's a short drive to the most stunning lighthouse in the region, **Pemaquid Point Light.**

If history is your thing, you'll find plenty of it in the relatively untouristed Bath-Brunswick area, home to the **Maine Maritime Museum** and several smaller but interesting museums at Bowdoin College. If you have more than a few days to explore the area, it's almost mandatory to get out onto the open ocean. For many people that means going to one of the islands in Penobscot Bay, where you can leave the bustle of the mainland behind and breathe

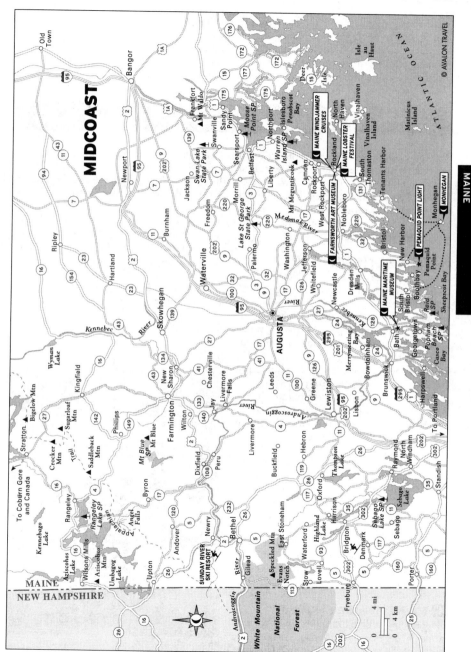

MAINE

MIDCOAST

© AVALON TRAVEL

in the salt air of quiet fishing villages. While each island has its advocates, perhaps the most unusual is **Monhegan Island,** a longtime artists colony that has neither cars nor electricity. If you can't decide which island to visit, book a **Windjammer Cruise** on one of the many schooners that leave from Camden. Ranging from several days to a week, the cruises will let you be blown by the wind to whatever anchorages happen to come.

Southern Midcoast

God must have been bored when he scribbled out this tortuous stretch of coastline, full of long and skinny peninsulas and saltwater bays. Thankfully the scenic highway of Route 1 cuts through the area to hit the main population centers—though a detour down at least one rocky peninsula is essential.

BATH-BRUNSWICK AREA

Erase your image of the pristine New England college town. Even though the prestigious liberal arts school Bowdoin anchors Brunswick, it has co-existed with an equally powerful institution, the Brunswick Naval Air Station, which keeps the town from becoming too precious. Recently the Pentagon dealt this town a difficult blow, however, when it declared the naval station to be closed by 2011. Town fathers have vowed to use the opportunity to reinvent Brunswick, highlighting attractions that include historic churches and homes, along with the gorgeous campus of the college.

A similar tension between art and industry informs Bath, the next town up the coast. Here, it's the vast shipbuilding complex of Bath Iron Works that has launched destroyers into the ocean, at the same time lending a solid base to the economy. The picturesque downtown may, in fact, be more your conception of college life. Over the years, Bath has gained a reputation for attracting artists and liberal types, so that workmen's bars sit cheek-and-jowl with funky art galleries and vegetarian cafés.

◀ Maine Maritime Museum

Shipbuilding in Bath didn't begin with the iron works. More than a century ago, the bustling center of Percy & Small Shipyards launched the five-masted schooners that carried Mainers into all corners of the world. The 20 acres of the former shipyard now form the campus of this museum (243 Washington St., Bath, 207/443-1316, www.mainemaritimemuseum. org, 9:30 a.m.–5 p.m. daily, $12 adults, $11 seniors, $9 children 5–17, free children under 5), which features masterfully curated exhibits tackling all aspects of seafaring.

The various buildings of the shipyard itself each have informative exhibits on the different stages in the building process, while tours of the fishing schooner *Sherman Zwicker* allow visitors to explore the finished

an exhibit at Maine Maritime Museum

MAINE AND THE CIVIL WAR

It has been said that the Civil War both began and ended in Brunswick, Maine. Harriet Beecher Stowe, whose book *Uncle Tom's Cabin* was a major galvanizing force behind the war, came up with the idea for the book while listening to an abolitionist sermon by her husband at the **First Parish Church** (9 Cleaveland St., Brunswick, 207/729-7331, www.firstparish.net). Across the street is the **Joshua L. Chamberlain Museum** (226 Maine St., Brunswick, 207/729-6606, http://community.curtislibrary.com/pejepscot.htm, 10 A.M.-4 P.M. Mon.-Fri., free), the home of the Civil War general who was chosen by General Grant to accept the surrender of the Confederacy at Appomattox Courthouse. A war hero who fought in 20 battles and was beloved by his men, Chamberlain was only recently given his proper due, when two films, *Gettysburg* and *Gods and Generals*, and Ken Burns' *Civil War* documentary all highlighted his heroic role in the Battle of Little Round Top. (Interestingly, he was played by Jeff Daniels in both feature movies.) Different rooms in the 1825 house highlight periods of his life, from his Civil War days to his later role as president of Bowdoin College.

© MICHAEL BLANDING

Civil War hero Joshua Chamberlain

product. Don't miss the lobstering exhibit tucked into a corner of the grounds; full of historical photographs and fishing gear, it's bound to give you a deeper appreciation of that night's meal.

Other Sights

On the campus of Bowdoin College, the small but fascinating **Peary-MacMillan Arctic Museum** (9500 College Station, Brunswick, 207/725-3416, http://academic.bowdoin.edu/arcticmuseum, 10 A.M.–5 P.M. Tues.–Sat.; 2–5 P.M. Sun., free) traces the Arctic adventures of two Bowdoin graduates and explorers, Donald MacMillan and Robert Peary. Exhibits include stuffed arctic animals and one of the original dog sledges Peary used to "discover" the North Pole.

Events

Most of the year, **Bath Iron Works** (700 Washington St., Bath, 207/443-3311, www.gdbiw.com) is off-limits to the public. That changes during one of its infrequent but spectacular ship launchings. Then the whole town comes out for the celebration and flags, food, and local dignitaries fill the waterfront to break champagne on the hull.

Food

Dr. Seuss characters cavort on the wall outside of **Starlight Cafe** (15 Lambard St., Bath, 207/443-3005, 7 A.M.–2 P.M. Mon.–Sat., $5–8), a casual basement eatery that captures the funky side of Bath. Locals congregate every morning for giant pancakes and fresh omelets, then come back for daily lunch specials. From

MAINE

the outside, **Scarlet Begonias** (212 Maine St., Brunswick, 207/721-0403, www.scarletbegoniasmaine.com, 11 A.M.–8 P.M. Mon.–Thu.; 11 A.M.–9 P.M. Fri.; noon–9 P.M. Sat., $8–15) looks and sounds like a flower shop, with vines and flowers crowding the window. In reality, it's a quaint country bistro full of mismatched furniture and the smell of garlic in the air. The menu includes gourmet sandwiches and pasta specials like the "Scarlet Harlot" (linguine with puttanesca sauce). It's BYOB, so make sure to tote a bottle of vino if you want some with dinner. A landmark restaurant for more than half-a-century, **Cook's Lobster House** (Rte. 24, Bailey Island, 207/833-2818, www.cookslobster.com, 11:30 A.M.–9 P.M. daily year-round, $7–33) serves up the best and freshest lobsters in the area, along with fried seafood and classic gut-busters like baked stuffed lobster and seafood Newburg. It is located on the tip of Bailey Island, south of Brunswick, and offers amazing water views, especially at sunset. For special occasions, **Robinhood Free Meetinghouse** (210 Robinhood Rd., Georgetown, 207/371-2188, www.robinhood-meetinghouse.com, 5:30–8 P.M. Tue.–Sun. late May–mid-Oct.; 5:30–8 P.M. Thu.–Sat. mid-Oct.–late May, $24–28) is a destination restaurant in a converted former church, with pews mixing among the tables in a dining room upstairs. Superstar chef Michael Gagne puts together a creative menu that goes beyond regional seafood with specialties like "two-textured duck"—confit and duck breast served with honey berry butter and caramelized apples.

Shopping

Downtown Bath is perfect for browsing and gallery carousing. Patchwork quilts hang in the window of **Mariner's Compass Quilt Shop** (11 Centre St., Bath, 207/443-2900, www.marinerscompass.com, 10 A.M.–5 P.M. Tue.–Sat.), a shop that has classes and circles as well as quilts and other blankets for sale. The young (at heart and otherwise) love **Baby Magnolia** (129 Front St., Bath, 207/443-8989, www.magnoliagiftstore.com, 10 A.M.–5 P.M. Mon.–Sat.), for its trove of baby gifts and accoutrements, but also

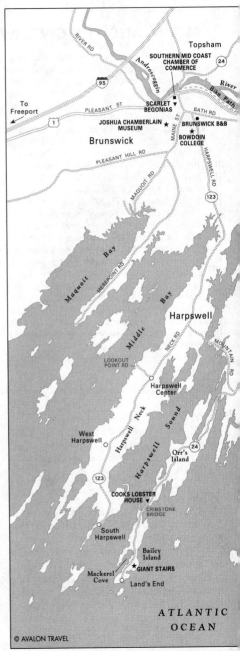

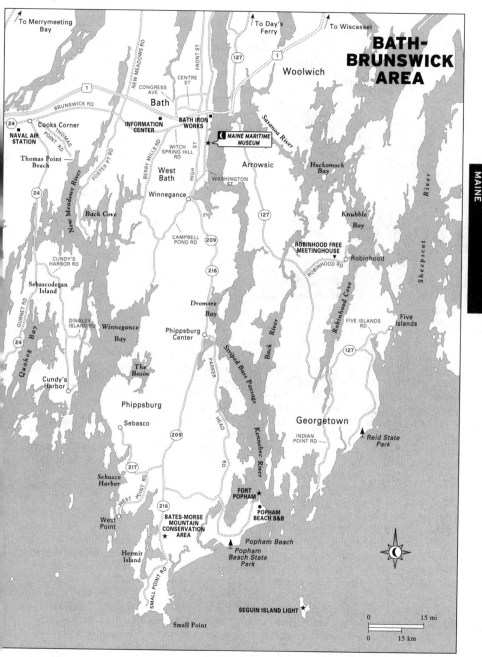

BATH-BRUNSWICK AREA

To Merrymeeting Bay

To Day's Ferry

To Wiscasset

NEW MEADOWS RD

FRONT ST

CENTRE ST

127

1

Woolwich

CONGRESS AVE

Bath

CENTRE ST

1

BRUNSWICK RD

24

Cooks Corner

NAVAL AIR STATION

INFORMATION CENTER

BATH IRON WORKS

MAINE MARITIME MUSEUM

Savanoa River

MAINE

Thomas Point Beach

POINT THOMAS RD

WITCH SPRING HILL RD

BERRY MILLS RD

HIGH ST

Arrowsic

Hockomock Bay

Sheepscot River

FOSTER PT RD

West Bath

WASHINGTON ST

Winnegance

127

Knubble Bay

24

Back Cove

CAMPBELL POND RD

209

ROBINHOOD FREE MEETINGHOUSE

Robinhood

CUNDY'S HARBOR RD

216

ROBINHOOD RD

Sebascodegan Island

DINGLEY ISLAND RD

Winnegance Bay

Dromore Bay

Back River

Robinhood Cove

FIVE ISLANDS RD

Five Islands

GURNET RD

Quahog Bay

24

Phippsburg Center

The Basin

PARKER RD

Striped Bass Passage

127

Cundy's Harbor

Phippsburg

Sebasco

209

HEAD RD

Kennebec River

Georgetown

INDIAN POINT RD

Reid State Park

217

Sebasco Harbor

WEST POINT RD

West Point

216

BATES-MORSE MOUNTAIN CONSERVATION AREA

FORT POPHAM

POPHAM BEACH B&B

Popham Beach

Hermit Island

SMALL POINT RD

Popham Beach State Park

Small Point

SEGUIN ISLAND LIGHT

0   15 mi

0   15 km

foliage on Bowdoin College campus

its more grown up stock of local jams, lavender sachets, and hand-woven blankets. Downtown Brunswick isn't as inviting for browsing, it's worth making a beeline to **Gulf of Maine Books** (134 Maine St., Brunswick, 207/729-5083, http://gulfofmainebooks.blogspot.com, 9:30 A.M.–5:30 P.M. Mon.–Sat.), a labor of love for local poet and publisher Gary Lawless and his wife Beth Leonard, who together have stocked the store with eclectic and unusual titles for 30 years.

Information and Services
The Bath-Brunswick area is served by the **Southern Midcoast Chamber of Commerce** (59 Pleasant St., Brunswick, 207/725-8797, www.midcoastmaine.com), which produces several useful guides to the area. The chamber runs a seasonal information center at 15 Commercial Street in Bath's former train station. The area's major hospital is **Mid-Coast Hospital** (123 Medical Center Dr., Brunswick, 207/729-0181, www.midcoasthealth.com), offering 24-hour emergency services. There are plenty of family-run and chain pharmacies in the region, though most are not open 24 hours. In 2006, more than half of downtown Brunswick became wired for free Internet access, so hopping online is now easy. Barring that, it's also available for free at **Bowdoin College Library** (3000 College Street Station, Brunswick, 207/725-3000) and at **Café Creme** (56 Front St., Bath, 207/443-6454). Find shipping services at **The UPS Store** (96 Maine St., Brunswick, 207/729-9891).

BOOTHBAY REGION
North of Bath, the Maine coast begins in earnest, with Route 1 turning into a two-lane divided highway snaking its way through pine forests and passing farm stands selling fresh berries on the side of the road. The route slows down both literally and figuratively at Wiscasset, a traffic bottleneck that also happens to be the most charming small town on the coast. The same can't quite be said of Boothbay Harbor, a summer resort community that's a study in organized chaos. The Boothbay Peninsula has its appeal, however, as the center for all manner of sailing and nature-cruising expeditions on the surrounding coast.

Sights
Much of downtown Wiscasset is listed on the National Register of Historic Places, and a ramble among the old captain's homes and Federal-style mansions is a delightful way to while away an afternoon. Particularly worth visiting is **Castle Tucker** (2 Lee St., Wiscasset, 207/882-7169, 11 A.M.–4 P.M. Wed.–Sun. Jun.–mid-Oct., $5), an 1807 captain's home overlooking the river, with Victorian furnishings and a stunning spiral staircase. More engaging (and expensive) is the **Musical Wonder House** (16–18 High St., Wiscasset, 207/882-7163, www.musicalwonderhouse.com, 10 A.M.–5 P.M. Mon–Sat., noon–5 P.M. Sun., tours $10–40), an 1852 mansion filled with antique music boxes and player pianos collected by its eccentric Austrian owner.

Halfway down the Boothbay Peninsula, the

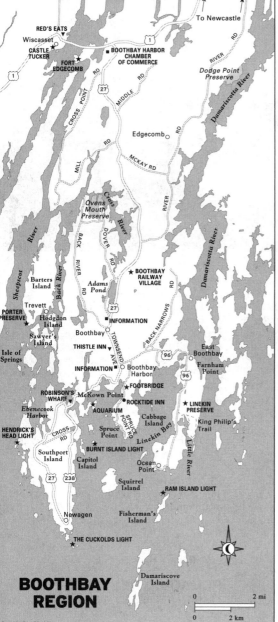

BOOTHBAY REGION

© AVALON TRAVEL

MAINE

Boothbay Railway Village (586 Wiscasset Rd., 207/633-4727, www. railwayvillage.org, 9:30 A.M.–5 P.M. daily, $9 adults, $5 children 3–16, free children under 3) is a required stop for families with children. Trains are, in fact, just the beginning of this 10-acre village that includes a town hall, church, and 26 other structures, as well as dozens of antique cars and firefighting equipment. The namesake railway is a narrow-gauge steam train that takes 20-minute rides around the village. Down at the end of the point, Boothbay Harbor is surrounded by four lighthouses that can be viewed by driving around Routes 27 and 96. During summer months, Balmy Day Cruises offers tours of **Burnt Island** (Pier 8, Boothbay Harbor, 207/633-2284, www.balmydayscruises.com, 7 A.M.–5:10 P.M. daily; 8 P.M. tours available Wed.–Sat. Jul.–Aug.; reduced schedules Mar.–Jun. and Sep.–Nov.; $14 adults, $7 children 3–11, free children under 3), where actors portray the family of an early-20th-century lighthouse keeper, who explains how the beacon actually works.

Shopping

Not surprisingly, Wiscasset is a major center for antiquing, with more than two dozen shops. A favorite is **The Marston House** (Main St. at Middle St., Wiscasset, 207/882-6010, www.marston-house.com, noon–5 P.M. daily May–Dec. and by appt.), which focuses on French country furniture. Across the bridge, potters at **Sheepscot River Pottery** (34 Rte. 1, Edgecomb, 207/882-9410, www.sheepscot.com, daily year-round) throw and fire their works

MAINE

COURTESY MAINE OFFICE OF TOURISM

Boothbay Harbor

in a studio adjoining the shop. Items for sale include plates hand-painted with Maine scenes. More artisan works are on display at the **Iron and Silk Forge and Gallery** (Rte. 27, Edgecomb, 207/882-4055), one-stop shopping for silk scarves and wrought-iron tools.

Food
There's almost always a line outside **Red's Eats** (41 Water St., Wiscasset, 207/882-6128, 11 A.M.–9 P.M. Mon.–Thu., 11 A.M.–11 P.M. Fri.–Sat., noon–6 P.M. Sun. late May–mid-Oct., $3–14), a little shack overlooking the bridge over the Sheepscot River—and with good reason. Locals and out-of-towners alike know it's the best place in town, if not the state, for lobster rolls, to say nothing of hot dogs and other handy snacks. (The view from the picnic tables by the river isn't bad either.) More opportunities for outdoor eating are rampant along the peninsula, which specializes in places for lobster-in-the-rough. Try **Robinson's Wharf** (20 Hendricks Hill Rd., 207/633-3830, www. robinsons-wharf.com, 11:30 A.M.–9 P.M. Tue.–Sat., $5–35) on Southport Island south of Boothbay Harbor. If it comes from the sea, they probably steam, fry, and serve it at

dozens of outdoor tables. (If you are around on Tuesday, it's two-for-one lobsters!) Standing out from the town's many family-style restaurants, the **Thistle Inn** (55 Oak St., Boothbay Harbor, 877/633-3541, www.thethistleinn. com, 5–10 P.M. daily late May–mid-Oct.; 4:30–9 P.M. Tue.–Sat. mid-Oct.–late May, $9–29) has an excellent dining room in its cozy captain's house. The menu is a solid mix of new American cuisine, including seared tuna, seafood bouillabaisse, and herb-encrusted rack of lamb. The pub next door serves Angus burgers and lighter fare; its bar is an 18-foot dory that once sailed the surrounding waters.

Information
The **Boothbay Harbor Region Chamber of Commerce** (Rtes. 1 & 27, 207/633-2353, www.boothbayharbor.com) runs an information center at the entrance to town, as well as a seasonal center on Route 1 right before the turnoff down the peninsula.

PEMAQUID REGION
Most travelers to the Pemaquid Peninsula get straight to the point to see one of the most famous lighthouses on the Maine coast. It's

worth taking your time driving down to the lighthouse, however. At the head of the peninsula, the little town of Damariscotta is a picturesque fishing village with a brick downtown full of galleries and gift shops. South of town, the area is full of old farmhouses that have been converted to bed-and-breakfasts and antiques shops.

◖ Pemaquid Point Light

No matter how many photographs have been taken of this venerable lighthouse (Bristol Park, end of Rte. 130, 207/677-2494, http://lighthouse.cc/pemaquid, $2), none quite captures the majesty of its perch on a rocky headland hundreds of feet above the crashing sea. In fact, it's such an iconic image of Maine, that it was chosen to grace the back of the state's quarter. Even more impressive is the climb on a wrought-iron spiral staircase to the top of the tower, from which you can get a seagull's-eye view of the rocks below, and inspect the Fresnel Lens close-up. The adjoining keeper's house is home to a **Fisherman's Museum**

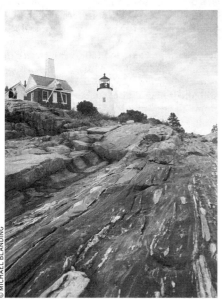
© MICHAEL BLANDING

Pemaquid Point Light

(207/677-2494, 10:30 A.M.–5 P.M. daily late May–mid-Oct., free), full of memorabilia on the lobstering trade. It has also recently opened a one-bedroom apartment, with two twin beds and a pullout double couch for weekly rentals (207/563-6500, www.mainecoastcottages.com, $1,150/week) for the ultimate "room with a view."

Other Sights

A detour before the lighthouse takes you to **Colonial Pemaquid Historic Site** (Colonial Pemaquid Dr., 207/677-2423, www.maine.gov, 10 A.M.–7 P.M. daily; closed off-season), where a reconstruction of the colonial-era Fort William Henry overlooks a quiet harbor. Historic demonstrations and battle reenactments detail the fascinating history of this forgotten frontier, where English and French settlers fought it out for supremacy in one of the first settlements in North America (settled permanently in 1625). Back on Route 1 on the other side of the peninsula, **Fawcett's Maine Antique Toy and Art Museum** (3506 Rte. 1, Waldoboro, 207/832-7398, http://home.gwi.net/~fawcetoy, 10 A.M.–4 P.M. Thurs.–Mon. and 12–4 P.M. Sat.–Sun. late May–mid-Oct.; 12–4 P.M. Sat.–Sun. mid-Oct.–Dec., $5, open by appt. anytime for $50 for six people) is a trip down memory lane for adults of a certain age, exhibiting memorabilia relating to Betty Boop, Felix the Cat, the Lone Ranger, and other bygone faves.

Entertainment

You never know what you are going to find at **Round Top Center for the Arts** (3 Round Top Lane, Damariscotta, 207/563-1507, www.roundtoparts.org), which might be staging community theater, a piano concerto, or banjo music on any given night. An art gallery and studio classes round out its offerings.

Shopping

In downtown the **Firehouse Gallery** (1 Bristol Rd., 207/563-7299, Damariscotta, www.thefirehousegallery.com, 10 A.M.–5 P.M., Tue.–Sat. May–Sept.) features contemporary art and

MAINE

MAINE

sculpture that goes far beyond coastal scenes and lighthouses. The eclectic **Weatherbird** (72 Courtyard St., Damariscotta, 207/563-8993, 8 A.M.–5:30 P.M. Mon.–Sat. year-round) is packed to the beak with gourmet foodstuffs, wine, jewelry, and women's clothing.

Food

The German heritage of Waldoboro is celebrated at **Morse's Kraut Haus** (3856 Washington Rd./Rte. 220, N. Waldoboro, 207/831-5569, www.morsessauerkraut.com, 8 A.M.–4 P.M. Thu.–Sun.; 10:30 A.M.–4 P.M. Mon.–Wed., $6–10), which is renowned as far away as Portland for its annual fall crop of homemade sauerkraut. The little café also serves old-world sandwiches, pierogies, and sausages. Situated in the center of town, **Damariscotta River Grill** (155 Main St., Damariscotta, 207/563-2992, 11 A.M.–9 P.M. daily; open at 10 A.M. on Sun.; close at 9:30 Fri.–Sat., $17–25) is a favorite dinner spot for locals, who tuck into dishes like Asian chicken salad, artichoke fondue, and local oysters on the half-shell in a dining room overlooking the river. The obligatory lobster-in-the-rough can be found at **Muscongus Bay Lobster** (28 Landing Rd., Round Pond, 207/529-2251, www.mainefreshlobster.com, $12–25), which also offers lobster and crab rolls and BYOB shore dinners with lobster, clams, and corn on the east side of the peninsula. The sprawling lobster pound has both outdoor and indoor seating.

Information

Info on the area is available through the **Damariscotta Region Chamber of Commerce** (15 Courtyard St., Damariscotta, 207/563-8340, www.damariscottaregion.com).

SPORTS AND RECREATION
Hiking and Biking

Egrets and ospreys are among the birdlife you might sight in **Bradley Pond Farm Preserve** (Bradley Pond Rd., 207/729-7694, www.btlt.org), a 160-acre preserve near Brunswick that has several miles of trails for traipsing around salt marshes, woods, and fields. The cyclists at **Bath Cycle & Ski** (115 Main St./Rte. 1, Woolwich, 207/442-7002, www.bikeman.com) are serious about cycling, sponsoring a mountain bike team and staging weekly rides along both roads and trails.

Beaches

With a rocky coastline and oftentimes frigid waters, the Midcoast doesn't offer much beachfront. The exception is **Popham Beach** (10 Perkins Farm Lane/Rte. 209, Phippsburg, 207/389-1335, www.maine.gov, $6 adults, $4 seniors, $1 children 5–11, free children under 5), a beautiful, sheltered expanse of sand and salt marsh south of Bath that draws families and college students to collect driftwood and stroll along the surf.

Boating and Fishing

Boothbay Harbor teems with sailing ships. *Lazy Jack* (Pier One, Boothbay Harbor, 207/633-3444, www.sailschoonerlazyjack.com, May–mid-Oct., $28) is a 1947 schooner offering two-hour sails of the harbor. Renowned ocean sailors Herb and Doris Smith have built five schooners, five of which were named Appledore. The exception is the **Windjammer *Eastwind*** (20 Commercial St., Boothbay Harbor, 207/633-6598, www.schoonereastwind.com, $25), which sets sail for two-and-a-half-hour cruises to see the seals at Seal Rocks. The Muscongus Bay is a favorite for sea kayaking. **Midcoast Kayak** (47 Main St., Damariscotta, 207/563-5732, www.midcoastkayak.com) rents kayaks ($35–55 for full day) and offers tours ($35–60) allowing you to poke in and out of salt marshes and harbors.

Camping

Located south of Boothbay Harbor over a bridge on a small island, **Gray's Homestead Campground** (21 Homestead Rd., Southport, 207/633-4612, www.graysoceancamping.com, $35–50) has a mix of 30 tent and RV sites, several with ocean views, the rest less than a 2-minute walk from a private sandy beach. The campground also has several cottages and condos available for rent by the week ($800–1000). Best of all, the campground goes lobstering with its own gear specifically for campers—and will even cook lobsters to order.

ACCOMMODATIONS
Under $100

Right in the center of the region, the **Wiscasset Motor Lodge** (596 Bath Rd./Rte. 1, Wiscasset, 800/732-8168, www.wiscassetmotorlodge.com, $72–108) offers rooms with knotty-pine walls and polyester bedspreads. But it's clean, comfortable, and among the cheapest places around.

$100-150

Sitting on piers overlooking Boothbay Harbor, the **Rocktide Inn** (35 Atlantic Ave., Boothbay Harbor, 207/633-4455, www.rocktideinn.com, $105–205) is an extraordinarily friendly hotel that caters to families and singles alike. The marina-side bar sports brightly colored vinyl seating, while the dining room is traversed by model trains. In keeping with the character, rooms are decorated with over-the-top flowers and plaids, with a harbor-side balcony running the length of the rooms.

$150-250

An eye for detail makes the **Brunswick Bed & Breakfast** (165 Park Row, Brunswick, 207/729-4914, www.brunswickbnb.com, $145–185) a favorite for parents and luminaries visiting Bowdoin. Innkeepers Steve and Mercie Normand have renovated an 1849 Greek Revival mansion in a clean, modern style, tied together with country accents and quilts. On chilly mornings, a fire burns in the cozy sitting room, where a full breakfast awaits. Built by a sea captain for his wife as a "compromise" for the years spent on the ocean, the █ **Bradley Inn** (3063 Bristol Rd., New Harbor, 800/942-

5560, www.bradleyinn.com, Apr.–Dec., $175–250) has an enviable location a short walk from Pemaquid Light. The twelve individually appointed rooms in the main house feature cathedral ceilings and cherry four-poster beds. The grounds feature gardens and seaside paths just inviting a romantic stroll. A former coast guard life-saving station, the **Popham Beach Bed & Breakfast** (4 Riverview Ave., Phippsburg, 207/389-2409, www.pophambeachbandb.com, $185–235) is directly on one of the most gorgeous beaches in Maine. The decor is beach-cottage clean, with nautical colors and ocean views. A three-course breakfast each morning should help you tackle whatever outdoor activities you have planned.

GETTING THERE AND AROUND

This is one area where a car is essential to exploring. While some towns, such as Bath and Boothbay Harbor, offer in-town trolley service, there are just too many inviting shoreline roads to limit yourself solely to public transport.

To drive to the region, take I-295 north from Portland to exit 28, then U.S. Route 1 north to Brunswick (25 mi., 30 min.). From Brunswick, continue north along U.S. Route 1 to Bath (8 mi., 12 min.) or Wiscasset (20 mi., 30 min.). For Popham Beach, take Route 209 south from Bath (15 mi., 30 min.). For Boothbay Harbor, head south along Route 27 from Wiscasset (15 mi., 30 min.). For Pemaquid Point, continue north from Wiscasset along U.S. Route 1 to Newcastle, then take Route 130 south to the lighthouse (25 mi., 40 min.).

In addition, buses run by **Concord Coach Lines** (800/639-3317, www.concordtrailways.com) service many towns along Route 1, including Brunswick (Mobil Mart, 101 Bath Rd./Rte. 24), Bath (Mail It 4 U, 10 State Rd.), Wiscasset (Huber's Market, 279 Rte. 1), and Damariscotta (Waltz Pharmacy, 167 Main St.).

Penobscot Bay

Scooped out of the middle of the Maine Coast, Penobscot Bay is Maine's center for both lobstering and pleasure-sailing. After miles of flirting with the coastline, Route 1 finally runs smack along the water as it passes through a series of picturesque Maine villages. This is prime lobster country, with each coastal community competing for bragging rights over who has the meatiest and juiciest of these eight-legged crustaceans. Not that these communities are all the same; portside Rockland gives way to upscale Camden and funky Belfast. In the bay, the various islands each have their own character, from the working lobstering island of Vinalhaven to the car- and electricity-free Monhegan.

ROCKLAND

Every seaside village in Maine boasts that their lobsters are the best—but none go as far to prove it as Rockland, which ships 10 million pounds of lobster around the world each year. The hub of the Penobscot area, Rockland has been a center of cod and lobster fishing for 200 years. It's only in the past decade or so that it has managed to clean up its gritty image and market its assets to attract tourists. Since that time, the town has gone through Maine's most successful renaissance to become a mandatory stop on the coast. Chief among the towns attractions is the fabulous Farnsworth Museum, which has expanded to fill three buildings in the downtown area and spawned dozens of smaller art galleries in its wake. That hasn't changed the industrial patina of the working waterfront, which is still home to a fleet of lobster boats and ferries steaming to the islands of the bay. The local chamber has proudly proclaimed Rockland to be "the Real Maine"—and so it is.

◖ Maine Lobster Festival

Rockland goes crazy for crustaceans every August in a festival (800/596-0376, www.mainelobsterfestival.com) that's been going

CLAW & ORDER

When it comes to choosing a lobster, is hard- or soft-shell better? Many lovers of the red beasts have no problem demolishing either one, but still have a preference; others will eat only one of the two, claiming the other type is a waste of time. First, though, a bit of background on the molting process itself: Lobsters shed their shells in and around July and September, growing a new, soft shell underneath before wriggling out of their old one. The new shell then takes several months to harden, which is why soft-shelled creatures are in such supply during summer and fall. Hardshells are the only kind available in winter months, and tend to have significantly more meat because they've had more time to fill out their shells. On the flip side, soft-shells often cost less since they weigh less, and are usually much easier to crack open. Purists, however, contend the issue is one of quality vs. quantity, saying that soft-shells have notably sweeter and more tender meat. Ultimately, it's a debate that ends with no winner, just lots of full stomachs and happy crustacean lovers.

for 60 years strong. The event begins with King Neptune's coronation of the Maine Sea Goddess on Wednesday night, followed by four full days of crafts exhibits, children's activities, a road race, a parade, and of course thousands of boiled lobsters, brought off the boats and prepared in the world's largest steamer. It ends on Sunday with the famed "Great International Lobster Crate Race," where fleet-footed contestants run across rickety lobster crates suspended in the harbor.

◖ Farnsworth Art Museum

Something about the light on the water and the rocks tumbling into the sea has inspired generations of Maine artists. The best of their work is showcased at this multi-faceted museum (16 Museum St., 207/596-6457, www.farnsworthmuseum.org, 10 A.M.–5 P.M. Thu.–Tue., 10 A.M.–8 P.M. Wed., late May–mid-Oct.; 10 A.M.–5 P.M. Wed.–Sun. mid-Oct.–late May, $12 adults, $10 seniors and students 17 and older, free children under 17 and free to all 5–8 P.M. Wed.), which features well-known Maine artists such as Winslow Homer and Andrew Wyeth. Behind its big modern galleries, the **Wyeth Center** highlights the very different works of Andrew's father, N. C., and his son Jamie. (The Wyeth Center is closed Jan–mid-May, but the rest of the museum remains open year-round.)

Andrew Wyeth's best-known work, *Christina's World,* isn't here (it's at MoMA in New York City), but the next best thing is—the house that inspired the arresting and melancholy character study. Docents can give you directions to the **Olson House** (Hathorn Pt. Rd., Cushing, $5), a half-hour drive away, which was once home to the crippled Christina and her eccentric brother Alvaro. Guides there tell the story of the painting, which was based on an actual event when Wyeth came across Christina crawling home from her parents' graves.

Other Sights

The **Rockland Breakwater Lighthouse** (207/785-4609, www.rocklandlighthouse.com, 10 A.M.–5 P.M. weekends and holidays late May.–mid-Oct., free) earns points for its location—at the end of a mile-long granite breakwater that protects Rockland Harbor. Walking the breakwater is an experience in itself, as sailboats, lobstermen, sea birds, and seals add to the scenery. For lighthouse fans, Rockland is also home to the **Maine Lighthouse Museum** (1 Park Dr., 207/594-3301, www.mainelighthousemuseum.com, 9 A.M.–5 P.M. Mon.–Fri., 10 A.M.–4 P.M. Sat.–Sun. Jun.–Oct.; or by appt., $5 adults, $4 seniors, free children under 12), which bills itself as the country's most extensive collection of lighthouse paraphernalia. A series of galleries attached to the local chamber of commerce are full of photos, models, lenses, and maps to help you strategize for light-sightseeing up the coast.

Shopping

The stretch of Main Street around the Farnsworth Museum has seen a profusion of small galleries. The cream of the crop is **Caldbeck Gallery** (12 Elm St., 207/594-5935, www.caldbeck.com, 11 A.M.–5 P.M. Tue.–Sat. or by appt.), which stages group and solo shows of contemporary Maine artists. Fine art, upmarket crafts, and handmade clothing are among the items for sale at **Archipelago** (386 Main St., 207/596-0701, www.thearchipelago.net, 9:30 A.M.–5:30 P.M. Mon.–Fri.; 9:30 A.M.–5 P.M. Sat.; 11 A.M.–4 P.M. Sun.), featuring works made by craftspeople living on Maine's many islands.

Food

The smell of roasting coffee fills **Rock City Books & Coffee** (328 Main St., 207/594-4123,www.rockcitycoffee.com, 6:30 A.M.–7 P.M. Mon.–Sat., 7 A.M.–7 P.M. Sun. daily year-round), a favorite gathering place for locals and purveyors of gourmet coffees, teas, pastries, sandwiches perfect for taking on the ferry, and daily soup specials. (It also features a good selection of new and used books, including sections on Maine artists and boatbuilding.) "Farm fresh" and "organic" are the buzzwords at **Primo** (2 S. Main St./Rte. 73, 207/596-0770, www.primorestaurant.com, 5–9 P.M. Wed.–Sun., $24–42), the number-one choice for destination dining in the region. Chef-owners Melissa Kelly and Price Kushner left New York to create their own restaurant in Maine, transforming a Victorian house into a series of intimate dining rooms surrounding an open-hearth kitchen. The elegance extends to the menu, which serves wholesome bistro fare such as char-grilled duck breast with buttered fiddlehead ferns and locally caught halibut with creamy white-bean puree and wilted dandelion leaves.

Information

The **Penobscot Bay Regional Chamber of Commerce** (1 Park Dr., 207/596-0376, www.therealmaine.com) runs a large and well-stocked information center in a new building by the harbor.

MAINE

ROCKPORT AND CAMDEN

The seaside town of Camden lent its visage to the 1957 movie *Peyton Place,* the classic film about a picturesque New England town with secrets seething behind its perfect lawns and colonial facades. Secrets aside, Camden could win an Academy Award for its role as a virtual museum of New England architecture, with its beauty providing a backdrop for generations of summer tourists. The town is framed dramatically by the Camden Hills, which—unusual for coastal Maine—march right up to the sea before plunging into a harbor forested with masts and sails.

The hills were sighted by Captain John Smith in 1614, but it wasn't until 1769 that the first settlers arrived, fostering a growing economy based on shipbuilding, anchor making, and limestone production. In 1891, a portion of the town broke off to form the quieter town of Rockport, which survives today as a working fishing village. Shortly thereafter, Camden entered a new phase when steamboat runs from New York and Philadelphia brought scads of tourists to breathe in its salt air. The boating crowd followed, founding a marina and summer yachting community that has become the

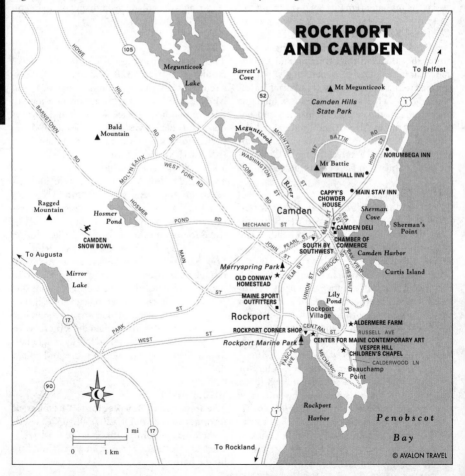

town's mainstay. Camden is decidedly old-money, and therefore not cheap; but no other town on the coast matches its combination of natural and man-made beauty.

◖ Maine Windjammer Cruises

The name of Maine's famous fleet of sailing ships comes from their uncanny ability to sail close-hauled into the wind—thus "jamming" it. Apart from their technical prowess, the fourteen ships of the **Maine Windjammer Association** (207/374-2993, www.sailmaine-coast.com) are true beauts, and an experience sailing aboard them is one of the pleasures of the coast. Guests book cruises from three to six days in length, with captains guiding the mostly engineless crafts wherever the wind takes them—poking around rocky islands, sailing into coves in search of seals, and racing lighthouses by night. Accommodations are spartan, meals family-style, and guests often put to work hauling up sails to the tune of sea-shanties. All of which makes the trip the antithesis of a luxury cruise, and thus

quintessentially Maine. Seven ships sail out of Rockland, including the three-masted *Victory Chimes,* which graces the state quarter; six sail from Camden, including the *Mary Day,* known as the "music boat" for its guitarist-captain; and one from Rockport. Costs for cruises vary widely depending on the size of the ship, experience of the captain, and length of the cruise. Expect to be set back $400–600 per person for a three-night excursion and in the neighborhood of $800–1,000 for a five-night trip.

Other Sights

The oldest house on the Midcoast, the **Old Conway Homestead** (Rte. 1, Camden, 207/236-2257, www.crmuseum.org, 11 A.M.–3 P.M. Tue.–Fri. July–Aug., $1.50) is an excellent example of an 18th-century Cape Cod–style home. Over the years, the local historical association has added to the site with a blacksmith shop, maple sap house, and interpretive center that details early Maine history. The homestead is located on Route 1, two-thirds of a mile south of Camden Village.

MAINE

COURTESY MAINE OFFICE OF TOURISM

the windjammer *Margaret Todd*

EDNA ST. VINCENT MILLAY IN CAMDEN

The first woman to receive the Pulitzer Prize for Poetry, 19th-century lyric poet and unabashed bohemian Edna St. Vincent Millay was born in Rockland and spent years of her youth in a small Camden house. Surrounded by meadows and of modest size, the house belonged to extended family, and in it she penned a number of her poems in her early teens, one of which – "Renascence" – used the view from the mountain behind the home as a device for charting her emotional development. (The poem's well-known first lines are: "All I could see from where I stood / Was three long mountains and a wood; / I turned and looked the other way, / And saw three islands in a bay.") Many of her early poems are filled with the imagery of Maine's rocky coastline and farms, but it was her first public reading of "Renascence" in 1912 that convinced one audience member to pay her way in full to Vassar College. After attending Vassar, Millay moved to Greenwich Village, where she became one of the most celebrated poets of her time, and wrote satire for *Vanity Fair*. That first reading took place at the still-existing **Whitehall Inn** (52 High St., Camden, 207/236-3391, www.whitehall-inn.com), and the room where it took place has been kept very much the way it was that evening, including a piano on which she played. Other memorabilia relating to her later career has since been added to the room, making it a mini-shrine to the poet. A statue of Millay by local sculptor Robert Willis graces the waterfront in Harbor Park.

Featuring Maine's best artists, the **Center for Maine Contemporary Art** (162 Russell Ave., Rockport, 207/236-2875, www.artsmaine. org, 10 A.M.–5 P.M. Tue.–Sat., 1–5 P.M. Sun. late May–Oct.; closed Tue.–Wed. in winter, $5 adults, free children) is always worth a look for its dozens of summer art shows held in a converted firehouse.

Entertainment and Events

Don't let the name fool you; the **Camden Opera House** (29 Elm St./Rte. 1, Camden, 207/236-7963, www.camdenoperahouse.com) is actually a multi-genre performing arts center that features folk and classical music performances and a popular summer lecture series.

Hotel rooms are hard to come by during Labor Day weekend, when **Camden Windjammer Festival** (207/236-4404, www. visitcamden.com) brings two dozen tall ships to grace Camden's harbor with boat parades, chowder contests, and fireworks.

Shopping

Before boarding your yacht, stop by **House of Logan** (32 Main St., Camden, 207/236-3943, www.houseoflogan.com, 9 A.M.–5 P.M. Mon.–Sat.), which stocks upscale clothing for men and women. One of Maine's best independent bookstores, **The Owl & Turtle Bookshop** (32 Washington St., Camden, 207/236-4769, www.owlandturtle.com, 9 A.M.–8 P.M. Mon.–Sat.; 10 A.M.–5 P.M. Sun.) has a "marine room" full of nautical books and charts, and a "children's room" with a view of the river below. Up the road, **Elysium Woodcarvings** (255 Masalin Rd., Lincolnville, 207/763-3175, www.tidewater.net/~elysium, open by appt. May–Dec.) specializes in another famous Maine half-breed—carved wooden "coon cats," a real-life cross between cat and raccoon.

Food

Despite Camden's location in lobster country, the specialty here is fresh crabmeat—worked into omelets, cakes, and even crab Benedict. Right on the Camden waterfront, **Cappy's Chowder House** (1 Main St., Camden, 207/236-2254, www.cappyschowder.com, 11:30 A.M.–10 P.M. Mon.–Thu.; 11:30 A.M.–11 P.M. Fri.; 10 A.M.–11 P.M. Sat.; 10 A.M.–10 P.M. Sun., $9–19) is a family-friendly restaurant that offers balloons and crayons to subjugate the kids and steaming bowls of award-winning chowder to please adults. Named for an old salt from nearby Eagle Island, the restaurant serves a range of seafood dishes, burgers, and sandwiches. If a salty waterfront repast is what you're after, there's simply no better place than **The Camden Deli** (37 Main St., Camden, 207/236-8343, www. camdendeli.com, 7 A.M.–7 P.M. daily, $8–17), thanks to the savory homemade panini and overstuffed sandwiches served on the rooftop deck in good weather (and in the casual, sunny café indoors in otherwise).

Information

The **Camden-Rockport-Lincolnville Chamber of Commerce** (Public Landing, 800/223-5459 or 207/236-4404, www.visit-camden.com) runs a helpful information center on the Camden waterfront.

BELFAST AND SEARSPORT

Travelers shooting up Route 1 from Camden to Acadia often miss the lovely little gem Belfast, which hugs the coast in a spot where the highway dives inland. Up until a few years ago, there was little reason to stop here anyway. Unlike the more touristy towns up the coast, Belfast was a working-class town with a gritty harbor full of fishing boats, and a few crunchy shops frequented by the back-to-the-landers who moved here to get away from it all in the 1970s. Something has happened here in the past few years, however, that has made the little town not only worth a look, but worth an overnight stay.

The renaissance began a few years ago when credit-card giant MBNA founded a branch on the outskirts of town, infusing needed capital into the sagging local economy. Since then, the town has taken a page from Rockland by cleaning up the harbor and marketing the working waterfront as an attraction, not an eyesore. At the same time, the town has embraced the arts as a way to boost community pride. It placed painted bear statues around the main streets in 2001 and reprised the effort in 2005 by asking local sculptors to create whimsical birdhouses around town. Local artists have responded to the overtures by inviting visitors into several quirky galleries on the main street leading up from the harbor, giving the town a lively, if unpolished, feel that's a welcome antidote to too-cute Camden.

Up Route 1 from Belfast, the small town of Searsport boasts a prestigious pedigree of historic buildings and captain's houses that hail from the era when it used to be a major shipbuilding center. Now the town's main claim to fame is an inviting maritime museum complex that preserves that part of Maine history. The stretch along Route 1 is also well-known for its profusion of antiques stores filled with the leavings from the attic of many a home here.

Sights

The quirky culture of Belfast extends even to its history. The **Belfast Museum** (10 Market St., Belfast, 207/338-9229, www.belfastmuseum.org, mid-June.–mid-Oct., free) contains a mishmash of interesting exhibits, including a recreated 19th century pharmacy and jail, and an homage to Belfast's most famous balloonist. While you are there, pick up a brochure for a self-guided walking tour of the many Victorian buildings in Belfast's downtown area.

While not as slick as the Maine Maritime Museum down the coast, the **Penobscot Marine Museum** (5 Church St., Searsport, 207/548-2529, www.penobscotmarinemuseum.org, 10 A.M.–5 P.M. Mon.–Sat.; noon–5 P.M. Sun., $8 adults, $3 children 7–15, free children 6 and under, $18 family) wins points for authenticity. Many of the original historic buildings in Searsport village have been preserved and filled with antiques and artwork gathered from the families of the captains who once sailed from the port. A particularly interesting exhibit in the old town hall traces the little-known history of Maine's contribution to international shipping during the golden years of the windjammers. Seventeen miles west of Belfast, the three-story **Liberty Tool Company** (57 Main St./Rte. 173, Liberty, 207/589-4771, www.jonesport-wood.com, 9 A.M.–5 P.M. daily Mar.–Dec.; 9 A.M.–5 P.M. Sat.–Sun. Jan.) is worth a detour for its astounding collection of 10,000 tools and countless nuts, bolts, and washers dutifully sorted into hundreds of tiny bins. Across the street, a museum showcases antique tools as well as artwork and Native American artifacts. Even further down Route 3, the deliciously quirky **Bryant's Stove & Music Museum** (27 Stovepipe Alley, Thorndike, 207/568-3665, www.bryantstove. com, 8 A.M.–4:30 P.M. Mon.–Sat., donations accepted) showcases the extraordinary collection of John Bryant, who has gathered more than a dozen antique cast-iron stoves, which are as much works of art as they are pieces of cooking equipment. Other exhibits in the ambitious museum include antique cars, music boxes, and a one-of-a-kind "doll circus."

Entertainment

A deck festooned with paper lanterns overlooks the waterfront at **Three Tides** (2 Pinchy Ln., Belfast, 207/338-1707, www.3tides.com, 4 P.M.–close Tue.–Sat.; 4 P.M.–9 P.M. Sun., $7–11), a tin-and-wood-beam shack that has been transformed into a hipster tapas bar. Teens and twentysomethings from around the area come here nightly to listen to jam bands and nosh on quesadillas and Pemaquid oysters.

Shopping

No store captures Belfast's funky side better than the **Belfast Co-op Store** (123 High St., Belfast, 208/338-2532, http://belfast.coop, 7:30 A.M.–8 P.M. daily), a natural-food co-op and community bulletin board that's been dispensing food and healthcare products for 30 years. Hand-knit Irish sweaters, Scottish kilt pins, and fine English china are among the items for sale at the **Shamrock, Thistle & Rose** (94 Main St., Belfast, 207/338-1864, www.shamrockthistlerose.com, 10 A.M.–6 P.M. Mon.–Sat., 11 A.M.–4 P.M. Sun. Jul.–Dec.; 10 A.M.–6 P.M. Sat.–Sun. Jan.–Nov.), a shop specializing in goods from the British Isles. Billing itself as the oldest shoe store in the country, **Colburn's Shoe Store** (79 Main St., Belfast, 207/338-1934, http://colburnshoe. com, 9 A.M.–5 P.M. Mon.–Sat.; 10 A.M.–3 P.M. Sun.) was founded in 1832, and originally sold

milk, spices, and rum in addition to footwear. Now the mammoth shop sells all the top name brands, as well as heavily discounted shoes in the basement.

If you can't find it at **Mainely Pottery** (Rte. 1, Belfast, 207/338-1108, www.mainely-pottery.com, 10 A.M.–5 P.M. daily May–Oct.; 10 A.M.–5 P.M. Mon.–Fri. Nov.–Dec.), then it isn't thrown and fired in Maine. Twenty-five different potters sell a range of stoneware, porcelain, earthenware, and raku. Part store, part gallery, **Bluejacket Ship Crafters** (160 E. Main St./Rte. 1, Searsport, 800/448-5567, www.bluejacketinc.com, 9 A.M.–5 P.M. Mon.–Sat. Jun.–mid-Oct.; 9 A.M.–4 P.M. Mon.–Fri. mid-Oct.–May) has row upon row of glass cases full of model sloops, dories, tugs, and military vehicles. It sells both kits for enthusiasts and wood and rigging material for scratch builders.

Food

An old diner-type establishment made funky with eclectic thrift store accoutrements, ◖ **Papa J's & the Lobster Bar** (191 Searsport Ave./Rte. 1, Belfast, 207/338-6860, www.mooringscamp.com, 4–10 P.M. Tue.–Sat., $12–25) is the brainchild of Jim and Ecko Baker, who also run the campground next door. Fresh hard-shelled lobsters from Wyman's lobster pound up the street are made decadent with a side of southern-style deep-fried corn. Equally rich is the lobster with a feta cheese/sun-dried tomato sauce served over penne. The restaurant draws a hopping crowd of campers. If you're wondering what the line is all about at **Dudley's Diner** (57 Main St., Belfast, 207/338-1884, 6 A.M.–9 P.M. Mon.–Sat.; 7 A.M.–9 P.M. Sun., $6–15), it's for the overstuffed omelets and sandwiches. The family-owned spot whips up a pastrami grilled Reuben that's become a local legend. Belfast's most upscale restaurant, the **Twilight Cafe** (39 Main St., Belfast, 207/338-0937, www. thetwilightcafe.com, 5–10 P.M. Tue.–Sat.; 5–9:30 P.M. Sun., $17–27) is a country kitchen with butter-cream walls and painted wooden tables, a few of which have a view of the harbor below. The food is all made from scratch and accented with creative flavors. Generous portions of fresh crabmeat in a crab cocktail is cut with the sweetness of mango salad; lobster cakes with ginger pumpkin crème fraiche are a little taste of autumn in Maine, no matter what time of year.

Information

The **Belfast Chamber of Commerce** (15 Main St., Belfast, 207/338-5900, www.belfastmaine.org) runs a small visitors information center near the harbor.

SPORTS AND RECREATION
Beaches

Penobscot's rocky coast isn't conducive to sunbathing. One exception is **Birch Point Beach State Park** (Ballyhac Rd., Owls Head, www.maine.gov), a forested state park with a sandy beach seven miles south of Rockland off Route 73.

Hiking and Biking

Breathtaking views of the ocean below are the stock-in-trade of **Camden Hills State Park** (280 Belfast Rd., Camden, 207/236-3109, www.maine.gov), a 5,700-acre park with strenuous rocky trails and meandering lowland paths overlooking the bay. The most popular trail leads to the stone observation tower at the top of Mount Battie. At the top is a plaque with a poem by Edna St. Vincent Millay, who was a frequent visitor to the spot. One of the largest uninhabited areas on the East Coast, **Sears Island** is accessible from a causeway off of Route 1 north of Searsport. The island is in a perpetual tug-of-war between conservationists and developers who want to site a resort or liquid natural gas terminal on the island. In 2009, the state forged an agreement to keep 600 of its 940 acres as a pristine location for seaside hiking and bird-watching. The fate of the rest of the island is still uncertain.

Boating

For sailing trips from Rockland and Camden, see *Windjammer Cruises* earlier in this chapter.

From Belfast, the 1901 Friendship sloop *Amity* (Belfast, 207/323-1443 or 207/469-0849, www.friendshipsloopamity.com, $20–30) offers morning and afternoon sails (unfortunately, the company cancelled sunset sails due to a dearth of wind off Belfast in the late afternoons). Fifth-generation descendent of a whaling captain and Maine Maritime grad Melissa Terry pilots the **M/V** *Good Return* (Thompson Wharf, Belfast, 207/322-5530, www.belfast-baycruises.com, $15–30 adults, $7–17 children), a cruise boat that takes lobster cruises in Belfast harbor to pull up traps, as well as day trips to Castine, and a cruise geared for kids to look for seals and porpoises. From Camden, the **M/V** *Lively Lady Too* (207/236-6672, late May–Sep.) also takes trips to haul lobster traps and look for nesting puffins, seals, and sea birds.

ACCOMMODATIONS
Under $100

If you are taking the ferry to one of the islands in the morning, you can't beat the convenience of the **Navigator Motor Inn** (520 Main St., Rockland, 207/594-2131, www.navigatorinn.com, mid-May–mid-Oct. $89–129), a three-story motel located right on Rockland Harbor near the ferry terminal. All rooms have mini-fridges, while the pricier rooms have water views.

$100-150

Located in a farmhouse outside of Belfast, the **Londonderry Inn** (133 Belmont Ave./Rte. 3, Belfast, 207/338-2763, www.londonderryinn.com, $95–140) is the labor of love of Marsha Oakes, who purchased the property 10 years ago and has filled it with an eclectic mix of furniture and antiques gathered from estate sales. The keyword here is hospitality, which takes the form of a three-course country breakfast, a 200-tape VHS lending library, and warm chocolate chip cookies served in the evenings.

$150-250

The historic ◀ **Captain Lindsey House** (5 Lindsey St., Rockland, 207/596-7950, www.lindseyhouse.com, $135–190) is not only the

MAINE

former home of a sea captain—it's also currently owned by two retired captains of a local schooner. Hosts Ellen and Ken Barnes delight in putting together itineraries for guests based on their intimate knowledge of the coast. Rich red and plaid decor, down couches, and a roaring fireplace create a comfortable country-inn atmosphere. Other perks include wireless Internet, Egyptian cotton towels, and a sherry and port hour before dinner.

Candles burn in the windows to welcome guests to the **Camden Maine Stay** (22 High St., Camden, 207/236-9636, www.mainestay.com, $130–280), a romantic bed-and-breakfast located in one of the oldest homes in town. The innkeepers have taken pains to create an antebellum ambience with period antiques and Oriental rugs scattered throughout the house. That doesn't mean sacrificing the modern age, however—a DVD player is attached to a communal TV in the sitting room, and the house is set up with wireless Internet access. For breakfast, guests have a choice of dining at a communal table or a private two-top on a sunny porch overlooking the garden.

$250 and Up

Undoubtedly the most special place to stay in the area is the **Norumbega Inn** (63 High St., 207/236-4646, www.norumbegainn.com, $195–350), a granite Victorian castle perched overlooking the bay. A typical room here features a picture window with a water view, a king-sized bed, stone fireplace, and claw-foot tub. In addition to a full breakfast in the morning, the kitchen also serves hors d'oeuvres in the evenings and offers "pantry privileges" for that midnight cookie jones.

GETTING THERE AND AROUND

Any trip to Penobscot Bay will take you far from the highway. For Rockland or Camden, take exit 28 off of I-295 to U.S. Route 1 and work your way up the coast to Newcastle. From Newcastle continue up Route 1 to Rockland (25 mi., 40 min.), Camden (30 mi., 50 min.), or Belfast (50 mi., 1 hr. 10 min.). Alternatively for Belfast, take I-95 to Augusta (exit 109), then U.S. Route 202 and Route 3 east to the coast (45 mi., 1 hr. 15 min.).

Concord Coach Lines (800/639-3317, www.concordtrailways.com) offers bus service to Rockland (Maine State Ferry Terminal, 517A Main St.), Camden/Rockport (Maritime Farms, 20 Commercial St./Rte. 1, Rockport), Belfast (Big Apple Convenience, 268 Main St.), and Searsport (Steamboat Gallery, 161 E. Main St./Rte. 1) on its three daily non-express trips up the coast.

In Rockland, **All Aboard Trolley Co.** (21 Limerock St., Rockland, 207/594-9300, www.aatrolley.com) circulates around the downtown area and stores. In the other towns, you are limited to taxis. Try **Schooner Bay Limo & Taxi** (Rockland, 207/594-5000), **Mid-Coast Limo** (Camden, 207/236-2424), and **Belfast Taxi Company** (Belfast, 207/338-2943).

Midcoast Islands

Trying to count the islands off the Maine coast on a map is a sure way to get a headache. Hundreds of spits in the ocean trail off the rock fingers of the coast. Many of them, of course, are little more than perches for tired seabirds. In the sheltered arms of Penobscot Bay, however, several larger islands have actually sprouted civilization, home to both hardy fishermen and wealthy summer folk. Like the mainland villages, each has its own personality, from the fishing island of Vinalhaven and the summer resort of Islesboro to the artists colony on Monhegan.

◖ MONHEGAN

If you aren't an artist before you touch down on this small, rocky island, you may be one by the time you leave. Just one and a half square

MAINE

Monhegan Harbor

miles in area, the island demands adjectives like "mystical" and "idyllic." Part of that is due to the island's vaunted natural beauty, which packs soaring pine trees, plunging 150-foot cliffs, 600 different species of wildflowers, and 100 types of birds into its microscopic area. But the island's special character is just as much a frame of mind energetically projected (and carefully protected) by the island's 100-or-so inhabitants and returning summer guests. Everyone who disembarks for the isle must agree to abide by 10 simple rules, most of which have to do with not disturbing the flora and fauna. You won't find many cars or streetlights here, so the other rule worth abiding is the one about bringing a flashlight to transverse the dirt walking paths at night.

The island's name comes from a Micmac or Maliseet word meaning "out-to-sea" island; it must have seemed fitting when Captain John Smith happened upon the rocky base all by itself in 1614. He founded a small fishing community here, which was wiped out in the French and Indian Wars. The island was resettled after the Revolution, but it wasn't until the turn of the 20th century that it really came into its own. That's when a clan of painters including Rockwell Kent, George Bellows, and Edward Hopper began basing studios here to capture the changing light on the rocks of what Kent called his "wonder island." In the 1950s, a forward-thinking summer resident founded a nonprofit to protect most of the island's land from development, keeping the few summer cottages gathered around the harbor.

Since then, generations of artists have been drawn by the island's siren song, and more than 30 of them have studios here often open to the public. It's the slow pace and freedom that keep bringing summer guests back here year after year, however. Children run in the streets or play with communal beach toys left on the island's one beach; adults linger over meals by kerosene lamp, rock on front porches of inns, or—if they are feeling inspired—pick up watercolor and brush to try and capture a bit of the island's beauty themselves.

Sights

As far as formal sights go, Monhegan has

MAINE

exactly one—but it's a great one. The **Monhegan Museum** (Lighthouse Hill, 207/596-7003, www.monheganmuseum.org, 11:30 A.M.–3:30 P.M. daily Jul.–Aug.; 1:30–3:30 P.M. late Jun. and Sep.) inhabits the keepers' house of the island's granite lighthouse, which is in turn perched on the bare crown of the island's highest point. As befitting the "artists' island," the museum contains paintings by many of Monhegan's most distinguished artists, as well as an exhibit on lobstering, old photographs, and antique children's toys scattered throughout its many rooms. Another exhibit tells the story of the Maliseet people, the island's earliest inhabitants.

Events
For a true taste of the "real Maine," head to Monhegan for the annual **Trap Day** (Oct. 1), the start of the lobstering season, in which the whole island turns out to help haul the traps, and the docks becoming a towering cityscape of wire and mesh. Don't think you'll go as a spectator, however—even visitors are pressed into service alongside lobstermen, -women, and -children.

Shopping
On any given day in the summer and early fall, several dozen artist studios are open for browsing. Flyers listing the open studios of the moment can be found throughout town—or you can just start knocking on doors. Many of the island's most acclaimed artists hang on the walls of the **Lupine Gallery** (Wharf Hill Rd., 207/594-8131, 11 A.M.–4:30 P.M. daily June–Aug.; call for off-season hours), which is open seasonally. The gallery also sells paint, brushes, and paper if you are feeling inspired.

Sports and Recreation
Though it's only a mile and a half long, Monhegan has 17 miles of trails and footpaths crisscrossing its forested landscape. One of the most popular is the hike through **Cathedral Woods,** where the island's children have built tiny "fairy houses" out of bark, moss, and dead wood. (There is some controversy about visitors

building their own houses—if you make one, be sure you only use materials that are on the forest floor.) Other trails, which can be found with the aid of trail maps distributed by any of the lodging houses, lead to the lighthouse and the dramatic 150-foot-high cliffs, the highest on the eastern seaboard. The only sandy beach on the island is the optimistically named **Swim Beach,** where only the hardiest of swimmers brave the Gulf of Maine's frigid waters. Most guests are content to sunbathe, play in the sand, or tide pool instead.

Accommodations
The rustic feel of the 1870 **Monhegan House** (1 Main St., 207/594-7983, www.monheganhouse.com, $135–165) is tempered by downhome accoutrements in the guest rooms, including gauzy white curtains and antique Victorian furniture. Guests congregate around a stone fireplace in the lobby or bump toothbrushes in the shared bathrooms on the second floor. Ask for a room with a lighthouse view. Flags wave from the turret of the **Island Inn** (on the harbor, 207/596-0371, www.islandinnmonhegan.com, $195–255), a grand turn-of-the-century hotel overlooking a harbor full of lobster boats. Inside are painted reproductions of the inn by Andrew Wyeth, Rockwell Kent, and other Monhegan artists. The inn's 34 rooms are simple without being rustic, featuring painted floors and furniture and fluffy duvets to keep guests warm on chilly Maine nights (like most of the accommodations on Monhegan, the inn is unheated). For a bit more seclusion, **Brackett's Oar House** (3 Fish Beach Ln., 207/594-9151, www.fishbeachmonhegan. com, $145) has an upper-floor apartment with a private balcony overlooking Fish Beach, the lighthouse, and the lobster boats bobbing in the harbor below. The apartment includes a full kitchen and outdoor grill. Its owner, Lisa Brackett, also rents other cottages around the island for longer stays.

Food
Right off the dock, the **Barnacle Cafe** (1 Wharf Rd., 207/594-7995, 8 A.M.–5 P.M. mid-

May–Oct., $4–6) is a mandatory first stop for espresso drinks, wraps, sandwiches, and legendary clam chowder. It has a few tables inside and on the porch. You can't get much saltier than **Fish House Fish** (Fish Beach, 207/594-9151, www.fishbeachmonhegan.com, lunch and dinner, $7–13), a lobster-in-the-rough eatery that serves unadulterated fresh fish, lobster, and freshly made chowder at a collection of picnic tables by the beach. The most popular restaurant on the island, perhaps, is the ◖ **Monhegan House Dining Room** (1 Main St., 207/594-7983, www.monheganhouse.com, dinner late Jun.–early Sep., $13–22), which serves gourmet New England comfort food like poached haddock with lemon butter and braised lamb shank with fennel and barley. The dining room overlooks a meadow with a view of the circling beam of the lighthouse above. A bit fancier, dinner at the **Island Inn Cafe** (on the harbor, 207/596-0371, www.islandinnmonhegan.com, breakfast from 7 A.M., lunch, and dinner from 6 P.M., $14–26) includes a stunning view of the whaleback silhouette of Manana Island, the next rock over. Seafood runs heavy on the menu here, including standout lobster bisque and fettuccine with steamed scallops. The café also packs trail lunches to go. Note that none of the island's restaurants serves alcohol—you can buy your own at **North End Market** (Village Center, 207/594-5546, 9 A.M.–5 P.M., June–Sept.; winter hours vary) and bring it with you to your meal.

Information

The best way to find information about Monhegan is on two websites run by islanders: **Monhegan Commons** (www.monhegan.com) and **A Visitor's Guide to Monhegan Island** (www.briegull.com/monheganwelcome). On the island itself, the rope shed by the meadow is the informal community board, where information and events are regularly posted.

Getting There and Around

Many private ferry boats make the trip to Monhegan from various points on the Midcoast. **Monhegan Boat Line** (207/372-8848, www.monheganboat.com) makes the trip year-round from Port Clyde. **Balmy Days Cruises** (207/633-2284 or 800/298-2284, www.balmydayscruises.com) runs a seasonal ferry from Boothbay Harbor; while **Hardy Boat Cruises** (207/677-2026 or 800/278-3346, www.hardyboat.com) makes the trip from New Harbor near Pemaquid Point. Most of these ferries leave in the morning and return in the evening, making a day trip a viable option. None of the island ferries accepts cars, and indeed there are few on the island. If you need transportation, however, several pickup trucks are available for hire. For walking around in town at night, a flashlight is essential.

ISLESBORO

The landscape of the thin double helix of Islesboro is notably different from the other islands in the bay. Twelve miles long, and only a few miles wide, much of the island is flat and forested, cut by a few round-the-island roads that almost cry out to meet the wheels of a bicycle. The population of the island measures a mere 658, though of course that is supplemented every year by the wealthy summer residents. The latter congregate at the southern end of the harbor in the evocatively named Dark Harbor, a moneyed resort community full of the imposing summer cottages owned by generations of wealthy families, and a smattering of Hollywood stars (John Travolta and Kirstie Alley being the most famous summer residents). Most of the island, however, is refreshingly down to earth, with quiet country lanes threading through the more modest homes of the year-round population, who offer plenty of waves as you bicycle past.

Currently there is no lodging available on the island, but its small size and pretty shoreline make it a worthwhile day trip.

Sights

The blocky **Grindle Point Lighthouse** (207/734-2253, www.lighthouse.cc/grindle) greets visitors coming into the harbor aboard the ferry. Built in 1875, the 39-foot tower is unusual for being constructed in the square

MAINE

Pacific West Coast style, instead of the round style common to the East Coast. Next door in the "one-and-a-half story" keeper's house, the **Sailors' Memorial Museum** (9:30 A.M.–4:30 P.M. Tues.–Sun. late June–early Sept., free) displays paintings of old sailing captains, model ships, and work by the local "artist of the week."

Shopping

The island has a few galleries and shops catering to the summer crowd. One of the best places to poke around is **Artisan Books & Bindery** (509 Pendleton Point Rd., 207/734-6852, www.artisanbooksandbindery.,com), where proprietor Craig Olson stocks a variety of used and rare books, as well as new books by Maine and Islesboro authors (yes, there are some). Be sure to call ahead, as the store's official hours are "by appointment or chance." Italian pottery, jewelry, and Maine-made crafts are part of the selection at **Hummingbird Hill** (1109 Meadow Pond Rd., 207/734-8193, 10 A.M.–5 P.M. daily), a small but delightful gift shop.

Sports and Recreation

For an island so perfect for bike-riding, it's odd that no bike rental facilities are available on-island. You can remedy that lapse by renting a bike at **Ragged Mountain Sports** (46 Elm St., Camden, 207/236-6664), and bringing it over on the ferry. Get an early start if you plan to cycle the length of the island, as the route is a full 20 miles each way. A shorter but still satisfying ride is the one from Dark Harbor to Pendleton Point, a distance of only eight miles. On the southeast tip of the island, **Pendleton Point** offers a small sandy beach in the sheltered arms of a rocky cove, perfect for tidepooling and collecting driftwood.

Food

In addition to selling groceries, T-shirts, and wine, **Durkee's General Store** (867 Main St., 207/734-2201, 8 A.M.–6 P.M. Mon.–Sat., 10 A.M.–2 P.M. Sun. year-round) serves pizza, burgers, and sandwiches. Or opt to dine in a

more relaxed setting at **Tarratine Golf Club Restaurant** (Golf Course Rd., 207/734-6970, 11:30 A.M.–8 P.M. daily June–Aug.; hours vary in off-season, $12–21). The menu (grilled salmon, barbecued chicken, and the like) is basic but dependable, and the views of the surrounding greens are worth a reservation in their own right.

Information

While there is no formal information center on Islesboro, be sure to pick up a guide to the island at the ferry landing in Lincolnville or the island's town office (150 Main Rd., 207/734-2253).

Getting There

The **Maine State Ferry Service** (Lincolnville, 207/789-5611, www.maine.gov) offers almost hourly service from the ferry terminal on Lincolnville beach (between Camden and Belfast). The ride takes only 20 minutes. Fares are $10 round-trip for adults, $4.75 round-trip for children ages 5–11. Children under 5 ride free. Plan well ahead if you want to bring a car over with you on the ferry, especially during the summer months when berths can be quite limited. Vehicle tickets are $27.50 round-trip. If you prefer to leave your wheels on the mainland, the best way to get around is by bicycle, which you should rent before you board at the **Tidewater Motel** (Main St., 207/863-4618). Bike tickets are $8.50 round-trip for adults and $5.50 for children. Otherwise, you'll have to make arrangements for a pick-up from your lodging, as there are no taxis on the island.

VINALHAVEN

This rocky island in the middle of the bay is blessed with two natural resources. The obvious one crawls along the ocean floor and is steamed and served with melted butter. Vinalhaven is famed for its lobster boats, which crowd the lanes of Carver's Harbor and air their traps on the docks. The island's other resource is the granite that was hewn out of stone quarries and made the island famous for girding the buildings in Boston and New York. In the early

20th century, Vinalhaven became a popular place for old-money families to summer; even today, plutocrats come every July and August to inhabit cottages on the secluded shores of the island and even quieter North Haven, the island immediately to the north. The combination of a working harbor, cosmopolitan summer crowd, and quiet natural beauty make the perfect place to get away from it all.

Sights

The **Vinalhaven Historical Society** (41 High St., 207/863-4410, www.vinalhavenhistoricalsociety.org, 11 A.M.–3 P.M. daily Jul.–Aug.; Tue.–Sat. early June–mid-Sept., free) has a small museum with artifacts from the lobster industry and the heyday of the granite trade. The hulking iron "galamander" used to haul the granite to shore still sits at the top of Main Street. On the harbor sits a 50-foot-long granite column that was commissioned for a war monument that was never built.

Entertainment and Shopping

One of the few places to grab a beer on the island is **The Sand Bar** (63 Main St., 207/863-4500, 11 A.M.–9 P.M. or later daily), a convivial dive frequented by lobstermen and teenagers alike, with a jukebox and occasional live music, as well as pub fare and pizzas.

The whole island comes out on Saturday mornings for **flea markets** in the open field by the galamander. Whether or not you find a treasure, it's a great way to meet the locals.

Sports and Recreation

The best way to explore the island is by bicycle, which can be rented with a signature and a promise at the **Tidewater Motel** (Main St., 207/863-4618). A good 10-mile loop traverses North Haven and Round the Island Roads. The island also has several great spots for hiking. A short rambling trail off of Old Harbor Road leads down to the **Basin,** where seals have been known to frolic in the surf. Overlooking Carver's Harbor, **Lane's Preserve** offers acres of conservation land with blackberry and raspberry bushes ripe for the picking. While the rocky island isn't known for its beaches, the granite trade has left an unexpected treasure— the abandoned quarries that are now filled with water. In the summertime, families and teenagers mob **Lawson's Quarry** (North Haven Rd.) and **Booth's Quarry** (Pequot Rd.) to dive into the deep, crystal-clear swimming holes. It's rumored there is another quarry where clothing is optional, but you'll have to ask a willing local for directions.

Accommodations

Built on a bridge by the ferry landing, the **Tidewater Motel** (207/863-4618, www.tidewatermotel.com, $165–195) offers friendly and basic accommodations. Owners Phil and Elaine Crossman are especially helpful in orientating guests to the island. Some rooms have kitchens and decks overlooking the harbor. For kids, the Crossmans offer a "crab grab bait bag" to help your little one snag a crab in the harbor. The stunning Victorian mansion of a granite baron is now the **Payne Homestead** (Main St., 207/863-9963, www.paynehomestead.com, $145–165), a bed-and-breakfast run by Texas-transplant Donna Payne. Each room is dramatically decorated in a different color, including rose, coral, and azure, and a full country breakfast is served each morning.

Food

A line forms every night in front of the ordering window at the ☕ **Harbor Gawker** (26 Main St., 207/863-9365, 11 A.M.–8 P.M. Mon.–Sat. Apr.–Oct., $2–18), a seafood shack on the harbor that features lobster literally fresh off the boat. Inside at simple tables, you are as likely to hear a conversation about fishing regulations as about Ivy League sports. Vinalhaven's nod to fine dining, **Haven** (49 Main St., 207/863-4969, 6–9 P.M. Tue.–Sat. Jun.–mid-Oct.; weekends only May and mid-Oct.–Dec., $16–24) offers two nightly seatings of chef-owner Tori Pratt's creative American cuisine. The restaurant has two rooms—a fine dining room by reservation only, and a more casual pub-style room simpler (and less expensive) entrées.

Information

The Vinalhaven Chamber of Commerce (www.vinalhaven.org) doesn't have an office, but does maintain a good informational website. The best place to pick up information on the island is **Carver's Harbor Market** (Main St., 207/863-4319), the informal local clearinghouse.

Getting There

The **Maine State Ferry Service** (207/596-2202, maine.govwww.maine.gov) runs between four and five ferries a day from Rockland, located on Port Terminal Road off Main Street. Fares are $17.50 round-trip for adults, $8.50 round-trip for children ages 5–11. Children under 5 ride free. Room for cars can be quite tight, especially in the summer when vehicles are often booked months in advance. Rates, if you can get a reservation, are $49.50 round-trip. Thankfully, cars aren't a necessity on Vinalhaven, especially if you plan on spending most of your time in and around Carver's Harbor, which is compact and easily walkable. If you want to venture farther afield, you'll need your own wheels, as there is no public transportation or taxis on the island. If you can't bring your car, rent a bike from the **Tidewater Motel** (Main St., 207/863-4618).

Western Lakes and Mountains

Nature plays the captivating diva in this unspoiled region of Maine, where lake after beautiful lake, mountain after mountain, and wood after clean-smelling wood are the manifestations of just what a showoff she can be. And man follows her cue: Thousands swarm every summer to the shores of Sebago Lake, to the slopes of Sunday River, and to the trails of the area's many parks and nature preserves. And in every setting, there's wildlife to be spotted—from moose and loons to trout and eagles.

None of which is to say the area is untouched by man. From the renowned music performances put on by Bates College and the festivals of Bethel to the mill-turned-artist studios of Lewiston, activity continues in the area year-round.

SEBAGO LAKE AREA

Welcome to camp central. Thanks to the endless water-related activities that Sebago Lake offers, its shores are home to seemingly countless family cabins, camping grounds, and children's summer camps. In summer and even into late winter, everyone and their uncle (literally) are here for the kayaking, canoeing, fishing, waterskiing, ice skating, and skiing (on nearby Shawnee Peak).

Of course, it wasn't always this crowded. Native Americans first settled around Sebago (which means "open water") and used it as a central trading area. Later, that business turned to pleasure; about a century after the area was settled by colonists in the mid-18th century, it transformed into a resort area. Today the small towns surrounding the lake (and the minor lakes surrounding it, known as the Long Lakes) are Naples, East Sebago, Windham, Harrison, Bridgton, Raymond, and Casco.

Sights

The nineteenth century mountain-man Rufus Porter was a man of many talents—in addition to founding *Scientific American* magazine, he was an icon of American landscape art, shaking it free of its European roots with murals painted on a grand scale, often right on the walls of private homes throughout New England. **The Rufus Porter Museum and Cultural Center** (67 North High St./Rte. 302 & 260 Main St., Bridgton, 207/647-2828, noon–4 P.M. Wed.–Sat., $5 adults, $4 seniors and students, free children 12 and under) pays homage to Porter's legacy, with several galleries dedicated to his evocations of the New England countryside, as well as a separate

WILD KINGDOM

Llamas work just great for trekking people and equipment over the rugged hills of the Andes, so why not in Maine? The **Telemark Inn** (591 Kings Hwy., Mason Township, 207/836-2703, www.telemarkinn.com, $125) answers that question with an on-property **llama farm** and regular expeditions up nearby hills and down paths to wooded swimming holes (get that llama to carry the towel!). But that's just the beginning of the animal experiences at this remote wilderness lodge, which sometimes seems more like a petting zoo than a place to spend the night. The lodge has cultivated a **hummingbird colony** with hundreds of birds, and offers guests the unique experience of feeding them directly from their own mouths. Then there is the kennel of rambunctious huskies that form the core of the lodge's **dog-sled team.** Even in summer, guests can participate in the "conditioning" of the dogs, who are kept on an active regimen of pulling wheeled carts and swim-training. The lodge also leads canoe trips to the nearby Androscoggin River and Umbagog Wildlife Sancturay. At day's end, bed down in an old-school Adirondack style lodge with woodstoves in some rooms. Two- to five-day packages including meals and all activities are $390-875 for adults and $300-675 for children 13 and under. Llama treks only are $75 for adults, $65 for children for a three-hour swimming hole excursion; and $600 for adults and $525 for children for a three-day trekking adventure.

exhibit of 15 impressive murals salvaged from a home outside of Boston. (Admission is charged separately for the two museums; there is a $1 discount to visit both.)

Events

One of the area's most crafty happenings—worth braving the summertime crowds for—is the annual **Chickadee Quilters Show** (Town Hall, Bridgton, 800/533-9595, second week of July), a showcase for spectacularly intricate handmade quilts. It's pure rural New England! In July and August, catch weekly classical concerts at the **Sebago-Long Lake Chamber Music Festival** (Deertrees Theatre, Harrison, 207/583-6747, www.sebagomusicfestival.org).

Food

A local institution for its tasty and homey dishes (if lobster casserole is on the menu, order it), **Olde Mill Tavern** (56 Main St., Harrison, 207/583-9077, www.oldemilltavern.com, 4 P.M.–8 P.M. Sun.–Thu.; 4 P.M.–9 P.M. Fri.–Sat., $12–24) is a cozy place to eat hefty plates of local fare in a historic renovated grist mill. If you're even hungry the next morning (and you may not be), head to **Ricky's Diner** (109 Main St., Bridgton, 207/647-2499, 5:30 A.M.–8 P.M. Sun.–Thu.; 5:30 A.M.–9 P.M. Fri.–Sat., $2–9) for simple and inexpensive omelets and a double helping of local gossip.

Information

The centrally located **Greater Bridgton Lakes Region Chamber of Commerce** (101 Portland Rd., Bridgton, 207/647-3472) runs an information center in downtown Bridgton with info on camping and boating, parks, and brochures on new restaurants and accommodations for the surrounding towns.

LEWISTON-AUBURN

The second-largest city in Maine, Lewiston is an enclave of student life, thanks to prestigious Bates College. Like many college towns, however, where there's well-respected academia, there's history, and Lewiston is no exception. Settlement for both Lewiston and Auburn started around 1770, around the river that runs between the towns. By the mid-19th century, industry had picked up in the form of Bates Mill, which used hydropower via the river. Milling continued to be a primary industry into the 20th century, by which point satellite mills had opened. Today, the mills are

MAINE

used more for tourist purposes, though they do turn out small runs of fabrics.

Sights

Spend an hour or two poking around the restored **Bates Mill Complex** (Canal St., Lewiston, 208/782-5355, www.ci.lewiston. me.us) and you'll get a smorgasbord of experiences—a little education (touring the old mill itself), a little shopping (in the retail stores), and a little aesthetic rejuvenation (in the art studios). The highlight is **Museum L-A** (35 Canal St., 207/333-3881, www.museumla.org, 10 A.M.–4 P.M. Mon.–Sat.,$3 adults, $2 students and seniors), a combination history/art museum that tells the story of the industrial revolution and Lewiston-Auburn's place in it. Unlike many history museums, this one focuses not on the lives of great generals or industrialists, but on the community made up of ordinary people, including immigrants who came from all over the world to work in the mills. Those modern exhibits are supplemented by more modern art exhibits, including student work from Bates College.

Another legacy from the same family that left the mill buildings behind, **Bates College** (2 Andrews Rd., Lewiston, 207/786-6255, www. bates.edu), is young by New England college standards—founded only in 1855. In the time since, however, it has come to be regarded as one of the top liberal arts schools in the country. The college holds regular lectures and concerts that are open to the public in the Olin Arts Center (75 Russell St., 207/786-6135).

It may be the state capital, but nearby Augusta is a quiet city. Its impressive Maine State Museum (83 State House Station, 230 State St., Augusta, 207/287-2304, www.mainestatemuseum.org, 9 A.M.–5 P.M. Tue.–Fri.; 10 A.M.–4 P.M. Sat., $2 adults, $1 seniors and children 6–18, free children under 6, family maximum $6), however, is well worth a detour. Check out the collections on the lumber, fishing, and shipbuilding industries—all designed to illustrate the state's history.

Events

The entire state, it seems, turns out and rallies each spring for the **Maine State Parade** (first Sat. of May), a giant May Day parade and celebration each year in Lewiston. Expect a crush of diverse Maine residents and an epic parade of colorful floats, music, and performers. Every summer, the **Bates Dance Festival** (207/786-6381, http://abacus.bates.edu/dancefest) attracts arts lovers from all over the country for its month-long spectrum of productions and workshops (be sure to call for dates and to reserve tickets—they sell out months ahead of time). In August, you can get airborne at the **Great Falls Balloon Festival** (207/786-6674, www.greatfallsballoonfestival.org) that takes over Lewiston and Auburn with festivities like pie-eating contests, concerts, crafts shows, and, of course, balloon rides.

Shopping

Open year-round, the **Nezinscot Farm Store** (284 Turner Center Rd., Turner, 207/225-3231, www.nezinscotfarm.com, 6 A.M.–6 P.M. Mon.–Fri.; 8 A.M.–5 P.M. Sat.) is a jackpot of fresh produce, baked goods, dried flowers, and other local products.

Food

Notably better than your average golf course restaurant, **Fore Seasons** (Rte. 117, North Parish Rd., Turner, 207/224-7090, http://fore-seasons.net, 11 A.M.–9 P.M. daily June–Aug.; 4 P.M.–9 P.M. Mon.–Sat., 12 P.M.–4 P.M. Sun. Sept.–May, $11–19), specializes in buffets filled with food that doesn't taste like buffet food. Head in for the weekend brunch buffet, and you'll be rewarded with homemade crab quiches, made-to-order omelets, and mountains of fresh fruit. Meals the way mom used to make them (in both their freshness and charmingly bygone-era recipes) are found at **Rolandeau's Restaurant** (755 Washington St., Auburn, 207/784-2110, www.rolandeausrestaurant.com, 11 A.M.–2:30 P.M. and 5 P.M.–9 P.M. Tues.–Fri., 5 P.M.–9 P.M. Sat., closed Sun., $4–9). When's the last time you had stuffed mushroom caps or rack of lamb with mint jelly for dinner? Or scallops with bacon for lunch? For quick-but-healthy lunches or early dinners, make a stop at **Nothing But The Blues** (81 College St., Lewiston, 207/784-6493, 11:30 A.M.–2 P.M. and 5 P.M.–8 P.M. Tue.–Fri.; 5–9 P.M. Sat., $8–14) for vegetarian-friendly pastas, stir-fries, and sandwiches.

Information

Get educated about both Lewiston and Auburn at the **Androscoggin County Chamber of Commerce** (415 Lisbon St., Lewiston, 207/783-2249, www.androscoggincounty.com). The office can help find accommodations, places to eat, and offers brochures and information on local businesses.

BETHEL

As pretty as this small historic town is spring through fall, it truly hits its stride in winter, when the Sunday River Ski Resort goes into full swing. That's when the area takes on snow-village status, with its covered bridges sporting snow, and activities everywhere you look—from skiing (of course) to snowshoeing. All that said, there's also quite a bit to do in warmer months—hiking and leaf-peeping, canoeing and shopping, just for starters.

Sights

For a dose of the Bethel of yore, tour the early 19th-century **Dr. Moses Mason House** (10–14 Broad St., 207/824-2908, www.bethelhistorical.org/museum.html, 1–4 P.M. Tues.–Sun., Jul.–early Sep.; 1–4 P.M. Tues.–Fri. Sep.–Jun., $3 adults, $1.50 children 6–12, free children under 6) and find an impressive collection of historic paintings and portraits, furniture, and other antiquities. The charming **Artist's Covered Bridge** (off of Sunday River Park Rd., follow the signs) was built in the late 19th century, and is one of nine of its kind in the state.

Events

Competitions are big year-round in Bethel, and it all starts in the winter, when a variety of ever-changing events are hosted by the local chamber of commerce. Spring sees the locally loved **April Fool's Pole, Paddle, and Paw**

Race (207/782-2302), a flurry of skiing, snow-shoeing, and canoeing. The latter gets an even bigger boost at July's **Androscoggin River Source to the Sea Trek-a-Thon** (207/527-2163, www.avcnet.org/arwc/trek.html). The multi-week event covers significant portions of the 170-mile distance from the headwaters.

Entertainment

Hit **The Foggy Goggle** (Sunday River Ski Resort, 207/824-3000) for a jumping après-ski drinking (and pick-up) scene. There's occasional live music there and at **Rooster's Roadhouse** (157 Mayville Rd., 207/824-0309, www.roostersroadhouse.com, 3 P.M.–closing, nightly), too, and mellow live piano (plus billiards) on weekends at **The Millbrook Tavern & Grille** (On the common, 207/824-2175, www.bethelinn.com, 11:30 A.M.–9 P.M. daily).

Shopping

Visit **Maine Line Products** (23 Main St., 207/824-2522,, www.mainelineproducts.com, 10 A.M.–5 P.M. Mon.–Fri.; 9 A.M.–5 P.M. Sat.) and find some gifts that are unique and tasteful (like the locally made caramel popcorn, fudge, and crafts) and some that are just downright weird (the wooden sticks said to predict the weather, for instance).

Food

Vegetarians can eat heartily at **Café DiCocoa** (125 Main St., 207/824-5282, 7 A.M.–7 P.M. daily, $6–11), what with the establishment's roster of organic, tofu-centric dishes. Far from your run-of-the-mill Maine fare, **Lake House Restaurant** (686 Waterford Rd./Rte. 35& 37, Waterford, 207/583-4182, www.lakehouse-maine.com, 6–9 P.M. Tue.–Sun. Jun.–Sept.; 6–9 P.M. Fri.–Sat. Oct.–May, $19–29) serves creations like lobster with Pernod béchamel in flaky pastry and roast duck with blackberry sauce. Set in an 18th-century farmhouse inn, the restaurant is about a 20-minute drive from Bethel, but well worth the car time.

Information

Get the lay of the land at **Bethel Area**

MAINE

MAINE

Chamber of Commerce (Cross St., 207/824-2282, www.bethelmaine.org). The friendly and well-organized office has everything you need to know about ski times and prices, restaurants, events, and directions.

SPORTS AND RECREATION
Beaches and Camping

The beautiful but crowded Sebago Lake Park (11 Park Access Rd., off US Route 302, Casco, 207/693-6613, $6.50 per day adults, $1 children 5–11, free children under 5) provides access to plenty of water, and is most popular for swimming, fishing, and sunbathing. Even with the hordes of fellow beachgoers, however, there's usually space for everyone; the park covers 1,300 acres. For those who'd like to spend more than a day at the beach, the state park has 250 wooded campsites ($25/night) as well as hiking trails through the forest.

Hiking and Biking

In Bridgton, the hiking trails of Pleasant Mountain (about 3 miles past the Shawnee Peak sign on Mountain Rd.; look for the Moose Trail sign) provide a solid range of options, from easy to challenging. Each can be done round-trip in an afternoon, and each rewards with stunning views of the area from the top. In Bethel, serious hikers head to The Mahoosucs, a mountain range full of pristine environments and difficult trails. Don't go unless you're an expert, have an extra few days, and are completely geared up. Ready to try? Head up to Grafton Notch State Park (1941 Bear River Rd., Newry, 207/824-2912, www.maine.gov), 3,000 acres of both short and long hikes, cut through the middle by the Appalachian Trail. Sound intimidating? Try nearby Step Falls Preserve (Rte. 26, Newry, 207/729-5181, www.nature.org) instead, filled with waterfalls, gorgeous fauna, and only moderately challenging hikes.

Boating and Fishing

Rent fishing boats of several sizes from Naples Marina (Rtes. 302 and 114, Naples, 207/693-6254, www.naplesmarinamaine.com) for use in the Sebago area. If you're headed out on Bethel's Androscoggin River, stop by Bethel Outdoor Adventure (121 Mayville Rd., Bethel, 207/824-4224, www.betheloutdooradventure.com) to rent canoes, arrange a drop-off or pick-up at the river, or get maps and directions.

Skiing

The 800-pound gorilla of Maine ski resorts, Sunday River Ski Resort (Sunday River Rd., Bethel, 207/824-3000, www.sundayriver.com, $74 adults, $63 youth 13–18, $51 seniors and children 6–12, free children under 6) has eight peaks and more than 125 trails to test the mettle of every level of skier, from beginner to advanced. In fact, Sunday River probably offers more diversity of terrain that any other resort in the northeast, with each peak taking on a distinctive character, from the precipitous White Cap (home to "White Heat," known as the "longest, widest, steepest trail in the east"), and wooded Oz with its fine glade skiing. Due to its location deep in Maine's western mountains, Sunday River gets plenty of natural snow—when that fails, however, it also has one of the best snowmaking systems in the northeast. The only drawback with the resort is its inaccessibility, a grueling 3.5 hour drive from Boston; for some, however, that's a plus, since the drive weeds out casual Sunday skiers, and keeps more powder for the die-hards.

ACCOMMODATIONS
Under $100

Though not exactly off the beaten path (it's close to everything in Bethel and a quick ride to Sunday River), The Chapman Inn (2 Church St., Bethel, 207/824-2657, www.chapmaninn.com, $60–130) manages to serve up some peace and quiet away from the slopes. Still need more incentive? The owners include a dynamite breakfast and all-you-can-eat cookies, all day long. The well-appointed rooms are very good value for the money; if you're on a budget, however, the inn has an even more economical bunkhouse ($33/night)—and guests there get the same gourmet breakfast.

$100-150

Restored by its owners to fit the era of its namesake, **The Victoria Inn** (32 Main St., Bethel, 207/-824-8060, www.thevictoria-inn.com, $109–159) is filled and finished with antiques and décor of the Victorian period. Breakfast is included.

$150 and Up

In the Sebago area, stay lakefront at **The Noble House** (81 Highland Rd., Bridgton, 207/647-3733, www.noblehousebb.com, $145–275), a prim yellow Victorian bed-and-breakfast filled with fireplaces, grand pianos, and canopy beds. At breakfast, the delicious ham-and-cheese strata, one of the owners' many specialties, will get your day started on a full stomach. Sunday River Ski Area's **Jordan Grand Hotel** (Sunday River, 207/824-3000, www.sundayriver.com, $140–240) is directly off the slopes, and houses a slew of perks and services, including several pools, babysitting, restaurants, and an arcade.

GETTING THERE AND AROUND

Public transportation isn't a huge priority in these woodsy areas, as most residents have cars. You are best off bringing one as well. To get to the Sebago Lake area from Portland, take U.S. Route 302 north to Bridgton (40 mi., 1 hr.), or Routes 25 and 114 north to Sebago (30 mi., 1 hr.). For Lewiston-Auburn, take I-95 north from Portland to exit 75, then drive north on Route 100 to the twin-city area (40 mi., 40 min.). For Bethel, head north up I-95 from Portland to exit 63, then north on Route 26 through the mountains (75 mi., 2 hrs.).

If you don't have wheels of your own, call at least a day ahead to **Bethel Express** (Bethel, 207/824-4646). Their vans will arrange to pick you up or drop you off between Bethel's Sunday River Ski Resort, its downtown, and Portland.

Bethel Express also runs taxi service within Bethel, from the town to the ski area and downtown. In Lewiston, the most dependable taxis are with **City Cab Company** (207/784-4521).

MAINE

DOWNEAST AND THE NORTH WOODS

Look at a map of inland northern Maine, and all of the squiggly lines disappear. Instead, they are replaced with a uniform grid of square timber plots stretching halfway up the state to the Canadian border. Inside that vast expanse are acres and acres of pine and spruce trees teeming with moose, black bear, and coyotes, with any places that might be considered "towns" few and far between. The North Woods encompasses some 3.5 million acres of forest, making it the largest area of undeveloped forestland in the United States. The area isn't quite "wilderness," however, since 3,000 miles of timber roads crisscross its boundaries and provide a livelihood for lumbermen and mills like they have for centuries.

Within this area of enticing remoteness, several areas have been designated for preservation and outdoor recreation. Maine's wilderness jewel is Baxter State Park, a rectangle of woods and mountains a third the size of Rhode Island. Flowing down from Canada, the extensive waterways of the Allagash and St. John's Rivers empty into Moosehead Lake, which gets its name from its uncanny similarity in shape to Maine's state animal, and draws many of its namesake quadrupeds to drink at its twisting banks and estuaries.

The southeast corner of Maine has a character—and remoteness—all its own. Named "downeast" by the ship captains who were carried downwind in that direction, the area is one of the least visited of the state and is also one of the poorest regions in New England. Those taking the time to get to know the Mainers here are rewarded with a salt-of-the-earth

© MICHAEL BLANDING

HIGHLIGHTS

(Fort Knox and the Penobscot Narrows Observatory: Some historians credit the impenetrability of this fort to the fact that it was never attacked. There's no better view of it than from the 400-foot platform on the bridge next door (page 581).

(Acadia National Park: It doesn't get any more Maine than the breathtaking rocky coastline and spruce-covered mountains of this unique island paradise (page 592).

(Stephen King Tour: The undisputed master of horror used the gritty town of Bangor as the backdrop for many a spine-tingling tale (page 598).

(West Quoddy Head Light: The Downeast candy-striper is one of the most popular lighthouses in the East (page 600).

(Moose Safari: There's no better place to see these eight-foot giants than on the lake that bears their name, Moosehead (page 606).

(Hiking Mount Katahdin: The northern end of the Appalachian Trail is an attractive day hike with a view of unfettered wilderness from the peak (page 611).

(Canoeing the Allagash: Mile after mile of pine-lined riverbank greets those intrepid enough to tackled its rapids (page 613).

LOOK FOR (TO FIND RECOMMENDED SIGHTS, ACTIVITIES, DINING, AND LODGING.

sensibility and flinty sense of humor that captures the best of the New England character. Downeast has its own star attraction in Acadia National Park, the only national park in the six-state region. Situated on the rocky cliffs of Mount Desert Island, it has some of the most dramatic scenery on the coast.

Those really looking for a coastal getaway head to the Blue Hill Peninsula, a rocky roller coaster of country lanes that skirt and plunge into the sea. Home base here is Castine, a colonial-era village that has become a haven for passing yachtsman. On the other side of one of the most stunning bridges in the world, Deer Isle is spoken of in quiet tones by its summer

devotees, who are understandably reluctant to share its magical shores with outsiders. In fact, Deer Isle may be the perfect mix of what visitors come to the region for, a low-key getaway that seems to accommodate everyone from rich boat owners to backwoods artists, and, of course, those two essential Maine ingredients: lobsters and lighthouses.

PLANNING YOUR TIME

The distances here are enormous, and pine trees can quickly become monotonous. Unless you want to spend the whole time in the car, it's wise to choose one or two destinations in the region—sticking either to Acadia and the

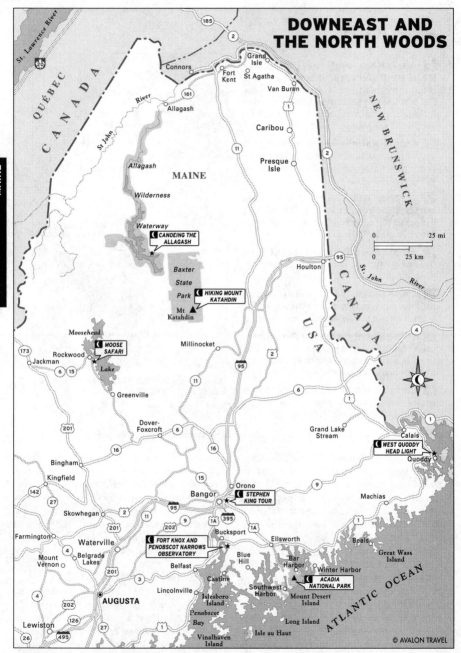

DOWNEAST AND THE NORTH WOODS

Downeast coast, or penetrating into the heart of the North Woods. On the coastal route, it's worth making the diversion to **Fort Knox,** which while never used for battle, is a fascinating journey into postcolonial America. No trip downeast is complete without a visit to **Acadia National Park.** At the very minimum, stay overnight in Bar Harbor and take an afternoon to drive the Park Loop Road. Three or four days, however, allows time to take a hike or two, ride the carriage roads, take a cruise, and explore some of the smaller villages of Mount Desert Island.

Another two or three days is sufficient to visit the beguiling Downeast coast. Stephen King fans shouldn't miss an opportunity to visit the horror writer's home town of Bangor, the largest city in these parts, where a **Stephen King Tour** visits sites mentioned in his novels. Along the coast northward is the heart of Maine blueberry country, where Maine's famous fruit is grown in a vast moonscape known as the blueberry barrens. At the far end of the Sunrise Coast, so-called because it is the first place the sun touches the United States, **West Quoddy Head Light** is as much a symbol of Maine as Pemaquid or Portland Head.

In the North Woods, you can count on seeing moose just by driving along the roads at night. A more surefire, and certainly less frightening, way to view them is on a **moose safari,** which pokes into the estuaries in Moosehead Lake where they are known to lurk. In Baxter State Park, the prime attraction is **Mount Katahdin,** the beginning of the Appalachian Trail and a pleasing day hike. But outdoors enthusiasts will want to spend several days in the park, allowing time to camp out on some of its more remote backwoods trails. The Allagash River is the most serious river in New England for serious canoeing, kayaking, and river rafting. A standard trip takes a week to travel the length of the river from Katahdin to Canada; three- or five-day trips take in shorter stretches of the river.

For all of these areas, keep in mind that Maine is significantly farther north than the rest of New England, and temperatures dip here early. The snows don't melt from the mountains until at least the end of April, and the region doesn't really get pleasant to visit until May. On the other side, leaves can start changing early, reaching their peak in early October or even late September in the northern reaches of the Allagash. By Halloween, the nights are frosty and dark—and the whole region shuts down between December and February.

MAINE

Blue Hill Peninsula

Flanking the west side of Penobscot Bay, the Blue Hill Peninsula has always been more accessible by sea than by land. Perhaps that explains why it is so causally bypassed by scores of summer tourists on their way up the coast. Those who take the turn discover a classic chunk of Maine coastline, with roller-coaster roads offering drop-dead views of the rocky coast. For more than 200 years, the rocky jut of land has been home to tiny fishing villages inhabited by hearty settlers. Now in summer its harbors are more likely to be filled with pleasure craft of the well-to-do, poking into the historic downtown of Castine or kayaking the magical coves of Deer Isle.

BUCKSPORT

Not the most picturesque of Maine coastal towns, the gritty town of Bucksport guards the entrance to the Penobscot River, historically one of the main trading routes for lumber and furs from Bangor and points north in Canada. The river mouth is marred by the smokestacks of a giant paper mill, but a key to its strategic importance is the formidable bulk of Fort Knox, one of the greatest surviving examples of the Civil War–era network of eastern coastal forts.

◖ Fort Knox and the Penobscot Narrows Observatory

Not to be confused with the one in Kentucky

MAINE

© MICHAEL BLANDING

Fort Knox

with all the gold, the building of this massive granite fort (Rte. 1, 207/469-6553, http://fortknox.maineguide.com, May–Oct., $3 adults, $1 children 5–11, free children under 5) began in 1844 and continued over the next 25 years. These days, it's difficult to conceive of anyone invading eastern Maine, but the British had done so twice, in 1779 and 1814, even briefly annexing the region on the latter occasion, and so the early Americans were determined that it not happen again. A model of strategic design, the fort is a delight to explore, either in the company of a state park tour guide or alone with a flashlight. Long, dark passageways lead down to cannons pitched over the river, and corridors flanking the entrance are rife with murder holes to pick off invading troops. Alas, before the fort was even completed, it was rendered obsolete by modern advances in warfare.

Complementing the fort is the adjoining **Penobscot Narrows Bridge and Observatory** (9 A.M.–5 P.M. daily, open until 6 P.M. Jul.–Aug.), which incorporates a public viewing deck a dizzying 437 feet above Penobscot Bay. Needless to say, the views 15 miles in every direction are breathtaking, making the bridge an instant tourist attraction onto which Bucksport has latched for its future revitalization. Entrances to the observatory are through Fort Knox; tickets are time-stamped, and the price includes entrance into the fort, so you can explore the historic site while you wait for your trip up the elevator.

Entertainment and Events

The old-time 1916 **Alamo Theatre** (379 Main St., 207/469-6910, www.oldfilm.org/alamo) is the headquarters of Northeast Historic Film, which shows both current and historical films in the renovated 120-seat theater, as well as staging occasional music concerts.

The labyrinthine corridors of Fort Knox are scary enough during the daytime, but they become positively frightful during **Fright at the Fort** (Bucksport, 207/469-6553, http://fortknox.maineguide.com/fright, $5–7), which fills up the fort with ghouls and goblins culled from the local teen population every Halloween.

COURTESY MAINE OFFICE OF TOURISM

Penobscot Narrows Bridge and Observatory

Food

A Bucksport institution for more than two decades, **Macleod's Restaurant** (93 Main St., 207/469-3963, 11 A.M.–8:30 P.M. Tue.–Sat.; 4–8 P.M. Sun., $10–21) is a cut above most of the local establishments. French chocolate silk pie is reason enough to stop in.

Information

You can learn more about Bucksport from the **Bucksport Chamber of Commerce** (52 Main St., 207/469-6818, www.bucksportbaychamber.com). The closest hospital is **Maine Coast Memorial Hospital** (50 Union St., Ellsworth, 207/664-5311, www.mcmhospital.org), and there are several pharmacies, including **Community Pharmacy** (75 Main St., 207/469-7030, www.communityrx.com), though none are open 24 hours. Free Internet access is offered at **The Buck Memorial Library** (Main St., 207/469-2650, www.buckmemoriallibrary.50megs.com).

CASTINE

It's hard to imagine a more perfect seaside town than tiny historic Castine. Despite its isolation (by land), the village is a favorite destination for day-sailers from around the Maine Coast, and the presence of the Maine Maritime Academy ensures a regular influx of cosmopolitan students from around the globe. Named after a French nobleman who married a local Native American woman and ran the town in the late 1600s, Castine values its history as a prize fought over by French, Dutch, British, and American seamen throughout the colonial period. After things settled down in the 1800s, it used its deep-water harbor and active East India trade to become the second-richest port in the country. Today its waterfront downtown is a mix of historic buildings, grand captain's houses, and swanky restaurants and galleries catering to the yachting set.

Sights

The far-ranging mind of Dr. John Howard Wilson, a Victorian-era geologist, forms the basis for the astounding collection in the **Wilson Museum** (107 Perkins St., 207/326-9247, www.wilsonmuseum.org, 2–5 P.M. daily late May–Sept., free). The menagerie inside includes African prehistoric artifacts, Balinese shadow puppets, fire department memorabilia, and old maps and ships' logs. A short and pleasant walk from downtown is **Dyce's Head Lighthouse,** a 19th-century classic tapered white tower. In the summer, midshipmen conduct tours of the *State of Maine,* the 500-foot training vessel owned by the **Maine Maritime Academy** (Pleasant St., Castine, 800/464-6565, www.mainemaritime.edu). Though not available for tours, be sure to notice the academy's other beauty, the schooner *Bowdoin,* which Maine explorer Adm. Donald MacMillan took on his many expeditions to the North Pole.

Shopping
The cheerfully appointed **Castine Historical Handworks** (9 Main St., 207/326-4460, http://castinehistoricalhandworks.com, 10 A.M.–6 P.M. Mon.–Sat.; 10 A.M.–5 P.M. Sun.) represents an impressive collection of work from artisans from all over Maine. Pick up handwoven baskets, carved animal and bird statues, painted seascapes, and traditionally crafted pottery.

Food
The rollicking **Dennett's Wharf** (15 Sea St., 207/326-9045, www.dennettswharf.net, 11 A.M.–10 P.M., $10–25) is the kind of place where rum-filled customers have pinned dollar bills to the ceiling. Students, families, and day sailors munch on baby-back ribs and lobster pie under an awning on the waterfront, then wash it all down with the restaurant's own Wharf Rat Ale. When thoughts of midday snacks start hitting, set your sights on **Bah's Bakehouse** (26 Water St., 207/326-9510, www.bahsworld. com, 7 A.M.–5 P.M., June–Sept.; hours vary in off-season, $2–9), where the cases are filled with strawberry and cream croissants, snickerdoodle cookies, and giant honey shortbreads.

The dining room of the ◖ **Pentagöet** (26 Main St., 207/326-8616, www.pentagoet. com, 8 A.M.–10 P.M. daily mid-May–Sept., $17–26) has a refined colonial ambience that somehow strangely sympathizes with the Ella Fitzgerald and Louis Armstrong crooning in the background. The menu is an impeccable mix of New England seafood and homemade pastas, highlighted by haute cuisine accents like white truffle oil, goat cheese cream, and tarragon bourride.

Information
A walking tour and shopping guide produced by the **Castine Merchants Association** (207/326-8526) is available at various locations downtown.

BLUE HILL
Smack dab between Castine and Bar Harbor, the town of Blue Hill is a charming combination of opposites. Founded late for the area, in 1762, the town struck pay dirt in the late 1900s when copper mines brought thousands of hungry speculators to the peninsula. A more sober trade developed with granite quarries, and the homes of the granite barons still grace the town. Later, during the Victorian era, the "rusticators" came to the town in the summers for its natural beauty. In the 1960s, the character of the town changed again as back-to-the-landers came to the peninsula year-round, bringing with them a funky spirit that remains today in the many art galleries and bookstores nestled among the food co-ops.

Sights
If Leonardo da Vinci had lived in Maine at the turn of the 19th century, he might have been Jonathan Fisher, a preacher who dabbled in painting, poetry, farming, and literally dozens of other fields. Memorabilia and items made by the man himself are on view at the **Jonathan Fisher House** (44 Mines Rd., 207/374-2459, www.jonathanfisherhouse.org, 1–4 P.M. Thurs.–Sat. July–mid-Oct., $5). With a small aquarium and exhibit space, the **MERI Center for Marine Studies** (55 Main St., 207/374-2135, www.meriresearch.org, 9 A.M.–5 P.M. Mon.–Fri., year-round, 9 A.M.–3 P.M. Sat., Jul.–Aug., free) provides a great introduction to the sealife of the peninsula and the surrounding coast. The back-to-the-land movement of the 1960s is on full display at the **Good**

Life Center (372 Harborside Rd., Harborside, 207/326-8211, www.goodlife.org, 1–4 P.M. Thu.–Mon. late Jun.–early Sept.; 1–4 P.M. Fri.–Sun. Sept., $5 donation), an homage to the farm of simple-living pioneers Helen and Scott Nearing. Tour guides now conjure up the days of *Mother Earth News* and explain the concepts and challenges involved in "going off the grid."

Entertainment

Three dozen members strong, the **Flash in the Pans** (207/374-2140, www.peninsulapan.org) brings a taste of the Caribbean to Maine with outdoor steel-band concerts around the peninsula all summer long. On alternate Mondays they instigates a street party in the small town of Brooksville.

Shopping

Better than the average gift shop, **New Cargoes** (49 Main St., 207/374-3733, www.newcargoes. com, 9:30 A.M.–5:30 P.M. Mon.–Sat.) sells a range of unique Maine-based gift items, toys, and housewares. The bronze Native American sculptures at the **Jud Hartmann Gallery** (79 Main St., 207/359-2544, www.judhartmann-gallery.com, 10 A.M.–5 P.M. Mon.–Sat., and Sun. if it is cloudy or raining, Jun.–mid-Sept.) give the word "majestic" a new definition

Food

A small sandwich place with picnic tables over-looking the water, **The Pantry** (27 Water St., 207/374-2229, breakfast and lunch, $2–6) serves excellent crab and lobster rolls along with other creative sandwiches. The sense of humor of the staff is exhibited in their specials, which include names like the Crabby Girls and the PMS (crabmeat salad with a dash of hot peppers, if you must know). From the outside, **Blue Moose** (50 Main St., 207/374-3274, www.thebluemooserestaurant.com, 10 A.M.–3 P.M. Mon.–Fri, 7:30 A.M.–3 P.M. Sat.–Sun, 5–9 P.M. Thu.–Mon., $9–19) looks like any old pub, and it feels like one on the inside too—that is, until you get a look at the innovative menu, which includes novelties like

Moroccan *tagine* stew, calypso rubbed pork, and Greek souvlaki.

Information

The **Blue Hill Chamber of Commerce** (107 Main St., 207/374-3242, www.bluehillpeninsula.org) provides information on the town and surrounding area in its office across from the post office.

DEER ISLE

It hits you like a dream—one minute you're driving along a scenic back road of the Blue Hill Peninsula, the next you are confronted with the awesome sight of the soaring suspension bridge that brings you across Eggemoggin Reach to the magical refuge of Deer Isle. A first-time visit to Deer Isle is filled with moments like these. The surprisingly large island was only connected to the mainland in 1939, and seems permanently stuck in that year. Even the profusion of pottery shops, art galleries, and low-key eateries on the waterfront of Deer Isle Village doesn't detract from the small-town quality or views of misty coves and smaller islands that surround it. While it has become a popular destination for moneyed tourists-in-the-know, Deer Isle is a working island first, with lobster boats and fishing gear crowding out the yachts in the Stonington harbor. For devotees who come here to get away from it all, it doesn't get any better than this.

Sights

Enough artifacts and curiosities to while away a rainy afternoon are contained in the **Deer Isle-Stonington Historical Society Museum** (416 Sunset Rd., Deer Isle, 207/367-2629, 1–4 P.M. Wed. and Fri. Jul.–mid-Sept.), which includes displays of period clothing, maritime instruments, ship models, and photos relating to the granite trade.

Entertainment

Originally built in 1893 as a dance hall, **The Stonington Opera House** (Fish Pier, Stonington, 207/367-2788, www.operahousearts.org) was recently renovated into a

MAINE

multi-purpose movie theater, performance center, and community space. Offerings on any given night might include a play-reading, chamber music, or black-and-white film.

Shopping

The island is particularly well-known for its many pottery studios. In the center of Deer Isle Village, **Blue Heron Gallery** (22 Morey Farm Dr., Deer Isle, 207/348-6051, www.blueherondeerisle.com, Jul.–Sept.) features work by faculty at the island's own Haystack School of Crafts, as well as other local potters. Of the island's many art galleries, the **Hoy Gallery** (80 Main St., Stonington, 207/367-2777, www.jillhoy.com, by appointment June–Sept.; closed in winter) is a standout for owner-artist Jill Hoy's colorful Maine seascapes. To really juice up your PB&J, stop by **Nervous Nellies Jams & Jellies** (589 Sunshine Rd., Deer Isle, 800/777-6845, www.nervousnellies.com, 9 A.M.–5 P.M. daily May–Dec.), a local jam maker producing fresh and fruit-filled concoctions with everything from hot peppers to local Maine blueberries for 25 years. Ninety percent of its production is sold out of their little shop on Deer Isle, which doubles as a miniature museum of imaginative sculptures—a lobster playing checkers, a 10-foot flamingo—made by the proprietors from materials foraged from the town dump.

Food

The Fisherman's Friend Restaurant (5 Atlantic Ave., Stonington, 207/367-2442, www.stoningtonharbor.com/fishermansfriend, 11 A.M.–9 P.M. Sun.–Thu., 9 A.M.–10 P.M. Fri.–Sat., late May–mid-Oct., $6–20) lives up to its name, serving the working men of the waterfront with hearty lobster stews, steamed mussels, and homemade pie à la mode. For years, the eclectic Mediterranean cuisine of the Cockatoo restaurant was a staple in Deer Isle vacations. Now chef/owner Susan Carter has moved upscale with a new restaurant at Goose Cove Lodge called, what else, the **C Cockatoo Portuguese Restaurant** (300 Goose Cove Rd., 207/348-2300, www.

goosecovelodgemaine.com, noon–10 P.M. daily, $17–25). Gone is Carter's pet cockatoo, which used to sing and cackle over seaside table. It's replaced by refined versions of Portuguese favorites like *bacalhau* and *paelha,* as well as prime beef and pork dishes. The seafood, caught daily by Carter's husband Bradley, is flapping fresh; and the sunset view over Goose Cove is out-of-this-world.

Information

The **Deer Isle-Stonington Chamber of Commerce** (207/348-6124, www.deerislemaine.com) runs a seasonal information center on Little Deer Isle, just over Singing Bridge.

SPORTS AND RECREATION
Hiking

The mile-long hike up the blueberry-covered **Blue Hill Mountain** lifts you almost 1,000 feet in just an hour or two of hiking. From the fire tower on the summit, a stunning panorama takes in Acadia, the Penobscot Bay islands, and the Camden Hills. The trailhead is located on Mountain Road, off Route 15. Deer Isle has several short hikes to quiet coves, mud flats, and tidal pools, where it's not unusual to spot nesting eagles and osprey. A trail map is available from the **Island Heritage Trust** (3 Main St., 207/348-2455, www.islandheritagetrust.org), which manages the preserves.

Boating

The rocky coves of the peninsula are ready-made for kayaking. **Castine Kayak Adventures** (17 Sea St., 207/866-3506, www.castinekayak.com) offers kayak rentals ($45–60/day), guided tours, moonlight paddles, and overnight trips, including expeditions in search of stunning phosphorescent plankton. Boats leave from Eaton's Wharf in Castine Harbor. Educational nature cruises around Blue Hill Bay and Eggemoggin Reach are offered by the scientists of the **Marine Environmental Research Institute** (www.meriresearch.org, 207/374-2135). Suitable for both children and adults, the three- and four-hour trips go in search of seals, seabirds, eagles, and porpoises.

ACCOMMODATIONS
Under $100
A quick walk from the beach (and equipped with the seaviews you'd expect), **Castine Cottages** (33 Snapp's Way., Castine, 207/326-8003, www.castinecottages.com, $75–150) are two-bedroom standalones with full kitchens, outdoor grills, and very cute décor.

$100-150
Maine Island style gets a dose of sophistication at **The Castine Inn** (33 Main St., Castine, 207/326-4365, www.castineinn.com, $95–195). Rooms are sunny and decorated in soothing tones, queen beds, and delicate window treatments (many of which frame views of the surrounding gardens and nearby harbor). Breakfast is included, and delicious—especially if the apple bread French toast is on offer.

$150-250
On a hill overlooking Castine's picturesque waterfront, the ⓒ **Pentagöet Inn** (26 Main St., Castine, 207/326-8616, www.pentagoet. com, $120–265) is one of the original inns built in the era when "rusticators" arrived via steamship from New York and Boston. The sprawling Queen Anne is full of period details, including vintage lithographs, claw-foot tubs, and elaborate Victorian headboards. A wraparound porch has plenty of rocking chairs for musing, while a wonderful bar area downstairs evokes the Golden Age of Sail with colonial antiques and portraits. Mornings are made easier with Maine blueberries, baked-apple French toast, and "featherbed" eggs. A rustic country lodge turned low-key resort, **Goose Cove Lodge** (Goose Cove Road, Sunset, 800/728-1963, www.goosecovelodgemaine. com, $125–200, cabins $175–550) is worth the price just for the views of its secluded Deer Isle cove. Decor calls to mind an old-school Adirondack hunting lodge, with wide fireplaces and high beamed ceilings. In addition to the main lodge, several luxurious cottages offer even more privacy on the forested grounds. An active children's program and separate dining hall ensure that even parents have time to enjoy the romance.

GETTING THERE AND AROUND
You're better off taking a boat than a bus or train to the Blue Hill Peninsula; public transportation generally bypasses the region on its way from the mid-coast to Acadia. The only viable option by land is to take your own car. To drive to Bucksport from Portland, take I-95 north to exit 109 at Augusta, then U.S. Route 202 and Route 3 east to connect with U.S. Route 1 north (120 mi., 3 hrs.). If you are already heading up U.S. 1 from the Midcoast region, Bucksport is another 20 miles (30 min.) from Belfast. From Bucksport to Castine, head south down Castine Road (15 mi., 20 min.); for Blue Hill head south down Route 15. For Deer Isle, continue south from Blue Hill down Route 15 to the intersection with Route 175, then take a left on Byards Point Road and head over the suspension bridge. From the bridge, continue south on Deer Isle Road to Stonington (25 mi., 45 min.).

ISLE AU HAUT
You'll have to wake up pretty early in the morning to secure passage to the small scrap of Acadia National Park located on this island in Penobscot Bay. In the summer even that won't help you. Only 48 day-trippers are allowed daily on the island—and spots are often booked weeks in advance. If you can get aboard, you'll find one of the most rugged and impossibly gorgeous of all the islands in Penobscot Bay. While it is right next door to Deer Isle and Vinalhaven, Isle Au Haut has remained remote and sparsely populated, mainly because of the parkland that covers its southern half. It gained some notoriety of late because of the book written by captain Linda Greenlaw (of *The Perfect Storm* fame) about her years growing up in a lobster village here, but even that has barely punctured its serenity. About the only thing to do here is hike in the pristine wilderness. The mile-long trail up **Duck Harbor Mountain** is a rigorous climb to

a spectacular vista, while the **Western Head** and **Cliff Trails** offer miles of ocean scenery.

Food and Shopping

You may feel like you've walked into a dream when you stumble across the **Black Dinah Café** (1 Moore's Harbor Rd., 207/335-5010, www. blackdinahchocolatiers.com, May–Sept.) at the end of a wooded trail at the base of an island mountain. You'll *know* you are dreaming when you bite into the decadent chocolates made on-site by **Black Dinah Chocolatiers.** The only way to prove it is real is to buy a bag of lavender dark-chocolate truffles to take home...The café also serves pastries from scratch using local and organic flours, eggs, and cream.

Accommodations

One of the more dramatic places to stay in Maine or anywhere else has long been **The Keeper's House** (Lighthouse Pt., 207/367-2261, www.keepershouse.com), a five-room inn attached by causeway to the gorgeous Robinson's Point Light. While the house has suspended inn operations for the time-being, it still rents out "The Woodshed" ($2000/week), a former storage shed that has been transformed into a snug and cozy cottage with renovated kitchen, bath, and music system. The house is completely off-the-grid, run by windmill and solar power. Water comes from the ocean by way of a desalinizer. For an even more rustic experience, Acadia National Park operates the **Duck Harbor Campground** (207/288-3338, www.nps.gov/acad, mid-May–mid-Oct.), a spartan campground with five lean-to shelters. Be sure to call ahead far in advance to reserve a spot; the park requires campers to fill-out a reservation request ahead of time. When your reservation is confirmed, you are issued a "special use permit" for $25, which you must bring to the island with you. There is no additional charge for the campground. Also, be aware that the mailboat only travels to Duck Harbor from mid-June to late September. Outside of that time period, you'll have to schlep your gear from the Town Landing.

Getting There

Passage to Isle Au Haut is through **Isle Au Haut Boat Company** (Sea Breeze Ave., Stonington, 207/367-5193 or 207/367-6516, www.isleauhaut.com), which operates a mailboat ferry to the island on a first-come, first-serve basis. During summer months, five ferries leave daily Monday through Saturday, and two on Sunday. During the rest of the year, trips shrink to three a day Monday through Saturday. Round-trip fares in-season are $35 adults, $19 children, and include a free return-trip on the same weekend. For an extra $20, you can reserve a bicycle ahead to be ready for when you arrive. The ferry arrives in Isle Au Haut at the town docks; during the summer it continues on to the National Park at Duck Harbor. Be advised, however, that only 48 day-trippers are allowed into the park daily (not including campers). Arrive early at the docks in Stonington.

Acadia Region

Anchored by the only national park in New England, Acadia has a way of fostering superlatives. Explorer Giovanni da Verrazano, when he sailed by in 1524, named the area after the dramatic shoreline of the part of Greece known as Arcadia. The first settlers of the area simply called their town Eden (which has since become the more prosaic Bar Harbor, a giant tourist trap that has become anything but paradise). Subsequent generations of artists and aristocrats sought out the area for its wilderness scenery, carving out and preserving the park for future generations.

The region's earliest settlers were a mix of French and British explorers who fought it out over the area. In fact, the pronunciation for Mount Desert is a hybrid of French and English, pronounced by the locals as "mount dessert." (The original name, l'Ile des Monts Déserts means "Island of Bare Mountains.") After generations of Native Americans, French missionaries, lobstermen, and granite traders had lived on **Mount Desert Island,** it was finally "discovered" in 1844. That's when painters such as Thomas Cole and Frederic Church first came from the Hudson River School to Acadia, and were struck by its natural beauty. Calling themselves "rusticators," the painters lived simply with native families and captured the cliffs and seacoast of the island with their brushes. When the well-to-do of the period saw these paintings, they decided to see this "eden" for themselves, and successive waves of Vanderbilts, Astors, Rockefellers, and Fords took the long steamship ride here from New York and Philadelphia. Most of the grand summer cottages they built sadly burned down in the great fire of 1947, which claimed some 200 buildings on the island. The Victorians' legacy, however, lives on in Acadia National Park, which was formed out of land that was bought up and preserved by the descendants of the summer folk.

While the national park takes up the bulk of the island, it is by no means the only thing on it. The boisterous summer community of Bar Harbor is a draw for families and teenagers; scattered around the island, other towns are a mix of yachting anchorages and lobstering villages.

ELLSWORTH AND TRENTON

For those on their way to Mount Desert Island (MDI), the towns of Ellsworth and Trenton are better known as summertime traffic bottlenecks. Ellsworth has been working hard to gentrify its gritty downtown; aside from a few historic homes, however, it still has a ways to go. Trenton, meanwhile, has pinned its fortunes to the passing parade of cars. The five-mile-long gauntlet along Route 3 offers a bewildering assortment of mini-golf courses, waterslides, paddle-boats, petting zoos, gift shops, lobster pounds, blueberry stands, and other enticements. Blindfold the children if you don't want to stop!

Sights

Named for its one-time owner, not its color, the 1828 Black House is now home to the **Woodlawn Museum** (Surry Rd/Rte. 172 & W. Main St., Ellsworth, 207/667-8671, www.woodlawnmuseum.com, 10 A.M.–5 P.M. Tues.–Sat., 1–4 P.M. Sun. June–Sept.; 1–4 P.M. Tues.–Sun. May and Oct., $10 adults, $3 children 5–12, free children under 5), one of Maine's best historic house museums. The Georgian home is full of antique furniture, rare books, and unique artifacts. Behind the home are barns full of more treasures and two miles of walking trails. Part authentic Maine and part P. T. Barnum, **The Great Maine Lumberjack Show** (Rte. 3/Bar Harbor Rd., Trenton, 207/667-0067, www.mainelumberjack.com, 7 P.M. daily mid-June–late Aug., $8.75 adult, $6.75 children) showcases the obscure sports of axe-throwing, log-rolling, speed climbing, and more.

Food

If you can't wait for Acadia to dig into your lobster, the **Trenton Bridge Lobster Pound** (1237 Bar Harbor Rd./Rte 3., Trenton, 207/667-2977, www.trentonbridgelobsterpound.com, Mon.–Sat., late May–mid-Oct., $8–25) has been serving steamed crustaceans to parkgoers for more than 40 years. It has a great view of Mount Desert Island over the bridge. The surest sign that Ellsworth is polishing its image is **Cleonice Mediterranean Bistro** (112 Main St., Ellsworth, 207/664-7554, www.cleonice.com, lunch from 11:30 A.M., dinner from 5 P.M. daily, $19–25), an old diner with high-backed wooden booths and a gleaming wooden bar that's been renovated into an upscale tapas bar and restaurant. Entrées draw from North African, Italian, and Iberian influences.

Information

The **Ellsworth Area Chamber of Commerce** (163 High St./Rte. 1, Ellsworth, 207/667-5584, www.ellsworthchamber.org) has a fine selection of brochures for the town and surrounding region.

MAINE

BAR HARBOR

It's hard to imagine a more appropriate foil for the beauty of Acadia than this tacky tourist town perched on the right-hand shoulder of Mount Desert Island. Around a central town common are streets clogged with T-shirt shops, ice cream parlors, pizza places, and gift shops. (Need something with a moose, lobster, or blueberry on it? You've come to the right place.) Then again, this is Maine after all, so nothing about the town is *too* garish. And if you've been traveling around the North Woods and craving action and nightlife, this just may be your oasis.

Sights

Yes, there really is a bar in Bar Harbor, and no, it's not the kind you are thinking of. When the tide recedes, it's possible to walk out to **Bar Island** in the middle of Frenchmen's Bay. Just be sure not to linger, lest the tide strand you for the next twelve hours (the bar is exposed for three to four hours at a time). Few traces remain of Maine's first inhabitants, the Wabanaki, or "People of the Dawn." What artifacts remain have been gathered at the **Abbe Museum** (26 Mount Desert St., 207/288-3519, www.abbemuseum.org, 10 A.M.–6 P.M. daily late May–early Nov.; 10 A.M.–4 P.M. Thu.–Sat. early Nov.–late May, $6 adults, $2 children 6–15, free children under 6 and Native Americans) a comprehensive and sensitively curated museum of Native American culture. Far from just a happy homage to the "noble savage," the museum both celebrates Native culture and complicates it with moving exhibits of the persecution and prejudice faced by Native peoples in New England.

Photographs of the well-to-do frolicking during Bar Harbor's Victorian heyday are on display at the **Bar Harbor Historical Society** (33 Ledgelawn Ave., 207/288-3807, www.barharborhistorical.org, 1–4 P.M. Mon.–Sat. June–Oct.; open by appt. in winter, free), founded just a year before the Great Fire of 1947. For a more hands- (and feet-)on view of history, take a walking tour of downtown Bar Harbor with **Mount Desert Island Tours** (207/460-

1682, www.mditours.com), which takes in the Gilded Age cottages that survived the fire with several different themed tours every summer, and also customizes tours for groups.

Learn all about lobsters at the **Mount Desert Oceanarium** (1351 Rte. 3, 207/288-5005, www.theoceanarium.com, 9 A.M.–5 P.M. Mon.–Sat. mid-May–late Oct., $15 adults, $10 children), a bayside nature center with lobster museum and hatchery, live seals, and marsh trails.

Entertainment

Dinner and a movie was never as enticing as at **Reel Pizza Cinerama** (33 Kennebec Pl., 207/288-3811, www.reelpizza.net, $15–23), which serves up piping-hot pies and beer and wine to go with mass-market and art-house films.

Shopping

Many of the shops in Bar Harbor sell variations on a theme—lobster and moose stuffed animals, T-shirts, Christmas ornaments, and other Maine-themed souvenirs. One exception is **In the Woods** (160 Main St., 207/288-4519, 10 A.M.–6 P.M. Sun.–Thu., 10 A.M.–8 P.M. Fri.–Sat., May–Oct.), a two-level store that sells everything you could imagine being made out of wood, from kitchen implements to toys to furniture imported from India. Before you go on a wildlife expedition, stop by **Sherman Books & Stationery** (56 Main St., 207/288-3161, www.shermans.com, 9 A.M.–9 P.M. daily May–Oct.; 9 A.M.–6 P.M. daily Nov.–Apr.), which carries an exceptional selection of bird-watching and wildlife guides and trail maps in addition to a full stock of books and cards. Almost as much a playground as it is a toy store, **Stone Soup** (113 Main St., 207/288-5219, www.stonesouptoys.com, 10 A.M.–6 P.M. Mon.–Fri., 10 A.M.–5 P.M. Sat.–Sun.) stocks plenty of high-quality gifts for kids, from wooden rocking horses and fantasy flight games to hand-knit sweaters.

Food

Northern Maine may be the last place you'd expect to find a good burrito. But **Gringo's**

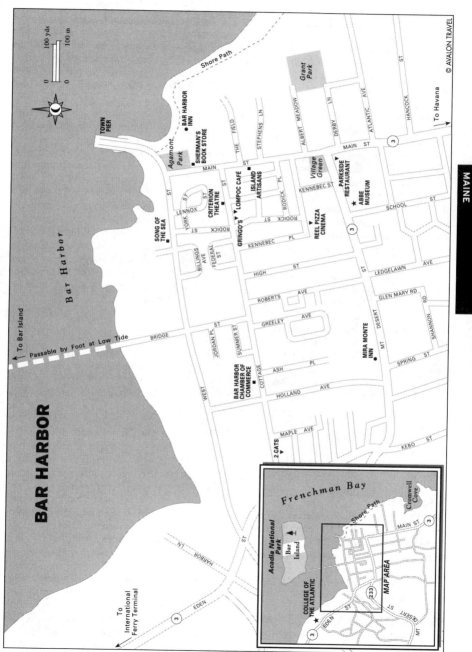

MAINE

© AVALON TRAVEL

(30 Rodick St., 207/288-2326, late May–mid-Oct.,$5–7) delivers with a range of flavors (pesto, mole, Thai), supplemented with addictive homemade salsas. The *only* place for brunch is **2 Cats** (130 Cottage St., 207/288-2808, 7 A.M.–1 P.M. daily year-round, $4–9), a funky spot acclaimed for its omelets and three kinds of eggs Benedict. At **Lompoc Cafe** (36 Rodick St., 207/288-9392, www.lompoc-cafe.com, 11:30 A.M.–1 A.M. daily mid-Apr.–Nov., $8–18) you could easily do a taste test of Maine-brewed beers. The friendly tavern has Bar Harbor's own Atlantic Brewing Co. as well as Casco Bay, Sea Dog, and Geary's on tap, along with a range of creative sandwiches and entrées. The young, local crowd is a welcome respite from the tourist bars. An outdoor patio and bocce court out back is especially popular in the summer.

Latin–New England fusion works at **Havana** (318 Main St., 207/288-2822, www.havana-maine.com, 5–10 P.M. nightly, Apr.–Oct. and mid-Dec.–early Jan., $16–35), a classy eatery with a great wine list and minimalist vibe. Dishes include lobster with lime-cilantro butter and black-bean-and-Dijon-crusted rack of lamb. Solid and classic dishes have made regulars out of many a local at **Parkside Restaurant** (185 Main St., 207/288-3700, www.theparksiderestaurant.com, 12 P.M.–3 P.M. and 5 P.M.–11 P.M., Mon.–Fri.; 5 P.M.–11 P.M. Sat.–Sun., $18–29). American staples like boiled lobster dinners and grilled steaks are the menu's biggest draws. Don't leave without a bite of blueberry pie.

Information

Everything you need to know about Bar Harbor can be learned at **Bar Harbor Chamber of Commerce** (93 Cottage St., 207/288-5103, www.barharbormaine.com). Before crossing the bridge, stop by the Acadia Welcome Center at 1201 Bar Harbor Rd. in Trenton for all the brochures you could ever want.

◖ ACADIA NATIONAL PARK

Sun sparkling on the water. Granite cliffs plunging dizzingly down to rocky coves dotted with lobster buoys. The smell of pine and campfire smoke in the crisp, salty air. The bald heads of the mountains poking through sweaters of spruce. Since the days of the first "rusticators," generations of visitors have fallen under Acadia's spell. Now nearly 3 million people visit the park (www.nps.gov/acad) every year, making it the most-visited national park in the system. Yet, even during the height of summer, its 46,000 acres leave plenty of room to spread out and enjoy the scenery. Glacial ponds, cliff-side walks, and mountainous hiking trails are all part of the mix. And while most of the park is located on MDI, the two sections off-island leave even more elbow room for roaming. The Schoodic Peninusla north of MDI is a perfect day trip to hiking trails on secluded coves. Plan ahead for the trip to Isle Au Haut, an undeveloped lobstering island where only 48 visitors are permitted each day (see the *Blue Hill Peninsula* section in this chapter for more information).

Park Loop Road

The best way to see the park on a short trip or to get an overview for longer stays is a drive on this highway, which does a lazy circle around the entire eastern side of the island. To enter the park, you'll need to get a visitors pass ($20/vehicle), which is good for a week from the purchase date. The **Acadia National Park Visitors Center** (Park Loop Rd., 207/288-3338, www.nps.gov/acad) not only provides maps and passes, it's also where you can pick up an audio tour to enhance the ride. (Note: while the visitors center is open year-round, most of the Park Loop Road, including Cadillac Mountain, is closed from December to mid-April.) The road rises steeply from the visitors center to **Sieur de Monts Spring,** where a garden and nature center give an overview of the park's flora and fauna. Along the rocky coast that follows, be sure to stop at **Thunder Hole,** a natural waterspout that is particularly active an hour or two before high tide. The horizon opens up with **Otter Cliffs,** granite cliffs shot through with crystals of quartz and feldspar that are the highest on the eastern seaboard.

ACADIA'S CARRIAGE ROADS

Worried that Mount Desert Island would get destroyed by the introduction of automobiles, starting in 1913 John D. Rockefeller Jr. oversaw the building of a vast network of roads that would be closed to motorized traffic. Today, the 57 miles of crushed-stone and paved roads are perfect for walking and biking. The roads curve gently through a forest of birch, beech, and maple trees, over hand-carved granite bridges and through tunnels and arches. A *Carriage Road User's Map* is available from the Park Service, and bicycles can be rented in Bar Harbor from **Acadia Bike** (48 Cottage St., 800/526-8615, www.acadiabike.com). If you'd rather see the roads the way they were meant to be seen, **Carriages in the Park** (Wildwood Stables, Park Loop Rd., 207/276-3622, $6-22) offers a range of tours in horse-drawn carriages, including tours of stone bridges, trips to Jordan Pond for popovers, and a sunset climb of Cadillac Mountain.

Short trails take hikers through the primeval forest that was spared by the great fire. After the turn back inland, the **Jordan Pond House** was the traditional stopping-off point for afternoon tea and hot popovers. A new building constructed in 1979 carries on the tradition. After Jordan Pond, be sure to note **Bubble Rock,** a glacial moraine that looks precariously balanced on the slope above. Finally, a side road rises through a series of switchbacks to the park's grand attraction, the 1,532-foot **Cadillac Mountain,** where thousands gathered for the millennium to be the first to see the sun in the United States. From the parking lot near the summit, visitors can take a short hike to the peak for a stunning view of the island-dotted waters of the Gulf of Maine below.

Hiking and Biking

In addition to the walk out to the bar, the ocean path to Otter Cliffs, and the Carriage Roads, the park has many more strenuous hikes. One of the more popular is the **Bubble Rock Trail,** a moderate, mile-long ascent to the tippy boulder. More harrowing is the aptly named **Precipice Trail,** the park's most challenging trail, which climbs iron rungs and ladders to the top of Champlain Mountain. Plan for a whole day to hike up to the summit of Mount Cadillac. The four-mile **North Ridge Trail** climbs gradually with spectacular views of Frenchman Bay. The more difficult **South Ridge Trail** climbs for almost eight miles up the granite cliff-face.

The **Bar Harbor Ferry** (207/288-2984, www.barharborferry.com) makes the trip to the tiny town of Winter Harbor in the Schoodic Peninsula section of the park (late Jun.–Aug.), where a 12-mile bike loop provides spectacular views of scenery and surf. You can rent a bike in Bar Harbor, or call the ferry to arrange a rental.

Swimming

If you are feeling the need to be chilled to the bone, visit **Sand Beach,** the island's only sandy stretch. More pleasant are the rocky ledges of **Echo Lake,** a glacial pond popular with swimmers and windsurfers. More secluded is the small **Lake Wood.** The rocks mid-way on the east side of the pond have been traditionally clothing-optional, though rangers have been cracking down on the practice.

Boating

No trip to Acadia is complete without getting out on the water in some way. Luckily, boat operators offer dozens of ways to do that. The four-masted *Margaret Todd* (207/288-4585, www.downeastwindjammer.com, $35 adult, $33 senior, $25 children 6–11, $5 children 2–5, free children under 2) will give you your windjammer fix with ranger-narrated cruises from Bar Harbor. (Bring a bone for the boat's first mate, Maggie.) The smaller lobster sloop *Chrissy* (207/288-2373, $38 adults, $28 children under 12) sails with a maximum of six passengers. Stop by **Maine State Sea Kayak**

(254 Main St., Southwest Harbor, 877/481-9500, www.mainestatekayak.com) to command a vessel of your own (half-day tour, $44). Canoes and kayaks from **National Park Canoe Rental** (Pretty Marsh Rd./Rte. 102, northern tip of Long Pond, 207/244-5854, www.nationalparkcanoerental.com, $44–52/day) plys the gentler waters of Long Pond.

Nature Cruises

One of the most entertaining ways you can spend an afternoon in Acadia is at the **Dive-In Theater** (College of the Atlantic, 105 Eden St., Bar Harbor, 207/288-3483, www.div-ered.com, $35 adults, $30 seniors, $25 children 5–11, $10 children under 5), during which the gregarious "Diver Ed" dives into the deep with an underwater camera while Ed's wife Edna narrates on board the R/V *Starfish Enterprise*. Back on the boat, Ed brings up lobsters, crabs, starfish and other critters for the kids to touch. Reservations required; park in the north lot of the College of the Atlantic, and meet Ed at the Door Museum of Natural History on campus. Captain John checks the traps on **Lulu Lobster Boat Ride** (55–56 West St., Bar Harbor, 207/963-2341, www.lululobsterboat.com, $30 adults, $27 seniors and military, $17 children 2–12, free children under 2) while sharing lobstering history and folklore. Leaving from Bass Harbor, **Island Cruises** (Shore Rd., Bass Harbor, 207/244-5785) takes low-key cruises to see ospreys, eagles, seals, and heron among the small islands of Blue Hill Bay.

Camping

The park has two campgrounds with a range of tent sites and lean-tos. Right on Park Loop Road, **Blackwoods Campground** (Rte. 3, 800/365-2267, www.nps.gov/acad, $20 per site May–Oct.; free Nov.–Apr.) requires reservations far in advance to secure a spot. In the southwest corner of the park, **Seawall Campground** (Rte. 102A, 207/244-3600, www.nps.gov/acad, $20 per drive-in site, $14 per walk-in tent site) is first-come, first-served, but plan on getting there early in the morning during busy summer months to have even a chance of snagging a spot.

ELSEWHERE ON MOUNT DESERT ISLAND

Not all of MDI is taken up by the wilds of Acadia. In fact, the half dozen small villages hugging its shores are a mix of fishing communities and playgrounds for the rich and famous. As summer resident Samuel Eliot Morrison once said, to live in Bar Harbor you needed "money but no brains," to live in Northeast Harbor you needed "brains but no money," and in Southwest Harbor you didn't need either. Times have changed a bit since then—money, and lots of it, is definitely required to spend much time in both Northeast Harbor and Southwest Harbor, the twin anchorages on corresponding sides of Somes Sound, a deep, glacially carved fjord that cuts the island in half. Of the two, Northeast Harbor is a bit more upscale, with yachts crowding out the harbor and upscale galleries and antiques shops lining Main Street. Southwest is calmer, with small boutiques and fishing vessels thrown into the mix.

At the tip of the fjord, Somesville was the first settlement on the island, dating back to 1761, and still has a number of historic buildings. The fishing villages of Bass Harbor and Tremont, to the west, are your best options for quiet seclusion, while Seal Harbor is the former location of Rockefeller's cottage, and provides an air of refined quietude.

Sights

Second to Audubon, no name perhaps is more sacred to bird-lovers than Wendell Gilley, who spent his life carving surprisingly realistic wooden birds. The **Wendell Gilley Museum** (Main St. & Herrick Rd., Southwest Harbor, 207/244-7555, www.wendellgilleymuseum.org, 10 A.M.–4 P.M. Tues.–Sun. June–Oct.; 10 A.M.–4 P.M. Fri.–Sun. May and Nov.–Dec.; by appt. Jan.–Apr., $5 adults, $2 children 5–12, free children under 5) showcases the best of his work, along with woodcarving demonstrations. The brass and chrome are blinding at

MAINE

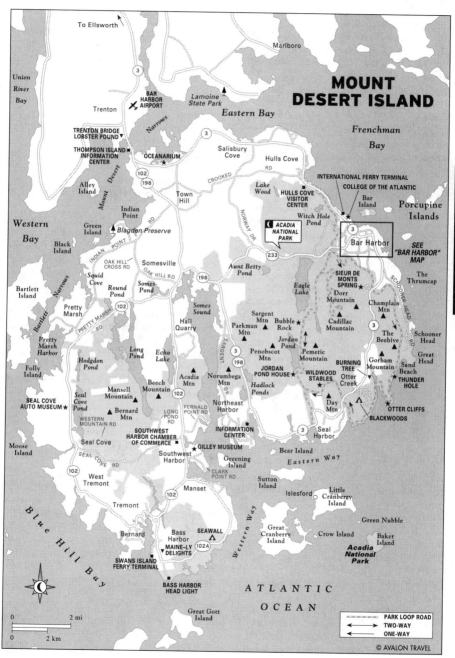

MOUNT DESERT ISLAND

To Ellsworth

Union River Bay

Marlboro

Trenton

Bar Harbor Airport

Lamoine State Park

Eastern Bay

Frenchman Bay

TRENTON BRIDGE LOBSTER POUND ▼
THOMPSON ISLAND INFORMATION CENTER ■

OCEANARIUM ★

Salisbury Cove

Hulls Cove

HULLS COVE RD

INTERNATIONAL FERRY TERMINAL
COLLEGE OF THE ATLANTIC

Bar Island

Porcupine Islands

Mount Desert Narrows

CROOKED RD

Lake Wood

HULLS COVE VISITOR CENTER

Witch Hole Pond

Bar Harbor

SEE "BAR HARBOR" MAP

The Thrumcap

Alley Island

Town Hill

ACADIA NATIONAL PARK

Western Bay

Green Island

Indian Point

Blagden Preserve ▲

Black Island

Somesville

OAK HILL CROSS RD

OAK HILL RD

Aunt Betty Pond

Eagle Lake

SIEUR DE MONTS SPRING ★

SCHOONER HEAD

Squid Cove

Round Pond

Somes Pond

Dorr Mountain ▲

Champlain Mtn ▲

Bartlett Island

Pretty Marsh

PRETTY MARSH RD

Hall Quarry

Somes Sound

Sargent Mtn ▲

Bubble Rock ★

Cadillac Mountain ▲

Schooner Head

The Beehive ▲

Pretty Marsh Harbor

Long Pond

Echo Lake

Parkman Mtn ▲

Jordan Pond

Penobscot Mtn ▲

Pemetic Mountain ▲

Great Head

Folly Island

Hodgdon Pond

Beech Mountain ▲

Acadia Mtn ▲

Norumbega Mtn ▲

JORDAN POND HOUSE ★

BURNING TREE

WILDWOOD STABLES ★

Gorham Mountain ▲

Sand Beach

THUNDER HOLE ★

SEAL COVE AUTO MUSEUM ★

Mansell Mountain ▲

Hadlock Ponds

Otter Creek

Seal Cove Pond

Bernard Mtn ▲

FERNALD POINT RD

Northeast Harbor

Day Mtn ▲

OTTER CLIFFS ★

BLACKWOODS ⚲

Moose Island

WESTERN MOUNTAIN RD

SOUTHWEST HARBOR CHAMBER OF COMMERCE ■

LONG POND RD

INFORMATION CENTER ■

Seal Harbor

Seal Cove

SEAL COVE RD

GILLEY MUSEUM ★

Southwest Harbor

Bear Island

Eastern Way

West Tremont

CLARK POINT RD

Greening Island

Sutton Island

Islesford

Little Cranberry Island

Green Nubble

Tremont

Manset

Bass Harbor

SEAWALL ⚲

102A

Western Way

Great Cranberry Island

Crow Island

Baker Island

Blue Hill Bay

Bernard

MAINE-LY DELIGHTS ▼

Acadia National Park

SWANS ISLAND FERRY TERMINAL

BASS HARBOR HEAD LIGHT

ATLANTIC OCEAN

Great Gott Island

0   2 mi

0   2 km

Great Cranberry Island

	PARK LOOP ROAD
←→	TWO-WAY
←	ONE-WAY

© AVALON TRAVEL

the **Seal Cove Auto Museum** (1414 Tremont Rd. & Pretty Marsh Rd., Southwest Harbor, 207/244-9242, www.sealcoveautomuseum. org, 10 A.M.–5 P.M. daily late May–mid-Oct., $5 adults, $4.50 seniors, $2 children 12 and under), which has more than 100 antique autos and dozens of vintage motorcycles on display. The red glow of **Bass Harbor Light** (Lighthouse Rd., off Rte. 102A, Bass Harbor) perches moodily on the rocks in the southwest corner of the island; it's a favorite for both photographers and romantics.

Shopping

Invest in the kind of artwork bound to become a family heirloom at **Clark Point Gallery** (46 Clark Point Rd., Southwest Harbor, 207/244-0290, www.clarkpointgallery.com, 12 P.M.–5 P.M. Tues.–Sat. mid-June to Labor Day; closed in winter). Here, paintings are all 19th and 20th century depictions of Maine—mostly Mount Desert Island. **Hatched on MDI** (360 Main St., Southwest Harbor, 207/244-9800, www.hatchedonmdi.com, 10 A.M.–5 P.M. Mon.–Sat. year-round) carries the cutest kids' clothes you are liable ever to see. It also sells adult sweaters emblazoned with NEH and SWH—so you can choose and display your allegiance. Part gallery, part gift shop, **Flying Mountain Artisans** (28 Main St., Southwest Harbor, 207/244-0404, www.flyingmountainartisans.net, 10 A.M.–5 P.M. Mon.–Fri., 10 A.M.–4 P.M. Sat.) lines its walls with watercolors and paintings by local artists in one corner, and stocks handmade, intricate quilts, pottery, jewelry, and children's clothing in the other.

Food

Karen Holmes Godbout started out selling hot dogs and donuts to fisherman; ◖ **Maine-ly Delights** (Grandville Rd., Bass Harbor, 207/244-3656, www.bassharbormaine.com, 11 A.M.–9 P.M. early Jun.–early Sept., $2–15) has now grown to a seafood shack par excellence, specializing in delicious crab rolls served in an unfussy environment. Sundays are known for her special crabmeat quiche. Bliss

out with a fantastic view of the water over basic-but-fresh fish specials at **Seafood Ketch** (1 McMullen Ave., Bass Harbor, 207/244-7463, 11 A.M.–9:30 P.M. Tues.–Sat., 11 A.M.–8 P.M. Sun.–Mon., June–Sept., $2–15). Popular with sailors, **Red Sky** (14 Clark Point Rd., Southwest Harbor, 207/244-0476, www.redskyrestaurant.com, 5:30–9 P.M. Tue.–Sat. May–Oct., $19–27) is a minimalist bistro that follows the current trend of all-natural food, simply prepared. Its signature dish is grey sole stuffed with lobster and Maine shrimp with béarnaise sauce. Between Bar Harbor and Northeast Harbor, **Burning Tree** (69 Otter Creek Dr./Rte. 3, Otter Creek, 207/288-9331, 5–10 P.M. Wed.–Mon. Jun.–mid-Oct.) has won raves for its out-of-the-ordinary seafood concoctions. Think curry pecan flounder and crab cakes bursting with fresh crab meat. The secret of this sophisticated hotspot is definitely out—be sure to make reservations.

Information

The **Southwest Harbor/Tremont Chamber of Commerce** (Rte. 102 and Seal Cove Rd., 207/244-9264, www.acadiachamber.com) covers the west side of the island. For information on the east side, pick up the **Northeast Harbor Port Guide** (207/276-5040, www.visitnortheastharbor.com), available from many area businesses.

ACCOMMODATIONS
Under $100

There are literally thousands of beds on MDI, which helps to keep prices low even in the summer. Some of the cheapest are at **Robbins Motel** (Rte. 3, Bar Harbor, 207/288-4659, www.acadia.net/robbins, May–mid-Oct., $58), which features the rates of yesteryear and rooms to match. Amenities, such as they are, include cable TV, a pool, and free Wi-Fi. Reserve ahead for the best rates.

$100–150

In the center of Southwest Harbor, **Penury Hall** (374 Main St., Southwest Harbor, 207/244-7102, www.penuryhall.com, $130) is a bed-and-breakfast located on the former site of Fort Prentice—signified by the replica of the cannon out front. The bright-green living room is full of puzzles, games, and a cat to keep guests occupied, while rooms are nautically themed and snug. Other perks include a canoe for borrowing and a sauna for relaxing after a hard day on the trails.

$150-250

Inhabiting one of the few surviving summer cottages in Bar Harbor, **⬛ Mira Monte Inn** (69 Mt. Desert St., Bar Harbor, 800/553-5109, www.miramonte.com, $170–245) captures an Old World feeling without any pretension. The rooms are full of little luxuries, like a wood stove, whirlpool tub, and warm towel racks, while an amazing breakfast spread ensures you'll have the energy for your outdoor pursuits. On that front, owner Marian Burns is one of the first bed-and-breakfast operators in town, and is full of advice on secret spots in the park. Gardens full of cranberries, blueberries, and thyme stretch out in back of the Victorian **Maison Suisse House** (144 Main St., Northeast Harbor, 207/276-5223, www.maisonsuisse.com, $175–395), which was named by a former owner from Switzerland. Located in Northeast Harbor village, the shingle-style summer cottage has fireplaces in the common rooms and tasteful, individually decorated guest rooms. Breakfast, either sit-down or take-out, is included from the restaurant/ bakery across the street.

$250 and Up

The grande dame of Bar Harbor is unquestionably the **Bar Harbor Inn** (Newport Dr., Bar Harbor, 207/288-3351 or 800/248-3351, www.barharborinn.com, $200–380), a grand resort hotel overlooking the waterfront. The main building was once the social club for Victorian-era vacationers, and features the requisite Queen Anne turrets and curving circular dining room. The inn has been expanded with a three-story row of rooms overlooking the water, which are luxuriously appointed, if a bit cookie-cutter in style.

GETTING THERE

To drive to Acadia from Portland, take I-95 north to exit 182A at Bangor, then U.S. Route 1A south to Ellsworth (150 mi., 2 hrs. 40 min.). For Bar Harbor, continue south from Ellsworth down Route 3 across the bridge to Mount Desert Island (20 mi., 40 min.).

It's relatively easy to reach Bar Harbor without wheels of your own. **US Airways** (800/428-4322, www.usairways.com) offers direct flights from Boston to Bar Harbor–Hancock County Airport, from whence you can get a free shuttle bus to town. From Canada, **Bay Ferries** (888/249-7245, www.catferry.com) offers once-daily high-speed-car-ferry service between Bar Harbor and Yarmouth, Nova Scotia.

Greyhound (800/552-8737, www.greyhound.com) has cancelled its Boston–Bar Harbor Route, but still operates bus service to Bangor. From there, you can take the **Bar Harbor–Bangor Shuttle** van service (207/479-5911, www.barharborshuttle.com, advance reservation required). You can also take a seasonal bus from Downeast Transportation (207/667-5796, www.downeasttrans.org).

GETTING AROUND

Surprisingly, a car is not necessary to explore Mount Desert Island. The **Island Explorer** (207/667-5796, www.exploreacadia.com) runs a fast, efficient and free fleet of propane-powered buses with routes all over the island, covering most of Park Loop Road and all the villages, hotels, campgrounds, and trailheads. Buses even have bike racks. And talk about cool—on the company website you can tap into a GPS-powered function that shows where each bus is on its route in real time. The same company offers regular bus service throughout Ellsworth and Trenton as well. **Acadia National Park Tours** (207/288-0300, www.acadiatours.com, $27.50 adults, $15 children 12 and under) runs a trolley contracted with the NPS to give sightseeing tours of the Park Loop Road. The two-and-a-half-hour narrated trip includes three 15-minute stops to stretch your legs. Tickets can be purchased from Testa's Restaurant (53 Main St., Bar Harbor).

Downeast

MAINE

Acadia provides a kind of mental barrier for those driving up the coast—southwest of Mount Desert Island is the Maine of picture postcards and windjammer cruises. To the northeast—or "downeast" if you follow the wind—is the *real* Maine, without all of those pretentious art galleries and hoity-toity restaurants. This is a land of honest, working folk and family-style restaurants that haven't changed their menus in decades.

The little-visited region of the state rewards with hidden beauty, both in its rocky, lighthouse-studded coastline, and its interior, honeycombed with blueberry barrens that light up the ground bright red in the fall. The best time to visit is August, when towns are bustling with workers to pick the year's crop, and Downeast towns hold fairs and carnivals to celebrate the harvest.

BANGOR

After Portland and Lewiston, Bangor is the third-largest city in Maine. Taken together with the suburb of Orono, it's also home to the state's largest public university, the University of Maine, which enrolls some 10,000 students. The young energy infuses some life into the city, making it a bit less dreary than its shuttered downtown might first suggest. But the city's heyday as a lumbering capital is far behind it. Founded by explorers looking for Norumbega, the lost city of gold, Bangor was the world's center of lumber production by the 1830s, when you could walk across the Penobscot River on logs floated down from its sawmills to the shipbuilding centers of the Midcoast. In the 20th century, the downtown was gutted by misguided urban renewal, and remains an uninviting place. In the shuttered storefronts and wind whistling beneath the bridges, you can almost imagine yourself in a novel by Stephen King, the city's favored son.

◖ Stephen King Tour

Born in Portland, Stephen King came to Orono

to attend college and has remained in the area ever since. His home, a creepy Victorian with a wrought-iron spider gate on West Broadway, is a must-see for any serious fan. But nothing really captures the spirit of the books like the wildly popular **Tommyknockers and More** (800/916-6673 or 207/947-5205, www.bangorcvb.org, $12), a monthly bus tour given by the local visitors bureau. The "master of horror" has been a huge booster of the city, filming many of the movie adaptations of his books here. Among the sites on the tour is the cemetery featured in the film *Pet Sematary,* in which King himself had a cameo as a minister, and many of the sites that inspired *It,* including "the barrens," the canal, and the standpipe where Pennywise the Clown may still lurk. The tour's schedule is sporadic, though you can count on its being offered at least once a month in summer. Due to its popularity, advance reservations are required.

Other Sights

A first-rate collection of contemporary work is housed at the **University of Maine Museum of Art** (Norumbega Hall, 40 Harlow St., 207/561-3350, www.umma.umaine.edu, 10 A.M.–5 P.M. Mon.–Sat., $3 adults, free children under 6), which features the art of Roy Lichtenstein, Richard Estes, and David Hockney.

Events

The city comes alive every August for the **American Folk Festival** (207/992-2630, www.americanfolkfestival.com), which brings 150,000 spectators to the Bangor waterfront to see the top names in folk and to tie up traffic for miles.

Shopping

The cramped **Betts Bookstore** (584 Hammond St., 207/947-7052, www.bettsbooks.com, 9 A.M.–3 P.M. Mon.–Fri.; 9:15 A.M.–2 P.M. Sat.) is a Stephen King fan's dream, with autographed first editions and

BIG PAUL

Minnesota can say whatever it wants, but as far as Maine is concerned, Paul Bunyan and his blue ox, Babe, hail from Bangor. The first stories of the mythical lumberjack started appearing in a newspaper in Detroit in 1910, when the larger-than-life figure became a symbol of the can-do spirit of American industry. But according to the traditional tall tales, Bunyan was born in Maine, where he weighed more than 100 pounds at birth, and as a child needed the milk of ten cows, fifty eggs, and ten pounds of potatoes every day just to sate his appetite. He grew so fast, his parents had to make him a new pair of boots daily just to keep his feet warm. Eventually, Bunyan began to work cutting trees, felling 20 trees with one swoop of his mighty axe. But he soon decided that if he stayed in New England he'd cut down all the trees and the other lumberjacks would be left without income for their families, so he reluctantly headed west to the Great Lakes. Lest anyone forget his roots, however, in 1959 Bangor's town fathers built a **statue of Paul Bunyan** in Bass Park for the city's 125-year anniversary, complete with a time capsule in the base to be opened in 2084. Of course, the statue is smaller than life size, since it's 31 feet high and only weighs 3,700 pounds.

stop restaurant, with lumberjack-sized portions of steak and seafood dishes, Dagwood sandwiches, free bottomless cups of coffee and "wicked good" homemade apple crisp. Authentic South Asian food is served at the family-run **Bahaar Pakistani Restaurant** (23 Hammond St., 207/945-5979, 11 A.M.–9 P.M. Mon.–Thu.; 11 A.M.–10 P.M. Fri.–Sat., $10–15)—with simple but spicy fare that may surprise palates used to Indian food with a markedly different spice combos. Good international fusion can be hard to find in northern Maine. Consider **Thistles Restaurant** (175 Exchange St., 207/945-5480, 11 A.M.–2:30 P.M. and 4:30–9 P.M. Tue.–Sat., $11–26) an oasis, with entrées drawn from South American, Mediterranean, and Greek influences—everything from fettuccini Bolognese to Argentinean-style skirt steak—served with white-tablecloth service. For value-conscious diners all plates are available in half-portions. Tango Tuesdays feature live tango music.

Information

The **Bangor Region Chamber of Commerce** (519 Main St., 207/947-0307, www.bangorregion.com) offers brochures and advice at a visitors center in the shadow of the Paul Bunyan statue.

SUNRISE COAST

Unlike the larger high-bush berries grown in the mid-Atlantic coast, Maine blueberries grow in low-lying bushes, and are much smaller. That doesn't mean, however, they aren't bursting with flavor, and the sweet, tart taste is an annual ritual of summer. The berries grow best in cold, wet climates like the area around the Downeast town of Cherryfield, where every August, acres and acres of blueberry barrens glow with the specks of blue that make them look from a distance like an Impressionist painting. Every year, some 20,000 migrant workers descend on the area for the annual harvest, which lasts for only a few weeks of frenzied activity.

Washington County is the poorest in Maine, and the largest town in the region, Machias, is

photos, as well as T-shirts and other King memorabilia. If you are in the market for a canoe, go to the source—**Old Town Canoe Factory Outlet** (125 Gilman Falls Ave., Old Town, 207/827-1530, 9 A.M.–5 P.M. Tues.–Sat.; closed Sun. and Mon.), headquarters for the world's most popular brand. The factory sells "seconds"—canoes with only slight flaws—at a steep discount, and cuts prices even more at annual spring and fall sales.

Food

Open 24 hours a day, **Dysart's** (Coldbrook Rd., I-95 exit 180, 207/942-4878, www. dysarts.com, $4–19) is the ultimate truck-

MAINE

understandably struggling. Around the area, however, the rugged coastline has an undeniable beauty that is made more stark by the lack of gawking crowds. Maine has only just started marketing this area to tourism. So far, it remains like much of the Maine coast used to be, populated with small, family-style restaurants and simple lodging houses. The pace of life is slow, even by Maine standards, and formal attractions are few and far between. It's easy to lose yourself in long hikes along the coast in the company of puffins and pine trees, or with lingered conversation over coffee in a neighborhood diner.

Sun comes early to the far eastern part of the region, known as "Way Downeast." Even though Calais and surrounding towns are in the same time zone as Boston, they are geographically in line with New Brunswick. It's not surprising that Canadian influence is strong here, as residents move back and forth across the border with relative ease. Native American influence is also felt heavily here. On their reservation on an island off of Eastport, the Passamaquoddy people have done a better job, perhaps, than any other tribe in New England at retaining their traditional way of life.

West Quoddy Head Light

Don't be fooled by the name: West Quoddy Head is actually the farthest east you can drive in the United States. Right at the end is one of the most distinctive lighthouses in the region—a tower that compares with Portland Head and Pemaquid Point as one of the most recognizable in the state. In point of fact, the 49-foot-high tower (Quoddy Head State Park, 973 South Lubec Rd., off Rte. 189, Lubec, 207/733-2180, www.westquoddy.com/, 10 A.M.–4 P.M. daily mid-May–mid-Oct., free) is one of only two in the country painted with red and white stripes—a common practice in Canada, where it helps them stand out against the snow. Depending on your frame of mind, it calls to mind an American flag, a candy cane, or Pippi Longstocking's hose. While the tower is not open to the public, the keeper's house

has a small museum, and the cliffs are prime viewing for seals, bald eagles, and sometimes even whales.

Other Sights

Built around 1818 by lumber magnate Thomas Ruggles, the **Ruggles House** (146 Main St., Columbia Falls, 207/483-4637, www.ruggleshouse.org, 9:30 A.M.–4:30 P.M. Mon.–Sat., 11 A.M.–4:30 P.M. Sun. June–mid-Oct., $5 adults, $2 children 6–12, free children under 6) is one of the best examples of Federal-style architecture in the region, if not the country. Highlights of the restored mini-mansion include the flying staircase in the entry hall and Palladian window upstairs; over half the furniture inside was owned by the Ruggles family.

Shortly after the battles of Concord and Lexington, enterprising Mainers seized the British ship *Margaretta*, in what is considered the first naval engagement of the Revolutionary War. The patriots gathered to plot their mission at **Burnham Tavern** (Rte. 192, one block off Rte. 1, Machias, 207/255-6930, www.burnhamtavern.com, 9:30 A.M.–4 P.M. Mon.–Sat. mid-June–Sept., $5 adults, $0.25 children under 12), now a museum telling the story of the encounter.

Blueberries aren't the only culinary specialty of the region. Now 100 years old, **Raye's Mustard Mill** (83 Washington St., Rte. 190, Eastport, 207/853-4451 or 800/853-1903, www.rayesmustard.com, 9 A.M.–5 P.M. daily, tours 1–3 P.M. Mon.–Fri. and sometimes Sat.) is the last U.S. producer using traditional "cold grind" techniques that preserves the subtle aromatics of seeds and spices. Tours take in the milling process and offer a chance to sample one of 15 varieties.

Entertainment and Events

The **Eastport Arts Center** (36 Washington St., Eastport, 207/853-4650, www.eastportartscenter.com) taps into local creativity with community theater and concerts.

The annual **Machias Wild Blueberry Festival** (Machias, 207/255-6665, www.machiasblueberry.com, late Aug.) starts with a huge blueberry-pancake breakfast and continues with a road race, fish fry, and a church service thanking God for a (hopefully) successful harvest.

Shopping

You can't miss the 50-foot-high bright-blue dome of **Wild Blueberry Land** (1067 Rte. 1, Columbia Falls, 207/483-2583, call for hours), which sells Maine's finest pureed into jams, jellies, syrups, honeys, and the best blueberry smoothies anywhere. Chocoholics nationwide rave about **Bayside Chocolate** (37 Water St., Lubec, 888/816-8880 or 207/733-8880, 8:30 A.M.–6 P.M. Mon.–Sat. May–Oct.; 8:30 A.M.–4 P.M. Mon.–Sat. Nov.–Apr.), a small local business that rivals (and some say surpasses) Godiva. **Bold Coast Smokehouse** (224 County Rd., Lubec, 207/733-8912, www.boldcoastsmokehouse.com, 8:30 A.M.–5 P.M. Mon.–Sat. year-round, 8:30 A.M.–5 P.M. Sun. Jun.–Sept.) carries on the region's smoked-fish tradition with "wicked good" smoked salmon made into lox, *gravlax,* and kabobs.

The fishing village of Eastport is rapidly being transformed into an artists community. Among its many galleries, **The Eastport Gallery** (74 Water St., Eastport, 207/853-4166, www.eastportgallery.com, hours vary) offers one-stop shopping for local work. Another worth visiting is **The Commons Eastport** (51 Water St., Eastport, 207/853-4123, www.commonseastport.com, 10: A.M.–6 P.M. Mon.–Sat., 1 P.M.–5 P.M. Sun. June–Sept.; 10: A.M.–5 P.M. Mon.–Sat., closed Sun. Oct.–May) for its arts as well as crafts—including locally made sweetgrass baskets.

Food

Most restaurants in the area have a sameness to the menu, sporting the tried-and-true surf, turf, and pasta dishes they have served for decades. (The silver lining in the deal is that prices haven't changed much over the years either.) In that category, **Uncle Kippy's** (County Rd., Rte. 189, Lubec, 207/733-2400, www.unclekippys.com, 11:30 A.M.–9 P.M. Mon.–Sat., closed Sun. June–Sept., $8–19) stands at the head of the pack for its fresh-caught seafood, charbroiled steaks, and homemade pizzas. All of Lubec seems to head into **Atlantic House Coffee Shop** (52 Water St., Lubec, 207/733-0906, www.atlantichouse.net, 7 A.M.–3 P.M. daily, $4–12) for breakfast on the weekends, and nearly half the town shows up on weekdays. Do so yourself, and be sure not to bypass the freshly made donuts.

Information

Machias Bay Chamber of Commerce (12 E. Main St., Machias, 207/255-4401, www.machiaschamber.org) has information on the city and surrounding area. **Eastport Area Chamber of Commerce** (72 Water St., Eastport, 207/853-4644, www.eastport.net) covers the towns of "way Downeast."

SPORTS AND RECREATION
Hiking and Biking

Downeast is an outdoors-lover's dream, with dozens of parks full of hiking trials. Many of its trails can be discovered with the help of *Cobscook Trails,* a 55-page booklet produced by the **Quoddy Regional Land Trust** (352 Rte. 1, P.O. Box 49, Whiting, 04691, 207/733-5509, www.qrlt.org). Copies can be mail-ordered for $10 or purchased for $7 at local stores. The little-visited **Maine Coastal Islands National Wildlife Refuge** (Pigeon Hill Rd., Steuben, 207/546-2124, www.fws.gov) has many trails along its miles of rocky coastline. On a clear day, you can see the 123-foot lighthouse on Petit Manan Island. The often fog-shrouded 1,579-acre **Great Wass Island Preserve** (Rte. 187, 207/729-5181, www.nature.org) protects the tip of Jonesport's peninsula with prime territory for bird-watching. Trails of between one and five miles hug the coastline. Named for the summer cottage where President Roosevelt spent time as a boy, the **Roosevelt Campobello International Park** (Campobello Island, off Rte. 189, Lubec, 506/752-2922, www.fdr.net, free) encompasses 2,800 acres on an island off of Lubec, jointly managed between the United States and Canada. Driving roads take in much of the park, but to really get prime views of the rugged Bay of Fundy coast, take the Liberty Point to Raccoon Beach trail, which skirts treacherous cliffs on its way to a sandy beach. For bikers, the **Downeast Route–East Coast Greenway** stretches 140 miles from Ellsworth to Calais, taking in gobs of ocean scenery on the way. Download a free mile-by-mile guide from the website of Maine Department of Transportation (207/624-3250, www.exploremaine.org/bike/downeast.html).

Nature Cruises

Many species of animals call this rugged coast home. The most unique is the Atlantic puffin, a colorful seabird that has perhaps unfairly won the nickname "clown of the sea" for its distinctive red-and-orange beak. **Bold Coast Charter Company** (Cutler, 207/259-4484, www.boldcoast.com, $100 adults, $60 children 14 and under) runs 5-hour trips in-season to Machias Seal Island in search of the gregarious seabirds; knowledgeable guide Andy Patterson explains their ecology en route. Tours leave from the Cutler town harbor; take Route 1 and 191 south into Cutler and look for a blue sign marked "Wharf Road"to locate the launch ramp. The Bay of Fundy is prime whale-watching territory. **Capt. Riddle's Whale Watch Cruises** (727 Friar Bay Rd., 0.5 mile past FDR Parkd., Campobello, New Brunswick, 506/752-2009, www.finback.com, CDN$55 adults, CDN$40 children) makes summertime cruises in search of finback, minke, right, and humpback whales, as well as seals, eagles and other sea creatures. Boats leave from Campobello Island, just over the border in New Brunswick, Canada.

Boating

For a close-up look at sealife and the awesome Bay of Fundy tides, **Cobscook Hikes & Paddles** (207/454-2130, www.cobscookhikesandpaddles.com) leads kayak tours exploring the area between Whiting and Calais. **Sunrise Canoe and Kayak** (68 Hoyttown Rd., Machias, 207/255-3375 or 877/980-2300, www.sunrisecanoeandkayak.com) leads trips on the Machias and St. Croix Rivers as well

as sea-kayaking trips to see Natve American petroglyphs in Machias Bay.

Camping

True to its name, the waterfront **Seaview Campground** (16 Norwood Rd., Eastport, 207/853-4471, www.eastportmaine.com) offers awesome views of the ocean from some of its 70 tent and RV sites on Harrington Cove ($25/tent, $38–48/RV, $43–53/RV with hookup).

ACCOMMODATIONS
Under $100

You won't find any luxury resorts Downeast (at least not yet), but you won't overpay for your room either. Cheap and clean describe the rooms at the **Bluebird Motel** (26 E. Main St., Rte 1, Machias, 207/255-3332, $75–80), an old-school motel with pine-paneled walls, cable TV, and air-conditioning. Outside of South America, not too many bed-and-breakfasts come with the opportunity for a llama trek after breakfast. The **Pleasant Bay B&B and Llama Keep** (386 West Side Rd., Addison, 207/483-4490, www.pleasantbay.com, $50–135), near Cherryfield, is actually located on a working llama farm and offers rides along its trails for $15. Rooms are comfortably decorated with country quilts and a mix of seafaring and llama paraphernalia. Walking into the **Home Port Inn** (45 Main St., Lubec, 207/733-2077, www.homeportinn.com, $95–115) is like entering the pages of a home design magazine. The seven guest rooms are designed with an artist's eye, incorporating pleasing color schemes, cozy quilts, antiques, and folk art. The oversized bed-and-breakfast in the center of Lubec also has an excellent restaurant on-site that serves local seafood and continental cuisine.

$100-150

Small and decked out in country florals and handmade quilts, **Riverside Inn** (Rte 1, East Machias, 207/255-4134, $90–135), lives up to its name with a pretty waterfront location surrounded by well-tended gardens. The inn's library is filled with good reads for cuddling up next to the fire with. Some bathrooms have clawfoot tubs, and rooms have queen-sized beds.

GETTING THERE AND AROUND

To drive to Bangor from Portland, take I-95 north to exit 182A (130 mi., 2 hrs. 10 min.). From Bangor to the Sunrise Coast, take U.S. Route 1A south to Ellsworth (20 mi., 40 min.). From there head north up U.S. Route 1 to Machias (65 mi., 1 hr. 40 min.). To continue along to Lubec, head north from Machias along U.S. 1, then east on Route 189 (30 mi., 45 min.). For Eastport, head north from Machias on Route 191, then east on Route 86 to rejoin U.S. Route 1 at Dennysville; then south on Route 190 at Perry (45 mi., 1 hr. 30 min.). For Calais, head north from Machias

along Route 191 to join U.S. 1 south (45 mi., 1 hr. 15 min.). Alternately to drive to Calais straight from Bangor, take Route 9 east to U.S. 1 south (95 mi., 2 hrs. 30 min.).

Flights arrive at **Bangor International Airport** (287 Godfrey Blvd., Bangor, 207/992-4623, www.flybangor.com) from several domestic carriers, including Delta (Atlanta, Boston, Cincinnati, New York-JFK), US Airways (Philadelphia), and Allegiant Air (Orlando and Tampa).By bus, **Greyhound** (800/552-8737, www.greyhound.com) makes several trips daily to Bangor from Boston, stopping in Portland en route.

West Bus Service (800/596-2823, ww.westbusservice.com) runs a daily bus between Bangorand Calais by way of Ellsworth and Machias. Stops are made by request in other towns along Route 1.

The North Woods

Longtime residents of the state will tell you there are actually "two Maines"—the relatively rich coastline of the south, populated by citified professionals and sunbaked summer folk; and the large, untrammeled acres of the north, sparsely inhabited by poor and working-class folk eking a living out of the land. Nowhere is this more apparent than the far northern expanse of spruce and pine known as the North Woods, which encompass almost 4 million acres of undeveloped wilderness. Talk to any of its residents for any length of time, and you are likely to find a somewhat justified disdain for their southern neighbors, who look upon the area as their own personal playground. The North Woods are unique for their size and wildness, encompassing much of the last old-growth forest in New England, and one of the last truly wild places in the country. Because of that, many Maine environmentalists have fought to lock down the land as a vast ecological preservation, a charge led by the environmental group RESTORE, which has pushed the dream of a three-million-acre

Maine Woods National Park, which would be larger than Yellowstone and Yosemite put together and bring more tourism to the area. That push, however, has been resisted by the residents who make their living from the timber and paper industry, which is still vibrant (though diminished from its 19th- and 20th-century heyday, mostly because of competition from Canada).

The more likely cause of encroachment into the North Woods, however, is likely to be private, not public. Around Moosehead Lake, in particular, a great experiment is currently in the works to develop a portion of the coastline into private homes, while preserving the rest in a pristine state. Environmentalists are critical of the plan, even while many year-round residents are salivating at the prospect of additional taxes and business from summer folk. New developments notwithstanding, visitors to this region come here for one thing: nature. The centerpiece of the North Woods, from an outdoors enthusiast's perspective, is Baxter State Park, which is larger than most national

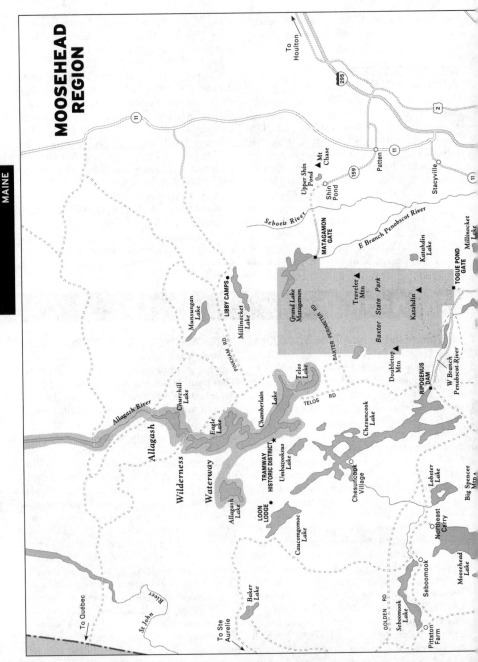

MAINE

MOOSEHEAD REGION

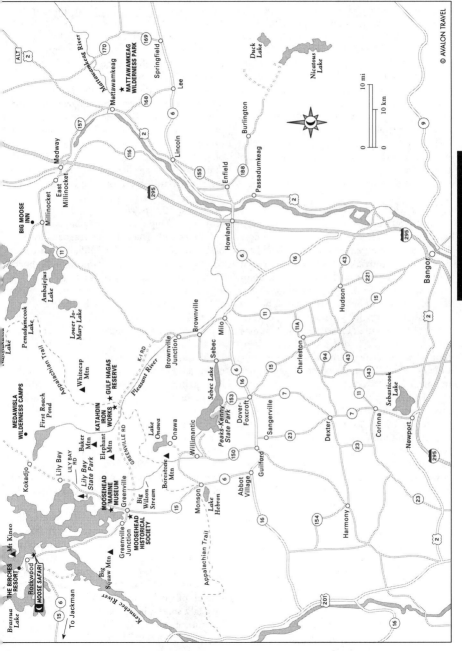

MAINE

parks and crisscrossed with hundreds of miles of trails. The centerpiece of the park, in turn, is Mount Katahdin, which pilgrims climb every year with the spring thaw to start their journey down the Appalachian Trail to Georgia. Further north, the Allagash River attracts more adventurous outdoors-lovers to canoe and kayak its exhilarating Class V rapids. As the state stretches towards Canada, roads become thinner and fewer between, and timber country takes over. In this area, many private hunting and fishing camps still exist, some of them accessible only by seaplane, for the ultimate in wilderness experience.

MOOSEHEAD REGION

It's as if God was putting down a big sign visible from 35,000 feet: Here there will be moose. Moosehead Lake, Maine's largest inland body of water, is unmistakably shaped like a giant antlered head of one of the state's great mammals, stretching from 32 miles from the tip of its top "antler" at Sebomook, to the bottom of its shaggy "mane" at the moose-obsessed town of Greenville. This is Moose Country, all right, with the resorts around the lake offering "moose cruises" and kayak trips up its estuaries to catch glimpses of these gentle, statuesque beasts. (Even though locals will admit they find them to be a nuisance when they meet them in their headlights at night.)

But there's more to the area than moose. The region surrounding the lake abounds with historical tales of riverboat captains, loggers, and fur trappers who over the years have made this rustic area their home. Relatively accessible compared to the forestland further north (it's only a five-and-a-half-hour drive from Boston), Moosehead is also the tourist gateway to the region. But so far that fact has done little to diminish its priceless natural beauty, with Mount Kineo rising majestically from an island in the middle of the lake, and loons cackling from its coves at night.

◖ Moose Safari

Moose are hardly endangered in Maine. Some 30,000 of them live throughout the state, with the vast majority making their home in the North Woods. Seeing them, however, is another matter. Despite their size, the animals are skittish around humans and are most likely to be seen at night by the side of the road—which isn't the safest vantage from which to view them. That's where water-based "moose safaris" come in. The animals linger around the estuaries fringing the lake for ready access to sweet overhanging branches and cooling water in the heat of the day—and better yet, are completely unafraid of any boats that might come their way, viewing them as largely uninteresting aquatic animals. From the vantage of the water, you can gawk to your hearts content at the majestic beasts, who are apt to go on obliviously munching their branchy breakfast.

Guides with **The Birches Resort** (off Rte. 6/15, Rockwood, 207/534-7305, www.birches. com) are expert at piloting large pontoon boats within a dozen feet of beasts. The resort offers a two-and-a-half-hour "moose cruise" at 7 A.M. ($35 adult, $25 children 4–12, free children under 4) and a longer "moose safari" in the afternoon at 4 P.M., which includes a cruise by the 800-foot cliffs of the lake's Mount Kineo ($45 adult, $30 children 4–12, free children under 4). The best time for sightings is in the late spring and early summer, when cruises can sometimes bag as many as a half-dozen moose.

If the thought of seeing moose with a dozen other humans is too much for you, **Northwoods Outfitters** (Maine St., Greenville, 207/695-3288, www.maineoutfitter.com) offers more intimate encounters from the vantage of your own canoe, for a rate of $30 to $50 per person.

An alternative to seeing moose by boat is seeing them by foot. **Maine-ly Photos** (353 Penobscot Rd., Millinocket, 207/723-5465, www.mainelyphotos.com, May–Oct., $50 adults, $45 per person for families of up to four people) leads van tours to parts of Baxter State Park and the West Branch of the Penobscot River, where tourists then take short walks to ponds moose are known to frequent. The tours offer a money-back guarantee that antlers will be sighted.

Other Sights

Maine's maritime legacy isn't confined to saltwater. More than 50 steamships once plied the waves of Moosehead, ferrying passengers and supplies between resorts, hunting camps, and logging bases. Their legacy is preserved at the **Moosehead Marine Museum** (12 Lily Bay Rd./Rte. 15, Greenville, 207/695-2716, www.katahdincruises.com, 10 A.M.–5 P.M. Tue.–Sat. Jun.–mid-Oct.), which includes photographs, models, engine parts, and other memorabilia dedicated to the old lake boats. The museum's prized possession is the *Katahdin*, a 110-foot vessel built by Bath Iron Works in 1914 and used to haul log booms. The last surviving steamboat on the lake, it now offers regular cruises between late June and early October to Sugar Island (Tue.–Sat. late Jun.–mid-Oct., $32 adults, $28 seniors, $17 children 11–16, free children under 11) and Mount Kineo (every other Wed., $37 adult, $33 senior, $20 children 11–16, free children under 11).

The region's other heroes—the lumberjacks—can be seen in spirit at the Moosehead Historical Society's **Lumberman's Museum** (444 Pritham Ave., Greenville, 207/695-2909, www.mooseheadhistory.org, 1–4 P.M. Wed.–Fri. early June–Sept., $4 adults, $2 children under 13), a house museum inside a renovated Victorian mansion that features axes and artifacts dedicated to the Paul Bunyans of the North Country. The museum also features a Victorian-era kitchen and dozens of Native American tools.

Though it was only active for 50 years, between 1843 and 1890, the **Katahdin Iron Works State Historic Site** (off Rte. 11, Brownville Junction, 207/941-4014, www.maine.gov, late May–early Sept., free) was once a massive operation, smelting up to 20 tons of iron ingots a day, mostly for use in rail-car wheels and farming implements. At its peak, the iron works was a thriving city, with its own post office and even a hotel. Today, all that remains of the business are two large stone structures—a beehive-shaped kiln that heated charcoal and a massive tower that formed part of the blast furnace itself and once spewed fire into the wilderness sky 24 hours a day. Interpretive panels re-create the history of the works, which is a popular spot for picnickers.

Events

The moose is the center of attention each spring during the month-long **Moose Mainea** (207/695-2702, www.mooseheadlake.org, mid-May–mid-June), which features a craft fair, "mooseball" supper, the Moose Tales slideshow, moose-calling demonstrations, Moose River Canoe Race, moose photo contest, and even some moose d'oeuvres to try. Jack London eat your heart out—every February, 20 sleds compete to be top dog in the **100 Mile Wilderness Sled Dog Race** (207/965-8120, www.100milewildernessrace.org), a competition in which teams race from Greenville, up Moosehead Lake, to Brownville and back for their share of a $5,000 purse. Hot chocolate flows at viewing points along the way. The weekend after Labor Day, hundreds of pontoon planes swoop into the lake for the **International Seaplane Fly-In** (Greenville, 207/695-2702, www.seaplanefly-in.org), the world's largest seaplane event. Events include flying and canoeing competitions, educational exhibits, and dancing.

Shopping

On the shores of Moosehead, the little town of Greenville exploits the local fauna with several moose-themed stores. **Moosin' Around Maine** (Pritham Ave., Greenville, 207/695-3929) is a mandatory stop for a moose T-shirt, mug, or magnet; it also features made-in-Maine pottery and blown glass. More unique finds can be unearthed at **Kamp Kamp** (Pritham Ave., Greenville, 207/695-0789, www.mooseheadlakeindianstore.com, daily Jun.–mid-Aug.; weekends only mid-Apr.–May and Sept.–Dec.), an old time "Indian store" re-created in exquisitely kitschy detail by the owners, who visited the lake frequently as children. In addition to camp furniture and souvenirs, it sells raccoon hats, rattlesnake eggs, slingshots, and other oddities.

Food

Rutting and foraging can be hard work—even the most overtaxed moose has to take a load off sometime. That's where the **Stress-Free Moose Pub & Cafe** (65 Pritham Ave., Greenville, 207/695-3100, 11 A.M.–9 P.M. Sun.–Thu.; 11 A.M.–9:30 P.M. Fri.–Sat., $5–8) comes in. The casual eatery in the center of Greenville features sandwiches and wraps along with an outdoor patio for enjoying them. Patrons can really kick back in an upstairs area with comfy couches and board games; the bar is one of the few in town that stays open late. A few doors down, **The Black Frog** (Pritham Ave., Greenville, 207/695-1100, www.theblackfrog.com, 11:30 A.M.–8 P.M. Sun.–Thurs., 11:30 A.M.–9 P.M. Fri. and Sat. $6–22) serves up a healthy dose of humor with such dishes as Moose Wings and Moose Balls (which are listed for $1,495). More to the point, the place makes a mean rack of BBQ ribs and a hearty lasagna loaded down with cheese and veggies. The dining room is built out on a dock over the lake and offers nice views of arriving seaplanes. On the west side of the lake, **The Birches Resort** (off Rte. 6/15, Rockwood, 207/534-7305, www.birches.com, 7 A.M.–9 P.M. daily $14–24) is the closest you'll find to fine dining this side of Portland. Entrées such as rib eye with black-bean-and-corn salsa; or salmon with raspberries and wine sauce go better with the giant moose head hovering over the room.

Information

The **Moosehead Lake Region Chamber of Commerce** (Indian Hill Plaza, 156 Moosehead Lake Rd./Rte. 15, Greenville, 207/695-2702 or 888/876-2778, www.mooseheadlake.org) runs a visitors center with brochures and the like. For more information on the North Woods, contact **The Maine Highlands** (207/947-5205 or 800/916-6673, www.themainehighlands.com) tourist information office.

SPORTS AND RECREATION

Let's face it, you didn't come to the Maine woods for the cuisine or the culture—you came to get out into the woods. The Moosehead region offers a good jumping-off point to get out into the wilderness, either to the two star attractions of Baxter State Park and the Allagash Wilderness Waterway or to whitewater rapids or skiing or snowmobiling trails, depending on the season.

It's impossible to shop for groceries or fill up on gas without coming across a flyer for a wilderness guide or outfitter. Many hotels and resorts also lead hiking, rafting, or canoeing trips as a side venture. While guides vary in skill and experience, you can't go wrong with a **Registered Maine Guide** (www.registeredmaineguides.com), a member of a tradition that stretches back to Cornelia Thurza "Fly Rod" Crosby, who established a system of training and vetting guides more than 100 years ago. Within that designation, some guides also belong to the **Maine Professional Guides Association** (www.maineguides.org), whose website offers the ability to search for guides in specific geographical areas or areas of interest on its website.

Hiking

Aside from the obvious draw of Baxter State Park, many smaller parks and preserves offer excellent hiking opportunities in the Moosehead region. One of the most obvious is **Mount Kineo,** the dramatic cliff-sided island in the middle of the lake. The easiest way to get to the trailhead is to take a boat across from Rockwood. It's also possible to drive from the opposite side of the lake. The route is a short, steep hike up the naturally stratified layers of rock that rewards hikers with a view of the lake on all sides. Another popular hike is the one to the fire tower atop **Big Squaw Mountain,** east of the lake, an easy four-mile round-trip hike that affords spectacular views. If you are feeling lazy, a chairlift from Big Squaw ski resort will whisk you up to the tower in 15 minutes. Another mountain popular with hikers doesn't even have a trail up to its peak. **Elephant Mountain** is named for obvious reasons—its massive bulk uncannily resembles a pachyderm. But the mountain's biggest draw is the wreck of a B-52 bomber, which crashed here during training maneuvers in high winds in January 1963. Of the nine passengers, two were rescued in a heroic attempt to reach them through 15 feet of snow the next day. The bomber's remains, which can be reached by an easy half-hour trail, are scattered across the mountainside, with guns and wing sections peeking out through the trees and a row of American flags marking the fallen soldiers at the fuselage.

Rafting and Canoeing

While the St. John and the Allagash might

WILDERNESS CAMPS

These days, getting away from it all is such a bandied-about rubric, we practically use it to describe a trip to the mall. But the term gets a reinvestment of meaning during a weekend at one of hundreds of rustic camps that dot the shores of remote rivers and lakes throughout the North Woods, some accessible by backwoods roads and others only by floatplane. The tradition of Maine's wilderness camps dates back to before the Civil War, when in the spring families would open up cabins deep in the middle of nowhere to cater to fishermen, and then stay open throughout the hunting season. Camps are owned under a variety of arrangements, by private owners and resort operators who set up drive-in and fly-in vacations for groups to fish, paddle, or just get lost in the rhythms of the woods and dance of the Northern Lights. Some offer home-cooked meals and canoe or motorboat rentals along with cabins stocked with cook stoves and refrigerators. To find a camp, check out the listings on the website of the **Maine Sporting Camps Association** (www.mainesportingcamps.com). Or check out one of the three options below:

- The cream of the crop are the **Libby Camps** (Ashland, 207/435-8274, www.libbycamps.com, $175-385 per day), to which you're flown via seaplane, to stay at any of ten antiques-filled outpost cabins. Run by the third generation of a backwoods sportfishing dynasty, the camps are known primarily for their superb fly-fishing in Millinocket Lake (back in the day, Teddy Roosevelt was said to be a fan), but also offer something far more elusive than the one that got away: total seclusion. Rates include gear, boats, three meals, maid service, and sometimes at least one flyout to a remote fishing pond.

- Now owned by the Appalachian Mountain Club, **Medawisla Wilderness Camps** (Kokadjo, 207/695-2690, www.outdoors.org, $31-144 per person) dot the shore of Second Roach Pond in the deep woods west of Moosehead. The camp is named after a Native American word for loons and is famous for its breeding population, which was recorded for use in the soundtrack of the film *On Golden Pond*. The seven sturdy housekeeping cabins are popular with fishermen, who come to angle for landlocked salmon, lake trout, and brook trout; and bird-watchers, who thrill to more than 100 species on the pond. It also has direct access to hiking trails and a 60-mile network of cross-country ski trails in winter. Rates include use of canoes and kayaks, as well as sometimes meals and housekeeping.

- You can't get much more remote than **Loon Lodge** (Round Pond, 207/745-8168, www.loonlodgemaine.com, $50-100 pp), which prides itself on being a two-and-a-half-hour drive in from "town" (the nearest being Greenville and Millinocket, each 75 miles away). It's also possible to fly in by seaplane from Greenville. Accommodations consist of knotty-pine cabins with propane stoves on the shore of Round Pond, each decorated in a different animal theme. Packages include use of canoes and rowboats and hearty home-cooked meals in the main lodge. In addition to Lake Trout and Salmon, the pond boasts the rare Blueback Trout, and big feisty Muskie. For non-fishermen, the lodge offers nature tours in which guides use "moose calls" to attract bull moose, and a trip out to a feeding station popular with black bears.

MAINE

be the wildest rivers in the area, they are not the most exhilarating. That honor goes to the Lower **West Branch of the Penobscot River,** a bruising 14-mile white-water flume between Baxter and Moosehead that takes in multiple Class IV and Class V rapids from the put-in at Ripogenus Dam. (Class V is defined as "extremely difficult, with large vertical drops, strong hydraulics, very swift, irregular currents in heavily obstructed channels." Still game?) The fun starts right away with a Class V at Ripogenus Gorge, then churns through other spills with names like Troublemaker and Exterminator Staircase before coming out at a long lake with beautiful views of Mount Katahdin to the east and finishing with a bang at a Class IV called Big Pockwockamus. Needless to say, the stretch can only be attempted by rafters and experienced canoeists in white-water craft. The Upper West Branch, by contrast, is a much more relaxing paddle between two large lakes in a region teeming with moose.

On the other side of Baxter State Park, the **East Branch of the Penobscot River** is a fast-running and precipitous river with many falls, short portages, and rapids, though none higher then Class III. The full trip from Telos Lake is 72 miles long and should take five to seven days. A shorter trip with excellent views of Traveler Mountain and several spectacular waterfalls starts at Grand Lake Matagamom and ends at Whetstone Falls, a distance of some 26 miles over three to four days.

Flowing southwest out of Moosehead Lake, the **Kennebec River** is popular with white-water rafters for its combination of gnarly rapids (rising up to Class V with the churning Magic Falls) and a long stretch of quiet water good for spotting wildlife as the adrenaline subsides. Farther south, don't let the name of the **Dead River** deter you. The 16-mile rafting run is touted as the "longest continuous stretch of white water in the east" and is great fun for its nonstop action. The course takes in Class IV rapids at Humpty Dumpty and Elephant Rock, before ending with a bang at the Class V Big Poplar Falls.

Many local guides offer trips on all of the above rivers. Close friends and 20-year canoeing partners David Butler and Tim Emery guide groups on the Upper West and East Branches of the Penobscot through their outfit **Maine Path & Paddle Guides** (877/632-2663, www.canoemaine.com). They also specialize in trips for families with very young children and seniors. **Allagash Canoe Trips** (207/237-3077, www.allagashcanoetrips.com) offers similar trips on the Penobscot along with daylong white-water trips to the Kennebec and Dead Rivers when the water is running slowly enough to make them canoeable.

One-stop shopping for white-water rafting is **Raft Maine** (207/723-8633, www.raftmaine.com), an association of 14 professional outfitters who have banded together to offer day trips to the Kennebec ($80–120 pp), Penobscot ($90–130) and Dead ($90–140) Rivers. The association also offers packages including lodging or camping and other wilderness activities.

Fishing

The North Woods teem with fishing opportunities on every type of water imaginable, from fast-running rivers to secluded woodland ponds. Among the species ripe for the catching are brook, rainbow, brown, and lake trout; salmon; small- and largemouth bass; and northern pike. Many fishermen head to remote wilderness camps that cater especially to anglers (see sidebar *Wilderness Camps*). Others book trips with resorts or outfitters such as **Maine Fishing Adentures** (207/944-1691, www.mainefishingadventures.com), which offers guided fishing trips on the Kennebec, Androscoggin, Rangely and Penobscot Rivers, as well as secluded trout ponds.

Skiing and Snowmobiling

On the eastern shore of Moosehead, **Lily Bay State Park** has eight miles of groomed trails for cross-country skiing. The most challenging trails weave up and down hills on the edge of the lake. On the western side of the lake, it's worth going out of the way for the 30 miles of groomed trails at **The Birches Resort,** which has two winter yurts along the trails for overnight stays. More adventurous skiers should venture out to **Hagas Bay,** known as the "Grand Canyon of Maine" for its craggy ravine, which offers some 15 miles of trails with vertiginous scenery, best explored in a three-day trip with stopovers at the Appalachian Mountain Club's Lyford Pond Camps. Skis can be rented from **Northwoods Outfitters** (Maine St., Greenville, 207/695-3288, www.maineoutfitter.com) for $15 a day.

Northwoods also rents snowmobiles to take advantage of the extensive trail system created for sleds every winter. The lakes and logging roads of the region are crisscrossed with trails maintained by the **Maine Snowmobile Association** (207/622-6983, www.mesnow.com) as part of its Interconnected Trail System. Some of the same outfitters involved with Raft Maine put on their long johns in the winter and become **Sled Maine** (800/275-3363, www.sledmaine.com), an association that arranges snowmobile rentals and overnight trips in the Moosehead/Katahdin region.

BAXTER STATE PARK

Looking at a map of Maine, it's impossible not to notice the large green rectangle that sits sandwiched between the rivers and lakes smack in the northern part of the state. The straight lines are deceptive—within the shape are more than 200,000 acres of the wildest lands in New England, a paradise for hikers and campers who are willing to work for their wilderness. In fact, the original charter of the park dedicates it to exactly "those who love nature and are willing to walk and make an effort to get close to nature." Because of that, the park has few roads, rewarding hikers who make the effort with 200 miles of remote trails pockmarked with waterfalls, fishing streams, ruined lumber camps, and mountain peaks with views of green as far as the eye can see.

◖ Hiking Mount Katahdin

In the Penobscot language, Katahdin means "the greatest mountain," and it would be hard to find a natural feature more accurately named. The great peak lords over the surrounding countryside for miles around, visible as far away as Moosehead Lake to the west and the Canadian border to the east—more than 50 miles in either direction. Not only is the mountain Maine's highest, but its size is also augmented by its unusual shape, long and lean with four natural bowls scooped out of the granite by glaciers. In fact, "Katahdin" is actually the name of a massif with several peaks along the ridges. At 5,267 feet, Baxter Peak is the highest, both in the park and in Maine.

As soon as the snow thaws in April, thousands of intrepid souls raid its slopes to bag the peak on the beginning of their trip down the Appalachian Trail to Sringer Mountain in Georgia, more than 2,000 miles away. Not that the hike is easy. For sheer difficulty, Katahdin is one of the toughest climbs in New England, especially up the steep ridge between Baxter and Chimney Peaks known as the Knife's Edge. As the name implies, that trail skirts the top of a narrow ridge sometimes only two feet wide, with almost vertical sides careening down hundreds of feet on either side. It's not a trail to be attempted on windy or rainy days. Several other trails, including the Arbol and Hunt Trails, offer only slightly less challenging routes to the summit. Check in at the park visitors center for trail maps and information on conditions. Whatever route you take, leave as early as possible—the round trip can take more than nine hours.

Other Hikes

The parking lot for Katahdin fills up quickly in summer months; by contrast other peaks in the park see less than a dozen pairs of boots a day. Just a few miles west of Baxter Peak, the three-mile **Owl Trail** presents several almost-vertical ascents along with views of Katahdin's treeless summit from its own two modest peaks (known as the "ears" of the Owl). Another lesser-known trail, **The Marston Trail** climbs the peaks of North and South Brother Mountains in a challenging nine-mile circuit north of Katahdin. The trail ends with a gambol through the Klondike wetland, where moose are plentiful.

Near the north entrance to the park, **Horse Mountain** is an easy hike to an abandoned fire tower with gorgeous views of the Penobscot's East Branch. The **Freezeout Trail,** which leaves from Trout Brook Farm Campground, is a 24-mile marathon hike through an area rich in wildlife and sparse in human life. From South Branch Campground, trails such as **North Traveler** traverse the Traveler Mountain range, which were formed by volcanic activity 400 million years ago, and afford hikers the chance to walk along beds of ancient lava. For more information on hiking and camping within the park, contact the **Friends of Baxter State Park** through their website (www.friendsofbaxter.org).

Camping

The park operates ten campgrounds, eight of which have drive-in sites. The byzantine reservation system employed by the park is complicated enough to stymie the most experienced tax law attorney. The upshot is that reservations can be made by mail or in person at the **park's headquarters** (64 Balsam Dr., Millinocket) until 10 days before the date of arrival, and by phone (207/723-5140) up to 14 days before arrival. Most of the campgrounds are open from mid-May to October, and popular sites, such as Roaring Brook and Abol campgrounds, fill up fast. Rates for lean-to and tent spaces are $10 per person per night with a $20 minimum; cabins are $27 per person, with minimums depending on their size. Gaslights and firewood are included in the fee. Also scattered throughout the backcountry are dozens of lean-to sites available to hikers for free; advance reservations are required.

Events

In mid-summer, the small town of Medway hosts the annual **Katahdin Area Wooden Arts/Canoe Festival** (Rte. 157, Medway, 207/723-4443, www.katahdinmaine.com) with displays by local boat manufacturers, white-water races, live animal exhibits, and fireworks.

Food

It's slim pickings on fine dining in the park,

but there are several modest eateries in nearby Millinocket that dish out good fare. Italian immigrants flooded this area during the logging heyday. Their legacy lives on at **Orvieto** (67 Prospect St., Millinocket, 207/723-8399, www.dicensiinc.com, 7 a.m.–6 p.m. Mon.–Fri.; 7 a.m.–2 p.m. Sat., $5–7), an authentic Umbrian deli and sandwich shop that will fulfill your craving for prosciutto, *capicola*, or provolone. Catering to hikers and hunters alike, the **Appalachian Trail Cafe** (210 Penobscot Avenue; 207/723-6720, www.appalachiantraillodge.com, 5 a.m.–9 p.m., $6–9) serves burgers and flapjacks at a smoky coffee counter downtown. Breakfast is available all day. For a splurge, **Fredericka's at the Big Moose Inn** (Rte. 157, Millinocket, 207/723-8391, www.bigmoosecabins.com, 5:30–9 p.m. Wed.–Sat. year-round, open Sun. Jul.–Aug., $17–24) can throw down with any big-city menu with sophisticated entrées like five-spice-dusted pork loin topped with crispy bacon and truffle oil. Its spacious dining room is all about blond wood and forest views.

Information

For trail maps and updated information about the park, stop at **Baxter State Park Authority Headquarters** (64 Balsam Dr., Millinocket, 207/723-5140, www.baxterstateparkauthority.com) on the way to the park's southern entrance. For information about the surrounding area, stop by the **Katahdin Area Chamber of Commerce** (1029 Central St., Millinocket, 207/723-4443, www.katahdinmaine.com).

ALLAGASH WILDERNESS WATERWAY

The vast majority of rivers in the United States flow south—not so the twin rivers of the Maine wilderness, the Allagash and St. John, which have their headwaters west of Katahdin and flow a hundred miles *north* into Canada. Along the way, they pass through vast stretches of wilderness without roads, making a trip upriver the wildest experience in New England. Other rivers in the region might have more gnarly rapids, but nowhere east of the

Mississippi will you be able to find a more wilderness paddling experience than the stretches of the Upper St. John.

Of course, that wildness is an illusion. The rivers' watersheds are the property of paper companies—and even today it's possible to hear the drone of a saw in the distance as you paddle. But by long-standing agreement, the companies have left hundreds of feet on either side of the river untrammeled. At night when the trucks go home and the sky is dense with stars, you can imagine what it was like in New England when only moose and indigenous people roamed among the pines.

Canoeing the Allagash

Of the two rivers, the Allagash is both more popular and offers more variety, with a trio of large lakes, Chamberlain, Eagle, and Churchill, leading off the route from its beginning on the edge of Baxter State Park. (Be sure to look for the two rusted-out steam locomotives that used to belong to the Eagle Lake and Umbazooksus Railroad and now sit on the edge of Eagle Lake.) If it's white water you are after, you might want to put in further up the river at Churchill Dam, where the rip-roaring Chase Rapids (a Class II) kicks off the second half of the waterway. From here, the river is a good mix of narrow lakes and rushing river currents. The waterway culminates in the spectacular 40-foot-high Allagash Falls (which of course you'll have to portage around), right before the intersection with the St. John River.

The entire waterway is 92 miles long and takes about 7 to 10 days to complete, depending on your bicep strength and penchant for daydreaming. The river doesn't "ice-out" until about May 15, so the paddling season lasts from mid-May to mid-October. Remember, however, that this is Maine, so cold-weather clothing is a must at all times of the year. The best times for a trip are May and June when the flowing meltwater makes for faster currents. If you venture out during the warmer months of July and August expect plenty of company; you'd do well to get up and set up camp early, lest you find yourself having to paddle another five miles downstream to find an unclaimed site.

Access is by private roads owned by paper companies; these can be entered via Greenville or Millinocket, or farther north from Ashland. Stay alert, as logging trucks can come barreling down the road without warning, and they have right-of-way at all times. The waterway has nine different entry points, including put-ins at Chamberlain Lake, Eagle Lake, Churchill Dam, Umsaskis Lake, and Round Pond. Along the way are some 20 well-maintained campsites, for which there is an $8 fee per site per night, payable to the North Maine Woods ranger when you enter the river. All canoeists are required to register with a ranger at first opportunity.

Canoeing the St. John

Compared to the Allagash, the St. John River is more remote, less crowded, and more difficult. For those reasons, it's best attempted by experienced canoeists or those traveling with a registered Maine guide. The traditional point of access is Fifth St. John Pond, accessible by a logging road north of Rockwood on the west side of Moosehead Lake. From there, the river begins its wild ride northward, taking in several Class I and II rapids in its 114-mile course. The river saves the best for last—right before the take-out point in Dickey are the aptly named "Big Rapids," a Class III.

Because the river isn't dammed, it is only navigable by paddlers for a brief period in May and June. The best time to hit the river is in early May before the black flies hatch—otherwise, bring plenty of Deet. Like the Allagash, the river is lined by a number of well-maintained camping areas, available for an $8 fee per night.

Guide Services

While it's more than feasible for experienced canoeists to brave either river by themselves, hiring a guide can make a trip more fun by providing information on natural and human history, and smoothing the logistics of boat travel in a remote area. A good choice is **Allagash**

Canoe Trips (207/237-3077, www.allagash-canoetrips.com), a family-run business whose guides have more than 100 years of experience on the river between them. Chip Cochrane, his wife, Lani, and his father, Warren, lead week-long trips on the Allagash ($930 adults, $750 children under 18) that begin at Chamberlain Lake and include several scenic hikes along the way. They also offer a shorter trip on the Allagash starting at Churchill Dam ($825 adults, $660 children), and a trip down the St. John River ($930 adults or teens) in early spring that begins with a floatplane ride to the upper ponds. Trips leave from Greenville with a shuttle service available from Bangor.

Information

The Allagash Wilderness Waterway is operated by the northern headquarters of the state of Maine's **Bureau of Parks and Lands** (207/941-4014, www.maine.gov), which has lots of useful information for paddlers on its website, including a Natural History Guide to the river's flora, fauna, and geology in PDF format. The land around the St. John River is managed by **North Maine Woods** (207/435-6213, www.northmainewoods.org), a nonprofit consortium, which produces a handy booklet, *Pocket Guide for the Canoeist on the St. John River,* available at the road checkpoint for $3. Another essential map is the fold-out *Allagash & St. John,* produced by DeLorme Mapping and available at outdoors stores and supermarkets throughout the area.

ACCOMMODATIONS
Resorts

The word "resort" might not immediately come to mind when you see **The Birches Resort** (off Rte. 6/15, Rockwood, 207/534-7305, www.birches.com), hidden down the end of a dirt road on the secluded west side of Moosehead Lake. Accommodations are rustic to say the least, consisting of a main lodge with no-frills rooms going for $85–125 a night, and a collection of cabins laid out along the lakeside, many with private porches overlooking the water ($180–330). Nowhere else around,

however, offers the range of options for enjoying the great outdoors, whether that means the on-site marina with canoes and sailboats for rent; the rafting and snowmobiling trips organized by the on-site expedition company; the miles of cross-country skiing trails, complete with their own wilderness yurts for trailside overnights; and the popular "moose cruises" on the lake. The result is the essence of Maine—friendly and unpretentious but with everything you need to get outside. Recently, the resort added a few more-upscale house rentals ($220–480) that feature outdoor hot tubs and private beaches.

Closer to Katahdin, **Big Moose Inn** (Rte. 157, Millinocket, 207/723-8391, www.bigmoosecabins.com) offers a good home base for those on a budget. The main inn has a dozen simple but cozy bedrooms ($53–56 pp) filled with antique photographs and wrought-iron beds. These rooms are particularly well-suited for families, as several have multiple beds (including, strangely enough, the Bridal Suite). Also on the premises are a number of rustic cabins ($49 pp) and tent and lean-to sites ($10–13 pp). While the inn doesn't itself arrange expeditions, it is headquarters to two white-water rafting companies, and can help arrange snowmobile delivery. The resort also has canoes for rent on a nearby lake and provides snowshoes to guests for use on its own network of trails.

Under $100

On the doorstep of Baxter State Park, the **Appalachian Trail Lodge** (33 Penobscot Ave., Millinocket, 207/723-4321, www.appalachiantraillodge.com, $35, $25 dormitory) is a favorite hostel for backpackers going all the way on the Appalachian Trail or day hikers looking for a place to group before or after tackling Katahdin. The bright-red family home has been converted into a bed-and-breakfast with single and double rooms, as well as a larger apartment for groups of up to six hikers. If you are looking for advice on hiking or climbing in the park, owners Don and Joan Cogswell have the accumulated knowledge of 15 years of hikers, along with an eagerness to advise new arrivals.

$100-150

The **Pleasant Street Inn** (26 Pleasant St., Greenville, 207/695-3400, www.pleasantstreetinn.com, $110–160), a Victorian bed-and-breakfast located in Greenville center, is owned and run by three artist friends who decided to entertain guests while they perfected their crafts. The attention to detail shows throughout the inn, which has an unerring sense of romance in the design and photorealist paintings made by one of the innkeepers hung throughout the house. Another of the hosts is a professionally trained chef who prepares gourmet breakfasts and, with advanced notice, will also cook a personalized dinner. The best detail of the house is the tall tower offering 360-degree views of the town and the lake. The inn offers romance packages that include moose safaris or pre-arranged cruises aboard the *Katahdin*.

$150-250

Someone had to cut the trees; someone had to own them. In 1885, lumber baron William Shaw took the profits from logging and poured them into a sprawling Victorian mansion with premium views over Moosehead Lake's East Cove. Many of the lavish details that Shaw built into his mansion, such as stamped tin walls and stained glass, have survived its renovation into the **Greenville Inn** (40 Norris St., Greenville, 207/695-2206, www.greenvilleinn.com, $155–265), one of the most luxurious lodgings in the area. After a hard day of rafting or snowmobiling, guests are pampered with plush duvets and marble showers in rooms decorated with strong, masculine colors. The new owners, who came to Maine to retire a few years ago, have added their own family heirlooms to the collection of Victorian antiques, and cook a full breakfast each morning. Private

cottages out back are paneled with wood inside for a more rustic feel without sacrificing the level of luxury.

GETTING THERE AND AROUND

To really explore the North Woods you'll need your own car with a good draft on its undercarriage—or better yet a four-wheel-drive vehicle. To drive to the Moosehead region from Portland, head north on I-295 to I-95, then take exit 157 at Newport. From there, take Route 11 north to Corinna, Route 7 north to Dover-Foxcroft, and Route 15 north to Greenville (150 mi., 3 hrs. 30 min.). To drive to the Katahdin area from Portland, take I-295 to I-95 north, then take exit 244 to Route 159 west to Millinocket (200 mi., 4 hrs.).

If you don't have a car of your own, many of the resorts and guide services in the area will arrange a pick-up from **Bangor International Airport** (207/992-4600, www.flybangor.com), a two-and-a-half-hour drive or half-hour seaplane flight from the Moosehead/Katahdin region. To fly to the North Woods, **Folsom's Air Service** (Greenville, 207/695-2821) provides air taxi from Bangor to Moosehead by seaplane and to the new 4-runway **Greenville Municipal Airport** (Airport Rd., Greenville, 207/695-2421, www.greenvilleme.com), while **Katahdin Air Service** (Millinocket, 866/359-6246, www.katahdinair.com) services a seaplane base near Baxter State Park. There is no regular bus or train service to the area.

Several private shuttle services provide transportation around Baxter State Park. Try **Minutemen Taxi** (Millinocket, 207/723-2000) or **Maine-ly Photos** (Millinocket, 207/723-5465, www.mainelyphotos.com). Many guide services also provide shuttle service for a nominal fee.

MAINE

BACKGROUND
AND ESSENTIALS

BACKGROUND

The Land

Few areas on earth squeeze such a varied topography into such a small space. New England covers an area of just over 70,000 square miles—making the region smaller than 20 of the U.S. states. Within that area, however, the region contains a multitude of landforms and habitats. Along the coastline, it runs from the sandy beaches of Connecticut and Rhode Island to the barrier beach of Cape Cod to the granite headlands north of Boston and the thousands of rocky fingers of Maine. In the interior, the terrain varies from the cranberry bogs and cedar swamps of Rhode Island to the soaring peaks of New Hampshire's White Mountains. In between, it tucks into fertile farmland, deep pine forests, rolling mountains covered with old-growth oak and maples, and—of course—part of the most densely populated urban corridor in the country.

GEOLOGY

In an eschatological mood, New England poet Robert Frost once mused about whether the world would end in fire or ice. Without taking sides on that question, it's fair to say that both fire and ice played equally dramatic roles in the *beginnings* of New England. Fire came first, in the form of molten hot lava that bubbled up violently from the earth's core starting some half a billion years ago. At that time, most of what

COURTESY OF STATE OF VERMONT

would become New England was underwater, just off the leading edge of a proto-continent known as Laurentia. As the tectonic plate that held Laurentia moved slowly eastward, it folded under its neighbor and melted, causing an upwelling of magma beneath the surface of the ocean. That upwelling formed a chain of island peaks off the coast of the continent. Eventually, the land mass of Laurentia crashed into these islands during the Ordovician Era around 440 million years ago, pushing them up into what is now the Taconic Mountains of far western Massachusetts and southwestern Vermont.

About a hundred million years later, in the Devonian Era, Laurentia crashed into a subcontinent called Avalonia to the south, rolling over the smaller landmass to create more upwelling of magma. At the same time, the continent collided with its neighboring continent Baltica—the precursor to Europe—causing the ocean floor between them to buckle and fold back over the continent. The combination created the Berkshire Hills, which have backbones of volcanic rock topped with older "basement rock" of gneiss and quartz that once sat at the floor of the sea. The ocean, meanwhile, was squeezed out over Avalonia to create a vast delta of sedimentary rock that now forms the bulk of Eastern Connecticut, Rhode Island, and Eastern Massachusetts. A bit later, during the Triassic period, a great fault opened up in the middle of the region, creating a 100-mile-long rift valley that would later become the Connecticut River.

At this time, all of the world's continents briefly joined together in a giant landmass called Pangaea. The commingling didn't last long, however. By the Jurassic Era, 200 million years ago, the continents were again on the move, and North America and Europe split up to create the Atlantic Ocean. Around the same time, a field of volcanoes opened up in the area of New Hampshire, spewing hot magma in plutons and ring dikes to form the massive granite peaks of the White Mountains. The Whites are the youngest mountains in the region, and the last evidence of volcanic activity, which ended about 130 million years ago.

New England's fiery birth was followed by a long period of erosion and settling before fire handed off its job to ice, and the last great ice age began.

Temperatures began to cool gradually about a million years ago. By the Pleistocene era, some 80,000 years ago (a mere hiccup in geological time), a massive ice sheet began to build up over Canada, more than a mile thick in places. As it did, the sheer weight of the ice caused it to flow southward in a huge glacier, leveling the earth, gouging out valleys, and breaking off mountaintops as it flowed. The farthest glacier reached all the way down to New York City, depositing millions of tons of rocks in a terminal moraine that forms Long Island, Block Island, Martha's Vineyard, and Nantucket. (Since so much of the earth's water was tied up in ice, sea levels were lower, and all of those islands were once mountains.) A more intense, but less far-reaching, glacier left a second terminal moraine around 20,000 years ago to form the northern spur of Long Island, along with Cape Cod and the Elizabeth Islands.

While the terminal moraines are the most visible result of the glaciers, all of New England was definitively shaped by the ice, which rolled and ebbed across the region for thousands of years. Mountains were pushed over and broken, so that even today in the Whites, the northern slopes offer more gradual ascents for hikers, while the steep southern faces present grueling challenges for rock climbers. Mountaintops and boulders, meanwhile, were picked up by the advancing ice sheet, and often deposited miles away from their origins. In some places, these huge glacial boulders, also known as "erratics," have become local landmarks, such as the 5,000-ton Madison Boulder in New Hampshire's lake region, the largest erratic in New England.

The glaciers changed the land in other ways as well. As it advanced, the ice sheet pushed away the softer substrate, exposing the harder, immovable granite. In many places, lone mountains called "monadnocks" remain to lord over the surrounding plains. The most famous of these is Mount Monadnock in southern New

Hampshire, whose views as far as Boston on a clear day make an irresistible magnet for hikers. In Rhode Island, the advancing ice gouged away the softer substrate in Narragansett Bay to expose granite islands, including the island on which Newport is located and from which the state gets its name.

The last of the glaciers retreated by 15,000 years ago. In its wake, however, it closed off the Connecticut River Valley and filled it with meltwater to create a huge inland lake named Lake Hitchcock. For more than 2,000 years, the lake stretched 200 miles from Connecticut to Vermont's Northeast Kingdom. (It was probably quite a sight, colored the striking azure blue of the glacial lakes that now grace Canada and Patagonia.) The layers of silt deposited by the drying lake helped create the rich, loamy soil of Massachusetts' Pioneer Valley—which stands in marked contrast to the rocky, glacial till of the rest of New England. Another glacial lake, Lake Vermont, formed to the west of New England, and drained into modern-day Lake Champlain.

Other land features marked by glaciers include long straight grooves in the earth known as "glacial scarring"; teardrop shaped hills called "drumlins," which are especially common in Rhode Island and Southeastern Massachusetts; and round depressions known as "kettle holes," which were caused by standing water from glacial melt drilling down into the earth, and often serve as local swimming holes. Global warming notwithstanding, some geologists surmise that our present period is just a brief interlude between ice ages—and Frost might get his answer when the glaciers roll down from Canada again.

CLIMATE

The snow started to fall during the afternoon of March 31, 1997. By the next morning, New Englanders across the region woke up to as much as two feet of the white stuff—setting the record for the most snow in one day in some areas. The so-called April Fool's Snowstorm melted quickly, but won't be soon forgotten by those who had to shovel out from

it. They got their payback, however, when March 31 of the next year posted temperatures in the 90s around Boston. Welcome to New England, where the saying goes, "If you don't like the weather, wait a minute!" With such extremes of wet, hot, cold, and windy, sometimes deciding what coat to wear can take the better part of a morning.

The changeability in New England's weather comes courtesy of its location on the dividing line between cold polar air mass to the north and the warm tropical air currents from the south. Sometimes one wins out, sometimes the other; but neither goes without a fight. Add a constant supply of moisture from the ocean, and you are guaranteed an unpredictable mix. Despite the regular precipitation, however, New England sees more than its fair share of clear days, when the sky is blue and you can see for miles from the peak of Mount Washington. Moreover, the moderating effect of the warm Gulf Stream ocean currents ensures that New England doesn't see the same extremes of temperature that affect the middle part of the country. Both summers and winters are comparatively mild—though it might not seem that way in the middle of a frigid January cold snap or the sweltering dog days of August.

As much as it's possible to generalize about weather in New England, a typical year starts with the mercury at its lowest. The coldest part of the year often occurs between Christmas and New Year's, when the thermometer can drop to single digits for more than a week in Boston, much to the chagrin of First Night revelers. Of course, in New Hampshire and northern Maine, that's de rigueur for the season. That snap of extreme cold is often followed by a period of milder weather known as the January thaw. But that only sets the stage for February, when the region sees the bulk of its snowfall. The number and severity of winter storms vary with the wind. The hardest hitters come when a zone of low pressure sits off to the east, bringing cold, wet air counter-clockwise down from the Maritimes to form a classic "nor'easter." Spend much time in the region, and you are bound to hear about the famous Blizzard of '78, a nor'easter that buried areas in up to five feet of snow and caused rises in tides of up to 15 feet.

After such lashings, you'd think New Englanders would deserve a nice spring—but sadly, they rarely get it. Rather, winter tapers off into a prolonged cold season known in New Hampshire, Vermont, and Western Massachusetts as "mud season." Despite the melting snow and thawing topsoil, the deeper subsoil often remains frozen, leaving the resulting water nowhere to go but into soupy puddles and shoe-linings. This is the weather that the famous L. L. Bean made his boots for.

Just when New Englanders think they can't take it anymore (somewhere around mid-April in Rhode Island and late May in Maine), summer finally bursts gloriously upon the scene, bypassing spring entirely and instilling a collective amnesia in New Englanders, who promptly forget the cold ever existed. Though temperatures rarely get above the 80s, the humid air can make the sunny days hot and sweaty indeed—especially in August when prolonged heat waves can rock the region. Many natives take refuge on the shore, where cool ocean breezes moderate the temperature, and can even make nights a bit nippy. Woe be unto him who forgets his sweater or windbreaker on the coast. Variations in heat absorption between the land and sea cause a daily land breeze in the mornings and a sea breeze every afternoon.

Finally after Labor Day comes many New Englanders' favorite season—fall. There's a reason so many Hollywood movies have been filmed against a backdrop of a New England autumn. The days are crisp but not yet cold, and the air is often dry and pleasantly breezy. As the green chlorophyll leeches out of the tree leaves, it leaves the spectacular reds, oranges, and yellows of New England's star attraction—its famed fall foliage. Not that this season is without its perils, however. While hurricanes aren't as common here as in southern states, every few years in August or September a humdinger speeds over the Gulf Stream and crashes into the Connecticut or Rhode Island coast. The infamous Hurricane of 1938 killed 600 people and swept away miles of oceanfront homes. More recently in 1991, Hurricane Bob single-handedly destroyed Massachusetts' apple crop. As October approaches, the days quickly get colder and darker. Before they surrender to winter, however, New England is virtually guaranteed at least one week of Indian Summer, when the mercury climbs back into the 70s and 80s for one last spectacular respite from the cold. For many, this combines the best of New England weather—sun, dry air, and fiery foliage.

Of course, the foregoing describes a typical year in central New England. Keep in mind that the region stretches 400 miles from the Canadian border to Long Island Sound—the same distance roughly between New York City and Columbia, South Carolina. Correspondingly, temperatures can vary as much as 20 degrees or more from north to south. Boston, for example, averages a high of 36 for January and a high of 82 for July. Compare that to Caribou in far northern Maine, which averages a high of just 19 in January and just 76 in July. The wise traveler comes prepared for anything.

Flora and Fauna

FLORA

Accustomed to the denuded European landscape, early settlers to New England were bowled over by the deep forests full of timber and game as far as the eye could see. Soaring pines, stretching oaks, and stately chestnuts filled the new land, prompting superlatives in many a Puritan's travel journal. While centuries of lumbering have taken their toll on the woods of the region, much of New England is still appealingly forested. In recent decades, abandoned farms have been reclaimed by the trees, creating even more wooded landscape. And unlike clear-cut land out West, the North Woods of Maine have for centuries been home to sustainable logging practices that have kept the wilderness wild.

Trees

Traditionally, the forests of the region have been divided into three zones: an oak-chestnut forest in Connecticut, Rhode Island, and far eastern Massachusetts; a hemlock–white pine–transition hardwood forest in central and western Massachusetts, southern New Hampshire, Vermont, and Maine; and a spruce–northern hardwood forest in northern New Hampshire, Vermont, and Maine. Of course, this greatly simplifies a landscape in which 50 different species of trees each have their own range and habitat—but it does provide a good working framework for understanding local fauna.

Chestnuts roasting on an open fire may have been part of the holidays for early New Englanders, but those days are sadly gone. After surviving in New England for millions of years, the mighty chestnut was wiped out by a blight imported from Japan in the early part of the 20th century. The forests of southern and eastern New England, however, are still abundant with red oak, scarlet oak, hickory, maple, birch, and beech. In the wetlands of Rhode Island and southeastern Massachusetts, the landscape is dominated by red maple and Atlantic white cedar, which thrives in swampy ground. Along the coast, larger trees give way to hardy pitch pine and scrub oak more suited to salty air and sandy soils.

Central New England has a good mix of broadleaf trees and evergreens. The forest here is dominated by oak and maple—including the famous sugar maple that yields the region's annual crop of maple syrup every spring. The most common tree is the white oak, named for the color of its bark and prized both for its straight timber and wide-spreading canopy. Arguably, this is the best region for leaf-peeping, since maples produce some of the brightest colors, while oaks are slower to turn, extending the season and providing a range of colors at any one time. White pine becomes more common as you travel north, where it can frequently be found growing on reclaimed agricultural land. That tree has smoother bark than its cousin, the red or Norway pine; to tell them apart, count the needles: White pines grow in clusters of five (W-H-I-T-E), while red grow in clusters of three (R-E-D). Other trees growing in this region include hemlock and ash.

In the Great North Woods of northern New England, the deciduous trees eventually give way to endless tracts of boreal forest, consisting of spruce and fir. Unlike pines, whose needles grow in clusters, spruce and fir needles are directly attached to the stem. These coniferous trees are better suited to the short growing season and nutrient-poor soil of Maine, and provided an endless source of timber for shipbuilding and fuel. Mixed in with the evergreens is an understory of hardy broadleaf trees, including aspen, beech, and birch. Few New England scenes are more iconic than a stand of white-and-black-striped birch trees in winter, or festooned with canary-yellow leaves in fall.

Flowers

The jewel of the New England woodlands is the delicate lady slipper, a member of the orchid family that grows in wetland areas and gets its name from down-curving flowers that resemble women's shoes. The translucent flower, found in pink, white, and yellow varieties, is notoriously difficult to transplant or grow, since it relies on companionable fungi in the soil for its nutrients. If you are lucky enough to see one in the wild, take care not to disturb it, since some species are endangered, and some are even illegal to pick in Massachusetts.

Much more common, if no less beloved by naturalists, is trillium, so called because of its distinctive three-petal flowers. The flower grows in many colors throughout the New England woods, including bright white, deep red, and the particularly beautiful painted trillium, which sports a magenta center tapering off to white edges. One of the first flowers to bloom in April is the bloodroot, which carpets the ground with clusters of white flowers. As the season progresses, other wildflowers visible in the fields and meadows include the fuchsia-colored, anemone-like New England aster; orange clusters of wood poppy; wild bleeding heart; bright-red wild columbine with its distinctive tube-like flowers; and the ghostly sharp-lobed hepatica, which grows in deep woods and swamps and features eight blue-purple petals arranged around an explosion of fine white stamens.

FAUNA

The best opportunities for seeing wildlife in New England occur along the water. Many animal tours offer chances to see seals and seabirds off of the New England coast. Even inland, you are much more apt to stumble upon a moose or black bear from the vantage of a kayak than hiking along a trail. Most of New England's fauna is harmless—the charismatic megafauna of the western states has been mostly hunted to extinction, despite dubious reports of mountain lion sightings that crop up periodically. Even so, use caution when approaching a moose or black bear—especially if its young are in the area. You don't want to get on the receiving end of antlers or claws.

Land Mammals

The lord of the forest is a gentle giant—and a good thing, too, since coming face-to-face with a moose is a humbling experience. Up to six feet tall, nine feet long, and with an antler span of five and a half feet, a bull moose often startles those unprepared for just how *big* it is. Because of that, the herbivore has few enemies—natural or otherwise. Signs all over New Hampshire and Maine warn drivers about "moose crossings," since countless times each season a car is totaled after hitting one of the 2,000-pound beasts, which then serenely walks away from the accident. Take care when driving in those regions at night, especially during the spring and summer months, when the giant animals range widely in search of food. In the autumn, moose retreat to the deep forest, where they are much harder to encounter.

Not quite as imposing, but majestic in their own way, are the white-tailed deer that are common in the backwoods of all six states. In some places, such as the island of Nantucket, deer are so plentiful that they have even become a nuisance. The last documented specimen of mountain lion—also called catamount—was taken in Maine in 1938, the giant cat is generally accepted to be extinct from the region. Every year, however, there are some 100 supposed mountain lion sightings; among the most credible was one in 2009 by a Fish and Game employee outside Concord, New Hampshire. None of the sightings to date, however, have yielded any tracks, fur, or scat that would definitely confirm that mountain lions are back in the region, leaving their fabled existence on par with UFOs or Sasquatch. The smaller bobcat, however, is quite commonly sighted, often mistaken for a small dog. And in far northern New Hampshire and Maine hikers even occasionally spot a slightly bigger lynx, identifiable by the pointed tufts on its ears.

Not to be confused with the more aggressive grizzlies of western states, the timid black bear is a reclusive tree-inhabiting animal, which can sometimes be seen exploring garbage dumps of northern New England at night. Red fox inhabit both open fields and mixed forest, while the larger gray fox prefers the deep woods of southern New England. Coyotes are more apt to be heard than seen. And gray wolves make only rare visits to northern Maine from their habitat in Canada. No breeding populations currently exist in the region.

The most common mammals, by far, are rodents, which exist in multitudes throughout the six-state area. Gray and red squirrels, chipmunks, and raccoons are familiar sights in both suburban and rural areas. Wilderness locales are home to skunk, marten, mink, ermine, seven types of shrew, three types of mole, mouse, rabbit (including cottontail, jackrabbit, and snowshoe hare), flying squirrel, beaver, vole, otter, and porcupine. One of the lesser-known rodents is the fisher, a large mink-like animal known for its vicious temperament that has been becoming more common in past years. In addition to smaller rodents, it's been known to prey on raccoon, porcupine, and even small deer. Finally, New England is home to nine different species of bat, which roost in abandoned barns and trees, and can often be heard screeching at night in search of insects to eat.

Reptiles and Amphibians

The streams and ponds of New England thrive with frogs, toads, turtles, and other amphibians. Anyone who has camped near standing water in New England is familiar with the deep-throated sound of the bullfrog, which can seem like competing bullhorns at night as the eight-inch-long males puff up their resonant throat sacks in competition for mates. An even more cherished sound in parts of New England is the high-pitched chirping of the spring peeper frogs, which heralds the beginning of warm weather. A dozen different types of turtle inhabit the area; most common is the painted turtle, which sports colorful mosaics of yellow stripes on its neck and shell. More rare is the common snapping turtle, which can live up to its name if provoked. Wetland areas and swamps are also home to many species of salamander, which outdo each other with arresting shades of red, blue, and yellow spots and stripes. The most striking of all is the Day-Glo orange body of the red-spotted newt.

The most commonly encountered snake is the common garter snake, a black-and-green striped snake that is ubiquitous throughout the region, even on offshore islands. Aquatic habitats are inhabited by ribbon snake and the large northern water snake, which is harmless despite its aggressive demeanor. Woodland habitats are home to the eastern hognose, ringneck, and milk snake, among other species. Only two types of snake in New England are venomous. The northern copperhead is a yellow color with brown diamond-shaped markings on its back; it is extremely rare, located only in the lower Connecticut River Valley and coastal region of Connecticut, with another small population around Plymouth, Massachusetts. The timber rattler is even more rare, existing only in remote, isolated pockets in New Hampshire, Vermont, Massachusetts, and Connecticut. Thankfully, rattlers tend to shun areas inhabited by humans—and hibernate a full eight months out of the year, from September to April. If hiking in the backcountry of the Berkshires or Taconics, however, be wary of their distinctive dry rattling sound.

Insects and Arachnids

Ask any New Englander about native insects, and he's apt to immediately identify two: the mosquito and the black fly. The former find ample breeding ground in the wetlands of the region and feast annually on the blood of hikers and beachgoers. The black fly is, if anything, even more vicious. Thankfully it is more limited in both range and time period, thriving only in the late spring and early summer in northern New England. The other regional scourge is the gypsy moth, which every ten years or so appears in the form of thousands of tiny caterpillars that decimate the foliage. Many attempts have been made to curtail the menace, including introduction of a parasitic fly that eats gypsy moth larvae. Unfortunately, the fly also eats larvae of the luna moth, a delicate greenish moth with a wingspan of up to five inches that is New England's most beautiful insect. In recent years, the luna moth has made a comeback and it is a more common nighttime visitor in the region.

Due to all of the variations in habitat, New England is a rich breeding ground for creepy-crawlies, most of which are absolutely harmless. There are more spiders in New York and New England than there are bird species in all of North America. The only poisonous variety, however, is the black widow, which is recognizable by its jet-black body with a broken red hourglass on its abdomen. These spiders are extremely rare; and while their venom is a neurotoxin, only about 1 percent of bites end in death.

Sealife

Cape Cod didn't get its name for nothing; early settlers to New England were overwhelmed by its rich fishing stocks, thanks to the shallow-water glacial deposits of Stellwagen Bank north of Cape Cod and Georges Bank south of Nantucket. Both are rich breeding grounds for cod, stripers, bluefish, and other species. They are also popular stopovers for migratory whale species including humpback, fin, mike, and North American right whales. Other visitors to New England's oceans include white-sided and bottlenose dolphins, harbour porpoises, leatherback sea turtles, and grey seals, which are especially prevalent on Cape Cod in summer. Despite the filming of *Jaws* on Martha's Vineyard, Great White sharks are very rare; boaters and divers are more apt to see a harmless basking shark, which likes to feed on surface plankton.

Closer to shore, the most popular animal is the New England clam, of which there are two varieties, the soft-shelled clam or steamer; and the hard-shell clam or quahog, which is also known as littleneck or cherrystone depending on its size, and is generally found in deeper waters. Tidepoolers are apt to encounter both rock crabs and hermit crabs, along with sea stars, urchins, and periwinkle snails. New England's most famous sea dweller, the lobster, inhabits deep, rocky underwater coves all over the eastern United States. Ninety percent of lobsters, however, are found in Massachusetts, Rhode Island, and Maine. Contrary to popular belief, they are usually brown, blue, or green in color, and only turn red upon cooking. The biggest lobster ever caught was over two feet long, and weighed almost 40 pounds.

Birds

New England's location on the Atlantic Flyway from Canada makes the region prime bird-watching country. The region is home to some 200 species of birds that breed, winter, or live year-round in the region. Some common species like the black-and-white chickadee, blue jay, and cardinal are spotted commonly in both rural and urban areas. Others, like the elusive wood thrush, inhabit only the deep forest, where its liquid warblings reward hikers with a mellifluous serenade. Likewise, the ghostly "laughing" of the common loon is a common sound on lakes in Maine, where the bird also graces the state license plate. Several decades ago, bald eagles were introduced into the cliffs around the Quabbin Reservoir in central Massachusetts; now there are some 40 birds in the area, making them a relatively common sight for hikers and boaters.

Likewise, efforts have been made to preserve the coastal breeding grounds of 30 species of shorebirds, including plovers, sandpipers, and oystercatchers. Seabirds that are commonly seen near land include sea ducks, gulls, terns, and cormorants, while farther out to sea, boaters can spy petrels, puffins, jaegers, and auks. Many of the area's wildlife refuges have active communities of bird-watchers who track recurring species on both land and water.

ENVIRONMENTAL ISSUES

The biggest issue in southern New England is urban sprawl, caused by the region's increasing population coupled with a lack of developable space. The home-rule governments in much of New England routinely squelch any larger regional planning initiatives, along with so-called "smart growth" plans that would cluster population around town centers and public transit. As a result, much of the area around Boston is hampered by a lack of affordable housing and an encroachment on open space that has caused tensions between developers and conservationists. (That may slowly change, however, as Massachusetts has finally pushed through the first major reforms to its zoning laws in 30 years, requiring every town to have a master plan to manage growth.)

At the same time, species that were once seen only in the deep woods have been increasingly spotted in the suburbs, where foxes, coyotes, fishers and other animals have posed a threat to family pets. In northern New England, its not urban sprawl but tourist development that has threatened the wide tracts of open space. With the decline of the timber industry, which generally had a good relationship with outdoorsmen and environmentalists, residents of Maine and New Hampshire have looked for new sources of income from the tourist trade, and struck uneasy bargains to preserve some tracts of land while developing others for roads and resorts.

New England's regulatory economy has ensured that much of the area enjoys clean air and water, even as efforts have been made to clean up the pollution of the mills and factories that boosted the economy in the 20th century. Isolated chemical factories and power plants continue to cause problems in some specific areas. One of the country's first nuclear power plants was commissioned at Seabrook in coastal New Hampshire, which became the site of a protest in the late 1970s that sparked the national movement against nuclear power. Despite that protest and periodic rumblings by environmentalists, Seabrook is still an operating power plant and a tourist destination to boot.

One of the most contentious ongoing issues in the region is controversy over how to effectively manage the coastal stock of fish and shellfish. Rampant overfishing decimated the stock of cod, flounder, and other groundfish species by the mid-1980s. At that point, the federal government seized the entire region's fisheries and began a desperate bid to restore populations using quotas and periodic bans. While the effort has been successful at restoring some species, such as haddock and bluefish, others still languish at severely reduced levels—with cod even less plentiful than in the 1980s. And along with the fish stocks, many fishermen have languished as well. Tensions between fishermen and regulators have led to angry protests and outright flouting of quotas, as well as disputes over the numbers used by scientists and environmentalists to justify them. At this point, the two sides are cooperating in an uneasy peace. And while New England's fishing community is nowhere near as vibrant as it once was, it has nevertheless managed to survive.

History

EARLY HISTORY
Native Inhabitants

Hard on the heels of the last glaciers retreating northwards, humans began to move into the area now known as New England about 10,000 years ago. By the time European settlers began to poke around the coasts, there were already anywhere from 25,000 to 100,000 Native Americans inhabiting the region. Unlike the Iroquois Confederacy in upstate New York or the mighty Algonquin tribes of Quebec, however, most New England tribes were small and unaffiliated with larger governments, making them both extremely mobile and vulnerable to manipulation and extermination by European settlers.

Romantic images of a dense wilderness inhabited by primitive savages are somewhat off the mark. Especially in southern New England, tribes such as Wampanoags, Narragansetts, and Pequots were quite civilized, growing corn, beans, squash, tobacco, and other crops to supplement their hunting and fishing. These tribes even cultivated the forest itself, burning wide

Wampanoag re-enactors at Plimoth Plantation

swaths to get rid of the undergrowth and allow park-like land that was ideal for hunting game and harvesting berries.

North of the Saco River in Maine, tribes such as the Micmacs, Abenakis, Penobscots, and Passamaquoddys were more nomadic by nature, subsisting entirely on hunting, fishing, and gathering. In the spring, they made use of fishing grounds on the coast for shellfish and birds; then in the summer they moved inland to ply the rivers with birch-bark canoes in search of larger game like elk and moose.

Early Explorers

Viking longships might have sailed the rivers of New England as early as the 11th century; if they did, however, they left no traces to definitively prove it. Instead, legends of Norse visitors from Iceland and Greenland remain just that—legends—supplemented only by highly dubious reports of "discoveries" of Viking rune stones in areas of the Maine and Massachusetts coast. As late as 50 years ago, however, historians also doubted that Vikings had colonized Newfoundland—until a settlement was unearthed there in 1960. This settlement was thought by many to be Vinland, a land mentioned in the Viking sagas as founded by Eric the Red west of Greenland. Others, however, have noted that grapes don't grow that far north and instead surmise that the actual location of Vinland is farther south in New England, perhaps on Cape Cod or in the area of Popham Beach, Maine.

The first documented European mariner to spy the New England coast was Giovanni da Verrazano, who sailed up from New York in 1524 and explored Block Island and Narragansett Bay, and rounded Cape Cod to Maine before returning to France. The first settlements in the region, however, didn't come until a half-century later, when Bartholomew Gosnold formed a small outpost southeast of Cape Cod (which he named) on what is now Cuttyhunk Island in 1602. That settlement was abandoned, however, when the explorers returned home in the winter.

To the north, French captain Samuel de Champlain sailed along the coast of Maine and New Hampshire, gave his name to Lake Champlain in 1609, and founded several small fur-trading settlements north of New England along the St. Lawrence River in Quebec. Other settlements followed down the coast, mostly small French and English fishing villages on the islands and peninsulas of the Maine coast, which were also abandoned when holds were filled with enough salt cod or beaver pelts to make a profitable crossing back to Europe.

Pilgrims and Puritans

In the end, it was spiritual rather than commercial desires that made the settlement of New England possible. After years of fighting between Catholics and Protestants in England, Queen Elizabeth I passed the Act of Uniformity in 1559, making it illegal not to attend official Church of England services. Throughout the next few decades, an increasingly persecuted minority of separatists advocated a break with the official church. After several of their leaders were executed, the separatists fled to Holland

FEELING BLUE?

There's a reason we call them Puritans. The early inhabitants of New England had one of the strictest codes of laws known to man. And just a glance through their annals could leave one with the impression that they were originators of modern sadomasochism as well. Punishments regularly doled out included whipping, dunking, hanging, and forcing lawbreakers to stand for hours in the stocks – not necessarily in that order. The first few laws listed in their 1647 law book are nothing if not consistent. Having false gods: death. Witchcraft: death. Conspiracy: death. Murder: death. Poisoning, kidnapping, sodomy, beastiality: death. Talking back to your parents after you turn 16: death (a fun fact to share with your kids during vacation). In 1692, laws were passed against "unnecessary and unseasonable" walking in the streets on Sundays, being French, and using witchcraft to "entertain, employ, feed, or reward any evil and wicked spirit." Just in case anyone was still having fun, the civic fathers in 1711 made it illegal to sing, dance, fiddle, pipe, or use a musical instrument at night. In 1787, a law was passed to jail pipers, fiddlers, runaways, and "stubborn children." The part about stubborn children wasn't deleted until 1973. While most of these colonial prohibitions have long since disappeared, some have survived in the form of so-called **"blue laws"** that still put the damper on fun. Connecticut, for example, still has laws against buying or selling alcohol on Sunday. In Massachusetts, "happy hour" drink specials are forbidden. And then there are the early bar closing times (by 1 or 2 A.M. in Boston) that have rankled generations of New England college students. They should just be happy they weren't born in 1650!

in 1608. But the Netherlands' alliance with England against Spain meant that persecutions continued there, and the separatists eventually hatched a plan to journey beyond the reach of the Queen by founding a colony in the New World. They received backing from the Virginia Company to set sail aboard the *Mayflower* in 1620.

The Pilgrims, as they called themselves, originally intended to set sail for the nascent colony of Jamestown in Virginia. Blown off course, however, they landed in what is now Plymouth, Massachusetts, outside of the jurisdiction of their backers. Before disembarking, they drafted the Mayflower Compact, a hastily arranged document that established the government of their new Plymouth Bay Colony. The primary author of the document, Rev. William Bradford, became governor. Of the 102 passengers aboard ship, almost half of them were not Pilgrims at all, but adventurers who hitched a ride to the New World, including the capable Captain Myles Standish, hired to be military commander for the colony. His skills were not initially needed, since Wampanoag people under their chief Massasoit were friendly to the new colonists, helping them plant corn and hunt. The cold and scarcity of resources took a harsh toll on the colonists, however, causing more than half of them to die in the first year. By the time Bradford called for celebration of the first Thanksgiving in the fall of 1621, he was thanking God not only for the bountiful harvest, but also for the colony's very survival.

The real settlement of New England didn't begin until the arrival a decade later of another band of religious seekers, the Puritans. Unlike the Pilgrims, the Puritans did not advocate a complete break from the Church of England. Rather, they believed the church could be reformed from within by returning to a stricter interpretation of the Bible and dispensing with many of the trappings and rituals that the Church of England had picked up from Catholicism. An increasingly dictatorial King Charles I, however, abolished parliament and began cracking down on any religion that didn't subscribe to the official tenets of the Church of England. In 1629, settlers under minister and orator John Winthrop decided to leave England altogether to found a new "shining city on a hill" that would serve as a paragon of morality to the rest of the world.

The following year, 1630, a full complement of eleven ships carrying more than 1,000 passengers landed on the tip of Cape Cod near Provincetown. Finding scarce resources, they moved on to land on another small peninsula that the Native Americans called Shawmut, or "Land of Living Waters," due to the teeming schools of fish in its harbor. There they resolved to found their city, which they named Boston, after the city in East Anglia where many of them had originated.

Boston wasn't exactly uninhabited—the first English settler of the peninsula was the Reverend William Blackstone, a hermit who came there alone around 1623 and built a house by a freshwater spring beneath three hills he called the "trimountain." But he was happy to sell the land to the new arrivals, and Winthrop and his crew declared Boston the new capital of the Massachusetts Bay Colony in 1632. Immediately, they proceeded to enforce a strict moral code that imposed death as punishment for crimes ranging from taking the Lord's name in vain to talking back to your parents. From that center, colonists quickly spread out north and west to form dozens of new cities and towns, fueled by waves of thousands of new immigrants over the next decade. The settlement of New England had officially begun.

More Settlers Arrive

At the same time that the Pilgrims and Puritans were settling Massachusetts, a hardier band of hunters and woodsmen finally established beachheads in northern New England. English aristocrat Sir Ferdinando Gorges established the Council of New England in 1621 and began making land grants and sending groups to hunt and fish the area. An early grant called the Laconia Company spanned the Merrimack and Kennebec Rivers north of Massachusetts

Bay. While the company was disbanded a few years later, many of the settlers remained, forming a loose confederation of parishes in what would later become New Hampshire and Maine. In 1624, they sent the first shipment of white pine to England, starting what would later become a rich trade in lumber for ships' masts.

Meanwhile, as the persecuted Puritans became themselves persecutors, religious "heretics" left Massachusetts Bay in search of new colonies where they could themselves worship in peace. A Salem minister named Roger Williams, an early proponent of the separation of church and state, was found guilty of heresy and banished in 1636. Traveling southwest, Williams and a few followers settled on Narragansett Bay and founded the city of Providence. A few years later, the English crown dispensed an official charter for the Colony of Rhode Island. From the beginning, this colony proved infinitely more tolerant than others in New England, recognizing freedom of religion, freedom of speech, and other rights we recognize today. Williams also enjoyed friendly relations with Narragansett people, who were proving more hostile to the Puritans.

Soon after Williams founded Providence, another group led by Anne Hutchinson, a teacher who believed that inspiration came directly from God without need of a Church, came to Rhode Island to found the city of Portsmouth in 1638. Some of these settlers later moved further south to found the city of Newport. At the same time, Hutchinson's fellow iconoclast, the Rev. John Wheelwright, took his congregation north to settle in what would later become New Hampshire. Originally founding the town of Strawbery Banke (which would later become Portsmouth), Wheelwright was kept moving by the expanding boundaries of Massachusetts Bay Colony, founding the towns of Exeter, New Hampshire, and eventually Wells, Maine.

Finally, several factions within the Puritan sect split off to form their own colonies. Discouraged with the strictures on government participation in Boston, the Rev. Thomas

Hooker set out to found Hartford along the Connecticut River in 1636, and set up a more inclusive form of government in which every male member of the church could vote. Farther south, a pair of English merchants formed the colony of New Haven in 1638. The two colonies merged to form the colony of Connecticut in 1662.

King Philip's War

Unlike in Rhode Island, however, the new inhabitants of Connecticut didn't enjoy friendly relations with the native inhabitants. Soon after Europeans made incursions into the area, a pair of British merchants were found killed by Pequots on the Connecticut River. That incident set off an escalation that led to raids and reprisals on both sides and eventually a plan by the settlers to wipe out their native enemies. The Pequot War of 1637 was in reality a quick business, in which 130 settlers together with Narragansett and Monhegan allies wiped out the entire Pequot tribe.

That war was only a skirmish in the upcoming Indian Wars that would completely alter the colonies in the next few decades. After the deaths of Plymouth Colony's Governor Bradford and his Natve American ally Massasoit, tensions between settlers and the Wampanoag people along the Massachusetts–Rhode Island border began to simmer. They eventually boiled over in 1675 in what would become known as King Philip's War. The conflict began when colonists arrested Massasoit's son Alexander on spurious charges. During the march he was forced to make to Plymouth, he sickened and died. Seeing the writing on the wall, Massasoit's younger son Metacomet (whom the colonists called Philip) launched a preemptive raid on the Massachusetts town of Swansea. The colonists counter-attacked by invading the Wampanoag camp at Mount Hope in Bristol, forcing 1,500 of the Wampanoag to escape by floating rafts across the river.

The war that followed drew together many of the Natve American tribes in New England in a last-gasp attempt to push back English expansion. Despite burning Providence and many other towns in the year-long campaign, the Natve Americans were defeated by their lack of supplies and treachery among warring tribes as much by the English force of arms. By the time peace was signed in 1676, Philip and more than 5,000 Natve Americans had been killed, with many more sold into slavery; on the English side, 500 colonists had been killed. After the war, many area tribes were permanently relocated to Rhode Island's South County, near the town of Charlestown, effectively spelling an end to autonomous Natve American presence in Southern New England in all but the far western frontier of Massachusetts.

The Colonial Period

Following King Philip's War, the residents of New England continued to expand and prosper. At the same time, England's Puritan-friendly regent Oliver Cromwell was replaced by the restoration of the monarchy under James II, who saw an opportunity to bring greater control over the bustling colonies. The ill-fated Dominion of New England, as the new government was called, only lasted two years—in some sense, however, it began the conflict between England and its colonies that would end in war a century later. In 1685, James named Sir Edmund Andros as viceroy over Massachusetts, Plymouth, Rhode Island, Connecticut, New Hampshire, and New York. After he levied taxes on the colonists, however, there were widespread protests against the arrangement. When William and Mary overthrew James in England's "Glorious Revolution," New Englanders also overthrew Andros, returning the colonies to direct rule by governors (including a united Massachusetts colony when Massachusetts Bay and Plymouth merged in 1691).

For the next century, New England's seemingly limitless supply of natural resources ensured that the region soon became a major player in the world's economy. In Massachusetts, religious zealotry gave way to a new dominion—not of God, but of cod. The "almighty codfish" was full of meat, could be salted and dried for long voyages by sea, and filled the waters around Massachusetts Bay by the schoolful. Based on the rich trade in the fish, along with lumber, furs, and rum, Boston became the third-busiest port in the entire British Empire by the early 1700s (after London and Bristol). By mid-century, Boston and other New England ports, including Portsmouth, Salem, Newport, and New Haven bustled with ships bringing in coffee, tea, textiles, and luxury goods imported from England.

Along with the benefits of being a colony, however, New Englanders had to shoulder the responsibilities. In 1754, when the mother country became embroiled in a dispute with France over trading rights in the Ohio Valley they were drawn into the fray. The resulting conflict, known as the French and Indian Wars, was fought in New York, Pennsylvania, and Quebec and eventually spelled the end of French claims to North America when it was resolved by the Treaty of Paris in 1763. However, many New Englanders fought in the conflict, and its aftermath was strongly felt in the region. The war directly benefited traders in Maine, New Hampshire, and the burgeoning territory of Vermont by eliminating competition from the French in the fur and lumber trade. Because the Natve Americans allied with the French, the war also caused the defeat of the Algonquin and Mohawk tribes who badgered inhabitants in western and northern New England with periodic raids. The most important effect of the war, however, was economic. Saddled with debt from its mammoth military undertakings, England decided to levy taxes on the colonies to pay for the war. After all, the crown reasoned, hadn't the colonies been the ones who benefited the most from the defeat of the French and Natve American tribes? Unfortunately for England, the colonists saw things differently.

WAR AND REVOLUTION
Early Rumblings

A decade before the outbreak of the Revolutionary War, few American colonists even considered independence from the Crown. Relations with England, while sometimes tense, were mutually beneficial for both parties, giving the colonies protection and a ready market for their goods, and giving England a source of raw materials and income. Millions of words have been spilled over what caused the

THE FORGOTTEN PATRIOT

Amid the graves in Boston's Granary Burying Ground is the final resting place of the man who has been called the Father of the Revolution, but who is virtually forgotten today. Born in 1725, **James Otis** was the most gifted speaker of the colonial era. More than a decade before the shots were fired at Lexington, he made a five-hour speech in court arguing against the Writs of Assistance (which allowed the Crown to search for smuggled goods on colonial vessels) and stated for the first time that "taxation without representation is tyranny." No less a figure than John Adams pinpointed the moment as the start of resistance against England. Otis later led the charge against the Stamp Act and the Townshend Acts with Samuel Adams. During a tavern brawl in 1769, however, he was hit on the head by a British soldier and literally lost his senses. For the rest of his life, he ran around the streets of Boston half-clothed, half-drunk, shooting off his musket at odd hours, and generally becoming an embarrassment to his fellow Sons of Liberty. He did at least get one final wish. Before his madness, he had written to his sister that he hoped when God decided to "take me out of time into eternity, that it will be by a flash of lightning." In May 1783, just a month after Congress officially declared victory in the Revolution, Otis was struck by lightning in Andover, Massachusetts, and died, virtually forgotten and disowned by the country he helped start. Not even his gravestone in Boston makes mention of the role he played in the beginnings of America.

quick snowball to war, but it essentially comes down to one: taxes. Even before the French and Indian Wars, the colonies had been curtailed by the Navigation Acts, which prohibited the colonies from trading directly with countries other than England (smugglers carrying molasses from the West Indies, of course, had no trouble circumventing these laws). Another provision that reserved any tree over 24 inches in diameter for use of the Royal Navy rankled northern woodsmen. But it wasn't until after the war that the British crown levied a tax directly on the colonies in the form of a stamp required for licenses and legal services. The protests against the Stamp Act of 1765 were surprising to the crown in their vehemence—throughout the colonies, citizens fumed about taxation without representation in parliament and took to the streets to show their displeasure. The furor was so great that the law was repealed a year later.

In its place, however, Parliament enacted a series of laws that were even more damaging to the maritime trade of New England—the Townshend Acts of 1767. Named for the British Chancellor of the Exchequer, these acts levied a series of taxes on imports including paint, lead, paper and, most outrageous to the colonists, tea. Merchants in Boston immediately responded with boycotts of British products, convincing their colleagues in New York and Philadelphia to follow suit. In 1770, Bostonians even sent back thousands of pounds of British goods back to England on a ship owned by rich merchant John Hancock. Eventually Parliament capitulated and repealed all of the taxes except one—the tax on tea.

In this atmosphere of heightened animosity, a simple argument about the payment of a barber's bill by a British soldier led to a confrontation with an angry mob that left five colonists dead. An early instance of the use of propaganda, the act was dubbed the Boston Massacre by Whig politician Samuel Adams and used to stir up resentment against British troops quartered in the city. Adams was a member of the Sons of Liberty, a radical underground group of activists who sought greater autonomy from the British Empire. After the incident, he scored a victory when British troops were removed from Boston. However, the incident did little to advance the cause of independence. The troops were defended by Adams's cousin John Adams and acquitted of murder at trial.

Elsewhere in New England, incidents displayed the growing sentiment of the colonists against the British. In Connecticut, the local branch of the Sons of Liberty succeeded in deposing the colonial governor and installing one of their own members, Jonathan Trumbull, in his place. In 1772, a group of patriots in Providence, Rhode Island, raided and set fire to the Royal Navy ship *Gaspee.* But the road to revolution was by no means sure until the night of December 16, 1773. That year, Parliament passed an even more stringent law on the importation of tea. Colonists fought back by dressing up as Natve Americans and stealing aboard three British ships at night. There they dumped 90,000 pounds of tea into the harbor in an act provocatively dubbed as the Boston Tea Party.

British retribution was swift. Upon receiving word of the act, Parliament passed the so-called Intolerable Acts, which set up a blockade of Boston Harbor and consolidated more power over the colonies in the hands of the crown. Sympathetic governments in Rhode Island and Connecticut delivered aid to the residents of Boston during the blockade. The following September, delegates from all of the 13 colonies met in Philadelphia in the first Continental Congress and escalated the tension, declaring their opposition to *any* British law enacted without representation from the colonies. The stage was set for war.

From Lexington to Bunker Hill

After the Boston Tea Party, Sam Adams, rich merchant John Hancock, and the rest of the Sons of Liberty moved quickly to prepare for the eventuality of armed conflict. With Hancock's money and Adams's fiery rhetoric, they were able to prepare colonists around the region both physically and emotionally for battle. They also began caching arms and ammunition in various storehouses close to Boston, and helped to organize militia companies that could join battle at a moment's notice—calling them "minutemen." For their part, the British army commanders knew that they were severely outnumbered by the colonists if war should break out, and realized that their best hope lay in seizing the caches of arms before the general populace could be whipped up to a war frenzy.

When British troops finally marched out from Boston to capture the ammunition stores in Concord in April 1775, setting alight the Revolutionary War, it wasn't the first time they had tried. A few months earlier, British General Thomas Gage had ordered a scouting party north of Boston in Marblehead to search for munitions stored in Salem. Despite a tense standoff with local minutemen, that day ended without bloodshed. In response, the Sons of Liberty set up an elaborate warning system to alert the populace should the troops try again. Two months later, on April 16, riders including Paul Revere had already raised the alarm ahead of the 700 soldiers that marched out of the city en route to Concord. At the time, Adams and Hancock were staying with a friend in the nearby town of Lexington. They hastily organized a show of resistance before themselves escaping back to Boston. By the time an advance party of 300 men under Major John Pitcairn marched into town, they found several dozen minutemen and veterans of the French and Indian Wars ranged on the town common warily clutching their muskets. Someone fired a shot, and by the time the smoke cleared eight colonists were dead. The first battle of the American Revolution took only a few moments, but it was only the beginning of a day of increasing bloodshed.

The Battle of Lexington was followed by another battle a few hours later in Concord. There several hundred minutemen had assembled from neighboring towns on the hill overlooking the North Bridge. Seeing smoke rising in the distance, some feared that the British had set fire to the town, and began to march toward the bridge. A British platoon opened fire, killing two of the colonists. As word spread of the casualties to their comrades, minutemen by the thousands began taking up positions behind houses, trees, and stone walls between Concord and Boston. After destroying what they could of the colonial munitions (most had been hidden before British arrival), the tired British began marching back to Boston through a deathtrap. In the long march back, 73 British soldiers were killed, with another 200 wounded or missing. On the rebels' side, only 49 were dead, with 44 wounded or missing. The implications of the battles, however, went far beyond the actual results. By proving that they could stand up to the most fearsome army in the world and win, the patriots recruited many other colonists to their cause.

Their next test occurred two months later at the Battle of Bunker Hill. The battles at Concord and Lexington were mere skirmishes compared to the bloody confrontation that occurred in Charlestown on June 17, 1775. A few days before, the newly formed Continental Army took up a position in Charlestown, just across the harbor from the British forces in Boston. For General Gage that was too close, and he decided it was time to knock out the colonials once and for all. Due to a last-minute change in plans, the so-called Battle of Bunker Hill actually occurred on Breed's Hill. Before the battle began, the colonists' commanding officer Colonel William Prescott, noting that his troops were low on powder, supposedly made the famous statement: "Don't fire until you see the whites of their eyes." The ensuing battle succeeded in dislodging the colonists, forcing them to retreat back to Cambridge. But like Concord and Lexington, the battle showed the force of the inexperienced Americans over the superior fighting power of the British. In three assaults up the hill, the British lost more than 1,000 men, while the colonists only lost half that. Perhaps wishing to even the score, the British commander Howe later said that the death of popular American General Joseph Warren was equal to the death of 500 patriots. Nevertheless, the Battle of Bunker Hill showed the world that the American Revolution was definitely *on*.

A grey circle of bricks marks the site of the Boston Massacre.

The Siege of Boston

After Lexington, Concord, and Bunker Hill, the British Army found itself in a precarious position, holed up in Boston surrounded on all sides by countryside teeming with hostile colonists. Schooled by the French and Indian War, many of the colonists were skilled fighters and military strategists. One of them, George Washington, now assumed command of the Continental Army in Cambridge, Massachusetts, in June 1775, and began a tense standoff with British General William Howe, who had replaced Gage as commander. Not eager to risk another bloody battle like the one at Breed's Hill, Washington commissioned Boston bookseller Henry Knox to drag 59 cannons to Boston from Fort Ticonderoga in upstate New York, which had been captured the previous month by a force of Massachusetts and Connecticut soldiers under the command of Benedict Arnold, and Ethan Allen's Green Mountain Boys of Vermont. Knox arrived at the fort in December 1775, and took more than two months to complete the journey across

more than two hundred miles of snow and ice. On the night of March 14, 1776, Washington's forces quietly dragged the cannons to the top of Dorchester Heights, where they commanded a deadly vantage over the city. A few days later, on March 17, 1776, Gage evacuated the city by ship to Nova Scotia without firing a shot—leaving much of New England free from British forces on land.

Battles Across New England

After the early successes in Massachusetts, the most important engagements of the war continued in the southern and mid-Atlantic states. However, over the next seven years of fighting, each of the New England states except New Hampshire would see blood spilt on its soil. Before he famously turned traitor, Benedict Arnold took his troops through the woods of northern Maine in an ill-fated attempt to attack Quebec City on December 31, 1776. Undone by hunger and smallpox, Arnold was defeated in his attacks on the city. Most of the fighting that did occur in Maine itself happened off its coast. Even before Dorchester Heights, ships of the fledgling Maine Navy captured the loyalist sloop *Margaretta* off the coast of Machias in what is regarded as the first naval battle of the war. In response, the British sent a fleet of six ships to bombard Falmouth, Maine (outside of Portland), nearly burning the entire town to the ground. Later in the war, in 1779, Maine saw one of the conflict's largest naval battles, when more than 20 colonial ships attacked a fleet of British warships stationed in Castine in Penobscot Bay. The campaign ended in disaster, however, in part due to the foolhardy actions of one Paul Revere, who was captaining a ship at the end of the Continental line and broke ranks, foiling the fighting formation. In one of the ironies of history, the commanding officer of the British fleet was General Peleg Wadsworth, the grandfather of Henry Wadsworth Longfellow, who years later would immortalize Revere in his poem "The Midnight Ride of Paul Revere."

Amazingly, even after the Battle of Bunker Hill, colonists were still split on the virtues

historical re-enactors at Concord Bridge

of declaring full independence from Great Britain. First among the colonies, Rhode Island bit the bullet to declare itself a sovereign nation on May 4, 1776, two months before the Declaration of Independence. The state did not fare well in the ensuing war, however. In December 1776, after a sea battle off the coast of Point Judith, the British fleet blockaded Narragansett Bay, trapping much of the Continental Navy in Providence. For the next few years, they occupied Newport, terrorizing the populace and bringing shipping to a standstill. In 1778, Washington attempted to liberate the port by sending Massachusetts General John Sullivan and 8,000 men to attack. However, a fierce storm prevented allied French ships from landing with reinforcements, and Sullivan was unable to take the city. The British remained in Newport until 1779, when they voluntarily withdrew to aid fighting farther south.

Of all the New England states, the hardest hit during the war was Connecticut, which was an enticing target due to its rich industrial base and its proximity to British strongholds in New York. In April 1777, 2,000 British troops sacked Danbury, defeating 200 militiamen (again led by Arnold), and destroying vast amounts of tents, food, and other stores that would have come in handy for Washington when he was freezing in Valley Forge that winter. To help the troops survive, Connecticut Governor Jonathan Trumbull helped round up cattle and drive them down to Pennsylvania for Washington's troops. Over the next few years, Connecticut was pillaged several more times, at Greenwich, New Haven, Fairfield, and Norwalk. The most devastating attack took place in September 1781, towards the end of the war, in Groton and New London. There Benedict Arnold—now fighting on the British side—took 2,000 troops and decimated the forts in both cities, burning much of New London to the ground.

The Battle of Bennington

When the war broke out, Vermont wasn't even yet an independent colony. Much of what would become Vermont was occupied by settlers in land grants from the governor of New Hampshire, who fought competing claims against encroachers from New York. In January 1777, an assembly declared Vermont an independent republic, initially called New Connecticut. (Even so, neither Vermont nor Maine were among the original 13 states. Vermont wasn't admitted into the union until 1791. Maine remained part of Massachusetts until 1820.) The fledgling republic gained new legitimacy a few months later during the Battle of Bennington, which proved to be the first battle in which the colonials beat the British in combat. The crucial victory led to the turning point of the war a few months later at Saratoga, and helped convince France and Spain to intervene on the side of the Americans.

The battle took place in two parts in August 1777, when, fresh from victory at Fort Ticonderoga, the British General John "Gentleman Johnnie" Burgoyne was marching down the Hudson River Valley to meet up with British troops from New York. The plan was to cut off New England from receiving supplies and reinforcements from the rest of the colonies, thereby setting it up for easy capture. Feeling the pinch of lack of supplies himself, however, the general made a fatal mistake when he decided along the way to capture a large storehouse of food and munitions in the small town of Bennington, Vermont.

Under command of the German Colonel Friedrich Baum, Burgoyne sent some 500 troops—including several hundred of the dreaded Hessian mercenaries—to raid the town. Unbeknownst to him, however, the American Colonel John Stark had previously set off from New Hampshire with 1,500 troops of his own. On August 16, Stark took the battle to the enemy, swarming up a ridge along the Wolloomsac River to attack Baum's position. In a short but bloody battle, his militiamen killed Baum and captured many of his men. Certain of victory, the excited Americans began pursuing the enemy, when they were surprised by a relief column of another 600 Hessian soldiers under Lieutenant Colonel Von Breymann.

Stark was pushed to retreat back towards Bennington. The tide of the battle turned once more, however, with the arrival of Colonel Seth Warner and 300 of his Green Mountain Boys, who had marched from Manchester, Vermont. In the second engagement, the Germans were routed and fled back to the Hudson, while the Americans claimed victory.

The battle was an embarrassing defeat for Burgoyne, whose army suffered some 900 casualties to Stark's 70. At a time in the war when American morale was low, the battle also proved once again that backcountry farmers and militiamen could defeat the most disciplined troops of Europe. Just two months later, with his forces depleted and short on provisions, Gentleman Johnnie was forced to surrender at Saratoga.

War's Aftermath

As any history book will tell you, the Revolutionary War was won not by the Americans, but by the French and Spanish, who entered the war after the victory at Saratoga and blockaded American ports against the British, swinging the tide of battle in favor of the newly independent republic. In 1783, a full decade after the Boston Tea Party, British General Cornwallis surrendered at Yorktown, leaving 13 newly independent states. Like most of the rest of the country, New England was in rough shape by war's end, hamstrung by debt from the massive amounts of money needed for the war effort. Because of its unique position, however, it was able to bounce back more quickly than other areas. Since most of the fighting had occurred farther south, New England ended up with its infrastructure intact—in fact, once its blockades were lifted, it even benefited from the lack of competition from New York and Philadelphia, which were still embroiled in fighting. Initially the region felt the loss of the Tory upper class, which fled once fighting started. In their place, however, rose a new American merchant class who had made fortunes in previous decades smuggling molasses and financing privateers against the British. They quickly assumed control of New

England and set about doing what Yankees did best—making money.

19TH CENTURY
The Federal Period

No longer hampered by British strictures on trade, this new class of bourgeoisie was soon sending ships to the far ports of the world in search of trading goods. For a time, the city of Salem was the richest in the world from its cornering of the trade in pepper with the East Indies. Whaling ships from Nantucket and New Bedford sailed the South Seas in search of whales, growing rich themselves off the trade in spermaceti oil and whalebone corsets, which were all the rage on the Continent. Boston, meanwhile, remained the largest port in the United States, vying for supremacy with Philadelphia and New York in the years after the Revolution. All over the region, signs of the new wealth appeared in the form of stunning brick mansions and elm-lined streets.

Politically, New England also vied with the other colonial powerhouses, Pennsylvania, New York, and Virginia, to determine the path of the new country. Many prominent Bostonians, including John Hancock, Samuel Adams, and John Adams were part of the founding fathers at the Constitutional Convention in 1789, where they pushed for a stronger federal government to raise armies, tax the populace, and set trade policies. The Federalists, as they came to be known, had their strongholds in New England and New York and reached their apogee when John Adams was elected president in 1796. A national backlash, however, soon found the southern agrarians in power under Virginian Thomas Jefferson and the influence of the Federalists waned. Many New England states opposed the War of 1812 with Britain and abstained from sending troops (thankfully, a push to secede and form the New England Confederacy around this time failed). Over the ensuing decades, the Federalists competed with the more agrarian southern states to push policies that would benefit the manufacturers that became the underpinning of the northern economy.

Industrialization

The "dark satanic mills" (as English Romantic poet William Blake called them) sprouted throughout England in the 18th century, transforming Europe into an industrialized economy. North America was slow to follow suit until after the war. In 1790, a British engineer named Samuel Slater was called in to rebuild the machinery at Moses Brown's textile mill in Pawtucket, Rhode Island. The innovations he put in place transformed the factory and began a trend that would blanket New England with mills at a record pace over the next few decades. In many ways the region was ideally suited for manufacturing, with many fast-running rivers to generate power, a steady supply of raw materials thanks to the shipping trade, and poor soil for the competing industry of farming. In short order, cities were transformed into mill towns with sturdy brick factories and blocks of rowhouses for low-wage workers who toiled endlessly spinning and weaving textiles. Along with the textile mills, other cities in the region won fame for production of consumer goods including shoes, paper, and clocks. A Scottish visitor to New England in the 1830s declared Niagara Falls and the mill town of Lowell, Massachusetts, the two greatest wonders of America.

As the New England factories churned out the goods, a new class of aristocrats emerged on Beacon Hill and in the seaport and manufacturing towns. Called Brahmins, they were known as much for their wealth as for their enlightened sense of noblesse oblige. Many were educated at universities such as Harvard, Yale, and Brown, which became national centers of learning and spawned scholars and researchers in natural science. Espousing Yankee values of thrift and modesty, many of the Brahmins eschewed more garish forms of wealth for the prestige of philanthropy and the arts. After all, many of their fortunes were one generation removed from rum-running and opium trading. Many Brahmins never forgot how they came by their wealth and took measures to redeem themselves, founding the first public library in Boston, and museums such as the Museum of Fine Arts.

Abolitionists and Transcendentalists

When Oliver Wendell Holmes Jr. declared in 1858 that Boston was the "hub of the solar system," he was referring not only to its wealth and financial influence, but also its intellectual influence. Over the two centuries since the Puritans arrived, Bostonians had gradually shed their strict morals and small-minded prejudices to develop a new, more all-embracing religious philosophy. The austerity of Puritanism—which taught that people were either elected to be saved or they were destined to be damned—may have commanded fear and respect in the days of the colonies, but post-Revolutionary New England was a prosperous, urbane culture, proud of its status as a national center of ideas.

Called Unitarianism, the new religion taught that God's salvation was available to anyone, not just those chosen few who were predestined for heaven. One by one, the New England Congregational churches "went Unitarian" and embraced this new philosophy, which emphasized an intellectual approach to the divine. And along with it came a new national conscience. Although early Unitarians were socially conservative, on political issues they were emphatically liberal. Congregants such as suffragist Susan B. Anthony were instrumental in organizing the women's movement. And prodded by ministers like William Ellery Channing and firebrand Theodore Parker, Boston stood at the forefront of the abolitionist movement.

Ever since the end of the Revolutionary War, the nation had faced a growing tension over slavery. Vermont and Maine, in fact, were admitted to the union only in compromises that also admitted southern, slave-owning states (Kentucky and Missouri, respectively). It was inevitable that it would eventually come to a boil. Once again, Rhode Island led the way, passing a law in 1784 for emancipation of all children born into slavery. No one, however, would have more effect on the abolitionist movement than William Lloyd Garrison, a preacher from Newburyport, Massachusetts, who tirelessly advocated for emancipation in his newspaper *The Liberator*. Forming the Anti-Slavery Society, Garrison was instrumental in making New England a center for abolitionist sentiment—which was championed in Washington by Massachusetts congressman John Quincy Adams. He was aided by Frederick Douglass, an escaped slave who settled on Beacon Hill and spoke tirelessly in support of emancipation throughout New England.

At the same time that Unitarianism was spreading across the country, it spawned a rebellion against itself in the form of a new philosophy, transcendentalism. In many ways, transcendentalism took the fundamental tenet of Unitarianism, that anyone could be saved, and took it a step father, declaring that churches themselves were unnecessary since people could experience a direct connection to the divine. Transcendentalists found this in a mystical communion with the natural world. Buoyed by a mystical communion with nature, its adherents called for a radical individualism that would break free from the tired conventions of Europe. From their home base in Concord, its two chief adherents, Ralph Waldo Emerson and Henry David Thoreau, laid down its philosophy and formed a nucleus of writers, including Bronson Alcott (and his daughter Louisa May) and Nathaniel Hawthorne, who would begin the flowering in American literature.

New England in the Civil War

No amount of philosophizing, however, could prevent the inevitable political clash of the Civil War. While none of the actual fighting of the war took place in New England, it could be argued that it was a New Englander who fired the first shot. Outraged by the passage of the Fugitive Slave Act, which demanded that captured slaves be returned to southern masters, Brunswick, Maine, resident Harriet Beecher Stowe wrote the novel *Uncle Tom's Cabin*, which galvanized public support in favor of the war. Tens of thousands of New Englanders enlisted in the fight, forming regiments from all six New England states. Among the most acclaimed was the Massachusetts 54th, the nation's first all-Black regiment, which was led by Bostonian Colonel Robert Gould Shaw, and suffered tremendous casualties in the heroic but tragic assault on Fort Wagner in July 1863. That same month, another New Englander, Joshua Chamberlain, won renown for his role in the Battle of Gettysburg. A professor at Bowdoin College, also in Brunswick, Maine, Chamberlain led the heroic defense of Little Round Top, saving the Union line through a dramatic flanking maneuver that caught the enemy by surprise. Two years later, in 1865, he received the flag of truce from the Confederate Army. Thus it's said in Maine that Brunswick both started and ended the war.

MODERN TIMES
The Immigrants Arrive

After the Civil War, the Golden Age of Sail gave way to the Age of Steam, as the railroad emerged to transport goods long distances. Increasingly isolated in the corner of a vast and growing country, New England gradually gave up its advantages in trade and manufacturing. New York surpassed Boston as the nation's largest port, and the opening up of the West and California decreased New England's dominance in the China trade. Even so, New England's Brahmin class continued to preside over vast amounts of wealth from their factories, and they began to show it in more and more elaborate ways. In addition to travel to other parts of the country, the railroad opened up many parts of New England to tourism, and grand Victorian "summer cottages" (read: mansions) and hotels were built along the coasts of Rhode Island and Maine, in the mountains of New Hampshire, and in the valleys of the Berkshires.

By the turn of the century, however, changes were occurring in the population. The first waves of immigrants from Ireland began in the early 1800s, but they intensified during the Great Hunger of 1850, during which two million people emigrated from the country. Many of them found their way to Boston, the closest major American city, and from there

Boston Irish Famine Memorial sculpted by artist Robert Shure

THE UNITED NATIONS OF NEW ENGLAND

Most of the place names in New England, not surprisingly, come from English or Native American roots. The rest of the world, however, is well represented in the names of small towns scattered throughout the region, which point to the origins – or imaginations – of their settlers:

- Athens, ME
- Athens, VT
- Belfast, ME
- Belgrade, ME
- Berlin, CT
- Berlin, MA
- Berlin, NH
- Bremen, ME
- Calais, ME
- Calais, VT
- China, ME
- Damascus, ME
- Denmark, ME
- Dublin, NH

sign in Lynchville, ME

- East Berlin, CT
- Egypt, ME
- Florence, VT

dispersed throughout the region. Poor but hard-working, many of them were welcomed in the mills. As their numbers swelled, however, a violent anti-Irish backlash began to coalesce among traditional Yankees anxious to hold on to their power and influence. In the mid-1850s, political groups called Know-Nothings burned Catholic churches and terrorized Irish communities.

The Irish won out by sheer numbers. By 1850, they comprised one-third of the city of Boston, with other cities boasting similar percentages. The new immigrants also organized themselves politically, forming a network of patronage politics in urban wards. Within just

a few generations, they completely changed the political make-up of the region, as represented in Boston by the colorful politician James Michael Curley. Curley spent almost as much time in prison as in political office in his early years—but eventually worked his way up to get elected to the U.S. House of Representatives in 1911. After failing to get reelected, he returned to Boston, where he presided over the city as mayor or governor for 30 years. A hugely popular and hugely corrupt politician, he was eventually convicted of mail fraud and pardoned by President Truman in 1947.

Waves of other immigrants followed the Irish, including Italians and French-Canadians

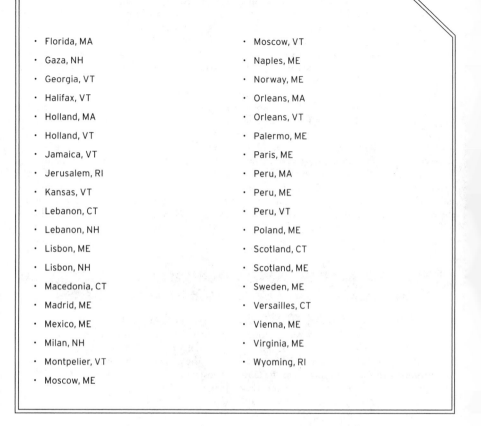

- Florida, MA
- Gaza, NH
- Georgia, VT
- Halifax, VT
- Holland, MA
- Holland, VT
- Jamaica, VT
- Jerusalem, RI
- Kansas, VT
- Lebanon, CT
- Lebanon, NH
- Lisbon, ME
- Lisbon, NH
- Macedonia, CT
- Madrid, ME
- Mexico, ME
- Milan, NH
- Montpelier, VT
- Moscow, ME
- Moscow, VT
- Naples, ME
- Norway, ME
- Orleans, MA
- Orleans, VT
- Palermo, ME
- Paris, ME
- Peru, MA
- Peru, ME
- Peru, VT
- Poland, ME
- Scotland, CT
- Scotland, ME
- Sweden, ME
- Versailles, CT
- Vienna, ME
- Virginia, ME
- Wyoming, RI

who also found work in the factories of the region. Not as complacent as the mill girls of a century earlier, the new immigrants helped push for improvements in working conditions. A 21-year-old Irish woman led her fellow female immigrants of more than two dozen different nationalities in walking out of a mill in Lawrence, Massachusetts, to perpetrate the Bread and Roses strike, one of the most significant watersheds in the labor movement. On the darker side, two Italian anarchists, Nicola Sacco and Bartolomeo Vanzetti, were unfairly accused of robbery and murder in 1920. Their case became a national cause célèbre, stirring up strong sentiments and prejudices about communists, immigrants, the labor movement, and the death penalty. Despite shoddy evidence and the intervention of prominent intellectuals such as Upton Sinclair and H. L. Mencken, however, they were found guilty and executed in 1927. Exactly 50 years later, Massachusetts governor Michael Dukakis issued a proclamation exonerating them.

Decline and Rebirth

By the time of World War II, New England was already in a period of slow decline. Many of the mills and factories that generated New England's wealth had become obsolete, and companies left the region in search of cheaper labor in other states and countries. At the same time, the urban centers that thrived in the previous century were abandoned by the middle class, who settled in streetcar suburbs on their outskirts. Despite various schemes to resurrect their cores, "urban renewal" was mostly a disaster, further hollowing out cities by bulldozing neighborhoods and erecting lifeless skyscrapers in their wakes. The sole bright spot in the postwar era was the election of one of New England's native sons, the charismatic war hero John Fitzgerald Kennedy as president in 1960. Even that hope was dimmed, however, when Kennedy was killed by an assassin's bullet three years later. After struggling with the rest of the nation through the 1960s and 1970s, however, the region rebounded in the 1980s by playing to one of its strengths: knowledge.

New England was one of the first regions of the country to realize the potential of the computer to transform American society. Led by a wealth of well-educated engineers from Massachusetts Institute of Technology and other area colleges, small technology firms grew into huge computer companies within a decade. The so-called Massachusetts Miracle revitalized the region and began a reversal of fortunes that injected wealth and self-confidence back into the cities. Since then, New England has been at the forefront of other technological revolutions, including the Internet and biotechnology, which has further bolstered its population and industrial base and left it well-poised for the 21st century. Indeed, when one of the worst recessions in the nation's history hit the country in 2008, New England fared better off than most regions due to its diversified economy and its scarcity of housing that kept up demand.

Government and Economy

GOVERNMENT AND POLITICS

It's been said that democracy was founded in Greece and perfected in New England. Many of the region's towns and villages are still run by town meetings that form the closest approximation to participatory democracy seen anywhere in the world. In cities, meanwhile, Democratic (with a big "D") machines founded by Irish and Italian immigrants still hold enormous sway. In fact, in many parts of New England, it can be assumed that residents are Democrats, if not even farther to the left. But there is more political diversity to the region than immediately meets the eye, from the Republican strongholds of southern Connecticut to the radical populists of Vermont, and the fiercely independent (and maddeningly mercurial) voters of New Hampshire. Even in liberal Massachusetts, the majority of voters are registered Independents, not Democrats, highlighting the individualism that has run through the political fiber of the region since the Revolution.

In national politics, Massachusetts casts a shadow much longer than its small size. Since the constitution was signed, prominent congressmen from the state have helped determine the course of the country, from Daniel Webster's compromise of 1850 to Tip O'Neill's long tenure over the House of Representatives in the 1980s to Ted Kennedy's unabashed liberalism in the Senate, where he loomed large in influence for 43 years. With the Democratic takeover of Congress in 2006, New England politicians found themselves chairing several major committees in the House and Senate. Typically, politicians from New England sit to the left on economic issues such as minimum wage and welfare, as well as national wedge issues such as abortion, gun control, and immigration. Even its Republican politicians, such as longtime Maine Senators Olympia Snowe and Susan Collins, often serve as voices of moderation within the party and temper the right-wing impulses of more radical conservatives.

New England recently rocked the nation in 2004, when the Massachusetts Superior Court declared that gays could not be prevented from

© MICHAEL BLANDING

Our smallest state, Rhode Island, has one of the more impressive state houses.

marrying. Since then, the issue has set off a furor nationally, with politicians in many states pushing through preemptive laws and constitutional amendments against gay marriage. In New England, however, the opposite has happened—since Massachusetts's court decision, Connecticut courts have also ruled gay marriage legal, and legislators in Vermont and New Hampshire have proactively passed laws allowing same-sex marriage (Maine lawmakers approved same-sex marriage, but the law was overturned by voters). As a result, now four of the five states in which gay marriage is legal are now in the region (the other is Iowa). Since these laws and court decisions, the initial outcry by many opposed to gay marriage has mostly died down. As gay men and lesbian women have become married and adopted children, many of the state's most prominent politicians and businesspeople have come out in favor of their unions. Even social conservatives mostly shrugged their shoulders when the promised apocalypse didn't happen, falling back on a typically Yankee sentiment of "live and let live."

Finally, New England has continued to influence the national dialogue on the most pressing national issue of the day—healthcare. Starting in 2005, Massachusetts began a grand experiment in requiring every citizen to obtain healthcare insurance, at the same time subsidizing care for those who couldn't afford it. The jury is still out on the system—it has cost significantly more than expected, and universal coverage still hasn't been achieved. However, the percentage of people without coverage in Massachusetts is down to 5 percent, and the state is now being used as a model for national healthcare legislation.

The region's stereotype as a bastion of liberalism, of course, means that politicians don't always fare well on the national stage. In several recent presidential races, New England candidates have gone down in flames: including Michael Dukakis, who lost in 1988 to George Bush; Paul Tsongas, who lost in the 1992 Democratic primary to Bill Clinton; Vermonter Howard Dean, who lost in the 2004 primary to Bay Stater John Kerry; and

NEW ENGLAND PRESIDENTS

JFK may be the best-known president from New England, but he's hardly the only one. Here's a handy guide to those Commanders-in-Chief hailing from the six-state area.

NAME	PARTY	YEARS	BIRTHPLACE	BEST-KNOWN FOR
John Adams	Federalist	1797–1801	Quincy, MA	Being Founding Father, Alien and Sedition Acts, providing material for future biographers
John Quincy Adams	Democratic-Republican	1825–1829	Quincy, MA	High tariffs, Republican infrastructure improvements, not living up to legacy of his father
Franklin Pierce	Democrat	1853–1875	Hillsborough, NH	Kansas Border War, alcoholism, being most unpopular president in history
Chester Arthur	Republican	1881–1885	Fairfield, VT	Rooting out corruption, becoming "Father of Civil Service"
Calvin Coolidge	Republican	1923–1929	Ludlow, VT	Presiding over Roaring Twenties, saying very little
John F. Kennedy	Democrat	1961–1963	Brookline, MA	Peace Corps, Cuban Missile Crisis, being assassinated while in office
George H. W. Bush	Republican	1989–1993	Milton, MA	First Gulf War, Fall of Berlin Wall, "Read my lips: no new taxes"
George W. Bush	Republican	2001–2009	New Haven, CT	Global War on Terrorism, Iraq War, frequent malapropisms

Kerry himself, who eventually lost in the general election to George W. Bush. The region is still looking for its standard-bearer to regain the Kennedy legacy in the White House.

ECONOMY

Four industries dominate the modern New England economy: technology, academia, medicine, and finance—with tourism a close fifth. The area is second only to Silicon Valley in its concentration of technology firms, which tends to make booms bigger and recessions deeper than other parts of the country. The great number of colleges and universities in the area has spawned a cottage industry of professors and researchers, who have also contributed to the region's status as a hub of medical innovation. In recent years, New England has become a hub of biotechnology and pharmaceutical firms, with Merck, AstraZeneca, and Novartis situating their worldwide research headquarters in the area. In a more traditional vein, the financial industry has always thrived with Yankee know-how. The mutual fund was invented in Boston, and there are probably more actuaries in Hartford than any other city on earth.

In addition to these urban pursuits, the area still has substantial concentrations of farming (particularly dairy), fruit cultivation (cranberries, apples, blueberries) and fishing (whitefish and lobster). All these industries, however, are failing under competition from cheaper imports from other countries or overfishing of fragile stocks. Where there is hope for local farms, it lies in the burgeoning sectors of organic foods and community-supported agriculture, which are in high demand among health-conscious and environmentally aware New Englanders.

People and Culture

Those who call New Englanders "cold" just haven't spent enough time with them. It's true that hellos and good days may not be as forthcoming here as in the South or the West, but New Englanders make up for a lack of superficial friendliness with a straightforwardness that lets you know exactly where you stand in their hearts. And if you do find your way into those hearts, you'll find an intense loyalty and camaraderie that is as surprising as the surface flintiness is off-putting. More than anything, New Englanders are bred on tradition, whether that's the rural pride of its farm-folk or the convivial parochialism of the South Boston Irish. But generations have not stood still; with the burgeoning technological, financial, and medical sectors, many of the cities in the region are filled with young professionals and culture vultures on the cutting edge of hip.

New Englanders' attitudes are very much a product of their backgrounds. With the Puritans' laws and mores embedded in their history and social traditions, Yankees are considered somewhat more restrained than people in many other parts of America. But that's often tempered by the other characteristics of their birthplace—a widespread reverence for higher education, a philosophical and artistic dedication to self-expression, and the ever-widening influence of its international citizens.

STATISTICS

New England is home to some 14 million people, who are unevenly distributed around the region. The majority of New England's population is centered in southern New England. Massachusetts is most populated, with 6.4 million people (or almost half of the region's population) within its borders. Connecticut is next with 3.5 million, followed by New Hampshire and Maine with a 1.3 million each, Rhode Island with a little over 1 million, and Vermont with just 600,000 people. That's the same number of residents who live in Boston, New England's largest city. The central Massachusetts city of Worcester is the region's second-largest city, with a population of 175,000. Just behind

STATE NICKNAMES

Each of the New England states – except one – has a nickname based on its most prominent feature. Massachusetts is called the Bay State after the giant ocean bay that stretches from Marblehead to Provincetown, one of the largest bays in the Atlantic Ocean, which gave its name to the original colony here. Rhode Island is called the Ocean State, after its 400 miles of coastline in a state with only 1,200 square miles of land area. New Hampshire is named the Granite State after the sheer granite peaks of the White Mountains – even though Barre, Vermont, and Vinalhaven, Maine have purer granite for commercial purposes. Vermont, naturally, is called the Green Mountain State, which is essentially just an Anglicization of its Francophone name. And Maine is named the Pine Tree State after its state tree, the White Pine, which lent its arrow-straight trunk to many a colonial-era ship's mast.

For its part, Connecticut's official nickname is the Constitution State, after the Fundamental Orders of 1638, which some scholars believe was the world's first constitution. A more common name for the state, however, is the Nutmeg State, a curious choice since nutmeg grows on the spice islands of the Caribbean. Some historians speculate that the name comes from the importance of the spice trade to early Connecticut seaports. Others contend that it was a derogatory term applied to Connecticut traders who slyly sold wooden nutmegs to unsuspecting buyers. Still others insist that those traders were maligned by country bumpkins who just didn't realize that the nutmegs had to be ground to release the spice, and mistakenly just thought they were being sold wooden nuts. Whatever the origins, Nutmeg has since trumped Constitution as the state nickname of choice for many residents, and all over the state you'll find proud references to local inhabitants as "nutmeggers."

that are the cities of Providence, the capital of Rhode Island (171,000); and Springfield, in Western Massachusetts (150,000); followed by Connecticut's largest cities, Bridgeport (136,000), New Haven (123,000), and the state capital of Hartford (124,000). Connecticut's smaller cities—Stamford and Waterbury—both ring in just a tad over 100,000, as does Manchester, New Hampshire, the only city of any size in northern New England. Portland, Maine's largest city, counts 62,000 people, while Burlington, Vermont, has just 39,000.

At present, the Gross Domestic Product of New England is about $640 billion—equal to about 20 percent of the economic output of the United States, and equivalent to whole countries such as India or Mexico. Individual citizens tend to be better off than their countrymen as well. At $68,000, the annual median household income for Connecticut is the highest in the country—with Massachusetts ($65,000) and New Hampshire ($64,000) not far behind. (Maine, on the other hand, struggles

near the bottom of the list with $46,000.) The average wage for workers spans between $900 and $1200 per week, comfortably above the national average (wages in Eastern Massachusetts and Connecticut are the highest, Rhode Island and Western Massachusetts the lowest). And the unemployment rate in New England was 8.1 percent at the height of the recession in 2009, well below the national average of 9.7 percent (Vermont is lowest with 6.8 percent).

As could be expected from a region that prides itself on its medical sector, New England is also healthier than the rest of the country. Buoyed by Massachusetts' new law requiring mandatory health insurance, the percentage of people without medical insurance is about 10 percent region-wide, compared with a national average of 15 percent—and disease statistics are correspondingly lower as well. And as might be expected from a socially liberal populace, marriage rates are among the lowest in the nation, at about 10 percent, compared with a national average of 16 percent. That said, once New Englanders do marry, they tend to stay together—the divorce rate for the region is just over 1 percent, compared to a national average that's twice that high.

The relative affluence of the region does have its downsides. New England's cost of living is the highest in the country (with the exception of Alaska), with goods and services averaging about 25 percent higher than the national average. One contributor to that is the high cost of housing—due to lack of space and high regulations on development, home prices in New England have shot up in recent years, with the median home price in some affluent towns around Boston topping $1 million. In part because of costs, the region has seen an exodus of population in past decades, with a net loss of tens of thousands of residents to the so-called Sun Belt of the South and Southwest United States. The region's population losses, however, have been offset by an influx of recent immigrants, especially from Central and South America and Eastern Europe, making the net change in population almost zero.

ETHNICITY

The most recent census figures reveal that New England averages slightly higher than the rest of the country in its numbers of Caucasian residents: just above 86 percent, compared to the nation's 75 percent. The second-largest group of inhabitants in the region is Latino at roughly 6 percent (which is only half the national average), followed by African Americans at approximately 5 percent, and Asian American at nearly 3 percent.

The northern states (Maine, New Hampshire, and Vermont) are more predominantly White (96 percent), while the southern states (Connecticut, Massachusetts, and Rhode Island) are more ethnically mixed (83 percent White). Within the Caucasian demographic of New England, the largest non-mixed groups tend to be Irish, Portuguese, and Polish. The

THE NEW ENGLAND DIALECT

It may be referred to most commonly as simply the Boston accent, but the eastern New England dialect can in fact be overheard all over the region in slightly different forms. Overlapping with the accents of Rhode Island, New Hampshire, southern Maine, and northeastern Connecticut, it is known among linguists primarily for one key feature: a phenomenon known as "non-rhoticity" (often demonstrated in films – think Ben Affleck in *Good Will Hunting*). This technical term essentially amounts to the phonetic elimination of the "r" following vowels in many words. (Hence the phrase, "Pahk youh cah in Hahvahd Yahd.")

Herewith, a brief key for deciphering some common New England-speak:

- **The Ahbs:** Nickname for the Arnold Arboretum, the Harvard University-owned park filled with rare and beautiful trees.

- **Ahnt:** Your uncle's wife.

- **Bubblah:** A water fountain.

- **Cawnah:** The place where two streets meet.

- **Cawnah stowah:** The convenience shop located on the place where two streets meet.

- **The Gahden:** Nickname for the Boston Garden or the TD Banknorth Garden, where concerts and events are held throughout the year, including home games of the Boston Celtics and the Boston Bruins.

- **Keggah:** A party with lots of beer (i.e., kegs), most common on college campuses.

- **Khakis:** What you start your car with.

- **Pahluh:** Front room (usually the living room) in a three-story apartment building.

NEW ENGLAND ON FILM

The kaleidoscopic foliage and picturesque old seaports of New England have proven irresistible to filmmakers ever since celluloid was invented. Hundreds of movies have been filmed around the region. For film pilgrims, here is a partial list of favorites.

- *Peyton Place* (1957): Camden, Maine, stands in for the quintessential New England village in this 1950s classic starring a ravishing Lana Turner.

- *Alice's Restaurant* (1969): Arlo Guthrie's epic story of taking out the trash, which inspired a Thanksgiving song ritual, was filmed in and around Great Barrington, Massachusetts.

- *Jaws* (1975): Martha's Vineyard was a perfect stand-in for Amity Island in the aquatic horror film that made director Steven Spielberg's reputation.

- *On Golden Pond* (1981): Squam Lake, New Hampshire, is still known as Golden Pond after taking a star turn in this tearjerker with Katherine Hepburn and Henry Fonda.

- *Pet Sematary* (1981): It's fitting that Maine's master of horror, Stephen King, would film this adaptation of his novel in his hometown of Bangor, Maine. (Acadia National Park also has a cameo.)

- *Federal Hill* (1994): Director Michael Corrente captures the grittier side of Providence, Rhode Island, in this on-location film about a young man torn between college and the mob.

- *The Spitfire Grill* (1996): This dark sleeper hit about a woman out of prison who finds work at a restaurant in a small Maine town was filmed in Peacham, in Vermont's Northeast Kingdom.

- *The Ice Storm* (1997): An all-star cast including Kevin Kline, Joan Allen, and Sigourney Weaver perfectly evoke the quiet desperation of 1970s suburban Connecticut, in this film shot on location in New Canaan.

- *Good Will Hunting* (1997): Matt Damon and Ben Affleck won screenwriting Oscars for

bulk of the region's Latino population traces its origins to the Caribbean and South America.

CULTURE

Two major strands of culture typify the region: the thriving rural culture that keeps alive farming, fishing, and livestock traditions, and the educated, intellectual culture that flows out from the colleges and universities. The most typical New England towns contain evidence of both: county fairs that still generate excitement in the populace, and cultural institutions such as museums, theaters, and art galleries that can be found in even the most remote corners of the region.

RELIGION

The region's earliest settlers may have been strict English Protestants, but due to waves of immigrants from French Canada, Italy,

Ireland—and most recently, from Latin and South America—Catholics are now far and away New England's largest religious group.

The most popular branches of Protestantism (members of which make up roughly one-third of the area's population) are Episcopalian, Congregational, Baptist, Methodist, and Pentecostal. Meanwhile, one of the world's most sizeable concentrations of practicing Jews calls Massachusetts home, and groups of the liberal-minded Unitarian Universalist church can also be spotted throughout New England. Sizeable Muslim and Hindu populations can be found in many of the region's cities.

LANGUAGE

English is by far the most widely spoken tongue in each of New England's states, with pockets of other languages also heard in towns known for large immigrant populations. (New their moody story about a genius janitor at MIT, filmed in Boston and Cambridge.

- *Amistad* (1997): The Massachusetts State House, Mystic Seaport, and locations in Newport and Providence all appear in Steven Spielberg's acclaimed tale of a 19th-century slave ship mutiny.

- *The Cider House Rules* (2003): Even though this adaptation of John Irving's novel is set in Maine, it was filmed just about everywhere else in New England, including Brattleboro and Bellows Falls, Vermont, and Lenox and Northampton, Massachusetts. The critically celebrated film stars Tobey Maguire, Charlize Theron, and Michael Caine.

- *Mystic River* (2003): Clint Eastwood filmed much of this Boston-based mob movie, adapted from a book by Boston-author Dennis Lehane, in and around the city; Sean Penn and Tim Robbins won best actor and supporting actor awards for the intensity of their performances.

- *Fever Pitch* (2005): Jimmy Fallon plays an obsessive Red Sox fan, and Drew Barrymore the woman who puts up with him, in scenes filmed at Fenway Park and other Boston locations. What the film lacks in plot and acting, it makes up for in capturing the fanaticism of Red Sox Nation.

- *The Departed* (2006): Martin Scorsese won his first Best Picture Oscar for another Lehane adapation, loosely based on the real-life story of Boston mobster Whitey Bulger, and the corrupt law enforcement agents who protected him. Jack Nicholson crews the scenery alongside Matt Damon and Leonardo DiCaprio.

- *Gone Baby, Gone* (2007): Ben Affleck's rookie outing as a director is not only a terrific suspense film with a surprise ending, but it is also one of the most accurate portrayals of Boston on film in years. Ben's brother Casey stars, along with Morgan Freeman, Alec Baldwin, Martin Sheen, and Dorchester homeboy Mark Wahlberg. The Quincy granite quarries have a memorable cameo.

Bedford, for example, where Portuguese is widely spoken; and Chinatown in Boston, where numerous Chinese dialects can be overheard on any given corner.)

Even within English, however, local idioms prevail in New England—particularly in Boston, where slang can be undecipherable to outsiders. Key terms to know include: "bang a U" (to make a U-turn while driving); "frappe" (known outside New England as a milkshake); and "wicked pissa" (meaning "very cool").

THE ARTS

A love of music and the arts has dominated New England's cultural scene for centuries, and thanks to the legacy of the Boston Brahmins (those blue-blooded families who ruled the city's society and industry in the 19th century) there are plenty of places to appreciate all of them—from large institutions like the Peabody-Essex Museum, Boston Symphony Orchestra in Massachusetts, and the Portland Museum of Art in Maine, to the small theatres of North Conway, New Hampshire, and independent art galleries of Burlington, Vermont.

Literature is also a big part of New England's abundant arts community—historically and in the present day. Writers Nathaniel Hawthorne, Edith Wharton, and Henry David Thoreau helped define the American character as they saw it from New England, and scribes such as Arthur Miller and John Updike have continued the tradition.

But much of the culture found in this area of the country is just as easily found in its streets, pubs, and parks. In and around Boston, Providence, and Portland, a thriving rock and folk music scene dominates the nightclubs and bars. (Boston in particular is the birthplace of bands ranging from The Pixies to Aerosmith.)

Further afield, in rural areas, you'll find plenty of folk-inspired performances—perhaps most notably distinct are the Acadian and Quebecois dance and folk music in northern areas of Maine.

SHOPPING

There's very little that even jaded shoppers can't find to buy in New England, thanks to the proliferation of designer boutiques and department stores in the cities (particularly Boston, Providence, and Portland) and galleries and independent stores selling artists' wares and crafts all over the six states. Handmade pottery and blown glass, for instance, are found throughout Vermont and Maine; wood-carving experts are plentiful in New Hampshire.

Designer outlets offering significant discounts on brand names are also a popular draw, and many have seen resort towns, hotels, and other attractions sprout up around them. The biggies are in Wrentham, Massachusetts; Manchester, Vermont; North Conway, New Hampshire; and Kittery and Freeport, Maine.

HOLIDAYS AND FESTIVALS

Rather than waiting for the weather to cooperate, New Englanders make their celebrations a year-round activity; even in the coldest temperatures, winter festivals abound. January's Stowe Winter Carnival in Vermont, for example, features snow golf, snowshoe-racing, ice-carving, snow volleyball, hockey, and parades. In the major cities, New Year's festivities get underway with arts festivals indoors and fireworks out.

In March, Boston is the place to be to toast St. Patrick's Day—both in the city's myriad Irish pubs and by watching its famed parade. June's highlights include the Arts & Ideas Festival in New Haven, Connecticut (the annual week-long celebration spotlights hundreds of performances, from opera on the green to hip-hop mini-festivals), and Boston's Harborfest, full of maritime history of the area along with fireworks, concerts, and historic reenactments.

In August, the world-famous Newport Jazz Festival takes over Rhode Island's seaside resort town, pulling in some of the world's biggest names in jazz. That same month, the Wild Blueberry Festival in Maine applauds the state's beloved crop with a children's parade, fish fries, a blueberry-pancake breakfast, crafts, and pie-eating contests.

Autumn is the region's prime time for tourism (and arguably its most beautiful season), so it's no wonder the festivals hit during those months. Vermont's Killington Foliage Weekend gets going every September, with a Brew Festival and gondola rides. Also in September is the Newport International Boat Show in Rhode Island, where nautical buffs can ogle 13 acres of sailboats, equipments, and demonstrations. October's Sea Harvest at Mystic Seaport includes a Chowderfest and plenty of fall foliage, and at the end of the month, Salem, Massachusetts brings in the crowds for Haunted Happenings—a packed schedule of witch trials and haunted harbor cruises.

The holidays gear up early in New England, with an impressive Christmas Craft Market in Rockport, Maine, stocked with locally made crafts from more than 70 vendors and artists. Then, come December, the quaint streets of Portsmouth, New Hampshire take a Rockwellian turn during the Candlelight Stroll at Strawbery Banke, as festively decorated period homes open their doors to tours, cider is passed around, and 1,000 candles are lit throughout the town.

ESSENTIALS

Getting There

New England is easily accessible by road, rail, and air (and even sea if you are coming by ferry from New York or Canada). While Logan Airport is the most obvious entrance, several of the region's smaller airports may offer cheaper flights from some cities. Amtrak's rail network isn't very extensive, but it does connect to most major New England cities. Those that aren't on the train routes are easily accessible by bus or car.

BY AIR

With up to 1.5 million passengers passing through its gates each month, **Boston-Logan International Airport** (One Harborside Dr., East Boston, 617/428-2800, www.massport.

com/logan) is the largest and busiest transportation hub in the region. The airport serves nearly 50 airlines, of which 13 are international, including Aer Lingus, Air Canada, Air France, Alitalia, British Airways, Finnair, Iberia, Icelandair, Lufthansa, SATA (Azores Express), Swiss, TACV, and Virgin Atlantic Airways. International flights arrive in Terminal E. From the airport, a variety of options take passengers to downtown Boston, which is only a mile away.

Several of the area's smaller regional airports are a good option for travelers looking to save a few bucks or get to other New England states without having to pass through Boston first.

Rhode Island's **Providence/T. F. Green Airport** (2000 Post Rd., Warwick, 401/737-8222, www. pvdairport.com) is served by all of the major domestic carriers and Air Canada. The airport is about a 30-minute drive to Providence. Another option for southern New England is **Bradley International Airport** (Schoephoester Rd., Windsor Locks, CT, 860/292-2000, www. bradleyairport.com), located halfway between Springfield, Massachusetts and Hartford, Connecticut; it's about a 45-minute drive from either city. In New Hampshire, **Manchester Airport** (1 Airport Rd., Manchester, 603/624-6556, www.flymanchester.com) has competed aggressively with Logan in the areas of prices and convenience. It's located about an hour-and-a-half drive from the White Mountains, and a half-hour from Portsmouth, and carries a half-dozen domestic airlines as well as Air Canada.

While not usually cheaper, several other regional airports offer easy access to northern New England. **Burlington International Airport** (1200 Airport Dr., S. Burlington, VT, 802/863-1889, www.burlingtonintlairport. com) is located right in downtown Burlington, and offers limited flights from cities including Atlanta, Cleveland, Detroit, New York, and Washington, D.C. **Portland International Jetport** (207/774-7301, www.portlandjetport. com) also offers several domestic routes from cities in the eastern United States to those looking for easy access to south and Midcoast Maine. Both Burlington and Portland are served by discount flights from New York on JetBlue airlines. Lastly, far northern Maine is home to **Bangor International Airport** (207/992-4600, www.flybangor.com), which offers flights from a handful of cities including Atlanta, New York, Philadelphia, Cincinnati, Detroit, and Minneapolis. The airport is also served by shuttles from Boston via American Eagle and Delta Connection. Despite their names, none of the three northern New England airports offer commercial international flights.

BY RAIL

Amtrak (800/872-7245, www.amtrak.com) runs frequent trains along the Northeast corridor to Boston, including the **Acela Express,** the United States' first high-speed service, from New York (3.5 hours) and Washington, D.C. (6 hours). Despite all of the hype when Acela opened a few years ago, however, design flaws in the construction of the tracks have limited speeds of the trains, and therefore the amount of time shaved off the journey. Unless you are in a rush, it can often make more sense to save $100 and take the **Regional** service, which also runs to Boston from New York (4.5 hours) and Washington (7 hours), stopping along the way in New Haven, New London, Providence, and several smaller cities on the Connecticut and Rhode Island coasts.

For travelers heading to northern New England, Amtrak offers the aptly named **Vermonter** route, which runs to St. Albans from New York (10 hours) and Washington, D.C. (14 hours). Along the way, it passes through a number of cities in the Connecticut River Valley, including New Haven, Hartford, Amherst, Brattleboro, Waterbury, and Burlington. Also, Amtrak's **Ethan Allen** route offers once-a-day service to Rutland, Vermont, from New York City (10 hours) by way of Albany.

From the west, Amtrak's **Lake Shore Limited** route offers service to Boston from Buffalo (12 hours) and Cleveland (15 hours), stopping along the way in Springfield and Worcester. Connecting to that route, Amtrak's **Adirondack** route offers service to Boston from Montreal, Quebec (12 hours), with a change of train in Albany.

BY BUS

New England is accessible from many domestic and Canadian locations via **Greyhound Bus Lines** (800/231-2222, www.greyhound.com). Nearby major cities offering service to Boston include New York (4.5 hours), Philadelphia (7.5 hours), Montreal (7.5 hours), Washington (10.5 hours), Buffalo (10.5 hours), Toronto (14 hours), and Cleveland (16 hours). While not the quickest way to travel, the bus can be an attractive alternative for those on a budget or traveling to more rural or remote regions not served by rail or air. For travelers coming from New York, an even cheaper bus option is **Fung Wah Transportation** (212/925-8889, www.fungwahbus.com), a bus that leaves from New York's Chinatown and offers prices as low as $15 each way. Buses, which run hourly, travel from 139 Canal Street in New York to Boston's South Station.

For those who really want to leave the driving to someone else, several economical bus tours offer trips around the region, especially for fall foliage season. **Atlas Travel Network** (800/942-3301, www.escortedfallfoliagetours. com) offers tours from New York and Boston from a consortium of tour companies. While itineraries differ, both take in a rough circle around the region over the course of 8–10 days for between $1,000 and $2,000 per person. The Vermont-based **New England Vacation Tours** (802/464-2076, www.sover.net/~nevt) offers a slightly more expensive fall foliage tour that includes round-trip airfare from anywhere in the country, in addition to summer tours of the coast and winter ski tour packages.

BY CAR

The major auto route into New England is I-95, which enters the southeast corner of Connecticut and snakes up the coast to Boston. The drive takes about three hours from the New York border without stops—four hours from New York or eight hours from Washington, D.C. This direct route, however, can often get clogged with truck traffic, especially through areas of eastern Connecticut and Rhode Island where it drops to two lanes each way. Many travelers prefer to take a detour at

New Haven north on I-91, then west on I-84 and I-90 to Boston; while slightly longer, this route is often quicker.

From the west, the main route into New England is I-90, also known as the Massachusetts Turnpike (or Mass Pike for short). I-90 is a toll road, and it takes a little over two hours to drive its length from the border of Western Massachusetts to Boston. From Canada, there are two border crossings into Vermont; one is at I-89, which offers quick access to Burlington and central Massachusetts and Connecticut by way of connection to I-91. The other crossing at the far northern end of I-91 offers quicker access to New Hampshire and Boston via connection to I-93. Several smaller highways offer border crossings into the wilderness of northern Maine.

BY SEA

Travelers coming from Atlantic Canada can take the express route from Yarmouth, Nova Scotia, to Bar Harbor (3 hours) or Portland, Maine (5.5 hours) aboard **The CAT** (877/359-3760, www.catferry.com), a high-speed car ferry that makes round trips on each route daily. Two year-round car ferries also make the trip to Connecticut from New York's Long Island. **Cross Sound Ferry Services** (860/443-5281, www.longislandferry.com) offers several daily trips from Orient Point to New London (1.5 hours). The **Bridgeport & Port Jefferson Steamboat Company** (631/473-0286, www. bpjferry.com) offers trips between those two cities (1.25 hours) every hour.

Getting Around

In terms of transportation infrastructure, New England is either the height of efficiency or mired in the past, depending on your point of view. In the last century, the area developed an unparalleled network of major highways and rail lines that makes almost any corner of the region accessible within a few hours. In the past few decades, however, the network

has stagnated from lack of investment, making highways frequently crowded at rush hour around major cities. Many of the old rail lines, meanwhile, have simply been ripped up (though fortuitously, some old railway right-of-ways have been transformed into attractive bike paths). While it's possible to visit most areas by public transportation, the region's bus routes are often slow and cumbersome, with connections in towns out of the way of your final destination. The added expense of renting a car is often worth it for the convenience and freedom of cruising the back roads, especially in foliage season. A 4x4 vehicle, however, is only necessary on the logging roads of far northern Maine.

BY AIR

Puddle-jumpers between Boston and many of the area's regional airports offer a quick and easy way to shoot around the region. Be forewarned, however, that relying on air travel for inter-city travel isn't cheap. It's just as expensive to fly to Burlington from Boston, for example, as it is to fly there from Atlanta or Detroit. And flying to Burlington from Manchester or Providence can be even more expensive. In most cases you'll save money by flying direct from your home to a regional airport, rather than stopping in Boston first. Better yet, it's often more economical to rent a car or travel by bus between cities.

The exceptions to the rule are flights to the islands, where high demand keeps costs in check, and the added expense can more than make up for the hassle of driving to the ferry and spending time at sea (to say nothing of the exorbitant rates ferries charge for automobile transit). Contact **Cape Air** (800/352-0714, www.capeair.com) for flights to Nantucket or Martha's Vineyard, or **New England Airlines** (800/243-2460, www.block-island.com/nea) for Block Island.

BY RAIL

In addition to the routes coming in from outside New England, **Amtrak** (800/872-7245, www.amtrak.com) offers the regional **Downeaster** service from Boston to Portland (2.5 hours). The train stops in several smaller towns along the way, including Dover, New Hampshire; and Wells and Old Orchard Beach, Maine. Note, however, that it's not possible to buy a one-ticket ride from New York to Portland, since the southern train runs to South Station, and the Downeaster embarks

from North Station. (Legend has it that inconvenience was by design, the scheme of enterprising Boston businessmen to lure travelers into the city.) Travelers from the South Shore to Maine must take a short subway trip between the two Boston stations to continue their trip.

The **Massachusetts Bay Transportation Authority** (617/222-5000, www.mbta.com) runs commuter rail service around Boston, with trains venturing to Worcester, Providence, and throughout the North and South Shores. The regional railways and commuter rails that once crisscrossed all six New England states, however, have all but disappeared. Despite attempts by some state governments and private companies to revive them for transportation, the fragments that remain (such as the scenic railway in Conway, New Hampshire and the narrow-gauge railroad in Portland, Maine) are more tourist attractions than actual options for transportation.

BY BUS

It may not be the fastest way to tour New England, but **Greyhound** (800/231-2222, www.greyhound.com) maintains a comprehensive web of routes that touches most cities, colleges, and tourist attractions in the region. Until recently, the Springfield-based **Peter Pan Bus Lines** (800/343-9999, www.peterpanbus.com) was an independent company that competed with the national behemoth. Now the two companies share routes and schedules, however, making travel on either interchangeable. Peter Pan also runs **Bonanza Bus Lines** (800/556-3815, www.bonanzabus.com), which serves Connecticut, Rhode Island, and Cape Cod. Other smaller, regional carriers serve out-of-the-way parts of northern New England—the largest being Concord Coach Lines (800/639-3317 or 603/228-3300, www.concordtrailways.com). Other carriers have slowly been disappearing in recent years, snatched up by the Greyhound behemoth—often at a loss of regional routes with low ridership. (See the appropriate destination chapters for more details.)

BY CAR

Getting around New England by car is a fairly painless exercise. Highways are efficient and in general well maintained, and traffic moves briskly outside of rush hour around major cities. The region is bisected north to south by I-91, which runs along the Connecticut River Valley along the border of New Hampshire and Vermont and down through central Massachusetts and Connecticut. In Vermont it connects with I-89 and in New Hamsphire with I-93, which runs all the way to Boston. An alternative to I-93 is U.S. 3, which parallels the interstate in New Hampshire, and then runs through Boston along the South Shore to Cape Cod. Skirting around the city, I-95 is the main coastal thoroughfare from the Connecticut–New York border all the way to northeast Maine. For inland Maine, travelers are relegated to slower undivided highways, including U.S. 201 to the Moosehead Lake region, and Route 11 to the Allagash.

East to west, the region is bisected by I-90, otherwise known as the Massachusetts Turnpike or Mass Pike, which runs the length of Massachusetts. To the south, the Pike connects near Worcester to I-84, which then runs east–west through Connecticut. North of the Pike, the highway is paralleled by Route 2, which is slower but can be a more efficient way to get to the northern Berkshires and southern Vermont. Traveling east or west in northern New England, meanwhile, can be a frustrating exercise, since all major roads lead north–south to Boston. Several federal highways, including U.S. 2 and U.S. 4, aid to accomplish the task, but if you use them be sure to leave more time for small-town stoplights and mountain switchbacks.

CAR RENTAL COMPANIES

The following companies have branches at major cities and airports:

- **Alamo** 800/462-5266
  www.alamo.com

- **Avis** 800/331-1212
  www.avis.com

- **Budget** 800/527-0700
  www.budget.com

- **Dollar** 800/800-4000
  www.dollar.com

- **Enterprise** 800/261-7331
  www.enterprise.com

- **Hertz** 800/654-3131
  www.hertz.com

- **National** 800/227-7368
  www.nationalcar.com

- **Thrifty** 800/367-2277
  www.thrifty.com

BY SEA

Ferries run from the mainland to many offshore islands, including Block Island, Nantucket, Martha's Vineyard, Monhegan, and various islands in Penobscot Bay. Additionally, other ferries run from Boston to the South Shore, Marblehead, and Provincetown. (See destination chapters for details.)

Sports and Recreation

The abundance of mountains, lakes, beaches, parks, and ocean all over New England means there is very little recreation that can't be enjoyed here. Of course, what you do depends on season and geography—in winter, skiers flock to the snowy peaks of the White Mountains in New Hampshire, Maine, and the Green Mountains of Vermont; fall and summer bring hunters, and fishermen, hikers, and mountain bikers to those same trails and streams. (Spring, on the other hand, is often far too muddy for any of the latter.)

Serious sea-lovers head to the coasts and islands of Maine, Rhode Island, and Massachusetts—areas with a longstanding and venerable history of fishing and boating, and plenty of resources to show for it. Meanwhile, the widely varied parks and preservation lands throughout New England are excellent grounds for bird-watching of all kinds, year-round.

HIKING AND CAMPING

New Englanders love camping, and prove it year after year by filling their region's campsites in droves—so much so that on holiday weekends, the challenge isn't finding a camping ground (there are plenty all around the mountainous areas as well as by the lakes and coast), but finding one with available sites. On such popular dates, it pays to arrive early in the morning (preferably before the weekend begins) or make a reservation in advance. Also, not all campgrounds offer sites for both RVs and tents; call ahead to be sure.

BIKING

Bikers in rural New England are blessed with countless terrain options: much of Cape Cod and its islands have bike paths and lanes carved out on picturesque bays; the entire region's small country towns sport wide and pretty roads meandering through historic villages; and the trails in northern New England make for excellent mountain biking (especially during fall foliage season). The cities are a different story. While it's certainly possible to bike around places like Boston, Portland, Hartford, and Providence, an abundance of traffic and a lack of bike paths mean that even experienced bikers should ride with extra caution.

ROCK CLIMBING

Northern New England is a veritable playground for mountaineers, who flock in all seasons to the area's challenging rock-climbing faces. Popular climbs are found in Maine's Acadia National Park, and in New Hampshire's White Mountains, including Franconia Notch, Cathedral Ledge, Ragged Mountain, and Cannon Cliff.

KAYAKING AND CANOEING

Wherever there's a coast in New England, there are usually plenty of places to put in a kayak and head out to sea for a salty run. Meanwhile, river rafting opportunities abound in every New England state, for nearly every level of paddler.

Vermont's highlights include the Class II Batten Kill, which is best run in the summer and flows under four picturesque covered bridges; Otter Creek, a Class II, north-running river into Lake Champlain; the Class II Winooski River runs past stunning natural scenery and small waterfalls; and the Lamoille River, which ranges from flat water to Class III.

In New Hampshire, the Class II Connecticut River runs through logging country. Massachusetts' Concord and Charles Rivers run past historic sites and wild ducks and geese, and offer flexible put-in and take-out spots, while the Deerfield River in Western Massachusetts takes paddlers through dense forests and open farmland. And with rapids rising in places to Class IV, it is the most accessible of the real white-water paddles in New England.

In Connecticut, the Housatonic River is an excellent Class II–III run in early spring and summer; and in Rhode Island, Great Swamp runs past wild ospreys and breathtakingly serene ponds.

The most pristine rivers in the region are in northern Maine, where the St. John and Allagash Rivers offer more than 100 miles of interconnected lakes and rivers, most of which are a gentle Class I or II in difficulty. The same can't be said of the Penobscot and Kennebec Rivers slightly farther south near Baxter State Park. This is where *serious* kayakers and rafters go to get wet, with rapids rising to Class IV, and one stretch of Class V on the Penobscot that will test even the most experienced paddlers.

SAILING

Coastal New England is quite literally awash in sailing culture—from spectators who merely use its proximity as an excuse to don preppy gear to lifelong, bona fide seadogs. With New England winters as harsh as they are, sailing communities tend to come alive in the late spring, summer, and fall. For the largest concentrations of charters and docks (public and private), sailing schools and outfitters, head in the direction of those towns with a long tradition of seafaring. Newport, Rhode Island; Nantucket, Massachusetts; and Portland, Maine, are examples of such well-known spots, but even the smaller and less touristy communities up and down the coast often offer excellent waters and perfectly accommodating berths.

HUNTING, FISHING, AND BIRD-WATCHING

Every season, without fail, droves of dedicated sportsmen and sportswomen descend upon the backwoods and seas of New England, seeking to watch, catch, or take home some of its bounty. Local regulations and licensing requirements can be strict; certain animals (marine mammals, for example) are protected in certain districts, and specific rules apply to most species for trapping, baiting, shooting, and catching. So be certain to check with the local fish and game offices of your area of interest before planning your trip.

Hunting areas are well regulated and plentiful, particularly in northern New England, where animals from woodcock and deer to turkey and moose roam.

Deep-sea fishing is one fruitful option in the summer and fall. Fish such as cod, striped bass, tuna, and lobster are popular catches—though many forms of fishing (particularly lobstering) are largely chartered activities. Moving-water fishing, meanwhile, takes place mostly in summer and early fall. Serious trout and bass anglers gravitate toward the Rapid and Kennebec Rivers in Maine; the Androscoggin, Saco, and Mohawk Rivers in New Hampshire; and Missisquoi, Batten Kill, and Connecticut Rivers in Vermont. In winter, ice fishing is popular in many small, northern towns—particularly in the area around Lake Champlain, Vermont. The sport requires hardy enthusiasts to cut holes in the ice above ponds and lakes, and catch fish as they cruise beneath the hole.

Any time of year, bird-watchers can feast their eyes in any number of wildlife refuges. Some of the best include Maine's Moosehorn and Petit Manan refuges; the Pleasant Valley Sanctuary in Massachusetts' Berkshires; Rhode Island's Wildlife Sanctuaries; and Vermont's Missisquoi and Silvio O Conte refuges.

SKIING AND WINTER SPORTS

Skiing in New England is more than a mere sport; it's what makes New England winters bearable for many residents. The pastime keeps entire small-town economies revved up from December through March (and for true addicts, April), and every year, pulls many an urbanite out from their city bubble and into face-to-face, downhill encounters with nature.

New England slopes vary greatly in difficulty and the crowds they draw. As would be expected, the more southern resorts and better-known, big-name spots tend to get packed with day-trippers from Boston, whereas the out-of-the-way and independently owned and operated resorts often have small, dedicated followings of skiers. Every New England state (except Rhode Island) boasts its share of good slopes, though some are undeniably better than others. In

Connecticut, Mohawk Mountain, Woodbury, and Powder Ridge are small but respectable runs. Favorites in Maine include Sugarloaf, Sunday River, Big Squaw, and Saddleback. New Hampshire's mountains are plentiful, offering a wealth of downhill options. The best are Bretton Woods, Attitash, Loon Mountain, Waterville Valley, and Wildcat. Skiing in Massachusetts revolves mostly around the bigger resorts at Wachusett and Nashoba Valley, which tend to get crowded. Vermont, meanwhile, draws some of the region's most serious skiers—to top mountains like Stowe, Stratton, Okemo, Killington, and Mad River Glen.

In addition to skiing, the majority of resorts allow snowboarding, though some do so in designated areas, and many offer special snowshoeing trails. (The latter can also be found on many hotel properties.) Snowmobiles can be found come winter in many an area state forest; strict regulations, however, require enthusiasts to be careful about where they motor.

Ice skating, too, is a popular winter activity—done in town and city parks, and recreation rinks. Most are open to the public, usually charge a small fee, and are listed with local town halls. Local parks are also full of sledding opportunities.

Accommodations and Food

Throughout the text, accommodations listings include the range of rates for a standard double room in high season (roughly May–Oct.). Depending on location, prices can be much higher during peak times (e.g., foliage or ski season) and steeply discounted in winter and spring. Food listings include the range of prices for dinner entrées, including sandwiches but not salads. Lunch is often significantly cheaper.

ACCOMMODATIONS

Many tourist destinations celebrate their peak seasons in the summer when the weather is the nicest; not so in New England. Peak travel here is in the fall, particularly in late September and October when the foliage is at its most dramatic and students are pouring into area colleges. Many hotels jack up their prices by a factor of two or even three during this brief crowded season. The same can be said, on a smaller scale for ski season, especially around February vacation, when rates in some locations in Northern New England can reach a peak higher than their nearby ski mountains. If leaf-peeping and skiing aren't your thing, you can save a lot of money by traveling in late August or early September when the summer humidity has dissipated, but hotel prices

haven't yet skyrocketed. Of course, the opposite holds true for beach destinations. New Englanders make the most of their brief period of heat between Memorial Day and Labor Day. Do yourself a favor and schedule your beach vacation on either side of these magical dates, when you'll beat both the crowds and high prices—and the weather is often just as nice (of course, you are gambling that New England's mercurial climate will cooperate).

Along with the rest of the country, New England has seen a steady rise in the price of accommodations at all levels, making it difficult to find any bargains among the major-name hotels. Bed-and-breakfasts, especially in more rural areas, can be an attractive alternative; often run by couples or families, they can offer dirt-cheap prices without sacrificing amenities or hominess. Those who prefer the anonymity of a motel will find more bargains (though less consistency) in independent operations. Gone are the days when a Super 8 or Motel 6 offers a $39 double—$139 is more like it. By contrast, you can still find a room in the $60–80 range at places like the Minuteman or Lamplighter. If in doubt, don't be shy about asking to see a room before committing.

For families, New England abounds in large country inns that serve as an economical alternative to the big-name hotels. Often historic properties that have seen slightly better days, they make up in charm what they lack in polish. Beware, however, of properties in high-traffic tourist destinations that have not been renovated since the Revolution. And don't immediately rush to the inn that shares the name of the town—that fact alone can boost prices by 20 percent or more.

NEW ENGLAND CUISINE

Traditional New England fare revolves around the seafood of the area's coast, but pays homage to the cooking methods of its British origins—the likes of boiled lobsters, baked-stuffed shrimp, fried cod, and steamed clams. Other foodstuffs native to the region also play a big part in the regional cuisine—cranberry sauce, maple syrup, cornbread, and baked beans, for starters.

These days, the culinary options in New England are as diverse as the population; you're as apt to find Thai-inspired bouillabaisse and tapas-style Punjabi specialties as you are classic clam chowder. But if you're up for trying the region's specialties at their source, don't miss these traditional New England dishes:

The clambake: A smorgasbord of seafoods (steamed lobster, mussels, and clams) served with vegetables (usually corn on the cob and potatoes). Traditionally these are steamed together in a hole dug on a beach, but are more often found in restaurants, cooked in a kitchen.

Lobster: Steamed or broiled, this native crustacean is a messy but glorious affair. The meat lies inside a tough shell, which is cracked by the diner using metal crackers and a small fork, and dipped in melted butter before eating.

Clams: Generally divided into types (hard shell or soft shell), clams are a true New England delicacy. Soft shells, or steamers, are usually eaten either steamed or fried. (If steamed, diners pull them from the shell, remove and discard the neck casing, and dip

HOW TO EAT A LOBSTER

For some, it's an intimidating and off-putting exercise in utter messiness. For others, it's a deliciously visceral process with a delightful end: some of the sweetest crustacean meat on the planet. However you view the process of eating a lobster, experts agree that the best way to tackle the creature is from the outside in, and working from small to big. Note that while plenty of creative preparations of the delicacy do exist, purists swear by a simple boiled specimen – its precious meat dressed only in a squeeze of lemon and dipped in drawn butter.

1. Start by breaking off the legs, holding the lobster by its back and pulling/twisting off the legs individually. Snap each in half at its joint and chew out the meat.

2. Next, take off the claws, tearing them at the joint closest to the body (twisting if necessary), then again at the joint closest to the claw itself. Use your fork to push out all the meat (many say the knuckle meat is the most delicious). Next use your crackers to crush the large claw, extracting all the meat, ideally in one large piece.

3. Grasp the tail with one hand, and the back with the other hand, then twist and gently pull to separate the two sections. Some people also choose to eat the green tomalley (the digestive gland) and, in a female lobster, the roe (the unfertilized eggs). Whether you follow suit depends on your personal palate.

4. Hold the tail with both hands, your thumbs placed just on the inside on the white cartilage, your index fingers wrapped around the red shell on the tail's back. Pressing in with your index fingers and out with your thumbs, split the tail down the middle, revealing the whole of the tail. Pull out with a fork or your fingers and devour.

them in broth and drawn butter before eating.) Hard shell clams are served differently: The smallest ones, known as littlenecks and cherrystones, are most frequently served raw with horseradish and cocktail sauce; the largest hard shells are chopped up and used primarily in chowders and stuffings.

Clam chowder: Dating back to the 18th century, New England clam chowder is by far the most popular of the region's creamy fish stews. Most restaurants have their own recipes, using a bit more potatoes here, a different ratio of bacon to cream there (but not tomatoes—that is what distinguishes Manhattan clam chowder and is therefore heresy in New England). Sampling and finding your favorite is the real fun.

Boston Baked Beans: Not for nothing is Boston nicknamed Beantown. This dish—made of dried beans baked slowly with salt pork and molasses—was a staple in colonial times, and remains a favorite today.

© MICHAEL BLANDING

Vermont farmers market

Practicalities

TIPS FOR TRAVELERS
Health and Safety

People travel to New England from all over the globe simply to receive care from the area's doctors and hospitals, which are widely regarded as among the best there is. So rest assured, should you need any medical attention while here, you'll be in good hands. That said, certain precautions will help you stay as safe as possible.

Compared with the rest of the nation, New England is relatively low in crime, and many of its rural areas are virtually crime-free. Cities are, not surprisingly, a different story. But even in capitals like Boston, Portland, Providence, and Hartford, if you follow the basic rules of common sense (take precautions in watching your belongings, avoid walking alone late at night, and be aware of your surroundings), odds are safety won't be a problem.

In the New England countryside, one of the biggest threats to visitors' safety can be the natural world they seek. When hiking the White Mountains or canoeing the endless rivers, it is essential to know about the dangers of exposure to the elements. Visit the local tourism offices for specific tips on preparing for an outing, and if you are at all unsure of your outdoors skills, consider hiring a guide to take you on your excursion.

Student Travelers

You'll be hard-pressed to find an area of the country more welcoming to students; with such a hefty roster of colleges and universities, New England teems with—and oftentimes caters to—young people.

Cafés (both those with Internet access and without it) are in abundance in cities and college towns, and youth hostels can be found in Boston, Cape Cod, Maine, and New Hampshire. Plenty of discounted tours are also offered throughout each state through the tourist boards, and many hotels offer student discounts with identification cards.

Gay and Lesbian Travelers

At this point in America's social history, few regions in the country are more friendly to gay and lesbian visitors than New England. Not only is the area home to five out of the six states where gay marriage is legal (Rhode Island recognizes out-of-state gay marriages, though doesn't perform them), but cities like Boston, Portland, and Providence have significant and thriving gay and lesbian communities. Meanwhile, resort towns such as Provincetown, Massachusetts, and Ogunquit, Maine are such magnets for gay and lesbian visitors that straight tourists are often the minority.

Gay and lesbian couples traveling to Massachusetts with the intention of getting married should be aware that, while marriage is legal in Massachusetts, if the two parties reside in a state in which same-sex marriage is illegal, the ceremony will not be binding.

Travelers with Disabilities

Public transportation in the vast majority of New England is wheelchair-accessible, as are most hotels, museums, and public buildings. Even many beaches and campgrounds in Massachusetts are accessible, though the more remote the destination, the greater the possibility that it will not be. As common sense would dictate, call ahead and plan accordingly.

Women Traveling Alone

In the vast majority of towns and cities, solo female travelers will feel perfectly at home and can travel safely and without harassment. In larger cities—Boston, Providence, Hartford, and Portland—it's wise to avoid strolling out late at night, though even in such circumstances, incidents are quite rare.

Traveling with Children

Travel all over New England is extremely family-friendly. Most hotels offer cribs in the room upon request, and public transportation and attractions offer discounted fares for children. The majority of restaurants are happy to offer high chairs, and many have kids' menus.

The one exception to this rule of family-friendliness is found at the occasional exclusive resort, which usually makes a point of labeling itself adults-only.

INFORMATION AND SERVICES
Internet Access

Cities in every state are peppered with Internet cafés which rent computer terminals (usually in 15-minute increments), as well as regular cafés that offer wireless Internet access (sometimes free, sometimes free only with a food purchase, and sometimes for a nominal fee) to those who bring their own laptops. Even outside cities, most midsize towns have cafés that charge either the cost of a cup of coffee or an hourly rate (a few dollars is average). You'll also find plenty of access sites (several large-scale transportation buildings offer it for free) that charge a few dollars per hour, and these days, almost all hotels offer wireless access for either free or a $5 to $10 per-day charge. Local libraries are also a good place to find easy Internet access, as many (if not all) offer free terminal use in varying time increments.

In smaller country towns, finding Internet service can be difficult. Thankfully, more and more lodging options are coming with wireless Internet standard. It's not just exclusive resorts either—even chain motels and small bed-and-breakfasts often advertise a wireless router as an added perk to their guests.

Business Hours

Business hours vary widely between cities and towns, but most stores and offices in state capital cities follow a schedule of 9 A.M.–5 or 6 P.M. on weekdays; 10 A.M.–6 P.M. on Saturdays; and noon–5 P.M. on Sundays. In smaller cities and town, particularly those in rural areas, expect more erratic weekend hours—or the possibility that they may simply stay closed until Monday. Opening hours are the one vestige of New England's Puritan past. As recently as two decades ago, it was difficult to find retail stores open on Sunday—and liquor stores in some states were even forbidden by law to open. Thankfully, those so-called "blue laws" have eased in recent years, so that Sunday is now like any other shopping day. Visitors from other parts of the world, however, are often shocked by local laws ensuring that most bars and clubs close their doors by 2 A.M. at the latest (and oftentimes by 1 A.M.). New Englanders have learned to adjust by starting their partying early.

Tipping

A 15 to 20 percent tip is customary in all but the most rural areas of New England (which are usually accustomed to just slightly lower percentages), in restaurants, bars, and hair salons and spas, if you are satisfied with the level of your service. At hotels, $1 per bag for porters is the norm, doormen usually receive $1 for hailing a taxi, maids usually receive $1–2 per night, and concierges are given anywhere from a few dollars to $20, depending on the services they have provided. In taxis, 10 to 15 percent is customary.

Magazines

Several regional magazines provide useful information for travelers, including: *New England Travel,* an annual but comprehensive magazine exploring all of the region's attractions and *Yankee Magazine,* for events, festivals, landmarks, restaurants, and tours all over New England. Several states and cities and even sub-regions produce their own magazines as well, including *Boston, Cape Cod Magazine*, *Rhode Island Monthly*, *Vermont Life,* and *Down East,* the monthly periodical dedicated to all things Maine.

RESOURCES

Suggested Reading

REFERENCE

Feintuch, Bert, ed. *The Encyclopedia of New England*. New Haven, CT: Yale University Press, 2005. A good book to read *before* you go, this 1,600-page, eight-pound tome will tell you everything you want to know about New England and then some, including entries on Walden Pond, fried clams, Ben & Jerry's, and the Red Sox. Instead of a disjointed alphabetical arrangement, the book cogently organizes contents by subject matter.

HISTORY

Canellos, Peter, *Last Lion: The Fall and Rise of Ted Kennedy*, New York: Simon & Schuster, 2009. Published by a team of writers from the *Boston Globe* just before his death, this is the definitive biography of Massachusetts's longtime U.S. Senator, who was as beloved in New England as he was flawed.

Cronon, William. *Changes in the Land: Indians, Colonists, and the Ecology of New England*. New York: Hill and Wang, 1983. The classic study of early New England history debunks myths and shatters preconceptions about Pilgrims and Native Americans and how each interacted with the landscape.

Demos, John. *The Unredeemed Captive: A Family Story from Early America*. New York: Vintage, 1994. A fascinating tale of the capture of Rev. John Williams and his family in the 1704 Deerfield Raid sheds light on the complicated relations between colonists and Native Americans. While Williams's wife and two children were killed, one daughter actually ended up marrying one of her captors.

Fairbrother, Trevor. *Painting Summer in New England*. New Haven, CT: Yale University Press, 2006. From a recent exhibition of the same name at the Peabody-Essex Museum, this beautiful art book includes dozens of paintings by American Impressionists, along with stories about the artists.

Forbes, Esther Hoskins. *Paul Revere and the World He Lived In*. Boston: Mariner Books, 1942. The Pulitzer Prize–winning story of Boston's original Renaissance man is just as fascinating now as when it was written 50 years ago.

Hill, Frances. *A Delusion of Satan: The Full Story of the Salem Witch Trials*. Cambridge, MA: Da Capo Press, 2003. A British novelist and historian, Hill has written the definitive account of the collective madness that overtook a small New England town in 1692.

Howard, Brett. *Boston: A Social History*. New York: Hawthorn, 1976. Detailing the impact of the city's leaders and most prominent families over the centuries, Howard shows the impact Boston Brahmins have had on local politics and cultural landscape.

Jennings, Francis. *The Invasion of America: Indians, Colonialism, and the Cant of Conquest*. New York: Norton, 1975. A classic "revisionist" history of the settling of New England makes the Pilgrims into the bad guys, instigating war with Native Americans in a cynical bid for land.

Labree, Benjamin Woods. *The Boston Tea Party.* Boston: Northeastern University Press, 1964. An exhaustive examination of the context and chronology of the single most important event leading up to the Revolutionary War.

Lager, Fred. *Ben & Jerry's: The Inside Scoop: How Two Real Guys Built a Business with a Social Conscience and a Sense of Humor.* New York: Three Rivers Press, 1999. If you just can't get enough Chunky Monkey or Cherry Garcia, pick up this book detailing the history of the Vermont local legends.

Lukas, J. Anthony. *Common Ground: A Turbulent Year in the Lives of Three American Families.* New York: Vintage, 1986. Written about the racially motivated busing crisis of the 1970s, this may be the best nonfiction book ever written about Boston.

McCullough, David. *1776.* New York: Simon & Schuster, 2005. Rather than writing a start-to-finish account of the Revolution, McCullough drills down to the pivotal year in which the fortunes of George Washington turned, from the tense stand-off of the siege of Boston to the ultimate victories at Trenton and Princeton.

McCullough, David. *John Adams.* New York: Simon & Schuster, 2001. The fascinating history of the least heralded of our nation's founding fathers—who may have had more lasting effect than any of his "brothers"—doubles as a glimpse into New England during our country's coming-of-age.

Miller, Perry. *The New England Mind: From Colony to Province.* Cambridge, MA: Belknap Press, 1983. A scholarly and vastly detailed look at a century that saw New Englanders go from Puritans in their thinking to true Yankees.

Paine, Lincoln P. *Down East: A Maritime History of Maine.* Gardiner, ME: Tilbury House Publishers, 2000. A look back at more than four centuries of pirates, privateers, lobstermen, and windjammers from a maritime historian and native Downeaster.

Rappeleye, Charles. *Sons of Providence: The Brown Brothers, the Slave Trade, and the American Revolution.* New York: Simon & Schuster, 2006. A fascinating journey into the heart of colonial America, told through the history of the most enlightened city in the New World—which nevertheless founded its fortune on the slave trade.

Schultz, Eric B., and Michael J. Tougias. *King Philip's War: the History and Legacy of America's Forgotten Conflict.* Woodstock, VT: Countryman Press, 2000. A detailed history of the early clashes between colonists and Native Americans that some believe indirectly caused the Revolutionary War a century later.

Scotti, R. A. *Sudden Sea: The Great Hurricane of 1938.* Boston: Back Bay Press, 2003. New England's original "perfect storm"—and one of the worst natural disasters in U.S. history—is brought alive in suspenseful detail, from the first clouds gathering over Long Island Sound to the 180-mph winds that ripped through the Connecticut coast.

Stanton, Mike. *The Prince of Providence: The Rise and Fall of Buddy Cianci, America's Most Notorious Mayor.* New York: Random House, 2004. Thuggish demagogue or brilliant urban mechanic, Buddy Cianci never failed to elicit strong emotions in Rhode Islanders. Freelance journalist Stanton tells Cianci's flamboyant story with wit and insight that sheds light on the insular culture of the smallest state.

Tourtellot, Arthur Bernon. *Lexington and Concord: the Beginning of the War of the American Revolution.* New York: Norton, 2000. This exhaustive and very readable account of the events leading up to the Revolutionary War brings alive the characters of Sam Adams and John Hancock with all of their gifts and foibles.

Vowell, Sarah. *The Wordy Shipmates* New York: Riverhead, 2007. The popular essayist and National Public Radio contributor not only writes one of the most irreverent and entertaining histories of the early days of Puritan and Pilgrim New England, but she also makes those ancient times surprisingly relevant to our own America.

Woodard, Colin. *The Lobster Coast: Rebels, Rusticators, and the Struggle for a Forgotten Frontier.* New York: Viking, 2004. From early Scotch-Irish woodchoppers to 20th-century oil painters, this clearly written account populates the map of Maine with colorful historical characters.

Zobel, Hiller B. *Boston Massacre.* New York: Norton, 2000. A thoroughly researched accounting of the misnamed event that helped precipitate the Revolution; it exposes Sam Adams as a cynical propagandist who skillfully incited an angry mob.

NATURAL HISTORY AND ECOLOGY

Albers, Jan. *Hands on the Land: A Natural History of the Vermont Landscape.* Boston: MIT Press, 2002. In a gorgeous oversized book, Albers details the various factors—geological, ecological, and economic—that have transformed the Green Mountain State.

Beston, Henry. *The Outermost House: A Year of Life on the Great Beach of Cape Cod.* New York: Owl Books, 1928. Beston's attempt to "go Thoreau" by living for a year in a small house in the dunes remains the most joyous evocation of Cape Cod's unique ecology.

Corson, Trevor. *The Secret Life of Lobsters: How Fishermen and Scientists Are Unraveling the Mysteries of Our Favorite Crustacean.* New York: HarperCollins, 2004. More than just a natural history of lobstering, Corson weaves in a detective story about the decline in lobster stocks and the increasingly hostile disputes between scientists and fishermen about its cause.

Degraff, Richard, and Mariko Yamasaki. *New England Wildlife: Habitat, Natural History, and Distribution.* Hanover, NH: University Press of New England, 2001. A no-nonsense guide to every last species of mammal, reptile, amphibian, and bird in the region, along with seasonal information and distribution maps. Note, however, that the book is limited to land species.

Kessler, Brad. *Goat Song: A Seasonal Life, A Short History of Herding, and the Art of Making Cheese* New York: Scribner, 2009. A lovely and earnest little book, longtime writer Kessler sets out to live the dream that tugs at many of us: leaving the city to go back to live a simpler life out on the farm. What he finds in two years of raising goats is nothing short of connection to our most mythic religious archetypes.

Kurlansky, Mark. *Cod: A Biography of the Fish that Changed the World.* New York: Penguin, 1998. The settlement and economic rise of New England is inseparable from the plentiful groundfish that once populated its waters in astounding numbers.

Muir, Diana. *Reflections in Bullough's Pond: Economy and Ecosystem in New England.* Hanover, NH: University Press of New England, 2002. With a sweeping meditation on people's effects on their environment, Muir casts her fishing pole back over 400 years of New England history while maintaining an effortless, back-porch style.

National Audubon Society. *National Audubon Society Regional Guide to New England.* New York: Knopf, 1998. The amateur naturalist would do well to pick up this guide, which details many local species of trees, wildflowers, reptiles, and mammals with 1,500 full-color illustrations.

Wessels, Tom. *Reading the Forested Landscape: A Natural History of New England.* Woodstock, VT: Countryman Press, 2005. A good read before heading off into the hills, this book helps put features of the landscape into their proper context.

Zielinski, Gregory A., and Barry D. Keim. *New England Weather, New England Climate.* Hanover, NH: University Press of New England, 2005. From nor'easters to Indian Summer, this book patiently explains the meteorological underpinnings to New England's famously wacky weather.

LITERATURE

Delbanco, Andrew. *Writing New England: An Anthology from the Puritans to the Present.* Cambridge, MA: Belknap Press, 2001. From John Winthrop to John Updike, all the great writers who have called New England home are gathered in one place. Through thoughtful subject arrangements, the editor tries to answer the question: what is the common spirit of New England?

Douglass, Frederick. *Narrative of the Life of Frederick Douglass, An American Slave: Written By Himself.* 1845, Signet Classics, 2005. The quintessential slave narrative includes details of Douglass's life as an abolitionist in Boston.

Hawthorne, Nathaniel. *The House of Seven Gables.* 1851, Signet Classics, 2001. The tragic story of several interlocking families is set in a house that still exists in Salem.

James, Henry. *The Bostonians.* 1886, Modern Library Classics, 2003. Beacon Hill comes alive in this evocation of 19th-century Boston.

Melville, Herman. *Moby-Dick.* 1851, Penguin Classics, 2002. Captain Ahab, the White Whale, and Ishmael along for the ride...what more could you ask for? Look for opening scenes set in New Bedford, Massachusetts.

Thoreau, Henry David. *Walden.* 1854, Modern Library Classics, 2000. The classic account of Thoreau's two years living a hermit's life on Walden Pond is a philosophical treatise, a timeless glimpse into 19th-century rural New England, and inspiration for the modern-day environmental movement. Look for an edition that includes *The Maine Woods* and *Cape Cod,* travelogues that blend the author's sharp eye and wry sense of humor.

CONTEMPORARY FICTION AND MEMOIR

Brown, Dan. *The Dante Club.* New York: Random House, 2004. This best-selling novel is inspired by a real-life club of Boston academics, including Henry Wadsworth Longfellow and Oliver Wendell Holmes, who worked to translate Dante's *Divine Comedy.* For a twist, Brown turns the scholars into sleuths working to solve a string of hellish murders.

Greenlaw, Linda. *The Lobster Chronicles: Life on a Very Small Island.* New York: Hyperion, 2003. The sword boat captain featured in Sebastian Junger's nonfiction book *The Perfect Storm* returns with a fascinating memoir of her return to her family's home on Isle Au Haut in Maine to try her hand at the lobstering business.

Irving, John. Many of the most popular books of this cult American novelist are set in New England. For example, *The Cider House Rules* is centered around an orphanage in Maine, *The World According to Garp* takes place in part at a New England boarding school, and *A Prayer for Owen Meaney* concerns several generations of a troubled New England family.

King, Stephen. No list of New England fiction would be complete without mentioning the modern master of the macabre, who set many of his novels and short stories in Maine and other New England states. Several, including *It* and *The Tommyknockers,* take place in the fictional Maine town of Derry—which bears remarkable resemblance to the city of Bangor.

Levin, Ira. *The Stepford Wives.* 1972, New York: HarperTorch, 2004. The dark side of suburbia is explored in this wry parody about the sinister town of Stepford, Connecticut, where there's something not quite right about the women. Of the two movie adaptations of the book, cult movie fans prefer the original 1975 version with Katharine Ross to the 2004 remake with Nicole Kidman and Bette Midler.

MacDonald, Michael Patrick. *All Souls: A Family Story from Southie.* New York: Ballantine, 2000. In writing his moving memoir of Irish-American life, MacDonald does for South Boston what Frank McCourt did for Dublin.

Metalious, Grace. *Peyton Place.* 1956, Northeastern University Press, 1999. The book about a small New England town and the secrets it holds behind not-so-closed-doors was a sensation when it was published in the 1950s, going on to inspire a TV show and movie.

McMahon, Jennifer. *Promise Not To Tell.* Harper, 2007. A haunting thriller set in Vermont, this recent debut novel expertly weaves between two child murders, one in the past, one in the present.

Russo, Richard. *Empire Falls.* New York: Vintage, 2001. A slow-paced evocation of blue-collar life in a Maine mill town, this book was made into an HBO mini-series starring Paul Newman and Ed Harris in 2005.

Shreve, Anita. *The Weight of Water.* New York: Little, Brown & Co., 1998. This haunting story uses the real-life murders on New Hampshire's Isle of Shoals 100 years ago to explore the complex relationship between a journalist and her husband.

Updike, John. *The Witches of Eastwick.* New York: Knopf, 1984. Three randy witches scandalize a small Rhode Island town in this popular favorite, based on Updike's former hometown of Ipswich, Massachusetts (where part of the movie starring Jack Nicholson was filmed).

OTHER GUIDEBOOKS

Appalachian Mountain Club Books (www.outdoors.org/publications/), or ACM, publishes dozens of guides considered gospel by outdoors enthusiasts in the region. They are jam-packed with no-nonsense directions for hiking and canoeing every inch of the New England wilderness. Among them are the *White Mountain Guide* and *Maine Mountain Guide,* as well as several guides for canoeing and kayaking.

Corbett, William. *Literary New England: A History and Guide.* New York: Faber and Faber, 1993. An excellent guide to sights associated with poets and writers who called New England home, it includes detailed directions to hard-to-find graves, historic sites, and houses.

Crouch, Andy. *The Good Beer Guide to New England.* Hanover, NH: University Press of New England, 2006. Don't know your Whale's Tail from your Smuttynose? This detailed guide to breweries in the region is the ultimate New England pub crawl.

Dojny, Brooke. *The New England Clam Shack Cookbook.* North Adams, MA: Storey Publishing, 2003. In addition to providing recipes for stuffed quahogs and other favorites, this book offers a guide to some of the best clam shacks, lobster pounds, and chowder houses in all six states.

Hartnett, Robert. *Maine Lighthouses Map & Guide.* Howes Cave, NY: Hartnett House Map Publishing, 2000. A foldout map that provides detailed directions to every lighthouse along the rocky fingers of the Maine coast. Hartnett also publishes a map to lighthouses in Massachusetts and New Hampshire (yes, there are two).

Jasper, Mark. *Haunted Inns of New England.* Yarmouth Port, MA: On Cape Publications, 2000. The author gives up the ghost on some of the spookiest—and most luxurious—accommodations in the region.

Kershner, Bruce, and Robert Leverett. *The Sierra Club Guide to the Ancient Forests of the Northeast.* San Francisco: Sierra Club Books, 2004. Despite centuries of human habitation and exploitation, a surprising number of old-growth stands still exist in New England. This guide takes you inside their mossy interiors, and explains what makes old-growth forests so unique.

Marcus, Jon. *Lighthouses of New England.* Osceola, WI: Voyageur Press, 2001. Written by a former editor of *Boston* magazine, this guide provides interesting facts and stunning photos of dozens of lighthouses along the New England coast.

Tourville, Jacqueline. *Moon New England Hiking.* Berkeley, CA: Avalon Travel, 2010. By the same publisher as Moon Handbooks, this guide features plenty of hiking trails to get your boots muddy.

Tree, Christina. *How New England Happened.* New York: Little, Brown & Co., 1976. Less a history book than a comprehensive guide to historic sites, written by a *Boston Globe* travel writer and arranged in chapters by chronological eras. While slightly out-of-date, there is no better back-road companion for the history buff.

Internet Resources

Sandwiched between the slew of websites hawking hotel discounts and vacation packages are some legitimately useful ones, full of updates and resources for planning a trip—from often-comprehensive information to maps and events.

GENERAL NEW ENGLAND WEBSITES
Boston.com
www.boston.com
The official site of the *Boston Globe,* the city's paper of record, it covers the day's news in Massachusetts, as well as news, events, and lifestyle happenings regionally.

Discover New England
www.discovernewengland.org
The site highlights seasonal events and current happenings in every corner of New England, and suggests driving tours and weather information, plus a brief primer on each state.

NewEngland.com
www.newengland.com
The site, run by the folks behind *Yankee* magazine, is packed with local landmarks, recommended itineraries, foliage reports, event listings, and vacation planners.

New England Towns
www.newenglandtowns.org
Read through the history of small New England towns, plus little-known facts and statistics.

FALL FOLIAGE REPORTS

Get in-depth and up-to-date foliage reports on each state, starting in early September and throughout autumn, from the following websites.

Vermont Fall Foliage Report
www.vtonly.com/foliage.htm

Updated twice per week, the site tracks and updates Vermont's changing foliage with a map showing where the changes are happening.

New Hampshire
Weekly Foliage Report
http://foliage.visitnh.gov

This weekly, seasonal report monitors the progress of foliage around the state with maps and color-coded timelines.

Connecticut Fall Foliage Report
http://dep.state.ct.us

Keep tabs on Connecticut's foliage progress throughout autumn with the site's consistently updated map, indicating where the most foliage can be found around the state.

Maine's Fall Foliage
www.maine.gov/doc/foliage/

Follow the fall foliage happening all season in Maine; the site provides current conditions, photos, and a kids page.

Massachusetts Fall Foliage
www.mass-vacation.com

Get in-depth and up-to-date foliage reports on Massachusetts, starting in early September and continuing throughout autumn.

MAJOR DESTINATION WEBSITES

Attracting visitors in the thousands (if not hundreds of thousands) every year, the region's best-known attractions have become increasingly web-savvy. Expect to find basic background information about the destination, plus essentials such as hours, location, entrance fees, driving directions, and special deals or packages currently offered.

Massachusetts
Greater Boston Convention & Visitors Bureau
www.bostonusa.com

The site provides a full a list of events throughout the year, and visitor information on lodging, restaurants, sights, shopping, and transportation.

The Freedom Trail Foundation
www.thefreedomtrail.org

Find tourist info, historical background, and latest news on tours and events for the 16 historical sites that make up Boston's Freedom Trail.

Boston Museum of Science
www.mos.org

Find out the Museum's current exhibits, buy tickets, get membership information, directions, and maps of the Museum.

The Berkshires
www.berkshires.org

This site offers lots of advice on dining and lodging in the area, plus other diversions such as spas, concerts, family outings, outdoor excursions, plus a list of current getaway deals.

Plimouth Plantation
www.plimoth.org

From historic background and online ticket purchasing to hours of operation and a list of current events happening at the Plantation, the site is full of practical information, including directions and a guide to respecting native cultures.

Cape Cod Chamber of Commerce
www.capecodchamber.org

The site contains full business listings, information on where to stay and eat, background on the 15 towns that make up Cape Cod, help on getting around the area, plus information on golfing, baseball, football, and other sporting in the area.

Nantucket Island
www.nantucket.net

Plan your island vacation with this site's easy listings of local restaurants, hotels and inns, beaches, and museums. There's also plenty of information on where and how to go boating, fishing, golfing, and biking, plus a section on where to take kids around the island.

Martha's Vineyard Island
www.mvol.com

From diving and sailing to horseback riding and beach-going, this site details all there is to do on and around Martha's Vineyard. It also lists accommodations and restaurants, posts a calendar of events and festivals, and provides information on car rentals and ferries, and vacation rentals.

Rhode Island
Providence Chamber of Commerce
www.provchamber.com

This site offers information not just on visiting Providence, but on moving there as well.

Newport, RI
www.gonewport.com

Find full listings of local businesses on the site, along with useful visitor information such as events, historic sights, and shows by area and neighborhood.

The Preservation Society
of Newport County
www.newportmansions.org

The Preservation Society operates the majority of mansions that are open to the public in Newport. Find out more about the history and character of each one on this in-depth site—plus essentials such as events, hours, and online ticketing.

Connecticut
Connecticut Tourism
www.tourism.state.ct.us

Built primarily for visitors to the state, the site lists weekend getaway itineraries and events happening throughout the year. It also offers help on getting to and around the different counties, and special deals on hotels.

Mystic, CT
www.mystic.org

The town's official site lists everything currently happening within it, from the Aquarium's exhibits to the Seaport's presentations. Also find restaurant, hotel, and shopping listings.

Vermont
Killington Chamber of Commerce, VT
www.killingtonchamber.com

Here you'll find information on nightlife and dining, shopping, accommodations, ski resorts, local churches and businesses, plus help on getting around the area by public transportation and finding local festivals.

Vermont Country Store
www.vermontcountrystore.com

The state's most beloved (and most marketed) quirky country store sells its hard-to-find stock online—everything from penny candy to sock monkey sheets.

New Hampshire
New Hampshire Tourism
www.visitnh.gov

Find all kinds of visitors' information on the state, including local foliage reports, travel itineraries, online photo galleries, deals on seasonal travel packages, and lodging and restaurant listings.

Mt. Washington Valley, NH
www.mtwashingtonvalley.org

Just about anything happening in the Valley shows up on this site: local events throughout the year, dog sledding and cross-country skiing—plus how to find the best local craftsmen and artists, as well as shopping, restaurant, and hotel listings.

Maine
Maine Tourism
www.visitmaine.com
The site offers information on everything to see and do in Maine, including fall foliage, outdoor recreation, family-friendly outings, restaurants, shopping, events, and accommodations.

Index

XYZ

List of Maps

Acknowledgments

A project of this magnitude could never have been completed without the assistance of a great many people. A big thank you to everyone around New England who helped us plan itineraries, fill in information, check facts, track down photos, fill our bellies, or sleep in comfort during the process of researching.

Merely a partial list of everyone who helped us, in ways large and small, includes Rehana Abbas, Kristen Adamo, John Alzapiedi, Sam Ankerson, Bob and Pennie Beach, Stacy Bell, Marian Burns, Rachel Carter, Julie Cook, Jeff David, William DeSousa-Mauk, Donna Desrochers, Irene Donnell, David Durfee, Ann Ewing, Shannon Farrell, Marlo Fogelman, Linda Fondulas, Ed Gannon, Mali Gero, Marli Gloeckner, Bill Griffith, Susan Grogan, Julie Grundy, Patricia Harris and David Lyon, Robert Gregson, Neil Humphrey, Kristin Hutton, Steve Jermanok, Barry Jessurun, Kelsey Keith, John Michael Kennedy, Traci Klepper, Kerri LaRoe, Jim Leonard, Didi Lutz, Jaisa MacAdam, Michael MacIntyre, Tavia Malone, Claire Mangers, Laurie Maw, Kristin Yantis Mettler, Nicole Maffeo Russo, Martha Morano, Rachael O'Brien, Marsha Oakes, Chris Pappas, Bruce and Debbie Pfander, Melissa Pinkerton, Billy and Patti Pusey, Namita Raina, Bradley Reichard, Whitney Riepe, Glen Sanokklis, Erika Schermerhorn, Lou Sideris, Robin Swett, Jen Thorn, Leslie Waters, Rebecca Werner, Rose Whitehouse, Rebecca Widness, Brill Williams, Charlene Williams, and Sophie Zunz-Burnett.

A special thanks goes to our indefatigable research assistants, without whom we would quite probably still be filling in addresses and websites: Emily Dyess, Melissa Lee, Casey O'Connell, Danielle Ossher, and Talia Ralph. Thanks also to Deb Squire, who generously donated several of her excellent photographs.

Special acknowledgements as well to everyone at Avalon Travel Publishing who made our words look and sound so good, including Jodee Krainik, Jehan Seirafi, Leah Gordon, Albert Angulo, Kathryn Osgood, Darren Alessi, Jamie Andrade, and everyone else behind the scenes. Meanwhile, we owe the biggest thanks of all to editor Kevin McLain for his guidance, to be sure, but most of all for his patience with our free-flowing approach to deadlines.

Last but not least, this book is dedicated to our wonderful children, Zachary Martin and Cleo Simone, two of the best-traveled and most-loved kids in New England.

www.moon.com

DESTINATIONS | ACTIVITIES | BLOGS | MAPS | BOOKS

MOON.COM is ready to help plan your next trip! Filled with fresh trip ideas and strategies, author interviews, informative travel blogs, a detailed map library, and descriptions of all the Moon guidebooks, Moon.com is all you need to get out and explore the world—or even places in your own backyard. While at Moon.com, sign up for our monthly e-newsletter for updates on new releases, travel tips, and expert advice from our on-the-go Moon authors. As always, when you travel with Moon, expect an experience that is uncommon and truly unique.

MOON IS ON FACEBOOK—BECOME A FAN!
JOIN THE MOON PHOTO GROUP ON FLICKR